GOOD BEER GUIDE 1998

EDITED BY JEFF EVANS

SPONSORED BY

Hømefire
Smokeless Coal

CAMRA

BOOKS

Campaign for Real Ale Ltd.
230 Hatfield Road, St Albans,
Hertfordshire AL1 4LW

CONTENTS

Editor: Jeff Evans. **Deputy Editor:** Jill Adam. **The HQ Team:** (Campaigns) Stephen Cox, Mike
Benner, Iain Loe, Ben Wardle, Mel Taylor; (Administration) Malcolm Harding, Kirk Winkler,
Cressida Feiler, Jean Jones, Mick Green, Gary Fowler, Karen Lynch, Anna Romano, Caroline
Mozley, Paula Oxley, Steve Powell. **Design:** Rob Howells. **Cover Photograph:** Tom Dobbie.
Maps: Perrott Cartographics, Machynlleth.

Published by Campaign for Real Ale Ltd., 230 Hatfield Road, St Albans, Hertfordshire AL1 4LW.
Tel. (01727) 867201. E-mail: camra@camra. org.uk Home Page: http:// www. camra.org.uk
Typeset by Tradespools Ltd., Frome, Somerset. **Printed by** Clays Ltd., Bungay, Suffolk.

ISBN 1 85249 131 0 (paperback)   ISBN 1 85249 133 7 (hardback)
© **Campaign for Real Ale Ltd. 1997/8**

Many thanks to all CAMRA members who helped with pub surveys and who provided information
on beers and breweries. Thanks, too, to CAMRA's Regional Directors for their assistance.

INTRODUCTION

I F HAROLD WILSON'S famous claim that a week is a long time in politics is true, then 25 years in the brewing industry is equivalent to a geological era. The publication in your hand first reached the bookstalls in a different age, at a time when Britain had just joined the EEC, and fought a cod war with Iceland. The aforementioned Mr Wilson was about to take Labour into power for the first time in four years. In the pop charts, Slade and Suzi Quatro were the Oasis and Spice Girl of the day and on television among the most watched programmes were *The Benny Hill Show* and *Love Thy Neighbour*. There were equally offensive offerings in the pub. The brewers matched Benny's birds with sexist adverts featuring buxom barmaids and *Love Thy Neighbour*'s Eddie Booth found an easy ally in obnoxious keg bitter – the liquid equivalent of a volley of personal insults.

Things change. Today it's not the EEC which is a hot issue, but the single currency within it. Clashes over cod have given way to battles over beef, and it is New Labour, rather than Old, which now pulls the Governmental strings. On TV, Benny and Eddie have been consigned to the backwaters of satellite broadcasting and in the more politically correct pub 1970s-style keg bitter has thankfully been given the elbow.

Make no mistake: the British pub has changed dramatically in the last quarter-century, and in most ways significantly for the better. Okay, instead of the 15 pence a pint beer used to cost 25 years ago we may be paying a scandalous £2.15 in places, but there have been great improvements, too. Take the fact that pubs can now open all day – a far more sensible system than the old skinny drinking slots at lunchtime and evening which encouraged quick consumption before the bell rang. And where were the family room, the wheelchair loo and the no-smoking area 25 years ago? On the beer front, you wouldn't have had much joy trying to buy a guest beer in a tied house in those days. Most importantly, you cannot overlook the fact that, back then, real ale was the exception in pubs but today it is the norm. Handpumps have sprouted on bars across the country and, far from having to seek out a real ale pub, most people have real ale right on their doorstep.

Twenty-five years on from the first edition of the *Good Beer Guide*, this is no time for modesty. Many of the improvements highlighted above have been achieved because of the efforts of CAMRA, the Campaign for Real Ale, and this publication, CAMRA's flagship. With each new edition the Campaign has been able to highlight issues which have been of greatest concern at the time. By focusing on subjects like licensing hours, pub refurbishments and guest beers, the *Guide* has more than played its part in bringing about overdue changes.

When the first edition was published, it was a struggle to find real ale and the *Guide* fulfilled the role of pointing drinkers to the few pubs where real ale could be enjoyed. True, it was, to a degree, selective (not that there was much to be selective about). There were certain pubs which sold real ale, but not good real ale, and these were quickly dismissed. The same applies today. We may have an abundance of real ale pubs but there are relatively few which merit high recommendation on the quality of the beer they sell. With over 60,000 pubs in the UK, only around 5,000 find their way into this book.

So, far from being tired and stale after 25 years on the shelves, the *Good*

The quest for a decent pint

Every drinker has heard it said that there is no bad beer, but some is just better than the rest. It's an old tale, which has never borne any truth. But today it is even further off the mark than ever.

Two major developments are threatening to kill off good ale once and for all:

● the large-scale promotion of characterless keg and tank beers at an advertising cost of millions of pounds a year; and

● the transfer from traditional methods of serving draught beer to pumps using carbon dioxide pressure, which makes ale gassy and sickly.

On top of which, the clo...... dozen...... brewer......
......nd Wal...... ......
......of

Beer Guide is as active and vibrant as ever. Anyone who enjoys a pint of beer will appreciate being shown where the best ale is to be found, and anyone who ever visits a pub will understand that there is still much to fight for. As Stephen Cox reveals in his feature beginning on page 8, CAMRA and the *Good Beer Guide* have scored some notable successes in the past year alone – saving the guest beer from European intervention and helping to block the Bass/Carlsberg-Tetley merger are just two. And there are many other battles which continue – to save the tied house, to cut beer duty, to prevent classic pubs being vandalised by marketing whiz-kids and to improve the quality of beer in all pubs.

CAMRA would be pleased to shut up shop and close down the *Good Beer Guide* if everything in the beer garden was rosy. Everyone knows that it is not. There is much to applaud and appreciate, but much to condemn and constructively criticise. The *Good Beer Guide* will continue to do both, for another 25 years if necessary.

BACK TO BASICS

It seems appropriate at this 25-year mark to reflect on the founding principles of the *Good Beer Guide* which continue to shape the book to this day. The first properly published edition (there was a photocopied prototype a year or so before) identified two major developments which were threatening to kill off good ale once and for all:
● the large-scale promotion of characterless keg and tank beers at an advertising cost of millions of pounds a year; and
● the transfer from traditional methods of serving draught beer to pumps using carbon dioxide pressure, which makes ale gassy and sickly.

The second point referred to traditionally brewed beer which was spoiled at the point of sale by using gas to force it into the glass ('top pressure'). This practice is nowhere near as prevalent as it was 25 years ago, but it still survives in places. However, the first point is as relevant today as in the *Good Beer Guide's* youth. Although gassy, cheerless keg

4

beer, as known at the time, has largely faded away (except in conservative pockets of the country), keg is still around in the form of new-fangled 'nitrokeg'. Less fizzy than its predecessor it may be, thanks to the use of nitrogen alongside carbon dioxide in its dispense, but it is just as characterless and still enjoys millions of pounds of advertising spend.

So what is the difference between keg, or nitrokeg, and real ale? In short, keg beer is a pasteurised, convenience product, about as interesting as processed cheese or sliced white bread. Being dead, it needs to have gas added to give it some artificial life. Real ale is a living, maturing beer which enjoys a fuller, fresher taste and various dimensions of flavour. It has its own natural gentle effervescence. But to best explain the difference we need to go back to the brewery and the start of the brewing process.

HOW BEER IS BREWED

All beer begins with malted barley. This is barley grain which has been partially germinated to help release vital sugars needed for the brewing process and then kilned to prevent further germination. The degree of kilning also dictates the character of the malt; the more 'baked' the malt, the darker the colour and the roastier the taste. Some are toasted black for bitter, coffeeish flavours; others are merely lightly crisped for a sweeter or nuttier taste. At the brewery the malt is crushed and then combined in a vessel called a mash tun with hot water (known as 'liquor' in the trade). This liquor has usually been treated to remove unsuitable chemicals or to emulate the natural brewing waters of towns like Burton upon Trent.

After an hour and a half's mashing and stirring, a thick, sweet liquid called wort is formed. This is then run off from the mash tun and diverted into a boiler known as a copper, leaving behind the spent grain, which is sprayed – or 'sparged' – to extract any last sugars and then sold for animal fodder. In the copper, the wort is boiled up with hops which add bitterness and sometimes herby, spicy or floral characters. Like malts, hops come in many varieties. Some are very bitter; others milder. Some make themselves known in the aroma; others are expressed in the taste. Hops also act as a preservative. They can be added as whole hop flowers or as compressed pellets. Some brewers use hop oils (concentrated hop extract), but it is widely considered that such oils can be too astringent. The hops are added at various stages of the boil. Sometimes 'adjuncts' are used. These include sugars, which add to the fermentability of the wort, and maize, which helps produce a good head on the finished beer, but such additives (and other less wholesome ingredients) are hotly opposed by purists.

After an hour or two in the copper, the hops are strained out and the hopped wort is run off and cooled. When the temperature has dipped sufficiently, the wort is pumped into a fermenting vessel, yeast is added ('pitched' is the technical term) and fermentation begins. Yeast is a single-celled fungus whose value to the brewer lies in its ability to turn the sugars in the wort into alcohol and carbon dioxide (which gives beer its natural effervescence). Each yeast, however, also has its own character which is skilfully harnessed and preserved by brewery chemists. Many breweries use the same yeasts for decades, ensuring that the brewery maintains its own style and individuality. The yeast is re-processed and re-used after each brew, with any excess generated sold to companies like Marmite.

During the first few days of fermentation, the yeast works furiously with the wort, growing quickly and covering the wort with a thick, undulating duvet of foam. Most is skimmed off, but some sinks into the brew and continues to work, eating up the sugars and generating more carbon dioxide and alcohol. A few days later, this 'primary fermentation' is deemed over and real ales and keg and nitrokeg beers go their separate ways. Those are the bare bones of the first stages of beer brewing. Each brewery, of course, has its own subtly different methods and uses recipes which combine various types of malts with various types of hops, in greater or lesser quantities. By varying brewing temperatures and fermenting times, and by introducing the ingredients at different stages, brewers contrive to produce, collectively, a magnificent array of flavours. Even beers using exactly the same base ingredients can taste dramatically different. It's one of the joys of beer drinking.

In the final stages at the brewery, keg and nitrokeg beers are chilled, filtered and pasteurised, effectively killing off and removing any living yeast still in the brew. They are then carbonated and put into sealed containers, called kegs. Real ales having been given time to mature at the brewery, so that harsher flavours are rounded out, are then put into casks (racked). Finings are added to ensure that the yeast is drawn out of suspension and down to the bottom of the cask. These finings are a glutinous substance usually made from the swim bladder of a fish and they attract yeast particles like a magnet. Like the yeast, you don't tend to drink them as they are left in the cask when beer is drawn off. Sometimes extra hops are added to the cask ('dry-hopping') and then the beer is shipped out for sale.

Once in the pub real ale has to be carefully stillaged and looked after. The casks have to be tapped but first vented to allow excess carbon dioxide produced by the still working yeast to escape. However, some must remain in suspension in the beer to provide its 'condition' or effervescence. (Some publicans then apply a blanket of gas to the cask to help keep the beer drinkable for a longer period of time, but CAMRA does not approve of any use of applied gas with cask beer as it may make the beer too fizzy or may prevent the beer maturing properly. It is better for the pub to order smaller casks which have a faster turnover.)

In the cellar, the beer continues to ferment and mature ('cask-condition'), so the beer should not be rushed onto sale, even if it quickly looks settled and clear ('drops bright'). Draught Bass, for instance, is at its best if kept for at least eight days after delivery before going on sale. (See *The CAMRA Guide to Cellarmanship* for much more information about keeping and serving real ale.) Keg or nitrokeg beer, meanwhile, needs little attention. It can be served straight away by connecting a cylinder of gas to the keg to force the contents to the bar. With no maturing process, it's hardly surprising that this type of beer is so one-dimensional, especially when it is also heavily chilled to mask any flavour it might have.

Real ale – served at a cool 12–13° C, rather than cold – is drawn to the bar by the use of simple pumps – a mechanical handpump, a pump driven by an electric motor or one using air pressure (it should never be carbon dioxide or other gas). It can also be served straight from the cask by opening the tap and letting the beer flow into the glass by gravity. These methods of dispense are highlighted in each pub entry in the *Good Beer Guide*.

Times, indeed, change. After a quarter of a century, the pub may be different in character and the laws which govern its use modified, but one thing has remained constant: a well-brewed beer, carefully looked after and properly served is one of life's greatest pleasures. Have a pint with us to celebrate our first 25 years!

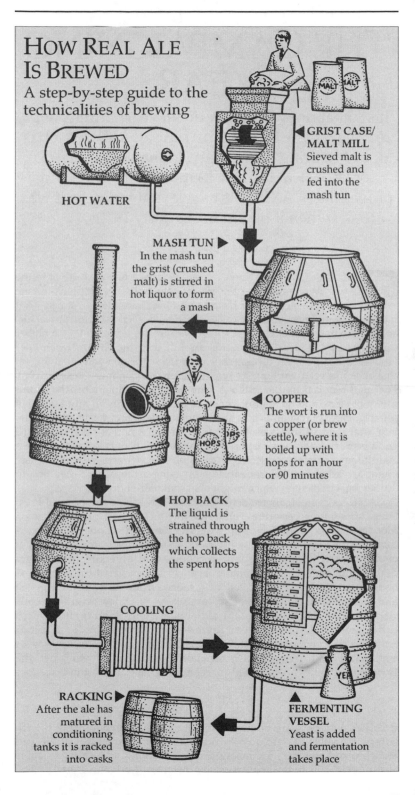

HOW REAL ALE IS BREWED

A step-by-step guide to the technicalities of brewing

HOT WATER

GRIST CASE/ MALT MILL
Sieved malt is crushed and fed into the mash tun

MASH TUN ▶
In the mash tun the grist (crushed malt) is stirred in hot liquor to form a mash

◀ COPPER
The wort is run into a copper (or brew kettle), where it is boiled up with hops for an hour or 90 minutes

◀ HOP BACK
The liquid is strained through the hop back which collects the spent hops

COOLING

RACKING ▶
After the ale has matured in conditioning tanks it is racked into casks

▲ FERMENTING VESSEL
Yeast is added and fermentation takes place

7

THE CAMPAIGNING YEAR

Just what does CAMRA do all year? Surely, with real ale on sale in so many pubs, CAMRA's job is done? Retiring Campaigns Manager *Stephen Cox* looks back at his last 12 months in office and proves that CAMRA is as relevant today as it was when it began in the early 1970s.

AUGUST

THE DAY before CAMRA opens the largest real ale festival in the world, the European Commission announces that it plans to take legal action against the British guest beer law. The guest beer, as it stands in legal terms, has to be cask-conditioned, such as a British real ale, and the Commission is worried this 'discriminates against other member states'. To say the least, our hands are full with the Great British Beer Festival. But we have a contingency plan ready, being aware that a legal challenge has been working its way through the Commission since 1993. The guest beer is being contested despite the fact that Britain has the widest choice of beers, and the widest choice of foreign imports, of any European country. The law is vital, as it helps Britain's smaller brewers get their beers into local pubs. It seems obvious to most observers that opening up the guest beer so that it can be any beer whatsoever will only benefit Guinness and the major lager producers. Worse still, an 'anything goes' guest beer might actually breach European law on tying arrangements, leading to further legal challenges which might abolish it outright!

CAMRA's campaigning machine swings into action; the Festival Press Office goes into hyper-drive. Television interviews begin at lunchtime on Monday and run until the evening on Tuesday. Ten national newspapers cover CAMRA's opposition. Behind our spokespeople stand the rows of cooled casks of real ale – the very choice and diversity that a legal challenge might seriously damage. Leaflets and posters hit the event 48 hours later and we get an excellent response from the public. I wake at four in the morning. T-shirts! They are ready by Friday, with the subtle slogan 'Brussels threatens real ale choice'. Our Belgian and Dutch colleagues are happy to wear them – they can see the logic of our argument. We've researched the guest beer issues over the last two years and have been briefing British officials. Round one is over when the Government comes out with a blunt rebuttal of the Commission case.

SEPTEMBER

CAMRA members are bombarding the European Commission with letters. CAMRA has already won the support of over 30 MEPs, and branches and members are meeting more. A hundred local newsletters and nearly 200 local branches are raising the issue locally. The

Commission takes a step back and puts the legal challenge on hold for a while. Over 150,000 leaflets are circulated – including to delegates at the three main political party conferences. We expect this to be a long haul.

OCTOBER

With publication of *Good Beer Guide 1997*, CAMRA highlights the threat to our most historic pub interiors. Again, heavy coverage follows in the national press. But, even as we publish, pubs on our list of pubs to save are being placed under threat of destruction. Planning and listing anomalies are thrown into the spotlight. Planning law does not stop someone turning a pub into a kebab shop, and new listing guidelines mean that even the most important pubs are not always eligible for listed status. The next few months are full of local campaigns against pub refurbishments as we speak out against grotesque changes which are often made without the support of, or consultation with, the local public. The press, on the other hand, seems obsessed with changes to pub names. We point out that pub names are just the icing on the cake. It's easy to change a name back, but it takes genius to rebuild a real pub.

NOVEMBER

Budget month. The media wake up to the Budget, although we have put our submission in three months ago. We are campaigning for a cut in beer duty, the tax our brewers pay to the Treasury, a levy which helps makes our beer the price it is today. The issue is simple: French drinkers pay a sixth of the beer tax we do. Calais supermarkets are cheaper because they pay so much less tax, leading to ten million pints of cheap foreign beer being imported into the UK every week. British pubs are losing business and it is the smallest community pubs which are struggling the most. The Treasury's own economic model shows that a cut in beer duty would be self-financing, as it would eliminate bootlegging, reduce inflation and safeguard pub and brewery jobs. What happens in the Budget? The Chancellor cuts duty on Scotch and leaves beer tax as it is. As beer is eight times more important to pub profits than spirits, CAMRA points out the Scotch cut will do nothing for struggling pubs.

CAMRA hosts a major trade seminar on the quality of beer. There's a lot of good beer about, but also a lot which is not so good. Quality is a complex issue, with problems starting in the marketing department ('let's make it blander to sell more'), the brewing department ('let's make it more of a convenience beer because we can't assume the publican can look after it'), passing through the distribution chain (where long journeys, warm lorries and poor storage may take their toll), and finally to the pub (where poor training and tight budgets can lead to all sorts of short cuts and nasty practices). It is a curious mark of CAMRA's status in the industry that some people try to blame us for the quality of beer – the one group of people who don't actually have the power to do anything directly to combat the problem.

DECEMBER

At the end of the calendar year, we've extracted some concessions from the European Commission. British MEPs are lobbying hard on the guest beer law and pointing to the range of eligible cask beers brewed in other

European countries. Our campaigning takes many different forms, from the local beer festival showing what interesting beers are available, down to the high profile campaign in Brussels.

JANUARY

CAMRA has prepared a manifesto, so drinkers' interests can be raised during the forthcoming General Election. The manifesto demands full-measure pints, a ban on take-overs and mergers, strengthening the guest beer law, a fundamental review of licensing law and a drastic cut in beer duty. CAMRA is, of course, strictly non-party political and so does not endorse candidates.

FEBRUARY

While the guest beer row rumbles on, the issue of the tied house also continues to concern the European Commission. CAMRA supports the tied house principle – it keeps smaller brewers in business and a good tenancy arrangement can benefit both the tenant and the customer. On the other hand, the introduction of long leases in the last ten years and the high-handed attitude of some companies ensure that thousands of tenants are justifiably pretty angry about their lot.

The Green Paper on tying arrangements produced by the Commission is better than it could have been, but some of the proposals could be very damaging to British pubs. I whiz off to Strasbourg for a briefing of MEPs by brewers, tenants and CAMRA. The meeting confirms that there is a lot of common ground, but tenants, rightly, want more protection and better terms. One tenant leader declares: 'If everyone ran their pubs like the family brewers there wouldn't be a problem'. Giant pub company Inntrepreneur's new code of practice is hailed as wonderful by tenant leaders, who express their regret that Inntrepreneur didn't take the same partnership approach when its first leases were offered ten years ago.

MARCH

Victory on the guest beer! The British Government proposes to extend the guest beer to bottle-conditioned ales. This benefits the speciality Continental beer trade, the growing market for British brewers in bottled beers and, ultimately, the beer consumer. The Commission has been forced to compromise by the high profile campaign, and the sterling work by British MEPs behind the scenes. The press highlights CAMRA's role in this important victory for beer drinkers.

The Monopolies and Mergers Commission hands its report on the proposed Bass/Carlsberg-Tetley link up to the Secretary of State. Bass plans to buy Carlsberg-Tetley, giving itself almost 40 per cent of the UK beer market. Two brewers would then have three-quarters of beer production in the UK. Choice would inevitably diminish; prices would ultimately rise. CAMRA has lobbied hard against the merger, but any decision must now wait until after the General Election.

APRIL

CAMRA's membership hits 50,000, the highest in its history. Ten years ago it was under 20,000. It proves that drinkers don't think we've achieved our aims. They realise there is still a lot to do and are flocking to join. CAMRA combines being a democratic voluntary organisation run by its members with a solid professional core. It operates as a local social organisation which does lots of fun things and yet has national and even international relevance. The membership subscription is the best £14 you could ever spend!

MAY

A General Election delivers a landslide Labour majority. The optimists among us look for full measure, as promised by the new Consumer Affairs Minister, a tougher line on take-overs and mergers, and perhaps a higher profile for consumer protection and information. The pessimists wonder if licensing law reform will figure high enough on the agenda, and wonder if Iron Chancellor Gordon Brown is likely to cut beer tax, penned in by tight spending plans and a short-sighted Treasury. Branches begin to work on convincing the record number of new MPs.

JUNE

President of the Board of Trade Margaret Beckett blocks the Carlsberg-Tetley take-over, as we wished. She resists a slightly half-baked proposal from the MMC to let it through provided Bass sells off half its pubs in a convoluted compromise. Dennis Turner MP floats a Private Member's Bill to abolish short measuring. Will it get enough time to be debated? The 'guest bottle' provision goes before Parliament.

JULY

Chancellor Gordon Brown announces a review of alcohol duties, but he also raises duty by a penny a pint. Could the review herald an outbreak of common sense, or is it just an excuse to put taxes up again? Fortunately we had pencilled in September for a campaign on tax and this will coincide quite nicely.

There's no prospect of a quick decision on the tied house from Brussels. Another lobbying meeting is planned. Preparation for the Great British Beer Festival is well under way. The campaigning year continues...

Stephen Cox was CAMRA's Campaigns Manager from 1988 to August 1997.

GOOD BEER GUIDING: 25 YEARS ON

Barrie Pepper looks back at the history of the
Good Beer Guide and enjoys its successes
– and its failures!

A SLIM, blue, spiral-bound folder graces my office bookshelf. I paid £11 for it at an auction about five years ago and it is titled *Where to Find Real Draught Beer*. It was published by CAMRA and, whilst it doesn't count in this retrospective survey of 25 years of the *Good Beer Guide*, it acted as a forerunner and holds a treasured place in my collection which takes in the next 24, from 1974 to 1997, and will soon contain this edition.

That prototype guide was a real mish-mash, listing only six pubs in the whole of Yorkshire and all of those in the Huddersfield area. There were 16 entries in Henley-on-Thames, all serving Brakspear's ales, and other small towns well represented were Salisbury with eight and Amersham, Devizes and Great Missenden with six each. Even Little Missenden had a couple. London and Manchester had the largest number of entries but there were none at all for Bristol, Birmingham, Leeds, Liverpool and Sheffield.

Quite frankly not a lot changed for the first of the 'real' *Good Beer Guides*, published in 1974. There was a better geographic spread for this edition, with Henley down to just five pubs and only four of them belonging to Brakspear. The large cities made their first entries and were well represented, but the choices were haphazard and it was not until 1975 that CAMRA branches played a big part in selecting the entries. Since that time, it has gone from strength to strength.

CAMPAIGNING SUCCESSES

The *Good Beer Guide* has been a terrific campaigning tool down the years. It has upset a lot of folk along the way but it can chalk up achievements which include longer pub opening hours, the fight for more choice which led to the setting up of the Monopolies and Mergers Commission investigation in the late 1980s, the struggle for a full pint which still goes on, and other ongoing crusades such as the preservation of our best pubs and the need for better pubs and quality service within them.

Its influence has been felt in so many ways, not just here but abroad, too, where, particularly in the United States and the Low Countries, it is a big seller. In 1983 a selection of Dutch pubs, mostly selling Fuller's ESB, was included. And in the previous year Irish pubs made their first entry into the *Guide*. I remember dashing into the famous Davy Byrnes to drink Theakston Best Bitter at almost twice the price I paid back home in Yorkshire.

Many famous folk have been induced to write feature articles for the guide. Miles Kington, Oz Clarke and Colin Dexter (of Inspector Morse fame) have all made their point. In 1991 Joe Ashton, the Labour MP for Bassetlaw and a CAMRA member since its inception, wrote a plaintive piece deploring the lack of real ale in the Houses of Parliament. His original efforts had led to bottles of Grolsch and Pilsner Urquell finding a place on the bars, but under sufferance. In his own words: '... there was a strict warning from the wine gang that, if they didn't sell, they would be withdrawn'. They sold and not too long afterwards real ale made its first (modern day) appearance on the bars of the best club in Britain. Nowadays, beers from many small independent and regional brewers are sold there and I trust the large influx of new MPs who find real ale as the norm will drink a toast to the *Good Beer Guide* and buy Joe Ashton a pint.

A WOBBLY START

1974

...orth: Dev...
...he of the best.
Ward: Sheffield.
Reasonably reliable.
Watney: Mortlake, London
Whitechapel, London.
Avoid like the plague.
Webster (Wa): Halifax.
Still a lot of real ale.
Wells, Charles: Bedfor...
...orth: Devize...
One of the best.
Ward: Sheffield.
Reasonably reliable.
Watney: Mortlake, Londo...
Whitechapel, London.
Avoid at all costs.
Webster (Wa): Halifax.
Still a lot of real ale.
Wells, Charles: Bedfo...
...one-in-three cha...

John Hanscomb was the editor of the 1974 guide. This was the one that had two editions, one of which told us to avoid Watney's beer 'like the plague'. The publishers, John Waddington of Leeds, thought this was libellous; Hanscomb's response was 'poppycock'. Nevertheless, the *Guide* was withdrawn on the eve of publication and Waddingtons stood the cost of a new cover which altered the description to 'Avoid at all costs'. A few lucky souls, including myself, have copies of both editions.

Another tale of John was that, when he got together all the pub entries, he found that there were none for Huntingdonshire (we were still with the old counties). So the following Sunday he took a two-hour lunchtime pub crawl along the A45 and came back with seven.

Michael Hardman, a founder member of CAMRA and editor of the next three editions of the *Guide*, recalled these incidents

13

in an article after twenty years of publication and there gave credit to Chris Hutt, author of *The Death of the English Pub*, for suggesting the name *Good Beer Guide*.

Hardman was followed by Roger Protz who put together six editions; Neil Hanson with five; Andrea Gillies, who compiled two; and, from 1991 to this present guide, Jeff Evans, the longest serving incumbent. Hanson's period of editorship, which started with the 1984 edition, coincided with the introduction of the *Guide's* first sponsorship, by British Coal, which lasted for nine years. A symbol signifying that the pub has a 'real fire' was introduced and has enhanced significance in this Silver Anniversary edition, with Homefire as the *Guide's* new sponsor.

BEWARE OF IMITATORS

The *Good Beer Guide* has been much copied. Perhaps the best example is *The Good Pub Guide* which was originally published in 1983 by the Consumers' Association. It is not a strict rival, having different aims and intentions, with the overall qualities of the public house to the fore. Descriptions are fulsome and there is no brewery section. Beer, it seems, is not as important as food. But it certainly has its place and is complementary to its elder brother.

The influence on other guides has taken time to show. *Egon Ronay's Pubs and Inns* guide has its adherents, although any guide which manages to leave out an entry for York must be questioned. Again it concentrates on food and only discovered in its 1994 edition that: '... cask ales (living beer) are becoming more and more popular'. I wonder where they had been for the previous twenty years?

1976

pleasant atmosphere

Outwoods

11–3 ; 6–10.30 (11 F,S)
Village Tavern
On A5
☎ *Great Chatwell 216*
Marston ② ❷ H
A welcoming pub which has changed little in 50 years
Ⓖ 🍺 🚲 🚃

Outwoods

11–3 ; 6–10.30 (11 F,S)
Village Tavern
Off A518
National Grid : 787181
☎ *Great Chatwell 216*
Marston ② ❷ H
A homely farmers' pub which should be treated with respect ♣ 🚃 Ⓡ

lleston

BUT NOBODY'S PERFECT

The *Good Beer Guide* itself is far from perfect, as anyone involved with the publication will freely admit. But its heart is in the right place and where it has slipped up it has done so in style. Take the 1976 edition, for instance, when one pub appeared twice, in both Salop (as Shropshire was temporarily known) and Staffordshire. The Village Tavern at Outwoods was on the A5 in Salop, and off the A518 in Staffs. In Salop it was described as 'a welcoming pub that has changed little in 50 years', and it had a garden. In Staffs it was 'a homely farmers' pub which should be treated with respect', and it had pub games and a room for meetings. In both counties it had a car park and sold Marston's beers.

I followed the affairs of the Village Tavern with interest over the years. It found life only in Staffordshire in later *Guides* and by 1980 it was 'a tiny village pub'. In 1987, the last entry for some years, the description read: 'Intimate, traditional village local, worth finding', and, by this time, it had taken on some of the newer qualities of the *Good Beer Guide* – it had a real fire and was a quiet pub. I checked the 1988 edition to see if the pub had

**CARTOONS HAVE PLAYED A BIG PART IN THE *GOOD BEER GUIDE* STORY.
THIS CLASSIC, BY BILL TIDY, IS FROM THE 1986 EDITION**

found its way back to the now renamed Shropshire but no such luck. However, it returned in 1994 after becoming CAMRA Staffordshire *Pub of the Year* and has retained its place ever since. It is now a free house and has a house beer brewed by Enville Ales. One day I must visit it.

Allegedly, tucked away in one edition is a county that never existed. I searched for Humbersetshire or something similar but never found it. There is also a pub that was a complete spoof and another that required a walk of half a mile along a canal towpath but claimed a car park. One Suffolk pub was on the London Underground. They are there for the finding along with a few other quirks.

But it is this book's purpose as a guide that is all important and if this edition of the *Good Beer Guide* gives you as much pleasure as the previous 24 have given to me then you will be a very content person. Happy reading and happy drinking.

*Barrie Pepper is Chairman of the British Guild of Beer Writers
and author of many books on beer and pubs.*

15

THE WARM WELCOME

'Oh, how lovely, a real coal fire.'

HOW MANY times have you said that yourself when you enter a pub – or a home – with a real fire burning brightly in the hearth. It creates a warm and welcoming atmosphere that no other form of heating can match.

Few things go together better than real ale and a real fire. This year's *Good Beer Guide* features well over 2,000 pubs which already appreciate the true value of a real coal fire and its unique ability to draw in customers, especially on a cold winter's day.

Homefire smokeless coal, sponsors of the *Good Beer Guide*, is one of a range of fuels from Coal Products Limited, Britain's leading manufacturer and distributor of solid fuel.

For over 30 years Homefire has been a favourite smokeless coal for open fires and multi-fuel stoves. It's made to conform to the latest environmental standards, so it's cleaner to make and cleaner to use. And each piece burns uniformly giving maximum heat with minimum waste.

Homefire and other fuels in the Coal Products' range are available loose or in pre-pack bags from all leading coal merchants. There are some 2,000 merchants who supply solid fuels to the homes of Britain. This distribution by a small army of independent retailers is one of the ways in which solid fuel differs from gas and electricity. Some

merchants' businesses are impressively large; many remain small personal and family concerns.

British Fuels and Charringtons Solid Fuel, both part of the Coal Products Group, are the two largest merchants, with well over 100 depots, giving nationwide service. In common with the overwhelming majority of merchants, they operate a Code of Practice known as the Approved Coal Merchant Scheme, which looks after customers' interests by insisting its members take all reasonable steps to ensure that customers' needs are met and they receive a high quality service.

You can find the location of your nearest Approved Coal Merchant stockist by calling the CPL Customer Helpline, on (0800) 716656.

SPECIAL OFFER FROM HOMEFIRE

If you have not used Homefire or its value for money partner Homefire Ovals, here's your chance to try them. CPL are offering a voucher worth £5 off the price of a 25kg bag to the first 500 *Good Beer Guide* readers who write in before 31 March 1998. (Please state the fuel you currently use and whether you have an open fire or multi-fuel stove.)

And that's not all. CPL has produced its own *Good Fuel Guide*. Fully illustrated, it lists the products for use on open fires, multi-fuel stoves, roomheaters, boilers and cookers, as well as providing hints on lighting a fire, maintaining appliances and other relevant information. And the guide is free.

For your Homefire voucher and/or CPL's *Good Fuel Guide* write with your name and address to:

Mr DAVID BURNHOPE
COAL PRODUCTS LTD.
FREEPOST SF 706
CHESTERFIELD S42 6BR

And keep the Homefires burning.

THE SILVER SELECTION

These are the select few, pubs which have sold consistently excellent beer for 25 years and have featured in every edition of the *Good Beer Guide* – no mean achievement!

ENGLAND

Bedfordshire
Cock, Broom
Fleur de Lis, Bedford
Rose & Crown, Ridgmont
Sow & Pigs, Toddington

Cambridgeshire
Queen's Head, Newton

Cheshire
Rising Sun, Tarporley

Cornwall
Blue Anchor, Helston

Devon
New Inn, Kilmington
Ship Inn, Axmouth

Dorset
Square & Compass,
Worth Matravers

Hertfordshire
Farriers Arms, St Albans

Kent
Jolly Drayman, Gravesend

Lancashire
Empress Hotel, Blackpool

Greater London
Buckingham Arms, SW1
Fox & Hounds, SW1
Star Tavern, SW1

Merseyside
Roscoe Head, Liverpool

Northumberland
Star, Netherton

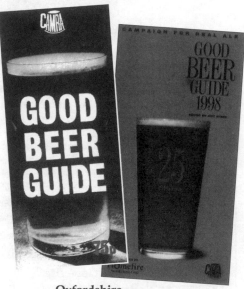

Oxfordshire
Crown & Tuns, Deddington

Shropshire
All Nations, Madeley (Telford)

Suffolk
Butt & Oyster, Pin Mill

WALES

Gwent
Cherry Tree, Tintern

SCOTLAND

Tayside
Fisherman's Tavern,
Broughty Ferry*

*24 editions only: Scotland was not
included in the first Good Beer Guide*

SUPERPUBS: BOON OR BLIGHT?

Giant, new chain pubs are taking over our city centres. Should we be over the Moon, sick as a Parrot or just Firkin angry? *Ted Bruning* considers the merits of the Superpub.

B RITAIN'S town and city centres today are very different from what they were 20 or even ten years ago. Supermarkets have emigrated to greenfield sites on ringroads and by-passes. Department stores are moving off the high street and into giant shopping centres such as Merry Hill and Meadowhall. Cinemas are either converted into bingo halls or boarded up, while their multi-screen replacements rub shoulders with ice-rinks and bowling-alleys on purpose-built leisure sites. Even humble ironmongers and motor spares shops have transformed themselves into DIY and car accessory superstores and resettled on self-contained retail parks. It used to be thought that these developments would leave high street pubs stranded among the charity shops, in an uninhabited wasteland bereft of customers. But it hasn't happened like that. In fact town-centre pubs are thriving as they haven't done since the 1970s, many of them themed as Hogsheads, Scruffy Murphy's, Rat & Parrots or O'Neills, while old car showrooms, furniture stores and, especially, banks have been converted into Wetherspoons, Brannigans, Firkins and God knows what else, often at a cost of over a million pounds a unit. And what's more, all these pubs – or Superpubs, as they have been dubbed – are doing a roaring trade.

Town Pubs Reborn

So why did brewers and, increasingly, non-brewing pub operators, invest so much in an environment which not so long ago seemed doomed, and how come it's all paid off so handsomely? A little history first.

The inventor of the Superpub as we know it is one Timothy Martin, a barrister who opened his first pub in North London back in the 1970s, at about the same time that David Bruce was founding the Firkin chain of brew pubs. Probably neither man really knew what he was starting, but I have an idea that Tim had a shrewder idea of where it would all lead than David did. Tim was driven by the inadequacy of the town-centre pubs he knew. They were ugly, scruffy, down at heel. The beer choice was strictly limited by the tie, and its quality was at best indifferent. The food was usually inedible. The pubs were loud with jukeboxes and one-armed bandits. They were uncomfortable. They were expensive.

Converting disused shoe shops, mini-marts and car showrooms into comfortable, no-frills, no-music alehouses, Tim Martin's JD Wetherspoon Organisation (named after one of his old teachers) spread slowly across North London, with Tim repeatedly deploying his legal skills to beat off objections to licences for his new pubs from entrenched interests. People liked his pubs. They were unthreatening. They sold a range of beers that most folk hadn't heard of. The food was at least good enough. The pubs had no music, but they still had a buzz. In the early 1980s I was a student living in Harringay. The choice was the Salisbury, a giant, once-splendid, Victorian gin-palace slowly collapsing into its own grease and spit, or the Suffolk Punch, a Wetherspoon which had once been a small supermarket. We all used the Wetherspoon.

TIM MARTIN, FOUNDER OF WETHERSPOONS AND INVENTOR OF THE SUPERPUB

Like an airliner, Tim's company gathered enough speed to take off, and if there was a precise point of departure it was August 1988, when the Licensing Act permitted all-day pub opening and, overnight, transformed the economics of the business. It was now worth setting out a truly lavish stall to attract whole new markets. The investment per pub began to rival the investment that the brewers of a century earlier had poured into their city-centre pubs – indeed, many of today's Superpubs started life as late Victorian Superpubs. The abandonment of city-centres by so many

institutions – supermarkets, department stores, shops, banks – did not hinder the progress of the Superpub: it merely created a great pool of comparatively inexpensive sites for Tim Martin and his growing army of imitators to fight over. And it turned out to be a myth that the migration of so much retail would hollow out the nation's town centres. As it transpired, department store shoppers hadn't been great pub users anyway; the town-centre drinkers came from offices, from small shops, from universities and colleges, from restaurants, all of them unaffected by the rush to the 'burbs.

The Superpub, with all its conveniences, created much of its own market, too, making pub-goers of many who wouldn't have used a traditional pub at all, especially female workers who found the Newt & Cucumber a good deal friendlier, cleaner and more suited to their requirements than the Dog & Duck had ever been. (And how many traditional Charrington or Watney houses had boasted wheelchair ramps and loos for people with disabilities?)

SO WHAT'S THE PROBLEM?

CAMRA was very enthusiastic about the new breed of pubs in the early days. They were a real breath of fresh air – literally, since Tim Martin also pioneered the smoke-free area, and especially in the range of real ales from regional and small independent brewers they offered. The pages of the

Good Beer Guide were soon crammed with Moon Under Waters, White Lion of Mortimers, JJ Moonses, and other characteristic Wetherspoon monikers. But you can have too much of a good thing, and soon everyone was getting in on the act, with Grosvenor Inns, Whitbread, Allied, Bass, Scottish Courage, Regent Inns, Greene King, Greenalls and even microbrewer Wychwood setting up 'brands' (as they have decided Superpubs are to be known) of their own. Town centres filled to bursting with Superpubs soon became an eveningtime magnet for so-called 'circuit' drinkers, youths moving from Superpub to Superpub in knots and gangs in a brutish parody of the Mediterranean passeggio. Too late, the police weighed in with objections to the proliferation of town-centre licences, and planning and licensing authorities discovered that floodgates, once opened, were almost impossible to close. Only now is the spread slowly coming under control.

Is CAMRA being curmudgeonly in its turn against the invasion of the Superpub? In some cases, perhaps. After all, anything that brings good ale and civilised surroundings to a forlorn wasteland like Slough (and this is not mere prejudice: I know how awful Slough's high street pubs used to be because I worked there) can only be wholeheartedly welcomed, surely? But we are justifiably outraged when some ancient inn, some treasure-house of our common past and shared identity, such as the Running Horse in Leatherhead, Surrey, is, on the whim of a marketing executive, bastardised, vandalised and reduced to the lowest common denominator of trash-culture.

We object when a venerable medieval institution like the Boot in St Albans is painted over to become a Scruffy Murphy's, a mock-Mick keg emporium which not only scorns the Irish, hijacking a genuine culture to create a horrible plastic pastiche, but also insults us by assuming that that's how we perceive the Irish. (CAMRA won that time.) We quail when we learn that a genuine Victorian pub is to be stripped out and reconstructed as what some half-trained architect thinks of as Victorian, with so-called 'specialist' glaziers hired to remove the original brilliant-cut- and acid-etched-glass from windows and partitions 'for safety during renovation work', only to mysteriously smash it. We fear for our lives when we see how, after 8pm, our town centres are transformed into so-called circuits, no-go areas for ordinary people, where clouds of drunken youths drift from Supervenue to Supervenue, half-finished bottles of beer in hand. And worse, we lovers of genuine pubs, when we see a cinema close and a Superpub open, know where the money to pay for the job will often have come from: rack-rented traditional tenants with full-repairing leases forced upon them, the only tradespeople in the land who pay full list-price for their beer, squeezed till their pips not only squeak but actually implode – that's where the money will have come from.

Town-centres need big pubs: there's a big market for them, and it's only natural that the investment should follow the demand. They can be great pubs, too: Wetherspoons' Commercial Rooms in Bristol holds the current CAMRA/English Heritage design award. But need so many Superpubs be so brash? Need they be so heavy-handedly themed? Need they make our town-centres so dangerous at night? And need they be so many?

Ted Bruning is a freelance journalist specialising in the brewing industry. He is assistant editor of What's Brewing and author of The CAMRA Guide to Real Cider amongst other titles.

BREWING IN PUBLIC

As the number of pubs which brew their own beer continues to increase, *Brian Glover* charts the history of the home-brew house.

W HEN CAMRA produced its first *Good Beer Guide* there were just four home-brew pubs left in Britain. They were regarded as the last remnants of a distant age, historical oddities left behind by the onward march of the brewing industry.

Once almost every household brewed its own beer. It was a domestic, kitchen craft, like cooking food. Public houses obviously brewed more. Larger commercial, or common, brewers who supplied a number of pubs were only able to expand with the development of steam power in the 18th century. The railway revolution that followed let them trade across the land, but the most significant date in the history of commercial breweries is 1830.

The Duke of Wellington's Beer Act that year allowed any householder to sell beer. The number of pubs doubled in less than a decade, some 25,000 houses flinging open their doors. Most had no facilities to brew on a large enough scale and instead bought in their ale from the common brewers. It was the beginning of the end for the golden age of pub brewing.

The eager brewing firms soon persuaded more established licensees to forego the pleasure of rising in the chill early hours to brew beer. Some simply bought up home-brew pubs as they developed their own tied estates. In 1841 almost half the pubs in England and Wales – around 27,000 out of a total of 57,000 – had brewed their own beer. By 1900 this figure had slumped to under 3,000 out of more than 73,000 pubs, with the practice mainly surviving in Yorkshire, the Midlands and Wales.

LAST INN LEGACY

The slide in the number of home-brew houses was accelerated by the rigours and restrictions of two world wars, and by the early 1970s the steam had stopped rising from most of the few remaining home-brew houses in the last stronghold of the Midlands. Pubs like the Druid's Head in Coseley near Wolverhampton, the Friary Hotel in Derby, Britannia in Loughborough and Nag's Head in Belper all gave up the ghost. Only four were left.

One was in the Black Country, near Dudley. The Old Swan at Netherton was popularly known as Ma Pardoe's, after the redoutable old lady who kept faith with the pub's battered mash tun. Two were tucked away in rural Shropshire: the Three Tuns at Bishop's Castle, with its imposing brick brewhouse still standing proud in the ancient market town, and the

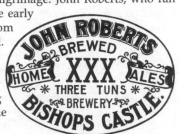

All Nations at Madeley, which owed its survival to another energetic woman, Eliza Lewis. She ladled the beer by hand, all 260 gallons of it, from the coal-fired copper into the fermenting vessel. The fourth was in the far south-western tip of England in Cornwall. Perhaps its distance from mainstream developments explained why the Blue Anchor at Helston not only continued to brew its own beers, but maintained their alcohol content at potent levels enjoyed before World War I. Geoff Richards was the third generation of his family to brew at the thatched stone pub which dates back to 1400. In a rapidly changing world, his Spingo Ales had barely altered. Their staggering strength caught unwary visitors by surprise.

The famous four became places of pilgrimage. John Roberts, who ran the Three Tuns at Bishop's Castle in the early 1970s, recalled: 'These three chaps from Southampton put a tent up in the field. When I opened that night, they were waiting at the door. Next morning the same thing. And so it went on. Nobody saw them in the town, but at opening time it was just as if they'd heard some call from a minaret.'

A Revolution Brewing

No-one believed that the tide was about to turn. But these were not the last drops of beer from the brew pub barrel before it ran dry. Instead, they helped to provide the heady inspiration for a revolution.

The first to re-launch the dying art was a former rocket engineer, Paul Leyton, at the Miners Arms in Priddy, Somerset, in 1973. He produced just five gallons a week of a bottle-conditioned beer called Own Ale in his kitchen. A mention in the fledgling *Good Beer Guide* brought eager drinkers flocking to the door – only to discover that the Miners Arms was a restaurant not a pub, and Own Ale could only be enjoyed with a meal.

The first proper pub was the Masons Arms at South Leigh in Oxfordshire in 1974, with its dark Sowlye Ale. A few others followed, like the Fighting Cocks at Corby Glen in Lincolnshire, the New Fermor Arms at Rufford in Lancashire and the Miskin Arms near Pontyclun in South Wales. But all served their beer under pressure and some used malt extract. The first revived brew pubs were often seen to be cutting corners rather than breaking new ground.

The new brewers who captured the drinkers' imagination were the bold free trade ventures like Litchborough, Blackawton, Godson, Butcombe, Pollard, Smiles and Penrhos. The only new home-brew pub with a profile to match was the John Thompson Inn at Ingleby in Derbyshire, where the JTS XXX began flowing in 1977. This proved so popular that it was soon sold to other pubs as Lloyds Country Bitter.

**DAVID BRUCE, FIRKIN FOUNDER,
IN ONE OF HIS BREWERIES**

FROM GAGS TO RICHES

The man who really put the revived home-brew pub on the map was David Bruce. This was partly because his Goose & Firkin in 1979 was the first to open in London, but also because of Bruce's enterprising marketing. Drinkers were not just offered home-brewed beer, but a rustic, bare-boards style of eccentric decor and a ton of groaning puns promoting ales like Dogbolter.

It proved to be a gags to riches story. Soon he had spread his successful concept from his first cramped cellar in Southwark – where the tiny malt extract plant had used his wife's tights as a hop strainer – to larger houses in the capital using full-mash equipment. Pubs like the Fox & Firkin in Lewisham also for the first time brought the brewery into the bar, allowing the drinker to see his beer being brewed behind glass panels.

By 1983 David Bruce was running six Firkin home-brew houses. The major brewers gazed in envy and amazement at his success. Brew pubs had become fashionable and big business. The tenth *Good Beer Guide* published that year listed 38 of them and the number swelled rapidly as large companies jumped on the small brewery bandwagon. Just two years later there were 70. Whitbread set up 11 home-brew pubs, Grand Metropolitan (Watney's) seven and Allied Breweries 12. Two retired Whitbread executives, Peter Shardlow and Robin Richards, established their own firm, Inn Brewing, in 1982 to meet the growing demand for equipment and advice. In their first year alone they installed ten breweries. In 1988 Bruce sold his Firkin chain – now numbering 12 pubs – for £6.6 million.

LULL BEFORE THE STORM

However, as the novelty faded, some of the leading companies pulled the plug on their mini mash tuns. Others were hit by the recession. The number fell from a high of 76 in the 1986 *Good Beer Guide* to 46 by the 1991 edition.

But the revival was merely delayed not ended. As the economy began to improve, so a brewery on the premises was again seen as a way to stimulate trade. From 1994 the gradual upward trend started to foam vigorously. And this time it was led by a wide range of entrepreneurs. The 1995 *Good Beer Guide* recorded 78 independent concerns brewing on the premises. Encouraged by the new guest beer law, some also expanded their business to supply other pubs. The divide between brew pubs and free trade brewers was increasingly breaking down. Some became substantial success stories.

In 1986 a former Watney brewer, John Gilbert, had begun brewing at a small street-corner pub, the Wyndham Arms in Salisbury. His Hop Back beers proved so popular that in 1992 he was forced to move the brewery out of the pub yard to larger premises. In the same year his powerful, straw-coloured Summer Lightning was voted the *Best Strong Bitter* at the Great British Beer Festival. Production rose to more than 6,000 barrels in 1994 and Hop Back bought four more pubs, one of which, the Hop Leaf in Reading, opened its own brewery in 1995.

BRANDS NOT BREWERIES

Many other brew pubs were breaking out of their bars but the only major company still involved in a big way was Allied, which in 1991 had taken over the Firkin group. However, the giant combine no longer saw Firkin as essentially a brewing company but just another brand image for a chain of pubs. The bare boards and bare-faced cheek were retained, but many of the new Firkin houses failed to receive a brewery. In 1996 more than a third of the 60 Firkins did not brew their own beer, while the company's insensitive treatment of historic houses angered many drinkers.

Last year's *Good Beer Guide* recorded a grand total of 137 home-brew pubs, 97 of which are independent. The pub brewery revolution is booming, with many more opening this year. The revival has come a long way from the meagre four survivors listed 25 years ago.

Brian Glover is a former editor of CAMRA's newspaper, What's Brewing, and the author of numerous books on beer. He won the prestigious gold tankard at the British Guild of Beer Writers awards in 1993.

HOW TO USE THE GOOD BEER GUIDE

I N ITS 25 YEARS the *Good Beer Guide* has assumed an identity of its own. It is quite unlike other pub guides in that it focuses not on the food, the wallpaper or the roses growing around the door (although these are not forgotten) but primarily on the quality of the beer on sale. It is also unlike most other guidebooks in that it does not employ professional inspectors who visit pubs only once or twice during the course of the year. Entries, instead, are chosen by local CAMRA members, beer enthusiasts who use the pubs in their area week-in, week-out. They decide which pubs should be submitted for the *Guide* at special branch selection meetings. At these meetings, they evaluate all the likely contenders and vote on which pubs to include in the book. Some clubs and off-licences may also be included, if the branch considers that they make significant contributions to the local real ale scene. These and the pubs are formally surveyed each year and the information is passed to CAMRA head office for processing. Branches see proofs of their entries and can recommend changes right up to the last possible moment before the *Guide* goes to press. We believe this provides the most up to date research system employed by any guidebook.

SELECTION CRITERIA

The chief criterion for inclusion in the *Good Beer Guide* is, of course, good beer – cask-conditioned real ale, traditionally well-kept without the application of life-extending gases. Whatever other attributes a pub may have, unless the beer is first class it will not be selected. Readers' recommendations are extremely useful and sometimes offer another viewpoint which our branches are always keen to bear in mind when considering their selections, but reader recommendation alone does not guarantee entry to the *Guide*, as it does with some other publications.

Central to the *Guide* is the fact that, first and foremost, CAMRA is a consumer organisation, dedicated to raising standards in the pub and brewing world. This occasionally means that other factors enter the selection equation. A pub which indulges in anti-consumer practices, like consistently short-measuring its customers, is unlikely to find favour. The use of deliberately misleading dispense equipment, such as fake handpumps which make you think you're getting real ale or real cider but which serve only keg versions, is another reason why pubs are not selected.

HOW THE GUIDE IS ORGANISED

Pubs are listed in areas which largely follow the county/local authority system. In some instances, where the new authorities are small, they have been amalgamated into larger regions. The Key Map on the inside back cover shows the subdivisions used in the book. English pubs are listed first, followed by pubs in Wales, Scotland, Northern Ireland and the offshore islands. For Wales and Scotland, where counties and regions have been largely abolished in recent years, details of the precise local authority areas covered by each section are given on the first page. *Good Beer Guide* areas are arranged alphabetically, with Greater London and Greater Manchester under L and M respectively. All areas have a location map, pinpointing where all the pubs are situated and also marking the independently-owned breweries and brew pubs. Breweries and brew pubs owned by the national brewers are not included in the maps.

THE PUB ENTRIES

Within each county, pubs are included in alphabetical order of place name, then alphabetically within each location. An at-a-glance guide to reading the pub entries is included below and repeated on the inside front cover but, basically, each entry provides the following information: name of pub, address, directions and Ordnance Survey map reference number (if tricky to find), telephone number (if available), opening hours, a brief description of the pub and its major features and, finally, a row of symbols highlighting its key facilities. For meals and accommodation, no assessment of quality is made, unless mentioned in the pub description. Evening meals should be assumed to be available until at least 9pm, unless otherwise stated. Opening times first confirm the hours in operation most of the week, followed by the hours on days which differ from the norm. Seasonal variations are shown in brackets. As Sunday opening is still relatively new, Sunday hours are once again individually stated this year. Look out, too, for the star symbol next to a pub's name. This indicates that the pub offers a fine example of an unspoilt, historic interior and is high on the list of CAMRA's pubs to preserve (see page 117 for more details).

Central to each entry is the list of real ales sold. These are arranged alphabetically by brewery and where more than one beer from a brewery is sold its beers are listed in ascending order of strength. Seasonal beers, such as winter ales, are included but are clearly only available at certain times of the year. For further information on all beers, check The Breweries and The Beers Index at the back of the book.

Locality ▶	**Much Blarney**	
Address and telephone number ▶	**Grubby O'Reilly's** Down Market (a long way from Tipperary) ☎ (01234) 567890	◀ Pub name
Draught beer available and dispense method ▶	11.30–3, 5.30–11; 11–11 Fri & Sat **Mick Taker's Special; Paddy's Bitter** Ⓗ	◀ Opening hours
	Formerly the Dog & Duck, a popular local; now everything an Irish bar isn't, with a crass new name to boot. Enjoy the mock Celtic decor, diddly music and the chance to drink nitrokeg stouts and 'Irish' ales at exorbitant prices. Count the shamrocks! As genuine as a two-punt note and coming soon to a pub near you. ◖ ▶ ㅤ ⇌	◀ Description of pub ◀ Facilities
Other good outlets worth trying ▶	**Try also: Rovers Return,** Benidorm (Britkeg)	

THE
GOOD BEER GUIDE

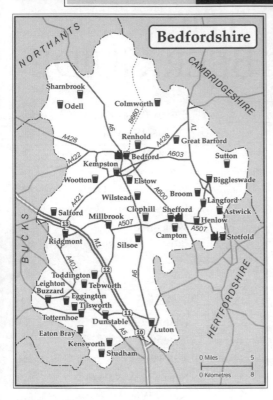

Fine, traditional pub near the town centre. A wide range of food at lunchtime includes home-made specials and a full breakfast (no food Sun).
❀ ◖❶ ♣ P

Biggleswade

Brown Bear

29 Hitchin Street (NW corner of market square)
☎ (01767) 316161
11–11; 12–10.30 Sun
Beer range varies Ⓗ
Medium-sized, backstreet pub, near the town centre, with a regularly changing beer selection. It has a well decorated, open-plan bar / lounge bar with a separate, no-smoking dining area at the rear. Children's certificate. Eve meals Thu–Sat. Cider in summer. ❀ ◖❶ ⇌ ♣ ☐

Try also: **Rose**, High St (Free)

Broom

Cock ☆

23 High Street
☎ (01763) 314411
11–3, 6–11; 11–11 Sat; 12–10.30 Sun
Greene King IPA, Abbot, seasonal beers Ⓖ
Grade II-listed building where the beer is served from the casks straight out of the cellar. A real gem: no bar but many small rooms off a central corridor which must be seen. Good food.
🛏 ⛺ ❀ ◖❶ ❶ Å ♣ P

Campton

White Hart

Mill Lane (off A507)
☎ (01462) 812657
12–3, 6–11; 11–11 Sat; 12–3, 7–10.30 Sun
Hook Norton Best Bitter; Morland Old Speckled Hen; Theakston Best Bitter, XB; guest beers Ⓗ
300-year-old, Grade II-listed, brick-and-beam pub with quarry-tiled floors and inglenooks. Live folk music every Wed. Petanque played. Lunches Mon–Fri.
🛏 ❀ ◖❶ Å ♣ P

Clophill

Stone Jug

Back Street (off A6)
☎ (01525) 860526
11–3, 6–11; 11–11 Sat; 12–10.30 Sun

Astwick

Tudor Oaks

1 Taylors Road (A1 northbound between Letchworth and Biggleswade)
☎ (01462) 834133
11–11; 12–3, 6–10.30 Sun
Boddingtons Bitter; guest beer Ⓗ
Pub serving an ever-changing range of guest beers (over 500 in the last two years), and the only pub in the area to sell draught perry. The cider bar is unique and must be seen. Exceptional value food, served every day until late eve.
🛏 ❀ 🛏 ◖❶ ♣ ☐ P ☐

Bedford

Anchor

397 Goldington Road (A428 Goldington Green)
☎ (01234) 353606
11–2.30 (3 Sat), 6–11; 12–4, 7–10.30 Sun
Greene King XX Mild, IPA, Abbot Ⓗ
Two-lounge pub with nautical decor, serving a varying range of reasonably priced food, with English and German dishes (not served Sun eve or Mon).

No-smoking area in the restaurant.
Q ❀ ◖❶ ❶ ♿ ♣ P

Fleur de Lis

12 Mill Street (E off A6 High St)
☎ (01234) 211004
10.30–11; 12–10.30 Sun
Wells Eagle; guest beer Ⓗ
Very well-run, one-bar, town-centre pub with a wide mix of clientele. Parking difficult lunchtimes. In every edition of the *Guide*. Occasional live music Tue eve and Sun afternoon. No food Sun.
◖

Hogshead

High Street (A6)
☎ (01234) 353749
11–11; 12–10.30 Sun
Boddingtons Bitter; Flowers Original; Fuller's London Pride; Marston's Pedigree; Wadworth 6X; guest beers Ⓗ
Popular, one-bar pub serving good food. Busy at weekends and Thu–Sat eves. ❀ ◖❶

Three Cups

45 Newnham Street (down Mill St from High St)
☎ (01234) 352153
11–11; 12–3, 7–10.30 Sun
Greene King IPA, Abbot, seasonal beers Ⓗ

🔺 INDEPENDENT BREWERIES

B&T: Shefford

Abel Brown's: Stotfold

Wells: Bedford

B&T Shefford Bitter; John Smith's Bitter; guest beers Ⓗ
Popular free house, a *Guide* regular, convenient for the Greensand Ridge walk. Check before arriving with children. No food Sun. ⚙ ◖ ♣ P

Colmworth

Wheatsheaf
Wilden Road (¾ mile E of B660)
OS101574 ☎ (01234) 376370
11–3, 6.30–11; 12–3, 7–10.30 Sun
Draught Bass; guest beers Ⓗ
17th-century country inn south of the village. Beware the low beams! Guest beers change frequently, with at least three normally on sale. Children's play area in the garden. Good, varied bar meals; franchised restaurant.
🏚 Q ⚙ ◖ ◗ ⊟ ♣ P

Dunstable

Victoria
69 West Street
☎ (01582) 662602
11–11; 12–10.30 Sun
Tetley Bitter; guest beers Ⓗ
Friendly local near the town centre. The L-shaped bar has one end for pub games; the other is dominated by Sky Sports. Three ever-changing guest beers, also a house beer brewed by Tring. S Beds CAMRA *Pub of the Year* 1996. Good value lunches.
⚙ ◖ ♣

Eaton Bray

Hope & Anchor
63 Bower Lane
☎ (01525) 220386
11–3, 5.30–11; 12–4, 7–10.30 Sun
Tetley Bitter; Vale Notley Ale, Wychert Ale; guest beer Ⓗ
Old, low-beamed, village inn, now refurbished and extended beyond recognition to combine a large restaurant and an urban-style main bar. Popular with locals. Occasional live music or disco. ⚙ ◖ ◗ ♣ P

Eggington

Horseshoes
High Street ☎ (01525) 210282
12–2.30, 6–11; 12–3, 7–10.30 Sun
Wadworth 6X; guest beers Ⓗ
Picture-postcard village pub with an upstairs gallery. An imaginative range of food is on offer (not lunch Mon), also an extensive wine list.
🏚 ⚙ ◖ ◗ ♣ P

Elstow

Swan
High Street ☎ (01234) 352066
11.30–3, 6–11; 12–3, 7–10.30 Sun
Greene King IPA, Abbot Ⓗ
Old village pub near Elstow Abbey: one L-shaped room plus a restaurant. Fresh produce is always used so Sun lunch must be booked (no food Sun eve). 🏚 ⚙ ◖ ◗ ♣ P

Great Barford

Golden Cross
2–4 Bedford Road (A421 at crossroads)
☎ (01234) 870439
12–11; 12–4, 7–10.30 Sun
Greene King IPA; guest beers Ⓗ
Cosy free house with a wide range of food plus four guest beers usually available. Live music Tue eve. Wheelchair access to the restaurant, where children are welcome (no-smoking area). No food Sun eve. Q ⛵ ⚙ ◖ ◗ ♣ P

Henlow

Engineers Arms
68 High Street
☎ (01462) 812284
2 (11 Fri & Sat)–11; 12–10.30 Sun
Marston's Bitter, Pedigree, HBC; Taylor Landlord Ⓗ
Pub where guest beers come direct from micros. Although they are served through a swan neck and tight sparkler, the staff are happy to serve them traditionally. Most staff members have attended hygiene and cellarmanship courses. 🏚 ⚙ ⊟ ♣ ⊟

Kempston

King William IV
56 High Street
☎ (01234) 854533
11.30–3, 5.30 (6 Sat)–11; 12–10.30 Sun
Wells Eagle, Bombardier; guest beer Ⓗ
Attractive, genuine, oak-beamed building which caters for a mixed clientele in one bar and a games room. The large garden has children's attractions. Children's certificate. Eve meals Tue–Sat.
⚙ ◖ ◗ ♣ P

Kensworth

Farmer's Boy
216 Common Road
☎ (01582) 872207
11–11; 12–10.30 Sun
Fuller's London Pride, ESB, seasonal beers Ⓗ
Friendly, well-kept village pub with a small public bar, a comfortable lounge and a separate dining area (excellent, home-cooked food). Children's certificate for the lounge and dining areas; play area in the garden. 🏚 ⚙ ◖ ◗ ♣ P

Langford

Red Cow
High Street
☎ (01462) 700642
11–11 (may vary); 12–3, 7–10.30 Sun
Greene King IPA Ⓗ
Traditional village local, a games-oriented pub where you enter a stranger and leave as a friend. Summer weekend barbecues.
🏚 ⚙ ♣ P

Leighton Buzzard

Globe
Globe Lane, Stoke Road, Old Linslade (1 mile NW of town centre, off A4146)
☎ (01525) 373338
11–3, 6–11; 12–4, 7–10.30 Sun
Brains SA; Fuller's London Pride; Marston's Pedigree; guest beers Ⓗ
Originally a farmhouse but converted to an inn when the Grand Union Canal, which passes within ten feet, was built. Split-level drinking area; large restaurant. Camping facilities at the rear.
🏚 Q ⚙ ◖ ◗ ♿ ♠ P

Hunt Hotel
19 Church Road, Linslade (opp. station)
☎ (01525) 374692
11–2.30, 5.30–11; 11–11 Sat; 12–3, 7–10.30 Sun
Draught Bass; Fuller's London Pride; Tetley Bitter; guest beers Ⓗ
Ochre-coloured hotel with a quiet bar which has recently been pleasantly refurbished. Two ever-changing guest beers available (at a price!). Occasional live music. Separate restaurant. Disabled access is via the entrance from the car park.
Q ⛵ 🛏 ◖ ◗ ♿ ⇌ P

Stag
1 Heath Road
☎ (01525) 372710
11–2.30 (3 Sat), 6–11; 12–3, 7–10.30 Sun
Fuller's Chiswick, London Pride, ESB, seasonal beers Ⓗ
Wedge-shaped, heavily renovated, street-corner local, formerly owned by Benskins. The landlord was Fuller's champion cellarman in 1995. Tiny car park. Good food (not served Sun). ◖ ◗ P

Luton

Bird & Bush
Hancock Drive, Bushmead
☎ (01582) 480723
12–11; 12–10.30 Sun
Draught Bass; Fuller's London Pride; Highgate IPA; guest beer Ⓗ

31

Modern estate pub with attractive Yorkshire flagstone and quarry-tiled floors. Good bar food includes vegetarian options (no food Sun eve).
✿ ◖ ▶ ᵶ ♣ P

Bricklayers Arms

16–18 High Town Road
☎ (01582) 611017
12–2.30, 5–11; 12–11 Fri & Sat;
12–10.30 Sun
Everards Mild, Beacon, Tiger, Old Original; guest beer Ⓗ
Friendly, unpretentious town pub with basic furnishings, including a variety of old wooden casks scattered throughout – the ones above the bar are from the short-lived Mickles microbrewery.
✿ ⇄ ♣ P

Mother Redcap

80 Latimer Road
☎ (01582) 730913
11–3, 5–11; 11–11 Fri & Sat; 12–3,
7–10.30 Sun
Greene King IPA, Abbot, seasonal beers Ⓗ
Well-renovated, one-bar pub with a games area separated from the lounge by a chimney breast. No food Sun.
✿ ◖ ♣ P

Two Brewers

43 Dumfries Street
☎ (01582) 723777
12–11; 12–10.30 Sun
B&T Shefford Bitter, Dragonslayer, SOS, seasonal beers; guest beers Ⓗ
Friendly, backstreet local with a good mix of customers. Good value beer in no-frills surroundings. ᵶ ✿ ♣

Wheelwrights Arms

34 Guildford Street
☎ (01582) 759321
10.30–11; 12–10.30 Sun
Flowers IPA; Fuller's Chiswick, London Pride, ESB, seasonal beers; guest beers Ⓗ
Lively, one-bar, town-centre free house, handy for the bus and rail stations, and Arndale shoppers. It opens at 7am to serve good-value breakfasts.
✿ ◖ ▶ ♣ ↻

Millbrook

Chequers

☎ (01525) 403835
11.30–2.30, 6–11; 12–2.30, 7–10.30 Sun
Adnams Broadside; Banks's Mild; Wadworth 6X; Wells Eagle Ⓗ
Popular pub overlooking Marston Vale, near Ampthill; frequented by testers from the nearby vehicle proving track. The restaurant area serves a wide variety of meals, including Sun roasts (no eve meals Sun). ◖ ▶ ♣ P

Odell

Bell

Horsefair Lane
☎ (01234) 720254
11–2.30, 6–11 (11–11 Sat spring & summer); 12–3, 7–10.30 Sun
Greene King IPA, Abbot, seasonal beers Ⓗ
Popular, thatched, multi-room village pub serving good food. The large garden near the River Ouse has an aviary of unusual birds. A riverside footpath leads into Harrold Country Park. Sun lunches 12–2; no food Sun eve in winter. ᵶ ✿ ◖ ▶ P

Renhold

Three Horseshoes

42 Top End (1 mile N of A421)
☎ (01234) 870218
11–2.30, 6–11; 11–11 Sat; 12–5, 7–10.30 Sun
Greene King XX Mild, IPA, Abbot Ⓗ, **Winter Ale** Ⓖ, **seasonal beers** Ⓗ
Friendly village pub with a children's play area in the garden. The public bar has traditional games. Good value food includes fresh steaks and soup. No eve meals Sun or Tue. A long-standing outlet for mild.
ᵶ Q ✿ ◖ ▶ ⊟ ᵶ ♣ P

Ridgmont

Rose & Crown

89 High Street
☎ (01525) 280245
10.30–2.30, 6–11; 12–4, 7–10.30 Sun
Adnams Broadside; Mansfield Riding Bitter; Wells Eagle, Bombardier Ⓗ
Popular, welcoming pub. The lounge bar has a 'Rupert' theme; the public has a separate games area with table football. The extensive grounds offer not only camping and caravanning facilities but also open-air table tennis. Featured in every edition of the *Good Beer Guide*.
ᵶ ◖ ▶ ⊟ ᴬ ♣ P

Salford

Red Lion Country Hotel

Wavendon Road (main Cranfield–Woburn Sands road)
☎ (01908) 583117
11–2.30, 6–11; 12–4, 7–10.30 Sun
Wells Eagle, Bombardier Ⓗ
350-year-old building with a comfortable lounge bar and a popular, separate restaurant. The accommodation features four poster beds. Good garden for children.
ᵶ Q ✿ ⇖ ◖ ▶ P

Sharnbrook

Swan With Two Nicks

High Street ☎ (01234) 781585
11–3, 5–11; 11–11 Sat; 12–10.30 Sun
Wells Eagle, Bombardier; guest beers Ⓗ
Friendly village local with a small rear patio. Home-cooked food includes daily specials and a vegetarian choice.
ᵶ ✿ ◖ ▶ ⊟ ♣ P

Shefford

Brewery Tap

North Bridge Street
☎ (01462) 851782
11–11; 12–10.30 Sun
B&T Shefford Bitter, Dragonslayer, SOS, seasonal beers; guest beer Ⓗ
Timber-clad, wooden-floored, hospitable pub, B&T's brewery tap. Children are welcome, as are well-behaved dogs. Filled rolls are usually available (no food Sun). Interesting collection of breweriana.
✿ ◖ ♣ ↻ P

Silsoe

Star & Garter

14–16 High Street
☎ (01525) 860250
11–3, 5.30–11; 12–3, 6–10.30 Sun
B&T Shefford Bitter; Boddingtons Bitter; Flowers IPA; Wadworth 6X Ⓗ
Dating in part from the 16th century: a large, comfortable lounge bar with a raised restaurant area and a smaller, more traditional, public bar adjoining. ᵶ ✿ ◖ ▶ ⊟ ♣ P

Stotfold

Stag

35 Brook Street
☎ (01462) 730261
6 (11 Fri & Sat)–11; 12–10.30 Sun
Abel Brown's Jack of Herts, Little Billy, Knucklehead, seasonal beers; Lloyds Bitter; Wadworth 6X; guest beers Ⓗ
Abel Brown's brewery is based here and was recently expanded. A beer house in every sense of the word, it offers up to four guests at all times. Real cider is served cool straight from the cellar. A real ale festival every week!
ᵶ ✿ ↻ P ⊓

Studham

Red Lion at Studham

Church Road
☎ (01582) 872530
11.30–3, 5.30–11; 11.30–11 Sat;
12–10.30 Sun
Adnams Bitter; Greene King Abbot; Marston's Bitter, Pedigree; guest beer Ⓗ

Well-furnished, comfortable pub facing the village common, with an L-shaped lounge bar, a dining room and a snug. Convenient for Whipsnade Zoo. 🏚 🏡 ◖▶ ♣ P

Sutton

John O'Gaunt Inn

30 High Street
☎ (01767) 260377
12–3, 7–11; 12–3, 7–10.30 Sun
Greene King IPA, Abbot Ⓗ
Attractive, rural pub close to the village ford. An interesting range of bar meals includes Sun lunch (no food Sun eve). The Northamptonshire skittle table and floodlit petanque court are well used by local leagues. 🏚 Q 🏡 ◖▶ 🍴 ♣ P

Tebworth

Queen's Head

The Lane ☎ (01525) 874101
11–3 (3.30 Sat), 6 (7 Sat)–11; 12–3, 7–10.30 Sun
Adnams Broadside Ⓖ; **Wells Eagle** Ⓗ
Fine village local with two small bars and jovial hosts; popular with locals and visitors alike. Good value food (not served Sun).
🏚 🏡 ◖▶ 🍴 ♣ P

Tilsworth

Anchor

1 Dunstable Road
☎ (01525) 210289
11–11; 12–10.30 Sun
Marston's beers Ⓗ
Lively village free house with a large, L-shaped lounge bar catering for all ages. The spacious garden features a popular adventure playground. The pub was

bought by Marston's in summer 1997 but the beer range had not been confirmed as we went to press.
🏚 🏡 ◖ ▶ & ♣ P

Try also: Red Lion, Stanbridge (Free)

Toddington

Bedford Arms

64 High Street
☎ (01525) 873503
12–3, 6–11 (11–11 summer Sat); 12–4, 7–10.30 (12–10.30 summer) Sun
Wells Eagle Ⓗ
Attractive pub both outside and in with two warm, comfortable lounge bars and a large garden with good facilities for children. Other beers are occasionally available.
🏚 🏡 ◖▶ ♣ P

Sow & Pigs

19 Church Square
☎ (01525) 873089
11–11; 12–10.30 Sun
Greene King IPA, Abbot, seasonal beers Ⓗ
19th-century commercial inn, little changed in many ways. The decor is strong on pigs, including a stained-glass window in the bar. Occasional live music. In every edition of the Guide. 🏚 Q 🏡 ♣ P

Totternhoe

Cross Keys

261 Castle Hill Road
☎ (01525) 220434
11.30–3.30, 6–11; 11.30–11 Sat; 12–3.30, 7–10.30 Sun
Boddingtons Bitter; Flowers IPA; guest beers Ⓗ
Picturesque, thatched pub dating back to the early 15th century and still with many

original beams. The large garden features a damson orchard and a children's play area and has extensive views over the Aylesbury Vale. No food Sun eve. 🏚 Q 🏡 ◖▶ ♣ P

Old Farm

16 Church Road
☎ (01582) 661294
12–3, 6–11; 12–4, 7–10.30 Sun
Fuller's Chiswick, London Pride, ESB, seasonal beers Ⓗ
Old village pub with a popular public bar, featuring a low, boarded ceiling, and a dining area with a large inglenook.
🏡 ◖▶ 🍴 ♣ P

Wilstead

Woolpack

2 Bedford Road
☎ (01234) 741694
12–3, 6–11; 12–11 Sat; 12–10.30 Sun
Greene King IPA, Abbot Ⓗ
Traditional village pub, well modernised to reflect the history of this 300-year-old building. Good range of meals in the restaurant area.
🏚 🏡 ◖▶ & ♣ P

Wootton

Chequers

47 Hall End Road (Wootton turn off A421, past school, then ½ mile on right)
☎ (01234) 768394
11–2.30 (4 Sat), 5.30 (6 Sat)–11; 12–4, 7–10.30 Sun
Wells Eagle, Bombardier; guest beers Ⓗ
16th-century coaching inn and restaurant, boasting three real fires, oak beams and brasses. Large garden. Boules played in summer. Monthly guest beers. No meals Mon.
🏚 Q 🏡 ◖▶ 🍴 ♣ P

Charles Wells Brewery of Bedford chalking up another advertising success.

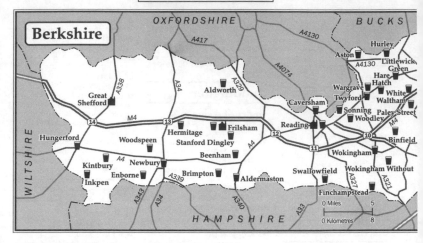

Berkshire

Aldermaston

Hind's Head
Wasing Lane
☎ (0118) 971 2194
11–2.30, 5–11; 12–3, 7–10.30 Sun
Courage Best Bitter; Fuller's London Pride; guest beer Ⓗ
Imposing, red-brick inn popular as an overnight stop for businessmen (quality accommodation) and offering a varied and ever-changing menu of good food. Evidence of a former brewery can still be seen and a miniature gaol is still in use, although it has not been used since 1865.
🏧 Q 🕸 🚲 ◖ ▶ P

Aldworth

Bell Inn ☆
☎ (01635) 578272
11–3, 6–11; 12–3, 7–10.30 Sun; closed Mon
Arkell's 3B, Kingsdown; Morrells Bitter, Mild; West Berkshire Good Old Boy Ⓗ
Ancient, unspoiled village pub popular with walkers from the nearby Ridgeway. It features a big garden, two simple bars with a single, central servery, and an outside gents, and has been run by the same family for 200 years. No carpets, fruit machines or piped music, but excellent filled rolls and a friendly welcome. Good Old Boy is sold as Old Tyler.
🏧 Q 🕸 ◖ ▶ ♣ P

Ascot

Stag
63 High Street (A329)
☎ (01344) 21622
11–3, 5.30–11; 11–11 Fri & Sat; 12–3, 7.30–10.30 Sun
Greene King IPA, Abbot, seasonal beers Ⓗ

Victorian-style, one-bar pub, handy for the racecourse. No meals Sun. 🕸 ◖ ▶ ✸

Aston

Flower Pot Hotel
Ferry Lane (off A4130 at Remenham Hill)
☎ (01491) 574721
11–3, 6–11; 12–3, 7–10.30 Sun
Brakspear Mild, Bitter, Old (winter), Special, OBJ Ⓗ
Follow narrow country lanes to find this splendid village pub which also has river access and its own moorings on the Thames. The locals' bar has a fishing theme, while the lounge/dining room has an interesting piece of furniture! Busy at regatta time. No eve meals Sun.
🏧 Q 🎄 🕸 🚲 ◖ ▶ 🍴 ♣ P

Beenham

Stocks Inn
☎ (0118) 971 3127
12–2 (2.30 Sat), 7–11; 12–3, 7–10.30 Sun
Archers Village; Hook Norton Best Bitter; Shepherd Neame Spitfire; Wells Bombardier; guest beer Ⓗ
Country pub dating back to 1720, built with Flemish bonded brick. Huddle in front of the fireplace and admire the landlord's WWII memorabilia. Renowned Sun roast lunch. Eve meals if booked.
🏧 Q 🕸 ◖ ♣ P

Try also: **Six Bells** (Free)

Binfield

Victoria Arms
Terrace Road North (300 yds N of Binfield crossroads)
☎ (01344) 483856
11.30–3, 6 (6.30 Sat)–11; 12–3, 7–10.30 Sun

Fuller's Chiswick, London Pride, ESB, seasonal beers Ⓗ
Village pub with an open-plan bar, well patronised by locals and office staff from nearby Bracknell. Note the large bottle collection on the rafters in the main seating area. No food Sun eve (quiz instead). 🕸 ◖ ▶ ♣ P

Brimpton

Three Horseshoes
Brimpton Lane
☎ (0118) 971 2183
11–3, 6–11; 12–3, 7–10.30 Sun
Fuller's London Pride, ESB; Wadworth 6X or Adnams Bitter Ⓗ
Pleasant Victorian, two-bar village pub built by Mays of Basingstoke. The panelled lounge with fine old clock and old prints contrasts with a larger public bar offering darts, pool and a jukebox. No meals Sun. Q 🕸 ◖ 🍴 ♣ P

Caversham

Clifton Arms
12 Gosbrook Road (off A4155)
☎ (0118) 947 1775
11–11; 12–10.30 Sun
Brakspear Bitter, Special, seasonal beers Ⓗ
Recently refurbished local with two comfortable bars and a friendly atmosphere, just off the shopping centre and not far from the Thames. Sun lunches served 12–6 (no meals Sun eve). Q 🕸 ◖ ▶ 🍴 ♣ P

Colnbrook

Punchbowl
Old Bath Road
☎ (01753) 682683
12–3, 5–11; 12–11 Fri; 11–11 Sat; 12–4, 8–10.30 Sun
Highgate Saddlers; guest beer Ⓗ

Small pub serving an industrial estate and the local community. The first and last pub in Berkshire. Eve meals end at 8. ❀ ◖ ▶ ♣ P

Datchet

Royal Stag
The Green ☎ (01753) 548218
11–11; 12–10.30 Sun
Ind Coope Burton Ale; Marston's Pedigree; Tetley Bitter; guest beer Ⓗ
A pub since the mid-17th century, popular with all ages. A mysterious blue hand print appears in the window next to the church yard.
🚲 ❀ ◖ ▶ 🚲 ⇌ ♣ P

Enborne

Craven Arms
Redihill OS427647
☎ (01635) 253336
11–11; 12–10.30 Sun
Wadworth IPA, 6X, Old Timer, seasonal beers; guest beers Ⓗ
Attractive, old country pub serving good food and catering well for families (fully-equipped, large family garden). Its one main bar has smaller areas off, including a family area with toys. No food winter Sun eves.
🚼 ❀ ◖ ▶ & ♣ P

Eton

Watermans Arms
Brocas Street (off High St, near Windsor Bridge)
☎ (01753) 861001
11–2.30 (3 Sat), 6–11; 12–3, 7–10.30 Sun
Brakspear Bitter; Courage Best Bitter, Directors; John Smith's Bitter; Theakston Best Bitter, Old Peculier Ⓗ
Popular, riverside local with a busy restaurant and an

extensive menu (try the pies). No food Sun eve. The no-smoking room has a boating theme. Families welcome.
🚲 Q ◖ ▶ ⇌ (Windsor Central/Riverside) ♣ ⚭

Finchampstead

Queens Oak
Church Lane (off B3016)
☎ (0118) 973 4855
11.30–2.30, 6–11; 12–3, 7–10.30 Sun
Brakspear Bitter, Old, Special, OBJ (winter)**; Theakston XB** Ⓗ
Attractive rural pub in a quiet village setting with a long-established no-smoking room. Interesting key fob collection. The large garden is great for families and there are regular summer barbecues. No food Sun eve. Q ❀ ◖ ▶ 🍴 ♣ ⚭

Frilsham

Pot Kiln
On Yattendon–Bucklebury road; ignore signs to Frilsham
OS552731 ☎ (01635) 201366
12–2.30 (not Tue), 6.30–11; 12–3, 7–10.30 Sun
Arkell's 3B; Morland Original, Old Speckled Hen; West Berkshire Brick Kiln Bitter Ⓗ
CAMRA regional *Pub of the Year* 1997: a proudly old-fashioned rarity, isolated among meadows and woodland. No fruit machines nor jukebox, but the walls of the four small bars often ring with the sounds of good company. Brick Kiln Bitter, brewed in the grounds, is found only here. Filled rolls only Sun and Tue.
🚲 Q ❀ ◖ ▶ P ⚭

Hare Hatch

Queen Victoria
Blakes Lane (off A4)
☎ (0118) 940 2477
11–3, 5.30–11; 12–10.30 Sun
Brakspear Bitter, Old, Special Ⓗ
Convivial, low-ceilinged, 17th-century pub, an oasis of calm civility just off the busy main road. Drinkers and diners mix well and well-behaved children are accepted. Rugby banter is also encouraged!
❀ ◖ ▶ ♣ P ⚭

Hermitage

Lamb
Long Lane (B4009)
☎ (01635) 200348
11 (11.30 Sat)–2.30, 6 (5.30 Fri)–11; 12–3, 7–10.30 Sun
Boddingtons Bitter; Flowers IPA, Original; guest beer Ⓗ
This area was noted for fine brickmaking and this building is an attractive example of local

Flemish bond. The three bars inside are now knocked into one comfortable lounge, but the atmosphere is determinedly a village local.
❀ ◖ ▶ P ⚭

Holyport

Belgian Arms
Holyport Street
☎ (01628) 34468
11–3, 5.30 (7 winter Sat)–11; 12–3, 7–10.30 Sun
Brakspear Bitter, Special Ⓗ
Unspoilt village pub overlooking a duck pond. Once past the 100-year-old wisteria, you enter an L-shaped bar leading to a conservatory and dining area. Over the years the pub has been a hat maker's, a fire station and a Wesleyan chapel. No food Sun eve.
🚲 Q ❀ ◖ ▶ P

Hungerford

Downgate
13 Down View, Park Street (off A338) ☎ (01488) 682708
11–3, 6–11; 12–3, 7–10.30 Sun
Arkell's 3B, Kingsdown, seasonal beers Ⓗ
Quiet pub on the edge of Hungerford Common, with a friendly village inn atmosphere. A small, intimate dining area is a few steps down from the bar. No eve meals Sun or Mon. Pleasant summer drinking.
🚲 Q ❀ ◖ ▶ ⇌ ♣ P

Hungerford Club
3 The Croft (off Church St, turn right under rail bridge)
☎ (01488) 682357
7–11; 12–3, 7–11 Sat; 12–3, 7–10.30 Sun
Flowers Original; Morland Original; guest beers Ⓗ
From the outside this club looks like a private house on the lovely church green. Inside is a comfy, pub-type lounge where friendly conversation is unavoidable. In summer, watch the bowls or tennis. Show this guide or CAMRA membership to be signed in.
❀ ⇌ ♣ P

Hurley

Red Lion
Applehouse Hill, Henley Road (A4130) ☎ (01628) 824433
11–3, 5.30–11; 12–3, 7–10.30 Sun

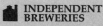

INDEPENDENT BREWERIES

Butts: Great Shefford

Reading Lion: Reading

West Berkshire: Frilsham

Brakspear Bitter, Old, Special H
Quiet, spacious, comfortably furnished, single-bar pub with a large garden. Set in pleasant countryside, it is especially popular in summer. Good selection of meals (not served Sun or Mon). ♨ Q ❀ ◖ ▶ P

Inkpen

Swan

Craven Road, Lower Inkpen (Hungerford–Combe road)
OS359643 ☎ (01488) 668326
12–2.30 (11–3 Sat), 7–11; 12–3, 7–10.30 Sun; closed Mon and winter Tue
Adnams Mild, Bitter; Butts Bitter, Barbus Barbus; guest beers H
Large, 16th-century inn near famous Combe gibbet in an area popular with walkers. Organic food is a speciality; the pub shop (open Wed–Sun) sells organic food and drink. Good range of games. Three open fires.
♨ Q ❀ ◖ ▶ ♣ ⌂ P ⟋

Kintbury

Dundas Arms

53 Station Road (off A4)
☎ (01488) 658263
11–2.30, 6–11; 12–2.30, 7–10.30 Sun
Draught Bass; Morland Original; Shepherd Neame Spitfire; guest beer H
18th-century inn by Kennet & Avon Canal (lock 78), with a good outside area from which horse-drawn barges can be seen in summer. Very good (if pricey) home-made bar and restaurant meals (no food Sun or Mon eve)
Q ❀ ⇘ ◖ ▶ ⇌ P

Littlewick Green

Cricketers

Coronation Road
☎ (01628) 822888
11–3, 5.30–11; 11–11 Sat; 12–10.30 Sun
Brakspear Bitter; Fuller's London Pride; guest beers H
Charming pub overlooking the green in a picturesque village. Decorated with cricketing memorabilia, it is split into three drinking areas, one with a pool table, another with a large log fire. ♨ ❀ ◖ ▶ ♣ P

Maidenhead

Hand & Flowers

15 Queen Street
☎ (01628) 23800
11–3, 5 (7 Sat)–11; 12–3, 7–10.30 Sun
Brakspear Bitter, Old, Special, OBJ H
Small, lovingly preserved, Victorian town-centre pub with no music or machines. The food is excellent, though understated. ♨ Q ◖ ⇌ ♣

Vine

20 Market Street
☎ (01628) 782112
11–11; 12–10.30 Sun
Brakspear Bitter, Old, Special H
Town-centre pub of average appearance and size. No eve meals Sun. ❀ ◖ ▶ ⇌ ♣

Moneyrow Green

White Hart

☎ (01628) 21460
11–11; 12–3, 7.30–10.30 Sun
Morland Original, Old Speckled Hen; guest beer H
Large, attractive, well-furnished, 400-year-old rural pub with two bars, a recent winner of Morland's cellarmanship award. No food at weekends.
♨ ❀ ◖ ⇘ ⟺ ♣ P

Newbury

Lock, Stock & Barrel

104 Northbrook Street (next to canal bridge)
☎ (01635) 42730
11–11; 12–10.30 (12–3, 7–10.30 winter) Sun
Fuller's Chiswick, London Pride, ESB; guest beer H
Spacious, one-bar pub just off the main shopping street, with a pleasant patio on the Kennet & Avon Canal and a rooftop terrace. No-smoking area lunchtimes. Wheelchair WC next to the bar.
❀ ◖ ▶ ⇘ ⇌ ⟋

Oakley Green

Old Red Lion

Oakley Green Road (B3024, off A308)
☎ (01753) 863892
11–3.30, 5–11; 12–10.30 Sun
Ansells Bitter; Draught Bass; Flowers IPA; Tetley Bitter H
Popular, 400-year-old country inn where the separate restaurant boasts an extensive menu of home-cooked food. Aunt Sally can be played in the garden in summer. No fruit machines or loud music. The real fire dominates the entrance to the bar.
♨ Q ❀ ◖ ▶ ⇘ P

Old Windsor

Jolly Gardeners

92–94 St Lukes Road
☎ (01753) 865944
11–11; 12–5, 7–10.30 (12–10.30 summer) Sun
Courage Best Bitter; Ushers Founders, seasonal beers H
Traditional village pub with one U-shaped bar. Games include shove-ha'penny. Small car park. ❀ P

Oxford Blue

Crimp Hill Road (off A308)
☎ (01753) 861954
11–11; 12–10.30 Sun
Adnams Bitter; Tetley Bitter; Wadworth 6X H
Pub established in 1802 by a retired soldier who named it after his regiment. Split into a number of drinking areas, one of which functions as a family room, and one as a restaurant (food all day). Large collection of aircraft memorabilia.
⇘ ❀ ⇘ ◖ ▶ ♣ P

Paley Street

Royal Oak

On B3024, 1 mile W of A330
☎ (01628) 20541
11.30–3, 5.30–11; 12–3, 7–10.30 Sun
Fuller's Chiswick, London Pride, ESB H
Small, single-bar pub in a rural location, with a separate restaurant area. Reliant on lunchtime trade, the bar is cosy and quiet eves. ♨ Q ◖ ▶ P

Reading

Corn Exchange

10 Forbury Road (opp. rail station) ☎ (0118) 951 2340
11–11; 12–3, 7–11 Sat; closed Sun
Fuller's Chiswick, London Pride, ESB, seasonal beers H
An old corn merchant's building imaginatively converted into a split-level pub, with much of the old equipment still in place. Mainly business people at lunchtime/early eve, but a good mix otherwise. The lower bar can be hired for functions. No eve meals Fri or Sat.
◖ ▶ ⇘ ⇌ ⟋

Dove

119 Orts Road (near canal, E of centre; behind college, off King's Rd) ☎ (0118) 935 2556
11–2.30, 5.30–11; 11–11 Sat; 12–3, 7–10.30 Sun
Brakspear Bitter, Old, Special H
One of few surviving pubs in the partially re-developed Newtown area: a friendly, community local with a reputation for live music – blues Wed, Irish folk Thu, American old time Fri, various Sat. Bar billiards and pool played. No meals Sat or Sun.
◖ ♣ P

Fisherman's Cottage

224 Kennetside (on canal bank, E of centre; off Orts Rd, near college) ☎ (0118) 957 1553
11.30–3 (may extend summer), 5.30–11; 11–11 Fri & Sat; 12–3, 7–10.30 Sun

Fuller's Chiswick, London Pride, ESB, seasonal beers Ⓗ
Extended pub by Blakes Lock on the Kennet & Avon Canal – a pleasant walk from the town centre and popular with locals, students and river users. No eve meals Tue.
🏠 ☎ 🏠 🌣 ◖ ▶ ♣ P

Hop Leaf
163–165 Southampton Street (A33 one-way system heading towards centre)
☎ (0118) 931 4700
12 (4 Mon)–11; 12–10.30 Sun
Hop Back GFB, Summer Lightning, Thunderstorm; Reading Lion Hop Leaf, seasonal beers; guest beers Ⓗ
Very friendly, community pub which attracts and welcomes all. The Reading Lion ales are brewed on site. Well worth the walk up the hill from the centre. ☎ ♣ ○

Horse & Jockey
120 Castle Street (A4, just W of inner ring road, near the police station)
☎ (0118) 959 0172
11–11; 12–10.30 Sun
Archers Village; guest beers Ⓗ
Friendly, one-bar pub, local CAMRA *Pub of the Year 1996*, serving three changing guest ales. Excellent food at sensible prices. Well worth finding.
🏠 ◖ ▶ ○ 🍺

Retreat
8 St John's Street (E of centre, close to King's Rd/Queen's Rd jct)
☎ (0118) 957 1593
11–11; 12–10.30 Sun
Flowers IPA; Marston's Pedigree; Wadworth 6X; guest beers Ⓗ
The name says it all – an unspoilt local which provides a welcome escape from the designer pubs of the town centre. Guest ales often come from Hampshire Brewery.
🍺 ♣

Try also: Back of Beyond, King's Rd (Wetherspoons); **Hobgoblin,** Broad St (Wychwood)

Slough

Moon & Spoon
86 High Street (opp. library)
☎ (01753) 531650
11–11; 12–10.30 Sun
Courage Directors; Theakston Best Bitter, XB; Younger Scotch; guest beers Ⓗ
Large Wetherspoons pub converted from building society premises in 1995. Good mix of clientele; it can get crowded weekend eves. Welcoming and safe for lone women. Q ◖ ▶ ⇌ ○ P 🍺

Red Cow
140 Albert Street
☎ (01753) 522614
11.30–3, 5 (7 Sat)–11; 12–4, 7–10.30 Sun
Courage Best Bitter, Directors; guest beers Ⓗ
Oak-beamed ex-farmhouse built in 1547, now a true community local. Quiz Tue.
🌣 ◖ ▶ ♣ P

Three Tuns
124 Bath Road (A4/A355 jct)
☎ (01753) 521911
11–11; 12–10.30 Sun
Courage Best Bitter; John Smith's Bitter; Theakston Best Bitter, XB Ⓗ
Friendly, one-bar local, a mile west of the centre. 🌣 ◖ ▶ ♣ P

Wheatsheaf
15 Albert Street
☎ (01753) 522018
11–11; 12–10.30 Sun
Fuller's Chiswick, London Pride, ESB, seasonal beers Ⓗ
Single bar pub attracting mainly thirty-somethings. The garden is tented over and heated in winter. Note the red phone box in the bar and pillar box in the garden. Try the 'Pies to Die For'. Live music weekend eves. 🌣 ◖ ▶

Sonning

Bull
High Street (off A4)
☎ (0118) 969 3901
11–3, 5.30 (6 Sat)–11; 12–3, 7–10.30 (12–10.30 summer) Sun
Gale's Best Bitter, IPA, HSB, seasonal beers; guest beers Ⓗ
Beautiful, historic inn in a lovely setting by a church and near the Thames. Its classic olde-English interior has beams and an inglenook and is divided into a locals' bar and a lounge and no-smoking restaurant. The type of pub Americans adore!
🏠 ☎ 🌣 🏠 ◖ ▶ 🍺 P

Stanford Dingley

Bull
☎ (0118) 974 4409
12–3 (not Mon), 7–11; 12–3, 7–10.30 Sun
Draught Bass; Brakspear Bitter; West Berkshire Skiff, Good Old Boy Ⓗ
Unspoilt, two-bar pub with a timber-framed tap room, dating back to the 15th century. Excellent menu. Well worth finding. 🏠 Q 🌣 ◖ ▶ ♣ P

Sunninghill

Duke's Head
Upper Village Road (off Oriental Rd, off B3020)
☎ (01344) 26949
11–11; 12–10.30 Sun

Greene King IPA, Abbot, seasonal beers; Marston's Pedigree Ⓗ
Comfortable, nicely furnished village local with friendly staff and an extensive menu – but it's a pub first. Children welcome in the no-smoking snug. No eve meals Sun.
Q 🍺 ◖ ▶ P 🍺

Swallowfield

Crown
The Street (off B3349)
☎ (0118) 988 3260
11–3, 6–11; 12–3.30, 7–10.30 Sun
Morland Original, seasonal beers *or* guest beers Ⓗ
The long-serving licensees (over 30 years) ensure that all are welcome in this traditional village pub which has two well-kept bars where good banter is appreciated. Sea anglers are especially welcome. Veggy/vegan and genuine, home-made food is available (eve meals Thu–Sat).
🏠 Q 🌣 ◖ ▶ 🍺 P

Twyford

Duke of Wellington
High Street ☎ (0118) 934 0456
11.30–2.30 (3 Sat), 5 (6 Sat)–11; 12–3, 7–10.30 Sun
Brakspear Mild, Bitter, Old (winter), Special, OBJ Ⓗ
Ever-popular local with a good mix of clients in its small, cosy lounge and recently extended bar. The large garden at the rear is ideal for families.
🌣 ◖ 🍺 ⇌ P

Wargrave

Bull
High Street ☎ (0118) 940 3120
11.30–2.30, 6–11; 12–3, 7–10.30 Sun
Brakspear Bitter, Special Ⓗ
15th-century village pub with a huge open fire and oak beams. There is a strong food trade but drinkers are always welcome. No eve meals Sun. 🏠 Q 🌣 🏠 ◖ ▶ ⇌ (summer only Sun)

White Waltham

Beehive
Waltham Road
☎ (01628) 822877
11–2.30 (3 Sat), 5.30–11; 12–3, 7–10.30 Sun
Brakspear Bitter; Flowers IPA, Original; guest beers Ⓗ
Thriving, friendly local opposite the cricket pitch and near a former WWII airfield. Sympathetically refurbished, it retains two bars and stages wide-ranging social events, including beer and cider festivals and brewery trips. Good value food.
🏠 Q 🌣 ◖ ▶ 🍺 ♣ ○ P

Windsor

Prince Christian
11 Kings Road
☎ (01753) 860980
11–3, 6–11; 12–2.30, 7–10.30 Sun
**Brakspear Bitter; Fuller's
London Pride** H
Free house just off the tourist
trail, with a somewhat Irish
flavour. Popular with staff
from nearby council offices.
No food weekends.
◖ ⇌

Swan
9 Mill Lane, Clewer Village
(just off A308 near A332 jct)
☎ (01753) 862069
6–11; 12–3, 6–11 Sat; 12–3, 7–10.30
Sun
**Boddingtons Bitter;
Courage Best Bitter; Fuller's
London Pride; guest
beer** (occasional) H
Haunted, 16th-century pub.
The function room was once a
court house with an attached
mortuary (now the kitchen). A
small and friendly community
inn with a YHA hostel close by.
Skittles is occasionally played.
✿ ⌂ ▲ ♣ P

Vansittart Arms
105 Vansittart Road
☎ (01753) 865988
11–11; 12–10.30 Sun
**Fuller's Chiswick, London
Pride, ESB, seasonal beers** H
Comfortable pub away from
the town centre, but it can get
very crowded. A good range of
reasonably priced food is
available.
♨ ✿ ◖ ▶ ♣

Wokingham

Duke's Head
56 Denmark Street
☎ (0118) 978 0316
11.30–3, 5.30 (5 Fri, 6 Sat)–11; 12–3,
7–10.30 Sun
Brakspear Bitter, Special H
Comfortable town pub
originally converted from three
cottages around 1791. Its one
bar has distinct drinking areas.
Skittle alley available for group
hire. No food Sun. ✿ ◖ ⇌ ♣ P

Queen's Head
23 The Terrace (A329, top of
Station Rd) ☎ (0118) 978 1221
11–3, 5.30–11; 12–3, 7–10.30 Sun
**Morland IPA, Original, Old
Masters, Old Speckled Hen,
seasonal beers** H
Charming, late-16th-century
pub in an elevated position.
The low-ceilinged bar is used
by locals and business regulars
who take an active role in the
many sporting activities.
Hidden garden at the rear
(Aunt Sally played). Excellent
lunches Mon–Sat. ✿ ◖ ⇌ ♣

Try also: Ship, Peach St
(Fuller's)

Wokingham
Without

Crooked Billet
Honey Hill (off B3430 2 miles
SE of Wokingham) OS826667
☎ (0118) 978 0438
11–11; 12–10.30 Sun
**Brakspear Mild, Bitter,
Special, OBJ** H
Splendid country pub
approached in one direction by

a ford and with a fishing lake
at the rear. The single bar
serves the main drinking area
and also a separate restaurant
which has an imaginative
menu at reasonable prices. No
eve meals Sun. A pub worth
finding! ♨ Q ✿ ◖ ▶ ♿ ♣ P

Woodley

Inn on the Park
Woodford Park, Haddon Drive
(off Butts Hill Rd)
☎ (0118) 962 8655
11–2.30, 6–11; 11–11 Tue, Fri & Sat;
12–10.30 Sun
**Brakspear Bitter, Special;
guest beers** H
Comfortable, modern lounge
bar in a sports centre, with a
good mix of locals and visiting
'athletes'. The beer range is
excellent for the area although
the three guest ales tend to
come from the major brewers.
✿ ♿ P

Woodspeen

Five Bells
Lambourn Road (2 miles NW
of Newbury on the old
Lambourn road) OS451687
☎ (01635) 48763
11.30–2.30, 6–11; 12–3, 7–10.30 Sun
**Morland Original; guest
beers** H
Rural one-bar Victorian pub
near the famous Watermill
Theatre, with walks along the
Lambourn Valley close at
hand. Good selection of bar
and restaurant meals all day.
Guest beers are from the
Morland list.
Q ✿ ♨ ◖ ▶ ♿ ♣ P ✗

WRING THE SWAN'S NECK

The plague of the dreaded tight sparkler continues to sweep across
southern Britain. The swan neck beer engine spout, with its
plastic sparkler at the end, is doing untold damage to fine southern
brews. This means of whipping up a thick, creamy head, perfect for
the enjoyment of northern brews like Boddingtons Bitter and Tetley
Bitter, is increasingly being applied to beers which are not produced
for such heavy-handed treatment. Classic southern ales like Brakspear Bitter, Young's Bitter and Fuller's London Pride are being
mangled by the tight sparkler, which reduces bitterness levels and
knocks all the natural fizz out of the beer and into the foaming head.
The gesture of removing the sparkler on request is often not enough
to save the beer, if much of its natural gas has been vented off in the
cellar in preparation for the sparkler frenzy to follow. Flat beer is no
good to anyone. So CAMRA's plea to publicans is this: Please don't
aim to serve all beers with a big head. Treat each beer on its merits
and with respect. Your customers will return the compliment.

Buckinghamshire

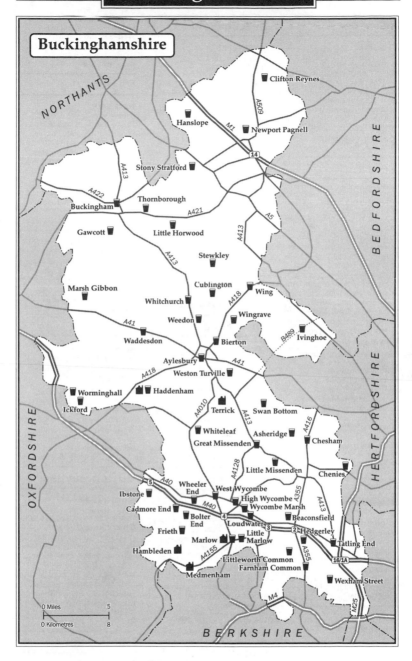

Buckinghamshire

NORTHANTS

BEDFORDSHIRE

HERTFORDSHIRE

OXFORDSHIRE

BERKSHIRE

Clifton Reynes
Hanslope
Newport Pagnell
Stony Stratford
Buckingham
Thornborough
Gawcott
Little Horwood
Stewkley
Marsh Gibbon
Cublington
Wing
Whitchurch
Wingrave
Weedon
Ivinghoe
Waddesdon
Bierton
Aylesbury
Weston Turville
Worminghall
Haddenham
Ickford
Terrick
Swan Bottom
Whiteleaf
Asheridge
Great Missenden
Chesham
Little Missenden
Chenies
Ibstone
Wheeler End
West Wycombe
Cadmore End
High Wycombe
Wycombe Marsh
Bolter End
Beaconsfield
Frieth
Loudwater
Hedgerley
Marlow
Little Marlow
Tatling End
Hambleden
Littleworth Common
Farnham Common
Wexham Street
Medmenham

0 Miles 5
0 Kilometres 8

A509 · M1 · 14 · A413 · A422 · A421 · A5 · A413 · A413 · A418 · B489 · A41 · A418 · A4010 · A413 · A4128 · A416 · A40 · M40 · A355 · A413 · A4155 · A355 · 16/1A · M4 · M25 · 5 · 4 · 3 · 2

INDEPENDENT BREWERIES

Chiltern: Terrick	**Rebellion**: Marlow	**Vale**: Haddenham
Old Luxters: Hambleden	**Trueman's**: Medmenham	

39

Asheridge

Blue Ball
1½ miles NW of Chesham
☎ (01494) 758263
12–2.30, 5.30 (4 Fri)–11; 12–11 Sat;
12–4, 7.30–10.30 Sun
Beer range varies Ⓗ
Set in beautiful countryside,
this family-run pub is a true
free house with a range of four
constantly changing beers. Try
the home-made soup.
🍴 ❀ ◖ ▲ ♣ P

Aylesbury

Aristocrat
1–5 Wendover Road
☎ (01296) 415366
11–3, 4.45–11; 11.30–11 Fri; 11–11 Sat;
12–3, 7–10.30 Sun
**Fuller's Chiswick, London
Pride, ESB, seasonal beers** Ⓗ
This welcoming, popular pub
caters for all ages with a mix of
quizzes, discos and karaoke and
live music. Attractive garden
area, complete with hanging
baskets. No food Sun.
❀ 🛏 ◖ ▶ ♿ ⇌ ♣ P

Buckinghamshire
Yeoman
Cambourne Avenue, Bedgrove
☎ (01296) 86615
11–11; 12–10.30 Sun
**ABC Best Bitter; Marston's
Pedigree; Tetley Bitter** Ⓗ
Large, estate pub built in the
1960s. It caters for families,
offering the 'Feasting Fox'
range of good value meals.
Very sports-oriented (it fields
two football teams).
🛏 ❀ ◖ ♣ P

Queen's Head
1 Temple Square
☎ (01296) 415484
11–3, 5.30–11; 12–3, 8–10.30 Sun
**Greenalls Bitter, Original;
Shipstone's Bitter; guest
beers** Ⓗ
Friendly, village-type pub
dating back to the 16th century,
in the old part of Aylesbury:
two bars, one featuring an
interesting collection of water
jugs, and a small dining area.
❀ 🛏 ◖ ▶ ⇌

Ship
59 Walton Street
☎ (01296) 21888
11.30–2.30 (3 Fri), 5–11; 11.30–11 Sat;
12–3, 7–10.30 Sun
**Greene King Abbot;
Marston's Pedigree; Vale
Notley** Ⓗ
Cosmopolitan, friendly town
pub by the canal basin on the
Grand Union Canal, opposite
the 'Blue Leanie' office block.
Discos Thu; occasional bands.
The beer range may vary
slightly.
❀ ◖ 🛏 ♿ ⇌ ♣ P

Beaconsfield

Greyhound
35 Windsor End
☎ (01494) 673823
11–3, 5.30–11; 12–3, 7–10.30 Sun
**Courage Best Bitter; Fuller's
London Pride; Wadworth 6X;
guest beers** Ⓗ
Originally a drovers' inn, this
pub now has a popular
beamed lounge bar and a
restaurant area (no eve meals
Sun). No mobile phones!
Q ❀ ◖ ▶

Bierton

Bell
191 Aylesbury Road
☎ (01296) 436055
11–3, 6–11 (11–11 winter Sat); 12–3,
7–10.30 Sun
**Fuller's Chiswick, London
Pride, ESB, seasonal beers** Ⓗ
Small, two-bar pub within easy
reach of Aylesbury. Thriving
food trade, with an emphasis
on fish. All meals home-
prepared. ❀ ◖ ▲ ♣ P

Bolter End

Peacock
On B482 ☎ (01494) 881417
11.45–2.30, 6–11; 12–3 (closed eves)
Sun
**Draught Bass; Brakspear
Bitter; Tetley Bitter; guest
beer** Ⓗ
Pub dating from 1620, just west
of Lane End: one large room
with several distinct areas. The
emphasis is on freshly
prepared, home-cooked meals.
🍴 Q ❀ ◖ ▶ ♣ P ⚲ 🍺

Buckingham

New Inn
18 Bridge Street
☎ (01280) 815713
11–11; 12–3, 7–10.30 Sun
**Greene King IPA, Abbot,
seasonal beers** Ⓗ
Enterprising town pub with
regular jazz and blues sessions,
and a superbly equipped
children's room. It specialises
in Sri Lankan curries.
🛏 ❀ ◖ ♣ ♣

Try also: **Whale**, Market Hill
(Fuller's)

Cadmore End

Old Ship
Marlow Road (B482)
☎ (01494) 883496
12–2.30 (3 Sat), 6–11; 12–3, 7–10.30
Sun
**Brakspear Bitter, Old, Special,
OBJ** Ⓖ
Tiny, unspoilt, traditional
country pub where all beer is
carried up from the cellar. One

of the classic pubs in the
Hambleden Valley. Eve meals
Wed–Sat. Limited parking
nearby. Positioned below road
level – don't miss it!
🍴 Q ❀ ◖ ▶ ♣

Chenies

Red Lion
Off A404 ☎ (01923) 282722
11–2.30, 5.30–11; 12–3, 7–10.30 Sun
**Benskins BB; Vale Notley;
Wadworth 6X** Ⓗ
Friendly, busy, village free
house, which attracts drinkers
and diners (no chips!). Look for
the snug to the rear of the
dining room. House beer from
Rebellion. Q ❀ ◖ ▶ P

Chesham

King's Arms
1 King Street ☎ (01494) 774466
11–2.30, 5.30–11; 12–4, 7–10.30 Sun
**Brakspear Bitter; Marston's
Pedigree; guest beer**
(summer) Ⓗ
Traditional old pub also
serving Hoegaarden White
beer on draught.
🍴 ❀ ◖ ▶ ⊖ ♣

Queen's Head
120 Church Street, Old
Chesham ☎ (01494) 783773
11–2.30 (3 Sat), 5 (6 Sat)–11; 12–3,
7–10.30 Sun
**Brakspear Bitter, Special;
Fuller's London Pride,
seasonal beers** *or* **guest
beers** Ⓗ
Traditional, popular pub
which can be very busy. Thai
restaurant upstairs.
🍴 Q ❀ ◖ ▶ 🍴 ⊖ ♣ P ⚲

Clifton Reynes

Robin Hood
☎ (01234) 711574
12–2.30, 6.30–11; 12–2.30, 7–10.30 Sun
Greene King IPA, Abbot Ⓗ
An unpretentious frontage
hides a 16th-century pub with
two bars and a conservatory
extension (family room). A
very large garden houses a pet
corner and a horse paddock.
Note the fine leaded Greene
King window in the lounge.
Meals Tue–Sat.
🍴 Q 🛏 ❀ ◖ 🍴 ♣

Cublington

Unicorn
High Street ☎ (01296) 681261
12–3 (not Mon), 5.30–11; 12–3, 7–10.30
Sun
Beer range varies Ⓗ
Excellent, low-beamed village
local with open fires at each
end of a long bar, plus a dining
room (no meals Sun eve). Five
changing ales.
🍴 Q ❀ ◖ ▶ ▲ P

Farnham Common

Yew Tree
Collinswood Road (A355, 1 mile N of village)
☎ (01753) 643723
11–11; 12–10.30 Sun
Morland IPA, Original, Old Speckled Hen; guest beer Ⓗ
300-year-old, deservedly popular, country pub with a small, basic, public bar and a larger, food-dominated saloon (award-winning pies). Open at 7 Mon–Sat for breakfast. No-smoking dining area.
🏠 ❀ ◖ ▶ ⊟ ▲ ♣ P

Frieth

Prince Albert
Moor End (100 yds from Lane End–Frieth road) OS798906
☎ (01494) 881683
11–3 (2.30 Mon), 5.30 (6 Mon)–11; 12–3, 7–10.30 Sun
Brakspear Mild, Bitter, Old, Special Ⓗ
Pub which has appeared in the *Guide* 23 times, with a superb atmosphere, location and hospitality. Josie's platefuls are a bonus at lunchtime (no food Sun). 🏠 Q ❀ ◖ ♣

Gawcott

Cuckoo's Nest
Back Street ☎ (01280) 812092
11–3 (not Mon), 6–11; 12–2.30, 7–10.30 Sun
Hook Norton Best Bitter; guest beer Ⓗ
Good, traditional, two-bar village local. No food, but you may bring your own. Occasional live folk sessions. Limited parking.
🏠 Q ❀ ⊟ ♣ P

Great Missenden

Cross Keys
40 High Street
☎ (01494) 865373
11–3, 5–11; 12–3, 7–10.30 Sun
Fuller's Chiswick, London Pride, ESB, seasonal beers Ⓗ
400-year-old pub with high-back settles in the bar. The restaurant is the only eating area in the eve, thus preserving a good atmosphere elsewhere.
Q ❀ ◖ ▶ ⇌ ♣ P

Haddenham

Red Lion
2 Church End
☎ (01844) 291606
11.30–3, 6–11; 11–11 Sat; 12–10.30 Sun
ABC Best Bitter; Marston's Pedigree; Worthington Bitter Ⓗ
Straightforward, two-bar local, overlooking the village pond.
🏠 Q ❀ ◖ ♣ P

Rising Sun
9 Thame Road
☎ (01844) 291744
11–3, 5.30–11; 11–11 Fri & Sat; 12–3, 7–10.30 Sun
Wells Eagle; guest beers Ⓗ
Small village local, usually serving two interesting guest beers. Real cider in summer. No food Sun. ❀ ◖ ⇌ ♣ ○

Try also: **Bottle & Glass**, Gibraltar (Morrells)

Hanslope

Globe
50 Hartwell Road, Long Street OS795480 ☎ (01908) 510336
12–2.30 (11–3 Sat), 6 (5 Wed)–11; 12–3, 7–10.30 Sun
Banks's Bitter Ⓗ/Ⓔ; **guest beer** Ⓗ
Comfortably-appointed, two-bar pub with a dining room. Beer can be bought in two-pint jugs to avoid a crush at the bar. The lounge bar has a children's certificate. No meals Tue.
Q ❀ ◖ ▶ ♣ ○ P ⊟

Hedgerley

One Pin
One Pin Lane
☎ (01753) 643035
11–3.30, 5.30–11; 12–10.30 Sun
Courage Best Bitter, Directors; Morland Old Speckled Hen Ⓗ
Traditional, two-bar local with a loyal clientele. The landlord has been in residence for over 30 years. Wheelchair access is through the garden doors. Check out the Thai menu.
🏠 Q ❀ ◖ ▶ ⊟ & ♣ ○ P

White Horse
Village Lane ☎ (01753) 643225
11–3, 5.30 (6 Sat)–11; 12–3, 7–10.30 Sun
Greene King IPA; guest beers Ⓖ
Picturesque, family-owned free house with two rooms: a comfortable lounge and a wonderful, stone-floored, rustic bar. All food is home-cooked (eve meals Fri and Sat). At least four guest beers; cider in summer.
🏠 Q ❀ ⇌ ◖ ▶ ♣ ○ P

Try also: **Brickmould**, Village Lane (Free)

High Wycombe

Rose & Crown
Desborough Road
☎ (01494) 527982
11.30–3, 5–11; 11–11 Fri & Sat; 12–10.30 Sun
Courage Best Bitter; Gale's HSB; Marston's Pedigree; Wadworth 6X; guest beers Ⓗ
Wycombe's most interesting selection of beers, in an L-shaped, corner pub with a busy office trade lunchtime. Weekday meals.
🏠 ◖ ⇌ ♣ ○

Wycombe Wines
20 Crendon Street
☎ (01494) 437228
10–10; 12–2, 7–10 Sun
Adnams Broadside; Brakspear Special; Fuller's ESB; Hook Norton Old Hooky; guest beers Ⓖ
Popular off-licence with five or six beers and more at weekends. Bottled beers include a Belgian selection. ⇌

Ibstone

Fox
The Common (off M40 jct 5) OS752940 ☎ (01491) 638289
11–3, 6–11; 12–3, 7–10.30 Sun
Brakspear Bitter; Fuller's London Pride; guest beers Ⓗ
Popular pub, high up in the Chilterns, with quality hotel accommodation, and food in both the bar and restaurant. Large garden in superb countryside.
🏠 Q ❀ 🛏 ◖ ▶ ♣ P

Ickford

Rising Sun
Worminghall Road
☎ (01844) 339238
12–2.30 (3 Sat), 6–11; 12–3, 7–10.30 Sun
Greene King IPA; Hancock's HB; Tap & Spile Premium; guest beer Ⓗ
Attractive, 15th-century, timber-framed, thatched coaching inn. The varied menu includes an 'eat as much as you like' lunchtime buffet, and a children's selection.
🏠 ❀ ◖ ♣ P

Ivinghoe

Rose & Crown
Vicarage Lane
☎ (01296) 668472
12–2.30 (3 Sat), 6–11; 12–3, 7–10.30 Sun
Adnams Bitter; Greene King IPA; Morrells Mild; guest beer Ⓗ
Hard-to-find, street-corner local with a comfortable lounge and a lively atmosphere in bars on different levels. High quality food (no meals Wed lunch or Sun eve).
🏠 Q ❀ ◖ ▲ ♣

Little Horwood

Shoulder of Mutton
Church Street
☎ (01296) 712514
11–2.30 (not Mon), 6–11; 12–3, 7–10.30 Sun
ABC Best Bitter; Marston's Pedigree Ⓗ

Grade I, thatched building dating from the 19th century: an L-shaped bar with a tiled floor, low beams and a small dining area, and a friendly lived-in feel. Meals served Tue–Sat, plus Sun lunch.
Q ✿ ◁ ▶ P

Little Marlow

King's Head

Church Road (A4155)
☎ (01628) 484407
11–3, 5.30–11; 12–3, 7–10.30 Sun
Brakspear Bitter; Fuller's London Pride; guest beers Ⓗ
One-bar village pub with much character, where varied home-cooked meals are always available (new dining room). Families very welcome. Wheelchair WC.
🍺 ✿ ◁ ▶ ♿ P ⚥

Little Missenden

Crown

Off A413 ☎ (01494) 862571
11–2.30, 6–11; 12–3, 7–10.30 Sun
Adnams Broadside; Hook Norton Best Bitter; Morrells Varsity; guest beer Ⓗ/Ⓖ
Fine, traditional pub with a genuine welcome, in the same family for nearly 100 years. Large garden. Lunches Tue–Fri. 🍺 Q ✿ ◁ ♣ P

Littleworth Common

Beech Tree

Dorney Wood Road OS934860
☎ (01628) 661328
11–11; 12–10.30 Sun
Boddingtons Mild; Flowers IPA; Greenalls Bitter Ⓗ
Traditional pub in Burnham Beeches, one of the few in the area regularly serving mild. Unusual tables have inset crib boards. A good place to finish a country walk. No meals Sun eve. 🍺 ✿ ◁ ▶ ♣ P

Blackwood Arms

Common Lane OS936861
☎ (01753) 642169
11–2.30, 5.30–11; 11–11 Fri & Sat;
12–10.30 Sun
Beer range varies Ⓗ
A beer drinker's paradise: six handpumps dispense up to a thousand guest beers a year, all from independent breweries, in a single L-shaped bar where good value food is always available. Cider varies.
🍺 Q ✿ ◁ ▶ ⭕ P

Loudwater

Derehams Inn

5 Derehams Lane (N of A40)
OS903907 ☎ (01494) 530965
11–3, 5.30–11; 12–3, 7–10.30 Sun

Brakspear Bitter; Fuller's London Pride; Morrells Graduate; Taylor Landlord; Wadworth 6X; Young's Bitter Ⓗ
Cosy pub, recently extended at the back. Hard to find, it is very much a local. Weekday lunches. 🍺 ✿ ◁ ♣ P

Marlow

Carpenters Arms

15 Spittal Street
☎ (01628) 473649
11–11; 12–10.30 Sun
Morrells Bitter, Varsity Ⓗ
Thriving workingman's local of considerable character, acquired by Morrells in 1992. Fresh, home-made sandwiches always available. Small patio.
🍺 Q ✿ ⇌ ♣

Clayton Arms

161 Oxford Road, Quoiting Square (off A4155)
☎ (01628) 478620
11–3 (3.30 Sat), 5.30 (6 Sat)–11;
12–3.30, 7–10.30 Sun
Brakspear Bitter, Old, Special Ⓗ
Genuine local, unspoilt by its refurbishment. The public bar atmosphere has been retained (darts at one end); the function room now doubles as an area for families and bar billiards.
🍺 Q ✿ ◁ ⇌ ♣

Prince of Wales

1 Mill Road ☎ (01628) 482970
11–11; 12–10.30 Sun
Brakspear Bitter; Fuller's London Pride; guest beers Ⓗ
Friendly, backstreet local with two connecting bars – a comfortable public and a lounge with a dining area. Families welcome. Quiz Sun eve (no food Sun eve).
✿ ◁ ▶ ⇌ ♣ P

Marsh Gibbon

Greyhound

West Edge ☎ (01869) 277365
12–3.30, 6–11; 12–10.30 Sun
Fuller's London Pride; Greene King Abbot; Hook Norton Best Bitter Ⓗ
Listed building, probably of Tudor origin, with 17th-century brickwork (rebuilt after a fire in 1740). Popular for its Thai cuisine, steaks and quick business lunches. 🍺 Q ✿ ◁ ▶ P 🍴

Newport Pagnell

Bull

33 Tickford Street
☎ (01908) 216617
11.30–2.30 (3 Sat), 5.15 (6.15 Sat)–11;
12–3, 6.15–10.30 Sun
Beer range varies Ⓗ
Small, popular, two-bar free house near the Aston Martin

works. The adventurous variety of ales includes a house beer from Morrells. Reasonably priced meals (not served Sun eve). Cider in summer.
Q ✿ 🚫 ◁ ▶ ♣ ⭕

Cannon

50 High Street
☎ (01908) 211495
11–11; 12–10.30 Sun
Draught Bass; M&B Brew XI; Highgate Saddlers; guest beer Ⓗ
Town-centre free house with military decor. 🍺 ♣ P

Stewkley

Swan

High Street North
☎ (01525) 240285
12–3, 6–11; 12–3, 7–10.30 Sun
Courage Best Bitter, Directors; Wadworth 6X Ⓗ
Fine Georgian pub situated in the village centre. Good atmosphere in an old beamed interior with a dining area. Live music most Sun eves.
✿ ◁ ▶ 🔲 ♣ P

Stony Stratford

Vaults (Bull Hotel)

High Street ☎ (01908) 567104
12–11; 12–3, 6.30–10.30 Sun
Draught Bass; Eldridge Pope Royal Oak; Fuller's London Pride; Wadworth 6X; Worthington Bitter Ⓗ
Narrow, wood and brick, 18th-century bar with a warm welcome, featuring much Victoriana and breweriana.
✿ 🚫 ◁ ▶ ♿ ♣ P

Swan Bottom

Old Swan

OS902055 ☎ (01494) 837239
12–3, 6–11; 12–11 Sat; 12–10.30 (3 winter, closed eve) Sun
Adnams Bitter; Brakspear Bitter; Butcombe Bitter; Fuller's London Pride Ⓗ
Old country pub, tucked away in the Chilterns in a lovely setting, with a large garden. Opening times may vary. Eve meals Tue–Sat (daily summer).
🍺 Q ✿ ◁ ▶ ♣ P

Tatling End

Stag & Griffin

Oxford Road (A40)
☎ (01753) 883100
11.30–11; 12–10.30 Sun
Viking Stiffin Ale, Ale; guest beers Ⓗ
Pleasant roadside pub and restaurant. Five ales are usually available and the beer engines are visible through a glass panel in the bar. Various drinking areas. ✿ ◁ ▶ 🅰 ♣ P

Thornborough

Lone Tree
Buckingham Road (A421, S of village) ☎ (01280) 812334
11–2.30, 6.30–11; 12–2.30, 7–10.30 Sun
B&T Shefford Bitter; Black Sheep Best Bitter; Marston's HBC; guest beers H
Tiny roadside pub which is primarily food-oriented (booking essential), but has an ever-changing range of real ales, many rare in this area, plus Biddenden cider.
🏚 ❀ ◖ ▶ P ⌿ 🍺

Waddesdon

Lion
High Street ☎ (01296) 651227
12–2.30, 5.30–11; 12–3, 7–10.30 Sun
Draught Bass; Fuller's London Pride; guest beer H
Free house specialising in good quality meals, served at a leisurely pace, from a daily changing menu. Ample portions and plenty of elbow room at the large wooden tables (no meals Sun eve).
🏚 Q ❀ ◖ ▶ P

Weedon

Five Elms
Stockaway ☎ (01296) 641439
12–2.30 (3.30 Sat), 6–11; 12–4, 7–10.30 Sun
Greene King IPA; Wadworth 6X; guest beer H
Charming 16th-century house with small bars and a fire in each. The pub's history has been published in a 40-page book. No meals Sun.
🏚 Q ☎ ❀ ◖ ▶

Weston Turville

Chequers
☎ (01296) 613298
11.30–3 (not Mon), 6–11; 12–3, 7–10.30 Sun
Adnams Bitter; Greene King IPA; Marston's Pedigree; Vale Notley; Wadworth 6X H
Pub with a stone-flagged bar with a large open fireplace and a serene atmosphere, despite being busy at times. Popular restaurant (no eve food Sun or Mon; bar meals only Sat lunch; Sun lunches in the restaurant).
🏚 ❀ ◖ ▶ P

West Wycombe

George & Dragon
☎ (01494) 464414
11–2.30, 5.30–11; 11–11 Sat; 12–10.30 (12–3, 7–10.30 winter) Sun

Courage Best Bitter; guest beers H
18th-century coaching inn with an original timbered bar; noted for its food and garden.
🏚 Q ☎ ❀ 🚪 ◖ ▶ P

Wexham Street

Plough
☎ (01753) 663814
11–11; 12–10.30 Sun
Benskins BB; Greene King Abbot; Marston's Pedigree; Tetley Bitter; guest beer H
Pub originally three cottages dating from the 17th century, with a listed frontage. Children welcome in the restaurant for meals (not served winter Sun eves). 🏚 ☎ ❀ ◖ ▶ P ⌿

Try also: Rose & Crown, Stoke Poges (Morland)

Wheeler End

Chequers
Bullocks Farm Lane OS806926 ☎ (01494) 883070
11–2.30 (not Mon), 5.30–11; 11–11 Sat; 12–10.30 Sun
Draught Bass; Brains Dark; Brakspear Bitter; Fuller's London Pride; Greene King IPA; guest beers H
350-year-old, friendly country pub, with a good atmosphere. Very popular for lunches (not served Mon). Live music Tue eve. 🏚 Q ❀ ◖ ♣ P

Whitchurch

White Swan
10 High Street ☎ (01296) 641228
11–11; 12–3, 7–10.30 Sun
Fuller's Chiswick, London Pride, ESB, seasonal beers H
Attractive, part-thatched, traditional village local with a large, mature garden. Note the distinctive wood panelling in the lounge and the splendid grandfather clock. Small dining/meeting room. No meals Sun eve. 🏚 ❀ ◖ ▶ ♣ P

Whiteleaf

Red Lion
Upper Icknield Way (off A4010) ☎ (01844) 344476
11.30–3, 5.30 (6 Sat)–11; 12–3, 7–10.30 Sun
Brakspear Bitter; Hook Norton Best Bitter; Morland Old Speckled Hen; guest beer H
17th-century, secluded free house, with settles and interesting antiques (some

nautical). Ask to see the unusual wooden puzzles and games.
🏚 Q ❀ 🚪 ◖ ▶ P

Wing

Cock Inn
High Street ☎ (01296) 688214
11–3, 6–11; 12–3, 7–10.30 Sun
Draught Bass; Stones Bitter; guest beers H
Former coaching inn, partly dating back to the 16th century. Six ales, with a bias towards microbreweries; seasonal beer festivals. The 60-seater restaurant offers an extensive menu.
🏚 Q ❀ ◖ ▶ ♿ ♣ P

Wingrave

Rose & Crown
The Green ☎ (01296) 681257
11.30–3, 5.30–11; 11.30–11 Sat; 12–10.30 Sun
ABC Best Bitter; Draught Bass or Flowers Original; Tetley Bitter; guest beer H
Excellent, unspoilt, early 17th-century, three-bar local: a stone-flagged public bar, a small snug and a lounge. No meals Sun eve.
🏚 Q ❀ ◖ ▶ 🚭 ♣ P

Worminghall

Clifden Arms
75 Clifden Road OS640083 ☎ (01844) 339273
11.30 (12 winter)–3, 6 (7 winter)–11; 12–3, 7–10.30 Sun
Adnams Broadside; Fuller's ESB; Hook Norton Best Bitter; guest beer H
Picturesque village local, named after Viscount Clifden, lord of the manor. Off the beaten track, it prides itself on not offering 'fast food', only good food cooked as quickly as possible. Aunt Sally in the garden.
🏚 ❀ ◖ ▶ 🚭 ♿ ♣ P

Wycombe Marsh

General Havelock
114 Kingsland Road OS889915 ☎ (01494) 520391
11–2.30 (3 Fri), 5.30 (5 Fri)–11; 11–11 Sat; 12–4, 7–10.30 Sun
Fuller's Chiswick, London Pride, ESB, seasonal beers H
Traditional family pub, smart, friendly and noted for its lunches (eve meals Fri and Sat).
🏚 ❀ ◖ ▶ ♣ P

For further details of the beers listed in the pub entries, consult The Beers Index and The Breweries at the back of this book.

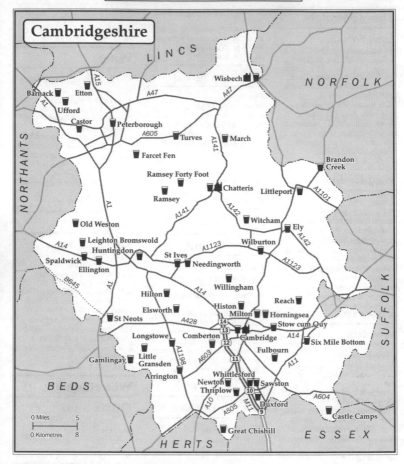

Cambridgeshire

LINCS

NORFOLK

Wisbech

Barnack • Etton
Ufford
Castor
Peterborough
A605
Turves • March
Farcet Fen
Ramsey Forty Foot
Chatteris • Littleport
Ramsey
Witcham
Old Weston
Ely
Leighton Bromswold
Huntingdon
Spaldwick
Ellington
St Ives
Needingworth
Willingham
Hilton
Reach
Elsworth
Histon • Milton
Horningsea
St Neots
Stow cum Quy
Longstowe
Comberton
Cambridge
Gamlingay
Fulbourn
Six Mile Bottom
Little Gransden
Arrington
Whittlesford
Newton
Thriplow
Sawston
Duxford
Castle Camps
Great Chishill
HERTS
ESSEX

NORTHANTS

BEDS

SUFFOLK

Brandon Creek

Wilburton

0 Miles 5
0 Kilometres 8

Arrington

Hardwicke Arms
96 Ermine Way (A1198)
☎ (01223) 208802
11–2, 6.30–11; 12–3, 7–10.30 Sun
**Greene King IPA; Hook
Norton Old Hooky; guest beer**
(occasional) Ⓗ
Welcoming hotel bar in a
roadside inn used by local and
passing trades. No food Sun
eve.
Q ☎ ⚜ ⇔ ◑ ▶ P ⚥

Barnack

Millstone
Millstone Lane (opp. Hills and
Hollows Common)
☎ (01780) 740296
11–2.30, 5.30 (6 Sat)–11; 12–4, 7–10.30
Sun
**Adnams Bitter; Everards
Tiger, Old Original; guest
beers** Ⓗ
Award-winning pub, in the
Guide since 1976: a stone-built
local with several alcoves.

Wheelchair WC. Separate
restaurant; function room at
the rear.
Q ☎ ⚜ ◑ ▶ ♿ P ⚥

Brandon Creek

Ship
On A10
☎ (01353) 676228
11–3, 6–11; 12–3, 7–10.30 Sun
Beer range varies Ⓗ
Smart, friendly, riverside inn;
Cambridge CAMRA *Pub of the
Year* 1996. The six handpumps
often feature local brews; cider
in summer.
🍴 ⚜ ◑ ▶ ⚡ P

Cambridge

Bird in Hand
73 Newmarket Road
☎ (01223) 354034
11–3, 5–11; 11–11 Fri & Sat; 12–3,
7–10.30 Sun
**Greene King XX Mild, IPA,
Abbot, seasonal beers** Ⓗ
Characterful, early 20th-
century, one-bar pub offering a

range of malt whiskies and
cheap mild Thu. Try the chilli
vodka. No food Sat.
🍴 ⚜ ◑ ♠ 🍴

Cambridge Blue
85–87 Gwydir Street (off Mill
Road)
☎ (01223) 361382
12–2.30 (4 Sat), 6–11; 12–3, 7–10.30
Sun
**Nethergate IPA, Bitter,
Golden Gate, Old Growler;
guest beers** Ⓗ
Characterful terraced pub
where a no-smoking bar, a tiny
snug and a conservatory

INDEPENDENT BREWERIES

Ancient Druids:
Cambridge

City of Cambridge:
Cambridge

Elgood's: Wisbech

Fenland: Chatteris

complement the main bar. The large garden features a model railway. Children's certificate. Guest beers always include a mild.
🏨 Q 🌰 🏵 ◖▮ ⇌ ♣ 👌 ⚹

Castle

38 Castle Street
☎ (01223) 353194
11.30–3, 5–11; 11.30–11 Sat; 12–3, 7–10.30 Sun
Adnams Mild, Bitter, Old, Broadside; guest beers ⊞
The Adnams western flagship, a superb example of sensitive pub renovation with five drinking areas on the ground floor and more upstairs. Suntrap patio. Six guest beers usually on tap.
🏨 🌰 🏵 ◖▮ 👌 ⚹

Champion of the Thames

68 King Street
☎ (01223) 352043
11–11; 11–4, 7–10.30 Sun
Greene King XX Mild, IPA ⊞**, Abbot** Ⓖ
Small pub of immense character where fine etched windows depict the 'Champ' in action. A rare city centre outlet for mild. Weekday lunches. ◖

Cow & Calf

14 Pound Hill
☎ (01223) 576220
12–3, 5–11; 12–3, 7–11 Sat; 12–3, 7–10.30 Sun
Courage Best Bitter; Elgood's Cambridge; Nethergate Bitter; Ruddles Best Bitter; Samuel Smith OBB; guest beer ⊞
A traditional pub atmosphere prevails in one of Cambridge's few true free houses. Four pub cats. Good value lunches (not served Sat). 🏨 🏵 ◖ ♣

Empress

72 Thoday Street (off Mill Rd)
☎ (01223) 247236
11–2.30, 6.30–11; 12–2.30, 7–10.30 Sun
Castle Eden Ale; Flowers Original; Marston's Pedigree; guest beers ⊞
Thriving backstreet pub, heaving eves, but always friendly and welcoming. Surprisingly large, it has three distinct drinking rooms, plus segregated games areas. Conversation prevails over the jukebox. 🏵 ♣ 👌

Free Press

Prospect Row
☎ (01223) 368337
12–2.30, 6–11; 12–3, 7–10.30 Sun
Greene King XX Mild, IPA, Abbot ⊞
Unspoilt, backstreet gem, completely no-smoking; with a very snug snug. Interesting food includes unusual vegetarian options. Eve meals finish at 8.30. 🏨 Q 🏵 ◖▮ ⚹

Jug & Firkin (off-licence)

90 Mill Road
☎ (01223) 315034
10.30–1.30, 3–10; 10–10.30 Sat; 12–2.30, 7–9.30 Sun
Beer range varies Ⓖ
Off-licence offering an amazing selection of bottled beers (many bottle-conditioned), plus at least five real ales. 👌

Live & Let Live

40 Mawson Road
☎ (01223) 460261
11–2.30, 5.30–11; 12–2.30, 7–10.30 Sun
Adnams Bitter; Everards Tiger; guest beers ⊞
Small, friendly backstreet pub, popular with regulars, students and tourists. The menu offers mostly home-made food. Always a mild available. 🏨 ◖▮ ♿ ⇌ 👌

Red Bull

11 Barton Road, Newnham
☎ (01223) 352788
11–11; 12–10.30 Sun
Boddingtons Bitter; Flowers IPA, Original; Marston's Pedigree; Wadworth 6X; guest beers ⊞
Busy, friendly pub decked out in the customary Whitbread alehouse style. Eve meals Mon–Fri, till 8pm.
🏵 ◖▮ P

St Rhadegund

129 King Street
☎ (01223) 311794
12–2.30, 5.30–11; 12–11 Sun; 6–10.30 Sun
Adnams Bitter; Fuller's London Pride; Nethergate Bitter; guest beer ⊞
Pub which more than makes up in character for what it lacks in size. Ask about the Veil Ale.

Tap & Spile (Mill)

14 Mill Lane ☎ (01223) 357026
11–11; 12–10.30 Sun
Adnams Bitter; Jennings Cumberland; guest beers ⊞
Recently redecorated pub retaining a sturdy but attractive alehouse-style interior. It overlooks the mill pond where punts can be hired. Eight ales on tap.
◖▮ 👌

Wrestlers

337 Newmarket Road
☎ (01223) 566554
12–3, 5–11; 12–3, 7–10.30 Sun
Adnams Broadside; Badger Tanglefoot; Morland Old Speckled Hen; Shepherd Neame Spitfire; Wells Eagle, Bombardier ⊞
Bustling, buoyant pub, full of life and offbeat charm. Live music twice a week. Authentic Thai bar meals and take-aways (no food Sun). 🏨 ◖▮ 👌

Castle Camps

Cock

High Street ☎ (01799) 584207
12–2, 7–11; 12–11 Sat; 12–3, 7–10.30 Sun
Greene King IPA, Abbot; Nethergate Bitter; guest beer ⊞
Friendly two-bar local serving fresh fish and chips Fri eve. Monthly folk nights.
🏨 🏵 ◖▮ ⊟ ♣ P

Castor

Royal Oak

24 Peterborough Road (off A47 bypass) ☎ (01733) 380217
11.30–3, 6–11; 11–11 Fri & Sat; 12–10.30 Sun
Draught Bass; Tetley Bitter; guest beers ⊞
Rural, 17th-century, thatched pub, enjoying a cosy atmosphere generated by low beamed ceilings, open fires and a maze of passages and rooms. Lunches Tue–Sat.
🏨 Q ◖ ♣ P

Chatteris

Honest John

24A–26 South Park Street
☎ (01354) 692698
11–2.30, 5.30–11; 12–2.30, 5.30–10.30 Sun
Brakspear Bitter; guest beers ⊞
Former Labour Exchange, now a comfortable pub with a large well-divided main room and a dining area. Q 🏵 ◖▮ ♣ P ⚹

Walk the Dog

34 Bridge Street (off A141)
☎ (01354) 693695
12–2.30, 6.30–11; 12–2.30, 7–10.30 Sun
Adnams Bitter; Draught Bass; Hancock's HB; guest beer ⊞
Small, friendly pub with a warm atmosphere.
🏨 🏵 ♣ P ⛫

Comberton

Grapevine

5 Green End ☎ (01223) 263059
6–11; 12–3, 6–11 Sat; 12–3, 7–10.30 Sun
Greene King IPA; Nethergate Golden Gate; guest beers ⊞
Unpretentious, food-free local whose garden adjoins the village pond. Disco Sun night.
🏨 🏵

Duxford

Plough

Plough Street
☎ (01223) 833170
11–3, 5.30–11; 11–11 Sat; 12–3, 7–10.30 Sun
Adnams Bitter; Everards Tiger, Old Original; guest beer ⊞

17th-century thatched pub offering a warm welcome and excellent value food (eve meals Tue–Sat). Handy for the Air Museum. 🛏 🏮 ◑ ▶ P

Ellington

Mermaid

High Street (off A14)
☎ (01480) 891450
12–2.30, 7–11; 12–3, 7–10.30 Sun
Draught Bass; guest beers (occasional)
Single-bar village pub that has seen few changes in recent years. Friendly atmosphere; worth finding.
🛏 Q 🏮 ◑ ♣ 🍺

Elsworth

Poacher

1 Brockley Road
☎ (01954) 267219
12–2.30, 6–11; 12–3, 7–10.30 Sun; closed Mon
Adnams Bitter *or* **Everards Tiger** Ⓗ
Generously-beamed, one-bar country inn with an enviable reputation for its food. Children welcome.
🛏 🏮 ◑ ▶ P

Ely

Fountain

1 Silver Street
☎ (01353) 663122
12–2.30, 5 (6 Sat)–11; 12–2.30, 7–10.30 Sun
Adnams Bitter, Broadside; Woodforde's Wherry; guest beers Ⓗ
Pub which has undergone a wholesale refurbishment but which is still a comfortable street-corner meeting place. Splendid new timber bar counter without a swan neck in sight. Children's certificate.
🛏 Q 🏮 ◑ 🍺

Prince Albert

62 Silver Street
☎ (01353) 663494
11.30–3 (3.30 Thu–Sat), 6.30–11; 12–3.30, 7–10.30 Sun
Greene King XX Mild, IPA, Abbot, seasonal beers Ⓗ
Classic town local where the emphasis is on good ale and chat. Your own food can be brought into the delightful garden as long as drinks are bought. Alternatively, the pub has quality snacks. Public car park opposite. Q 🏮 🍺 ♣

West End House

16 West End ☎ (01353) 662907
11–2.30 (3 Sat), 6–11; 12–3, 7–10.30 Sun
Courage Directors; Marston's Pedigree; Ruddles Best Bitter; Theakston XB, Old Peculier; Webster's Yorkshire Bitter Ⓗ
Well-appointed, backstreet local with low ceilings, beams

and brasses in an unspoilt tumble of drinking areas.
🛏 🏮 ♿ ♣

Etton

Golden Pheasant

1 Main Street ☎ (01733) 252387
11–11; 12–10.30 Sun
Draught Bass; Woodforde's Wherry; guest beers Ⓗ
19th-century manor house with a roomy, comfortable lounge, a family room and a restaurant. The large garden features an aviary.
🛏 Q 🍺 🏮 ◑ ♿ 🅰 ♣ P ⚥

Farcet Fen

Plough

Milk and Water Drove, Ramsey Road (B1095)
☎ (01733) 844307
11–3 (4 Thu–Sat), 6–11; 12–4, 7–10.30 Sun
Highgate Dark; John Smith's Bitter; guest beers Ⓗ
Good example of an unspoilt, isolated, fenland pub. No frills; Sun lunches the only food served. Brasses and kettles decorate the single bar.
🛏 Q 🏮 ♣ P 🍺

Fulbourn

Six Bells

9 High Street ☎ (01223) 880244
11.30–2.30, 6–11; 12–11 Sat; 12–10.30 Sun
Flowers IPA; Ind Coope Burton Ale; Tolly Cobbold Mild; guest beer Ⓗ
Thriving village pub run by local people, offering a warm welcome in both bars. Regular live jazz includes monthly jazz brunches in the function room. Home-cooked bar meals (not served Sun/Mon eves).
🛏 🏮 ◑ ▶ 🅰 ♣ P

Gamlingay

Cock

25 Church Street
☎ (01767) 650255
11.30–3, 5.30–11; 11–11 Sat; 12–3, 7–10.30 Sun
Greene King IPA, Abbot Ⓗ
Timber-framed pub of some interest: both bars have extensive wood panelling; display of cocks in the public bar. Popular for food at the weekends.
🛏 🍺 🏮 ◑ ▶ 🍺 ♣ P

Great Chishill

Pheasant

24 Heydon Road
☎ (01763) 838535
12–3, 6–11; 12–3, 7–10.30 Sun
Adnams Bitter; Ruddles Best Bitter; guest beers Ⓗ
Well-appointed country pub with an inglenook, beams,

flagstones and a lovely raised garden. Quite 'foody', but still a nice place for a drink.
🛏 🏮 ◑ ▶ P

Hilton

Prince of Wales

Potton Road (B1040)
☎ (01480) 830257
11–2.30 (3 Sat; not Mon), 6 (7 winter Sat)–11; 12–3, 7–10.30 Sun
Draught Bass; Oakham JHB; guest beer (occasional) Ⓗ
Welcoming, well-run, two-bar village local with a log fire. Good accommodation. No food Mon.
🛏 🛏 ◑ ▶ ♿ ♣ P 🍺

Histon

King William IV

8 Church Street
☎ (01223) 233930
11.30–3, 5 (6 Sat)–11; 12–3, 6–10.30 Sun
Boddingtons Bitter; Greene King IPA, Abbot; Hook Norton Old Hooky; Ruddles County Ⓗ
Pub with a cosy, beamed lounge and a youth-oriented public bar. The excellent food has a Mexican/American flavour (book Sun lunch).
🛏 🏮 ◑ ▶ ♣ P

Red Lion

27 High Street
☎ (01223) 564437
11.30–3, 5 (4 Fri)–11; 11.30–11 Sat; 12–5, 7–10.30 Sun
Everards Beacon, Tiger; Nethergate Bitter; Whitbread Fuggles IPA; guest beers Ⓗ
Enterprising free house offering a choice between a comfy lounge and a boisterous public. No food Sun.
🏮 ◑ 🍺 ♣ P

Horningsea

Crown & Punchbowl

High Street ☎ (01223) 860643
12–2.30 (not Sat), 6.30–11; 12–3, 7–10.30 Sun
Adnams Extra; Elgood's Cambridge; Greene King IPA; guest beer Ⓗ
17th-century inn at the centre of a picturesque village on the River Cam, close to the A14. The cosy quarry-tiled 'old' bar contrasts with the snug; the candle-lit dining room features stained-glass screens.
🛏 🍺 🏮 🛏 ◑ 🍺 ♣ P

Huntingdon

Old Bridge Hotel

1 High Street (off ring road)
☎ (01480) 452681
11–11; 12–10.30 Sun
Adnams Bitter; guest beers Ⓗ
Relaxing, sumptuous, splendid hotel bar serving excellent

cuisine and interesting guest
beers. ♨ Q ❀ ⇔ ◖ ▶ ≈ P

Leighton Bromswold

Green Man

37 The Avenue (off A14)
☎ (01480) 890238
12–3 (not Tue–Thu), 7–11; 12–3,
7–10.30 Sun; closed Mon
**Nethergate IPA; Taylor
Landlord; guest beers** Ⓗ
Comfortable, welcoming
village free house with an
expanding collection of
brewery memorabilia, a wide
range of beers and good value
food. Hood skittles played.
Deservedly popular.
☎ ❀ ◖ ▶ ♿ ♣ P

Little Gransden

Chequers

71 Main Road
☎ (01767) 677348
12–2, 7–11; 11–11 Sat; 12–10.30 Sun
Adnams Bitter; guest beers Ⓗ
Worth searching for, this three-
roomed village pub maintains
its rustic charm; recent
improvements have only
enhanced its qualities. Friendly
and welcoming.
♨ ❀ ⊟ ♣ P

Littleport

George & Dragon

13 Station Road
☎ (01353) 862639
11.30–11; 12–3, 7–10.30 Sun
**Badger Dorset Best; Fuller's
London Pride; guest beers** Ⓗ
Now boasting three separate
rooms following
refurbishment, this
enterprising establishment
continues to offer a relaxed,
friendly atmosphere.
❀ ◖ ▶ ⊟ ≈ ♣ P

Longstowe

Golden Miller

54 High Street (B1046)
☎ (01954) 719385
12–2.30, 6.30–11; 12–3, 7–10.30 Sun
Adnams Bitter Ⓗ,
Broadside Ⓖ; **Bateman XB** Ⓗ
Friendly village pub named
after the 1934 Grand National
winner. Separate dining room
(no eve meals Tue).
❀ ◖ ▶ ♣ P ⊟

March

Rose & Crown

41 St Peters Road
☎ (01354) 52879
11.30–2.30 (not Wed), 7–11; 12–3,
7–10.30 Sun
**John Smith's Bitter; guest
beers** Ⓗ
Friendly, traditional, two-
roomed pub, the only true free

house in March. The guest
beers include milds and stouts;
the cider varies. Q ❀ ♣ ⇔ P

Milton

Waggon & Horses

39 High Street
☎ (01223) 860313
12–3, 5–11; 12–11 Sat; 12–10.30 Sun
Bateman XB; guest beers Ⓗ
Friendly pub selling five guest
beers, four ciders from the
cellar, and a malt whisky
selection. No-smoking
restaurant area. Limited
parking. ♨ ❀ ◖ ▶ ♿ ♣ ⇔ P

Needingworth

Queens Head

30 High Street (off A1123)
☎ (01480) 463946
12–11; 12–3, 7–10.30 Sun
**Smiles Golden Brew;
Woodforde's Wherry; guest
beers** Ⓗ
Friendly, two-bar village local,
with a strong dominoes
following. Always a good
range of guest beers (the
handpumps are in the public
bar). ❀ ◖ ▶ ⊟ ♣ P

Newton

Queen's Head

Fowlmere Road
☎ (01223) 870436
11.30–2.30, 6–11; 12–2.30, 7–10.30 Sun
**Adnams Bitter, Broadside,
Tally Ho** Ⓖ
Classic village inn which has
appeared in every edition of
the *Guide*. The Queen in
question is Anne of Cleves.
♨ Q ⊟ ⇔ P

Old Weston

Swan

Main Street (B660, off A14)
☎ (01832) 293400
6.30–11; 12–3, 7–11 Sat; 12–3, 7–10.30
Sun
**Adnams Bitter, Broadside;
Morland Old Speckled Hen;
guest beers** Ⓗ
Three-roomed village pub, full
of character, with a warm,
welcoming atmosphere. The
beer range always includes a
mild. Hood skittles played.
♨ ☎ ❀ ◖ ▶ ▲ ♣ P

Peterborough

Blue Bell

Welland Road, Dogsthorpe (1
mile off A47) ☎ (01733) 54890
11–3, 6–11; 12–3, 7–10.30 Sun
**Elgood's Cambridge, Pageant
Ale, Golden Newt,
Greyhound, seasonal beers;
guest beers** Ⓗ
One of the oldest pubs in town,
converted from a farmhouse in
1665. Two large rooms with

real fires; the lounge also has
an oak-panelled snug. Five ales
are always available, maybe
more. The best pint of Elgood's
in Peterborough.
♨ Q ❀ ◖ ▶ ♣ P

Blue Bell

6 The Green, Werrington (½
mile off A15) ☎ (01733) 571264
11–3, 5–11; 12–10.30 Sun
**Elgood's Cambridge,
Greyhound** Ⓗ
Attractive white building, circa
1890 (extended in 1985) with a
friendly public bar and a very
comfortable lounge. Fresh food
daily, home cooked by the
landlord who is highly quality
conscious. ❀ ◖ ▶ ⊟ ♣ P

Bogarts

17 North Street (opp.
Queensgate shopping
complex) ☎ (01733) 349995
11–11; closed Sun
**Draught Bass; Oakham JHB;
guest beers** Ⓗ
Traditional, no-frills pub
whose atmosphere appeals to
discerning ale drinkers: no
pool or jukebox, just good ale
(seven handpumps) and chat.
Small suntrap garden.
❀ ◖ ≈ ⇔

Charters

Town Bridge (steps down from
S end of bridge)
☎ (01733) 315700
12–11; 12–10.30 Sun
**Draught Bass; Everards Tiger;
Fuller's London Pride;
Oakham JHB, Bishops
Farewell, Old Tosspot; guest
beers** Ⓗ
Real ale flagship: a large,
converted Dutch barge. Over
550 different beers were sold in
1996 from 12 handpumps.
Spacious restaurant upstairs.
❀ ◖ ▶ ≈ ⇔ ⊟

Cherry Tree Inn

9–11 Oundle Road, Woodston
(near city centre town bridge)
☎ (01733) 345812
12–3, 6–11; 12–11 Sat; 12–10.30 Sun
**Draught Bass; Marston's
Pedigree; Morland Old
Speckled Hen; Tetley Bitter,
Imperial; guest beer** Ⓗ
Recently refurbished house
which has not lost its local feel.
A good food menu
complements the beer range. A
popular weekend music venue,
with live bands.
♨ ❀ ◖ ▶ ≈ ♣ P

College Arms

40 The Broadway
☎ (01733) 319745
11–11; 12–10.30 Sun
**Courage Directors; Younger
Scotch; guest beers** Ⓗ
Impressive conversion of a
former technical college,
offering a vast selection of
guest beers. One beer is always

discounted. Food until one hour before closing.
Q ❀ ◖ ▶ ♿ ⌂ P ✄

Fountain
2 Burghley Road (just N of centre) ☎ (01733) 54533
11–2.30, 7–11; 12–3, 7–10.30 Sun
Draught Bass; Everards Beacon, Tiger, Old Original; guest beers Ⓗ
Friendly pub close to the city centre. Real fire in the very comfortable lounge; pool table in the public bar. No food Sun.
🏨 ❀ ◖ ▶ ♣

Hand & Heart
12 Highbury Street (off Lincoln Rd, Millfield)
☎ (01733) 707040
10.30–3, 6–11; 12–3, 7–10.30 Sun
Courage Directors; Elgood's Black Dog Mild; Marston's Pedigree; Morland Old Masters; John Smith's Bitter; guest beer Ⓗ
Fine example of a 1930s backstreet local, featuring original Warwicks windows.
🏨 Q ⊞ ♣ ⌂

Ramblewood Inn
The Village, Orton Longville (off Oundle road, opp. Orton Staunch) ☎ (01733) 394444
12–11; 12–10.30 Sun
Adnams Broadside; Draught Bass; Fuller's London Pride; guest beers Ⓗ
Formerly the stables of Orton Hall, which is now an hotel. This pub has a cosy atmosphere, attractive gardens and a highly regarded, good value restaurant. 🍴 ◖ ▶ ♿ Å ⇌ (Nene Valley Rlwy) P

Woolpack
29 North Street, Stanground (1 mile from centre by road, ½ mile by river) ☎ (01733) 54417
11.30–3, 5–11; 11–11 Fri & Sat; 12–10.30 Sun
Boddingtons Bitter; Castle Eden Ale; guest beers Ⓗ
Built in 1711; popular with locals and the passing boat trade. Note the exhibition of militaria in an outside barn and the remains of a medieval wall in the picturesque garden. An inglenook was rediscovered ten years ago. ❀ ◖ ♣ ♣

Ramsey

Jolly Sailor
43 Great Whyte
☎ (01487) 813388
11–3, 5.30 (7 Sat)–11; 12–3, 7–10.30 Sun
Flowers Original; Ind Coope Burton Ale; Tetley Bitter; guest beer (weekend) Ⓗ
Small, friendly and unspoilt town pub. The Great Whyte River flows through an adjacent culvert. 🏨 Q ❀ P

Ramsey Forty Foot

George Inn
1 Ramsey Road
☎ (01487) 812775
12–4, 6–11; 12–4, 7–10.30 Sun
Beer range varies Ⓗ
Traditional fenland village free house whose cosy atmosphere is enhanced by an inglenook fireplace. It stands adjacent to Fortyfoot Drain which is popular for fishing and boat moorings.
🏨 ❀ Å P

Reach

Kings
Fair Green ☎ (01638) 741745
12–3 (not Mon), 7–11; 12–3, 7–10.30 Sun
Fenland FBB; Greene King IPA; guest beers Ⓗ
Comfortable, split-level beamed pub, handy for the Devil's Dyke and the annual Reach Fair; converted from a farmhouse 22 years ago. Home-made soups are a speciality on the cosmopolitan menu (no food Mon; eve meals Tue–Sat). 🏨 ❀ ◖ ▶ ♣ P

St Ives

Nelsons Head
7 Merryland (off Bridge St)
☎ (01480) 463342
10.30–2.30 (11–3 Sat), 6–11; 12–3, 7–10.30 Sun
Greene King IPA, Abbot, seasonal beers Ⓗ
Formerly the Three Tuns, this town-centre pub is tucked away down a sidestreet: a large front bar, with a small rear drinking area and a dining room; popular and welcoming. Wheelchair access is via the side gate. 🏨 ❀ ◖ ♿ ♣

St Neots

Blue Ball
Russell Street
☎ (01480) 386195
11–11; 12–3, 7–10.30 Sun
Greene King XX Mild Ⓖ, IPA, Abbot Ⓗ
Backstreet, two-bar pub, full of interesting breweriana. Always a warm welcome.
🏨 ❀ ⊞ ♣ P

Sawston

Greyhound
2 High Street ☎ (01223) 832260
11–3, 5–11; 12–3, 7–10.30 Sun
Boddingtons Bitter; Flowers IPA, Original; Fuller's London Pride; Wadworth 6X; guest beer Ⓗ
Large, comfortable, family-oriented pub with a spacious conservatory-cum-dining area. No food Sun eve. 🏨 ❀ P

Six Mile Bottom

Green Man Inn
London Road
☎ (01638) 570373
11.30–2.30 (later if busy), 4.30–11; 11.30–11 Fri & Sat; 12–7 Sun
Adnams Bitter; Eccleshall Slaters Bitter; Greene King IPA; guest beers Ⓗ
Bustling roadhouse which has gained a loyal local following for its quality food and drink and haphazard charm. The restaurant is gaily bedecked with flowers and candles (no food Sun eve or Mon). Pool area. 🏨 ❀ 🍴 ◖ ▶ P

Spaldwick

George
High Street ☎ (01480) 890293
12–3, 6–11; 12–3, 7–10.30 Sun
Adnams Broadside; Wells Eagle, Bombardier Ⓗ
Comfortable, Grade II-listed Georgian coaching inn, built from ships' timbers. Good value food from a varied menu. Large garden.
🏨 ❀ ◖ ▶ ⊞ ♣ P

Stow cum Quy

White Swan
Main Street ☎ (01223) 811821
11–3, 5.30–11; 12–3, 7–10.30 Sun
Adnams Bitter; Courage Directors; Fuller's London Pride; Greene King IPA; John Smith's Bitter; guest beer Ⓗ
Comfortable local at the heart of a quiet village; a pub since the 16th century. Outstanding home-cooked meals are served in the bar or adjoining no-smoking restaurant (Tue–Sun). Popular with traditional games players. ❀ ◖ ▶ ♣ P

Thriplow

Green Man
☎ (01763) 208855
12–3, 6–11; 12–3, 7–10.30 Sun
Hook Norton Best Bitter; Taylor Landlord; guest beers Ⓗ
Village free house saved from closure by West End musical director Roger Ward. No lunches Sat or eve meals Sun. 🏨 ❀ ◖ ▶ P

Turves

Three Horseshoes
344 March Road (off A604, through Coates)
☎ (01733) 840414
12–2.15, 7–11; 12–3, 7–10.30 Sun; closed Tue
Courage Best Bitter; guest beers Ⓗ

Pub boasting a wood-panelled bar and a 40-seater restaurant with an extensive menu (good food). The large garden has a play area, patio and barbecue. 🏚 Q 🍴 🏵 ◐ ♿ ♣ P

Ufford

Olde White Hart
Main Street ☎ (01780) 740250
11–2.30, 6–11; 12–3, 7–10.30 Sun
Theakston Best Bitter, Old Peculier (winter); **Wadworth 6X; guest beers** Ⓗ
17th-century, former farmhouse with a homely feel and lots of character. Popular restaurant at the back, with a cocktail bar; smallish, comfortable front bar.
🏚 Q 🏵 ◐ ▶ 🛏 ♣ P

Whittlesford

Bees in the Wall
36 North Road
☎ (01223) 834289
6–11; 12–2.30, 6–11 Sat; 12–4, 7–10.30 Sun
Bateman XB; Fuller's London Pride; Hook Norton Best Bitter; guest beer Ⓗ

Old-fashioned beer house heated only by an open fire. There really are bees in the wall. The beer range can vary.
🏚 Q 🏵 🛏 ♣ P

Wilburton

King's Head
49 High Street
☎ (01353) 741029
12–2.30 (3 Sat), 6–11; 12–3, 7–10.30 Sun
Adnams Bitter; Greene King IPA; guest beer Ⓗ
Pub which accurately describes itself as 'a nice place for nice people'; effectively two bars, one with a fine tiled floor. Interesting menu (no food Sun eve). 🏚 🏵 ◐ ▶ ♣ P

Willingham

Three Tuns
Church Street
☎ (01954) 260437
11–2.30, 6–11; 12–2.30, 7–10.30 Sun
Greene King XX Mild, IPA, Abbot, seasonal beers Ⓗ
Unchanging epitome of the English village local. Basic lunchtime snacks. Q 🏵 🛏 ♣ P

Wisbech

Rose Tavern
53 North Brink
☎ (01945) 588335
12–2.30, 6 (5.30 Thu & Fri)–11; 12–3, 7–10.30 Sun
Butterknowle Banner Bitter; Everards Beacon; guest beers Ⓗ
Cosy, one-roomed pub on the riverside, in a listed 200-year-old building, close to Elgood's brewery. A summer beer festival is held in an outbuilding. 🏵 ♣

Witcham

White Horse
7 Silver Street
☎ (01353) 778298
12–3 (not Mon), 6.30–11; 12–3, 7–10.30 Sun
Greene King IPA; Nethergate IPA; guest beers Ⓗ
Run with panache and enthusiasm, this pub has developed a well-deserved reputation for both its food and ale. No meals Sun eve.
🏵 ◐ ▶ ♣ P ⌖

Elgood's, the oldest brewery in Cambridgeshire, dating from the 18th century, like many established regional brewers is now facing competition from neighbouring new microbreweries, in this case Fenland in Chatteris and City of Cambridge in Cambridge.

Cheshire

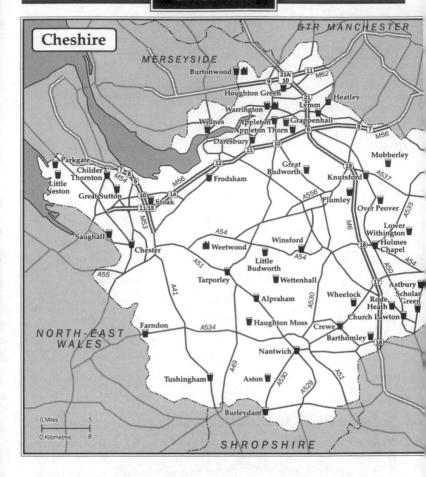

Alpraham

Travellers Rest ☆
Chester Road (A51)
☎ (01829) 260523
6–11; 12–3, 6–11 Sat; 12–3, 7–10.30
Sun
**McEwan 70/-; Tetley Mild,
Bitter** H
Quiet village local, like a
private house, unaffected by
change over 30 years. Bowling
green to the rear. Q ❀ ♣ ♠ P

Appleton

Birchdale Hotel
Birchdale Road (signed from
A49 at London Bridge)
☎ (01925) 263662
6 (8.30 Sat)–11; 8.30–10.30 Sun
**Boddingtons Bitter; guest
beer** H
Quiet residential hotel: a large
comfortable lounge and a
games room. A pleasant, quiet
place for an evening drink.
Q ❀ ⌂ ♣ P ⬚

Appleton Thorn

Appleton Thorn
Village Hall
Stretton Road
☎ (01925) 261187
8.30–11; 8.30–10.30 Sun; closed
Mon–Wed
Beer range varies H
Attractive, mainly sandstone,
former school converted to a
village hall; CAMRA *Club of the
Year* 1995. It also opens 12–3 on
the first Sun of the month.
Q ❀ ♿ P

Astbury

Egerton Arms
Off A24
☎ (01260) 273946
11.30–11; 12–10.30 Sun
Robinson's Best Bitter E,
Frederics H
Comfortable, roomy, 14th-
century pub near the 'picture
book' village green. Good
selection of food in the
restaurant or as bar snacks.
No-smoking family room;
garden play area.
🏪 Q ⬚ ❀ ⌂ ◑ ▶ P ⅀

Aston

Bhurtpore Inn
Wrenbury Road (off A530)
☎ (01270) 780917
12–2.30 (3 Sat), 6.30–11; 12–3, 7–10.30
Sun
**Hanby Drawwell; guest
beers** H
Pub attracting clientele from
miles around with at least nine
guest beers, a huge range of
foreign beers in bottle and on
draught, plus various ciders;
1400 guest beers in the last five
years. An annual beer festival
is held the weekend before
Easter. Good variety of bar
food, from light snacks to full
meals, with all main courses
freshly home-made; separate
restaurant.
🏪 Q ❀ ◑ ▶ 🍴 ♿ ⚓ ⇌
(Wrenbury) ♣ ⌂ P

Barthomley

White Lion
Audley Road (off B5078, ½ mile from M6 jct 16)
☎ (01270) 882242
11.30 (5 Thu)–11; 12–10.30 Sun
Burtonwood Bitter, Forshaw's, Top Hat, Buccaneer H
Popular, black and white, thatched pub at the centre of a small, picturesque village. Dated 1616, it displays a list of 16 landlords and three landladies. A new bunk house (bring your own sleeping bag) is available. Bar snacks finish at 2pm. ♨ Q ✿ ❀ ➡ ♣ P

Bollington

Meridian
48 Palmerston Street
☎ (01625) 573883
12–11; 12–10.30 Sun
Boddingtons Bitter; Burtonwood Mild, Bitter H
Typical multi-roomed pub that time forgot, popular with all ages; skittles played. ⊞ ♣

Queens
40 High Street
☎ (01625) 573068
2–11; 12–3, 7–10.30 Sun
Robinson's Hatters Mild, Best Bitter H
Solidly built, stone pub, set back slightly from the rest of the terrace and modernised in typical Robinson's style. Very popular. ✿ ◖ ▶

Try also: **Church House**, Chapel St (Free)

Burleydam

Combermere Arms
On A525, 3 miles from Audlem
☎ (01948) 871223
11 (12 winter)–11; 12–10.30 Sun
Draught Bass; Worthington Bitter; guest beer H
Reputedly haunted, 16th-century free house with a varied clientele. Several beer festivals are held each year. Two guest beers in summer. Good food (served all day Sat–Sun). Children's indoor adventure play centre.
♨ ✿ ✿ ◖ ▶ ♣ P

Burtonwood

Bridge Inn
Phipps Lane ☎ (01925) 225709
11.30–11; 12–10.30 Sun
Burtonwood Mild, Bitter H
Four-roomed pub, oriented towards local sports; the licensee's memorabilia from his rugby league playing days is displayed. Children welcome in the conservatory. No food Sun. ✿ ✿ ◖ ♣ P

Chester

Albion
Park Street ☎ (01244) 340345
11.30–3, 5.30–11; 11.30–11 Fri; 12–4, 7–10.30 Sun
Cains Bitter; Greenalls Bitter, Original; guest beer H
Victorian, street-corner pub retaining three rooms, including a snug. Flags, enamel signs and other items relating to the Great War are displayed. Home-cooked food, with some unusual dishes at reasonable prices, is served up to 8pm (not Mon). ♨ Q ◖ ▶

Centurion
Oldfield Drive, Vicars Cross (off A51, 1 mile from city)
☎ (01244) 347623
11.30 (11 Sat)–11; 12–10.30 Sun
Jennings Bitter; Robinson's Best Bitter; Tetley Dark Mild, Bitter; guest beers H
Friendly, modern pub where beer festivals and charity fund-raising events are regularly held; nominated as *Community Pub of the Year*. Children's play area in the garden. Well worth a visit. ✿ ⊞ ♣ P

Harkers Arms
1 Russell Street
☎ (01244) 344525
11.30–3, 5–11; 12–11 Sat; 12–3, 7–10.30 Sun
Boddingtons Bitter; Cheriton Diggers Gold; Fuller's London Pride; Taylor Landlord; guest beer H
Decidedly upmarket, converted canalside warehouse with solid wooden furniture and airy windows. Bare boards and a gallery of decorative prints add to the ambience. Very popular at weekends, despite premium prices. Diverse menu (eve meals Sun–Thu). Door policing Wed–Sat.
Q ◖ ▶ ⇌

Mill Hotel
Milton Street (off ring road)
☎ (01244) 350035
11–11; 12–10.30 Sun
Boddingtons Bitter; Weetwood Best Bitter; guest beers H
Local CAMRA *Pub of the Year*; a busy hotel bar with up to five guest ales, one of which is always a mild. The house beer is brewed by Coach House. Parking is often difficult. The hotel stands next to the Shropshire Union Canal.
✿ ⊨ ◖ ▶ ♿ ⇌ P

Olde Custom House
Watergate Street
☎ (01244) 324435
11–11; 12–10.30 Sun
Banks's Mild; Marston's Bitter, Pedigree, HBC H
Recently refurbished, three-roomed, 17th-century pub within the city walls, near Roodee racecourse. Good variety of bar meals (eve meals end 8.30). ✿ ◖ ▶ ⊞ ♣

Talbot
33 Walter Street, Newton (near fire station)
☎ (01244) 317901
11–11; 11–5, 7–11 Sat; 12–5, 7–10.30 Sun
Burtonwood Mild, Bitter H
Small, unspoilt, street-corner, terraced local with a convivial atmosphere. Games, played in both rooms, include bagatelle.
⊞ ♿ ⇌ ♣

INDEPENDENT BREWERIES
Beartown: Congleton

Burtonwood: Burtonwood

Coach House: Warrington

Weetwood: Weetwood

Childer Thornton

White Lion
New Road (100 yds off A41)
☎ (0151) 339 3402
11.30–3, 5–11; 11.30–11 Fri & Sat;
12–4, 7–10.30 Sun
Thwaites Best Mild, Bitter H
Friendly, unspoilt, two-room
country local on the outskirts
of Ellesmere Port. Families
welcome in the snug at
lunchtime. No food Sun.
🏚 Q ❀ ◖ P

Church Lawton

Lawton Arms Hotel
Liverpool Road West (A50,
near A34 jct) ☎ (01270) 873743
11.30–3, 5.30 (6.30 Sat)–11; 11–11 Fri;
12–3, 7–10.30 Sun
**Robinson's Hatters Mild, Best
Bitter** E
Two-roomed, welcoming pub
with a dining room.
◖ ▶ ⬚ ♣ P

Congleton

Moss Inn
140 Canal Road
☎ (01260) 273583
11–11; 12–10.30 Sun
**Bateman Mild; Marston's
Bitter, Pedigree** H
Welcoming, cosy pub where
the walls are laden with
interesting artefacts. A thriving
local trade is boosted by
cyclists, walkers and boaters
from the canal (100 yards).
Extensive smoke filter and
extraction system. Eve meals
6–8, Tue–Fri.
❀ ◖ ▶ ⬚ ♣ ⇌ P

Waggon & Horses
Newcastle Road, West Heath
☎ (01260) 274366
11.30–3, 6–11; 12–3, 7–10.30 Sun
Marston's Bitter, Pedigree H
Large, well-established inn on
the western edge of town,
standing at the confluence of
the A34, A54 and A534 –
outside drinking is somewhat
akin to sitting in the middle of
a roundabout. No food Sun.
🏚 ◖ ♣ P

Crewe

Albion
1 Pedley Street (off Mill St)
☎ (01270) 256234
7 (4 Mon, 12 Sat)–11; 12–3,
7–10.30 Sun
**Tetley Mild, Bitter; guest
beers** H
Street-corner local with an
emphasis on darts and
dominoes. The frequently
changing guest beers come
from small independent
breweries; 500 different guest
beers in the last two years.
Cider varies. ⬚ ⇌ ♣ ○

King's Arms
56 Earle Street
☎ (01270) 584134
11.30–11; 12–10.30 Sun
**Boddingtons Bitter; Chester's
Mild; Whitbread Trophy** H
Multi-roomed pub, close to the
town centre; a useful retreat
from the Grand Junction Retail
Park. ❀ 🛏 ⬚ ♣

Daresbury

Ring 'O' Bells
Old Chester Road (off A56)
☎ (01925) 740256
12–11; 12–10.30 Sun
**Boddingtons Bitter; Greenalls
Mild, Bitter, Original; guest
beer** H
Large pub in the village where
Lewis Carroll was born.
Refurbished in Greenalls' rural
style, it has an emphasis on
food but still room for
drinkers. The guest beer (from
Greenalls' list) can be pricey.
🏚 Q ⛲ ❀ ◖ ▶ ⬚ ♣ P

Disley

Dandy Cock Inn
15 Market Street
☎ (01663) 763712
12–11; 12–10.30 Sun
**Robinson's Hatters Mild, Old
Stockport, Best Bitter** H
Once a home for cock fighting,
this traditional local sits in the
heart of the village on the busy
A6. The cosy lounge bar and
restaurant area create a good
mix. Quality food – from
blackboard bar meals to full à
la carte – is available till 8pm,
except Mon. ❀ ◖ ▶ ⇌ P

Eaton

Plough
Macclesfield Road
☎ (01260) 280207
12–3, 7–11; 12–3, 7–10.30 Sun
**Banks's Bitter; Marston's
Pedigree; guest beers** H
Village-centre pub, revitalised
in recent years by ex-brewer
Clive Wincle. Much emphasis
is on food and it can get busy
as a consequence. This does not
detract from the welcoming
atmosphere.
🏚 ❀ 🛏 ◖ ▶ ♣ P

Farndon

Farndon Arms
High Street ☎ (01829) 270570
11–11; 12–10.30 Sun
**Boddingtons Bitter;
Worthington Bitter; guest
beers** H
Comfortable, well-furbished
village pub and restaurant
where meals are available at all
times (steak and kidney pies a
speciality). Close to the River
Dee.
🏚 Q ❀ 🛏 ◖ ▶ ⬚ ♣ ♠ P ⚲

Frodsham

Netherton Hall
Chester Road (A56)
☎ (01928) 732342
12–11; 12–10.30 Sun
**Marston's Pedigree; Tetley
Bitter; guest beers** H
Former farmhouse, now a
large, open-plan pub serving
excellent food, in a good
walking area handy for the
Frodsham and Helsby Hills.
Play area for children.
❀ ◖ ▶ ⬚ ♣ P ☗

Queen's Head
92 Main Street
☎ (01928) 733289
11 (11.30 Tue & Wed)–11; 11.30–3,
6.30–11 Mon; 12–10.30 (12–3.30,
7–10.30 Jan–Mar) Sun
**Greenalls Mild, Bitter; guest
beer** H
Popular pub with various
rooms. Built in 1550, it has
plenty of history. A folk club
meets in the rear stables.
Excellent for pub games. The
guest beer is from Greenalls'
list. ◖ ⇌ ♣ P

Rowland's Bar
31 Church Street
☎ (01928) 733361
11–11; 12–10.30 Sun
**Boddingtons Bitter;
Weetwood Best Bitter; guest
beers** H
Popular, single-room pub
found in the main shopping
area, stocking 12 guest beers a
week, from independent
breweries. Good food served,
but not Sun eve. The cider
varies. ◖ ▶ ⇌ ○ ☗

Grappenhall

Grappenhall
Community Centre
Bellhouse Lane (200 yds from
A50) ☎ (01925) 268633
7.30–11; 12–5, 7.30–11 Sat; 12–10.30
Sun
**Ruddles Best Bitter; Tetley
Bitter; Webster's Yorkshire
Bitter; guest beer** H
Large private club and social
centre in an old farmhouse and
barn which supports a wide
range of activities; close to the
Bridgewater Canal. Two to
three guest beers per week;
annual beer festival in April. A
CAMRA membership card
allows admission.
Q ❀ ⬚ ♣ P

Great Budworth

Cock O' Budworth
Warrington Road (A559)
☎ (01606) 891287
11–11; 12–10.30 Sun

Holt Mild, Bitter H
Clean, attractive country pub:
two bars include a tap room
with darts and dominoes.
Wide selection of food
(children's and vegetarian
dishes). Originally a working
farm; note the old cobblestones
in front.
🏚 Q 🍴 🕭 🕪 ♣ P

George & Dragon
High Street (off A559)
☎ (01606) 891317
11.30–3, 6–11; 11.30–11 Sat; 12–10.30
Sun
Tetley Bitter; guest beers H
Set opposite the church in a
picturesque village, this former
local CAMRA *Pub of the Year*
serves two guest beers.
🍴 🕭 🕪 ♣ P

Great Sutton

White Swan
Old Chester Road
☎ (0151) 339 9284
11.30–11; 12–10.30 Sun
**Burtonwood Mild, Bitter;
guest beers** H
Welcoming pub with a bar and
a split-level lounge. Note the
nostalgic prints of Ellesmere
Port and the vintage model
vehicle collection. With up to
five guest ales a week, this is an
oasis for variety. No food Tue.
🕭 🕪 ♣ P

Handforth

Railway
Station Road ☎ (01625) 523472
11–3, 5.30–11; 12–10.30 Sun
**Robinsons's Hatters Mild,
Best Bitter** E
Large, multi-roomed pub
facing the station; a thriving
local which is popular with all.
Q 🕭🕭 🕇 ♣ P

Haughton Moss

Nag's Head
Long Lane ☎ (01829) 260265
11–3 (not Mon), 6.30–11; 12–3, 7–10.30
Sun
**Marston's Bitter, Pedigree;
guest beer** H
Attractive, black and white
country pub with a friendly
atmosphere and good food.
The bowling green provides
good entertainment in
summer. 🏚 🕭 🕪 🖤 ♣ P

Heatley

Railway
Mill Lane (B5159)
☎ (01925) 752742
12 (11.30 Sat)–11; 12–10.30 Sun
**Boddingtons Bitter; Taylor
Landlord; guest beer** H
Large and still traditional pub,
serving as a focal point for the
community. Local society
meetings are catered for in the

many different rooms; folk
club Thu. The large open
garden sits alongside the
Trans-Pennine Trail. No food
Sun. The guest beer is from
Greenalls' list.
Q 🕭🕭 🕭 🕪 🕇 ♣ P

Higher Hurdsfield

George & Dragon
61 Rainow Road
☎ (01625) 424300
12–3 (not Sat), 7–11; 12–3, 7–10.30 Sun
Beer range varies H
Small, friendly, stone pub set
back off the main road. Part of
the pub is 400 years old. Bus
stop outside. 🕭 ♣

Holmes Chapel

Swan
29 Station Road
☎ (01477) 532259
11–11; 12–10.30 Sun
Samuel Smith OBB H
Former coaching inn with good
food (huge pizzas a speciality).
An interesting old black stove
is on display. The car park is
reached by driving under the
pub. 🏚 🕭 🕭 🕪 🕇 🕇 P

Houghton Green

Plough
Mill Lane ☎ (01925) 815849
11.30–11; 12–10.30 Sun
**Boddingtons Bitter; Greenalls
Mild, Bitter, Original; guest
beer** H
Expanded in the early 1990s to
cater for a large residential
area, this pub has a strong
emphasis on food. Live music
Tue, quiz night Thu. Bowling
green at the back. The guest
beer is from Greenalls' list.
🕭 🕪 🕇 P

Knutsford

Angel
96 King Street
☎ (01565) 651165
11.30–11; 12–10.30 Sun
Holt Mild, Bitter H
Large, smart, town-centre inn
which was moved from its
previous site across the road in
the late 18th century and is
decorated in the style of that
period, with a number of
wood-panelled rooms and
heavy-framed pictures. Cosy
and welcoming.
🏚 Q 🕭 🕪 🕇 🕇 🕇

Builders Arms
Mobberley Road
☎ (01565) 634528
11.30–3, 5.30–11; 12–2, 7–10.30 Sun
**Banks's Mild; Marston's
Bitter, Pedigree** H
Delightful pub in an attractive
terrace on the outskirts of the
town centre. A former Taylor's

Eagle Brewery house, now a
busy pub with a keen games
following. Best approached
from the road opposite the
Legh Arms. Q 🕭 🕇 🕇

Freemasons
Silk Mill Street
☎ (01565) 632368
11–11; 12–10.30 Sun
**Burtonwood Bitter,
Buccaneer** H
Large, white, three-storey
building, just off Princess St.
Silk Mill St was the birthplace
in 1715 of Edward Penny RA, a
founding member and first
professor of painting at the
Royal Academy.
🏚 🕭 🕪 🕇 🕇 🕇

Try also: White Bear, Canute
Place (Greenalls)

Little Budworth

Shrewsbury Arms
Chester Road (A54)
☎ (01829) 760240
11.30–3, 6–11; 12–3, 7–10.30 Sun
**Robinson's Best Bitter,
Frederics** H
Just 20 mins' from Chester and
five from Oulton Park motor
racing circuit, this neat country
pub comprises a snug, a
lounge, a large garden and a
small dining room (bookable)
where families are welcome.
No food Mon eve. Q 🕭 🕭 🕪 P

Little Neston

Harp Inn
Quayside (from Burton Rd
down Marshlands Rd; left
along Marsh Rd)
☎ (0151) 336 6980
11–11; 12–10.30 Sun
**Chester's Mild; Flowers IPA;
Taylor Landlord; Whitbread
Trophy** H
Delightful, two-roomed, ex-
miners' pub served by one bar.
The superb public bar has a
real fire and low beams. It may
be difficult to get to, but it's a
joy to find. Beware high tides!
Eve meals finish at 7.30.
🏚 Q 🕭 🕭 🕪 P

Lower Withington

Red Lion
Trap Street, Dicklow Cob (off
B5392) ☎ (01477) 571248
11.45–2.30 (3 Sat), 5.30–11; 12–3,
7–10.30 Sun
**Robinson's Dark Mild, Best
Bitter** H
Large rural pub on the village
green, with a restaurant, a
lounge bar and a tap room for
locals; close to Jodrell Bank
radio telescope. Although the
pump clips say Robinson's Best
Mild, it is actually a very rare
outlet for the dark.
🏚 🕭 🕪 🕇 🕇 ♣ P

CHESHIRE

Lymm

Spread Eagle
47 Eagle Brow
☎ (01925) 755939
11.30–11; 12–10.30 Sun
Lees GB Mild, Bitter H,
Moonraker E
Pub in a picturesque village
near the Bridgewater Canal: a
split-level lounge, a cosy snug
with a real fire and a bar with
TV; no piped music. Friendly
welcome and service from the
staff and Rodney, the pub cat.
Good, home-cooked food.
Limited parking.
🏠 Q ◑ 🕭 P

Macclesfield

Baths
40 Green Street
11–4 (not Mon–Thu), 6.30–11; 12–3,
7–10.30 Sun
**Banks's Hanson's Mild,
Bitter; Boddingtons Bitter** H
Small, but thriving local, just
off the A537 Buxton road, a few
mins' walk from the
station. A local bowling green
inspired its original name
(Bowling Green Tavern), and a
public bath its present. The
pub has outlived both.
🕭 ≈ ♣

Boarhound
37 Brook Street (off Silk Rd)
☎ (01625) 421200
11–11; 12–10.30 Sun
**Robinson's Hatters Mild, Best
Bitter** H
Originally called the
Commercial, this large brick
local is a few mins' walk from
Waters Green. Recently
refurbished, its large upstairs
meeting room is popular with
groups. 🌸 ≈ ♣

British Flag
42 Coare Street
☎ (01625) 425500
12–3, 5.30–11; 12–3, 7–10.30 Sun
**Robinson's Hatters Mild, Best
Bitter** H
Comfortable local with an
excellent pool room. In the
1860s, the pub boasted ginger
beer manufacturing and had a
reputation as the local King's
School 'brewery tap', as it was
frequented by school staff!
🕭 ≈ ♣

George & Dragon
Sunderland Street
☎ (01625) 421898
11–3 (4 Mon & Thu, 5 Sat), 5.30 (7
Sat)–11; 11–11 Fri; 12–3, 7–10.30 Sun
**Robinson's Hatters Mild, Best
Bitter** E
Friendly pub serving good
value food early eve. Pool,
darts and skittles are played.
Near the bus and rail stations.
🌸 ▶ ≈ ♣

Railway View
Byrons Lane
☎ (01625) 423657
5.30–11; 12–3, 6–11 Fri & Sat; 12–3,
7–10.30 Sun
**Bateman Mild, XB, XXXB;
guest beers** H
Pleasant pub, 100 yards from
the main London road.
Excellent range of guest beers;
house beer from Coach House.
Q ▶ ♣

Waters Green Tavern
96 Waters Green
☎ (01625) 422653
11.30–3.30, 5.30 (7 Sat)–11; 12–3,
7–10.30 Sun
**Mansfield Riding Bitter; guest
beers** H
Close to the bus and rail
stations, this pleasant pub was
originally three storeys; the
half-timbered frontage is false.
Popular at lunchtime (good
food); excellent range of guest
beers. ◑ ≈ ♣

Try also: **Chester Road
Tavern**, Chester Rd (Greenalls)

Mobberley

Bull's Head
Town Lane (off B5085)
☎ (01565) 873134
11–11; 12–10.30 Sun
**Boddingtons Bitter; Tetley
Mild, Bitter; guest beer** H
Large, picturesque community
pub of late 17th- and early
18th-century origin, with an
open-plan lounge and a central
fireplace. Folk music first Fri
each month. The house beer is
by Coach House. A terrace
overlooks the bowling green at
the rear. 🏠 🌸 ◑ ▶ 🕭 ♣ P

Try also: **Roebuck**, Town Lane
(Free)

Nantwich

Frog & Ferret
4 Oatmarket
☎ (01270) 629324
11–11; 12–3, 7–10.30 Sun
**Banks's Bitter; Camerons
Strongarm; guest beers** H
Popular, open-plan pub,
student-oriented yet making
older customers feel welcome;
a main venue for Nantwich's
jazz and folk festivals.
Extremely busy Fri and Sat
eves. The house beers come
from Banks's and Coach
House. 🌸 ◑

Oddfellows Arms
Welsh Row (A534)
☎ (01270) 624758
11–3.30, 5.30–11; 12–3.30, 7–10.30 Sun
**Burtonwood Mild, Bitter,
Forshaw's** H
Cosy, single-roomed bar, with
beams and low ceilings.
🏠 Q 🌸 ◑ ♣

Wilbraham Arms
58 Welsh Row (A534)
☎ (01270) 626419
11–11; 12–10.30 Sun
**Theakston Best Bitter; guest
beers** H
Former Georgian coach house,
recently refurbished but
retaining a friendly
atmosphere and a strong local
following. Occasional cider.
🏠 ◑ ▶ 🕭 P

Newbold

Horseshoe
Fence Lane ☎ (01260) 272205
11–3, 6–11; 12–3, 7–10.30 Sun
**Robinson's Hatters Mild, Best
Bitter** E, **Frederics** H
Isolated country pub, formerly
part of a farmhouse and still
enjoying a farming
atmosphere; difficult to find
but worth the effort. Superb
children's play area. Good
local trade; welcome for
walkers and canal-boaters.
🏠 Q 🛏 🌸 ♣ P

Over Peover

Parkgate Inn
Stocks Lane ☎ (01625) 861455
11–11; 12–4, 7–10.30 Sun
Samuel Smith OBB H
Very smart, ivy-clad old pub
with several small, wood-
panelled rooms, including a
tap room. It stages an annual
gooseberry competition (Aug)
and the winners are in a frame
on the wall. Occasional visits
from local morris dancers.
🏠 Q 🌸 ◑ ▶ 🕭 ♣ P

Parkgate

Red Lion
The Parade ☎ (0151) 336 1548
12–2.30, 5–11; 12–11 Fri & Sat;
12–10.30 Sun
**Ind Coope Burton Ale; Tetley
Bitter; Walker Mild; guest
beer** H
Wirral CAMRA *Pub of the Year*
1996: a traditional lounge and
bar with a superb view of the
Welsh hills across the Dee
estuary and marsh (famous for
bird life). Local numbers are
swelled by many summer
visitors. Nelson, the parrot,
guards the bar. Q ◑ 🕭 ♣

Plumley

Golden Pheasant
Plumley Moor Lane (off A556)
☎ (01565) 722261
11–3, 5.30–11; 12–10.30 Sun
Lees GB Mild, Bitter H
Large hotel pub in the heart of
the Cheshire countryside with
a large, open-plan lounge, a
smaller public bar and a
restaurant. Bowling green.
🏠 🌸 🏠 ◑ ▶ 🕭 ♿ ≈ ♣ P ⚲

54

Prestbury

Admiral Rodney
New Road
☎ (01625) 828078
11–3, 5.30–11; 12–3, 7–10.30 Sun
Robinson's Hatters Mild, Best Bitter Ⓗ
Popular inn in an attractive village terrace, a Grade II-listed building. The original front door became the back door when the new road was built through the village.
🏚 Q ◖ ⇌ P

Rainow

Highwayman
Whaley Bridge Road (B5470)
☎ (01625) 573245
11–3, 7–11; 12–3, 7–10.30 Sun
Thwaites Bitter Ⓗ
Remote and windswept inn, known as the Blacksmith's Arms until 1949 and locally as the 'Patch'. Breathtaking views from the front door; inside is a maze of connecting rooms with a small tap room in the far corner. Three blazing open fires in winter. 🏚 Q ◖ ▶ ⊟ P

Rode Heath

Royal Oak
41 Sandbach Road (A533)
☎ (01270) 875670
12–3 (not Mon), 5.30 (5 Fri)–11; 12–11 Sat; 12–10.30 Sun
Ansells Mild; Draught Bass; Greene King Abbot; Marston's Pedigree; Tetley Bitter; Titanic Premium; guest beer Ⓗ
Two-roomed pub consisting of a comfortable lounge plus a games room. Tetley's Tapster's Choice beers sold. No food Sun eve or Mon. Q ❀ ◖ ▶ ♣ P

Saughall

Greyhound Inn
Seahill Road
☎ (01244) 880205
11–3, 5–11; 11–11 Sat; 12–3, 7–10.30 Sun
Boddingtons Bitter; Castle Eden Ale; guest beers Ⓗ
Served from a central bar, this multi-area pub is popular with locals. The Curry and Pint deal on Mon eve is good value; quiz night Thu. Two guests are sometimes available. No food Sun eve; other eves till 8.30.
Q ❀ ◖ ▶ ⊟ ⅙ ♣ P

Scholar Green

Rising Sun
112 Station Road (off A34)
☎ (01782) 776235
12–3, 7–11; 12–3, 7–10.30 Sun
Marston's Bitter, Pedigree, HBC Ⓗ

Three-roomed pub between Scholar Green and the Macclesfield Canal; a Victorian pub, enlarged in 1939. Good food at reasonable prices.
🏚 ⛝ ◖ ▶ ⊟ ♣ P

Stoak

Bunbury Arms
Little Stanney Lane (1 mile S of M53 jct 10) OS422733
☎ (01244) 301665
12–3, 6–11; 12–11 Sat; 12–10.30 Sun
Boddingtons Bitter; Cains Bitter; Higsons Bitter Ⓗ
Quiet, traditional pub with a small original public bar. The lounge is aimed at the traditional pubgoer wanting a quiet meal and a pint. Children welcome for meals (served all day Sun; eve meals finish at 8).
Q ❀ ◖ ▶ ⊟ Ⓐ ♣ P

Tarporley

Rising Sun
38 High Street (A51)
☎ (01829) 732423
11.30–3, 5.30–11; 11.30–11 Sat; 12–10.30 Sun
Robinson's Hatters Mild, Best Bitter Ⓗ
This authentic old pub scores heavily on almost all fronts and is a *Guide* perennial. Meals in the lounge bar and restaurant are renowned for quality and value, but one bar is reserved for drinkers. Children welcome at lunchtime (and eves in the restaurant). The TV is for sport only. Q ◖ ▶ P

Swan Hotel
50 High Street (A51)
☎ (01829) 733838
11–3, 6–11; 11–11 Sat; 12–3, 7–10.30 Sun
Ruddles Best Bitter, County; Wadworth 6X; guest beers Ⓗ
Elegant, family-run free house, an 18th-century building at the centre of picturesque Tarporley. Two oak-beamed bars boast open fires. Extensive range of English and French cuisine in the brasserie.
🛏 ◖ ▶ ⅙ P

Tushingham

Blue Bell Inn
100 yds from A41, 4 miles N of Whitchurch
☎ (01948) 662172
12–3, 6–11; 12–3, 7–10.30 Sun
Hanby Drawwell; guest beers Ⓗ
Welcoming, characterful, 17th-century pub with a wealth of beams. Friendly locals; cracking atmosphere. Guest beers are normally from small independents.
🏚 Q ❀ ◖ ▶ Ⓐ ♣ P

Warrington

Bull's Head
33 Church Street
☎ (01925) 635680
12–11; 12–10.30 Sun
Draught Bass; Cains Bitter; Flowers Original; Greenalls Mild, Bitter; guest beer Ⓗ
Rambling, 17th-century community pub. The modest frontage conceals not only five rooms but also a bowling green and a function room to the rear. An understandably popular pub which sets a standard for other Greenalls pubs. The guest beer is from Greenalls' list.
❀ ◖ ⊟ ⇌ (Central) ♣

Lord Rodney
67 Winwick Road
☎ (01925) 234296
12–11; 12–10.30 Sun
Boddingtons Bitter; Tetley Bitter; guest beers Ⓗ
Tetley Festival Ale House with weekly changing guest beers (up to eight). Live music (can be loud) Fri eve; quiz Tue eve. Weekday lunches.
◖ ⇌ (Central) ♣

Lower Angel
27 Buttermarket Street
☎ (01925) 633299
11–4, 7–11; 12–3, 7–10.30 Sun
Ind Coope Burton Ale; Walker Mild, Bitter, Best Bitter; guest beer Ⓗ
Real town-centre pub, concentrating on beer not food, with an ever-changing guest beer. Note the collection of old and odd bottled beers in the bar; spot the resident ghost in the lounge.
⊟ ⇌ (Central) ♣

Old Town House
Buttermarket Street
☎ (01925) 242787
11.30–11; 12–10.30 Sun
Courage Directors; John Smith's Bitter; Theakston XB; guest beers Ⓗ
Single-bar pub, set back from the main road, with usually around six guest beers a week, mainly from micros. Up to three guest ciders are served by gravity. Live music Fri eve. Eve meals Mon–Fri. ❀ ◖ ▶ ⇌ (Central) ♣ ⌂

Saracen's Head
381 Wilderspool Causeway (A49, 1 mile S of town centre)
☎ (01925) 634466
11.30–11; 12–10.30 Sun
Greenalls Mild, Bitter, Original; guest beer Ⓗ
Large, multi-roomed pub opposite the old Greenalls Brewery (the guest beer is from Greenalls' list); a community pub with quiz nights and

family days. Food available until 9 (large portions at reasonable prices); the restaurant is open seven days a week. Bowling green and farm animals in the grounds.
P

Wettenhall

Little Man
Winsford Road OS601628
(01270) 528203
12–3 (not Tue), 7–11; 12–3.30, 7–10.30 Sun
Boddingtons Bitter; guest beers H
Friendly local which can be busy; five cask ales and good pub grub make it well worth a visit. Darts and dominoes are played. Near the local marina and equestrian centre.
P

Wheelock

Commercial Hotel ☆
Game Street (off A534, near Bridge 154 of Trent & Mersey Canal)
(01270) 760122
8–11; 12–2, 8–10.30 Sun
Boddingtons Bitter; Marston's Pedigree; Thwaites Bitter; guest beer H
Listed Georgian building that has been run by the same family for 75 years. Four distinct rooms include a games room with a full-sized snooker table. Spontaneous music performances Thu eve, when a guest beer is sold.
Q P

Widnes

Millfield
Millfield Road
(0151) 424 2955
11–11; 11–5, 7–11 Sat; 12–3, 7–10.30 Sun
Webster's Yorkshire Bitter; Wilson's Mild H
Traditional, unspoilt, busy backstreet pub, with a recently redecorated lounge and a small bar.

Wilmslow

Farmers Arms
71 Chapel Lane
(01625) 532443
11–11; 12–10.30 Sun
Boddingtons Mild, Bitter; guest beer H
Traditional, Victorian town pub: several rooms with brasses and antiques. Very busy at times due to its good atmosphere. Eye-catching finery around the etched lounge windows. The garden is kept in beautiful condition. The family room is upstairs. No food Sun.
P

Wincle

Ship
Off A54, near Danebridge
(01260) 227217
12–3, 7–11; 12–4, 7–10.30 Sun (closed winter Mon)
Boddingtons Bitter; guest beer H
Attractive, 16th-century, sandstone village inn overlooking the scenic Dane Valley. The 18-inch thick stone walls are designed to withstand the rigours of local winters. The sign above the door is of the *Nimrod*, the ship in which Shackleton sailed to the Arctic. Popular with walkers. Good food.
Q P

Winsford

Prince's Feathers
Station Road (off A54, new bypass) (01606) 594191
11–3, 6–11; 11–11 Fri & Sat; 12–10.30 Sun
Cains Bitter; Chester's Mild; Flowers IPA; guest beers H
Local CAMRA *Pub of the Season* 1996: a two-roomed, lively town pub with boxing memorabilia in the bar. Cask ale nights (Tue) feature cheap beer promotions. Traditional meals available Sat lunch.
P

Brewers all across the country agree: excessive UK beer duty is killing jobs. Pat Read of London's Young's Brewery leads this demonstration against high beer tax.

THE NEW BREWERIES

The 1998 *Good Beer Guide* introduces no less than 48 new independent breweries and brew pubs. Full details can be found in The Breweries, beginning on page 415, but here is a county by county checklist of the new producers.

ENGLAND

CAMBRIDGESHIRE
City of Cambridge, Cambridge
Fenland, Chatteris

CORNWALL
Keltek, Tregony
Skinner's, Truro

CUMBRIA
Derwent, Cockermouth
Drunken Duck, Barngates
Lakeland, Kendal
Strawberry Bank, Cartmel Fell

ESSEX
Mighty Oak, Hutton

HAMPSHIRE
Beckett's, Basingstoke
Itchen Valley, Alresford

HEREFORDSHIRE
Shoes, Norton Canon
Woodhampton, Aymestrey

HERTFORDSHIRE
Verulam, St Albans

ISLE OF WIGHT
Ventnor, Ventnor

LANCASHIRE
Blackburn, Blackburn

LEICESTERSHIRE & RUTLAND
Man in the Moon, Ashby Magna
O'Gaunt, Burrough on the Hill

LINCOLNSHIRE
Blue Cow, South Witham
DarkTribe, Gunness
Deeping, Market Deeping
Duffield, Harmston
Oldershaw, Grantham

GREATER MANCHESTER
Mash & Air, Manchester
Old Pint Pot, Salford
Saddleworth, Uppermill

MERSEYSIDE
Beecham's, St Helens

NORFOLK
Blue Moon, Hingham

NOTTINGHAMSHIRE
Fiddlers, Old Basford

SHROPSHIRE
Six Bells, Bishop's Castle

STAFFORDSHIRE
Stony Rock, Waterhouses

SUFFOLK
Brettvale, Bildeston

SURREY
Hale & Hearty, Farnham
Leith Hill, Coldharbour

TYNE & WEAR
Four Rivers, Newcastle upon Tyne
Riverside, Sunderland

WARWICKSHIRE
Queen's Head, Iron Cross

WEST MIDLANDS
Beowulf, Birmingham
Jones & Mather, Brierley Hill

YORKSHIRE
Abbeydale, Sheffield
Barnfield, Slaithwaite
Fernandes, Wakefield
Swaled Ale, Gunnerside

WALES

NORTH-EAST WALES
Travellers Inn, Caerwys

WEST WALES
Flannery's, Aberystwyth

SCOTLAND

DUMFRIES & GALLOWAY
Sulwath, Southerness

TAYSIDE
Inveralmond, Perth

OFFSHORE BRITAIN

ISLE OF MAN
Old Laxey, Laxey

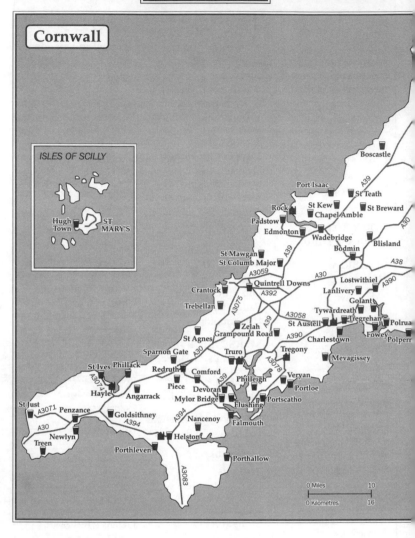

Cornwall

ISLES OF SCILLY

Hugh Town — ST MARY'S

Boscastle
Port Isaac — St Teath
Rock — St Kew — St Breward
Chapel Amble
Padstow
Edmonton
Wadebridge — Blisland
Bodmin
St Mawgan
St Columb Major
A3059
Quintrell Downs
Crantock
Lostwithiel
Lanlivery
Golant
Trebellan
Tywardreath
Zelah
St Austell — Tregrehan — Polrua
Grampound Road
St Agnes
Charlestown — Fowey — Polperr
Sparnon Gate
Truro
Tregony
Mevagissey
St Ives — Phillack
Redruth
Comford
Veryan
Hayle
Piece
Phillegh
Portloe
Angarrack
Devoran
Portscatho
St Just
Mylor Bridge
Flushing
Penzance
Goldsithney
Nancenoy
Falmouth
Newlyn
Helston
Treen
Porthleven
Porthallow

0 Miles 10
0 Kilometres 16

Angarrack

Angarrack Inn
32 Steamers Hill (off A30)
☎ (01736) 752380
11–3, 6–11; 12–3, 7–10.30 Sun
**St Austell Bosun's, Tinners,
HSD** Ⓗ
Attractive, welcoming and
comfortable village pub,
offering an extensive and good
value menu of home-cooking
(no food winter Mon eve).
🅼 ✿ ◖ ▶ Å P

Blisland

Blisland Inn
The Green ☎ (01208) 850739
12–3, 6–11; 11–11 Fri & Sat; 12–4,
7–10.30 Sun
Beer range varies Ⓗ/Ⓖ
Set on the only village green in
Cornwall, this fine granite free
house (formerly the Royal
Oak) offers up to five guest
beers plus a house beer from
Sutton Brewery; the cider
changes regularly. Friendly
atmosphere; large family/
games room. Good, home-
cooked local produce.
🅼 Q ➳ ✿ ◖ ▶ ♣ ◔ P

Bodmin

Mason's Arms
5–9 Higher Bore Street
☎ (01208) 72607
11–3, 5–11; 11–11 Sat; 12–10.30 Sun
**Draught Bass; Fuller's London
Pride; Worthington Bitter;
guest beers** Ⓗ

Historic, two-bar town pub,
reputed to hold the oldest
continuous licence in
Cornwall. The lounge is quiet.
Very good value food. Good
for families.
Q ➳ ✿ ◖ ▶ ⊞ ♣ P

Boscastle

Wellington Hotel
The Harbour
☎ (01840) 250202
11–3, 5.30–11 (11–11 summer); 12–3,
6–10.30 (12–10.30 summer) Sun
**Draught Bass; Dartmoor Best
Bitter; Flowers IPA;
Whitbread Fuggles IPA; guest
beers** Ⓗ
Attractive, 16th-century
coaching inn. The long bar is

Callington

Coachmakers Arms
Newport Square
☎ (01579) 382567
11–3, 6.30–11; 12–3, 7–10.30 Sun
Draught Bass; Greene King Abbot; guest beer H
300-year-old coaching inn, offering a warm atmosphere, a popular, small bar and a good range of food. Q 🛏 ◑ ▸ ♣ P

Chapel Amble

Maltster's Arms
☎ (01736) 752380
11–3, 5.30–11; 12–2.30, 7–10.30 Sun
Fuller's London Pride; Greene King Abbot; Sharp's Cornish Coaster; guest beer H
17th-century, olde-worlde pub with low beams, wood panelling and a slate floor in the bar. Excellent menu – fish is a speciality. The house beer is brewed by Sharp's. Family room upstairs. Cider in summer.
🛏 Q ♿ 🐕 ◑ ▸ ♣ ♻

Charlestown

Rashleigh Arms
☎ (01726) 73635
11–11; 12–10.30 Sun
Draught Bass; Ruddles County; St Austell Tinners; Sharp's Own or Doom Bar; Tetley Bitter; Wadworth 6X; guest beers H
Large, friendly inn overlooking the famous port, comprising two large bars and a family room.
🐕 ❀ 🛏 ◑ ▸ 🍴 ♿ Å ♣ P

Comford

Fox & Hounds
On A393 ☎ (01209) 820251
11–3, 6–11 (varies summer); 12–3, 7–10.30 Sun
Draught Bass; St Austell XXXX Mild (winter), Tinners, HSD, Winter Warmer G
Comfortable country pub with a restaurant specialising in home cooking. All ales are served from the casks behind the bar. Look for the frieze in the snug. The pub and garden are a blaze of colour in summer. 🛏 ❀ ◑ ▸ Å ♣ P

Crantock

Old Albion
Langurroc Road
☎ (01637) 830243
12–11; 12–10.30 Sun
Draught Bass; Courage Best Bitter; John Smith's Bitter; guest beers H
Picture postcard village inn serving food to suit all tastes; Sun lunches are popular. Set in a pleasant walking area, with a safe sandy beach nearby.
🛏 Q 🐕 ❀ ◑ ▸ Å ♻ P

Devoran

Old Quay Inn
St John's Terrace (off A39)
☎ (01872) 863142
11.45–2.30, 6–11; 12–3, 7–10.30 Sun
Draught Bass; Flowers IPA; guest beer H
Welcoming village inn offering an ever-changing guest ale, plus beer festivals in Oct and Feb. Fine views over Devoran quay and creek. Limited parking. Good, home-cooked food. 🛏 ❀ 🛏 ◑ ▸ ♣ P

Edmonton

Quarryman
Just off A39 ☎ (01208) 816444
11–11; 12–10.30 Sun
Draught Bass; guest beers H
Pub built in the mid-18th century as a school house for quarry workers' families. Their cottages are now part of a holiday and sports complex, with a bistro.
🛏 Q ❀ 🛏 ◑ ▸ ♣ P ✄

Falmouth

Quayside Inn
41 Arwenack Street
☎ (01326) 312113
11–3, 7–11 (11–11 summer & upstairs bar); 12–10.30 Sun
Draught Bass G**; Courage Directors; Flowers Original; Fuller's London Pride; Ruddles County; Sharp's Doom Bar; Tetley Bitter** H**; guest beers** G
Pub where the bar at street-level has comfortable surroundings and is popular for lunches, while the bar at quay-level has bare floors and all beers on view. The downstairs serves beer, cider and wine only.
❀ ◑ ▸ ⇌ (The Dell) ♻

Seven Stars ☆
The Moor ☎ (01326) 312111
11–3, 6–11; 12–3, 7–10.30 Sun
Draught Bass G**; Morland Old Speckled Hen** H**; Sharp's Own** G
Pub whose unspoilt interior has remained unchanged for

adorned with lamps from St Juliot's church, placed there by Thomas Hardy. The stained-glass windows date from 1846. Splendid food. Live folk music Mon eve.
🛏 Q 🐕 ❀ 🛏 ◑ ▸ ♣ P

Botus Fleming

Rising Sun
½ mile off A388, near Saltash
☎ (01752) 842792
7–11; 12–4, 7–11 Sat; 12–4, 7–10.30 Sun
Adnams Bitter; Draught Bass; Cottage Golden Arrow; Fuller's ESB; guest beers H
Unspoilt gem tucked away in a small village near Saltash. Outside boules pitch. Inch's cider.
🛏 ❀ ♿ Å ♣ ♻ P

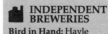

five generations: a lively tap room and quiet snug. The present landlord is an ordained priest. Q ✿ ⌂

Flushing

Royal Standard
St Peter's Hill (off A393; also via passenger ferry from Falmouth) ☎ (01326) 374250
11–2.30 (3 Fri & Sat), 6.30–11; 12–3, 7–10.30 (varies winter) Sun
Draught Bass; Flowers IPA; Sharp's Doom Bar H
The present landlord has run this local for over 30 years. Home-made pasties and apple pies are specialities. Fine views of the Penryn River from the front patio. ▨ ✿ ◖ ▶ ♣

Fowey

Galleon
12 Fore Street
☎ (01726) 833014
11–11; 12–10.30 Sun
Draught Bass; Flowers IPA; Sharp's Cornish Coaster; guest beers (summer) H
400-year-old pub on the river, refurbished but retaining its Cornish character. Fine views from the lounge and patio areas. Wide range of bar meals (fish a speciality). Trad jazz Sun lunch; live music Fri eve.
✿ ⌂ ◖ ▶ ৬ ▲ ♣ ☼

Golant

Fisherman's Arms
Fore Street (off B3269)
☎ (01726) 832453
11–11 (12–3, 6–11 winter); 12–4, 7–10.30 Sun
Ushers Best Bitter, Founders, seasonal beers H
Charming village pub, in a lovely waterside setting, with views across the River Fowey. Good, home-cooked food. Beware of being cut off!
▨ Q ౿ ✿ ◖ ▶ ♣ P

Goldsithney

Crown
Fore Street
☎ (01736) 710494
11–3, 6–11 (11–11 summer); 12–10.30 Sun
St Austell XXXX Mild, Trelawny's Pride, HSD H
Attractive, comfortable, village pub with a very popular restaurant (booking advisable); excellent, home-cooked bar meals, too.
▨ ✿ ⌂ ◖ ▶

Grampound Road

Four Burrow Inn
The Square (off A390, between Grampound and Probus)
OS484935 ☎ (01726) 882296

7–11; 11.30–3, 7–11 Sat; 12–3, 7–10.30 Sun
Sharp's Doom Bar, Own H
Free house, a recently extended and refurbished former village coaching stables; now a lively pub. ৬ P

Gunnislake

Rising Sun Inn
Calstock Road
☎ (01822) 832201
11–3, 5–11; 11–11 Sat; 12–3, 7–10.30 Sun
Draught Bass; Princetown Jail Ale; St Austell HSD; Sharp's Cornish Coaster; guest beers H
Friendly inn with pleasing decor, serving an excellent beer choice and superb food. Helpful bar staff. Views over the Tamar Valley.
▨ Q ✿ ⌂ ◖ ▶ ▲ ⇌ ♣ P

Helston

Blue Anchor
Coinagehall Street
☎ (01326) 562821
11–11; 12–10.30 Sun
Blue Anchor Middle, Best, Special, Extra Special H
The flagship of pub breweries: a rambling, unspoilt, 15th-century, granite building with a thatched roof and its own brewery at the rear. No jukeboxes or bandits; occasional cider. The basic family room doubles as a skittle alley.
▨ Q ౿ ◖ ▲ ☼

Isles of Scilly:
St Mary's

Bishop & Wolf
Main street, Hugh Town
☎ (01720) 422790
11–11; 12–10.30 Sun
St Austell XXXX Mild, Tinners, HSD H
Named after the two famous local lighthouses, this lively pub features marine decor in its large bar, pool room and upstairs restaurant. The beer is fined at the pub, after its sometimes arduous sea crossing. Children welcome.
◖ ▶ ▲ ♣

Kilkhampton

New Inn
☎ (01288) 321488
11–2.30, 6–11; 12–3, 7–10.30 Sun
Hancock's HB; Sharp's Own; guest beers H
Spacious, 15th-century village pub: a quiet front bar and a family room with a skittle alley. Good, home-cooked meals (no Sun lunch in summer).
▨ Q ౿ ✿ ◖ ▶ ♣ P

Kingsand

Rising Sun
The Green ☎ (01752) 822840
11–11; 12–10.30 Sun
Draught Bass or Sharp's Own; Courage Best Bitter; guest beer (summer) H
Popular, yet quiet and cosy pub: a former customs house in a village of narrow streets, on the Coastal Path. Friendly hosts. Parking for four cars. Excellent food (meals served all day Sat–Sun).
▨ Q ✿ ⌂ ◖ ▶ ▲ ♣ P

Lanlivery

Crown
Off A390, 2 miles W of St Austell ☎ (01208) 872707
11–3, 6.30–11; 12–3, 6.30–10.30 Sun
Draught Bass; Sharp's Own; Worthington Bitter H
12th-century pub, a listed building with two restaurants, one no-smoking. Very pleasant country surroundings; friendly staff. The accommodation is adapted for wheelchair users.
▨ Q ౿ ✿ ⌂ ◖ ▶ ⌂ ৬ ▲ ♣ P

Lostwithiel

Royal Oak
King Street (off A390)
☎ (01208) 872552
11–11; 12–10.30 Sun
Draught Bass; Fuller's London Pride; Marston's Pedigree; Sharp's Cornish Coaster; guest beers H
Historic, 13th-century inn, situated in the old capital of Cornwall. A stone floored public bar contrasts with a comfortable lounge and restaurant. Unusual bottled beers. ▨ Q ౿ ✿ ⌂ ◖ ▶ ⌂ ▲ ⇌ ♣ P

Mevagissey

Fountain Inn
Fore Street
☎ (01726) 842320
11.30–11; 12–10.30 Sun
St Austell Tinners, Trelawny's Pride, Winter Warmer H
Friendly, two-bar, olde-worlde inn, with slate floors, beams and historic photos. The upstairs restaurant is open March–Oct.
▨ Q ⌂ ◖ ▶ ▲ ♣

Mylor Bridge

Lemon Arms
Off A393 at Penryn
☎ (01326) 373666
11–3, 6–11; 12–3, 7–10.30 Sun
St Austell Tinners, HSD H, **Winter Warmer** G

Friendly, one-bar pub at the village centre. Good home-cooked meals. Popular with sailing enthusiasts; families very welcome.
🏰 ❀ ◖ ▶ ▲ ♣ P

Nancenoy

Trengilly Wartha Inn
Off B3291 OS731282
☎ (01326) 340332
11–3, 6.30–11 (may vary summer); 12–3, 7–10.30 Sun
Dartmoor Best Bitter G; **Sharp's Cornish Coaster; guest beers** G/H
Delightful, remote inn, serving ever-changing guest beers and an excellent quality menu. Good country walks nearby. 🏰
Q ⍾ ❀ 🛏 ◖ ▶ ▲ ♣ ⌂ P ⌇

Newlyn

Fisherman's Arms
Fore Street ☎ (01736) 63399
10.30–3, 5.30–11; 12–3, 7–10.30 Sun
St Austell Bosun's, Trelawny's Pride, HSD H
Popular old local with superb views over Mount's Bay and the harbour. Note the inglenook and intriguing memorabilia. Good simple food. Very limited parking.
🏰 ❀ ◖ ▶

Padstow

Old Ship Hotel
Mill Square ☎ (01841) 532357
11–3, 6–11 (11–11 summer); 12–3, 7–10.30 (12–10.30 summer) Sun
Draught Bass; Brains SA; Flowers IPA H; **guest beers** H/G
Comfortable hotel just off the busy harbour with a large outdoor drinking area. The front bar is nicely wood panelled and has nautical pictures. Regular live music.
Q ⍾ ❀ 🛏 ◖ ▶ ▣ ♣ P

Penzance

Globe & Ale House
1 Queen Street
☎ (01736) 64098
11–11; 12–10.30 Sun
Draught Bass; Flowers Original; Sharp's Own H; **guest beers** G
Greenalls alehouse with a good beer choice and a range of simple dishes. Dylan Thomas held his wedding reception here. ◖ ▶

Mount's Bay Inn
Promenade, Wherrytown
☎ (01736) 63027
11–3, 5.30–11; 12–3, 7–10.30 Sun
Draught Bass; Worthington Bitter; guest beers H
Small, friendly, free house on the seafront towards Newlyn. The dining area is in the bar

(no meals Sun or Tue eves in winter). 🏰 Q ◖ ▶

Phillack

Bucket of Blood
14 Churchtown Road
☎ (01736) 752378
11–2.30, 6–11; 12–4, 7–10.30 Sun
St Austell XXXX Mild, Trelawny's Pride, HSD H
Historic, friendly pub close to Hayle beaches; its name is derived from a 'gory' legend! Meals in summer.
🏰 Q ⍾ ❀ ◖ ▶ ♣ ⌂ P

Philleigh

Roseland Inn
On King Harry Ferry road
☎ (01872) 580254
11.30–3, 6.30–11 (11.30–11 summer); 12–3, 7–10.30 Sun
Draught Bass; Greenalls Bitter; Marston's Pedigree; guest beer H
Classic, 17th-century country inn at the heart of the Roseland Peninsula, with slate floors, beams, a restaurant, a bar, and a locals' snug. Good menu of home-cooked food. Cider in summer. 🏰 Q ❀ ◖ ▶ ⌂ P

Piece

Countryman
On Four Lanes–Pool road
☎ (01209) 215960
11–11; 12–10.30 Sun
Courage Best Bitter, Directors; Morland Old Speckled Hen; Sharp's Own; Theakston Old Peculier; guest beer H
A former count house for the local tin-mining community, this welcoming, popular, country pub provides good food and regular entertainment.
🏰 ❀ ◖ ▶ ⅄ ▲ ♣ P

Polperro

Blue Peter
The Quay ☎ (01503) 272743
11–11; 12–10.30 Sun
St Austell Tinners, HSD; Sharp's Doom Bar; guest beers H
Small pub on the Coastal Path reached by a flight of steps at the end of the quay; very lively and friendly, hosting live music Sat, and Sun morning. No food, but you may take in sandwiches. 🏰 ▲ ♣ ⌂

Crumplehorn Inn
The Old Mill (on A387)
☎ (01503) 272348
11–11; 12–2.30, 7–10.30 Sun
Draught Bass; St Austell XXXX Mild, HSD; guest beers H
Inn converted from an old mill mentioned in the *Domesday Book*, in a very popular area

with tourists. The beer is fined when it reaches the inn. Good food. 🏰 Q ⍾ ❀ 🛏 ◖ ▶ ▣ ▲ ♣ ⌂ P

Polruan

Lugger
The Quay ☎ (01726) 870007
11–11; 12–3, 7–10.30 Sun
St Austell Bosun's, XXXX Mild, Tinners, Trelawny's Pride, HSD H
Fine pub, boasting nautical decor and a friendly atmosphere. Q ◖ ▶ ▣ ♣

Porthallow

Five Pilchards
☎ (01326) 280256
12–2.30 (2 winter, 3 Sat), 6.30 (7.30 winter)–11; 12–2.30, 7.30–10.30 Sun (closed Sun eve & Mon in winter)
Greene King Abbot; guest beers H
Attractive rural pub by the beach, with fine views towards Falmouth. A collection of ships' lamps, model ships and wreck histories is on display. Parking nearby. 🏰 ❀ 🚗 ◖

Porthleven

Atlantic Inn
Peverell Terrace
☎ (01326) 562439
12–11; 12–10.30 Sun
Boddingtons Bitter; Brakspear Bitter; Fuller's London Pride; Wadworth 6X; Whitbread Fuggles IPA; guest beers H
Friendly, strong community local overlooking the harbour. Live music.
🏰 ⍾ ❀ ◖ ▶ ▲ ♣ ⌂ P

Port Isaac

Shipwright
The Terrace ☎ (01208) 880305
12–2.30 (3.30 Sat & summer), 7–11; 12–3, 7–10.30 Sun
Draught Bass; Flowers IPA; guest beer H
Friendly, family-run pub and bistro. A fine place to sit and enjoy the excellent sea view. The bar is decorated with flags, masts and old shipwright's tools. ❀ 🚗 ◖ ▶ ♣

Portloe

Ship Inn
☎ (01872) 501356
11.30–2.30 (3 Sat), 6.30–11 (11–11 summer); 12–3, 7–10.30 (12–10.30 summer) Sun
St Austell XXXX Mild, Tinners, Trelawny's Pride (summer) H
Friendly, two-bar local in a small fishing village featuring old village photos and a collection of knots on the beams. Good, home-cooked

food. Convenient for the Coastal Path.
🏨 Q ♿ ☼ 🛏 ⌖ ◐ ◗ ♣ ⌂ P

Portscatho

Plume of Feathers
☎ (01872) 580321
11.30–2.30, 6.30–11 (11–11 summer); 12–3, 7–10.30 Sun
St Austell XXXX Mild, Tinners, Trelawny's Pride Ⓗ
Popular village local on the Roseland Peninsula Coastal Path. Two bars feature open beams and a cosy atmosphere; a meeting place for local clubs. Good food. ☼ ◐ ◗

Quintrell Downs

Two Clomes
East Road (A392)
☎ (01637) 871163
12–3, 7–11 (11–11 summer); 12–3, 7–10.30 (12–10.30 summer) Sun
Otter Bitter; Sharp's Doom Bar, Special; guest beers Ⓗ
18th-century free house which takes its name from the clome ovens either side of the open log fire. No lunches Mon.
🏨 Q ♿ ☼ ◐ ◗ ♿ ▲ ⇌ P

Redruth

Tricky Dickie's
Tolgus Mount (off old Redruth bypass) ☎ (01209) 219292
11–3, 6–11 (midnight Tue & Thu); 12–3, 7–10.30 (all day if busy) Sun
Flowers IPA; Greene King Abbot; Sharp's Own; Wadworth 6X; guest beer Ⓗ
Renovated old tin mine smithy offering squash and exercise facilities. Live jazz Tue; other live entertainment Thu. The emphasis is on meals. Children welcome. 🏨 ☼ ◐ ◗ ♿ ♣ P

Rilla Mill

Manor House Inn
N of Liskeard on B3254; turn right at Upton Cross OS295731
☎ (01579) 62354
12–3, 7 (6.45 Sat)–11; 12–3, 7–10.30 Sun
Draught Bass; guest beers Ⓗ
Very busy, comfortable 17th-century inn and restaurant in the Lynher Valley. Two guest beers are offered, plus cider in summer. Excellent food.
Q ♿ ☼ 🛏 ◐ ◗ ⌂ P ✦

St Agnes

Driftwood Spars
Trevaunance Cove
☎ (01872) 552428
11–11 (midnight Fri & Sat); 12–10.30 Sun
Draught Bass; Ind Coope Burton Ale; Sharp's Own; Tetley Bitter; guest beers Ⓗ

Rambling, 17th-century hotel with a nautical theme in an old tin mining area. Live entertainment at weekends.
🏨 ♿ ☼ 🛏 ◐ ◗ ⌂ P

St Austell

Carlyon Arms
Sandy Hill (1 mile E of town on Bethel road) ☎ (01726) 72129
11–3, 5–11; 11–11 Sat; 12–10.30 Sun
St Austell XXXX Mild, Tinners, Trelawny's Pride, HSD Ⓗ
Friendly local serving good home-cooked food (eve meals Tue–Sat). Regular live music.
🏨 ☼ 🛏 ◐ ◗ ♿ ♣ P

St Breward

Old Inn
☎ (01208) 850711
12–3, 6–11; 12–3, 7–10.30 Sun
Draught Bass; Ruddles County; Sharp's Doom Bar; guest beers Ⓗ
Sturdy, granite-built, moorland pub next to the highest church in Cornwall. A slate flagstone floor and a large open fireplace are features.
🏨 Q ♿ ☼ ◐ ◗ 🍴 ♣ P

St Cleer

Stag Inn
Fore Street ☎ (01579) 342305
12–11; 12–10.30 Sun
Draught Bass; Greene King Abbot; Sharp's Cornish Coaster, Own; Wadworth 6X; guest beers Ⓗ
Welcoming inn on the edge of Bodmin Moor, offering a good range of beers and regular events. A family room is available when the pub is not too busy. Beer festival last weekend in June.
🏨 Q ♿ ☼ ◐ ◗ ♣ P

St Columb Major

Ring O'Bells
3 Bank Street
☎ (01637) 880259
12–3, 5–11; 12–4, 7–10.30 Sun
Draught Bass; Sharp's Cornish Coaster, Own Ⓗ**; guest beers** Ⓖ
Pub with a narrow frontage which belies an extensive interior of three bars catering for all tastes, from loud rock to an intimate restaurant (supper licence until midnight).
🏨 ☼ ◐ ◗ P

St Ives

Sloop Inn
The Wharf
☎ (01736) 796584
11–11; 12–10.30 Sun
Boddingtons Bitter; Courage Best Bitter; Morland Old

Speckled Hen; Ruddles County; John Smith's Bitter; Theakston Old Peculier Ⓗ
One of Cornwall's oldest (1312) and most famous inns, situated right on the harbour front. Popular with locals, fishermen, artists and tourists all year round. Seafood a speciality. Beware the low ceilings.
Q ♿ ☼ 🛏 ◐ ◗ ⇌ ♣

St Just

Star Inn
Fore Street
☎ (01736) 788767
11–3, 6–11 (11–11 summer); 12–10.30 Sun
St Austell XXXX Mild, Tinners, Trelawny's Pride, HSD Ⓗ
Fine, old granite pub in a tin mining area; a typical Cornish local with friendly staff. Cider in summer. 🏨 ♿ 🛏 ◐ ◗ ⌂

St Kew

St Kew Inn
Churchtown
☎ (01208) 841259
11–2.30, 6–11; 12–2.30, 7–10.30 Sun
St Austell Tinners, HSD Ⓖ
Busy pub with a reputation for good food; a delightful 15th-century inn next to the village church, with a large beer garden. Note the worn flagstone floor in the public bar and dining rooms.
🏨 Q ☼ 🛏 ◐ ◗ 🍴 P

St Mawgan

Falcon
☎ (01637) 860225
11–3, 6–11; 12–10.30 Sun
St Austell Tinners, Trelawny's Pride, HSD Ⓗ
Attractive pub at the centre of a quiet village, only a few miles from the bustle of Newquay and the airport. Popular for meals.
🏨 Q ♿ ☼ 🛏 ◐ ◗ ▲ P

St Teath

White Hart Hotel
The Square
☎ (01208) 850281
11–2.30, 6–11; 12–3, 7–10.30 Sun
Draught Bass; Ruddles County; Ushers Best Bitter Ⓗ
Busy, 18th-century, village-centre pub, with three bars, ranging from a quiet snug to a loud public bar with satellite TV. Separate dining areas.
🏨 Q ♿ ☼ 🛏 ◐ ◗ 🍴 ♣ P

Saltash

Two Bridges
Albert Road ☎ (01752) 848952
12–11; 12–10.30 Sun

Courage Best Bitter; Ushers Best Bitter, Founders, seasonal beers H
Lively pub with a cosy, country cottage interior. The large garden benefits from fine river views. Regular live music. 🏰 ⊛ ⇌ ♣ ⌂

Sparnon Gate

Cornish Arms
On old Portreath road
☎ (01209) 216407
12–2.30, 4.30 (5 summer)–11; 12–3, 7 (6.30 summer)–10.30 Sun
Sharp's Doom Bar G, Special H
17th-century free house with welcoming owners who offer proper food. This cosy pub has a small, basic bar and a comfortable main bar. Unspoilt, it boasts stone walls, beams, brasses and mining photos. 🏰 Q ⊛ ◖▶ ♿ ▲ P

Stratton

King's Arms
Howells Road (A3092)
☎ (01288) 352396
12–2.30, 6.30–11; 12–11 Fri & Sat; 12–10.30 Sun
Exmoor Ale; Sharp's Cornish Coaster, Own; guest beers H
Delightful, popular, 17th-century village pub with two bars and a slate flag floor. Changing range of guest beers; cider in summer.
🏰 ⊛ 🛏 ◖▶ ♣ ⌂ P

Trebellan

Smuggler's Den Inn
Take Cubert Road off A3075, left to Trebellan
☎ (01637) 830209
12–2, 6–11 (may vary; 11–11 summer); 12–3, 7–10.30 Sun
Fuller's London Pride; Morland Old Speckled Hen H; Sharp's Doom Bar G; guest beers H/G
Tucked down a narrow lane, it is a joy to find this old thatched pub with its extensive, good value menu.
🏰 ⛴ ⊛ ◖▶ ▲ P

Treen

Logan Rock Inn
☎ (01736) 810495
10.30–11; 12–10.30 Sun
St Austell Bosun's, Tinners, Trelawny's Pride, HSD H

Outstanding small pub near some superb coastal scenery and the Minack Open Air Theatre. The bar is full of character and offers good food.
🏰 ⛴ ⊛ ◖▶ P

Tregrehan

Britannia
On A390, 3 miles E of St Austell
☎ (01726) 812889
11–11; 12–10.30 Sun
Draught Bass; Morland Old Speckled Hen; St Austell Tinners; Sharp's Doom Bar, Own; guest beers H
Large, 16th-century inn, open all day for food. Safe garden and play area.
Q ⛴ ⊛ ◖▶ ⊟ ♿ ▲ P

Truro

City Inn
Pydar Street (B3284, signed Perranporth)
☎ (01872) 272623
11–11; 12–3, 7–10.30 Sun
Draught Bass; Courage Best Bitter, Directors; Theakston Best Bitter; guest beers H
Popular local with a friendly atmosphere and excellent value food. Large garden.
⊛ 🛏 ◖▶ ♣

Old Ale House
7 Quay Street
☎ (01872) 271122
11–11; 12–3, 7–10.30 Sun
Draught Bass G; Boddingtons Bitter; Sharp's Doom Bar H, Own G; guest beers H/G
Popular 'alehouse' theme pub where sawdust abounds. No electronic games or screens, hence conversation rules, except Mon and Thu when loud live music takes over. Acoustic music Sat; pleasantly quiet other nights. No food Sun. ◖▶

Tywardreath

New Inn
Fore Street
☎ (01726) 813901
11.30–3, 6–11; 11–11 Sat; 12–4, 7–10.30 Sun
Draught Bass; St Austell XXXX Mild G, Tinners, HSD H
Popular, classic village local near the coast, with a secluded garden and a games/children's

room. Limited parking.
🏰 Q ⛴ ⊛ ◖▶ ⊟ ▲ ⇌ (Par) ♣ ⌂ P

Upton Cross

Caradon Inn
On B3254
☎ (01579) 362391
11.30–11; 12–3, 7–10.30 Sun
Draught Bass G; Boddingtons Bitter; Flowers Original; St Austell HSD; Sharp's Own H
Friendly, 17th-century, slate-clad country inn enjoying a reputation for good value food. Pool and a jukebox in the public bar; quieter lounge. Cider in summer. Near Sterts Open Air Theatre.
🏰 Q ⊛ ◖▶ ♿ ▲ ♣ ⌂ P

Veryan

New Inn
Near A3078 on Roseland Peninsula
☎ (01872) 501362
11.30–3, 6.30–11; 12–3, 7–10.30 Sun
St Austell Tinners, HSD G
Comfortable, welcoming hostelry in the village centre. Ales are served from wooden casks behind the bar. Good range of food. 🏰 Q ⊛ 🛏 ◖▶

Wadebridge

Molesworth Arms
Molesworth Street
☎ (01208) 812055
11–11; 12–10.30 Sun
Morland Old Speckled Hen; Ruddles County; John Smith's Bitter; Webster's Green Label H
Grand, 16th-century coaching inn with a central archway and bars on either side. The public bar is small and basic compared to the smarter saloon. ⊛ 🛏 ◖▶ ⊟ ♣

Zelah

Hawkins Arms
☎ (01872) 540339
11–3, 6–11; 12–3, 7–10.30 Sun
Draught Bass; Dartmoor Best Bitter; Greene King Abbot; Tetley Bitter; guest beers H
Popular village local off the A30, offering home-cooked meals and good value B&B. No-smoking dining area.
🏰 ⛴ ⊛ ⊛ ◖▶ ♿ ♣ ⌂ P 🍴

In addition to the *Good Beer Guide*, CAMRA produces a range of local (mostly county-based) pub guides. A full list of the latest titles is available on request from CAMRA head office: tel. (01727) 867201.

Cumbria

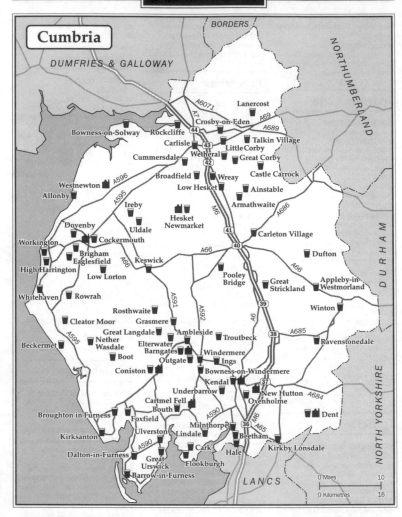

Cumbria

BORDERS
NORTHUMBERLAND
DUMFRIES & GALLOWAY
A6071
Lanercost
A7
Crosby-on-Eden
A69
A689
Bowness-on-Solway
Rockcliffe
44
Talkin Village
Carlisle
43
Little Corby
Cummersdale
Wetheral
Great Corby
42
Broadfield
Wreay
Castle Carrock
Westnewton
A596
Low Hesket
Ainstable
Allonby
Armathwaite
A686
Ireby
A595
Hesket
Newmarket
Dovenby
Uldale
Carleton Village
DURHAM
Workington
Cockermouth
41
Brigham
A66
40
Dufton
Eaglesfield
Keswick
High Harrington
Low Lorton
A66
Whitehaven
Rowrah
Pooley
Bridge
Great
Strickland
Appleby-in-
Westmorland
Rosthwaite
A591
A592
39
Winton
Cleator Moor
Grasmere
Great Langdale
Ambleside
Troutbeck
A685
Ravenstonedale
Nether
Wasdale
Elterwater
A6
38
Beckermet
A595
Barngates
Windermere
Boot
Outgate
Ings
Coniston
Bowness-on-Windermere
NORTH YORKSHIRE
Kendal
37
Underbarrow
New Hutton
A684
Cartmel Fell
Oxenholme
Broughton in Furness
Bouth
Dent
Foxfield
Milnthorpe
36
Kirksanton
Ulverston
Lindale
M6 A65
Beetham
Dalton-in-Furness
A590
Cark
Hale
Kirkby Lonsdale
Great
Urswick
Flookburgh
LANCS
Barrow-in-Furness
0 Miles 10
0 Kilometres 16

Ainstable

New Crown
☎ (01768) 896273
11 (12 winter)–3, 6–11; 7–10.30 (closed lunch) Sun
Tetley Bitter; guest beers Ⓗ
Worth visiting, cosy village local with a dining room (no food Mon).
🏫 Q ❀ 🛏 ◁ ▷ ♣ P

Allonby

Ship
☎ (01900) 881017
11–3, 7–11; 12–3, 7–10.30 Sun
Yates Bitter, Premium; guest beer Ⓗ
Peaceful, comfortable hotel in a quiet seaside village on the beautiful Solway coast, with stunning views of Scotland

across the Firth. The only tied house of Yates Brewery, whose occasional brews are stocked.
🏫 Q ❀ 🛏 ◁ ▷ ▲ ♣ P

Ambleside

Golden Rule
Smithy Brow (100 yds off A591, towards Kirkstone)
☎ (0153 94) 32257
11–11; 12–10.30 Sun
Robinson's Hatters Mild, Old Stockport, Hartleys XB, Best Bitter Ⓗ
Deservedly popular with locals, walkers and students, this is a 'proper' pub – no jukebox or cooking smells, just 'crack' and well filled rolls/ pork pies. The bar has two side rooms.
🏫 Q ❀ ♣ ♣

🍺 **INDEPENDENT BREWERIES**

Bitter End: Cockermouth

Cartmel: Kendal

Coniston: Coniston

Dent: Dent

Derwent: Cockermouth

Drunken Duck: Barngates

Hesket Newmarket: Hesket Newmarket

Jennings: Cockermouth

Lakeland: Kendal

Old Cottage: New Hutton

Strawberry Bank: Cartmel Fell

Yates: Westnewton

Queens Hotel

Market Place
☎ (0153 94) 32206
11–11; 12–10.30 Sun

Boddingtons Bitter; Jennings Bitter; Theakston XB; guest beers Ⓗ

Village-centre hotel with an enlarged lounge bar, a dining room and Victoria's Restaurant, offering a wide selection of meals. The no-smoking cellar hosts live music. Guest beers often come from Cumbrian micros.

🏠 🌣 � 🌜 ▶ 🍴 ♣ ✕

Appleby-in-Westmorland

Golden Ball

High Wynd
☎ (0176 83) 51493
12–3, 6–11; 12–3, 7–10.30 Sun (may vary)

Jennings Bitter, Cumberland Ale Ⓗ

Popular, friendly, honest, no-frills, town-centre pub of a type that is now all too rare. Children's certificate.

🍴 ➔ ♣

Royal Oak Inn

Bongate ☎ (0176 83) 51463
11–3, 6–11; 12–10.30 Sun

Black Sheep Best Bitter; Theakston Best Bitter; Yates Bitter; Younger Scotch; guest beers Ⓗ

Stylish, edge-of-town former coaching inn, boasting a superb wood-panelled tap room, a comfortable lounge and a dining room. The house beer is brewed by Hesket Newmarket; up to four guest beers. 🏠 Q 🌣 🚉 🌜 ▶ 🍴 ♣

Armathwaite

Fox & Pheasant

☎ (0169 74) 72400
11–11; 12–10.30 Sun

Hesket Newmarket Doris's 90th Birthday Ale; Mitchell's Lancaster Bomber; guest beer (summer) Ⓗ

17th-century coaching house with a small hotel at the front, featuring an oak-beamed lounge and a slate-floored stable bar. Good food. The village is on the Settle–Carlisle railway line.

🏠 Q 🌣 🚉 🌜 ▶ ➔ ♣ P

Barngates

Drunken Duck

☎ (0153 94) 36347
11.30–3, 6–11; 12–3, 6–10.30 Sun

Jennings Bitter; Mitchell's Lancaster Bomber; Theakston Old Peculier; Yates Bitter, Premium Ⓗ

Isolated, but very popular pub, with mountain views: no

jukebox, machines or TV. Good quality meals include imaginative vegetarian choices. A house beer is brewed at the pub.

🏠 Q 🌣 🚉 🌜 ▶ ♣ P ✕

Barrow-in-Furness

Albion Hotel

29 Dalton Road
☎ (01229) 820089
11–3, 6–11; 11–11 Fri & Sat; 12–3, 7–10.30 Sun

Theakston Best Bitter; Younger No. 3; guest beers Ⓗ

Friendly, town-centre local, popular with all ages, with two distinctive rooms. Good quality lunches, Mon–Fri.

🌣 🚉 🌜 🍴 ➔ ♣

Farmers Arms

Hollow Lane, Newbarns
☎ (01229) 870802
2.30–5, 7.30–11; 1–11 Sat; 12–10.30 Sun

Beer varies Ⓗ

One-roomed pub, mostly nitrokeg, but with one guest beer enjoying a good turnover. Q

King's Arms

Quarry Brow, Hawcoat (100 yds W of Hawcoat Lane crossroads)
☎ (01229) 871303
7–11; 12–4, 7–11 Sat; 12–4, 7–10.30 Sun

Robinson's Hatters Mild, Old Stockport, Hartleys XB, Best Bitter Ⓗ

Traditional, two-roomed local, with a staunchly loyal regular clientele. Quiz alternate Suns.

Q 🚉 ♣ 🍺

Beckermet

Royal Oak

☎ (01946) 841551
11–3, 6–11; 11–11 Sat; 12–10.30 Sun

Jennings Bitter, Cumberland Ale Ⓗ

Low-ceilinged, welcoming country pub: a panelled games room and a cosy, central bar for conversation. Excellent food (with unusual specials) at fair prices. Children's certificate.

🏠 Q 🌣 🌣 🚉 🌜 ▶ P

Beetham

Wheatsheaf Hotel

☎ (0153 95) 62123
11–3, 7–11; 12–3, 7–10.30 Sun

Boddingtons Bitter; Tetley Bitter Ⓗ

Unpretentious, village hotel just off the A6. Three bars include a stone-flagged tap room and a dining room upstairs. Families welcome until 8.30pm.

🏠 🌣 🚉 🌜 ▶ 🍴 🅰 ♣ P

Boot

Burnmoor Inn

☎ (01947) 23224
11–3, 5–11; 12–3, 5–10.30 Sun

Jennings Bitter, Cumberland Ale Ⓗ

Charming inn set in a fold of the hills near the foot of Scafell, close to the terminus of La'al Ratty narrow gauge steam railway. Surrounded by beautiful scenery, it is perennially popular. Families welcome.

🏠 Q 🌣 🚉 🌜 ▶ 🅰 ♣ P

Bouth

White Hart Inn

☎ (01229) 861229
12–2 (3 Sat; not Mon), 6–11; 12–3, 6–10.30 Sun (may stay open all day summer weekends)

Boddingtons Bitter; Highgate Dark; Tetley Bitter; Theakston Black Bull; guest beer Ⓗ

Village pub in a pleasant, unspoilt area on the edge of the Lake District, featuring old Lakeland photographs and paintings.

🏠 Q 🌣 🌣 🚉 🌜 ▶ 🅰 ♣ P

Bowness-on-Solway

King's Arms

☎ (0169 73) 51426
7–11; 11–3, 7–11 Sat; 12–3, 7–10.30 Sun

Jennings Bitter, Cumberland Ale, Cocker Hoop Ⓗ

Traditional, basic, village pub, at the western end of Hadrian's Wall. 🏠 Q 🌣 🅰 ♣

Bowness-on-Windermere

Village Inn

Lake Road ☎ (0153 94) 43731
11–11; 12–10.30 Sun

Boddingtons Bitter; Cartmel Lakeland Gold; Castle Eden Ale; Jennings Cumberland Ale; guest beers Ⓗ

Busy, village-centre pub with a restaurant offering good value meals all day. Guest beers often come from Cumbrian brewers. Originally the manse to the parish church opposite.

🌣 🌜 ▶ ♿ P

Brigham

Lime Kiln

Low Road ☎ (01900) 825375
12–3, 6.30–11; 12–3, 7–10.30 Sun

Robinson's Hartleys XB Ⓗ

Pleasant, two-roomed village local, popular for meals, especially curries (no food Mon except bank hols). Children welcome.

Q 🌣 🚉 🌜 ▶ 🅰 ♣ P

Broadfield

Crown
4 miles S of Carlisle racecourse
☎ (0169 74) 73467
12–3, 6.30–11; 12–3, 7–10.30 Sun
Theakston Best Bitter; guest beer Ⓗ
Roadside country pub: three rooms knocked into one, with a friendly welcome. Excellent meals; changing guest beer.
🏨 ❀ ◖▸ ♣ P ♒

Broughton in Furness

Manor Arms
The Square
☎ (01229) 716286
12–11; 12–10.30 Sun
Draught Bass; Butterknowle Banner Bitter; Flowers Original; Yates Bitter, Premium; guest beers Ⓗ
Bustling, 18th-century, family-run free house in a quiet village square: local CAMRA *Pub of the Year* for the last seven years. Snacks served all day. Accommodation discounts for CAMRA members (all rooms are en suite).
🏨 Q ❀ 🛏 ♣ ♒

Cark

Rose & Crown
☎ (0153 95) 58501
11–11; 12–3, 7–10.30 Sun
Robinson's Hartleys XB, Best Bitter Ⓗ
Good, solid drinking pub, with a working well inside.
🏨 Q ❀ ◖▸ ♿ ▲ ⇌ (Cark & Cartmel) P

Carleton Village

Cross Keys
On A686
☎ (01768) 866233
11–3, 6–11; 12–3, 7–10.30 Sun (may vary)
Ward's Best Bitter; guest beer Ⓗ
17th-century inn on the outskirts of Penrith; rumoured to be haunted.
Q ❀ ◖▸ ▲ ♣ P ♒

Carlisle

Boardroom
Paternoster Row
☎ (01228) 27695
11–11; 12–2, 7–10.30 (12–10.30 summer) Sun
Theakston Mild, Best Bitter, XB; Younger Scotch; guest beer Ⓗ
Old pub, nestling alongside the 11th-century cathedral, near the city centre; popular with students and office workers.
◖ ⇌

Caledonian Cask House
17 Botchergate (opp. station)
☎ (01228) 30460
11–11; 12–10.30 Sun
Boddingtons Bitter; guest beers Ⓗ
Large, city-centre pub with up to five guest beers, changed regularly. Good value, home-cooked food. ◖ ⇌ ◔

Carlisle Rugby Club
Warwick Road
☎ (01228) 21300
7 (5.30 Fri, 6 Sat)–11 (12.30–11 Sat in football season); 12–3, 7–10.30 Sun
Tetley Bitter; Yates Bitter; guest beer Ⓗ
Welcoming club with a cosy lounge and a large bar; often crowded when Carlisle Utd are at home. Show the *Guide* or CAMRA membership to be signed in. 🏨 ♨ ❀ ♣ P

Howard Arms
Lowther Street
☎ (01228) 32926
11–11; 12–10.30 Sun
Theakston Best Bitter, XB Ⓗ
Busy pub, and a regular *Guide* entry; partitions give a multi-roomed effect. Unchanged for many years, it bears evidence of the State Management scheme. ❀ ◖ ⇌

Jacksons
Fisher Street ☎ (01228) 596868
11–2am (6 Mon; nightclub opens at 10pm Tue–Sat); closed Sun
Federation Buchanan's Best Bitter, Buchanan's Original; Hesket Newmarket Doris's 90th Birthday Ale; guest beer Ⓗ
Two venues in one: an all-day pub/café bar upstairs (with food); real ale also in the nightclub downstairs (door charge; students free with card). 🏨 ◖▸ ⇌

London Tavern
2 Alexander Street
☎ (01228) 32752
1 (12 Sat)–11; 12–4, 7–10.30 Sun
Thwaites Bitter; guest beer Ⓗ
One-room corner local; Thwaites's most northerly tied house. ⇌ ♣

Castle Carrock

Duke of Cumberland
☎ (01228) 70341
12–3 (not Mon), 7–11 (12–11 summer Sat); 12–3, 7–10.30 (12–10.30 summer) Sun
Boddingtons Bitter; Jennings Bitter, Cumberland Ale; guest beer Ⓗ
Pleasant, village-centre pub with a friendly welcome: a bar and a lounge with a pool room to the rear. Good, home-cooked food (not served Mon). Camping by arrangement.
🏨 Q ❀ ◖▸ ▲ ♣ P

Cleator Moor

New Victoria
Ennerdale Road
☎ (01946) 62986
11–11 (5 Tue & Wed); 12–10.30 Sun
Boddingtons Bitter; Jennings Bitter, Cumberland Ale; guest beer Ⓗ
Comfortable pub on the main street of this small town. Strong community atmosphere; welcome for all.
❀ ♣

Cockermouth

Bitter End
15 Kirkgate
☎ (01900) 828993
11.30–3, 5.30–11; 12–3, 7–10.30 Sun
Bitter End Cockersnoot, Skinners Old Strong; Jennings Bitter; guest beers Ⓗ
Interesting brew pub created out of a derelict shell by licensees with a proven commitment to real ales and superb food (not served Sun eve). Brewing (some!) takes place in a small room, visible through glass from the lounge. Children welcome for meals.
🏨 Q ◖▸ ▲

Bush Hotel
Main Street (B5292)
☎ (01900) 822064
11–11; 12–10.30 Sun
Jennings Mild, Bitter, Cumberland Ale, Cocker Hoop, Sneck Lifter, seasonal beers; guest beers Ⓗ
The nearest thing to a brewery tap, this popular pub has a loyal following. Winner of a local CAMRA award; now selecting rarer guest ales.
🏨 ◖▸

Swan Inn
Kirkgate ☎ (01900) 822425
11–3, 7–11; 12–3, 7.30–10.30 Sun
Jennings Bitter Ⓗ
Popular, friendly pub on a cobbled Georgian square in a conservation area. The beers (from Jennings) may vary.
Q ♣

Coniston

Black Bull Hotel
Yewdale Road
☎ (0153 94) 41335
11–11; 12–10.30 Sun
Coniston Bluebird, Old Man Ale; Theakston Old Peculier Ⓗ
16th-century coaching inn at the heart of Coniston which features original photographs of Donald Campbell's ill-fated *Bluebird*. The microbrewery on the premises also brews a winter special.
🏨 Q ❀ 🛏 ◖▸ ▲ P

Sun Hotel

☎ (0153 94) 41248
11–11; 12–10.30 Sun
**Coniston Old Man Ale;
Jennings Cumberland Ale;
Tetley Bitter** H
Simply furnished and
decorated public bar, featuring
a local stone fireplace, high-
backed settles and old sewing
machine tables. Popular with
walkers and climbers.
🏚 ❀ 🛏 🌢 ▶ Å P

Crosby-on-Eden

Stag Inn

☎ (01228) 573210
11.30–3, 6–11; 12–3, 6.30–10.30 Sun
**Jennings Mild, Bitter,
Cumberland Ale, Sneck
Lifter; guest beer**
(occasional) H
Superb, olde-worlde pub with
low-beamed ceilings and
stone-flagged floors. Good
value home-cooked food is
served in both the bar and the
upstairs restaurant. The village
has now been bypassed, but is
worth a detour.
Q ❀ 🌢 ▶ ♣

Cummersdale

Spinners Arms

☎ (01228) 32928
6.30 (12 Sat)–11; 12–4, 7–10.30 Sun
**Theakston Black Bull, Best
Bitter; guest beer** H
Village local, designed (like
other State Management pubs)
by Harry Redfern, with an
L-shaped bar and a small
lounge area. 🏚 ❀ ▶ ♣

Dalton-in-Furness

Masons Arms

101 Market Street
☎ (01229) 462678
11–11; 12–10.30 Sun
Beer varies H
Cosy, friendly, unassuming
town pub on the main road.
Busy at the weekend, hosting
live music. Weekly guest beer.
No food Wed.
🌢 ♿ ⇌ ♣ P

Dent

Sun Inn

Main Street ☎ (0153 96) 25208
11–2.30, 7–11; 11–11 Sat & summer;
12–10.30 Sun
**Dent Bitter, Ramsbottom,
T'Owd Tup; Younger
Scotch** H
Traditional pub on the cobbled
main street of this pleasant
village. Good value food in the
quiet bar which has a no-
smoking annexe. The games
room has a jukebox, etc. Dent's
George & Dragon, nearby, is
also recommended.
🏚 Q ❀ 🛏 🌢 ▶ Å ♣ P ✄

Dovenby

Ship Inn

Main Street ☎ (01900) 828097
11–3, 5.30–11; 11–11 Sat; 12–10.30 Sun
Jennings Bitter H
Cosy, friendly country pub
where families are welcome
(play equipment in the
garden). A second Jennings
beer is available in summer.
🏚 Q ❀ 🛏 🌢 ▶ ♣ P

Dufton

Stag Inn

☎ (0176 83) 51608
12–3 (not winter Mon), 6–11 (11–11
summer); 12–3, 7–10.30 (12–10.30
summer) Sun
**Black Sheep Best Bitter;
Boddingtons Bitter; guest
beers** H
Friendly, three-room local in
an attractive village on the
Pennine Way. Popular with
visitors and locals, it has an
unusual kitchen range in the
front bar. Good value food; up
to three guest beers. Children's
certificate.
🏚 ❀ 🛏 🌢 ▶ Å ♣ P

Eaglesfield

Black Cock

☎ (01900) 822989
11–3, 6–11; 12–4, 7–10.30 Sun
Jennings Bitter H
Gem of a pub run by a gem of a
landlady; well worth a detour.
Unspoilt and unaltered, it
stands in a delightful village
with a history. 🏚 Q ☜ ❀ ♣

Elterwater

Britannia Inn

☎ (0153 94) 37210
11–11; 12–10.30 Sun
**Coniston Bluebird; Jennings
Bitter; guest beers** H
Set in the heart of probably the
most popular Lakes valley, the
'Brit' has a bar to the right of
the entrance hall, a dining
room to the left and a cosy back
room. 🏚 Q ❀ 🛏 🌢 ▶ Å

Flookburgh

Crown Inn

45 Market Street
☎ (0153 95) 58248
12–4, 7–11; 12–4, 7–10.30 Sun
**Robinson's Old Stockport,
Hartleys XB, Best Bitter** H
Bustling and friendly, roomy
village local. 🏚 ❀ Å ⇌ (Cark
& Cartmel) ♣ P

Foxfield

Prince of Wales

By station ☎ (01229) 716238
7 (11.30 Fri & Sat)–11; 12–10.30 Sun
(winter hours: 5 (11.30 Sat)–11; 12–

10.30 Sun; closed Tue–Thu); closed
Mon all year
Beer range varies H
Comfortable pub, well-run by
the owners of Tigertops
Brewery, with always a
Tigertops beer available from a
choice of three or more.
🏚 Q ❀ ⇌ ♣ P 🍺

Grasmere

Travellers Rest

☎ (0153 94) 35604
11–11; 12–10.30 Sun
Jennings Mild (summer),
**Bitter, Cumberland Ale,
Sneck Lifter; Marston's
Pedigree** H
Family-run pub with a small
bar, big fire, lots of dining
space (meals all day Easter–
Oct) and a games room. Two
letting cottages nearby on the
Coast to Coast Walk. The
King's Head, six miles north on
the A591, is owned by the
family and also recommended.
🏚 ❀ 🛏 🌢 ▶ Å ♣ P

Great Corby

Queen Inn

☎ (01228) 560731
12–2.30, 6.30–11; 12–3, 7–10.30 Sun
(may vary winter)
Beer range varies H
Superb village pub within ten
mins' walk of Wetheral station,
across the imposing railway
viaduct over the River Eden.
🏚 Q ❀ ⇌ (Wetheral) ♣ P

Great Langdale

Old Dungeon Ghyll

☎ (0153 94) 37272
11–11; 12–10.30 Sun
**Jennings Mild, Cumberland
Ale; Theakston XB, Old
Peculier; Yates Bitter; guest
beers** H
Universally known as a basic
bar serving the needs of
walkers, climbers and campers.
Steaming socks around the
blazing range are a common
sight. A more sedate diners'/
residents' bar is adjacent. Book
for the restaurant.
🏚 Q ❀ 🛏 🌢 ▶ Å 🍺

Great Strickland

Strickland Arms

Off A6, between M6 jcts 39 and
40 ☎ (01931) 712238
12–3 (not Wed), 6–11; 12–10.30 Sun
**Ind Coope Burton Ale;
Jennings Bitter; Tetley Bitter;
guest beer** H
Fine, two-bar village pub
serving the community and
visitors to the splendid
countryside. Separate games
room; good value meals; large
garden with a play area.
🏚 Q ❀ 🛏 🌢 ▶ Å ♣ P

CUMBRIA

Great Urswick

Derby Arms
☎ (01229) 586348
12–3, 5.30–11; 12–11 Sat; 12–10.30 Sun
Robinson's Hatters Mild, Old Stockport, Hartleys XB Ⓗ
Village local with a comfortable atmosphere. Good 'crack'. ♨ ❀ ♣ P

Try also: **General Burgoyne** (Robinson's)

Hale

Kings Arms
☎ (0153 95) 63203
11–3, 6–11; 12–10.30 Sun
Mitchell's Original, Lancaster Bomber, seasonal beer (summer) Ⓗ
Single-bar pub with a pool room, plus a function/family room upstairs and a bowling green next door. Good value meals.
♨ ⛵ ❀ 🖼 🚮 ◗ ▲ ♣ P

Hesket Newmarket

Old Crown
1 mile SE of Caldbeck
OS341386 ☎ (0169 74) 78288
12–3 (not Mon–Fri except school hols), 5.30–11; 12–3, 7–10.30 Sun
Hesket Newmarket Great Cockup, Blencathra, Skiddaw Special, Doris's 90th Birthday Ale, Catbells Pale Ale, Old Carrock Ⓗ
Superb fellside village pub, offering fine food. Hesket Newmarket Brewery is in the converted barn at the back. Eve meals finish at 8.30 (no eve meals Sun or Mon, except bank hols). ♨ Q ❀ ◗ ▲ ♣

High Harrington

Galloping Horse
Main Road
☎ (01900) 830083
11–3, 5.30–11; 12–3, 7–10.30 Sun
Jennings Mild, Bitter Ⓗ
Large, comfortable pub with several rooms. Tasty, reasonably priced meals include a renowned steak pie. Large games room; children's certificate until 9.30.
Q ⛵ ❀ ◗ ▶ ♣ P ⚲

Ings

Watermill Inn
☎ (01539) 821309
12–2.30, 6–11; 12–3, 6–10.30 Sun
Black Sheep Special; Coniston Bluebird; Lees Moonraker; Theakston Best Bitter, XB, Old Peculier; guest beers Ⓗ
Popular, family-run free house offering up to eight guest beers and good value meals using local produce. CAMRA

Westmorland *Pub of the Year* several times. A must.
♨ Q ❀ 🖼 ◗ ▶ ▲ ♣ ♋ P ⚲

Ireby

Paddy's Bar
The Square
☎ (0169 73) 71460
11 (5.30 winter Sat)–11; 12–3, 6.30–10.30 Sun
Jennings Bitter; Yates Bitter; guest beers Ⓗ
Irish character pub, with a village shop and post office, situated on the old market square – not a 'theme' pub. Meals Tue–Sun. ♨ Q ▶

Kendal

Castle Inn
Castle Street
☎ (01539) 729983
11–11; 12–10.30 Sun
Tetley Bitter; Theakston Best Bitter; guest beers Ⓗ
Two-roomed pub, popular with office staff for good value lunches and as a genuine local. Note the framed Duttons window on an inside wall. Families welcome until 6pm.
❀ 🖼 ◗ ≋ ♣

Ring O'Bells ☆
39 Kirkland
☎ (01539) 720326
12–3 (not Tue), 6–11 (may vary summer); 12–3, 7–10.30 Sun (may vary)
Vaux Lorimer's Best Scotch, Bitter, Samson; Ward's Best Bitter; guest beer Ⓗ
Largely unspoilt, two-bar pub on consecrated ground. The snug is a gem – complete with a coffin table.
♨ ❀ 🖼 ◗ ▶ ♣

Keswick

Bank Tavern
47 Main Street
☎ (0176 87) 72663
11–11; 12–10.30 Sun
Jennings Mild, Bitter, Cumberland Ale, Sneck Lifter Ⓗ
Popular local, maintaining a community spirit and a welcome for visitors.
Q ⛵ ❀ 🖼 ◗ ▲ ♣

George Hotel
St Johns Street
☎ (0176 87) 72076
11–11; 12–10.30 Sun
Theakston Best Bitter, XB, Old Peculier; Yates Bitter Ⓗ
Delightful, little-altered coaching inn with stone-flagged floors and old local prints. The oldest inn in Keswick, it was here the Earl of Derwentwater had his last pint before dying in the 1715 rebellion.
♨ Q ⛵ 🖼 ◗ ▶ ♣ P

Lake Road Inn
Lake Road ☎ (0176 87) 72404
11–3, 6–11 (11–11 summer); 12–10.30 Sun
Jennings Bitter, Cumberland Ale, Cocker Hoop; guest beers Ⓗ
Cosy, attractive, refurbished town pub, popular with visitors and locals. Winner of the *Keswick in Bloom* (pubs) competition. Eve meals finish at 8.30 (not served winter Wed). Children's certificate.
♨ ❀ ◗ ▶ ▲ ♣

Kirkby Lonsdale

Snooty Fox Tavern
Main Street
☎ (0152 42) 71308
11–11; 12–10.30 Sun
Robinson's Hartleys XB; Taylor Landlord; Theakston Best Bitter Ⓗ
Pub where the front bar has interesting memorabilia. Good value, quality meals are served in the dining room. The part-flag-floored back bar has a jukebox.
♨ Q ❀ 🖼 ◗ ▶ ▣ ▲ P

Kirksanton

King William IV
☎ (01229) 772009
12–3, 7–11; 12–3, 7–10.30 Sun
Tetley Bitter; guest beers Ⓗ
Friendly village local whose walls are adorned with photos and pictures for sale. Away from the Lake District 'honeypot' areas and worth a visit. Tiny car park.
♨ Q ❀ 🖼 ◗ ▶ ♣ P

Lanercost

Blacksmiths Bar at Abbeybridge Inn
2 miles from Brampton
☎ (0169 77) 2224
12–2.30, 7–11; 12–2.30, 7–10.30 Sun
Yates Bitter; guest beers Ⓗ
An absolute gem. The split-level bar area has a spiral staircase, leading up to a restaurant. Two or three changing guest beers. Close to Lanercost Priory.
♨ Q ❀ 🖼 ◗ ▶ ♣ P

Lindale

Royal Oak Inn (Top House)
☎ (0153 95) 32882
12–3.30, 6–11 (may vary); 12–3.30, 6.30–10.30 Sun
Robinson's Hartleys XB, Best Bitter Ⓗ
Bustling, roomy, local providing excellent food in both the bar and dining area. Large garden.
Q ❀ 🖼 ◗ ▶ ♣ P

Little Corby

Haywain
Off A69 ☎ (01228) 560598
12–3, 7 (6 Fri)–11 (11–11 summer Sat);
12–3, 7–10.30 (12–10.30 summer) Sun
**Robinson's Old Stockport,
Hartleys XB, Best Bitter** Ⓗ
Homely pub with a warm
welcome. Three rooms: a
lounge, a bar and a snug. Good
food. Q ❀ ◑ ▶ ♣ P

Low Hesket

Rose & Crown
On A6 ☎ (0169 74) 73346
11.30–3, 6–11; 12–3, 7–10.30 Sun
**Jennings Mild, Bitter,
Cumberland Ale** Ⓗ
Comfortable village pub with a
friendly atmosphere and good
value food, including a
vegetarian option from a
varied menu (no food Mon eve
except bank hols). One of the
few real mild pubs in the area.
🏚 Q ❀ ◑ ▶ ♣ P

Low Lorton

Wheatsheaf Inn
☎ (01900) 85268
12–3, 6–11 (11 summer); 12–3,
7–10.30 (12–10.30 summer) Sun
**Jennings Bitter, Cumberland
Ale, Cocker Hoop, Sneck
Lifter** Ⓗ
Pleasant country pub with
superb food (restaurant or bar
meals), a children's certificate
and an enclosed garden. Lots
of interesting artefacts, maps,
books and teddies on display.
Q ☙ ❀ ◑ ▶ ▲ ♣ P

Milnthorpe

Coach & Horses
Haverflatts Lane
☎ (0153 95) 63210
11–3, 6–11; 11–11 Fri & Sat; 12–10.30
Sun
**Mitchell's Original, seasonal
beer** (summer) Ⓗ
Spacious, unpretentious local
with a strong pool and darts
following, and a TV and
jukebox in the bar. Good value
pub grub at all reasonable
hours in the dining area.
🏚 ❀ ✇ ◑ ▶ ♣ P

Nether Wasdale

Screes Hotel
☎ (0194 67) 26262
12–3, 6–11; 12–3, 6–10.30 Sun
**Jennings Bitter; Theakston
Best Bitter; Yates Bitter; guest
beers** Ⓗ
Homely hotel with split-level
bars, set in a delightful hamlet,
a mile west of beautiful
Waswater; much loved by
walkers, climbers and campers.
Regular live music and guest

ale nights. The garden boasts
superb views.
🏚 Q ☙ ❀ ✇ ◑ ▶ ▲ ♣ P

Outgate

Outgate Inn
On B5286, Hawkshead–
Ambleside road
☎ (0153 94) 36413
11–3, 6–11; 12–3, 7–10.30 Sun
**Robinson's Hartleys XB, Best
Bitter, Frederics** Ⓗ
Spacious, two-roomed country
pub, away from it all but busy
on summer weekends. Live
jazz every Fri.
🏚 ❀ ✇ ◑ ▶ ▲ P

Oxenholme

Station Inn
500 yds up hill from the station
☎ (01539) 724094
11–3, 6–11; 11–11 Sat; 12–10.30 Sun
**Boddingtons Bitter, Flowers
Original; Theakston Best
Bitter; guest beer** Ⓗ
Lively local on the edge of the
village. Guest beers come from
the Whitbread Cask Collection.
Excellent garden with a play
area (there is one inside, too).
Last food orders 8.30pm.
🏚 ❀ ✇ ◑ ▶ ▲ ⇌ ♣

Pooley Bridge

Sun Inn
☎ (0176 84) 86205
12–11; 12–10.30 Sun
**Jennings Bitter, Cumberland
Ale, Sneck Lifter; guest
beer** Ⓗ
Pub where the cosy, wood-
panelled lounge bar is popular
with diners; the lower level,
more basic bar has Sky TV (by
request), jukebox, machines,
and pool (winter).
🏚 ❀ ✇ ◑ ▶ ⊟ ♣ P

Ravenstonedale

Black Swan
☎ (0153 96) 23204
11.30–3, 6–11; 12–3, 7–10.30 Sun
**Black Sheep Best Bitter;
Jennings Bitter; Younger
Scotch; guest beers** Ⓗ
Well-appointed, Victorian
hotel with a locals' bar, a
comfortable lounge and a
dining room. Some bedrooms
are adapted for guests with
disabilities.
🏚 Q ❀ ✇ ◑ ▶ ⊟ ♿ ♣ P

Rockcliffe

Rose & Crown
☎ (01228) 74044
11–3, 6–11; 6–10.30 (closed lunch) Sun
**McEwan 70/-; Theakston Best
Bitter; guest beer** Ⓗ
Multi-level, country pub with a
rustic feel. Extensive menu.
❀ ◑ ▶ ♣ P ⚥

Rosthwaite

Riverside Bar, Scafell
Hotel
☎ (0176 87) 77208
11–11; 12–10.30 Sun
**Theakston Best Bitter, XB,
Old Peculier** Ⓗ
Refurbished real ale bar at the
rear of a country hotel in a
beautiful valley, popular for
outdoor pursuits. Children,
walkers and climbers welcome.
🏚 Q ☙ ❀ ✇ ◑ ▶ ▲ P

Rowrah

Stork Hotel
On A5086
☎ (01946) 861213
11–3, 6–11; 12–3, 7–10.30 Sun
**Boddingtons Bitter; Jennings
Bitter, Cumberland Ale** Ⓗ
Family-run local, near a go-
kart track and the Coast to
Coast Walk/Cycleway.
🏚 Q ☙ ❀ ✇ ♣ P

Talkin Village

Hare & Hounds
From B6413 take village turn,
not tarn turn
☎ (0169 77) 3456
7 (12 Sat)–11 (opens 12–2.30 Mon–Fri
school and bank hols); 12–10.30 Sun
**Boddingtons Bitter; Jennings
Cumberland Ale; guest
beers** Ⓗ
Charming, two-roomed inn,
close to the lovely Talkin tarn:
a classic village pub with
beams, stone fireplaces, etched-
glass and bags of atmosphere.
🏚 ❀ ✇ ◑ ▶ ▲ ♣ P

Troutbeck

Queens Head Hotel
Townhead ☎ (0153 94) 32174
11–11; 12–10.30 Sun
**Boddingtons Bitter; Mitchell's
Lancaster Bomber; Tetley
Bitter; guest beers** Ⓗ
Award-winning pub on
several levels. The four-poster
bed frame bar, Mayor's Parlour
and fine quality meals are
notable features. It usually has
a guest beer from a local micro.
Good mountain views from the
slate-flagged patio.
🏚 ❀ ✇ ◑ ▶ ▲ P

Uldale

Snooty Fox
☎ (0169 73) 71479
12–3, 6.30–11; 12–11 Sat; 12–10.30 Sun
Theakston Best Bitter Ⓗ
Charming inn, nestling in a
peaceful village in the northern
fells, within the National Park,
offering views of Skiddaw. Uld
Ale comes from Hesket
Newmarket Brewery.
Q ❀ ✇ ◑ ▶ ♿ ♣ P

Ulverston

King's Head Hotel
14 Queen Street
☎ (01229) 582892
10.30–11; 12–10.30 Sun
**Morland Old Speckled Hen;
John Smith's Bitter;
Theakston Best Bitter, XB;
guest beers** H
Cosy, friendly, town-centre
local with a bowling green at
the rear. It can get very busy at
weekends. ♨ ✿ 🛏 ⇒ ♣

Stan Laurel Inn
The Ellers
☎ (01229) 582814
12–3, 7–11; 12–3, 7–10.30 Sun
**Jennings Cocker Hoop; Tetley
Dark Mild, Bitter; guest
beers** H
Friendly local featuring Laurel
and Hardy memorabilia: a
lounge, bar/games room and a
dining area. The six
handpumps offer three guest
beers, including Carlsberg-
Tetley's Tapster's Choice.
🍴 ✿ ♨ ◑ ▣ ♿ ⇒ ♣ P

Underbarrow

Punchbowl Inn
☎ (0153 95) 68234
12–3.30, 6–11 (may extend summer);
12–3.30, 7–10.30 Sun
**Draught Bass; Boddingtons
Bitter; guest beer** H
Traditional village local with a
dark-beamed bar area. Good
value meals (last orders 8.30);
fresh fish a speciality on Fri.
No lunches Tue, except after
bank hols. Part of a priest's
hole can be seen behind the
bar. ♨ ✿ ◑ ♪ ♣ P

Wetheral

Crown Hotel
Station Road
☎ (01228) 561888
12–2, 5.30–11; 12–3, 5.30–10.30 Sun
Thwaites Bitter H

Very comfortable hotel with
excellent amenities, including a
leisure club and conference
centre. The homely bar is
popular with locals and
visitors. 🛏 ◑ ♪ ⇒ ♣ P

Whitehaven

Central
Duke Street ☎ (01946) 692796
11–11; 12–10.30 Sun
**Theakston Mild, Best Bitter,
XB; guest beers** H
Busy, two-roomed, town-
centre pub, popular with all.
The lounge has a railway
theme; the back bar is popular
with sporty types. Lunches
Thu–Sun. ◑ ▣ ⇒ ♣

Stump
50 High Road, Kells
☎ (01946) 693365
7 (12 Fri & Sat)–11; 12–10.30 Sun
Robinson's Best Bitter H
On a hill south of the harbour,
with panoramic views of the
town centre, this pub is built
on the stump of an old
windmill. Friendly welcome
for all. Q 🍴 ✿ ♣ P

Windermere

Grey Walls Hotel
(Greys Inn)
Elleray Road
☎ (0153 94) 43741
11–11; 12–10.30 Sun
**Theakston Mild, Best Bitter,
Old Peculier; guest beers** H
Busy pub with a strong local
following; pool and TV in the
games area; a no-smoking area
(until 9.30) is next to the family
room (with a TV). Food all day
Sun (dining room).
♨ 🍴 ✿ 🛏 ◑ ♪ ⇒ ♣ P ✗

Winton

Bay Horse
☎ (0176 83) 71451
12–3 (not Mon in winter, or Tue), 7 (6
summer)–11; 12–3, 7–10.30 Sun

**Theakston Best Bitter;
Younger Scotch; guest beers** H
Traditional local overlooking
the village green. The stone
floor bar (where dogs are
welcome) has a games area up
a couple of steps; comfortable
lounge bar. Guest beers come
from micros or small
regionals.
🍴 Q ✿ 🛏 ◑ ♪ ▣ ♣ P

Workington

Commercial
5 Market Place
☎ (01900) 603981
12–5, 6.30–11; 12–4, 7–10.30 Sun
Jennings Bitter H
Popular, well-run pub, close to
the lively town centre.
♣ ✗

George IV
Stanley Street
☎ (01900) 602266
11–3, 7–11; 12–2, 7–10.30 Sun
Jennings Bitter H
Cosy, end of terrace, quiet,
friendly local, on probably the
oldest street in town,
convenient for RL, football and
greyhound stadia, and next to
an attractive harbour
development.
♨ Q ⇒ ♣ ♣

Wreay

Plough Inn
☎ (0169 74) 73504
7 (6.30 summer Fri)–11; 12–3, 6.30–11
Sat; 12–3, 7–10.30 Sun; closed
weekday lunchtimes, except bank hols
**Black Sheep Best Bitter;
Tetley Bitter** H
Two-roomed village local, with
a pool room at the rear and a
beer garden behind. Note the
collection of claypipes
belonging to the 12 Men of
Wreay who date back to the
1600s. Lunches served
weekends and bank hols.
Q ✿ ◑ ♪ ♣ ⌂ P

LOOK FOR A STAR

Keep your eyes peeled for a star next to a pub's name in this book.
It indicates that the pub features on CAMRA's National
Inventory of heritage pubs – pubs which have unspoilt interiors of
outstanding historic importance. Not all pubs on the complete list
feature in the *Good Beer Guide*, but many do, combining a classic
setting with the best of British beer. The pubs come from all eras and
a visit may transport you back decades or even centuries, to see how
pub life used to be. You'll also see just why these couple of hundred
pubs must be preserved at all costs. For a copy of the full National
Inventory, send a stamped, self-addressed, large envelope to
CAMRA, 230 Hatfield Road, St Albans AL1 4LW.

Derbyshire

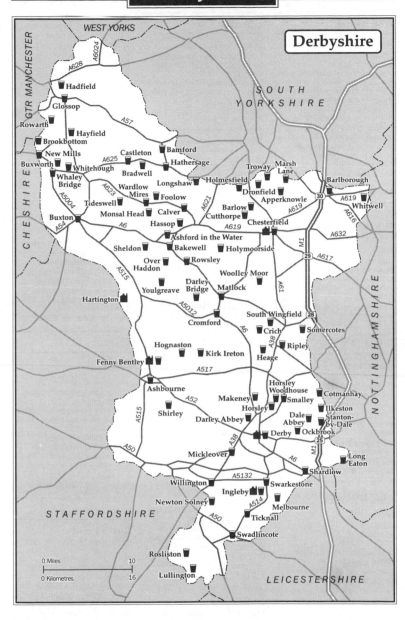

INDEPENDENT BREWERIES

Black Bull: Fenny Bentley

Brunswick: Derby

John Thompson Inn/ Lloyds: Ingleby

Leatherbritches: Fenny Bentley

Townes: Chesterfield

Whim: Hartington

Apperknowle

Yellow Lion
High Street ☎ (01246) 413181
12–3, 5–11; 12–3, 7–10.30 Sun
Draught Bass; Greene King Abbot; Stones Bitter; guest beers Ⓗ
Busy, stone, village free house with a large lounge and a no-smoking restaurant.
Q ❀ ⇚ ◑ ▶ ♣ P

Ashbourne

Bowling Green
2 North Avenue (A515)
☎ (01335) 342511
11–3, 5–11; 11–11 Thu & Sat; 12–10.30 Sun
Draught Bass; Mansfield Old Baily; Worthington Bitter; guest beers Ⓗ
Pub with a spacious bar and a smaller lounge housing oriental artefacts. Wide food choice – all home cooked – fresh fish is a speciality. Children welcome in the restaurant. There is always a mild on tap.
🏠 ◖ ▶ ⬜ ♣ P

Ashford in the Water

Bull's Head
Church Street
☎ (01629) 812931
11.30–3, 6–11; 12–3, 7–10.30 Sun
Robinson's Old Stockport, Best Bitter Ⓗ
Unspoilt country pub with a beamed ceiling in the main bar. Popular with walkers. No Mon eve meals.
🏠 Q ❀ ◖ ▶ ⬜ ▲ ♣ P

Bakewell

Peacock
Market Place
☎ (01629) 812994
11–11; 12–10.30 Sun
Ward's Best Bitter; guest beer Ⓗ
Busy town-centre pub where visitors are welcome. Eve meals in summer.
🏠 Q ❀ ◖ ▶ ▲ ♣ P

Bamford

Derwent
Main Road
☎ (01433) 651395
11–11; 12–10.30 Sun
Stones Bitter; Ward's Best Bitter; guest beer Ⓗ
Unspoilt, Peak District hotel dating from 1890, with a tap room, two lounge areas and a dining room (good home-cooked food).
🛏 ❀ 🏠 ◖ ▶ ⬜ ▲ ⇌ ♣ P

Barlborough

Rose & Crown
High Street
☎ (01246) 810364
12–3, 5.30–11; 12–3, 7–10.30 (12–10.30 summer) Sun
Hardys & Hansons Best Bitter, seasonal beer Ⓗ
Tidy village pub set behind an historic Norman cross by the Elizabethan manor house.
❀ ◖ ▶ ⬜ ♣ P ✗ 🍴

Barlow

Hare & Hounds
32 Commonside Road (200 yds off B6051) ☎ (0114) 289 0464
11–11; 12–4, 7–10.30 Sun
Draught Bass; Stones Bitter Ⓗ
Friendly, multi-roomed, cosy local. The rear lounge has views across the valley.
🏠 Q ⬥ ❀ ♣ P

Bradwell

Valley Lodge
Church Street
☎ (01433) 620427
8 (7 summer)–11; 12–3, 7–11 Sat; 12–3, 7–10.30 Sun
Barnsley Bitter; Stones Bitter; guest beers Ⓗ
Large, three-roomed pub in a scenic Peak District village. The tap room has a pool table and is separated from the comfortable lounge by a small foyer bar.
🏠 Q ❀ 🏠 ◖ ▶ ⬜ ▲ ♣ P

Brookbottom

Fox Inn
Brookbottom Road (access on foot from Strines station or by narrow road from New Mills)
☎ (0161) 427 1634
11.30–3, 7 (5.30 summer)–11; 12–3, 7–10.30 Sun
Robinson's Hatters Mild, Best Bitter Ⓗ
Whitewashed, low-ceilinged, stone pub in a quiet hamlet.
🏠 ❀ ◖ ▲ ⇌ (Strines) P

Buxton

Bakers Arms
26 West Road (near Fiveways jct) ☎ (01298) 24404
12–3, 6–11; 12–3, 7–10.30 Sun
Ind Coope Burton Ale; Tetley Bitter; guest beer Ⓗ
Unspoilt, traditional pub: a two-roomed, no-frills alehouse. Tapster's Choice guest beer.
Q ▲ ♣ P

Cheshire Cheese
37–39 High Street
☎ (01298) 73135
12–11; 12–10.30 Sun
Hardys & Hansons Best Bitter, Classic, seasonal beers Ⓗ
Busy pub, catering for all. A bay-fronted entrance leads to a long, low-beamed interior. Meals Tue–Sun. ◖ ▶ ⇌ P

Duke of York
123 St Johns Road, Burbage
☎ (01298) 24006
12–3, 5–11; 12–11 Fri, Sat & summer; 12–10.30 Sun
Ind Coope Burton Ale; Tetley Bitter; guest beer Ⓗ
Old coaching inn, much larger inside than it looks: two main

rooms are served by a central bar. Popular with walkers. Tapster's Choice guest beers.
Q ◖ ▶ ▲

Swan Hotel
41 High Street ☎ (01298) 23278
11–11; 12–10.30 Sun
Tetley Bitter; Theakston Best Bitter Ⓗ
Friendly, three-roomed local with one room devoted to all things Scottish. Over 100 different whiskies; house beer from Coach House.
Q ▲ ⇌

Buxworth

Navigation Inn
Brookside Road (off B6062, by canal basin) ☎ (01663) 732072
11–11; 12–10.30 Sun
Marston's Pedigree; Taylor Landlord; Webster's Yorkshire Bitter; guest beer Ⓗ
Excellent, multi-roomed pub with an extensive restaurant, alongside the only remaining UK canal tramway interchange.
🏠 Q ⬥ ❀ 🏠 ◖ ▶ ⬜ ♣ P 🍴

Calver

Bridge Inn
Calver Bridge (A623)
☎ (01433) 630415
11.30–3 (4.30 Sat), 5.30–11; 12–4.30, 7–10.30 Sun
Hardys & Hansons Best Bitter, Classic, seasonal beers; Stones Bitter Ⓗ
Unspoilt village local: a spacious lounge and a tap room with a games area. Meals end 8.30 (not served eves Mon or winter Sun).
🏠 Q ❀ ◖ ▶ ⬜ ▲ ♣ P ✗

Castleton

Bull's Head
Cross Street ☎ (01433) 620256
12–3 (5 summer), 6–11; 12–3, 7–10.30 Sun
Robinson's Best Bitter, Old Tom Ⓗ
Friendly local in a tourist village: a large lounge, a pool room and a restaurant (book eve meals). ❀ 🛏 ◖ ♣ P

Chesterfield

Boythorpe Inn
Boythorpe Road, Boythorpe
☎ ((01246) 235280
11–11; 12–10.30 Sun
Hardys & Hansons Best Bitter, Classic, seasonal beers; Stones Bitter Ⓗ
Large, friendly pub on the edge of the centre, close to Queens Park. Bowling green.
🏠 ❀ ◖ ♣ P 🍴

Derby Tup
387 Sheffield Road,
Whittington Moor
☎ (01246) 454316
11.30–11; 11–3, 5–11 Mon; 12–4,
7–10.30 Sun
**Bateman XXXB; Marston's
Pedigree; Taylor Landlord;
Tetley Bitter; Theakston XB,
Old Peculier; guest beer** H
Superb, unspoilt, free house
with three rooms, offering 15
guest beers a week. Eve meals
end at 7.30.
Q ◖ ▶ ♣ ⚲

Market Hotel
95 New Square
☎ (01246) 273641
11–11; 12–2, 7–10.30 Sun
**Ind Coope Burton Ale;
Marston's Pedigree; Tetley
Bitter; guest beers** H
Busy Tetley Festival Ale
House, stocking an excellent
range of guest beers. No meals
Sun. ◖ ⇌ ♣

Red Lion
570 Sheffield Road,
Whittington Moor
☎ (01246) 450770
11–3, 7–11; 12–3, 7–10.30 Sun
**Old Mill Bitter, seasonal
beer** H
Pleasant local with a small
lounge, a larger public bar and
a central bar. No food Sun.
Q ❀ ◖ ⊞ ♣ P

Royal Oak
43 Chatsworth Road,
Brampton (A619, opp. B&Q)
☎ (01246) 277854
11–11; 12–10.30 Sun
**Theakston Best Bitter, XB,
Old Peculier; Townes
Sunshine, Best Lockoford;
guest beer** H
Busy local hosting regular live
music. Eight cask ales,
plus bottle-conditioned and
Belgian beers.
🚌 ❀ ⊞ ⇌ ♣ P

Rutland Arms
16 Stephenson Place
☎ (01246) 205857
11–11; 12–10.30 Sun
**Boddingtons Bitter; Castle
Eden Ale; Marston's
Pedigree** H**; guest beer** H/G
Popular open-plan Hogshead
tavern, stocking a wide choice
of guest ales and bottle-
conditioned beers.
❀ ◖ ▶ ⇌ ♣ ○

Victoria Inn
21–23 Victoria Street West,
Brampton (off A619)
☎ (01246) 273832
12–4 (5 Sat), 7–11; 12–5, 7–10.30 Sun
**Vaux Samson; Ward's Thorne
BB, Best Bitter; guest beer** H
Friendly, two-roomed local.
Live music Sat eve. Weekend
lunches served. ⌕ ❀ ◖ ⊞ ♣ P

Cotmanhay

Bridge Inn
Bridge Street
☎ (0115) 932 2589
11–11; 12–10.30 Sun
**Hardy & Hansons Best Mild,
Best Bitter** E
Traditional two-room local by
the Erewash Canal.
Q ❀ ⊞ ♣ P ⚲

Crich

Cliff Inn
Cromford Road
☎ (01773) 852444
11–3, 6–11; 12–3, 7–10.30 Sun
Hardys & Hansons Classic H
Cosy, popular, two-roomed
stone pub near the Tramway
Museum. Q ⌕ ◖ ▶ ▲ P

Cromford

Boat Inn
Scarthin ☎ (01629) 823282
11.30–3, 6.30–11; 12–3, 7–10.30 Sun
Draught Bass; guest beer H
18th-century local near a mill
pond, serving reasonably-
priced, home-made food. The
house beer is from Townes.
🚌 Q ❀ ◖ ▶ ⇌ ♣

Cutthorpe

Gate Inn
Overgreen ☎ (01246) 276923
11.30–3, 6 (6.30 Mon & Tue)–11; 12–3,
7–10.30 Sun
**Boddingtons Bitter; Flowers
Original; Mansfield Bitter;
guest beer** H
Well-preserved village pub,
popular for food; eve meals
Wed–Sat. Fine view over the
valley. 🚌 ◖ ▶ ▲ P

Dale Abbey

Carpenters Arms
½ mile off A6096
☎ (0115) 932 5277
12–3, 6 (7 Sat)–11; 12–4, 7–10.30 Sun
**Ansells Bitter; Ind Coope
Burton Ale; Marston's
Pedigree; guest beer** H
Popular, food-oriented pub off
the beaten track in a pretty
hamlet.
🚌 ⌕ ❀ ◖ ▶ ⊞ ♣ P

Darley Abbey

Abbey
Darley Street (near river)
☎ (01332) 558297
11.30–2.30, 6–11; 12–10.30 Sun
Samuel Smith OBB H
15th-century ecclesiastic
building, skilfully rescued
from dereliction and now the
focal point of this conservation
area. Features include a stone-
flagged floor. 🚌 ◖ ♣ P

Darley Bridge

Three Stags' Heads
Main Road
☎ (01629) 732358
12–3, 6.30–11; 12–11 Sat; 12–3, 7–10.30
Sun
**Hardys & Hansons Best Mild,
Best Bitter, seasonal beers** H
250-year-old, busy village
local; handy for the moors and
riverside walks.
🚌 ❀ ◖ ♣ P

Derby

Alexandra Hotel
203 Siddals Road
☎ (01332) 293993
11–11; 12–3, 7–10.30 Sun
**Bateman XB; Bramcote
Hemlock Bitter; Marston's
Pedigree; guest beers** H
Friendly, two-roomed pub,
with an excellent bottled beer
and whisky selection, plus at
least seven guest beers. No
food Sun.
Q ❀ 🚲 ◖ ⊞ ⇌ ♣ ○ P

Brunswick
1 Railway Terrace
☎ (01332) 290677
11–11; 12–10.30 Sun
**Brunswick Recession, First
Brew, Second Brew, Railway
Porter, Old Accidental; Taylor
Landlord; Theakston Old
Peculier** H**; guest beers** H/G
Traditional railwaymen's pub
with an on-site brewery and 17
handpumps selling its own
beers and a countrywide
selection of independent
brews.
Q ⌕ ❀ ◖ ▲ ⇌ ♣ ○ ⚲

Drill Hall Vaults
1 Newlands Street
☎ (01332) 298073
7–11; 12–2.30, 7–10.30 Sun
Marston's Pedigree H
Friendly, multi-sectioned,
single-roomed pub. No food
Sun. 🚌 ◖ ♣

Flowerpot
25 King Street
☎ (01332) 204955
11–11; 12–10.30 Sun
**Draught Bass; Marston's
Pedigree** H/G**; Taylor
Landlord** H**; guest beers** H/G
Lively, extended pub offering
ten beers and live music. Eve
meals (Mon–Sat) finish early.
There is always one mild on
sale. Q ❀ ◖ ▶ ♣

Furnace Inn
9 Duke Street
☎ (01332) 331563
11–11; 12–3, 6.30–10.30 Sun
**Hardy & Hansons Best Mild,
Classic; guest beer** H
Traditional local with an open-
plan interior. ❀ ⊞ ♣

New Zealand Arms
2 Langley Street
☎ (01332) 370387
12–2.30, 5.30–11; 12–11 Fri & Sat;
12–10.30 Sun
**Marston's Pedigree; Tetley
Bitter H; guest beers H/G**
Festival Ale House of open-
plan design featuring wood
panelling and stone floors.
Good food. ◖ ▶ ὦ ♣ ⌂ P

Peacock
87 Nottingham Road (across
river from market place and
through underpass)
☎ (01332) 340712
11–11; 12–10.30 Sun
Marston's Bitter, Pedigree H
17th-century, stone coaching
inn with a bustling front bar
and a games room. Meals
served 11–7. ὦ ♣ ◖ ⊞ ⇌ ♣

Ram Inn
84 Bridge Street
☎ (01332) 371871
12–11; 12–10.30 Sun
**Marston's Pedigree; Tetley
Bitter; guest beer**
(occasional) **H**
Refurbished local. Meals
served till 6pm Mon–Fri. A
house beer, Ram Ale, is also
sold. ◖ ♣

Smithfield
Meadow Road (cross bridge
from market place, follow river
to right) ☎ (01332) 370429
11–11; 12–10.30 Sun
**Bass Offilers Bitter, Draught
Bass; Marston's Pedigree;
guest beers H**
Bow-fronted riverside pub
with a big bar and two smaller
rooms, one with table skittles.
The ten handpumps frequently
feature Derbyshire brewers.
Meals served until 6.45.
⋈ Q ὦ ♣ ◖ ⊞ ⇌ ♣ P

Try also: Station Inn, Midland
Rd (Bass)

Dronfield

Victoria
Stubley Lane ☎ (01246) 412117
12–2, 4.30–11; 12–11 Thu & Fri; 11–11
Sat; 12–10.30 Sun
**Banks's Mild, Bitter, seasonal
beers; Marston's Pedigree H**
Genuine local with a
comfortable L-shaped lounge
and a darts area. ὦ ◖ ⇌ ♣ ⊟

Fenny Bentley

Bently Brook Inn
On A515 ☎ (01335) 350278
11–11; 12–10.30 Sun
**Leatherbritches Ashbourne
Ale; guest beers H**
Imposing country house, the
home of Leatherbritches
Brewery.
⋈ Q ὦ ⋈ ◖ ▶ ▲ P

Coach & Horses
☎ (01335) 350246
11.30–3, 6.30–11; 12–3, 6.30–10.30 Sun
**Black Bull Dovedale, Best
Bitter H**
Charming pub and restaurant
featuring low ceilings and
panelled walls.
⋈ Q ὦ ◖ ὦ ▲ P ⅄

Foolow

Bull's Head
☎ (01433) 630873
12–3 (not Mon), 7 (6.30 summer)–11
(closed winter Mon eve); 12–3 (closed
eve) Sun
**Black Sheep Best Bitter;
Ward's Best Bitter; guest
beer H**
Successful, family-run pub and
restaurant situated by the
village pond.
⋈ Q ◖ ▶ ▲ P ⊟

Glossop

Bull's Head
102 Church Street
☎ (01457) 853291
2 (12 Sat)–11; 12–10.30 Sun
**Robinson's Old Stockport,
Best Bitter, Old Tom H**
Listed, 16th-century, roadside
inn, at the foot of the Pennines,
renowned for its Indian
cuisine. Traditional 'northern'
tap room.
ὦ ὦ ▶ ⇌ ♣

Crown Inn
142 Victoria Street
☎ (01457) 862824
11.30–11; 12–10.30 Sun
Samuel Smith OBB H
Friendly local with two
comfortable snugs (one no-
smoking), a lively games room
and a central bar. The cheapest
pub pint in town.
⋈ Q ὦ ὦ ⇌ ♣ ⅄

Friendship
3 Arundel Street
☎ (01457) 855277
12.30–3 (4 Sat), 5 (7 Sat)–11; 12–3,
7–10.30 Sun
**Robinson's Hatters Mild, Best
Bitter H**
Stone, corner local with a
wood-panelled interior
featuring a semi-circular bar.
An open-plan lounge and a
back tap room are served by a
hatch. Families welcome.
⋈ Q ⊞ ⇌ ♣

Prince of Wales
Milltown (off A57)
☎ (01457) 864679
11.30–3, 5–11; 11.30–11 Thu–Sat; 12–5,
7–10.30 Sun
**Banks's Mild; Marston's
Bitter, Pedigree, HBC H**
Thriving community pub with
four drinking areas and
sociable staff. Eve meals Fri
and Sat.
⋈ ὦ ὦ ◖ ▶ ⊞ ὦ ⇌ ♣ P ⊟

Star Inn Ale House
2 Howard Street
☎ (01457)
12–11; 12–10.30 Sun
**Boddingtons Bitter; Lees
Bitter; guest beers H**
Town-centre alehouse with
polished wooden floors. Up to
five guest beers.
⊞ ὦ ⇌ ♣

Hadfield

Spring Tavern
Woolley Bridge (A57)
☎ (01457) 852967
11.30–3, 5.30–11; 12–3, 7–10.30 Sun
**Theakston Best Bitter; guest
beers H**
Small, friendly, family-run free
house serving reasonably
priced bar food.
Q ὦ ◖ ▶ P

Hassop

Eyre Arms
On B6001
☎ (01629) 640390
11.30–3, 6–11; 12–3, 6.30–10.30 Sun
**Marston's Pedigree; John
Smith's Bitter; guest beer H**
17th-century inn with two
unspoilt rooms featuring
beams and settles. Varied
menu (local specialities).
⋈ Q ὦ ◖ ▶ P

Hathersage

Scotsman's Pack
School Lane
☎ (01433) 650253
12–3, 6–11; 12–11 Sat; 12–10.30 Sun
**Burtonwood Bitter, Forshaw's,
Top Hat, seasonal beers H**
Comfortable village pub with
three lounge areas served by a
central bar. 'Little John's Chair'
was made for a giant.
Q ὦ ⋈ ◖ ▶ ▲ ⇌ ♣ P

Hayfield

Kinder Lodge
10 New Mills Road
☎ (01663) 743613
3 (5.30 Mon, 12 Fri, 11.30 Sat)–11
(11–11 Fri & Sat in summer); 12–10.30
Sun (may vary)
**Ind Coope Burton Ale; Tetley
Bitter; guest beer H**
Three-storey, stone pub near
Hayfield visitor centre; hikers
and cyclists welcome. Good
games room. Q ὦ ◖ ♣ P

Royal Hotel
Market Place
☎ (01663) 742721
12–11; 12–10.30 Sun
**Marston's Pedigree; John
Smith's Bitter; guest beers H**
Former vicarage next to the
River Sett, the village church
and the cricket ground.
Original oak panels and pews

are features. Regular live
music.
🏠 Q ✿ 🍴 ◑ & Å P

Heage

Black Boy
Old Road (set back from B6013)
☎ (01773) 856799
11.45–3, 6.45–11; 12–4, 7–10.30 Sun
Mansfield Bitter; guest beer H
Large, homely, open-plan
stone building with a
restaurant above. No food Sun
eve or Mon lunch.
🏠 ✿ ◑ ▶ Å ♣ P 🍴

Hognaston

Red Lion Inn
Main Street (off B5035)
☎ (01335) 370396
12–3 (not Mon), 6–11; 12–3, 6–10.30
Sun
**Marston's Bitter, Pedigree,
HBC; Morland Old Speckled
Hen** H
Friendly, stone village pub
with a single bar,
sympathetically improved a
few years ago. Excellent home-
made food is served (no
chips!). It overlooks Carsington
Reservoir.
🏠 ☜ 🍴 ◑ & Å ♣ P

Holmesfield

Traveller's Rest
Main Road ☎ (0114) 289 0446
12–11; 12–4, 7–10.30 Sun
**John Smith's Bitter; Stones
Bitter; Younger No. 3** H
Pleasant pub with a pool table
in the tap room and a spacious
lounge. Regular live music.
✿ 🍴 Å ♣ P

Holymoorside

Lamb
16 Loads Road
☎ (01246) 566167
12–3 (not Mon–Thu), 7–11; 12–3,
7–10.30 Sun
**Draught Bass; Home Bitter;
Theakston XB; guest beer** H
Cosy, two-roomed pub
near the National Park. Up to
four guest ales. Local CAMRA
Pub of the Year 1996.
🏠 Q ✿ ♣ P

Horsley

Coach & Horses
47 Church Street (Off A609)
☎ (01332) 880581
11.30–3, 6–11; 11.30–11 Sat; 12–4,
7–10.30 Sun
Marston's Bitter, Pedigree H
Homely, open-plan village pub
with a beamed ceiling, a
conservatory and home-
cooked food (not served Sun
eve).
🏠 Q ☜ ✿ ◑ ▶ & Å ♣ P

Horsley Woodhouse

Old Oak
176 Main Street
☎ (01332) 780672
5.30–11; 12–3, 6–11 Sat; 12–3, 7–10.30
Sun
**Everards Tiger; Mansfield
Bitter; Marston's Pedigree;
guest beer** H
Two-roomed village local in
traditional style. No food Tue
eve. 🏠 Q ✿ ▶ ♣ P

Ilkeston

Dewdrop Inn
Station Street (Off A6096)
☎ (0115) 932 9684
11.30–3.30 (not Sat), 7–11; 12–4,
7–10.30 Sun
**Vaux Mild, Waggle Dance;
Ward's Best Bitter; guest
beers** H
Friendly, unchanged, multi-
roomed Victorian boozer with
a high-ceilinged lounge. Good
whisky selection. Regional
CAMRA *Pub of the Year 1997.*
🏠 Q ☜ ✿ 🍴 ◑ ▶ ♣ ♁

Durham Ox
25 Durham Street
☎ (0115) 932 4570
11–11; 12–10.30 Sun
**Vaux Mild, Waggle Dance;
Ward's Best Bitter; guest
beer** H
Cosy, backstreet, award-
winning local which used to be
a prison. Skittles played.
🏠 ✿ ♣

Ingleby

John Thompson Inn
☎ (01332) 862469
10.30–2.30, 7–11; 12–2.30, 7–10.30 Sun
Draught Bass; JTS XXX H
Converted, 15th-century
farmhouse, now a brew pub,
housing many antiques and
paintings. 🏠 ☜ ✿ ◑ & ♣ P

Kirk Ireton

Barley Mow   ☆
Main Street ☎ (01335) 370306
12–2, 7–11; 12–2, 7–10.30 Sun
**Hook Norton Best Bitter;
Marston's Pedigree; guest
beers** G
Tall, gabled, Jacobean building,
with a rambling interior. Multi-
roomed, it features low,
beamed ceilings, slate tables
and well-worn woodwork.
🏠 Q ✿ 🍴 ♣ ♁ P ⚥ 🍴

Long Eaton

Hole in the Wall
Regent Street
☎ (0115) 973 4920
10.30–3 (3.30 Mon & Thu), 5.45–11;

10.30–11 Fri & Sat; 12–4.30, 7–10.30
Sun
**Draught Bass; Worthington
Bitter; guest beers** H
Excellent two-roomed local: a
bar with TV and pool, a
lounge, plus an off-sales hatch.
The garden has a skittle alley
and a barbecue. Guest beers
and ciders are changed weekly.
An award-winning, town-
centre pub. ✿ ◑ 🍺 ➾ ♣ ♁

Old Ale House
Tamworth Road
☎ (0115) 973 5265
12–11; 12–10.30 Sun
**Draught Bass; Greene King
Abbot; Shipstone's Bitter;
Tetley Bitter** H**; guest beers** G
Spacious, open-plan, games
oriented pub on the outskirts
of town, opposite the Erewash
Canal. Weekend meals 12–7.
✿ ◑ 🍺 ♣ P

Longshaw

Grouse Inn
On B6054 ☎ (01433) 630423
12–3, 6–11; 12–3, 7–10.30 Sun
**Vaux Waggle Dance; Ward's
Best Bitter; guest beer** H
Pub built as a farmhouse in
1804, and the hayloft, barn
doors and stone trough
survive: a large lounge, a
conservatory and a tap room.
Eve meals Wed–Sun.
🏠 Q ☜ ✿ ◑ ▶ 🍺 ♣ P

Lullington

Colvile Arms
Main Street ☎ (01827) 373212
7–11; 12–3, 7–11 Sat; 12–3, 7–10.30
Sun
**Draught Bass; Marston's
Pedigree; guest beers**
(occasional) H
Busy, 18th-century free house
in a pleasant village: a basic,
wood-panelled bar, two
lounges and a bowling green.
🏠 ✿ 🍺 ♣ P

Makeney

Holly Bush Inn
Holly Bush Lane OS352447
☎ (01332) 841729
12–3, 6–11; 11–11 Sat; 12–10.30 Sun
**Marston's Pedigree; Ruddles
County; guest beers** G
Old pub with many rooms in a
Grade II-listed building. The
beer comes from the cellar in
jugs. House beer from
Brunswick. 🏠 Q ☜ ✿ ◑ ♣ P

Marsh Lane

George Inn
46 Lightwood Road (off B6056)
☎ (01246) 433178
12–4, 7–11; 12–3, 7–10.30 Sun
**Stones Bitter; Ward's Best
Bitter; guest beers** H

Popular local boasting good views over the Rother Valley. Townes beer is often available. Q ❀ ⊞ ♣ P ⛁

Matlock

Boat House
110 Dale Road
☎ (01629) 583776
11.30–11; 12–10.30 Sun
Hardys & Hansons Best Mild, Best Bitter, Classic, seasonal beers Ⓗ
Basic, friendly, three-roomed local by the River Derwent.
🏨 ⛟ ❀ 🛏 ◖ ▶ ⊞ ⇌ ♣ P

Thorn Tree
48 Jackson Road, Matlock Bank (behind County Hall)
☎ (01629) 582923
11.30–3 (not Mon or Tue), 7–11; 12–3.30, 7–10.30 Sun
Draught Bass; Mansfield Bitter, Old Baily; guest beer Ⓗ
Welcoming, 18th-century local with two cosy rooms. Extensive views across the valley. Q ❀ ◖ ♣

Melbourne

Blue Bell Inn
53 Church Street
☎ (01332) 862606
11–11; 12–10.30 Sun
Draught Bass; Everards Tiger; Marston's Pedigree Ⓗ
Small, friendly village local. No food Sun eve. ⛟ ❀ ◖ ▶ ⊞ ♣

Lamb Inn
High Street ☎ (01332) 862779
12–3, 4.30–11; 12–11 Fri & Sat; 12–10.30 Sun
Draught Bass; guest beers Ⓗ
Attractive mock-Tudor pub with a comfortable interior.
❀ ◖ ⊞ ♣ P

Mickleover

Honeycomb
Ladybank Road
☎ (01332) 515600
12–2.30 (3 Sat), 6.30–11; 12–3, 7–10.30 Sun
Everards Beacon, Tiger, Old Original; guest beer Ⓗ
Popular, honeycomb-shaped pub on two levels. Meals Tue–Sat. ❀ ◖ ⊞ ♣ P

Monsal Head

Monsal Head Hotel
On B6465 ☎ (01629) 640250
11–11; 12–10.30 Sun
Courage Directors; Marston's Pedigree; Theakston Best Bitter, XB, Old Peculier; Whim Hartington Bitter; guest beers Ⓗ
150-year-old country hotel with an elegant lounge. Real ales are in the stable bar, with

its stall seating and inglenook. House beer from Lloyds.
🏨 Q ❀ 🛏 ◖ ▶ ▲ ♣ P

New Mills

Beehive
Albion Road
11–2 (3 Sat), 5.30 (7 Sat)–11; 12–3, 7–10.30 Sun
Boddingtons Bitter; Flowers IPA; guest beer Ⓗ
Unusual, triangular, stone pub with a small lounge, a larger vault, and a tiny restaurant. Popular with boaters on the Peak Forest Canal.
◖ ▶ ⊞ ⇌ (Newtown) ♣

Newton Solney

Unicorn
Repton Road (B5008)
☎ (01283) 703324
11.30 (12 Sat)–3, 7–11; 12–3, 7–10.30 Sun
Draught Bass; Marston's Pedigree; guest beer Ⓗ
Lively village local popular for games. No food Sun eve.
❀ 🛏 ◖ ▶ ᶑ ♣ P

Ockbrook

Royal Oak
Green Lane ☎ (01332) 662378
11.30–2.30, 7–11; 12–2.30, 7–11; 12–3, 7–10.30 Sun
Draught Bass; Worthington Bitter; guest beers Ⓗ/Ⓖ
Lively, friendly village local with small cosy rooms. Good value lunches; children's play area. 🏨 Q ❀ ᶑ ♣ P

Over Haddon

Lathkil Hotel
½ mile S of B5055
☎ (01629) 812501
11.30–3, 6.30–11; 12–3, 7–10.30 Sun
Ward's Best Bitter; guest beer Ⓗ
Free house in an idyllic setting (view of Lathkil Dale), with a fine, oak-panelled bar. Excellent food (not served Sun). 🏨 Q ❀ 🛏 ◖ ▶ ▲ P ⛁

Ripley

Three Horseshoes
Market Place ☎ (01773) 743113
11–3, 5–11; 11–11 Sat; 12–10.30 Sun
Bateman seasonal beers; guest beer Ⓗ
Typical, two-roomed local with a pool table. ◖ ♣ P ⛁

Rosliston

Bull's Head
Burton Road ☎ (01283) 761705
12–2.30, 7–11; 12–3, 7–10.30 Sun
Draught Bass; Marston's Pedigree Ⓗ

Turn-of-the-century village pub with a public bar and a smart, cosy lounge.
🏨 ◖ ⊞ ᶑ ♣ P

Rowarth

Little Mill Inn
Off Siloh Road
☎ (01633) 743178
11–11; 12–10.30 Sun
Banks's Bitter; Camerons Strongarm; Hardys & Hansons Best Bitter; Marston's Pedigree; guest beer Ⓗ
Large, multi-roomed pub of great character, boasting a working waterwheel. Adventure playground. Good food.
🏨 ⛟ ❀ 🛏 ◖ ▶ ᶑ ▲ P ⛁

Rowsley

Grouse & Claret
Station Road (A6)
☎ (01629) 733233
11–11; 12–10.30 Sun
Mansfield Riding Bitter, Bitter, Old Baily, seasonal beers Ⓗ
Imposing, ex-railway hotel, comfortably refurbished but retaining a tap room (hikers welcome). Wide range of home-cooked meals; family room in summer. 🏨 Q ⛟ ❀ 🛏 ◖ ▶ ⊞ ▲ ♣ P ⛀

Shardlow

Malt Shovel
The Wharf ☎ (01332) 799763
11–11; 12–3, 7–10.30 (12–10.30 summer) Sun
Marston's Bitter, Pedigree; guest beer Ⓗ
Multi-roomed, canalside tavern converted from an old maltings; full of character and popular with boaters. Good, home-cooked food (not served Sun). 🏨 Q ❀ ◖ ▲ ♣ P

Sheldon

Cock & Pullet
Main Street ☎ (01629) 814292
11–11; 12–10.30 Sun
Draught Bass; Stones Bitter; Tetley Mild Ⓗ
Converted barn, retaining original beams. The bar area and tap room have stone flags.
🏨 ❀ 🛏 ◖ ▶ ᶑ ▲ ♣ P

Shirley

Saracen's Head
☎ (01335) 360330
12–3, 7–11; 12–3, 7–10.30 Sun
Draught Bass; Hoskins & Oldfield Supreme; Marston's Pedigree; guest beers Ⓗ
Attractive pub, dating from 1791, in a delightful country village: an open lounge with a

snug, offering a good range of home-cooked food (not served Sun eve). Children welcome if dining. An ideal walking and cycling area.
🏠 Q ❀ 🛏 ◁ ▷ ⅏ Å ♣ P

Smalley

Bell Inn
Main Road
☎ (01332) 880635
11.30–2.30, 6–11; 12–2, 7–10.30 Sun
Bateman XB; Whim Hartington Bitter; guest beer H
Two-roomed, country-style pub, with a warm atmosphere.
🏠 Q ❀ 🛏 ◁ ▷ ⅏ Å P

Somercotes

Horse & Jockey
Leabrooks Road
☎ (01773) 602179
11–2, 7–11; 12–3, 7–10.30 Sun
Greene King IPA; Marston's Pedigree; guest beer H
Busy, unspoilt, multi-roomed local. ❀ ⅏ ♣

South Wingfield

Old Yew Tree
Manor Road
☎ (01773) 833763
5–11; 12–3, 6.30–11; 12–3, 7–10.30 Sun
Marston's Pedigree; guest beers H
Popular pub near Wingfield Manor, boasting oak panelling. No meals Sun eve.
🏠 Q ❀ ◁ ▷ Å ♣ P

Stanton-by-Dale

Chequers
Dale Road
☎ (0115) 932 0946
11–2.30, 6–11; 11–11 Sat; 12–10.30 Sun
Draught Bass E
Busy local featuring an old water pump in its single bar. No meals Sun.
❀ ◁ ♣ P

Swadlincote

Springfield
25 North Street
☎ (01283) 221546
11–11; 12–4, 7–10.30 Sun
Draught Bass; Marston's Pedigree H
Pleasing, two-roomed, popular local. ❀ ◁ ⅏ ♣ P

Swarkestone

Crewe & Harpur
Swarkestone Road
☎ (01332) 700641
11–11; 12–10.30 Sun
Marston's Bitter, Pedigree; guest beer H

200-year-old coaching inn by the River Trent, with a roomy interior. Popular with diners.
🏠 ❀ ◁ ▷ ⅏ P

Ticknall

Chequers Inn
27 High Street
☎ (01332) 864392
12–2.30, 6–11; 12–3, 7–10.30 Sun
Marston's Pedigree; Ruddles County; guest beers H
Small, friendly, two-roomed local with an inglenook.
🏠 Q ❀ ♣ P

Tideswell

George Hotel
Commercial Road
☎ (01298) 871382
11–3, 7–11; 12–3, 7–10.30 Sun
Hardys & Hansons Best Bitter, Classic, seasonal beers H
Substantial stone hotel next to the church – the 'Cathedral of the Peak'. A large L-shaped lounge, a snug and a tap room. No eve meals winter Mon.
🏠 ❀ 🛏 ◁ ▷ ⅏ Å ♣ P

Troway

Gate Inn
Main Road
☎ (01246) 413280
12–3, 7–11; 12–3, 7–10.30 Sun
Burtonwood Bitter, Forshaw's, Top Hat H
Well-preserved, family-run village local overlooking the Moss Valley. Children welcome. 🏠 Q ❀ ⅏ ♣ P 🗓

Wardlow Mires

Three Stags' Heads ☆
At A623/B6465 jct
☎ (01298) 872268
7 (12 Sat & bank hols)–11; 12–10.30 Sun
Abbeydale Matins, Absolution, Black Mass; Springhead Bitter H**; guest beer** G
Carefully restored, unspoilt, two-roomed, 17th-century farmhouse pub. The stone-flagged bar is heated by a range. 🏠 Q ❀ ◁ ▷ Å P

Whaley Bridge

Shepherd's Arms
7 Old Road
☎ (01663) 732384
11–3, 5.30–11; 12–3, 7–10.30 Sun
Banks's Mild; Marston's Bitter, Pedigree H
Ageless local, near the High Peak Canal terminus. The lounge is quiet; the vault is lively and convivial, with scrubbed tables and a flagged floor. 🏠 Q ❀ ⅏ ⇌ ♣ P

Whitehough

Oddfellows
Whitehead Lane
☎ (01663) 750306
12–3 (not winter Mon–Thu), 5–11; 12–11 Fri & Sat; 12–10.30 Sun
Bateman Mild; Marston's Bitter, Pedigree H
Classic, stone, conversational pub in a picturesque Peak District village near Chinley. Three small rooms cluster around the bar, creating a homely atmosphere. A centre for the community. Eve meals end at 8. ❀ ◁ ▷

Whitwell

Jug & Glass
13 Portland Street
☎ (01909) 720289
11–3, 6.30–11; 12–3, 6.30–10.30 Sun
John Smith's Bitter, Magnet H
Unspoilt, listed building: a two-roomed local with a wooden bar and open fires in an ex-mining community.
🏠 Q ❀ ⅏ ♣ P 🗓

Willington

Green Dragon
The Green
☎ (01283) 702327
11–3, 6 (5 Fri)–11; 12–3, 7–10.30 Sun
Marston's Pedigree; Tetley Bitter; guest beer H
Cosy village pub in a quiet location close to the Trent & Mersey Canal. Popular with diners (no meals Sun eve).
❀ ◁ ▷ ⇌ P

Woolley Moor

White Horse Inn
Badger Lane
☎ (01246) 590319
11.30–2.30 (3.30 Sat), 6–11; 12–3.30, 5–10.30 Sun
Draught Bass; guest beer H
Proper village pub dating from the 17th century. The extensive garden, with a children's play area, affords a view of the Amber Valley. Award-winning restaurant.
Q ❀ ◁ ▷ ⅏ Å ♣ P

Youlgreave

George Hotel
Church Street
☎ (01629) 636292
11–2.30, 6.30–11; 11–11 Sat; 12–10.30 Sun
John Smith's Bitter; Theakston Mild; guest beer H
Large, lively local opposite a fine church. Hikers welcome. Good range of home-cooked food.
Q ❀ 🛏 ◁ ▷ ⅏ Å ♣ P

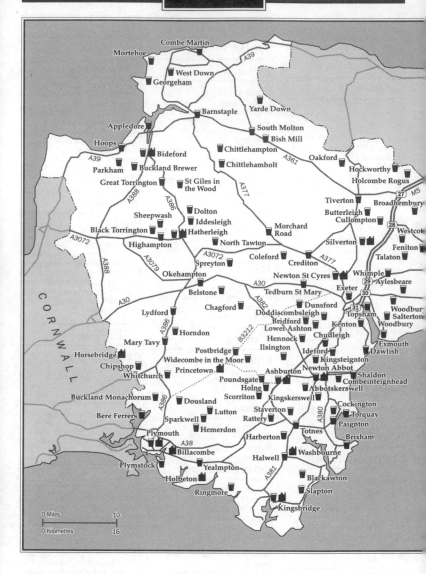

Devon

Abbotskerswell

Two Mile Oak
Totnes Road (A381)
☎ (01803) 812411
11–3, 5–11 (11–11 summer); 12–3,
7–10.30 (12–10.30 summer) Sun
Draught Bass G; **Eldridge
Pope Royal Oak; Flowers
IPA** G/ H
Pub with a superb public bar
with a real fire and bare
floorboards, where the beer is
served on gravity if you ask.
There's also a well-established
bar menu and a restaurant.
Taunton Traditional cider is
stocked, too.
🏘 Q 🕸 ◑ ▷ ▲ ♣ ⏲ P

Appledore

Coach & Horses
5 Market Street
☎ (01237) 474470
12–3, 7–11; 12–3, 7–10.30 Sun
Beer range varies H
Jazz- and blues-oriented, very
popular local with a good
range of ales. Live music Wed
eve. 🏘 ☕ ◑ ▷

Ashburton

London Hotel
11 West Street
☎ (01364) 652478
11–2.30, 5.30–11 (11–11 summer);

12–2.30, 7–10.30 (12–10.30 summer)
Sun
**Thompson's Best Bitter, IPA,
Figurehead, Man 'o' War,
Celebration Porter** H
Quiet, old coaching inn with
two bar areas with open fires,
beamed ceilings and a no-
smoking dining area.
🏘 Q ☕ 🛏 ◑ ▷

Axminster

Axminster Inn
Silver Street
☎ (01297) 34947
11–11; 12–10.30 Sun
Palmers BB, IPA H
Popular, straightforward town

S O M E R S E T

Clayhidon

Luppitt
Stockland

Kilmington

Axminster

DORSET

Colyton

Branscombe

Axmouth

Sidmouth
East
Budleigh

Devon

Aylesbeare

Halfway Inn
Sidmouth Road (A3052/B3180
jct) ☎ (01395) 232273
11.30–3, 5.30–11; 12–10.30 Sun
**Draught Bass; Flowers
Original; Worthington Bitter;
guest beer** Ⓗ
Two-bar country pub and
restaurant at a busy crossroads.
Good value food; friendly
management.
Q ✿ ◑ ▶ ▲ P

Barnstaple

Check Inn
14 Castle Street
☎ (01271) 75964
11–3 (may vary), 7–11; 12–3, 7–10.30
Sun
Beer range varies Ⓗ
Small town pub near the cattle
market, with live jam sessions
Thu eves. Five handpumps
serve Cotleigh beers and other
independent ales. The off sales,
at the rear, is known as the
'Check Out'.
🛏 ◑ ▶ ≋ ♣ P

Corner House
108 Boutport Street
☎ (01271) 43528
11–3, 5 (7 Wed)–11; 11–11 Fri & Sat;
12–3, 7–10.30 Sun
Draught Bass Ⓖ/Ⓗ**; guest
beers** Ⓖ
Convivial, wood-panelled
town-centre pub with
outstanding Bass on
handpump and at times
gravity. Q ➳ ₺ ≋ ♣

Rolle Quay
Rolle's Quay
☎ (01271) 45182
11–11; 12–10.30 Sun
Beer range varies Ⓗ
Locally renowned pub for its
ale range and hospitality, close
to the town centre and fronting
an historic working quay.
Cotleigh beers are usually
available. Wide range of good
value meals.
Q ✿ ◑ ▶ ⊟ ₺ ▲ ♣ ⌂

Belstone

Tors
2 miles SE of Okehampton
OS619936 ☎ (01837) 840689
11–2.30, 6–11; 12–4, 7–10.30 Sun
Otter Bitter, Ale; guest beer Ⓗ
Large granite building in an
unspoilt village on the
northern edge of Dartmoor,
situated on the Tarka Trail. A
good base for country walks.
The accent is on Devon ales.
Home-cooked food.
🛏 ✿ 🛏 ◑ ▶ ♣

Bere Ferrers

Old Plough
☎ (01822) 840358
12–3, 7–11 (closed Mon Nov–end Feb);
12–3, 7–10.30 Sun
Draught Bass Ⓖ**; Flowers
IPA** Ⓗ**; Sutton Dartmoor
Pride** Ⓖ**; Wadworth 6X** Ⓗ
16th-century village inn, by the
River Tavy in an area of
outstanding beauty. Cider in
summer. 🛏 ✿ ◑ ▶ ≋ ♣

Bideford

Ship on Launch
14 Barnstaple Street, East the
Water ☎ (01237) 472426
11–11; 12–4, 7–10.30 Sun
Beer range varies Ⓗ
Handy pub for the Tarka Trail
with a classic, unspoilt, old
front bar featuring old ships'
masts as ceiling joists.
🛏 Q ➳ ✿ ◑ ▶ ⊟ ⌂ P

White Hart
Queen Street ☎ (01237) 473203
11–11; 12–3, 7–10.30 Sun
**Jollyboat Mainbrace; guest
beer** Ⓗ
Friendly old town pub,
featuring excellent jazz and
blues music Wed–Fri eves. No
eve meals in winter. ✿ ◑ ▶

Bish Mill

Mill Inn
From S Molton take B3137 to
Tiverton ☎ (01769) 550944

---

pub with a friendly welcome.
🛏 Q ➳ ✿ 🛏 ◑ ⊟ ₺ ≋ ♣
⌂ P

Axmouth

Ship Inn
☎ (01297) 21838
11–2.30, 6–11; 12–2.30, 7–10.30 Sun
Draught Bass; Flowers IPA Ⓗ
Well-known pub serving
excellent food in a large dining
room (no eve meals winter
Tue). Convalescing owls make
unusual drinking companions.
One of only two pubs in Devon
in every edition of the *Guide*.
🛏 Q ✿ ◑ ▶ ⊟ ₺ ▲ ♣ P

12–2.30, 6.30–11; 11–11 Sat &
summer; 12–10.30 Sun
**Draught Bass; Cotleigh
Tawny; guest beer**
(occasional) H
17th-century inn featuring a
settle next to a log fire. It opens
at 7.30 in summer for breakfast.
Children welcome in the
games room. Cider in
summer.
🏠 Q ❀ 🛏 ◑ ♿ ⛟ ♣ ➘ P

Blackawton

George Inn
Main Street
☎ (01803) 712342
12–2.30, 7–11; 12–10.30 Sun
**Princetown IPA H; guest
beers H/G**
This traditional village pub has
a very good atmosphere and a
regularly changing beer list;
mini-festivals are held
throughout the year. Large
selection of foreign beers.
Good value food. 🏠 Q ❦ ❀
🛏 ◑ ♿ ⛟ ♣ ➘ P ☗

Black Torrington

Torridge Inn
Signed on A3072
☎ (01409) 231243
11–3, 6–11; 12–4, 7–10.30 Sun
**Brakspear Bitter; Fuller's
London Pride; guest beer**
(occasional) H
Friendly pub, offering good
food (no food Sun; no lunches
Tue or Wed). A focus for local
activities.
🏠 ❦ ❀ 🛏 ◑ ♣ P

Branscombe

Fountain Head
☎ (01297) 680359
11.30–2.30, 6.45–11 (11–3, 6–11
summer); 12–2.30, 7–10.30 (12–3,
6–10.30 summer) Sun
**Branscombe Vale Branoc,
Olde Stoker; guest beers**
(occasional) H
14th-century pub with huge
log fires in its bars; the lounge
was formerly a blacksmith's
forge. Wood-panelled walls
and a stone-flagged floor
are features. Good value
food.
🏠 Q ❀ 🛏 ◑ ♣ ➘ P

Bridford

Bridford Inn
☎ (01647) 252436
12–2.30 (not Tue), 7–11; 12–3, 6.30–11
Sat; 12–3, 7–10.30 Sun
Draught Bass; guest beers H
Delightful, 13th-century
building which was converted
in the 1960s to a village pub
with one large room. Terrific
atmosphere. Greek food is a
speciality.
🏠 Q ❦ ❀ 🛏 ◑ ♿ ♣ ➘ P ✗

Brixham

Blue Anchor
83 Fore Street
☎ (01803) 859373
11–11; 12–10.30 Sun
**Blackawton 44 Special,
Headstrong; guest beers** H
Popular with tourists and
locals, this historic, 16th-
century, harbourside pub, a
former sail loft, offers live
music and reasonably-priced
food. 🏠 Q ◑ ♣

Broadhembury

Drewe Arms
☎ (01404) 841267
11–2.30, 6–11; 12–2.30, 7–10.30 Sun
**Otter Bitter, Ale, Bright,
Head** G
A picturesque exterior and a
relatively unspoilt, old-
fashioned interior are features
of this thatched Grade II-listed
village inn, set amongst
thatched whitewashed cottages
(no food Sun eve).
🏠 Q ❀ ◑ ♣ ➘ P

Buckland Brewer

Coach & Horses
Take A386, then A388, from
Bideford ☎ (01237) 451395
11.30–3, 6–11; 12–3, 7–10.30 Sun
**Flowers Original; Fuller's
London Pride; guest beer**
(summer) H
Thatched inn dating back to
the 15th century and later used
as a staging post and retreat by
Royalists during the Civil War.
Two bars and a pool room;
good atmosphere and good
food. 🏠 ❀ 🛏 ◑ ♣ ➘ P

Buckland Monachorum

Drake Manor Inn
The Village ☎ (01822) 853892
11.30–2.30 (3 Sat), 6.30–11; 12–3,
7–10.30 Sun
**John Smith's Bitter; Ushers
Best Bitter, Founders, seasonal
beers** H
16th-century local in a
picturesque village serving
over 70 whiskies and a varied
menu with home-made
specials. 🏠 Q ❀ ◑ ♣ ⛟ P

Butterleigh

Butterleigh Inn
☎ (01884) 855407
12–2.30, 6 (5 Fri)–11; 12–2.30, 7–10.30
Sun
**Cotleigh Barn Owl, Tawny;
guest beers**
Friendly, unspoilt, village inn
popular for food and
accommodation. Local
CAMRA *Pub of the Year* 1995.
🏠 Q ❀ 🛏 ◑ ♿ ♣ P

Chagford

Globe Inn
High Street ☎ (01647) 433485
11–3, 7–11; 11–11 Sat; 12–3, 7–10.30
Sun
**Courage Best Bitter, Directors;
guest beers** H
Friendly, 16th-century, two-bar
coaching inn in the centre of a
delightful country town. Cider
in summer.
🏠 Q 🛏 ◑ ♿ ⛟ ♣ ➘ ☗

Chipshop

Chipshop Inn
Off A384, 3 miles W of
Tavistock OS437751
☎ (01822) 832322
12–2.30, 5–11; 12–11 Sat; 12–10.30 Sun
**Draught Bass; Exmoor Ale;
guest beers** H
Welcoming, one-bar pub on a
remote crossroads, boasting a
notable collection of mirrors.
Free, popular skittle alley.
🏠 Q ◑ ⛟ ♣ P

Chittlehamholt

Exeter Inn
Take B3226 to Crediton from S
Molton, 4 miles then right
☎ (01769) 540281
11.30–2.30, 6–11; 12–3, 7–10.30 Sun
Dartmoor Best Bitter G;
**Marston's Pedigree; Tetley
Bitter** H
16th-century, thatched,
beamed coaching inn with a
friendly atmosphere.
🏠 ❦ ❀ 🛏 ◑ ♿ ⛟ ♣ ➘

Chittlehampton

Bell Inn
The Square (off B3227)
☎ (01769) 540368
11–3, 7–11; 11–11 Sat; 12–3, 7–10.30
Sun
**Draught Bass; Greene King
Abbot; guest beers** H
Friendly pub in the village
square. Note the jug and bottle
etched in a window of the hall.
Over 120 whiskies are
displayed in the bar.
❀ ◑ ♣ ➘

Chudleigh

Bishop Lacy
Fore Street ☎ (01626) 852196
11–11; 12–10.30 Sun
**Boddingtons Bitter; Flowers
IPA; Fuller's London Pride;
guest beers** H/G
No records exist to show the
age of this pub, but the Grade
II star-listed building with
medieval decor, is believed to
be 14th-century. The back bar
has ales on stillage. No-
smoking dining area.
🏠 ❀ ◑ ♣ ➘ P

Clayhidon

Half Moon Inn
☎ (01823) 680291
12–2.30, 7–11; 12–3.30, 7–10.30 Sun
Cotleigh Tawny; Otter Bitter, Ale Ⓗ
Old, but well cared for village local with nice views across the Culm Valley.
🏚 Q 🍺 ❀ ◖ ▶ 🍴 ♣ 🛏 P

Cockington

Drum Inn
☎ (01803) 605143
11–3, 7 (6 summer)–11 (11–11 summer school hols); 12–3, 7–10.30 (12–10.30 summer) Sun
Dartmoor Best Bitter; guest beer Ⓗ
Large, popular village pub, in beautiful surroundings. Thatcher's cider in summer.
🏚 Q 🍺 ❀ ◖ ▶ 🍴 🛏 P ⚦

Coleford

New Inn
☎ (01363) 84242
12–2.30, 6–11; 12–2.30, 7–10.30 Sun
Badger Dorset Best; Otter Ale; Wadworth 6X Ⓗ
Large, well-appointed pub/ restaurant with one bar in a 13th-century, Grade II-listed building with a splendid thatched roof. Friendly atmosphere; talkative parrot. Rather expensive, but good quality food.
🏚 ❀ 🚐 ◖ ▶ ♣ P

Colyton

Gerrard Arms
St Andrews Square
☎ (01297) 52588
11.30–3, 6–11; 12–3, 7–10.30 Sun
Draught Bass; Otter Bitter; guest beer Ⓗ
Pleasant, friendly village pub near the church.
❀ ◖ ▶ 🍴

Combeinteignhead

Wild Goose
Between Newton Abbot and Shaldon on road S of Teign estuary ☎ (01626) 872241
11.30–2.30, 6.30–11; 12–3, 7–10.30 Sun
Beer range varies Ⓗ
17th-century farmhouse in a quiet village near the River Teign, hosting jazz Mon. Good food; cider in summer. Local CAMRA *Pub of the Year* 1996.
🏚 Q ❀ ◖ ▶ 🍴 🛏 P

Combe Martin

Castle
High Street ☎ (01271) 883706
12–3, 6.30–11 (12–11 summer); 12–10.30 Sun
Draught Bass; Worthington Bitter; guest beers Ⓗ
Instantly welcoming local with good conversation and a tremendously strong line in guests from independent breweries. Thatcher's cider in summer.
🍺 ❀ 🚐 ◖ ▶ 🍴 ♣ P

Crediton

Crediton Inn
28A Mill Street (Tiverton road)
☎ (01363) 772882
11–11; 12–2, 7–10.30 Sun
Draught Bass; guest beers Ⓗ
Friendly pub just off the town centre, serving three ales in a convivial atmosphere. A modest menu of cooked meals and a skittle alley feature.
◖ ▶ ⇌ ♣ P

Cullompton

White Hart
19 Fore Street
☎ (01884) 33260
11–11; 12–10.30 Sun
Courage Best Bitter, Directors; John Smith's Bitter Ⓗ
Busy, town-centre pub with a welcoming fire and good value food.
🏚 🚐 ◖ ▶ ♣ P

Dawlish

Marine Hotel
Marine Parade
☎ (01626) 865245
11–11; 12–10.30 Sun
Draught Bass; Dartmoor Best Bitter; guest beer (occasional) Ⓗ
Pleasant, seafront hotel bar, close to the centre and station.
🚐 ◖ ▶ ⇌

Prince of Wales
Old Town Street
☎ (01626) 862145
11–11; 12–10.30 Sun
Draught Bass; Flowers IPA Ⓖ
Fairly basic pub, but with a good atmosphere, similar to Exeter's Double Locks in character, featuring irreverent cartoon murals in the WCs. Blues music is a speciality. Inch's cider is served.
🏚 ❀ ◖ ▶ ♣ 🛏

Doddiscombsleigh

Nobody Inn
☎ (01647) 252394
12–2.30, 6–11; 12–3, 7–10.30 Sun
Draught Bass Ⓖ**; Branscombe Vale Branoc; guest beers** Ⓗ
Large village pub dating from the 15th century. Four ales are available plus over 600 wines, 250-plus whiskies and a huge selection of cheeses. Popular with visitors, but it can be hard to find.
🏚 Q ❀ 🚐 ◖ ▶ 🛏 P ⚦

Dolton

Union Inn
Take B3220 from Gt Torrington, then B3217
☎ (01805) 804633
12–2.30 (not Wed), 6–11; 12–2.30, 7–10.30 Sun
Dartmoor Best Bitter; St Austell HSD Ⓗ
16th-century Devon cob longhouse with two bars, a cosy restaurant and a function room opening out on to a courtyard garden. Great village atmosphere.
🏚 Q ❀ 🚐 ◖ ▶ P

Dousland

Burrator Inn
☎ (01822) 853121
11–11; 12–10.30 Sun
Draught Bass; Flowers IPA; Wadworth 6X; guest beers Ⓗ
Victorian country inn, near Burrator Reservoir. The large restaurant serves good value food. 🏚 🍺 ❀ 🚐 ◖ ▶ 🍴 ♣ P

Dunsford

Royal Oak
☎ (01647) 252256
12–2.30, 6.30 (7 Mon)–11; 12–2.30, 7–10.30 Sun
Flowers IPA; Fuller's London Pride; Greene King Abbot; guest beers Ⓗ
Popular local in an attractive village on the edge of Dartmoor National Park, featuring Victorian decor in a single bar, plus dining and games areas. Good range of reasonably-priced, home-cooked food; local cider.
🏚 Q ❀ 🚐 ◖ ▶ 🍴 ♣ 🛏 P

East Budleigh

Rolle Arms
☎ (01395) 442012
11–2.30, 6–11; 12–3, 7–10.30 Sun
Boddingtons Bitter; Flowers IPA Ⓗ
Pleasant, one-bar, village pub with a games room. Excellent, home-produced food. Very popular with nearby agricultural college students. The house beer comes from Branscombe Vale.
Q 🍺 🚐 ◖ ▶ 🍴 🛏 P

Exeter

Brook Green
Well Street (near St James Park football ground)
☎ (01392) 496370
12–2.30 (3 Sat), 6–11; 12–3, 7–10.30 Sun
Beer range varies Ⓗ
Enterprising Whitbread tenancy making full use of the guest beer rules. Whitbread beers are kept under mixed gas

cask breathers but guest beers are served properly. Snacks available.

≈ (St James Pk) ♣ P

Cowick Barton

Cowick Lane, St Thomas
☎ (01392) 270411
11–2.30, 6.30–11; 12–3, 7–10.30 Sun
Draught Bass; Courage Best Bitter, Directors H
16th-century, Grade II star-listed pub with a cosy, friendly atmosphere; described as a 'country pub in a city'. Good value food in the restaurant.

✿ ◖▶ ⊟ P

Double Locks Hotel

Canal Banks, Marsh Barton
(follow next to incinerator, over canal, turn right)
OS932900
☎ (01392) 56947
11–11; 12–10.30 Sun
Adnams Broadside G**;
Everards Old Original** H**;
Smiles Golden Brew** G**, Best,
Heritage** H**; guest beers** G
Large canalside pub with an eccentric air, an atmospheric bar and huge grounds. Frequent live music. Generally ten cask ales available.

▥ ▰ ✿ ◖▶ ᕀ ▲ ♣ ◔ P

Great Western Hotel

Station Approach
☎ (01392) 74039
11–11; 12–10.30 Sun
Draught Bass; Smiles Golden Brew; Stones Bitter; guest beers H
Comfortable hotel/pub serving good value food. Trade has built up and it now offers at least six cask ales. Limited parking.

▰ ◖▶ ≈ (St David's) P

Jolly Porter

St David's Hill (near station)
☎ (01392) 54848
11–11; 12–10.30 Sun
Courage Best Bitter, Directors; John Smith's Bitter; guest beers H
Popular, long, narrow pub on several levels, offering good value food. Jazz Wed eve; two-week autumn beer festival.

◖▶ ≈ (St David's) ◔

On the Waterfront

The Quay
☎ (01392) 210590
12–2.30, 5.30–11 (12–11 summer); 12–3, 6–10.30 (12–10.30 summer) Sun
Boddingtons Bitter; Courage Directors; guest beer H
Pub formed from two warehouses, cut into the cliff behind the quay. Well known for its pizzas, it is now run by Greenalls and remains unspoilt. Wheelchair WC.

✿ ◖▶ ♿ ≈ (St Thomas/Central)

Well House

Cathedral Yard
☎ (01392) 434831
11–11; 7–10.30 (closed lunch) Sun
Draught Bass; guest beers H
Federation Buchanan's Original is sold as Cathedral Cask at this popular, city-centre pub which serves a good range of local and unusual guest beers. Ask to see the historic cellar. ◖ ≈ (Central)

Exmouth

Country House Inn

Withycombe Village Road
☎ (01395) 263444
10.30–11; 12–10.30 Sun
Draught Bass; Boddingtons Bitter; Flowers IPA, Original H
Suburban local, hosting summer barbecues beside a stream. Excellent food lunchtimes Mon–Sat and Fri–Sat eves (booking advisable). Skittle alley and a games room available. Formerly a blacksmith's. ✿ ◖▶ ♣

Grove

The Esplanade
☎ (01395) 272101
11–3, 5.30–11; 11–11 Sat & summer; 12–10.30 Sun
Boddingtons Bitter; Brakspear Special; Flowers Original; Greene King Abbot; Wadworth 6X; guest beer (occasional) H
Friendly, family, seafront pub near the docks. Good value food includes locally caught seafood. Live music Fri; monthly mini-beer festivals Oct–May. Safe play area for children. Wheelchair WC.

▰ ✿ ◖▶ ♿ ≈ P

Feniton

Nog Inn

Ottery Road
☎ (01404) 850210
11–3, 6–11; 12–3, 7–10.30 Sun
Cotleigh Tawny; guest beers H
Friendly village pub, with a varied range of mostly local beers. ✿ ▰ ᕀ ≈ ♣ P

Georgeham

King's Arms

Chapel Street
☎ (01271) 890240
12–3, 7–11 (midnight Fri & Sat in summer); 12–3, 7–10.30 Sun
Marston's Pedigree; Thompson's Celebration Porter; guest beers G
Conversational pub serving a stunning range of constantly changing guest ales from independent breweries. Skittles played.

▥ ✿ ▰ ◖▶ ▲ ♣

Great Torrington

Black Horse Inn

High Street ☎ (01805) 622121
11–3, 5.30–11; 11–11 Sat; 12–4, 7–10.30 Sun
Courage Best Bitter, Directors; John Smith's Bitter; guest beer H
Pub famous for its use as an office during the Civil War by first the Royalists then the Parliamentarians; modernised in places but still mostly 16th century. ▥ ▱ ▰ ◖▶ ▲ ♣

Halwell

Old Inn

Follow A381 out of Totnes towards Kingsbridge
☎ (01803) 712329
11–3, 6.30–11; 11–11 Fri & Sat; 12–10.30 Sun
Beer range varies H
Village pub with a warm atmosphere. There has been a pub on this site since 1104.

▥ Q ▱ ✿ ▰ ◖▶ ♣ ◔ P

Harberton

Church House Inn

☎ (01803) 863707
12 (11.30 Sat)–3, 6–11; 12–3, 6–10.30 Sun
Draught Bass; Courage Best Bitter; guest beers H
Beautiful, typical South Devon church house. Dating from the 12th century, the pub has many old features, including a medieval oak screen behind which is the family room.

▥ Q ▱ ✿ ▰ ◖▶ ▲ ♣ ◔ P

Hatherleigh

George Hotel

4 Market Street
☎ (01837) 810454
11–11; 12–3, 7–10.30 Sun
Draught Bass; Boddingtons Bitter; Wadworth 6X; guest beer H
14th-century inn which originally served as a rest house and sanctuary for local monks, and later as a coaching inn. It retains all its historic charm, with many rooms, including a farmers' bar open in summer.

▥ Q ▱ ✿ ▰ ◖▶ ♣ ◔ P

Hemerdon

Miners Arms

☎ (01752) 343252
11–2.30, 5.30–11; 12–3, 7–10.30 Sun
Draught Bass H/G**;
Boddingtons Bitter; Sutton XSB; Ushers Best Bitter; guest beers** H
Former tin miners' pub on the hill overlooking Plympton.

▥ Q ▱ ✿ ◖▶ ♣ ◔ P

Hennock

Palk Arms
Off A38 at Chudleigh
Knighton, follow signs
☎ (01626) 833027
12–3 (11–3.30 summer), 7–11; 12–
10.30 Sun
Beer range varies G
17th-century country pub,
boasting a good local trade, a
good atmosphere and fantastic
views of the Teign Valley.
Regular storytelling eves;
home-cooked food.
🏠 Q 🕿 ❀ ◁ ▶ ▲ ♣ 🛢

Highampton

Golden Inn
On A3072 ☎ (01409) 231200
11.30–3, 6.30–11; 12–3, 7–10.30 Sun
**Draught Bass; Butcombe
Bitter** H
16th-century inn with a low-
beamed ceiling and a hops-
strewn bar. Good atmosphere.
🏠 Q ❀ ◁ ▶ ▲ ♣ P

Hockworthy

Staplecross Inn
☎ (01398) 361374
6.30 (11 Sat)–11; 12–10.30 Sun
Cotleigh Tawny; guest beer H
Unspoilt, 400-year-old country
pub on the Somerset border:
two bars both with traditional
stone floors. Eve meals Thu–
Sat. 🏠 Q ❀ ▶ ▲ ♣ 🛢 P

Holcombe Rogus

Prince of Wales
☎ (01823) 672070
11.30–3 (not Tue), 6.30–11; 12–3,
7–10.30 Sun
**Cotleigh Tawny; Otter Ale;
guest beers** H
Pleasant country pub, not far
from the Grand Western Canal.
Note the cash register
handpumps. Local cider in
summer.
🕿 ❀ ◁ ▶ ▲ ♣ 🛢 P ✍

Holne

Church House Inn
☎ (01364) 631208
11.30–3, 6.30–11; 12–3, 7–10.30 Sun
**Butcombe Bitter; Dartmoor
Best Bitter; Morland Old
Speckled Hen; guest beers** H
14th-century inn at the village
centre, within the Dartmoor
National Park: two bars and a
dining area. Gray's Farm cider.
🏠 Q 🕿 ❀ 🍴 ◁ ▶ ▲ ♣ 🛢 ✍

Hoops

Hoops Inn
On A39 ☎ (01237) 451222
11–11; 12–10.30 Sun
**Draught Bass; Dartmoor Best
Bitter; guest beers** H

Real gem of a coaching inn,
built in the 13th century. Cosy,
with log fires at both ends of
the main bar, it was once a
meeting place for smugglers.
🏠 ❀ 🍴 ◁ ▶ ▲ ♣ P

Horndon

Elephant's Nest Inn
Off A386, 1½ miles E of Mary
Tavy ☎ (01822) 810273
11.30–2.30, 6.30–11; 12–2.30, 7–10.30
Sun
**Boddingtons Bitter; Palmers
IPA; St Austell HSD; guest
beers** H
Picturesque, 16th-century
moorland pub with a relaxed
atmosphere, serving a good
value, varied menu. Local
CAMRA *Pub of the Year* 1996.
🏠 Q 🕿 ❀ ◁ ▶ 🛢 P

Iddesleigh

Duke of York
On B3217 ☎ (01837) 810253
11–11; 12–10.30 Sun
**Adnams Broadside; Cotleigh
Tawny; Smiles Golden Brew;
guest beers** G
Welcoming, 12th-century inn
with rocking chairs by the
fireside. A deserved local
CAMRA *Pub of the Year*.
Freshly prepared food is
always available. Local guest
ciders. 🏠 Q ❀ 🍴 ◁ ▶ ♣ 🛢

Ideford

Royal Oak
☎ (01626) 852274
12–3, 7–11; 12–10.30 Sun
Draught Bass; Flowers IPA H
Small, unspoilt thatched pub,
full of wartime souvenirs.
🏠 Q ❀ P

Ilsington

Carpenters Arms
☎ (01626) 661215
11–2.30, 6–11; 12–3, 7–10.30 Sun
Flowers IPA G; **Wadworth
6X** H
Old village pub with a friendly
local atmosphere, used mainly
by farmers and villagers.
🏠 Q ❀ ◁ ▶ 🛢

Kenton

Devon Arms Hotel
Fore Street ☎ (01626) 890213
11–3, 5–11; 12–3, 7–10.30 Sun
**Draught Bass; Flowers IPA;
Wadworth 6X** H
Large, friendly, village pub
with a good food menu. Built
in the 16th century, it only
became a pub in 1822. Children
welcome in the skittle alley in
summer.
Q ❀ 🍴 ◁ ▶ 🍴 ♣ 🛢 P 🛢

Kilmington

New Inn
The Hill ☎ (01297) 33376
11–3, 6–11; 12–3, 7–10.30 Sun
Palmers BB, IPA H
This 14th-century Devon
longhouse has been a pub since
at least 1800; Grade II-listed, it
is a friendly village inn with a
large, safe garden. One of two
pubs in Devon to be in every
edition of the *Guide*. The
venting of casks is via a water
trap.
🏠 Q 🕿 ❀ ◁ ▶ 🍴 🛢 ♣ P

Kingsbridge

Ship & Plough
The Promenade
☎ (01548) 852485
11–11; 12–10.30 Sun
**Blewitts Best, Wages, Head
Off** H
Lively, town-centre pub
offering home-brewed beers
and food at reasonable prices.
Dating from the 18th-century,
it boasts beamed ceilings and
other historic features. Cider in
summer.
🏠 🕿 ❀ ◁ ▶ ▲ ♣ 🛢

Kingskerswell

Bickley Mill
Follow signs to Stoneycombe,
past church ☎ (01803) 873201
11–2.30, 6–11; 12–3, 7–10.30 Sun
**Draught Bass; Wadworth 6X;
guest beer** H
Once a flour mill, dating from
the 13th century, in
Stoneycombe Valley, now a
friendly, rambling, one-bar
pub, where non-smoking
drinkers share an area with
diners.
🏠 🕿 ❀ 🍴 ◁ ▶ ♣ P ✍

Kingsteignton

Ten Tors Inn
Exeter Road (near A380)
☎ (01626) 65434
11–2.30, 5–11; 12–3, 7–10.30 Sun
**Draught Bass; Brains SA;
Eldridge Pope Royal Oak** H
Spacious pub, popular with
locals and tourists. The relaxed
atmosphere is complemented
by a wide range of home-
cooked meals.
🏠 Q 🕿 ❀ ◁ ▶ 🛢 ▲ P

Lower Ashton

Manor Inn
Off B3193 ☎ (01647) 252304
12–2.30, 6 (7 Sat)–11; 12–2.30, 7–10.30
Sun; closed Mon
**Hampshire Lionheart;
Teignworthy Reel Ale;
Theakston XB** H; **Wadworth
6X** G; **guest beer** H

Set in an attractive hamlet of
listed buildings, this pub has a
deserved reputation for good
value food. Unspoilt bar area.
🏨 Q ✿ ◖ ▶ ▲ ♣ ⌂ P

Lutton

Mountain
Old Church Lane
☎ (01752) 837247
11–2.30, 7 (6 Thu–Sat & summer)–11;
12.30–3.30, 7 (6 summer)–10.30 Sun
**Morland Old Speckled Hen;
Sutton XSB; guest beers** H
Cob walls and a large fireplace
make this pub in the Dartmoor
National Park worth visiting.
Families welcome. The house
beer is specially brewed by
Summerskills. Cider in
summer.
🏨 Q ☙ ✿ ◖ ▶ ♣ ⌂ P

Lydford

Castle Inn
☎ (01822) 820241
11.30–3, 6–11; 12–3, 7–10.30 Sun
**Blackawton Bitter; Fuller's
London Pride** H**; guest
beers** G
Cosy, 16th-century inn, next to
the castle. The Tinners Bar and
Foresters Restaurant feature
low ceilings, slate floors, large
stone fireplaces and many
curios. Award-winning food.
🏨 Q ✿ 🛏 ◖ ▶ P

Mucky Duck Inn
Next to Whitelady Falls
☎ (01822) 820208
12–2.30 (3 Sat; 11–3 summer), 6–11;
12–3, 7–10.30 Sun
**Sharp's Cornish Coaster,
Own; guest beers** H
Accommodating and much
improved inn, with slate floors
and exposed stone walls, a
large family room and a pool
area. 🏨 Q ☙ ✿ 🛏 ◖ ▶ P

Mary Tavy

Mary Tavy Inn
Lane Head (A386, 2 miles from
Tavistock) ☎ (01822) 810326
11.45–3, 6–11; 12–3, 7–10.30 Sun
**Draught Bass; St Austell
XXXX Mild, HSD; guest
beer** H
Cosy, two-bar pub built in the
16th century on the edge of
Dartmoor. Good value food.
🏨 Q ☙ ✿ 🛏 ◖ ▶ ⊞ ▲ ♣ P

Morchard Road

Sturt Arms
On A377 ☎ (01363) 85102
11.30 (12 winter)–3, 5.30–11; 12–3,
7–10.30 Sun
Beer range varies H
Former roadside pub now
partly converted to a
restaurant, with a friendly
atmosphere and pleasant
decor. All food is home-made.

Sturt Ale comes from
Branscombe Vale. 🏨 ✿ 🛏 ◖ ▶
⇌ (limited service) ♣ ⌂ P

Mortehoe

Ship Aground
The Square ☎ (01271) 870856
11–11; 12–10.30 Sun
**Cotleigh Tawny; Flowers
Original; guest beers** H
Friendly village local boasting
a lovely fireplace. Skittles
played in winter. Hancock's
cider in summer.
🏨 ☙ ✿ ◖ ▶ ▲ ♣ ⌂

Newton Abbot

Golden Lion
4 Market Street
☎ (01626) 67062
11–3 (4 Sat), 5.30 (6 Sat)–11; 12–3,
7–10.30 Sun
**Teignworthy Reel Ale; guest
beers** H
The oldest pub in town: a long
single bar, plus a games room.
✿ 🛏 ◖ & P

Try also: **Dartmouth Inn**, East
St (Free)

Newton St Cyres

Beer Engine
Follow signs from A377
☎ (01392) 851282
11–11; 12–10.30 Sun
**Beer Engine Rail Ale, Piston
Bitter, Sleeper Heavy,
seasonal beers** H
Friendly, popular brew pub by
the station, serving good value
food with an emphasis on local
produce. The brewery may be
viewed when the downstairs
bar is open. 🏨 Q ✿ ◖ ▶ ⇌
(limited service) P

North Tawton

Railway
Whiddon Down Road (1 mile S
of village) ☎ (01837) 82789
12–2, 6–11; 12–3, 7–10.30 Sun
Beer range varies H
Converted, 19th-century
farmhouse but still part of a
working farm next to the old
North Tawton railway station.
The bar decor recalls the
station in past years. The
changing beers come from SW
micros. 🏨 ✿ 🛏 ◖ ▶ ▲ ♣ P

Oakford

Red Lion
Rookery Hill ☎ (01398) 351219
5 (11 Sat)–11; 12–10.30 Sun
Juwards Bitter; guest beers H
17th-century, Grade II-listed
coaching inn with a single bar
and a warm welcome. Close to
Exmoor for walkers.
🏨 Q ✿ 🛏 & ▲ ♣ P

Okehampton

Plymouth Inn
26 West Street ☎ (01837) 53633
12–3, 7–11; 12–11 Sat; 12–10.30 Sun
**Sharp's Cornish Coaster;
guest beers** G
Old coaching inn with a cosy
bar, a good restaurant and a
fine family room.
Q ☙ ✿ ◖ ▶ & ♣

Paignton

Devonport Arms
42 Elmbank Road
☎ (01803) 558322
11–11; 12–10.30 Sun
**Theakston Old Peculier; guest
beers** H
Backstreet local, near the zoo;
well worth finding.
🏨 Q ☙ ✿ ◖ ▶ & ⇌ ⌂ P

Polsham Arms
35 Lower Polsham Road
☎ (01803) 558360
11–11; 12–10.30 Sun
**Boddingtons Bitter; Castle
Eden Ale; Greene King Abbot;
Morland Old Speckled Hen;
Wadworth 6X; Whitbread
Fuggles IPA** H
Two-bar pub: pool, skittles and
music in one bar, and a quiet
lounge. Bikers welcome.
🏨 Q ✿ ◖ ▶ ⊞ ⇌ ♣ P

Parkham

Bell Inn
Off A38 ☎ (01237) 451201
Draught Bass G**; Flowers IPA;
guest beer** H
13th-century inn, thoughtfully
modernised, with a good,
friendly atmosphere and
excellent food. Family room in
summer. 🏨 Q ☙ ◖ ▶ P

Plymouth

Clifton Hotel
35 Clifton Street, Greenbank
☎ (01752) 266563
5 (11 Fri & Sat)–11; 12–10.30 Sun
Badger Tanglefoot G**/**H**;
Draught Bass; Flowers IPA;
Summerskills Indiana's
Bones** H**; guest beers** G**/**H
A house beer, Clifton Classic, is
brewed by Summerskills
specifically for this warm,
friendly pub, said to be the
luckiest in the UK due to three
lottery millionaires drinking
here. Unusual guest beers.
& ⇌ ♣

Dolphin Hotel
14 Barbican ☎ (01752) 660876
10–11; 12–10.30 Sun
Draught Bass; guest beers
(occasional) G
The last unspoilt pub on the
ancient Barbican, frequented

by fishermen, artists and actors. Original works by Beryl Cook are displayed. 🏠 Q

London Inn

8 Church Road, Plympton St Maurice
☎ (01752) 337025
11–11; 12–10.30 Sun
Courage Best Bitter; Ruddles County; guest beers Ⓗ
17th-century coaching inn, reputedly haunted by Civil War ghosts.
🏠 ❀ ◖ ▶ ⊟ ♣ P

Providence Inn

20 Providence Street, North Hill
☎ (01752) 228178
12–11; 12–5, 7–10.30 Sun
Ind Coope Burton Ale; Tetley Bitter; guest beer Ⓗ
Cosy, one-bar, street-corner local in a terraced residential area, not far from the centre.
◖ ♣

Royal Albert Bridge Inn

960 Wolseley Road, Saltash Passage
☎ (01752) 361108
10.30–11; 12–10.30 Sun
Draught Bass; Courage Best Bitter Ⓗ
Riverside local with a friendly atmosphere, close to the Brunel rail bridge, offering picturesque views over the River Tamar to Cornwall.
❀ ◖ ▶ ⊟ ⇌ (St Budeaux/ Ferry Rd) ♣

Shipwright's Arms

13 Sutton Road, Coxside
☎ (01752) 665804
11–3, 6 (5.30 Fri)–11; 12–3, 7–10.30 Sun
Courage Best Bitter, Directors Ⓗ
Small sidestreet local which is friendly and very cosy.
🏠 ❀ ◖ ᕒ ♣ P

Tap & Spile

21 Looe Street
☎ (01752) 662485
11.30–3, 5–11; 11–11 Sat; 12–10.30 Sun
Beer range varies Ⓗ
Formerly the Barbican Arms; now refurbished and enlarged, it has become a popular pub renowned for its constantly varying beer range. Good value meals. ❀ ◖ ▶

Thistle Park Tavern

32 Commercial Road, Coxside
☎ (01752) 667677
11–11; 12–10.30 Sun
St Austell HSD; Sutton Dartmoor Pride, XSB, Old Pedantic; guest beers Ⓗ
Popular with students and locals, this pub is a little worn but very friendly. Sutton Brewery is next door.
◖ ▶ ♣

Plymstock

Boringdon Arms

Boringdon Terrace, Turnchapel
☎ (01752) 402053
11–11; 12–10.30 Sun
Butcombe Bitter; RCH Pitchfork; Smiles Best; Summerskills Best Bitter; guest beers Ⓗ
Friendly, 18th-century, terraced, popular local, hosting a bi-monthly beer festival. All day food; cider in summer. This charming waterside village lies near the coastal path.
🏠 Q ᕒ ❀ ᕾ ◖ ▶ ⊟ ♣ ᗕ

New Inn

Boringdon Road, Turnchapel
☎ (01752) 402765
12 (11 Sat)–11; 12–10.30 Sun
Beer range varies Ⓗ
Refurbished village local with a very welcoming atmosphere, establishing a reputation for fine food. Excellent view over the Cattewater and marina.
🏠 ◖ ▶ ♣ P

Postbridge

Warren House Inn

On B3212 ☎ (01822) 880208
11–3, 5.30–11 (11–11 summer); 12–10.30 Sun
Badger Tanglefoot; Butcombe Bitter; Gibbs Mew Bishop's Tipple; guest beers Ⓗ
The third highest pub in England, isolated on the moor; ideal for walkers. A log fire has been burning continuously since 1845.
🏠 Q ᕒ ❀ ◖ ▲ ♣ ᗕ P

Poundsgate

Tavistock Inn

☎ (01364) 631251
11–3, 6–11; 12–3, 7–10.30 Sun
Courage Best Bitter; Ushers Best Bitter, Founders Ⓗ
700-year-old, traditional moorland pub: a rugged front bar, and a small side room. Very popular in summer months.
🏠 Q ᕒ ❀ ◖ ▶ ▲ ♣ P

Rattery

Church House Inn

☎ (01364) 642220
11–2.30, 6–11 (6.30–10.30 winter Mon–Thu); 12–2.30, 7–10.30 Sun
Dartmoor Best Bitter; Greene King Abbot; Marston's Pedigree; guest beer (occasional) Ⓗ
Historic, Grade II star-listed inn, beside the church, originally used to house the monks who built it in 1028: a long, single, low-beamed bar with two inglenooks and a

good reputation for food. Luscombe cider in summer.
🏠 ❀ ◖ ▶ ᗕ P

Ringmore

Journey's End Inn

☎ (01548) 810205
11.30–3, 6–11; 12–10.30 Sun
Exmoor Ale; Otter Ale Ⓖ; **guest beers** Ⓗ/Ⓖ
Wonderful, 13th-century, friendly village inn where nothing is too much trouble. The main bar is wood-panelled; the snug bar has flagstones. Children welcome.
🏠 Q ❀ ❀ ◖ ▶ ᗕ P ⊟

St Giles in the Wood

Cranford Inn

Cranford Street (B3227, 3 miles from Gt Torrington)
☎ (01805) 623309
12–2.30, 6–11; 12–3, 7–10.30 Sun
Beer range varies Ⓖ
Converted farmhouse offering a warm welcome and good food. Q ❀ ⇌ ◖ ▶ ♣ P

Scorriton

Tradesman's Arms

☎ (01364) 631206
12–3, 7–11; 12–3, 7–10.30 Sun
Draught Bass; Princetown Dartmoor IPA; guest beer (summer) Ⓗ
Quiet, 300-year-old pub, built to serve tin miners from the moor. Good atmosphere. No-smoking family room. No meals Mon eve.
🏠 Q ᕒ ❀ ⇌ ◖ ▶ ▲ ᗕ P ✁

Shaldon

Clifford Arms

34 Fore Street
☎ (01626) 872311
11–3, 5–11; 11–11 Sat; 12–3, 7–10.30 Sun
Draught Bass; guest beers Ⓗ
One of Devon's prettiest pubs, much photographed for its fabulous summer floral displays. 18th-century, olde-worlde atmosphere; excellent food. Q ❀ ◖ ▶ ▲

Sheepwash

Half Moon Inn

Take A386 from Gt Torrington to Hatherleigh
☎ (01409) 231376
11–2.30, 6–11; 12–2.30, 7–10.30 Sun
Courage Best Bitter; Jollyboat Mainbrace; Marston's Pedigree Ⓗ
A splendid example of a local hostelry, this inn has connections with local fishing and shooting activities. Tidy dress required.
🏠 Q ᕒ ❀ ❀ ⇌ ⊟

Sidmouth

Radway

1 Radway Place
☎ (01395) 578305
11–3.30, 7–11; 12–4, 7–10.30 Sun
Draught Bass; Flowers IPΛ Ⓗ
Friendly, one-bar local near the
cinema; Grade II listed.
◖◗ & ⌂

Silverton

Silverton Inn

Fore Street ☎ (01392) 860196
11.30–3, 6–11; 12–10.30 Sun
**Exe Valley Dob's Best Bitter;
Fuller's London Pride; guest
beers** Ⓗ
One-bar village local with no
silly frills. Recommended
restaurant upstairs (booking
advisable). Live music Sun at
3pm. ⚬ ◖◗

Slapton

Tower Inn

☎ (01548) 580216
12–3, 6–11; 12–3, 7–10.30 Sun
**Badger Tanglefoot; Dartmoor
Best Bitter; Exmoor Ale; Gibbs
Mew Bishop's Tipple** Ⓗ**;
guest beers** Ⓗ/Ⓖ
14th-century inn in the shadow
of an old monastery bell tower.
Featuring wooden/flagstone
floors, it is split into four areas.
Cider in summer; the beer
range may be reduced in
winter. Small, awkward car
park.
⚬ Q ⛄ ⚙ ⇔ ◖◗ ▲ ⌂ P

South Molton

George Hotel

Broad Street ☎ (01769) 572514
11 (12.30 winter)–3, 6–11; 12–3,
7–10.30 Sun
**Draught Bass; Dartmoor Best
Bitter; guest beer** Ⓗ
Friendly, family-run,
16th-century posting inn
hosting regular folk and jazz
eves. ⚬ Q ⛄ ⚙ ⇔ ◖◗ ▲ P

Sparkwell

Treby Arms

☎ (01752) 837363
11–3, 6–11; 12–3.30, 7–10.30 Sun
Draught Bass; guest beer Ⓗ
Deservedly popular village
pub dating from around 1750,
close to Dartmoor Wildlife
Park. The dining area serves
home-cooked food. Treby Best
Bitter is Mildmay Colours Best.
⚬ ⚙ ◖◗ & ♣ P

Spreyton

Tom Cobley Tavern

☎ (01647) 231314
12–2.30 (not Mon), 6–11; 12–2.30,
7–10.30 Sun

**Butcombe Bitter; Cotleigh
Tawny; guest beer** Ⓗ
Quiet, mildly eccentric village
local with a superb function/
family room. All food is home-
made (special curry nights); no
food Mon. Table tennis played.
⚬ Q ⚙ ⇔ ◖◗ ♣ P

Staverton

Sea Trout Inn

☎ (01803) 762274
11–3, 6–11; 12–3, 7–10.30 Sun
Draught Bass Ⓖ**; Dartmoor
Best Bitter; Wadworth 6X;
guest beer** Ⓗ
15th-century inn of attractive
appearance, situated close to
the River Dart.
⚬ Q ⚙ ⇔ ◖◗ & ♣ P

Stockland

King's Arms

☎ (01404) 881361
12–3, 6.30–11; 12–3, 7–10.30 Sun
**Exmoor Ale; Otter Ale; John
Smith's Bitter; Theakston
XB** Ⓗ
Carefully enlarged and
modernised, Grade II-listed
free house with a friendly
atmosphere. Excellent menu.
Q ⇔ ◖◗ ⊟ ▲ ♣ ⌂ P

Talaton

Talaton Inn

☎ (01404) 822214
12–2.30, 7–11; 12–3, 7–10.30 Sun
Otter Bitter; guest beers Ⓗ
Popular village local offering a
range of fresh, home-made
food in both the bar and the
16th-century, beamed lounge.
⚬ ⛄ ⚙ ⇔ ◖◗ ⊟ ♣ P ⊬

Tedburn St Mary

King's Arms

☎ (01647) 61224
11–3, 6–11; 11–11 Fri & Sat; 12–3,
7–10.30 Sun
**Draught Bass; Cotleigh
Tawny; guest beer** Ⓗ
Attractive coaching house,
with exposed beams, serving a
good range of food including
local produce (the restaurant
doubles as a family room when
quiet). The public bar area has
a pool table. The house beer is
Federation Buchanan's Best
Bitter.
⚬ ⚙ ⇔ ◖◗ ⊟ ▲ ♣ P

Tiverton

Racehorse

Wellbrook Street
☎ (01884) 252606
11–11; 12–10.30 Sun
**Courage Best Bitter;
Theakston XB; Ushers Best
Bitter; Webster's Yorkshire
Bitter** Ⓗ
Popular local with a large
function room-cum-skittle

alley at the rear. The children's
garden has play and pets areas.
Food served all day. Limited
parking.
⚬ ⛄ ⚙ ◖◗ & ♣ ⌂ P

White Horse

Gold Street ☎ (01884) 252022
11–11; 12–10.30 Sun
Draught Bass; guest beer Ⓗ
Small, split-level, friendly,
town-centre pub with good
value food. ⇔ ◖◗ & ♣

Topsham

Bridge Inn ☆

Bridge Hill ☎ (01392) 873862
12–2.30, 6–10.30 (11 Fri & Sat); 12–2,
7–10.30 Sun
**Adnams Broadside; Badger
Tanglefoot; Branscombe Vale
Branoc; Exe Valley Devon
Glory; Fuller's London Pride;
guest beers** Ⓖ
Well-known, 15th-century,
Grade II-listed pub, unchanged
for most of this century and in
the present family for 100
years. The Barn Bar was once a
maltings and brewery but the
original building was a lodging
house for cathedral masons.
Up to ten beers available.
⚬ Q ⚙ ◖◗ ⇌ P

Globe Hotel

34 Fore Street
☎ (01392) 873471
11–11; 12–3, 7–10.30 Sun
**Draught Bass; Hancock's HB;
Worthington Bitter; guest beer**
(occasional) Ⓗ
16th-century, Grade II-listed
coaching house, boasting many
original beams, giving an
olde-worlde atmosphere. Good
food.
Q ⛄ ⚙ ◖◗ & ⇌ ♣ P

Torquay

Chelston Manor Hotel

Old Mill Road
☎ (01803) 605142
12–3, 6–11; 12–3, 7–10.30 Sun
**Boddingtons Bitter; Flowers
IPA, Original; guest beers** Ⓗ
This beautiful, 17th-century
pub is famed locally for its
excellent range of ales and
generous meals. The building
has many historical
connections.
Q ⛄ ⚙ ⇔ ◖◗ & ⇌ P

Crown & Sceptre

2 Petitor Road, St Marychurch
☎ (01803) 328290
11–3 (4 Sat), 5.30 (6.30 Sat)–11; 12–3,
7–10.30 Sun
**Courage Best Bitter, Directors;
Marston's Pedigree; Morland
Old Speckled Hen; Ruddles
County; Theakston XB; guest
beers** Ⓗ
200-year-old, stone coaching
house with a very friendly
atmosphere, very popular with

the locals. Well worth a visit.
No food Sun.
🏚 Q 🌠 🕭 🕮 🕭 🕭 🖈 ♣ P

Devon Dumpling
108 Shiphay Lane, Shiphay
☎ (01803) 613465
11–2.30, 6–11; 11–11 Sat; 12–10.30 Sun
**Courage Best Bitter, Directors;
Ruddles County; John Smith's
Bitter; guest beer** H
Lively local, popular for its
excellent, home-cooked food.
An attractive thatched roof
adds character and charm to
this beautiful historic building.
🏚 Q 🌠 🕭 🕮 P

Pig in Black
168–170 Union Street
☎ (01803) 213848
11–11; 12–10.30 Sun
**Courage Best Bitter, Directors;
John Smith's Bitter; guest
beers** H
Lively town-centre pub,
popular with business people
at lunchtimes, and younger
folk eves and weekends.
Interesting guest beers.
Formerly the Wig & Pen.
🕮 🕭 (Torre) ♣

Totnes

Rumours
30 High Street
☎ (01803) 864682
10am–11; 5–10.30 Sun
**Draught Bass; Dartmoor Best
Bitter; Ind Coope Burton Ale;
guest beer** H
Small, friendly wine bar with a
restaurant licence (book for
meals). Q 🕭 🕮 🕭 ✄

Westcott

Merry Harriers
On B3181, S of Cullompton
☎ (01392) 881254
11.30–2.30, 6–11; 12–3, 7–10.30 Sun
Draught Bass H
Friendly roadside inn where
the restaurant enjoys a
reputation for high quality,
home-cooked food.
🏚 Q 🌠 🕮 🕭 🕭 A P

West Down

Crown
The Square ☎ (01271) 862790
12–3, 6 (7 winter)–11; 12–3, 6–10.30
Sun
Wadworth 6X; guest beers H

This proudly scrubbed little
pub is a real gem, with
gleaming brasswork, a friendly
landlord and one of the finest
pub gardens you're ever likely
to see, all set in the village's
listed square. Cider in
summer.
🏚 🕭 🌠 🕮 A ♣ 🖒 P

Whimple

New Fountain Inn
Church Road (signed from old
A30) ☎ (01404) 822350
11.30–2.30, 6.30–11; 12–10.30 Sun
**Cotleigh Tawny; Teignworthy
Reel Ale; guest beers** H
Welcoming village inn, serving
good value, home-cooked
food. Well-equipped, safe
garden.
🏚 Q 🌠 🕮 🕭 🕭 ⇌ ♣ 🖒 P

Whitchurch

Whitchurch Inn
Church Hill
☎ (01822) 615383
11–3, 5 (6 Tue & Thu)–11; 11–11 Sat;
12–4, 6–10.30 Sun
**Draught Bass; Worthington
Bitter; guest beers** H
Village pub and restaurant
near the moor: a single bar
housing exposed beams and a
large fireplace with a built-in
bread oven. A friendly
atmosphere prevails.
Q 🕮 🕭 ♣ P

Widecombe in the Moor

Rugglestone Inn ☆
Signed from village centre, ½
mile OS721766
☎ (01364) 621327
11.30–2.30, 6 (7 winter)–11; 11–3, 6–11
Sat; 12–3, 7–10.30 Sun
Draught Bass (summer);
**Butcombe Bitter; Flowers IPA;
guest beer** (occasional) G
Named after a local 'Logan'
stone, this traditional
Dartmoor pub has changed
little. No children under 14 are
allowed in, but a shelter is
provided for them in bad
weather. Mind the stream
when walking to the toilets.
Lower Whiddon cider. No
food Sun–Mon eve in winter
months.
🏚 Q 🌠 🕮 A ♣ 🖒 P

Woodbury

White Hart
Church Stile Lane
☎ (01395) 23221
11–3, 6–11; 11–11 Sat; 12–3, 7–10.30
Sun
Draught Bass; Otter Ale H
Formerly housing the church
builders, this pub is over 500
years old and Grade II listed. It
is well-known for its home-
produced food. Large games
room.
🏚 Q 🕭 🌠 🕮 🕭 🖈 ♣ P

Woodbury Salterton

Diggers Rest
☎ (01395) 32375
11–2.30, 6.30–11; 12–2.30, 7–10.30 Sun
**Draught Bass; Dartmoor Best
Bitter** H
14th-century, Grade II-listed,
thatched pub, known for its
food. Unusual handpumps
dispense the beer. A skittle
alley at the rear doubles as a
family room in summer
months.
🏚 Q 🕭 🕮 🕭 🖈 ♣ 🖒 P

Yarde Down

Poltimore Arms
Off A399 OS725357
☎ (01598) 710381
12–2.30, 6.30–11; 12–2.30, 7–10.30 Sun
**Cotleigh Tawny; guest
beers** G
Welcoming hostelry on the
western reaches of the Exmoor
National Park, popular with
the hill farming community.
Varied range of good value
food.
🏚 Q 🕭 🌠 🕮 A P

Yealmpton

Volunteer
Fore Street (A379)
☎ (01752) 880463
11–3, 5–11; 11–11 Fri & Sat; 12–10.30
Sun
**Courage Best Bitter, Directors;
John Smith's Bitter;
Summerskills Best Bitter** H
Friendly, two-bar, village local:
a lounge bar, and a public bar
with a large collection of naval
crests on the beams. Greatly
improved food.
🏚 🌠 🕮 🕭 ♣ 🖒

CAMRA BOOKS

To complement the *Good Beer Guide*, CAMRA also publishes a series of other beer- and pub-related titles. These range from pub food and accommodation guides to overseas beer guides and even home-brewing manuals. See the back of the book for further details.

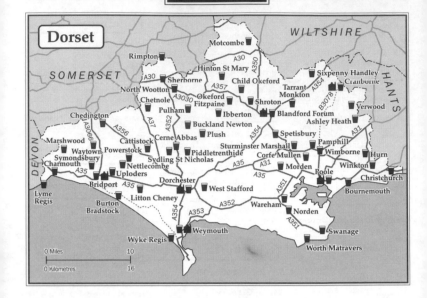

Ashley Heath

Struan Hotel

Horton Road (½ mile N of
A31 / A338 jct)
☎ (01425) 473553
11–3, 6–11; 12–3, 7–10.30 Sun
**Badger Dorset Best,
Tanglefoot** H
Originally a 1920s manor
house, now a smart lounge bar
and a restaurant. Jazz Thu
eves. Wells Eagle is sold as
Struan Bitter. 🏚 ❀ 🛏 ◖ ▶ P

Blandford Forum

Damory Oak Inn

Damory Court Street
☎ (01258) 452791
11–11; 12–2.30, 7–10.30 Sun
**Badger Dorset Best,
Tanglefoot** H
Friendly local with a two-
roomed bar. 🏚 ❀

Dolphin

42 East Street ☎ (01258) 456813
11–3, 6–11; 11–11 Sat & summer; 12–3,
7–10.30 Sun
**Draught Bass; Gibbs Mew
Wiltshire, Salisbury, Wake
Ale, Bishop's Tipple;
Theakston Best Bitter** H**; guest
beers** H/G
Friendly, small town pub,
comfortably refurbished and
re-named, serving unusual
beers for this town. No food
Sun eve. 🏚 ◖ ▶ ◖

King's Arms Hotel

Whitecliff Mill Street
☎ (01258) 452163
11–11; 12–10.30 Sun

**Draught Bass; Ringwood
Best Bitter; Worthington
Bitter** H
Historic Georgian hotel on the
former site of JL Marsh
Brewery. 🏚 ❀ 🛏 P

Stour Inn

☎ (01258) 451276
11–2.30, 6–11; 12–3, 7–10.30 Sun
Badger Dorset Best H
The Badger Brewery tap, on
the banks of the River Stour:
one large, comfortable room.
🏚 Q ❀

Bournemouth

Cottonwood Hotel

82 Grove Road
☎ (01202) 553183
11.30–3, 5–11; 12–10.30 Sun
**Draught Bass; Ringwood Best
Bitter; guest beer**
(occasional) H
Smart hotel bar, open to non-
residents, on the East Clifftop.
The verandah offers splendid
views of the Purbeck Hills.
Pianist Thu and Sun; jazz Fri.
❀ 🛏 ◖ ▶ ᇿ ≈ P

Dean Court
Supporters' Club

King's Park, Boscombe
(adjoining AFC Bournemouth
ground)
☎ (01202) 398313
11–3, 7–11; 12–3, 7–10.30 Sun
**Wadworth 6X; Worthington
Bitter; guest beer** H
Large, two-roomed club
serving interesting guest beers.
Show this guide or CAMRA
membership to enter (limited
admittance match days).
ᇿ ♣ P

Goat & Tricycle

27–29 West Hill Road
☎ (01202) 314220
12–3, 5.30–11; 12–3, 7–10.30 Sun
**Wadworth IPA, 6X; guest
beers** H
Split-level, comfortable pub,
close to the town centre. Up to
13 beers; large range of food
with good portions. Covered
patio at the side. Note the large
display of headgear inside.
🏚 ❀ ◖ ▶ ᇿ

Moon in the Square

4–8 Exeter Road
☎ (01202) 314940
11–11; 12–10.30 Sun
**Ringwood Fortyniner;
Theakston Best Bitter;
Younger Scotch; Wadworth
6X; guest beers** H
Popular Wetherspoons pub
close to the beach but amongst
the big stores. Upstairs are
photos of old Bournemouth
and its famous townsfolk.
❀ ◖ ▶ ᚖ

 **INDEPENDENT
BREWERIES**

Badger: Blandford Forum

Cranborne: Cranborne

Goldfinch: Dorchester

Hardy: Dorchester

Palmers: Bridport

Poole: Poole

Quay: Weymouth

Porterhouse

113 Poole Road, Westbourne
☎ (01202) 768586
11–11; 12–3, 7–10.30 Sun
**Ringwood Best Bitter, True
Glory, Fortyniner, XXXX
Porter, Old Thumper; guest
beer** Ⓗ
Local CAMRA *Pub of the Year*
1996, the best example of a
proper pub in town, serving
interesting guest beers at keen
prices. Keep an eye open for
the ghost! ◖ ♣ ᗡ

Punch & Judy

31 Poole Hill
☎ (01202) 290016
11–3, 5–11; 11–11 Sat; 12–3, 7–10.30
Sun
**Marston's Bitter, Pedigree,
HBC** Ⓗ
Friendly, popular pub, a short
walk from Bournemouth
Square. Good value food.
◖ ፊ

Bridport

Crown

West Bay Road (A35)
☎ (01308) 422037
11–3, 7–11; 12–3, 7–10.30 Sun
Palmers BB, IPA, 200 Ⓗ
Popular, friendly pub in the
south of town. Busy at
weekends with diners.
❀ ፊ Å ♣ ᗡ P

Woodman Inn

61 South Street
☎ (01308) 456455
11–3, 6–11; 12–4, 7–10.30 Sun
Draught Bass; guest beers Ⓗ
Popular free house offering a
diverse range of beers.
Welcoming staff; excellent food
(no eve meals Sun–Thu in
winter). ❀ ◖ ▶ ፊ ♣

Buckland Newton

Gaggle of Geese

☎ (01300) 345249
12–2.30, 6.30–11; 12–3, 7–10.30 Sun
**Badger Dorset Best; Draught
Bass; Oakhill Best Bitter;
Wadworth 6X; guest beer** Ⓗ
Large country pub offering
good food in a friendly
atmosphere. A goose auction is
held in May and Sept.
🏚 ❀ ◖ ▶ ፊ Å ♣ P

Burton Bradstock

Anchor Inn

High Street ☎ (01308) 897228
11–3, 6–11 (varies summer); 12–3,
7–10.30 Sun
**Ushers Best Bitter, Founders,
seasonal beers** Ⓗ
Friendly pub at the heart of the
village. Popular for food, it has
a pleasant, separate dining
area, ideal for families.
🏚 Q ᔓ ◖ ▶ ◿ ᗡ

Dove Inn

Southover ☎ (01308) 897897
11.30–2.30, 6–11; 12–3, 7–10.30 Sun
House beers Ⓗ
Pleasant, friendly pub, close to
the coastal footpaths: a
400-year-old inn with a table in
the bar made from a wrecked
schooner. Cider in summer.
The Dove beers come from
Teignworthy.
🏚 Q ᔓ ❀ ◖ ▶ ᗡ P

Try also: **Three Horseshoes**,
High St (Palmers)

Cattistock

Fox & Hounds Inn

Duck Street ☎ (01300) 320444
12–2.30 (not Mon), 7–11; 12–3, 7–10.30
Sun
**Fuller's London Pride;
Oakhill Best Bitter; guest
beers** Ⓗ
Former medieval longhouse
opposite the church. Two large
fireplaces dominate the main
bar. A flagstone floor,
panelling and window seats
add more character.
🏚 Q ❀ ◿ ◖ ▶ ♣ P

Cerne Abbas

Red Lion

Long Street ☎ (01300) 341441
11.30–3, 6.30–11; 12–3, 7–10.30 Sun
**Wadworth IPA, 6X; guest
beer** Ⓗ
An unusual frontage marks
this pub out in this popular
village beneath the Cerne
Giant. Unusual, good food
(children's portions).
🏚 Q ❀ ◖ ▶ ፊ Å

Charmouth

George

The Street ☎ (01297) 560280
11–3, 7–11; 12–3, 7–10.30 Sun
**Otter Bitter; Ruddles Best
Bitter; John Smith's Bitter** Ⓗ
Friendly, busy, family-run
local at the village centre.
🏚 ◖ ▶ ♣

Chedington

Winyards Gap Inn

On A356 ☎ (01935) 891224
11–2.30, 7–11 (11–3, 6.30–11 summer
Sat); 12–3, 7–10.30 Sun
**Flowers Original; Wadworth
6X; guest beers** (summer) Ⓗ
Pub with an extensive menu
(specialising in fish), plus
magnificent views from the
garden. Putting green
opposite. 🏚 ❀ ◿ ◖ ▶ ♣ P

Chetnole

Chetnole Inn

☎ (01935) 872337
11–2.30, 6.30–11; 12–3, 7–10.30 Sun
**Otter Bitter; Palmers IPA;
guest beers** Ⓗ

Popular, friendly local in
lovely countryside opposite
the church. Excellent selection
of beers and food. Easter beer
festival.
🏚 Q ❀ ◖ ▶ ◿ ፊ Å ⇌ ᗡ P

Child Okeford

Saxon Inn

Gold Hill (narrow lane N end
of village) ☎ (01258) 860310
11.30–2.30, 7–11; 12–2.30, 7–10.30 Sun
Beer range varies Ⓗ
Quiet, friendly, two-roomed
pub, converted from two
cottages in 1949 but looking
much older. 🏚 Q ◖ ▶ ፊ

Christchurch

Olde George Inn

2A Castle Street
☎ (01202) 479383
10.30–2.30 (3 Sat), 6 (7 Sat)–11; 12–3,
7–10.30 Sun
**Flowers Original; Ringwood
Fortyniner; guest beers** Ⓗ
Friendly, Tudor coaching inn:
two low-ceilinged bars and a
pleasant courtyard. The music
room hosts folk and blues Wed
and jazz Thu eve. ❀ ◖ ⇌ P

Corfe Mullen

Coventry Arms

Mill Street (A31, 2 miles W of
Wimborne) ☎ (01258) 857284
11–2.30 (3 Sat), 5.30–11; 12–3,
5.30–10.30 Sun
**Draught Bass; Courage
Directors; Ringwood Best
Bitter, Fortyniner, Old
Thumper; guest beer** Ⓖ
Pub dating back to 1426, built
on a site mentioned in the
Domesday Book. It is famous for
its 500-year-old mummified
cat. Excellent food; large
riverside garden.
Q ❀ ◖ ▶ ፊ Å ♣ P

Cranborne

Sheaf of Arrows

The Square ☎ (01725) 517456
11.30–2.30 (3.30 Sat), 6–11; 12–3,
7–10.30 Sun
**Cranborne Quiver, Porter,
Summer Ale; Ringwood Best
Bitter** Ⓗ
Thriving village local, the
home of Cranborne Brewery:
two contrasting bars and a
skittle alley.
Q ❀ ◿ ◖ ▶ Å ♣ ᗡ

Dorchester

Blue Raddle

Church Street
☎ (01305) 267762
11.30–3, 7–11; 12–3, 7–10.30 Sun
**Greene King Abbot; Otter
Bitter; guest beers** Ⓗ
Sidestreet free house serving
good value food. Local

CAMRA *Pub of the Year* 1996.
No food Mon eve.
Q ◖ ▶ ≋ (South/West) ♣

Tom Brown's
47 High East Street
☎ (01305) 264020
11–11, 12–3, 7–10.30 Sun
Goldfinch Tom Brown's, Flashman's Clout, Midnight Blinder Ⓗ
Wooden-floored home of the Goldfinch Brewery. Eve meals end early.
🛏 ◖ ▶ ≋ (West)

Hinton St Mary

White Horse
☎ (01258) 472723
11.30–2.15, 6.15–11; 12–3, 7–10.30 Sun
Beer range varies Ⓗ
Friendly village free house offering a range of activities. Always one session bitter and a stronger beer on tap.
🛏 Q ❀ ◖ ▶ Ⓔ & ♣ P

Hurn

Avon Causeway Hotel
Off B3073 ☎ (01202) 482714
11–11; 12–10.30 Sun
Ringwood Best Bitter, Old Thumper Ⓔ; **Wadworth IPA, 6X, Farmers Glory** Ⓗ; **guest beers** Ⓗ/Ⓔ
Old Hurn railway station, now a large, comfortable pub. The bar food is varied and good value. Jazz night Tue. The railway carriage restaurant hosts Murder Mystery eves Fri and Sat (book).
🎵 ❀ 🛏 ◖ ▶ & ▲ P ⤢

Ibberton

Crown
Church Lane (4 miles SW of A357) OS788077
☎ (01258) 817448
11–2.30, 7–11; 12–2.30, 7–10.30 Sun
Draught Bass; M&B Brew XI; Wadworth 6X Ⓗ
Idyllic country pub with a flagstone floor and a large inglenook, well off the beaten track, nestling below Bulbarrow Hill.
🎵 Q ⛺ ❀ ◖ ▶ & ♣ ○ P

Litton Cheney

White Horse
☎ (01308) 482539
11.30–3, 6.30–11; 11.30–11 Fri, Sat & summer; 12–10.30 Sun
Palmers BB, IPA, 200 Ⓗ
Pub on the outskirts of the village next to the YHA and a babbling brook: a panelled bar with a stone floor. Interesting menu. Children are welcome in the skittle alley. No eve meals winter Sun.
🎵 Q ❀ ◖ ▶ & ▲ ♣ P

Lyme Regis

Cobb Arms
Marine Parade
☎ (01297) 443242
11–11; 12–10.30 Sun
Palmers BB, IPA, 200, Tally Ho! Ⓗ
Harbourside pub, recently upgraded, a focus for marine activities. Children's certificate.
🎵 ❀ 🛏 & & ○

Nag's Head
Silver Street ☎ (01297) 442312
11–3, 6–11; 11–11 Sat; 12–10.30 Sun
Draught Bass; Ringwood Fortyniner; guest beers Ⓗ
Friendly free house offering a wide range of guest beers and local games. Very good, traditional food in an upstairs restaurant with sea views.
🎵 ❀ 🛏 ◖ ▶ Ⓔ & ▲ ♣

Volunteer
31 Broad Street
☎ (01297) 442214
11–3, 7–11; 12–3, 7–10.30 Sun
Draught Bass Ⓗ; **Branscombe Vale Branoc** Ⓖ; **Wadworth 6X** Ⓗ; **guest beer** Ⓖ
Pub with a single, welcoming bar and a restaurant (children welcome). The house beer 'Donegal Ale' is from Branscombe Vale.
Q 🛏 ◖ ▶ ▲ ♣ ⤢

Marshwood

Bottle Inn
On B3165 ☎ (01297) 678254
11–3, 6–11; 12–2.30, 7–10.30 Sun
Otter Bitter; Wadworth 6X Ⓗ
Genuine village local: two small rooms around a central bar in a 16th-century thatched building.
🎵 Q ❀ 🛏 ▶ ▲ ♣ P

Morden

Cock & Bottle
East Morden (B3075)
☎ (01929) 459238
11–2.30, 6–11; 12–3, 7–10.30 Sun
Badger IPA, Dorset Best, Tanglefoot Ⓗ
Friendly, 400-year-old village pub in a rural setting, with a sympathetic restaurant extension. Good range of good value food. 🎵 ❀ ◖ ▶ & ♣ P

Motcombe

Coppleridge Inn
OS842266 ☎ (01747) 851980
11–11; 12–10.30 Sun
Butcombe Bitter; Shepherd Neame Spitfire; guest beer Ⓗ
Converted farmhouse (18th-century) outside the village, with views over Blackmore Vale. Adventurous food. Customers may play cricket or tennis in the extensive grounds.
🎵 Q ⛺ ❀ 🛏 ◖ ▶ & ♣ P ⤢

Nettlecombe

Marquis of Lorne
Off A3066 ☎ (01308) 485236
11–2.30, 6–11; 12–3, 7–10.30 Sun
Palmers BB, IPA Ⓗ, **200** Ⓖ
Quiet, friendly, 16th-century pub nestling under Eggardon Hill: two bar areas and a spacious garden with spectacular views. Cider in summer.
🎵 Q ⛺ ❀ 🛏 ◖ ▶ ♣ ○ P

Norden

Halfway Inn
Wareham Road (A351)
☎ (01929) 480402
11–3, 6–11; 12–3, 7–10.30 Sun
Beer range varies Ⓖ/Ⓗ
Ancient Purbeck, multi-roomed house which specialises in Greek Cypriot and English food. Near Swanage steam railway and the Blue Pool. ❀ ◖ ▶ P

North Wootton

Three Elms
☎ (01935) 812881
11–2.30, 6.30 (6 Fri & Sat)–11; 12–3, 7–10.30 Sun
Butcombe Bitter; Fuller's London Pride; Shepherd Neame Spitfire; guest beers Ⓗ
Popular pub, serving eight ales and a wide range of good food (especially vegetarian). 1100 model vehicles on show. The house beer is Ash Vine Bitter.
Q ❀ 🛏 ◖ ▶ ♣ ○ P

Okeford Fitzpaine

Royal Oak
Lower Street (A357)
☎ (01258) 860308
12 (11 Sat)–2.30, 6.30–11; 12–2.30, 7–10.30 Sun
Ringwood Best Bitter; Wadworth 6X; guest beer Ⓗ
Friendly, thriving village local, offering a comfortable lounge and a flagstone bar, with an upstairs skittle alley and a back room for pool. Good value, home-cooked food.
🎵 Q ◖ ▶ Ⓔ ♣ ○ P

Pamphill

Vine Inn
Vine Hill (off B3082) OS995003
☎ (01202) 882259
11–2.30, 7–11; 12–3, 7–10.30 Sun
Beer range varies Ⓗ/Ⓖ
Friendly, split-level, two-bar pub in a rural area near Kingston Lacy House; the pub is also NT property. Lovely patio; limited parking.
Q ❀ Ⓔ ○ P 🍺

Piddletrenthide

Piddle Inn
☎ (01300) 348468
11.30–2.30, 6.30–11; 11.30–11 Sat; 12–3, 7–10.30 Sun
Draught Bass; Ringwood Best Bitter; Wadworth 6X Ⓗ
Traditional village pub, licensed since 1770, featuring a collection of 160 chamber pots. The garden is on the River Piddle.
⛫ ♉ ❀ ◖ ◗ ♿ ♣ ⌓ P

Plush

Brace of Pheasants
Off B3143 ☎ (01300) 348357
12–2.30, 7–11; 12–2.30, 7–10.30 Sun
Fuller's London Pride; Smiles Golden Brew Ⓖ
Traditional thatched pub in a quiet village, serving an extensive range of good food. Wheelchair access is via the fire door. ⛫ Q ❀ ◖ ◗ ♿ ♣ P

Poole

Albion
470 Ringwood Road, Parkstone
☎ (01202) 732197
11–3, 5–11; 11–11 Sat; 12–4, 7–10.30 Sun
Badger Dorset Best, Tanglefoot Ⓗ
Two-bar pub on the main road into Poole: a spacious public bar with a pool table and a comfortable lounge. No eve meals Sun. ❀ ◖ ◗ ⊟ ♣ P

Bermuda Triangle
10 Parr Street, Lower Parkstone
☎ (01202) 748087
11–3, 5.30–11; 12–3, 7–10.30 Sun
Beer range varies Ⓗ
Small, but popular free house, offering four changing ales, plus foreign bottled beers. Artefacts on the Bermuda Triangle theme are displayed.
⇌ (Parkstone)

Blue Boar
29 Market Close
☎ (01202) 682247
11–3, 5–11; 12–3, 7–10.30 Sun
Draught Bass; Courage Best Bitter, Directors; John Smith's Bitter; guest beers Ⓗ
Former merchant's house in the old town, sympathetically converted: a comfortable lounge on the ground floor and an extensive cellar bar, admitting children lunchtimes (closed Sun lunch). No lunches Sun. ◖ ⊟ ⇌ ♣

Branksome Railway Hotel
429 Poole Road, Parkstone (opp. station)
☎ (01202) 769555
11–11; 12–10.30 Sun
Brakspear Bitter; Fuller's London Pride; guest beer Ⓗ
Large, one-bar pub in Victorian style with high ceilings.
♉ ⇌ (Branksome) P

Brewhouse
68 High Street (near Dolphin shopping centre)
☎ (01202) 685288
11–11; 12–10.30 Sun
Poole Best Bitter, Holes Bay Hog, Bosun, Bedrock Ⓗ
Long-roomed, basic brewery tap for Poole Brewery, with probably the lowest beer prices in Dorset. ⇌

Sandacres Free House
3 Banks Road, Sandbanks
☎ (01202) 707244
10–3, 6–11; 12–3, 7–10.30 Sun
Poole Bosun; Ringwood Best Bitter, Old Thumper; Wadworth 6X; guest beers Ⓗ
Popular free house handy for Sandbanks beach, with spectacular views over Poole harbour. A large comfortable lounge often shows Sky Sports; a games room admits children until 9. ◖ ◗ ♿ ♣ P

Powerstock

Three Horseshoes
☎ (01308) 485328
11–3, 6–11; 12–3, 7–10.30 Sun
Palmers BB, IPA Ⓗ
Pub in a picturesque village, with a welcoming drinking area and a restaurant (excellent food). ⛫ Q ❀ ⛿ ◖ ◗ ▲ P

Pulham

Halsey Arms
☎ (01258) 817344
11.30–2.30 (not Wed), 6–11; 12–3, 7–10.30 Sun
Courage Best Bitter; Exmoor Ale; guest beers Ⓗ
Friendly country pub with an impressive range of ales. Outdoor children's play area; skittle alley/function room.
⛫ Q ♉ ❀ ◖ ◗ ♿ ♣ ⌓ P ⊓

Rimpton

Whitepost
On B3148 ☎ (01935) 850717
12–3, 6.30–11; 12–3, 7–10.30 Sun
Draught Bass; Butcombe Bitter; guest beer Ⓗ
Free house straddling the Somerset border, offering excellent value food.
Q ❀ ◖ ◗ ♣ ⌓ P

Sherborne

Digby Tap
Cooks Lane ☎ (01935) 813148
11–2.30, 5.30–11; 12–2.30, 7–10.30 Sun
Beer range varies Ⓗ
Basic, traditional, town drinking house; stone-flagged floors, panelling and old photos add to the atmosphere. No food Sun. Over 20 different beers a week. ⛫ ◖ ⇌

Skippers
Horsecastles ☎ (01935) 812753
11–2.30, 5.30–11; 12–3, 7–10.30 Sun
Adnams Bitter; Draught Bass; Wadworth IPA, 6X; guest beer Ⓗ
Refurbished, end of terrace, former cider house.
Q ❀ ◖ ◗ ⇌ ♣ P

Shroton

Cricketers
W of A350 ☎ (01258) 860421
11–3, 7–11; 12–3, 7–10.30 Sun
Beer range varies Ⓗ
Large, friendly village pub near the Iron Age fort of Hambledon Hill; popular with walkers. ⛫ Q ❀ ◖ ◗ ♣ P

Sixpenny Handley

Roebuck
22 High Street
☎ (01725) 552002
11–2.30 (not Mon), 6–11 (closed winter Mon); 12–3, 7–10.30 Sun
Ringwood Best Bitter, Fortyniner, XXXX Porter; guest beers Ⓗ
Pub with a comfortable L-shaped bar with a cosy fireside. The beer is often brought from the cellar in a jug. No food Mon.
⛫ Q ♉ ❀ ◖ ◗ ♣ P

Spetisbury

Drax Arms
High Street (A350)
☎ (01258) 452658
11.30–2.30 (3 Sat), 6.30–11; 12–3, 7–10.30 Sun
Badger Dorset Best, Tanglefoot Ⓗ
Popular roadside inn rebuilt in 1926: two communicating bars, one with darts and a shove-ha'penny board. ❀ ◖ ◗ ♣ P

Sturminster Marshall

Red Lion
Church Street (1 mile E of A350) ☎ (01258) 857319
11–2.30, 6–11; 12–3, 6–10.30 Sun
Badger Dorset Best, IPA, Tanglefoot Ⓗ
Popular, friendly pub where the skittle alley doubles as a family room and no-smoking area. ⛫ ♉ ❀ ◖ ◗ ♣ P ⚟

Swanage

Red Lion
63 High Street
☎ (01929) 423533
11–11; 12–10.30 Sun
Flowers Original; Ringwood Fortyniner Ⓖ

Popular, down-to-earth, two-bar pub. The public bar adjoins the ground-floor cellar from where the beers are dispensed. A lounge leads to a large garden and children's room. Eve meals Fri and Sat only (steak nights).
♉ ❀ ◖ ◗ ⊞ ♣ ⌓ P

Sydling St Nicholas

Greyhound Inn
High Street
☎ (01300) 341303
11–3, 7–11; 12–3, 7–10.30 Sun
Eldridge Pope Hardy Country; Princetown Jail Ale; guest beers [H]
Large, renovated pub and restaurant. Families welcome throughout. Wheelchair entry is via the conservatory.
♨ ❀ ◖ ◗ ♿ ▲ ♣ P

Symondsbury

Ilchester Arms
☎ (01308) 422600
11–2.30, 7–11; 12–3, 7–10.30 Sun
Palmers BB, IPA, 200 [H]
Attractive, welcoming village local overlooked by Comers Hill.
♨ Q ♉ ❀ ⛟ ◖ ◗ ▲ ♣ ⌓ P

Tarrant Monkton

Langton Arms
Off A354 ☎ (01258) 830225
11.30–3, 6–11; 11.30–11 Sat; 12–3, 7–10.30 Sun
Smiles Best [H]**; guest beers** [H]/[G]
17th-century country pub with three frequently changing ales in the lounge (and on request in the public bar). Children's play areas, a skittle alley and a local, varied menu are additional features.
♨ Q ♉ ❀ ⛟ ◖ ◗ ⊞ ♿ P

Uploders

Crown
☎ (01308) 485356
11–2.30, 6.30–11; 12–3, 7–10.30 Sun
Palmers BB, IPA, Tally Ho! [H]
Friendly pub with an excellent garden. Play Ring the Bull. ♨ Q ❀ ⛟ ◖ ◗ ⊞ ♿ ▲ ♣ ⌓ P

Verwood

Albion
Station Road (B3081, W side of town) ☎ (01202) 825267
11–2.30, 5 (6 Sat)–11; 12–2.30, 7–10.30 Sun
Gibbs Mew Salisbury, Wake Ale, Bishop's Tipple [H]
Superb, cosy pub built in 1866 as Verwood's station. Good value food. ❀ ◖ ◗ P

Wareham

Duke of Wellington
7 East Street ☎ (01929) 553015
11–3, 6–11; 12–3, 7–10.30 Sun
Marston's Pedigree; Ringwood Best Bitter; guest beers [H]
Local in a quiet part of town, with a restaurant area. En route to the Saxon East Walls.
◖ ◗ ⇌

Waytown

Hare & Hounds
☎ (01308) 488203
11.30–2.30, 6.30–11; 12–3, 7–10.30 Sun
Palmers BB, IPA, Tally Ho! *or* **200** (summer) [G]
Popular, small country pub with lovely views from the garden. Children's play area. No food Sun eve or winter Mon lunch.
♨ Q ♉ ❀ ◖ ◗ ⊞ ♣ ⌓ P

West Stafford

Wise Man
☎ (01305) 263694
11–3, 6–11; 12–3, 7–10.30 Sun
Draught Bass; Marston's Pedigree; guest beer [H]
Lovely, 400-year-old, ivy-draped, thatched pub in a quiet village. It has retained its public and lounge bars and boasts a fine display of Toby jugs. ♨ ❀ ◖ ◗ ⊞ ♿ ♣ ⌓ P

Weymouth

Weatherbury Hotel
7 Carlton Road North
☎ (01305) 786040
11–2.30, 5.30–11; 11–11 Fri & Sat; 12–10.30 Sun
Draught Bass; guest beers [H]
Comfortable local in a residential area. Big on team games so it can get crowded.
❀ ⛟ ◖ ◗ ♣ P

Wimborne

Crown & Anchor
Wimborne Road, Walford (B3078, N of town)
☎ (01202) 841405
10.30–2.30, 6–11; 12–3, 7–10.30 Sun
Badger Dorset Best [H]
Friendly local, with a garden alongside the River Allen. Handy for the craft centre at Walford Mill. ♨ Q ❀ ◖ ▲ P

Winkton

Lamb Inn
Burley Road ☎ (01425) 672427
11–2.45, 5.30–11; 11–11 Sat; 12–3, 7–10.30 Sun
Marston's Pedigree; Ringwood Best Bitter, Fortyniner; Wadworth 6X [H]
Cheerful country pub with good value food. Children's play area in the garden.
❀ ◖ ◗ ⊞ ▲ ♣ P

Worth Matravers

Square & Compass ☆
Off B3069 OS974777
☎ (01929) 439229
11–3, 6–11; 11–11 Sat; 12–3, 7–10.30 Sun
Badger Tanglefoot; Ringwood Fortyniner; guest beers [G]
Run by the Newman family, in their 90th year at this ancient stone pub. Flagstone floors, serving hatches, views of medieval field patterns and the sea, plus fossil finds, result in a fascinating visit.
♨ Q ❀ ♣ ⌓ P

Wyke Regis

Wyke Smugglers
76 Portland Road
☎ (01305) 760010
11–2.30, 6–11; 12–3, 7–10.30 Sun
Boddingtons Bitter; Flowers Original; Smiles Heritage; guest beers [H]
Popular, dart-players' local on the road to Portland. Two guest beers from micro/regional brewers. Disco Fri/Sat. ❀ ♿ ♣ P

CHECK OUT THE BREWERIES

Theakston Best Bitter, Flowers Original, Boddingtons Bitter? For full details of who brews what and where, and, more significantly, who owns whom, see The Breweries at the back of this book. Use The Beers Index to quickly pinpoint every beer.

Durham

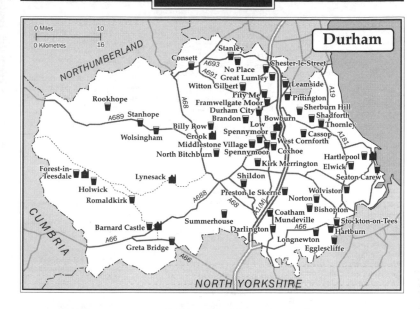

Barnard Castle

King's Head ('Dickens Inn')
14 Market Place
☎ (01833) 690333
11–11; 12–10.30 Sun
Butterknowle Conciliation Ale; John Smith's Bitter Ⓗ
Wood-panelled, town-centre pub comprising two rooms: one large front room and a spacious side room.
❀ ♠ P

Try also: Three Horseshoes, Galgate (Bass); **Old Well**, The Bank (Free)

Billy Row

Dun Cow (Cow's Tail)
Old White Lea (down lane by Royal George pub)
☎ (01388) 762714
7.30–11; 12–2, 7.30–10.30 Sun
Butterknowle Banner Bitter, Conciliation Ale Ⓗ
Unspoilt gem, well off the beaten track but worth a visit; a two-roomed pub with an open fire and range. One of the few original inns left in the county, owned by the same family since 1830. Butterknowle's bottle-conditioned ales stocked. Note: closed weekday lunchtime. ♨ Q ❀ ♣ P ⌀

Bishopton

Talbot
The Green
☎ (01740) 630371
11–3, 5.30–11; 12–3, 7–10.30 Sun

Camerons Strongarm; Ind Coope Burton Ale; guest beer Ⓗ
Pleasant village local with a strong emphasis on meals; in the *Guide* for 24 consecutive years, under the same landlord. ♨ Q ❀ ◑ ▶ P

Brandon

Brawns Den
Winchester Drive (300 yds from A690) ☎ (0191) 378 1687
11–3, 7–11; 12–4.30, 7–10.30 Sun
Tetley Bitter; guest beers Ⓗ
Modern pub on the outskirts of Durham City, by the Brandon–Bishop Auckland walkway. Walkers and cyclists are always welcome. The guest beers are from the Tapster's Choice list. ❀ ♿ ♣ P

Cassop

Victoria Inn
Front Street, North Cassop (B169) ☎ (01429) 821410
5 (11 Sat)–11; 12–10.30 Sun
Worthington Bitter Ⓗ
250-year-old village inn, a friendly, family pub with plenty of country walks nearby and a panoramic view of the vale and Durham Cathedral. It fields darts, dominoes and football teams. Good food; lunches Sun. ❀ ◑ ▶ ⊞ ♿

Chester-le-Street

Butchers Arms
Middle Chare
☎ (0191) 388 3605
11–3, 6.30–11; 12–3, 7–10.30 Sun

Camerons Bitter, Strongarm; Marston's Pedigree Ⓗ
Contemporary town pub with traditional decor, popular with all ages: a single room with a side area affording more privacy. Busy at lunchtime (full food menu). Darts and dominoes are played.
Q ⇔ ◑ ♣

Smiths Arms
Brecon Hill, Castledene (just off B1284)
☎ (0191) 385 6915
4 (12 Sat)–11; 12–3, 7–10.30 Sun
Draught Bass; Stones Bitter; Theakston XB; guest beer (weekends) Ⓗ
Comfortable lounge and a smaller bar in a traditional, country-style pub, plus a small, neat rear room for families, pool and games machines. Almost under the A1(M): miles from anywhere, minutes from everywhere.
♨ Q ♥ ⊞ ♣ P

🏠 **INDEPENDENT BREWERIES**

Butterknowle: Lynesack

Camerons: Hartlepool

Durham: Bowburn

High Force: Forest-in-Teesdale

Hodge's: Crook

Middleton's: Barnard Castle

Coatham Mundeville

Foresters Arms
Brafferton Lane (A167, ¼ mile S of A1(M) jct) ☎ (01325) 320565
11–3, 4.45–11; 11–11 Fri & Sat; 12–10.30 Sun
John Smith's Bitter, Magnet ⊞
Welcoming pub with a strong Irish flavour, serving well-prepared food (no meals Sun eve). Happy hour 5–7 during the week. Occasional live music. See the Vietnamese pot-bellied pig in the garden.
🏮 ☀ ◖ ⊨ P

Consett

Grey Horse
115 Sherburn Terrace (off A692) ☎ (01207) 502585
12–5, 7–11; 12–10.30 Sun
Draught Bass; guest beers ⊞
Pub with a traditional bar, with a pool room off to one side, and a cosy lounge hosting organ music Fri night. It caters for all ages with friendly service.
🏮 Q

Coxhoe

Cricketers
Victoria Terrace, Cornforth Lane ☎ (0191) 377 0510
12·2 (4 Sat), 7·11; 12·10.30 Sun
Vaux Lorimer's Best Scotch, Samson ⊞
Attractive, one-bar village local. Well-upholstered, it boasts a beamed ceiling and plenty of bric-a-brac in the bar and lounge areas. Q ☀ ♣

Darlington

Binns Department Store (off-licence)
1–7 High Row ☎ (01325) 462606
9–5.30 (6 Sat); closed Sun
House of Fraser department store with a well-stocked bottled beer section in the basement. Over 200 quality beers to take away, including dozens of British and Belgian bottle-conditioned ales. Good selection of special glasses.

Britannia
1 Archer Street ☎ (01325) 463787
11.30–3 (may extend), 5.30–11; 12–3, 7–10.30 Sun
Camerons Strongarm; Tetley Imperial; guest beer ⊞
Relaxed, uncomplicated old local, on the fringe of the town centre but a million miles from the hectic weekend 'circuit'. A bastion of cask beer for 130 years, it is still recognisable as the private house it originally

was. Guest beers from the Tapster's Choice range.
Q ♣ P ⊓

Glittering Star
Stonebridge ☎ (01325) 353191
11.30–3, 5.30–11; 11–11 Fri & Sat; 12–10.30 Sun
Samuel Smith OBB ⊞
Town-centre local, remodelled faithfully on traditional pub design principles with not a hint of pastiche or gimmickry.
◖ ⊞ ⊨ ♣

Golden Cock
5 Tubwell Row ☎ (01325) 468843
11–11; 12–10.30 Sun
Courage Directors; John Smith's Magnet ⊞
Bustling, town-centre pub, totally refurbished in 1995: a split-level bar with a pool area to the rear and a small snug to one side. ◖ ▶ ⇌ ♣

Number Twenty-2
22 Coniscliffe Road ☎ (01325) 354590
11–11; closed Sun
Hambleton Nightmare; Village White Boar, Bull, Old Raby; guest beers ⊞
Very popular, classy new pub in a former restaurant. Huge curved windows and a high ceiling give it an airy spaciousness even when packed. Catering for 'thirty-somethings', it turns over 15-plus independent ales per week, but has no spirit licence. No food Mon eve. NE CAMRA *Pub of the Year* 1997.
Q ◖ ▶ & ⊖ ⊓

Old Yard Tapas Bar
98 Bondgate ☎ (01325) 467385
11–2.30, 7 (5 Fri)–11; 11–11 Sat; 7–10.30 (closed lunch) Sun
McEwan 80/-; John Smith's Magnet; Younger No. 3; guest beer ⊞
This Mediterranean-style taverna exudes an atmosphere of holiday destinations a thousand miles from the bustle of Darlington! Traditional Spanish Tapas and Greek Mezes are always available, also a specials menu. Regular live theme nights, e.g. Flamenco. ◖ ▶ ⇌

Pennyweight
8 Bakehouse Hill, Market Place ☎ (01325) 464244
11–11; 12–10.30 Sun
Vaux Samson, Waggle Dance, Double Maxim; Ward's Best Bitter; guest beers ⊞
Busy, one-roomed Market Place pub with a modern layout but traditional furnishings. It can be noisy (and pricey) Fri and Sat eve, but offers an adventurous range of beers for a Vaux tied house. Pavement tables in summer. ☀ ◖ ⇌

Tap & Spile
99 Bondgate ☎ (01325) 381679
11.30–11; 12–10.30 Sun
Beer range varies ⊞
Traditional English alehouse, hosting weekly live entertainment in the function room. Up to eight guest beers; traditional pub food Mon–Sat.
☀ ◖ ⇌ ♣ ⊖ ⊭

Durham City

Brewer & Firkin
58 Saddler Street ☎ (0191) 386 4134
11–11; 12–10.30 Sun
Boddingtons Bitter; Castle Eden Ale; Flowers Original; Marston's Pedigree; guest beer ⊞
Theme pub offering live music upstairs (not loud) with real ale; young lager drinkers downstairs at weekends. Popular with students, tourists and locals. Popular lunchtime food. ◖ &

Dun Cow
37 Old Elvet (opp. jail) ☎ (0191) 386 9219
11–11; 12–10.30 Sun
Boddingtons Bitter; Castle Eden Ale; guest beer ⊞
Pub with a tiny bar, popular with regulars; sport-oriented Sunday patrons and a strong student contingent in the lounge. It boasts the highest cask sales of Castle Eden in the country. ◖ &

Old Elm Tree
12 Crossgate ☎ (0191) 386 4621
12–3, 6–11; 12–11 Sat; 12–3, 7–10.30 Sun
Vaux Samson, Waggle Dance; Ward's Best Bitter; guest beers ⊞
Built in 1601, an open, friendly pub, well used by all ages and lively at weekends. Note the old elm tree in the bar.
☀ & ⇌ ⊖

Shakespeare ☆
63 Saddler Street ☎ (0191) 386 9709
11–11; 12–10.30 Sun
Courage Directors; McEwan 80/-; Theakston Best Bitter, XB; guest beer (occasional) ⊞
Listed building, formerly very quiet; following a recent update it now has a TV and a bandit – but no jukebox. Good backroom; antique snug; busy bar. Popular with students and tourists. ☎ ◖

Victoria ☆
86 Halgarth Street ☎ (0191) 386 5269
11–3, 6–11; 12–2, 7–10.30 Sun
Hodge's Original; McEwan 80/-; Marston's Pedigree; Theakston Best Bitter; guest beer ⊞

Attractive city pub featuring original authentic Victorian furnishings and decor. Three different styles in its bar, snug, and small meeting room, without TV or jukebox, give a traditional, warm atmosphere, enjoyed by locals and students. ⚌ Q ⋈ & P

Try also: Colpitts, Hawthorn Tce (Samuel Smith); **Half Moon**, Old Elvet (Bass)

Egglescliffe

Pot & Glass
Church Road (off A135)
☎ (01642) 651009
12–3, 5.30–11; 12–4.30, 7–10.30 Sun
Draught Bass; Worthington Bitter; guest beer Ⓗ
Fine old village pub with notable bar fronts. The side room is suitable for families. The pub is the focus of village life, even fielding its own cricket team. Amongst its residents is a group of ghostly nuns. Book Sun lunch.
Q ⏃ ☀ ◑ ⤜ ♣ P

Elwick

McOrville
The Green (off A19)
☎ (01429) 273344
11.30–3, 7–11; 11–11 Sat; 12–4, 7–10.30 Sun
Boddingtons Bitter; Castle Eden Ale; guest beers Ⓗ
Country tavern on the village green serving an excellent, home-cooked lunchtime menu, with eves set aside for drinkers. Quiz Wed; monthly live jazz (Thu). See the expanding collection of pigs. ⚌ ☀ ◑ & ♣ P

Try also: Spotted Cow, The Green (Camerons)

Forest-in-Teesdale

High Force Hotel
☎ (01833) 622222
11–5, 7–11 (may vary); 12–10.30 Sun
High Force Low Force, Teesdale Low Force, Forest XB, Cauldron Snout; Theakston Best Bitter Ⓗ
Small, unpretentious, stone-built old hotel, one of the highest in England, next to the spectacular falls. The public bar has two linked rooms serving beers from the hotel's own brewery. The landlord is happy to show visitors the brewhouse.
⚌ Q ⏃ ☀ ◑ ⋈ ◑ ▶ ♣ P

Framwellgate Moor

Tap & Spile
27 Front Street (½ mile off A167 bypass) ☎ (0191) 386 5451
11.30–3, 6 (5 Fri)–11; 12–3, 7–10.30 Sun

Tap & Spile Premium; Village White Boar; guest beers Ⓗ
Three rooms in basic 'Tap & Spile' style, including a no-smoking lounge. The back room combines games and family facilities. Real cider on gravity dispense. Up to seven guest ales, including a mild and a porter or stout.
Q ⏃ ♣ ◑ ✠

Try also: Marquis of Granby, Front St (Samuel Smith)

Great Lumley

Old England
Front Street ☎ (0191) 388 5257
11–11; 12–10.30 Sun
Beer range varies Ⓗ
Pub with a large, lively bar popular with youngsters and some older clientele. The quiet, comfortable lounge has a friendly atmosphere and is popular with locals. Lunches served Fri–Sun, eve meals Mon–Sat. Q ◑ ▶ ⊞ ♣ P

Greta Bridge

Morritt Arms Hotel
Signed off A66
☎ (01833) 627232
11–11 (Sir Walter Scott bar opens 8); 12–10.30 Sun
Butterknowle Conciliation Ale; Taylor Landlord; Tetley Bitter; Theakston Best Bitter Ⓗ
Two very different hostelries exist here, in a fine setting, secluded from the nearby A66. The main bar, in the magnificently traditional country house hotel, has Dickens murals by 'Guinness artist' John Gilroy. The detached Sir Walter Scott bar serves the local trade with Conciliation only.
⚌ Q ☀ ⋈ ◑ ▶ ⊞ & ♣ P

Hartburn

Masham Hotel
87 Hartburn Village
☎ (01642) 580414
11–11; 12–3, 7–10.30 Sun
Draught Bass; Black Sheep Special; guest beer (occasional) Ⓗ
Unspoilt pub in the centre of a tree-lined village street. Several separate drinking areas; warm welcome from the landlord and locals alike. Q ☀ ⊞ ♣ P

Hartlepool

Jacksons Arms
Tower Street ☎ (01429) 862413
11–11; 12–10.30 Sun
Draught Bass; Boddingtons Bitter; Theakston XB; guest beers Ⓗ
Traditional, street-corner local catering for a wide range of

clients; close to the town centre and museum/art gallery complex. Q ◑ ⊞ ⤜ ♣

Tap & Spile
66 Church Street
☎ (01429) 222400
11–3, 6–11; 11–11 Sun; 7–10.30 (closed lunch) Sun
Camerons Strongarm; guest beers Ⓗ
Fine restoration of a 19th-century drinking house, featuring an internal balcony, in one of the town's main drinking areas, convenient for the award-winning museums and art gallery. ◑ & ⤜ ♣ ◑

Touchdown
245 West View Road
☎ (01429) 266320
7 (12 Sat)–11; 12–4, 7–10.30 Sun
Camerons Strongarm Ⓗ
1950s estate pub on the northern edge of town; the focal point of the community. Note: closed weekday lunch.
⊞ & P ⊞

Try also: Blacksmiths Arms, Stranton (Camerons)

Holwick

Strathmore Arms
Off B6277 OS909268
☎ (01833) 640362
12 (7 Mon)–11; 12–10.30 Sun
Ruddles Best Bitter; Theakston Best Bitter, Black Bull; guest beer Ⓗ
17th-century, stone-built hostelry near the Pennine Way: a cosy, unspoilt bar with an open hearth and an upstairs bar for functions. Regular live music. Families (and their dogs) welcome. Camping field to the rear, beneath the magnificent Holwick Scar. No food Mon.
⚌ Q ☀ ⋈ ◑ ▶ ▲ ♣ P

Kirk Merrington

Half Moon
Crowther Place
11–11; 12–10.30 Sun
Durham Magus or Celtic; Stones Bitter; guest beer (occasional) Ⓗ
Pub which goes a long way to being all things to all men: one split room divided into a quiet side and a boisterous side by a central bar. ⚌ ◑ ▶ & ⊟

Leamside

Three Horse Shoes
Pithouse Lane (off A690)
☎ (0191) 584 2394
12–3 (not Mon–Wed), 7 (5 summer)–11; 12–3, 7–10.30 Sun
Theakston Best Bitter; guest beers Ⓗ
Friendly, country inn comprising a large bar with a lounge at one end and a family

room off the other. Regular charity nights. Up to three guest beers.
🏚 ⛺ ❀ ◐ ▶ A ♣ P

Longnewton

Vane Arms
Off A66 ☎ (01642) 580401
11.30–3, 5.30–11; 11.30–11 Fri & Sat; 12–10.30 Sun
Stones Bitter; Worthington Bitter; guest beers Ⓗ
Old, end-of-terrace village local, drawing a mixed clientele to its plush lounge and more basic bar. Eve meals Fri and Sat. ❀ ◐ ▶ ⊟ P

Low Spennymoor

Frog & Ferret
Coulson Street (1 mile from A167) ☎ (01388) 818312
11–11; 11–4, 7–11 Sat; 12–3, 7–10.30 Sun
Boddingtons Bitter; Camerons Strongarm; Courage Directors; Theakston XB; guest beers Ⓗ
Current Durham CAMRA *Pub of the Year*; this small, one-roomed, street-corner pub has a good reputation. Its easy-going atmosphere and changing guest beers make for a good time. Not recommended for families. Note the original pub sign.
Q

Middlestone Village

Ship Inn
Low Row ☎ (01388) 810904
11–11; 12–10.30 Sun
Vaux Samson; Ward's Best Bitter; guest beer Ⓗ
The Ship, closed by Vaux and re-opened following a vigorous campaign by local CAMRA members, has been completely refurbished and offers a warm welcome to all. Restaurant and bar meals.
Q ⛺ ◐ ▶ ♣ P

No Place

Beamish Mary Inn
600 yds from A693
☎ (0191) 370 0237
12–3, 6–11; 12–11 Fri & Sat; 12–10.30 Sun
Black Sheep Best Bitter; Courage Directors; Jennings Cumberland Ale; Theakston Best Bitter, XB, Old Peculier Ⓗ
Close to Beamish Open Air Museum, this very popular, characterful pub gets very busy. Live music three times weekly; beer festival Jan. The house beer comes from Big Lamp. CAMRA National *Pub of the Year* 1995.
🏚 ❀ 🛏 ◐ ▶ ⊟ ♿ A ♣ ⌂ P

North Bitchburn

Red Lion
North Bitchburn Terrace
☎ (01388) 763561
12–3, 7–11; 12–3, 7–10.30 Sun
Courage Directors; Marston's Pedigree; John Smith's Bitter; guest beer Ⓗ
Friendly, traditional village pub where the welcome is as warm as the open fires. Very popular for its excellent meals and wide range of guest beers – a regular guest is the pub's own Mane Brew, brewed by Hambleton. CAMRA regional *Pub of the Year* 1995.
🏚 Q ❀ ◐ ♣ ⌂ P ⊟

Norton

Red Lion
Harland Place (A193)
☎ (01642) 554858
11.30–11; 12–3, 7–10.30 Sun
Theakston Best Bitter; Younger No.3 Ⓗ
Large, old, corner pub with Victorian-style decor; parts are over 300 years old. Very much a local. Q ◐ ⊟ ♣

Unicorn
High Street ☎ (01642) 553888
11.30–3, 5.30–11; 11–11 Sat; 12–3, 7–10.30 Sun
John Smith's Magnet Ⓗ
Friendly, old, street-corner, village local with several rooms: a basic, but welcoming bar and side rooms where families are welcome. Locally known as Nellie's.
Q ⛺ ❀ ◐ ⊟ ♣

Pittington

Village Tavern
☎ (0191) 372 1188
11–11; 12–10.30 Sun
Tetley Bitter; Vaux Samson; guest beer Ⓗ
Popular public bar adjoining the Hallgarth Manor Hotel on the village outskirts. It is decorated in a country farmhouse style, complete with a cast iron range.
Q ❀ 🛏 ◐ ▶ ♣ P

Try also: Blacksmith's Arms (Vaux)

Pity Me

Lambton Hounds
63 Front Street (off A167)
☎ (0191) 386 4742
11–11; 12–4, 7–10.30 Sun
Vaux Lorimer's Best Scotch; Ward's Best Bitter; guest beer Ⓗ
250-year-old coaching inn on the Great North Road, with a bar, a lounge, a snug room with bell service and a dining room. Quoits played in

summer near the garden area. The guest beer is supplied by Vaux.
🏚 Q ⛺ ❀ 🛏 ◐ ▶ ⊟ ♣ P

Preston le Skerne

Blacksmith's Arms
Ricknall Lane (1 mile E of A167, on Newton Aycliffe–Stainton road)
☎ (01325) 314873
12–3, 5.30–11; 12–3, 7–10.30 Sun
Black Sheep Best Bitter; John Smith's Magnet; guest beers Ⓗ
Locally known as the 'Hammers', the Blacksmith's is a family-run free house offering a range of home-cooked meals, plus locally brewed guest ales. The large garden features a children's play area and a collection of ducks and hens. No food Sun eve. Q ❀ ◐ ▶ ♣ P

Romaldkirk

Kirk Inn
The Green
☎ (01833) 650260
12–3 (not Tue), 6–11; 12–3, 7–10.30 Sun
Boddingtons Bitter; Castle Eden Ale; High Force Teesdale Bitter; guest beers Ⓗ
Charming, single-room pub, situated on the village green, with a welcoming atmosphere. It doubles as a part-time post office. Excellent meals are produced by the landlord.
🏚 Q ❀ ◐ ▶ ♣

Rookhope

Rookhope Inn
☎ (01388) 517215
7–11; 12–3, 7–11 Sat; 12–3, 7–10.30 Sun
Butterknowle Bitter; Hexhamshire Devil's Water; Tetley Bitter; guest beer (summer) Ⓗ
Pleasant country pub on the Coast-to-Coast walk in Weardale. Friendly licensees offer good food. Paved area for outdoor drinking.
🏚 ❀ 🛏 ◐ ▶ ♣ P

Seaton Carew

Seaton Hotel
Church Street
☎ (01429) 266212
11–11; 12–10.30 Sun
Boddingtons Bitter; Castle Eden Ale; guest beers Ⓗ
Reputedly haunted seafront pub dating from 1792. The lounge is decorated with pictures of old Seaton. The clientele is a mix of regulars and tourists.
Q ⛺ ❀ 🛏 ◐ ▶ ♣ P

Shadforth

Plough Inn
South Side (B1283)
☎ (0191) 372 0375
6.30–11; 12–5, 6.30–11 Fri; 12–11 Sat;
12–4, 7–10.30 Sun
**Draught Bass; Stones Bitter;
guest beers** Ⓗ
Traditional, two-bar, country
pub popular with all. The beer
range is changed weekly.
Durham CAMRA *Pub of the
Year 1996.* 🏠 Q ✿ ◑ ▶ ♣ P

Sherburn Hill

Moor Edge
Front Street
☎ (0191) 372 1618
12–4, 7–11; 12–3, 7–10.30 Sun
**Vaux Lorimer's Best Scotch,
Bitter; guest beer** Ⓗ
18th-century village inn where
the bar and lounge boast coal
fires, reflecting the warm
atmosphere. A haven for the
dominoes enthusiast; quoits
played in summer.
🏠 Q ✿ 🍴 ♣ P 🍴

Try also: Burley Edge, Front St
(Vaux)

Shildon

Timothy Hackworth
107 Main Street (B6282 jct)
☎ (01388) 772525
12–11; 12–10.30 Sun
Camerons Strongarm Ⓗ
Friendly village local, named
after a famous steam engine
builder. The decor features
pictures of old Shildon and
steam engines built by
Hackworth at the nearby Soho
works (now a museum).
Q ♣ P

Spennymoor

Ash Tree
Carr Lane (½ mile from centre
on Greenways Estate)
☎ (01388) 814490
12–2 (not Mon or Tue), 6–11; 12–11
Sat; 12–10.30 Sun
**Vaux Samson, Double Maxim;
guest beers** Ⓗ
Estate pub, the hub of the
community, selling real ale
since opening in 1980 and
appealing to all.
✿ ♣ P 🍴

Stanhope

Grey Bull
17 West Terrace
☎ (01388) 528177
11.30–2.30, 7–11 (11–11 May–Dec);
12–2 (4 May–Dec), 7.30–10.30 Sun
**Newcastle Exhibition;
Theakston Best Bitter** Ⓗ
Friendly, down-to-earth local
with one large room; built in

the 1780s as a combined pub
and violin-maker's.
🏠 Q ✿ ♣ P

Try also: Queen's Head, Front
St (Camerons)

Stanley

Blue Boar Tavern
103 Front Street (off A693)
☎ (01207) 231167
11–3, 7–11; 11–11 Thu–Sat; 12–10.30
Sun
**Draught Bass; Stones Bitter;
guest beers** Ⓗ
Originally a coaching house,
this pub is popular lunchtimes
and weekends, mainly with
couples, but caters for all ages.
The four guest ales are
changed thrice-weekly.
🏠 ◑ ▶ ♿

Stockton-on-Tees

Fitzgerald's
9–10 High Street
☎ (01642) 678220
11.30–3 (3.30 Fri, 4 Sat), 6.30–11;
7–10.30 (closed lunch) Sun
**Draught Bass; McEwan 80/-;
Taylor Landlord; Younger
No.3 or Theakston Old
Peculier; guest beers** Ⓗ
The imposing stone facade
looks much too grand for a
pub, but the open-plan, split-
level interior has typical
Fitzgerald's touches. Regular
beer festivals. ◑ ⇌ ♣

Senators
Bishopton Road West (by
Whitehouse Farm shopping
centre) ☎ (01642) 672060
11–3 (4 Fri & Sat), 7–11; 12–3, 7–10.30
Sun
**Vaux Double Maxim; Ward's
Thorne BB; guest beer** Ⓗ
Smart, modern pub drawing a
strong local trade in a single,
split-level bar with a raised
dining area. The free quiz Tue
night is a real crowd-puller! No
eve meals Tue or Sun; booking
advised for Sun lunch.
✿ ◑ P

Sun Inn
Knowles Street (off High St)
☎ (01642) 615676
11–4, 5.30–11; 11–11 Wed, Fri & Sat;
12–10.30 Sun
Draught Bass Ⓗ
Classic town-centre pub with
an unswerving commitment to
real ale. It claims the UK's
largest sales of Draught Bass,
which comes as no surprise to
those who've sampled it. Folk
club Mon. 🍴 ⇌ ♣

Theatre
Yarm Lane ☎ (01642) 674478
11–11; 7–10.30 (closed lunch) Sun
**Theakston Best Bitter, XB,
Old Peculier** Ⓗ
Refurbished, one-bar, town
pub with a Victorian interior;

often busy at weekends. Meals
Sun eve–Thu. ◑ ▶ ♣

Summerhouse

Raby Hunt
On B6279
☎ (01325) 374604
11.30–3, 6.30–11; 12–3, 7–10.30 Sun
**Newcastle Exhibition;
Theakston Black Bull; guest
beer** Ⓗ
Neat, welcoming, old stone
free house, in a pretty
whitewashed hamlet, with a
homely lounge and a busy
locals' bar. Good, home-
cooked lunches (not served
Sun). 🏠 Q ✿ ◑ 🍴 ♣ P

Thornley

Crossways Hotel
Dunelm Road (A181)
☎ (01429) 821248
11–11; 12–10.30 Sun
Beer range varies Ⓗ
Family-owned and -run hotel:
two public bars serving drinks
and food, plus an à la carte
restaurant. It currently sells
Scottish Courage products,
with guest ales from the
Whitbread portfolio.
✿ 🛏 ◑ ▶ ♿ P

West Cornforth

Slake
Slake Terrace (½ mile off A177)
☎ (01740) 650975
7–11; 12–5, 7–11 Sat; 12–5, 7–10.30
Sun
Stones Bitter; Theakston XB Ⓗ
Bright, comfortable and
friendly village local – a
drinkers' pub. Note: closed
weekday lunch. ✿ ♣ P

Square & Compass
7 The Green
☎ (01740) 654606
7–11; 11–3, 7–11 Sat; 12–10.30 Sun
Draught Bass; Stones Bitter Ⓗ
Cosy pub affording good
views over the village green
and the surrounding
countryside. Its decor includes
historic photographs of the
village. Quiz Thu. Note closed
weekday lunch. No eve meals
Sun. 🏠 Q ✿ ◑ ▶ ♿ ♣ P

Witton Gilbert

Glendenning Arms
Front Street
☎ (0191) 371 0316
12–4, 7–11; 12–4, 7–10.30 Sun
Vaux Samson Ⓗ
Twenty-two years in the *Guide*,
this friendly local thankfully
never changes. The two rooms
include a very comfortable
lounge. Racing memorabilia
decorates the bar. Outside
seating is in the car park.
🏠 Q ✿ ♣ P

Traveller's Rest

Front Street ☎ (0191) 371 0458
11–3, 6–11; 12–3, 7–10.30 Sun
McEwan 80/-; Theakston Best Bitter, XB, Old Peculier; Younger No.3 Ⓗ
Popular village pub with attractive traditional decor, featuring a split-level no-smoking room and a conservatory ideal for children. Boules played summer eves and Sun. Wide variety of good food. 🏿 Q ☎ ✿ 🍴 ◑ ♣ P ⚊

Wolsingham

Bay Horse

Main Street (B6296, ½ mile up dale from the village centre)

☎ (01388) 527220
11–11; 12–10.30 Sun
Ruddles County; Tetley Bitter Ⓗ
19th-century pub with numerous extensions, serving good food in an attractive rural setting. The bar has two linked rooms; the restaurant is open all day. Children welcome.
Q ✿ 🍴 ◑ ▣ ▲ ♣ P ⊟

Mill Race

Front Street, West End
☎ (01388) 526551
11–11; 12–10.30 Sun
Courage Directors; McEwan 80/-; Marston's Pedigree; John Smith's Magnet; Theakston XB; guest beers Ⓗ
Warm, friendly, family pub

offering ales from Scottish Courage. Food is served all day. Children's certificate.
🏿 Q ☎ ✿ 🍴 ◑ ♣ P

Wolviston

Wellington

31–33 High Street
☎ (01740) 644439
11–11; 12–10.30 Sun
Draught Bass; Worthington Bitter; guest beers Ⓗ
Traditional village pub with plenty of character: one area has a fine collection of chamber pots. Folk club Thu. Wheelchair access is from the rear car park.
Q ✿ ◑ ▶ ♣ P

Hartlepool's Lion Brewery roars back! Camerons MD Derek Andrew (left) receives the prestigious **Dan Kane Award** *from CAMRA director Jim Fox. The award, presented for initiatives to improve beer quality, was in recognition of the brewery's revival of original, unadulterated beer recipes.*

THE CAMRA GUIDE TO CELLARMANSHIP

IT TAKES superb cellar skills to serve a perfect pint of cask ale. The work of a master brewer can be ruined within hours if a cask is not properly looked after in the pub cellar. The beer needs to be stored for the right period of time at the correct temperature, and carefully stillaged, vented and tapped for the best results.

Now the cellarman's skills have been revealed in *The CAMRA Guide to Cellarmanship*, by expert beer keeper Ivor Clissold. This handy little book provides vital information about looking after and serving beer, with tables and diagrams to ensure even the most technical of information is easy to follow. A special appendix provides precise guidelines on how to care for over 300 of Britain's most popular ales. How long should Draught Bass be kept before serving? Or Tetley Bitter? The answers to these questions and other brewery 'secrets' are all now at hand.

Whether you're a publican looking to earn a place in the *Good Beer Guide*, or just a beer lover hoping to set up a cask for a party, *The CAMRA Guide to Cellarmanship* is essential reading. Order your copy, at £6.99 inclusive of postage, from CAMRA, 230 Hatfield Road, St Albans, Hertfordshire AL1 4LW; tel. (01727) 867201. Discounts are available for CAMRA members.

Essex

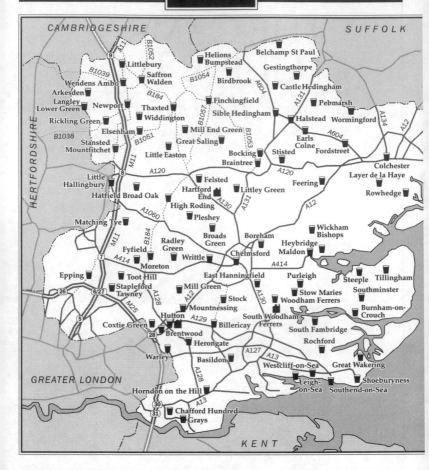

Aingers Green

Royal Fusiliers
Aingers Green Road (1 mile S of Gt Bentley Green) OS119204
☎ (01206) 250001
11–2.30 (3.30 Sat), 5.30–11; 12–4, 7–10.30 Sun
Beer range varies H
Friendly free house with bricks and beams in its two bars. A pool table and darts are away from the bar. Cider is available in summer.
🏚 Q ✿ ⌂ P ⊟

Arkesden

Axe & Compasses
☎ (01799) 550272
11–2.30, 6–11; 12–3, 7–10.30 Sun
Greene King IPA, Abbot H
Superb, 17th-century, traditional local, always offering a friendly welcome from its staff and regulars. Thriving food trade (good range of meals).
🏚 Q ✿ ◖ ▸ ⊕ ♣ P

Basildon

Moon on the Square
1–15 Market Square (near A176) ☎ (01268) 520360
11–11; 12–10.30 Sun
Courage Directors; Theakston Best Bitter, XB; Younger Scotch; guest beer H
Attractive Wetherspoons pub, a recent shop conversion. Bouncers man the doors after 12.30 Sat. Q ◖ ▸ ⅙ ⇌ ⌿

Belchamp St Paul

Cherry Tree Inn
Knowl Green OS784413
☎ (01787) 237263
12–3, 7–11; 12–11 Sat; 12–3, 7–10.30 Sun; closed Tue
Adnams Bitter; Greene King IPA; guest beer H
Cosy, friendly, isolated pub, comfortably refurbished. Excellent value beer and home-cooked food. Good play area for children.
🏚 Q ✿ 🚐 ◖ ▸ ♣ P

Billericay

Coach & Horses
36 Chapel Street (near B1007)
☎ (01277) 622873
10–11; 12–3.30, 7–10.30 Sun
Greene King IPA, Abbot; Shepherd Neame Master Brew Bitter; guest beers H
Friendly, comfortable, one-bar pub off the high street, appealing to a mixed clientele of all ages with a common interest in good beer and conversation. Darts, dominoes and crib are played. The collections of jugs and elephants are impressive. No food Sun.
🏚 ✿ ◖ ⇌ ♣ P

Birdbrook

Plough
The Street (1 mile off B1054)
☎ (01440) 785336
12–3, 6–11; 12–3, 7–10.30 Sun
Adnams Bitter; Greene King IPA; guest beer H

Essex

Lawford
Manningtree A120 Harwich
Little Bentley Little Oakley
A133 Tendring
Aingers Green
Wivenhoe Little Clacton
Brightlingsea Walton-on-the-Naze
Great Clacton Great Holland
St Osyth

0 Miles 10
0 Kilometres 16

Traditional village local with a friendly atmosphere. Shove-ha'penny played.
🏰 Q ❀ ◁ ▶ ⊟ ♣ P

Bocking

Angel
36 Bocking End
☎ (01376) 321549
11–3, 5.30–11; 11–11 Sat; 12–10.30 Sun
Beer range varies H
Approximately 15th-century pub with a lively atmosphere and a beer club. Sport-oriented, it shows live football.
◁ & P

Boreham

Queen's Head
Church Road (near B1137)
☎ (01245) 467298
10.30 (10 Sat)–3, 5 (6 Sat)–11; 12–4, 7–10.30 Sun
Greene King IPA, Abbot H
Friendly village local with two contrasting bars. Good value Sun lunch.
Q ❀ ◁ ▶ ⊟ ♣ P

Braintree

King William IV
114 London Road (near B1053/A120 jct)
☎ (01376) 330088
11–3, 6–11; 11–11 Sat; 12–3, 7–10.30 Sun
Ridleys IPA G
Cosy, two-bar local with a very friendly atmosphere; darts and quizzes are popular. Award-winning flower displays in summer. 🏰 ❀ ⊟ ♣ P

Wagon & Horses
53 South Street (B1256)
☎ (01376) 553356
11–3 (4 Sat), 5.30 (6 Sat)–11; 12–3, 7–10.30 Sun
Greene King IPA, Abbot, seasonal beers H
Comfortable pub with a large lounge, a raised dining area and a friendly snug. Look for the well. No eve meals Wed or Sun. ❀ ◁ ▶ ⊟ ⇌ ♣ P

Brentwood

Swan
123 High Street (A1023)
☎ (01277) 211848
11–11; 12–10.30 Sun
Boddingtons Bitter; Flowers IPA, Original; Mighty Oak Burntwood; Wadworth 6X; Whitbread Abroad Cooper H; guest beers H/G
1930s-style pub but dating back to the 15th century. Always up to 12 cask beers on, four dispensed straight from the cask as in all Hogshead Ale Houses. Good atmosphere; well-trained staff and friendly management.
🏰 Q ❀ ◁ ⇌ ♣ P

Victoria Arms
50 Ongar Road (A128)
☎ (01277) 223371
11–11; 12–10.30 Sun
Greene King IPA, Abbot; guest beers H
Friendly pub on the edge of the town centre, stocking a very wide range of whiskies. Tiny car park. ❀ ◁ P

Brightlingsea

Railway Tavern
58 Station Road (near B1029)
☎ (01206) 302581
5 (12 Fri & Sat)–11; 12–3, 7–10.30 Sun
Beer range varies H
Friendly, two-bar pub near the promenade, popular with visitors and locals. The walls are adorned with railway memorabilia. Variety of games. 1997 local CAMRA Pub of the Year, it holds a cider festival every May. A mild is always available.
🏰 Q ☞ ❀ ⊟ & ▲ ♣ ⌂

Broads Green

Walnut Tree
1 mile W of B1008 OS694125
☎ (01245) 360222
11.30–2.30, 6.30–11; 12–2.30, 7–10.30 Sun
Ridleys IPA G
Former local CAMRA Pub of the Year: a well-preserved, Victorian, agricultural community pub overlooking the village green, with an unspoilt public bar and a snug. A later extension houses the lounge. Other Ridleys' beers are sometimes available.
🏰 Q ❀ ◁ ▶ ⊟ ♣ P

Burnham-on-Crouch

Olde White Harte Hotel
The Quay
☎ (01621) 782106
11–11; 12–10.30 Sun
Adnams Bitter; Crouch Vale Best Bitter; Tolly Cobbold Bitter H
Riverside pub with 1950s roadhouse decor in hammered oak in the bar area. Frequented by locals and yachtsmen; bustling on summer eves, particularly at weekends. Enjoy a pint on the jetty.
🏰 Q ☞ ❀ ⊨ ◁ ▶ ▲ ⇌ P

Castle Hedingham

Bell Inn
10 St James Street (B1058)
☎ (01787) 460350
11.30–3, 6–11; 12–3, 7–10.30 Sun
Greene King IPA, Abbot; Shepherd Neame Master Brew Bitter G
Excellent, genuine-timbered, many-roomed pub with casks behind the bar. Occasional live music; good value food (not served Mon eve, except bank hols). Comfortable family room.
🏰 Q ☞ ❀ ◁ ▶ ⊟ ▲ ♣ P ⊬

Chafford Hundred

Chafford Hundred
100 Fleming Road (by B186, via Pilgrims Lane roundabout)
☎ (01375) 481153
11–11; 12–10.30 Sun
Boddingtons Bitter; Flowers Original; guest beers H

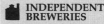

INDEPENDENT BREWERIES

Crouch Vale: South Woodham Ferrers

Mighty Oak: Hutton

Ridleys: Hartford End

This pub is like a licensed family restaurant with a children's games room. A good value menu offers daily specials; baby seats available in the restaurant. Wheelchair WC. Q ☕ ⊛ ◑ ▶ ᕕ ⇌ P

Chelmsford

Bird in Hand

New Writtle Street (near B1007) ☎ (01245) 600002
12–3, 6–11; 12–11 Fri & Sat; 12–10.30 Sun
Ridleys IPA, Rumpus ⊞
Friendly, backstreet local close to the cricket and football grounds. No meals Sun lunchtime. ⊛ ◑ ⊟ ♣ P

Endeavour

351 Springfield Road (B1137) ☎ (01245) 257717
11–11; 12–2.30, 7–10.30 Sun
Greene King XX Mild, IPA, Abbot; Shepherd Neame Master Brew Bitter; guest beers ⊞
Friendly, quiet, three-roomed Gray's pub serving a wide selection of good, home-cooked food (not Sun), with daily specials. A rare outlet in the area for the mild. Note the unusual pub sign.
ᗰ Q ◑ ▶ ⊟ ♣

Original Plough

28 Duke Street (near A138) ☎ (01245) 250145
11–11; 12–3, 7–10.30 Sun
Beer range varies ⊞
Popular, lively pub offering a changing selection of six guest beers. It attracts mature ale enthusiasts and young trendies alike. ⊛ ◑ ⇌ ♣ P

Partners

30 Lower Anchor Street (near B1007) ☎ (01245) 265181
11–3, 5.30–11; 11–11 Sat; 12–10.30 Sun
Crouch Vale Best Bitter; Greene King IPA; guest beers ⊞
Friendly, one-bar local with an ever-changing range of guest beers (at least three). Weekday meals. ☕ ⊛ ◑ ♣ P

White Horse

25 Townfield Street (near A138) ☎ (01245) 269556
11–3, 5.30 (7 Sat)–11; 12–10.30 Sun
Beer range varies ⊞
Convivial backstreet free house, offering ten beers. Background blues music is often played; good conversation. Big screen TV for sports. ◑ ⇌ ♣

Colchester

Beer House

126 Magdalen Street (A134) ☎ (01206) 792642
12–2.30 (not Mon–Wed), 5.30–11; 12–11 Fri & Sat; 12–10.30 Sun

Greene King IPA; guest beers ⊞
Traditional, one-bar pub, hosting live music Sun lunch. The beer range is constantly changing, with five guests. ⊛ ⇌ (Town) ♣

Bricklayers

27 Bergholt Road (B1508/A134) ☎ (01206) 852008
11–3, 5.30–11; 11–11 Sat; 12–3, 7–10.30 Sun
Adnams Bitter, Old, Broadside; guest beers ⊞
Pub with a refurbished, split-level saloon bar and a public bar, serving four, constantly changing guest beers. CAMRA award-winning landlord. Good value Sun lunch.
⊛ ◑ ⊟ ⇌ (North) ♣ P

British Grenadier

67 Military Road ☎ (01206) 791647
11–2.30 (3 Fri & Sat), 7–11; 12–3, 7–10.30 Sun
Adnams Mild or **seasonal beer, Bitter** ⊞, **Old** ⒼG
The highest pub in town; a two-bar, friendly local with a strong darts and pool following. ⊟ ⇌ (Town) ♣

King's Arms/Hogshead

61–63 Crouch Street (near A134) ☎ (01206) 572886
11–11; 12–10.30 Sun
Boddingtons Bitter; Castle Eden Ale ⒼG; **Flowers Original; Whitbread Abroad Cooper** ⊞
Popular, large, open-plan pub, well refurbished. Sun eve quiz; bank hol beer festivals.
ᗰ ⊛ ◑ ⌂ P

Odd One Out

Mersea Road (B1025) ☎ (01206) 578140
4 (11 Fri & Sat)–11; 12–10.30 Sun
Archers Best Bitter; Ridleys IPA; guest beers ⊞
Excellent, genuine free house: three basic bars and a no-smoking, quiet back room. Up to five guest beers usually include a mild; Crones and Thatcher's cider. Possibly the cheapest pub in town.
ᗰ Q ⊛ ⇌ (Town) ♣ ⌂ ✄

Rose & Crown

51 East Street (A137) ☎ (01206) 866677
11–2.30, 6–11; 12–2.30, 7–10.30 Sun
Adnams Broadside; Tetley Bitter; Tolly Cobbold IPA ⊞
Comfortable single bar in a very old hotel in this historic town. The house beer is supplied by Tolly. The heavily-beamed Tudor Bar welcomes locals. ⇌ ◑ ▶ P

Stockwell Arms

18 West Stockwell Street (by side of town hall) ☎ (01206) 575560

10.30–11; 10.30–3.30, 6.30–11 Sat; 12–3, 7–10.30 Sun
Nethergate Bitter; Ruddles Best Bitter, County; Theakston XB, Old Peculier; Webster's Green Label, Yorkshire Bitter ⊞
Historic, friendly family pub in the old Dutch quarter. Book eve meals and Sun lunch.
Q ⊛ ◑ ▶ ⇌ (North) ♣ ⊟

Coxtie Green

White Horse

173 Coxtie Green Road OS564959
☎ (01277) 372410
11.30–3, 5.30–11; 12–4, 7–11 Sat; 12–3, 7–10.30 Sun
Beer range varies ⊞
Small, comfortable, two-bar pub with a very large garden, featuring a children's play area. Usually six real ales; beer festival July. No food Sun.
Q ⊛ ◑ ▶ ⊟ P

Earls Colne

Bird in Hand

Coggeshall Road (B1024) ☎ (01787) 222557
12–2.30, 6–11; 12–2.30, 7–10.30 Sun
Ridleys IPA ⊞, **ESX** or **Rumpus, Witchfinder** or **Winter Ale** ⒼG
Excellent Ridleys country pub. Built around 1896, it has two bars and an off-sales hatch. The public bar is unspoilt, with many original features; the saloon is comfortable and relaxing. Gravity beers are served from polypins. Good value food.
ᗰ Q ⊛ ◑ ▶ ⊟ ♣ ▲ P

East Hanningfield

Windmill Tavern

The Tye, Main Road ☎ (01245) 400315
11–11; 12–10.30 Sun
Boddingtons Bitter; Crouch Vale Best Bitter; Marston's Pedigree; guest beer ⊞
Friendly, original free house opposite the village green. The guest beer changes weekly. Home-made food includes a set menu and specials (no food Mon eve).
ᗰ ⊛ ◑ ▶ ♣ P

Elsenham

Crown

High Street (B1051) ☎ (01279) 812827
11–2.30, 6–11; 12–2.30, 7–10.30 Sun
Beer range varies ⊞
Deservedly popular, friendly village pub with a pargetted exterior and a good reputation for excellent food (no meals Sun eve).
ᗰ ⊛ ◑ ▶ ⊟ ♣ P

Epping

Forest Gate
111 Bell Common (off B1393, Ivy Chimneys road) OS451011
☎ (01992) 572312
10–3, 5.30–11; 12–3, 7–10.30 Sun
Adnams Bitter H,
Broadside G; **Ridleys IPA** H,
ESX; guest beers G
On the edge of Epping Forest, a single-bar, traditional, 17th-century pub which has been run by the same family for many years. The guest beers come from local independent brewers. A renowned turkey broth is sold lunchtime.
🏠 Q ❀ ♣ ➼ P

Feering

Sun Inn
3 Feering Hill (B1024)
☎ (01376) 570442
11–3, 6–11; 12–3, 6–10.30 Sun
Courage Directors; guest beers H
Former mansion, heavily timbered, with carved beams and log fires. Large patio and beer garden. Beer fests May and Aug Bank Hol. Good food. Phone to camp. 🏠 ❀ ◖ ▶ ▲
⇌ (Kelvedon) ♣ ➼ P

Felsted

Chequers
Braintree Road (B1417)
☎ (01371) 820226
12–2.30, 6–11; 12–11 Fri, Sat & summer; 12–10.30 Sun
Ridleys IPA H
Victorian pub in a sleepy village, with public, lounge and function/family rooms. The nearby public school lends a sporty atmosphere (particularly cricket). The landlady is Ridleys' longest serving tenant.
🏠 ⛺ ❀ ◖ ▶ ⊟ ♿ ♣ P

Finchingfield

Red Lion
Church Hill ☎ (01371) 810400
12–3, 6–11; 12–11 Sat & bank hols; 12–10.30 Sun
Ridleys IPA, ESX H
Friendly local with a restaurant in one of the most picturesque villages in Essex.
🏠 ❀ ◖ ▶ ♣ P

Fordstreet

Coopers Arms
On A604, 3 miles W of Colchester ☎ (01206) 241177
12–3, 7–11; 12–3, 7–10.30 Sun
Greene King IPA; Woodforde's Wherry; guest beers H
Friendly pub with comfortable leather chairs and sofas,

hosting a fishing club and a golf society. Q ❀ ◖ ▶ ♣ P

Fyfield

Queen's Head
Queen's Street (off B184)
☎ (01277) 899231
11–3, 6–11; 11–11 Sat; 12–3, 7–10.30 Sun
Adnams Bitter; Mansfield Bitter; Smiles Best; guest beers H
Genuine free house, the focal point of the village, popular with all ages. The long bar has spacious alcoves. Regularly changing guest beers (at least three), from small independents. The garden overlooks the River Roding. Famed Essex Huffers feature on the menu (no food Sat eve).
🏠 ❀ ◖ ▶ ♣ P

Gestingthorpe

Pheasant
Audley End OS813376
☎ (01787) 461196
12–3, 6–11; 12–3, 7–10.30 Sun
Adnams Bitter; Draught Bass; Greene King IPA; guest beers H
Multi-roomed, traditional village local. No meals Sun eve.
🏠 ❀ ◖ ▶ ♣ P

Grays

Theobald Arms
141 Argent Street
☎ (01375) 372253
10.30–3, 5–11; 10.30–11 Fri & Sat; 12–10.30 Sun
Courage Best Bitter; guest beers H
Traditional, family-run, two-bar pub. The public bar features an unusual revolving pool table. Popular with office workers at lunchtime.
❀ ◖ ▶ ♿ ⇌ ♣ P

Great Clacton

Plough
1 North Road (near B1032)
☎ (01255) 429998
11–11; 12–6, 7–10.30 Sun
Flowers Original; Greene King IPA; Tetley Bitter; guest beers H
17th-century listed building, once three cottages, now a popular local. Live music at weekends. The lounge bar is ideal for conversation.
🏠 ❀ ◖ ▶ ⊟ ▲ ♣

Great Holland

Lion's Den
Little Clacton Road (by B1032)
☎ (01255) 675137
11–3, 6–11; 12–3, 7–10.30 Sun
Greene King IPA, seasonal beers; guest beers H

Old-fashioned wayside pub which has mellowed with time. A large sleeping lion (stuffed) cuddles the piano, while the log fire crackles and spits in winter. Local Hogshead cider.
🏠 ❀ ◖ ▶ ♣ ➼ P

Great Saling

White Hart
The Street (2 miles N of A120) OS701254 ☎ (01371) 850341
12–3.30, 5.30–11; 12–11 Sat; 12–10.30 Sun
Ridleys IPA, Rumpus H
Superb 16th-century, beamed Tudor pub, with a raised timbered gallery, in *Lovejoy* country. A speciality is the Essex Huffer – a large roll with a choice of fillings (which the pub claims to have invented). The restaurant is in a restored bakehouse at the rear. It can get crowded at weekends, particularly in summer.
🏠 Q ❀ ◖ ▶ ⊟ P

Great Wakering

Anchor
23 High Street (B1017)
☎ (01702) 219265
11–11; 12–10.30 Sun
Draught Bass; Ridleys IPA; guest beers H
Friendly, family-run pub with two bars, very popular with all ages. Note the collection of walking sticks above the bar.
🏠 ❀ 🛏 ◖ ▶ ♿ ♣ ➼ P

Halstead

Dog Inn
37 Hedingham Road (A604)
☎ (01787) 477774
12–2.30 (3 Sat), 6–11; 12–3, 7–10.30 Sun
Adnams Bitter; Nethergate Bitter; guest beer H
Friendly, 17th-century local offering reasonably priced en suite accommodation and bar meals, close to the town centre. Over 350 guest ales to date. Phone to camp.
🏠 Q ⛺ ❀ 🛏 ◖ ▶ ▲ P

Harwich

Alma
25 King's Head Street (off the quay) ☎ (01255) 503474
11.30 (11 Sat)–3, 7–11; 12–3, 7–10.30 Sun
Flowers Original; Greene King IPA; Tolly Cobbold Mild; guest beer H
Pub with a large room featuring nautical artefacts and a central, horseshoe bar, curiously reminiscent of a Wild West saloon. Small corridor snug behind the main bar.
🏠 Q ❀ ◖ ⇌ (Town) ♣

Hanover Inn

65 Church Road
☎ (01255) 502927
10.30–2, 6.30–11; 12–3, 7–10.30 Sun
Tolly Cobbold Mild, Old Strong H
Popular town pub; the back room has a pool table and loud music. It sells a rare example of a Tolly Cobbold house beer.
🚃 ᕦ ≉ (Town) ♣

Hatfield Broad Oak

Cock

High Street (B183)
☎ (01279) 718273
12–3, 6–11; 12–3 (may extend), 7–10.30 Sun
Fuller's London Pride; Greene King IPA; guest beers H
Ancient, traditional rural pub, in the village centre, well restored to improve facilities (disabled access, new public bar and a no-smoking room). Very popular for food; private dining room available. Usually four guest beers, all from independents. No food Sun eve.
🚃 Q ⊛ ᗊ ▶ ᕦ ♣ ⇔ P ⅏

Helions Bumpstead

Three Horseshoes

Water Lane OS650414
☎ (01440) 730298
11.45–2.30, 7–11; 12–2.30, 7–10.30 Sun
Greene King IPA, Abbot, seasonal beers H
Fine, friendly, remote pub boasting superb, award-wining gardens. No food Mon/Tue eve or Sun.
🚃 Q ᗊ ▶ ᕦ Ａ ♣ P

Herongate

Green Man

11 Cricketers Lane (A128)
☎ (01277) 810292
11–2.30 (3 Sat), 6–11; 12–10.30 Sun
Adnams Bitter; Ind Coope Burton Ale; Marston's Pedigree; Tetley Bitter; guest beer H
Pleasant, large main bar with a number of rooms set back; one is designated as a no-smoking area and one as a family room. Good, recently renovated, children's garden play area. Darts and shove-ha'penny are played.
🚃 ㄥ ⊛ ᗊ ▶ ♣ ⅏

Old Dog Inn

Billericay Road (1 mile E of A128) OS641910
☎ (01277) 810337
11 (12 Sat)–2.30, 6–11; 12–3.30, 7–10.30 Sun
Adnams Extra; Greene King Abbot; Ridleys IPA; guest beers H/G
Friendly, low-beamed country pub. ㄥ ⊛ ᗊ ▶ ᕦ ♣ P

Heybridge

Maltsters Arms

Hall Road ☎ (01621) 853880
11.30–3.30, 6–11; 12–3.30, 7–10.30 Sun
Greene King IPA, Abbot G
Backstreet local where the public and saloon bars enjoy a 1960s atmosphere. Note the tilting stillages for gravity serving and the antique till. ♣

High Roding

Black Lion

The Street (B184)
☎ (01371) 872847
12–3, 6–11 (11.30 Fri & Sat); 12–3, 7–10.30 Sun
Ridleys IPA, seasonal beers G
A *Guide* entry for many years, this 15th-century, traditional, timber-framed pub continues to maintain its deserved reputation. The highly regarded food is cooked to order. 🚃 Q ㄥ ⊛ ᗊ ▶ ᕦ ♣ P

Horndon on the Hill

Bell Inn

High Road (near B1007)
☎ (01375) 673154
11–2.30 (3 Sat), 6–11; 12–3, 7–10.30 Sun
Draught Bass G; **Fuller's London Pride; Highgate IPA; guest beers** H
Busy, 15th-century, coaching inn in an attractive old village, now bypassed. Quality food is served in the bar and restaurant.
🚃 Q ⊛ ⋈ ᗊ ▶ ᕦ P

Hutton

Chequers

213 Rayleigh Road (A129)
☎ (01277) 224980
12 (11 Sat)–11; 12–10.30 Sun
Draught Bass; Harveys BB; guest beer H
Small, cosy pub with beams. The guest beer is usually from an independent brewery not usually available locally (including Mighty Oak).
⊛ ᗊ ᕦ ≉ (Shenfield) ♣ P

Langley Lower Green

Bull

OS436345 ☎ (01279) 777309
12–2.30, 6–11; 12–3, 7–10.30 Sun
Adnams Bitter, Broadside; Greene King IPA H
Classic, Victorian rural pub in one of the smallest Essex villages, with a local clientele. A pitch-penny game is concealed under a bench in the saloon bar. 🚃 Q ⊛ ᕦ ♣ P

Lawford

Station Buffet

Manningtree Station Buffet, Station Road (near A137)
☎ (01206) 391114
10.30–11; 12–3 (closed eve) Sun
Adnams Bitter; Shepherd Neame Spitfire; guest beers H
Very small, one-bar pub on the station platform. Breakfasts are served from 5.30am during the week; home-cooked food. The listed building boasts an original marble bar.
⊛ ᗊ ▶ ≉ (Manningtree)

Layer de la Haye

Donkey & Buskins

High Road (B1026)
☎ (01206) 734774
11–2.30, 6–11; 12–3, 7–10.30 Sun
Adnams Bitter; Flowers IPA, Original; guest beer H
Two-bar country pub; one bar is used as a dining room where fish and home-made dishes feature on the menu. Sparklers will be removed if you ask. The beer is a little pricy. The large garden is suitable for children.
⊛ ᗊ ▶ P

Leigh-on-Sea

Broker

213–217 Leigh Road
☎ (01702) 471932
11–3, 6–11; 12–3, 7–10.30 Sun
Shepherd Neame Spitfire; guest beers H
Family-run free house serving a varied range of beers and bar or restaurant meals (eve meals weekends). Children welcome until 7.30 in a sectioned-off, no-smoking area of the bar.
ㄥ ⊛ ᗊ ▶ ≉ (Chalkwell)

Elms

1060 London Road (A13)
☎ (01702) 74687
10–11; 12–10.30 Sun
Courage Directors; Theakston Best Bitter; Younger Scotch; guest beers H
Old, large, rambling building refurbished by Wetherspoons, but more like a local than usual.
Q ⊛ ᗊ ▶ ᕼ ⇔ P ⅏

Little Bentley

Bricklayer's Arms

Rectory Road (near A120)
☎ (01206) 250405
12.30–3.30, 6.30–11; 12–3, 7–10.30 Sun
Greene King IPA; Mauldons Squires H
Cosy pub in a country setting serving fine, home-made food. Interesting plate rack.
Q ⊛ ᗊ ▶ P

Littlebury

Queen's Head
High Street (B1383)
☎ (01799) 522251
12–11; 12–3, 7–10.30 Sun
Draught Bass; guest beers Ⓗ
600-year-old village local with
traditional food and good
accommodation. The landlord
is an accomplished chef (no
food Sun eve). The six-plus real
ales change frequently; the
Easter beer festival offers over
70 beers.
🏠 ⊛ 🛏 ◖▶ ♣ P

Little Clacton

Apple Tree
The Street (B1441)
☎ (01255) 861026
11–3, 6–11; 12–3, 7–10.30 Sun
**Fuller's ESB; Wells Eagle;
guest beers** Ⓗ
Real ale oasis featuring beams,
brass and a bare-brick interior.
One of the area's leading live
music pubs at weekends.
⊛ ◖▶ P

Little Easton

Stag
Duck Street (1 mile W of B184)
☎ (01371) 870214
11–2.30 (later if busy), 6–11; 12–3,
7–10.30 Sun
Ridleys IPA Ⓗ
Friendly, refurbished, village
local, enjoying fine views over
the Chelmer Valley from its
large garden (excellent
children's play area).
🏠 ⊛ ◖▶ 🅰 ♣ P

Little Hallingbury

Sutton Arms
Bishop's Stortford Road, Hall
Green (by A1060)
☎ (01279) 730460
11–2.30, 6–11; 12–11 Sat; 12–10.30 Sun
**B&T Shefford Bitter; Ind
Coope Burton Ale; Tetley
Bitter; guest beer** Ⓗ
Two-roomed pub: the small
snug bar retains a village local
atmosphere. Very popular for
its range of food, it can get very
busy at weekends.
🏠 ⊛ ◖▶ 🅰 ♣ P

Little Oakley

Olde Cherry Tree
Clacton Road (B1414)
☎ (01255) 880333
11–2.30, 5–11; 12–3, 7–10.30 Sun
**Adnams Bitter, Broadside;
Draught Bass; Wells Eagle;
guest beers** Ⓗ
Surprisingly unlisted pub,
despite its antiquity; a frequent
haunt of fuchsia freaks and
aero-modellers. Come at

Christmas to see the
decorations. 🏠 ⊛ ◖▶ ♣ P

Littley Green

Compasses
Turn off B1417 opp. Ridleys
Brewery OS699172
☎ (01245) 362308
11.30–3, 6–11; 12–3, 7–10.30 Sun
**Ridleys IPA, ESX,
Witchfinder, Rumpus, Winter
Ale** Ⓖ
Victorian, cottage-style pub,
difficult to find; local CAMRA
Pub of the Year 1996 for the sixth
time. The bar food speciality is
the Essex Huffer (a very large
bap). Good range of whiskies.
A real gem. 🏠 Q ⊛ ◖▶ ♣ P

Maldon

Blue Boar Hotel
Silver Street ☎ (01621) 852681
11–2.30 (3 Fri & Sat), 6–11; 12–3,
7–10.30 Sun
Adnams Bitter; guest beers Ⓖ
Friendly, two-room bar in the
town centre, full of character
with a ceiling of exposed
beams. Home-cooked food.
🏠 Q 🍽 ⊛ 🛏 ◖▶ ♣ P

Queens Head
The Hythe ☎ (01621) 854112
10.30–11; 12–10.30 Sun
**Greene King IPA, Abbot;
Shepherd Neame Master
Brew Bitter; guest beers** Ⓗ
Traditional, quiet, three-bar
pub overlooking the quayside
with its Thames barges; strong
maritime atmosphere. Large
outdoor drinking area. Enjoy a
stroll along the prom. Lunches
Mon–Fri. 🏠 Q ⊛ ◖ ♣ P

Manningtree

Crown Hotel
51 High Street (B1352)
☎ (01206) 396333
11–11; 12–10.30 Sun
**Greene King XX Mild, IPA,
Abbot, seasonal beers** Ⓗ
16th-century, three-bar
coaching inn with panoramic
views over the River Stour.
Nautical bric-a-brac reflects the
history and life of
Manningtree. No food Mon
eve. 🍽 ⊛ ◖▶ 🍴 ♨ ⇌ ♣ P

Matching Tye

Fox Inn
The Green OS515113
☎ (01279) 731335
12–3, 7–11; 12–10.30 Sun; closed Mon
**Draught Bass; Ridleys
seasonal beers; Shepherd
Neame Spitfire; guest beer** Ⓗ
Large, old pub with three
rooms (one used as a no-
smoking dining area) adorned
with foxy artefacts. Food is
available all hours. The

extensive garden has a
petanque piste.
Q ⊛ ◖▶ 🍴 ♿ ♣ P

Mill End Green

Green Man
1 mile E of B184 OS619260
☎ (01371) 870286
11.30–3, 6–11; 12–3, 7–10.30 Sun
**Adnams Bitter; Greene King
IPA; Ridleys IPA** Ⓗ; **guest
beer** Ⓖ
Friendly, 15th-century, oak-
studded, low-beamed, country
pub featured in TV's *Lovejoy*
series. Superb gardens and an
outdoor area for families. Good
value food (not served Sun
eve). 🏠 Q ⊛ 🛏 ◖▶ 🅰 ♣ P

Mill Green

Viper
Mill Green Road OS641018
☎ (01277) 352010
11–2.30, 6–11; 12–3, 7–10.30 Sun
Ridleys IPA; guest beers Ⓗ
Hidden away in the woods
(excellent walks), this is the
only pub of this name in the
country. Three bars: a basic
public, a cosy snug and a
comfortable lounge. Thirty
years with the same landlord
has preserved this rural gem.
🏠 Q ⊛ 🍴 ♣ P

Moreton

Nag's Head
Church Road
☎ (01277) 890239
12–3, 6.30–11; 12–3, 6.30–10.30 Sun;
closed Mon
**Brakspear Bitter; Hook
Norton Best Bitter; Tolly
Cobbold Original; guest
beer** Ⓗ
Large free house with an
L-shaped bar, a lounge on a
split level and a restaurant. The
menu includes several unusual
dishes, but is a bit pricy.
Q ⊛ ◖▶ P

White Hart
Church Road
☎ (01277) 890228
1–3, 5.30–11; 11–11 Sat; 12–10.30 Sun
**Adnams Bitter; Belchers Best
Bitter; Courage Best Bitter,
Directors; Shepherd Neame
Master Brew Bitter;
Theakston XB** Ⓗ
Late-medieval building with
much original wood exposed.
The lounge bar has a snob
screen which came from a
former London pub.
Restaurant to the rear (no food
Sun eve). 🏠 Q ⊛ ◖▶ 🍴 ♣ P

Mountnessing

Prince of Wales
199 Roman Road (B1002)
☎ (01277) 353445
11–3, 6–11; 12–3, 7–10.30 Sun

Ridleys IPA, Mild, ESX,
Rumpus, seasonal beers Ⓗ
Fine, old, beamed pub near the
windmill, serving superb,
home-cooked food (not Mon
eve). Local CAMRA *Pub of the
Year* 1996. 🏰 ❀ ◖ ❁ ♣ P

Newport

Coach & Horses

Cambridge Road (B1383)
☎ (01799) 540292
11–11; 12–10.30 Sun
Young's Bitter; guest beers Ⓗ
Warm, welcoming, 16th-
century coaching inn. Excellent
restaurant and bar food; four
guest ales. Pleasant garden.
🏰 ⚲ ❀ ◖ ❁ & A P

Pebmarsh

King's Head

The Street (1½ miles E of A131)
OS851335 ☎ (01787) 269306
12–2, 7 (5 Fri)–11; 12–3, 7–10.30 Sun
Beer range varies Ⓗ
Real ale drinker's paradise
with a 1470, oak-beam interior
and a constantly changing
line-up of at least four beers.
Skittle alley in a barn.
🏰 Q ⚲ ❀ ◖ ❁ & A ♣ P

Pleshey

White Horse

The Street OS663143
☎ (01245) 237281
12–3, 7–11; 12–4, 7–10.30 Sun
Beer range varies Ⓗ
Attractive, old, beamed pub
with an extensive menu and a
new drinkers' bar extension.
Usually two or three beers
available, plus an occasional
cider. 🏰 ❀ ◖ ❁ A ⬤ P ✗ ⊟

Purleigh

Bell

The Street (near B1010)
OS841020 ☎ (01621) 828348
11–3, 6–11; 12–3, 7–10.30 Sun
Adnams Bitter; Benskins BB;
Greene King IPA; guest
beer Ⓗ
Spacious country pub on a
14th-century site, overlooking
the Blackwater estuary, with a
large inglenook. No music;
friendly atmosphere. The
garden is unfenced. No food
Tue eve. 🏰 Q ❀ ◖ ♣ P

Radley Green

Cuckoo

500 yds from A414, Writtle–
Norton Heath road OS622054
☎ (01245) 248356
12–2.30, 6–11; 12–4, 7–10.30 Sun
Ridleys IPA, Witchfinder,
Rumpus, seasonal beers Ⓗ
Remote country pub (formerly
the Thatchers Arms),
surrounded by farmland;

popular with caravanners. Safe
outdoor areas for children.
🏰 Q ❀ ◖ A ♣ P

Rickling Green

Cricketers Arms

½ mile off B1383, near
Quendon OS511290
☎ (01799) 543210
12–3, 6–11; 12–3, 6.30–10.30 Sun
Flowers IPA; guest beers Ⓖ
Enlarged old pub in an idyllic
setting, overlooking the cricket
green. Guest beers always
include a mild or a dark beer
and a strong ale. Excellent,
imaginative food.
🏰 ⚲ ❀ ❀ ◖ ❁ ♣

Rochford

Golden Lion

35 North Street
☎ (01702) 545487
12–11; 12–10.30 Sun
Fuller's London Pride; Greene
King Abbot; Hancock's HB;
Theakston Old Peculier; guest
beers Ⓗ
Traditional, no-nonsense, free
house offering a selection of
guest beers. The building is a
300-year-old ex-tailor's shop.
Local CAMRA *Pub of the Year*
awards are displayed. A real
cider (Zum-Zum) is always
available. ❀ ◖ ⇌ ♣ ⌂

New Ship

7–9 East Street
☎ (01702) 544244
11–11; 12–5, 7–10.30 Sun
Worthington Bitter; guest
beer Ⓗ
Basic local – older than the Old
Ship. Try the home-made
soups. ❀ ◖ ⇌ ♣ P

Old Ship

12–14 North Street
☎ (01702) 544210
11–11; 12–10.30 Sun
Eldridge Pope Royal Oak;
Marston's Pedigree; guest
beers Ⓗ
Large, traditional pub serving
a good range of beers
(including a house beer) and
excellent value food (Mon–Fri).
First appearance in the *Guide*.
❀ ◖ ⇌ ♣ P

Rowhedge

Walnut Tree

Fingringhoe Road (1 mile E of
B1025) OS021216
☎ (01206) 728149
8 (7.30 Fri)–11; 12–3, 7–11 Sat; 12–3,
7.30–10.30 Sun; closed Mon & Wed
Beer range varies Ⓗ
Friendly, lively pub on the
outskirts of Colchester,
boasting a real vinyl jukebox.
Usually four ales on. Cheese
club Fri eve from 9pm;
reasonably-priced food. Check
opening times. ❀ ◖ ♣ P

Saffron Walden

Cross Keys

32 High Street
☎ (01799) 522207
10.30–11; 12–10.30 Sun
Benskins BB; Ind Coope
Burton Ale; Tetley Bitter Ⓗ
Dating from 1450, this single
bar (plus restaurant and pool
room) pub enjoys a good
lunchtime trade and can be
busy eves and weekends.
❀ ⚲ ◖ ❁ &

Eight Bells

18 Bridge Street (B184)
☎ (01799) 522790
11–3, 6–11; 12–10.30 Sun
Adnams Bitter; Friary Meux
BB; Ind Coope Burton Ale;
Tetley Bitter; guest beers Ⓗ
16th-century, oak-beamed inn.
The single bar has a family
room off; the rest of the pub is
given over to food.
⚲ ❀ ◖ ❁ P

St Osyth

White Hart

71 Mill Street
☎ (01255) 820318
11–3, 7–11; 12–4, 7–10.30 Sun
Adnams Bitter; guest beers Ⓗ
Heavily disguised,
19th-century pub. A
fascinating pictorial history of
the Essex coastline can be
viewed on the way to the
toilets. 🏰 ⚲ ❀ ◖ ♣ P

Shoeburyness

Angel Inn

Parsons Corner, North
Shoebury (A13/B1017 jct)
☎ (01702) 589600
11–3, 5.30–11; 12–3, 7–10.30 Sun
Greene King IPA, Abbot;
Mighty Oak Burntwood;
guest beers Ⓗ
Superb restoration of a group
of 17th-century, timber-framed
buildings (Grade II-listed) to
form a truly traditional pub
with a thatched restaurant.
Many of the interior features
were salvaged from former
churches. Note the genuine
flagstones and carved bar with
angels. A gem.
Q ❀ ◖ & P

Sible Hedingham

Sugar Loaves

175 Swan Street (A1017, old
A604) ☎ (01787) 462720
12–11; 12–10.30 Sun
Adnams Bitter, Broadside;
guest beer Ⓗ
Restored, 15th-century, oak-
beamed inn: a friendly local
with a basic public bar. Thai
food is a speciality.
🏰 ⚲ ❀ ◖ ❁ ❁ ♣ P

Southend-on-Sea

Bakers Bar
15–17 Alexandra Street (off High St) ☎ (01702) 390403
10.30–midnight (1am Tue & Wed, 2am Fri & Sat); closed Sun
Courage Directors; Shepherd Neame Master Brew Bitter; guest beers G
Underground bar located in a former Victorian bakery, usually serving up to six ales. Popular with the younger set.
❀ ◖ ▶ ≠ (Central/Victoria)

Cork & Cheese Ale House
10 Talza Way (below Victoria Plaza shopping centre)
☎ (01702) 616914
11–11; closed Sun
Beer range varies H
Pub which specialises in independent and microbrewers' beers; 1,000 different ales in five years. A real cider is always available. Local CAMRA *Pub of the Year* for the third time in 1997. Good value. ❀ ◖ ▶ ≠ (Victoria/Central) ♣ ⌂

Last Post
5 Weston Road (opp. central station)/8–10 Clifftown Road
☎ (01702) 431682
10–11; 12–10.30 Sun
Courage Directors; Marston's Pedigree; Theakston Best Bitter; Younger Scotch; guest beers H
Massive, town-centre Wetherspoons pub on the site of a former post office. Popular with all ages; very busy at weekends. Occasional festivals offer a good range of guest ales and ciders at very reasonable prices. Q ❀ ◖ ▶ ≠ (Central/Victoria) ✍

Liberty Belle
10–12 Marine Parade
☎ (01702) 466936
10–11; 12–10.30 Sun
Courage Best Bitter, Directors; guest beers H
Traditional refurbishment of a local, formerly the Borough Hotel; 18 times in the *Guide* in the last 21 years. See the chalkboards for guest beer and real cider details. Chess, darts, pool, dominoes and cards are played. Not your usual seafront pub. ☜ ❀ ◖ ◖ & ≠ (Central/Victoria) ♣ ⌂

South Fambridge

Anchor
Fambridge Road
☎ (01702) 203535
11–3, 6–11; 11–11 Sat; 12–10.30 Sun
Crouch Vale IPA; Greene King Abbot; guest beers H

Riverside inn with darts and pool upstairs. Good food.
Q ❀ ◖ ▶ ♣ P

Southminster

Rose Inn
Burnham Road (B1012, ½ mile S of village) ☎ (01621) 772915
12–2.30, 5–11; 12–2.30, 5–10.30 Sun
Greene King IPA, Abbot H
Small, quiet, simple, two-bar pub: a wayside alehouse made from two cottages.
⚒ Q ◖ P

Station Arms
39 Station Road (near B1020/B1021)
☎ (01621) 772225
12–2.30, 6–11; 12–11 Sat; 12–4, 7–10.30 Sun
Crouch Vale Best Bitter; Fuller's London Pride; guest beers H
Friendly and informal, weatherboarded high street pub offering up to four guest beers, plus beer festivals in May, July and Aug. No eve meals Sun or Wed.
⚒ Q ☜ ❀ ◖ ▶ ≠ ♣ ⌂

Stansted Mountfitchet

Dog & Duck
58 Lower Street (B1351)
☎ (01279) 812047
10–2.30, 5.30–11; 12–3, 7–10.30 Sun
Greene King IPA, Abbot H
Typical Essex weatherboarded village local, with devoted regulars. No food Sun.
Q ❀ ◖ ◖ ≠ ♣ P

Queen's Head
3 Lower Street (B1351)
☎ (01279) 812458
11–3, 5.30 (7 Sat)–11; 12–3, 7–10.30 Sun
Draught Bass; Flowers IPA; Morland Old Speckled Hen; Wadworth 6X H
Bright, friendly village pub, popular with locals. The building is mostly 17th century. No food Sun.
❀ ◖ ≠ ♣

Stapleford Tawney

Moletrap
Tawney Common (1 mile W of Toot Hill, take single track road S) OS501014
☎ (01992) 522394
12–2.30 (11.30–3 summer), 7 (6 summer)–11; 12–5, 7–10.30 Sun
McMullen AK; guest beers H
Isolated, 400-year-old free house which has three guest beers. Popular with all ages, it is principally a farming community pub and was once owned by the inventor of a type of moletrap. Difficult to find, but worth the effort.
⚒ Q ❀ ◖ ♣ P

Steeple

Star
The Street ☎ (01621) 772646
12–3, 6.45–11; 12–3, 7–10.30 Sun
Adnams Bitter; guest beers H
This pub welcomes everyone including sailors, bikers and caravanners. The guest beers come from independents and local micros. ☜ ❀ ◖ ▶ & ▲ P

Stisted

Dolphin
Coggeshall Road (A120)
☎ (01376) 321143
11–3, 6–11; 12–3, 7–10.30 Sun
Ridleys IPA, ESX G
Charming, 15th-century olde-worlde pub with exposed beams. Formerly farm workers' cottages, it has been a hostelry for 100 years. No eve meals Tue or Sun.
⚒ Q ❀ ◖ ▶ ⊞ ♣ P

Stock

Hoop
21 High Street (B1007)
☎ (01277) 841137
10–11; 12–10.30 Sun
Adnams Mild, Bitter; guest beers H/G
Very popular, small, timber-framed pub with usually six ales (including one from Nethergate), plus cider and often a perry. A good selection of home-made food is available all day. Famed for its May beer festival in the large garden.
Q ❀ ◖ ▶ ♣ ⌂

Stow Maries

Prince of Wales
Woodham Road (near B1012)
OS830993 ☎ (01621) 828971
11–11; 12–10.30 Sun
Fuller's Chiswick; guest beers H
Beautifully restored rural gem with a changing range of five or six esoteric ales (always a mild and a stout or porter), and a working Victorian baker's oven. A CAMRA award-winner and runner-up in national *Pub of the Year* awards.
⚒ Q ☜ ❀ ◖ ▶ ▲ ♣ ⌂ P

Tendring

Cherry Tree
Crow Lane (B1035)
☎ (01255) 830340
11–3, 6–11; 12–8 (10.30 summer) Sun
Adnams Bitter; Greene King IPA, Abbot; guest beer H
Two converted 17th-century cottages form this village pub, now popular for its food. Growing real ale reputation. Beams, brass and bricks feature. ⚒ Q ◖ ▶ ▲ P

Thaxted

Rose & Crown Inn
31 Mill End (near B184)
☎ (01371) 831152
11–3, 5–11 (12–2.30, 6–11 winter);
12–3, 7–10.30 Sun
Ridleys IPA; guest beer Ⓗ
Friendly, well-run local in an
historic town with a
magnificent church, Guildhall
and windmill. It is believed to
have been built on the site of a
monks' hostelry. The cosy
dining area offers excellent
food.
✿ 🛏 ◖ ▶ 🏠 ☂ ♣ P

Star
Mill End (B184)
☎ (01371) 830368
11–11; 12–4, 7–10.30 (12–10.30
summer) Sun
**Adnams Mild, Bitter, Old,
Broadside; guest beer** Ⓗ
Popular local with a keen darts
following. Exposed beams and
vast brick fireplaces feature in
both bars. Safe children's play
area. Popular with local morris
men. Good value food.
🏚 ✿ ◖ ▶ 🏠 ♣ P

Tillingham

Cap & Feathers
South Street
☎ (01621) 779212
11.30–3, 6–11; 11.30–11 Sat, summer
& bank hols; 12–4, 7–10.30 Sun
**Crouch Vale Dark, IPA, Best
Bitter; guest beer** Ⓗ
This splendid, 15th-century
pub is the only one owned by
Crouch Vale and has the full
range of their beers, as well as a
guest and a cider. Enjoy lively
folk eves or quiet fireside
conversation with the
welcoming locals.
🏚 Q ☺ 🛏 ✿ ◖ ▶ ♣ ⌂ P

Toot Hill

Green Man
☎ (01992) 522255
11–3, 6–11; 12–3, 7–10.30 Sun
**Crouch Vale Best Bitter; guest
beers** Ⓗ
Early 19th-century inn serving
popular, home-cooked food in
its new-style restaurant.
Charming floral courtyard in
summer. Two guest beers from
small independents.
🏚 Q ✿ ◖ ▶ ♣ P

Walton-on-the-Naze

Royal Marine
3 Old Pier Street (near B1034)
☎ (01255) 674000
10 (11 winter)–11; 12–10.30 Sun
**Adnams Bitter; Marston's
Pedigree** Ⓗ

Walton's long-established
classic pub: a haunt of folk
singers and sailors.
🏚 ▶ ▲ 🚌 ♣

Warley

Brave Nelson
138 Woodman Road (off B186)
☎ (01277) 211690
12–3, 5.30–11; 12–11 Sat; 12–4, 7–10.30
(12–10.30 summer) Sun
**Nethergate Bitter; Ruddles
Best Bitter; Webster's
Yorkshire Bitter; guest beer** Ⓗ
Comfortable, friendly local
with a nautical theme, a rare
local outlet for Nethergate
beer. The safe garden for
children hosts summer
barbecues and petanque
games. No food Sun.
✿ ◖ 🏠 ♣ P

Wendens Ambo

Bell
Royston Road (B1039)
☎ (01799) 540382
11.30–2.30, 6–11 (may vary summer);
12–3, 7–10.30 Sun
**Adnams Bitter; Ansells Mild;
guest beers** Ⓗ
Welcoming, cosy traditional
pub, a focal point for many
village events. Children
welcome in the restaurant and
extensive gardens. No food
Mon eve. Petanque played. 🏚
✿ ◖ ▶ 🚌 (Audley End) ♣ P

Westcliff-on-Sea

Cricketers Inn
228 London Road (A13/Milton
Rd jct)
☎ (01702) 343168
11.30–11; 12–10.30 Sun
**Greene King IPA, Abbot;
guest beers** Ⓗ
Thriving, main road, drinkers'
pub: a Gray's house with a
wide range of guest beers
available to the licensee.
◖ ▶ 🏠 ♣ ⌂ P

Palace Theatre Bar
430 London Road (A13)
☎ (01702) 347816
12–2.30, 6–11; 7–10.30 (closed lunch)
Sun
**Courage Directors; Greene
King IPA; guest beers** Ⓗ
Theatre foyer bar hosting live
music Sun eve. Eve meals
available on show nights.
✿ ◖ ♿ 🚌

Wickham Bishops

Mitre
2 The Street OS846123
☎ (01621) 891378
11.30–3.30, 5.30–11; 12–10.30 Sun
**Ridleys IPA, Rumpus,
seasonal beers** Ⓗ
Lively village local staging
regular social events. Busy
restaurant. 🏚 Q ✿ ◖ ▶ 🏠 P

Widdington

Fleur de Lys
High Street (1 mile E of B1383)
☎ (01799) 540659
12–3, 6–11; 12–4, 7–10.30 Sun
**Adnams Bitter, Broadside;
Draught Bass; Ridleys IPA;
guest beers** Ⓗ
Friendly village local with a
good choice of ales and meals
(Tue–Sun). Live music Fri eve.
🏚 Q ☺ 🛏 ◖ ▶ ♣ P

Wivenhoe

Horse & Groom
55 The Cross (B1028)
☎ (01206) 824928
10.30–3, 5.30 (6 Sat)–11; 12–3.30,
7–10.30 Sun
**Adnams Mild, Bitter, Old;
guest beers** Ⓗ
Adnams house just outside a
pretty fishing village. Good
value, home-cooked food
Mon–Sat.
Q ✿ ◖ 🏠 🚌 ♣ P

Woodham Ferrers

Bell
Main Road (B1418, 1 mile N of
B1012 jct)
☎ (01245) 320443
11–3, 6–11; 12–3, 7–10.30 Sun
**Adnams Bitter; Ridleys IPA;
guest beers** Ⓗ
Mostly dating from 1885, this is
quite a large village pub,
attracting all ages. The patio,
with pond and waterwheel,
provides a hilltop view of SE
Essex. ✿ ◖ ▶ ♣ P

Wormingford

Crown
Colchester Road (B1508 to
Sudbury)
☎ (01787) 227405
11.30–3, 6–11; 12–3, 7–10.30 Sun
Greene King IPA Ⓗ**, Abbot;
Marston's Pedigree** Ⓖ
Pub with a comfortable lounge
bar with attractive oak
panelling, contrasting with a
basic public bar, popular with
walkers.
Q ✿ 🛏 ◖ ▶ 🏠 ♿ P

Writtle

Wheatsheaf
70 The Green (near A1060)
☎ (01245) 420695
11–2.30 (3 Fri), 5.30–11; 11–11 Sat;
12–10.30 Sun
**Greene King IPA, Abbot;
guest beers** Ⓗ
Traditional, cosy, two-bar
village pub, popular with
locals, bell ringers and morris
dancers. Q ✿ 🏠 ♣ P

**Try also: Inn on the Green,
The Green (Free)**

Gloucestershire & Bristol

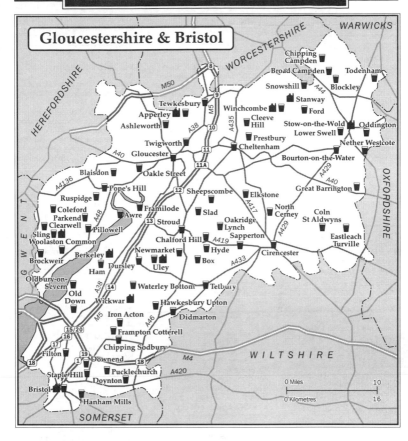

Gloucestershire & Bristol

Apperley

Coal House Inn
Gabb Lane (off B4213)
OS854283 ☎ (01452) 780211
11–2.30 (3 Sat), 6 (7 winter)–11; 12–3,
7–10.30 Sun
**Wadworth 6X; Wickwar
Coopers' WPA; guest beers** H
Originally a coal wharf, now a
welcoming, recently
refurbished pub on the banks
of the River Severn, half a mile
from the village centre.
Moorings provided.
🏠 Q 👥 ❀ ◑ ▸ ▲ ♣ P ⌇

Ashleworth

Boat Inn
The Quay OS819251
☎ (01452) 700272
11–2.30, 6 (7 winter)–11; 12–3, 7–10.30
Sun
**Arkell's 3B; Brandy Cask
Whistling Joe; Oakhill
Yeoman; Smiles Best** G
Delightful old pub beside the
Severn, a miracle of survival
owned by the same family for
over 400 years; the interior has
hardly changed in a century.

SW CAMRA region *Pub of the
Year* 1996. Lunchtime snacks.
Moorings available.
Q ❀ ♣ ⌂ P

Try also: Queen's Arms (Free)

Awre

Red Hart
Signed off A48, S of Newnham
OS709080 ☎ (01594) 510220
12–2.30, 7–11; 12–2.30, 7–10.30 Sun;
closed Mon
Beer range varies H
Off the beaten track, this cosy
pub has a well in the bar. Pride
taken in the food; families
welcome. Worth finding. No
food Sun eve. ❀ ◑ ▸ ♿ ♣ P

Blaisdon

Red Hart
2 miles off A48/A40
☎ (01452) 830477
12–3, 6–11; 12–3, 7–10.30 Sun
**Hook Norton Best Bitter;
Tetley Bitter; Theakston Best
Bitter; guest beers** H
Attractive, stone-flagged,
one-bar pub at the heart of the
village, with an adventurous
guest beer policy. Children's
certificate; large outdoor area.
Good, home-cooked food.
Twice CAMRA
Gloucestershire *Pub of the Year*.
🏠 ❀ ◑ ▸ ♣ ⌂ P

🍺 INDEPENDENT BREWERIES

Berkeley: Berkeley

Donnington:
Stow-on-the-Wold

Farmers Arms: Apperley

Freeminer: Sling

Goff's: Winchcombe

Ross: Bristol

Smiles: Bristol

Stanway: Stanway

Uley: Uley

Wickwar: Wickwar

Blockley

Crown

High Street (off B4479)
☎ (01386) 700245
11–11 (11–3, 6.30–11 winter); 12–10.30
Sun
**Goff's Jouster; Hook Norton
Best Bitter; guest beers** Ⓗ
Elizabethan hostelry in a large,
quaint and quiet, Cotswold
village, popular with locals
and tourists. Sample the
regularly changing guest beers
in very comfortable
surroundings. A pub which is
well worth a visit.
🚲 Q ✿ 🛏 ◖ ▷ P

**Try also: Great Western,
Station Rd (Hook Norton)**

Bourton-on-the-Water

Old Manse Hotel

Victoria Street
☎ (01451) 820082
10–11; 12–10.30 Sun
**Courage Directors; Goff's
Jouster; Morland Old
Speckled Hen; Ruddles
County** Ⓗ
Built in 1748 and since
extended and modernised into
an hotel and restaurant. The
Cotswold stone public bar has
a good atmosphere and is very
popular with locals and
tourists. The garden is situated
by the River Windrush.
🚲 ✿ 🛏 ◖ ▷ ♿ ♣ ↻ P

Box

Halfway House

☎ (01453) 832631
11.30–3, 6 (5.30 Fri & Sat)–11; 12–3,
7–10.30 Sun
**Adnams Bitter; Marston's
Bitter, Pedigree; Taylor
Landlord; guest beer** Ⓗ
Friendly, relaxing pub on the
edge of a common, between
Minchinhampton and
Nailsworth: a centre of activity
for the local community
offering an enterprising range
of guest beers. Skittle alley and
a function room available.
✿ ◖ ▷ ♿ ♣ P ✂

Bristol

Albert

1 West Street, Bedminster
☎ (0117) 966 1968
12–2.30, 7.30–11; 12–3, 7–10.30 Sun
**Courage Best Bitter; Smiles
Best; guest beers** Ⓗ
Popular, two-bar pub. The
main bar is papered with
record sleeves and
photographs; regular live
jazz and folk music.
◖ 🍴

Annexe Inn

Seymour Road, Bishopston
☎ (0117) 949 3931
11.30–2.30, 6–11; 11.30–11 Sat; 12–
10.30 Sun
**Courage Georges BA, Best
Bitter; Marston's Pedigree;
Smiles Best; Theakston Best
Bitter; Wadworth 6X; guest
beer** Ⓗ
Very pleasant, low-level pub in
the shadow of another larger
one, about 200 yards from the
county cricket ground. A no-
smoking conservatory doubles
as the family room. A new
restaurant is planned for eve
meals. 🐕 ✿ ◖ ▷ ♣ ✂ 🍴

Bell

21 Alfred Place, Kingsdown
☎ (0117) 907 7563
5.30 (12 Sat)–11; 12–4, 7–10.30 Sun
**Wickwar BOB, Olde
Merryford** Ⓗ
Compact, comfortable, wood-
panelled local. Candles on
tables add to the cosy
atmosphere at night. Do not be
fooled by Ushers signs on the
exterior.

Bridge

16 Passage Street
☎ (0117) 949 9967
11.30–11; 12–2.30, 8–10.30 Sun
**Bath Gem, Barnstormer;
Courage Best Bitter** Ⓗ
Very small pub, between
Temple Meads station and
Broadmead. Very close to the
Courage Brewery, it claims to
be Bristol's smallest public
house. Satellite TV.
Q ◖ ⇌ (T Meads)

Cadbury House

68 Richmond Road, Montpelier
☎ (0117) 924 7874
12–11; 12–10.30 Sun
**Courage Best Bitter; Wickwar
BOB, Olde Merryford,
seasonal beers** Ⓗ
Busy, cosmopolitan pub. The
pleasant garden is popular in
summer. Original Space
Invaders is played here, and
old one-armed bandits are
features. Meals served
12–7pm.
🚲 ✿ ◖ ⇌ (Montpelier) ♣ ↻

Commercial Rooms

43–45 Corn Street
☎ (0117) 927 9681
11–11; 12–10.30 Sun
**Butcombe Bitter, Wilmot's;
Courage Directors; Theakston
Best Bitter; Younger Scotch;
guest beers** Ⓗ
Superb Wetherspoons
conversion of a former
gentlemen's club in the
banking area. National
CAMRA/English Heritage
award-winner in 1996 for
refurbishment. A high bar
counter, a no-smoking room
and gas lights feature.

Wheelchair access (via a side
door) is awkward when busy.
Q ◖ ▷ ♿ ↻ ✂

Cornubia

142 Temple Street
☎ (0117) 925 4415
11.30–8.30 (11 Fri); closed Sat & Sun
**Courage Best Bitter; Wickwar
BOB; guest beers** Ⓗ
This former Courage
hospitality pub was reopened
to the public in 1996. Tucked
away in a small street near the
brewery, it always has two
other beers from small local
brewers. Opening hours vary –
check. Eve meals Mon–Thu.
Q ◖ ▷ ⇌ (T Meads) P

Hare on the Hill

41 Thomas Street North
☎ (0117) 908 1982
12.30–2.30, 5–11; 12–11 Fri & Sat;
12–10.30 Sun
**Bath SPA, Gem, Barnstormer;
guest beer** Ⓗ
Bath Ales's first pub, formerly
known as the Masons Arms.
Friendly and welcoming, it is
located up a steep hill close to
Stokes Croft. Meals may soon
be available. ♣

Highbury Vaults

164 St Michaels Hill,
Kingsdown
☎ (0117) 973 3203
12–11; 12–10.30 Sun
**Brains SA; Smiles Golden
Brew, Best, Heritage, seasonal
beers; guest beers** Ⓗ
Renowned, two-bar,
traditional pub with a large,
attractive, heated, semi-
covered patio garden at the
rear. Its timber-panelled
interior has low-level lighting
and no jukebox. Popular with
students. Good food (eve meals
Mon–Fri till 8.30).
✿ ◖ ▷ ♣

Hope & Anchor

38 Jacobs Wells Road, Hotwells
☎ (0117) 929 2987
12–11; 12–10.30 Sun
Beer range varies Ⓗ
Popular, genuine free house,
with four regularly changing
ales. The secluded rear garden
gets busy in summer.
Interesting range of bar meals,
plus barbecues in summer.
✿ ◖ ▷

Kellaway Arms

140 Kellaway Avenue, Horfield
☎ (0117) 949 7548
11–2.30, 6–11; 11–11 Sat; 12–3, 7–10.30
Sun
**Courage Georges BA, Best
Bitter; Marston's Pedigree;
Smiles Best** Ⓗ
Friendly, two-bar local near
Horfield Common: a large
lounge and a smaller public
bar, plus a sizeable garden.
No food Sun.
Q ✿ ◖ 🍴 ♣

Lamb

69 West Street, Bedminster
11–4, 5.30 (7 Sat)–11; 12–3, 7–10.30 Sun

Butcombe Bitter G; **Courage Best Bitter; Ruddles County** H
Friendly local boasting a collection of china plates. Darts and crossword aficionados number among the regulars. Limited parking. ❀ ♣ P

Mechanics Arms

123 Cloudshill Road, St George
☎ (0117) 955 6915
4 (12 Sat)–11; 12–10.30 Sun

Butcombe Bitter, Wilmot's; Courage Georges BA H
Popular local converted from three rooms into one. Note the circular window incorporating a rose design behind the bar. Regular live music. It can get smoky. ❀ ♣

Post Office Tavern

17 Westbury Hill, Westbury-on-Trym ☎ (0117) 940 1233
11–11; 12–3, 7–10.30 Sun

Draught Bass G; **Fuller's London Pride; Otter Bitter; Shepherd Neame Spitfire; Smiles Golden Brew, Best** H; **guest beers** G/H
Busy pub with a post office theme. A large menu includes home-made pizzas. Wickwar BOB is sold as Pot Bitter, one of ten beers normally on.
Q ◖ ▶ ✄

Prince of Wales

84 Stoke Lane, Westbury-on-Trym ☎ (0117) 962 3715
11–3, 5.30–11; 11–11 Sat; 12–3.30, 7–10.30 Sun

Bath SPA; Courage Best Bitter; Smiles Best; Theakston XB H
Friendly pub in a residential area, displaying decorative mirrors and sporting cartoons. French boules is played in summer in the large garden. Boys Bitter is Courage Georges BA; the beer range may vary; good wine list. No-smoking area lunchtime. ❀ ◖ ♣ ✄

Quinton House

2 Park Place, Clifton
☎ (0117) 907 7858
11.30–3, 5.30–11; 11.30–11 Fri & Sat; 12–10.30 Sun

Courage Best Bitter; Ushers Best Bitter, Founders, seasonal beers H
Traditional, single-room pub off Queens Road, with wooden panelling and floors. Bar meals include daily specials (no food Sun). ◖

Railway Tavern

Station Road, Fishponds
☎ (0117) 965 8774
12–11; 12–3.30, 6–11 Mon; 12–10.30 Sun

Ind Coope Burton Ale; Smiles Best; Tetley Bitter; guest beer H

Popular, large, one-bar, friendly local with a skittle alley. Handy for the Bristol-Bath cycle track. Guest beers come from the Tapster's Choice range; sparklers removed on request.
❀ ◖ ♣

Reckless Engineer

Temple Gate (opp. station)
☎ (0117) 929 0425
12–11; 12–3, 7.30–11 Sat; 12–10.30 Sun

Tetley Bitter; guest beers H
Formerly the Isambard, transformed in 1996 into a bare-floorboarded alehouse specialising in local and stronger ales. Live rock bands every Sat and some Fri (show CAMRA card for free entry). Over 100 guest beers in 1996.
◖ ▶ ≩ (T Meads) ✄

Seven Ways

22 New Street, St Judes
☎ (0117) 955 6862
11.30–3, 6.30–11; 12–3, 7–10.30 Sun

Courage Best Bitter; Ushers Best Bitter, seasonal beers H, **seasonal beers** H/G
Friendly, two-bar local in the old market drinking area. Busy lunchtimes; quiet eves. No food Sat; Sun lunches must be booked. Stonehouse cider available. Q ◖ ⚏ ♣ ⌣

Victoria

20 Chock Lane, Westbury-on-Trym ☎ (0117) 950 0441
12–3, 5.30–11; 12–4, 7–10.30 Sun

Adnams Broadside; Badger Tanglefoot; Draught Bass; Wadworth IPA, 6X H, **seasonal beers** G/H
Built in the 1700s and once used as a court house, this comfortably furnished pub is out of the way, down a quiet lane. Boules played. Only pizzas served eves and weekends. ❀ ◖ ♣

Try also: Bag O'Nails, St Georges Rd, Hotwells (Free); **King's Head**, Victoria St (Scottish Courage)

Broad Campden

Bakers Arms

Off B4081 ☎ (01386) 840515
11.30–2.30, 6–11; 12–3, 7–10.30 Sun

Marston's Pedigree; guest beers H
Stone-built village local with oak beams and an open fire, plus an adventurous guest beer policy. ⚏ Q ❀ ◖ ♣ ⌣ P

Brockweir

Brockweir Country Inn

Off A466, over bridge
☎ (01291) 689548
12–2.30, 6–11; 12–11 Sat; 12–3, 7–10.30 Sun

Freeminer Bitter; Hook Norton Best Bitter; guest beers H
Unspoilt village pub near the banks of the Wye. Its beams come from a ship built in Brockweir many years ago. Popular with walkers; Tintern Abbey and Offa's Dyke are nearby. Good B&B and food. Cider in summer.
⚏ ❀ ⇌ ◖ ▶ ⚏ ▲ ♣ ⌣ P

Chalford Hill

Old Neighbourhood Inn

Midway (up Neighbourhood Hill from A419)
☎ (01453) 883385
11–3, 6–11; 12–3, 7–10.30 Sun

Archers Village; Draught Bass; Webster's Green Label; guest beers H
Two main bars, a games room and a restaurant in an attractive, welcoming pub.
⚏ ❀ ◖ ▶ ♣ P

Cheltenham

Adam & Eve

8 Townsend Street
☎ (01242) 690030
10.30–3, 5–11; 10.30–11 Sat; 12–3, 6–10.30 Sun

Arkell's Bitter, 3B, Kingsdown, seasonal beers H
Friendly, nicely redecorated, two-bar pub near the Tesco superstore, 15 mins' walk from the centre. A cheerful welcome makes this pub a pleasure to drink in. Lunchtime snacks.
Q ❀ ⚏ ⅙ ♣

Bayshill Inn

92 St George's Place (behind bus station) ☎ (01242) 524388
11–3, 5–11; 11–11 Sat; 12–3, 7–10.30 Sun

Badger Tanglefoot; Wadworth IPA, 6X, Old Timer; guest beer H
Deservedly popular, town-centre pub without frills. Good value lunches (not served Sun).
Q ❀ ◖ ♣ ⌣

Hewlett Arms

Harp Hill ☎ (01242) 228600
11–3 (5 Sat), 4 (6 Sat)–11; 12–5, 7–10.30 Sun

Boddingtons Bitter; Gale's HSB; Goff's Jouster; guest beers H
Suburban, single-bar local, with good food inside and a pleasant garden outside.
❀ ◖ ▶ ♣ P

Kemble Brewery Inn

27 Fairview Street (off ring road in Fairview)
☎ (01242) 243446
11.30–2.30, 5.30–11; 11.30–11 Sat; 12–4, 7–10.30 Sun

Archers Village, Best Bitter, Golden; guest beer H

Comfortable, backstreet local
near the centre. Small, it can
get crowded, but is the only
Archers tied house in the area.
Good value food (popular for
its Sun lunches).
⌀ ◖ ♣

Suffolk Arms
Suffolk Road
☎ (01242) 524713
12–3, 6.30–11; 11–11 Sat & summer;
12–10.30 Sun
**Draught Bass; Boddingtons
Bitter; Brakspear Bitter; Goff's
Jouster; Wadworth 6X; guest
beer** ⊞
Single-bar local, formerly an
hotel. Situated near the Bath
Rd shops, it offers
straightforward, good value
food. The large skittle alley
also serves as a function room.
⌀ ◖ ♣

Tailor's
Cambray Place
☎ (01242) 255453
11–11; 12–2, 7–10.30 Sun
**Badger Tanglefoot; Draught
Bass; Wadworth IPA, 6X,
Farmers Glory, Old Timer;
guest beer** ⊞
Creeper-clad, two-level pub in
the centre. Sofas and armchairs
provide a comfortable setting
upstairs; the downstairs bar
(open Fri and Sat) is popular
with students. Eve meals Mon–
Thu. ⌀ ◖ ◗

Try also: **Exmouth Arms**, Bath
Rd (Arkell's)

Chipping Campden

Volunteer
Lower High Street
☎ (01386) 840688
11.30–3, 5–11; 12–3, 7–10.30 Sun
**Highgate Saddlers; Stanway
Stanney Bitter; Theakston XB;
guest beers** ⊞
Stone-built pub with a
courtyard and a pleasant
garden, located slightly out of
the village centre, to the west.
Ninety-six guest beers sold in
1996.
⌗ Q ⌀ ⛵ ◖ ◗ ⌔ ♣ ♠

Try also: **Eight Bells**, Church
St (Free)

Chipping Sodbury

Beaufort Hunt
72 Broad Street
☎ (01454) 312871
10.30–3, 5 (6.30 Sat)–11; 12–3, 7–10.30
Sun
**Draught Bass; Tetley Bitter;
guest beers** ⊞
Homely, two-bar, high street
local in a pleasant market
town. Ornately decorated, it
has an attractive outdoor
drinking area. Guest beers
change weekly. Q ⌀ ◖

Cirencester

Drillman's Arms
34 Gloucester Road, Stratton
(A417)
☎ (01285) 653892
11–3, 5.30–11; 11–11 Sat; 12–3.30,
7–10.30 Sun
**Archers Village, Best Bitter;
Boddingtons Bitter;
Wadworth 6X; guest beer** ⊞
Convivial Georgian inn
perched beside the main road.
A small, low-beamed lounge,
with a good log fire, leads to a
much enlarged rear bar and
skittle alley where families are
welcome. The house beer is
Archers Village; cider in
summer. A mini-beer festival is
staged over Aug Bank Hol.
⌗ ⛵ ⌀ ◖ ◗ ⌔ ♣ ⌣ P

Oddfellows' Arms
12–14 Chester Street (left at
traffic lights off A417
roundabout, 2nd right)
☎ (01285) 641540
11–3, 5.30–11; 12–3, 7–10.30 Sun
Beer range varies ⊞
Many make the effort to find
this haven for ale enthusiasts,
tucked away in a backstreet,
offering six guest beers and a
good range of home-cooked
food (not served Sun eve);
resist the puddings if you can!
Good family room extension at
the rear.
⌗ ⛵ ⌀ ◖ ◗ ⌔

Twelve Bells
12 Lewis Lane (straight on at
traffic lights off A417
roundabout)
☎ (01285) 644549
11–11; 12–10.30 Sun
**Archers Best Bitter; guest
beers** ⊞
Beer drinkers' haven, lovingly
resurrected by the owner/
landlord, with a genuine
atmosphere. The lively front
bar leads to quieter panelled
rooms at the rear. Five guest
beers (200 a year) include a
local session beer. A small
menu offers very reasonably
priced food.
⌗ Q ⛵ ⌀ ◖ ◗ ⌔ ♣ ⌣ P

Try also: **Corinium Court**,
Gloucester St (Free)

Clearwell

Lamb
The Cross, High Street
☎ (01594) 835441
6–11; 12–3, 6–11 Fri & Sat; 12–3,
7–10.30 Sun
**Freeminer Bitter; guest
beers** Ⓖ
Small, friendly, cosy bar with a
larger lounge; always at least
one guest beer. Well-behaved
children welcome.
⌗ Q ⌀ ♣ ⌣ P

Cleeve Hill

High Roost
On B4632 ☎ (01242) 672010
11.30–2.30 (3.30 Sat), 7–11; 12–4,
7–10.30 Sun
**Hook Norton Best Bitter, Old
Hooky; guest beers** ⊞
One-bar pub set on the highest
hill in the county, reached up a
flight of stone steps. Two large
bay windows give good views
of the Severn Valley. Children
allowed in until 8pm. Facilities
include a jukebox, dartboard
and bar skittles.
⌀ ⌂ ◖ ◗ ♣ P

Coleford

Angel
Market Place ☎ (01594) 833113
11–11; 12–10.30 Sun
Beer range varies ⊞
Comfortable, town-centre hotel
dating from around 1608. The
Malt & Hops Real Ale Bar
stocks five ales. Well-behaved
children welcome.
⌀ ⌂ ◖ ◗ ⌔ ♣ P

Coln St Aldwyns

New Inn
☎ (01285) 750651
11–2.30, 5.30–11; 11–11 Sat &
summer; 12–10.30 Sun
**Hook Norton Best Bitter;
Morland Original; Wadworth
6X** ⊞
Picturesque, 16th-century
coaching inn built around a
courtyard. Its pleasant, smart
rustic bars feature an open fire
and a stove. Award-winning
restaurant.
⌗ Q ⛵ ⌀ ⌂ ◖ ◗ ♣ P

Didmarton

Kings Arms
The Street ☎ (01454) 238245
11.30–3 (not Mon), 6–11; 12–3, 7–10.30
Sun
**John Smith's Bitter; Smiles
Best; Uley Hogshead; guest
beers** ⊞
17th-century former coaching
inn, recently renovated
throughout. It was leased in
1745 for 1000 years from the
Beaufort estate at six pence per
year! Meals Tue–Sat.
⌗ Q ⌀ ⌂ ◖ ◗ ⌔ ▲ ♣ P

Downend

White Swan
70 North Street
☎ (0117) 975 4154
11–11; 12–5, 7–10.30 Sun
Ushers Best Bitter ⊞**,
Founders** Ⓖ**, seasonal beers** ⊞
Friendly, 200-year-old local,
formerly a farmhouse; very
popular with cider drinkers
(four real ciders) and darts and

cribbage teams. Lunchtime snacks. Open-plan, it can get smoky, but retains separate drinking areas.
❀ ♣ ○

Doynton

Cross House
High Street ☎ (0117) 937 2261
11–3, 6–11; 12–3, 7–10.30 Sun
Draught Bass; Courage Best Bitter H
Busy village local, worth seeking out. ❀ ◖ ▶ ♣ P

Dursley

Old Spot Inn
Hill Road ☎ (01453) 542870
11–3, 5–11; 11–11 Fri & Sat; 12–10.30 Sun
Draught Bass; Bath SPA; Uley Old Ric, Old Spot; guest beer H
Excellent town pub that began life in the 18th century as a farm cottage. Recently refurbished and extended, it is popular with locals and Cotswold Way walkers. Folk/blues Wed; chess and boules played. Old Ric beer sausages and home-made pies are specialities. Public car park opposite. ♨ Q ❀ ◖ ♣ ✂

Eastleach Turville

Victoria
OS198052 ☎ (01367) 850277
11–3, 7 (6 summer)–11; 12–3, 7–10.30 Sun
Arkell's 3B, Kingsdown H
Comfortable, 16th-century pub, overlooking the village. Renowned for its springtime daffodil display.
♨ ❀ ◖ ▶ ⌖ ♣ P ⌷

Elkstone

Highwayman Inn
Beech Pike (A417)
☎ (01285) 821221
11–2.30, 6–11; 12–2.30, 7–10.30 Sun
Arkell's Bitter, 3B, Kingsdown H
Comfortable, 16th-century coaching inn on the Ermin Way, featuring a long bar with a roaring log fire at one end, plus a restaurant and a family room. Good selection of food.
♨ ⚏ ❀ ⛵ ◖ ▶ P

Filton

Ratepayers Arms
Filton Recreation Centre, Elm Park (at mini-roundabout turn off A38, left by police station)
☎ (0117) 908 2265
11.30–2 (2.30 Thu & Fri), 6.30 (4 winter Sat)–11; 12–3 (2 summer), 7–10.30 Sun
Butcombe Bitter; Ind Coope Burton Ale; Smiles Best; Tetley Bitter; guest beer H

Comfortable, well-laid-out bar in the recreation centre, open to the public, with a skittle alley, snooker room and occasional live music (Sun eve). The name stems from it being owned by the town council. Q ⌖ ⚏ (Filton Abbey Wood) ♣ P

Ford

Plough Inn
On B4077 OS088294
☎ (01386) 584215
11–11; 12–10.30 Sun
Donnington BB, SBA H
Splendid, unspoilt, country pub, where the cellar used to be a gaol. Note the rhyme on the front wall. No food Sun eve; open 9am for breakfast.
♨ ❀ ⛵ ◖ ▶ ⌖ ⚏ ♣ ○ P

Framilode

Ship Inn
By B4071 from A38 and M5 jct
13 OS751103 ☎ (01452) 740260
11–3, 7 (6 Fri & Sat)–11; 12–3, 7–10.30 Sun
Draught Bass; Bath Barnstormer; Tetley Bitter H
Superbly situated at the Severn entrance to the old Stroudwater Canal, this has been a pub since the canal's opening in 1779. Welcoming atmosphere and excellent menus in both bar and restaurant. Children's play area in the spacious grounds.
♨ ⛴ ❀ ⚏ ◖ ▶ 🅰 ♣ ○ P ✂

Frampton Cotterell

Rising Sun
43 Ryecroft Road
☎ (01454) 772330
11.30–3, 7–11; 12–3, 7–10.30 Sun
Draught Bass; Butcombe Bitter; Smiles Best; Wadworth 6X; Wickwar Coopers' WPA; guest beer H
Deservedly popular pub with a skittle alley and an upper-level dining area: a genuine free house which supports local brewers. Local CAMRA *Pub of the Year* 1995. Q ◖ ♣ P

Gloucester

Black Swan Inn
68–70 Southgate Street
☎ (01452) 523642
11–11; 12–2.30, 7–10.30 Sun
Donnington BB; guest beers H
Mid-19th-century, listed building in a conservation area, adjacent to Blackfriars. The two-roomed bar has neo-colonial decor and horse racing pictures. The only outlet for Donnington in Gloucester. Refurbished accommodation at a reasonable price.
Q ⚏ ◖ P

Prince of Wales
25 Station Road
☎ (01452) 524390
11.30–2.30 (3 Fri; 11–3 Sat), 6–11; 12–4, 7–10.30 Sun
Gale's HSB; Morland Old Speckled Hen H; **guest beers** H/G
Lively Victorian pub, near the rail and bus stations. Up to four guest beers; bargain food and accommodation.
❀ ⚏ ◖ ⚏ ♣ P

Regal
King's Square
☎ (01452) 332344
11–11; 12–10.30 Sun
Butcombe Bitter; Courage Directors; Theakston Best Bitter, XB; Younger Scotch; guest beers H
Wetherspoon superpub in a former cinema where major architectural features have been retained: the screen has been replaced by a wall of glass. No music or machines; food all day; beer at bargain prices. Q ❀ ◖ ▶ ⚏ ⌖ ○ ✂

Whitesmiths Arms
81 Southgate Street (opp. main entrance to Historic Docks)
☎ (01452) 414770
11–11; 12–3, 7–10.30 Sun
Arkell's Bitter, 3B, Kingsdown, seasonal beers H
Named after maritime metal-workers, this fine pub has been sensitively extended to incorporate the medieval building next door.
♨ ❀ ◖ ▶ ⌖ ♣

Try also: Windmill, Eastgate St (Free)

Great Barrington

Fox Inn
1 mile N of A40
☎ (01451) 844385
11–11; 12–3, 7–10.30 (12–10.30 summer) Sun
Donnington XXX (summer), **BB, SBA** H
Excellent, stone-built pub with flagstone floors and lots of atmosphere, in a beautiful location by the River Windrush (riverside barbecues in summer). Popular with walkers and locals. No eve meals winter Mons.
♨ Q ⛴ ❀ ⚏ ◖ ▶ ♣ P

Ham

Salutation
OS680983 ☎ (01453) 810284
11 (10 Sat)–2.30, 6–11; 12–3, 7–10.30 Sun
Draught Bass; Berkeley Old Friend, Dicky Pearce H
Smart, welcoming, two-bar country pub, just south of Berkeley Castle, boasting a large, attractive garden and a children's play area. The new

skittle alley provides a venue for functions.
Q ❀ ◑ ◗ ⊟ ♿ ♣ ⌓ P

Hanham Mills

Old Lock & Weir
From Hanham, go to foot of Abbots Rd, turn right
☎ (0117) 967 3793
11–11; 12–10.30 Sun
Draught Bass; Exmoor Gold; Marston's Pedigree; guest beer H
300-year-old, welcoming, single-bar, multi-roomed riverside pub, mentioned in Conan Doyle's *Micah Clark*. Much stone and wood in evidence; friendly staff; families welcome. Book for the excellent Sun lunches. Local CAMRA *Pub of the Year* 1996.
❀ ◑ ◗ ♣ P

Hawkesbury Upton

Beaufort Arms
High Street (500 yds from A46)
☎ (01454) 238217
12–3, 5.30–11; 12–11 Sat; 12–10.30 Sun
Wickwar BOB; guest beers H
18th-century, two-bar free house with Victorian modifications and a stable converted to a dining area (good quality food); close to the Cotswold Way. Families, walkers, and cyclists are all welcomed.
⛼ Q ❀ ◑ ◗ ⊟ ▲ ♣ ⌓ P

Hyde

Ragged Cot
OS887012
☎ (01453) 884643
11–2.30 (3 Sat), 6–11; 12–3, 7–10.30 Sun
Draught Bass; Theakston Best Bitter; Uley Old Spot; Wadworth 6X H
Busy, comfortable 16th-century free house in open countryside near Minchinhampton Common and Gatcombe Park. It stocks 36 malt whiskies. Booking advisable for meals.
⛼ Q ❀ ⛟ ◑ ◗ ▲ ♣ ⌓ P

Iron Acton

Rose & Crown
High Street
☎ (01454) 228423
5–11; 12–2.30, 6–11 Sat; 12–3, 7–10.30 Sun
Draught Bass; Flowers IPA; Marston's Pedigree; Wickwar Olde Merryford; Uley Pig's Ear H
Very friendly pub with two distinct bars, in an attractive village near Yate. The building dates from 1680.
⛼ Q ❀ ⛟ ♣

Lower Swell

Golden Ball
Main Road ☎ (01451) 830247
11–3, 6–11 (may close earlier winter); 12–3, 7–10.30 Sun
Donnington BB, SBA H
Friendly, unspoilt, 17th-century Cotswold village pub, popular with tourists and locals, serving good food (not Wed or Sun eves in winter). Aunt Sally in the garden.
⛼ ❀ ⛟ ◑ ◗ ♣ ⌓ P

Nether Westcote

New Inn
Off A424 OS225205
☎ (01993) 830827
11.30–2.30, 7 (6 Fri & Sat)–11; 12–3, 7–10.30 Sun
Morrells Bitter, Mild, Varsity, Graduate H
Delightful Cotswold stone pub on the north side of a secluded village; the only Morrells pub in Gloucestershire. Enjoy the welcoming, relaxed atmosphere and the excellent, varied food menu. Outstanding value.
⛼ Q ❀ ◑ ◗ ▲ ♣ P

Newmarket

George
OS839997 ☎ (01453) 833228
11–3, 6–11; 11–11 Fri; 12–3, 7–10.30 Sun
Draught Bass; Brains Bitter; Uley Old Spot H
Pleasant, stone-built pub looking southwards over the valley above Nailsworth. Traditional food is cooked by an award-winning chef (booking advised). Limited parking. Q ❀ ◑ ◗ ▲ P

North Cerney

Bathurst Arms
On A435 ☎ (01285) 831281
11–3, 6–11; 12–3, 7–10.30 Sun
Arkell's 3B; Hook Norton Best Bitter; Wadworth 6X; guest beer H
Attractive, 17th-century village pub with flagstone floors, settles and a stove in an inglenook. Everything you would expect from a Cotswold pub – even the tiny River Churn runs through the garden. Excellent food and good accommodation.
⛼ Q ❀ ⛟ ◑ ◗ ⊟ ♿ ▲ ♣ P

Oakle Street

Silent Whistle
Off A48, 5 miles from Gloucester ☎ (01452) 750294
11.30–2.30, 7–11; 12–4, 7–10.30 Sun
Draught Bass; Hook Norton Best Bitter H
Former railway hotel, renamed in memory of a lost station. Good value food. Well-behaved children welcome (play area in the adjacent field).
⛼ ❀ ◑ ◗ ▲ ♣ P

Oakridge Lynch

Butchers' Arms
Follow Oakridge signs from Bisley OS915038
☎ (01285) 760371
11–3, 6–11; 12–3, 7–10.30 Sun
Archers Best Bitter; Goff's Jouster; Hook Norton Best Bitter; Tetley Bitter; Theakston Best Bitter H
Stone-built, former butcher's shop, now a popular three-bar local. The restaurant is used as a skittle alley Mon and Tue, but food is still available in the bars. ⛼ Q ♘ ❀ ◑ ◗ ♿ ♣ P

Oddington

Horse & Groom
Upper Oddington (off A436)
☎ (01451) 830584
11.30–2.30, 6–11; 12–2.30, 7–10.30 Sun
Fuller's London Pride; Hook Norton Best Bitter, seasonal beers H
Small, 16th-century free house surrounded by narrow country lanes, unspoilt countryside, honey-coloured stonework and a meandering river. Inside a large inglenook, old beams and tasteful furnishings feature. The restaurant has an excellent, extensive menu.
⛼ Q ❀ ⛟ ◑ ◗ ⊟ ♣ ⌓ P

Oldbury-on-Severn

Anchor Inn
Church Road
☎ (01454) 413331
11.30–2.30 (3 Sat), 6.30 (6 Sat)–11; 12–3, 7–10.30 Sun
Draught Bass G**; Black Sheep Best Bitter; Butcombe Bitter; Theakston Best Bitter** H**, Old Peculier** G**; Worthington Bitter** H
Popular, welcoming village pub in converted mill buildings with traditional decor, a dining area offering an inventive menu, and a garden with benches and boules pitches. Wheelchair WC.
⛼ Q ❀ ◑ ◗ ⊟ ♿ ♣ P

Old Down

Fox Inn
The Inner Down
☎ (01454) 412507
12–3, 7–11; 12–11 Sat; 12–5, 7–10.30 Sun
Draught Bass; Mole's Best Bitter; guest beer H
Cosy, stone village pub with an L-shaped bar. The picturesque terrace/garden has children's play equipment and a boules

pitch. Bar snacks available. The house beer is John Smith's.
🏰 Q 🌟 ○ P

Parkend

Fountain
Off B4234
☎ (01594) 562189
12–3, 6–11; 12–11 Sat; 12–3, 7–10.30 Sun
Freeminer Bitter; guest beers H
One-bar pub at the heart of the Forest of Dean and near its railway. Old tools and implements hang from beams. The home-cooked food includes vegetarian and children's menus. A self-catering lodge is available for groups (booking advised).
🏰 Q 🌟 🚅 🌓 ♣ ○ P

Pillowell

Swan
400 yds E of B4234
☎ (01594) 562477
7–11; 12–3, 7–11 Sat; 12–3, 7–10.30 Sun
Thwaites Bitter; guest beers H
Comfortable and friendly local, on a sharp bend in the road, near a disused railway line. Sandwiches available. No children allowed.
Q ♣ ○ P

Pope's Hill

Greyhound
On A4151, halfway between Elton and Littledean
☎ (01452) 760344
11–3, 5.30–11; 12–3, 7–10.30 Sun
Blackbeard Stairway to Heaven; Freeminer Speculation; guest beer H
Pub boasting beams, brasses and a roaring fire in winter. Note the montages made from clock and watch parts: some are for sale. Good value beers and food. The large garden has a play area.
🏰 🐕 🌟 🌓 ♣ ○ P

Prestbury

Royal Oak
The Burgage
☎ (01242) 522344
11.30–2.30, 5.30–11; 12–3.30, 7–10.30 Sun
Archers Best Bitter; Boddingtons Bitter; Wadworth 6X H
Attractive, 16th-century Cotswold stone pub with two bars, in apparently the most haunted village in England. It retains a traditional atmosphere despite its close proximity to Cheltenham. Meals Mon–Sat.
Q 🌟 🌓 ♣ P

Pucklechurch

Rose & Crown
68 Parkfield Road
☎ (0117) 937 2351
11.30–2.30, 5.30–11; 11–11 Sat; 12–3, 6.30–10.30 Sun
Adnams Broadside G; **Draught Bass; Wadworth IPA, 6X** H, **Old Timer** G
Large, attractive, two-bar local: a small public bar, a sprawling lounge with an unusual fireplace, plus a restaurant (no-smoking). Some beers are served direct from the cellar. The garden has a play area.
🏰 Q 🌟 🌓 🥨 ♣ P ✗

Ruspidge

New Inn
On B4227 ☎ (01594) 824508
7 (12 Sat)–11; 12–4, 7–10.30 Sun
Wye Valley Bitter; Ruddles Best Bitter; guest beer H
Comfortable, friendly village pub open eves only during the week. The games room offers an interesting selection, including table skittles.
🏰 🌟 ♣ P

Sapperton

Daneway Inn
Daneway (W of village)
OS939034 ☎ (01285) 760297
11–2.30 (5 Sat), 6.30–11; 12–5, 7–10.30 Sun
Wadworth IPA, 6X; guest beer H
Superb pub built in 1784 for canal workers near one end of the now disused Sapperton tunnel. The comfortable lounge is dominated by a magnificent Dutch carved fireplace. Large garden. Cider in summer.
🏰 Q 🐕 🌟 🌓 🥨 ♣ ○ P ✗ 🍺

Sheepscombe

Butchers Arms
OS892104 ☎ (01452) 812113
11–3.30, 6–11 (11.30–3, 6.30–11 winter); 11–11 Sat; 12–4, 7–10.30 Sun
Fuller's London Pride; Hook Norton Best Bitter; Uley Old Spot H
18th-century village inn with a restaurant area. A collection of memorabilia, including a wood-burning stove are features. Good range of food. In a picturesque village location, it is surrounded by good walking country.
🏰 Q 🌟 🌓 🥨 ○ P ✗

Slad

Woolpack
On B4070 ☎ (01452) 813429
12–3 (11–3.30 Sat), 6–11; 12–2.30, 7–10.30 Sun
Boddingtons Bitter; Fuller's London Pride; Uley Old Spot, Pig's Ear; Wadworth 6X H
Three-bar, 16th-century Cotswold pub on the edge of the scenic Slad Valley. A games room is on the lower level. Quoits and shove-ha'penny are played. Made famous by late author Laurie Lee.
🏰 Q 🐕 🌟 🌓 ♣ ○ P

Sling

Miners Arms
On B4228
☎ (01594) 836632
11–11; 12–3, 7–10.30 Sun
Freeminer Bitter, Speculation H
Basic, no-frills local, the Freeminer brewery tap, serving a good range of its beers (usually four). Hot pies available. Large area for camping (no caravans).
🏰 🌟 🥨 ♣ ○ P

Snowshill

Snowshill Arms
☎ (01386) 852653
11.30 (11 summer)–2.30, 6.30 (6 summer)–11; 12–2.30, 7–10.30 Sun
Donnington BB, SBA H
Typical Cotswold country pub, catering for both locals and tourists. The adjacent manor house (NT) should not be missed. The pub has a skittle alley, a large garden with a play area and some superb views.
🏰 Q 🌟 🌓 🥨 ♣ ○ P 🍺

Staple Hill

Humpers Off-Licence
26 Soundwell Road
☎ (0117) 956 5525
12–2 (3 Sat & Sun), 5–10.30 (12–10.30 summer Sat & Sun)
Ash Vine Hop & Glory; Draught Bass; Butcombe Bitter; Smiles Best; Wickwar BOB H; **guest beers** G
Undoubtedly Bristol's premier off-licence for real ale, with five regular and up to three guest beers from far and wide, often strong brews. All beers are well below pub prices. Large range of polypins at Christmas. Thatcher's cider is sold plus many bottled beers.
○

Stroud

Duke of York
22 Nelson Street
☎ (01453) 758715
12–3, 7–11; 11.30–4, 6–11 Fri; 11.30–11 Sat; 12–10.30 Sun
Draught Bass; Wells Eagle; guest beers H
Hospitable town pub by a public car park. No food Sun.
🌓 🍺 ♣

Tetbury

Crown Inn
Gumstool Hill
☎ (01666) 502469
11–3, 5.30–11; 12–10.30 Sun
Boddingtons Bitter; Flowers IPA, Original; guest beers H
Superb Cotswold stone pub: a comfortable lounge bar with a conservatory behind. Public car park adjacent.
🏾 ⊛ 🛏 🌒 ▶ ➘ ⊁

Tewkesbury

Old Black Bear
65 High Street
☎ (01684) 292202
11–11; 12–10.30 Sun
Greenalls Bitter H, **Original** E; **Wadworth 6X** H; **guest beers** G
The oldest inn in the county, featuring rambling bar areas with a pleasant terrace overlooking the River Avon (moorings available). No food Sun eve.
⊛ 🌒 ▶ ♠ ♣

White Bear
Bredon Road (off High St)
☎ (01684) 296614
11–11; 12–10.30 Sun
Wye Valley Bitter; guest beers H
One-bar, lively local serving changing guest ales. Tewkesbury Winter Ale Festival is held in the skittle alley in Feb.
⊛ ♠ ♣ ➘ P

Todenham

Farriers Arms
☎ (01608) 650901
12–3, 6.30–11; 12–3, 7–10.30 Sun
Hook Norton Best Bitter; Theakston Best Bitter, XB; guest beers H
Cosy, friendly, red brick pub on the main road through the village. Games include Aunt Sally in the car park. No food Sun eve.
🏾 Q 🐂 ⊛ 🛏 🌒 ▶ 🔥 ♠ ♣ P

Twigworth

Twigworth
Tewkesbury Road (A38)
☎ (01452) 730266
11.30–11; 12–10.30 Sun
Boddingtons Bitter; Greenalls Bitter; Tetley Bitter; guest beer H
The former Twigworth Hotel, enlarged by Greenalls to become a Premier Lodge (over 50 rooms) and pub. The spacious interior offers a pleasant ambience with its mock-Victorian decor. Excellent facilities for children; 'Miller's Kitchen' dining area.
🐂 ⊛ 🛏 🌒 ▶ 🔥 ♣ P ⊁

Uley

Old Crown
17 The Green (B4066)
☎ (01453) 860502
11.30–2.30, 7 (6 summer)–11; 12–3, 7–10.30 Sun
Boddingtons Bitter; Federation Buchanan's Best Bitter; Uley Bitter, Pig's Ear; guest beer H
Single-bar Cotswold village pub, built in 1638 as farm cottages. It has been improved internally recently and has a games room up a spiral staircase. Close to Uley Brewery and the Cotswold Way. En suite accommodation.
🐂 ⊛ 🛏 🌒 ▶ ♣ P

Waterley Bottom

New Inn
Signed from N Nibley OS758964
☎ (01453) 543659
12–2.30, 7–11 (12–11 summer Sat); 12–2.30, 7–10.30 (12–10.30 summer) Sun
Cotleigh Tawny; Greene King Abbot; Smiles Best H; **Theakston Old Peculier; guest beer** G
Free house with a setting and welcome that handsomely repay the navigational effort needed to find it. Limited

menu and accommodation. The house beer (WB) is a variation of Cotleigh Harrier. Cream teas are served at weekends, May–Sept.
🏾 ⊛ 🛏 🌒 ▶ 🔥 ♣ ➘ P

Winchcombe

Bell Inn
37 Gretton Road (½ mile from centre)
☎ (01242) 602205
11–11; 12–10.30 Sun
Brains Dark; Donnington BB, SBA; Eldridge Pope Royal Oak; Greene King Abbot; Shepherd Neame Spitfire H
Former Donnington pub, now a free house: a cosy local with active darts and cribbage teams. Bar snacks lunchtime.
🏾 Q ⊛ 🛏 ♣ ➘ P

Plaisterers Arms
Abbey Terrace (B4632)
☎ (01242) 602358
11–11 (11–3, 6–11 Mon–Thu in winter); 12–10.30 Sun
Goff's Jouster, White Knight; Tetley Bitter; Wadworth 6X H
Two-bar, multi-level pub in the centre of this ancient Saxon town. Piped music plays but there are quiet areas. The large garden at the rear has a patio and a children's play area. Good food.
🏾 Q ⊛ 🛏 🌒 ▶ 🔥 ♠ ♣

Woolaston Common

Rising Sun
1 mile off A48 OS590009
☎ (01594) 529282
12–2.30 (not Wed), 6.30–11; 12–3, 7–10.30 Sun
Crown Buckley Best Bitter; Theakston Best Bitter; guest beer (summer) H
Lovely country pub with excellent views and a friendly landlord. Wide range of good value, home-cooked food. Swings in the garden; children are allowed inside lunchtime and early eve.
Q ⊛ 🌒 ▶ 🔥 ♠ ♣ P

CALLING ALL SURFERS

Internet users will be pleased to discover CAMRA's home page. This includes details of the major developments in the brewing world and CAMRA's response to them, plus all the latest campaigning news. There's a full up to date listing of CAMRA's many beer festivals (including dates and venues) and the low down on CAMRA's other activities, plus a full catalogue of CAMRA books and products, and much more. Check it out now.

Address: http://www.camra.org.uk

HERITAGE PUB INTERIORS
CAMRA'S NATIONAL INVENTORY

THE 1997 EDITION of the *Good Beer Guide* broke new ground by introducing the special 'star' symbol for pubs with historically-outstanding interiors and made a feature of CAMRA's National Inventory, the Campaign's pioneering initiative to flag up and raise awareness of the very best of Britain's pub heritage.

Continuing threats to the nation's dwindling stock of genuine historic pubs, and the need for serious national stocktaking, were keynote themes at the launch of the 1997 *Guide* and attracted keen attention from national and local media. In subsequent feedback from readers of the *Guide* there has been a very positive welcome for this extra dimension to CAMRA's flagship publication and a very clear message that CAMRA's concern for the historic pub heritage is shared by a much wider public. So positive has been the reception that the heritage 'star' symbol appears again in this, the 1998 *Good Beer Guide*.

As for the National Inventory itself, this started life in 1991 as an emergency listing of the country's finest and rarest pub interiors – historic gems whose loss or despoliation ought (in an enlightened world) to provoke a national outcry. It accounts for perhaps the top ten per cent of all historically-important pub interiors in the UK and the pubs it includes are notable for their 'intactness' (of historic plan-form and fittings) or great rarity value. It is seen as a first step towards a structured statement of Britain's national pub preservation priorities (the next step being more comprehensive regional listings of other important pubs which may be less intact but badly need protection). It has been the subject of wide consultation with statutory and amenity bodies, with brewers, pub operators and the licensed trade, and it seems quite probable that this process of awareness-raising has been a factor in 'saving' at least three irreplaceable pub interiors from damaging alteration in the last two years alone. Pub owners are now likely to think twice before embarking on any changes to a pub's fabric. The selection of pubs to be included in the National Inventory is kept under regular review, as are the selection criteria themselves, and CAMRA sees it as an evolving concept, open to comment and refinement at any time.

NATI

ENGLAND

BEDFORDSHIRE
Broom: Cock

BERKSHIRE
Aldworth: Bell

CHESHIRE
Alpraham: Travellers
Gawsworth:
Harrington Arms
Macclesfield: Castle
Stockton Heath: Red
Wheelock: Com erc

CORNWA
Falmouth: S

■ *To obtain the full list of pubs that currently constitutes CAMRA's National Inventory, please send a large, stamped, self-addressed envelope to:*
Pubs Group, CAMRA, 230 Hatfield Road, St Albans, Hertfordshire AL1 4LW.

Hampshire

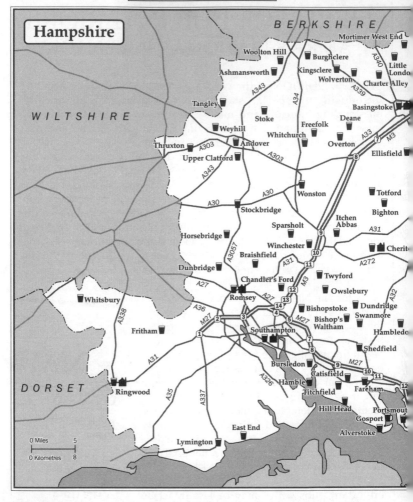

Hampshire

BERKSHIRE

WILTSHIRE

Mortimer West End
Woolton Hill
Burghclere
Ashmansworth
Kingsclere
Little Londo
Wolverton
Charter Alley
Tangley
Stoke
Deane
Basingstoke
Weyhill
Freefolk
Whitchurch
Thruxton
Andover
Overton
Ellisfield
Upper Clatford
Totford
Wonston
Bighton
Stockbridge
Itchen
Abbas
Sparsholt
Cherit
Horsebridge
Winchester
Braishfield
Dunbridge
Twyford
Chandler's Ford
Owslebury
Whitsbury
Romsey
Bishopstoke
Dundridge
Swanmore
Fritham
Southampton
Bishop's
Waltham
Hambledo
Shedfield
Bursledon
Catisfield
Ringwood
Hamble
Titchfield
Fareham
Hill Head
Portsmout
Gosport
East End
Alverstoke
Lymington

DORSET

0 Miles 5
0 Kilometres 8

Aldershot

Duke of York
248 Weybourne Road (B3007
Farnham road)
☎ (01252) 21150
11–11; 12–4, 7–10.30 Sun
**Courage Best Bitter, Directors;
guest beer** Ⓗ
Pub where an extensive menu
includes home-made curries
and children's choices.
Children are welcome in the
restaurant area. No food
served Sun eve.
Q ⛟ ✿ 🛏 ◑ ▶ ⬡ P

Garden Gate
4 Church Lane East
☎ (01252) 21051
11.30–3, 5.30–11 (11.30–11 summer);
12–4, 6–10.30 (12–10.30 summer) Sun
**Greene King XX Mild, IPA,
Abbot, seasonal beers** Ⓗ
An unusual U-shaped layout
keeps drinkers and dart

players apart in this smart,
one-bar pub. The small back
room is used for families,
meals or functions; regular live
blue grass music.
⛟ ✿ 🛏 ◑ ▶ ≉ ♣ P

Red Lion
Ash Road ☎ (01252) 403503
12–11; 12–3, 7–10.30 Sun
**Courage Best Bitter; guest
beers** Ⓗ
Imposing pub on the main
road; in the early 19th century
its cellars were used as
overnight cells for prisoners
from London courts bound for
Portsmouth. The single bar
retains three distinct drinking
areas. Weekday lunches.
🏚 ✿ ◑ ≉ P

Royal Staff
37A Mount Pleasant Road (off
High St) ☎ (01252) 22932
12–2 (3 Wed–Fri), 5.30 (5 Tue)–11;
12–11 Sat; 12–4, 7–10.30 Sun

**Fuller's Chiswick, London
Pride, ESB, seasonal beers** Ⓗ
Backstreet local refurbished in
the best Victorian style. A
strong community spirit
prevails in this one-bar pub,
with the emphasis on games in
one half. There is also a good
children's garden.
✿ ◑ ≉ ♣

Alton

Railway Hotel
Anstey Road
☎ (01420) 84208
11–2, 4.45–11; 12–3, 7–10.30 Sun
**Courage Best Bitter; Ushers
Best Bitter, seasonal beers** Ⓗ
Friendly boozer, the closest
pub to the station. Oversized
glasses are used for Ushers
beers. The jukebox is very
occasionally loud. Limited
parking available.
≉ P 🍺

118

Fuller's London Pride; Marston's Bitter; Taylor Landlord; guest beer H
Traditional, two-bar town pub with a welcome for all, especially for horse racing, cricket and real ale fans.

Lamb
21 Winchester Street
☎ (01264) 323961
11–3, 6 (5 Fri, 7 Sat)–11; 12–3, 7–10.30 Sun
Wadworth IPA, 6X, Old Timer H
Welcoming, three-roomed pub on the edge of the town centre. The lounge is particularly cosy and quiet (and the beer is cheaper). No food Sun.

Ashmansworth

Plough
Off A343 ☎ (01635) 253047
12–2.30 (3 Sat; not Mon or Tue); 6–11; 12–3, 7–10.30 Sun
Archers Village, Golden; guest beers G
Hampshire's highest pub (700 ft above sea level): completely unspoilt, with casks on stillage behind the bar. Friendly and popular.

Basingstoke

Bounty Inn
81 Bounty Road
☎ (01256) 320071
11–11; 12–10.30 Sun
Ushers Best Bitter, Founders, seasonal beers H
Two-bar local next to Mays Bounty cricket ground. The characterful, friendly public bar boasts a collection of sporting memorabilia, Sky TV and a hexagonal pool table. Tiny car park.

Queen's Arms
Bunnian Place
☎ (01256) 465488
11–3, 5–11; 11–11 Fri & Sat; 12–3, 7–10.30 Sun
Courage Best Bitter, Directors; John Smith's Bitter; Wadworth 6X; guest beer H
Often busy pub now dwarfed by office blocks, but retaining character. A welcoming stop for train travellers, office workers and locals alike.

Skewers
Lytton Road ☎ (01256) 464139
11–11; 12–10.30 Sun
Courage Best Bitter; Theakston XB (summer), Old Peculier (winter) H
Friendly, modern estate pub with a new extension used as a no-smoking, family and dining

room (no meals Sun eve). Spacious and very relaxing.

Soldiers Return
80 Upper Sherborne Road
☎ (01256) 322449
11–2.30, 5.30–11; 11–11 Fri & Sat; 12–5, 7–10.30 Sun
Courage Best Bitter; guest beers H
Turn-of-the-century, family local bordering Oakridge Estate, with a modernised interior, but a Grade I-listed exterior. A well-appointed, no-smoking children's room is off the public bar. Guest beers are from Hampshire Brewery.

Bentworth

Sun Inn
Sun Hill (off A339, midway between Basingstoke and Alton) ☎ (01420) 562338
12–3, 6–11; 12–3, 7–10.30 Sun
Cheriton Pots Ale; Courage Best Bitter; Marston's Pedigree; Ringwood Best Bitter; guest beers H
Picturesque inn dating from the 17th century in a small village, serving an extensive, home-cooked food menu (no food winter Sun eve). The house beer is by Hampshire Brewery.

Bighton

Three Horseshoes
Off A31/B3047 OS616344
☎ (01962) 732859
11–2.30, 6–11; 12–3, 7–10.30 Sun
Gale's Butser, Winter Brew, HSB H
Delightful, rural local, where the art of good conversation is still practised. A pub since 1615, it has a quiet, relaxing lounge, whilst the bar houses a country crafts collection. Handy for the Mid-Hants

Alverstoke

Alverbank
Stokes Bay Road
☎ (01705) 510005
11–11; 12–10.30 Sun
Ringwood Best Bitter; guest beers H
Originally a Victorian country house overlooking Stokes Bay, once frequented by Lillie Langtry. It normally has a quiet relaxing atmosphere during the week, but be prepared for wedding receptions and functions at weekends.

Andover

Blacksmith's Arms
134 New Street
☎ (01264) 352881
11.30–2.30 (not Tue), 5–11; 12–3, 7–10.30 Sun

⛪ INDEPENDENT BREWERIES
Beckett's: Basingstoke
Cheriton: Cheriton
Gale's: Horndean
Hampshire: Romsey
Hedgehog & Hogshead: Southampton
Itchen Valley: Alresford
Ringwood: Ringwood
Spikes: Portsmouth
Winfields: Portsmouth
Worldham: East Worldham

Railway (Ropley station two miles). No food Sun or Mon.
🏠 Q ⊛ ◖ ⊞ & ♣ P

Bishopstoke

Forester Arms

1 Stoke Common Road
☎ (01703) 620287
12–3, 7–11; 12–3, 7–10.30 Sun
Gibbs Mew Wiltshire, Salisbury, Wake Ale, Deacon (summer), Bishop's Tipple; guest beer Ⓗ
Friendly pub fielding numerous games teams. The public bar has a pool annexe; the lounge bar has a log fire. Reputedly haunted. Lunches by arrangement.
🏠 Q ⊛ 🛏 ◖ ⊞ ♣ ⌂ P 🍴

Bishop's Waltham

Bunch of Grapes

St Peter's Street
☎ (01489) 892935
10–2, 6–11; 12–2, 7–10.30 Sun
Courage Best Bitter; Ushers Best Bitter Ⓖ**, Founders, seasonal beers** Ⓗ
In a narrow street leading to the parish church, this small pub has been run by the same family since 1913. The bar and the back room, unaltered for many years, are rare.
Q ⊛ 👶

Braishfield

Newport Inn

Newport Lane
☎ (01794) 368225
10–2.30, 6–11; 12–2.30, 7–10.30 Sun
Gale's Butser, Best Bitter, Winter Brew, HSB Ⓗ
A gem in a time-warp – worth a detour. The doorstep sandwiches and ploughmans are famous throughout the county. Communal singing around the piano Sun eve (be ready to join in). Large, rambling garden.
🏠 Q ⊛ ◖ ♣ P

Burghclere

Carpenters Arms

Harts Lane (E of A34)
☎ (01635) 278251
11–3, 6–11; 12–5, 7–10.30 Sun
Arkell's Bitter, 3B, Kingsdown, seasonal beer Ⓗ
Large, one-bar pub with an attractive conservatory at the rear. The garden has extensive views to the south.
🏠 Q ⊛ ◖ ▶ & P

Queen

Harts Lane (1 mile E of A34)
☎ (01635) 278350
11–3, 6–11; 12–3, 7–10.30 Sun
Adnams Bitter, Broadside; Arkell's 3B Ⓗ
Spacious, one-bar, traditional village local, with a friendly

welcome and a pleasant atmosphere. Plenty of games; strong interest in horse racing. No food Sun. Q ⊛ ◖ ♣ P

Buriton

Five Bells

48 High Street
☎ (01730) 263584
11–2.30 (3 Fri & Sat), 5.30–11; 12–3, 7–10.30 Sun
Ballard's Best Bitter; Friary Meux BB; Greene King IPA; Ind Coope Burton Ale; Ringwood Best Bitter, Old Thumper Ⓗ
Very popular, traditional village pub with two beamed bars, each with imposing woodburning fires; well known for its good quality food. Live music Wed eve.
🏠 Q ⊛ 🛏 ◖ ▶ ⊞ & ♣ P

Bursledon

Jolly Sailor

Land's End Road, Old Bursledon ☎ (01703) 405557
11–11; 12–10.30 Sun
Badger IPA (summer), Dorset Best, Tanglefoot; Wadworth 6X Ⓗ
16th-century riverside pub of TV's *Howards' Way* fame, with a beamed ceiling, flagstone floor and a restaurant area offering an extensive menu. Access is difficult – the beer arrives via its own cliff railway! Moorings on the River Hamble. ⊛ ◖ ▶ 🛏 ⇌

Linden Tree

School Road (off A27 / A3025)
☎ (01703) 402356
11–2.30 (3 Sat), 6 (5 Fri)–11; 12–3, 7–10.30 Sun
Draught Bass; Wadworth IPA, 6X, Farmers Glory (summer), Old Timer Ⓗ
Excellent, comfortable, one-bar pub with no obtrusive gaming machines. A children's play area and pergola make it ideal for summer; a blazing log fire extends a warm welcome in winter. High quality, home-cooked lunches (not served Sun). 🏠 Q ⊛ ◖ ♣ P

Catisfield

Limes

34 Catisfield Lane
☎ (01329) 842629
12–2.30 (3 Sat), 5 (7 Sat)–11; 12–3, 7–10.30 Sun
Gale's HSB; Gibbs Mew Salisbury, Bishop's Tipple; Ringwood Fortyniner Ⓗ**, Old Thumper** Ⓖ
Large Victorian building converted to a pub with two bars and a function room, which hosts a number of clubs. The garden has a petanque terrain. Q ⊛ ◖ ▶ ⊞ ♣ P

Chalton

Red Lion

OS731160 ☎ (01705) 592246
11–3, 6–11; 12–3, 7–10.30 Sun
Gale's Butser, Best Bitter, IPA, HSB, seasonal beers; guest beers Ⓗ
Considered the oldest pub in Hampshire, this began life in 1147 as a workshop during the building of the local church, becoming a pub in 1503. On the South Downs, it is one of the most idyllic pubs in the South.
🏠 ⊛ ◖ ▶ ⊞ P

Chandler's Ford

Cleveland Bay

1 Pilgrim Close
☎ (01703) 269814
11–11; 12–10.30 Sun
Wadworth IPA, 6X, seasonal beers Ⓗ**; guest beers** Ⓔ
Newly built pub in the midst of a giant housing development. Guest beers are served by free-flow through imitation wooden casks. 🏠 ⊛ ◖ ▶ & P

Charter Alley

White Hart

White Hart Lane (1 mile W of A340) ☎ (01256) 850048
12–2.30 (3 Sat), 7–11; 12–3, 7–10.30 Sun
Greene King Abbot; Harveys BB, Morrells Mild; guest beers Ⓗ
Large village pub with a skittle alley in the main bar. It attracts a strong local following for its range of beers; local CAMRA *Pub of the Year* 1996. Cider in summer. No food Mon eve.
🏠 Q ⊛ ◖ ♣ ⌂ 🍴

Cheriton

Flower Pots

W of B3046 at S end of village
☎ (01962) 771318
12–2.30, 6–11; 12–3, 7–10.30 Sun
Cheriton Pots Ale, Best Bitter, Diggers Gold Ⓖ
Charming village local: intimate bars, recently seamlessly extended, and an attractive garden provide the ideal location for sampling the beers produced here. Good value food (no meals Sun eve).
🏠 Q ⊛ 🛏 ◖ ▶ ⊞ & ♣ ⌂ P

Cove

Plough & Horses

90 Fleet Road
☎ (01252) 545199
11–11; 12–10.30 Sun
Ansells Mild; Friary Meux BB; Ind Coope Burton Ale; Tetley Bitter; guest beer Ⓗ
Large, well-furnished 'Big Steak' pub with three main bar

areas, one mainly for food; friendly, welcoming and busy. Children welcome; large garden. ♿ ❀ ◖ ♣ P

Crookham Village

Black Horse
The Street ☎ (01252) 616434
11–3, 5–11; 12–3, 7–10.30 Sun
Courage Best Bitter; Hogs Back TEA; Marston's Pedigree; guest beer (occasional) H
Welcoming local offering a friendly atmosphere and good food in a charming, unspoilt, low-beamed building. Near good walks by the Basingstoke Canal. Q ❀ ◖ ♣

Deane

Deane Gate Inn
On B3400 ☎ (01256) 780226
11–3, 5–11; 12–3, 7–10.30 Sun
Courage Best Bitter; Ushers Best Bitter, Founders, seasonal beers H
17th-century pub with low beams in the older part.
♨ ❀ ⊨ ◖ ♣ ♿ ♠ P

Dunbridge

Mill Arms
Barley Hill (by station)
☎ (01794) 340401
11–3, 6–11; 12–3, 7–10.30 Sun
Beer range varies H
Rambling old building with many rooms, including a fine skittle alley. Up to four beers include a house beer from Poole Brewery.
♨ ♿ ❀ ◖ ♣ ♿ ♠ ♣ P ✄

Dundridge

Hampshire Bowman
Dundridge Lane (1½ miles off B3035) OS578185
☎ (01489) 892940
11–2.30 (3 Sat; 12–2 Mon), 6–11; 12–3, 7–10.30 (12–4, 6–10.30 summer) Sun
Archers Village, Golden; Ringwood Fortyniner; guest beers G
Excellent country pub along a winding single track country lane, with one traditional, brick-floored bar and a small serving counter. Camping on a Caravan Club site. No food Sun eve or Mon.
♨ Q ❀ ◖ ♠ ♣ ⊖ P

East End (Lymington)

East End Arms
Lymington Road (3 miles E of IOW ferry) OS362968
☎ (01590) 626223
11.30–2.30 (3 Sat), 6–11; 12–4, 7–10.30 Sun
Adnams Broadside G; **Ringwood Best Bitter** H

Fortyniner, Old Thumper; guest beers G
Popular country pub, rather remote but worth finding. A basic front public bar is used mainly by locals and a comfortable lounge more for dining; a varied menu includes game pies. The landlord won *Tapper of the Year* 95–96 for selling the most Ringwood beer. ♨ ❀ ◖ ⊨ ♠ ♣ P

Ellisfield

Fox
Green Lane (off A339, 3 miles E of Basingstoke)
☎ (01256) 381210
11.30–2.30 (3 Sat), 6.30–11; 12–3, 7–10.30 Sun
Badger Tanglefoot; Fuller's London Pride; Gale's HSB; Hampshire King Alfred's; Marston's Pedigree; Theakston Old Peculier; guest beer H
Neat country local set in a leafy lane 'twixt woods and farmland; beware of deer on the surrounding lanes. The menu features good fish and game dishes.
Q ❀ ◖ ⊨ ♣ P

Fareham

White Horse
North Wallington (½ mile from Delme roundabout)
☎ (01329) 235197
11–3, 5 (6 Sat)–11; 12–3, 7–10.30 Sun
Draught Bass G/H; **Hop Back Summer Lightning; M&B Brew XI; guest beers** G
Pub by the River Wallington and home of Wallington Cricket Club. Smart/casual dress required. No food Mon eve. Up to six guest beers.
♨ ❀ ◖ ⊨ ♣

Farnborough

Prince of Wales
184 Rectory Road
☎ (01252) 545578
11–3, 5–11; 10.30 Sun
Badger Tanglefoot; Fuller's London Pride; Hogs Back TEA; Ringwood Fortyniner; Wadworth 6X; guest beers H
The best free house for miles, selling ten beers, including four unusual guests. Friendly staff and a convivial atmosphere in an invariably busy pub. Excellent food.
Q ❀ ◖ ⇌ (North) P

Freefolk

Watership Down Inn
On B3400 ☎ (01256) 892254
11.30–3, 6–11; 12–3.30, 7–10.30 Sun
Archers Best Bitter; Brakspear Bitter; guest beers H
One-bar house dating back to the 19th century, renamed after

the Richard Adams book set locally, but the locals still know it as the Jerry. The spacious garden has many amenities. Food is home made. Games include antique penny arcade machines. ❀ ◖ ♣ P

Fritham

Royal Oak
1 mile S of B3078 OS232141
☎ (01703) 812606
11–3, 6–11; 12–3, 7–10.30 Sun
Ringwood Best Bitter; Wadworth IPA; guest beer (summer) G
Tiny, unspoilt, thatched pub at the end of a New Forest track, with a small front bar and a tiny snug. A centre for country activities – the owners are commoners of the forest.
♨ Q ❀ ♠ ♣

Gosport

Queens Hotel
143 Queens Road
☎ (01705) 525518
11.30–2.30, 7–11; 11.30–11 Sat; 12–3, 7–10.30 Sun
Archers Village; Hook Norton Old Hooky; Ringwood Fortyniner; guest beers H
Award-winning pub which sets the standard for the area, but may be difficult to find. Three drinking areas, with the fire, and its carved wood surround, the focal point. A real ale paradise. No food Sun.
♨ ◖ ♣

Wheatsheaf
225 Brockhurst Road
☎ (01705) 581546
12–2, 5.30–11; 11–11 Fri & Sat; 12–10.30 Sun
Flowers Original G
Unspoilt local with two bars and a games room, near historic Fort Brockhurst. Elephants feature in the decor. No food Sun. ❀ ◖ ♣ ♣ P

Greatham

Silver Birch Inn
Petersfield Road
☎ (01420) 573262
11.30–3, 5.30–11; 12–3.30, 7–10.30 Sun
Beer range varies H
Single-bar pub with a log fire. Dogs are welcome; special corner for parrots. Extensive dining area; food includes pasta dishes.
♨ Q ❀ ⊨ ◖ ♠ P

Hamble

King & Queen
High Street ☎ (01703) 454247
11–11; 12–10.30 Sun
Boddingtons Bitter; Fuller's London Pride; Wadworth 6X; guest beer H

Unpretentious, single-bar pub serving locals and mariners. Home-cooked bar food (book Sun lunch); a bistro attached to the pub is open Tue–Sat from 7. Brakspear's Bitter is sold as Totally Pissed. ₳ ❀ ◖ P

Hambledon

Bat & Ball

Broadhalfpenny Down (2½ miles from village on Clanfield road) OS677167
☎ (01705) 632692
11.30–3, 6–11; 12–3, 7–10.30 Sun
Gale's Butser, Best Bitter, HSB Ⓗ
Old pub, high up on Broadhalfpenny Down, regarded by some as the birthplace of cricket and thankfully restored as a museum of the game. Eve meals in the restaurant.
₳ ❀ ◖ & ♣ P ⦰

New Inn

West Street ☎ (01705) 632466
12–2.30, 7–11; 12–2.30, 7–10.30 Sun
Ballard's Trotton; Ringwood True Glory, Fortyniner, Old Thumper Ⓗ
Friendly village pub where the art of conversation has not been lost. A genuine free house, easy to miss, due to the lack of pub signs.
₳ Q ❀ ⊞ & ♣ P

Hammer Vale

Prince of Wales

Hammer Lane OS868326
☎ (01428) 652600
11–3, 6–11; 12–3, 7–10.30 Sun
Gale's Best Bitter, HSB, seasonal beers; guest beer Ⓖ
Inter-war roadhouse, built on the incorrect assumption that the A3 was to be constructed only yards away. This isolated pub boasts a stillage behind the bar, three open fires, a wood-burning stove and old Ameys Brewery windows. No food Sun eve. ₳ ❀ ◖ Ⅰ ▲ P

Hartley Wintney

Waggon & Horses

High Street (A30)
☎ (01252) 842119
11–11; 12–3, 7–10.30 Sun
Courage Best Bitter; Gale's HSB; Wadworth 6X; guest beer Ⓗ
Friendly, village-centre pub, with a cosy lounge, a lively public bar and always an imaginative guest beer on tap. No food Sun. ₳ Q ❀ ◖ ⊞ ♣

Havant

Old House at Home

2 South Street
☎ (01705) 483464
11–11; 12–10.30 Sun

Gale's Butser, Best Bitter, HSB, seasonal beers; guest beers Ⓗ
Attractive, 17th-century, half-timbered building, in a quiet corner of town, next to the church. Originally five cottages, it became a pub/bakery, then finally a comfortable two-bar pub. The public bar houses some interesting antiques.
₳ ❀ ◖ ⊞ ⦰ ☂ ♣

Hawkley

Hawkley Inn

Pococks Lane OS747292
☎ (01730) 827205
12–2.30 (3 Sat), 6–11; 12–3, 7–10.30 Sun
Ballard's Trotton; Cheriton Pots Ale; guest beers Ⓗ
Popular free house in a village well off the beaten track, attracting walkers and furnished in a very individual style (note the moose head). Six ales from independent breweries. No eve meals Sun.
₳ Q ❀ ◖ Ⅰ ⦰

Hill Head

Osborne View

Hill Head Road
☎ (01329) 664623
11–11; 12–10.30 Sun
Badger IPA, Dorset Best, Tanglefoot; Gribble Reg's Tipple, Blackadder II Ⓗ
Large, open-plan bar with panoramic views of the Solent. Although the emphasis is on food, there is plenty of room for drinkers.
₳ ❀ ◖ Ⅰ ♣ P ⦰

Horndean

Brewers Arms

1 Five Heads Road (100 yds off old A3)
☎ (01705) 591325
12–2 (3.30 Fri, 4 Sat; not Mon), 5 (6 Sat)–11; 12–4, 7–10.30 Sun
Flowers Original; Worthington Bitter; guest beers Ⓗ
Friendly, traditional, two-bar local with up to five beers.
Q ❀ ⊞ ♣ P

Horsebridge

John O'Gaunt

½ mile W of A3057, S of King's Somborne ☎ (01794) 388394
11–2.30 (3 Sat), 6–11; 12–3, 7–10.30 Sun
Palmers IPA; Ringwood Best Bitter, Fortyniner; guest beer (occasional) Ⓗ
Fine village pub in the lovely Test Valley – good walking country. The guest beer is often from Adnams and all the beers are good value. Shove-

ha'penny is taken seriously. No food Tue eve.
₳ Q ❀ ♣ P

Itchen Abbas

Trout Inn

Main Road (B3047)
☎ (01962) 779537
12–3, 6–11; 11–11 Sat; 12–4, 7–10.30 Sun
Marston's Bitter, Pedigree, Owd Rodger, HBC Ⓗ
Smart, lively country inn in the lovely Itchen Valley, with quality en suite accommodation. The two bars are adorned with breweriana and local views. The lounge forms part of the dining room; the bar has a jovial atmosphere. Children's play area in the garden.
₳ Q ❀ ⋈ ◖ Ⅰ ⊞ ♣ P

Kingsclere

Swan

Swan Street (B3051, off A339)
☎ (01635) 298314
11–3, 6–11; 12–3, 7–10.30 Sun
Greene King Abbot; Hampshire King Alfred's; Tetley Bitter; Theakston XB; guest beer Ⓗ
Family-run country pub in a scenic village. Popular with diners (separate eating area, but no food Sun).
₳ Q ⋈ ◖ Ⅰ ♣ P

Little London

Plough Inn

Silchester Road (1 mile E of A340) ☎ (01256) 850628
12–2.30, 6–11; 12–3, 6–10.30 Sun
Brakspear Bitter; Ringwood Best Bitter; guest beers Ⓗ
Small, unspoilt, village local with a quarry tiled floor and a large open fire. A rare example of a genuine country pub. No food Sun. ₳ Q ❀ & ♣ P

Long Sutton

Four Horseshoes

The Street OS748471
☎ (01256) 862488
11–3 (extends summer), 5–11; 12–3, 7–10.30 Sun
Gale's Butser, Best Bitter, HSB; guest beer Ⓗ
Quiet village local offering a friendly atmosphere and excellent food in a charming, unspoilt, low-beamed building with an attractive conservatory. ₳ Q ❀ ◖ Ⅰ P

Lymington (Pennington)

Musketeer

26 North Street
☎ (01590) 676527
11.30–2.30, 5.30–11; 12–3, 7–10.30 Sun

Brakspear Bitter; Ringwood Best Bitter, Fortyniner; guest beer Ⓗ
Good-looking pub with leaded windows, a friendly village local with a log fire and comfortable atmosphere. The menu includes unusual, home-made specials; eve menu Sat only (book); no food Sun.
🏘 Q ☜ 🏠 ◖ ♣ P

Medstead

Castle of Comfort
Castle Street (2 miles N of A31 at Four Marks)
☎ (01420) 562112
11–2.30, 6–11; 12–3, 6–10.30 Sun
Courage Best Bitter; Ushers Best Bitter, Founders, seasonal beer Ⓗ
Unspoilt village local, split into a comfortable lounge and a refurbished public bar. The regulars make you welcome. Steam trains run on the nearby Watercress Line.
🏘 Q ❀ 🏠 ♣ P 🛏

Mortimer West End

Turners Arms
West End Road
☎ (0118) 933 2961
12–2.30, 6–11; 12–3, 7–10.30 Sun
Brakspear Mild, Bitter, Special Ⓗ
Good local with proper wooden beams, but fake brickwork on the bar. Food in both the bar and restaurant, where children are allowed. A nice country pub. 🏘 ❀ ◖ ▶ P

North Warnborough

Lord Derby
Bartley Heath (A287, 1 mile from M3 jct 5)
☎ (01256) 702283
11.30–11; 11–3, 6–11 Sat; 12–3, 7–10.30 Sun
Fuller's London Pride; guest beers Ⓗ
Large, open-plan pub, with a good local following.
❀ ◖ ▶ 🏠 & ♣ P

Oakhanger

Red Lion
Off B3004 ☎ (01420) 472232
11–3, 6–11; 12–3, 7–10.30 Sun
Courage Best Bitter, Directors; Ringwood True Glory; guest beer (occasional) Ⓗ
True village pub with an excellent restaurant.
🏘 Q ◖ ▶ 🏠 P

Overton

Old House at Home
Station Road (100 yds N of B3400) ☎ (01256) 770335
11–2, 6–11; 11–11 Sat; 12–10.30 Sun

Courage Best Bitter Ⓗ; Ushers Best Bitter Ⓖ, Founders, seasonal beers Ⓗ
Recently extended village local where games are enthusiastically played. Good family garden. Limited parking. Q ❀ 🏠 ▶ ♣ P

Owslebury

Ship Inn
Off B2177, 1½ miles N of Marwell Zoo
☎ (01962) 777358
11–3, 6–11; 11–11 Sat; 12–10.30 Sun
Bateman Mild; Marston's Bitter, Pedigree, HBC Ⓗ
Lively, busy, two-bar country inn. The comfortable main bar has nautical and cricketing memorabilia; a second bar has a dining area serving good, home-cooked food. A large garden boasts a pond, a marquee, a children's play area, animals and a bowling green. 🏘 Q ❀ 🏠 ◖ ▶ ♣ P

Petersfield

Good Intent
46 College Street (near old A3/A272 jct)
☎ (01730) 263838
11–3, 6–11; 12–3, 7–10.30 Sun
Gale's Butser, Best Bitter, IPA, HSB, Festival Mild, seasonal beers; guest beers Ⓗ
Friendly, traditional, 16th-century local hosting live music Sun eve. Excellent, home-cooked food includes locally produced HSB sausages. No meals Sun or Mon eves.
🏘 ☜ ❀ ◖ ▶ & ⇌ ♣

Portsmouth

Apsley House
13 Auckland Road West, Southsea ☎ (01705) 821294
11–11; 12–10.30 Sun
Archers Golden; Ringwood Best Bitter; Tetley Bitter; guest beers Ⓗ
Backstreet pub, hidden away but handy for Southsea's shopping area. Named after the Duke of Wellington's London home (address No. 1 London, as featured on the pub sign). ❀ ◖ ▶ ⌂ ⌦

Connaught Arms
119 Guildford Road, Fratton
☎ (01705) 646455
11.30–2.30, 6–11; 11.30–11 Fri & Sat; 12–4, 7–10.30 Sun
Brains SA; Fuller's London Pride; guest beers Ⓗ
Gem of a pub of attractive brewer's Tudor design, occupying a corner site; justly famed as Portsmouth's 'pasty pub'. A must.
❀ ◖ ⇌ (Fratton) ♣ ⌂

Eldon Arms
15–17 Eldon Street, Southsea
☎ (01705) 851778
11.30–2.30 (3 Sat), 5 (6 Sat)–11; 11.30–11 Fri; 12–3, 7–10.30 Sun
Draught Bass; Eldridge Pope Hardy Country, Royal Oak; Webster's Green Label; guest beers Ⓗ
Large, but friendly local; one room split into five distinct areas. Excellent range of superb food – the specials would fill Goliath. Bar billiards, shove-ha'penny, darts and pool played.
❀ ◖ ▶ ⇌ ♣ ⌂

Fifth Hants Volunteer Arms
74 Albert Road, Southsea (near King's Theatre)
☎ (01705) 827161
12–11; 12–10.30 Sun
Gale's Best Bitter, IPA, HSB, seasonal beers; guest beer Ⓗ
Lively, two-bar local; the saloon displays a large collection of military memorabilia. Lunches are available at weekends only.
Q ◖ ▶ ♣

Florist
324 Fratton Road, Fratton
☎ (01705) 820289
11–3, 6–11; 11–11 Sat; 12–10.30 Sun
Wadworth IPA, 6X, Farmers Glory or seasonal beers Ⓗ
Attractive, two-bar, Grade II-listed corner local with a brewer's Tudor exterior and a witch's hat tower. The rear lounge is quiet; the public bar has darts, pool, a jukebox and a TV. Run by the same family for over 35 years.
Q 🏠 ⇌ (Fratton) ♣

Leopold Tavern
154 Albert Road, Southsea
☎ (01705) 829748
11–11; 12–10.30 Sun
Burts VPA; Wadworth 6X Ⓗ
Pub whose exterior offers a classic example of the former United Brewery's glazed tile-work. Inside is much larger than expected, with original carved wood bar fittings and old photos of Portsmouth.
♣

Old Oyster House
291 Locksway Road, Milton, Southsea (off A288, near university's Langstone site)
☎ (01705) 827456
12–11; 12–10.30 Sun
Brains Dark; Fuller's London Pride; guest beers Ⓗ
Large single bar based around a nautical theme, plus a lounge bar which is now a family room, standing by the only remaining section of the Portsea Canal. Two ciders and a mild are usually available.
☜ ❀ ◖ ▶ ♣ ⌂

Red White & Blue

150 Fawcett Road, Southsea
☎ (01705) 780013
11–11; 12–10.30 Sun
Gale's Butser, Best Bitter, IPA, Winter Brew, HSB Ⓗ
Compact corner local, patriotic to two nations. It can get crowded on games eves. Decorations include various naval plaques.
≋ (Fratton) ♣

RMA Tavern

58 Cromwell Road, Eastney, Southsea (opp. old Royal Marine barracks)
☎ (01705) 820896
10.30–11; 12–10.30 Sun
Gale's Butser, HSB, seasonal beers; guest beers Ⓗ
Two main bars, plus a function room, are housed in this surprisingly large corner local: the only pub in the city with a permanent skittle alley. Numerous games played. Blues music Thu.
Q ◖ ▶ ⊞ ♣ ↺

Sir Loyne of Beefe

152 Highland Road, Eastney, Southsea
☎ (01705) 820115
11–11; 12–5.30, 7–10.30 Sun
Draught Bass; Fuller's London Pride; Hop Back Summer Lightning; guest beers Ⓗ
First in a chain of 'SLOBS' which extends from Portsmouth to Brighton: a large public bar, a snug and a very comfortable lounge, near the site of the former Eastney tram depot. Up to five guest beers are available.
Q ⊞ ♣

Sir Robert Peel

Astley Street
☎ (01705) 345708
11.45–3.30 (4.30 Sat), 7–11; 12–4.30, 7–10.30 Sun
Beer range varies Ⓗ
1960s-style, two-bar, friendly, genuine free house. Don't be deterred by the exterior: inside it features a 'posh' end and a 'rough' end. Inexpensive, wholesome bar meals (not served Sun). Six ales.
◖ ▶ ⊞ ≋ ♣ ↺ P

Wetherspoons

2 Guildhall Walk
☎ (01705) 295912
11–11; 12–10.30 Sun
Courage Directors; Hop Back Summer Lightning; Ringwood Fortyniner; Theakston Best Bitter; Younger Scotch; guest beers Ⓗ
Well-refurbished as one bar, the old Portsmouth & Gosport Gas Co. offices now offer a friendly, pleasant venue for a meal or a drink. The staff are welcoming, even when the pub is very busy.
◖ ▶ & ≋ ↺ ⚲

Priors Dean

White Horse (Pub With No Name)

400 yds off main road, signed E Tisted OS714290
☎ (01420) 588387
11–2.30 (3 Sat), 6–11; 12–3, 7–10.30 Sun
Ballard's Best Bitter; Draught Bass; Gale's HSB; Ringwood Fortyniner; guest beers Ⓗ
Famous old pub hidden down a gravel track in a field (second track from the main road), with no pub sign – it fell down years ago, hence the nickname. Ten beers are on offer, two of which are house beers: the stronger from Ringwood, the other from Gale's. ⚇ Q ✿ ◖ ▶ ⊞ ♠ P

Ringwood

London Tavern

Linford Road, Poulner
☎ (01425) 473819
11.30 (11 Sat)–3, 5.30 (5 Sat)–11; 11.30–11 Fri; 12–4, 7–10.30 Sun
Fuller's London Pride; Ringwood Best Bitter; guest beers Ⓗ
Attractive, 19th-century local; a frequent prize-winner in the *Ringwood in Bloom* competition. No food Sun.
⚇ ✿ ◖ ♣ P

Romsey

Tudor Rose

3 Cornmarket
☎ (01794) 512126
10–11; 12–4, 7–10.30 Sun
Courage Best Bitter, Directors Ⓗ
One-bar, no-frills pub in the town centre. The courtyard is very attractive in summer, with flower baskets and tubs. Regular 'folk music with attitude'. Eve meals in summer; no food winter Sun.
⚇ ✿ ◖ ▶ ≋ ♣

Rotherwick

Falcon

The Street ☎ (01256) 762586
11–11; 12–10.30 Sun
Brakspear Bitter; Flowers Original; Morrells Varsity; guest beers Ⓗ
Friendly, popular, two-bar village local where a wonderful collection of beer bottles decorates the walls. Cider in summer. Good food, but it can be a bit pricey.
⚇ Q ☍ ✿ ◖ ▶ & ♠ ♣ ↺ P

Selborne

Queens Hotel

High Street ☎ (01420) 511454
11–11; 12–10.30 Sun
Courage Best Bitter; Ushers Best Bitter, Founders, seasonal beers Ⓗ
Two-bar village pub: a characterful public and a saloon bar with an attached restaurant. It can get noisy; occasional live jazz. The landlord organises horse and carriage trips to other pubs.
⚇ ✿ ☍ ◖ ▶ ⊞ & P

Selborne Arms

High Street ☎ (01420) 511247
11–3, 5.30–11; 11–11 Fri & Sat; 12–10.30 Sun
Courage Best Bitter; Flowers IPA *or* **Original; Wadworth 6X; guest beers** Ⓗ
Comfortable pub with plenty for children in the garden (substantial gated play area and a mini-farm of small animals). Home-made food from an interesting menu. Popular with ramblers.
⚇ Q ✿ ◖ ▶ P

Shedfield

Wheatsheaf

Botley Road (A334)
☎ (01329) 833024
12–11; 12–10.30 Sun
Archers Village Ⓖ; **Beer Seller Hampshire Hog** Ⓗ; **Cheriton Pots Ale** Ⓖ; **Hop Back Summer Lightning** Ⓗ; **guest beers** Ⓖ
Traditional roadside inn with two comfortable bars; a former Marston's house, now an excellent free house without gimmicks. Home-made food. The house beer is brewed by Hampshire. Cider in summer.
Q ✿ ◖ ⊞ ♠ ↺ P

Southampton

Bevois Castle

63 Onslow Road, Bevois Valley
☎ (01703) 330350
11–3, 6.30–11; 11–11 Sun; 12–10.30 Sun
Eldridge Pope Traditional, Country Bitter; guest beers Ⓗ
Friendly, traditional, one-bar pub in a popular area. Good value, home-cooked food (barbecues in summer); no eve meals Sun/Mon – other eves till 7.30. Good selection of cognacs. ✿ ◖ ▶ ♠ P

Bosun's Locker

Castle Square, Upper Bugle Street ☎ (01703) 333364
11–3, 6–11; 11–11 Fri & Sat; 12–3, 7–10.30 Sun
Boddingtons Bitter; Fuller's London Pride; Poole Bosun; guest beer Ⓗ
Spacious Tudor-style pub on the city walls. The interior sports a nautical theme. Interesting, home-cooked food. One extra guest beer plus a cider in summer.
⚇ ☍ ◖ ▶ ↺

Crown

9 Highcrown Street
☎ (01703) 315033
11–3, 5–11; 11–11 Fri & Sat; 12–4,
7.30–10.30 Sun
**Flowers Original; Fuller's
London Pride; Wadworth 6X;
guest beers** H
Single-bar pub with a rustic
feel, close to the university and
the common; popular with
students and locals. It is a base
for a number of clubs, ranging
from scuba diving to squash.
Real cider occasionally in
summer. ❀ ◑ ▶ ◔ P

Duke of Wellington

36 Bugle Street (near Tudor
House Museum)
☎ (01703) 339222
11–11; 12–10.30 Sun
**Boddingtons Bitter; Courage
Best Bitter** H**, Directors** G**;
Theakston Best Bitter;
Wadworth 6X** H**; guest
beers** H**/**G
Two-bar, backstreet pub,
dating from the 13th century,
the oldest continuously
inhabited building in town.
🏨 ◑ ▶ ◔

Eagle

1 Palmerston Road
☎ (01703) 333825
11–11; 12–10.30 Sun
**Boddingtons Mild, Bitter;
Flowers Original; Fuller's
London Pride; Ringwood Old
Thumper; Wadworth 6X** H**;
guest beers** H**/**G
Large, one-bar, city pub
featuring stone floors and
wooden beams. Jazz sessions
Tue eve. Selection of Belgian
beers; five guest beers, three on
gravity. Meals served 12–7
(vegetarian option).
◑ ♣ ◔

Freemantle Arms

Albany Road
☎ (01703) 320759
10.30–3, 6–11; 10.30–11 Fri & Sat;
12–10.30 Sun
**Banks's Mild; Marston's
Bitter, Pedigree, HBC** H
Friendly, two-bar local in a
quiet cul-de-sac, offering a
relaxing atmosphere in
contrast to the nearby bustle of
Shirley Road. ❀ ◱ ♣ ◻

Hobbit

134 Bevois Valley Road
☎ (01703) 232591
6–11 (midnight Thu, 1am Sat); 5–1am
Fri; 7–10.30 Sun
**Boddingtons Bitter; Flowers
Original; Hop Back
Thunderstorm; Whitbread
Best Bitter; guest beers** H
Popular, lively young persons'
pub with live music in the
downstairs bar. Barbecued
food available Fri and Sat eves.
The large multi-level garden
stages charity music festivals

bank hols. The house beer is by
Hampshire.
❀ ▶ ⇌ (St Denys) ♣

Miller's Pond

2 Middle Road, Sholing
☎ (01703) 444755
11–11; 12–10.30 Sun
Adnams Broadside (summer)**;
Wadworth IPA, 6X, Old
Timer; guest beers** H
Street-corner local, run by the
same family since 1972. The
entrance to the single bar is via
the terrace overlooking the
garden, which has climbing
frames and swings.
❀ ◑ ⇌ (Sholing) P

Park Inn

37 Carlisle Road, Shirley
☎ (01703) 787835
11–3 (3.30 Sat), 5 (6.30 Sat)–11; 12–3,
7–10.30 Sun
**Badger Tanglefoot; Wadworth
IPA, 6X, Old Timer, seasonal
beers; guest beers** H
Friendly, one-bar local near the
shopping precinct, boasting
some interesting mirrors.
Dominoes, cribbage and other
games are played.
❀ ◑ ♣

Richmond Inn

108 Portswood Road,
Portswood
☎ (01703) 554523
11–11; 12–10.30 Sun
**Banks's Mild; Marston's
Bitter, Pedigree, Owd Rodger**
(Christmas)**, HBC** H
Popular, two-bar pub in a
busy suburb, dating from the
1870s. The public bar has Sky
TV and live Irish music Thu
eve. The lounge features an
old LSD cash register and
a good whisky selection.
❀ ⊞ ♣

Salisbury Arms

126 Shirley High Street, Shirley
(opp. precinct)
☎ (01703) 774624
10–11; 12–10.30 Sun
**Banks's Mild; Marston's
Bitter, Pedigree, HBC** H
Friendly, well-refurbished pub
in the shopping area with a
central bar and a skittle alley.
Sparklers are not used but are
available. ◑ ♣ ⚲

Waterloo Arms

101 Waterloo Road, Freemantle
☎ (01703) 220022
12–11; 12–3, 7–10.30 (12–10.30
summer) Sun
**Hop Back GFB, Entire Stout,
Thunderstorm, Summer
Lightning; guest beers** H
Popular, one-bar local with a
mixed clientele and no
gimmicks. The walls are
festooned with awards for Hop
Back beers. Ten mins' walk
from Central station. Sausages
feature prominently on the bar
food menu.
❀ ◑ ▶ ⇌ (Millbrook) ♣ ◔

Sparsholt

Plough

☎ (01962) 776353
11–3, 6–11; 12–4, 6–10.30 Sun
**Wadworth IPA, 6X, Old
Timer; guest beer** H
Well-extended and refurbished
country pub with a strong
emphasis on high quality food,
but still popular with drinkers.
Facilities for children in the
garden.
🏨 ⋈ ❀ ◑ ♿ ♠ P ⚲

Standford

Robin Hood

Standford Lane (B3004)
☎ (01428) 751508
11–11; 12–10.30 Sun
**Draught Bass; Gibbs Mew
Salisbury, Bishop's Tipple** H
Pub dating from 1904, hosting
live music Fri and Sat eves and
a folk club Wed. Children
allowed in the left-hand part of
the bar.
❀ ◑ P

Stockbridge

Three Cups Inn

High Street
☎ (01264) 810527
11–2, 6–11; 12–2, 7–10.30 Sun
**Draught Bass; Fuller's London
Pride; guest beers** H
15th-century coaching inn,
closed as a pub 1910–1996 and
used as an undertaker's, cream
tea shop and builders' store in
the intervening years. Rambles
nearby in the pretty Test
Valley. No food Sun eve.
🏨 ❀ 🛏 ◑ ▶ ♠ P

Stoke

White Hart

Off B3048, 1 mile from St Mary
Bourne
☎ (01264) 738355
12–2 (3 Sat), 6.30–11; 12–3, 7–10.30
Sun
**Fuller's London Pride;
Hampshire King Alfred's** H
Vital amenity set in a pretty
village in the Bourne Valley.
Interesting, home-cooked
meals (no food Sun eve, or
Mon). 🏨 Q ⋈ ❀ ◑ ▶ ♣ P

Swanmore

New Inn

Chapel Road
☎ (01489) 893588
11–3, 6–11; 12–3, 7–10.30 Sun
**Bateman Mild; Marston's
Bitter, Pedigree, HBC** H
Good, welcoming village local:
one bar to suit all tastes. Good,
home-made food, including
pies (no meals Sun eve or Tue).
Q ❀ ◑ ▶ ♠ ♣ P

Tangley

Cricketers
At Tangley Bottom OS326528
☎ (01264) 730283
11–3, 6–11; 12–3.30, 7–10.30 Sun
Draught Bass; Cheriton Pots Ale, Diggers Gold; guest beer Ⓖ
Remote, 18th-century drovers' inn with a friendly village atmosphere in the bar area. A large family/dining room at the rear serves good quality home cooking (book at weekends). Caravan Club field for camping behind.
🚫 Q ⛺ 🌳 ◑ ▲ ♣ P

Thruxton

White Horse
Off A303 westbound towards E Cholderton ☎ (01264) 772401
11–3, 6–11; 12–4, 7–10.30 Sun
Fuller's London Pride; Smiles Golden Brew Ⓗ
Charming old thatched pub with a beamed ceiling. A carving above the fireplace dates it from 1451. It is situated below the A303, but once inside, you'd never know. The family room is the pool room. No food Sun/Mon eves.
🚫 🌳 ⛺ ◑ ♣ ⌂ P

Titchfield

Wheatsheaf
East Street ☎ (01329) 842965
12–3, 6–11; 11–11 Fri; 12–3, 7–10.30 Sun
Fuller's London Pride; guest beers Ⓗ
16th-century building in a conservation area near the river. The American hosts have sympathetically extended the interior to include a snug and a small function room. No food Tue eve. 🚫 Q ⛺ ◑ ▶

Totford

Woolpack
On B3046, S of Brown Candover ☎ (01962) 732101
11.30–3, 6–11; 11.30–3, 7–10.30 Sun
Cheriton Pots Ale; Eldridge Pope Hardy Country; Gale's HSB; Palmers IPA Ⓗ
16th-century, spacious and friendly, country inn and restaurant serving a good, varied menu. Large, pleasant garden with a duck pond. Children welcome in the restaurant.
🚫 Q ⛺ 🏡 ◑ ♣ P

Twyford

Phoenix
High Street (B3335, 1 mile S of M3 jct 11) ☎ (01962) 713322
11.30–3, 6–11; 12–3, 7–10.30 Sun

Banks's Mild; Marston's Bitter, Pedigree Ⓗ
Busy, friendly village inn serving a wide range of good value food. The skittle alley/function room is a family room at lunchtime.
🚫 🌳 ⛺ ◑ ♣ P

Upper Clatford

Crook & Shears
Off A343 ☎ (01264) 361543
11.30–3.30, 6–11; 12–3.30, 7–10.30 Sun
Flowers Original; Fuller's London Pride; Gale's HSB; guest beers Ⓗ
Thriving, two-bar thatched pub. The low ceilings, open fireplace and rambling wisteria all add to its charm. The skittle alley/function room is popular, as is the excellent food (not served eves Sun/Mon).
🚫 Q ⛺ ◑ 🍴

Weyhill

Star Inn
Weyhill Road (A342)
☎ (01264) 772356
11–3, 6–11; 11–11 Fri & Sat; 12–10.30 Sun
Butts Jester, Bitter; Hampshire King Alfred's, Lionheart; guest beer Ⓗ
Friendly, two-bar roadside pub on the site of a 16th-century drovers' inn. Recent alterations have revealed some of the older structure in the family area. An Italian restaurant extends from the lounge.
🚫 🌳 ⛺ ◑ 🍴 P

Weyhill Fair
Weyhill Road (A342)
☎ (01264) 773631
11–3, 6 (5 Fri, 6.30 Sat)–11; 12–3, 7–10.30 Sun
Morrells Bitter, Varsity, Graduate; guest beers Ⓗ
Very popular free house offering three rapidly changing guest beers, including a mild, plus an inviting menu of home-cooked food at modest prices (not served Sun eve).
🚫 Q 🌳 ⛺ ◑ ▲ ♣ P ✂ 🍴

Whitchurch

Prince Regent
104 London Road (B3400)
☎ (01256) 892179
11–11; 12–10.30 Sun
Archers Best Bitter; Hop Back GFB; guest beer (occasional) Ⓗ
Friendly, welcoming, one-room bar, overlooking the Test Valley. Book Sun lunch.
🚫 ⛺ ◑ ♣ ⌂ P

Red House
London Street (B3400)
☎ (01256) 895558
11–3, 5–11; 12–2, 6–10.30 Sun
Cheriton Pots Ale, Diggers Gold; Courage Best Bitter; Theakston XB Ⓗ

Pub with two bars, both with log fires, plus a restaurant serving good food.
🚫 Q ⛺ ◑ ▶ 🍴 ⚘ ♣ ≠ P 🍴

Whitsbury

Cartwheel
Whitsbury Road OS129138
☎ (01725) 518362
11–2.30, 6–11; 12–3, 7–10.30 Sun
Beer range varies Ⓗ
200-year-old, Grade II-listed building in a remote village on the outskirts of the New Forest, less than two miles from Breamore's Anglo Saxon church. Six beers are usually available (always a Hop Back and a Ringwood). Excellent, varied menu (not served Tue eve in winter). 🚫 ⛺ ◑ ▶ ♣ P

Winchester

Albion
2 Stockbridge Road
☎ (01962) 853429
11–11; 12–10.30 Sun
Draught Bass; Hook Norton Best Bitter; Worthington Bitter; guest beer (occasional) Ⓗ
Anti-Tardislike, this substantial corner pub is quite small inside, meaning it's standing room only at busy times. Good range of lunches; many table games: skittles, shove-ha'penny, etc. Cider in summer. Q ◑ ≠ ♣ ⌂

Foresters Arms
71 North Walls
☎ (01962) 861539
12–11; 12–10.30 Sun
Marston's Bitter, Pedigree, HBC Ⓗ
Busy, boisterous town pub, recently refurbished to create a more single-bar format. Handy for Winchester sports centre.
≠ ♣

Hyde Tavern
57 Hyde Street (400 yds N of Theatre Royal)
☎ (01962) 862592
11.30–2.30, 5–11; 11–3, 6–11 Sat; 12–3, 7–10.30 Sun
Marston's Bitter, Pedigree Ⓗ
Charming, cosy, two-bar local tucked away in a quiet street, but very close to the centre. The pub dates from the 15th century and has low ceilings and sloping floors. No swan necks. Q ◑ ≠

Wykeham Arms
75 Kingsgate Street
☎ (01962) 853834
11–11; 12–10.30 Sun
Draught Bass; Eldridge Pope Traditional, Hardy Country, Royal Oak Ⓗ
Very busy, award-winning, Georgian pub, hard under the walls of Winchester College, decorated with a vast clutter of

odd furniture and artefacts. Extensive menu; wine list of 75-plus choices. Limited parking. 🏠 🦽 🐕 ◑ ▶ P ✄

Wolverton

George & Dragon
Towns End (1 mile off A339)
☎ (01635) 298292
12–3, 5.30–11; 12–3, 7–10.30 Sun
Brakspear Special; Fuller's London Pride; Hampshire King Alfred's; Wadworth IPA, 6X Ⓗ
Cosy country inn with oak beams and a feature fireplace. Good, home-made food

includes regular specials. An ideal stop on country walks; large garden. Skittle alley for hire. 🏠 Q 🐕 ◑ ▶ P

Wonston

Wonston Arms
Stoke Charity Road (off A30 at Sutton Scotney)
☎ (01962) 760288
11–3, 6.30–11; 12–3, 6.45–10.30 Sun
Beer range varies Ⓗ
Pleasant, welcoming country pub, dog- and children-friendly. A step back in time and a proper beer drinker's pub. 🏠 Q 🐕 ♿ ♣ P

Woolton Hill

Rampant Cat
Broad Layings (off A343, then road opp. 'The Stores' in village centre)
☎ (01635) 253474
12–3 (not Mon), 7–11; 12–3, 7–10.30 Sun
Archers Best Bitter, Golden; Arkell's 3B; guest beer Ⓗ
Pleasant, welcoming country pub with a large, L-shaped bar. The restaurant leads to a patio and large garden. Popular with ramblers. No meals Sun eve or Mon. 🏠 Q 🐕 ◑ ▶ ♣ P

EXTRA! ADNAMS EXTRA! DON'T READ ALL ABOUT IT!

Do you find it odd that the national drink of France receives more coverage in British newspapers than the national drink of the UK? Most beer enthusiasts do. In fact, there are four times as many articles published about wine than there are about beer, as CAMRA discovered when it commissioned an independent survey of press clippings in autumn 1996.

The survey was jointly funded by Whitbread, such is the concern across the industry that beer – and British beer in particular – does not enjoy fair treatment in the media. Most national newspapers have one or more wine writers who contribute weekly columns. Few newspapers have a regular beer writer and any beer coverage – apart from newsy items like duty increases in the Budget – is usually squeezed into the drinks (aka wine) column.

All this is very galling for those of us who appreciate beer and want to read more about it. It is also a very strange state of affairs, considering that in Britain we drink three times as much beer as wine and that the beer market is worth nearly three times more financially than the wine market.

The attitude of press food and drink editors is, frankly, blinkered: they simply do not recognise that there is a market for words on beer. Perhaps they need reminding that CAMRA sells thousands and thousands of beer books each year.

Where regular beer coverage is permitted, writers like Michael Jackson and Roger Protz enjoy a wide and appreciative readership. The British Guild of Beer Writers, now ten years old, is always ready to supply the right writer for the right beer story, so editors cannot simply blame lack of supply. As Protz, *Glenfiddich Drinks Writer of the Year* 1997, stated: 'Beer at its best is a more complex drink than wine. Journalists should be looking at beer as a serious contender'.

So come on media, give us what we want – more items on what the Brewers Society once correctly labelled 'The best long drink in the world'!

Herefordshire

Aymestrey

Riverside Inn
On A4110 ☎ (01568) 708440
12–3, 6.30–11; 12–3, 7–10.30 Sun
Beer range varies H
Formerly the Crown: a
friendly, 16th-century,
riverside inn where the bar
area leads through to a lounge
and restaurant. The guest beer
policy is adventurous, usually
including Otter Ale. The 'tap'
for Woodhampton brewery.
🏚 🏵 🛏 🕽 🕽 🛦 P

Bishop's Frome

Chase Inn
On B4214 ☎ (01885) 490234
12–3.30, 6–11; 12–3.30, 7–10.30 Sun
**Hook Norton Best Bitter; Wye
Valley Bitter** H
Uncomplicated and keenly-
run, village green pub that
caters for all tastes: an ideal
B&B stop and popular for Sun
roasts. Locals dominate the

two bars and welcome all-
comers. The landlord supports
Herefordshire breweries. Good
value. 🏚 🏵 🛏 🕽 🕽 🛦 ♣ P

Bromyard

Rose & Lion
5 New Road
☎ (01885) 482381
11–3, 6–11; 11–11 Sat; 12–3, 7–10.30
Sun
**Wye Valley Bitter, HPA,
Supreme; guest beer** H
Friendly, unpretentious and
popular with locals: a three-bar
pub with much character,
based around a courtyard.
Wye Valley's only tied outlet
outside Hereford is constantly
improving. Q 🏵 🕽 ♣ P

Colwall

Chase Inn
Chase Road, Upper Colwall
(off B4218 Walwyn Road at
higher hairpin bend)
☎ (01684) 540276

12–2.30 (not Tue), 6–11; 12–2.30,
7–10.30 Sun
**Donnington BB, SBA;
Hobsons Best Bitter; Wye
Valley seasonal beer** H
Two-bar free house discretely
tucked away in a wooded
backwater of the Malvern
Hills. A splendid garden
affords views to the west.
Limited, but very wholesome,
menu lunchtimes (not Sun or

> ### 🍺 INDEPENDENT BREWERIES
> **Fromes Hill:** Fromes Hill
>
> **Ledbury:** Ledbury
>
> **Marches:** Leominster
>
> **Shoes:** Norton Canon
>
> **SP Sporting Ales:**
> Stoke Prior
>
> **Woodhampton:**
> Aymestrey
>
> **Wye Valley:** Hereford

Tue). Worth the 25-min uphill walk from Colwall station.
🔔 ◗ 🍺 ♣ P

Fromes Hill

Wheatsheaf Inn
On A4103
☎ (01531) 640888
12–11; 12–10.30 Sun
Fromes Hill Buckswood Dingle, Overture; M&B Brew XI ⊞
Refurbished, single-bar roadside house that is home to the Fromes Hill brewery. The L-shaped bar is divided into a bar area (with TV) and a semi-dining area, the former frequented by locals. Large garden. 🏨 🔔 ◗ 🍴 🅰 ♣ P

Hereford

Barrels
69 St Owen Street
☎ (01432) 274968
11–11; 12–10.30 Sun
Wye Valley Bitter, HPA, Supreme, Brew 69, seasonal beers; guest beer ⊞
Herefordshire CAMRA *Pub of the Year* 1996 and everything an independent brewery tap should be; one of the last multi-room pubs in Hereford. No food, no frills, just good beer and company. Popular at weekends. Charity beer fest Aug Bank Hol.
🔔 🍺 🚲 ♣ 🍶

Lichfield Vaults
11 Church Street
☎ (01432) 267994
11–11; 12–10.30 Sun
Ansells Mild; Marston's Pedigree; Tetley Bitter; guest beers ⊞
Pleasantly refurbished pub in a lane close to the cathedral and shops. The single bar divides into two drinking areas and is popular with city drinkers at weekends. A Festival Ale House, it usually has three guest beers. Patio at the rear. No parking in the immediate vicinity. 🔔 ◗ ♣

Spread Eagle
King Street
☎ (01432) 272205
11–3, 6–11; 11–11 Fri, Sat & summer; 12–10.30 Sun
Draught Bass; Boddingtons Bitter; Fuller's London Pride; Greene King Abbot; Wadworth 6X; guest beers ⊞
Single-bar pub stretching back from the street. It divides into three areas, which, with wooden floors and beams, reveal its past. The metropolitan feel (younger clientele) is reflected a little in the prices. Worth a stop on a city crawl. 🔔 ◗ 🍴

Three Elms Inn
1 Canon Pyon Road
☎ (01432) 273338
11–11; 12–10.30 Sun
Boddingtons Bitter; Flowers Original; Marston's Pedigree; guest beers ⊞
One large, L-shaped bar dominates this refurbished, deservedly popular pub. Good for families and/or a meal stop (Berni menu), this pub always has six beers, including independent guests. Wheelchair WC; children's play pen. Handy for the racecourse.
🚲 🏨 🔔 ◗ 🍴 🚲 ♣ P

Treacle Mine
83–85 St Martins Street (south of river)
☎ (01432) 266022
11–3.30 (12–3 Mon), 6–11; 11–11 Fri & Sat; 12–10.30 Sun
Banks's Mild, Bitter; guest beers ⊞
Deservedly well-patronised, stylishly refurbished, small, one-bar pub. Old and new meet in an original mix of beams, old brickwork and satellite TV. A lively local trade means there is rarely a dull moment. Guest beers come from both larger and smaller breweries. Cider (various brands) is available in summer.
♣ 🍶

Victory
88 St Owen Street
☎ (01432) 274998
11–11; 12–10.30 Sun
Wye Valley Bitter, HPA, Supreme, seasonal beers; guest beer ⊞
Successful Wye Valley house that has an unusual galleon theme running through the long single bar. Always popular, it is busy without being unwelcoming. A mixed clientele is attracted by the excellent range of beers. The best bet for Wye Valley's Dorothy Goodbody's Stout. Parking is tricky.
🔔 🚲 ♣ 🍶

Kington

Olde Tavern ☆
22 Victoria Road
☎ (01544) 231384
7.30–11; 11.30–3, 7.30–11 Sat & Bank Hols; 12–2.30, 7–10.30 Sun
Ansells Bitter ⊞
An outstanding example of old Kington – a must for connoisseurs of the English pub. Two bars, complete with settles, benches and curios, are to be discovered behind a Victorian facade. This award winner is friendly and unique. No food is available.
Q 🍺 🅰 ♣

Old Fogey
37 High Street
☎ (01544) 230685
5.30 (11 Sat)–11; 12–10.30 Sun
Wood Special; guest beers ⊞
Small, one-bar pub with a basic and unspoilt interior. Having negotiated the tight entrance doors, a snug and cosy pub with friendly locals will make any visit worthwhile. The only noise is good conversation and laughter. 🔔 ♣

Queen's Head
Bridge Street
☎ (01544) 231106
12 (12.30 winter)–2.30, 5–11; 12–11 Sat; 12–3, 7–10.30 Sun
Hobsons Best Bitter; Three Tuns XXX Bitter; guest beer ⊞
Two-bar, typical town pub with a wooden-floored public bar, complete with a games machine, and a quieter lounge. The Dunn Plowman brewery at the rear has now relocated to the Three Tuns at Bishop's Castle, from where the Dunn Plowman house beer comes. An SP Sporting Ale is also sold. The menu specialises in pizzas.
🔔 ◗ 🍺 🅰 ♣

Lea

Crown Inn
Gloucester Road (A40)
☎ (01989) 750407
12–11; 12–10.30 Sun
John Smith's Bitter; RCH Pitchfork; guest beers ⊞
Revitalised roadside local that specialises in guest beers, usually from RCH and Wye Valley. The main bar area is broken up by an old fireplace into separate areas, including a games room. 🏨 🔔 ♣ P

Ledbury

Horseshoe Inn
The Homend
☎ (01531) 632770
12–11; 12–10.30 Sun
Boddingtons Bitter; Flowers IPA; Wadworth 6X; guest beers ⊞
A flight of stone steps leads into a single-bar pub that, despite 20th-century refurbishment and trappings, still retains some character. It sells the most adventurous beers in the Ledbury area.
🏨 🔔 ◗ 🚲 ♣

Prince of Wales
Church Lane (off Market Sq)
☎ (01531) 632250
11–3.30 (4 Sat), 6.30–11; 12–3.30, 6.30–10.30 Sun
Banks's Hanson's Mild, Bitter ⊞
16th-century, archetypal, black and white-timbered town pub in the delightful setting of the cobbled Church Lane. Two

main bar areas mix comfort and some character. The pub is professionally run by a landlord keen on games and live folk (Wed). Cider in summer (Weston's). No-smoking area lunchtime. Eve meals served in summer, Fri–Sun.
Q ❀ ◁ ▷ ⇌ ♣ ⌂ ✗

Royal Oak Hotel

The Southend
☎ (01531) 632110
11.30–2, 5–11 (11.30–11 summer); 12–3, 6–10.30 (12–10.30 summer) Sun
Ledbury Goldings Best, Challenger SB, Chinook IPA, seasonal beers ⊞
Home of the Ledbury Brewery Co., this hotel is not aesthetically or architecturally outstanding, but good food and beer win the day. Keenly-run, its main bar has dining chairs; a lower cellar bar is more drinking-oriented. Runner-up for Herefordshire CAMRA *Pub of the Year* 1996.
♨ ⊨ ◁ ▷ ♣ ⌂ P ⊟

Leominster

Black Horse

74 South Street
☎ (01568) 611946
11–2.30, 6–11; 11–11 Sat; 12–3, 7–10.30 Sun
Hobsons Town Crier; Marches BHB; guest beers ⊞
Excellent free house which serves the best selection of ales for miles: a lively public bar and a quieter lounge and restaurant (no meals Sun eve; booking is advisable). Increasingly popular with locals and visitors alike, it is the 'tap' for Marches ales.
❀ ◁ ▷ ⊟ ♣ P

Grape Vaults

4 Broad Street
☎ (01568) 611404
11–3, 5–11; 12–4, 6.30–10.30 Sun
Banks's Mild; Marston's Bitter, Pedigree; guest beers ⊞
Cosy, well-run pub where a plain facade conceals a wonderfully intact and well-restored interior. Fireplaces feature in the bar and snug, with much etched-glass and wood panels. Above average bar snacks (until 9pm). One of two guest beers is from Marston's. ♨ Q ◁ ▷

Letton

Swan Inn

On A438 ☎ (01544) 327304
11–11; 11–3, 6–11 Mon & Tue; 12–3, 7–10.30 Sun
Draught Bass ⊞
Pleasant roadside inn situated in the Wye Valley. The main bar caters for diners and locals alike (food is always available in a separate eating area). Old Swan Bitter is the house beer from Wye Valley.
♨ ❀ ⊨ ◁ ▷ ⊟ ♣ P

Much Dewchurch

Black Swan

On B4348 ☎ (01981) 540295
12 (11.30 summer)–2.30, 6 (5.30 summer)–11; 12–3, 7–10.30 Sun
Courage Directors; Taylor Landlord; guest beers ⊞
Reputedly the oldest pub in Herefordshire, successful in both dining and beer trades. Four different areas include a public bar and games room. The lounge has settees, a piano and many nice features. Always two guest beers; Courage Best is sold under a house name.
♨ ❀ ⊨ ◁ ▷ ♣ ⌂ P

Risbury

Hop Pole Inn (Bert's)   ☆

½ mile E of village on Pencombe Road OS554549
11–3, 6–11; 12–3, 7–10.30 Sun
Wood Parish *or* Special Ⓖ
Isolated farmhouse that time has forgotten. Bert, the landlord since 1929, hasn't been tempted by such vulgar modernisms as keg beer or lager. In the single bar, beer is served from the cask and coach seats provide the furniture. If the door is locked, knock – and wait! ♨ Q ❀ ♣ P

Ross-on-Wye

Crown & Sceptre

Market Place ☎ (01989) 562765
11–11; 12–10.30 Sun
Archers Best Bitter; Draught Bass; Greene King Abbot; Morland Old Speckled Hen; guest beers ⊞
The real ale pub in Ross: this single-bar, town-centre pub is

popular, especially at the weekends, and is frequented by a young clientele, but there's a good mix. Good food (no eve meals Jan–March). Beer festival Easter. A previous local CAMRA *Pub of the Year*. Parking is a problem.
♨ ❀ ◁ ▷ ♣ ⌂

St Owen's Cross

New Inn

At A4173/B4521 jct
☎ (01989) 730274
12–2.30 (3 Fri & Sat), 6–11; 12–3, 7–10.30 Sun
Draught Bass; Fuller's London Pride; Smiles Best Bitter; Tetley Bitter; Wadworth 6X; guest beer (summer) ⊞
18th-century country pub close to the A40 and A49, famous for its hanging baskets in summer. It boasts many splendid furnishings and features, including a fine fireplace. Separate restaurant. Accommodation consists of two rooms with four-posters.
♨ ❀ ◁ ▷ ♠ ♣ P

Tillington

Bell Inn

Tillington Road (at village crossroads) ☎ (01432) 760395
11–3, 6–11; 11–11 Sat; 12–10.30 Sun
Beer range varies ⊞
Neat and tidy inn with a restaurant, at the heart of the village. A lively public bar, with a jukebox, contrasts with a mellow lounge which divides into bar and patio-style areas. Families are welcomed; excellent garden area. Always at least four beers on tap. No meals winter Sun eves.
♨ ❀ ◁ ▷ ♠ ♣ ⌂ P

Woolhope

Crown Inn

☎ (01432) 860468
12–2.30, 6.30 (7 Mon–Thu in winter)–11; 12–2.30, 7–10.30 Sun
Hook Norton Best Bitter; Smiles Best Bitter; Tetley Bitter; guest beer (occasional) ⊞
Food-oriented pub, very popular with out-of-town diners. A small area of the bar is set aside for discerning beer drinkers.
Q ❀ ⊨ ◁ ▷ ♣ ⌂ P

KEGBUSTER
REMEMBERS

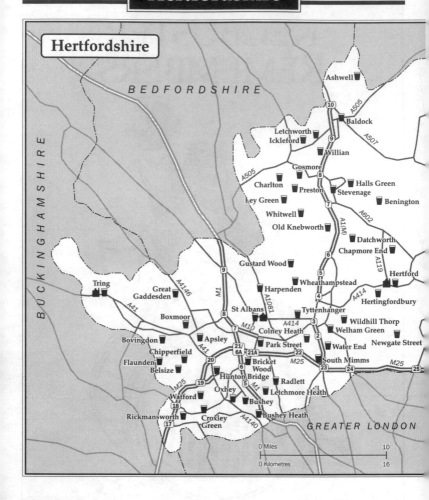

Hertfordshire

BEDFORDSHIRE

BUCKINGHAMSHIRE

Ashwell
Baldock
Letchworth
Ickleford
Willian
Gosmore
Charlton
Preston
Halls Green
Stevenage
Benington
Ley Green
Whitwell
Old Knebworth
Datchworth
Chapmore End
Gustard Wood
Wheathampstead
Hertford
Tring
Great Gaddesden
Harpenden
Hertingfordbury
Boxmoor
St Albans
Tyttenhanger
Wildhill Thorp
Welham Green
Colney Heath
Bovingdon
Apsley
Park Street
Water End
Newgate Street
Chipperfield
Bricket Wood
South Mimms
Flaunden
Belsize
Hunton Bridge
Radlett
Oxhey
Letchmore Heath
Watford
Bushey
Rickmansworth
Croxley Green
Bushey Heath

GREATER LONDON

0 Miles 10
0 Kilometres 16

Apsley

White Lion

44 London Road
☎ (01442) 68948
11–11; 12–10.30 Sun
Fuller's Chiswick, London Pride, ESB, seasonal beers H
Very friendly, street-corner local on the busy London road with a London pub type atmosphere. Lunches are served Mon–Fri.
🏨 🏵 🌢 ⇌ ♣ P

Ashwell

Bushel & Strike

Mill Street
☎ (01462) 742394
11–3, 6 (5.30 Fri)–11; 11–11 Sat; 12–10.30 Sun
Wells Eagle, Bombardier; guest beers H
With 17th-century origins, this pub is now much extended and boasts a restaurant and a sizeable garden. The tallest church steeple in the county overshadows the pub, which is set within a charming old village.
🏵 🌢 ▶ ♣ ⟷ P ⚲

Baldock

Old White Horse

1 Station Road (A505/A507 jct)
☎ (01462) 893168
11–3, 5.30–11; 11–11 Fri & Sat; 12–10.30 Sun
Adnams Bitter; Boddingtons Bitter H; **Fuller's London Pride** H/G; **Wadworth 6X** H; **Woodforde's Wherry; guest beers** H/G
Popular, former coaching inn on the old Great North Road. Jamaican cuisine available (book eve meals). The garden has a play area for children and a patio.
🏵 🌢 ▶ ⇌ ♣ P

Belsize

Plough

Dunny Lane (Sarratt–Chipperfield road) OS034008
☎ (01923) 262800
11–3, 5.30–11; 12–3, 7–10.30 Sun
ABC Best Bitter; Greene King IPA; Young's Bitter H
Isolated pub with a children's certificate. Good food (no meals Sun eve). Ask if anyone can demonstrate the game invented by a customer.
🏨 🏵 🌢 ▶ ♣ P

Benington

Lordship Arms

42 Whempstead Road (3 miles E of Stevenage via B1037) OS308227 ☎ (01438) 869665
12–3, 6–11; 12–3, 7–10.30 Sun
Fuller's ESB; McMullen AK; Young's Special; guest beers H

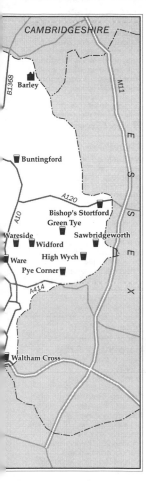

Smartly renovated village local serving a changing range of interesting guest beers and home-cooked food. Telephone memorabilia includes a working red phone box in the garden. The cider varies.
🏠 🌣 ◑ ♣ ⌂ P

Bishop's Stortford

Tap & Spile
31 North Street
☎ (01279) 654978
11–3, 5.30–11; 11–11 Fri & Sat; 12–3, 7–10.30 Sun
Bateman XXXB; Tap & Spile Premium; guest beers Ⓗ
17th-century inn on three levels, with two bars. Live music in the function room most weekends. The six ever-changing guests always include a mild and a cider. Relaxed atmosphere. Limited parking.
🏠 Q 🌣 ◑ ♣ ⌂ P

Bovingdon

Wheatsheaf
High Street ☎ (01442) 832196
11–2.30 (3 Sat), 6–11; 12–3, 7–10.30 Sun
Boddingtons Bitter; guest beer Ⓗ
Fine example of a traditional village pub – friendly, cosy and unspoilt. Dating back to the 15th century, it features lots of brass, old photos of the village, and sewing machine tables. Fresh food. Q 🌣 ♣ P

Boxmoor

Boxmoor Vintners (off-licence)
25–27 St Johns Road
☎ (01442) 252171
9.30–1, 4.30–9.30; 12–2, 7–9 Sun & bank hols
Adnams Bitter, Broadside; guest beer Ⓗ
Independent off-licence, the only one in the area with draught ales. Low prices and unusual guest ales, plus a good selection of British bottled beers.

Bricket Wood

Moor Mill
Smug Oak Lane (off A5183 by M25 bridge) OS152024
☎ (01727) 875557
11–11; 12–10.30 Sun
Beer range varies Ⓗ
Very popular, restored Anglo-Saxon mill on the River Ver (mentioned in the *Domesday Book*), featuring a massive water-wheel. Swan neck dispense but the sparkler will be removed on request. Book for meals in the restaurant.
🏠 Q 🛏 🌣 ◑ ◗ 🍴 ♿ P

Buntingford

Crown
17 High Street
☎ (01763) 271422
12–3, 5.30–11; 12–11 Sat; 12–3.30, 7–10.30 Sun
Courage Best Bitter; Mauldons Best Bitter; Wadworth 6X; guest beer Ⓗ
Traditional town pub with a strong commitment to real ale but also serving good food. The family area is a covered patio. 🏠 Q 🛏 🌣 ◑ ◗

Bushey

Swan
25 Park Road (off A411)
☎ (0181) 950 2256
11–11; 12–10.30 Sun
Benskins BB; Ind Coope Burton Ale Ⓗ
Single public bar in a pub appealing to all which has hardly changed since its appearance in the first *Guide*.
🏠 ♣

Bushey Heath

Black Boy
19 Windmill Street
☎ (0181) 950 2230
11.30–3 (4 Sat), 5.30–11; 11.30–11 Fri; 12–4, 7–10.30 Sun
Adnams Bitter; Benskins BB; Chiltern Beechwood; guest beers Ⓗ
Local CAMRA *Pub of the Year* 1996: a backstreet pub well worth finding. Up to five beers are available and good food is served daily. Real cider occasionally. 🌣 ◑ ◗ ⌂ P

Chapmore End

Woodman
30 Chapmore End (off B158 near A602 jct) OS328164
☎ (01920) 463143
12–3, 6–11; 12–4, 7–10.30 Sun
Greene King IPA, Abbot, seasonal beers Ⓖ
A traditional gem, South Herts CAMRA *Pub of the Year* 1996. Real ales are served by gravity from cooled casks in a 'cellar' behind the bar – try a pint of 'Mix'. Bar meals include pizza and balti (not served Sat eve/Sun). A large garden has a mini zoo and a children's play area.
🏠 Q 🌣 ◑ ◗ 🍴 ♣ P

Charlton

Windmill
Charlton Road (off A602) OS178281
☎ (01462) 432096
11–3, 5.30–11; 12–3, 7–10.30 Sun
Wells Eagle, Bombardier; guest beer Ⓗ
Village pub where the garden leads down to the River Hiz (resident ducks). Good, home-cooked food (Mon–Sat). Monthly guest beer. 🌣 ◑ ◗ P

Chipperfield

Royal Oak
1 The Street
☎ (01923) 266537
12–3, 6–11; 12–3, 7–10.30 Sun
Draught Bass; Flowers Original; Young's Bitter, Special Ⓗ**; guest beer (occasional)** Ⓖ

🏭 **INDEPENDENT BREWERIES**

Dark Horse: Hertford

Fox & Hounds: Barley

McMullen: Hertford

Tring: Tring

Verulam: St Albans

Smart, friendly pub, 17 years in the *Guide*. Highly polished wood and brass abound. Good food (eve meals by arrangement only; sandwiches only Sun). 🚫 Q ⊛ ◖▶ ♣ P

Colney Heath

Crooked Billet
88 High Street
☎ (01727) 822128
11–2.30, 5.30–11; 11–11 Sat; 12–10.30 Sun

Draught Bass; Courage Directors; Fuller's London Pride; Greene King Abbot; Theakston Best Bitter; guest beers Ⓗ
Cottage-style pub with two bars, serving good, home-made meals from a new kitchen. The large garden overlooks open fields.
🚫 Q ⊛ ◖▶ P

Croxley Green

Coach & Horses
The Green (off A412)
☎ (01923) 774457
11–11; 12–10.30 Sun

Adnams Broadside; Marston's Pedigree; Tetley Bitter; Young's Special; guest beers Ⓗ
Traditional village local in a pleasant setting on the green. Always six real ales available, as well as home-cooked food (12–10 each day; 12–3.30 Sun in winter). Monthly food theme eves. Petanque played.
🚫 ⊛ ◖▶ ♣ P

Datchworth

Plough
5 Datchworth Green (1 mile from B197 at Woolmer Green) OS269182 ☎ (01438) 813000
11.30–3, 6–11; 12–4, 7–10.30 Sun

Greene King IPA, Abbot, seasonal beers Ⓗ
Small, welcoming local, just off the green: one room with a large, central fireplace. A former Simpson's of Baldock house. No food Sun.
🚫 Q ⊛ ◖▲ ♣ P

Tilbury
1 Watton Road (1 mile from B197 at Woolmer Green) OS270183 ☎ (01438) 812496
11–3, 5–11; 11–11 Thu–Sat; 12–10.30 Sun

Draught Bass; guest beers Ⓗ/Ⓖ
Friendly, two-bar pub with a no-smoking dining room. The regular beers (including two house beers from the Bass Museum) are complemented by unusual ales from small independents; some occasionally served by gravity in the Ale Bar, which displays

brewery memorabilia. Wide range of home-cooked food.
Q ⊛ ◖▶ ⊟ ▲ ♣ P

Flaunden

Bricklayers Arms
Hogpits Bottom
☎ (01442) 833322
11.30–2.30 (3 Sat), 6–11 (11–11 summer Sat); 12–3, 7–10.30 (12–10.30 summer) Sun

Brakspear Bitter; Fuller's London Pride; guest beers Ⓗ
Smart, food-oriented, country pub which is still drinker-friendly, offering a varied range of ales. Pleasant garden.
🚫 Q ⊛ ◖▶ P

Gosmore

Bird in Hand
High Street (Hitchin turn from A1(M) jct 8; 2nd left at 1st roundabout) OS187272
☎ (01462) 432079
12–3, 5.30–11; 12–11 Sat; 12–10.30 Sun

Greene King XX Mild, IPA, Abbot Ⓗ
Refurbished pub in a quiet village setting, used by locals but visitors are made most welcome. Eve meals 6–8.30 (not served Sun). ⊛ ◖▶ ♣ P

Great Gaddesden

Cock & Bottle
Off A4146 ☎ (01442) 255381
11.30–3, 5.30–11; 12–3, 7–10.30 Sun

Fuller's ESB; Hop Back Summer Lightning; Morland Old Speckled Hen; Taylor Landlord; guest beer Ⓗ
Set in the Gade Valley, close to Hemel Hempstead, this ever-improving pub welcomes drinkers, diners and families. Very reasonable prices. Booking is advised for Sun lunch and some eve meals.
🚫 Q ⊛ ◖▶ ♣ P ⌿

Green Tye

Prince of Wales
Off B1004 ☎ (01279) 842517
11.30–3, 5.30–11; 11–11 Sat; 12–3, 7–10.30 Sun

Flowers IPA; McMullen AK; guest beers Ⓗ
Traditional country pub in a picturesque village, a good halt featured in several rambling guides. Two guest beers are changed monthly; occasional beer festivals.
🚫 ⊛ ◖♣ P

Gustard Wood

Cross Keys
Ballslough Hill (off B651, 1 mile N of Wheathampstead) OS174165 ☎ (01582) 832165
11–3.30, 6–11; 12–4.30, 7–10.30 Sun

Fuller's London Pride; Greene King IPA; Ind Coope Burton

Ale; Marston's Pedigree; Taylor Landlord; Tetley Bitter; guest beers Ⓗ
Roomy, one-bar, 17th-century pub with a large open fire and many wall clocks. The dining room serves good, reasonably priced meals. A large garden has tables. The family room is not always open.
🚫 Q ⏾ ⊛ ⊠ ◖♣ P

Halls Green

Rising Sun
Weston Road (minor road to Cromer) OS275287
☎ (01462) 790487
11–2.30, 6–11; 12–3, 7–10.30 Sun

Draught Bass; Courage Directors; McMullen AK, Country, Gladstone, seasonal beers Ⓗ
Beautiful, one-bar pub in the country. The enormous garden has children's play equipment and a petanque pitch. The conservatory acts as a restaurant; families are most welcome. Unusual range of Polish flavoured vodkas.
🚫 ⏾ ⊛ ◖▶ ♣ P

Harpenden

Carpenters Arms
Cravells Road, Southdown (off A1081)
☎ (01582) 460311
11–3, 5.30–11; 12–3, 7–10.30 Sun

Courage Best Bitter; Ruddles County; Webster's Yorkshire Bitter; guest beer Ⓗ
200-year-old homely pub with motoring memorabilia. It features locally-brewed house beers from small and independent breweries. No food Sun.
🚫 Q ⊛ ◖⊟ ♣ P

Cross Keys
39 High Street (A1081)
☎ (01582) 763989
11.30–2.30, 5–11; 12–3, 7–10.30 Sun

Boddingtons Bitter; Brakspear Bitter; Flowers Original; Taylor Landlord Ⓗ
300-year-old pub boasting a flagstoned floor, oak beams and masses of pewter, including the bar top. A rare gem, unchanged for 35 years. No meals winter Sun.
🚫 Q ⊛ ◖▶ ⇌ ♣

Red Cow
171 Westfield Road (off B653 E Hyde–Batford road)
☎ (01582) 621058
11–11; 12–10.30 Sun

Courage Directors; Ruddles County Special; Verulam Ⓗ/Ⓖ
Grade II-listed, 16th-century building. Note the 80 plaques carrying drinking quotations and rhymes.
🚫 ⊛ ◖▶ ♣ P ⊟

Hertford

Sportsman
117 Fore Street
☎ (01992) 551621
12–3, 5.30–11; 12–11 Fri & Sat; 12–3,
7–10.30 Sun
**Adnams Bitter; Everards
Tiger; Marston's Pedigree;
Ruddles Best Bitter;
Wadworth 6X** Ⓗ
Busy, town-centre pub staging
live music at least one Sat eve a
month. It used to be the
brewery tap of Youngs of
Hertford and was formerly
known as the Blue Coat Boy
after the local school. Thu is
student night.
◖ ▶ ⇌ (East)

White Horse
30 Castle Street
☎ (01992) 501950
12–2.30 (3 Sat), 5.30 (5 Fri, 6 Sat)–11;
12–3.30, 7–10.30 Sun
**Dark Horse Ale, Sunrunner;
Fuller's London Pride; Hook
Norton Best Bitter** Ⓗ**; guest
beers** Ⓗ/Ⓖ
Hertford's leading free house,
the Dark Horse Brewery tap,
offering ale from all noted
micro/small brewers (up to
nine beers usually on), plus a
wide choice of fruit wines. An
upstairs no-smoking area is
open to children. Lunches are
served daily, including
specials.
🏚 Q ◖ ⌷ ⇌ (East/North) ⚲

Hertingfordbury

Prince of Wales
244 Hertingfordbury Road (400
yds from A414)
☎ (01992) 581149
11–2.30 (3 Sat), 5.30 (6 Sat)–11; 12–4,
7–10.30 Sun
**Dark Horse Sunrunner;
Fuller's London Pride;
McMullen AK; Wadworth 6X;
guest beers** Ⓗ
Local CAMRA *Pub of the Year*
runner-up 1996, this one-bar
local is the focus of village life.
No meals Sun eve.
⚇ ⌷ ◖ ▶ ♣ P

High Wych

Rising Sun
1 mile W of Sawbridgeworth
☎ (01279) 724099
12–2.30 (3 Fri & Sat), 5–11; 12–3,
7–10.30 Sun
**Courage Best Bitter, Directors;
guest beers** Ⓖ
A *Guide* regular for over 20
years, affectionately known as
'Sid's', this small, basic, no
frills, traditional pub has been
run by the same family for
generations. Warm welcome
(especially if the woodburner
is alight).
🏚 Q ⓫ ⚇ ♣ P

Hunton Bridge

Kings Head
Bridge Road (off A41)
☎ (01923) 262307
11–3, 5.30–11; 12–3, 7–10.30 Sun
**Benskins BB; Marston's
Pedigree; Tetley Bitter; guest
beer** Ⓗ
Friendly pub on different
levels (it's two cottages joined
together). The old stables, by
the Grand Union Canal, house
a skittle alley (family room in
summer). 🏚 Q ⓫ ⚇ ◖ ▶ ♣ P

Ickleford

Cricketers
107 Arlesey Road (800 yds
from A600)
☎ (01462) 432629
11–3, 5.30–11; 11–11 Sat; 12–10.30 Sun
Beer range varies Ⓗ
Very friendly free house in the
village centre, offering a good
choice of beer to suit all tastes,
home-cooked food and good
accommodation. Local
CAMRA *Pub of the Year* 1994.
🏚 Q ⚇ ⛺ ◖ ▶ ♣ ⌂ P

Plume of Feathers
Upper Green (400 yds from
A600, down Turnpike Lane)
☎ (01462) 432729
11–3 (4 Sat), 6–11; 12–5, 7–10.30 Sun
**Boddingtons Bitter; Fuller's
London Pride; King & Barnes
Sussex; Wadworth 6X; guest
beers** Ⓗ
Friendly village local run by
two sisters; changed over the
years but not spoilt. Good
quality, home-cooked food.
Lively, but not noisy.
Q ⚇ ◖ ▶ ♣ P

Letchmore Heath

Three Horseshoes
The Green
☎ (01923) 856084
11–3, 6–11; 11–11 Sat; 12–10.30 Sun
**Benskins BB; Tetley Bitter;
guest beers** Ⓗ
Two-bar, 17th-century pub
next to the pond, facing the
green: a flagstoned public bar
and a horse brass-bedecked
beamed lounge. Extensive
menu. 🏚 Q ◖ ▶ ⓫ P

Letchworth

Arena Tavern
3 Arena Parade
☎ (01462) 686400
10.30–11; 12–3, 7–10.30 Sun
**John Smith's Bitter; guest
beers** Ⓗ
Cosy, town-centre free house
near the cinema. Three beers
are always available; varied
lunch menu. Regular jazz/
blues nights. Large public car
park opposite. ◖ ⇌

Ley Green

Plough
Plough Lane OS162243
☎ (01438) 871394
11–11; 12–4, 7–10.30 Sun
Greene King IPA, Abbot Ⓗ
Country pub overlooking
farmland, with chickens and
ducks. 🏚 Q ⛍ ⚇ ◖ ▶ ▲ ♣ P

Newgate Street

Coach & Horses
61 Newgate Street Village
☎ (01707) 872326
11–3, 5.30–11; 11–11 Sat; 12–10.30 Sun
**Draught Bass; Benskins BB;
Dartmoor Best Bitter; M&B
Brew XI; Tetley Bitter** Ⓗ
Genuine, old, ivy-covered pub
next to the church, the meeting
place of many different clubs.
The car park has been
extended without ruining the
character of the pub. Children
welcome in the function room.
🏚 Q ⛍ ⚇ ◖ P

Old Knebworth

Lytton Arms
Park Lane OS229202
☎ (01438) 812312
11–3, 5–11; 11–11 Fri & Sat; 12–10.30
Sun
**Draught Bass; Fuller's London
Pride; Theakston Best Bitter;
Woodforde's Wherry; guest
beers** Ⓗ
Large, 19th-century Lutyens
building on the edge of
Knebworth Park. The 12 beers
usually include a mild and
beers from the Millennium
Brewing Co., which are
contract-brewed. Large
selection of foreign bottled
beers and malt whiskies.
Children's certificate.
🏚 Q ⚇ ◖ ▶ ⚅ ♣ ⌂ P ⚲

Oxhey

Victoria
39 Chalk Hill
☎ (01923) 227993
11–3, 5.30–11; 12–4.30, 7–10.30 Sun
**Benskins BB; Tetley Bitter;
guest beer** Ⓗ
Two-bar pub at the bottom of
Chalk Hill; very much a
community pub which even
has its own ski club. Barbecues
summer Sun when the pub
stays open all afternoon. Tiny
car park.
⚇ ◖ ⇌ (Bushey) ♣ P

Park Street

Overdraught
86 Park Street
☎ (01727) 874200
11–11; 12–3, 7–10.30 Sun
**Marston's Bitter, Pedigree;
guest beers** Ⓗ

Friendly village local with two bar areas offering two guest beers from micro-breweries and good value, home-made food (eve meals finish early). Children's certificate.
🏚 Q ☸ ⊿ ⇌ ⌂ P

Preston

Red Lion
The Green ☎ (01462) 459585
12–3 (2.30 Fri), 5.30–11; 12–11 Sat; 12–3, 7–10.30 Sun
Draught Bass; Greene King IPA; Robinson's Frederics; guest beer H
Georgian-style public house owned by the villagers. Good, home-cooked food served daily. 🏚 ⥒ ☸ ⊿ ▶ ♣ P

Pye Corner

Plume of Feathers
On High Wych road, between Harlow and Sawbridgeworth
☎ (01279) 424154
11.30–3, 5.30 (7 Sat)–11; 12–4, 7–10.30 Sun
Courage Best Bitter; Marston's Pedigree; guest beers H
Former court house and coaching inn with a resident ghost. Three regularly changing guest beers and occasional live music are features. Family-oriented, it has a small public bar and an enclosed rear patio which is popular on summer eves.
🏚 ⊿ ▶ ⊟ ♣ P

Radlett

Cat & Fiddle
14 Watling Street (A5183)
☎ (01923) 424154
11–11; 12–10.30 Sun
Adnams Broadside; Courage Best Bitter, Directors; guest beers H
18th-century pub with many oak-panelled bars giving the feel of a country inn. Large collection of china cats.
🏚 Q ☸ ⊿ ⇌ P

Rickmansworth

Fox & Hounds
183 High Street
☎ (01923) 441119
11–11; 12–10.30 Sun
Courage Best Bitter, Directors; guest beer H
Comfortable Victorian pub retaining a traditional feel in two separate bars. Interesting guest beers.
🏚 Q ☸ ⇌ ⊖ ♣ P

St Albans

Farmers Boy
134 London Road
☎ (01727) 857473
11–11; 12–10.30 Sun

Verulam Special, IPA H**, Farmer's Joy** H/G**; guest beers** H
One-bar pub with its own brewery attached. A real log fire and large, friendly dogs give a country atmosphere.
🏚 ☸ ⊿ ▶ ⌂

Farriers Arms
35 Lower Dagnall Street (off A5183)
☎ (01727) 851025
12–2.30 (4 Sat), 5.30 (7 Sat)–11; 12–3, 7–10.30 Sun
McMullen AK, Country, Gladstone, seasonal *or* guest beer H
A perennial entry in the *Guide*. Recent decoration has not spoilt this backstreet local which is home to many sports and games teams. Lunches served Mon–Fri. Tricky parking. Q ⊿ ♣

Lower Red Lion
34–36 Fishpool Street
☎ (01727) 855669
12–2.30, 5.30–11; 11–11 Sat; 12–4, 7–10.30 Sun
Adnams Bitter; Fuller's London Pride; guest beers H
17th-century coaching inn, a genuine free house with five guest beers from micro-breweries. The house beer comes from Tring. No food Sun. Good B&B.
🏚 Q ☸ ⨝ ⊿ ♣ P

Mermaid
98 Hatfield Road
☎ (01727) 854487
11–3, 5.30–11; 12–5 Sun
Everards Beacon, Tiger, Old Original; guest beer H
Small, one-bar pub drawing a mixed clientele – students, suits and locals. Quizzes and backgammon are specialities. Meals Mon–Fri. Closed Sun eve. ☸ ⊿ ♣ P

Sawbridgeworth

Gate Inn
81 London Road
☎ (01279) 722313
11.30–2.30, 5.30 (5 Fri & Sat)–11; 12–3, 7–10.30 Sun
Adnams Bitter; Brakspear Special; Castle Eden Ale; Fuller's London Pride; guest beers H
Pub dating back to Napoleonic times, on the site of the town's Parsonage Gate; popular with all ages. Guest beers, including milds, are regularly changed (total exceeds 1,000). No food Sun. Q ⊿ ⥒ ⇌ ⌂ P

South Mimms

Black Horse
65 Blackhorse Lane (200 yds from B556) ☎ (01707) 642174
11–3, 5.30–11; 11–11 Fri & Sat; 12–3, 7–10.30 Sun

Greene King XX Mild, IPA, Abbot, seasonal beers H
Lively local with a friendly welcome. Darts in the public bar; comfortable lounge.
🏚 ☸ ⊿ ♣ P

Stevenage

Our Mutual Friend
Broadwater Crescent (1 mile off A1(M) jct 7, off A602 roundabout) ☎ (01438) 312282
11–11; 12–10.30 Sun
Boddingtons Bitter; Flowers Original; guest beers H
Estate pub near Stevenage Borough FC, named after a long-gone local pub of the same name (derived from Dickens's last novel). Good selection of games. Frequent beer festivals.
☸ ⊿ ▶ ⊟ & ♣ P

Tring

Kings Arms
King Street (near Natural History Museum)
☎ (01442) 823318
12 (11.30)–2.30 (3 Fri), 7–11; 12–4, 7–10.30 Sun
Adnams Bitter; Brakspear Special; Wadworth 6X; guest beers H
Backstreet local, always very busy even though hard to find. Constantly changing and varied range of ales and cider. No-smoking area lunchtime. Healthy menu.
🏚 Q ☸ ⊿ ▶ ♣ ⌂ ⊬

Robin Hood Inn
1 Brook Street
☎ (01442) 824912
11.30–2.30, 5.30–11; 11–3, 6.30–11 Sat; 12–3, 7–10.30 Sun
Fuller's Chiswick, London Pride, ESB, seasonal beers H
Superb, olde-worlde pub, always gleaming. The excellent menu specialises in seafood (all fresh). The licensee has a Fuller's cellarmanship award and has also won Fuller's *Country Pub of the Year* award.
🏚 ☸ ⊿ ▶ ♣

Tyttenhanger

Plough
Tyttenhanger Green (off A414 via Highfield Lane)
☎ (01727) 857777
11–2.30 (3 Sat), 6–11; 12–3, 7–10.30 Sun
Fuller's London Pride, ESB; Greene King Abbot; Marston's Pedigree; Taylor Landlord; Woodforde's Wherry; guest beer H
Popular free house serving good value lunches. Large collection of bottled beers; the house beer is brewed by Mansfield. The garden is

popular in summer (good play equipment). 🏨 Q ❀ ◗ P

Waltham Cross

Vaults
160 High Street
☎ (01992) 631600
11–11; 12–3, 7–10.30 Sun
Beer range varies 🅷
Pub converted from a former bank, offering a choice of six beers, five from small independents (southern brewery beers may sometimes be on sparklers). Bands play Thu; jazz Sun. Car park access is off Monarch Way (northerly direction). ❀ ◗ ◗ 🍺 ♣ P

Ware

Albion
12 Crib Street (behind St Mary's church)
☎ (01920) 463599
11–11; 12–3, 7–10.30 Sun
Adnams Bitter; Boddingtons Bitter; Flowers IPA 🅷
Oak-beamed bar in a 16/17th-century, half-timbered building which features wonderful floral displays outside in summer. A superb cosy and popular local. No food Sun. 🏨 ◗ 🍺

Worppell
35 Watton Road
☎ (01920) 462572
11.30–2.30, 5–11; 11–11 Fri & Sat; 12–3, 7–10.30 Sun
Greene King IPA, Abbot, seasonal beers 🅷
Formerly the New Rose & Crown: the present name is that of a builder who bought and rebuilt the pub in the 1800s. Though recently altered, it maintains its very friendly atmosphere.
◗ 🍺 ♣

Wareside

Chequers
☎ (01920) 467010
12–3, 6–11; 12–11 Sat; 12–10.30 Sun
Adnams Bitter; Greene King Abbot; guest beer 🅷
Relaxed and cosy, old cottage-style pub with many old beams and features exposed. The house ale is brewed by the Dark Horse Brewery. A good choice of food is available; no eve meals Sun.
🏨 Q ❀ 🛏 ◗ ◗ 🍴 🛱 ♣ P

Water End (North Mymms)

Old Maypole
43 Warrengate Road (off B197)
OS230041
☎ (01707) 642119

11–2.30 (3 Sat), 5.30–11; 12–3, 7–10.30 Sun
Greene King IPA, Abbot, seasonal beers 🅷
16th-century, split-level pub with an inglenook and a separate room for non-smoking families. Handy for the Royal Veterinary College. No food Sun.
🏨 Q 🛏 ❀ ◗ P ♨

Woodman
Warrengate Road (off B197)
☎ (01707) 650502
11–3, 5.30 (5 Fri)–11; 12–10.30 Sun
Courage Best Bitter, Directors; Marston's Pedigree; Wadworth 6X 🅷
250-year-old, two-bar, brassed and beamed pub with a quiet back garden. Only snacks available Sun. 🏨 ❀ ◗ ◗

Watford

Estcourt Arms
2 St John's Road (350 yds SW of Junction station)
☎ (01923) 220754
11–11; 12–10.30 Sun
Tetley Bitter; guest beers 🅷
Friendly, street-corner town pub generating a genuine Irish atmosphere. A small snug complements the larger bar. Home-cooked food Mon–Fri. Adnams Bitter and Fuller's London Pride often feature among the guest beers. Patio with two tables for outside drinking.
❀ ◗ 🍺 (Junction)

Welham Green

Hope & Anchor
2 Station Road
☎ (01707) 262935
11–2.30 (3 Sat), 5.30 (6 Sat)–11; 12–3, 7–10.30 Sun
Courage Best Bitter, Directors; John Smith's Bitter 🅷
Village local with two contrasting bars. It was recorded as a beer house in 1838, when the North Mymms bellringers were paid in beer. No food Sun.
Q ❀ ◗ 🍺 ❀ P

Wheathampstead

Nelson
135 Marford Road
☎ (01582) 832196
11.30–11; 12–3, 7–10.30 Sun
Adnams Bitter; Fuller's London Pride; Greene King IPA; Tetley Bitter; guest beers 🅷
Roadside pub with three areas (an open fire between two of them) and a glass-covered well behind the bar. Good, reasonably priced lunches are served (Mon–Sat). The 'quiet' symbol refers to lunchtimes only. 🏨 Q ❀ ◗ ♣ P

Whitwell ✦

Maidens Head
67 High Street
☎ (01438) 871392
11.30–2.30 (may be later), 5–11; 12–3, 7–10.30 Sun
Draught Bass; McMullen AK, Country; guest beer 🅷
Excellent village local of character, with friendly locals and staff, plus good, home-cooked food. East Anglia CAMRA *Pub of the Year* 1996; the landlord has won the McMullen Master Cellarman award four years running.
🏨 ❀ ◗ ◗ ♣ P

Widford

Green Man
High Street
☎ (01279) 842454
12–11; 12–10.30 Sun
Courage Directors; McMullen AK, Gladstone, seasonal beers 🅷
Attractive village local with a long bar and an open-plan interior. Largely due to the efforts of the tenants, it attracts a mixture of local and passing trade. The Sun eve jazz is very popular. Food is always available.
🏨 ❀ ◗ ◗ 🛏 🅰 ♣ P

Wildhill Thorp

Woodman
45 Wildhill Lane (between A1000 and B158) OS265068
☎ (01707) 642618
11.30–2.30, 5.30–11; 12–2.30, 7–10.30 Sun
Greene King IPA, Abbot, seasonal beers; McMullen AK; guest beers 🅷
Genuine local, first registered as a beerhouse in 1851 and now offering an enterprising selection of guest ales from small independent breweries at reasonable prices. Chip-free lunches (not served Sun). Sky TV in the snug for Spurs supporters.
Q ❀ 🛱 ◗ ♣ P

Willian

Three Horseshoes
Baldock Lane (tiny lane opp. the church, 1 mile off A1(M) jct 9 towards Letchworth) OS225308
☎ (01462) 685713
11–11; 12–10.30 Sun
Greene King IPA, Abbot, seasonal beers 🅷
Comfortable, single-bar pub with a friendly atmosphere. A converted barn serves as a function room hosting bridge and darts tournaments.
🏨 ❀ ◗ ◗ ♣ ❀

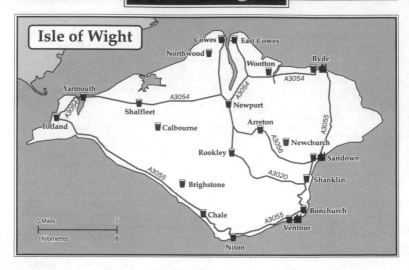

Isle of Wight

Cowes · East Cowes · Northwood · Wootton · Ryde · A3054 · Yarmouth · A3054 · Newport · Shalfleet · A3054 · Calbourne · Arreton · Totland · A3054 · Rookley · A3056 · Newchurch · A3055 · Sandown · Brighstone · A3020 · Shanklin · Chale · A3055 · Bonchurch · Ventnor · Niton

0 Miles 5
0 Kilometres 8

Arreton

White Lion

Main Road
☎ (01983) 528479
11–3, 7–11; 12–3, 6–10.30 Sun
Draught Bass H/G;
Boddingtons Bitter H;
Flowers Original; Goddards
Fuggle-Dee-Dum H/G
Excellent refurbishment of a
traditional country pub, with a
well-laid-out interior. Good
food. Near many places of
interest to island visitors.
🏨 Q ⛵ ❀ ◑ ▶ ♿ ♣ P ✚

Bonchurch

Bonchurch Inn

The Shute (off Sandown Road)
☎ (01983) 852611
11–4 (3 winter), 6.30–11; 12–3, 7–10.30
Sun
Courage Best Bitter,
Directors G
Superbly preserved, stone pub,
tucked away in a courtyard,
formerly the stables of the
adjacent manor house. The
floors came from a ship's deck,
the chairs from a liner.
Authentic Italian food.
Q ⛵ ❀ ◑ ▶ ♿ ♣

Brighstone

Countryman

Limerstone Road
☎ (01983) 740616
11–3, 7–11 (11–11 summer); 12–3,
7–10.30 Sun
Badger Dorset Best,
Tanglefoot H
Spacious and friendly country
roadhouse with a large lounge
bar, a public bar and an
extensive function room. A
good family stop-over with a

reputation for good food. Near
many holiday attractions.
🏨 Q ❀ ◑ ▶ ♿ ♣ P ✚

Calbourne

Blacksmith's Arms

Calbourne Road
☎ (01983) 529263
11–3, 6–11 (11–11 summer); 12–10.30
Sun
Archers Golden; Black Sheep
Riggwelter; Cotleigh Tawny;
Ventnor Golden H
CAMRA regional *Pub of the
Year* 1997, serving an excellent
and constantly varying range
of ales, plus an extensive range
of German and other bottled
beers. Popular for its German
food, too. Panoramic Solent
views.
🏨 Q ⛵ ❀ ◑ ▶ P ✚

Chale

Wight Mouse

Newport Road (B3399)
☎ (01983) 730431
11–11; 12–10.30 Sun
Boddingtons Bitter; Gale's
HSB; Marston's Pedigree;
Morland Old Speckled Hen;
Wadworth 6X; guest beer H
Very busy, old stone pub with
an adjoining hotel, near
Blackgang Chine theme park.
An award-winning family and
whisky pub, it has a garden
play area and three family
rooms. Food all day (late
supper licence). Live music
every night.
🏨 Q ❀ ◑ ▶ ♿ ♣ P ✚

Cowes

Anchor

High Street ☎ (01983) 292823
11–11; 12–10.30 Sun

Badger Tanglefoot; Flowers
Original; Fuller's London
Pride; Greene King Abbot;
Goddards Fuggle-Dee-Dum H
Extended town pub, very
popular with locals and
yachtsmen. Live music, good
food (interesting and varied
menu, with barbecues in
summer) and a good variety of
ales are all available.
🏨 ❀ ◑ ▶ 🍴

East Cowes

Ship & Castle

21 Castle Street
☎ (01983) 290522
11–11; 12–10.30 Sun
Badger Dorset Best; Courage
Directors; Ind Coope Burton
Ale; guest beers H
Pleasant, one-bar town pub
which serves some interesting
beers. No food Tue.
◑ ♣

Newchurch

Pointer Inn

High Street (N of A3056, 2
miles W of Sandown)
☎ (01983) 865202
11–4, 6–11; 12–4, 7–10.30 (12–10.30
summer) Sun
Gale's Best Bitter, HSB H
Thriving village pub by the
church, serving home-cooked
food.
Q ⛵ ❀ ◑ ▶ 🍴 ♿ ▲ ♣ P

🏭 **INDEPENDENT
BREWERIES**

Burts: Sandown

Goddards: Ryde

Ventnor: Ventnor

Newport

Castle
91 High Street
☎ (01983) 522528
10.30–11; 12–10.30 Sun
Boddingtons Bitter; Flowers Original; Greene King Abbot Ⓗ
Characterful, 17th-century, stone, single-bar pub replete with flagstones and beams, it has served as a venue for cockfighting, a marriage parlour and a thieves' sanctuary. ♨ ◖ ▶ ♿

Prince of Wales
Town Lane
☎ (01983) 525026
10.30–11; 12–3, 7–10.30 Sun
Ushers Best Bitter, Founders, seasonal beers Ⓗ
Street-corner, town local with an excellent reputation amongst local drinkers. Good, interesting, home-cooked food.
🏚 ◖ ▶ 🍽 ♿ ♣ ▭ ☐

Railway Medina
Sea Street ☎ (01983) 528303
11–3, 6–11; 12–4, 7–10.30 Sun
Gale's HSB; Goddards Special; Webster's Green Label Ⓗ
Cosy, backstreet local with much railway memorabilia; now a free house with a relaxing atmosphere.
☀ ◖ ▶ 🍽 ♣ ☐

Niton

White Lion
High Street ☎ (01983) 730293
11–3.30, 5–11; 12–3, 7–10.30 Sun
Castle Eden Ale; guest beer Ⓗ
Beautiful, historic village inn with a large function room. Good, home-cooked food.
🏚 Q ♨ 🌸 ◖ ▶ 🍽 Ⓐ P ✗

Northwood

Travellers Joy
Pallance Road (follow signs for Porchfield off A3020)
☎ (01983) 298024
11–2.30, 5–11 Fri & Sat; 12–3, 7–10.30 Sun
Badger Dorset Best; Goddards Special; Marston's Pedigree; Ruddles County; Theakston Old Peculier; guest beers Ⓗ
Well-renovated country inn offering a fine choice of ales. Local CAMRA *Pub of the Year* for many years. The large garden has a children's play area. ♨ 🌸 ◖ ▶ Ⓐ ♣ ▭ P ✗

Rookley

Chequers
Niton Road (off A3020)
☎ (01983) 840314
11–11; 12–10.30 Sun

Courage Best Bitter, Directors; John Smith's Bitter; guest beer Ⓗ
Country pub at the heart of the island: a lounge bar, a large restaurant, and a flagstoned public bar with spacious children's play areas inside and out. Extensive menu of home-cooked food; fresh fish always available.
🏚 Q ♨ 🌸 ◖ ▶ 🍽 ♿ Ⓐ ♣ P ✗

Ryde

Falcon
17 Swanmore Road
☎ (01983) 563900
11–3, 6–11; 12–3, 7–10.30 Sun
Gale's Best Bitter, HSB Ⓗ
Stone-built, town local in a residential area, run by the long-standing ex-landlord of the Castle. 🌸 🍽 ☀ ➔ ♣

Hole in the Wall
68 St Johns Road
☎ (01983) 615405
11–3, 6–11; 11–11 Sat; 12–3, 7–10.30 Sun
Burts Nipper, Newport Nobbler, Crustache; guest beers Ⓗ
Nicely extended and refurbished, street-corner local, attracting a growing following for its interesting beer selection. 🏚 ♨ 🌸 ▶ ➔

Sandown

Caulkheads
Avenue Road
☎ (01983) 403878
10.30–11; 12–10.30 Sun
Boddingtons Bitter; Flowers Original; Morland Old Speckled Hen; Wadworth 6X Ⓗ
Lively, family-oriented pub with a restaurant seating 180. Indoor children's play area; large garden.
♨ ◖ ▶ 🍽 ♿ Ⓐ ♣ P ✗

Shalfleet

New Inn
Main Road ☎ (01983) 531314
12–3, 6–11 (12–11 summer); 12–3, 7–10.30 Sun
Boddingtons Bitter; Flowers Original Ⓗ
Ancient quayside inn, specialising in seafood. Very popular with islanders and visiting yachtsmen alike.
Q ♨ 🌸 ◖ ▶ ♣

Shanklin

Chine Inn
Chine Hill ☎ (01983) 865880
11.30–3, 7.30–11 (11–11 summer); 12–3, 7–10.30 (12–10.30 summer) Sun
Draught Bass; Goddards Fuggle-Dee-Dum; Worthington Bitter Ⓗ

This building has stood since 1621, and has lately recovered much of the charm of the old Burts house it used to be. Cosy in winter; fine views over Sandown Bay in summer.
🏚 Q ♨ 🌸 🍽 ◖ ▶

Totland

Highdown Inn
Highdown Lane (1½ miles E of Alum Bay old road) OS324858
☎ (01983) 752450
11–3, 7–11 (11–11 summer); 12–10.30 Sun
Ushers Best Bitter, Founders Ⓗ
Country pub near some fine walks. Once a notorious smuggling den, it is now an excellent stopping-off point during a bracing visit to Tennyson Down. Good food.
🏚 Q 🌸 🍽 ◖ ▶ 🍽 Ⓐ ♣ P ☐

Ventnor

Volunteer
Victoria Street
☎ (01983) 852537
11–11; 12–3, 7–10.30 Sun
Badger Dorset Best; Hampshire King Alfred's; Ventnor Mild Ⓗ
Traditional, friendly town local, renovated to preserve its original character and displaying interesting memorabilia. A superb pub.
🏚 Q ♣

Wootton

Woodmans Arms
119 Station Road
☎ (01983) 882785
11–3, 6–11; 12–3, 7–10.30 Sun
Draught Bass; Flowers Original; Fuller's London Pride; guest beers Ⓗ
Friendly country pub, very popular with locals, near the steam railway. Good value food. ♨ 🌸 ◖ ▶ ♿ Ⓐ ➔ ♣ P

Yarmouth

Wheatsheaf
Bridge Road ☎ (01983) 760456
11–3, 6–11; 11–11 Sat & summer; 12–3, 7–10.30 Sun
Flowers Original; Goddards Fuggle-Dee-Dum; Morland Old Speckled Hen Ⓗ
Old coaching house, now with additional rooms; spacious and comfortable for families, with good value food and beer.
🏚 Q ♨ 🌸 ◖ ▶ 🍽 ♣

Protect your pleasure – join CAMRA today! See the back of this book for membership details.

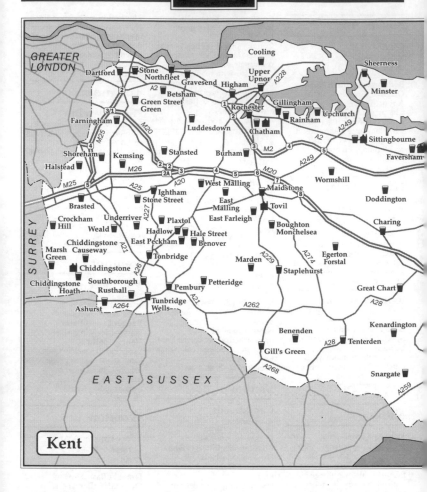

Kent

Ashford

Hooden Horse on the Hill

Silver Hill Road, Willsborough
☎ (01233) 662226
12–3, 6–11; 12–3, 7–10.30 Sun
**Goacher's Light; Hook Norton
Old Hooky; Hop Back
Summer Lighting; guest
beers** H
Standing on the one-way road
from Hythe, this pub has a
large garden. The menu offers
a good choice of spicy meals
with a Mexican theme.
Biddenden cider. ❀ ◖ ◗ ⇔ P

Hooden on the Water

Rugby Gardens, Torrington
Road
☎ (01233) 633404
12–2.30, 6–11; 12–3, 7–10.30 Sun
**Goacher's Light; Hook Norton
Old Hooky; Hop Back
Summer Lightning; guest
beer** H

The sixth pub in the Hooden
Horse chain continues the
tradition of hopped ceilings,
bare floor boards, good
service and a great
atmosphere.
❀ ◖ ◗ ⇌ ⇔ P

Ashurst

Bald Faced Stag

On A264, 5 miles W of
Tunbridge Wells
☎ (01892) 740321
11 (12 winter)–3, 6–11; 11–11 Sat;
12–10.30 Sun
**Draught Bass; Greene King
IPA; Harveys BB; guest
beers** H
Friendly, single-bar, free house
on the main Tunbridge Wells–
East Grinstead road, on the
Sussex border. Popular with
locals and passing trade alike.
Ever changing range of guest
beers.
⛺ ❀ ◖ ◗ ▲ ⇌ ♣ P

Badlesmere

Red Lion

Ashford Road
☎ (01233) 740320
11.30–3, 6–11; 11.30–11 Fri & Sat;
12–10.30 Sun
**Fuller's London Pride; Greene
King XX Mild, Abbot;
Shepherd Neame Master
Brew Bitter; guest beers** H
Excellent free house on the
Faversham to Ashford road,
well known for its weekend
folk and ale festivals in June
and August. Extensive outside
drinking area with two pot-
bellied pigs. Live music every
Fri eve. Eve meals Tue–Sat.
⛺ ❀ ◖ ◗ ▲ ♣ ⇔

Barfreston

Yew Tree Inn

☎ (01304) 831619
11–11; 12–10.30 Sun
Black Sheep Best Bitter;

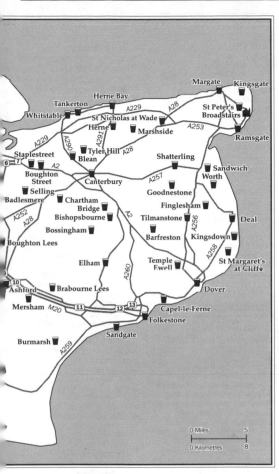

Master Brew Bitter;
Wadworth 6X; guest beers Ⓗ
Village pub named after a local
WWI VC hero: a popular
convivial local with quiz nights
and Bat and Trap and
petanque teams. Good food
(not served Sun or Mon eves).
The large garden has a
children's play area.
🏛 ◐ ▶ ⊞ ♣ P

Bishopsbourne

Mermaid
The Street (off A2 S of
Canterbury)
☎ (01227) 830581
11–3, 6–11; 12–3, 7–10.30 Sun
Shepherd Neame Master
Brew Bitter, seasonal beers Ⓗ
Attractive, unpretentious pub
in a typical Kentish village,
once the home of author Joseph
Conrad. The pub is named
after the coat of arms of a local
family. In the *Guide* for 16
consecutive years.
🏛 Q 🏛 ◐ ♣

Blean

Royal Oak
140 Blean Common (A290)
☎ (01227) 471247
11–11; 12–10.30 Sun
Shepherd Neame Master
Brew Bitter; guest beers Ⓗ
Popular, Victorian pub with a
conservatory restaurant, a
games room, library and a
large screen TV for sporting
events. Meals Wed–Sun.
🏛 🏛 ◐ ▶ ♣ P

Bossingham

Hop Pocket
The Street
☎ (01227) 709866
12–3, 7–11; 12–3, 7–10.30 Sun
Shepherd Neame Master
Brew Bitter, Spitfire; guest
beers Ⓗ
19th-century, candlelit pub, its
ceiling hung with hops;
popular for its excellent food
(conservatory dining area).
Selection of fruit wines.
🏛 🏛 ◐ ▶ Ⓐ ♣ P

Fuller's ESB; Greene King XX
Mild, IPA; Taylor Landlord;
guest beers Ⓗ
Lively village local appealing
to a wide cross-section of
drinkers. Well worth the long
walk from Shepherdswell
station. A rare outlet for real
cider (Thatcher's).
🏛 🏛 ◐ ▶ ♣ ◡ P

Benenden

King William IV
The Street ☎ (01580) 240636
10.30–3, 6–11; 12–3, 7–10.30 Sun
Shepherd Neame Master
Brew Bitter, Spitfire, Bishops
Finger (occasional), seasonal
beers Ⓗ
Excellent, two-bar village local
with a friendly and relaxed
atmosphere and good food (no
meals Sun or Mon eve).
Families welcome in the public
bar. 🏛 Q 🏛 ◐ ▶ ⊞ P

Try also: Woodcock, Iden
Green (Beards)

Benover

Woolpack
Benover Road (B2162 1 mile S
of Yalding) ☎ (01892) 730356
11–2.30 (3.30 Sat), 6–11 (11–11
summer Sat); 12–3.30, 7–10.30 (12–
10.30 summer) Sun
Shepherd Neame Master
Brew Bitter, Spitfire, Bishops
Finger Ⓗ
Tile-hung, 17th-century
country pub with two
interlinked bars separated by
an open fireplace and
decorated with hops and old
farming implements.
🏛 🏛 ◐ ▶ ♣ P

Betsham

Colyer Arms
Station Road (B262, 1 mile S of
A2) ☎ (01474) 832392
11.30–11; 11.30–4.30, 7–11 Sat; 12–4,
7–10.30 (12–10.30 summer) Sun
Courage Best Bitter; Ruddles
County; Shepherd Neame

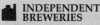
141

Boughton Lees

Flying Horse Inn
☎ (01233) 620914
11–3, 6–11 (11–11 summer); 12–3,
7–10.30 (12–10.30 summer) Sun
**Courage Best Bitter, Directors;
Marston's Pedigree; Morland
Old Speckled Hen; Wadworth
6X; guest beer** H
It's well worth a visit to this
pub, four miles outside
Ashford on the Faversham
road. Its one bar offers a good
range of home-cooked food.
Ask to see the wells.
🏠 🍴 ❀ 🐾 🛏 ♣ P

Boughton Monchelsea

Red House
Hermitage Lane (S off B2169
down Wierton Rd and East
Hall Hill) OS783488
☎ (01622) 743986
12–3 (not Tue), 7–11; 12–11 Sat;
12–10.30 Sun
**Greene King Abbot;
Hampshire Lionheart; Hop
Back Summer Lightning;
Otter Bitter; Viking Thor's
Thunder; guest beers** H
Welcoming, country free
house, with a good selection of
guest beers, plus an extensive
range of imported bottled
beers and fruit wines. The large
garden and campsite are
handy for the beer festival in
May.
🏠 🍴 ❀ 🍺 🛏 🛐 🛏 ♣ ⌂ P

Boughton Street

Queen's Head Inn
111 The Street, Boughton-
under-Blean
☎ (01227) 751369
11–4, 6–11; 12–4, 7–10.30 Sun
**Shepherd Neame Master
Brew Bitter, Spitfire, Porter** H
Coaching inn on the old A2,
noted for its good food and
comfortable accommodation.
No eve meals Sun.
Q ❀ 🏠 🍺 🛏 ♣ P

Brabourne Lees

Plough
Lees Road ☎ (01303) 812169
11 (4 winter Tue)–11; 12–10.30 Sun
**Shepherd Neame Master
Brew Bitter, Spitfire, Bishops
Finger, Porter** H
16th-century village pub with a
log fire and easy chairs. Bat
and Trap, a pets' corner and an
animal rescue sanctuary are
housed in the grounds. Food at
all sessions until 30 mins before
time: the speciality, an Indian
banquet, is a must (order in
advance).
🏠 ❀ 🍺 🛏 ♣ P

Brasted

Bull Inn
High Street
☎ (01959) 562551
10.30–2.30, 5.30–11; 10.30–11 Sat &
bank hols; 12–3, 7–10.30 Sun
**Shepherd Neame Master
Brew Bitter, Spitfire, Bishops
Finger** H
Small, friendly pub on the A25
at the west end of a village of
antique shops. Popular for
food. ❀ 🍺 🛏 ♣ P

Bridge

Plough & Harrow
86 High Street
☎ (01227) 830455
11–3, 6–11; 11–11 Sat; 12–3, 7–10.30
Sun
**Shepherd Neame Master
Brew Bitter** H
Traditional village local – the
centre of activities; good for
games. Shepherd Neame's *Pub
of the Year*. 🏠 ♣ P

Broadstairs

Bradstowe Bar (Royal Albion Hotel)
6–12 Albion Street
☎ (01843) 868071
11–3, 6.30–11 (11–11 summer); 12–3,
7–10.30 (12–10.30 summer) Sun
**Courage Directors; Shepherd
Neame Master Brew Bitter;
Webster's Yorkshire Bitter;
guest beer** (summer) H
Locals mix with residents at
this friendly hotel bar, boasting
a large garden and superb
views over Viking Bay. The
imposing hotel has a restaurant
and a children's certificate.
Meals in summer.
🏠 Q 🍴 ❀ 🏠 🍺 🛐 P

Burham

Toastmasters Inn
65 Church Street
☎ (01634) 861299
12–11; 12–10.30 Sun
**Greene King IPA; Young's
Special; guest beers** H
This tucked-away local
features two different parts: the
front bar has the real ales on
seven handpumps; at the rear
is an Asian restaurant. Well
worth travelling to. 🍺 🛏 ♣ P

Burmarsh

Shepherd & Crook
Shear Way, Thorndyke Road
OS101320 ☎ (01303) 872336
11.30–3, 7–11; 12–3, 7–10.30 Sun
**Adnams Bitter; Greene King
IPA, seasonal beers; guest
beers** H
Traditionally-run pub: a
comfortable saloon filled with

old phones, muskets and RAF
memorabilia. 🏠 Q ❀ 🍴 🛏 🍺 P

Canterbury

Bishop's Finger
13 St Dunstan's Street (between
West station and Westgate)
☎ (01227) 768915
11–11; 12–3, 7–10.30 Sun
**Shepherd Neame Master
Brew Bitter, Spitfire, Bishops
Finger** H
Friendly, popular pub with a
panelled interior and a
pleasant patio at the rear.
❀ 🍺 🛏 🛐 (West)

Canterbury Beer Shop
83 Northgate ☎ (01227) 472288
11–1, 5.30–10; 11–10 Sat; closed Sun &
bank hols
**Adnams Broadside; Fuller's
London Pride, ESB; Marston's
Owd Rodger; Taylor
Landlord; guest beers** G
Off-licence selling a very wide
range of draught and bottle-
conditioned beers. 🛐 (West)

Canterbury Tales
12 The Friars (opp. Marlowe
Theatre) ☎ (01227) 768594
11–11; 12–10.30 Sun
**Goacher's Light; Shepherd
Neame Master Brew Bitter;
guest beers** H
Busy, enterprising pub
specialising in Kent beers but
also with a wide range of
guests from elsewhere. Live
music includes jazz Sun
afternoons. Mexican restaurant
on the first floor.
🍺 🛏 🛐 (West) ⌂

Jolly Sailor
75 Northgate ☎ (01227) 463828
11–11; 12–10.30 Sun
**Boddingtons Bitter; Flowers
Original; Whitbread Abroad
Cooper; guest beers** H
19th-century pub, converted
three years ago to a Hogshead
alehouse. Always four guest
beers on tap. ❀ 🍺 ♣

New Inn
19 Havelock Street
☎ (01227) 464584
11.30–3, 6 (5 Wed & Fri)–11; 12–4,
7–10.30 Sun
**Greene King IPA; Harveys
BB; guest beers** H
Victorian, mid-terraced,
traditional town pub with a
modern conservatory. A local
for the nearby college.
🍴 ❀ 🍺 🛐 🛐 (East)

Tap & Spile
76 St Dunstan's Street (near
Westgate) ☎ (01227) 463583
11–11; 12–10.30 Sun
**Tap & Spile Premium; guest
beers** H
Cosy, two-bar, revamped,
typical Tap & Spile outlet with
period photos of bygone pubs.

Third of a pint glasses are available for sampling the many guest beers.
❀ ≈ (West) ♣ ↻

Capel-le-Ferne

Royal Oak

New Dover Road (B2011, E of village) ☎ (01303) 244787
11.30–3 (4 Sat), 6 (7 Sat)–11; 12–4, 8 (7 summer)–10.30 Sun
Shepherd Neame Master Brew Bitter; guest beers Ⓗ
Old, split-level pub standing over the Channel crossing: a cosy, snug bar with a games room behind. No food Wed eve. ♨ Q ❀ ◖▶ ▲ ♣ P

Charing

Bowl Inn

Egg Hill Road OS950514
☎ (01233) 712256
5 (12 Fri & Sat)–11; 12–10.30 Sun
Fuller's London Pride; King & Barnes Sussex; guest beers Ⓗ
Ever-popular, remote, 16th-century inn: Kent CAMRA *Pub of the Year* 1994. ♨ ❀ ▲ ♣ P

Chartham

Cross Keys

Bolts Hill (from A28 take Shalmsford St turn, after ½ mile turn left)
☎ (01227) 738216
12–3, 6–11; 11–11 Sat; 12–10.30 Sun
John Smith's Bitter; Viking Ale; guest beers Ⓗ
Village local, dating from the 18th century, popular for games. It usually stocks two guest beers plus an occasional cask cider.
♨ Q ❀ ≈ ♣ ↻ P

Chatham

Alexandra

43 Railway Street
☎ (01634) 843959
11–11; 12–3, 7–10.30 Sun
Shepherd Neame Master Brew Bitter, Spitfire, Bishops Finger, Porter Ⓗ
Superb Victorian building set out on its own in the middle of a one-way traffic system. A haven for commuters from the nearby station with its single bar and friendly welcome.
♨ ❀ ≈ ♣

Chiddingstone Causeway

Little Brown Jug

On B2027, opp. Penshurst Station ☎ (01892) 870318
11.30–3, 6–11; 12–3, 7–10.30 Sun
Harveys BB; guest beers Ⓗ
Busy, friendly, family-run, free house offering three ever-changing guest beers (many unusual) and an excellent

range of good food. Spacious garden. ♨ Q ❀ ◖▶ ≈ (Penshurst) P ⊬

Chiddingstone Hoath

Rock

From Chiddingstone village follow road through Wellers Town ☎ (01892) 870296
11.30–3, 6–11; 12–3, 7–10.30 Sun
Larkins Bitter, Porter; Shepherd Neame Master Brew Bitter Ⓗ
16th-century, rural pub in an isolated setting. A worn red brick floor features in the main bar, which is heated by a wood-burning stove. The Larkins is brewed just down the road. Ring the Bull played.
♨ Q ❀ ◖▶ ♣ P

Cooling

Horseshoe & Castle

Main Road ☎ (01634) 221691
11.30–3, 7 (5 Fri)–11; 12–10.30 Sun
Adnams Bitter; Draught Bass, Flagship Ensign Ⓗ
Pub nestled in a sleepy village with Dickensian connections. The cellar is apparently haunted. ❀ ◖▶ ♣ P ⊬

Crockham Hill

Royal Oak

Main Road (B2026/B269 jct)
☎ (01732) 866335
11–2.30, 6–11; 12–3, 7–10.30 Sun
Shepherd Neame Master Brew Bitter, Best Bitter, Spitfire, seasonal beer Ⓗ
Attractive, small, country pub at the centre of village life. The pleasant landlord and landlady make visitors welcome. Families may eat. Eve meals Tue–Sat. ♨ ❀ ◖▶ P

Dartford

Dart

30 Chastilian Road
☎ (01322) 225510
4.30 (12 Fri & Sat)–11; 12–10.30 Sun
Flowers Original; John Smith's Bitter; guest beer Ⓗ
Well-appointed community local in a large housing area near Dartford Heath (at the Crayford end), featuring a comfortable lounge bar and a public bar, popular for darts and pool. Regularly changing guest beer. ❀ ⊞ ♿ P

Paper Moon

55 High Street
☎ (01322) 281127
10–11; 12–10.30 Sun
Courage Directors; Fuller's London Pride; Theakston Best Bitter; Younger Scotch; guest beers Ⓗ

Town-centre, corner pub, formerly a bank, converted in typical Wetherspoons style. Two guest beers from a wide portfolio are usually available.
Q ◖▶ ♿ ≈ ⊬

Tiger

28 St Albans Road (off A226, East Hill) ☎ (01322) 293688
11–11; 12–10.30 Sun
Courage Best Bitter; Shepherd Neame Master Brew Bitter; guest beer Ⓗ
Small, cosy, sidestreet local fielding darts, pool and football teams. The guest beer is often from a local microbrewery. No meals Sat–Sun. ❀ ◖ ≈ ♣

Wat Tyler

80 High Street
☎ (01322) 272546
10–11; 12.30–10.30 Sun
Courage Best Bitter; Theakston Old Peculier; Young's Special, Winter Warmer; guest beers Ⓗ
Historic, town-centre free house and convivial meeting place, named after the 14th-century leader of the Peasants' Revolt. Good range of constantly changing guest beers at competitive prices. Occasional live music weekends. Q ◖ ≈

Deal

Admiral Penn

79 Beach Street
☎ (01304) 374279
11–3, 6–11; closed Sun
Draught Bass; Mansfield Bitter; Wells Bombardier Ⓗ
Cosy, relaxing, seafront bar with much ceiling bric-a-brac.
♨ ◖ ≈ ♣

Alma

126 West Street
☎ (01304) 360244
10–3, 6–11; 12–3, 7–10.30 Sun
Shepherd Neame Master Brew Bitter; guest beers Ⓗ
Lively town pub with changing guest ales from far and wide. ≈ ♣

Antwerp

45 Beach Street
☎ (01304) 374843
10.30–5, 7–11 (not Tue eve); 12–4, 7–10.30 Sun
Viking Ale; guest beers Ⓗ
Light, airy, seafront bar looking out on to the town pier. Microbrews feature regularly. ◖ ≈ ♣

Saracen's Head

1 Alfred Square
☎ (01304) 381650
10.30–11; 12–10.30 Sun
Shepherd Neame Master Brew Bitter, Spitfire, Bishops Finger Ⓗ

Large, single-bar pub towards the northern end of historic Deal. 🏠 🛏 ◖ ♣

Doddington

Chequers
The Street
11–3.45, 7–11; 11–11 Fri & Sat; 12–3, 7–10.30 Sun
Shepherd Neame Master Brew Bitter, Bishops Finger Ⓗ
Excellent, welcoming, village pub, South-East CAMRA *Pub of the Year* 1995. Games include an unusual Kentish dartboard. Well worth a visit.
🏠 Q ❄ ❀ ◖ ◖ ♣ P

Dover

Blakes
52 Castle Street
☎ (01304) 202194
11–3, 7–11; 12–3 (closed eves) Sun
Fuller's London Pride; Hancock's HB; M&B Brew XI; guest beer (occasional) Ⓗ
Smart cellar bar and bistro with a relaxing atmosphere, plus a wood-panelled street-level bar.
❀ ◖ ▶ ⇌ (Priory)

Boar's Head
46–48 Eaton Road
☎ (01304) 204490
11–3, 6–11; 12–3, 7–10.30 Sun
Greene King IPA; seasonal beers; guest beers Ⓗ
Traditional, suburban local showing strong community spirit. Microbreweries are often favoured. Skittle alley.
🏠 ❀ ♣

Castle
Russell Street (off A20, next to bus garage) ☎ (01304) 202108
11–11; 12–10.30 Sun
Whitbread Fuggles IPA Ⓗ
Managed town pub improving its image with new decor and good value meals. The ale can be served without a sparkler on request. ❄ ◖ ⇌ (Priory)

Mogul
Chapel Place (off seafront, above A20) ☎ (01304) 205072
11–11; 12–10.30 Sun
Viking Ale; guest beers Ⓗ
A decade after rebuilding following a fire, this pub is now a firm supporter of local brews. ⇌ (Priory) ♣

Try also: **Louis Armstrong**, Charlton Green (Bass)

East Farleigh

Farleigh Bull
Lower Road ☎ (01622) 726282
11–11; 12–10.30 Sun
Boddingtons Mild, Bitter; Flowers Original; Wadworth 6X; guest beers Ⓗ
Comfortable, Victorian pub offering a warm welcome, with

an open wood and coal fire. The grounds house a small farm with a pot-bellied pig. A focus for the village community. Children's certificate. 🏠 ❄ ❀ ◖ ▶ ⚬ ▲
⇌ ♣ ⌂ P ⚥

Victory
Farleigh Bridge (next to station) ☎ (01622) 726591
11–11; 12–10.30 Sun
Goacher's Dark; Tetley Bitter; guest beer Ⓗ
Friendly local near the River Medway. The large garden boasts picturesque views. Popular for its Sun lunches.
❀ ◖ ▶ ▲ ⇌ ♣ P

East Malling

Rising Sun
125 Mill Street
☎ (01732) 843284
12–11; 12–10.30 Sun
Goacher's Light; Morland Old Speckled Hen; Shepherd Neame Master Brew Bitter; guest beer Ⓗ
This regular entry is a family-owned pub, noted for its competitive prices and good value lunches. Warm welcome for games teams in the large bar; Sky Sports on TV. No food weekends. ❀ ◖ ⇌

East Peckham

Bush, Blackbird & Thrush
194 Bush Road (½ mile N of village) ☎ (01622) 871349
11–11 (11–3, 7–11 winter weekdays); 12–10.30 (12–5, 7–10.30 winter) Sun
Shepherd Neame Master Brew Bitter, Spitfire, seasonal beers Ⓖ
Picturesque, 14th-century village inn set in the heart of hop country, boasting oak beams, a two-acre garden, excellent food and fine wines. Bat and Trap in summer.
🏠 ❀ ◖ ▶ ▲ ♣ P

Try also: **Swan**, West Peckham (Free)

Egerton Forstal

Queen's Arms
OS893464 ☎ (01233) 756386
11.30 (11 summer)–2, 6.30–11; 12–3, 7–10.30 Sun
Harveys BB; Rother Valley Level Best; Wells Bombardier; guest beers Ⓖ
Quiet village local with beamed ceilings; hard to find but well worth it. Wells Bombardier was named after the landlady's father – Bombardier Billy Wells. Good, home-cooked food (not served Tue); steaks cooked to order.
🏠 Q ❀ ◖ ▶ ♣ ⌂ P

Elham

Rose & Crown
High Street ☎ (01303) 840226
11–3, 6–11; 12–3, 7–10.30 Sun
Ruddles Best Bitter; guest beers Ⓗ
Traditional pub serving three guest beers; a rare outlet for mild. Good range of home-cooked food (children allowed in the eating areas). Accommodation is in a converted stable.
🏠 Q ❀ 🛏 ◖ ▶ ♣ P

Farningham

Chequers
High Street ☎ (01322) 865222
11–11; 12–10.30 Sun
Fuller's London Pride, ESB; Morland Old Speckled Hen; Taylor Landlord; guest beers Ⓗ
Welcoming, comfortable, popular corner local in a picturesque village. Up to four guest ales available. Recommended home-made food (not served Sun).
◖ ♣

Faversham

Anchor
52 Abbey Street
☎ (01795) 536471
11–3, 5.30–11; 11–11 Fri & Sat; 12–4, 7–10.30 Sun
Shepherd Neame Master Brew Bitter, Spitfire, Porter, Bishops Finger (summer) Ⓗ
First recorded as a pub in 1676, this superb two-bar pub was once owned by the monks of the erstwhile Faversham Abbey. It stands next to the Standard Quay with its collection of former commercial sailing vessels. Continental sausages are a speciality. Eve meals on request. 🏠 ❀ ◖

Crown & Anchor
41 The Mall ☎ (01795) 532812
10.30–3 (4 Sat), 5.30 (6 Sat)–11; 12–3, 7–10.30 Sun
Shepherd Neame Master Brew Bitter Ⓗ
Locals' pub close to the station. The landlord's goulash is authentic – he is Hungarian.
◖ ▶ ⇌ ♣

Shipwrights Arms
Hollowshore (from Davington turn right at pub sign into Ham Road) OS017636
☎ (01795) 590088
11–11; 12–10.30 Sun
Goacher's Mild; Shepherd Neame Master Brew Bitter, Spitfire; guest beer Ⓖ
Isolated and romantically-set pub, outside Faversham at the confluence of two creeks; a

gem with an excellent vantage point for observing seabirds. Pawley Farm Cider. No-smoking family room.
🏚 Q ⛄ ⊛ ◑ ▶ ♣ ♠ ⭢ P ⚲

Finglesham

Crown

The Street ☎ (01304) 612555
11–3, 6–11; 12–3, 7–10.30 Sun
Brakspear Special; Ruddles County; Shepherd Neame Master Brew Bitter; Webster's Yorkshire Bitter; guest beers Ⓗ
Award-winning, popular local with a dining area (booking advised for meals). Caravan site adjacent. 🏚 ⊛ ◑ ▶ ▲ P

Folkestone

Harveys Wine Bar

10 Langhorne Gardens
☎ (01303) 253758
11.30–11; 12–10.30 Sun
Draught Bass; Worthington Bitter Ⓗ**; guest beers** Ⓗ/Ⓖ
Cellar pub beneath the Langhorne Gardens Hotel offering four guest beers.
🏚 ⊛ 🍴 ◑ ⇌ (Central) ⭢

Lifeboat Inn

42 North Street (bottom of Tram Rd, 1st left under railway, left again)
☎ (01303) 243958
12–3, 6–11; 11–11 Fri & Sat; 12–3, 7–10.30 Sun
Draught Bass; Fuller's London Pride; guest beers Ⓗ
Classic backstreet pub serving up to six beers, with guests from independent micros.
⊛ ◑ ♣

Gillingham

Barge

63 Layfield Road
☎ (01634) 850485
12–3, 7–11; 12–11 Sat; 12–10.30 Sun
Wadworth 6X; guest beers Ⓗ
Single-bar, end-of-terrace pub where the interior depicts 'life below decks' as painted by a local artist. Free folk club every Mon. Good scenic views of the River Medway. Four guest handpumps offer beers from independents only. Eves are candlelit. ⊛ ◑ ♣

Dog & Bone

21 Jeffrey Street
☎ (01634) 576829
11–11; 12–10.30 Sun
Beer range varies Ⓗ
Spacious, two-bar town pub which offers a friendly welcome, and three handpumps offering a good selection. Close to Gillingham FC (away supporters welcome). 🏚 ⊛ ◑ ▶ ⇌ ♣

Falcon

95 Marlborough Road
☎ (01634) 850614
12–3, 5.30–11; 12–11 Sat; 12–5, 7–10.30 Sun
Ruddles Best Bitter; John Smith's Bitter; guest beers Ⓗ
Single-bar, compact town house, busy most eves; friendly atmosphere. Two, usually independents' guest ales; occasional barbecues.
⊛ ◑ ⇌ ♣

King George V

1 Prospect Row, Brompton (off end of High St)
☎ (01634) 842418
11–11; 12–3, 6–10.30 Sun
Draught Bass; guest beers Ⓗ
One-bar local with strong naval links from the days of Chatham Dockyard. Many artefacts adorn the walls. Good value food (no meals Sun).
⊛ 🍴 ◑ ♣

Prince of Guinea

49 Medway Road
☎ (01634) 851534
11–11; 12–4, 7–10.30 Sun
Harveys Pale Ale, BB, Armada, seasonal beers Ⓗ
One-bar, detached house with no keg bitters. Multi-lingual clientele (thanks to the local docks). Good value food.
◑ ▶ ♣

Roseneath

79 Arden Street
☎ (01634) 852553
11.30–11; 12–10.30 Sun
Beer range varies Ⓗ
The house ale, Snakehound, is brewed by Goacher's for this busy, one-bar, terraced pub, while the five guest beers mostly come from microbreweries.
⊛ ⇌ ♣

Will Adams

73 Saxton Street
☎ (01634) 575902
12–3, 7–11; 12–3, 7–10.30 Sun
Fuller's London Pride; guest beers Ⓗ
The mural in the bar of this friendly pub depicts the life of Will Adams (shipbuilder and adventurer). It stays open Sat when Gillingham FC are at home. Good value food; good selection of single malts and up to three guest beers.
⊛ ◑ ⇌ ♣ ⭢

Gill's Green

Wellington Arms

Off A229, N of Hawkhurst
☎ (01580) 753119
12–3, 6–11 (12–11 summer); 12–3, 7–10.30 (12–10.30 summer) Sun
Harveys BB; Wadworth 6X; guest beers Ⓗ
Hidden-away pub, popular with ramblers and those seeking wholesome food in pleasant, friendly

surroundings. It dates back to Elizabethan times.
🏚 ⊛ ◑ ▶ P

Goodnestone

Fitzwalter Arms

The Street OS255546
☎ (01304) 840303
11–3, 6 (6.30 winter)–11 ; 12–3, 7–10.30 Sun
Shepherd Neame Master Brew Bitter Ⓗ
Pub originally a gate lodge for the local landowner, hence the distinctive design. 🏚 Q ◑ ♣

Gravesend

Jolly Drayman

1 Love Lane, Wellington Street
☎ (01474) 352355
11.30 (12 Sat)–3, 6 (7 Sat)–11; 12–3, 7–10.30 Sun
Draught Bass; Fuller's London Pride; guest beers Ⓗ
Part of the old Wellington brewery, a comfortable lounge-style, town-centre pub with low beams; a regular *Guide* entry, known locally as the Coke Oven. Lunches Tue–Fri.
⊛ ◑ ▶ ⇌ ♣

Somerset Arms

10 Darnley Road (near station)
☎ (01474) 533837
11–11 (midnight Thu–Sat); 12–4, 7.30–10.30 Sun
Beer range varies Ⓗ
Country-style-decorated town-centre pub with wooden church pews. Discos Thu–Sun eves; eve meals Mon–Wed. Six continually changing ales from all over Britain. ◑ ▶ ⇌

Great Chart

Hooden Horse

The Street ☎ (01233) 625583
11.30–2.30, 6–11; 12–3, 7–10.30 Sun
Goacher's Light; Hook Norton Old Hooky; Hop Back Summer Lightning; Ringwood Old Thumper; guest beers Ⓗ
Hop-strewn ceilings and candlelit tables feature in this tiled, timber-floored pub, the original in the Hooden Horse chain. Food is served up to half an hour before closing time.
⊛ ◑ ▶ ⭢

Green Street Green (Darenth)

Ship

Green Street Green Road (B260, 1½ miles E of Longfield)
☎ (01474) 702279
11–2.30, 5.30–11 (11–11 summer Sat); 12–3, 7–10.30 (12–10.30 summer) Sun
Courage Best Bitter, Directors; Young's Bitter; guest beers Ⓗ
Imposing, 17th-century pub, overlooking the village green, offering excellent value

lunches and regular gourmet eves. Try the back bar – but beware of the ghost!
🏨 🐌 ⌀ ♣ P

Hadlow

Fiddling Monkey
Maidstone Road (A26)
☎ (01732) 850267
11–2.30, 6–11; 11–11 Fri & Sat; 12–10.30 Sun
Harveys BB; Larkins Bitter; guest beer (occasional) Ⓗ
Large, friendly, one-bar village local which sets out to please all tastes, with a games area, a quiet snug around the fire and good value food (eve meals Sat–Sun). The large garden has a pond and play equipment.
🏨 ☀ ⌀ ♣ P

Hale Street

Harp
218 Hale Street
☎ (01622) 872334
11–11; 12–10.30 Sun
Fuller's London Pride; Harveys BB; guest beer Ⓗ
Pub with two bar areas featuring old oak beams and brasses. A good atmosphere is enhanced by events, games and excellent food.
🏨 Q ☀ ⌀ ♿ ♣ ⌂ P

Halstead

Rose & Crown
Otford Lane ☎ (01959) 533120
11.30–3, 4.30–11; 11.30–11 Sat; 12–10.30 Sun
Courage Best Bitter; Larkins Traditional Ale; guest beers Ⓗ
200-year-old, flint, two-bar pub with an open fire and no music or machines in the quiet bar. Larkins' and various Harveys' brews are regular beers, supported by an interesting and changing range of guests. Children welcome in the games room. 🏨 Q ☀ ⌀ ♿ �) (Knockholt) P

Herne

Smugglers Inn
1 School Lane (A291)
☎ (01227) 741395
11–3.30, 6–11; 11–11 Sat; 12–4, 7–10.30 Sun
Shepherd Neame Master Brew Bitter, Spitfire Ⓗ
Friendly, listed, Grade II pub in an attractive village, five miles from Canterbury on a bus route. Its name alludes to a local smuggling legend. Newly-opened garden. No food Sun.
🏨 ☀ 🛏 ⌀ ♿ ♣ ♠ ♣

Try also: Fox & Hounds, Herne Common (Shepherd Neame)

Herne Bay

Share & Coulter
Thornden Wood Road (off A299 via Greenhill)
☎ (01227) 374877
11–3, 6–11; 12–4, 7–10.30 Sun
Shepherd Neame Master Brew Bitter, Bishops Finger Ⓗ
Two-bar country pub with traditional decor; worth finding. Bat and Trap and petanque are played. No food Sun.
🏨 Q ☀ ⌀ ♿ ♠ ♣ P

Try also: Diver's Arms, Central Parade (Shepherd Neame)

Higham

Stone Horse
Dillywood Lane (50 yds off B2000 towards Cliffe Woods)
☎ (01634) 722046
11–3, 6–11; 11–11 Sat; 12–3, 7–10.30 Sun
Courage Best Bitter Ⓗ
Attractive, 17th-century, isolated country inn with two bars. Various pub games feature throughout the year. Home-cooked lunches; French-style fixed price meals eves. A varying Flagship beer complements the Courage.
☀ ⌀ ♿ ♣ P

Ightham

Old House
Redwell Lane (½ mile SE of village, between A25 and A227) OS590559
☎ (01732) 882383
7–11 (9 Tue); 12–3, 7–11 Sat; 12–3, 7–10.30 Sun
Brakspear Bitter Ⓖ**; Flowers IPA** Ⓗ**; Hook Norton Old Hooky; guest beer** Ⓖ
Difficult to find pub without a sign. Partly 16th-century, it has two unspoilt bars, no music and a large open fireplace. A rare outlet for gravity dispensed beers.
🏨 Q ♣

Kemsing

Rising Sun
Cotmans Ash Lane OS563599
☎ (01959) 522683
11–3, 6–11; 12–10.30 Sun
Flowers Original; Morland Old Speckled Hen; guest beers Ⓗ
Isolated country pub, popular in summer with families and hikers. The main bar is a converted hunting lodge. Good quality food; local ciders and guest beers from Kent breweries.
🏨 Q 🐌 ☀ ⌀ ♣ ⌂ P

Kenardington

World's Wonder
Kenardington Road OS977329
☎ (01233) 732431
11.30–2.30, 6.30–11; 12–3, 7–10.30 Sun
Bateman XXXB; Harveys BB; Shepherd Neame Spitfire Ⓗ
Welcoming, hospitable, unpretentious country pub. Eve meals Tue–Sat.
🏨 ☀ ⌀ ♿ P

Kingsdown

King's Head
Upper Street ☎ (01304) 373915
11–2.30, 7–11; 12–2.30, 7–10.30 Sun
Draught Bass; Hancock's HB; Worthington Bitter Ⓗ
Welcoming village local at the eastern end of the white cliffs. Booking advised for eve meals (Wed–Sun). ☀ ⌀ ♿ ♣ ♠

Kingsgate

Nineteenth Hole
George Hill Road OS386702
☎ (01843) 869548
11–3, 6–11; 11–11 Sat; 12–10.30 Sun
Viking Island Ale, Thor's Thunder; guest beers Ⓗ
Comfortable, one-bar pub at a road junction, with a wedge-shaped interior. No food Sun.
☀ 🛏 ⌀ ♣ ♠

Luddesdown

Cock Inn
Henley Street OS664672
☎ (01474) 814208
12–11; 12–10.30 Sun
Adnams Bitter; Young's Special Ⓗ**; guest beers** Ⓗ/Ⓖ
Well-run, two-bar free house offering a wide range of beers, always including a local mild and local ciders. Classic car memorabilia in the public bar; no music or children. Accessible by footpath from Sole Street station and thoroughly recommended.
🏨 Q ☀ ⌀ ♣ ⌂ P

Maidstone

Hare & Hounds
45–47 Lower Boxley Road (opp. prison) ☎ (01622) 678388
11–3 (3.30 Fri), 5.30 (7 Sat)–11; 12–3, 7–10.30 Sun
Flowers IPA; Fuller's London Pride Ⓗ
Friendly, one-bar pub, two mins' walk from Maidstone East station. Eve meals (Mon–Fri) end at 7. No lunch Sun.
☀ ⌀ �) (East) ♣

Pilot
23–25 Upper Stone Street (A229 southbound) ☎ (01622) 691162
11–3, 6 (7 Sat)–11; 12–3, 7–10.30 Sun

Harveys XX Mild, BB,
Armada, seasonal beers H
Welcoming, no-frills pub with
a log fire. The food is simple
but good – no chips! No meals
Sun lunch. A country pub in
the town, full of character.
🏠 ⊛ ◖ ▶ ≠ (East/West) ♣

Wheelers Arms

1 Perry Street (off A229 behind
Shell garage) ☎ (01622) 752229
12–11; 12–10.30 Sun
**Shepherd Neame Master
Brew Bitter** H
Street-corner local with a bar
billiards table. Popular for Sun
lunches (no food Mon–Fri eves
except by arrangement).
Usually one other Shep's beer
is available.
⊛ ◖ ▶ ≠ (East) ♣

Marden

Stilebridge Inn

Staplehurst Road (A229)
☎ (01622) 831236
11.30–3, 6–11; 12–10.30 Sun
Beer range varies H
Stylish and comfortable pub
with a very friendly welcome
in several bar areas, plus a
beamed restaurant which
offers excellent food. Up to
seven beers are served, with a
bias towards rare micros.
Q ⊛ ◖ ▶ P ⊁

West End Tavern

West End ☎ (01622) 831956
11–3, 6–11; 11–11 Sat; 12–3, 7–10.30
Sun
**Adnams Bitter, Old;
Brakspear Special; Flowers
Original; Harveys BB;
Wadworth 6X** H
18th-century, timber-beamed
free house with a welcoming,
log-burning inglenook and a
large, U-shaped bar.
🏠 ⊛ ◖ ▶ ▲ ≠ ♣ P

Margate

Spread Eagle

25 Victoria Road (50 yds off
B2055 by St John's church)
☎ (01843) 293396
11.30–3, 5.30–11; 11–11 Fri & Sat;
12–10.30 Sun
**Adnams Broadside; Fuller's
London Pride; Greene King
IPA; Viking Thor's Thunder;
guest beer** H
Excellent, award-winning,
backstreet corner local,
CAMRA SE region 1997 *Pub of
the Year*. Good value food (not
served Sun). Children's
certificate. Q ⊱ ⊛ ◖ ▶

Marsh Green

Wheatsheaf Inn

On B2028 ☎ (01732) 864091
11–3, 5.30–11; 11–11 Sat; 12–3, 7–10.30
Sun

Adnams Bitter; Harveys BB;
Larkins Bitter; Taylor
Landlord; guest beers H
Popular, friendly, multi-bar
pub with a conservatory at the
rear. Nine real ales – many
changing weekly – and
excellent value, good quality
food.
🏠 Q ⊱ ⊛ ◖ ▶ ⅙ ♣ ⌒ P ⊁

Marshside

Gate Inn

Boyden Gate (Chislet turn off
A28 in Upstreet)
☎ (01227) 860498
11–2.30 (3 Sat), 6–11; 12–3, 6–10.30
Sun
**Shepherd Neame Master
Brew Bitter, Spitfire, Porter** G
Splendid country pub, now 21
times in the *Guide*. It features
apple trees, duck-racing,
cricket, rugby, food theme eves
and a beer festival in August.
Excellent food; no-smoking
area at lunchtime.
🏠 Q ⊱ ⊛ ◖ ▶ ⅙ ▲ ♣ P ⊁

Mersham

Farriers Arms

Flood Street ☎ (01233) 720444
11–2.30, 6.30–11; 12–4, 7–10.30 Sun
Friary Meux BB; guest beer H
Comfortable, two-bar pub next
to a mill stream. Ever-changing
guest beer.
🏠 ⊛ 🛏 ◖ ▶ ▲ ♣ P

Minster (Sheppey)

British Queen

115 Chequers Road
☎ (01795) 873131
12–4, 7–11; 12–4, 7–10.30 Sun
**Shepherd Neame Master
Brew Bitter, Spitfire** H
Classic, gimmick-free, two-bar
pub where a friendly welcome
is assured. Enthusiastic fund
raising for local charities.
Q ⊛ ⊡ ♣ P

Northfleet

Rose

Rose Street (modern estate by
station) ☎ (01474) 365791
11–11; 12–3, 7–10.30 Sun
**Shepherd Neame Master
Brew Bitter, seasonal beers** H
Very friendly, one-bar local
with a lively atmosphere.
Occasional live music. Well-
kept outside drinking area.
⊛ ⅙ ≠ ♣

Pembury

Black Horse

12 High Street
☎ (01892) 822141
11–11; 12–3, 7–10.30 Sun
Courage Directors (winter);
**Morland Old Speckled Hen;
Theakston Best Bitter, XB** H

Old village pub with an open
fire and a central bar which
divides the room into two
areas. Popular seafood
restaurant in the grounds. A
house beer is also available.
🏠 ⊛ ◖ ▶

Petteridge

Hopbine

Petteridge Lane (N of A21)
OS668412 ☎ (01892) 722561
12 (11 Sat)–2.30, 6–11; 12–3, 7–10.30
Sun
**King & Barnes Mild, Sussex,
Broadwood, Festive, seasonal
beers** H
Little-altered, brick and
weatherboarded pub, not
easily found. Friendly
atmosphere; monthly folk and
story-telling event. King &
Barnes's only house in Kent.
No food Wed.
🏠 ⊛ ◖ ▶ ⅙ ♣ ⌒ P

Plaxtol

Golding Hop

Sheet Hill (follow road W out
of village)
11–3, 6–11; 12–4, 7–10.30 Sun
**Adnams Bitter; Young's
Special; guest beers** G
Attractive, 15th-century inn
with three areas, one with an
open log fire. Originally a cider
house. 🏠 Q ⊛ ◖ ♣ ⌒ P

Rainham

Mackland Arms

213 Station Road
☎ (01634) 232178
10–11; 12–10.30 Sun
**Shepherd Neame Master
Brew Bitter, Best Bitter,
Spitfire** H
Terraced pub with a single
L-shaped bar, a rare outlet for
the Best. Friendly atmosphere.
≠ ♣

Rose Inn

249 High Street (A2)
☎ (01634) 231047
11–11; 12–10.30 Sun
**Shepherd Neame Master
Brew Bitter** H
Friendly, two-bar corner local.
Good value, home-prepared
food (including a vegetarian
dish) is served until 8pm (2.30
Sat); no food Sun. ◖ ▶ ⊡ ♣ P

Ramsgate

Addington Arms

45 Ashburnham Road
☎ (01843) 591489
11–11; 12–10.30 Sun
**Fuller's London Pride; Viking
Ale** H
Recently refurbished to a high
standard, this popular local
appeals to all ages. Plenty of
amusements, including Sky
TV. ⊱ ⊛ ◖ ♣

Artillery Arms
36 Westcliffe Road (near hospital) ☎ (01843) 853282
12–11; 12–10.30 Sun
Beer range varies H
Superb, small, corner local, Thanet CAMRA joint *Pub of the Year* 1996. It is said to have been a brothel in Victorian times. Adventurous choice of beers. ⇌

Honeysuckle
31 Honeysuckle Road (off Hereson Rd) ☎ (01843) 597532
11–2.30, 5.30–11; 12–3, 7–10.30 Sun
Ruddles County; Viking Ale; guest beers H
Village-style pub in a backstreet. A pub has stood on the site since 1789; it gained its present name in 1800.
🛏 ❀ ◖ ♣ P

Montefiore Arms
1 Trinity Place (off Hereson Rd) ☎ (01843) 591489
12–3, 7–11; 12–3, 7–10.30 Sun; closed Wed
Viking Ale, seasonal beers; Young's Bitter H
Backstreet, one-bar, local fielding active sports teams. 🛏

Rochester

Granville Arms
83 Maidstone Road
☎ (01634) 845243
11.30–11; 12–10.30 Sun
Greene King IPA, Abbot H
Friendly, vibrant local, a few mins' walk from the historic city centre. Sun lunch is served from 4pm to 6pm! No food Wed. ♨ ❀ ◖ ⇌ ♣ P

Greyhound
Rochester Avenue
☎ (01634) 844120
10–3, 6–11; 10–11 Sat; 12–10.30 Sun
Shepherd Neame Master Brew Bitter H
Beautiful, backstreet local, a long-running *Guide* entry. Basic public bar; the lounge bar has chaises-longues. Bottle-conditioned Spitfire available. Book for food. ♨ ◖ ⊟ ⇌

Man of Kent
6–8 John Street
☎ (01634) 818771
12–11; 12–10.30 Sun
Beer range varies H
This lively pub is a must, specialising in Kent produce and only selling Kent microbrewery beer, cider and wine. Bikers welcome; live music Tue. Food is not always available. ♨ ❀ ◖ ⇌ ♣ ◌

Star Inn
Star Hill ☎ (01634) 826811
11–11; 12–3 Sun
Beer range varies H
Cosy, single-bar pub with seven changing beers. Busy Fri

and Sat eves. Weekday lunches. ♨ ◖ ⇌

Try also: White Horse, Borstal (Greene King)

Rusthall

Toad Rock
1 Harmony Street (off A264, 1 mile W of T Wells)
☎ (01892) 520818
11–3, 6–11; 11–11 Sat; 12–3, 7–10.30 Sun
Adnams Bitter; Fuller's London Pride; Harveys BB; guest beers H
Friendly, two-bar pub dating from the 16th century, opposite a local landmark (Toad Rock). Good value food includes vegetarian and a specialist sausage menu. Ever changing selection of guest ales.
♨ ❀ ◖ ♣ P

St Margaret's at Cliffe

Hope Inn
High Street ☎ (01304) 852444
11–11; 12–3, 7–10.30 Sun
Shepherd Neame Master Brew Bitter, Spitfire H
Attractive village local in a popular holiday area. Skittle alley. ♨ ❀ ◖ ▲ ♣ P

St Nicholas at Wade

Bell Inn
The Street ☎ (01843) 847250
11.30 (11 summer)–3, 6.30 (6 summer)–11; 12–4, 7–10.30 Sun
Draught Bass; Flowers IPA; Highgate Dark; Wadworth 6X; guest beers H
Noted for food, the Bell has a number of cosy rooms dating from Tudor times, and a larger games room at the rear. No eve meals Sun.
♨ Q 🛏 ❀ ◖ ▲ ♣ P

St Peter's

Red Lion
2 High Street ☎ (01843) 861402
11–3, 7–11; 11–11 Sat; 12–4, 7–10.30 Sun
Boddingtons Bitter; Flowers IPA; Viking seasonal beers H
Pub on a site opposite a Norman church. Built in the early 1800s, its large, open bar maintains the style of a traditional village local.
🛏 ◖ ⅃ ♣ P

Sandgate

Ship Inn
65 High Street
☎ (01303) 248525
11–11; 12–10.30 Sun
Courage Directors; Fuller's London Pride; Greene King

IPA; Hampshire Pendragon; Theakston Old Peculier; guest beers G
Nautical and Napoleonic memorabilia adorns this pub whose fish lady ghost is mainly seen by women. Various ciders. ❀ ◖ ▶ ⊟ ◌

Sandwich

George & Dragon
24 Fisher Street
☎ (01304) 613106
11–3, 6–11; 12–3, 7–10.30 Sun
Shepherd Neame Master Brew Bitter, Spitfire; Viking Thor's Thunder; guest beers H
Completely refurbished old inn with brick and pine much in evidence. The emphasis is on home-cooked food (not served Sun eve). ❀ ◖ ▶ ⇌

Market Inn
7 Cattle Market
☎ (01304) 611133
10–11; 12–10.30 Sun
Shepherd Neame Master Brew Bitter, Spitfire H
Classic old market pub which has been restored to its proper role as a meeting place.
◖ ⇌

Selling

Rose & Crown
Perry Wood (1 mile S of Selling) OS041551
☎ (01227) 752214
11–2.30 (3 Sat), 6.30–11; 12–3, 7–10.30 Sun
Adnams Bitter; Goacher's Dark; Harveys BB; guest beers H
Popular, 16th-century free house set against 150 acres of natural woodland. It has an attractive garden with an aviary and a children's play area, also a Bat and Trap pitch – the traditional pub game of Kent. Eve meals Tue–Sat.
♨ 🛏 ❀ ◖ ▲ ♣ P

Shatterling

Frog & Orange
Pedding Hill (A257)
☎ (01304) 812525
12–3, 6–11; 12–3, 7–10.30 Sun
Shepherd Neame Master Brew Bitter, Spitfire; Vaux Waggle Dance; guest beers H
Recently refurbished roadhouse, serving locals and tourists alike, renamed from the Green Man. Local cider.
❀ ◖ ▲ ◌ P

Sheerness

Red Lion
61 High Street, Bluetown (off A249) ☎ (01795) 663165
12–3, 6 (8 Sat)–11; 12–3, 8–10.30 Sun
Beer range varies H

Small, friendly, two-bar, free house where the long-serving landlord sedulously avoids national brands.
Q ◖ ⊞ ⇌ ♣

Shoreham

Royal Oak

2 High Street
☎ (01959) 522319
10.30–3, 6–11; 12–3, 7–10.30 Sun
Adnams Mild, Bitter, Broadside; Brakspear Bitter; guest beers Ⓗ
Highly recommended hostelry in the heart of an attractive Darent Valley village: the hub of local life and welcoming to strangers; a good stopping point for ramblers. Good value food; unusual games; no music.
🏚 Q ❀ ◖ ▮ ⊞ ⇌ ♣ ⏰

Try also: Old George Inn, Church St (Free)

Sittingbourne

Fountain Inn

Station Street
☎ (01795) 472015
11–3, 5.30–11; 11–11 Fri & Sat;
12–10.30 Sun
Shepherd Neame Master Brew Bitter, Spitfire *or* **Porter** Ⓗ
Spacious, welcoming pub. The nearest pub to Sittingbourne Steam Railway.
🏚 ❀ ◖ ⇌ ♣ P

Old Oak

68 East Street
☎ (01795) 472685
10.30–2.30, 7–11; 12–2.30, 7–10.30 Sun
Beer range varies Ⓗ
Unpretentious, friendly, one-bar town local. ❀ ◖ ▮ ♣

Ship Inn

22 East Street ☎ (01795) 425087
11–3 (4 Fri & Sat), 6.30–11; 12–4,
7–10.30 Sun
Courage Best Bitter; Viking Island Dark Mild; guest beer Ⓗ
This two-bar local boasts one of Sittingbourne's longest-serving landlords. The only real mild outlet in town. Snacks available eves.
☎ ◖ ⊞ ⇌ P

Snargate

Red Lion ☆

OS990286 ☎ (01797) 344648
11–3, 7–11; 12–3, 7–10.30 Sun
Goacher's Light; Rother Valley Level Best; guest beers Ⓖ
Unspoilt pub: no carpets, outside loos, and a marble top counter, run with love and devotion not by accountants. A *Guide* regular.
🏚 Q ❀ ♣ ⏰ P

Southborough

Bat & Ball

141 London Road
☎ (01892) 518085
11–11; 12–10.30 Sun
Beer range varies Ⓗ
Small, single-bar, free house on the main road. Many of the beers are rare for the area. Chess played. 🏚 ♣

Stansted

Black Horse

Tumblefield Road
☎ (01732) 822355
11–3, 6 (7 winter)–11; 11–11 Sat;
12–10.30 Sun
Larkins Traditional Ale; Young's Special, Winter Warmer; guest beers Ⓗ
Revitalised and under new ownership; the centre of village life and an excellent staging post for hikers. Good value food is served until 10pm. Strictly no music.
🏚 Q ❀ ◖ ▮ A ♣ ⏰ P ⚥

Staplehurst

Lord Raglan

Chart Hill Road (off A229)
OS786472 ☎ (01622) 843747
12–3, 6–11; 12–4 (closed eve) Sun
Goacher's Light; Harveys BB; guest beers Ⓗ
Popular, unspoilt country pub with a large garden set amongst orchards. The bar area is adorned with local hops. The guest ales are usually strong. Excellent value and quality food. Children welcome.
🏚 Q ❀ ◖ ▮ P

Staplestreet

Three Horseshoes

The Street ☎ (01227) 750842
11–3 (4.30 Sat), 5 (6 Sat)–11; 11–11 Fri;
12–3, 7–10.30 Sun
Shepherd Neame Master Brew Bitter Ⓖ
Delightful rural pub, half a mile from Boughton Street. A very rare outlet for gravity-dispensed ale. No meals Sun eve or Fri lunchtime.
🏚 Q ◖ ▮ ♣

Stone (Dartford)

Bricklayers Arms

62 London Road (A226, 1 mile E of Dartford)
☎ (01322) 284552
11–11; 12–10.30 Sun
Courage Best Bitter; guest beers Ⓗ
Small, welcoming, terraced pub on the eastern edge of Dartford, serving two regularly changing beers from small independents and microbreweries. Live music

often on Sat eve. A popular games pub, with Bat and Trap in summer. ❀ ♣

Stone Street

Padwell Arms

☎ (01732) 761532
12–3, 6–11; 12–3, 7–10.30 Sun
Badger Dorset Best; Hook Norton Old Hooky; guest beers Ⓗ
Award-winning country pub offering a traditional atmosphere as well as a choice of seven ales, all from small breweries. Two ciders in summer. Well worth finding.
🏚 ❀ ♣ ⏰ P

Tankerton

Tankerton Arms

Tower Hill
☎ (01227) 272024
12–11; 12–10.30 Sun
Fuller's London Pride; Shepherd Neame Master Brew Bitter; guest beers Ⓗ
Pub displaying a traditional, wood and mirror bar back and an interesting carved bar at the rear. Sea views. Live jazz most Tue eves. An imaginative menu offers a vegetarian choice. 🏚 Q ☎ ❀ ◖ ▮ ♣

Temple Ewell

Fox

High Street (off B2060)
☎ (01304) 823598
11–3, 6.30–11; 12–3, 7–10.30 Sun
Marston's Pedigree Ⓗ
Traditional village local which retains its community function. Quiet side bar; skittle alley.
🏚 ❀ ⇌ (Kearsney) ♣ P

Tenterden

White Lion Hotel

High Street
☎ (01580) 765077
11–11; 12–10.30 Sun
Draught Bass; Harveys BB; guest beer (occasional) Ⓗ
Modernised, 350-year-old coaching inn opposite the Kent & East Sussex Steam Railway.
❀ ⇝ ◖ ▮ P

Tilmanstone

Ravens

Upper Street (off A256)
☎ (01304) 617337
11–2.30, 7–11; 12–3, 7–10.30 Sun
Flowers Original; Ind Coope Burton Ale; Marston's Pedigree; guest beers Ⓗ
Refurbished village local, popular with the farming community. Booking is advised for meals.
🏚 ❀ ◖ ▮ ♣ P

Tonbridge

New Drum
54 Lavender Hill (off A26)
☎ (01732) 365044
11–11; 12–5, 7–10.30 Sun
**Fuller's London Pride;
Harveys BB; guest beers** Ⓗ
Family-run, free house offering
a friendly welcome. Six real
ales, including a house beer
from a West Country brewer;
two-pint steins used. No bar
food Sun. ✿ ◑ ≒ ♣

Primrose
112 Pembury Road
☎ (01732) 358699
11.30–11; 12–10.30 Sun
**Flowers Original; Harveys BB;
Marston's Pedigree; Morland
Old Speckled Hen; Young's
Special** Ⓗ
Weatherboarded, one-bar pub
with a warm, welcoming
atmosphere. Good food.
✿ ◑ & ≒ ♣ P ▯

Stag's Head
Stafford Road
☎ (01732) 352017
11–3, 6–11; 11–11 Thu–Sat; 12–3,
7–10.30 Sun
**Flowers Original; Taylor Best
Bitter; guest beer** Ⓗ
One-bar, backstreet pub;
friendly, but it tends to have
loud jukebox music.
✿ ≒ ♣ P

Tunbridge Wells

Bedford Hotel
2 High Street
☎ (01892) 526580
11–11; 12–7 Sun
**Greene King XX Mild, IPA,
Abbot, seasonal beers** Ⓗ
Single-bar pub, opposite the
station, near the Pantiles.
Popular with office workers
and shoppers during the day;
commuters and regulars in the
eves. No food Sun.
◑ ≒ ♣

Tyler Hill

Ivy House
27 Hackington Road
☎ (01227) 472200
11–11; 11–2.30, 6–11 Mon–Wed;
12–10.30 Sun
**Shepherd Neame Master
Brew Bitter, Spitfire** *or*
Bishops Finger Ⓗ
A pub since 1830 in a building
dating from 1701. Good value
food; eve meals till 8pm (no
food Sun eve). Typical village
pub atmosphere.
🅼 ✿ ◑ ▶ ♣ P

Underriver

White Rock
Carters Hill ☎ (01732) 833112
11–3, 6–11; 12–3, 7–10.30 Sun
**Harveys BB; King & Barnes
Sussex; guest beer** Ⓗ
Welcoming, attractive country
pub: one large bar with pool,
darts and machines, plus a
small, quiet bar with a log fire,
and an excellent restaurant.
🅼 Q ✿ ◑ ♣ P

Upchurch

Brown Jug
Horsham Lane
☎ (01634) 235287
11–2.30 (3 Sat), 6–11; 12–3, 7–10.30
Sun
**Shepherd Neame Master
Brew Bitter** Ⓗ
Step back in time at this classic,
two-bar pub where a large
collection of jugs covers the
ceilings. The pub's fascinating
history is worth a leisurely
read in the peaceful saloon.
🅼 Q ⛺ ✿ 🍴 ♣ P

Upper Upnor

Tudor Rose
High Street ☎ (01634) 715305
11.30–3.30, 7–11; 12–3.30, 7–10.30 Sun
**Young's Bitter, Special; guest
beers** Ⓗ
Friendly, multi-roomed pub
near Upnor Castle,
overlooking the River Medway
and the former dockyard.
Good value food (not served
Sun, or Mon eve).
🅼 ⛺ ✿ ◑ ▶ ♣

Weald

Windmill
Windmill Road (exit off A21
for Tonbridge N)
☎ (01732) 463330
11–11; 12–3, 7–10.30 Sun
**Greene King IPA, Abbot,
seasonal beers** Ⓗ
Two-bar village pub with
entertainment kept in the
public bar. For the country
rambler there are free maps to
consult in the lounge.
🅼 Q ✿ ◑ ▶ 🍴 ♣ ♠

West Malling

Joiner's Arms
High Street ☎ (01732) 840723
11–3, 5–11; 11–11 Fri & Sat; 12–3,
7–10.30 Sun
**Shepherd Neame Master
Brew Bitter, Bishops Finger,
seasonal beers** Ⓗ

Friendly, two-bar local in a
small, bustling town. Good
value lunches (no food Sun).
Bar billiards. 🅼 ✿ ◑ ≒ ♣

Whitstable

Alberres
Sea Street
☎ (01227) 273400
11.30–4, 7–11; 11.30–11 Fri & Sat;
12–10.30 Sun
**Ind Coope Burton Ale; Tetley
Bitter; guest beer** Ⓗ
Former Tomson & Wotton pub
– note the windows. A sign in
the bar shows the 1953 flood
level. ♣

East Kent
72 Oxford Street
☎ (01227) 272018
11–11; 12–10.30 Sun
**Shepherd Neame Master
Brew Bitter, Spitfire** (summer),
Porter Ⓗ
Traditional, three-bar town
pub with a spacious bar area.
Games, live music, and local
events are hosted. Families
welcome. No food Sun.
⛺ ✿ ◑ ≒ ♣ P

Noah's Ark
83 Canterbury Road
☎ (01227) 272332
11–3, 6–11; 12–3, 7–10.30 Sun
**Shepherd Neame Master
Brew Bitter** Ⓗ
Two-bar pub with a mainly
local trade, run by the longest-
serving landlord in town.
✿ 🍴 ♣

Wormshill

Blacksmith's Arms
The Street ☎ (01622) 884386
12–2.30, 7 (6 Fri & Sat)–11; 12–3,
7–10.30 Sun
**Shepherd Neame Master
Brew Bitter; guest beers** Ⓗ
Welcoming, 16th-century free
house boasting beams, a tiled
floor, a real fire and good food.
Swale CAMRA *Pub of the Year*
1996/7. No eve meals Sun or
Mon. 🅼 Q ✿ ◑ ▶ ♠ P

Worth

St Crispin
The Street ☎ (01304) 612081
11–2.30, 6–11; 12–4.30, 7–10.30 Sun
**Fuller's London Pride; Gale's
HSB; Harveys XX Mild;
Shepherd Neame Master
Brew Bitter** Ⓗ**; guest beers** Ⓖ
Well-established and
refurbished local with a
popular restaurant and chalet
accommodation.
🅼 ✿ 🛏 ◑ ♣ P

Protect your pleasure – join CAMRA today!

BEER FESTIVAL CALENDAR 1998

CAMRA beer festivals provide wonderful opportunities for sampling beers not normally found in the locality. Festivals are staffed by CAMRA members on a voluntary basis and offer a wide range of interesting real ales from breweries all over the country, plus live entertainment and much more. The biggest event is the Great British Beer Festival in August, where over 500 different beers can be enjoyed. For further details of this and the major regional events outlined below, together with precise dates and venues, contact CAMRA on (01727) 867201, or see your local press.

JANUARY
Atherton
Exeter

FEBRUARY
Basingstoke
Battersea
Bradford
Burton upon Trent
Dorchester
Dover
Durham
Falmouth
Fleetwood
Merseyside
Plymouth
Rugby
Sussex

MARCH
Camden (London Drinker)
Darlington
Dukeries (N Notts)
Ealing
Eastleigh
Gosport
Leeds
Walsall
Wigan

APRIL
Bury St Edmunds
Castle Point
Chippenham
Coventry
Dunstable
Farnham
Huddersfield
Mansfield
Newcastle upon Tyne
Oldham
Perth

MAY
Alloa
Barnsley
Cambridge
Chester
Cleethorpes
Colchester
Dewsbury
Doncaster
Dudley

Frodsham
Lincoln
Northampton
Ongar
Oxford
Paisley
Reading
Sudbury
Wolverhampton
Woodchurch
Yapton

JUNE
Barnsley
Catford
Exeter
Leighton Buzzard
Salisbury
Stockport
Surrey
Thurrock (Grays)

JULY
Ardingly
Canterbury
Chelmsford
Cotswolds
Derby
Grantham
Larling
Lewes
Milton Keynes
Southampton
Tameside Canals
Woodcote

AUGUST
Great British Beer Festival
Birmingham
Clacton
Peterborough
Portsmouth

SEPTEMBER
Belfast
Burton upon Trent
Carmarthen
Chappel (Essex)
Chichester
Darlington
Durham
Feltham

Glasgow
Harbury
Ipswich
Keighley
Letchworth
Maidstone
Northampton
Northwich
St Ives (Cambs)
Severn Valley Railway
Sheffield
Shrewsbury
Tamworth

OCTOBER
Alloa
Bath
Bedford
Cardiff
East Lancs
Edinburgh
Falmouth
Guernsey
Holmfirth
Hull
Keighley
Loughborough
Middlesbrough
Newton Abbot
Norwich
Nottingham
Overton
Rhyl
St Albans
Scunthorpe
Stoke-on-Trent
Swindon
Wakefield

NOVEMBER
Aberdeen
Bury
Dudley
Jersey
Luton
Mid Wales
Rochford
Wirral
Woking
York

DECEMBER
London (Pig's Ear)

Lancashire

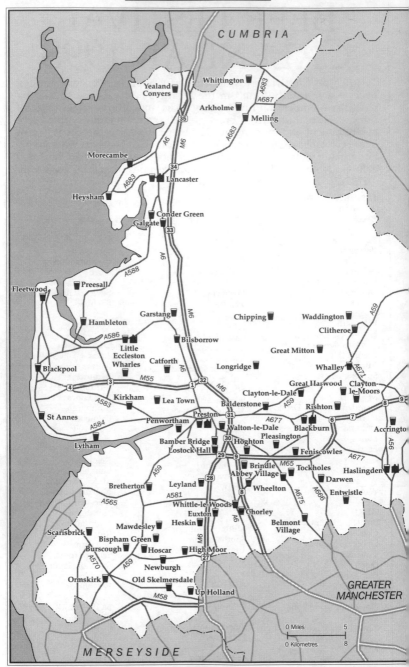

CUMBRIA

Yealand Conyers
Whittington
Arkholme
Melling
A687
A683
35
A6
M6
A683

Morecambe
34
Lancaster
Heysham
Conder Green
Galgate
33
A6

A588
Fleetwood
Preesall
Garstang
M6
Chipping
Waddington
Clitheroe
A59

Hambleton
Bilsborrow
Great Mitton
A586
Little Eccleston Wharles
Catforth
Longridge
Whalley
A671
Blackpool
M55
A6
Great Harwood
Clayton-le-Moors
4
3
Kirkham
Lea Town
32
Clayton-le-Dale
A59
Rishton
8
9
A583
1
M6
Balderstone
Great Harwood
St Annes
Penwortham
Preston
31
A677
Blackburn
6
7
Accrington
A584
Walton-le-Dale
Pleasington
A56
Lytham
Bamber Bridge
30
Hoghton
Feniscowles
A677
Lostock Hall
29
9
Brindle
M65
Tockholes
Haslingden
28
Abbey Village
Darwen
A59
Leyland
8
Wheelton
Entwistle
Bretherton
A581
Whittle-le-Woods
A675
A565
Euxton
Chorley
A666
Heskin
M6
Belmont Village
Scarisbrick
Mawdesley
A6
Bispham Green
Burscough
Hoscar
High Moor
27
Newburgh
Ormskirk
Old Skelmersdale
A570
A59
Up Holland
M58

GREATER MANCHESTER

0 Miles   5
0 Kilometres   8

MERSEYSIDE

🏭 INDEPENDENT BREWERIES

Blackburn: Blackburn	**Mitchell's**: Lancaster	**Thwaites**: Blackburn
Hart: Little Eccleston	**Moorhouse's**: Burnley	
Little Avenham: Preston	**Porter**: Haslingden	

152

Lancashire

NORTH YORKSHIRE

A59

Salterforth

A56

Blacko

Barrowford

M65

13

Colne

12

Brierfield

11

0

Burnley

Cliviger

A646

WEST YORKSHIRE

A671

Abbey Village

Hare & Hounds
129 Bolton Road (A675/Dole Lane jct) ☎ (01254) 830534
12–2.30, 5–11; 12–11 Sat; 12–10.30 Sun
Boddingtons Bitter; Taylor Landlord; guest beers Ⓗ
Popular country inn: one large main room with a central bar and a games room at the back. Good local. Handy for Walks. Food served all day Sat and Sun until 8.30.
🛏 🚭 🕸 ◑ ▷ ♣ P

Accrington

Arden Arms
85 Abbey Street (A680)
☎ (01254) 385971
12–11; 12–10.30 Sun
Boddingtons Bitter; Marston's Pedigree; Moorhouse's Premier; guest beer Ⓗ
Multi-roomed, semi-open-plan pub close to the town centre.
≳ ♣

Brooks Club
Infant Street (off A680)
☎ (01254) 234039
11–5, 7–11, 12–3, 7–10.30 Sun
Boddingtons Bitter; guest beer Ⓗ
Modern, purpose-built club with a lounge, a games area and a concert room. Show the *Guide* or CAMRA membership card to be signed in. One of the few local outlets for real cider.
≳ ♣ ⌣

Arkholme

Bay Horse
☎ (0152 42) 21425
11.30–3, 6–11; 12–3, 7–10.30 Sun
Mitchell's Original, Lancaster Bomber, seasonal beers Ⓗ
Small, old-fashioned country inn dating back to 1705, in a tourist-free village. Three rooms; one is used by families, one for games. No muddy boots. Own bowling green.
🕸 ◑ ▷ ♣ P

Balderstone

Myerscough
Whalley Road (A59)
☎ (01254) 812222
11.30–3, 5.30–11; 12–3, 7–10.30 Sun
Robinson's Hatters Mild, Best Bitter Ⓗ
Pleasant country inn close to the main entrance of Samlesbury Aerodrome, with a cosy wood-panelled lounge and another small room. Quality meals (finish at 8.30). A third Robinson's beer is also sold. 🛏 Q 🕸 🍴 ◑ ▷ P

Bamber Bridge

Olde Original Withy Trees
157 Station Road (A6)
☎ (01772) 330396
11–11; 12–10.30 Sun
Burtonwood Bitter, seasonal beers Ⓗ
Busy local: a refurbished former farmhouse with a strong darts following. Children's play area outside.
🛏 🚭 ◑ ♣ P

Barrowford

White Bear
Gisburn Road (A682)
☎ (01282) 615646
11–3, 5.30–11; 11–11 Fri & Sat; 12–10.30 Sun
Draught Bass; Worthington Bitter; guest beer Ⓗ
One bar, two rooms and a dining room in a 17th-century village inn, steeped in local history and associated with the John Wesley Methodist church. The varied menu is served all day Sun. 🚭 ◑ ▷ P

Belmont Village

Black Dog Inn
2 Church Street (A675)
☎ (01204) 811218
12–4 (3 Mon–Wed), 7–11; 12–4, 6.30–10.30 Sun
Holt Mild, Bitter Ⓗ
Popular, homely, traditional, moorland village pub, multi-roomed and decorated with antiques. Eve meals for residents only Mon–Tue.
🛏 Q 🚭 🕸 🍴 ◑ ▷ P

Bilsborrow

White Bull
Garstang Road (A6)
☎ (01995) 640324
12–11; 12–10.30 Sun
Theakston Mild, Best Bitter; guest beer (summer) Ⓗ
Unspoilt, traditional village pub by the Lancaster Canal, serving good, home-cooked food 12–6 (12–8 Fri–Sun). Children welcome in a designated area till 9.
🛏 🚭 ◑ ♿ ⚓ ♣ P

Bispham Green

Eagle & Child
Maltkiln Lane (off B5246)
☎ (01257) 462297
12–3, 5.30–11; 12–10.30 Sun
Coach House Gunpowder Mild; Flowers Original; Theakston Best Bitter; Thwaites Bitter; guest beers Ⓗ
Vibrant, well-renovated village local with a reputation for good food. Bowling green.
🛏 Q 🚭 🕸 ◑ ▷ ♣ ⌣ P ⚥

Blackburn

Adelphi Beer Engine
33 Railway Road (by bus station)
11–11; 12–10.30 Sun
Boddingtons Mild, Bitter; Castle Eden Ale; Flowers IPA;

153

Marston's Pedigree; Whitbread Trophy H
Large, town-centre pub offering a good range of beer in a comfortable atmosphere, but it can be expensive. ♿ ◖ & ⇌

Cellar Bar
39 King Street
☎ (01254) 698111
11–11 (midnight Wed–Sat); 7–10.30 (closed lunch) Sun
Blackburn BBC 3, BBC 2, BBC 1 H
Very large building (1778), just off the town centre and popular with students. All beers are brewed behind.
🍴 ❀ ◖ ⇌

Florence Hotel
149 Moss Street, Daisyfield (opp. new TA barracks)
☎ (01254) 53100
11.30–3, 6.30–11; 11.30–11 Fri & Sat; 12–10.30 Sun
Thwaites Best Mild, Bitter H
Refurbished, street-corner pub, popular with local workers lunchtimes. All food is home cooked. Menagerie in the garden. ❀ ◖ ♣

Havelock
Stancliffe Street (off Preston old road) ☎ (01254) 53208
12–11; 12–10.30 Sun
Thwaites Best Mild, Bitter H
Cosy, traditional local with a games room and a tiny snug. Coal fires in the bar and lounge. Close to Ewood Park. Lunches Sat.
🍴 ❀ ◖ ⇌ (Mill Hill) ♣ P

Navigation Inn
Canal Street, Mill Hill
☎ (01254) 53230
11–11; 12–10.30 Sun
Thwaites Best Mild, Bitter H
Well-patronised, traditional boozer next to the Leeds–Liverpool Canal. Handy for Ewood Park.
◖ ⇌ (Mill Hill) ♣

Blacko

Cross Gaits
Beverley Road (off A682 at Blacko school)
☎ (01282) 616312
12–3 (not Mon–Wed), 5.30–11; 12–4, 7–10.30 Sun
Burtonwood Bitter, Top Hat; guest beer H
Comfortable, popular country pub with the date 1647 above the door. Excellent food Fri–Sun lunch and Wed–Sat eve. Children's play area in the garden. 🍴 Q ❀ ◖ ▶ ♣ P

Blackpool

Bispham Hotel
Red Bank Road (near Sainsbury's) ☎ (01253) 351752
11–11; 12–10.30 Sun
Samuel Smith OBB H

Distinctively designed, busy local near the seafront. No food Sun or Mon.
Q ◖ ⊕ & ⊖ (Red Bank Rd)

Counting House
10 Talbot Square (opp. north pier) ☎ (01253) 290979
10.30–11; 12–10.30 Sun
Boddingtons Bitter; Cains Bitter; guest beer H
Spacious, converted bank on two floors, offering excellent views of the prom and sea. It can get very busy at weekends. Food served every day until 7.45. Families welcome until 8 in an upstairs room. Wheelchair WC. ◖ ▶ & ⇌ (North) ⊖ (North Pier) ♣ ⊬

Empress Hotel
59 Exchange Street
☎ (01253) 751347
11–11 (12.30am Fri & Sat in summer); 12–10.30 Sun
Thwaites Best Mild, Bitter H
Spacious, Victorian, old-fashioned, basic hotel with a large games room, a dance floor boasting a Wurlitzer organ, and a big screen TV. Food lunchtimes for non-residents. Lancashire's only ever-present *Guide* entry. ♿ 🛏 ◖ ⊕ & ⇌ (North) ⊖ (Pleasant St) ♣

Pump & Truncheon
13 Bonny Street
☎ (01253) 21869
11–11; 12–10.30 Sun
Boddingtons Mild, Bitter; Whitbread Abroad Cooper; guest beers H
Welcoming alehouse in the bare floorboards style, with police paraphernalia, behind the promenade. Children welcome until 5 Mon–Fri (3 Sat–Sun).
🍴 ◖ ⊖ (Central Pier) ♣ ♢

Raikes Hall
16 Liverpool Road
☎ (01253) 294372
11–11; 12–10.30 Sun
Bass Mild, Draught Bass; Stones Bitter; Worthington Bitter; guest beer H
Pub built in 1750 as part of the Raikes Hall estate; home to bowls tournaments and an R&B club. Popular games room. Food served until 7.30 (6.30 Sat–Sun). Families welcome in a designated area. Wheelchair WC.
Q ❀ ◖ ⊕ & ♣ P

Saddle Inn
286 Whitegate Drive (A583)
☎ (01253) 798900
12 (11.30 Sat)–11; 12–10.30 Sun
Draught Bass; Worthington Bitter; guest beers H
Small, but cosy, three-roomed, popular local; the oldest continuously licensed house in Blackpool (1776). Up to eight guest beers per week.

Children's play area. The dining room offers good value lunches.
🍴 Q ❀ ◖ ▶ P ⊬

Stanley Beer Engine
139 Church Street
☎ (01253) 26582
11–11; 12–10.30 Sun
Boddingtons Bitter; Flowers IPA; Whitbread Trophy; guest beers H
Basic, popular, Whitbread alehouse near the Winter Gardens, full of Blackpool FC memorabilia. Wholesome food and up to eight independents' guest beers are served. Difficult parking.
◖ ⇌ (North) ⊖ (Tower) ♣ ♢

Wheatsheaf
194–196 Talbot Road (A586, opp. station)
☎ (01253) 25062
10.30–11; 12–10.30 Sun
Theakston Mild, Best Bitter, XB, Old Peculier; guest beer H
Traditional, lively, town-centre local, full of character. A wide range of single malts and wines and, unusually, fresh fruit and vegetable juices are available. A CAMRA award-winning pub.
🍴 & ⇌ (North) ♣

Bretherton

Blue Anchor
South Road (B5247)
☎ (01772) 600270
11.30–3, 5–11; 11.30–11 Fri & Sat; 12–10.30 Sun
Boddingtons Bitter; Flowers IPA; guest beers H
Well-kept inn with a large garden. Excellent value meals (served all day Sat and Sun), and interesting guest beers.
Q ❀ ◖ ♣ P

Brierfield

Lane Ends Inn
High Reedley Road
☎ (01282) 612072
12–11; 12–10.30 Sun
Vaux Bitter, Samson H
Welcoming pub on the outskirts of town, a rare outlet for Vaux beers in the area. Wide variety of reasonably priced food.
❀ ◖ ▶ ♣ P

Poultry Fanciers WMC
39 Railway View
☎ (01282) 612404
7.30–11; 8.30–10.30 Sun
Moorhouse's Premier; Thwaites Bitter; guest beers H
Welcoming, workingmen's club, offering the best real ale selection around. Show the *Guide* or CAMRA membership card to be signed in. Guest beers come from Thwaites.
& ⇌ ♣ P ⊟

Brindle

Cavendish Arms
Sandy Lane (B5256)
☎ (01254) 852912
11–2.30, 5.30–11; 12–4, 7.30–10.30 Sun
Burtonwood Bitter, seasonal beers H
Outstanding, traditional village pub, refurbished in the 1930s, with stained-glass and wood carvings. Close to Hoghton Towers.
🏚 ⛲ ⊛ ◖ 🍺 P

Burnley

Coal Clough
41 Coal Clough Lane (200 yds E of M65 jct 10)
☎ (01282) 423226
11–11; 12–10.30 Sun
Draught Bass; Boddingtons Bitter; Worthington Bitter H
Friendly, end-of-terrace, busy, community local. The games room is popular and traditional. A Bass national award-winner.
🍺 ⇌ (Barracks) ♣

Sparrow Hawk Hotel
Church Street
☎ (01282) 421551
11–3, 6–11; 11–11 Sat; 12–3, 7–10.30 Sun
Moorhouse's Premier, Pendle Witches Brew; Theakston Best Bitter; guest beers H
Pub considered to have the oldest licence in Burnley, as well as the finest range of ales: a welcoming establishment offering superb bar meals. Occasional cider. No real ale in the no-smoking bar. ⊨ ◖ &
⇌ (Central) ♣ ⌂ P ⊬

Tim Bobbin Hotel
319 Padiham Road (A678)
☎ (01282) 424165
11–11; 12–10.30 Sun
Samuel Smith OBB H
Busy, main road pub with a large, comfortable lounge and a games room. Named after a local dialect poet.
⊛ 🍺 ⇌ (Barracks) ♣ P

Burscough

Martin Inn
Martin Lane (off B5242)
☎ (01704) 892302
11.30–3, 5.30–11; 12–4, 7–10.30 Sun
Boddingtons Bitter; Marston's Pedigree; Tetley Dark Mild, Bitter; Walker Best Bitter; guest beers H
Welcoming inn, close to the Leeds–Liverpool Canal and the Martin Mere Wildfowl Trust. A central bar serves a large, stone-floored bar area. Good choice of food.
🏚 ⊛ ⊨ ◖ 🍴 A P

Catforth

Bay Horse Hotel
Catforth Road (off B5269)
☎ (01772) 690389
11–11; 12–10.30 Sun
Boddingtons Bitter; Burtonwood Bitter; Forshaw's H
Good, homely, village local with a friendly atmosphere, offering 'good food, good drink, good humour'. Children welcome in a designated area (until 9). Wheelchair WC.
🏚 Q ⛲ ⊛ ◖ 🍺 & A ♣ P

Running Pump
Catforth Road (off B5269)
☎ (01772) 690265
11–3, 5–11; 11–11 Sat; 12–10.30 Sun
Robinson's Hatters Mild, Hartleys XB, Best Bitter, Old Tom (winter) G
Charming country pub of great character, offering full à la carte dining (restaurant open Wed–Sun) and excellent, home-cooked bar meals. Families welcome in a designated area. Well worth finding. 🏚 Q ⊛ ◖ 🍴 ♣ P

Chipping

Sun Inn
2 Windy Street
☎ (01995) 61206
11–11; 12–10.30 Sun
Boddingtons Mild, Bitter H
Stone pub in a prize-winning village, used by locals and visitors to the Trough of Bowland: a wood-panelled bar with three rooms off, one having a Ring the Bull game.
🏚 ⊛ ◖ 🍴 A ♣

Chorley

Duke of York
124 Bolton Street (A6)
☎ (01257) 275001
12–11; 12–10.30 Sun
Holt Mild, Bitter H
This became a Holt's pub in 1996 (formerly Greenalls): a split-level lounge with a large public bar. Note the windows from the long-closed Sumners Brewery. ⊛ ◖ 🍺 ⇌ ♣

Malt 'n' Hops
50–52 Friday Street (near station) ☎ (01257) 260967
12–11; 12–10.30 Sun
Boddingtons Bitter; Cains Mild; Taylor Landlord; guest beers H
Single-bar pub of character, furnished with Victoriana. Unusual exterior for the area. Four guest beers. ⇌

Prince of Wales
New Market Street (near bus station) ☎ (01257) 232348

11–11; 12–10.30 Sun
Vaux Samson, Waggle Dance; Ward's Thorne BB; guest beer H
Pub re-opened in 1995 after lying derelict for five years: a large single bar with three central piers. Meals served 10–7 (3 Sun). ◖ ⊬

Railway
20–22 Steeley Lane (behind station)
☎ (01257) 411449
12–11; 12–10.30 Sun
Draught Bass; Stones Bitter; Theakston Mild, Best Bitter; guest beers H
Lively local, decorated in Edwardian style, with a single bar, large alcoves and an unusual display of model vehicles. 🏚 ⇌ ♣

Tut 'n' Shive
Market Street
☎ (01257) 262858
11–11; 12–10.30 Sun
Boddingtons Bitter; Castle Eden Ale; guest beers H
Formerly the Royal Oak Hotel: a split-level bar upstairs with a downstairs bar open at weekends. Meals are served 12–2 and 5–7.
◖ 🍴 ⇌

Clayton-le-Dale

Royal Oak
Longsight Road (A59, ½ mile from B6245 jct)
☎ (01254) 812453
12–3, 6–11; 12–11 Sat; 12–10.30 Sun
Vaux Samson; Ward's Best Bitter, seasonal beers; guest beers H
Attractive rural inn and restaurant, popular with walkers, anglers and equestrians. Children's play area in the garden.
🏚 Q ⊛ ⊨ ◖ 🍴 & A ♣ P

Clayton-le-Moors

Albion
243 Whalley Road (A680)
☎ (01254) 238585
12 (5 Mon & Tue)–11; 12–10.30 Sun
Porter Mild, Bitter, Rossendale, Porter, Sunshine, seasonal beers H
Open-plan pub, close to the mid-point of the Leeds–Liverpool Canal; microbrewer Dave Porter's second pub, serving excellent value beers.
Q ⊛ ◖ & ♣ P

Clitheroe

New Inn
Parson Lane (B6243)
☎ (01200) 23312
11–11; 12–10.30 Sun
Black Sheep Best Bitter; OB Bitter; guest beers H

Friendly local opposite the castle with a traditional interior of four rooms.
🏃 Q 🍴 ≋ ♣ P

Cliviger

Queens Hotel

412 Burnley Road
1–11; 12–10.30 Sun
John Smith's Bitter; Webster's Green Label; guest beers H
Small, two-roomed village local: a tap room and a best room. A good old fashioned boozer – no music but plenty of talking. Hikers welcome.
🏃 Q ♣

Colne

Golden Ball Inn

Burnley Road
☎ (01282) 861862
11.30–3.30, 7–11 (11.30–11 summer); 11 (11.30 summer)–11 Fri & Sat; 12–10.30 Sun
Marston's Pedigree; Tetley Mild, Bitter; guest beers H
Popular roadside inn, busy at lunchtimes due to the mill shop at the rear. Superb meals. Live entertainment Thu.
🏃 🍴 ◐ & ♣ P

Conder Green

Stork

On A588 ☎ (01524) 751234
11–11; 12–10.30 Sun
Boddingtons Bitter; Tetley Bitter; guest beers H
Long, panelled, beamed building with several small rooms (children welcome) and, down a level, the main bar area and a restaurant. Handy for the Lune Estuary path. Two guest beers include seasonals from Whitbread.
🏃 🏃 🍴 ◐ ▶ ▲ ♣ P

Darwen

Bowling Green

386 Bolton Road (A666)
☎ (01254) 702148
11.30–4, 7–11; 11.30–11 Fri & Sat; 12–10.30 Sun
Matthew Brown Bitter; Theakston Mild, Best Bitter; guest beer H
Community local with a good games following. Weekend barbecues. 🏃 🍴 & ♣ P

Greenfield

Lower Barn Street
☎ (01254) 703945
12–3, 5.30–11; 12–11 Fri & Sat; 12–10.30 Sun
Boddingtons Bitter; Taylor Landlord; Thwaites Best Mild, Bitter; guest beers H
Open-plan pub next to the Sough tunnel: Darwen's prime beer house, serving good value, home-cooked food (all day Sun till 7, no eve meals

Tue). Four guest beers usually include a porter. Q 🍴 ◐ ▶

Punch Hotel

Chapels ☎ (01254) 702510
12–11; 12–10.30 Sun
Chester's Mild; Whitbread Trophy; guest beers H
Large, multi-roomed, friendly games pub. The only outlet for cider (and occasionally perry) in town. 🍴 🏃 ◐ ▶ & ♣ ⌂ P

Entwistle

Strawbury Duck

Overshores Road (signed on the Edgworth–Darwen old road) OS852013
☎ (01204) 852013
12–3 (not Mon), 7–11; 12–11 Sat; 12–10.30 Sun
Boddingtons Bitter; Marston's Pedigree; Moorhouse's Pendle Witches Brew; Taylor Landlord; guest beers H
Old, isolated but busy, country pub next to the station. A good base for walks in hill country. Children welcome till 8.30, but no motorcyclists.
🏃 Q 🏃 🍴 ◐ ▶ ≋ ♣ P ⊬

Euxton

Euxton Mills Hotel

Wigan Road (A49/A581 jct)
☎ (01257) 264002
11.30–3, 5.30–11; 12–10.30 Sun
Burtonwood Mild, Bitter, Forshaw's, Buccaneer H
Part-18th-century pub, serving excellent meals (except winter Mon). Three bars; children are welcome in the dining area.
Q 🍴 ◐ 🍴 ♣ P ⊬

Feniscowles

Feildens Arms

Preston Old Road (A674/A6062 jct)
☎ (01254) 200988
12–11; 12–10.30 Sun
Boddingtons Bitter; Chester's Mild; Flowers IPA; Higsons Mild; Tetley Bitter; guest beers H
Attractive, quiet local, catering for all ages and retaining a tiny vault. Guest beers are often from independents. Lunches Tue–Sun. 🏃 Q 🍴 ◐
≋ (Pleasington) ♣ P

Fleetwood

North Euston Hotel

The Esplanade (near bus and tram termini)
☎ (01253) 876525
11–11; 12–10.30 Sun
Boddingtons Bitter; Ruddles County; Webster's Yorkshire Bitter; Wilson's Mild, Bitter; guest beer H
Large, stone-fronted Victorian building overlooking the Wyre estuary and Morecambe Bay.

Spacious rooms; the family room closes at 7.
Q 🏃 🍴 ◐ & ⊖ P ⊬

Ship

24–26 Warren Street (near council offices)
☎ (01253) 778415
11–11; 12–10.30 Sun
Boddingtons Bitter; Gray's Bitter H
Busy, friendly pub with a central bar, a comfortable lounge and a pool table.
🏃 🏃 🍴 ◐ & ⊖ (Lord St) ♣

Steamer

1–2 Queens Terrace
☎ (01253) 771756
11–11; 12–10.30 Sun
Theakston Mild, Best Bitter; guest beer H
Victorian riverside pub next to the traditional market. One bar serves two lounges and a room for games. 1950s and '60s music Sat eve. No children after 5. Lunches in summer.
🏃 🍴 ◐ (Ferry) ♣ P

Wyre Lounge Bar

Marine Hall, The Esplanade
☎ (01253) 771141
12–4, 7–11; 12–4, 7–10.30 Sun
Courage Directors; Moorhouse's Premier; Pendle Witches Brew; guest beers H
Part of the attractive Marine Hall and Gardens complex; twice local CAMRA *Pub of the Year*, famous for its choice of guest beers.
Q 🍴 & ⊖ (Ferry) P

Galgate

Plough

Main Road (A6)
☎ (01524) 751337
11–11; 12–10.30 Sun
Boddingtons Bitter; guest beers H
Modernised, open-plan pub with a distinct cosy 'lounge' end. A robust masculine atmosphere is augmented on Sat by sports teams. Handy for the canal. 🏃 🍴 ◐ P

Garstang

Royal Oak

Market Place ☎ (01995) 603318
11–3 (4 Thu), 7–11; 11–11 Fri & Sat; 12–10.30 Sun
Robinson's Hatters Mild, Hartleys XB, Best Bitter, Frederics H
Partly a 15th-century farmhouse, but this is mostly a 1670 coaching inn, thoughtfully renovated, with intimate drinking areas.
🍴 🍴 ◐ ▶ ♣ P

Th'Owd Tithe Barn

Church Street
☎ (01995) 604486
11–3, 6–11 (11–11 summer); 12–10.30 Sun

Mitchell's Original, Lancaster Bomber, seasonal beers ℍ
Real old tithe barn in an attractive canalside setting. Most of the space is a restaurant in cod-medieval style; one end is more pubby. Upstairs is a small canal museum.
🏃 Q 🍴 🕭 ▶ ♣ P

Great Harwood

Dog & Otter
The Cliffe ☎ (01254) 885760
12–3, 6–11; 12–10.30 Sun
Jennings Mild, Bitter, Cumberland Ale, Sneck Lifter ℍ
Comfortable, open-plan pub and restaurant serving a good range of beers and food; opposite the cricket ground. Families welcome.
🕭 ▶ ♠ P

Royal Hotel
Station Road ☎ (01254) 883541
12–1.30 (not Mon & Tue), 7–11; 12–3, 7–10.30 Sun
Moorhouse's Premier; guest beers ℍ
Victorian, open-plan pub, stocking a wide range of bottled beers and four guest ales. Home-cooked meals. Winner of several CAMRA awards. Parking for residents.
Q 🍴 🛏 🕭 ▶ ♣ 🛢

Great Mitton

Owd Ned's River View Tavern
Mitton Hall, Mitton Road (B6246, 2 miles from Whalley) ☎ (01254) 826544
11–11; 12–10.30 Sun
Boddingtons Mild, Bitter; Castle Eden Ale; Flowers Original; Jennings Cumberland Ale; Wadworth 6X; guest beers ℍ
Overlooking the River Ribble, in picturesque country, this pub places an emphasis on food and good facilities for children. Open 7.30 for breakfast.
🏃 Q 🐕 🍴 🛏 🕭 ▶ ♦ ♣ P

Hambleton

Shard Bridge Inn
Old Bridge Lane
☎ (01253) 700208
12–3, 6–11 (11–11 summer); 12–3, 7–10.30 Sun
Robinson's Best Bitter; Walker Best Bitter; guest beers ℍ
Formerly the ferry booking office, dating back to 1786, this pub houses paraphernalia from the ferry service and the defunct toll bridge. Enjoy the view over the river.
🍴 🕭 ▶ 🍷 🔥 ▲ ♣ P ⚥

Haslingden

Griffin Inn
86 Hud Rake ☎ (01706) 214021
12–11; 12–10.30 Sun
Porter Mild, Bitter, Rossendale, Porter, Sunshine ℍ
Open-plan pub with views over the valley; great for conversation. 🏃 Q ♣

Heskin

Farmers Arms
85 Wood Lane (B5250)
☎ (01257) 451276
12–11; 12–10.30 Sun
Boddingtons Bitter; Castle Eden Ale; Flowers IPA; Morland Old Speckled Hen; Taylor Landlord; guest beers ℍ
Country pub with an emphasis on food; a comfortable, split-level lounge and a dining area, plus a good public bar for drinkers. Families are welcome (large play area); near Camelot Theme Park.
🏃 Q 🐕 🍴 🕭 ▶ 🍷 ▲ ♣ P

Heysham

Old Hall
Heysham Road
☎ (01524) 851209
11–11; 12–10.30 Sun
Mitchell's Original, Lancaster Bomber, seasonal beers ℍ
Actually an old hall, dated 1584, rescued from dereliction in 1958 and fitted out in Mitchell's usual style: a single large bar with the counter at one end. Note the stained-glass. 🐕 🕭 ▶ ♿ P

Royal
7 Main Street ☎ (01524) 859298
11–11; 12–10.30 Sun
Mitchell's Original, Lancaster Bomber ℍ
Old, four-roomed, low-ceilinged pub near St Patrick's Chapel and rock-hewn graves. Busy local trade; packed with holidaymakers in the season. Children admitted to the games room until 7.30.
🏃 🐕 🕭 ▶ ♣ P

High Moor

Rigbye Arms
2 Whittle Lane
☎ (01257) 462354
12–3, 5.30–11 (12–11 Thu–Sat in summer); 12–10.30 Sun
Ind Coope Burton Ale; Tetley Dark Mild, Mild, Bitter; guest beer ℍ
Remote rural pub that is popular with ramblers and can be busy. Deserved reputation for food; the upstairs

restaurant is open Fri and Sat 5.30–11 (bar food all day Sun). Bowling green.
🏃 Q 🐕 🕭 ▶ 🍷 P

Hoghton

Black Horse
Gregson Lane (off A675 at Higher Walton)
☎ (01254) 852541
11.30–11; 12–10.30 Sun
Matthew Brown Bitter; Theakston Mild, Best Bitter, XB; guest beer ℍ
Large, friendly, open-plan village pub with a games area, catering mainly for drinkers, but serving good food (children allowed in for food).
🏃 🐕 🕭 ▶ ♣ P

Royal Oak Hotel
Blackburn Old Road, Riley Green (A675/A6061 jct)
☎ (01254) 201445
11–3, 5.30–11; 11–11 Sat; 12–10.30 Sun
Thwaites Best Mild, Bitter, seasonal beers ℍ
Traditional, low-ceilinged country pub, formed from a row of cottages, with several cosy drinking areas and a dining area. 🏃 Q 🐕 ▶ P ⚥

Hoscar

Railway Tavern
Hoscar Moss Road
☎ (01704) 892369
12–3, 5–11; 12–11 Sat; 12–10.30 Sun
Jennings Bitter; Tetley Mild, Bitter; guest beers ℍ
Refurbished, but unspoilt local next to Hoscar station. Excellent, home-cooked food. Popular with cyclists. Easter beer festival.
🏃 Q 🐄 🐕 🕭 ▶ 🍷 🚆 ♣ P

Kirkham

Queen's Arms
7 Poulton Street (opp. market place) ☎ (01772) 686705
11–11; 12–10.30 Sun
Theakston Best Bitter, XB; guest beer (occasional) ℍ
Excellent, lively, town-centre local, full of character. Children welcome in a designated area and the safe garden. Pool room; wheelchair WC. 🐕 🕭 ♿ ♣

Swan Hotel
115 Poulton Street
12–11; 12–10.30 Sun
Matthew Brown Bitter; Theakston Best Bitter; Wells Bombardier; guest beers ℍ
Popular, friendly, two-bar, town-centre local providing a large screen TV plus entertainment at weekends. Three guest beers; over 100 whiskies. 🐕 🛏 🍷 ♣ P

Lancaster

Bowerham
Bowerham Road
☎ (01524) 65050
11–5, 6–11; 12–10.30 Sun
Mitchell's Original, Lancaster Bomber, seasonal beers H
Large, turn-of-the-century, suburban pub with several rooms, drawing a mostly local trade. Bowling green.
❀ ⬚ ♣

George & Dragon
24 St George's Quay
☎ (01524) 844739
11.30–11; 12–10.30 Sun
Ward's Thorne BB, Best Bitter; guest beers
Narrow, single-bar pub, decorated in modern style, close to the Maritime Museum. All beers are served through a tight sparkler. ❀ ◖ ▶ ⇌ P

Golden Lion
Moor Lane (near brewery)
☎ (01524) 63198
12–3, 7–11; 7–10.30 (closed lunch) Sun
Theakston Best Bitter, Black Bull, XB, Old Peculier; guest beer H
A pub since at least 1612: an L-shaped bar and an adjoining games room, plus a no-smoking 'heritage' room.
⬛ ♣ ✏

John O' Gaunt
35 Market Lane (off A6)
☎ (01524) 65356
11–3 (5 Sat); 6 (7 Sat)–11; 11–11 Thu & Fri; 12–3, 7–10.30 Sun
Boddingtons Bitter; Ind Coope Burton Ale; Jennings Bitter; Tetley Bitter; guest beers H
Small pub, often packed, with a handsome original frontage. Frequent live music – the landlord is a jazz enthusiast. Snacks only Sun lunch. ❀ ◖ ▶

Moorlands
Quarry Road ☎ (01524) 33792
12–3.30, 6–11; 12–11 Sat; 12–10.30 Sun
Mitchell's Original, Lancaster Bomber, seasonal beers H
Large, inner-suburban, turn-of-the-century local, modernised but retaining much of the original layout and features, including stained-glass. ⬚ ♣

Lea Town

Smith's Arms (Slip Inn)
Lea Lane (opp. BNFL East Gate) ☎ (01772) 726906
12–3, 4.30–11; 12–10.30 Sun
Thwaites Best Mild, Bitter H
Superb country gem, one of the last proper drinkers' pubs. However, lunches are good and cheap (not served Sat). Popular with workers from the

BNFL factory.
⬛ Q ⬥ ❀ ◖ ⓐ ♣ P

Leyland

Dunkirk Hall
Dunkirk Lane (B5248/B5253)
☎ (01772) 422102
11–3, 5–11; 11–11 Fri & Sat; 12–10.30 Sun
Courage Directors; John Smith's Bitter; Webster's Green Label H
Converted farmhouse dating from 1662, west of the town centre: a listed building with flagged floors, panelled walls and beams. No food Mon.
Q ❀ ◖ ▶ P

Eagle & Child
30 Church Road (B5248)
☎ (01772) 433531
11.45–11; 12–10.30 Sun
Burtonwood Bitter, Forshaw's, Top Hat, Buccaneer; guest beer H
Ancient inn near the historic cross. One long bar is divided into several drinking areas. Weekday meals. ❀ ◖ ♣ P

George IV
63 Towngate ☎ (01772) 464051
11–11; 12–10.30 Sun
Boddingtons Bitter; Greenalls Bitter; Tetley Bitter; guest beers H
Attractive town pub hosting live bands some eves; popular with young people at weekends. ◖ ⬚ ♣ P

Little Eccleston

Cartford Hotel
Cartford Lane (by toll bridge, ½ mile off A586)
☎ (01995) 670166
12–3, 7 (6.30 summer)–11; 12–4, 6–10.30 Sun
Beer range varies H
Delightfully situated free house by the River Wyre. An extensive bar menu includes children's meals. Six changing guest beers; Hart brewery is behind the pub (at least two Hart beers available). A local CAMRA award-winner.
⬛ ❀ ⌂ ◖ ▶ ᘓ ♣ ⊙ P

Longridge

Alston Arms
Inglewhite Road
☎ (01772) 783331
11.30–11; 12–10.30 Sun
Courage Best Bitter; John Smith's Bitter; Theakston Mild, Best Bitter; guest beer H
Superb family pub; the garden features a double decker bus and a mini-farm. Impressive floral frontage in summer. New conservatory for meals.
⬛ Q ⬥ ❀ ◖ ▶ ⓐ ♣ P

Forrest Arms
2 Derby Road
☎ (01772) 782610
12–2 (not Tue & Wed), 5 (7 Tue & Wed)–11 (may extend in summer); 12–11 Fri & Sat; 12–10.30 Sun
Boddingtons Bitter; guest beers H
Excellent, terraced pub handy for the town centre; three rooms serve a varied clientele. Guest beers may be unusual and/or cheap. A local CAMRA award-winner. ❀ ◖ ⓐ ♣

Towneley Arms
41 Berry Lane
☎ (01772) 782219
11–11; 12–10.30 Sun
Tetley Mild, Bitter H
Former railway station buildings, now a friendly, multi-roomed, well-preserved pub, displaying CAMRA mirrors. ⬛ ⬚ ⓐ ♣ P

Lostock Hall

Victoria
Watkin Lane ☎ (01772) 335338
11–3, 6–11; 11–11 Sat; 12–10.30 Sun
John Smith's Bitter; guest beers H
Large pub set back from the main road; a true community local, the meeting place for several clubs. ◖ ⬚ ⇌ ♣ P

Lytham

Hole in One
Forest Drive (off B5261)
☎ (01253) 730598
11–3, 6–11; 11–11 Fri & Sat; 12–10.30 Sun
Thwaites Bitter H
Busy, friendly modern local near Fairhaven Golf Course, with a large games room. Good home-made food; children most welcome. Wheelchair WC. Q ❀ ◖ ⬚ ᘓ ♣ P

Ship & Royal
91 Clifton Street
☎ (01253) 736186
11–11; 12–10.30 Sun
Boddingtons Bitter; Greenalls Bitter, Original; Stones Bitter; Theakston Best Bitter H
Well-refurbished, busy pub where families are welcome. Eve meals 6–8 (not Sun). Wheelchair WC.
⬥ ◖ ▶ ᘓ ⇌ ✏

Taps
12 Henry Street (off Lytham Sq) ☎ (01253) 736226
11–11; 12–10.30 Sun
Beer range varies H
Busy, friendly, basic alehouse, serving a wide choice of changing guest beers. The only licensee to win local CAMRA *Pub of the Year* in two different pubs. Difficult parking. Wheelchair WC.
⬛ Q ❀ ◖ ᘓ ⇌ ⊙

Mawdesley

Black Bull

Hall Lane (off B5246) OS499151
☎ (01704) 462202
12–11; 12–10.30 Sun
**Greenalls Mild, Bitter,
Original; Tetley Bitter; guest
beer** H
Welcoming, 417-year-old
country pub with an excellent
menu. Winner of the county's
Best Kept Village Pub of the Year
1996.
🏮 Q ☎ ⊛ ◑ ▶ ♣ P ⊁

Robin Hood

Bluestone Lane OS506163
☎ (01704) 821761
11–3, 6–11; 11–11 Sat; 12–10.30 Sun
**Boddingtons Bitter; Castle
Eden Ale; Flowers IPA;
Robinson's Hartleys XB;
Taylor Landlord; guest
beers** H
Food-oriented, isolated
country pub located at a
crossroads between Croston,
Eccleston and Mawdesley.
Seven ales and a warm
welcome are always on offer.
☎ ⊛ ◑ ▶ P ⊁

Melling

Melling Hall

☎ (0152 42) 22022
12–3, 6–11; 11–11 Sat; 12–10.30 Sun
**Boddingtons Bitter; Taylor
Golden Best (occasional),
Landlord; Theakston Best
Bitter** H
17th-century manor house
which became a hotel in the
1940s. Two contrasting bars;
garden play area.
🏮 ⊛ ◑ ▶ ♠ ♣ P

Morecambe

Davy Jones Locker

76 Marine Road West
☎ (01524) 410180
11–11; 12–10.30 Sun
**Mitchell's Original, Lancaster
Bomber** H
Independent cellar bar beneath
the Clarendon Hotel, with
nautical decor. Other Mitchell's
beers are stocked.
🏮 ⊛ ♣

Smugglers' Den

Poulton Road
☎ (01524) 421684
11–3, 7–11; 11–11 Fri & Sat (& Tue–Thu
in summer); 12–10.30 Sun
**Boddingtons Bitter; Jennings
Bitter; Tetley Bitter; guest
beer** H
The smugglers are long gone
but stained-glass and nautical
knick-knacks remind
customers of this low-beamed,
stone-floored pub's past. Busy
in summer.
🏮 ⊛ ⊟ ♣ P

Newburgh

Red Lion Hotel

Ash Brow (A5209)
☎ (01257) 462336
11–11; 12–10.30 Sun
**Burtonwood Mild, Bitter,
Forshaw's, Buccaneer; guest
beer** H
Former coaching inn, opposite
the village green, popular for
its food. The background
music and satellite TV can be
intrusive. ⊛ 🚗 ◑ ▶ P

Old Skelmersdale

Horse Shoe Inn

137 Liverpool Road (B5312)
☎ (01695) 731676
11–11; 12–10.30 Sun
**Cains Bitter; Walker Mild;
guest beers** H
Victorian community pub built
to serve local miners. Excellent
value food includes breakfasts
(served from 7.30 weekdays
and 9.30 weekends). Good
reputation for guest beers.
🏮 Q ☎ ⊛ ◑ ⊟ A P

Ormskirk

Golden Lion

39 Moor Street (edge of
pedestrian zone)
☎ (01695) 572354
11–11; 12–10.30 Sun
**Tetley Mild, Bitter; guest
beer** H
Refurbished town-centre pub
with a central bar serving two
rooms, and a split-level lounge.
The house beer is brewed by
Carlsberg-Tetley; Tapster's
Choice guest beer. Good value
lunches. ◑ ⊟ ⇌

Hayfield

22 County Road (A59)
☎ (01695) 571157
12–11; 12–10.30 Sun
**Courage Directors; John
Smith's Bitter; Theakston Best
Bitter; guest beers** H
Popular free house,
comfortably furnished, serving
up to ten guest beers and
excellent value meals. Eve
meals end at 8.30 (8 Sun). Good
wheelchair access. Worth the
short walk from the centre.
⊛ ◑ ▶ ⅙ ⇌ P ⊟

Penwortham

St Teresa's Parish Centre

Queensway (off A59)
☎ (01772) 743523
7 (2 Sat)–11; 1–4, 7–10.30 Sun
**Burtonwood Mild, Bitter,
Forshaw's; Ind Coope Burton
Ale; Tetley Mild, Bitter; guest
beers** H
Popular Catholic club in a
residential area: a lounge, a

games room and a large
function room, each with its
own bar. A former CAMRA
Club of the Year. Show a
CAMRA card for admission
(non-members 25p). Children
admitted at lunchtime. Annual
beer festival each Feb.
☎ ⊛ ⊟ ♣ P ⊁

Pleasington

Railway Hotel

Pleasington Lane
☎ (01254) 21520
12–5, 6.30–11; 12–11 Sat; 12–10.30 Sun
**Boddingtons Bitter; Matthew
Brown Bitter; Wilson's Mild,
Bitter; guest beer** H
Farmhouse converted to a pub
about 1870. Quiet, it caters for
all ages. Reasonably-priced
beers; bowling green. Quiz Tue
eve.
🏮 Q ☎ ⊛ ◑ ▶ ⇌ ♣ P

Preesall

Black Bull

192 Park Lane
☎ (01253) 810294
12–3 (not Mon), 6 (7 Mon)–11; 12–3,
7–10.30 Sun
**Tetley Mild, Bitter; guest
beers** H
Historic, low-ceilinged,
friendly, rural village pub.
Food is served every day
except Mon, although the main
emphasis is on the beer. Eve
meals 6–9 (7–8.30 Sun). Mainly
mature local clientele. Children
are welcome in the two back
rooms until 8pm.
Q ◑ ▶ A ♣ P

Preston

Ashton Institute & Social Club

10–12 Wellington Road (off
A583/A5085)
☎ (01772) 726582
7 (4 Fri & Sat)–11; 12–10.30 Sun
**Boddingtons Bitter; guest
beers** H
Enterprising club, now with a
relaxed tie, offering three guest
bitters and a guest mild. The
oldest club in Preston still
occupying its original premises
(since 1944). Show CAMRA
membership card or the *Guide*
for entry. ⊛ ♣

Black Horse ☆

166 Friargate
10.30–11; 7–10.30 (closed lunch) Sun
**Robinson's Old Stockport,
Hartleys XB, Best Bitter,
Frederics, Old Tom** H
With its large tiled bar, mosaic
floors, wood panelling, hall of
mirrors and other original
features, this listed building
has won an English Heritage
award for *Best Refurbishment*.
⊛ ◑ ⇌

Hogshead
99 Fylde Road (A583)
☎ (01772) 252870
11–11; 12–10.30 Sun
Boddingtons Bitter; Whitbread Abroad Cooper; guest beers H/G
Former doctor's surgery and home, restored as a cask alehouse. Its good, friendly atmosphere attracts a wide range of customers. Food served all day until 7 (Sun 12–3). Very busy weekend eves. Up to 12 beers.
Q ❀ ◖ ◗ ♿ 🚭

Lamb & Packet
91A Friargate
☎ (01772) 251857
11.30–11; 11.30–3, 6.30–11 Sat; 12–10.30 Sun
Thwaites Bitter; guest beer H
Busy one-roomer which has more than held its own in Preston's changing pub scene. At lunchtimes the good value food ensures a mix of students and office workers, but students take over eves. Meals until 6.30. Guest beers are supplied by Thwaites. ◖

Mitre
90–91 Moor Lane
☎ (01772) 251918
12–3, 5.30–11; 12–11 Sat; 12–10.30 Sun
Vaux Samson; Ward's Best Bitter; guest beers H
Welcoming pub with a comfortable lounge and a vault with pool and darts. Close to the town centre. No food Sat.
◖ ♣ P

Moorbrook
370 North Road
☎ (01772) 201127
4 (12 Sat)–11; 12–3, 7–10.30 Sun
Thwaites Bitter H
Friendly local, just outside the town centre, with two small rooms off the main bar area. A folk club meets Fri eve.
Q ❀ ♣

New Britannia
6 Heatley Street (off Friargate)
☎ (01772) 253424
11–3 (4 Sat), 6–11; 7–10.30 (closed lunch) Sun
Boddingtons Bitter; Castle Eden Ale; Flowers Original; Marston's Pedigree; guest beers H
Small, cosy, single bar in a terraced town-centre pub, close to the university. Note the splendid Britannia windows. Weekday food. ❀ ◖ ⇌ ♣ ⌓

Old Black Bull
35 Friargate (Ringway jct)
☎ (01772) 254402
10.30–11; 12–10.30 Sun
Boddingtons Bitter; guest beers H
Tudor-fronted pub with a snug, a games area and a lounge off the main bar, and a tiny vault at the front. The alehouse theme is supported by seven changing guest beers. No food Sun.
❀ ◖ ⊞ ⇌ ♣ ⌓

Olde Blue Bell
114 Church Street
☎ (01772) 251280
11–3.30 (4 Sat), 6 (7 Sat)–11; 12–4, 7–10.30 Sun
Samuel Smith OBB H
The oldest pub in Preston: like a country cottage with two small rooms off the main bar area. Good for conversation but busy Fri/Sat nights. Good value food. ♨ ❀ ◖

Olde Dog & Partridge
44 Friargate ☎ (01772) 252217
11–3, 6–11; 12–3, 7–10.30 Sun
Draught Bass; Highgate Dark, Old; Worthington Bitter; guest beers H
Preston's internationally renowned rock pub. Its basic decor has not changed in over ten years. Excellent value lunches (not served Sun). Popular with all, especially rockers and students. ◖ ⇌ ♣

Plungington Tavern
85 Plungington Road
☎ (01772) 252339
12 (11 Sat)–11; 12–3, 7–10.30 Sun
Bass Toby Cask; Hancock's HB; Highgate Dark; Stones Bitter H
Good value, basic, street-corner pub in a terraced area reached by bus no. 23 from the centre. Note the impressive tiled frontage. ⊞ ♣

Real Ale Shop
47 Lovat Road (off A6 N of town) ☎ (01772) 201591
11–2, 5–10; 12–2, 6–10 Sun
Beer range varies H/G
Superb off-licence which, besides its four beers on draught, has an extensive range of bottled beers.
⌓

Sumners
Watling St Road, Fulwood (B6242) ☎ (01772) 705626
11.30–11; 12–10.30 Sun
Boddingtons Mild, Bitter; guest beer H
Large, busy, modern pub, handy for the football ground, with a wood-panelled lounge, a no-smoking dining area and a spacious games room. Meals served all day until 7. The guest beer comes from Greenalls' list.
❀ ◖ ◗ ⊞ ♿ ♣ P

Rishton

Rishton Arms
Station Road ☎ (01254) 886396
7 (11 Sat)–11; 12–10.30 Sun
Thwaites Best Mild, Bitter, seasonal beer H
Pleasant, two-roomed pub boasting a grandfather clock in the lounge. ⇌ ♣ P

St Annes

Victoria Hotel
Church Road (off B5233)
☎ (01253) 721041
11–11; 12–10.30 Sun
Beer range varies H
Popular, busy pub with a large vault which celebrated its centenary in 1997. Food served 12–2. ❀ ◖ ⊞ ♿ ♣ P

Salterforth

Anchor Inn
Salterforth Lane
☎ (01282) 813186
12–11; 12–10.30 Sun
Bass Mild, Draught Bass; Theakston Best Bitter; Worthington Bitter; guest beers (summer) H
Welcome stopping place on the Leeds–Liverpool Canal. Semi-open-plan, it dates back to 1655. Good value food (children's menu). Garden play area. ♨ ❀ ◖ ◗ ▲ ♣ P

Scarisbrick

Heatons Bridge Inn
2 Heatons Bridge Road (B5242, by Leeds–Liverpool Canal)
☎ (01704) 840549
11–11; 12–10.30 Sun
Tetley Mild, Bitter; guest beers H
Popular, welcoming canalside inn, extended at the rear without loss of character. The small rooms off the small bar area are ideal for conversation. Excellent value food (all day Sun); children welcome in the dining area.
♨ Q ❀ ◖ ◗ ♣ P 🚭

Tockholes

Royal Arms
Tockholes Road
☎ (01254) 705373
12–3, 7–11; 12–11 Fri, Sat & summer; 12–10.30 Sun
Thwaites Best Mild, Bitter, seasonal beers H
Very cosy, attractive moorland pub with a fire in each of its four rooms. Handy for walks. Recommended food.
♨ Q ♉ ❀ ◖ ◗ ♣ P 🚭

Up Holland

Delph Tavern
Tontine ☎ (01695) 622239
11.30–11; 12–10.30 Sun
Boddingtons Bitter; Flowers IPA; Moorhouse's Premier; guest beers H

Lively pub, catering for all ages, with a large lounge area. ➠ ❀ ◁ ▯ & ♣ P

Old Dog
6 Alma Hill
8–11; 8–10.30 Sun
Draught Bass; Boddingtons Bitter; Burtonwood Mild; Worthington Bitter Ⓗ
Pub with three small, intimate rooms off an even smaller bar.
Q ➠ ♣

Waddington

Buck Inn (Lower)
Church Road
☎ (01200) 28705
11–3, 6–11; 11–11 Thu–Sat; 12–3, 7–10.30 Sun
Ruddles County; Taylor Best Bitter, Landlord; Younger No. 3 Ⓗ
Very friendly, little-altered, old coaching house dating from 1760. Excellent, home-cooked food.
🏨 Q ➠ ❀ ⌸ ◁ ▯ 🛏 & ▲ P

Walton-le-Dale

Yew Tree
100 Victoria Road (A6/A675 jct)
☎ (01772) 555103
11–3, 5.30–11; 11–11 Sat; 12–10.30 Sun
Boddingtons Bitter; Taylor Landlord; Theakston Best Bitter; guest beer Ⓗ
Extended roadside pub, with a bar eating area and a restaurant, handy for the cinema complex south of Preston. ➠ ❀ ◁ ▯ & ♣ P

Whalley

Swan
62 King Street
☎ (01254) 822195
11–11; 12–10.30 Sun
Boddingtons Bitter; Moorhouse's Premier; Taylor Landlord; Thwaites Bitter; Wadworth 6X; guest beer Ⓗ
Excellent pub in the centre of an historic village. Good value food. 🛏 ◁ ▯ ♣ P

Wharles

Eagle & Child
1 Church Road (3 miles NE of Kirkham) OS448356
☎ (01772) 690312
12–3 (not winter Mon–Fri), 7–11; 12–4, 7–10.30 Sun
Beer range varies Ⓗ
Pleasant, country free house with a thatched roof, beamed ceilings and antique furniture.
🏨 Q ♣ P

Wheelton

Red Lion
196 Blackburn Road (off A674)
☎ (01254) 830378
12–11; 12–10.30 Sun
Boddingtons Bitter; Theakston Best Bitter; guest beers Ⓗ
Popular, village-centre pub with a split-level interior: a comfortable bar and a games room. A short walk from the Leeds–Liverpool Canal at Johnsons Hillock. Lunches Fri–Sun. 🏨 ◁ ♣ P

Whittington

Dragon's Head
☎ (0152 42) 72383
11–11; 12–10.30 Sun
Mitchell's Original Ⓗ
Old-fashioned village inn. Off the cosy bar is a dining room, a pool room and a post office.
🏨 ❀ 🛏 ◁ ▲ ♣ P

Whittle-le-Woods

Royal Oak
216 Chorley Old Road
☎ (01257) 276485
12–10.30 Sun
Matthew Brown Bitter; Hanby Black Magic; Ruddles County; Theakston Black Bull; Wells Bombardier Ⓗ
Splendid, small, one-bar, terraced village pub: a real local and a meeting place for mature motorcycle enthusiasts. Note the Nuttalls cut-glass windows. Bar billiards (rare in this area). 🏨 Q ❀ ♣

Yealand Conyers

New Inn
40 Yealand Road
☎ (01524) 732938
11–3, 5.30–11; 11–11 Sat & summer; 12–10.30 Sun
Robinson's Hatters Mild, Hartleys XB, Best Bitter, Frederics, Old Tom Ⓗ
Old village inn, popular for food. The conversion of a barn to a restaurant should free the attractive bar for drinking.
🏨 ❀ ◁ ▯ ♣ P

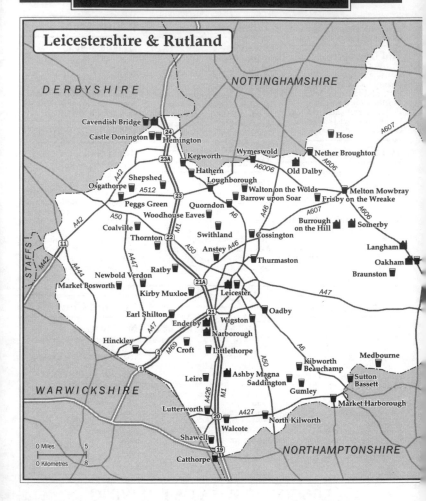

Leicestershire & Rutland

Anstey

Old Hare & Hounds
34 Bradgate Road (opp.
church) ☎ (0116) 236 2496
11–3.30, 6.30–11; 12–3, 7–10.30 Sun
**Marston's Bitter, Pedigree,
HBC** Ⓗ
Split-level pub with three
rooms and one central bar; a
popular local. Q ❀ ♣ P

Barrowden

Exeter Arms
Main Street (off A47)
☎ (01572) 747247
12–2 (not Mon), 6–11; 12–3, 7–10.30
Sun
**Marston's Bitter, Pedigree;
guest beers** Ⓗ
Stone pub on the village green
opposite a duck pond. Local
CAMRA *Pub of the Year* 1995, it
has one long room with bare

walls and oak beams. Cider in
summer. ♨ ❀ ◑ ♣ ◔ ⚲

Barrow upon Soar

Navigation Inn
Mill Lane
☎ (01509) 412842
11–3, 5.30–11; 11–11 Sat; 12–3, 7–10.30
Sun
**Marston's Pedigree;
Shipstone's Mild, Bitter; guest
beers** Ⓗ
Popular village local alongside
the canal; limited parking but
still worth a visit. Barbecues
Sat/Sun in summer otherwise
no food Sat or Sun.
♨ Q ❀ ❀ ◑ ♣

Braunston

Old Plough Inn
High Street
☎ (01572) 722714
11–3, 6–11; 12–3, 6–10.30 Sun

**Grainstore Cooking, Triple B;
Ruddles Best Bitter, County;
Theakston XB** Ⓗ
Country pub with a cosy
lounge. The conservatory
restaurant has a false ceiling
made from parasols. It
sometimes sells all three
Rutland breweries' beers at the
same time. ♨ ❀ ◑ ▲ ♣ P

Castle Donington

Nag's Head
Hilltop
☎ (01322) 850652
11.30–2.30, 5.30–11; 12–3, 7–10.30 Sun
**Banks's Mild; Marston's
Bitter, Pedigree** Ⓗ
Small country inn on the hilltop side of the village. Food is
served in no-smoking, bistro-
style dining rooms, with plenty
of oak beams and open fires.
No eve meals Sun.
♨ Q ❀ ◑ ▶ ♿ P

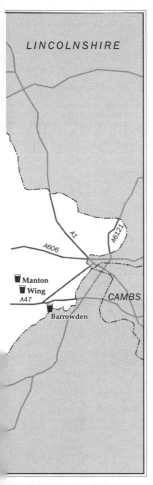

LINCOLNSHIRE

A1

A606

A6121

Manton

Wing

A47

CAMBS

Barrowden

Catthorpe

Cherrytree
Main Street ☎ (01788) 860430
12–3 (not Mon or Tue), 5–11; 12–3,
7–10.30 Sun
**Ansells Bitter; Draught Bass;
Hook Norton Best Bitter;
guest beer** Ⓗ
Friendly village boozer
frequented by all types. The
one-roomed bar is adjoined by
a games room and an eating
area. ❀ ◑ ♣ P

Cavendish Bridge

Old Crown
400 yds off A6 at Trent bridge
☎ (01332) 792392
11–3, 5–11; 12–3.30, 7–10.30 Sun
**Draught Bass; Marston's
Pedigree; guest beers** Ⓗ
Friendly, atmospheric village
pub with a collection of
breweriana. Three guest beers;

cider in summer. Home-
cooked lunches. A gem.
❀ ◑ ♣ ◌ P

Coalville

Pick & Shovel
2 High Street (opp. clock
tower) ☎ (01530) 835551
11–11; 12–3, 7–10.30 Sun
**Banks's Mild, Taphouse
Bitter; Camerons Strongarm;
Marston's Pedigree; guest
beers** Ⓗ
Lively pub in a central
position, attracting all ages:
three old properties knocked
together, with the atmosphere
of a 100-year-old drinking
house. Red tiled and wood
floors feature, with some cubby
holes for privacy. Good cheap
food. Regular live music, Thu–
Sun.
🏨 ❀ ◑ ▶ ♿ ♣ ✕ 目

Cossington

Royal Oak
105 Main Street
☎ (01509) 813937
12–2.30 (3 Sat; not Mon), 6–11; 12–3,
7–10.30 Sun
**Everards Beacon, Tiger, Old
Original; guest beers** Ⓗ
Small, tastefully refurbished
village local with one, wooden-
panelled, L-shaped room with
plain wooden tables. Two
guest beers from Everards Old
English Ale Club. Popular with
diners (book vegetarian meals).
❀ ◑ ▶ ♣

Croft

Heathcote Arms
Hill Street ☎ (01455) 282439
12–2 (2.30 Fri), 5.30–11; 12–11 Sat;
12–3, 7–10.30 Sun
**Everards Mild, Beacon, Tiger,
Old Original; guest beers** Ⓗ
Unspoilt, friendly village pub
with three rooms, on a hilltop
overlooking the river. Table
and long alley skittles. Guest
beers come from Everards Old
English Ale Club. Enjoy the
relaxed atmosphere.
🏨 Q ◑ ♣ P

Earl Shilton

Red Lion Inn
168 High Street
☎ (01455) 840829
11–2.30 (may extend), 5.30–11; 12–3,
7–10.30 Sun
Draught Bass; M&B Mild Ⓗ
Basic, beer drinkers' pub with
three rooms around one central
bar. ❀ ♣ P

Frisby on the Wreake

Bell Inn
2 Main Street
☎ (01664) 434237
12–2.30, 6–11; 12–2.30, 7–10.30 Sun
**Draught Bass; Bateman XB,
XXXB; Marston's Pedigree;
Tetley Bitter; guest beer** Ⓗ
Large, friendly village local
dating from 1759, once an
Allied tied house but now free.
At least two guest beers;
popular with diners.
🏨 Q ♿ ❀ ◑ ▶ P

Gumley

Bell Inn
Main Street
☎ (0116) 279 2476
11–3, 5.30–11; 12–3, 7–10.30 Sun
**Draught Bass, Boddingtons
Bitter; Ridleys IPA; Wadworth
6X; guest beer** Ⓗ
Welcoming, beamed village
local with an L-shaped
drinking area and a separate
restaurant. No eve meals Sun/
Mon. No children under 5.
Q ❀ ◑ ▶ ♣ P

Hathern

Three Crowns
Wide Lane (A6 from
Loughborough, 1st right after
traffic lights)
☎ (01509) 842233
12–2.30, 5.30–11; 12–11 Sat; 12–3,
7–10.30 Sun
**Draught Bass; Highgate Dark;
M&B Mild; Worthington
Bitter; guest beer** Ⓗ
Lively village local with three
bars, a skittle alley and a large

🏭 **INDEPENDENT BREWERIES**

Belvoir: Old Dalby	**Oakham:** Oakham
Everards: Narborough	**O'Gaunt:** Burrough on the Hill
Featherstone: Enderby	
Grainstore: Oakham	**Parish:** Somerby
Hoskins: Leicester	**Ruddles:** Langham
Hoskins & Oldfield: Leicester	**Shardlow:** Cavendish Bridge
Man in the Moon: Ashby Magna	

163

garden. An Enterprise Inns house.

🏨 Q ✿ ⊕ Å ♣ P ✗ ⊟

Hemington

Jolly Sailor

Main Street (off A6, near M1 jct 24) ☎ (01332) 810448
11–11; 12–10.30 Sun
Draught Bass; M&B Mild; Mansfield Bitter; Marston's Pedigree; guest beers ⊞
Two-roomed, small village local, heavily timbered. Artefacts adorn the walls and ceilings. Four guest beers; occasional cider in summer.

🏨 Q ☷ ✿ ♣ ○ P

Hinckley

Railway Hotel

Station Road ☎ (01455) 615285
11.30–2.30 (4 Sat), 5 (6.30 Sat)–11; 12–4, 7–10.30 Sun
Banks's Mild; Marston's Bitter, Pedigree ⊞
Spacious, three-roomed local with a basic bar and a comfortable lounge with a conservatory housing a pool table. Unrefurbished for many years; a typical beer drinkers' pub. Q ☷ ✿ 🏨 ◖ ⇌ ♣ P

Hose

Black Horse

21 Bolton Lane
☎ (01949) 860336
12–2.30, 6.30–11; 12–4, 7–10.30 Sun
Everards Mild; Home Bitter; John Smith's Bitter; guest beers ⊞
Three-roomed village pub with a traditional lounge, an unspoilt bar and a wood-panelled restaurant with 'naughty' forties prints on the wall. Eve meals Wed–Sun.

🏨 Q ✿ ◖ ▶ ⊕ Å ♣ P

Rose & Crown

43 Bolton Lane
☎ (01949) 860424
12–3, 7–11; 12–3, 7–10.30 Sun
Beer range varies ⊞
Traditional village free house where the eight guest beers vary and are normally from independents or microbreweries. The pub has a large single room with a separate function and dining room (good food).

🏨 ✿ ◖ ▶ Å ♣ P ✗ ⊟

Kegworth

Cap & Stocking

20 Borough Street (left at chemist in village centre; left and left again)
☎ (01509) 674818
11.30–3 (2.30 winter), 6.30–11; 12–3, 7–10.30 Sun
Draught Bass Ⓖ**; Hancock's HB; M&B Mild; guest beer** ⊞

Traditional, three-room village pub with coal fires in two; close to E Midlands airport and Donington Park. The Bass is brought from the cellar in jugs.

🏨 Q ✿ ◖ ⊕ & ♣ P

Red Lion

24 High Street
☎ (01509) 672466
11–11; 12–10.30 Sun
Draught Bass; Bateman XB; Marston's Pedigree; Theakston Best Bitter; guest beers ⊞
Village local, full of character and characters, with four separate rooms, a large garden and children's play area. HQ of the Tynemill pub group, always selling a guest mild. Good food. 🏨 Q ☷ ✿ ◖ ▶ ⊕ & Å ♣ ○ P ✗

Kibworth Beauchamp

Coach & Horses

2 Leicester Road (A6)
☎ (0116) 279 2247
11.30–2.30, 5–11; 11–11 Sat; 12–3, 7–10.30 Sun
Ansells Mild, Bitter; Draught Bass; Tetley Bitter ⊞
Cosy, old coaching inn, featuring coin-filled beams and horse brasses; popular with local and passing custom. Traditional, home-cooked food (separate restaurant).

🏨 ◖ ▶ ♣ P

Kirby Muxloe

Royal Oak

35 Main Street
☎ (0116) 239 3166
11–2.30, 6–11; 12–3, 7–10.30 Sun
Adnams Bitter; Everards Mild, Beacon, Tiger; guest beer ⊞
A modern exterior conceals a comfortable, traditionally-styled lounge with a restaurant, popular with business folk and locals. The guest beer is from Everards Old English Ale Club.

✿ ◖ ▶ P

Leicester

Black Boy

35 Albion Street (corner of Chatham St, off Granby St)
☎ (0116) 254 0222
11–11; 12–10.30 Sun
Draught Bass; Highgate Dark; Worthington Bitter; guest beers ⊞
Classic city-centre local, with a charming Victorian feel and a cosmopolitan clientele. The cosy lounge has wood panelling, an oval bar and an ornate, decorative ceiling; the bar is basic. Traditional food (daily specials available). Popular with theatregoers.

Q ☷ ✿ ◖ ⇌ ♣

Black Horse

1 Foxon Street, Braunstone Gate
☎ (0116) 254 0030
5.30–11; 12–2.30, 5.30–11 Mon; 12–11 Fri & Sat; 12–10.30 Sun
Everards Beacon, Tiger; guest beers ⊞
120-year-old beer drinkers' pub close to the city centre and popular with students: two rooms untouched by refurbishment with one central bar. Guest beers come from the Everards Old English Ale Club (always two). ✿

Clarendon

7–9 West Avenue, Clarendon Park (near London Road, A6)
☎ (0116) 270 7530
12 (11.30 Sat)–11; 12–10.30 Sun
Draught Bass; M&B Mild; guest beers ⊞
Friendly, two-roomed, corner pub in a terraced residential area. Popular with students eves. Eve meals end at 7.30; no food Sat or Sun. No-smoking area eves only.

Q ✿ ◖ ▶ ✗

Fuzzock & Firkin

203 Welford Road (A50)
☎ (0116) 270 8141
12–11; 12–10.30 Sun
Firkin Fuzzock, Ass, Dogbolter; guest beers ⊞
The Stork's Head until 1993: the first of six Firkin pubs now in Leicestershire, the beer coming from the Phantom & Firkin in Loughborough. The basic wooden flooring and furniture are popular with the young at night and with all during the day. Meals 12–6. The cider available varies.

✿ ◖ ♣ ○ P

Hat & Beaver

60 Highcross Street (400 yds W of clock tower, off High St)
☎ (0116) 262 2157
11–3.30, 6–11; 12–3, 7–10.30 Sun
Hardys & Hansons Best Mild, Best Bitter, Classic ⊞
Basic, two-roomed local with a relaxed atmosphere; formerly a Bass house. TV in the bar; well-filled cobs usually available. Close to The Shires shopping centre.

✿ ⊕ ♣

Joiners Arms

73 Sanvey Gate
☎ (0116) 262 6420
12–3, 5.30–11; 11–4, 7–11 Sat; 12–3, 7–10.30 Sun
Banks's Mild ⊞**, Bitter** Ⓔ
Sixties building with a large, basic bar, a comfortable lounge and a games room. To the left of the pub stands the front wall of the original Joiners Arms. Beware: the non-handpulled mild is nitrokeg.

◖ ♣ P ⊟

Salmon

19 Butt Close Lane
☎ (0116) 253 2301
11–11; 12–4 Sun (closed eve)
**Banks's Hanson's Mild,
Bitter** Ⓔ
Small, city-centre pub with a
modern interior: one large,
U-shaped room serves a varied
clientele. Note: the Banks's
Mild is now nitrokeg, though
the font is similar to cask-
conditioned. Close to St
Margaret's bus station and The
Shires shopping centre.
☀ ◖ ⬒

Three Cranes

82 Humberstone Gate (500 yds
E of clock tower)
☎ (0116) 251 7164
11–11 (doors closed Sat afternoons
when Leicester City FC are at home);
12–10.30 Sun
**Draught Bass; M&B Mild;
Worthington Bitter; guest
beers** Ⓗ
City-centre free house popular
with beer drinkers. Its large,
U-shaped bar always offers at
least four guest beers from
small brewers. Meals served
till 8pm. Discount B&B for
CAMRA members.
☀ ⇞ ◖ ▶ ♣

Vaults

1 Wellington Street
☎ (0116) 255 5506
5 (12 Fri & Sat)–11; 12–3, 7–10.30 Sun
**Steamin' Billy Mild, Bitter;
guest beers** Ⓗ
Cellar bar with a Bohemian
atmosphere, selling beers
mainly from microbrewers,
including one from
Leatherbritches, changing
daily. Live blues Sun eve
(entrance sometimes charged).
⬦ ⚲

Victoria Jubilee

112 Leire Street (off Melton Rd,
A46) ☎ (0116) 266 3599
11–2.30 (3.30 Sat), 6–11; 12–4, 7–10.30
Sun
Marston's Bitter, Pedigree Ⓗ
Friendly, two-roomed, corner
local with a basic bar and a
comfortable lounge, situated in
a Victorian terraced area.
Called the Full Moon until
Queen Victoria's Jubilee in
1887. ☀ ♣

Wilkie's Continental Bar

29 Market Street (off Horsefair
St near town hall)
☎ (0116) 255 6877
12–11; closed Sun
**Adnams Extra; Boddingtons
Bitter; Marston's Pedigree;
Shepherd Neame Spitfire;
guest beers** Ⓗ
Well-established, friendly
continental bar stocking up to
six ales, three German beers,
cider and guest Belgian beers
on draught, plus over 100
bottled beers. Spanish and
German food at reasonable
prices. ◖ ⇞ ⬦

Leire

Queens Arms

Main Street ☎ (01455) 209227
12–3, 5.30–11; 12–11 Sat; 12–10.30 Sun
**Marston's Bitter, Pedigree,
HBC** Ⓗ
Warm, traditional, rural village
local: one open bar with a
beamed lounge. Barbecues in
summer. Good facilities for
visitors with disabilities.
⇞ Q ⚑ ☀ ◖ ▶ ♿ ♣ P

Littlethorpe

Plough

Station Road
☎ (0116) 286 2383
11–2.30 (3 Sat), 6–11; 12–3, 7–10.30
Sun
**Everards Beacon, Tiger, Old
Original; guest beers** Ⓗ
Friendly, thatched village local
featuring a cosy lounge, a bar
and a dining area. Long alley
skittles by arrangement; no
jukebox or machines. The wide
variety of customers come for
the food and hospitality. Q ☀ ◖
▶ ♿ ⇞ (Narborough) ♣ P

Loughborough

Gate Inn

99 Meadow Lane (near canal
bridge) ☎ (01509) 263779
11.30–2.30 (3 Sat), 6–11; 12–3, 7–10.30
Sun
**Banks's Mild; Marston's
Pedigree** Ⓗ
Popular, friendly local with
three rooms, close to the Grand
Union Canal. Large darts
following (12 teams).
Q ☀ ◖ ⇞ ♣ P ⬒

Swan in the Rushes

21 The Rushes
☎ (01509) 217014
11–11; 12–10.30 Sun
**Archers Golden; Greene King
Abbot; Marston's Pedigree;
Tetley Bitter; guest beers** Ⓗ
Traditional pub with an
unspoilt tap room and bar.
Regular music in an upstairs
room; separate dining room.
⇞ Q ☀ ⇞ ◖ ▶ ♿ ⇞ ♣ ⬦
P ⚲

Tap & Mallet

36 Nottingham Road
☎ (01509) 210028
11.30–2.30, 5–11; 11.30–11 Sat; 12–
10.30 Sun
**Courage Best Bitter, Directors;
Theakston Mild; guest
beers** Ⓗ
Popular true free house
between the town centre and
the station. The interesting
guest beers (at least four,
mostly from microbreweries)
are discounted to CAMRA

members. Large patio and
garden with children's play/
pets area. ⇞ ☀ ⇞ ♣ ⬦

Windmill

62 Sparrow Hill
☎ (01509) 264071
11–2.30 (3 Fri & Sat), 5 (7 Sat)–11;
12–3, 7–10.30 Sun
**Banks's Mild; Marston's
Bitter, Pedigree, HBC** Ⓗ
Two-roomed, traditional pub,
the oldest in Loughborough,
attracting a mixed age group
and supposedly haunted.
Function room for small
groups. No eve meals Fri or
Sun. ⇞ Q ☀ ◖ ▶ ♿ ⇞ ♣ P

Lutterworth

Off-licence and Beer Room

35 Station Road
10–10; 12–2, 7–10 Sun
Beer range varies Ⓖ
Specialist bottled beer off-
licence with over 300 different
international beers. Draught
cask ale and cider changes
weekly. ⬦

Manton

Horse & Jockey

2 St Mary's Road (off A6003)
☎ (01572) 737335
11–3, 7–11; 12–3, 7–10.30 Sun
**Mansfield Riding Bitter, Old
Baily** Ⓗ
A rarity near Rutland Water –
an unspoilt 250-year-old
village local. Cycle repair
outfits on sale.
⇞ ☀ ◖ ▶ ⬒ ♣

Market Bosworth

Red Lion

1 Park Street ☎ (01455) 291713
11–2.30, 7–11; 11–11 Sat; 12–3, 7–10.30
Sun
**Banks's Mild, Bitter;
Camerons Bitter; Marston's
Pedigree; Theakston XB, Old
Peculier; guest beers** Ⓗ
Village pub popular with locals
and tourists from the nearby
Bosworth Railway and
battlesite. A large, split-level,
L-shaped pub, once Hoskins's
sole tied house.
⇞ ☀ ◖ ⓐ ♣ P

Market Harborough

Red Cow

58–59 High Street
☎ (01858) 463673
11–3 (4 Sat), 6 (7 Sat)–11; 12–3,
7–10.30 Sun
**Marston's Bitter, Pedigree,
HBC** Ⓗ
Unspoilt, town-centre pub
with a small single bar. No
frills or music, just games and
conversation. Q ♣

Medbourne

Nevil Arms
12 Waterfall Way
☎ (01858) 565288
12–2.30, 6–11; 12–3, 7–10.30 Sun
Adnams Bitter; Ruddles Best Bitter, County; guest beers H
Pub built in 1876 as a coaching inn on the village green, standing next to an attractive stream. A popular weekend venue for families (tame ducks). Unusual pub games by arrangement. Two guest beers; lovely food.
🏚 ♿ 🏵 🛏 ◖ ▶ ▲ ♣ P

Melton Mowbray

Anne of Cleves
12 Burton Street
☎ (01664) 481336
10–11; 12–10.30 Sun
Everards Beacon, Tiger, Old Original; guest beer H
Very sympathetically restored, Grade II-listed building that is 612 years old and once belonged to Anne of Cleves as part of her divorce settlement from Henry VIII. Excellent food. 🏚 Q ♿ ◖ ▶ ⇌ P ✦

Crown
10 Burton Street
☎ (01664) 64682
11–3.30, 7–11; 11–11 Sat; 12–3.30, 7–10.30 Sun
Everards Beacon, Tiger, Old Original, seasonal beers; guest beer H
Two-roomed town pub popular with office workers and shoppers lunchtimes and a mixed-age crowd at night.
🏚 ♿ 🏵 ◖ 🛏 ⇌ ♣

Nether Broughton

Red Lion Hotel
23 Main Road
☎ (01664) 822429
11–3, 6–11; 11–11 Sat; 12–10.30 Sun
Home Mild, Bitter; John Smith's Bitter; Tetley Bitter; Theakston XB; guest beers H
Large, two-roomed hotel with a skittle alley, a petanque pitch and an enclosed grass drinking area where animals run free. The bar is traditionally beamed. No eve meals Sun.
🏚 Q ♿ 🏵 🛏 ◖ ▶ 🛏 ▲ ♣ P

Newbold Verdon

Jubilee Inn
80 Main Street
☎ (01455) 822698
11–2.30 (not Tue or Wed), 7 (6 Wed)–11; 11–11 Fri & Sat; 12–2.30, 7–10.30 Sun
Marston's Bitter, Pedigree H
Friendly, two-roomed village local, cosy and unspoilt.
🏚 🏵 ♣ P

North Kilworth

White Lion
Lutterworth Road (main road)
☎ (01858) 880260
12–2.30, 5–11; 12–11 Sat; 12–10.30 Sun
Marston's Bitter, Pedigree, HBC H
Former coaching inn close to the Grand Union Canal: a large single bar with distinct areas. Outside features include a garden, farmyard animals, a barbecue area and a skittle alley. No eve meals Mon.
🏚 🏵 ◖ ▶ ♣ P

Oadby

Cow & Plough
Stoughton Farm Park, Gartree Road (signed 'Farmworld' off A6) ☎ (0116) 272 0852
5–9; 5 (7 winter)–9 Sun
Fuller's London Pride; Hoskins & Oldfield HOB Bitter; Steamin' Billy Mild, Bitter; guest beers H
Former E Midlands CAMRA *Pub of the Year*, part of a leisure park during the day. These atmospheric vaults are adorned with breweriana. Beers mainly come from microbrewers.
Q ♿ 🏵 🏵 🛏 ♿ ♣ ◔ P ✦

Oakham

Grainstore Brewery Tap
Station Approach (by station on outskirts of town)
☎ (01572) 770065
11–2.30, 6 (5 Fri, 4 Sat)–11 (all day on request); 12–2.30, 7–10.30 Sun
Grainstore Cooking, Triple B, Ten Fifty, seasonal beer; guest beers H
Large downstairs bar with Grainstore Brewery above. Original wooden floors and brick walls feature in this ex-grain warehouse of Oakham railway station. Baguettes lunchtime. Wheelchair WC.
Q ♿ 🏵 ♿ ⇌ ♣ P 🍴

White Lion
30 Melton Road (A60, near station) ☎ (01572) 724844
11.30–3, 6–11; 12–3, 7–10.30 Sun
Draught Bass; Worthington Bitter; guest beers H
Split-level pub in a Grade II-listed building. Good food.
🏚 🛏 ◖ ▶ ⇌ P

Osgathorpe

Royal Oak
20 Main Street
☎ (01509) 222443
7–11; 12–3, 7–10.30 Sun
M&B Mild; Marston's Pedigree H

Friendly, quiet local in a picturesque valley. Good accommodation. Note closed lunchtimes Mon–Sat.
🏚 Q ♿ 🏵 🛏 ♿ ▲ ♣ P

Peggs Green

New Inn
200 yds from A512
☎ (01530) 222293
12–2.30, 7–11; 12–3.30, 7–10.30 Sun
Draught Bass; M&B Mild; Marston's Pedigree; Wadworth 6X H
Traditional, multi-roomed local in a quiet village.
🏚 Q ♿ 🏵 🛏 ♣ P

Quorndon

Blacksmiths Arms
29 Meeting Street (left at Quorn cross from Leicester)
☎ (01509) 412751
12–2 (11–2.30 Sat), 5.30–11; 12–3, 7–10.30 Sun
Marston's Bitter, Pedigree H
Traditional, old village alehouse.
🏚 Q 🛏 ♣ P

Ratby

Plough Inn
6 Burroughs Road
☎ (0116) 239 2103
11–3, 6–11; 12–3, 7–10.30 Sun
Bateman Mild; Marston's Bitter, Pedigree, HBC H
Large, 600-year-old, refurbished regulars' pub, also popular with diners.
🏚 ♿ 🏵 ◖ ▶ ♣ ◔ P

Saddington

Queen's Head
Main Street ☎ (0116) 240 2536
11–3, 5.30–11; 12–3, 7–10.30 Sun
Adnams Bitter; Everards Beacon, Tiger; guest beer H
From the front this looks like just a good village local, but behind lovely views of the Laughton Valley and Saddington Reservoir can be enjoyed from the large garden or conservatory-style restaurant. No eve meals Sun.
🏚 Q 🏵 ◖ ▶ ▲ P

Shawell

White Swan Inn
Main Street ☎ (01788) 860357
12–2.30 (not Sat), 7–11; 12–3, 7–10.30 Sun; closed Mon
Adnams Bitter; Marston's Bitter, Pedigree; Morland Old Speckled Hen H
Traditional, 17th-century panelled and beamed pub and restaurant, popular with locals. Friendly landlord.
🏚 Q ♿ 🛏 ◖ ▶ ▲ ♣ P 🍴

Shepshed

Black Swan

21 Loughborough Road
☎ (01509) 506783
12–3, 5.30–11; 12–4, 7–10.30 Sun
**Draught Bass; M&B Mild;
Worthington Bitter; Tetley
Bitter; guest beer** H
Smart, large, multi-roomed
pub satisfying both beer
drinkers and foodies. Children
welcome in the restaurant.
Good food (no eve food Sun or
Mon unless booked). ◑ ▶ P

Bull & Bush

61 Sullington Road
☎ (01509) 506783
12–3, 5.30–11; 12–4, 7–10.30 Sun
**Banks's Mild; Marston's
Pedigree** H
Friendly, traditional and
largely unspoilt local with a
fine carved-wood servery in its
only room. ❀ ♣ P

Crown

Market Place
☎ (01509) 502665
11–3 (not Mon or Tue), 6 (5 Mon &
Tue)–11; 11–11 Fri & Sat; 12–10.30 Sun
**Everards Beacon, Tiger; Old
Original** H
Busy town pub, popular with
locals and due to be extended.
♨ ❀ ♣ P

Richmond

48 Forest Street
☎ (01509) 503309
12–2, 7–11; 12–2, 7–10.30 Sun
**Draught Bass; M&B Mild;
Marston's Pedigree; guest
beer** H
Hospitable local with a
sporting emphasis. Recent
improvements have not altered
the character. ♿ ♣

Sutton Bassett

Queen's Head

Main Street (B664)
☎ (01858) 463530
11.45–3, 6.30–11; 12–3, 7–10.30 Sun
**Adnams Bitter; Ruddles Best
Bitter, County; guest beers** H
Rural village pub which offers
a minimum of five guest beers
and tries to maintain variety:
regular beer festivals. Separate
restaurant. ♨ ❀ ◑ ▶ P

Swithland

Griffin Inn

174 Main Street
☎ (01509) 891096
12–2.30 (3 Sat), 6–11; 12–3, 7–10.30
Sun
**Adnams Bitter; Everards
Beacon, Tiger, Old Original;
guest beers** (occasional) H

Friendly village local with
three comfortable rooms, a
small games/family room and
long alley skittles. The landlord
is an ex-footballer. Don't miss
the photos in the passageway.
No meals Sun eve or Mon/Tue
eves in winter.
♨ Q ➴ ❀ ◑ ▶ Å ♣ P

Thornton

Bricklayers Arms

Main Street
☎ (01530) 230808
12–3 (not Jan–Mar), 7 (6 summer)–11;
12–3, 7–10.30 Sun
**Everards Mild, Tiger, seasonal
beers; guest beers** H
Unspoilt village local partly
dating from the 16th century: a
basic, quarry-tile-floored bar
area and a cosy lounge
overlooking Thornton Trout
Fisheries. Guest beers are from
Everards Old English Ale Club.
Wheelchair access at the rear.
♨ Q ➴ ❀ ♿ ♣ P

Thurmaston

Unicorn & Star

796 Melton Road (old main
road) ☎ (0116) 269 2849
11–3, 6–11; 12–3, 7–10.30 Sun
Shipstone's Mild, Bitter H
Known to locals as the 'Top
House': a basic, beer-drinkers'
bar with no frills, and a
comfortable lounge.
❀ ♣ P

Walcote

Black Horse

Main Street ☎ (01455) 552684
12–2 (not Mon or Tue), 6.30–11;
12–2.30, 7–10.30 Sun
**Hook Norton Best Bitter;
Hoskins & Oldfield HOB
Bitter; Taylor Landlord; guest
beers** H
Single-bar free house close to
M1 jct 20; well worth the
detour. Excellent, home-
cooked Thai food; guest beers
from independents. Occasional
cider. ♨ Q ◑ ▶ ⊖ P

Walton on the Wolds

Anchor

2 Loughborough Road
☎ (01509) 880018
12–3, 7 (6.30 summer)–11; 12–3,
7–10.30 Sun
**Marston's Bitter, Pedigree;
Taylor Landlord; guest
beers** H
Large, single-roomed village
pub, featuring a garden at the
front with a large patio area,
and a grass area at the rear.

Excellent food (themed nights);
no meals Sun eve.
Q ❀ ◑ ▶ ♣ ⊖ P

Wigston

Star & Garter

114 Leicester Road
☎ (0116) 288 2450
11–2.30, 5–11; 11–11 Sat; 12–3, 7–10.30
Sun
**Everards Mild, Beacon, Tiger;
guest beer** H
Friendly two-roomed pub
catering for all ages with a
wood-panelled bar and a cosy,
beamed lounge. Long alley
skittles by arrangement. The
guest beer is from Everards
Old English Ale Club.
❀ ◑ ⊟ ♣ P

Wing

Cuckoo

Top Street
☎ (01572) 737340
11.30–3 (not Tue), 6.30–11; 12–4,
7–10.30 Sun
**Marston's Pedigree; guest
beers** H
Whitewashed, unspoilt village
local which stages a steam rally
and beer festival in summer.
Curries a speciality.
♨ ❀ ◑ ▶ Å ♣ P

Woodhouse Eaves

Wheatsheaf

Brand Hill (½ mile from
village)
☎ (01509) 890320
12–2.30, 7 (6.30 Fri & Sat)–11; 12–3,
7–10.30 Sun
**Draught Bass; Boddingtons
Bitter; Marston's Pedigree;
Ruddles County; Taylor
Landlord; guest beers** H
Comfortable country pub and
restaurant near the Great
Central Steam Railway. Good
range of guest beers; Gale's
fruit wines. No food Sun eve.
♨ Q ❀ ◑ ▶ ⊖ P

Wymeswold

Hammer & Pincers

5 East Road (A6006)
☎ (01509) 880735
12–2.30 (3 Sat), 6–11; 12–3, 7–10.30
Sun
**Draught Bass; Marston's
Pedigree; Ruddles County;
Tetley Bitter; Theakston XB;
guest beer** H
Former coaching inn offering a
large selection of home-cooked
food at all sessions. Spacious
outside drinking area (semi-
covered); children welcome
inside, too.
Q ❀ ◑ ▶ P ⚥

Join CAMRA and help save pubs and breweries!

Lincolnshire

Lincolnshire

Aby

Railway Tavern
Main Road ☎ (01507) 480676
12–3, 7–11 (midnight Sat); 12–3,
7–10.30 Sun; closed Tue
Bateman XB; guest beers Ⓗ
Pub with an open-plan
restaurant and bar with an
adjoining games room. The
walls are adorned with railway
and rural memorabilia. Home
of the Desperate Dan cow pie.
🏚 ⊛ ◑ ◗ ♿ ♣ P

Alford

Half Moon
West Street ☎ (01507) 463477
10–11 (1am Fri, 2 Sat); 12–10.30 Sun
**Draught Bass; Vaux Samson;
Worthington Bitter; guest
beers** Ⓗ
Welcoming, ever-expanding,
lively pub, situated in a market
town famed for its craft fairs.
An ideal base for visiting the

Wolds and Tennyson country.
Popular restaurant; large
garden. ☎ ⊛ ◑ ◗ ◫ ♣ P

Allington

Welby Arms
The Green ☎ (01400) 281361
12–2.30 (3 Sat), 5.30 (6.30 Sat)–11;
12–4, 7–10.30 Sun
**Draught Bass; John Smith's
Bitter; Taylor Landlord; guest
beers** Ⓗ
Local CAMRA *Village Pub of the
Year 1997*. Drinkers and diners,
in separate areas, enjoy
imaginative guest beers and
excellent value, home-cooked
food. Close to the A1.
🏚 Q ⊛ ◑ ◗ ♿ P

Althorpe

Dolphin Inn
27 Trunk Road (A18)
☎ (01724) 784510
12–3, 5–11; 12–11 Fri & Sat; 12–4,
7–10.30 (12–10.30 summer) Sun

**Vaux Samson, Double Maxim;
Ward's Thorne BB** Ⓗ
Roadside pub with an
emphasis on, and an excellent
reputation for, food (not served
Mon eve). Well-equipped
family room.
Q ☎ ⊛ ◑ ◗ ▲ ➤ P

Ashby

Malt Shovel

219 Ashby High Street
☎ (01724) 843318
11–11; 12–10.30 Sun
**Barnsley Bitter; John Smith's
Bitter; Theakston Old
Peculier; guest beers** H
Former snooker hall in a busy
shopping area. The single
room has an olde-worlde feel,
with wooden beams, bare
brickwork and floral
furnishings. Good value meals.
Guest beers come from
independents. Licensed
snooker club next door.
🏰 ◖ ▶

Aubourn

Royal Oak

Royal Oak Lane
☎ (01522) 788291
12–2.30, 7–11; 12–2, 7–10.30 Sun
**Bateman XB, XXXB; Samuel
Smith OBB; guest beers** H
Welcoming village free house
where brasses and pumpclips
adorn the lounge. Large
garden at the rear. At least two
guest beers available.
🏰 ❀ ◖ ▶ ⊞ ♣ P

Barholm

Five Horseshoes

Horseshoe Lane
☎ (01778) 560238
5–11; 12–3, 5–11 Sat; 12–10.30 Sun
**Adnams Bitter; Theakston XB;
guest beers** H
Wonderfully refurbished,
stone-built hamlet pub;
Peterborough CAMRA *Pub of
the Year* 1996. Two guest beers.
Barbecues summer Sun lunch.
🏰 Q ⛴ ❀ P

Barrow upon Humber

Squash Club

Manor Farmhouse, Thorngarth
Lane (behind church)
☎ (01469) 530686
6.30–11; 7–10.30 Sun
**Ward's Thorne BB, Best Bitter;
guest beer** H
Members-only club where
card-carrying CAMRA
members are freely admitted.
Guest beers are from the Vaux
collection. 🏰 ♣ P

Barton-upon-Humber

Wheatsheaf Hotel

3 Holydyke ☎ (01652) 633175
11–3 (4.30 Sat), 6–11; 12–10.30 Sun
**Vaux Mild, Waggle Dance;
Ward's Thorne BB, Best
Bitter** H

Friendly, quiet, three-roomed
pub in the town centre.
Possibly the best pub food in
Barton.
Q ⛴ ❀ ◖ ▶ ⊞ ▲ ⇌ P

Bicker

Red Lion

Donington Road (100 yds off
A52) ☎ (01775) 821950
11–3, 6–11; 11–11 Sat; 12–10.30 Sun
Draught Bass; Bateman XB H
Renovated, 17th-century,
friendly, village pub serving
quality home-cooked food at
reasonable prices.
🏰 ❀ ◖ ▶ ⛾ P

Blyton

Black Horse Inn

93 High Street (A159)
☎ (01427) 628277
11.45–3.30 (not Mon), 7 (5 Fri)–11;
12–4, 7–10.30 Sun
Mansfield Bitter; guest beer H
Traditional, small, cosy and
welcoming village local: two
distinct drinking areas served
by a single bar, with real fires
in both, plus a dining room (no
food Mon). Two guest beers
normally in summer.
🏰 ❀ 🛏 ◖ ▶ ♣ P

Boston

Ball House

Wainfleet Road (A52, 1 mile N
of town) ☎ (01205) 364478
11–3, 6.30–11; 12–3, 7–10.30 Sun
**Draught Bass; Bateman Mild,
XB** H
Mock-Tudor **pub** boasting
award-winning summer floral
displays. Excellent, home-
cooked food is popular
(booking advised weekend
eves). Its unusual name is
reputedly derived from its site
– a former cannonball store.
🏰 ⛴ ❀ ◖ ▶ ⛾ ♣ P

Carpenter's Arms

20 Witham Street
☎ (01205) 362840
11–3, 7–11; 11–11 Fri & Sat; 12–10.30
Sun
**Draught Bass; Bateman XB;
guest beer** H
Traditional, multi-roomed
local in the maze of sidestreets
off the medieval Wormgate. It
can be very noisy Fri and Sat
eves. 🏰 ❀ ⇌ ♣

Coach & Horses

Main Ridge East
☎ (01205) 362301
11–3, 7–11; 11–11 Sat; 12–3, 7–10.30
Sun
**Draught Bass; Bateman Mild,
XB** H
Traditional, basic, welcoming
local near the football ground
and busy on match days.
🏰 ⇌ ♣

Eagle

144 West Street (by station)
☎ (01205) 361116
11–2.30, 6 (5 Thu & Fri)–11; 11–11 Sat;
12–3, 7–10.30 Sun
**Adnams Broadside; Fuller's
London Pride; Taylor
Landlord; guest beers** H
Outpost of Lincoln's Small
Beer Company, offering a
changing choice of three guest
beers (one low-priced). The
function room hosts societies,
including Boston Folk Club.
🏰 ❀ ⊞ ⇌ ♣ ◔

Olde Magnet Tavern

South Square
☎ (01205) 369186
11.30 (11 Thu–Sat)–11; 12–4, 7–10.30
Sun
**Draught Bass; Bateman XB;
M&B Mild; Stones Bitter;
Taylor Landlord; Theakston
Old Peculier** H
Friendly, popular town pub, by
the river. It stands amongst
warehouses that have been
converted to an arts centre and
for residential use, opposite the
Guildhall. The lounge has a
flagstone floor.
❀ 🛏 ◖ ▶ ⊞ ⇌

Ropers Arms

33 Horncastle Road
☎ (01205) 355741
2 (11 Sat & summer)–11; 12–10.30 Sun
Bateman Mild, XB H
Corner local refurbished in
traditional style. It can be
lively, particularly Sun
afternoons (live football on a
large screen TV). ❀ 🛏 ⇌ ♣

Bottesford

Bottesford Town Football & Social Club

Birch Park, Ontario Road
☎ (01724) 871883
7.30 (2.30 Sat)–11; 12–3, 7.30–10.30
Sun
Bateman Mild, XB H
Popular sports club in a
residential area. The single
room is divided into a small
bar area and a large,
comfortable lounge. Families
welcome. Its only local outlet
for Bateman's beers. Guests are
welcome, but must be signed
in. ❀ ⛾ ♣ P

Brant Broughton

Generous Britain

High Street ☎ (01400) 242119
12–3, 7–11; 12–11 Fri & Sat; 12–10.30
Sun
Beer range varies H
Proper village pub with a
friendly local atmosphere.
Maypole beers are well
represented and include the
house ale.
🏰 ❀ ◖ ▶ ⊞ ▲ ♣ P ⛫

Butterwick

Five Bells
1 Church Road
☎ (01205) 760282
12–3, 7–11; 12–11 Fri & Sat; 12–4,
7–10.30 Sun
Bateman Mild, XB Ⓗ
Welcoming, family-run pub,
known as 'Horry's Folly'. It
was built as a station hotel,
complete with platform
buildings, in anticipation of the
railway which eventually
followed a different route.
🏰 ❀ ◑ ▸ ♿ ♣ P

Caythorpe

Red Lion Inn
62 High Street
☎ (01400) 272632
11–3, 6–11; Sun hours vary
Draught Bass; Bateman XB Ⓗ;
guest beers Ⓗ/Ⓖ
Friendly village pub with two
bar areas and a restaurant.
Varying guest beer selection;
extensive menu of home-
cooked meals. The 'beer and
curry' festivals are
recommended. Varied ciders.
🏰 Q 🛏 ❀ ◑ ▸ ♿ ♠ ♣ ♡ P

Chapel St Leonards

Ship
109 Sea Road ☎ (01754) 872640
12–3.30, 7–11; 12–3, 7–10.30 Sun
**Bateman Mild, XB; guest
beers** Ⓗ
Refurbished, welcoming local
away from the bustle of the
resort. The cosy bar/lounge
features two real fires. The
'guest beers' are all from
Bateman and the brewery's full
range is often available in
summer. 🏰 🛏 ❀ ♠ ♣ P

Cleethorpes

Crow's Nest Hotel
Balmoral Road
☎ (01472) 698867
11.30–3, 6–11; 12–3, 7–10.30 Sun
Samuel Smith OBB Ⓗ
Large, 1950s estate pub with a
quiet, comfortable lounge and
a basic, occasionally lively,
public bar. The only Sam's
house for miles and the
cheapest pint in the area. No
meals Wed.
Q 🛏 ❀ � ◑ 🔌 ♣ P

Kings Royal
20 Kingsway ☎ (01472) 691012
11–11; 12–10.30 Sun
**Ruddles Best Bitter;
Theakston XB; Younger
Scotch, No. 3; guest beer** Ⓗ
Pub whose Victorian lounge
bar has a cosy atmosphere, in
contrast to the Irish bar which
has regular live music.
❀ � ◑ ▸ ♣

No. 2 Refreshment Room
Station Approach (on the
station)
☎ (01472) 697951
11–11; 12–10.30 Sun
**Mansfield Riding Mild; John
Smith's Magnet; guest
beers** Ⓗ
Tiny, one-roomed basic bar not
to be missed when you get off
the train. ⇌ ♣

Smugglers
12–14 High Cliff Road
☎ (01472) 200862
11–11; 12–10.30 Sun
**Banks's Mild; Bateman Mild;
Marston's Bitter, Pedigree,
Owd Rodger; guest beer** Ⓗ
Attractive, open-plan pub,
refurbished in traditional style;
popular with locals and
tourists. Meals are served all
day in summer months.
❀ ◑ ▸ ♠ ⇌

Willy's Pub & Brewery
17 High Cliff Road
☎ (01472) 602145
11–11; 12–10.30 Sun
**Bateman XB; Willy's Original;
guest beers** Ⓗ
Refurbished seafront bar,
popular with all ages and
lively in the eve. All food is
home-cooked. The brewery can
be seen from the bar. A
popular beer festival is held
every year in Nov.
◑ ⇌

Coleby

Tempest Arms
Hill Rise (off A607, 7 miles S of
Lincoln)
☎ (01522) 810287
11.30–2.30, 6.30–11; 12–3, 7–10.30 Sun
**Bateman XB; Courage
Directors; Wells Bombardier;
guest beer** Ⓗ
Welcoming village local on the
Viking Way footpath, with
views over the Vale of Trent
towards Newark. A centre of
village life, hosting fundraising
events; guest beers tend to
coincide with events. Eve
meals Thu–Sun.
❀ ◑ ▸ ♿ ♣ P

Coningsby

Leagate Inn
Leagate Road (B1192)
☎ (01526) 342370
11.30–3, 7 (6 winter Sat)–11; 12–3,
7–10.30 (12–10.30 summer) Sun
**Bateman XB; Boddingtons
Bitter; Marston's Pedigree** Ⓗ;
guest beers Ⓗ/Ⓖ
Built in 1542, this largely
unchanged pub, with a priest
hole and antique furniture,
offers a superb atmosphere
and excellent food. The garden
is popular with children.
🏰 Q ❀ ◑ ▸ ♿ P

Corby Glen

Woodhouse Inn
2 Bourne Road
☎ (01476) 550316
12–3, 5.30–11; 12–4, 7–10.30 Sun
**Ruddles Best Bitter, County;
Theakston Best Bitter, XB,
Old Peculier; guest beer** Ⓗ
Comfortable pub in a village
famous for its sheep fair. The
chatty landlord is happy to
advise on the more exotic
dishes on offer. Close to the A1.
🏰 Q ❀ � ◑ ▸ ♿ P ☂

Denton

Welby Arms
Church Street
☎ (01476) 870304
11–3, 6–11; 12–3, 7–10.30 Sun
**Mansfield Riding Bitter,
Bitter, Old Baily; guest
beers** Ⓗ
Old farmhouse-type pub with
two bars, open fires, and an
oak-panelled lounge. A good
range of food features local
specialities. Guest beers come
from Mansfield. A post office is
incorporated into the pub.
🏰 Q ❀ ◑ ▸ 🔌 P

Dyke

Wishing Well
Main Street ☎ (01778) 422970
11–3, 6–11; 12–3, 7–10.30 Sun
**Everards Tiger; Greene King
Abbot; guest beers** Ⓗ
Popular village pub offering a
house beer, 'Going Down
Well', and over 685 guest beers
in the last three years. The
wishing well, still containing
water, can be seen in the
restaurant (book for eve
meals).
🏰 ❀ � ◑ ▸ 🔌 ♿ ♠ ♣ P

East Butterwick

Dog & Gun
High Street ☎ (01724) 783419
7 (5 Thu & Fri, 11 Sat)–11; 12–10.30
Sun
DarkTribe Full Ahead or
Terrier or **Galleon; John
Smith's Bitter** Ⓗ
Remote, unrestored, basic
village pub beside the Trent.
The first pub to serve
DarkTribe Brewery's beers
(one at a time). Good beer
prices.
🏰 Q ❀ ♠ ♣ P

East Kirkby

Red Lion
Main Road ☎ (01790) 763406
11–3, 7–11; 12–3, 7–10.30 Sun
**Bateman XB; John Smith's
Bitter; guest beers** Ⓗ
Popular pub, adorned with
clocks, old tools and

breweriana, close to a wartime airfield and air museum. The pool room was once a butcher's shop.
🏨 ⛺ 🏮 ◑ ▶ ▲ ♣ P

Eastoft

River Don Tavern
Sampson Street (A161)
☎ (01724) 798225
12–2.30, 7–11; 12–4, 7–10.30 Sun
John Smith's Bitter; guest beers (summer) H
Friendly, family-run, 250-year-old village local. Good food (not served Tue eve).
🏨 Q ⛺ 🏮 ◑ ▶ ♣ P

Epworth

Red Lion Hotel
Market Place ☎ (01427) 872208
11–11; 12–10.30 Sun
Ind Coope Burton Ale; Tetley Bitter; guest beers H
Residential, olde-worlde coaching inn serving good food in the bar or delightful restaurant, from an extensive menu (sizzling steaks a speciality). 🏨 ⛺ 🏮 🛏 ◑ ▶ P

Freiston

King's Head
Church Road
☎ (01205) 760368
11–2.30, 7–11; 11–11 Sat; 12–3, 7–10.30 Sun
Draught Bass; Bateman Mild, XB H
15th-century, traditional village pub with a homely atmosphere. The Lancaster Restaurant (open Tue–Sat eves) serves quality, home-cooked food. 🏨 Q ⛺ 🏮 ◑ ▶ ♣ P

Frognall

Goat
155 Spalding Road (A16, outskirts of village)
☎ (01778) 347629
11–2.30, 6–11; 12–3, 7–10.30 Sun
Adnams Bitter; Draught Bass; guest beers H
Pub offering 200+ beers each year, frequently from micros; beer festival (May Bank Hol). Home-made pies a speciality on an extensive menu.
🏨 Q ⛺ 🏮 ◑ ▶ ♿ ▲ P ✂

Fulbeck

Hare & Hounds
The Green ☎ (01400) 272090
11.30–2.30, 5–11; 12–3, 7–10.30 Sun
Draught Bass; Bateman XB; Fuller's London Pride; guest beers H
Friendly village pub serving five ales and an excellent choice of food.
🏨 Q ⛺ 🛏 ◑ ▶ ♿ P

Gainsborough

Eight Jolly Brewers
Ship Court, Silver Street (off market place)
☎ (01427) 677128
11–3, 7–11; 11–11 Sat; 12–5, 7.30–10.30 Sun
Old Mill Bitter; guest beers H
A folk club regularly meets at this small pub, which is bursting with life. It always sells six guest beers, plus a house beer from Highwood. Lunches Mon–Fri. CAMRA *Pub of the Year* finalist 1996.
Q ⛺ 🏮 ◑ ▶ ✂ 🍴

Melrose Sports & Social Club
51 Melrose Road (off A159, Morton Tce) ☎ (01427) 613015
12–4, 8–11, including Sun
Mansfield Bitter, Old Baily; Ward's Best Bitter; guest beer H
Busy social club allowing free entry on production of this guide or a CAMRA membership card. Wheelchair ramp at the back. Q ⛺ ♣ P

Peacock Hotel
Corringham Road (B1433, ½ mile from centre)
☎ (01427) 615859
11.30–3, 5–11; 11.30–11 Fri & Sat; 12–10.30 Sun
Marston's Bitter, Pedigree, HBC H
Large, friendly refurbished, community pub, serving good value food.
⛺ ◑ ▶ 🛏 ♿ ≈ ♣ P

Garthorpe

Bay Horse
Shore Road ☎ (01724) 798306
12–2 (3 Sat), 7–11; 12–3, 7.30–10.30 Sun
Mansfield Riding Bitter, Old Baily H
Comfortable, traditional pub with a small entrance bar, a public bar, a small family room and a lounge bar. Live entertainment Sat. Good value, home-cooked food Thu–Sun.
🏨 ⛺ 🏮 ◑ ▶ 🛏 ♣ P

Gedney Drove End

New Inn
Main Road (end of B1359)
☎ (01406) 550389
7–11; 11–3.30, 7–11 Sat & bank hols; 12–3.30, 7–10.30 Sun
Elgood's Cambridge Bitter H
Lively village local where the landlady has built up an extensive collection of pigs during her 20 years here. A stall in the car park sells produce from the pub's smallholding.
🏨 ⛺ 🏮 ◑ ▶ ▲ ♣ P

Gedney Dyke

Chequers
Main Street ☎ (01406) 362666
12–2.30, 7–11; 12–2.30, 7–10.30 Sun
Adnams Bitter; Draught Bass; Elgood's GSB; Greene King Abbot; Morland Old Speckled Hen H
Comfortable country pub and restaurant with the accent on food (in CAMRA's *Good Pub Food* guide). Situated in a quiet village, it dates back to 1795 and is popular with diners and drinkers alike.
🏨 ⛺ ◑ ▶ P

Gosberton Risegate

Duke of York
106 Risegate Road (B1397, 1½ miles from Gosberton)
☎ (01775) 840193
12–11; 12–4, 7–10.30 Sun
Bateman XB; John Smith's Bitter; guest beers H
Village local with a widespread reputation for good value food (no-smoking dining room) and bar snacks. 🏨 ⛺ ◑ ▶ ▲ ♣ P

Grainthorpe

Black Horse
Mill Lane (off A1031)
☎ (01472) 388229
12–3 (not winter Mon–Fri), 7–11 (12–11 summer Sat); 12–3, 7–10.30 Sun
Bateman Mild, XB; Boddingtons Bitter; guest beers H
Friendly, cosy pub where a quiet lounge contrasts with the bar. Old Blackie is brewed by Highwood.
🏨 Q ⛺ ◑ ▶ 🛏 ▲ ♣ P

Grantham

Angel & Royal Hotel
High Street ☎ (01476) 565816
5 (12 Fri)–11; 11–4, 7–11 Sat; 12–3, 7–10.30 Sun
Banks's Bitter; Camerons Strongarm; Morrells Varsity, Graduate H
Reputedly England's oldest coaching inn, established in the 13th century and associated with Richard III. It boasts fine masonry, timbered ceilings, tapestries and a real fire in winter. 🏨 Q 🛏 🏮 P

Beehive
10–11 Castlegate
☎ (01476) 567794
11.30–3 (5 Sat), 5–11; 11.30–11 Thu & Fri; 7–10.30 (closed lunch) Sun
Beer range varies H
Busy town-centre local, popular with students. It is renowned as the pub with a living sign. One Bateman and two guest beers are stocked.
⛺ 🏮 ♿ ≈

Blue Bull

64 Westgate ☎ (01476) 570929
11–3 (4 Sat), 7–11; 12–3, 7–10.30 Sun
**Higsons Bitter; Marston's
Pedigree; guest beers** H
Local CAMRA *Pub of the Year*
1997: a friendly 1850s pub with
two bars and a restaurant
serving good, home-cooked
food (no food Mon and Sun
eves). Wide selection of guest
beers; varying ciders.
Q ❀ ◖ ≢ ♣ ➾ P

Tollemache Inn

17 St Peters Hill
☎ (01476) 594696
11–11; 12–10.30 Sun
**Banks's Mild; Courage
Directors; Marston's Pedigree;
Theakston Best Bitter;
Younger Scotch; guest beers** H
Busy, town-centre pub. The
absence of music and the
availability of food all day,
makes this a popular venue
with all ages.
Q ❀ ◖ & ≢ ➾ ⚥

Great Limber

New Inn

High Street (A18)
☎ (01469) 560257
11–3, 6.30–11; 11–11 Sat; 12–10.30 Sun
**Boddingtons Bitter;
Highwood Tom Wood Old
Timber; Samuel Smith OBB;
Worthington Bitter** H
Country village pub, popular
for its good food, served in the
lounge and dining room,
whilst retaining a friendly,
traditional public bar.
♨ Q ❀ ⇔ ◖ ⊟ ♣ P

Grimsby

Hope & Anchor

148 Victoria Street
☎ (01472) 342565
11–11; 12–10.30 Sun
**Fuller's London Pride; Tetley
Mild, Bitter, Imperial; guest
beers** H
Popular, two-roomed, town-
centre pub. Three guest beers.
No food Sun. ❀ ◖ ⊟ ≢ ♣

Rutland Arms

26–30 Rutland Street
☎ (01472) 241345
11–11; 12–4.30, 8–10.30 Sun
**Old Mill Mild, Bitter, Old
Curiosity** H
Pub with one room: a large
lounge with a pool table
and darts. & ♣

Swigs

21 Osborne Street
☎ (01472) 354773
11–11; 7–10.30 (closed lunch) Sun
**Bateman XB; Willy's Original;
guest beers** H
Popular continental café bar
featuring good quality lunches
(not served Sun). Quiet
lunchtime and early eves,

noisier later on. In the *Guide*
since opening. ◖ ≢ (Town)

Tap & Spile

Haven Mill, Garth Lane
☎ (01472) 357493
12–4, 7–11; 12–11 Fri & Sat; 12–3,
7–10.30 Sun
Beer range varies H
Large, one-roomed, open-plan
former flour mill retaining old
stone, brick and woodwork. It
is well used, with a good
atmosphere. Up to eight ales,
usually including a
Tomlinson's brew.
❀ ◖ & ≢ (Town) ♣ ➾

Hainton

Heneage Arms

Louth Road ☎ (01507) 313553
12–2.30 (not Mon), 7–11; 12–3, 7–10.30
Sun
**Highwood Tom Wood Best
Bitter, Harvest, seasonal beer;
guest beer** (summer) H
Pub where the comfortable
main bar has two real fires,
affording a warm welcome
which is echoed from behind
the bar. Note the old petrol
pump in the car park.
Occasional cider in summer.
♨ Q ☙ ❀ ⇔ ◖ & ➾ P

Haltoft End

Castle

Wainfleet Road (A52, 2 miles
NE of Boston)
☎ (01205) 760393
11–11; 12–10.30 Sun
**Bateman Mild, XB; guest
beer** H
Friendly, roadside local with a
deserved reputation for good
value meals. A keen darts and
dominoes pub, it hosts matches
most eves. Excellent adventure
playground for children.
♨ ❀ ⇔ ◖ ⏵ ♣ P

Haxey

Loco

31–33 Church Street
☎ (01427) 752879
7 (6 Fri)–11; 12–5, 7–10.30 Sun
**Courage Directors; John
Smith's Bitter** H
Stone-floored village pub, full
of railway memorabilia and
antiques; the bar was a church
pulpit and the front section of a
steam locomotive adds
interest. Eve meals (Thu–Sat)
and Sun lunch served. ☙ ⏵

Heighington

Butcher & Beast

High Street ☎ (01522) 790386
11–3.30 (5 Sat), 7–11; 12–5, 7–10.30
Sun
**Draught Bass; Bateman XB,
XXXB; guest beers** H
Friendly, popular village pub.
Award-winning floral displays

outside; summer barbecues.
No food Sun/Mon eves.
♨ ☙ ❀ ◖ ⏵ ♣ P ⚑

Hemingby

Coach & Horses

☎ (01507) 578280
12–3 (not Mon or Tue), 7 (6
Wed–Fri)–11; 11–11 Sat; 12–10.30 Sun
**Draught Bass; Bateman XB;
guest beer** H
Pleasant, welcoming pub on
the west edge of the village,
next to the church. Look out for
low beams! Eve meals served
6–8 Wed–Fri, 7–10 Sat; book
Sun lunch. ♨ ❀ ◖ ⏵ ▲ ♣ P

Holbeach St Marks

New Inn

Main Road ☎ (01406) 701231
12–2.30, 7–11 (midnight Sat); 12–4.30,
7–10.30 Sun
**Bateman Mild; Boddingtons
Bitter; Tetley Bitter; guest
beers** H
Popular village local with a
cosy atmosphere. A lively
music venue, it also hosts
regular art exhibitions. Close to
the Wash marshlands and
nature reserves.
♨ Q ❀ ⇔ ◖ ⏵ ▲ ♣ P

Horbling

Plough

Spring Lane ☎ (01529) 240263
12–3, 7–11; 12–3, 7–10.30 Sun
**Greene King IPA, Abbot;
guest beer** H
Late 17th-century building
owned by the parish council.
Regular speciality eves in the
restaurant (booking advised).
♨ ❀ ◖ ⏵ ⊟ ♣ P

Horncastle

Black Swan

South Street ☎ (01507) 522378
11–3, 6.30–11; 12–3, 7–10.30 Sun
**Courage Directors; John
Smith's Bitter; Theakston XB;
guest beer** H
Known as the 'Mucky Duck',
this multi-roomed pub features
regular live music and a
changing guest beer. It attracts
the younger set eves.
♨ ❀ ♣ P

Fighting Cocks

West Street ☎ (01507) 527307
11–4, 7–11; 12–3, 7–10.30 Sun
**Draught Bass; Bateman XB;
Courage Directors; Fuller's
London Pride; Marston's
Pedigree; John Smith's
Bitter** H
Modernised, 200-year-old pub
with a cheerful and bustling
atmosphere. Reputed to be
haunted by a cat and a cavalier.
The restaurant is closed Sun.
Q ❀ ⇔ ◖ ⏵ & ▲ P

Hubbert's Bridge

Wheatsheaf
Station Road ☎ (01205) 290347
11–2.30, 5–11; 11–11 Sat; 12–3.30,
7–10.30 Sun
**Vaux Samson; Ward's Thorne
BB; guest beers** H
Welcoming, family-run,
bankside pub, ideal for fishing
and near good golfing
facilities. Excellent food in the
bar and restaurant, with
imaginative vegetarian dishes
and cheap lunchtime specials.
🏘 ❀ 🛏 ◑ ▶ ▲ ≈ ♣ P

Kirkby on Bain

Ebrington Arms
Main Street ☎ (01526) 354560
12–3, 7–11 (11–11 summer); 12–4,
7–10.30 (12–10.30 summer) Sun
**Bateman XB, XXXB; guest
beers** H
Traditional village local with a
changing choice of guest beers
(usually from small breweries).
Beer festivals Easter and Aug
Bank Hol weekends. The
Bainside Restaurant has a good
reputation.
🏘 ❀ ◑ ▶ ♿ ▲ ♣ ◔ P ✗

Laughterton

Friendship
Main Road ☎ (01427) 718681
11.30–2.30 (3 Sat), 6–11; 12–3, 7–10.30
Sun
**Draught Bass; Bateman XXXB;
Ward's Best Bitter; guest
beer** H
Comfortable village pub, with
its own art gallery; popular
with golfers. Good plain food
(try 'Mum's Pie'). Caravan
club-only campsite.
❀ ◑ ▶ ▲ ♣ P

Lincoln

Dog & Bone
10 John Street
☎ (01522) 522403
12–3, 7 (5 summer Fri)–11; 11–11 Sat;
12–10.30 Sun
**Draught Bass; Bateman XB,
XXXB; Salem Porter;
Marston's Pedigree; guest
beer** H
Friendly, one-roomed
(formerly two-roomed) pub.
Popular with students, it stages
fun nights during term-time
and boasts an array of antiques
and old relics with a touch of
humour. Big screen TV for
sport. Wheelchair entrance
from the rear car park.
🏘 ❀ ◑ ♿ ≈ ♣ P

Golden Eagle
21 High Street
☎ (01522) 521058
11–3, 5–11; 11–11 Fri & Sat; 12–10.30
Sun
**Bateman XB; Everards Beacon;
Fuller's London Pride; Taylor
Landlord; guest beers** H
Friendly, two-bar pub close to
the football ground, part of the
Small Beer group: a lively,
sporty bar and a quiet lounge.
Guest beers from far and wide;
regular festivals; annual cider
event. ❀ ◑ ♣ ◔ P

Jolly Brewer
26 Broadgate ☎ (01522) 528583
11–11; 12–10.30 Sun
**Draught Bass; Shepherd
Neame Spitfire; Theakston
XB; Younger Scotch, No. 3;
guest beers** H
Art-Deco prevails throughout
this pub which attracts a varied
clientele. No food Sun. A
regular *Guide* entry.
🏘 ❀ ◑ ≈ ♣ ◔ P

Lord Tennyson
72 Rasen Lane
☎ (01522) 530690
11–2.30 (3 Sat), 5.30–11; 12–3, 7–10.30
Sun
**Vaux Samson, Waggle Dance;
Ward's Best Bitter; guest
beer** H
Popular pub, close to the
tourist area but far enough
away to retain a local feel;
named after the Lincolnshire
Poet Laureate. The food is of
excellent quality and variety
with good value special offers.
No food Sun eve. ❀ ◑ ▶ ♣ P

Morning Star
11 Greetwellgate
☎ (01522) 527079
11–11; 12–5, 7–10.30 Sun
**Draught Bass; Ruddles Best
Bitter; guest beers** H
Revitalised uphill pub, near the
cathedral, pleasant for outdoor
drinking in summer. The only
noise is conversation. It is run
by the aptly named Mr & Mrs
Beers. Piano night Sat. Fine
collection of aircraft paintings.
🏘 Q ❀ ◑ ♣ P 🖵

Peacock Inn
23 Wragby Road
☎ (01522) 524703
11.30–11; 12–10.30 Sun
**Hardys & Hansons Best Mild,
Best Bitter, Classic, seasonal
beers** H
Popular local on the edge of the
tourist area. Eve meals Fri–Sun
in summer. 🏘 ❀ ◑ ▶ ♣ P

Portland Arms
50 Portland Street (near Ritz
Cinema) ☎ (01522) 513912
11–11; 12–10.30 Sun
**Draught Bass; Bateman XXXB;
Courage Directors; John
Smith's Bitter; guest beers** H
Simple, friendly, town pub
with absolutely no ties: a lively
tap room/games area and a
cosy, quiet, best room. It
usually serves six guest beers
(including a mild) from across

the UK, plus a cider. Worth
seeking out.
Q ❀ 🍴 ≈ ♣ ◔ P

Queen in the West
12–14 Moor Street
☎ (01522) 880123
12 (11 Sat)–4, 5.30 (7 Sat)–11; 11–11
Fri; 12–4, 7–10.30 Sun
**Courage Directors; Morland
Old Speckled Hen; Ruddles
Best Bitter; John Smith's
Bitter; Theakston XB; Wells
Bombardier; guest beer** H
Traditional, stone-built corner
pub extended into adjacent
houses: a comfortable lounge
and a public bar housing
games. Popular with local
workers lunchtimes and
residents eves. ◑ 🍴 ♣

Sippers
26 Melville Street (opp. bus
station) ☎ (01522) 527612
11–2.30, 5 (4 Fri, 7 Sat)–11; 7–10.30 Sun
(closed lunch) Sun
**Courage Directors; Marston's
Pedigree; Morland Old
Speckled Hen; John Smith's
Bitter; Wilson's Mild; guest
beer** H
Handy pub for both the rail
and bus stations; popular
lunchtimes with local workers,
quieter eves. Usually two guest
beers from small brewers are
sold. The excellent food is not
available Sat eve or Sun.
◑ ▶ ≈ ♣

Victoria
6 Union Road (by W gate of
castle) ☎ (01522) 536048
11–11; 12–10.30 Sun
**Bateman XB; Everards Old
Original; Taylor Landlord;
guest beers** H
Small, characterful pub,
offering up to seven guests
(always a mild). It stages
regular brewery feature nights
and beer festivals, summer and
winter. Good lunches.
Q ❀ ◑ 🍴 ♣ ◔

Louth

Malt Shovel
21 Northgate ☎ (01507) 608904
11–2 (4.30 Wed, Fri & Sat; not Mon),
7–11; 12–3, 7–10.30 Sun
**Bass Mild, Draught Bass;
Stones Bitter; guest beers** H
Edwardian building, now a
welcoming single bar with a
lounge and a games area.
🏘 Q ♿ ♣ P

Masons Arms
Cornmarket ☎ (01507) 609525
11–11; 12–3, 7–10.30 Sun
**Draught Bass; Bateman Mild,
XB, XXXB; Salem Porter;
Marston's Pedigree; guest
beer** H
Local CAMRA *Pub of the Year*: a
friendly, family-run,
18th-century posting inn
offering home-made fare and

charming accommodation. Children's certificate.
Q ⇔ ◁ ▶

Newmarket Inn

Newmarket Road
☎ (01507) 605146
6–11; 12–3, 7–10.30 Sun
Castle Eden Ale; Flowers IPA; Highwood Tom Wood Best Bitter; guest beer Ⓗ
Formerly known as the Brown Cow, renamed in 1972 by the present owner's family: a pleasantly decorated, two-roomed pub with a dining room (eve meals Fri and Sat). Popular with all ages. Limited parking. ₥ Q ⊛ ◁ & ♣ P

Wheatsheaf Inn

62 Westgate ☎ (01507) 603159
11–3, 5–11; 11–11 Sat; 12–4, 7–10.30
(12–10.30 summer) Sun
Draught Bass; Boddingtons Bitter; Flowers Original; guest beers Ⓗ
Attractive, traditional, old inn dated 1612, in a Georgian terrace, with three bars, all with real fires. The house beer, Tipsy Toad, is not brewed on the premises. Children welcome until 9pm.
₥ Q ⊛ ◁ & P

Woolpack

Riverhead ☎ (01507) 606568
11–3 (4 Sat), 5–11; 12–4, 7–10.30 Sun
Bateman Mild, XB, Valiant, XXXB; Marston's Pedigree; guest beers Ⓗ
18th-century wool merchant's house with a bar, lounge and snug. Real fires, excellent food and traditional games feature. ₥ Q ⊛ ◁ ▲ ♣ P

Mablethorpe

Montalt Arms

George Street (off High St)
☎ (01507) 472794
11.30–3, 7–11; 12–3, 7–10.30 Sun
Bateman XB; Courage Directors; guest beer Ⓗ
Real ale oasis named after a 13th-century knight: a large, friendly lounge bar with an adjoining restaurant. Popular in summer with holidaymakers. No food Sun eve or Mon. Tiny car park.
₥ ◁ ▶ P

Maltby le Marsh

Crown Inn

Beesby Road (A157/A1104 jct)
☎ (01507) 450349
12 (11 summer)–3, 7–11; 12–3, 7–10.30
Sun
Bateman XB, XXXB Ⓗ
Characterful, 17th-century, oak-beamed, two-roomed pub in a rural village, with an extensive collection of pottery.
Q ⊛ ◁ ▶ ▲ P

Market Deeping

Bull

19 Market Place
☎ (01778) 343320
11–2.30, 5–11; 11–11 Fri & Sat;
12–10.30 Sun
Adnams Bitter; Everards Tiger, Old Original; guest beer Ⓗ
14th-century coaching inn, featuring a below-ground-level dug-out and an upstairs room. Memorabilia from landlord Bert Murray's footballing days adds to the atmosphere. The guest beer is from the Everards list. Book eve meals in the restaurant. ⊛ ◁ ▶ ▲ ♣

Messingham

Horn Inn

High Street ☎ (01724) 762426
11–11; 12–10.30 Sun
Highwood Tom Wood Shepherd's Delight or **seasonal beer; John Smith's Bitter; guest beer** Ⓗ
Friendly village local on the main road. The single room gives an impression of separate drinking areas. Live music Wed. Excellent lunches. Wheelchair ramp at the rear.
₥ ⊛ ◁ & ♣ P

Nettleham

Black Horse

Chapel Lane ☎ (01522) 750702
11.30–3 (4.30 Sat), 7 (5 Fri)–11;
12–5.30, 7–10.30 Sun
Boddingtons Bitter; Tetley Bitter; Theakston Best Bitter, XB; Wilson's Mild; guest beers Ⓗ
18th-century, stone pub in a pretty village. Monthly live music, with top-drawer folk performers. All Nettleham's pubs sell real ale.
Q ▨ ◁ ⊞ ♣

North Kelsey

Butcher's Arms

Middle Street
☎ (01652) 678002
12–11; 12–10.30 Sun
Highwood Tom Wood Best Bitter, Harvest, Old Timber, seasonal beer Ⓗ
Friendly, basic, old village pub, recently reopened and refurbished. The wood-burning open fire is tempting on winter nights. No hot eve meals. ₥ Q ◁ ▶ & ♣ P

North Kelsey Moor

Queen's Head

Station Road (near disused N Kelsey station) OS070018
☎ (01652) 678055

12–2 (4 Sat; not Mon, Wed or Thu),
7–11; 12–4, 7–10.30 Sun
Theakston Best Bitter; guest beers Ⓗ
Excellent three-room free house offering a good range of food, plus changing guest beers. Popular quiz Thu eve; Tue is free Old Peculier sausage night. Pensioners special lunches Tue and Fri. No meals Sun eve.
₥ Q ⊛ ◁ ▶ ⊞ & ▲ ♣ P

Oasby

Houblon Arms

Village Street
☎ (01529) 455215
12–2.30, 6.30 (6 Fri & Sat)–11; 12–3,
7–10.30 Sun
Draught Bass; Bateman Mild, XB; guest beers Ⓗ
Charming old village inn with low, beamed ceilings and antique furnishings.
₥ Q ⊛ ⇔ ◁ ▶ P

Owston Ferry

Crooked Billet

Silver Street
☎ (01427) 728264
11.30–3 (not Mon except bank hols), 6
(7 Mon & Sat)–11; 12–3, 7–10.30 Sun
Ward's Thorne BB; guest beer Ⓗ
Friendly local by the River Trent, with its own boxing club. Weekend sing-alongs. A new summer outdoor drinking area overlooks the river. Good food: lunches Tue–Sun, eve meals Tue–Fri (till 8).
₥ ⊛ ◁ ▶ & P ⊟

Quadring

Red Cow Inn

128 Main Road
☎ (01775) 821143
12–3, 6.30–11; 11.30–11 Sat; 12–10.30
Sun
Vaux Samson; Ward's Best Bitter; guest beers Ⓗ
Comfortable and friendly village local, with an unusual tiled bar hood.
₥ ♣ P ⊟

Raithby

Red Lion

Main Street
☎ (01790) 753727
7–11; 12–3, 7–11 Sat & bank hols; 12–3,
7–10.30 Sun
Tetley Bitter; guest beers Ⓗ
Inviting, friendly pub in an attractive Wolds village with a deserved reputation for excellent, interesting food. Comfortable accommodation. An adjoining barn houses a small full mash brewery expected to be brewing soon.
₥ Q ⊛ ⇔ ◁ ▶ ♣ P

Rothwell

Nickerson Arms

Hill Rise (off A46, near Caistor)
☎ (01472) 371300
12–3, 7–11; 12–4, 7–10.30 Sun
Bateman XB, XXXB; Courage Directors; Fuller's London Pride; Marston's Pedigree; guest beer H
Deservedly popular country pub in a pretty Wolds village. A wide range of draught and bottled foreign beers complements the excellent food in the bar and restaurant.
🏨 ✿ ◖ ❩ ♣ P

Ruskington

Black Bull

10 Rectory Road
☎ (01526) 832270
11.30–2.30 (3 Fri & Sat), 6.30–11; 12–3, 7–10.30 Sun
Draught Bass; Bateman XB; guest beer H
Friendly, lively village pub, comfortably furnished, hosting thriving quiz nights Wed and Sun. Note the sculpture over the entrance. Book for Sun lunch and eve meals.
✿ 🏚 ◖ ❩ 🍴 ᖕ ⇌ ♣ P

Sandtoft

Reindeer Inn

☎ (01724) 710774
6–11; 12–4, 7–11 Fri & Sat; 12–4, 7–10.30 Sun
Draught Bass; John Smith's Bitter; Worthington Bitter H
Cosy, inviting country pub with a private function room. Traditional home-cooked food is always available. Popular at weekends. 🏨 ᗡ ✿ ◖ ♣ P ▯

Saxilby

Ship Inn

21 Bridge Street
☎ (01522) 702259
11.30–2.30 (3 Fri & Sat), 7 (5.30 summer)–11; 12–3, 7–10.30 Sun
John Smith's Bitter H
Friendly village pub, popular with sports enthusiasts, opposite the Fossdyke Navigation, England's oldest canal. Home-cooked food at reasonable prices. Book eve meals and to camp in the garden. ✿ ◖ ❩ ▲ ⇌ ♣ P

Scunthorpe

Crosby

Normanby Road
☎ (01724) 843830
12–11 bar; 7–11 lounge; 12–10.30 Sun
Marston's Bitter, Pedigree, HBC H
Refurbished ex-Bass hotel just off the town centre. A brash games bar attracts a young clientele; the large lounge is more sedate but has live music weekends and Sun afternoon jam sessions. Excellent, home-cooked food.
✿ ◖ ❩ 🏚 ᖕ ⇌ ♣ P

Warren Lodge

Luneburg Way, Skippingdale
☎ (01724) 271314
11–11; 12–10.30 Sun
Ind Coope Burton Ale; Marston's Pedigree; Tetley Bitter, seasonal beers H
Large, modern pub, extended in the Big Steak House/Wacky Warehouse style with indoor and outdoor play areas.
ᗡ ◖ ❩ P

Skegness

Vine Hotel

Vine Road, Seacroft
☎ (01754) 763018
11–11; 12–10.30 Sun
Bateman Mild, XB, Valiant, XXXB H
An oasis of peace and calm in a secluded wooded setting, away from the hurly-burly of the resort. Leafy gardens in summer; roaring fires in winter. Good food and accommodation.
🏨 Q ✿ 🏚 ◖ ❩ ᖕ ♣ P

Sleaford

Carre Arms

Mareham Lane
☎ (01529) 303156
11–3, 5.30–11; 12–3, 7–10.30 Sun
Draught Bass; M&B Brew XI H
Town local hotel with a comfortable bar and lounge/ restaurant. ✿ 🏚 ◖ ❩ 🏚 ⇌ P

Rose & Crown

2 Watergate
☎ (01529) 303350
11–2.30, 7–11; 12–4, 7.30–10.30 Sun
Mansfield Bitter, Old Baily H
Refurbished, busy town pub, with a good-sized games area on a lower level from the bar. No food weekends.
✿ ◖ ⇌ ♣ P

South Ferriby

Hope & Anchor

Sluice Road
☎ (01652) 635242
12–3, 6–11; 11–11 Sat & summer; 12–3, 7–10.30 (12–10.30 summer) Sun
Adnams Bitter; Mansfield Riding Mild, Riding Bitter; Morland Old Speckled Hen H
Pub on the bank of the Humber at the confluence of the River Ancholme, next to the lock gates: superb views of the Humber Bridge. Three rooms and a children's outdoor play area. ᗡ ✿ ◖ ❩ ᖕ ♣ P

Spalding

Lincoln Arms

4 Bridge Street
☎ (01775) 722691
11–3, 7–11; 12–3, 7–10.30 Sun
Mansfield Riding Mild, Riding Bitter, Bitter, Old Baily H
Comfortable, 18th-century, riverside pub with a warm welcome that attracts a wide range of customers. A meeting place for numerous clubs.
🏚 ⇌ ♣

Lincolnshire Poacher

11 Double Street
☎ (01775) 766490
11–3, 5–11; 11–11 Sat; 12–3, 7–10.30 (12–10.30 summer) Sun
Theakston Best Bitter, XB, Old Peculier; guest beers H
Pleasant, busy pub on the riverside with a lively atmosphere. Three or four guest beers; varied menu.
✿ ◖ ❩ ᖕ ⇌

Olde White Horse

Churchgate ☎ (01775) 766740
11.30–2.30, 5–11; 11–4, 7–11 Sat; 12–4, 7–10.30 Sun
Samuel Smith OBB H
Imposing, 14th-century, thatched building by the town bridge; refurbished with stone-flagged floors and a comfortable lounge. Extensive bar meal menu.
🏨 Q ✿ ◖ ❩ ⇌ P ⌗

Ship Albion

37 Albion Street
☎ (01775) 769644
11.30–11; 12–10.30 Sun
Draught Bass; Bateman XB; Boddingtons Bitter; guest beers H
Friendly, comfortable pub offering reasonably priced food. Home of Spalding folk club. 🏨 ✿ 🏚 ◖ ❩ ♣ P

Springthorpe

New Inn

16 Hill Road ☎ (01427) 838254
12–2 (not Sat), 7–11; 12–2, 7–10.30 Sun; closed Mon
Bateman XXXB; Marston's Pedigree; guest beer H
Basic village local serving excellent home-cooked food.
🏨 Q ✿ ◖ ❩ 🏚 P

Stamford

Daniel Lambert

20 St Leonard's Street
☎ (01780) 55991
11.30–2.30 (3 Sat), 6–11; 11.30–11 Fri; 12–3, 7–10.30 Sun
Adnams Bitter; Courage Directors; John Smith's Bitter; Taylor Landlord; guest beer H
Friendly, one-room pub with a cloister-type restaurant

beneath, named after one of Britain's heaviest men who died in Stamford and whose picture dominates the bar. Eve meals Tue–Sat. 🏾 Q ◖ ▶ ⇌ ♣

Dolphin

60 East Street
☎ (01780) 55494
11–3, 5.30–11; 12–3, 7–10.30 Sun
Wells Eagle, Bombardier; guest beers Ⓗ
300-year-old pub with four small rooms and a restaurant. Annual beer festival. Wheelchair WC.
🏾 ❀ 🛏 ◖ ▶ & ⇌ ♣ ☐

Green Man

29 Scotgate (5 mins' walk towards Oakham from centre)
☎ (01780) 53598
11–11; 12–10.30 Sun
Theakston Best Bitter, XB; guest beers Ⓗ
Friendly, refurbished, old-style local with wooden beams, flooring and furniture. Beer festivals Easter and summer; occasional cider.
🏾 ❀ 🛏 ◖ ⇌ ♣ ⌂ ☐

St Peter's Inn

11 St Peter's Street (5 mins' walk uphill from centre)
☎ (01780) 63298
12–2.30 (not Mon), 5.30–11; 12–11 Fri & Sat; 12–10.30 Sun
Marston's Bitter, Pedigree Ⓗ**; guest beers** Ⓗ/Ⓖ
Stone-built, spotless, 200-year-old pub with beers on gravity in the cloister bar downstairs (not open weekday lunch). ❀ ◖ ⇌ P

Stickney

Plough & Dove

Main Road ☎ (01205) 480965
11.30–3.30, 6.30–11; 12–3, 7–10.30 Sun
Bateman Mild, XB; guest beer Ⓗ
Lively village pub, hosting regular karaoke and shows. The guest beer (sold at a promotional price) is only available from Fri night, until sold out. 🏾 ❀ ◖ ▶ ♣ ☐

Surfleet

Mermaid

2 Gosberton Road (main road)
☎ (01775) 680275
11.30–2.30 (3 Sat), 6.30–11; 12–3, 7–10.30 Sun
Adnams Broadside; John Smith's Bitter; guest beers Ⓗ
Former brewery by the River Glen with a warm atmosphere. Sumptuous meals in the extended restaurant; large garden, perfect for children.
🏾 Q ❀ 🛏 ◖ ▶ P

Susworth

Jenny Wren

East Ferry Road (3 miles off A159 at Scotter, by River Trent)
☎ (01724) 784000
12–3, 5–11; 12–4, 6–10.30 Sun
John Smith's Bitter; guest beers Ⓗ
Excellently appointed, large, 18th-century village inn, featuring attractive rural decor, with bare brickwork and wooden beams. Despite the strong emphasis on food, the public bar is more of a drinkers' area, with three guest beers. 🏾 ❀ ◖ ▶ 🍴 & ♣ P ⚊

Thornton Curtis

Thornton Hunt

Main Street ☎ (01469) 531252
12–3, 7–11; 12–3, 7–10.30 Sun
John Smith's Bitter; Theakston Best Bitter; guest beer Ⓗ
200-year-old village pub partly dating back to Henry VIII, who is rumoured to have stayed here. ❀ 🛏 ◖ ▶ P

Threekingham

Three Kings

Salters Way (100 yds S of A52)
☎ (01529) 240249
11–11; 12–10.30 Sun
Draught Bass; guest beers Ⓗ
Welcoming village pub which reputedly, together with the

village, takes its name from the 9th-century battle of Stow Green where three Danish kings were killed. Look for the painted stone effigies above the front entrance.
🏾 ❀ ◖ ▶ 🍴 & ♣ P

Waddingham

Marquis of Granby

High Street (1½ miles E of A15)
☎ (01673) 818387
12–2 (3 summer), 7 (6 summer)–11; 12–3, 7–10.30 Sun
Ward's Best Bitter; guest beer (summer) Ⓗ
Very smart village local with one large room. Its rural atmosphere is enhanced by wood fittings, pottery jugs, pictures and brasses. Popular for meals; holder of brewery cellar and other awards. Occasional guest beers from Ward's Classic Cask Collection. 🏾 ❀ ◖ & ♣ P

Wainfleet

Jolly Sailor Inn

19 St John Street
☎ (01754) 880275
11–2, 4.30–11; 11–11 Fri & Sat; 12–2, 7–10.30 Sun
Bateman Mild, XB; guest beer (occasional) Ⓗ
Tucked away from the centre of town, this pub's cosy bar contains a large bottle collection, sporting and brewery photos and a heavy table made from old ship's timber. A large function room and restaurant are attached. Book meals in winter.
🏾 ❀ ◖ ▶ ⚊ ⇌ ♣

Royal Oak

73 High Street
☎ (01754) 880328
11–3 (may extend summer), 7–11; 11–11 Sat; 12–10.30 Sun
Bateman Mild, XB, XXXB Ⓗ
Cheerful pub whose building once housed the Bethlehem Hospital for the insane. Note the detailed model of *HMS Vanguard*.
🏾 ❀ 🛏 ◖ ▶ ⚊ ⇌ ♣ P ☐

SUPPORT YOUR LOCAL BEERFEST

For a chance to sample beers not normally found in your locality, pop along to your local CAMRA beer festival. These events are staffed entirely by unpaid CAMRA members, many of whom give up precious holiday time to do so.

If you support CAMRA's aims, and appreciate the work voluntary members put in, why not show it by visiting your local beer festival? More details about events and venues can be found on page 151.

THE CAMRA GUIDE TO REAL ALE IN A BOTTLE

CAMRA's *Good Beer Guide* has been promoting draught real ale for 25 years. Now CAMRA has turned its attention to real ale which can be drunk in the home as well as in the pub.

The CAMRA Guide to Real Ale in a Bottle focuses on bottle-conditioned beers – beers which contain yeast and continue to mature in the bottle for a fuller, fresher taste, just as real ales mature in the cask at the pub.

All Britain's bottle-conditioned beers are profiled, with tasting notes. There are details of bottled real ales from overseas and features on how to buy, keep and serve real ale in a bottle. The full story of this historic beer style and a feature on the bottled 'Classics' help set the scene.

Compiled by Jeff Evans, eight times editor of the *Good Beer Guide*, this is a book no serious beer drinker can afford to be without as the bottled beer revival continues apace. Let CAMRA be your guide through the supermarket aisles and along the off-licence shelves. Pick up your copy in your local bookshop, or order it direct, at £7.99 inclusive of postage, from CAMRA, 230 Hatfield Road, St Albans, Hertfordshire AL1 4LW; tel. (01727) 867201. Discounts are available for CAMRA members.

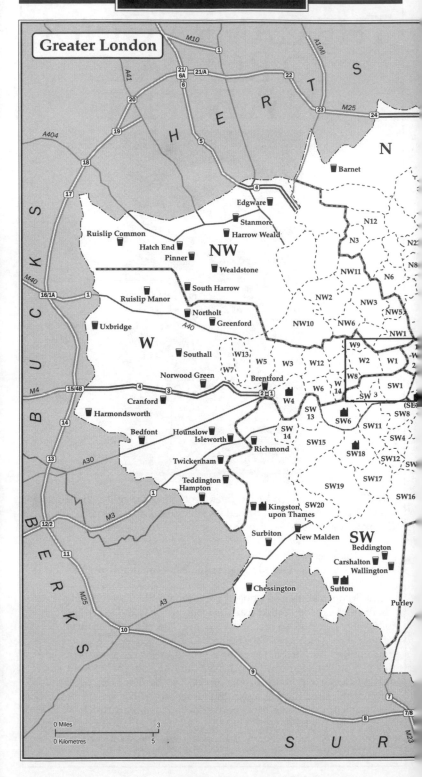

Greater London

HERTS

N

M10
A1(M)
A41
21/6A
21/A
6
22
20
23
M25
24
19
A404
5
18
Barnet
17
Edgware
N12
Ruislip Common
Stanmore
Harrow Weald
N3
N2
Hatch End
NW
N8
Pinner
Wealdstone
NW11
N6
M40
South Harrow
NW5
16/1A
1
Ruislip Manor
NW2
NW3
Northolt
NW10
NW6
NW1
Uxbridge
Greenford
A40
W9
1-W
W
Southall
W13
W5
W3
W12
W2
W1
2
Norwood Green
W7
W8
SW1
M4
15/4B
4
3
Brentford
W6
W14
SW3
Cranford
2 1
W4
(SE
Harmondsworth
SW13
SW6
SW8
Bedfont
Hounslow
SW14
SW11
SW4
Isleworth
SW15
SW12
SW
Richmond
SW18
A30
Twickenham
SW17
SW19
Teddington
SW20
SW16
Hampton
Kingston
upon Thames
SW
1
M3
Surbiton
New Malden
Beddington
12/2
Carshalton
Wallington
11
Chessington
Sutton
Purley
A3
10
9
7
8
7/8
SURREY
M23

BUCKS

BERKS

0 Miles   3
0 Kilometres   5

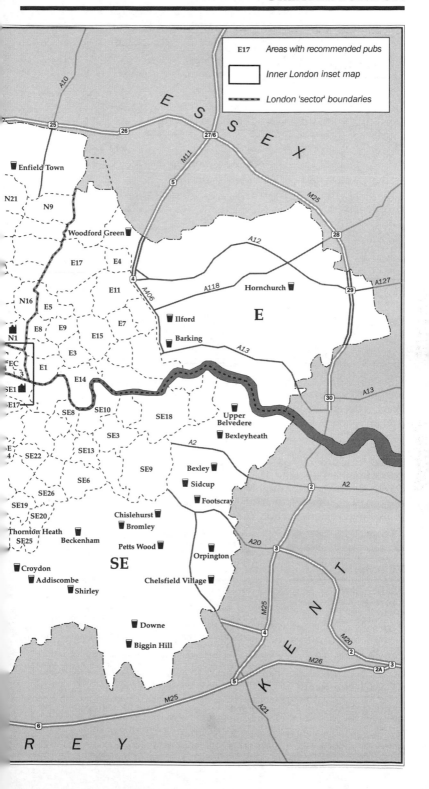

Legend:
- E17 — Areas with recommended pubs
- Inner London inset map
- London 'sector' boundaries

ESSEX

Enfield Town

N21

N9

Woodford Green

N16

E17   E4

E11

E5

A406

E8   E9

E7

N1

E15

EC

E3

E1

A118   Hornchurch

Ilford

Barking

E

A12

A13

A127

Upper Belvedere

SE8   SE10

SE18

SE3

Bexleyheath

SE13

A2

SE9

Bexley

SE22

Sidcup

SE6

Footscray

SE26

SE19

SE20

Chislehurst

Thornton Heath   Bromley

SE25   Beckenham

Petts Wood

SE

Orpington

Croydon

Addiscombe

Chelsfield Village

Shirley

Downe

Biggin Hill

KENT

M25

M20

M26

SURREY

179

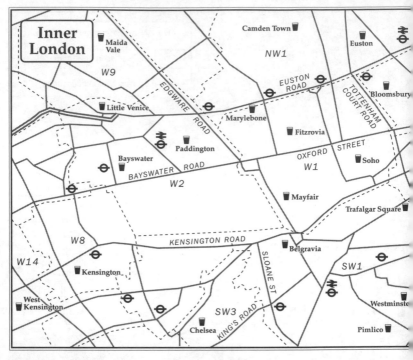

NB: Pubs within Greater London are divided into seven geographical sectors: Central, East, North, North-West, South-East, South-West and West, reflecting London postal boundaries (see Greater London map on previous pages). Look under Central London for postal districts EC1 to EC4, and WC1 and WC2. For each of the surrounding sectors, postal districts are listed in numerical order (E1, E4, etc.), followed in alphabetical order by the outlying areas which do not have London postal numbers (Barking, Hornchurch, etc.). The Inner London map, above, shows the area roughly covered by the Circle Line and outlines regions of London (Bloomsbury, Holborn, etc.) which have featured pubs. Some regions straddle more than one postal district.

Central London

EC1: Barbican

Shakespeare
101 Crescent House, Goswell Road
11–11; 11–3 Sat; closed Sun
Tetley Bitter; guest beers H
City pub serving several guest beers. The atmosphere can be smoky. Food served until 10pm. ◑ ▶ ⇌ ⊖

EC1: Clerkenwell

Artillery Arms
102 Bunhill Row
☎ (0171) 253 4683
11–11; 12–10.30 Sun
Fuller's Chiswick, London Pride, ESB, seasonal beers H
Small, one-bar pub attracting

both locals and office workers. Opposite Bunhill burial ground. ◑ ⇌ (Old St) ⊖

Britannia
94 Ironmonger Row
☎ (0171) 253 6441
11–11; 12–10.30 Sun
Boddingtons Bitter; Fuller's London Pride; Marston's Pedigree; guest beer H
The lunchtime office workers are replaced by locals and tourists from the nearby hotel eves and weekends in this immaculate pub. Live music Fri and Sat.
◑ ⇌ (Old St) ⊖ ♣

Leopard
33 Seward Street
☎ (0171) 253 3587
11–11; closed Sat & Sun
Gibbs Mew Salisbury; Greene King Abbot H; **guest beers** H/G

Imaginatively renovated pub off Goswell Rd with an interesting menu. Regular beer festivals. ⚌ ◑ ⊖ (Barbican)

Masque Haunt
168–172 Old Street
☎ (0171) 251 4195
11–11; 12–10.30 Sun
Courage Directors; Fuller's London Pride; Theakston Best Bitter; Younger Scotch; guest beers H
Large, one-bar pub with a raised drinking area at the rear. Wetherspoons beer festivals staged.
Q ◑ ◐ ⇌ (Old St) ⊖ ⊙ ⚲

O'Hanlon's
8 Tysoe Street
11–11; 12–10.30 Sun
O'Hanlon's Dry Stout, seasonal beers H
Small, comfortable Irish pub near Exmouth market. Six

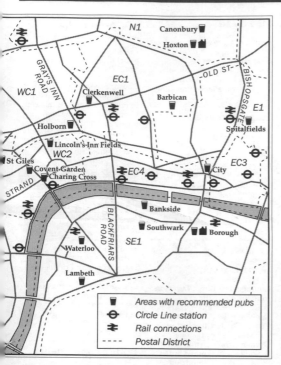

Large, modern pub by the
Thames, underneath Cannon
Street railway bridge. Eve
meals to order only.
✿ ◖ ♿ ≷ (Cannon St) ⊖

Old Bank of England
192 Fleet Street
☎ (0171) 430 2255
11–11; closed Sat & Sun
**Fuller's Chiswick, London
Pride, ESB, seasonal beers;
guest beers** Ⓗ
Superb conversion of a former
bank: a Fuller's Ale & Pie
house. Q ◖ ≷ (City
Thameslink) ⊖ (Temple)

WC1: Bloomsbury

Calthorpe Arms
252 Gray's Inn Road
☎ (0171) 278 4372
11–3, 5–11; 11–11 Wed–Sat; 12–10.30
Sun
**Young's Bitter, Special,
seasonal beers** Ⓗ
Friendly corner pub, popular
with locals and office workers
alike. The upstairs dining room
is open lunchtimes; eve meals
on request. ✿ ◖ ≷ (King's
Cross) ⊖ (Russell Sq)

King's Arms
11A Northington Street
☎ (0171) 405 9107
11–11; closed Sat & Sun
**Draught Bass; Fuller's London
Pride; Greene King IPA; guest
beer** Ⓗ
Traditional corner pub in a
sidestreet off Gray's Inn Rd:
one bar and two upstairs
rooms. Very popular with the
local legal community.
Q ✿ ◖ ≷ (King's Cross) ⊖ ✄

Lamb
94 Lamb's Conduit Street
☎ (0171) 405 0713
11–11; 12–4, 7–10.30 Sun
**Young's Bitter, Special,
Winter Warmer** Ⓗ
Dark green upholstery blends
with etched-glass snob screens
to create a resplendent interior
in this Grade II-listed,
Victorian local. Memorabilia of
the music hall, a working
polyphon and a comfortable
no-smoking snug feature.
Q ✿ ◖ ⊖ (Russell Sq) ♣ ✄

handpumps dispense a variety
of beers from the pub's own
brewery in South London.
Good quality food. Q ◖ ▶ ≷
(Farringdon) ⊖ (Angel)

Sekforde Arms
34 Sekforde Street
☎ (0171) 253 3251
11–11; 12–4 Sun
**Young's Bitter, Special,
seasonal beers** Ⓗ
Small corner pub with an
upstairs restaurant which
doubles as a function room
eves. ◖ ▶ ≷ (Farringdon) ⊖

EC3: City

Elephant
119 Fenchurch Street
☎ (0171) 623 8970
11–11; closed Sat & Sun
**Young's Bitter, Special,
seasonal beers** Ⓗ
Basic bar at street level, with a
smarter bar downstairs
(respectable dress requested).
It may close earlier eves if
quiet. Q ▶ ≷ (Fenchurch
St) ⊖ (Aldgate)

Lamb Tavern
10–12 Leadenhall Market
☎ (0171) 626 2454
11–9; closed Sat & Sun
**Young's Bitter, Special,
seasonal beers** Ⓗ
Large pub in Leadenhall
Market. The downstairs bar

has standing room only;
seating upstairs (no-smoking).
Q ◖ ▶ ≷ (Fenchurch St) ⊖
(Monument) ✄

Swan
Ship Tavern Passage, 77–80
Gracechurch Street
☎ (0171) 283 7712
11–11 (may close earlier); closed Sat &
Sun
**Fuller's Chiswick, London
Pride, ESB, seasonal beers** Ⓗ
Small, alley pub with a tiny
downstairs bar and the main
bar above. Q ◖ ▶ ≷
(Fenchurch St) ⊖ (Bank)

EC4: City

Banker
Cousin Lane
☎ (0171) 283 5206
11–9; closed Sat & Sun
**Fuller's Chiswick, London
Pride, ESB, seasonal beers** Ⓗ

Rugby Tavern
19 Great James Street
☎ (0171) 405 1384
11–11; closed Sat & Sun
Fuller's Chiswick, London Pride, ESB, seasonal beers Ⓗ
Corner pub whose horseshoe bar is in danger of being overwhelmed by a plethora of blackboards promoting both wares and pub activities. A function room is available for hire as is the whole pub at weekends. Benches outside in a pedestrianised area.
🏵 ◖ ⊖ (Russell Sq) ✦

WC1: Holborn

Cittie of Yorke ☆
22 High Holborn
☎ (0171) 242 7670
11.30–11; closed Sun
Samuel Smith OBB Ⓗ
This 15th-century inn and coffee house was rebuilt in 1923 using some of the original materials. The vast main bar to the rear boasts huge vats, screened compartments and a rare triangular stove. Very busy early eves.
🏛 ◖ ⇌ (Farringdon) ⊖ (Holborn)

Three Cups
21–22 Sandland Street
☎ (0171) 831 4302
11–11; closed Sat & Sun
Young's Bitter, Special, seasonal beers Ⓗ
Single-bar pub tucked away from the bustle of High Holborn. Eve meals on request.
Q 🏵 ◖ ▶ ⇌ (Farringdon) ⊖ (Holborn)

WC2: Charing Cross

Marquis of Granby
51 Chandos Place
11–11; 12–10.30 Sun
Adnams Bitter; Marston's Pedigree; Tetley Bitter Ⓗ
Pleasant, wedge-shaped pub just off the Strand. Note the unusual ceiling gas heaters.
◖ ⇌ ⊖

WC2: Covent Garden

Cross Keys
31 Endell Street
☎ (0171) 836 5185
11–11; 12–10.30 Sun
Courage Best Bitter, Directors; Marston's Pedigree Ⓗ
Small, pleasant pub whose enormous display of foliage almost hides the sign depicted in relief on the facade. Inside there is much bric-a-brac, including Beatles memorabilia.
◖ ⊖

Hogshead
21 Drury Lane
☎ (0171) 240 2489
11–11; 12–10.30 Sun
Beer range varies Ⓗ
Small, friendly pub opposite the New London Theatre. Baguettes available lunchtime.
⊖

Hogshead in Covent Garden
23 Wellington Street
☎ (0171) 836 6930
11–11; 12–10.30 Sun
Beer range varies Ⓗ
Corner pub opposite the newly rebuilt Lyceum Theatre, with an enterprising range of guest beers including microbreweries' products. There is also an upstairs bar.
◖ ⊖

Lamb & Flag ☆
33 Rose Street
☎ (0171) 497 9504
11–11 (10.45 Fri & Sat); 12–10.30 Sun
Courage Best Bitter, Directors; John Smith's Bitter; Wadworth 6X; guest beers Ⓗ
Reputed to be the oldest pub in Covent Garden, this historic pub was used by the poet Dryden (who was mugged in the side alley). Samuel Butler lived nearby. No food Sun.
◖ ⊖ (Leicester Sq)

Marquess of Anglesey
39 Bow Street
☎ (0171) 240 3216
11–11; 12–10.30 Sun
Young's Bitter, Special, Ram Rod, Winter Warmer, seasonal beers Ⓗ
Refurbished corner pub, handy for all local attractions. The upstairs bar and restaurant are frequented by musicians.
Q ◖ ▶ ⊖

Prince of Wales
150–151 Drury Lane
☎ (0171) 836 5183
11–11; 12–10.30 Sun
Courage Best Bitter, Directors; Theakston Best Bitter, XB, Old Peculier; guest beers Ⓗ
Roomy corner pub with bare floors; formerly 'Charlie's'.
◖ ▶ ⊖

WC2: Lincoln's Inn Fields

Seven Stars
53 Carey Street
☎ (0171) 242 8521
11–11; closed Sat & Sun
Courage Best Bitter, Directors Ⓗ
Small, spartan, beer house in the shadow of the Royal Courts of Justice. Unimproved and excellent, it is frequented by lawyers and their clients.
Q ◖ ▶ ⊖ (Chancery Lane)

WC2: St Giles

Angel
61 St Giles High Street
☎ (0171) 240 2876
11–11; closed Sun
Courage Best Bitter, Directors; Theakston Best Bitter, XB Ⓗ
Reputedly haunted local near Centre Point. Condemned felons were allegedly offered a drink here on the way to Tyburn from Newgate. Q 🏵 ◖ ▶ ⊖ (Tottenham Ct Rd) ✦

E1: Spitalfields

Alma
41 Spelman Street
☎ (0171) 247 5604
11–11; 12–3, 7–10.30 Sun
Fuller's London Pride; guest beers Ⓗ
Comfortable, backstreet pub with two ever-changing guest beers from small breweries. A 'museum' of local history, once a brewery. ◖ ⇌ (Liverpool St) ⊖ (Aldgate E) ✦

Pride of Spitalfields
3 Heneage Street
☎ (0171) 247 8933
11–11; 12–10.30 Sun
Crouch Vale Woodham IPA; Fuller's London Pride, ESB; guest beer Ⓗ
Small pub, just off Brick Lane, featuring many photographs of the old East End. The beer range may vary.
🏛 🏵 ◖ ⇌ (Liverpool St) ⊖ (Aldgate E)

E1: Wapping

White Swan & Cuckoo
97 Wapping Lane
☎ (0171) 488 4959
11–11; 12–10.30 Sun
Courage Best Bitter, Directors; Ruddles Best Bitter; Webster's Yorkshire Bitter; guest beer Ⓗ
Comfortable local decorated with old photos, ships' crests, wood panelling and bare floorboards. Thai dishes a speciality. Reasonable beer prices. ◖ ▶ ⊖

E1: Whitechapel

Black Bull
199 Whitechapel Road
☎ (0171) 247 6707
11–11; 12–10.30 Sun
Beer range varies Ⓗ
Down-to-earth East End boozer in the heart of Whitechapel. The beers usually come from Ridleys and Leyland breweries and often include a mild. ◖ ⊖

Lord Rodney's Head

285 Whitechapel Road
☎ (0171) 247 9795
11–11; 12–10.30 Sun
B&T Shefford Bitter, SOD, SOS, seasonal beers Ⓗ
Long, narrow, clock-filled pub of considerable character. It has a bar billiards table and hosts regular live music.
⊖ ♣ ⌂

E3: Bow

Coborn Arms

8 Coborn Road
☎ (0181) 980 3793
11–11 (may close winter afternoons); 12–10.30 Sun
Young's Bitter, Special, seasonal beers Ⓗ
Comfortable local decorated with old photos and old local maps. Wheelchair WC.
❀ ◐ Ɗ ﴾ ⊖ (Bow Rd) ♣

E4: Chingford

Bull & Crown

The Green ☎ (0181) 528 5773
11–11; 12–5, 7–10.30 Sun
Ridleys IPA; Tetley Bitter Ⓗ
Large 'French château'-style pub with one large bar.
Weekday lunches. ⋈ ◐ ⇌ P

King's Head

King's Head Hill
☎ (0181) 529 1655
12–11; 12–3, 7–10.30 Sun
Adnams Broadside; Ind Coope Burton Ale; Tetley Bitter; Young's Bitter, Special; guest beers Ⓗ
One-bar, comfortable pub of 18th-century origin. Occasional beer festivals. ❀ ◐ ⇌ ♣ P

E5: Clapton

Anchor & Hope

15 High Hill Ferry
☎ (0181) 806 1730
11–3, 5.30–11; 12–3, 7–10.30 Sun
Fuller's London Pride, ESB Ⓗ
Friendly pub, next to the river. Its very small bar gets busy.
❀ ⇌ ♣

Prince of Wales

146 Lea Bridge Road
☎ (0181) 533 3463
11–11; 12–10.30 Sun
Young's Bitter, Special, seasonal beers Ⓗ
Large riverside pub with a traditional public bar and a comfortable saloon bar.
❀ ◐ Ɗ ⊞ ⇌ ♣ P

E7: Forest Gate

Old Spotted Dog

212 Upton Lane
☎ (0181) 472 1794
11–3, 5.30 (7 Sat)–11; 12–4, 7–10.30 Sun
Marston's Pedigree; Ruddles County; guest beers Ⓗ

Large pub, with many nooks and crannies, of 16th-century origin. A large extension houses a family room and restaurant. Varied ciders and perries. ⋈ ☞ ❀ ◐ Ɗ ⇌ ⌂

E8: Hackney

Marksman

254 Hackney Road
☎ (0171) 739 7393
11–11; 12–10.30 Sun
Everards Old Original; Ruddles County; Wadworth 6X Ⓗ
Small, one-bar pub with a military theme; a popular local and an oasis in this area.
⇌ (Cambridge Heath)

Prince Arthur

95 Forest Road
☎ (0171) 254 3439
11.30–11; 11.30–4, 7–11 Sat; 12–3, 7–10.30 Sun
Fuller's London Pride; guest beers Ⓗ
Small, sidestreet pub with a paved outside drinking area: an ever-present Guide entry since 1984 (as Lady Diana).
❀ ◐ Ɗ ⇌ ♣

E9: Hackney

Penhurst Arms

25 Penhurst Road
☎ (0181) 986 8089
11 (1 winter Mon–Fri)–11; 12–10.30 Sun
Beer range varies Ⓗ
Backstreet local which may close lunchtime if quiet. The beers change regularly.
❀ ♣

Royal Inn on the Park

111 Lauriston Road
12–2.30, 6–11; 12–11 Sat & summer; 12–10.30 Sun
Boddingtons Bitter; Fuller's London Pride, ESB; guest beers Ⓗ
Large, one-bar pub on the edge of Victoria Park. Live music.
⋈ ❀ ◐ Ɗ

Royal Standard

84 Victoria Park Road
☎ (0171) 985 3224
12–3, 5.15–midnight; 12–midnight Fri & Sat; 12–10.30 Sun
Draught Bass; Courage Best Bitter; Fuller's London Pride, ESB; Marston's Pedigree Ⓗ
Large, comfortable local in a residential area. Modernisation has not spoilt its Victorian charm. Eve meals by arrangement. Q ❀ ◐ ♣ P

E11: Leytonstone

Bell

468 High Road
☎ (0181) 539 3704
11–11; 12–10.30 Sun
Draught Bass Ⓗ

Traditional, three-roomed pub, now in the colours of the 'East London Pub Company'.
Q ❀ ◐ Ɗ ⊞ ⇌ (High Rd) ♣

Birkbeck Tavern

45 Langthorne Road
☎ (0181) 539 2584
11–11; 12–10.30 Sun
Draught Bass; Courage Best Bitter; guest beers Ⓗ
Popular, backstreet, community pub with a pleasant garden. Busy on Leyton Orient match days. Local CAMRA Pub of the Year 1996. ❀ ⊞ ⊖ (Leyton) ♣

E11: Wanstead

Duke of Edinburgh

Nightingale Lane
☎ (0181) 989 0014
12–11; 12–10.30 Sun
Eldridge Pope Royal Oak; Young's Bitter; guest beer Ⓗ
Excellent, well-run, backstreet local, fielding two darts teams. Large screen satellite TV for sporting events. No food Sun.
❀ ◐ ⊖ ♣

E14: Isle of Dogs

Cat & Canary

Fishermans Walk, Canary Wharf ☎ (0171) 512 9187
11–9; 12–3 Sat; closed Sun
Fuller's Chiswick, London Pride, ESB, seasonal beers Ⓗ
Modern, single-bar pub, with split-levels and alcoves, furnished with old church pews. Very busy weekday lunchtime and eves. Right on the dockside, it boasts views of warehouses and preserved ships. ◐ Ɗ ⇌ (Limehouse) ⊖ (Canary Wharf DLR) ♣

E14: Limehouse

Oporto Tavern

43 West India Dock Road
11–11; 12–10.30 Sun
Fuller's London Pride; Greene King IPA; Jennings Bitter; guest beers Ⓗ
Small, single-bar pub, with a lively local atmosphere. The neat, wood-panelled decor features old prints of the area's docks and canals. ◐ ⇌ (Limehouse) ⊖ (West Ferry DLR)

E14: Stepney

Queen's Head

8 Flamborough Street
☎ (0171) 790 6481
11–2.30, 5.30–11; 12–3, 7.30–11 Sun; 12–3, 7–10.30 Sun
Young's Bitter, Special, seasonal beers Ⓗ
Backstreet local with a London 'Fives' dartboard. A real oasis; this is the pub where the Queen Mother pulled a pint –

see the plaque. ◖ ⊞ ⇌
(Limehouse) ⊖ (DLR) ♣

E15: Stratford

Goldengrove
146 The Grove
☎ (0181) 519 0750
11–11; 12–10.30 Sun
**Courage Directors; Fuller's
London Pride; Theakston Best
Bitter; Younger Scotch; guest
beers** H
Large, single-bar pub with a
good atmosphere; often busy.
Limited parking.
Q ❀ ◖ ▶ ⇌ ⊖ P ⌦

E17: Walthamstow

College Arms
807 Forest Road
☎ (0181) 531 8001
11–11; 12–10.30 Sun
**Fuller's London Pride; Gale's
HSB; Greene King IPA,
Abbot** H; **guest beers** H/G
Ex-Wetherspoons house,
probably the best pub
Wetherspoons has sold.
◖ ▶ ⇌ (Wood St)

Village
31 Orford Road
☎ (0181) 581 9982
11–11; 12–10.30 Sun
**Belhaven St Andrew's Ale;
Ward's Thorne BB, Best Bitter;
guest beers** H
Small pub, mainly used by a
younger clientele: an oasis in
this area.
Q ☼ ❀ ◖ ⇌ (Central) ⊖

Barking

Britannia
1 Church Road (near A123)
☎ (0181) 594 1305
11–3, 5–11; 11–11 Sat; 12–3, 7–10.30
(maybe all day) Sun
**Young's Bitter, Special, Ram
Rod, Winter Warmer, seasonal
beers** H
Three-bar pub: a roomy,
comfortable lounge with a
connecting private bar and a
more basic public. Note the
caryatids on the exterior. Local
CAMRA *Pub of the Year* 1997.
❀ ◖ ⊞ ⇌ ⊖ ♣ P

Hornchurch

Chequers
North Street (near A124)
☎ (01708) 442094
11–11, 11–3, 5.30–11 Fri & Sat; 12–
4.30, 7–10.30 Sun
**Friary Meux BB; Young's
Bitter; guest beer** H
Victorian pub with a friendly
atmosphere in a residential
area. The guest beer is usually
on the strong side; the house
beer comes from Ind Coope.
The beer prices are very
competitive. Weekday lunches.
◖ ⇌ (Emerson Pk) ♣ P

Pit Bar
(Queen's Theatre)
Billet Lane (near A124)
☎ (01708) 456118
12–3, 6–11; 12–3, 7–10.30 Sun
**Greene King IPA, Abbot,
seasonal beers** H; **Hop Back
Summer Lightning; guest
beers** G
Modern theatre bar open to the
public. Jazz Sun lunch, when
beer prices are increased from
their usual low level; closed
Sun eve if there's no
performance. Meals served
10–9.30. Q ☼ ◖ ▶ ⇌
(Emerson Pk) ⊖ P

Ilford

Prince of Wales
63 Green Lane (A1083, ½ mile E
of centre) ☎ (0181) 478 1326
11–3, 5.15–11; 11–11 Fri & Sat;
12–10.30 Sun
**Ind Coope Burton Ale; Tetley
Bitter** H
Pleasant local, attracting a
wide range of customers, with
three distinctive drinking areas
and a small, secluded garden.
The house beer is from
Carlsberg-Tetley. Weekday
lunches. ❀ ◖ ⊞ ♣ P

Rose & Crown
16 Ilford Hill (A118, near A406)
☎ (0181) 478 7104
11–11; 12–10.30 Sun
**Marston's Pedigree; Morland
Old Speckled Hen; Tetley
Bitter; guest beers** H
One-bar pub with distinct
drinking areas: the first Tetley
Festival Ale House in the
London area. Up to four
independent guest beers –
unusual for the area; the house
beer is from Carlsberg-Tetley.
No food Sun or Sat eve.
Limited parking.
❀ ◖ ▶ ⇌ ♣ ⌂ P

Woodford Green

Cricketers
299–301 High Road (A11)
☎ (0181) 504 2734
11–3, 5.30–11; 11–11 Sat; 12–10.30 Sun
**McMullen AK, Country,
Gladstone, seasonal beers** H
Pleasant, comfortable,
suburban local with a wood-
panelled lounge and a more
basic public bar. Good value
pensioners' lunches weekdays
(no food Sun). ❀ ◖ ⊞ P

Traveller's Friend
496–498 High Road (A104)
☎ (0181) 504 2435
11–11; 12–10.30 Sun
**Courage Best Bitter, Directors;
Ridleys IPA; guest beers** H
Excellent, small, friendly,
wood-panelled pub with many
original snob screens: a little
gem. Tiny car park.
Q ◖ ⊖ P

N1: Canonbury

Compton Arms
4 Compton Avenue
☎ (0171) 359 6883
12–11; 12–10.30 Sun
Greene King IPA, Abbot H
Small, friendly local in cottage
style; a country pub in central
London which can get very
busy at weekends. Meals
served 12–9. Small courtyard
garden.
Q ❀ ◖ ⇌ (Highbury &
Islington) ⊖

Earl of Radnor
106 Mildmay Grove
☎ (0171) 241 0318
11–11; 12–10.30 Sun
Fuller's London Pride, ESB H;
seasonal beers H/G
Cosy locals' bar with wrought
iron fittings and Art Deco
glass. Pavement tables for
outside drinking. ❀ ◖ ▶ ⇌
(Dalston Kingsland) ♣

Marquess Tavern
32 Canonbury Street
☎ (0171) 354 2975
11–11; 12–10.30 Sun
Young's Bitter, Special H,
Winter Warmer G/H
Magnificent, 19th-century local
serving home-cooked food.
Pavement tables outside.
🏚 Q ❀ ◖ ⇌ (Essex Rd) ⊖
(Highbury & Islington)

N1: Hoxton

Wenlock Arms
26 Wenlock Road
☎ (0171) 608 3406
11.30–11; 12–10.30 Sun
**Nethergate IPA; Tetley Bitter;
guest beers** H
North London's premier real
ale free house offers an ever-
changing range of ales, many
from new micros. Live jazz Sun
lunch. Handy for the Regent's
Canal. Local CAMRA *Pub of the
Year* 1995 and '96. Cider and
perry are both usually
available.
🏚 ⇌ (Old St) ⊖ ⌂ ⊟

N3: Finchley Central

Joiners Arms
51 Ballards Lane
☎ (0181) 346 8171
11–11; 12–10.30 Sun
**Draught Bass; Fuller's London
Pride** H
Comfortable, two-bar locals'
roadhouse retaining many
original fittings. A quiet refuge
from Tesco's next door.
❀ ◖ ⊞ ⊖

N6: Highgate

Gatehouse
1 North Road
☎ (0181) 340 8054
11–11; 12–10.30 Sun
Courage Directors; Fuller's London Pride; Theakston Best Bitter; Younger Scotch; guest beers H
Closed for many years, this famous, haunted pub was tastefully resurrected by Wetherspoons in 1994. It features a large bar with alcoves, plus an eating area displaying historical information. It can be very busy, especially in summer, and attracts a very cosmopolitan crowd.
Q ◑ ▶ ➍ ⑂

N8: Hornsey

Toll Gate
26–30 Turnpike Lane
☎ (0181) 889 9085
11–11; 12–10.30 Sun
Courage Directors; Fuller's London Pride; Theakston Best Bitter; Younger Scotch; guest beers H
Large Wetherspoons shop conversion with the standard, book-filled interior and accoutrements. It has a deservedly high reputation with locals, but it may be punishingly busy at weekends. Good range of guest beers.
❀ ◑ ▶ ➍ (Turnpike Lane) ⑂

N9: Lower Edmonton

Lamb
52–54 Church Street
☎ (0181) 887 0128
11–11; 12–10.30 Sun
Courage Directors; Fuller's London Pride; Theakston Best Bitter, XB; guest beers H
Familiar Wetherspoons conversion of restaurant premises, with wood-panelling much in evidence. The pub is named after the 19th-century poet who lived locally. Two guest beers. Wheelchair WC. Patio for outside drinking.
Q ❀ ◑ ▶ ♿ ➍ (Edmonton Green) ♣ ⌂

William IV
102 Hertford Road
☎ (0181) 807 2605
12–11; 12–10.30 Sun
Ind Coope Burton Ale; Young's Bitter; guest beer H
Attractive, Edwardian, street-corner local, noted for its floral displays, fine tiled exterior, etched glass and ironwork. The guest beer is a Tapster's Choice ale. No food is served at weekends. ❀ ◑ ▶ ♿ ➍ (Edmonton Green) ♣

N12: North Finchley

Tally Ho
749 High Road
☎ (0181) 445 4390
11–11; 12–10.30 Sun
Courage Directors; Fuller's London Pride; Theakston Best Bitter; guest beers H
Imposing pub, rescued by Wetherspoons from years of decline. The island bar serves three distinct drinking areas. The upstairs bar/restaurant is no-smoking.
🏠 🐾 ❀ ◑ ▶ ⌂ ⑂

N16: Stoke Newington

Rochester Castle
145 Stoke Newington High Street ☎ (0171) 249 6016
11–11; 12–10.30 Sun
Courage Directors; Fuller's London Pride; Greene King Abbot; Theakston Best Bitter; Younger Scotch; guest beers H
Large local: a friendly Wetherspoons conversion, boasting two full walls of original listed tiling; even the steps are listed. It recently reverted to its original name (formerly the Tanners Hall).
Q ❀ ◑ ▶ ➍ ⌂ ⑂

N21: Winchmore Hill

Dog & Duck
74 Hoppers Road
☎ (0181) 886 1987
12–11; 12–10.30 Sun
Boddingtons Bitter; guest beers H
Little pub with a loyal local following. The three guest beers usually include a Whitbread seasonal special. Shove-ha'penny played.
🏠 ❀ ➍ (Palmers Green) ♣

Orange Tree
18 Highfield Road
☎ (0181) 360 4853
12–11; 12–10.30 Sun
Adnams Bitter; Greene King IPA; guest beer H
Friendly, down-to-earth local, off the beaten track but worth seeking out. Limited parking.
❀ ◑ ➍ ♣ P

N22: Wood Green

Starting Gate
Station Road
☎ (0181) 889 9789
12–11; 12–10.30 Sun
Adnams Bitter; Ind Coope Burton Ale; Tetley Bitter; Young's Bitter; guest beers H
Named after the former Alexandra Palace racecourse, this pub has 1930s wood decor, alcoves with panoramic paintings, and exquisite etched-glass windows and interior panels. It attracts a local crowd, is often busy and may be very smoky. No food Sun.
❀ ◑ ➍ (Alexandra Palace)

Try also: Palace Gates, Palace Gates Rd (Free)

Barnet

King William IV
18 Hadley Highstone, Hadley
☎ (0181) 449 6728
11–3, 5.30–11; 12–4, 7–10.30 Sun
Benskins BB; Ind Coope Burton Ale; guest beer H
Unspoilt, 17th-century pub: three distinct drinking areas, mercifully free of fruit machines and piped muzak. Extensive lunchtime menu. The house beer is brewed by Ushers. 🏠 Q ❀ ◑ P

Olde Mitre
58 High Street
☎ (0181) 449 6582
11.30–11; 12–3, 7–11 Sat; 12–3, 7–10.30 Sun
Adnams Bitter; Ind Coope Burton Ale; Tetley Bitter; guest beers H
Attractive, 17th-century listed building, once a coaching inn. The rota of guest beers usually includes a stout. It may close Sat afternoon if Barnet FC are at home. No food Sun.
Q ◑ ➍ (High Barnet) ♣ P

White Lion
50 St Albans Road
☎ (0181) 449 4560
11–2.30, 5–11; 12–3, 6–11 Sat; 12–4, 7–10.30 Sun
Greene King IPA, Abbot; Marston's Pedigree; Morland Old Speckled Hen; Wadworth 6X; guest beer H
Comfortable, rejuvenated free house on the edge of town. The house beer, Healy's Sanctuary, is ABC Best Bitter. The beer range may vary. No food Sun.
❀ ◑ ♣ P

Enfield Town

Stag
1 Little Park Gardens
☎ (0181) 363 1836
11–11; 12–5, 7–10.30 Sun
Draught Bass; Fuller's London Pride; Greene King IPA; Tetley Bitter H
Deservedly popular, town-centre pub by the bus terminus. TV for major sports. The upstairs restaurant (open Wed–Sun) doubles as a function room. No food Sun eve.
❀ ◑ ▶ ➍ (Enfield Chase) ♣

North-West London

NW1: Camden Town

Spread Eagle
141 Albert Street
☎ (0171) 267 1410
11–11; 12–10.30 Sun
Young's Bitter, Ram Rod, Special, seasonal beers H
Friendly pub near Camden Lock market, built in 1858 and expanded into adjoining buildings in the 1930s and in 1963. Now altered into one bar, it retains different areas. Eve meals Sun–Thu.
❀ ◑ ▶ ≉ (Camden Rd) ⊖

NW1: Euston

Head of Steam
1 Eversholt Street (E side of bus station) ☎ (0171) 388 2221
12–11; 12–10.30 Sun
B&T Dragonslayer; Draught Bass; Highgate Dark; Hop Back Summer Lightning; O'Hanlon's Red Ale; guest beers H
Upstairs bar adjacent to Euston station, with much railway memorabilia. Guest beers are often from northern micros. Children's certificate until 9; eve meals until 8.30.
◑ ▶ ≉ ⊖ ♣ ♡ ✲

NW1: Marylebone

Perseverance
11 Shroton Street
☎ (0171) 723 7469
11–11; 12–3, 7–10.30 Sun
Draught Bass; Fuller's London Pride; guest beer H
Friendly, well-presented, former 19th-century coaching inn with a horseshoe bar. It has suffered from two major floods in the past year, but is still as good as ever. The guest beer is sometimes a mild. Eve meals are not always available.
❀ ◑ ▶ ≉ ⊖

NW2: Cricklewood

Beaten Docket
50–56 Cricklewood Broadway
☎ (0181) 450 2972
11–11; 12–10.30 Sun
Courage Directors; Fuller's London Pride; Greene King Abbot; Younger Scotch; guest beer H
Large Wetherspoons pub on the main road in an area not known for quality beer. It can get busy at weekends.
❀ ◑ ▶ ⅍ ≉ ✲

NW3: Belsize Park

Washington
50 Englands Lane
☎ (0171) 722 6118
11–11; 12–10.30 Sun
Ind Coope Burton Ale; Marston's Pedigree; Tetley Bitter; Young's Bitter; guest beer H
Magnificent Victorian 'gin palace', dating from 1865, with much original tilework, etched glass and mirrors. Home to several sports teams and the Hampstead Comedy Club. Open 10am for breakfast. Shove-ha'penny is played.
◑ ⊖ ♣

NW3: Hampstead

Duke of Hamilton
23–25 New End
☎ (0171) 794 0258
11–11; 12–10.30 Sun
Fuller's London Pride, ESB; guest beers H
Friendly, single-bar pub, just off busy Heath St, popular with locals and patrons of the New End Theatre next door.
❀ ⊖

Flask
14 Flask Walk
☎ (0171) 435 4580
11–11; 12–10.30 Sun
Young's Bitter, Special, seasonal beers H
Famous Victorian watering-hole in a picturesque location, with a rare, genuine public bar. It attracts young and old alike.
Q ❀ ◑ ◱ ⅍ ⊖

Holly Bush ☆
22 Holly Mount
☎ (0171) 435 2892
11–3 (4 Sat), 5.30–11; 12–3, 7–10.30 Sun
Benskins BB; Ind Coope Burton Ale; Tetley Bitter; guest beer H
Secluded local, converted from stables in 1896. The traditional front bar is gas-lit and features some interesting Benskins memorabilia. Regular live music. No food Mon. Shove-ha'penny is played.
♨ Q ⅏ ◑ ♣ ♠

NW5: Kentish Town

Pineapple
51 Leverton Street
☎ (0171) 209 4961
12 (11 Sat)–11; 12–10.30 Sun
Greene King IPA; Marston's Pedigree; Theakston Best Bitter H
Cosy, Victorian backstreet local with a loyal following. Occasional quiz nights and banjo music.
≉ ⊖ ♣

NW6: Kilburn

Queen's Arms
1 Kilburn High Road
☎ (0171) 624 5735
11–11; 12–10.30 Sun
Young's Bitter, Special, seasonal beers H
Pub built in 1958: three lounge bars knocked into one, with numerous old prints and wood panelling. Unusual roof garden. Eve meals weekdays. Small car park. ❀ ◑ ▶ ◱ ≉ (High Rd) ⊖ (Park) ♣ P

NW10: Harlesden

Grand Junction Arms
Acton Lane
☎ (0181) 965 5670
11–11; 12–10.30 Sun
Young's Bitter, Special, seasonal beers H
Spacious, three-bar pub with moorings on the Grand Union Canal. The garden contains children's play equipment. Good value food served all day.
Q ❀ ◑ ▶ ◱ ⅍ ≉ ⊖ ♣ P

NW11: Golders Green

White Swan
243 Golders Green Road
☎ (0181) 458 2036
11–11; 12–10.30 Sun
Ind Coope Burton Ale; Tetley Bitter; Young's Bitter H
Friendly, welcoming local in an under-pubbed area, retaining a public bar atmosphere. Attractive garden; excellent home-cooked food.
♨ ❀ ◑ ▶ ⊖ (Brent Cross) ♣ P

Edgware

Change of Hart
21 High Street
☎ (0181) 952 0039
11–11; 12–10.30 Sun
Marston's Pedigree; Tetley Bitter; guest beers H
Formerly the White Hart coaching inn, now three areas around an island bar. The outdoor drinking area is next to Dean's Brook. Eve meals until 7pm. Q ❀ ◑ ▶ ◱ ⊖ P

Harrow Weald

Seven Balls
749 Kenton Lane
☎ (0181) 954 0261
11–11; 12–10.30 Sun
Benskins BB; Tetley Bitter; guest beer H
Old coaching inn attracting a good mix of locals and passing trade. Tapster's Choice guest beer. ❀ ◑ ▶ ◱ ♣ P ✲

Hatch End

Moon & Sixpence
250 Uxbridge Road
☎ (0181) 420 1074
11–11; 12–10.30 Sun
Courage Directors; Fuller's London Pride; Theakston Best Bitter; Younger Scotch; guest beers 🄷
Popular, smaller than average, Wetherspoons pub, attracting a good mix. Pleasant garden. Up to two guest beers: occasional beer festivals.
Q ❀ ◖ ◗ ⇌ ⚡

Pinner

Queen's Head
31 High Street
☎ (0181) 868 9844
11–3.30, 5–11; 12–3.30, 7–10.30 Sun
Benskins BB; Ind Coope Burton Ale; Marston's Pedigree; Tetley Bitter; Young's Special 🄷
Grade I-listed building, first obtaining its licence to accommodate patrons of the first Pinner Fair way back in the early 14th century. A typically olde-worlde pub, it is well worth a visit.
♨ Q ❀ ◖ P

Try also: Oddfellows, Waxwell Lane (Carlsberg-Tetley)

Ruislip Common

Six Bells
Ducks Hill Road
☎ (01895) 639466
11–11; 12–10.30 Sun
Benskins BB; Tetley Bitter; Young's Bitter; guest beers 🄷
Grade I-listed building (including the outside gents), which has been tastefully extended in recent years. The original part has a very inviting open fireplace and a stone-flagged floor. There is also an outdoor skittle alley. Well worth a visit.
♨ Q ☕ ❀ ◖ ◗ ♿ ▲ ♣ P ⚡

South Harrow

Fornax & Firkin
Northolt Road
☎ (0181) 422 0505
11–11 (11.40 Thu, midnight Fri & Sat); 12–10.30 Sun
Firkin Starbright, Fornax, Golden Glory, Dogbolter; guest beer 🄷
Large, one-bar pub previously called the Constellation (Fornax means a constellation of seven stars). Popular with students; live rock music is staged Tue, Thu and Sat and a disco is held Fri.
❀ ◖ ◗ ♿ ⊖ ♣ ⌂ P ⚡

Stanmore

Malthouse
7 Stanmore Hill
☎ (0181) 420 7265
11–11; 12–10.30 Sun
Boddingtons Bitter; guest beers 🄷
Split-level, two-roomer which has greatly improved the real ale choice in the area. Often busy weekend eves, it is a real community pub. Up to three guest beers, which are usually from independents.
❀ ◖ ⊖ ♣

Vine
154 Stanmore Hill
☎ (0181) 954 4676
11–11; 12–10.30 Sun
Benskins BB; Marston's Pedigree; Tetley Bitter; guest beers 🄷
Old coaching inn pleasantly refurbished and retaining separate drinking areas.
❀ ◖ ♣ P

Wealdstone

Royal Oak
60 Peel Road
☎ (0181) 427 3122
11–11; 12–10.30 Sun
Adnams Bitter; Ind Coope Burton Ale; Tetley Bitter; guest beers 🄷
Fine example of a 1930s pub, extended into a pleasant conservatory. The large, airy lounge retains separate drinking areas. Small car park.
❀ ◖ ⊟ ♿ ⇌ (Harrow & Wealdstone) ⊖ ♣ P

Sarsen Stone
32 High Street
☎ (0181) 863 8533
11–11; 12–10.30 Sun
Courage Directors; Fuller's London Pride; Younger Scotch; guest beers 🄷
Long, narrow, town-centre pub frequented by both local workers and seasoned drinkers. Occasional beer festivals. Q ◖ ◗ ⇌ (Harrow & Wealdstone) ⊖ ⚡

South-East London

SE1: Bankside

Founders Arms
52 Hopton Street
☎ (0171) 928 1899
11–11; 12–10.30 Sun
Young's Bitter, Special, seasonal beer 🄷
Modern, riverside pub close to Blackfriars Bridge, with fine views across the Thames to St Paul's. No meals Sun or Mon eves.
❀ ◖ ◗ ♿ ⇌ ⊖

SE1: Borough

George Inn ☆
77 Borough High Street
☎ (0171) 407 2056
11–11; 12–10.30 Sun
Boddingtons Bitter; Castle Eden Ale; Flowers Original; guest beers 🄷
Large, 17th-century, galleried inn owned by the National Trust. Popular with tourists and commuters, although prices are high. A house beer from nearby Bishops Brewery is sold; monthly beer festivals. Restaurant open Mon, Wed and Fri. Q ❀ ◖ ◗ ⇌ (London Bridge) ⊖ ♣

Lord Clyde
27 Clennan Street
☎ (0171) 407 3397
11–11; 11–4, 7–11 Sat; 12–3, 7–10,30 Sun
Bishops Cathedral, Thirsty Willies; Ruddles Best Bitter; Webster's Yorkshire Bitter; Young's Bitter; guest beer 🄷
Traditional, two-roomed pub which supports the local brewery, Bishops. Superb tiled exterior.
◖ ⇌ (London Bridge) ⊖ ♣

Wheatsheaf
6 Stoney Street
☎ (0171) 407 1514
11–11; 12–3, 7–10.30 Sun
Courage Best Bitter; Bishops Thirsty Willies, Willies Revenge, seasonal beers; guest beers 🄷
Excellent, two-bar, market pub, a regular outlet for the nearby Bishops Brewery. A dark beer is always available. Occasional real cider. No food weekends.
◖ ⇌ (London Bridge) ⊖ ⌂

SE1: Lambeth

Windmill
44 Lambeth High Street
11–11; closed Sat & Sun
Courage Best Bitter, Directors; Wadworth 6X 🄷
Very friendly Courage local. The decor shows scenes of old Lambeth and lots of photos of the fire service (the pub is behind a large fire station).
◖ ◗ ⇌ (Vauxhall) ⊖ (Lambeth N)

SE1: Southwark

Ship
68 Borough Road
☎ (0171) 403 7059
11–11; 12–3, 8–10.30 Sun
Fuller's Chiswick, London Pride, ESB, seasonal beers 🄷
Popular, long, narrow, single-bar pub with a maritime decor. No food Sun eve. ❀ ◖ ◗ ⇌ (London Bridge) ⊖ (Borough)

SE1: Waterloo

King's Arms
25 Roupell Street
☎ (0171) 207 0784
11–11; 12–3, 8–10.30 Sun
Adnams Bitter; Marston's Pedigree; Ruddles Best Bitter; Tetley Bitter H
Small, two-bar pub in the shadow of Waterloo East station. No food weekends.
◑ ⬚ ≢ ⊖

SE3: Blackheath

Bitter Experience
129 Lee Road
11 (10 Sat)–9.30 (10 Fri & Sat)
Beer range varies G
Well-established, independent local off-licence which always has a choice of at least five real ales on tap and an extensive range of bottled beers from the UK and overseas. Helpful staff.
≢ (Lee)

Hare & Billet
Hare & Billet Road
11–11; 12–10.30 Sun
Boddingtons Bitter; Flowers Original; Whitbread Abroad Cooper H; **guest beers** H/G
Long-standing theme pub, an original Hogshead Ale House that has retained its charm and history. Well worth a visit.
Q ◑ ≢

SE6: Catford

Rutland
55 Perry Hill
☎ (0181) 291 9426
11–11; 12–10.30 Sun
Adnams Broadside; Draught Bass; Fuller's London Pride; Young's Bitter, Special, Winter Warmer H
Large, open-plan free house featuring live music most nights (mainly jazz). ◑ ≢

SE8: Deptford

Crystal Palace Tavern
105 Tanners Hill
4–midnight; 3–2am Fri; 1pm–2am Sat; 1–10.30 Sun
Beer range varies H
Friendly local hosting summer barbecues, plus live music Thu–Sat. Deservedly popular.
🎪 ⛺ ⊛ ≢ (New Cross Gate)
⟳ ⛨

Dog & Bell
116 Prince Street
☎ (0181) 692 5664
11.30–11; 12–10.30 Sun
Fuller's London Pride, ESB, seasonal beers; guest beers H
1993 and '96 SE London CAMRA *Pub of the Year*: a friendly, backstreet local. Home-cooked food (weekdays)

at reasonable prices includes a vegetarian choice. Occasional real ciders.
🎪 Q ⊛ ◑ ▮ ⬚ ≢ ♣

Old Manor House
58 Bush Road
11–11; 12–10.30 Sun
Young's Bitter, Special; guest beers H
Lovely little local amidst the modern Surrey Quays area.
⊖ (Surrey Quays) ♣

SE9: Eltham

Howerd Club
447 Rochester Way
☎ (0181) 856 7212
7.30–11; 12–3, 7.30–11 Sat; 12–2, 7.30–10.30 Sun
Fuller's London Pride; Shepherd Neame Master Brew Bitter; guest beer H
Well-turned-out community centre attached to St Barnabas church hall. It is named after Frankie Howerd who lived locally. CAMRA national *Club of the Year* 1996.
Q ⊛ ≢

SE10: Greenwich

Admiral Hardy
7 College Approach
☎ (0181) 858 6452
11–11; 12–10.30 Sun
Shepherd Neame Master Brew Bitter, Best Bitter, Spitfire; Marston's Pedigree; guest beers H
Friendly, town-centre pub, unusual for its central bar; a great place to rest while shopping in the market next door. Meals served 12–5.
⊛ ◑ ≢

Ashburnham Arms
25 Ashburnham Grove
☎ (0181) 692 2007
12–3, 6–11; 12–3, 7–10.30 Sun
Shepherd Neame Master Brew Bitter, Best Bitter, Spitfire, Bishops Finger or **Porter** H
Excellent, backstreet local with a good reputation for food (eve meals Tue and Fri). A former London CAMRA *Pub of the Year*. ⊛ ◑ ♣

Richard I ☆
52–54 Royal Hill
☎ (0181) 692 2996
11–11; 12–10.30 Sun
Young's Bitter, Special, seasonal beers H
Unspoilt, two-bar, bow-windowed pub, displaying an interesting collection of photographs and prints. A welcome relief from the bustle of Greenwich market. No food Sun; summer barbecues. Shove-ha'penny can be played.
Q ⊛ ◑ ⬚ ≢ ♣

SE13: Lewisham

Hogshead
354 Lewisham High Street
☎ (0181) 690 2054
11–11; 12–10.30 Sun
Boddingtons Bitter; Whitbread Fuggles IPA H; **guest beers** H/G
Busy pub near Lewisham Hospital with a very friendly atmosphere. No food Sun.
⊛ ◑ ≢ (Ladywell) ♣ ⟳

SE17: Walworth

Beehive
60–62 Carter Street
☎ (0171) 703 4992
11–11; 12–10.30 Sun
Courage Best Bitter, Directors; Fuller's London Pride; Wadworth 6X H
Popular local with a single island bar offering a large selection of malt whiskies and good food (served all day).
⊛ ◑ ▶ ⊖ (Kennington) ♣

Tankard
178 Walworth Road
☎ (0171) 703 4006
11–11; 12–10.30 Sun
Greene King IPA, Abbot H
Recently refurbished pub with a mock Tudor exterior, next door to the Labour Party HQ. No food Sat. Live music Sun.
◑ ≢ (Elephant & Castle) ⊖ ♣

SE18: Shooters Hill

Bull
151 Shooters Hill
11–3, 5.30–11; 12.30–3.30, 7–10.30 Sun
Courage Best Bitter, Directors H
Dating from 1749, and rebuilt in 1888, this is one of the few unspoilt pubs in an area dominated by houses acquired by Courage from the former Beasley Brewery. It has recently seen a revival. No food Sun. ◑

SE18: Woolwich

Edinburgh Castle
110 Samuel Street
☎ (0181) 317 0764
12–11; 12–10.30 Sun
Courage Best Bitter, Directors; guest beer H
300-year-old, family pub, hidden behind a council estate and well worth seeking out.
≢ (Woolwich Dockyard) ♣

Prince Albert (Rose's)
49 Hare Street
☎ (0181) 854 1538
11–11 (12–7 bank hols); 12–3 (closed eve) Sun
Beer range varies H

Popular, town-centre pub serving a good range of ales – normally three on at a time.
≋ (Arsenal/Dockyard) ♣

SE19: Crystal Palace

Railway Bell
14 Cawnpore Street
12–3.30, 5–11; 12–10.30 Sun
Young's Bitter, Special, seasonal beers Ⓗ
Cosy, friendly local with one bar. The garden has recently been improved – barbecues held summer weekends. No food Sun.
Q ❀ ◖ ≋ (Gypsy Hill) ♣

SE20: Penge

Maple Tree
52–54 Maple Road
☎ (0181) 778 8701
11–11; 12–10.30 Sun
Fuller's London Pride; Shepherd Neame Master Brew Bitter; Young's Bitter, Special; guest beers Ⓗ
Comfortable pub, serving local interests, with a games room. No food Sun. ❀ ◖ ♣

Moon & Stars
164–166 High Street
☎ (0181) 776 5680
11–11; 12–10.30 Sun
Courage Directors; Fuller's London Pride; Theakston Best Bitter; Younger Scotch; guest beers Ⓗ
Large Wetherspoons pub on the site of a former cinema: a favourite of local drinkers.
Q ❀ ◖ ▶ ♿ ≋ (Penge E/Kent House) ♻ P ✚

SE22: East Dulwich

Crystal Palace Tavern
193 Crystal Palace Road
☎ (0181) 693 4968
11–11; 12–10.30 Sun
Ind Coope Burton Ale; Tetley Bitter; Young's Bitter; guest beers Ⓗ
Popular local which retains evidence of its Victorian origins: one of the mainstays of real ale in the Dulwich area for two decades. Crystal Palace Bitter is a stock Ind Coope 'house' bitter. The guest beers are from the Tapster's Choice list. ⑤

SE24: Herne Hill

Lord Stanley
31 Hinton Road
11–11; 12–10.30 Sun
Fuller's London Pride; Ruddles Best Bitter; guest beers Ⓗ
Good value, friendly free house in an area not noted for real ale. Licence plates from

almost every US state are displayed. Good value meals at all times. Q ❀ ◖ ▶ ≋ (Loughborough Jct)

SE25: South Norwood

Alliance
91 High Street (A213)
☎ (0181) 653 3604
11–11; 12–10.30 Sun
Courage Best Bitter, Directors; Wadworth 6X; guest beers Ⓗ
In a prominent position by the clocktower, and easily found by bus and train, this well-tested mock-Tudor outlet of real ale is a must.
◖ ♿ ≋ (Norwood Jct) ♣

Clifton Arms
21 Clifton Road
☎ (0181) 771 2443
12 (11 Sat)–11; 12–10.30 Sun
Fuller's London Pride; Ind Coope Burton Ale; guest beers Ⓗ
Well-established pub that offers a variety of regionals'/micros' beers. It can be crowded when football is on.
❀ ◖ ≋ (Selhurst/Norwood Jct) ♣

Portmanor
1 Portland Road (A215)
☎ (0181) 655 1308
11–11; 12–10.30 Sun
Fuller's London Pride; Young's Special; guest beers Ⓗ
Lively, comfortable, one-bar pub with an extra serving area on the balcony in summer. It always serves six beers at competitive prices; guests generally come from small breweries. No food Sun.
❀ ◖ ≋ (Norwood Jct)

SE26: Upper Sydenham

Dulwich Wood House
39 Sydenham Hill
11–11; 12–10.30 Sun
Young's Bitter, Special, seasonal beers Ⓗ
Large, friendly, country-style pub noted for its extensive gardens and petanque pistes. Local CAMRA *Pub of the Year* 1995. Barbecues daily in summer. ♨ Q ❀ ◖ ≋ (Sydenham Hill) ♣ P

Addiscombe

Builder's Arms
65 Leslie Park Road (off A222, between Cherry Orchard Rd and Lower Addiscombe Rd)
☎ (0181) 654 1803
12–11; 12–10.30 Sun
Fuller's Chiswick, London Pride, ESB, seasonal beers Ⓗ

Recent modernisation and extension have enhanced this comfortable, friendly, backstreet local which was CAMRA Croydon *Pub of the Year* 1996. Eve meals end at 8.30; no food Sat eve or Sun.
❀ ◖ ▶ ⑤ ≋ (E Croydon) ♣

Claret Free House
5A Bingham Corner, Lower Addiscombe Road (A222, near Bingham Rd)
11.30–11; 12–10.30 Sun
Eldridge Pope Royal Oak; Palmers BB; Shepherd Neame Spitfire; guest beers Ⓗ
Small, comfortable bar in a shopping parade. It enjoys a loyal local following, but also attracts ale lovers from a wide area. ◖

Beckenham

Jolly Woodman   ☆
9 Chancery Lane
11–11; 12–10.30 Sun
Draught Bass; M&B Brew XI; Shepherd Neame Master Brew Bitter; guest beer Ⓗ
Popular, friendly, unspoilt country-style pub in the London suburbs. This Bass house was one of the last to get a spirit licence.
Q ❀ ◖ ≋ (Jct) ♣

Bexley

Black Horse
63 Albert Road
☎ (01322) 523371
11–3, 5 (6.30 Sat)–11; 11–11 Fri; 12–3, 7–10.30 Sun
Courage Best Bitter; guest beer Ⓗ
Fine example of a cosy, backstreet local. A house beer is sold. ❀ ◖ ≋

Cork & Cask (off-licence)
3 Bourne Parade, Bourne Road
☎ (01322) 528884
11–2, 4–10; 10–10 Sat; 12–3, 7–10 Sun
Beer range varies Ⓖ
Off-licence with usually five ales and two ciders available, plus an excellent range of British and foreign bottled beers. Containers sold.
≋ ♻

King's Head
65 Bexley High Street
☎ (01322) 526112
11–11; 11–4, 6–11 Sat; 12–4, 7–10.30 Sun
Courage Best Bitter; Greene King IPA, Abbot Ⓗ
Historic, 16th-century, timber-framed building with genuine oak beams, in the heart of old Bexley village. A very popular, welcoming pub.
❀ ◖ ≋ P

189

Bexleyheath

Robin Hood & Little John
78 Lion Road
☎ (0181) 303 1128
11–11; 12–10.30 Sun
**Courage Best Bitter, Directors;
Ruddles County; John Smith's
Bitter; Wadworth 6X; guest
beers** Ⓗ
Popular, two-bar, backstreet
local in a Grade II-listed
building. Home-made meals
and snacks (not served Sun).
The tables are made from
Singer sewing machines.
Over-21s only.
ᗐ ✿ ⌕ ♣

Royal Oak
(Polly Clean Stairs)
Mount Road
☎ (0181) 303 4454
11–3, 6–11; 12–3, 7–10.30 Sun
**Courage Best Bitter;
Wadworth 6X; guest beers** Ⓗ
The former Upton village store,
now a village-style local in a
residential area: a gem. No
food Sun. Q ✿ P

Biggin Hill

Crown
Leaves Green Road, Leaves
Green ☎ (01959) 572920
11–2.30, 5.30–11; 11–11 Sat; 12–3,
7–10.30 Sun
**Shepherd Neame Master
Brew Bitter, Spitfire, Bishops
Finger, seasonal beers** Ⓗ
Cosy, comfortable pub with
low-level piped music. Wide
range of food at reasonable
prices. ✿ ♿ P

Bromley

Bitter End
139 Masons Hill
☎ (0181) 466 6083
12–3, 5–10 (9 Mon); 11–10 Sat; 12–2,
7–9 Sun
Beer range varies Ⓖ
This excellent off-licence offers
an ever-changing range of beer
and cider and a wide range of
British and imported bottled
beers. ≠ (South) ▭

Red Lion
10 North Road
☎ (0181) 460 2691
11–11; 12–10.30 Sun
**Adnams Broadside; Beards
Best Bitter; Harveys BB; guest
beers** Ⓗ
Recently bought by Beards of
Sussex, this pub, away from
Bromley centre, has been
sympathetically refurbished:
note the clock, and the
stunning tiling uncovered
during the refit. Meals served
12–7, Mon–Sat.
♨ Q ✿ ⌕ ≠ (North)

Chelsfield Village

Five Bells
Church Road (1 mile from M25
jct 4)
☎ (01689) 821044
11–3, 6–11; 12–3.30, 7–10.30 Sun
**Courage Best Bitter; guest
beer** Ⓗ
Comfortable village pub with a
friendly atmosphere. Weekly
guest beer; good selection of
wine. It has been in the same
family for 65 years.
Q ✿ ⌕ ▣ ♣ P

Chislehurst

Bull's Head
Royal Parade (A208)
☎ (0181) 467 1727
11–11; 12–3, 7–10.30 Sun
**Young's Bitter, Special,
Winter Warmer** Ⓗ
Large, ivy-clad, listed pub
catering for all tastes in its
many bars (public/saloon/
lounge/cocktail). It can get
very busy. Large screen TV in
the public bar for sporting
events.
♨ Q ᗐ ✿ ◖ ⌕ ▣ P

Sydney Arms
Old Perry Street (off A222)
☎ (0181) 467 3025
11–3, 5.30–11; 11–11 Fri & Sat; 12–4,
7–10.30 Sun
**Courage Best Bitter, Directors;
guest beers** Ⓗ
Pleasant, well-hidden pub
hosting regular quiz nights.
Old photos of the pub are
displayed. Children welcome
in the conservatory.
Q ᗐ ✿ ◖ ⌕ ▣ ♣ P ✍

Croydon

Cricketers Arms
23 Southbridge Place (under
old town flyover)
☎ (0181) 405 4545
11–11; 12–10.30 Sun
**Fuller's London Pride;
Hancock's HB; Harveys BB;
guest beers** Ⓗ
Quiet, softly-lit, one-bar pub,
split into four areas with a
games room at the rear. Wide
choice of food (eve meals to
order only).
✿ ⌕ ≠ (Waddon) ♣ P

Crown
90 Stanley Road (between A23
and A235)
☎ (0181) 684 4952
11–11; 12–10.30 Sun
**Webster's Yorkshire Bitter;
Young's Bitter** Ⓗ
Excellent, street-corner local: a
single large bar with a
collection of plates and two
dartboards for the two teams.
Other games include dominoes
and Trivial Pursuit.
◖ ♣

Dog & Bull ☆
24–25 Surrey Street (off A235)
☎ (0181) 688 3664
11–11; 12–4, 8–10.30 Sun
**Young's Bitter, Special,
Winter Warmer, seasonal
beers** Ⓗ
Characterful, Grade II-listed
building with three drinking
areas, including one with a
food servery. The rear yard is
laid out as a well-equipped
garden.
Q ✿ ⌕ ≠ (East/West) ♣

Duke of Cambridge
7 Holmesdale Road
☎ (0181) 665 6440
11–11; 12–10.30 Sun
**Adnams Bitter; Draught Bass;
Fuller's London Pride;
Hancock's HB; guest beers** Ⓗ
Workaday local, easily
accessible by public transport,
and offering good service and
good value food. Basically one
bar with a variety of seating
areas; a good, friendly,
community pub.
✿ ◖ ♿ ≠ (Selhurst) ♣

George
17–21 George Street
☎ (0181) 649 9077
11–11; 12–10.30 Sun
**Courage Directors; Fuller's
London Pride; Theakston Best
Bitter; Younger Scotch; guest
beers** Ⓗ
Wetherspoons conversion of a
furniture shop, with two bar
areas (no-smoking at the rear).
Usually crowded, with
drinkers of all ages, it is
convenient for the main
shopping area. Weston's cider.
Q ◖ ♿ ≠ (East/West) ▭ ✍

Princess Royal
22 Longley Road
☎ (0181) 240 0046
11–3, 5.30–11; 11–11 Fri; 12–3, 7.30–11
Sat; 12–3, 8–10.30 Sun
**Greene King XX Mild, IPA,
Abbot, seasonal beers** Ⓗ
Cosy pub with a friendly
welcome. It has a country feel
and boasts a log fire in winter.
Also known as the Glue Pot
(see the pub sign and the
explanation inside). No food
Sun eve.
♨ ✿ ◖ ♣

Royal Standard
1 Sheldon Street (off High St)
☎ (0181) 688 9749
11.30–11; 12–10.30 Sun
**Fuller's Chiswick, London
Pride, ESB, seasonal beers** Ⓗ
Friendly, traditional, popular,
backstreet local with fine
etched-glass windows and a
serving hatch into the small
rear bar. The garden is across
the road. Greater London
CAMRA *Pub of the Year* 1996.
No food Sun.
Q ✿ ⌕ ≠ (East) ♣

Downe

George & Dragon
26 High Street
☎ (01689) 859682
11–3, 5.30–11; 12–10.30 Sun
Draught Bass; Greene King IPA; Hancock's HB; guest beers Ⓗ
Excellent village local with an imaginative choice of guest beers, generally from the north.
ⅿ ❀ ◖ ▶

Queen's Head
25 High Street
☎ (01689) 682145
11–3, 5.30–11; 11–11 Sat & Thu–Fri in summer; 12–10.30 Sun
Ind Coope Burton Ale; Marston's Pedigree; Tetley Bitter; guest beer (occasional) Ⓗ
Two-bar village local, with parts dating back to 1547. It supports the local cricket team and was reputedly frequented by Charles Darwin who lived in the village.
ⅿ Q ☎ ❀ ◖ ▶ ⊟ ⅃ P

Footscray

Seven Stars
High Street ☎ (0181) 300 2057
11–11; 12–3, 7–10.30 Sun
Bass Toby Cask, Draught Bass; Greene King IPA Ⓗ
16th-century pub retaining many original features. Live music Fri eve. ❀ ◖

Orpington

Cricketers
93 Chislehurst Road
☎ (01689) 812648
11–11; 12–10.30 Sun
Courage Best Bitter; guest beers Ⓗ
Comfortable pub on Broomhill Common. Small car park and beer garden. No food Sun. Good interest in guest beers.
❀ ◖ P

Harvest Moon
141 High Street
☎ (01689) 876931
11–11; 12–10.30 Sun
Courage Directors; Fuller's London Pride; Theakston Best Bitter, XB; Younger Scotch; guest beers Ⓗ
Single-bar pub, adjacent to the Walnuts shopping centre entrance; a typical Wetherspoons shop conversion. Food is served all day. ⅿ Q ◖ ▶ ⅃ ≉ ♣ ⅄

Petts Wood

Sovereign of the Seas
109–111 Queensway
☎ (01689) 891606
11–11; 12–10.30 Sun
Courage Directors; Fuller's London Pride; Theakston Best Bitter; Younger Scotch; guest beers Ⓗ
Large, one-bar pub: a familiar Wetherspoons shop conversion.
Q ❀ ◖ ▶ ⅃ ≉ ⅂ ⅄

Purley

Foxley Hatch
8–9 Russell Hill Parade, Russell Hill Road (A23 near A22/A235 jct) ☎ (0181) 763 9307
11–11; 12–10.30 Sun
Courage Directors; Fuller's London Pride; Theakston Best Bitter, XB; Younger Scotch; guest beers Ⓗ
Wetherspoons conversion of a former shop, popular with locals. Memorabilia relates to local history. Q ◖ ▶ ≉ ⅂ ⅄

Shirley

Sandrock
152 Upper Shirley Road
☎ (0181) 656 0712
11–11; 12–10.30 Sun
Draught Bass; Fuller's London Pride Ⓗ
Popular pub in the more up-market part of Croydon which, in spite of a strong emphasis on food, retains a good local following: one bar with a dining area behind. Handy for the Addington Hills.
❀ ◖ ▶ P

Sidcup

Alma
Alma Road
11–2.30, 5.30 (7 Sat)–11; 11–11 Fri; 12–3, 7–10.30 Sun
Courage Best Bitter; Young's Bitter, Special Ⓗ
Deservedly popular, backstreet local, retaining some of its Victorian-style interior.
Q ◖ ≉

Thornton Heath

Railway Telegraph
19 Brigstock Road
☎ (0181) 684 5809
11–11; 12–4, 7–10.30 Sun
Young's Bitter, Special, Winter Warmer Ⓗ
Attractive, street-corner pub opposite the station: two comfortable bars, both with real fires. The public bar has cheaper prices and a dartboard. No food Sun.
ⅿ ❀ ◖ ⊟ ≉ ♣

Upper Belvedere

Royal Standard
39 Nuxley Road
☎ (01322) 432774
11–11; 12–10.30 Sun

Adnams Bitter; Draught Bass; Caledonian Deuchars IPA; Fuller's London Pride Ⓗ; **Highgate Old** Ⓖ; **guest beers** Ⓗ
Central pub, offering regularly changing guest beers and three beer festivals a year (Scottish beers are featured over the Easter weekend).
☎ ❀ ◖ ⅃ P

South-West London

SW1: Belgravia

Fox & Hounds
29 Passmore Street
☎ (0171) 730 6367
11–3, 5.30–11; 12–2, 7–10.30 Sun
Adnams Bitter; Draught Bass; Greene King IPA; Harveys BB Ⓗ
Tiny, unchanging local with the last known beer and wine-only licence in London. Run by the same landlady for 26 years, it has been in every edition of the *Guide*.
Q ⊖ (Sloane Sq) ♣

Grouse & Claret
Little Chester Street
☎ (0171) 235 3438
11–11; 12–3 (closed eve) Sun
Badger Dorset Best, Tanglefoot; guest beers Ⓗ
Plush, upmarket corner pub in a quiet backstreet. The cellar wine bar/function room is connected to a first-floor restaurant via a central spiral staircase (no food weekends).
◖ ▶ ⊟ ≉ (Victoria) ⊖ (Hyde Pk Cnr) ♣

Nag's Head ☆
53 Kinnerton Street
☎ (0171) 235 1135
11–11; 12–10.30 Sun
Adnams Bitter; Tetley Bitter Ⓗ
Tiny, unspoilt historic pub off Wilton Place which seems caught in a time warp. The interior is on different levels. Note the ancient lever type slot machines for which old pennies can be obtained at the bar.
ⅿ ◖ ▶ ⊖ (Hyde Pk Crnr)

Star Tavern
6 Belgrave Mews West
☎ (0171) 235 3019
11.30–11; 11.30–3, 6.30–11 Sat; 12–3, 7–10.30 Sun
Fuller's Chiswick, London Pride, ESB Ⓗ
Attractive, unspoilt mews pub hidden off the west side of Belgrave Square. The side room has scrubbed tables and two real fires. In every edition of the *Good Beer Guide*.
Weekday meals.
ⅿ Q ◖ ▶ ⊖ (Hyde Pk Crnr)

SW1: Pimlico

Royal Oak

2 Regency Street
☎ (0171) 834 7046
11–11; 12–3, 8–11 Sat; 12–3, 8–10.30
Sun
**Young's Bitter, Special,
seasonal beers** H
Small, wedge-shaped, corner
local, recently narrowly saved
from demolition. Visit it and
celebrate!
Q ❀ ◖ ▌ ⊖ (St James's Pk)

SW1: Trafalgar Square

Lord Moon of the Mall

16–18 Whitehall
☎ (0171) 839 7701
11–11; 12–10.30 Sun
**Courage Directors; Fuller's
London Pride; Theakston Best
Bitter; Younger Scotch; guest
beers** H
Large Wetherspoons pub in
former bank premises, with a
magnificent vaulted ceiling;
next door to the Whitehall
Theatre. Wheelchair WC. There
are always two guest beers.
Q ◖ ▌ & ≠ (Charing Cross)
⊖ ↻

SW1: Westminster

Buckingham Arms

62 Petty France
☎ (0171) 222 3386
11–11; 12–6 Sun
**Young's Bitter, Special,
seasonal beers** H
Busy pub near the Passport
Office, with a corridor drinking
area behind the bar.
◖ ▌ ⊖ (St James's Pk)

Westminster Arms

9 Storeys Gate
11–11 (8 Sat); 12–6 Sun
Beer range varies H
Busy pub near Westminster
Abbey and the Houses of
Parliament. There is a
restaurant upstairs, plus a wine
bar downstairs.
◖ ▌ ⊖

SW2: Brixton

Crown & Sceptre

2 Streatham Hill
☎ (0181) 671 0843
11–11; 12–10.30 Sun
**Courage Directors; Fuller's
London Pride; Hop Back
Summer Lightning;
Theakston Best Bitter;
Younger Scotch; guest beers** H
Large Wetherspoons pub
standing on a busy crossroads:
a very popular local with a
wide cross-section of the
community. Two guest beers
are always available.
Q ❀ ◖ ▌ ↻ P ✂

SW3: Chelsea

Blenheim

27 Cale Street
☎ (0171) 349 0056
11–11; 12–10.30 Sun
**Badger Dorset Best,
Tanglefoot** H
Large, one-bar pub dominated
by a vast old-fashioned
sideboard. ◖ ▌

Crown

153 Dovehouse Street
☎ (0171) 352 9505
11–11; 12–10.30 Sun
Beer range varies H
Extremely popular community
pub just off Fulham Rd.
◖ ⊖ (S Kensington) ⛁

Wellesley Arms

70 Sydney Street
☎ (0171) 352 7924
11–11; 12–10.30 Sun
**Courage Best Bitter, Directors;
Theakston Best Bitter** H
Pleasant pub with etched-glass
windows and military
memorabilia. Meals served
12–9.30. Sky TV.
Q ◖ ▌ ♣

SW4: Clapham

Bread & Roses

68 Clapham Manor Street
11–11; 12–10.30 Sun
Adnams Bitter; guest beers H
Refurbished, bright, airy and
clutter-free pub serving food
till 10pm. The house beer,
Workers Ale, is brewed by
Smiles; independent brewery
guest beers. Local bands play
live eves. ⛌ ❀ ◖ ▌ & ⊖
(Common) ✂

Mistress P's

29 North Street, Old Town
☎ (0171) 622 5347
11–11; 12–10.30 Sun
**Flowers Original; Fuller's
London Pride; Wadworth
6X** H
Nice, friendly, cosy pub with
Sky Sports and piped music.
❀ ◖ ⊖ (Common)

SW6: Parsons Green

White Horse

1 Parsons Green
☎ (0171) 736 2115
11–11; 12–10.30 Sun
**Adnams Extra; Draught Bass;
Harveys BB; Highgate Dark;
guest beer** H
Large, busy pub with an
outside terrace facing the
green. It hosts many beer
festivals and tastings and
stocks all the Trappist bottled
beers. ⛌ ❀ ◖ ▌ ⊖

SW8: Battersea

British Lion

137 Thessaly Road
☎ (0171) 498 3648
11.30 (11 Sat)–11; 12–10.30 Sun
Courage Best Bitter H
Delightful pub featuring a
listed original Victorian bar
back. A regular local clientele
enjoys the free library and
homely atmosphere. All female
staff. A gem. No food Sun. ❀
▌ ≠ (Wandsworth Rd) ♣

SW8: South Lambeth

Surprise

16 Southville
☎ (0171) 622 4623
11–11; 12–10.30 Sun
**Young's Bitter, Special,
Winter Warmer** H
Unchanged and unchanging:
the archetypal backstreet local.
Families often spill over into
Larkhall Park in summer. No
food Sun eve.
⛌⛌ Q ❀ ◖ ▌ ⊖ ♣

SW8: Stockwell

Priory Arms

83 Lansdowne Way
11–11; 12–3, 7–10.30 Sun
**Harveys BB; Young's Bitter,
Special; guest beers** H
SW London CAMRA *Pub of the
Year* 1992, '94 and '96: a Grade
II-listed, refurbished, pub with
a wooden floor in the bar area.
Over 1,000 different real ales
from far and wide have been
sold. Friendly conversation;
quality background music. Eve
meals finish early. ❀ ◖ ▌ ≠
(Vauxhall) ⊖ (Stockwell) ♣
↻

SW11: Battersea

Bolingbroke

Cobham Close
☎ (0171) 228 7678
11–11; 12–10.30 Sun
**Draught Bass; Fuller's London
Pride; Greene King IPA** H
Attractive house built from
three cottages, now in a
modern cul-de-sac. The new
landlord is trying to expand
the beer range. Renowned for
Sat breakfasts and Sun roasts.
Music Sat eve. ◖ ▌ ♣

Duke of Cambridge

228 Battersea Bridge Road
☎ (0171) 223 5662
11–11; 12–10.30 Sun
**Young's Bitter, Special,
Winter Warmer, seasonal
beers** H
Victorian local with the best
beer for miles and a strong
local following.
❀ ◖ ▌ ⊕ ♣ ⛁

Fox & Hounds

66 Latchmere Road
☎ (0171) 228 2624
11–11; 12–4, 7–10.30 Sun
Draught Bass; Ruddles Best Bitter H
Good family house with a big garden and a nice U-shaped bar due for refurbishment.
❀ ≋ (Clapham Jct) ♣

SW11: Clapham

Beehive

197 St Johns Hill
☎ (0171) 207 1267
11–11; 12–10.30 Sun
Fuller's Chiswick, London Pride, ESB, seasonal beers H
Small, one-bar local boasting a collection of beehives behind the bar. SW London CAMRA *Pub of the Year* two years running. It has two TVs, but they are only turned on for sports. ❀ ◖ ♿ ≋ (Jct)

SW12: Balham

Prince of Wales

270 Cavendish Road
11–11; 12–10.30 Sun
Courage Best Bitter; Fuller's London Pride H
Well-designed, two-bar, 1950s pub: a lively public bar with darts and games, and a quiet, comfortable saloon. Home-cooked food 12–10pm.
Q ❀ ◖ ▮ ⊞ ≋ ⊖ ♣

SW13: Barnes

Coach & Horses

27 Barnes High Street
☎ (0181) 876 2695
11–11; 12–3.30, 7–10.30 Sun
Young's Bitter, Special, Winter Warmer H
Very cosy, welcoming, conversational, one-bar local with a huge log fire. There is a garden play area, plus a paddock room for children. No food Sun (except summer barbecues). 🏚 Q 🕭 ❀ ◖ ≋ (Barnes Bridge)

Red Lion

2 Castelnau ☎ (0181) 748 2984
11–11; 12–10.30 Sun
Fuller's Chiswick, London Pride, ESB, seasonal beers H
Large, impressive, Georgian-fronted pub, comfortably furnished and welcoming. The ornate restaurant provides a wide selection of meals. Large garden with a children's play area. 🏚 ❀ ◖ ▮ ≋ ♣

SW14: Mortlake

Hare & Hounds

216 Upper Richmond Road
☎ (0181) 876 4304
11–11; 12–10.30 Sun

Young's Bitter, Special, Winter Warmer H
Comfortable, roomy pub: the oak-panelled lounge has a pleasant atmosphere; part of the bar is set aside for snooker. A large, walled garden provides a children's play area and hosts barbecues. Wide choice of good value food. Live music Sun eve (when no meals are served). 🏚 Q ❀ ◖ ▮ ≋

SW15: Putney

Green Man

1 Putney Heath
☎ (0181) 788 8096
11–11; 12–3, 7–10.30 Sun
Young's Bitter, Special, Winter Warmer H
Unspoilt, country-style pub on the edge of Putney Heath with attractive outside drinking areas. Eve meals in summer. Ring the Bull played.
❀ ◖ ⊞ ♣

Spotted Horse

122 Putney High Street
☎ (0181) 288 0246
11–11; 12–3, 7–10.30 Sun
Young's Bitter, Special, Ram Rod, seasonal beers H
Popular pub serving a good mix of customers; trendy but not spoilt. ◖ ▮ ♿ ≋ ⊖ ♣

SW16: Streatham Common

Pied Bull

498 Streatham High Road
☎ (0181) 764 4003
11–11; 12–10.30 Sun
Young's Bitter, Special, seasonal beers H
Large, comfortable house with a single serving area but several drinking areas.
Q ◖ ▮ ⊞ ≋ ♣ P

SW17: Tooting

Castle

38 Tooting High Street
☎ (0181) 672 7018
11–11; 12–10.30 Sun
Young's Bitter, Special, Winter Warmer H
Large, single-bar pub on a busy crossroads but retaining a relaxed atmosphere. Parking may be charged for at times.
🏚 Q ❀ ◖ ♿ ⊖ ♣ P

King's Head

84 Upper Tooting Road
11–11; 12–10.30 Sun
Courage Best Bitter, Directors; Theakston Best Bitter, XB; guest beer (occasional) H
Sympathetically refurbished in 1996, this ornate, late-Victorian pub retains many original features – the etched glass is a delight. No meals Sun eve.
🕭 ❀ ◖ ▮ ⊞ ⊖ (Bec) ♣ P

Prince of Wales

646 Garratt Lane
☎ (0181) 946 2628
11–11; 12–4, 7–10.30 Sun
Young's Bitter, Special H
Reassuringly consistent, two-bar house; comfortable and spacious. The large family room has a dartboard for eve use. 🕭 P

SW18: Earlsfield

Country House

2 Groton Road
☎ (0181) 874 2715
12–11; 12–10.30 Sun
Courage Best Bitter, Directors; Morland Old Speckled Hen; John Smith's Bitter; Young's Bitter H
More like its name than a city pub; highly polished and retaining its character.
◖ ⊞ ≋ ♣ ⊟

SW18: Wandsworth

Old Sergeant

102–104 Garratt Lane
☎ (0181) 874 4099
11–11; 12–10.30 Sun
Young's Bitter, Special, Winter Warmer H
One of a dying breed – a friendly, cosy local, fielding sports and quiz teams.
◖ ⊞ ♣

Queen Adelaide

35 Putney Bridge Road
☎ (0181) 874 1695
11–11; 12–10.30 Sun
Young's Bitter, Special, seasonal beers H
Traditional, one-bar pub, dedicated to the queen of William IV. 🏚 ❀ ◖ ♣

SW19: Merton

Princess Royal

25 Abbey Road
☎ (0181) 542 3273
11–3, 5.30–11; 11–11 Fri & Sat; 12–4, 7–10.30 Sun
Courage Best Bitter, Directors; guest beers H
A haven of tranquillity: an early 19th-century, two-bar, corner pub, attractively decorated with autographed film star photos and old prints. Local, friendly clientele. The big garden is a bonus in summer.
❀ ◖ ⊞ ⊖ (S Wimbledon) ♣ ⊟

SW19: South Wimbledon

Sultan

78 Norman Road
☎ (0181) 542 4532
12–11; 12–4, 7–10.30 Sun

Hop Back GFB, Special, Stout, Thunderstorm, Summer Lightning, seasonal beers H
1950s building named after a famous racehorse. The pub was brought back from the dead and transformed into local CAMRA *Pub of the Year* 1995.
Q ✿ ♿ ♣ 🍺

SW19: Wimbledon

Brewery Tap
68–69 High Street
☎ (0181) 947 9331
11–11; 12–10.30 Sun
Brakspear Bitter; Flowers Original; Fuller's London Pride; guest beers H
No brewery ever existed here, but since this Victorian pub was redesigned and extended in 1995 it has stocked up to five beers in the small, angular bar. Quiet week nights.
🍺 ♿ ⇄

Hand & Racket
25–27 Wimbledon Hill Road
☎ (0181) 947 9391
11–11; 12–10.30 Sun
Boddingtons Bitter; Flowers IPA, Original; Fuller's London Pride; Marston's Pedigree; Wadworth 6X H**; guest beers** G
1995 Hogshead conversion, formerly a Boots store, with an attractive bar layout on split-levels with screens and recesses. Busy lunch and early eve with business people; popular later with students. Quiet music. Four guest beers are sold but prices are on the high side.
🏚 🍺 ♿ ⇄ ⊖ ⊙

Wibbas Down Inn
6–12 Gladstone Road
☎ (0181) 540 6788
11–11; 12–10.30 Sun
Courage Directors; Fuller's London Pride; Theakston Best Bitter; Younger Scotch; guest beers H
Cavernous Wetherspoons outlet, a conversion of half of a former Tesco's to a huge bar opposite the bus station, extending through to a smaller bar opposite the theatre. Frequently changing guest beers, mainly from micros.
Q ✿ 🍺 ♿ ⇄ ⊖ ⊙ ⍓

SW19: Wimbledon Common

Hand in Hand
7 Crooked Billet
☎ (0181) 946 5720
11–11; 12–10.30 Sun
Young's Bitter, Special, Winter Warmer, seasonal beers H
Large, mixed period pub, very popular with local

professionals and always very busy in summer. Q ⍓ ✿ 🍺

SW20: Raynes Park

Cavern
100 Coombe Lane
☎ (0181) 944 8211
11–11; 12–10.30 Sun
Boddingtons Bitter; Fuller's London Pride; Young's Bitter; guest beer H
Popular, vibrant, one-bar pub opened in 1991, featuring a tiled floor and raised, carpeted areas. Rock 'n' roll jukebox and memorabilia. *Best Dressed Bar* in the *Morning Advertiser* national awards 1995.
✿ 🍺 ⇄

Beddington

Plough
The Broadway, Croydon Road (A323/B272 jct)
☎ (0181) 647 1122
11–3, 5.30–11; 11–11 Fri & Sat; 12–10.30 Sun
Young's Bitter, Special, seasonal beers H
Large, one-bar pub with a central, circular bar, serving a wide range of food.
🏚 ✿ 🍺 ⇄ (Waddon) ♣ P

Carshalton

Racehorse
17 West Street (B278)
☎ (0181) 647 6818
11–11; 12–3, 7–10.30 Sun
Courage Best Bitter, Directors; King & Barnes Sussex, seasonal beers; guest beers H
Smart, two-bar pub with an eating area in the lounge bar; excellent food (not served Sun eve). All guest beers come from independent breweries.
Q ✿ 🍺 ⇄ ♣ P

Railway Tavern
47 North Street (B277, off A232)
☎ (0181) 669 8016
12–2.30, 5–11; 12–11 Sat; 12–4, 7–10.30 Sun
Fuller's London Pride, ESB, seasonal beers H
Popular, street-corner local adorned with railwayana and mirrors. Famous for its marble-playing teams and morris dancers. Q ⇄ ♣

Windsor Castle
378 Carshalton Road (A232)
☎ (0181) 669 1191
11–11; 12–10.30 Sun
Draught Bass; Fuller's London Pride; Hancock's HB; Worthington Bitter; guest beers H
Large, one-bar pub offering a good range of guest ales from microbreweries. Four-pint pitchers are sold for the price of three. The restaurant is closed Sun eve when live

music is staged. Q ✿ 🍺 ⇄ (Carshalton Beeches) ♣ P

Chessington

North Star
271 Hook Road (A243)
☎ (0181) 391 5248
12–11; 12–4, 7–10.30 Sun
Draught Bass; Hancock's HB; Highgate Dark H
Popular, lively, 150-year-old pub, a rare mild outlet for the area. Children's play facilities in the garden. Q ✿ 🍺 ♣ P

Kingston upon Thames

Bricklayers Arms
53 Hawks Road (off A2043)
☎ (0181) 546 0393
12–11; 12–10.30 Sun
Morland Original, Old Masters, Old Speckled Hen; guest beer H
Traditional, homely pub, with an accent on food; deservedly popular with diners.
Q ✿ 🍺 ⍓

Canbury Arms
49 Canbury Park Road (off A307) ☎ (0181) 288 1882
11–11; 12–10.30 Sun
Courage Best Bitter, Directors H**; Morland Old Speckled Hen; Wadworth 6X** G**; guest beers** H
One-bar pub near the station, featuring wooden beams, old local photos and a reference library. Food all day (12–3 Sun). ⍓ ✿ 🍺 ♿ ⇄ ♣ ⊙ P

Park Tavern
19 New Road
10.30–11; 12–3, 7–10.30 Sun
Boddingtons Bitter; Brakspear Special; Young's Bitter; guest beers H
Comfortable, friendly local near Richmond Park gate. Local CAMRA *Pub of the Year* 1997. Parking is difficult.
🏚 Q ♣ ♣

Two Brewers
19 Wood Street (A308)
☎ (0181) 549 3712
11–11; closed Sun except Dec when it opens 12–6
Courage Best Bitter; guest beers H
Pub on the one-way system but retaining a local feel; 1995/96 local CAMRA *Pub of the Year*. Its reasonably priced lunches are popular with shoppers.
🏚 🍺 ♣

Wych Elm
93 Elm Road
☎ (0181) 546 3271
11–3, 5–11; 11–11 Sat; 12–3, 7–10.30 Sun
Fuller's Chiswick, London Pride, ESB, seasonal beers H

Sensitively refurbished a few years ago, this pub is comprised of a smart saloon and a plain, neat public bar. Award-winning garden and window boxes. No food Sun.
🌢 ◖ 🍴 ♣

New Malden

Woodies
Thetford Road (South Lane exit off A3) ☎ (0181) 949 5824
11–11; 12–10.30 Sun
Flowers Original; Fuller's London Pride; Young's Bitter, Special; guest beers Ⓗ
Ex-cricket pavilion, housing a collection of sports, film and theatrical memorabilia. New large patio area. Excellent, substantial pub grub.
🏚 Q 🌢 🍴 ♣ P

Richmond

Coach & Horses
8 Kew Green, Kew
☎ (0181) 940 1208
11–11; 12–10.30 Sun
Young's Bitter, Special, seasonal beers Ⓗ
Large, traditional, edge-of-town coaching inn with many preserved features from the 19th century. Popular with families (particularly for Sun lunch; no food Sun eve) and visitors to Kew.
🏚 Q 🌢 🏚 ⇌ (Kew Bridge) ⊖ (Kew Gdns) P

Old Ship
3 King Street
☎ (0181) 940 5014
11–11; 12–10.30 Sun
Young's Bitter, Special, Winter Warmer Ⓗ
Attractive, well-kept, cosy town-centre pub with a nautical theme and a first-floor look-out bar. Wholesome food available most hours, except Sun eve. Board games Mon eve. 🏚 ◖ ◗ ⇌ ⊖

Orange Tree
45 Kew Road
☎ (0181) 940 0944
11–11; 12–10.30 Sun
Young's Bitter, Special, Winter Warmer Ⓗ
Fine, popular pub in a large Victorian building, with a fringe theatre upstairs and a restaurant downstairs. Good variety of excellent bar food in the lounge; no food Sun eve.
🏚 Q 🌢 ◖ ◗ ⇌ ⊖

Waterman's Arms
10–12 Water Lane
☎ (0181) 940 2893
11–3, 5.30–11; 11–11 Sat; 12–4, 7–10.30 Sun
Young's Bitter, Special, Winter Warmer Ⓗ
Small, Victorian pub in a cobbled stone lane leading to the river, with an attractive bar

in its cosy, two-room layout. Simple, home-made meals. Try the games – Horsey-Horsey and Shut the Box.
🏚 Q 🐂 🌢 ◖ ◗ ⇌ ⊖ ♣

White Cross Hotel
Water Lane ☎ (0181) 940 6844
11–11; 12–10.30 Sun
Young's Bitter, Special, seasonal beers Ⓗ
Extremely popular, Thames-side pub in a picturesque setting, offering excellent bar food and service. The riverside terrace bar is open in summer and sunny winter weekends.
🏚 Q 🌢 ◖ ⇌ ⊖ ♣

Surbiton

Black Lion
58 Brighton Road (A243)
☎ (0181) 399 1666
11–3, 5–11; 11–11 Fri & Sat; 12–10.30 Sun
Young's Bitter, Special, seasonal beers Ⓗ
Comfortable and traditional Young's pub; one long bar area with a more private room. No food Sun eve. Friendly staff.
Q 🌢 ◖ ◗ ⇌ ♣

Denby Dale
84 Victoria Road (off A243)
☎ (0181) 390 2778
11–11; 12–10.30 Sun
Fuller's Chiswick, London Pride, ESB, seasonal beers; guest beer Ⓗ
Fuller's Ale & Pie house in a former bank. Its new, old-fashioned look includes wood panelling, floorboards and leaded light windows. A pleasant and friendly place.
Q ◖ ◗ ⇌

Waggon & Horses
1 Surbiton Hill Road (A240)
11–2.30 (3 Fri), 5–11; 11–11 Sat; 12–4, 7–10.30 Sun
Young's Bitter, Special, seasonal beers Ⓗ
Imposing but comfortable, multi-roomed pub, appreciated for its traditional atmosphere and friendly welcome. Good food.
Q 🌢 ◖ 🏚 ♣ P

Sutton

Cock & Bull
26–30 High Street (one-way system, A232)
☎ (0181) 288 1516
11–11; 12–4, 8–10.30 Sun
Fuller's Chiswick, London Pride, ESB, seasonal beers; guest beer Ⓗ
Former Nat West bank, converted to a Fuller's Ale & Pie house with a plush, one-bar layout. Guest beers are usually from regional breweries. Good food (not served Sun eve).
◖ ◗ ♿ ⇌

Moon on the Hill
5–9 Hill Road (off A232)
☎ (0181) 643 1202
11–11; 12–10.30 Sun
Courage Directors; Fuller's London Pride; Theakston Best Bitter; Younger Scotch; guest beers Ⓗ
The Wetherspoons formula set in part of a former department store, featuring a split-level drinking area with a wide staircase leading to a no-smoking area and an outdoor terrace. Microbrewery guest ales. Q 🌢 ◖ ◗ ♿ ⇌ ○ ✝

New Town
7 Lind Road (off A232)
☎ (0181) 770 2072
11–3, 5–11; 11–11 Sat; 12–10.30 Sun
Young's Bitter, Special, seasonal beers Ⓗ
Popular, friendly, street-corner local in Sutton's new town area: a carpeted public bar (lower prices), and an unusual three-level saloon. No food Sun eve. Q 🌢 ◖ ◗ 🏚 ♣ ✝

Wallington

Duke's Head
6 Manor Road (A232)
☎ (0181) 647 1595
11–11; 12–3.30, 7–10.30 Sun
Young's Bitter, Special, seasonal beers Ⓗ
Pub with a small, traditional public bar, and a low-ceilinged, wood-panelled lounge, on the south side of the green. Eve meals end at 8; no food Sat eve or Sun. Q ◖ ◗ 🏚 ⇌ P

West London

W1: Fitzrovia

Duke of York
47 Rathbone Street
11–11 (5 Sat); closed Sun
Greene King IPA, Abbot, seasonal beers Ⓗ
Friendly corner local at the end of a pedestrian street.
◖ ⊖ (Goodge St)

Jack Horner
236 Tottenham Court Road
☎ (0171) 636 2868
11–11; closed Sun
Fuller's Chiswick, London Pride, ESB, seasonal beers; guest beer Ⓗ
Fuller's Ale & Pie house in a former bank near Oxford Street shops and London University. It can get very crowded eves. ◖ ♿ ⊖ (Tottenham Ct Rd)

Rising Sun
46 Tottenham Court Road
☎ (0171) 636 6530
11–11; 12–10.30 Sun
Courage Directors; Greene King Abbot; Theakston Best

Bitter, XB, Old Peculier; guest beers Ⓗ
Long corner pub in the T&J Bernard style, meaning all swan necks and sparklers. It can get busy weekday eves. Usually three guest beers and a selection of continental bottled beers.
⊛ ◖ ▶ ⊖ (Goodge St) ⏎

Ship
134 New Cavendish Street
11–11; closed weekends
Draught Bass; Boddingtons Bitter Ⓗ
Interesting pub, a shrine to the now closed Wenlock Brewery with its mirrors, brasswork and advertising. Worth a visit.
⊖ (Oxford Circus)

W1: Marylebone

Beehive
7 Homer Street
☎ (0171) 262 6581
11–3, 5.30 (7 Sat)–11; 11–11 Fri; 12–3, 7–10.30 Sun
Boddingtons Bitter; Fuller's London Pride Ⓗ
Tiny, welcoming, backstreet local, rebuilt in 1910. Weekday lunches.
Q ◖ ≈ ⊖ (Edgware Rd)

Golden Eagle
59 Marylebone Lane
☎ (0171) 935 3228
11–11; 11–3, 7–11 Sat; 12–10.30 Sun
Draught Bass; Brakspear Bitter; Fuller's London Pride; Marston's Pedigree Ⓗ
Small, cosy free house featuring a piano player weekend eves.
Q ◖ ⊖ (Baker St) ♣

Harcourt Arms
32 Harcourt Street
☎ (0171) 723 6634
11.30–11; 11–3, 5.30–11 Sat; 12–3, 5.30–10.30 Sun
Adnams Bitter; Marston's Pedigree; Tetley Bitter; guest beers Ⓗ
Sidestreet local, built in 1826. It boasts a rear garden – unusual for the area. ⊛ ◖ ▶ ≈ ⊖

Turners Arms
26 Crawford Street
☎ (0171) 724 4504
11–11; 11–3, 7–11 Sat; 12–3, 7–10.30 Sun
Shepherd Neame Master Brew Bitter, Best Bitter, Spitfire, Bishops Finger Ⓗ
Recently refurbished, brightly-lit pub. Q ⊛ ◖ ▶ ≈ ⊖

Wargrave Arms
42 Brendon Street
☎ (0171) 723 0559
11–11; 12–3, 7–11 Sat; 12–3, 7–10.30 Sun
Young's Bitter, Special, seasonal beers Ⓗ
Long, narrow, corner local, low-lit, with a food area at the side. An ex-Finch's pub, built in 1866.
Q ⊛ ◖ ▶ ≈ ⊖ (Edgware Rd)

Worcester Arms
89 George Street
☎ (0171) 935 6050
11–11; 12–10.30 Sun
Beer range varies Ⓗ
Narrow, corner pub with an impressive Courage Alton Brewery mirror. ◖ ▶ ≈

W1: Mayfair

Guinea
30 Bruton Place
☎ (0171) 409 1728
11 (6.30 Sat)–11; closed Sun
Young's Bitter, Special, seasonal beers Ⓗ
Typical, old-fashioned Young's house. The restaurant is renowned for its steak and kidney pudding. Q ◖

W1: Soho

King's Arms
23 Poland Street
☎ (0171) 734 5907
12 (11 Sat)–11; 12–10.30 Sun
Courage Directors; Theakston Best Bitter; guest beer Ⓗ
Friendly, gay pub, attracting mainly men and home to a number of groups. Quiet upstairs bar.
◖ ▶ ⊖ (Oxford Circus)

W2: Bayswater

Prince Edward
73 Princes Square
☎ (0171) 722 2221
11–11; 12–10.30 Sun
Boddingtons Bitter; Flowers Original; Fuller's London Pride; Marston's Pedigree Ⓗ
Large, pleasant pub near Queensway. Extensive food menu; wine bar downstairs.
◖ ▶ ⊖

W2: Little Venice

Bridge House
13 Westbourne Terrace Road
☎ (0171) 286 7925
11–11; 12–10.30 Sun
Draught Bass; Worthington Bitter Ⓗ
Pleasant canalside pub with a theatre upstairs.
◖ ▶ ⊖ (Warwick Ave)

W2: Paddington

Archery Tavern
4 Bathurst Street
☎ (0171) 402 4916
11–11; 12–10.30 Sun
Badger IPA, Dorset Best, Tanglefoot; Gribble Black Adder II Ⓗ
Wood-panelled pub with working stables in an adjoining mews. ◖ ▶ ≈ ⊖ ♣

Victoria
10A Strathearn Place
☎ (0171) 724 1191
12–11; 12–3, 7–10.30 Sun
Fuller's Chiswick, London Pride, ESB, seasonal beers Ⓗ
Pleasant, corner pub with nice woodwork and superb mirrors. Queen Victoria is reputed to have rested here on her way to open Paddington Station. Q ◖ ▶ ≈ ⊖

W3: Acton

Duke of York
Steyne Road ☎ (0181) 992 0463
11.30–11; 12–10.30 Sun
Fuller's Chiswick, London Pride, ESB; guest beers Ⓗ
Free house with a single, friendly bar, drawing a regular clientele, plus a dining area. Three guest beers; some swan necks used. Fresh food is served all day. ⍎ ⊛ ◖ ▶ ≈ (Central) ⊖ (Town)

King's Head
High Street ☎ (0181) 992 0232
11–11; 12–10.30 Sun
Fuller's Chiswick, London Pride, ESB, seasonal beers Ⓗ
Comfortable, single-bar pub, displaying old photos of the area. Food served until 7pm.
Q ◖ ▶ ≈ (Central) ⊖ (Town)

W4: Chiswick

Bell & Crown
11–13 Thames Street, Strand on the Green ☎ (0181) 994 4164
11–11; 12–10.30 Sun
Fuller's Chiswick, London Pride, ESB, seasonal beers Ⓗ
Riverside pub with two conservatories and a riverside terrace. No food Sun eve.
Q ⊛ ◖ ▶ ≈ (Kew Bridge)

Duke of York
107 Devonshire Road
☎ (0181) 994 2118
11–3, 5–11; 11–11 Fri & Sat; 12–10.30 Sun
Fuller's Chiswick, London Pride Ⓗ
Very much a local. Be sure to ask for handpumped Chiswick as the keg version is also sold. Weekday lunches.
⍩ ⊛ ◖ ⊖ (Turnham Green)

JJ Moon's
80–82 Chiswick High Road
☎ (0181) 742 7263
11–11; 12–10.30 Sun
Courage Directors; Fuller's London Pride; Morland Old Speckled Hen; Theakston Best Bitter; Younger Scotch; guest beers Ⓗ
Modern Wetherspoons pub with an old pub atmosphere, serving allegedly the cheapest beer locally. Q ◖ ▶ ♿ ⊖ (Turnham Green) ⏎

Old Pack Horse

434 Chiswick High Road
☎ (0181) 994 2872
11–11; 12–10.30 Sun
Fuller's Chiswick, London Pride, ESB H
A refuge from the busy High Road, a pub with an imposing exterior, but comfortable inside. It can be busy weekday lunchtimes.
❀ ◖ ▶ ❺ (Park)

W5: Ealing

North Star

43 The Broadway (A4020)
☎ (0181) 567 4848
11–11; 12–10.30 Sun
Ind Coope Burton Ale; Marston's Pedigree; Tetley Bitter; Young's Bitter; guest beer H
Large, old pub with little recent modernisation; three rooms and a friendly atmosphere.
⚏ Q ❀ ◖ ⇌ (Bdwy) ❺

Red Lion

13 St Mary's Road
☎ (0181) 567 2541
11–11; 12–10.30 Sun
Fuller's Chiswick, London Pride, ESB H
One-bar institution, opposite the Ealing Studios and adorned with film memorabilia. Award-winning, terrace-style garden. A gem.
Q ❀ ◖ ⇌ (Bdwy) ❺

TJ Duffy

282 Northfield Avenue
☎ (0181) 932 1711
11–11; 12–10.30 Sun
Draught Bass; Fuller's London Pride; guest beer H
One-bar pub with a warm, convivial atmosphere, run by an award-winning landlord. No food Sun eve. The guest beer is usually taken from the Bass guest list.
◖ ▶ ❺ (Northfields)

W6: Hammersmith

Andover Arms

57 Aldensley Road
☎ (0181) 741 9794
11–11; 12–10.30 Sun
Fuller's Chiswick, London Pride, ESB H
Pleasant local in Brackenbury village, well hidden and pleasantly furnished. Thai food is a speciality.
◖ ▶ ❺ (Ravenscourt Pk)

Brook Green

170 Shepherd's Bush Road
☎ (0171) 602 2643
11–11; 12–3, 7–10.30 Sun
Young's Bitter, Special H
Large pub facing Brook Green, handy for Tesco's superstore.
⚏ ◖ ▶ ❺

Hammersmith Ram

81 King Street
☎ (0181) 748 4511
11–11; 12–10.30 Sun
Young's Bitter, Special, seasonal beers H
Formerly the Builders, now extensively refurbished and featuring bare boards. Blues night Tue.
◖ ▶ ⅄ ❺

Salutation

154 King Street
☎ (0181) 748 3668
11–11; 12–10.30 Sun
Fuller's Chiswick, London Pride, ESB H
Popular high street pub, boasting one of West London's finest beer gardens.
❀ ◖ ⅄ ❺

W7: Hanwell

Fox

Green Lane
☎ (0181) 997 3912
11–11; 12–10.30 Sun
Courage Best Bitter, Directors; Marston's Pedigree; guest beers H
Large roadhouse near the canal and Brent Valley Park; popular with walkers.
❀ ◖ ⅄ ▲ ⇌ ♣ P

Viaduct Inn

221 Uxbridge Road (A4020)
☎ (0181) 567 1362
11.30–11; 12–10.30 Sun
Fuller's Chiswick, London Pride, ESB, seasonal beers H
Straightforward local, popular with nearby hospital staff. Mind low doorways. Meals served 12–8 (5 Sat and Sun).
❀ ◖ ▶ ⊞ ⇌ ♣ P

W8: Kensington

Britannia

1 Allen Street
☎ (0171) 937 1864
11–11; 12–10.30 Sun
Young's Bitter, Special, seasonal beers H
Two-bar pub, off the High Street, with a large conservatory (no-smoking lunchtimes) and wood panelled bars. No food Sun eve. Q ◖ ▶ ❺ (High St) ⅄

Churchill Arms

119 Kensington Church Street
☎ (0171) 727 4242
11–11; 12–10.30 Sun
Fuller's Chiswick, London Pride, ESB, seasonal beers H
Extremely busy pub with a collection of Churchillian memorabilia and photos of US presidents. It specialises in Thai food, also Sun roast lunches.
Q ◖ ▶ ❺ (Notting Hill Gate)

W9: Maida Vale

Truscott Arms

55 Shirland Road
☎ (0171) 236 0310
11–11; 12–10.30 Sun
Draught Bass; Brakspear Bitter; Greene King IPA; Theakston XB; Young's Special H
Large, lively pub with an impressive bank of handpulls.
◖ ❺ (Warwick Ave) ♣

Warrington Hotel ☆

93 Warrington Crescent
☎ (0171) 286 0310
11–11; 12–10.30 Sun
Brakspear Special; Fuller's London Pride, ESB; Young's Special; guest beer (occasional) H
Large 'gin palace' with elaborate woodwork, tiles and glass, and a semi-circular, marble-topped bar. In contrast, the former public bar is quite restrained. Thai restaurant upstairs (eves).
◖ ▶ ⊟ ❺ (Warwick Ave)

W12: Shepherd's Bush

Crown & Sceptre

57 Melina Road
☎ (0181) 743 6414
11–11; 12–10.30 Sun
Fuller's London Pride, ESB, seasonal beers H
Backstreet, two-bar pub: an oasis in a beer desert, displaying much QPR memorabilia. Meals served 12–10. Q ❀ ◖ ▶ ♣

Moon on the Green

172 Uxbridge Road
☎ (0181) 749 5709
11–11; 12–10.30 Sun
Courage Directors; Fuller's London Pride; Theakston Best Bitter; Younger Scotch H
Two-bar pub in ex-shop premises, overlooking the green. Glass-fronted, it features wood panelling throughout and especially in the basement.
Q ◖ ▶ ❺ ⌣ ⅄

W13: West Ealing

Drayton Court Hotel

2 The Avenue
☎ (0181) 997 1019
11–11; 12–10.30 Sun
Fuller's Chiswick, London Pride, ESB, seasonal beers H
Classic, late-Victorian edifice; its local nickname is Dracula's Castle. Live theatre Sun afternoon and Mon–Thu eves. Meals generally served 12–9 (12–3, 7–9 Sun). The landlord is a Fuller's *Cellarman of the Year*.
☎ ❀ ◖ ⊟ ⅄ ▲ ⇌ ♣

W14: West Kensington

Seven Stars
253 North End Road
☎ (0171) 385 3571
11–11; 12–10.30 Sun
Fuller's London Pride, ESB H
Comfortable, two-bar local
hiding behind an unusual,
1930s Art Deco exterior.
Strong, genuine Irish flavour.
🏠 ◖▮ ⌂ ♣ ♠

Warwick Arms
160 Warwick Road
☎ (0171) 603 3560
11–11; 12–10.30 Sun
**Fuller's Chiswick, London
Pride, ESB, seasonal beers** H
Traditional local, built in 1828
for the now-defunct canal
basin. Note the attractive
Wedgwood handpumps.
Handy for Earl's Court and
Olympia halls. Live piano Sat
eve. 🏠 Q ☀ ◖▮ ⇌
(Olympia) ⊖ (Earl's Ct) ♣

Bedfont

Beehive
333 Staines Road (A315)
☎ (0181) 890 8086
12–3, 5–11; 11–11 Fri & Sat; 12–4,
7–10.30 Sun
Fuller's London Pride, ESB H
Excellent pub with a friendly
atmosphere, an attractive
lounge and a well-kept garden.
Good value food from a Thai
and traditional menu (not
served Sun). ☀ ◖▮ P

Brentford

Beehive
227 High Street
☎ (0181) 560 2421
11–11; 12–10.30 Sun
**Fuller's Chiswick, London
Pride, ESB** H
Large, prominent, popular pub
at the centre of Brentford.
Wholesome food; the Sun roast
lunches are recommended. Bar
skittles played.
🏠 ☀ ◖▮ ⇌ ♣

Brewery Tap
47 Catherine Wheel Road
☎ (0181) 560 5200
11–11; 12–10.30 Sun
**Fuller's London Pride, ESB,
seasonal beers** H
Cosy, lively, Victorian local,
with three elevated bars, off
the High Street and by the
Grand Union Canal. Live
music, including trad jazz Tue
and Thu. Good value, home-
cooked food with man-sized
portions of Sun roasts
(bookings advisable). Eve
meals until 8 (not Sun).
☀ ◖▮ ⇌ ♣

Magpie & Crown
128 High Street
☎ (0181) 560 5658
11–11; 12–10.30 Sun
Nethergate IPA; guest beers H
1923 brewer's Tudor pub with
three independents' guest
beers, a cask cider (perry
occasionally) and continental
bottled beers. Food is served
weekdays to 7pm, plus Sun
lunchtime.
☀ 🛏 ◖▮ ⇌ ♣ ⌂

Cranford

Queen's Head
123 High Street
☎ (0181) 897 0722
11–11; 12–10.30 Sun
**Fuller's Chiswick, London
Pride, ESB, seasonal beers** H
Large, Tudor-style pub in the
aerodrome conservation area,
featuring one bar but two
distinct drinking areas. A
lounge to one side is used for
dining. Award-winning
hanging baskets.
🏠 Q ☀ ◖▮ ♣ P

Greenford

Black Horse
425 Oldfield Lane North
☎ (0181) 578 1384
11–11; 12–10.30 Sun
**Fuller's Chiswick, London
Pride, ESB, seasonal beers** H
Busy, friendly, canalside pub
with moorings on the Grand
Union's Paddington arm; set in
the middle of an industrial
area. The large garden has a
children's play area. No meals
Sun eve.
☀ ◖▮ ⇌ ⊖ ♣ P

Bridge Hotel
Western Avenue (A40/A4127
jct)
☎ (0181) 566 6246
11–11; 12–10.30 Sun
**Young's Bitter, Special,
seasonal beers** H
More of a hotel with a pub
attached than in its original
form.
Q ☀ 🛏 ◖▮ ⇌ ⊖ ♣ P

Hampton

White Hart
70 High Street
☎ (0181) 979 5352
11–3, 5.30–11; 11–11 Sat; 12–10.30 Sun
**Boddingtons Bitter; Greene
King Abbot; guest beers** H
True free house with an
impressive bank of
handpumps serving a good
choice of constantly changing
guest beers in a convivial
atmosphere. Dickens
mentioned it in *Oliver Twist*.
Local CAMRA *Pub of the Year*
1996.
🏠 Q ☀ ◖▮

Harmondsworth

Crown
High Street ☎ (0181) 759 1007
11–11; 12–10.30 Sun
**Brakspear Bitter; Courage
Best Bitter, Directors; Fuller's
London Pride** H
Despite its proximity to
Heathrow Airport, this is still a
true village local: convivial,
characterful and lively.
🏠 Q ☀ ◖▮ ♣

Hounslow

Cross Lances
236 Hanworth Road (A314)
☎ (0181) 570 4174
11–11; 12–10.30 Sun
Fuller's London Pride, ESB H
Early Victorian, traditional,
tiled local, with a popular
public bar. The saloon has a
large, welcoming fire.
Wholesome meals are served at
all hours on request (book Sun
lunch).
🏠 Q ☀ ◖▮ ⇌ ♣ P

Moon Under Water
84–88 Staines Road
☎ (0181) 572 7506
11–11; 12–10.30 Sun
**Courage Directors; Fuller's
London Pride; Theakston Best
Bitter, XB; Younger Scotch;
guest beers** H
Early Wetherspoons shop
conversion, since extended but
very welcoming, with up to
five guest beers. Near
Safeway's supermarket, at the
western end of Hounslow's
high street.
Q ☀ ◖▮ ⅃ ⊖ (Central) ⌂ ✂

Isleworth

Castle
18 Upper Square,
Old Isleworth
☎ (0181) 560 3615
11–11; 12–10.30 Sun
**Young's Bitter, Special,
seasonal beers** H
Prominent pub, a long-
standing *Guide* entry, housing
a large, comfortable bar, plus a
games area. Families are
welcome in the conservatory.
The building dates from before
1930 and replaces another pub
which once served the local
docks.
🏠 Q ⅃ ☀ ◖▮ ♣ P

Coach & Horses
183 London Road (A315)
☎ (0181) 560 1447
11–11; 12–4, 7–10.30 Sun
**Young's Bitter, Special,
seasonal beers** H
17th-century, two-level
coaching inn, mentioned in
Dickens's *Oliver Twist*. The bar
is in the upper part. 🏠 Q ☀ ◖
▮ ⅃ ⇌ (Syon Lane) ♣ P

Red Lion

92–94 Linkfield Road
☎ (0181) 560 1457
11–11; 12–10.30 Sun
Brakspear Bitter; Flowers IPA; Marston's Pedigree; guest beers H
Substantial pub, hidden away in a quiet terrace. The original pub was built in the 18th century to serve the local factory workers.
✿ ⌂ ◖ ▶ ⇌ ♣

Northolt

Crown

Ealing Road
☎ (0181) 845 1197
11–11; 12–3, 7–10.30 Sun
Boddingtons Bitter; Flowers Original H
Pub in the centre of Northolt village; it can be very busy.
✿ ◖ ▶ ⊖ P

Plough

Mandeville Road
☎ (0181) 845 1750
11–11; 12–10.30 Sun
Fuller's London Pride, ESB H
Friendly pub with a thatched roof on the edge of Northolt village. Thai food is a speciality. ✿ ◖ ⊞ ⊖ P

Norwood Green

Plough

Tentelow Lane (A4127)
☎ (0181) 574 1945
11–11; 12–10.30 Sun
Fuller's Chiswick, London Pride, ESB H
Salubrious inn of ancient origin with various nooks and crannies and a trim garden. A flagstoned area forms the only remotely public bar section, and here sport is often screened. Elsewhere, conversation dominates. Weekday lunches.
Q ✿ ◖ ♣ P

Ruislip Manor

JJ Moon's

12 Victoria Road
☎ (01895) 622373
11–11; 12–10.30 Sun
Courage Directors; Fuller's London Pride; Theakston Best Bitter; Younger Scotch; guest beers H
Traditional-style, mock-Victorian alehouse, converted from an old Woolworth's store. Very popular with all ages.
Q ◖ ▶ ⅙ ⊖ ⅟

Southall

Beaconsfield Arms

63 West End Road
☎ (0181) 843 1581
11–11; 12–10.30 Sun
Draught Bass; Greene King Abbot; Highgate Dark, Saddlers; Scanlon's Spike; guest beers H
Large, formerly three-bar, ex-Fuller's pub which closed in the 1970s and reopened as a free house 16 years ago. A rare cask mild outlet. Seasonal Greene King beers often guest.
✿ ⇌ ♣ P

Teddington

Queen Dowager

49 North Lane
☎ (0181) 943 3474
11–11; 12–10.30 Sun
Young's Bitter, Special, Winter Warmer H
Small, relaxing pub with an excellent garden, named after Queen Adelaide who resided nearby. No meals Sun. Local CAMRA *Pub of the Year* 1993.
Q ✿ ◖ ⊞ ⇌

Twickenham

Eel Pie

9–11 Church Street
☎ (0181) 891 1717
11–11; 12–10.30 Sun
Badger Dorset Best, Tanglefoot; Brakspear Special; Gribble Black Adder II; guest beer H
Popular pub in a shopping area, just yards from the river and town centre, enjoying a deservedly high reputation for its lunches (not served Sun). Roomy and comfortable.
◖ ⇌ ♣ ⌣

Pope's Grotto

Cross Deep (A310)
☎ (0181) 892 3050
11–3, 5.30–11; 11–11 Sat; 12–10.30 Sun
Young's Bitter, Special, Ram Rod, seasonal beers H
Large, post-war, three-bar pub overlooking a pretty riverside park. It enjoys a good reputation for food; the dining area is in the lounge. ⌂ Q ✿ ◖ ▶ ⊞ ⇌ (Strawberry Hill) ♣ P

Prince Albert

30 Hampton Road
☎ (0181) 894 3963
11–11; 12–10.30 Sun
Fuller's Chiswick, London Pride, ESB H

Small, Victorian pub with a friendly atmosphere. Structural alterations in 1997 have not affected the bar, the beer, or the homely feeling. No food Sun eve.
Q ✿ ◖ ▶

Prince Blucher

124 The Green
☎ (0181) 894 1824
11–11; 12–10.30 Sun
Fuller's Chiswick, London Pride, ESB, seasonal beers H
Large, single-bar pub which, although modernised, still retains much character. The TV lounge is very popular for sport (rugby and soccer on weekend afternoons). There's also a conservatory and a large garden with children's play equipment.
✿ ◖

Uxbridge

Crown

Colham Green Road
☎ (01895) 442303
11–11; 12–3, 7–10.30 Sun
Fuller's Chiswick, London Pride, ESB H
Comfortable local with a lively public bar, handy for Hillingdon Hospital. Well-laid-out patio garden.
⅞ ✿ ◖ ⊞ ♣ P

Load of Hay

Villiers Street
☎ (01895) 234676
11–3, 5.30 (7 Sat)–11; 12–3, 7–10.30 Sun
Beer range varies H
Town pub with a real country feel; the main bar was formerly a stabling area. The superb smaller front bar is opened occasionally and is available for functions. Local CAMRA *Pub of the Year* 1995 and '96. Eve meals Mon–Fri.
Q ✿ ◖ ▶ ♣ P ⅟

Queen's Head

Windsor Street
☎ (01895) 234174
11–11; 12–10.30 Sun
Courage Best Bitter; Greene King Abbot; Theakston Best Bitter, XB, Old Peculier; guest beers H
One-bar pub, popular with local workers and other folk: a T&J Bernard house, it also stocks a range of bottled foreign beers but the guest beers are expensive. It can get very busy, especially Fri. No food Sun.
◖ ⊖

Discover even more great London pubs in CAMRA's pocket guidebook, *Known Treasures & Hidden Gems*, priced £7.99.

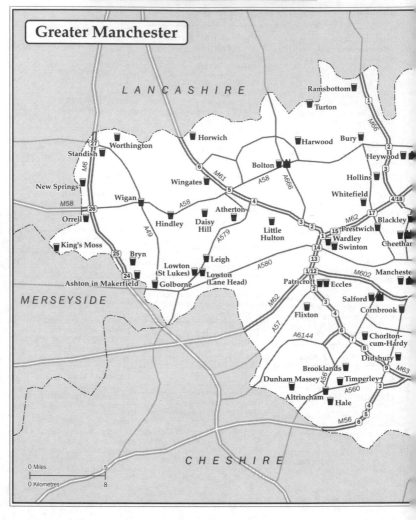

Greater Manchester

Altrincham

Hogshead
Old Market Place (A56)
☎ (0161) 927 7062
11.30–11; 12–10.30 Sun
**Boddingtons Bitter;
Whitbread Abroad Cooper;
guest beers** Ⓗ
Originally a coaching inn that
served as the town hall in the
late 19th century. All types of
live music are performed. Eve
meals 5–7; Sun food served
12–7. Nine guest beers;
Bulmers Old Hazy cider.
🏚 ֎ ◑ ▶ ⪰ ⊖ 🕙 ✕

Malt Shovels
68 Stamford Street
☎ (0161) 928 2053
11.30–11; 12–4, 7–10.30 Sun
Samuel Smith OBB Ⓗ

Friendly, cosmopolitan, town-
centre pub, famous for live trad
and modern jazz. Pool room
upstairs. No food Sun.
◑ ⪰ ⊖ ♣

Orange Tree
13–15 Old Market Place (A56)
☎ (0161) 928 2600
11.30–11; 12–10.30 Sun
**Courage Directors; Marston's
Pedigree; Morland Old
Speckled Hen; Wilson's
Bitter; guest beer** Ⓗ
Friendly, family-run local, very
accommodating to all. Note the
old photos of Altrincham and
neighbouring pubs long since
gone, and the exposed wattle
and daub construction. There
is an upstairs function room
for hire. Patio for outside
drinking.
🛏 ֎ ◑ ▶ ⪰ ⊖ ♣ ✕

Tatton Arms
3–5 Tipping Street (close to
Sainsbury's)
☎ (0161) 941 2502
11–11; 12–10.30 Sun
Boddingtons Bitter Ⓗ
Thriving, two-roomed,
football-oriented local where
pictures reflect the long-
serving landlord's nautical
background and the two
Manchester football clubs. The
outdoor drinking area is a sun
trap. No food Sun.
🏚 ֎ ◑ ⊞ ⪰ ⊖ ♣ P

Ancoats

Mitchell Arms
215 Every Street (A662)
☎ (0161) 273 3097
12–11; 12–3, 7–10.30 Sun
Banks's Mild, Bitter Ⓔ

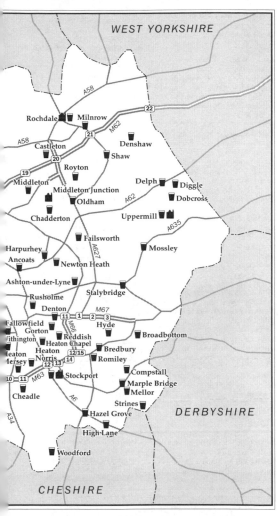

West Yorkshire
A58
22
M62
Rochdale   Milnrow
21
A58   Castleton
20   Denshaw
19   Royton   Shaw
Middleton   Delph   Diggle
Middleton Junction   Dobcross
Oldham   A62
Chadderton   Uppermill   A635
Failsworth
Harpurhey   Mossley
Ancoats   A627
Newton Heath
Ashton-under-Lyne
Rusholme   Stalybridge
Denton   M67
Fallowfield   11   1   2   3
Gorton   Hyde   Broadbottom
Withington   Reddish
Heaton Chapel   Bredbury
Heaton   12/15   Romiley
Heaton Norris   14
Mersey   12   13   Compstall
10   11   Stockport   Marple Bridge
M63   Mellor
Cheadle   Strines
A6   Hazel Grove   DERBYSHIRE
High Lane
A34   Woodford
Cheshire

Recent refurbishment has done nothing to diminish the appeal of this no-nonsense, corner pub. The small, smart lounge now competes with the popular and busy vault. ⬛ ♣ 🗍

Ashton in Makerfield

Commercial
21 Heath Road
☎ (01942) 726955
12–3 (not winter Mon–Thu), 7–11;
12–11 Fri & Sat; 12–10.30 Sun
Burtonwood Bitter, Buccaneer, seasonal beers Ⓗ
Popular backstreet local, handy for Haydock Park racecourse.
⬛

Ashton-under-Lyne

Dog & Pheasant
528 Oldham Road
☎ (0161) 330 4894
12–11; 12–6, 7.30–11 Sat; 12–4.30,
8–10.30 Sun
Banks's Mild; Marston's Bitter, Pedigree, HBC Ⓗ
Popular, friendly local close to Daisy Nook Country Park, serving good value food.
🏘 ⬛ ◑ ▶ P

Junction
Mosley Road (A670, near golf club) ☎ (0161) 343 1611
12–3, 5.30–11; 11–11 Fri & Sat; 12–4,
7–10.30 Sun
Robinson's Hatters Mild, Best Bitter, Frederics Ⓗ
Attractive, stone, terraced local where small rooms provide a

warm welcome. No meals Mon or Sat. ◑ ♣ P

Oddfellows
Kings Road, Hurst
☎ (0161) 330 6356
12–11; 12–10.30 Sun
Robinson's Hatters Mild, Best Bitter Ⓗ
Popular, multi-roomed local which boasts many traditional features, not least the splendid bar. Other beers from the Robinson's range appear regularly. A welcoming and sociable local. ⬛ ⨍

Station
2 Warrington Street
☎ (0161) 330 6776
11.30–11; 12–3 (4 summer), 7–11 Sat;
12–3, 7–10.30 Sun
Boddingtons Bitter; Marston's Pedigree; guest beers Ⓗ
Well-known free house which has established a reputation for serving well-kept beers from all around Britain, with an emphasis on new and smaller breweries. Six handpumps serve the quickly changing guest beers. ⬛ ◑ ⇌ ⌂

Atherton

Atherton Arms
6 Tyldesley Road
☎ (01942) 882885
11.30–11; 12–10.30 Sun
Holt Mild, Bitter Ⓗ
Immense pub: a huge, open lounge with a main bar; a large, sporty tap room catering for pool and snooker; a small bar in the corridor and a large function room with a stage and a bar. Occasional live music.
⬛ & ⇌ ♣ P

Letters Inn
2 Wigan Road
☎ (01942) 792094
12–11; 12–10.30 Sun
Lees Bitter; Tetley Mild, Bitter Ⓗ

Comfortable, edge-of-town-centre local with an L-shaped lounge and a tap room.
🍺 ♣ P

Pendle Witch

2–4 Warburton Place
☎ (01942) 884537
12–11; 12–10.30 Sun
Moorhouse's Black Cat, Premier, Pendle Witches Brew, seasonal beers; guest beers Ⓗ
Newly refurbished, one-roomed, popular local with a pool table, cosy seating and a loud jukebox. Busy at weekends. ❀ ≠ ♣

Blackley

Pleasant Inn

370 Chapel Lane (off A6104, end of Crab Lane)
☎ (0161) 740 3391
1 (12 Sat)–11; 12–10.30 Sun
Robinson's Hatters Mild, Best Bitter Ⓗ
Small, three-roomed, community pub in an ancient urban village. The lively vault, golf society room (known as the Pig Sty) and the lounge attract a loyal local clientele in this fairly remote location. Family room till 8pm.
⅄ ❀ 🍺 ♣

Bolton

Bob's Smithy

1448 Chorley Old Road
☎ (01204) 842622
12–3, 4.30–11; 12–4, 7–11 Sat; 12–4, 7–10.30 Sun
Boddingtons Bitter; Taylor Best Bitter; Walker Mild, Bitter; guest beers Ⓗ
Popular pub on the fringes of the moor, with panoramic vistas of Bolton; named after the local blacksmith who frequented it. ⚒ ❀ ◖ ♣ P

Clifton Arms

94 Newport Street
☎ (01204) 392738
11–11; 11–3, 7–11 Sat; 12–2, 7–10.30 Sun
Jennings Bitter; Marston's Pedigree; Moorhouse's Premier Ⓗ
Friendly, town-centre pub near the bus/rail interchange. Folk music Mon; quiz Wed; regular mini-beer festivals. No food Sun. ◖ ≠ ♣

Hen & Chickens

143 Deansgate
☎ (01204) 389836
11.30–11; 7.30–10.30 (closed lunch) Sun
Bass Toby Cask; Greenalls Mild, Bitter; Stones Bitter Ⓗ
Friendly local in the town centre, handy for the bus station. Excellent value, home-cooked lunches. ◖ ≠ ⅃ ♣

Lodge Bank Tavern

260 Bridgeman Street
☎ (01204) 531946
12–5, 7.30–11; 11–11 Fri & Sat; 12–10.30 Sun
Lees GB Mild, Bitter Ⓗ
Comfortable, welcoming local outside the town centre near Bobby Heywoods Park: one of the last pubs in Bolton to be granted a spirits licence.
❀ ≠ ♣ P

Lord Clyde

107 Folds Road
☎ (01204) 521705
12–11; 12–4, 7–10.30 Sun
Hydes' Anvil Dark Mild, Light, Bitter Ⓔ
Friendly, traditional, multi-roomed pub near the town centre: a small, L-shaped tap room, a small room at the rear and a large lounge. Home-cooked lunches Fri.
Q ❀ 🍺 ♣ P ⅃

Maxims

28 Bradshawgate
☎ (01204) 523486
11.30–4, 5.30–11; 7–10.30 (closed lunch) Sun
Vaux Samson, Waggle Dance; guest beer Ⓗ
Large, Victorian pub in the town centre. It has an upstairs disco at the weekends when it can be very busy and loud. Children welcome lunchtime. Pensioners' lunchtime specials served (no food Sun).
◖ ♿ ≠

Old Original British Queen

107 Blackburn Road (A666)
☎ 12–11; 12–3, 7–10.30 Sun
Holt Bitter Ⓗ
Main road local with a lounge and a games area. The name differentiates between two rival hostelries. ♣

Sweet Green Tavern

127 Crook Street
☎ (01204) 392258
11.30–3 (3.30 Sat), 7–11; 11.30–11 Thu & Fri; 12–3, 7–10.30 Sun
Tetley Bitter; guest beers Ⓗ
Large community pub on the fringe of the town centre which has not lost its character. Ideally situated near the bus/rail interchange. NB: Home fans only on BWFC home games. No food Sun.
⚒ ❀ ◖ ≠ ♣ P

Watermillock

Crompton Way, Astley Bridge (¼ mile from A58/A666 jct)
☎ (01204) 591798
11–3, 5–11; 12–10.30 Sun
Banks's Mild, Bitter; Camerons Strongarm; Marston's Pedigree; Morrells Varsity Ⓗ
Sympathetic conversion of a large Victorian house, a former nursing home. Built in late

Gothic style, it retains original fireplaces, mullioned windows and plaster ceilings. Bar meals in the Squires Bar; restaurant next door. ❀ ◖ ▶ ♿ ≠ (Hall i' th' Wood) P ⅃

Bredbury

Horsfield Arms

Ashton Road
☎ (0161) 430 6930
11.45–11; 11.45–3, 7–11 Sat; 12–3, 7–10.30 Sun
Robinson's Hatters Mild, Best Bitter Ⓔ
Pleasant pub with a well-appointed lounge and a games room. ❀ ◖ 🍺 ♣ P

Try also: Arden Arms, Castle Hill (Robinson's)

Broadbottom

Cheshire Cheese

65 Lower Market Street
☎ (01457) 762339
6 (12 summer Sat)–11; 12–10.30 Sun
Thwaites Best Mild, Bitter, seasonal beers; guest beers Ⓗ
Friendly village pub, popular with locals, surrounded by walking country. The beers are served without sparklers on request. Note the aviary in the ladies! ⚒ ❀ ♠ ≠ ♣ ⌂ ⅃

Brooklands

Brook

Brooklands Station Approach
☎ (0161) 973 7773
11.30–11; 12–10.30 Sun
Lees Bitter Ⓗ
Converted station master's house retaining a railway theme. The upstairs bistro is open Thu–Sun eve, 7–midnight; bar food every lunchtime.
❀ ◖ ▶ ⊖ P

Bryn

Bath Springs

455 Bryn Road
☎ (01942) 202716
11–11; 12–10.30 Sun
Ind Coope Burton Ale; Tetley Dark Mild, Bitter Ⓗ
Formidable redbrick building serving excellent value, home-cooked lunches. The pub is named after the defunct Bath Springs Brewery in Ormskirk. Weekday lunches. ◖ 🍺 ≠ ♣

Bury

Blue Bell

840 Manchester Road (A56, near Blackford Bridge)
☎ (0161) 766 2496
12–11; 12–10.30 Sun
Holt Mild, Bitter Ⓗ
Large, three-roomed pub with a traditional vault and a

friendly host. Popular with mature Man. Utd. supporters; the large, comfortable lounge is mostly patronised by friendly locals.
Q ❀ ♣ P

Bridge Inn

731 Manchester Road (A56 at Blackford Bridge)
☎ (0161) 796 8122
12–3, 5–11; 12–11 Sat; 12–3, 7–10.30 Sun
Courage Directors; Marston's Pedigree; John Smith's Bitter; guest beer Ⓗ
Cosy pub with brass ornaments and lots of knick-knacks. Plenty of choice of food at lunchtime (not served Sun), including specials. Small car park – no escape during rush hour! There is a patio at the front. ♨ ❀ ◖ ♣ P

Dusty Miller

87 Crostons Road (B6213/B6214 jct)
☎ (0161) 764 1124
12–11; 12–4, 7–11 Sat; 12–10.30 Sun
Moorhouse's Black Cat, Premier, Pendle Witches Brew; guest beers Ⓗ
One of only a handful of Moorhouse's tied houses, this pub has two rooms and an enclosed courtyard where children are admitted. Well worth the short walk from the town centre. No food Wed. Two regularly-changed guest beers.
❀ ◖ ♣

Old Blue Bell

2 Bell Lane (B6221/B6222 jct)
☎ (0161) 761 3674
12–11; 12–10.30 Sun
Holt Mild, Bitter Ⓗ
Impressive pub at a busy road junction on the outskirts of the town centre, with a traditional, multi-roomed layout featuring a busy, popular vault and several other rooms. The lounge has live music Thu and Sat afternoons and Sun eve; a quieter room is to the rear of the bar area. Children are welcome until 6pm.
Q ⛲ ♣

Try also: Tap & Spile, Manchester Old Rd (Free)

Castleton

Blue Pits Inn

842 Manchester Road (A664)
☎ (01706) 32151
12–4 (5 Fri & Sat), 7.30–11; 12–4, 7–10.30 Sun
Lees GB Mild, Bitter Ⓗ
Welcoming, friendly local in a former railway building, once used as a mortuary. Three distinct drinking areas. Winner of the JW Lees *Best Kept Cellar* award 1997. Large upstairs function room. ➹ P

Midland Beer Company

826 Manchester Road (A664)
☎ (01706) 750873
11.30–11; 12–10.30 Sun
Burtonwood Bitter; Moorhouse's Pendle Witches Brew; Thwaites Bitter; guest beers Ⓗ
Converted bank housing a modern, open-plan, continental-style bar in an area not known for its choice of real ale. One or more beers are sold cheaply. Weekday lunches.
◖ ➹

Chadderton

Horton Arms

19 Streetbridge (B6195, almost under A627M)
☎ (0161) 624 7793
11–11; 12–10.30 Sun
Lees GB Mild, Bitter Ⓗ
Comfortable pub which has a rural feel despite its easy access to Oldham and Rochdale: one quiet room and a large lounge, broken up neatly into distinct drinking areas. No food Sun.
❀ ◖ P

Hunt Lane Tavern

754 Middleton Road West (A669, ½ mile from centre)
☎ (0161) 627 2969
11.30–11 (11.30–3, 5–11 winter); 12–3.30, 7–10.30 Sun
Lees GB Mild, Bitter Ⓗ
Friendly, country-style pub in a suburban setting. Excellent value dining until 7.30, Mon–Fri). Quiz night Mon. Q ❀ ◖ ▮ ◖ ♣ P

Try also: Sun Mill Inn, Middleton Rd (Whitbread)

Cheadle

Queens Arms

177 Stockport Road (A560, 100 yds from M63 jct 11)
☎ (0161) 428 3081
12 (3 Mon)–11; 12–10.30 Sun
Robinson's Hatters Mild, Old Stockport, Best Bitter Ⓗ
Deceptively large pub close to the new AA centre. The old bowling green is now a safe play area for children and is very popular in summer. In winter, families can use the rear lounge. Weekday lunches in summer.
♨ Q ➹ ❀ ◖ ⊞ ♣ P ⊱

Cheetham

Queen's Arms

4–6 Honey Street (off A665, near A6010 jct)
☎ (0161) 834 4239
12–11; 12–10.30 Sun
Cains Mild *or* Taylor Mild; Phoenix Bantam; Taylor Landlord; guest beers Ⓗ

This pub features an Empress Brewery tiled facade, a large garden with a children's play area and a view of the Irk Valley and city centre. Ever-changing guest beers. ♨ ♨ ◖ ▮
➹ (Victoria) ⊖ ♣ ⌂

Chorlton-cum-Hardy

Beech Inn

72 Beech Road
☎ (0161) 881 1180
11–11; 12–10.30 Sun
Boddingtons Bitter; Flowers Original; Morland Old Speckled Hen; Taylor Best Bitter, Landlord; guest beers Ⓗ
Thriving, three-roomed pub, just off the village green. No food, no music, no gimmicks, but popular with all ages.
Q ❀ ⛁

Compstall

Andrew Arms

George Street
☎ (0161) 427 2281
11–11; 12–10.30 Sun
Robinson's Hatters Mild, Best Bitter Ⓗ
Ideally placed for Etherow Country Park: a perennial and deserved *Guide* entry with a relaxing atmosphere.
♨ Q ❀ ◖ ♣ P

Cornbrook

Hope Inn

297 Chester Road (A56)
☎ (0161) 848 0038
11–11; 11–5, 7–11 Sat; 12–5, 7–10.30 Sun
Hydes' Anvil Light, Bitter Ⓔ
Surviving example of a once plentiful Manchester bar-type pub: telly and chat with a mainly mature clientele in a friendly atmosphere. Pool table in the back room; children welcome until 5. It may stay open all day at weekends if busy. ♣ ⊟

Daisy Hill

Rose Hill Tavern

321 Leigh Road, Westhoughton (B5235) ☎ (01942) 815529
12–11; 12–10.30 Sun
Holt Mild, Bitter Ⓗ
Large, busy roadside pub, near the station, with a warm, friendly welcome. ❀ ➹ P

Delph

Royal Oak (Th' Heights)

Broad Lane, Heights (1 mile above Denshaw road)
OS982090 ☎ (01457) 874460
7–11; 12–3.30, 7–10.30 Sun

Boddingtons Bitter; Coach House Gunpowder Mild; guest beers Ⓗ
Isolated, 250-year-old, stone pub on an historic pack horse route overlooking the Tame Valley: a cosy bar and three rooms. Good, home-cooked food Fri–Sun eve (home-bred beef is often on the menu).
🏠 Q ✿ ▷ & P

Denshaw

Black Horse Inn
4 The Culvert, Oldham Road (A672, 2 miles from M62 jct 22)
☎ (01457) 874375
12–3, 6–11; 12–10.30 Sun
Banks's Mild, Bitter; Draught Bass; guest beer Ⓗ
Attractive, 17th-century, stone pub in a row of terraced cottages with a cosy, L-shaped bar area and two rooms (one available for functions and parties). Wide range of meals lunchtime and early eve.
Q ⏰ ✿ ◁ ▷ ♣ P 🍴

Try also: Junction, Rochdale Rd (Lees)

Denton

Chapel House
145 Stockport Road
11–11; 12–4, 7–10.30 Sun
Holt Mild, Bitter Ⓗ
Imposing redbrick building with a comfortable lounge and a traditional vault.
✿ 🍺 ♣ P

Jolly Hatters
67 Stockport Road
☎ (0161) 336 3682
2 (12 Fri & Sat)–11; 12–10.30 Sun
Hydes' Anvil Light, Bitter Ⓔ
Fine example of a multi-roomed urban local, comfortable and deservedly popular. The well-furnished lounge and snug are complemented by a public bar and a games room. A hub of the community, it boasts a medical bookshelf!
Q 🍺 ♣ 🍴

Didsbury

Station Hotel
682 Wilmslow Road (B5093)
☎ (0161) 445 9761
11–11; 12–10.30 Sun
Bateman Mild; Marston's Bitter, Pedigree, HBC; guest beers Ⓗ
Small, quiet, three-roomed pub converted from a bakery around 1890. One of the few remaining locals in a trendy village, it displays pictures of old Didsbury and is bedecked with flowering plants in summer. Q ✿ ♣

Diggle

Diggle Hotel
Station Houses (½ mile off A670) ☎ (01457) 872741
12–3, 5–11; 12–11 Sat; 12–3, 5–10.30 Sun
Boddingtons Bitter; Chester's Mild; Flowers Original; OB Bitter; Taylor Golden Best, Landlord Ⓗ
Popular and busy, especially in summer, 18th-century, stone pub in a pleasant hamlet, with a bar area and two other rooms. The accent is on a wide range of home-cooked meals (served all day Sat).
✿ 🏠 ◁ ▷ & P

Dobcross

Navigation
Wool Road (A670)
☎ (01457) 872418
11.30–3, 5–11; 11.30–11 Sat; 12–10.30 Sun
Banks's Hanson's Mild, Bitter; Marston's Bitter; guest beer Ⓗ
Next to the Huddersfield Narrow Canal: a stone pub, built in 1806 to slake the thirst of the navvies cutting the Standedge Tunnel under the Pennines. The open-plan lounge is a shrine to brass band music. Eve meals finish early (no eve meals Sun).
✿ ◁ ▷ ♣

Swan Inn
The Square
☎ (01457) 873451
12–3 (not Mon), 5–11; 12–3, 7–10.30 Sun
Marston's Pedigree; Moorhouse's Pendle Witches Brew; Phoenix Best Bitter; Theakston Mild, Best Bitter; guest beers Ⓗ
Stone-built, village local with an interesting history, dating from 1765: a renovated bar area with a flagged floor, plus three distinct drinking areas. Good value, home-cooked food includes Indian dishes (not served Sun or Mon eves). Well-appointed function room.
🏠 Q ✿ ◁ ▷ ♣ ✂

Dunham Massey

Vine Inn
Barns Lane (off B5160)
☎ (0161) 928 3275
11.30–11; 12–10.30 Sun
Samuel Smith OBB Ⓗ
Multi-roomed village local with a country pub feel, close to the Bridgewater Canal and Dunham Hall and Park (NT). Popular for Sun roast lunches; eve meals end at 8.30.
🏠 Q 🍺 ✿ ◁ ▷ ♣ P ✂

Eccles

Lamb Hotel ☆
33 Regent Road (A57, opp. bus station)
☎ (0161) 789 3882
11.30–11; 12–10.30 Sun
Holt Mild, Bitter Ⓗ
Unspoilt Edwardian gem: a listed building where Art Nouveau tiling lines the walls and staircase. A now rare full-sized billiards table stands in the games room. It can get very busy at weekends.
◁ 🍺 ⇌ ♣ P

Queen's Arms
Green Lane, Patricroft (by station)
☎ (0161) 789 2019
12–3, 7 (5 Fri)–11; 12–11 Sat; 12–4, 7–10.30 Sun
Boddingtons Mild, Bitter; guest beer Ⓗ
Britain's first railway pub, on the oldest passenger line, named after Queen Victoria's journey; it boasts a fine view of the track and trains. Listed by CAMRA members some years ago, it has just been sympathetically restored after further representations by the local CAMRA branch. Children are welcome until 8pm.
🍺 ✿ 🍺 ⇌ (Patricroft) ♣ P

Try also: Stanley Arms, Liverpool Rd (Holt)

Failsworth

Millgate
Ashton Road West (off A62)
☎ (0161) 688 4910
11.30–11; 12–10.30 Sun
Boddingtons Bitter; Holt Mild, Bitter; guest beers Ⓗ
Very popular, large, modern pub with a restaurant; very spacious and comfortably furnished. Ideal for families, the garden has adventure play equipment. Extensive menu in the restaurant (meals are served all day Sun).
🍺 ✿ ◁ ▷ 🍺 & P

Fallowfield

Friendship Inn
353 Wilmslow Road (B5093)
☎ (0161) 224 5758
11.30–11; 12–10.30 Sun
Hydes' Anvil Light, Bitter Ⓔ, seasonal beers Ⓗ/Ⓔ
Popular, main road pub in the heart of a vibrant student area, welcoming locals and students alike. A horseshoe-shaped bar serves one large area. Outdoor drinking on a raised patio is popular in summer.
✿ ◁ ▷ P 🍴

Flixton

Church Inn
34 Church Road (B5123, 200 yds from station)
☎ (0161) 748 2158
11–11; 12–10.30 Sun
Greenalls Mild, Bitter, Original; guest beer H
Former schoolhouse and courtroom, licensed for over 120 years; comfortably furnished with various seating areas. Well-behaved children are welcome till 7.30pm (small play area outdoors). The guest beer is usually from a small brewer. No food Sun.
Q ✿ ◖ ♣ P

Golborne

Railway
131 High Street
12–11; 12–10.30 Sun
Theakston Mild, Best Bitter; guest beers H
Smart, comfortable pub overlooking the main line with a lounge and a tap room. Occasional live music; constantly changing guest beers. The pub features seasonal beer festivals, a beer club, and its own newsletter. Traditional cider is occasionally available.
✿ ⊨ ⊕ ♣ ➾ P

Gorton

Coach & Horses
227 Belle Vue Street (600 yds E of A57/A6010 jct)
☎ (0161) 223 0440
5.30 (12 Sat)–11; 12–10.30 Sun
Robinson's Hatters Mild, Best Bitter H
The definitive pint of Robinson's is served in this warm-hearted, family-run community local. Cask beer greatly outsells other drinks amongst its loyal locals and passing trade from the cinema or speedway nearby. The TV in the vault is popular for sport, but otherwise talk and good fellowship prevail. Manchester 'log-end' dartboard.
⊕ ➾ (Belle Vue) ♣ P

Travellers Call
521 Hyde Road (by A57/A6010 jct)
☎ (0161) 223 1722
11.30–11; 12–10.30 Sun
Hydes' Anvil Mild, Bitter E
Now safe from demolition, this simple, old-style Manchester boozer may soon have some money spent on it, hopefully for sensitive refurbishment. The robust, but very friendly, atmosphere seems certain to survive. A true survivor to be cherished. ⊕ ♣

Waggon & Horses
736 Hyde Road (A57)
☎ (0161) 231 6262
11–11; 12–10.30 Sun
Holt Mild, Bitter H
Sensibly modernised to provide four linked drinking areas – a vault-style area, a games area, a main lounge and a 'back room' – this large, main road house attracts a busy trade for fine beer at low prices. Entertainment Sat eve, but otherwise it's a place for drinking and conversation.
➾ (Ryder Brow) ♣ P

Hale

Railway
128–130 Ashley Road
☎ (0161) 941 5327
11–11; 12–10.30 Sun
Robinson's Hatters Mild, Old Stockport, Hartleys XB, Best Bitter H, **Old Tom** G
Reputedly haunted, but friendly, unspoilt, 1930s, multi-roomed local, retaining much wood panelling. Families welcome until 8.30. No food Sun. Q ⍟ ✿ ◖ ♣
⊖ (Altrincham) ♣

Harpurhey

Junction
Queens Road, Hendham Vale (A6010) ☎ (0161) 202 5808
11–11; 12.30–10.30 Sun
Boddingtons Bitter; Holt Bitter; Lees Bitter H
Traditional Manchester pub with an unusual curved frontage. Good quality locally brewed beers at reasonable prices in a popular, Irish community pub.
⍟ ✿ ⊕ ⊖ (Woodlands Rd) ♣

Harwood

House Without a Name
75–77 Leegate
☎ (01204) 300063
11–11; 12–10.30 Sun
Boddingtons Bitter; Holt Bitter H
Small pub in a row of stone cottages dating from 1332; a lounge and a public bar. Originally an unlicensed brew pub, it was given its unusual name by an impatient magistrate. ✿ ⊕

Hazel Grove

Three Bears
Jacksons Lane (A5143)
☎ (0161) 439 0611
11.30–11; 12–10.30 Sun
Robinson's Hatters Mild, Hartleys XB, Best Bitter, Frederics H

Compact, modern pub facing open fields at the southern edge of the village. An attractive, cosy interior is divided into three distinct sections; welcoming and often busy. Eve meals end at 7.30; food served all day Sun. Children welcome until 8.
✿ ◖ ▶ ⅋ P ⏛

Heaton Chapel

Hind's Head
Manchester Road (A626)
☎ (0161) 431 9301
11.30–11; 12–10.30 Sun
Castle Eden Ale; Fuller's London Pride; Higsons Bitter; Marston's Pedigree; Taylor Landlord; guest beer H
Smart, welcoming, cottage-style pub with a conservatory-type restaurant. The lounge is divided into self-contained areas and the well-tended garden is a very pleasant place for a summer drink. Children welcome for meals (no food Sun eve; other eves till 8.45).
✿ ◖ ▶ ⅋ P

Heaton Mersey

Crown Inn
6 Vale Close, Didsbury Road (A5175) ☎ (0161) 442 4531
11–11; 12–10.30 Sun
Robinson's Hatters Mild, Best Bitter E
Traditional, two-bar local, near a conservation area, which claims to be the oldest pub in Stockport. Note the particularly attractive rear patio – a sun trap in summer. The food is very highly regarded (eve meals Tue–Fri).
✿ ◖ ▶ P ⏛

Griffin
552 Didsbury Road (A5145)
12–11; 12–10.30 Sun
Holt Mild, Bitter H
Often very busy, this multi-roomed, main road local is dominated by its superb mahogany and etched-glass bar. This old favourite has returned to winning ways, and is current local CAMRA *Pub of the Year*. Weekday lunches.
✿ ◖ P ⅋

Heaton Norris

Moss Rose
63 Didsbury Road (A5145)
☎ (0161) 432 5168
11.30–3 (4 Sat), 5.30 (7 Sat)–11; 11.30–11 Mon & Fri; 12–5, 7.30–10.30 Sun
Hydes' Anvil Light, Bitter E, **seasonal beers** H
Don't let the 1970s exterior put you off: this is a fine community local with a contrasting lounge and vault. Note: only the lower-gravity

seasonal beers tend to be stocked. No food Sun or Thu.
◁ ⌂ ♣ P ⛺

Nursery ☆

Green Lane (off A6, by Lex Rover garage)
☎ (0161) 432 2044
11.30–3, 5.30–11; 11.30–11 Sat & bank hols; 12–10.30 Sun
Hydes' Anvil Mild, Bitter Ⓔ, **seasonal beers** Ⓗ
Winner of a design award when built in 1939, this fine pub is little changed today. It is tucked away in a pleasant suburb and has its own bowling green. Excellent food (set lunches only Sun). Children welcome if dining.
Q ⊛ ◁ ▶ ♣ P ⛺

Heywood

Wishing Well

89 York Street
☎ (01706) 620923
12–11; 12–10.30 Sun
Jennings Bitter; Moorhouse's Premier, Pendle Witches Brew; Taylor Landlord; Tetley Bitter; guest beers Ⓗ
Excellent free house with a wonderful range of keenly-priced ales and a good atmosphere in five different drinking areas. The house beers are from Phoenix (Wigwam) and Moorhouse's (Millers Brook). ⌂ ◁ ♣ P

Try also: **Starkey Arms**, Manchester Rd (Holt)

High Lane

Royal Oak

Buxton Road ☎ (01663) 762380
12–11; 12–10.30 Sun
Burtonwood Bitter, Buccaneer, seasonal beers Ⓗ
Pub with always plenty of attractions – quizzes, live music and a children's play area with a bouncy castle. Eve meals finish at 7. ⍩ ⊛ ◁ ▶ ⇌ (Middlewood) ♣ P

Hindley

Minstrel

174 Wigan Road
☎ (01942) 519446
11–11; 12–10.30 Sun
Lees GB Mild, Bitter; Tetley Bitter; guest beers Ⓗ
Small, but characterful and friendly local. Built around the 1700s, it features a low, beamed ceiling in the bar area.
⊛ ◁ ▶ ⅙ ♣

Hollins

Hollins Bush Inn

257 Hollins Lane (off A56 at Blackford Bridge)
☎ (0161) 766 5692
12–3.30, 6–11; 12–11 Sat; 12–10.30 Sun

Lees GB Mild, Bitter Ⓗ
Friendly, three-roomed pub thought to be about 200 years old. It has a loyal following of locals and is handy for the Pilsworth shopping/cinema complex. No lunches Sun, or eve meals Tue. Q ◁ ▶ ♣ P

Horwich

Old Original Bay Horse

206 Lee Lane (B6226)
☎ (01204) 696231
11–11; 12–10.30 Sun
Boddingtons Bitter; Chester's Mild; Flowers Original; Lees Bitter; guest beer Ⓗ
Small, town-centre pub, very busy at weekends. Cosy, little vault. Q ⊛ ⌂ ♣ P

Toll Bar

2 Chorley New Road (A575)
12–4, 7–11; 12–11 Sat; 12–10.30 Sun
Thwaites Best Mild, Bitter, seasonal beers Ⓗ
Large, three-roomed pub opposite Lever Park. Note the unusual mural on the corner of the building. No food Sun.
⍩ ⛐ ⊛ ◁ ♣

Hyde

Sportsman Inn

57 Mottram Road
☎ (0161) 368 5000
11.30–11; 12–10.30 Sun
Plassey Bitter; Taylor Landlord; Whim Magic Mushroom Mild, Hartington Bitter; guest beers Ⓗ
Excellent free house with an expanding trade, following its purchase from Whitbread. It has been much improved by the new landlord who puts on an interesting range of guest beers and ciders from independent producers.
◁ ⌂ ⇌ (Newton) ♣ ⌢ P

White Lion

7 Market Place
☎ (0161) 368 2948
11–11; 11–5, 7–11 Sat; 12–4, 7–10.30 Sun
Robinson's Hatters Mild, Best Bitter Ⓔ, **Old Tom** Ⓗ
Bustling market pub in the centre of town, usually busy lunchtime. The opened-up interior is the hub of much community activity, whilst the other side of the long bar boasts a friendly, untouched, tap room. A rare all-year outlet for Old Tom. No food Sun.
◁ ⌂ ⇌ (Central) ♣ ⛺

King's Moss

Colliers Arms

Pimbo Road ☎ (01744) 892894
12–11; 12–10.30 Sun
Greenalls Mild, Bitter, Original; guest beers Ⓗ

This 1850, out-of-the-way village pub retains a stone flag floor and two fires; a family pub with a well-kept beer garden. Good home cooking.
⍩ Q ⊛ ◁ ▶ ⅙ P ⌿

Leigh

Musketeer

15 Lord Street
☎ (01942) 701143
11–11; 12–3, 7–10.30 Sun
Boddingtons Mild, Bitter; guest beer Ⓗ
Town-centre pub with two rooms, popular with locals.
◁ ▶ ♣

Railway

160 Twist Lane (A572/A579 jct) ☎ (01942) 203853
12–11; 12–10.30 Sun
Tetley Dark Mild, Bitter, Worthington Bitter; guest beer Ⓗ
Friendly, open-plan, traditional pub, popular with locals. Good value food from a basic menu (not served Sun eve). Strong local sports involvement. ⊛ ⍩ ◁ ▶ ♣

Victoria

68–70 Kirkhall Lane (opp. B&Q, off A579)
☎ (01942) 606114
2–5 (not Mon–Wed), 7.30–11; 12–11 Sat; 12–10.30 Sun
Lees Bitter; Tetley Mild, Bitter Ⓗ
Multi-roomed pub on two levels, popular with locals. Handy for Leigh RLFC. ♣

Little Hulton

Dun Mare

277 Manchester Road West (A6, near M61 jct 4)
☎ (0161) 790 5235
12–4, 7–11; 12–11 Sat; 12–4.30, 7–10.30 Sun
Walker Mild, Best Bitter Ⓗ
Attractive local, the only Walker outlet in the area. Check the 1964 framed price list – Bitter 1/7d, Mild 1/4d a pint.
Q ⊛ ⌂ ⅙ ♣ P

Lowton (Lane Head)

Red Lion

324 Newton Road
☎ (01942) 671429
12–3.30, 5.30–11; 12–11 Sat; 12–10.30 Sun
Davenports Bitter; Greenalls Mild, Bitter, Original; Tetley Bitter; guest beer Ⓗ
Recently re-designed and refurbished local with a raised seating area and a standing area in front of the re-sited bar. The dining area is away from the bar; the lounge leads to a bowling green and garden,

next to the landlord's war games centre. The mild pump is in the tap room bar.
✿ 🍴 🍺 ▶ 🍴 ♣ P

Lowton (St Lukes)

Hare & Hounds

1 Golborne Road
☎ (01942) 728387
12–11; 12–10.30 Sun
Tetley Mild, Bitter; guest beers Ⓗ
Large, open-plan pub in two halves: a lounge and tap room area with low beams, plus a lounge eating area away from the bar, catering for all. Busy at weekends. Children's playground outside.
✿ 🍺 ▶ 🍴 ♣ P

Manchester City Centre

Beer House

Angel Street (off A664)
☎ (0161) 839 7019
11.30–11; 12.30–10.30 Sun
Moorhouse's Pendle Witches Brew; guest beers Ⓗ
Busy, friendly, pub. A Laurel & Hardy society meets upstairs. Watch out for food promotions.
🍺 ▶ ⇌ (Victoria) ⊖ ◠

Castle

66 Oldham Street (near A62/A665 jct) ☎ (0161) 236 2945
11.30–11; 12–4, 7.30–10.30 Sun
Robinson's Dark Mild, Hatters Mild, Old Stockport, Hartleys XB, Best Bitter, Frederics, Old Tom Ⓗ
Robinson's only city-centre pub. A tiled facade and mosaic floor lead into the comfortable front bar with a cosy snug and games room to the rear. Manchester Draught Society meets on Wed; live blues Thu. Children's room open till 7. Q
♿ 🍴 ⇌ (Victoria/Piccadilly) ⊖ (Piccadilly Gdns/High St) ♣

Circus Tavern ☆

86 Portland Street
☎ (0161) 236 5818
12–11; 12–4 (closed eve) Sun
Tetley Bitter Ⓗ
Recognised as one of Britain's most unspoilt, traditional pubs, this tiny two-roomer is a Manchester institution, its intimacy encouraging conversation. Since it's so small (total capacity around 40), it may shut its doors when full at weekends.
🏚 Q ⇌ (Piccadilly) ⊖ (Piccadilly Gdns)

City Arms

48 Kennedy Street
11.30–11; 11.30–3, 7–11 Sat; closed Sun
Beer range varies Ⓗ

Very popular Festival Ale House, much frequented by the business community. Good value food. A listed building with a noteworthy frontage.
🍴 ♿ ⇌ (Oxford Rd) ⊖ (St Peters Sq)

Crown Inn

321 Deansgate
☎ (0161) 834 1930
11–11; 12–10.30 Sun
Vaux Mild, Samson; guest beer Ⓗ
Former Wilson's pub in the Castlefield area, the only mild outlet in the district. Its one bar manages to combine the atmosphere of both a lounge and a vault. Good value food (weekdays) and accommodation. 🏚 🍴 ⇌ (Deansgate) ⊖ (G Mex) ♣

Ganders Go South

Barton Arcade, Barton Square
☎ (0161) 832 8360
12–3, 5 (5.30 Sat)–11 (midnight Fri, 1am Sat); closed Sun
Marston's Bitter, Pedigree, HBC Ⓗ
Small bar below street level, well worth finding. Live jazz six nights a week, with famous names. Excellent Cajun and New Orleans food (set menu and à la carte). 🍴 ▶ ⇌ (Victoria) ⊖ (St Peters Sq)

Grey Horse

80 Portland Street
☎ (0161) 236 1874
11–11; 12–10.30 Sun
Hydes' Anvil Mild, Bitter Ⓗ
This much-loved city-centre haunt is now back to its best in the hands of a skilful and experienced licensee. The single-room interior is ideal for a drink and a chat, with just quiet radio or tapes to break the hush. No kitchen, but you may bring your own snacks.
⇌ (Piccadilly) ⊖ (Piccadilly Gdns)

Hare & Hounds

46 Shudehill (near Arndale Centre) ☎ (0161) 832 4737
11–11; 12–10.30 Sun
Tetley Dark Mild, Bitter; Highwood Tom Wood Harvest Bitter Ⓗ
19th-century pub whose decor echoes its name. A wealth of fine tiles and stained-glass separates the three rooms.
Q 🍴 ⇌ (Victoria) ⊖ (High St/Market St) ♣

Hogshead

64 High Street (near Arndale Centre) ☎ (0161) 832 4824
11–11; 12–3 Sun, closed Sun eve
Boddingtons Bitter; Castle Eden Ale; Flowers Original; Taylor Landlord; guest beers Ⓗ/Ⓖ
Typical Hogshead Ale House opened in 1993 (formerly the Wheatsheaf): a large, open-

plan bar area and partitioned seating areas. Up to four beers on gravity; good value lunches.
🏚 🍺 ♿ ⇌ (Victoria) ⊖ (High St) ♣ ◠

Jolly Angler

47 Ducie Street (near A665/A662 jct, by canal aqueduct)
☎ (0161) 236 5307
12–3, 5.30–11; 11–11 Sat; 12–4, 7–10.30 Sun
Hydes' Anvil Billy Westwoods, Bitter, seasonal beers Ⓗ
True Irish pub, without the clichés. Two basic rooms are served by a popular bar – great for music and chat.
🏚 ⇌ (Piccadilly) ⊖

Marble Arch

Rochdale Road (A664, 350 yds from A665 jct)
☎ (0161) 832 5914
12–11; 7–10.30 (closed lunch) Sun
Beer range varies Ⓗ
Featuring a Victorian tiled interior wall, a sloping floor and a 'must-see' wall frieze, this busy pub has a friendly atmosphere.
🏚 🍺 ⇌ (Victoria) ⊖ ◠

Pot of Beer

36 New Mount Street (off A664, near A665 jct)
☎ (0161) 834 8579
12–11; closed Sun
Boddingtons Bitter; Robinson's Dark Mild Ⓗ**; guest beers** Ⓗ/Ⓖ
Formerly the Harp & Shamrock, this pub was surplus to Marston's requirements. After a demolition threat, it was sold to the free trade and now offers a friendly, small pub atmosphere.
🏚 ⇌ (Victoria) ⊖

Waldorf

12 Gore Street (off A6)
☎ (0161) 228 3269
11–11; 12–10.30 Sun
Chester's Mild; Boddingtons Bitter; Marston's Pedigree; Taylor Landlord; guest beer Ⓗ
Much sought after by film location crews for its authentic looking London beer house-style appearance, the Waldorf is located in a rejuvenated sector of the city centre, close to the main rail termini.
Q ✿ 🍴 ▶ ⇌ (Piccadilly) ⊖

White Lion

43 Liverpool Road, Castlefield
☎ (0161) 832 7373
11.30–11; 12–10.30 Sun
Boddingtons Bitter; Taylor Landlord; guest beers Ⓗ
Pub at the heart of the Castlefield area, close to the canal basin and museums. Good value food is all made on the premises; the curries are highly recommended (no eve

meals Fri; food served Sun
until 6). ❀ ◖ ⬥ ⇌
(Deansgate) ⊖ (G Mex)

Marple Bridge

Travellers Call

134 Glossop Road
☎ (0161) 427 4169
12–11; 12–10.30 Sun
**Robinson's Hatters Mild, Best
Bitter** Ⓗ
Pub at the top of a long hill, but
worth the climb for the
warmest of welcomes and
Robinson's at its best.
Q ❀ ◖ ♿ P

Try also: **Pineapple**, Market St,
Marple (Robinson's)

Mellor

Oddfellows Arms

73 Moor End Road (3 miles
from Marple on back New
Mills road) ☎ (0161) 449 7826
11–3, 5.30–11; 12–3, 7.30–10.30 Sun
**Banks's Mild; Marston's
Bitter, Pedigree; guest beer** Ⓗ
Elegant, three-storey building,
sympathetically altered
internally, in a picture postcard
setting. Strong accent on
quality food; excellent choice
of beers. ♨ Q ❀ ◖ ▶ ♿ P 🍴

Middleton

Crown Inn

52 Rochdale Road (A664)
☎ (0161) 654 9174
11–11; 12–10.30 Sun
Lees GB Mild, Bitter Ⓗ
End of terrace pub with a small
locals' snug and a larger
lounge with much brass bric-a-
brac. Standing room only is
often the order of the day such
is its popularity. ♣ P

Tandle Hill Tavern

Thornham Fold, Thornham
Lane (unmetalled road, 1 mile
off A671 or A664) OS898091
☎ (01706) 345297
7 (5 summer)–11; 12–10.30 Sun
**Lees GB Mild, Bitter,
Moonraker** (winter) Ⓗ
Hidden gem, set amongst open
country in a small farming
community. Its two rooms and
bar have been redecorated
recently and have a welcoming
atmosphere. Sun lunch served.
♨ Q ☻

Try also: **Oddfellows Arms**,
Oldham Rd (Scottish Courage)

Milnrow

Crown & Shuttle

170 Rochdale Road, Firgrove
(A640) ☎ (01706) 48259
12–11; 12–10.30 Sun
Lees GB Mild, Bitter Ⓗ
A warm welcome always
awaits at this terraced pub, run

by a couple who make the
place seem like home. It fields a
ladies rounders team.
♨ ☻ ❀ ⬥

Mossley

Tollemache Arms

Manchester Road (A15)
☎ (01457) 832354
11.30–11; 12–3, 7–10.30 Sun
**Robinson's Hatters Mild, Best
Bitter** Ⓗ
Popular, cosy, sociable, stone
local next to Huddersfield
Narrow Canal. Compact, oak-
panelled rooms and a polished
bar feature. In the same family
since 1959. ♨ Q ❀ ♣ P

Try also: **Rising Sun**,
Stockport Rd (Free)

New Springs

Colliers Arms

192 Wigan Road, Aspull
☎ (01942) 831171
12.30–5.30 (not Thu), 7.30–11; 12–5,
7–10.30 Sun
Burtonwood Mild, Bitter Ⓗ
Unspoilt, 18th-century pub
near the Leeds–Liverpool
Canal. Tiny car park.
♨ ⬥ ♣ P

Newton Heath

Robin Hood

237 Droylsden Road (500 yds
from A62, Oldham road)
☎ (0161) 681 5167
12–4.30, 7–11; 12–11 Sat; 12–10.30 Sun
**Bateman Mild; Marston's
Bitter** Ⓗ
Comfortable, two-roomed pub
with a well-decorated lounge
and an extensive vault. It
appeals to a wide cross-section
of customers.
❀ ⬥ ⇌ (Dean Lane) ♣ P

Try also: **Railway**, Dean Lane
(Holt)

Oldham

Dog & Partridge

376 Roundthorn Road (off
B6194) ☎ (0161) 624 3335
7 (4 Fri, 11 Sat)–11; 12–2, 7–11 Tue;
12–10.30 Sun
Lees GB Mild, Bitter Ⓗ
Popular, comfortably
furnished, detached pub in a
semi-rural setting, with low,
beamed ceilings. Busy Sun
lunch with local football teams.
♨ ❀ ♣ ♣ P

Hogshead

36 Union Street
☎ (0161) 628 0301
11.30–11; 1–10.30 Sun
**Boddingtons Bitter; Castle
Eden Ale; Chester's Mild;
Whitbread seasonal beers;
guest beers** Ⓗ

Whitbread cask alehouse
providing a varied choice of
guest beers through its ten
handpumps. Special events
and live music at times. Food is
served until 7.30 (no meals
Sun). An oasis for the
discerning drinker in the
middle of Oldham.
♨ ◖ ▶ ⇌ (Mumps) ⌣ P

Try also: **Bank Top Tavern**,
King Sq (Lees)

Orrell

Bird i' th' Hand

Gathurst Road
☎ (01942) 212006
11–11; 12–3, 5.30–11 Mon; 12–10.30
Sun
**Theakston Mild, Bitter, Old
Peculier; Webster's Green
Label; Wilson's Mild** Ⓗ
Warm, friendly pub, pleasantly
decorated in country style,
with a good atmosphere and a
mix of all ages. At one time it
was used for local inquests.
❀ ◖ ▶ ♿ ▲ ⇌ (Gathurst) ♣ P

Patricroft

Grapes Hotel

439 Liverpool Road (A57 near
M63 jct 2) ☎ (0161) 789 6971
11–11; 12–10.30 Sun
Holt Mild, Bitter Ⓗ
Classic, Edwardian listed
building: the lavish
architecture has to be seen to
be believed. Its multi-roomed
layout has been used in various
TV drama productions.
⬥ ⇌ ♣ P

Prestwich

Woodthorpe

Bury Old Road (near A665/
A6044 jct) ☎ (0161) 795 0032
11–11; 11.30–4, 7–11 Sat; 12–4, 7–10.30
Sun
Holt Mild, Bitter Ⓗ
The original home of one of the
Holt brewing family: a lovely
old restored building set in its
own grounds. One guest room
has a four-poster bed. Home-
cooked food.
Q ❀ 🛏 ◖ ♣ P

Try also: **Red Lion**, Bury New
Rd (Holt)

Ramsbottom

Good Samaritan

13 Peel Brow (near station)
☎ (01706) 823314
11–11; 12–10.30 Sun
**Lees Bitter; John Smith's
Bitter; Wilson's Bitter; guest
beer** Ⓗ
Built in the 1840s as a coaching
house, this traditional pub is a
short walk from the town
centre across the railway line.

It has three drinking areas and is popular with locals. The guest beer is often a mild. Food served Fri, Sat and Sun.
❀ ◖ ≠ ♣ P

Reddish

Thatched Tavern

54 Stanhope Street (off B6167, 200 yds from Houldsworth Sq)
11–11; 12–10.30 Sun
Tetley Mild, Bitter Ⓗ
Homely, multi-roomed, street-corner local with a comfortable lounge and a traditional vault. Difficult to find, but well worth the effort. Note the pictures of the 19th-century pub when it really was thatched.
❀ ⊟ ♣

Rochdale

Albion

600 Whitworth Road (A671, 2 miles from centre)
☎ (01706) 48540
12–3 (not Mon–Wed), 4.30–11; 12–11; Sat; 12–10.30 Sun
Bateman Mild; Lees Bitter; Marston's Bitter, Pedigree; Taylor Landlord; guest beers Ⓗ
This cosy, little pub on the northern outskirts of town offers a wide variety of beers, with usually one from the nearby Phoenix Brewery. An interesting choice of food is available (lunches are served at weekends only).
♨ Q ❀ ◖ ▶

Cask & Feather

1 Oldham Road
☎ (01706) 7114/6
11–11; 12–10.30 Sun
McGuinness Feather Plucker Mild, Best Bitter, Special Reserve, Junction Bitter, Tommy Todd Porter, seasonal beers Ⓗ
Distinctive pub whose castellated frontage stands guard over a busy road junction. The comfortable interior is often busy with a wide range of clients drawn by the Thomas McGuinness beers (the brewery can be viewed at the rear) and the good value lunches which are served.
◖ ≠

Eagle

59 Oldham Road (A671/ Wood St jct)
☎ (01706) 47222
12–3 (4 Sat), 5 (7 Sat)–11; 12–11 Fri; 12–10.30 Sun
Samuel Smith OBB Ⓗ
Popular stone pub, away from the town centre, containing various interesting artefacts and period features.
≠ ♣

Healey Hotel

172 Shawclough Road (B6377)
☎ (01706) 45453
12–3, 5–11; 12–3, 5–10.30 Sun
Robinson's Best Bitter Ⓗ
Terraced pub in a rural area, near Healey Dell Nature Reserve: three drinking areas with a relaxing atmosphere, in a pub retaining much of its splendid tiled interior.
Q ❀ ◖ ▶

Merry Monk

234 College Road (near A6060/ B6222 jct) ☎ (01706) 46919
12–11; 12–3, 7–10.30 Sun
Marston's Bitter, Pedigree; guest beers Ⓗ
Friendly, unpretentious, free house selling up to four guest beers: local CAMRA *Pub of the Season*, winter 1997. Free jukebox; unusual Ring the Bull game. ♣ P

Spring Inn

183 Broad Lane (½ mile off A671) ☎ (01706) 33529
11–11; 12–10.30 Sun
Lees GB Mild, Bitter Ⓗ
Recently extended to become one of Lees restaurant-type pubs, serving interesting food; speciality food nights are held regularly. ◖ ▶ ⊟ P

Success to the Plough

179 Bolton Road, Marland (A58) ☎ (01706) 33270
12–11; 12–3, 7–10.30 Sun
Lees GB Mild, Bitter Ⓗ
Imposing, detached pub with a deceptively spacious interior, divided into separate areas. A splendid bowling green to the rear hosts several crown green competitions. Weekday lunches. ❀ ◖ P

Try also: Cemetery Inn☆, Bury Rd (Free)

Romiley

Duke of York

Stockport Road
☎ (0161) 430 2806
11.30–11; 12–10.30 Sun
Courage Directors; Ruddles County; John Smith's Bitter; guest beer Ⓗ
Long, low pub of harmonious proportions, close to the Peak Forest Canal. It is just as pleasing inside, with a beamed lounge and a good vault. Good, home-cooked food.
♨ ❀ ◖ ▶ ⊟ ≠ ♣ P

Royton

Dog & Partridge

148 Middleton Road (B6195)
☎ (0161) 628 4198
11–11; 12–10.30 Sun
Lees GB Mild, Bitter Ⓗ
Out-of-town-centre boozer where a warm welcome is

always guaranteed. Excellent selection of malt whiskies.
◖ ⊟

Marston Tavern

83 Rochdale Road (A671, near town hall) ☎ (0161) 628 0569
12–11; 12–3, 7–10.30 Sun
Bateman Mild; Marston's Bitter, Pedigree Ⓗ
Detached pub in the centre of Royton, with two distinct drinking areas. Regular quiz nights midweek, but there tends to be a much more lively atmosphere at weekends.
♣

Try also: Railway, Rochdale Rd (Lees)

Rusholme

Albert

5 Walmer Street (off B5117 at Shere Khan)
11–11; 12–4, 7–10.30 Sun
Hydes' Anvil Bitter Ⓔ
A little island of Irishness amongst the fragrant aromas of Manchester's 'Curry Mile', this friendly two-roomer's loyal regular trade is swollen at weekends by restaurant-goers, but Sun eve's traditional music session tunefully reasserts its true identity. ⊟ ♣ P 🕁

Salford

Crescent

20 Crescent (A6, near university)
☎ (0161) 736 5600
12 (7.30 Sat)–11; 1–4, 7.30–10.30 Sun
Beer range varies Ⓗ
Rambling three-roomed house with an extensive frontage. It has a 'lived-in' ambience and a thriving cat population. Popular with students during term-time. Six guest beers, plus a Titanic house beer. Weekday meals (eves until 8). ♨ ◖ ▶ ≠ (Crescent) ♣ ⌂ P 🕁

Dock & Pulpit

1 Encombe Place (off A6, near cathedral) ☎ (0161) 834 0201
12–3, 5–11; 12–11 Sat; 12–3, 7.30–10.30 Sun
Beer range varies Ⓗ
Small, friendly, gas-lit, one-room free house with a cast iron fireplace. It can be hard to find but is worth the effort. The odd name derives from the nearby former law courts and the church. Four guest beers plus a house beer from John Smith's.
♨ ≠ (Central) ♣ ⌂

Eagle Inn

19 Collier Street (off A6041)
☎ (0161) 832 4919
11–11; 12–10.30 Sun
Holt Mild, Bitter Ⓗ
Traditional backstreet gem, exposed by a new trunk road;

still not easy to find but worth seeking out. A genuine local, with a friendly atmosphere. ⌂ & ≹ (Victoria/Central) ⊖ (Victoria) ♣

Olde Nelson

285 Chapel Street (A6, opp. cathedral) ☎ (0161) 832 6189
12–3.30, 6.30–11; 11–5.15, 7–11 Sat; 12–10.30 Sun
Boddingtons Bitter; Chester's Mild; Lees Bitter; Whitbread Trophy Ⓗ
Multi-roomed Victorian gem with a large front vault and lots of etched glass. It sometimes closes for a few hours late Sun afternoon.
Q ⧖ ⚲ ⌂ ≹ (Central) ♣

Red Lion

279 Bolton Road, Irlams o' th' Height (former A6, between A666 and A5186 jcts)
☎ (0161) 736 9680
11–11; 12–10.30 Sun
Holt Mild, Bitter Ⓔ
Pre-war, three-roomed pub catering for the older drinker. The organist entertains on Tue, Wed and Sun eves. One of three Holt's pubs in the village.
Q ⌂ ♣ P

Union Tavern

105 Liverpool Street (midway between A5063 and A5066)
☎ (0161) 736 2885
11–11; 12–10.30 Sun
Holt Mild, Bitter Ⓗ
Popular Holt's outlet in the heart of Salford, now surrounded by industrial units. It fields seven darts teams. A no-frills, basic, honest boozer.
⌂ & ≹ (Crescent) ♣ P

Welcome

Robert Hall Street, Ordsall (off A5066, near B5461 jct)
☎ (0161) 872 6040
11.30–4, 7.30–11; 12–4, 7.30–10.30 Sun
Lees GB Mild, Bitter Ⓔ
A survivor in an inner city area where many pubs are boarded, burnt out or gone forever: a true community local with a comfortable lounge and a vault. The handpumps activate electric motors. Q ⌂ ♣ P

Shaw

Black Horse

203A Rochdale Road (B6194, ½ mile from centre)
☎ (01706) 847173
3.30 (12 Sat)–11; 12–10.30 Sun
Lees GB Mild, Bitter Ⓗ
Traditional, friendly, stone pub, a short walk from the station, with a comfortable lounge area and a vault.
♣ P

Try also: **Blue Bell**, Market St (Robinson's)

Stalybridge

Q

3 Market Street
☎ (0161) 303 9157
12–11; 12–5, 7–11 Sat; 12–4, 7–10.30 Sun
Exmoor Gold; Fuller's London Pride; Marston's Bitter, Pedigree; Taylor Landlord; guest beers Ⓗ
The pub with the shortest name in Britain (Stalybridge also has the pub with the longest name). Created out of a shop, and now expanded into the adjoining premises, it has a friendly atmosphere, a cocktail bar and a conservatory upstairs. Live jazz Mon. Sun lunch served. Q ≹

Rose & Crown

7 Market Street
☎ (0161) 303 7098
11–11; 12–3, 7–10.30 Sun
Vaux Mild, Bitter, Samson, seasonal beers *or* guest beer Ⓗ
Friendly, urban local recently refurbished to a high standard in keeping with the pub's history. Deservedly popular, it has a growing band of regulars. ⚌ ≹ ♣

White House

1 Water Street
☎ (0161) 303 2288
11–11; 12–4, 7–10.30 Sun
Bateman Mild; Marston's Bitter; guest beers Ⓗ
Enterprising, friendly and popular, free house with up to six beers, mostly from independent breweries, a fine selection of malt whiskies and a range of foreign bottled beers. No food Sun. Folk music Thu eve. ◖ ▮ ≹ P

Try also: **Station Buffet**☆, Platform 1, Stalybridge Station (Free)

Standish

Boars Head

Wigan Road (A49)
☎ (01942) 749747
11.30–3, 5.30–11; 12–3, 7–10.30 Sun
Burtonwood Mild, Bitter, Forshaw's, Top Hat, Buccaneer, seasonal beers Ⓗ
Old, characterful coaching house, recently refurbished at the rear to accentuate the patio garden. Its low ceilings are festooned with water jugs. Own bowling green; sport is always on TV.
⚌ ⧖ ۞ ⌂ ♣ P

Dog & Partridge

33 School Lane
☎ (01257) 401218
1–11; 12–10.30 Sun
Boddingtons Bitter; Tetley Dark Mild, Mild, Bitter Ⓗ

Lively, male-oriented, open-plan local, where sport is always on TV; the weekend's Wigan RLFC video is shown during the following week. Limited parking. ۞ ♣ P

Stockport

Armoury

Greek Street, Shaw Heath
☎ (0161) 480 5055
11–11; 11–4, 8–11 Sat; 12–3, 7–10.30 Sun
Robinson's Hatters Mild, Best Bitter Ⓔ
A classic 1920s interior hides behind the plain facade of this street-corner local. In the same family for two generations, it offers something for everyone with a warm lounge, darts room, lobby (with own bar counter) and a superb vault.
Q ⌂ ≹ ♣

Bakers Vaults

Market Place
☎ (0161) 480 3182
11–11; 12–4, 7–10.30 Sun
Robinson's Hatters Mild, Best Bitter Ⓔ
Cosy two-roomer in Stockport's historic market place. It boasts two bars and provides hot meals every lunchtime and Fri eve. Famed for its live music most nights.
◖ ≹

Crown

154 Heaton Lane (W of A6 under viaduct)
☎ (0161) 429 8646
12–11; 12–10.30 Sun
Boddingtons Bitter; Lees Bitter; guest beers Ⓗ
Comfortable, multi-roomed ale house, serving up to nine beers and a guest cider.
۞ ◖ ≹ ♣ ↺ ⚬

Florist

100 Shaw Heath
☎ (0161) 666 0405
11–11; 12–3, 7–10.30 Sun
Robinson's Hatters Mild, Best Bitter Ⓗ
Multi-roomed Victorian monolith, now revitalised under new licensees. Despite its busy road junction position, the pub can be difficult to spot – look for the name high up on the wall. Eve meals 5–7.
۞ ◖ ▮ ≹ ♣

Greyhound

27 Bowden Street, Edgeley
☎ (0161) 480 5699
11.30–11; 12–10.30 Sun
Boddingtons Mild, Bitter; guest beers Ⓗ
Classic community local – don't be put off by the estate pub exterior, inside it's a warm-hearted gem, improved by a 1995 refurbishment. Cask Boddingtons Mild is now a

rarity; two or three guest beers are usually available. 🍴 ⇌ ♣ P

Olde Woolpack

70 Brinksway (A560)
☎ (0161) 429 6621
11.30–3 (4 Sat), 5 (7 Sat)–11; 11–11 Fri; 12–10.30 Sun
Marston's Pedigree; Tetley Dark Mild, Pedigree; Theakston Best Bitter; guest beers Ⓗ
Semi-open-plan local with a good trade, despite the absence of nearby housing. It is dominated by a giant blue pyramid and handy for the motorway. The guest bitter changes regularly and the mild may vary, too. Good value food. 🍴 ♣ P

Railway

1 Avenue Street (off A560)
☎ (0161) 429 6062
12–11; 12–10.30 Sun
Porter Mild, Bitter, Rossendale Ale, Porter, Sunshine, seasonal beers Ⓗ
Single lounge, corner pub opposite the superstores; Porter's third tied house. No fruit machines, pool tables, TV or jukebox. Pub fare includes some speciality house dishes cooked to order. Low beer prices for the area. ❀ 🍴 ♣ 🍺

Unity Inn

41 Wellington Road South (A6, opp. station approach)
☎ (0161) 480 4310
11.30–11; 11 30–11 Sat; 7–11 Sat; 7–10.30 (closed lunch) Sun
Robinson's Hatters Mild, Best Bitter Ⓗ
Busy, town-centre pub with the feel of a real local. The hard-working landlady ensures a warm welcome for all. Good mix of customers. Handy for Grand Central leisure complex. 🍴 ⇌

Strines

Sportsman's Arms

105 Strines Road (1 mile from Marple on New Mills road)
☎ (0161) 427 2888
11.30–3, 5.30–11; 12–3, 7–10.30 Sun
Draught Bass; Boddingtons Bitter; Cains Mild, Bitter Ⓗ
Welcoming country pub with two rooms: a vault and a lounge/dining room. Impressive views over to Mellor. 🏔 Q ⛱ ❀ 🍴 ▷ & ▲ ⇌ P 🍴

Swinton

Cricketers' Arms

227 Manchester Road (A6, near A572 jct) ☎ (0161) 281 5382
11.30–11; 12–10.30 Sun
Holt Mild, Bitter Ⓗ
Smart, busy, two-roomed local, popular with older customers. 🍴 ♣

Newmarket

621 Bolton Road, Pendlebury (A666, opp. market)
☎ (0161) 794 3650
11–11; 12–10.30 Sun
Holt Mild, Bitter Ⓗ
Bustling, basic, market pub, catering for a wide cross-section of customers. Live entertainment Sun. 🍴 ⇌ ♣ P

White Swan

186 Worsley Road (A572, near A580 jct) ☎ (0161) 794 1504
12–11; 12–10.30 Sun
Holt Mild, Bitter Ⓗ
Large, smart, four-roomed late 1920s pub; a wood-panelled main room with a side room, retaining a vestige of a dividing wall. Separate vault with its own entrance and gents; large, sumptuous function room at the rear (children welcome Sun lunch). ❀ 🍴 ♣ P

Timperley

Quarry Bank Inn

Bloomsbury Lane (off B5165)
☎ (0161) 980 4345
11.30–11; 12–10.30 Sun
Hydes' Anvil Billy Westwoods, Mild, Bitter, seasonal beers Ⓔ
Thriving suburban pub with a lively vault and a popular, but quiet lounge. The conservatory is available as a family room until 7. Own bowling green; quiz night Wed; jazz Thu. Eve meals Fri and Sat only, 6–9.
Q ⛱ ❀ 🍴 ▷ 🍴 ♣ P 🍴

Turton

Bull's Head

857 Bradshaw Road
☎ (01204) 852411
12–3 (4 Sat), 6.30–11 (12–11 summer); 12–4, 7–10.30 (12–10.30 summer) Sun
Marston's Pedigree; Ruddles County; Theakston Best Bitter; guest beers Ⓗ
Stone pub rebuilt in 1891, on the original Watling Street (Roman road). Reputedly haunted, it enjoys excellent views across the moors. Regular piano nights. Busy summer food trade.
🏔 Q ❀ 🍴 ▲ P

Uppermill

Cross Keys

Off Running Hill Gate (off A670) ☎ (01457) 874626
11–11; 12–10.30 Sun
Lees GB Mild, Bitter, Moonraker Ⓗ
Attractive, 18th-century, stone building overlooking Saddleworth church. The public bar has a stone-flagged floor and a Yorkshire range. The hub of many activities,

including mountain rescue and a clay pigeon club. Folk night Wed. Children's certificate. Eve meals end 7.30.
🏔 Q ⛱ ❀ 🍴 ▷ 🍴 & ▲ ♣ P

Try also: Waggon Inn, High St (Robinson's)

Wardley

Morning Star

520 Manchester Road (A6)
☎ (0161) 794 4927
12–11; 12–10.30 Sun
Holt Mild, Bitter Ⓗ
Friendly community pub on the outskirts of town with a lively vault. Entertainment Sat and Sun eves. Weekday lunches.
❀ 🍴 🍴 ⇌ (Moorside) ♣ P

Whitefield

Coach & Horses

71 Bury Old Road (A665)
☎ (0161) 766 3024
11–11; 12–10.30 Sun
Holt Mild, Bitter Ⓗ
Happily unmodernised pub with a friendly atmosphere in its three rooms: a snug, a lounge and a surprisingly spacious tap, away from the central bar area.
Q ❀ ⊖ (Besses o' th' Barn) ♣

Eagle & Child

Higher Lane (near A667/A56 jct) ☎ (0161) 766 3024
11–11; 12–10.30 Sun
Holt Mild, Bitter Ⓗ
Large, black and white pub just set back from the road (limited space in front for parking): a spacious main bar room and unspoilt side rooms, plus a large bowling green. ⛱ ❀ 🍴 ⊖ (Besses o' th' Barn) P

New Grove Inn

183 Bury New Road (A56)
☎ (0161) 766 2190
11–11; 12–10.30 Sun
Holt Mild, Bitter Ⓗ
Spacious, modernised two-roomer where the interior belies its 1920s brick exterior. Strong social and sporting support ensures that both bars are well frequented.
⊖ ♣

Try also: Beehive, Bury New Road (Whitbread)

Wigan

Beer Engine

69 Poolstock Lane
☎ (01942) 321820
11–11; 12–10.30 Sun
Draught Bass; Exmoor Gold; Moorhouse's Pendle Witches Brew; John Smith's Bitter; Vaux Mild, Waggle Dance; guest beers Ⓗ
Former club with a comfortable lounge and a large

concert room which stages an
annual beer, pie and music
festival. Excellent bowling
green. ❀ ◖❙ ⇄ (North
Western/Wallgate) ♣ P

Bird i' th' Hand
(Th' En 'Ole)

102 Gidlow Lane
☎ (01942) 241004
12–11; 12–10.30 Sun
**Tetley Mild, Bitter; Theakston
Best Bitter; guest beer** ℍ
Impressive mosaic work above
the door fronts a great example
of a backstreet boozer: a
comfortable lounge and a
lively tap room.
❀ ◖❙ ⊟ ᕦ ♣ P

Bold Hotel

161 Poolstock Lane
☎ (01942) 241095
12–4.30, 7–11; 12–3, 7–10.30 Sun
Burtonwood Mild, Bitter ℍ
Small, unchanged local on the
edge of town. The tap room is
full of rugby memorabilia.
Q ⊟ ♣

Bowling Green

106–108 Wigan Lane (A49)
☎ (01942) 516004
12–11; 12–10.30 Sun
**Courage Directors; John
Smith's Bitter; Theakston
Black Bull; Younger No. 3;
guest beer** ℍ
Large, former Walker's outlet:
a buzzing vault with sport on
TV; waitress service in the busy
lounge. Out of the *Guide* for a
while, but back with a
vengeance. ᕤ ❀ ⊟ ♣ ☗

Orwell

4 Wigan Pier, Wallgate
☎ (01942) 323034
11–11 (11–5, 7–11 winter); 12–3,
7–10.30 Sun
Samuel Smith OBB ℍ/ᴳ**;
Tetley Bitter** ℍ**; guest
beers** ℍ/ᴳ
This large pub is unusual in
that it has been converted from
open-plan to separate rooms –
and has benefited from the
change. At the heart of the
Wigan Pier complex, right next
to the canal, it gets busy in
summer. ◖❙ ⊟ ᕦ ❀ (North
Western/Wallgate)

Springfield Hotel ☆

47 Springfield Road
☎ (01942) 242072
7 (12 Sat)–11; 12–10.30 Sun
**Tetley Dark Mild, Bitter;
Walker Best Bitter** ℍ
Large, friendly pub near
Wigan Athletic FC, featuring
the usual excellent Walker's
decor and admirable
woodwork; impressive inside
and out. It can be busy on
match days. ⊟ ♣ P

Swan & Railway

80 Wallgate
☎ (01942) 495032
11–11; 12–4, 7–10.30 Sun
**Banks's Mild, Bitter;
Marston's Pedigree; Morrells
Graduate** ℍ
Listed and saved from
becoming a theme pub, and
recently refurbished: as good
an old fashioned boozer as
you'll get these days.
Q ᕤ ᗕ ◖❙ ⊟ ⇄ (North
Western/Wallgate)

Tudor House

New Market Street (by bus
station)
☎ (01942) 700296
11–11; 12–10.30 Sun
**Draught Bass; Highgate Dark;
guest beers** ℍ
Earthy, town-centre boozer,
popular with the younger
crowd (across the road from
the college). It features a
rapidly changing range of
beers and good value food.
ᕤ ❀ ᗕ ◖❙ ⇄ (North
Western/Wallgate) ᗝ

Wingates

Waggon & Horses

170 Chorley Road,
Westhoughton (A6, off M61
jct 5)
☎ (01942) 812273
12–11; 12–10.30 Sun
**Burtonwood Bitter; guest
beers** ℍ
Spacious, multi-roomed pub
with a large restaurant,
offering a good welcome for
families. It also stocks a Bank
Top beer.
ᗕ ❀ ◖❙ ᕦ ♣ P

Withington

Red Lion

532 Wilmslow Road (B5093,
near Christie Hospital)
☎ (0161) 434 2441
11–11; 12–10.30 Sun
**Banks's Mild; Marston's
Bitter, Pedigree, Owd Rodger,
HBC** ℍ
Extremely busy main road
pub, popular with both locals
and students and famous for
its bowling green. An attractive
country-style exterior gives
way to waves of extensions to
the rear. Children welcome in
the conservatory until 8. Eve
meals Mon–Thu.
ᗕ ❀ ◖❙ ⊟ ♣ P

Woodford

Davenport Arms
(Thief's Neck)

550 Chester Road (A5102)
☎ (0161) 439 2435
11–3.30, 5.15–11; 11–11 Sat; 12–3,
7–10.30 Sun
Robinson's Hatters Mild ℍ**,
Old Stockport, Hartleys XB** ᴇ**,
Best Bitter, Old Tom** ℍ
Superb, unspoilt farmhouse
pub on the edge of suburbia. A
multi-roomed layout includes
a traditional tap room and a
no-smoking snug where
children are admitted at
lunchtime. Large, attractive
garden to the rear. Regional
CAMRA *Pub of the Year* 1997.
ᕤ Q ᗕ ❀ ◖ ⊟ ♣ P ✂

Worthington

White Crow

Chorley Road (A5106)
☎ (01257) 474344
12–11; 12–10.30 Sun
**Greenalls Mild, Bitter,
Original; Tetley Bitter; guest
beer** ℍ
Large pub, recently
refurbished in olde-worlde
style, with a deserved
reputation for its food (served
daily 12–9). Close to
Worthington Lakes. Children's
play area outside.
ᕤ ❀ ◖❙ ᕦ ♣ P

BREWERY BREAKS

Many breweries have branched out into the entertainment
business and are now offering fascinating tours and exhibitions for the casual visitor. To help you pinpoint the perfect beery
day out, Ted Bruning has compiled a CAMRA guide to brewery
attractions and visitors' centres. Entitled *Brewery Breaks*, it is priced
just £3.99 and is available from all good bookshops, or direct (and
post-free) from CAMRA, 230 Hatfield Road, St Albans, Hertfordshire AL1 4LW. Discounts are available for CAMRA members.

Merseyside

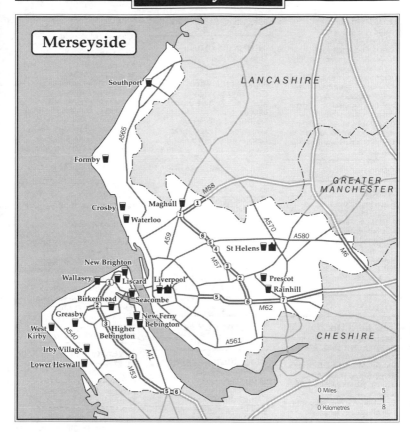

Merseyside

Bebington

Rose & Crown
57 The Village (opp. town hall)
☎ (0151) 643 1312
11–3, 5–11; 11–11 Fri & Sat; 12–10.30
Sun
**Thwaites Best Mild, Bitter,
seasonal beers** Ⓗ
Bustling, friendly, multi-
roomed local, popular with
office workers and shoppers at
lunchtime and with local
residents at night. No meals
Sun. Q ◖ ⊟ ⇌ ♣ P

Birkenhead

Chester Arms
20 Chester Street (near
Woodside ferry terminal)
☎ (0151) 650 0676
11–11; 12–10.30 Sun
**Cain's Mild, Bitter, FA,
seasonal beers; Tetley Bitter;
guest beers** Ⓗ
Town-centre pub: one bar
serving a large lounge. Food
available 12–7, except Sun
eve. A Robert Cain
Alehouse.
❀ ◖ ▶ ⇌ (Hamilton Sq) ♣

Commodore
25 Lord Street (behind
Hamilton Sq station)
☎ (0151) 647 6558
11–11; 12–10.30 Sun
**Marston's Pedigree; Phoenix
Wobbly Bob; John Smith's
Bitter; Theakston Best Bitter,
XB; guest beers** Ⓗ
Backstreet bikers' pub with a
licensee whose views do not
always accord with those of
CAMRA. Live bands Sat eve.
Up to four rotating guest beers;
Wirral's only outlet for Holt
Bitter, available on a fairly
regular basis. No food is
served Sun.
⛐ ❀ ◖ ⇌ (Hamilton Sq)

Crown Ale House
128 Conway Street (by Europa
Centre)
☎ (0151) 647 9108
11.30–11; 12–3, 7–10.30 Sun
**Cains Bitter; Greenalls Mild,
Bitter; Jennings Sneck Lifter;
guest beers** Ⓗ
Multi-roomed, town-centre
alehouse offering up to six
guest beers from independent
breweries. Varied menu (no
food Sun; eve meals Thu–Sat

until 8). Handy for the shops
and market. Local CAMRA
Pub of the Year 1997.
Q ❀ ◖ ▶ ⊟ ⇌ (Central) ⊖
(Hamilton Sq) ♣ ⏃

Old Colonial
167 Bridge Street (500 yds from
Hamilton Sq station)
☎ (0151) 666 1258
11–11; 12–10.30 Sun
**Cains Mild, Bitter, FA,
seasonal beers; Tetley Bitter;
guest beers** Ⓗ
A Robert Cain Alehouse,
undergoing a major traditional
refurbishment and offering a
wide range of rotating guest
beers.
Q ◖ ⇌ (Hamilton Sq) ♣ P

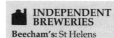

**INDEPENDENT
BREWERIES**

Beecham's: St Helens

Cains: Liverpool

Liverpool: Liverpool

Passageway: Liverpool

Stork Hotel
41–43 Price Street
☎ (0151) 647 7506
11.30–11; 12–3, 7–10.30 Sun
Flowers IPA; guest beer H
Splendid, four-roomed
Victorian pub built in 1840. It
features an island bar with a
tiled frontage, windows
depicting Threlfalls Salford
Ales and interesting
photographs of old dock and
ferry scenes. Weekday lunches.
☎ ✿ ◖ ⊞ ≠ (Hamilton Sq/
Central) ♣

Crosby

Crosby
75 Liverpool Road
☎ (0151) 924 2574
11–11; 12–10.30 Sun
Beer range varies H/G
Whitbread Hogshead pub,
large and busy. The landlord
ensures a wide range of beers
at all times. Eve meals 5–7
✿ ◖ ≠ (Blundellsands/
Crosby)

Formby

Freshfield Hotel
1 Massams Lane (½ mile from
B5424) ☎ (01704) 874871
12–11; 12–10.30 Sun
**Boddingtons Mild, Bitter;
Flowers IPA; Whitbread
Trophy, Abroad Cooper** H;
guest beers H/G
Hogshead Ale House, popular
with all ages. A large bar
serves 12 ales on handpump
and two on gravity. Weekday
lunches.
♨ ✿ ◖ ≠ (Freshfield) ◔ P

Greasby

Irby Mill
Mill Lane ☎ (0151) 604 0194
11.30–11; 12–10.30 Sun
**Cains Mild, Bitter; Jennings
Bitter; Tetley Bitter;
Theakston Best Bitter; guest
beers** H
Excellent, award-winning,
unspoilt country pub where
the licensee maintains the best
pub traditions; no jukebox or
slot machines. Q ✿ ◖ P

Higher Bebington

Travellers Rest
169 Mount Road
☎ (0151) 608 2988
12–11; 12–10.30 Sun
**Boddingtons Bitter; Cains
Bitter; Flowers IPA; Greene
King Abbot; Taylor Landlord;
guest beers** H
Pleasant village inn, dating
from 1720, popular with locals
and walkers. One bar serves an
open-plan lounge with cosy
partitioned areas. Wheelchair
WC. ♨ ◖ ♿

Irby Village

Shippons Inn
Thingwall Road
☎ (0151) 648 0449
11–11; 12–10.30 Sun
**Banks's Mild, Bitter;
Camerons Strongarm;
Marston's Pedigree; guest
beer** H
Traditional village pub,
converted in 1994 from an
18th-century farm building. It
features an inglenook with a
log fire, and attractions include
Mon folk music and a lively
Wed quiz.
♨ ✿ ◖ ♿ P

Liscard

Primrose Hotel
1 Withens Lane
☎ (0151) 637 1340
12–11; 12–10.30 Sun
Cains Mild, Bitter H
Unmistakeable, half-timbered
pub with wood-panelled walls
and an ornate ceiling.
✿ ♣ P

Liverpool: *City
Centre*

Blackburne Arms
24 Catherine Street
☎ (0151) 708 0252
12–11; 12–10.30 Sun
Cains Bitter H
Quiet pub, popular with locals,
close to the Anglican
Cathedral.

Bonapartes
21A Clarence Street
☎ (0151) 709 0737
12 (7 Sat)–12.30am; 7–10.30 (closed
lunch) Sun
**Vaux Samson, Waggle Dance;
Ward's Best Bitter** H
Pub popular with students for
its late licence. Bistro-style at
lunchtime. Music and candlelit
tables create atmosphere.
◖ ≠ (Lime St) ⊖

Cambridge
Mulberry Street (near
university)
11.30 (4 Sat)–11; 12–10.30 Sun
**Burtonwood Bitter, Forshaw's,
Top Hat, Buccaneer; guest
beer** H
Friendly local, very popular
with students in term-time. No
food Sat. Roadside outside
drinking area. ✿ ◖ ♣

Carnarvon Castle
5 Tarleton Street
11–11; closed Sun
**Draught Bass; Cains Mild,
Bitter** H
Small, but busy, two-roomed
pub, popular with shoppers
and regulars alike. Admire the
splendid display of Dinky/

Corgi toys. No food Sat.
♨ Q ◖ ≠ (Lime St) ⊖
(Central/Moorfields)

Everyman
9 Hope Street
☎ (0151) 708 9545
12–midnight; closed Sun
Beer range varies H
Bar and bistro beneath the
Everyman Theatre. The foyer
bar upstairs sells Cains FA;
downstairs there are usually
four guest beers. Unusual
menu with a large selection of
vegetarian options; an entry in
CAMRA's *Good Pub Food*.
Q ◖ ▷ ◔

Globe
17 Cases Street (opp. Central
station)
☎ (0151) 709 5060
11–11; 12–10.30 Sun
**Cains Mild, Brewery Bitter,
Bitter, FA** H
Former Higsons' pub now
under Greenalls' management
but signed as a Robert Cain
house, selling the full range of
Cains beers. A welcoming,
traditional atmosphere in a
pub with an incredible sloping
floor and a backroom snug.
≠ (Lime St) ⊖ (Central)

Liverpool Brewery Co.
21–23 Berry Street
☎ (0151) 709 5055
11–11; 12–10.30 Sun
**Liverpool Celebration,
Festival; guest beers** H
Pub brewery popular with
students, situated on the edge
of Liverpool's Chinatown. Beer
is brewed in the pub-front
brewery and kept in cellar
tanks. The upstairs room is a
music venue.
≠ (Lime St) ⊖ (Central)

Peter Kavanagh's
2–6 Egerton Street
☎ (0151) 709 8443
12–11; 12–10.30 Sun
**Cains Bitter; Courage
Directors; Ind Coope Burton
Ale; Tetley Bitter; guest
beer** H
Very friendly, quaint, Victorian
pub with an odd assortment of
bric-a-brac in the bar and two
lounges either side. It can be
very lively eves, especially Fri.
The pub celebrated its
centenary in 1997. The guest
beer is from Tetley's list.
Q ✿ ◖

Pig & Whistle
12 Covent Garden
☎ (0151) 236 4760
11.30–11; 12–9 Sat; 12–10.30 Sun
**Marston's Pedigree; Tetley
Bitter; Walker Bitter** H
Comfortable, traditional pub
opposite the Atlantic Tower
Hotel, famous for its
'emigrants served' brass plate
now secured in the bar.

Traditional folk music first Sun of each month. The upstairs bar is open lunchtimes.
Ⓖ ⇒ (Moorfields)

Post Office

2 Great Newton Street (from Lime St take London Rd to Pembroke Place)
☎ (0151) 707 1005
12 (1 Sat)–11; 1–10.30 Sun
Boddingtons Bitter; Cains Bitter; guest beers Ⓗ
Friendly pub with a quiet lounge and a bar with a jukebox and pool; popular with locals, hospital professionals, university lecturers and students. Its busiest times are lunch and early eve. Close to the Metropolitan Cathedral. Guest beers are obtained from Greenalls' list.
Q ❀ Ⓖ ⇒ (Lime St) ♣

Roscoe Head

24 Roscoe Street
☎ (0151) 709 4490
11–11; 12–10.30 Sun
Ind Coope Burton Ale; Jennings Bitter; Marston's Pedigree; Tetley Mild, Bitter Ⓗ
Ever-present in the *Guide*. The many awards displayed are testament to the success of the pub and its licensees. No music: three snugs create a friendly atmosphere where conversation thrives. Snacks only Sat lunch.
Q Ⓖ ⇒ (Lime St) ⊖ (Central)

Ship & Mitre

133 Dale Street
11.30 (12.30 Sat)–11; 12.30–10.30 Sun
Cains Mild; Matthew Clark Chadwick's Finest; guest beers Ⓗ
The city's foremost real ale pub, serving up to ten unusual guest beers, usually including two from the local Passageway Brewery. A friendly atmosphere, gas lighting, and a collection of vintage typewriters are features. Good value lunches (not served Sat or Sun). Ⓖ ⇒ (Lime St) ⊖ (Moorfields) ⇔ 🚻

Swan

86 Wood Street
☎ (0151) 709 5281
11.30–11; 12–10.30 Sun
Cains Mild, Bitter; Marston's Pedigree; Phoenix Wobbly Bob; guest beers Ⓗ
This basic, backstreet free house, which boasts the best rock jukebox in town, also attracts people for its good value, home-cooked food. No food Sat; breakfasts served Sun. There is also an upstairs bar. Up to two guest beers are available.
Ⓖ ⇒ (Central) ♣ ⇔

Wetherspoons

Unit 1, Charlotte Row
☎ (0151) 709 4802
11–11; 12–10.30 Sun
Banks's Mild; Cains Mild, Bitter; Courage Directors; Theakston Best Bitter; Younger Scotch; guest beers Ⓗ
Large, modern pub in the shell of an old department store. Good service; always one guest beer on offer. Occasional beer festivals.
Q Ⓖ ▶ ⅋ ⇒ (Lime St) ⊖ ⇔ ⼄

White Star (Quinns)

2–4 Rainford Gardens
☎ (0151) 236 4572
11–11; 12–3, 7–10.30 Sun
Draught Bass; Cains Bitter; guest beers Ⓗ
Traditional pub amongst the plethora of café-bars in the famous Matthew St area. Occasional beer festivals. One of the guest beers will be a Cain's special.
Ⓖ ⇒ (Lime St) ⊖

Liverpool: *East*

Albany

40–42 Albany Road
☎ (0151) 228 8597
11–11; 12–10.30 Sun
Cains Mild, Bitter Ⓗ
Lively, friendly local in a backstreet terrace. No food at weekends. Ⓖ ♣

Childwall Abbey

Score Lane, Childwall (off Childwall Valley Road)
☎ (0151) 722 5293
11.30–11; 12–10.30 Sun
Burtonwood Bitter, Top Hat, seasonal beers; guest beer Ⓗ
Fine 18th-century inn, opposite Childwall church. The name is a misnomer, since the church was never an abbey or priory. A country atmosphere prevails in Liverpool suburbia at this Grade I-listed building. Eve meals finish at 8. 🍴 ❀ Ⓖ ▶

Clubmoor

119 Townsend Lane
12–11; 12–10.30 Sun
Cains Mild, Bitter Ⓗ
Handsome, detached pub on a main road with a large lounge, and a public bar with darts and Sky TV. Not far from Everton and Liverpool FC grounds. Quiz night Wed. ❀ ⅋ ♣

Edinburgh

4 Sandown Lane
12–11; 12–10.30 Sun
Cains Bitter; Walker Mild, Bitter Ⓗ
A real gem, a tiny local hidden away from the busy Wavertree High Street: a small lounge and an even smaller bar, but a big welcome. Q ⅋

Kensington

189 Kensington
☎ (0151) 263 6807
12–11; 12–10.30 Sun
Cains Mild, Bitter Ⓗ
Classic street-corner local; a popular pub, often with table service in the lounge.
⅋ ♣

Mount Vernon

1 Irvine Street
12–11; 12–10.30 Sun
Beer range varies Ⓗ
Lively pub with an extremely friendly atmosphere, popular with locals, hospital staff, students and university lecturers. ♣ P

Wheatsheaf

186 East Prescot Road
☎ (0151) 228 5080
11.30–11; 12–10.30 Sun
Cains Bitter Ⓗ
Popular, traditional pub with table service in the two lounges. Busy L-shaped bar.
Q ⅋ P

Liverpool: *South*

Brewery Tap

35 Stanhope Street (by Cains Brewery) ☎ (0151) 709 2129
11–11; 12–10.30 Sun
Cains Mild, Bitter, FA; guest beers Ⓗ
CAMRA *Best Refurbishment* award-winning, heritage pub, deservedly popular, with a wide-ranging clientele; the base for Cains Brewery trips. It serves three guest beers and the Cains monthly special brews. Interesting breweriana features. Q ❀ Ⓖ P

Dealers Arms

79–81 St Mary's Road, Garston
☎ (0151) 427 9128
11.30–11; 12–10.30 Sun
Cains Mild, Bitter Ⓗ
Local on the main shopping street. A small, cosy back room at the rear has cable TV.
⅋ ⇒ ♣

Royal George

99 Park Road
☎ (0151) 708 9277
11–11; 12–10.30 Sun
Tetley Dark Mild, Bitter; guest beer Ⓗ
Very friendly, popular pub locally known as 'Blacks', offering a competitively priced guest beer. Cable TV. ⅋ ♣

Willowbank

329 Smithdown Road
11–11; 12–10.30 Sun
Ind Coope Burton Ale; Marston's Pedigree; Tetley Dark Mild, Bitter; Walker Bitter; guest beers Ⓗ
Comfortable pub, attracting a good mix of locals and students. Up to three guest beers. Barbecues in summer

and occasional beer festivals. Good food. ❀ ◑ ⊞ ♣ P

Lower Heswall

Dee View Inn
Dee View Road (300 yds from Heswall centre along the Mount) ☎ (0151) 342 2320
12–11; 12–10.30 Sun
Boddingtons Bitter; Cains Bitter; Thwaites Bitter; guest beer Ⓗ
Popular, traditional pub dating from the 19th century, with views over the River Dee and the Welsh hills. It stands opposite the war memorial on a hairpin bend. ◑ ♣ P

Maghull

Red House
31 Foxhouse Lane
☎ (0151) 526 1376
11–11; 12–10.30 Sun
Tetley Bitter; Walker Mild, Best Bitter; guest beers Ⓗ
Friendly, suburban local: an oasis for pub-lovers in Maghull. No food Sun.
❀ ◑ ⊞ ⇌ ♣ P

New Brighton

Clarence Hotel
89 Albion Street
☎ (0151) 639 3860
11.30–11; 12–10.30 Sun
Beer range varies Ⓗ
Warm, welcoming local in a residential area, drawing a good mix of clientele to its split-level lounge. Live music Tue. A Whitbread pub where the licensees like to try new beers and changes of menu. Cream teas on the agenda!
❀ ◑ ⊞ ⇌ ♣

New Ferry

Cleveland Arms
31 Bebington Road
☎ (0151) 645 2847
11.30–11; 12–10.30 Sun
Thwaites Best Mild, Bitter, seasonal beers Ⓗ
Popular, friendly, open-plan local in a pedestrianised area.
⇌ (Bebington) ♣ P

Travellers Rest
11 New Ferry Road
☎ (0151) 644 8653
11–11; 12–10.30 Sun
Banks's Mild, Bitter; Morrells Varsity Ⓗ
Friendly, traditional, community pub with a mixed clientele. Possibly the oldest existing pub in New Ferry, very little altered during the last 50 years, with its quarry tiled floor, it is more suited to a quiet country village than a busy town centre.
Q ⇌ ♣ P ⏇

Prescot

Clock Face
54 Derby Street
☎ (0151) 292 4121
11–11; 12–3, 7–10.30 Sun
Thwaites Bitter Ⓗ
Attractive, sandstone house converted to a pub in the 1980s, with a pleasant, relaxed atmosphere. Good value and excellent food. ❀ ◑ ⇌ P

Hare & Hounds
10 Warrington Road
11–11; 12–10.30 Sun
Cains Mild, Bitter; guest beer Ⓗ
Known as 'Tommy Hall's' and the 'Weighing Machine', this former Joseph Jones house, which was two-roomed and is now L-shaped, retains its traditional atmosphere. ⇌

Sun Inn
11 Derby Street
12–11; 12–10.30 Sun
Beer range varies Ⓗ
Traditional town pub in a terrace; friendly and welcoming, with cosy, unspoilt rooms and a public bar.
🚌 Q ⊞ ⇌ ♣

Rainhill

Commercial
Station Road
☎ (0151) 426 6446
12–11; 12–10.30 Sun
Cains Bitter; guest beers Ⓗ
Joseph Jones Knotty Ash pub with windows to match. This modernised Victorian pub still has three distinct drinking areas. ❀ ⊞ ⇌ ♣ P

St Helens

Abbey
Hard Lane ☎ (01744) 28609
12–11; 12–10.30 Sun
Holt Mild, Bitter Ⓗ
Large, multi-roomed ex-Greenalls pub on the edge of the town. ♣ P

Phoenix Inn
Canal Street ☎ (01744) 21953
11–11; 12–10.30 Sun
Taylor Landlord; guest beers Ⓗ
Pub whose busy, lively bar boasts a rugby league theme. Live music at weekends.
⊞ ♣ ⏇

Royal Alfred
Shaw Street ☎ (01744) 26786
11–11; 12–10.30 Sun
Cains Bitter; guest beer Ⓗ
Cosmopolitan, edge-of-town-centre pub, next to the station, offering some live music.
🚌 ⊞ ⇌ (Central) ♣ P

Turk's Head
Cooper Street
☎ (01744) 604426
11.30–11; 12–4, 7–10.30 Sun
Cains Mild, Bitter, FA; Holt Bitter; Tetley Bitter; guest beers Ⓗ
This unusual, half-timbered building hosts many clubs and teams and is at the heart of the community. It even owns a racehorse. The food is highly recommended.
🚌 ❀ ◑ ⊞ ⇌ ♣

Seacombe

Prince Alfred
3 Church Road
☎ (0151) 638 1674
11–11; 12–10.30 Sun
Boddingtons Mild, Bitter; Cains Mild (occasional), **Bitter** Ⓗ
The pub to visit for the area's best choice of beers; small, comfortable and friendly. Just up the road from the Mersey ferry terminal. ❀ ♿ ♣ ⏇

Southport

Barons Bar
Scarisbrick Hotel, Lord Street (opp. town hall)
☎ (01704) 543000
11–11; 12–10.30 Sun
Boddingtons Bitter; Morland Old Speckled Hen; Tetley Bitter; guest beers Ⓗ
Opulently furnished, friendly, traditional lounge bar within a centrally-located hotel. Varied clientele; busy at weekends. The house beer, Flag & Turret, is brewed by Little Avenham. Annual beer festival in May. Food available in the adjacent bars. ☒ 🚌 ◑ ⇌

Cheshire Lines
81 King Street
☎ (01704) 532178
11–11; 12–10.30 Sun
Tetley Bitter; Walker Mild, Bitter; guest beer Ⓗ
Town-centre, traditional pub in a street full of guest houses; named after the defunct railway, which is now a coastal path. 🚌 Q ❀ ⇌ ♣

Coronation
12 King Street (opp. market hall) ☎ (01704) 530611
11–11; 12–10.30 Sun
Boddingtons Bitter; Chester's Mild; Whitbread Abroad Cooper Ⓗ**; guest beers** Ⓗ/Ⓖ
Hogshead town-centre pub, busy at weekends, serving an ever-changing range of seven guest beers. A great addition to the central hostelries. Typical RSJ and bare brick decor. The home-produced chillied eggs are a must. Food served 11–7 (12–4 Sun). ◑ ▶ ⇌ ⏚

Guest House

16 Union Street (off Lord St, near fire station)
☎ (01704) 537660
12–11; 12–10.30 Sun
Draught Bass; Boddingtons Bitter; Cains Mild; Higsons Bitter; guest beers H
Traditional gem in the town centre: several rooms with a courtyard at the rear.
Q ❀ ⇌ ♣ ⚲

Up Steps

20 Upper Aughton Road, Birkdale
☎ (01704) 569245
11–11; 12–10.30 Sun
Matthew Brown Bitter; Courage Directors; Theakston Mild, Best Bitter, XB H
Superb example of a community local where a friendly welcome is guaranteed; winner of local CAMRA awards over the past few years. A good place to sit and read the paper in comfort.
❀ ⇌ (Birkdale) ♣ P

Zetland

53 Zetland Street
☎ (01704) 544541
11.30–11; 12–10.30 Sun
Burtonwood Mild, Bitter,

Forshaw's, Top Hat or **Buccaneer** H
Large, Victorian pub with its own bowling green (which can be hired). It retains separate rooms; the family room is open until 8.30. No food Mon.
☜ ❀ ◑ ⊟ P

Wallasey

Farmers Arms

225 Wallasey Village
☎ (0151) 638 2110
11.30–11; 12–10.30 Sun
Cains Bitter; Tetley Bitter; Theakston Best Bitter; guest beer H
Ever-popular, past local CAMRA *Pub of the Year*: a front bar, a side snug and a back lounge cater for all. No jukebox. The guest beer pump is in the bar. Quiz nights.
◑ ⊟ ⚹ ⊖ (Grove Rd)

Waterloo

Marine

3–5 South Road (off A565)
☎ (0151) 928 3358
12–11; 12–10.30 Sun
Cains Bitter H
Large, multi-roomed pub close to the marina and the coastal

walk. Its friendly atmosphere appeals to older clientele who create a lively conversational buzz. Occasional live music; barm cakes on request. A walled outdoor area at the rear features a bouncy castle in summer. ♨ Q ❀ ⊟ ⇌ ♣

Volunteer Canteen

45 East Street (near Crosby Marina) ☎ (0151) 928 6594
12–11; 12–10.30 Sun
Cains Bitter; Theakston Best Bitter H
A small, cosy lounge with waitress service complements the public bar in this traditional local.
♨ Q ⊟ ⇌ ♣

West Kirby

Hilbre Court

Banks Road ☎ (0151) 625 7811
11.30–11; 12–10.30 Sun
Tetley Dark Mild, Bitter; guest beers H
Popular, friendly pub with a restaurant. The lounge bar is open-plan with defined drinking areas. Try the excellent lunches. Close to the promenade, boating lake and the Wirral Way. ❀ ◑ ▶ ⇌ ♣ P

Raising Cain! The Robert Cain brewery in Liverpool, a sad relic after Whitbread's closure of Higsons in 1990, now thriving in the hands of Cains.

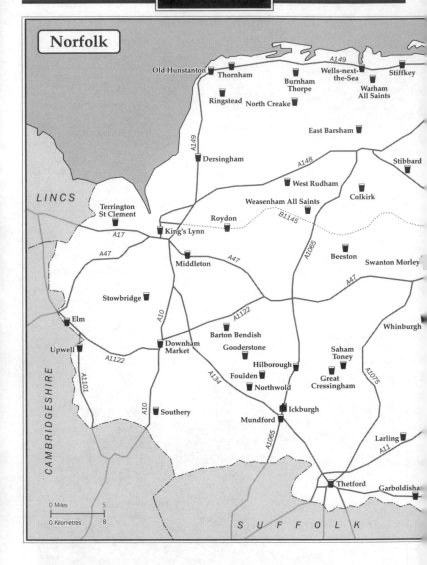

Norfolk

LINCS

CAMBRIDGESHIRE

SUFFOLK

Old Hunstanton · Thornham · Burnham Thorpe · Wells-next-the-Sea · Stiffkey · Warham All Saints · Ringstead · North Creake · East Barsham · Stibbard · Dersingham · West Rudham · Weasenham All Saints · Colkirk · Terrington St Clement · Roydon · King's Lynn · Beeston · Swanton Morley · Middleton · Stowbridge · Elm · Downham Market · Barton Bendish · Gooderstone · Whinburgh · Upwell · Hilborough · Saham Toney · Foulden · Northwold · Great Cressingham · Southery · Ickburgh · Mundford · Larling · Thetford · Garboldisham

A149 · A148 · A17 · A47 · A10 · A1122 · A1101 · A134 · A1065 · A1075 · A11 · B1145

| 0 Miles | 5 |
| 0 Kilometres | 8 |

Ashwellthorpe

King's Head
The Turnpike (B1113)
☎ (01508) 489419
11–11; 12–3, 7–10.30 Sun
**Greene King Abbot;
Woodforde's Wherry; guest
beer** Ⓗ
Genuine local with a 400-year
pedigree and a roaring log fire.
🏠 ❀ ◑ ▷ ♿ ♣ P

Attleborough

Griffin Hotel
Church Street
☎ (01953) 452149
10.30–3, 5.30–11; 12–3, 7–10.30 Sun

**Draught Bass; Greene King
Abbot; Wolf Bitter; guest
beers** Ⓗ
Welcoming old coaching inn
retaining much charm. Strong
guest beers from all over the
country; wide-ranging menu.
🏠 Q 🛏 ◑ ▷ ♿ Å ⇌ ♣ P

Barton Bendish

Spread Eagle
Church Road
☎ (01366) 347295
12–3 (not Mon), 7–11; 12–3, 7–10.30
Sun
**Greene King IPA, Abbot;
guest beer** Ⓗ
Friendly inn in a quiet village;
comfortable and traditional,

with a bar, restaurant, a games
room, and an attractive garden.
🏠 Q 🛏 ❀ 🛏 ◑ ▷ ♿ Å ♣ P 🍴

Bawburgh

King's Head
Harts Lane
☎ (01603) 744977
11–11; 12–10.30 Sun
**Adnams Bitter; Boddingtons
Bitter; Flowers IPA, Original;
Marston's Pedigree** Ⓗ
Two comfortable, low-
ceilinged bars with beams and
exposed brickwork. The
restaurant serves an
adventurous menu.
🏠 Q ❀ ◑ ▷ P

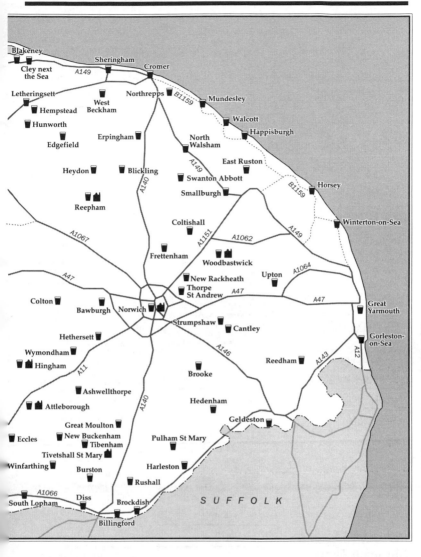

Beeston

Ploughshare
The Street ☎ (01328) 701845
12–2.30, 6–11; 12–11 Sat; 12–3, 7–10.30
Sun
**Greene King IPA, Abbot;
guest beer** Ⓗ
The oldest part of this popular
village pub dates from the 17th
century. Tasty home-cooked
food; Kingfisher cider in
summer. 🏚 ⚲ ✿ ◖ ◗ ⌂ P ⚲

Billingford

Horseshoes
Lower Street (A143, between
Scole and Harleston)
☎ (01379) 740414

11–3, 7–11; 12–3, 7–10.30 Sun
**Greene King Abbot; guest
beer** Ⓗ

Cosy, friendly pub enjoying a
rural location by an historic
windmill (key available). It
specialises in home-cooked
food in large portions, served
seven days a week. The garden

has a children's play area.
✿ 🛏 ◖ ◗ P ⚲

Blakeney

Manor Hotel
The Quay ☎ (01263) 740376
11–2.30, 6–11; 12–3, 6–10.30 Sun
Adnams Mild, Bitter, Extra Ⓗ

🏭 **INDEPENDENT BREWERIES**

Blue Moon: Hingham	**Wolf**: Attleborough
Buffy's: Tivetshall St Mary	**Woodforde's**: Woodbastwick
Chalk Hill: Norwich	
Iceni: Ickburgh	**York Tavern**: Norwich
Reepham: Reepham	

Pleasant hotel bar overlooking salt marshes, offering reasonably-priced beer and good food. Q ✿ ⊨ ◖ ▶ ▲ P

Blickling

Buckinghamshire Arms
☎ (01263) 732133
11–3, 6–11; 12–3, 7–10.30 Sun
Adnams Bitter, Broadside; Reepham Granary Ⓗ
Unspoilt pub next to Blickling Hall with its lovely walking and cycling routes: a delightful snug and a bar with a real fire. No food Sun eve.
♨ Q ✿ ⊨ ◖ ▶ P

Brockdish

Greyhound
The Street (off A143)
☎ (01379) 668775
7–11; 12–2, 7–11 Sat; 12–2, 7–10.30 Sun
Buffy's Bitter, Polly's Folly, Ale, Strong; Old Chimneys Great Raft Bitter; Woodforde's Wherry; guest beers Ⓖ
Attractive, friendly 17th-century inn serving unsophisticated, homely food, and secondhand books and records.
♨ Q ✿ ◖ ▶ ♣ P ⊁ 🗓

Brooke

White Lion
49 The Street (400 yds from B1332) ☎ (01508) 550443
12–2.30, 5.30–11; 12–11 Sat; 12–10.30 Sun
Adnams Bitter, Broadside; Boddingtons Bitter; Woodforde's Wherry; guest beers Ⓗ
Attractive pub in the centre of a quiet village, facing the mere. No food Mon.
♨ ⅀ ✿ ◖ ▶ ▲ ♣ P 🗓

Burnham Thorpe

Lord Nelson
Walsingham Road
☎ (01328) 738241
11–3, 6–11; 12–3, 7–10.30 Sun
Greene King XX Mild, IPA, Abbot; Woodforde's Wherry, Nelson's Revenge (summer) Ⓖ
Popular pub full of Nelson memorabilia – he actually supped here. There are no bars – all beer comes from the tap room.
♨ Q ⅀ ✿ ◖ ▶ ♣ P ⊁

Burston

Crown Inn
Crown Green
☎ (01379) 741257
11.30–3, 5.30–11; 12–3.30, 6–10.30 Sun

Adnams Bitter; Greene King Abbot; guest beer Ⓖ
16th-century pub with real beams and inglenooks in the lounge and restaurant. The public bar has a large pool and darts area. Book your meal, as all food is cooked from fresh local produce. Bowling green.
♨ Q ✿ ◖ ▶ 🍴 ♣ P

Cantley

Cock Tavern
Manor Road ☎ (01493) 700895
11–4, 6 (7 Sat)–11; 12–4, 7–10.30 Sun
Samuel Smith OBB; guest beers Ⓗ
Comfortable pub in a remote location north of the village. Guest beers often come from local brewers.
♨ ⅀ ✿ ◖ ▶ ♣ P

Cley next the Sea

George & Dragon Hotel
High Street ☎ (01263) 740652
11–3, 6–11; 12–2.30, 7–10.30 Sun
Greene King IPA, Abbot, seasonal beers Ⓗ
Birdwatchers' pub with two bars, plus a room for diners and families. Interesting George & Dragon memorabilia. No eve meals winter Mon/Tue. ✿ ⊨ ◖ ▶ P

Colkirk

Crown
Crown Road ☎ (01328) 862172
11–2.30, 6–11; 12–3, 7–10.30 Sun
Greene King XX Mild, Abbot, seasonal beers Ⓗ
Welcoming, popular, two-bar pub with an attractive dining area, and an open fire in a brick inglenook. Range of games; good food.
♨ Q ✿ ◖ ▶ ▲ ♣ P

Coltishall

Red Lion
Church Street
☎ (01603) 737402
11–3, 5–11; 12–3, 7–10.30 Sun
Adnams Bitter; Boddingtons Bitter; Brakspear Bitter; Fuller's Chiswick; Greene King Abbot; Morland Old Speckled Hen Ⓗ
Large, rambling pub split into many rooms on varying levels. Note the windows etched with the pub lions. The house beer is by Woodforde's.
Q ✿ ◖ ▶ 🍴 ♣ P

Colton

Ugly Bug Inn
High House Farm Lane
☎ (01603) 880794
12–3, 5.30–11.30; 12–3, 7–10.30 Sun

Hancock's HB; Morland Old Speckled Hen; guest beers Ⓗ
Single-bar pub converted from a barn, featuring a brick and beam interior and large gardens with ponds. The house beer is brewed by Iceni. No food Sun eve.
♨ ⅀ ✿ ⊨ ◖ ▶ க ♣ P

Cromer

Red Lion Hotel
Brooke Street
☎ (01263) 514964
11–11; 12–10.30 Sun
Adnams Bitter; Draught Bass; Greene King Abbot; Fuller's London Pride; Highgate IPA; McMullen AK Ⓗ
This family-run Victorian free house and hotel has seen many changes. The rich mahogany fittings in the Edwardian public bar complement the flint and brick interior. Sea views.
♨ Q ⅀ ⊨ ◖ ▶ க ▲ ≠ P

Dersingham

Feathers
Manor Road
☎ (01485) 540207
11–2.30, 5.30–11; 12–3, 7–10.30 Sun
Adnams Bitter; Draught Bass; guest beer Ⓗ
Pub with a stable bar for those who like it noisy and two bars and a restaurant for the rest. Close to Sandringham, with a large, safe garden with playthings for children.
♨ ✿ ⊨ ◖ ▶ 🗓 P

Diss

Cock Inn
63 Lower Denmark Street (off A1066)
☎ (01379) 643633
11.30–2.30, 5–11; 11.30–11 Fri & Sat; 12–10.30 Sun
Adnams Bitter, Broadside; Woodforde's Nelson's Revenge; guest beers Ⓗ
Attractive, heavily-beamed, 16th-century free house with five handpumps and a friendly atmosphere, in a pleasant location, overlooking a green.
♨ Q ✿ ⊨ ≠ ♣ P

Downham Market

Crown Hotel
Bridge Street
☎ (01366) 382322
11–11; 12–3, 7–10.30 Sun
Bateman XB; Courage Directors; Theakston Mild; guest beers Ⓗ
Genuine 17th-century coaching inn with a bar of renown and a comfortable meeting room. Something of interest is always on handpump.
♨ Q ✿ ⊨ ◖ ▶ P

East Barsham

White Horse Inn
Fakenham Road
☎ (01328) 820645
11–3, 7–11; 12–3, 7–10.30 (12–10.30 summer) Sun
Boddingtons Bitter; Greene King IPA, Abbot Ⓗ**; Woodforde's Wherry** ⒼComfortable, friendly 17th-century inn, with a large inglenook and two restaurants (one for non-smokers); a lovely pub in an unspoilt village with good accommodation and food. ♨ ✿ ⌂ ⓓ ▶ ♣ P

East Ruston

Butchers Arms
Oak Lane (1 mile from B1159)
☎ (01692) 650237
12–3, 7–11 (10 Mon–Thu in winter); 12–2.30, 7–10.30 Sun
Adnams Bitter; Draught Bass; guest beers ⒽComfortable, refurbished country pub and restaurant, displaying many old artefacts.
Q ✿ ⓓ ▶ Å ♣ P

Eccles

Old Railway Tavern (Eccles 'Tap')
Station Road
12–2.30, 5.30–11; 12–3, 7–10.30 Sun
Adnams Bitter; Greene King IPA Ⓗ**; guest beers** (occasional) ⒼTimeless village local with a relaxed atmosphere. Gravity dispensed Adnams is rare for the area.
♨ Q ✿ ⇌ (Eccles Rd, limited service) ♣ P ▯

Edgefield

Three Pigs
Norwich Road (B1149)
☎ (01263) 587634
11–2.30, 7–11; 12–2.30, 7–10.30 Sun
Adnams Bitter Ⓗ18th-century inn with a comfortable local atmosphere. No food Mon eve.
Q ✿ ⓓ ▶ ♣ P

Elm

Blacksmiths Arms
Elm High Road (A1101)
☎ (01945) 466422
11.30–2.30, 5–11 (11–11 summer Sat); 12–3, 7–10.30 (12–10.30 summer) Sun
Greene King IPA, Abbot, seasonal beers ⒽWell-refurbished and extended, 18th-century pub with a split-level bar and a conservatory dining area. Friendly service; extensive variety of freshly-cooked local produce (no meals Tue/Wed in winter). ♨ Q ✿ ⓓ ▶ ⅙ P

Erpingham

Spread Eagle
Eagle Lane (off A140 N of Aylesham)
☎ (01203) 761591
11–3, 6.30–11; 12–3, 7–10.30 Sun
Woodforde's Wherry, Gt Eastern, Norfolk Nog, Headcracker ⒽVery friendly local: a long bar with a games room at one end and a dining room leading on to the garden at the other. Good food. The stable block once housed Woodforde's Brewery who supply the house beers. ♨ ⛺ ✿ ⓓ ▶ Å ♣ P

Foulden

White Hart Inn
White Hart Street
☎ (01366) 328638
11–3, 6–11; 12–3, 7–10.30 Sun
Greene King XX Mild, IPA, Abbot; guest beers ⒽBusy village pub serving good value food. ♨ Q ✿ ⓓ ▶ ♣ P

Frettenham

Rose & Crown
Buxton Road OS239177
☎ (01603) 898341
7–11; 12–3, 7–11 Sat; 12–3, 7–10.30 Sun
Ansells Mild; Flowers IPA; Ind Coope Burton Ale; Tetley Bitter; guest beers ⒽLarge, single-bar, sporting local with wood panelling throughout. ♨ ✿ ♣ P

Garboldisham

Fox Inn
The Street
☎ (01953) 688151
11.30–3, 5–11; 11–11 Sat; 12–10.30 Sun
Adnams Bitter, Old, Extra, Broadside (summer)**; Greene King IPA; guest beer** Ⓗ17th-century pub with a lovely, old beamed interior with inglenooks. The games room has a pool table; small restaurant (no food Sun eve). Children welcome. ♨ ✿ ⓓ ▶ ♣ P ⅙

Geldeston

Wherry
7 The Street
☎ (01508) 518371
11–3, 7 (6 summer)–11; 12–3, 7–10.30 Sun
Adnams Bitter, Old, Broadside ⒽFriendly pub and restaurant which retains the charm of a small village inn, with its original old bar and a sympathetic modern extension. ♨ Q ⛺ ✿ ⓓ ▶ Å ♣ P

Gooderstone

Swan
☎ (01366) 328365
12–3, 7–11; 12–3, 7–10.30 Sun
Flowers IPA; guest beers ⒽCheery pub at the heart of Norfolk. The conservatory and enormous garden make a perfect venue for a summer's eve. The pub now doubles as the village post office.
♨ ✿ ⓓ ▶ Å ♣ P

Gorleston-on-Sea

Dock Tavern
Dock Tavern Lane
☎ (01493) 442255
11–11; 12–10.30 Sun
Adnams Broadside; Draught Bass; Greene King IPA, Abbot; guest beers ⒽAttractive, comfortable, open-plan, single-room local.
✿ ♣

Great Cressingham

Windmill
Water End (off A1065)
☎ (01760) 756232
11.30–3, 6–11; 12–3, 6.30–10.30 Sun
Adnams Bitter, Broadside; Draught Bass; Greene King IPA; Samuel Smith OBB; guest beer Ⓗ18th-century village pub with many rooms and bars, well known locally for its food.
♨ Q ⛺ ✿ ⓓ ▶ Å ♣ P

Great Moulton

Fox & Hounds
Frith Way
☎ (01379) 677506
12–2.30 (not Mon), 7–11; 12–3, 7–10.30 Sun
Adnams Bitter; Boddingtons Bitter; Greene King Abbot ⒽTruly historic, 15th-century building which has operated as a pub since 1789. In summer enjoy the garden, the horse paddock and pond. No food Mon. Children welcome.
♨ ✿ ⓓ ▶ ♿ Å ♣ P

Great Yarmouth

Mariners Tavern
69 Howard Street South
☎ (01493) 332299
11–3, 8–11; closed Mon–Wed eves and Sun
Draught Bass; Woodforde's Mardler's Mild, Norfolk Nog; guest beers ⒽFirst-class, friendly free house with no keg beer. Local sausages and kippers always available.
♨ Q ✿ ⓓ ▶ Å ⇌ ♣ P

Red Herring
24–25 Havelock Road
☎ (01493) 863384
11–3, 6–11; 12–3, 7–10.30 Sun
Woodforde's Mardler's Mild, Wherry, Emerald Ale; guest beers Ⓗ
19th-century free house in the midst of curing houses, with photos of old Yarmouth adorning the walls. This corner local is hard to find.
Q ☺ ❀ ◑ ◗ ♣ ⇔

Happisburgh

Hill House
Off B1159
☎ (01692) 650004
12–2.30, 7–11; 12–11 Sat & summer; 12–10.30 Sun
Adnams Bitter; Scott's Blues & Bloater; Shepherd Neame Spitfire; guest beers (summer) Ⓗ
16th-century village pub with exposed wooden beams, originally called the Windmill, but changed to Hill House in the 1700s. Conan Doyle wrote *The Dancing Men* here.
♛ ☺ ❀ ⛟ ◑ ◗ ▲ ♣ P

Harleston

Cherry Tree
74 London Road
☎ (01379) 852845
11.30–2.30 (2 Wed, 3 Sat), 6–11; 12–5, 7–10.30 Sun
Adnams Bitter, Old, Broadside; guest beer Ⓗ
Refurbished in 1995, this pub now has a dining area and carpets, but the two beamed bars are still separate. No food Mon; eve meals Wed, Fri and Sat only. ❀ ◑ ◗ ⊞ ♣ P

Hedenham

Mermaid
Norwich Road (B1332)
☎ (01508) 482480
11–3, 7–11; 12–3, 7–10.30 Sun
Adnams Bitter; Greene King IPA; guest beer Ⓗ
Comfortable, refurbished country pub, which has retained much original character. ♛ ❀ ◑ ◗ ▲ ♣ P

Hempstead

Hare & Hounds
Baconsthorpe Road
☎ (01263) 713285
11–3, 5.30–11; 12–3, 7–10.30 Sun
Adnams Bitter; Greene King Abbot; Woodforde's Wherry; guest beer Ⓗ
Long bar in a genuine, old, beamed pub with a wood burner in the inglenook. Friendly atmosphere.
♛ ❀ ⛟ ◑ ◗ P

Hethersett

King's Head
36 Old Norwich Road
☎ (01603) 810206
11–2.30, 5.30 (5 Fri, 6 Sat)–11; 12–3, 7–10.30 Sun
Courage Directors; Marston's Pedigree; Morland Old Speckled Hen; John Smith's Bitter; Woodforde's Wherry; guest beer Ⓗ
Traditional public bar and a comfortable lounge with a dining area, in an old village now almost a suburb of Norwich. ♛ Q ❀ ◑ ◗ ⊞ ♣ P

Heydon

Earle Arms
The Street ☎ (01263) 587376
12–2 (3 summer), 6.30 (7 summer)–11; 12–3.30, 7–10.30 Sun; closed Mon
Flowers IPA; Morland Old Speckled Hen; Woodforde's Wherry, Gt Eastern (summer), **Norfolk Nog** Ⓗ
Early 17th-century pub in good walking country, built by Erasmus Earle (Sergeant-at-Law to Charles I). No jukebox or fruit machines; cider in summer. No food Sun eve.
♛ Q ❀ ◑ ◗ ⊞ ♿ ▲ ♣ ⇔ P ⚡

Hilborough

Swan
Brandon Road
☎ (01760) 756380
11–3, 6 (7 winter)–11; 12–4, 6–10.30 Sun
Adnams Mild, Bitter; Greene King IPA; guest beer Ⓗ
Friendly, 18th-century roadside pub, also the village post office.
♛ Q ❀ ⛟ ◑ ◗ ▲ ♣ P

Hingham

White Hart Hotel
3 Market Place
☎ (01953) 850214
11–3, 6.30–11; 12–3, 7–10.30 Sun
Adnams Bitter; Marston's Pedigree; Webster's Yorkshire Bitter Ⓗ
An imposing hotel frontage hides a plush locals' bar, plus a no-smoking dining area, at the centre of Abraham Lincoln's ancestral village.
♛ Q ☺ ⛟ ◑ ◗ P

Horsey

Nelson Head
The Street (off B1159)
☎ (01493) 393378
11–2.30 (3 Sat), 6 (7 winter)–11; 12–3, 7–10.30 Sun
Woodforde's Wherry; Nelson's Revenge (summer) Ⓗ
Friendly, one-bar country pub with nautical artefacts, handy for the marshes, Horsey Mill, the Broads and beach. Original home-cooked food a speciality.
♛ Q ☺ ❀ ◑ ◗ ▲ ♣ P

Hunworth

Hunny Bell
The Green ☎ (01263) 712300
11–3, 5.30–11; 12–3, 7–10.30 Sun
Adnams Bitter; Greene King IPA, Abbot Ⓗ
Comfortable bar with a log fire and a warm atmosphere, offering a good, varied, bar menu, reasonably priced, and a restaurant. ♛ ☺ ❀ ◑ ◗ ♣ P

King's Lynn

Duke's Head (Lynn Bar)
Tuesday Market Place
☎ (01553) 774996
11–2.30 (3 Tue), 5 (6 Sat)–11; 12–2.30, 6–10.30 Sun
Banks's Bitter; Draught Bass; Marston's Pedigree; Woodforde's Gt Eastern Ⓗ
Cosy bar in a large hotel. The lack of music and machines, together with the comfortable armchairs, provides a relaxing atmosphere. Q ⛟ P

Fenman
Blackfriars Road
☎ (01553) 761889
11–11; 12–3, 7–10.30 Sun
Beer range varies Ⓗ
Pleasantly refurbished, popular pub with a railway theme, opposite the station.
⇌ ♣

London Porterhouse
78 London Road
☎ (01553) 766842
12–3, 6–11; 12–11 Sat; 12–10.30 Sun
Greene King IPA, Abbot Ⓖ
Tiny, lively pub close to the historic South Gates, with casks racked behind the bar.
Q ❀ ◑ ♣

Ouse Amateur Sailing Club
Ferry Lane ☎ (01553) 772239
11–3, 7–11; 7–11 (closed lunch) Sun
Draught Bass; Bateman XB, XXXB; guest beer Ⓖ
Small club by the West Lynn ferry landing stage, overlooking the river. Choice of five beers. CAMRA members and bearers of this guide are welcome.
♛ ❀ ◑ ◗ ♣

White Horse
9 Wootton Road, Gaywood
☎ (01553) 763258
11–3, 5.30–11; 11–11 Fri & Sat; 12–3, 7–10.30 Sun
Greene King IPA; John Smith's Bitter; Theakston XB; guest beer Ⓗ
Popular, two-roomed local near the Gaywood clock.

Pleasant and comfortable, this drinkers' pub is at the heart of the community. Limited parking. ⊞ P

Larling

Angel
On A11
☎ (01953) 717963
11–3, 5–11; 11–11 Fri & Sat; 12–10.30 Sun

Adnams Bitter; Tetley Bitter; guest beers H
The real ale turnover is ever-increasing in this family-run roadside free house. Local CAMRA Gold Award-winner 1997. ⚉ ❀ ⌂ ◁ ▶ ▲ ♣ P

Letheringsett

King's Head
Holt Road
☎ (01263) 712691
11–11; 12–10.30 Sun

Adnams Bitter; Greene King IPA, Abbot; guest beer H
Pub with two bars, each with a log fire, a games room and a restaurant serving home-cooked meals made from fresh local produce (children's menu). The garden has a play area and adventure castle.
⚉ ╰ ❀ ◁ ▶ ♣ P

Middleton

Gate Inn
Fair Green (off A47)
☎ (01553) 840518
12–3, 7 (5 Fri & Sat)–11; 12–3, 7–10.30 Sun

Boddingtons Bitter; Flowers IPA; guest beers H
Pleasant village local with good food and award-winning floral displays. No food Mon eve. ⚉ ❀ ◁ ▶ ♣ P

Mundesley

Royal Hotel
Paston Road
☎ (01263) 720096
11–3, 6–11; 12–3, 6–10.30 Sun

Adnams Bitter; Greene King IPA, Abbot; guest beer H
This hotel's Nelson Bar has comfortable, olde-worlde charm thanks to its inglenook and leather chairs.
⚉ Q ╰ ♨ ◁ ▶ ▲ P

Mundford

Crown Hotel
Crown Road
☎ (01842) 878233
11–11; 12–10.30 Sun

Samuel Smith OBB; Woodforde's Wherry; guest beers H
Flint village pub built in 1650. Very busy summer Suns. Good food. ⚉ Q ❀ ♨ ◁ ▶ P

New Buckenham

King's Head
Market Place ☎ (01953) 860487
12–3, 7–11; 12–3, 7–10.30 Sun

Adnams Bitter; Draught Bass; Iceni Fine Soft Day H
Unspoilt, two-bar pub near the village green that now hosts two fairs a year.
⚉ Q ❀ ◁ ▶ ♣

New Rackheath

Sole & Heel
2 Salhouse Road
☎ (01603) 720146
11.30–3, 6.30–11; 11–11 Sat; 12–4, 7–10.30 Sun

Boddingtons Bitter; Flowers IPA; Shepherd Neame Bishops Finger; guest beers H
Unpretentious, friendly village local with distinctive 1930s architecture. Up to five guest beers. ⚉ ❀ ♣ P

North Creake

Jolly Farmers
1 Burnham Road
☎ (01328) 738185
11.30–3, 7–11; 12–2.30, 7–10.30 Sun

Greene King Abbot; Tetley Bitter; guest bitter H
Old local in the village centre: a real public bar, a character lounge and a restaurant. Handy for the North Norfolk coast. ⚉ Q ❀ ◁ ▶ ⊞ ♣ P

Northrepps

Parson's Pleasure
Church Barn ☎ (01263) 579691
11–11; 12–10.30 Sun

Greene King IPA, Abbot H
Pub built in flint and beamed throughout, warmed by log fires. ⚉ ╰ ❀ ♨ ◁ ▶ ▲ P

North Walsham

Orchard Gardens
Mundesley Road
☎ (01692) 405152
11–11; 12–10.30 Sun

Chalk Hill Tap Bitter; Courage Directors; Woodforde's Wherry; guest beers H
Town pub combining local beers with friendly service. A games area and conservatory are features in this Victorian building. ❀ ≆ ♣ P

Northwold

Crown
30 High Street
☎ (01366) 727317
12–2.30, 6–11; 11.30–11 Sat; 12–3, 7–10.30 Sun

Greene King IPA, Abbot; guest beers H

18th-century 'chalk lump' pub, serving good food. A good place to find locally-brewed Iceni beers.
⚉ Q ❀ ◁ ▶ ♣ P

Norwich

Adam & Eve
17 Bishopgate
11–11; 12–10.30 Sun

Adnams Bitter; Marston's Pedigree; Theakston Old Peculier; Wadworth 6X H
Very old, split-level pub in a peaceful location, offering lots of nooks and crannies in which to enjoy a quiet pint.
Q ❀ ◁

Alexandra Tavern
16 Stafford Street
☎ (01603) 627772
10.30–11; 12–10.30 Sun

Adnams Bitter; Chalk Hill CHB, Dreadnought, Flintknapper's Mild; Marston's Pedigree; guest beer H
Classic, two-bar corner local with a pool table and a vinyl jukebox. Q ❀ ⌂

Billy Bluelight
27 Hall Road
☎ (01603) 623768
12–3, 7–11; 12–11 Sat; 12–10.30 Sun

Woodforde's Mardler's Mild, Wherry, Emerald Ale, Gt Eastern, Nelson's Revenge, Headcracker; guest beers H
The only Woodforde's house in Norwich; a popular one-bar pub, stocking almost the entire Woodforde's range.
⚉ ◁ ⅍ ♣

Coach & Horses
82 Thorpe Road
☎ (01603) 477077
11–11; 12–10.30 Sun

Chalk Hill Tap Bitter, CHB, Dreadnought, Flintknapper's Mild, Old Tackle; guest beers H
Friendly, lively pub with a large L-shaped drinking area. House beers come from the on-site Chalk Hill Brewery; varied guest beers are available.
⚉ ❀ ◁ ▶ ⅍ ≆ ♣ ⌂ P

Denmark Arms
43 Sandringham Road (1 mile W of centre, off Earlham Rd)
☎ (01603) 628986
7 (11 Sat)–11; 12–10.30 Sun

Adnams Bitter, Broadside; Courage Best Bitter; guest beer H
Classic example of a two-bar backstreet local; note the large collection of thimbles in the public bar. Folk music some eves. The pub may change its name in the near future. No keg bitters stocked; occasional cider in summer.
⚉ Q ❀ ⊞ ♣ ⌂

Eaton Cottage
75 Mount Pleasant
☎ (01603) 453048
11–11; 12–10.30 Sun
Adnams Bitter; Marston's Pedigree; John Smith's Bitter; guest beers H
Truly traditional, unspoilt corner local. Live entertainment some eves.
🏵 🍴 ♣

Fat Cat
49 West End Street
☎ (01603) 624364
12–11; 12–10.30 Sun
Adnams Bitter, Extra; Fuller's London Pride; Kelham Island Pale Rider; Woodforde's Gt Eastern H**; guest beers** H/G
Bustling and lively corner pub with 20 real ales, about half on gravity from the large tap room behind the bar. A must.
Q 🏵 ♣ 🍴

Horse & Dray
137 Ber Street
☎ (01603) 624741
11–2.30, 4.30–11; 11–11 Sat; 12–3, 7–10.30 Sun
Adnams Mild, Bitter, Old, Broadside; guest beer H
Friendly local, due for refurbishment, only a short distance from the centre.
🚍 🏵 🍴 ♿

Ribs of Beef
24 Wensum Street
☎ (01603) 619517
10.30–11; 12–10.30 Sun
Adnams Bitter; Flowers IPA; Marston's Pedigree; Reepham Rapier; Woodforde's Wherry; guest beers H
Something of a connoisseur's pub, offering good food in a friendly atmosphere, with a large range of guest ales.
🍴

St Andrew's Tavern
4 St Andrew's Street
☎ (01603) 614858
11–11; 12–10.30 Sun
Adnams Bitter, Broadside H**; guest beers** H/G
Well-established, city-centre pub where meals are served 12–6 Sun and 12–7 Sat (12–2.30 other days). Varied ales. No-smoking area lunchtimes.
🍴 ♣ 🍴 ♿ 🚬

Trafford Arms
61 Grove Road
☎ (01603) 628466
11–11; 12–10.30 Sun
Adnams Bitter; Boddingtons Bitter; Tetley Bitter; Woodforde's Mardler's Mild; guest beers H
Large, one-bar, open-plan pub serving a wide range of beers, including Woodforde's house beers. No-smoking area available lunchtime.
🍴 ♿ ♣ 🍴 🚬

Vine
7 Dove Street
☎ (01603) 629258
10.30–11; 12–10.30 Sun
Adnams Bitter, Extra, Broadside, seasonal beer; guest beer H
Possibly the smallest pub in Norwich, an ex-Courage pub, near the market place, offering a very friendly welcome. Regular quizzes and folk music. 🏵 ♣

Wig & Pen
6 St Martin at Palace Plain
☎ (01603) 625891
11.30 (12 Sat)–11; 12–4 Sun, closed Sun eve
Adnams Bitter; Buffy's Bitter; Scott's Hopleaf, Dark Oast H
Friendly bar near the law courts, serving local beers.
🚍 🍴

York Tavern
1 Leicester Street
☎ (01603) 620918
11–11; 12–10.30 Sun
Courage Best Bitter, Directors; Marston's Pedigree; Morland Old Speckled Hen; Wadworth 6X; York Tavern Old Duke H
Knocked-through corner pub aiming at the younger customer, boasting a large garden at the back, plus a big upstairs function room. Home to the York Brewing Company – you can see the small brewing plant at the rear. Food served all day at weekends.
🏵 🍴 ▶

Old Hunstanton

Ancient Mariner
Golf Course Road
☎ (01485) 534411
11–3, 6–11; 11–11 Sat & summer; 12–10.30 Sun
Adnams Bitter, Broadside; Draught Bass; guest beer H
Traditional pub attached to the Le Strange Arms hotel. Catering for all the family, it features bare boards, a seafaring atmosphere, and a conservatory with a grape vine.
🚍 🛥 🏵 🚪 🍴 ▶ ♿ ♣ P 🚬

Pulham St Mary

King's Head Inn
Station Road
☎ (01379) 676318
11–3, 5.30–11; 11–11 Sat; 12–10.30 Sun
Adnams Bitter; Buffy's Bitter; guest beers H
Relaxed, beamed, old village pub with an assortment of drinking and eating areas and an inglenook. Note the memorabilia of the locally-made Pulham Pigs (airships).
🚍 🏵 🚪 🍴 ▶ P

Reedham

Railway Tavern
17 The Havaker (B1140)
☎ (01493) 700340
11–3 (may extend), 6–11; 11–11 Fri & Sat; 12–10.30 Sun
Adnams Extra; Theakston Best Bitter; Woodforde's Gt Eastern; guest beers H
A good mix of customers and a warm welcome are features of this Grade II-listed Victorian building. Large selection of whiskies; guest beers often come from micros; cider in summer. 🚍 Q 🏵 🚪 ◀ ▶ ⚓ ➤
♣ 🍴 P 🚬

Reepham

King's Arms
Market Place
☎ (01603) 870345
11.30–3, 5.30–11; 11.30–11 Sat; 12–3, 7–10.30 Sun
Adnams Bitter, Broadside; Draught Bass; Greene King Abbot; Woodforde's Wherry; guest beer H
Attractive, early 18th-century coaching inn: two bars with three real fires. Good meals, live jazz in the courtyard in summer and bar billiards feature in this very traditional pub. Children welcome.
🚍 Q 🏵 ◀ ▶ 🍴 ♣ P

Ringstead

Gin Trap
High Street
☎ (01485) 525264
11.30–2.30 (may extend summer), 7–11; 12–2.30, 7–10.30 Sun
Adnams Bitter, Broadside; Greene King Abbot; Woodforde's Norfolk Nog H
Popular village local with good food (small restaurant) and a large garden. The decor includes gin traps. The house beer is by Woodforde's.
🚍 🏵 ◀ ▶ ♣ P

Roydon

Blacksmith's Arms
30 Station Road (off A148)
☎ (01485) 601347
11–11; 12–10.30 Sun
Greene King IPA H
100-year-old village pub, very popular with locals but with a friendly welcome for all. An Iceni beer is always available.
🏵 ♣ P

Rushall

Half Moon
The Street ☎ (01379) 740793
12–2.30, 6 (5 Sat)–11; 12–10.30 Sun
Adnams Bitter; guest beer H
16th-century pub with beams and inglenooks, largely food

oriented. The house beer is by
Woodforde's.
🏚 ॐ ⍟ 🍴 ◖ ▲ P

Saham Toney

Bell
1 Bell Lane ☎ (01953) 884934
12–3, 6 (7 Sat)–11; 12–3, 7–10.30 Sun
**Adnams Bitter; Fuller's
London Pride; guest beers** Ⓗ
Homely, welcoming, 'clay
lump' pub: one bar with a
dining area, plus bare boards
and beams from 1698.
🏚 ॐ ⍟ ◖ & ▲ ♣ P

Sheringham

Lobster
13 High Street
☎ (01263) 822716
11–11; 12–10.30 Sun
**Adnams Bitter; Marston's
Pedigree; John Smith's
Bitter** Ⓗ
Popular pub in a busy high
street, close to the seafront: the
cosy lounge bar has relics of
the sea and marine maps as
decoration; the public bar has a
pool table and darts. A family
favourite in the holiday season.
🏚 Q ॐ ⍟ ◖ 🍴 ⌑ ≈ ♣ P

Smallburgh

Crown
North Walsham Road
☎ (01692) 536314
12–3 (4 Sat), 5.30 (7 Sat)–11; 12–3 Sun,
closed Sun eve
**Boddingtons Bitter; Greene
King IPA, Abbot; Tetley
Bitter; guest beer** Ⓗ
Comfortable, two-bar village
pub and restaurant in a 15th-
century, thatched and beamed
building. The games room
opens on to a lovely garden.
🏚 ⍟ 🍴 ◖ ▲ ♣ P

Southery

Jolly Farmers
Feltwell Road (off A10)
☎ (01366) 377327
11–2.30, 6–11; 12–3, 7–10.30 Sun
**Adnams Bitter; Greene King
IPA, Abbot** Ⓗ
Large, modern, single-bar pub
with good quality food always
available, and the best value
for miles. Interesting display of
farm implements. ⍟ ◖ 🍴 & P

South Lopham

White Horse
The Street ☎ (01379) 687252
11–3, 6–11; 12–4, 6.30–10.30 Sun
**Adnams Bitter; Greene King
IPA, Abbot; guest beer** Ⓗ
Lovely, 300-year-old, beamed
local with inglenooks and a
dining area at one end. A large
outdoor green has play
apparatus, well away from the

pub – but in view. Children's
certificate. 🏚 ⍟ 🍴 ◖ & ♣ P

Stibbard

Ordnance Arms
Guist Bottom (A1067)
☎ (01328) 829471
11–2.30 (3 Sat), 5.30–11; 12–3, 5.30–
10.30 Sun
**Draught Bass; Greene King
IPA** Ⓗ
Comfortable, unspoilt, three-
bar pub with a pool table in
one room; a sociable drinkers'
pub with a Thai restaurant
(open Tue–Sat eves) at the rear.
Reasonably priced beers.
🏚 Q ⍟ ♣ P

Stiffkey

Red Lion
44 Wells Road
☎ (01328) 830522
11–2.30, 7 (6 summer)–11; 12–3,
7–10.30 Sun
**Greene King Abbot;
Woodforde's Wherry** Ⓖ; **guest
beers** Ⓗ
Friendly local with a
commitment to regional ales.
Several drinking areas of
character.
🏚 Q ॐ ⍟ ◖ ▲ ♣ P

Stowbridge

Heron
Station Road
☎ (01366) 384147
11–3, 7–11; 12–3, 7–10.30 Sun
**Adnams Bitter; Draught Bass;
Greene King IPA, Abbot;
guest beers** Ⓗ
Friendly, riverside pub
between the Great Ouse and
the relief channel, with a
comfortable lounge, a games
room, and a pleasant garden.
🏚 Q ⍟ 🍴 ◖ ▲ ♣ P

Strumpshaw

Shoulder of Mutton
Norwich Road (on Brundall–
Lingwood road)
☎ (01603) 712274
11–11; 12–10.30 Sun
**Adnams Bitter, Extra or
Broadside, seasonal beers;
Boddingtons Bitter** Ⓗ
Large, friendly, single-bar pub,
set back from the road: a
thriving local displaying a
number of games trophies. No
food Sun eve.
🏚 ⍟ ◖ 🍴 ♣ P

Swanton Abbott

Jolly Farmers
Aylsham Road
☎ (01692) 538542
11–11; 12–10.30 Sun
**Greene King IPA, Abbot;
guest beers** Ⓗ

Sociable local with a games
room and a parrot! Reasonably
priced food.
ॐ ⍟ ◖ ▲ ♣ P ⌿

Swanton Morley

Angel Inn
Greengate ☎ (01362) 637407
12–11; 12–3, 7–10.30 Sun
**Boddingtons Mild, Bitter;
Samuel Smith OBB; guest
beer** Ⓗ
Welcoming, old, beamed pub
with an inglenook and a pool
room. Abraham Lincoln's
ancestors reputedly lived here.
🏚 ⍟ ▲ ♣ P

Terrington St
Clement

County Arms
29 Marshland Street
☎ (01553) 828511
12–3, 7–11; 12–3, 7–10.30 Sun
**Greene King XX Mild, IPA,
Abbot; guest beers**
(occasional) Ⓗ
Large, friendly village local,
just off the old A17, not on the
normal tourist trail and
therefore a true local. Naval
memorabilia is featured.
🏚 ⍟ 🍴 P

Thetford

Albion
93–95 Castle Street (opp. Castle
Hill ancient monument)
☎ (01842) 752796
11–2.30 (3 Fri), 6 (5 Fri)–11; 12–2.30,
7–10.30 Sun
**Greene King IPA, Abbot,
seasonal beers** Ⓗ
Excellent value ale is sold in
this small, traditional local, set
back amongst flint cottages in a
quiet part of the town. Limited
parking. 🏚 ⍟ ♣ P

Dolphin Inn
Old Market Street (¼ mile from
centre, below Castle Hill)
☎ (01842) 752271
11–3, 6–11; 12–3, 7–10.30 Sun
**Greene King IPA; guest
beers** Ⓗ
Attractive, popular, one-bar,
17th-century inn where oak
beams feature throughout.
Friendly staff.
🏚 Q ⍟ ◖ & P

Thornham

Lifeboat
Ship Lane ☎ (01485) 512236
11–11; 12–10.30 Sun
**Adnams Bitter; Greene King
IPA, Abbot; Woodforde's
Wherry; guest beers** Ⓗ
Oil lamps still light the bar of
this 16th-century smugglers'
inn, which is full of warmth
and character. The large,
attractively furnished

conservatory is ideal for families. Weston's Old Rosie cider (rare in the area).
♨ Q ❀ 🛏 ◖ ◗ ▲ ♣ ⌓

Thorpe St Andrew

King's Head
36 Yarmouth Road
☎ (01603) 433540
11–11; 12–3, 7–10.30 (12–10.30 summer) Sun
Adnams Bitter; Flowers Original; Fuller's London Pride; Greene King IPA; Marston's Pedigree; Morland Old Speckled Hen; guest beer [H]
One-bar, 16th-century pub situated on the river, serving home-cooked specials and vegetarian meals. Seven ales at all times. Live entertainment summer weekends.
♨ Q ❀ 🛏 ◖ ◗ P

Tibenham

Greyhound
The Street ☎ (01379) 677676
11–4, 6–11; 11–11 Fri & Sat; 12–10.30 Sun
Adnams Bitter; Wadworth 6X; guest beer [H]
Local drinkers' pub with two adjoining bars in an old beamed building with a quarry tiled floor. Well worth finding.
♨ Q ❀ ▲ ♣ P

Upton

White Horse
17 Chapel Road
☎ (01493) 750696
11–11; 12–10.30 Sun
Beer range varies [H]
Friendly, cosy village local offering four real ales in a pleasant atmosphere. Cider in summer. ♨ ❀ ◖ ◗ ▲ ♣ ⌓ P

Upwell

Five Bells
1 New Road ☎ (01945) 772222
12–3 (not Mon), 6–11; 11–11 Fri & Sat; 12–3, 7–10.30 Sun
Draught Bass; John Smith's Bitter; Theakston Best Bitter; guest beer [H]
Lively village inn next to the church, featuring a bar counter in ecclesiastic style. The plush restaurant serves Chinese food.
♘ ❀ 🛏 ◖ ◗ ♿ ♣ P

Walcott

Lighthouse Inn
Coast Road (B1159)
☎ (01692) 650371
11–3, 6–11; 11–11 Sat & summer; 12–10.30 Sun
Adnams Bitter; Marston's Pedigree; Tetley Bitter; guest beers [H]
Friendly pub, popular with locals and visitors. Good value food is available at most times.
♨ ♘ ❀ ◖ ◗ ▲ ♣ P

Warham All Saints

Three Horseshoes ☆
The Street ☎ (01328) 710547
11.30–2.30, 6–11; 12–3, 6–10.30 Sun
Greene King IPA, Abbot; Woodforde's Wherry; guest beer [H]
Sympathetically enlarged and modernised, 1920s pub close to the coast. Ideal for birdwatching and the beaches, it specialises in local traditional food (eve meals end at 8.30).
♨ Q ♘ ❀ 🛏 ◖ ◗ ♿ ▲ ♣ P

Weasenham All Saints

Ostrich Inn
On A1065 ☎ (01328) 838221
11.30–2.30 (not Mon), 7–11; 12–3, 7–10.30 Sun
Adnams Bitter [H]
Genuine, old-fashioned, welcoming local.
♨ Q ❀ ⊞ ♣ P

Wells-next-the-Sea

Crown Hotel
The Buttlands
☎ (01328) 710209
11–2.30, 6–11; 12–2.30, 7–10.30 Sun
Adnams Bitter; Draught Bass; Marston's Pedigree [H]
Attractive old coaching inn with a Georgian facade, a comfortable bar, a restaurant, and a south-facing sun lounge.
♨ ♘ ❀ 🛏 ◖ ◗ P

West Beckham

Wheatsheaf
Church Road
☎ (01263) 822110
12–3, 7–11 (11–3, 6–11 summer); 12–3, 6–10.30 Sun
Draught Bass; Woodforde's Wherry, Nelson's Revenge [H], **Norfolk Nog, Headcracker** [G]; **guest beer** [H]
Old, brick and flint pub with a beamed interior; very popular with locals and summer visitors. Children are welcome, provided they remain with parents. Cider in summer. ♨ Q ❀ 🛏 ◖ ◗ ⊞ ♿ ♣ ⌓ P ⊬

West Rudham

Duke's Head
Lynn Road (A148)
☎ (01485) 528540
11–3, 6.30–11; 12–2.30, 7–10.30 Sun
Shepherd Neame Master Brew Bitter; Woodforde's Wherry; guest beers [H]
Conversational pub, an interesting example of vernacular architecture on the outside, with a comfortably modernised interior. Cricket library. ♨ Q ❀ ◖ ◗ ⊞ ♣ P

Whinburgh

Mustard Pot
Dereham Road
☎ (01362) 692179
11–3, 6.30–11; 12–3, 7–10.30 Sun
Woodforde's Wherry; guest beer [H]
Friendly village local, formerly a row of houses. Additional guest beer in summer.
♨ Q ❀ ◖ ◗ ♿ ♣ P

Winfarthing

Fighting Cocks
The Street ☎ (01379) 643283
4–11; 12–3, 7–10.30 Sun
Adnams Bitter; guest beer [G]
Large, 15th-century, beamed pub with inglenooks and a games room. Sun lunches are served. ♨ ❀ ◗ ▲ ♣ P

Winterton-on-Sea

Fisherman's Return
The Lane (off B1159)
☎ (01493) 393305
11–2.30, 6 (7 winter)–11; 11–11 Sat; 12–10.30 Sun
Adnams Bitter [G]; **guest beers** [H]
Popular, two-bar local, handy for the beach, offering a varying selection of beers, original home-cooked food and over 30 whiskies.
♨ ♘ ❀ 🛏 ◖ ◗ ♣ ⌓ P ⊬

Woodbastwick

Fur & Feather Inn
Slad Lane ☎ (01603) 720003
12–2 (11–3 summer), 6–11; 12–3, 7–10.30 Sun
Woodforde's Mardler's Mild, Broadsman, Gt Eastern, Norfolk Nog, Baldric, Headcracker [G]
Formerly a row of farm cottages across the yard from Woodforde's brewery, now a country pub, popular for its food. ❀ ◖ ◗ ⌓ P ⊬

Wymondham

Feathers Inn
13 Town Green
☎ (01953) 607675
11–2.30, 7 (6 Fri)–11; 12–2.30, 7–10.30 Sun
Adnams Bitter; Greene King Abbot; Marston's Pedigree; Samuel Smith OBB; guest beers [H]
Busy, friendly, local with one beamed bar and a good atmosphere, serving a good selection of home-cooked food, and decorated with tools and farming implements. The house beer is by Samuel Smith.
Q ❀ ◖ ◗ ♣

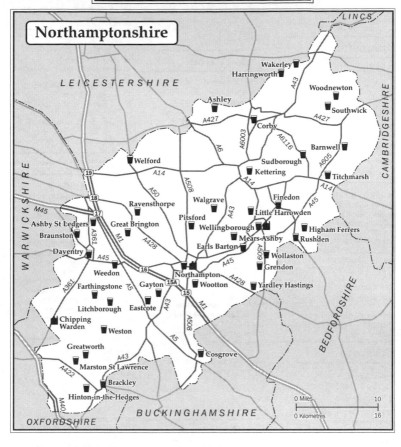

Northamptonshire

LINCS

LEICESTERSHIRE

Wakerley
Harringworth
Woodnewton
Ashley
Southwick
A427
Corby
A6003
A6116
Barnwell
Welford
Sudborough
Kettering
Titchmarsh
Ravensthorpe
Walgrave
Finedon
Pitsford
Little Harrowden
Ashby St Ledgers
Great Brington
Wellingborough
Braunston
Mears-Ashby
Higham Ferrers
Daventry
Earls Barton
Rushden
Weedon
Wollaston
Grendon
Farthingstone
Gayton
Northampton
Yardley Hastings
Litchborough
Eastcote
Wootton
Chipping Warden
Weston
Greatworth
Cosgrove
Marston St Lawrence
Brackley
Hinton-in-the-Hedges

WARWICKSHIRE
CAMBRIDGESHIRE
BEDFORDSHIRE
BUCKINGHAMSHIRE
OXFORDSHIRE

0 Miles 10
0 Kilometres 16

Ashby St Ledgers

Old Coach House Inn
Off A361 ☎ (01788) 890349
12–2.30, 6–11; 12–11 Sat; 12–3, 7–10.30 Sun
**Everards Old Original;
Flowers Original; guest
beers** H
Traditional, cosy pub with a
small snug bar and a games
room with many beams and
features. The main lounge has
a large wood fire and an old
range for winter. Eight guest
ales. 🏠 🌳 🏵 🍴 🍺 🍴 ⊞ P

Ashley

George
21 Main Street (off A427/B664)
☎ (01858) 565881
12–2.30, 6–11; 12–11 Sat; 12–10.30 Sun
**Mansfield Riding Bitter,
Bitter, Old Baily** H
Very friendly village local with
a superb tiled bar floor and
wooden settles in both the bar
and lounge. A skittles room
with a small serving hatch is to
the rear. A small extension

now means you don't get wet
when visiting the toilets! No
food Tue. 🏠 🍴 🍺 🍴 ⊞ ⌂ ♣ P

Barnwell

Montagu Arms
Off A605 by Oundle turn
☎ (01832) 273726
11–3, 6–11; 11–11 Fri & Sat; 12–10 Sun
Flowers IPA, Original H;
Hook Norton Old Hooky G;
Wadworth 6X G/H; **guest
beers** H
Reputedly haunted, 16th-
century, stone pub with a large
bar featuring a wealth of
exposed timbers, a new no-
smoking restaurant, a games
bar, en suite accommodation
and large gardens, including
children's play areas, crazy
golf and a camp site.
🏠 Q 🏵 �bed 🍴 🍺 🍴 ⊞ Å ♣ P

Brackley

Greyhound
101 High Street
☎ (01280) 703331
12–3, 7–11; 12–4, 7–10.30 Sun
Banks's Bitter; guest beers H

Traditional, town-centre pub
offering four guest beers plus a
house beer, 'Skinny Mutt',
brewed by Vale. Mexican food
is a speciality in the restaurant.
Over 40 malt whiskies to try.
Cider in summer.
🏠 🍴 🍺 ♣ ⌂

Red Lion
11 Market Place
☎ (01280) 702228
11–11; 12–10.30 Sun
**Wells Eagle, Bombardier;
guest beer** H
Stone-built, 16th-century pub
with a TV, pool table and a
lounge bar. Regular live music
events in the summer, in the

barn bar at the back. Eve meals served Mon–Thu.
🏚 ✿ 🛏 ◖▶ ♣

Braunston

Old Plough
High Street ☎ (01788) 890000
11.30–2.30, 6.30–11; 12–3, 7–10.30 Sun
Ansells Bitter; Ind Coope Burton Ale Ⓗ
A pub since 1672, featuring a cosy, semi-timbered lounge, with a real fire, and a separate bar with games. Good food.
🏚 ✿ ◖▶ ⌸ ♣ P

Corby

Knight's Lodge
Tower Hill Road (off A6003)
☎ (01536) 742602
12–3 (4 Fri & Sat), 6–11; 12–3.30, 7–10.30 Sun
Everards Beacon, Tiger, Old Original; guest beer Ⓗ
An oasis in this ex-steelworks town, this 17th-century, beamed farmhouse is sited on a 12th-century knights' lodging, once found in Rockingham Forest. If you are lucky, you may see one of the eight ghosts! No eve meals Sun.
🏚 ✿ ◖▶ ♣ P

Cosgrove

Navigation
Thrupp Wharf (signed from A508) ☎ (01908) 543156
11–3.30, 6–11; 12–3, 7–10.30 Sun
Morland Old Speckled Hen; guest beers Ⓗ
Stone pub set in rural countryside, with the garden alongside the Grand Union Canal. A balcony offers fine views of boats and summer sunsets. The restaurant serves excellent food and boasts two pianos. Impressive pump clip collection above the bar.
🏚 ✿ ◖▶ Å P

Daventry

Coach & Horses
Warwick Street
☎ (01327) 76692
11–2.30, 5–11; 12–3, 7–11 Sat; 12–3, 7–10.30 Sun
Ind Coope Burton Ale; Marston's Pedigree; Tetley Bitter; guest beers Ⓗ
An open fire, boarded floors and stone walls give a warm feel to this town-centre pub. The stables across the coaching yard host a jazz night alternate Thu. Changing guest beers. No food Sun. 🏚 Q ✿ ◖ ♣

Dun Cow
Brook Street ☎ (01327) 71545
10.30–3, 5–11; 10.30–11 Fri; 12–3, 7–10.30 Sun
Davenports Bitter; Greenalls Original Ⓗ

Early 17th-century coaching inn with an unspoilt snug bar. Monthly folk music. No food Sun. 🏚 Q ✿ ◖ P

Earls Barton

Stag's Head
25 High Street
☎ (01604) 810520
11–3, 6.30–11; 12–3, 7–10.30 Sun
Home Bitter; Marston's Pedigree; Morland Old Speckled Hen; Theakston Best Bitter, XB Ⓗ
Popular pub with a smart lounge area, a popular meeting place for many clubs (numerous function rooms).
Q ✿ ◖ & ♣ P

Eastcote

Eastcote Arms
6 Gayton Road (take Banbury Lane turn for Duncote)
☎ (01327) 830731
12–2.30 (not Mon), 6–11; 12–3, 7–10.30 Sun
Draught Bass; Fuller's London Pride; Jennings Bitter; Samuel Smith OBB; guest beer Ⓗ
Local CAMRA *Pub of the Year* runner-up 1995 and '96: an unspoilt, friendly village pub with high standards in all areas. A small, no-smoking dining room through the snug serves excellent, home-cooked food (Tue–Sun lunch, Thu–Sat eve). Book lunches Thu and Sun. 🏚 Q ✿ ◖▶ P

Farthingstone

King's Arms
Main Street ☎ (01327) 361604
12–2.30 (not Mon), 6.30–11; 12–3, 7–10.30 Sun
Hook Norton Best Bitter; Tetley Bitter; guest beers Ⓗ
An inglenook fire in this seemingly small bar gives a very home-like atmosphere. Comfortable armchairs are available next to the stairs leading to an upper area. A separate room offers Northants skittles. 🏚 Q ✿ ◖▶ ♣ P

Finedon

Bell Inn
Bell Hill ☎ (01933) 680332
11.30–3, 5.30–11; 12–3, 7–10.30 Sun
Hop Back Summer Lightning Ⓖ**; Ruddles Best Bitter, County; Vaux Samson; Ward's Best Bitter** Ⓗ
Super old pub, one of the oldest in England, dating back to 1042. The main bar has an inglenook with a wood burner. The back bar leads to a restaurant area. Shove-ha'penny played.
🏚 Q ✿ ◖▶ & ♣ P

Gayton

Eykyn Arms
20 High Street (A43)
☎ (01604) 858361
12–2 (not Mon), 7 (earlier summer)–11; 12–3, 7–10.30 Sun
Theakston XB; Wells Eagle, Fargo; guest beers Ⓗ
Good, basic, popular local with a bar and a lounge. The front bar has a nautical/aviation theme. Floral patio. Dogs welcome. 🏚 ✿ ◖ Å ♣ P

Great Brington

Fox & Hounds
High Street (off A428)
☎ (01604) 770651
12–2.30, 5.30–11; 12–10.30 Sun
Theakston Best Bitter, XB, Old Peculier; guest beers Ⓗ
350-year-old coaching inn with flagstoned floors, original beams and some wood panelling. The olde-worlde interior is split into three areas of character. Log fires create a welcoming atmosphere. The games room affords a view of casks in the cellar. Nine guest beers. 🏚 ✿ ◖▶ ♣ P

Greatworth

Inn
Chapel Road (1 mile off B4525)
☎ (01295) 710976
11.30 (12 Sat)–2.30 (not Mon), 6–11; 12–10.30 Sun
Hook Norton Mild, Best Bitter, seasonal beer *or* guest beer Ⓗ
Greatly improved, welcoming village local serving excellent, home-made organic food. Aunt Sally is played at the back. A games room with a pool table is in an old barn. No food Sun eve. 🏚 ◖▶ ♣ P

Grendon

Half Moon
42 Main Road
☎ (01933) 663263
12–3 (4 Sat), 6 (6.30 Sat)–11; 12–3, 7–10.30 Sun
Morland Old Speckled Hen; Shepherd Neame Spitfire; Wells Eagle Ⓗ
Traditional, oak-beamed pub in a pretty village. Regular themed food eves include Thai food nights (no food Sun eve). One of the beers may give way to a guest. 🏚 ✿ ◖▶ & ♣ P

Harringworth

White Swan
Seaton Road ☎ (01572) 747543
11.30–2.30, 6.30–11; 12–3, 7–10.30 Sun
Greene King IPA, Abbot; Marston's Pedigree Ⓗ

16th-century inn built of local limestone with a collyweston roof: a bar area, a games and drinking area and a restaurant. The stairs up to the accommodation have a trip step, an early form of burglar alarm. Close to the famous railway viaduct across the River Welland.
Q ✿ 🛏 ◑ ▶ ♣ P

Higham Ferrers

Green Dragon Hotel

4 College Street (A6)
☎ (01933) 312088
11.30–11; 12–10.30 Sun
Badger Tanglefoot; Banks's Bitter; Shepherd Neame Spitfire; Tetley Bitter; guest beers H
Stone-built, 17th-century, Grade II-listed pub on a conservation high street. Thirteen beers are available, including mild, stout or porter. Beer festivals May and Aug. Two acres of garden include a children's adventure playground. Cider in summer.
✿ 🛏 ◑ ▶ ♣ 🛓 ♣ ♻

Hinton-in-the-Hedges

Crewe Arms

☎ (01280) 703314
12–2.30, 7 (6.30 Fri & Sat)–11; 12–2.30, 7–10.30 Sun
Hook Norton Best Bitter; Marston's Pedigree; guest beers H
Cosy, stone-built local tucked away in a tiny hamlet. The bar has a well-used real fire and a snug contains a bar billiards table. Function room at the rear. 🏚 Q ✿ ◑ ▶ ♣ P

Kettering

Piper

Windmill Avenue (200 yds from Wicksteed Park, off A6)
☎ (01536) 513870
11–3 (4 Sat), 5 (6 Sat)–11; 12–10.30 Sun
Ansells Mild; Theakston Best Bitter, XB, Old Peculier; guest beer H
Popular 1950s pub. A pleasant lounge and a separate bar appeal to young and old alike. Water-colours in the lounge are for sale. The guest beer is changed weekly.
✿ ◑ ▶ ♣ ♣ P

Talbot Inn

Meadow Road (near B&Q and McDonalds) ☎ (01536) 514565
11–11; 12–10.30 Sun
Marston's Bitter, Pedigree, HBC H
Close to the town centre, this traditional boozer always has a warm atmosphere. Two plush lounges, a bar and new conservatory feature together

with limited accommodation. No food Mon.
🛏 ✿ 🛏 ◑ ▶ ♣ ♣

Try also: Old Market Inn, Sheep St (Free)

Litchborough

Red Lion

4 Banbury Road
☎ (01327) 830250
11–3, 6.30–11; 12–3, 6.30–10.30 Sun
Banks's Bitter E**; Marston's Pedigree; Morrells Graduate** H
Good-looking stone pub in a picturesque village, featuring an inglenook, real fire, flagstone floor and oak beams: a genuine pub with a landlord to match. Separate rooms for Northants skittles and pool. Popular with walkers. Food in good proportions Tue–Sat.
🏚 Q ✿ ◑ ▶ ♣ P

Little Harrowden

Lamb Inn

Orlingbury Road
☎ (01933) 673300
11–2.30, 7–11; 12–3, 7–10.30 Sun
Adnams Broadside; Badger Tanglefoot; Morland Old Speckled Hen; Wells Eagle, Bombardier; guest beer H
Traditional, oak-beamed village pub well-known for its food (no meals Sun eve). Northants skittles played. Good atmosphere.
Q ✿ ◑ ▶ ♣ P

Marston St Lawrence

Marston Inn

1½ miles off B4525
☎ (01295) 711906
12–3 (not Mon), 7 (6 Sat)–11; 12–3, 7–10.30 Sun
Hook Norton Mild, Best Bitter, Old Hooky, seasonal beer or guest beer H
Welcoming, stone village local. Recently extended, it now has two bars and a separate restaurant (excellent, home-made food). Aunt Sally is played in the garden. Camping, with caravans allowed, behind the pub. No food Sun eve or Mon.
🏚 Q ✿ ◑ ▶ ▲ ♣ ♻

Mears Ashby

Griffin's Head

☎ (01604) 812945
11.30–2.30, 5.30–11; 12–3, 6.30–11 Sat; 12–3, 7–10.30 Sun
Everards Beacon, Tiger; Marston's Bitter, Pedigree; guest beers H
Quality village inn with a classic bar with darts and skittles, plus a lounge and side restaurant with thick carpet

and tapestry-covered seating. Food is always excellent. Guest beers are often from Frog Island. 🏚 Q ✿ ◑ ▶ 🍴 ♣ P

Northampton

Bold Dragoon

48 High Street, Weston Favell
☎ (01604) 401221
11–3, 5.30–11; 11–11 Sat; 12–3, 7–10.30 Sun
Banks's Bitter; Boddingtons Bitter; Flowers IPA; Wadworth 6X; guest beers H
Popular pub with comfortable lounge, with a central fireplace, and a busy games room with a loud jukebox and, occasionally louder, rugby players. At least three guest ales. ✿ 🛓 🛓 ♣ P

Duke of Edinburgh

3–5 Adelaide Street (off Barrack Rd) ☎ (01604) 37903
11–3, 5–11; 11–11 Sat; 12–3, 7–10.30 Sun
Wells Eagle, Bombardier; guest beers H
Classic corner local with an L-shaped bar and a central serving area. Impromptu piano players are always welcome, as are any musicians. Live music Sat eve. Northants skittles played. 50–70s disco Fri.
✿ ♣

Fish Inn

11 Fish Street ☎ (01604) 234040
11–11; 7–10.30 (closed lunch) Sun
Courage Directors; Morland Old Speckled Hen; Theakston Best Bitter, XB; Younger No. 3; guest beers H
Traditional pub in a town-centre location. Good range of food lunchtime. T&J Bernard's famous pies available until 10. Regular beer festivals.
🛏 ◑ ⚖

Lamplighter

66 Overstone Road (400 yds E of bus station) ☎ (01604) 31125
11.30–3, 6–11; 11.30–11 Sat; 12–4, 7–10.30 Sun
Courage Best Bitter, Directors; Marston's Pedigree H
Street-corner local with a smart interior on different levels, giving the impression of several private alcoves. Value-for-money traditional Sun lunch. Music quiz Thu nights.
✿ ◑

Malt Shovel Tavern

121 Bridge Street
☎ (01604) 234212
12–3, 5–11; 12–3, 7–10.30 Sun
Banks's Bitter; Boddingtons Mild; Castle Eden Ale; Frog Island Natterjack; guest beers H
Outstanding inn, recently refurbished and packed with local breweriana. Forty bottled beers; 20 Scottish malts. Home-cooked food includes the

legendary 'Shovel Pie' (no lunches Sun). No noise; no sparklers. Very high standards in all areas. Q ☀ ◑ ▶ ⅙ ➴ ♣

Moon on the Square
The Parade ☎ (01604) 34062
11–11; 12–10.30 Sun
Courage Directors; Frog Island Shoemaker; Theakston Best Bitter, XB; Younger Scotch; guest beers ⊞
Large pub, on the busy market square, in typical Wetherspoons style. Rapid turnover of guest beers – sometimes several a week. Regular beer festivals (when real ciders may also be available). Q ◑ ▶ ⅙ ➴ ⅟

Old Black Lion
Black Lion Hill
☎ (01604) 39472
11–11; 12–3, 7–10 Sun
Frog Island Natterjack; Marston's Pedigree; Webster's Yorkshire Bitter; guest beers ⊞
Grade II-listed coaching inn (possibly older in parts) with a bar and a split lounge. Close to the railway station, it can be very busy on soccer and rugby match days. The upstairs room is home to a folk club. Northants skittles, pool and darts teams fielded.
◑ ➴ ♣

Victoria Inn
2 Poole Street ☎ (01604) 33660
12–3, 5.30–11; 11–11 Fri & Sat;
12–10.30 Sun
Fuller's London Pride; Whitbread Best Bitter; guest beers ⊞
Thriving real ale pub, a corner local with friendly staff and several changing guest beers. Occasional live music.
♣

Try also: **Crown & Cushion**, Wellingborough Rd (Free)

Pitsford

Griffin
High Street ☎ (01604) 880346
11–2.30 (not Mon), 5.30–11; 12–11 Sat
(if busy); 12–3, 7–10.30 Sun
Draught Bass; Fuller's London Pride; Theakston Old Peculier; Worthington Bitter ⊞
Listed, refurbished, stone-built village local, an ideal stop after a walk around the reservoir. Popular with sporting groups.
☀ ◑ ⊞ ♣ P

Ravensthorpe

Chequers
Church Lane (off A428)
☎ (01604) 770379
11–3, 6–11; 11–11 Sat; 12–3, 7–10.30 Sun

Fuller's London Pride; Mansfield Bitter; Samuel Smith OBB; Thwaites Bitter; guest beer ⊞
One of the county's few free houses, set in a village amidst rolling countryside and worth seeking out. A beamed, single, L-shaped bar is adorned with bric-a-brac. A restaurant conservatory to the rear serves good value food. Family room across the courtyard. Northants skittles can be played.
👶 ☀ ◑ ▶ ♣ P

Rushden

Rushden Historical Transport Society
Station Approach (A6, N end of town, on one-way system)
☎ (01933) 318988
7.30–11; 12–2.30, 7.30–10.30 Sun
Fuller's London Pride; guest beers ⊞
Midland Railway station saved by locals after the line closure in 1962. A private, gas-lit bar and an adjoining museum house transport memorabilia. A no-smoking carriage by the platform is often used as an extended bar.
👪 Q ☀ P ⅟ ⊡

Southwick

Shuckburgh Arms
Main Street
☎ (01832) 274007
12–2 (3 Sat; not Mon), 6–11; 12–3,
7–10.30 Sun
Adnams Bitter; Fuller's London Pride; guest beer (summer) ⊞
Cosy village local, dating from the 16th century: a through-bar with games and eating areas at one end, and a large fireplace at the other. Situated by the cricket pitch and close to Southwick Hall, it is popular with all sections of the community.
👪 Q 👶 ☀ ◑ ▶ ♣ P

Sudborough

Vane Arms
Main Street (off A6116)
☎ (01832) 733223
11.30 (12 Sat)–3 (not Mon), 5.30 (6
Sat)–11; 12–3, 7–10.30 Sun
Beer range varies ⊞
Northants CAMRA *Pub of the Year* 1995 and '96: an outstanding, two-bar free house of great character in a picturesque village. Nine constantly changing real ales plus draught Kriek and Frambozen. Mexican food is a speciality. Northants skittles played. There is a patio for outside drinking.
👪 Q 👶 ☂ ◑ ▶ ⊞ ♣ ☕ P

Titchmarsh

Dog & Partridge
6 High Street ☎ (01832) 732546
12–2.30, 6–11; 12–3, 7–10.30 Sun
Adnams Bitter, Broadside; Wells Eagle, Bombardier ⊞
18th-century village local with one large room incorporating quiet and games areas. Popular with all ages, and with hikers and ramblers. 👪 Q ☀ ◑ ♣ P

Wakerley

Exeter Arms
☎ (01572) 747817
12–2.30 (not Mon), 6–11; 12–3, 7–10.30
Sun
Adnams Bitter; Marston's Pedigree; Taylor Landlord ⊞
17th-century, stone pub with a comfortable lounge with a wood burning stove. Wheelchair access at the side door. 👪 ☀ ⊞ ◑ ▶ ⅙ ♣ P

Walgrave

Royal Oak
Zion Hill (off A43)
☎ (01604) 781248
11–3 (12–3.30 Sat), 6–11; 12–4,
6.30–10.30 Sun
Boddingtons Bitter; Morrells Bitter; Webster's Yorkshire Bitter; guest beers ⊞
Very popular village pub now free of its Manns shackles. Large bar to the front; at the rear is a smaller bar and weekend restaurant. Local newspaper *Pub of the Year* 1995. Excellent value food. Up to five guest beers. ☀ ◑ ▶ ⊞ ♣ P ⅟

Weedon

Globe Hotel
High Street (A5/A45 jct)
☎ (01327) 340336
11–11; 12–3, 7–10.30 Sun
Marston's Bitter, Pedigree; Webster's Yorkshire Bitter; guest beers ⊞
Very professionally-run country inn, maintaining a pub feel in the bar, which serves home-cooked fare. High quality food also features in the restaurant. Ideal for a weekend break (excellent B&B), or a drink whilst passing through.
👪 Q ⊞ ◑ ▶ ⅙ P

Try also: **Wheatsheaf**, High St (Banks's)

Welford

Shoulder of Mutton
12 High Street
☎ (01858) 575375
12–2.30 (not Thu), 7–11; 12–3, 7–10.30
Sun
Draught Bass; Worthington Bitter; guest beer ⊞

Friendly, 17th-century pub with a food emphasis (no meals Thu). Its large, single bar is effectively divided into separate areas through arches. Large garden with a children's play area. Northants skittles is available.
🏮 ◁ ▮ ♣ P

Wellingborough

Cannon
Cannon Street
☎ (01933) 279629
11–11; 12–10.30 Sun
Cannon Light Brigade, Pride, Florrie Night-in-Ale, Vivaldi, Fodder; Wells Eagle; guest beers Ⓗ
Very friendly brew pub on the edge of the town centre. The bar features an extensive collection of rare beer bottles, whilst the games room offers bar billiards. Lunchtime snacks. 🏚 🏮 ⌺ ♣ P

Vivian Arms
153 Knox Road (sidestreet, opposite church; between station and town)
☎ (01933) 223660
11–2.30, 6–11; 11–11 Sat; 12–10.30 Sun
Badger Dorset Best, Tanglefoot; Wells Eagle Ⓗ
Traditional, street-corner local, featuring a calm, wood-panelled bar, a cosy lounge and a large games room. Peace reigns in two of the three bars and there's not a diner in sight (unless you count the pies and toasties!).
🏚 Q 🏮 ⌺ ≷ ♣ P

Weston

Crown
2 Helmdon Road
☎ (01295) 760310
12–2.30, 6–11; 12–3, 7–10.30 Sun
Matthew Clark Twelve Bore; Marston's Pedigree; guest beers Ⓗ
Stone-built, beamed village pub, in part dating back to 1593. Family-run, it has that friendly, welcoming feel. Various areas for darts, etc.
🏚 Q 🛏 ◁ ▮ ♣

Wollaston

Crispin Arms
Hinwick Road
☎ (01933) 664303
12–11; 12–10.30 Sun
Fuller's London Pride; Greene King Abbot; Shepherd Neame Spitfire, Bishops Finger; Theakston Best Bitter; Woodforde's Wherry Ⓗ
Drinkers' pub which has a loyal clientele. Two main areas are separated by an archway. A document hanging in the main bar traces the pub's history back to the mid-19th century. Regular events. 🏚 Q 🏮 P

Woodnewton

White Swan
Main Street ☎ (01780) 470381
12–3, 6.30–11; 12–3.30, 7–10.30 Sun
Badger Tanglefoot; Fuller's London Pride; Oakham JHB; guest beer Ⓗ

Welcoming, 200-year-old village free house consisting of a single, long room and a restaurant serving excellent food from an extensive menu. Wheelchair WC.
🏮 ◁ ▮ ⌺ ♣ P

Wootton

Wootton Workingmen's Club
23 High Street
☎ (01604) 761863
12–2 (2.30 Fri & Sat), 7–11; 12–2.30, 7–10.30 Sun
Draught Bass; Wells Eagle; guest beers Ⓗ
East Midlands CAMRA *Club of the Year* 1993: a superb club with a separate games room. The function room hosts live entertainment at weekends, while the lounge offers a pub atmosphere. CIU restrictions apply. Excellent guest beers.
♣ P

Yardley Hastings

Red Lion
89 High Street (off Bedford Rd)
☎ (01604) 696210
11–2.30 (3 Sat), 6–11; 12–3, 7–10.30 Sun
Adnams Broadside; Wells Eagle Ⓗ
Cosy, village pub featuring gleaming brass and copperware in its low-beamed lounge. The bar has darts and Northants skittles. Excellent lunches (not served Sun).
🏚 Q 🏮 ◁ ⌺ ♿ ♣ P

THE GREAT BRITISH BEER FESTIVAL

If flicking through the pages of the *Good Beer Guide* has whetted your appetite for beers not normally found in your locality, fear not: you do not have to tread the length and breadth of the country in search of unusual ales. All that's needed to quench your thirst for the exotic is a trip to CAMRA's Great British Beer Festival, held each August.

In recent years the Festival has been staged at London's Olympia, filling two vast halls with over 300 ales, drawn from all parts of the UK. There are also special beers from other countries – compare an American India Pale Ale with its British equivalent, or discover continental lagers that make feeble UK versions blush with embarrassment. British bottle-conditioned beers vie for attention with foreign bottles, and the cider and perry stand is perennially popular.

To help the beer down, food of all types is available, from meaty sausages to imaginative vegetarian snacks. The modest admission fee also covers live entertainment.

For details of the 1998 Great British Beer Festival, contact CAMRA on (01727) 867201.

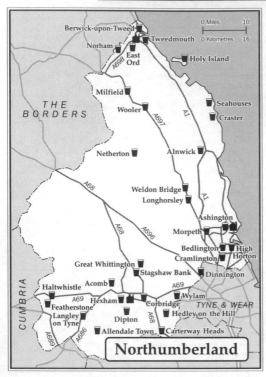

Northumberland

explanation can be found within the pub).

Ashington

Elephant
Newbiggin Road
☎ (01670) 814157
12–11; 12–10.30 Sun
Bateman XB, XXXB H
Bateman's first pub north of the River Tyne is an impressive building, formerly an hotel. Well worth a visit, it is friendly and welcoming. Good food.
🏨 ◖ ▶ P

Bedlington

Northumberland Arms
Eastend Front Street
☎ (01670) 822754
12–4, 7–11; 12–11 Fri & Sat; 12–10.30 Sun
Beer range varies H
Warm and welcoming, well-run pub offering a good range of constantly changing guest beers. Meals Thu–Sat.
🏨 ◖

Berwick-upon-Tweed

Barrels
59 Bridge Street
☎ (01289) 308013
11–3, 6–11; 7–10.30 Sun
Boddingtons Bitter; Border Farne Island; Castle Eden Ale; Flowers Original; Marston's Pedigree; guest beers H
Warm, comfortable pub at the northern end of the historic Berwick Bridge, renowned for the quality of its food and drink. ◖ ▶ ≠

Free Trade ☆
Castlegate ☎ (01289) 306498
11–2, 8–11 (may vary); 7–10.30 Sun
Vaux Lorimer's Best Scotch H
Excellent example of a Victorian town pub run with refreshing eccentricity. Later additions to interior fittings blend well with the antique wood and glass. Basic but brilliant. Q ⬛ ≠

Carterway Heads

Manor House Inn
On A68 6 miles S of Corbridge
☎ (01207) 255268
12–3, 6–11; 12–3, 7–10.30 Sun

Acomb

Miners Arms
Main Street ☎ (01434) 603909
12 (5 winter weekdays)–11; 12–10.30 Sun
Federation Buchanan's Best Bitter; guest beers H
18th-century traditional village inn near Hexham where locals and visitors are made to feel welcome. The house beer, Miners Lamp, is brewed by Big Lamp. One guest in winter, increasing to three in summer. Meals served in summer only.
🏨 Q ◖ ▶ ☐

Allendale Town

Golden Lion
Market Place ☎ (01434) 863225
4 (11 Sat)–11; 12–10.30 Sun
Boddingtons Bitter; Butterknowle Conciliation Ale; guest beers H
Quiet, friendly pub overlooking the market place.
🏨 Q ☎ ♣

King's Head Hotel
Market Place ☎ (01434) 863681
11–11; 12–10.30 Sun
Jennings Cumberland Ale; Marston's Pedigree;

Theakston Best Bitter, Old Peculier; guest beers H
Comfortable, busy hotel bar in a market town high in the Pennines, serving good food. An ideal base for exploring the wonderful surrounding countryside.
🏨 Q ☎ 🏨 ◖ ▶ ♣

Alnwick

John Bull
Howick Street
☎ (01665) 602055
11–3, 7–11; 12–2, 7–10.30 Sun
Tetley Bitter; guest beers H
Basic, 1820s pub in the middle of a terrace of houses. At one time it had its own maltings and brewery. Triominoes (three sided dominoes) is played. Q ♣

Old Cross
Narrowgate
☎ (01665) 602735
11–11; 12–10.30 Sun
Theakston Best Bitter; guest beers H
Welcoming listed building, over 200 years old, known locally as the 'Dirty Bottles' which refers to a sealed window of dirty bottles, believed to be cursed (a full

---

Big Lamp Bitter; Butterknowle Bitter; guest beers 🄷
Former CAMRA Northumberland *Pub of the Year* and a tourist board winner: a welcoming country inn enjoying splendid views of the Derwent Valley. In winter there is usually a guest stout or porter, plus guest ciders. Excellent menu of home-cooked food.
♨ Q 🛏 ◖ ◗ ⌓ P

Corbridge

Dyvells Hotel
Station Road ☎ (01434) 633633
7 (12 Sat)–11; 12–4, 7–10.30 (12–10.30 summer) Sun
Draught Bass; Black Sheep Best Bitter; guest beers 🄷
A warm welcome from the locals at this popular hotel bar makes this pub worth seeking out. An ideal base for exploring Hadrian's Wall country.
♨ ❀ 🛏 ◖ ◗ ⇌ ♣ P

Cramlington

Blagdon Arms
Village Square
☎ (01670) 713512
12–11; 12–10.30 Sun
Vaux Waggle Dance; Ward's Best Bitter 🄷
Pub at the heart of the old village, now refurbished to a high standard and divided into a number of different areas, which help to maintain the atmosphere. The cask beer is served from the lounge. No meals Sun eve. ❀ ◖ ◗ ⊟ ♿ ⇌

Plough
Middle Farm Buildings
☎ (01670) 737633
11–3, 6–11; 11–11 Fri & Sat; 12–10.30 Sun
Boddingtons Bitter; Theakston XB; guest beers 🄷
Fine stone pub created from former farm buildings. Usually four beers are served from handpumps in the lounge. The combination of well-kept beers and interesting surroundings is difficult to beat. ❀ ⊟ ⇌ P

Craster

Jolly Fisherman
Haven Hill ☎ (01665) 576461
11–3, 6–11 (11–11 summer & Sat); 12–10.30 Sun
Vaux Lorimer's Best Scotch; Ward's Thorne BB 🄷
Friendly, busy pub in a tiny coastal village famous for its kippers. Excellent seafood (try the crab sandwiches) and marvellous sea views.
♨ Q ♘ ❀ ◖ ◗ ▲ ♣ P

Dinnington

White Swan
Prestwick Road
☎ (01661) 820140
11–3, 6–11; 12–3, 6.30–10.30 Sun
Courage Directors; Ruddles Best Bitter, County; guest beers (summer) 🄷
Busy country pub offering a friendly welcome in pleasant surroundings and good food from an extensive menu.
❀ ◖ ◗ P

Dipton

Dipton Mill Inn
Dipton Mill Road
☎ (01434) 606577
12–2.30, 6–11; 12–4, 7–10.30 Sun
Hexhamshire Shire Bitter, Devil's Water, Whapweasel; Theakston Best Bitter; guest beers 🄷
An excellent advertisement for Hexhamshire Brewery, this inn is set in beautiful countryside; the garden has its own burn. Bar billiards is played in the back room. CAMRA Northumberland *Pub of the Year*.
♨ Q ♘ ❀ ◖ ◗ ▲ ♣ P 🍺

East Ord

Salmon Inn
☎ (01289) 305227
12–11; 12–10.30 Sun
Vaux Lorimer's Best Scotch; guest beers 🄷
A warm welcome from a friendly landlady and a real fire in winter are assured in this two-roomed local which has a bar and pool room. Hillfort remains and free fishing on the River Tweed are a short walk away. Eve meals Thu–Sun.
♨ Q ❀ ◖ ◗ ⊟ ▲ ♣ P

Featherstone

Wallace Arms
☎ (01434) 231872
12–2.30 (not Mon or Tue), 4–11; 11–11 Fri & Sat; 12–3, 7–10.30 Sun
Hexhamshire Shire Bitter, Whapweasel; guest beers (summer) 🄷
Friendly pub in beautiful countryside, not far from Featherstone Castle. Enjoyable music nights.
♨ Q ❀ ◖ ◗ ▲ ♣ P

Great Whittington

Queen's Head Inn
☎ (01434) 672267
12–2, 6–11; 12–3, 7–10.30 Sun
Hambleton Bitter; guest beers 🄷
This inn, set in lovely countryside close to Hadrian's Wall, dates from the 15th century and is reputedly the oldest in the county. Four handpumps serve a variety of guest beers, including a house beer brewed by Hambleton. Good quality food based on local produce. ♨ Q ◖ ◗ P

Haltwhistle

Black Bull
Market Place ☎ (01434) 320463
12–5, 7–11; 12–10.30 Sun
Jennings Bitter, Cumberland Ale, Sneck Lifter; Marston's Pedigree; guest beers 🄷
Very cosy, unspoilt, stone pub with low ceilings, beams and a tiny snug. Warm welcome.
♨ Q ◖ ⇌ ♣

Grey Bull
Wapping ☎ (01434) 321991
11–11; 12–3, 7–10.30 Sun
Stones Bitter; guest beers 🄷
Busy town pub, popular with locals who make visitors more than welcome. The front bar is lively, the panelled back bar quieter. Ever-changing guest beers. Quoits played. Q ♘ ❀
🛏 ◖ ◗ ⊟ ♿ ▲ ⇌ ♣ P

Hedley on the Hill

Feathers Inn
☎ (01661) 843607
6 (11 Fri & Sat)–11; 12–3, 7–10.30 Sun
Boddingtons Bitter; guest beers 🄷
Pleasant country pub with an attractive bar and lounge. Both rooms have real fires, adding to the cosy atmosphere. Changing guest beers; excellent food from an interesting menu which changes weekly. Lunches weekends only.
♨ Q ❀ ◖ ◗ P

Hexham

Tap & Spile
Battle Hill ☎ (01434) 602039
11–11; 12–10.30 Sun
Theakston Best Bitter; guest beers 🄷
Busy, recently refurbished market town pub with a changing range of real ales from far and wide. Regular live music – Northumberland traditional music is a favourite.
♨ ◖ ⇌

High Horton

Three Horseshoes
Hatherley Lane
☎ (01670) 822410
12–11; 12–10.30 Sun
Ind Coope Burton Ale; Marston's Pedigree; Tetley Bitter; guest beers 🄷
Large, friendly, 18th-century coaching inn, serving a wide

variety of guest ales and whiskies. 🌳 ◖ ▶ P

Holy Island

Ship

Marygate (across causeway – check tide tables)
☎ (01289) 389311
11–11 (may vary winter); 12–10.30 Sun
Beer range varies ℍ
Unspoilt, refurbished, 400-year-old pub with wood panelling and low beams, featuring old photos of the area. No lunches or real ale in winter. ⚒ Q 🌳 ◖ ▶

Langley on Tyne

Carts Bog Inn

On A686
☎ (01434) 684338
12–3, 7–11; 12–3, 7–10.30 Sun
Marston's Pedigree; Theakston Best Bitter; guest beers ℍ
1730s inn, unspoilt, family-owned and run, featuring guest beers from north-eastern microbreweries. An unusual menu offers Japanese, Chinese, Indian and Thai meals, all freshly made. Live music alternate Fri; music and beer festival in summer.
⚒ Q 🍽 🌳 ◖ ▶ ♣ P

Longhorsley

Linden Pub

Linden Hall Hotel (A697)
☎ (01670) 516611
11–3, 6–11; 12–3, 7–10.30 Sun
Theakston Best Bitter; guest beers ℍ
Interesting conversion from an old granary, in the grounds of Linden Hall Hotel. A large, open fire, right in the middle of the pub, is a feature.
🌳 🍽 ◖ ♿ P

Milfield

Red Lion Inn

Main Road (A697)
☎ (01668) 216224
11–11; 12–10.30 Sun
Draught Bass; Stones Bitter; guest beers ℍ
The oldest building in the village, a former coaching inn dating back to 1740. Its wide range of activities includes karaoke nights, guided walks, golf, fishing and horse riding; even gliding is available locally. ⚒ Q 🌳 🍽 ◖ ▶ P

Morpeth

Tap & Spile

Manchester Street
☎ (01670) 513540
12–2.30, 4–11; 12–11 Fri & Sat; 12–10.30 Sun
Beer range varies ℍ
Welcoming, comfortable pub, offering up to eight guest beers. Traditional pipe and fiddle music sessions are held. Weston's Old Rosie cider.
◖ ♣ ⌂

Netherton

Star Inn ☆

On B634 ☎ (01669) 630238
12–1.30, 7–11 (may vary winter); 12–1.30, 7–10.30 Sun
Castle Eden Ale Ⓖ
Marvellous, unspoilt gem where beer is served direct from the cellar. Popular with walkers. ⚒ Q 🌳 P

Norham

Masons Arms

16 West Street
☎ (01289) 382326
11–3, 7–11; 11–11 Sat (may vary winter); 12–3, 7–10.30 Sun
Vaux Lorimer's Best Scotch; guest beers ℍ
Lively locals from both sides of the border meet here in a bar full of knick-knacks, including a water jug collection, and photos of old Norham and its floods. Norham castle is nearby. Dining room and pool room. No food Sun eve.
⚒ Q 🍳 🌳 🍽 ◖ ▶ ♣

Seahouses

Olde Ship

Main Street ☎ (01665) 720200
11–3, 6–11; 12–3, 7–10.30 Sun
McEwan 80/-; Marston's Pedigree; Morland Old Speckled Hen; Theakston Best Bitter; guest beers (summer) ℍ
Family-owned treasure house of genuine nautical artefacts. Close to the harbour, it is popular with visitors and locals. ⚒ Q 🍳 🍽 ◖ ▲ P

Stagshaw Bank

Fox & Hounds

On A68 ☎ (01434) 633024
11–11; 12–10.30 Sun
Theakston Best Bitter; guest beers ℍ

Welcoming, old stone building near Hadrian's Wall. The large conservatory serves as a restaurant.
⚒ Q 🌳 🍽 ◖ ▶ ♣ P

Tweedmouth

Angel

11 Brewery Bank
☎ (01289) 306273
11–3, 6–11; 12–3, 7–10.30 Sun
Border Special, Rampart; Everards Tiger; Taylor Landlord; guest beers ℍ
The Border Brewery sign suggests this is the local brewery tap – a link less concrete than it seems, but still the best bet for Border beers: a friendly local with a lively atmosphere eves and match days (handy for Berwick Rangers FC). 🌳

Weldon Bridge

Anglers Arms

☎ (01665) 570271
11–3, 6–11; 12–3, 7–10.30 Sun
Theakston Best Bitter; guest beers ℍ
1760s coaching inn beside the picturesque Weldon Bridge. Fishing is available on the inn's private stretch of the River Coquet. Good food.
⚒ Q 🌳 🍽 ◖ ▶ P

Wooler

Black Bull

2 High Street ☎ (01668) 281309
11–11; 12–10.30 Sun
Draught Bass; Worthington Bitter; guest beers ℍ
17th-century coaching inn, now an hotel with bar/lounge, function room and a stable bar to the rear (venue for Fri and Sat night discos), in a quiet north Northumberland market town. Bronze and Iron Age settlements can be seen close by. ⚒ 🍽 ◖ ▶ ♣ P

Wylam

Boathouse

Station Road ☎ (01661) 853431
12–3, 6–11; 12–11 Fri & Sat; 12–3, 7–10.30 Sun
Marston's Pedigree; Morland Old Speckled Hen; Taylor Landlord; Theakston Best Bitter; guest beers ℍ
Friendly pub on the south bank of the Tyne, offering a wide choice of cask ales and good food. Guest ciders.
⚒ Q 🍳 🌳 ◖ ▶ 🍺 ⇌ ♣ ⌂ P

NEW BREWERIES

Catch up with the UK's new breweries: see page 57.

Nottinghamshire

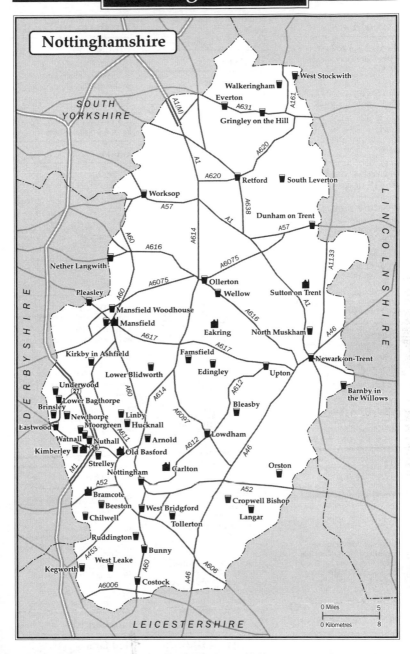

Nottinghamshire

West Stockwith
Walkeringham
Everton
Gringley on the Hill
SOUTH YORKSHIRE
A631
A161
A620
Retford
South Leverton
Worksop
A620
A638
Dunham on Trent
A57
A1
A57
A60
A616
A614
A6075
Nether Langwith
A6075
Ollerton
Wellow
Sutton on Trent
Pleasley
A60
Mansfield Woodhouse
Mansfield
Eakring
North Muskham
A616
A1
A1133
LINCOLNSHIRE
A617
Kirkby in Ashfield
Famsfield
A617
Newark-on-Trent
Lower Blidworth
Edingley
Upton
A46
Underwood
Lower Bagthorpe
A60
A614
A612
Bleasby
Barnby in the Willows
Brinsley
Newthorpe
Linby
A6097
Eastwood
Moorgreen
Hucknall
Lowdham
A46
Watnall
A611
Arnold
A612
Nuthall
Kimberley
Old Basford
Strelley
Carlton
Orston
Nottingham
A52
Bramcote
A52
Cropwell Bishop
Beeston
West Bridgford
Langar
Chilwell
Tollerton
Ruddington
A453
Bunny
A60
A606
Kegworth
West Leake
A46
A6006
Costock
DERBYSHIRE

0 Miles 5
0 Kilometres 8

LEICESTERSHIRE

INDEPENDENT BREWERIES

Bramcote: Bramcote

Fiddlers: Old Basford

Hardys & Hansons: Kimberley

Mallard: Carlton

Mansfield: Mansfield

Maypole: Eakring

Springhead: Sutton on Trent

Arnold

Druid's Tavern
109 High Street
☎ (0115) 926 5512
12–2.30 (3 Sat), 7–11; 12–3, 7–10.30 Sun
Hardys & Hansons Best Mild, Best Bitter E**, Classic, seasonal beers** H
Basic, popular no-frills pub, with a pool room and an outside skittle alley.
❀ ♣ P

Barnby in the Willows

Willow Tree
Front Street (off A17)
☎ (01636) 726613
12–3 (not Mon), 7–11; 12–3, 7–10.30 Sun
Marston's Pedigree; guest beers H
17th-century coaching inn, a free house serving freshly cooked food. House beer from Rudgate. Children's play area.
🏚 ⛲ ❀ 🛏 ◖ ▶ P

Beeston

Commercial Inn
19 Wollaton Road
☎ (0115) 925 4480
11–2.30, 5.30–11; 11–11 Fri & Sat; 12–10.30 Sun
Hardys & Hansons Best Mild E**, Best Bitter** H/E**, Classic, seasonal beers** H
Established, friendly local where the public bar has been recently extended. Despite appearances, the font-like electric pumps dispense real ale. ❀ ◖ ♣ P 🍽

Victoria Hotel
Dovecote Lane
☎ (0115) 925 4049
11–3, 5–11; 11–11 Fri & Sat; 12–4.30, 7–10.30 Sun
Bateman XB; Bramcote Hemlock Bitter; Courage Directors; Everards Tiger; Marston's Pedigree; guest beers H
Busy Victorian architectural gem. Fine food; over 100 whiskies.
🏚 ❀ ◖ ▶ ⛁ & ≉ ♣ ➪ P

Bleasby

Waggon & Horses
Gypsy Lane (1 mile S of station)
☎ (01636) 830283
12–3 (not Mon or Tue in winter), 6.30–11; 12–3, 7–10.30 Sun
Banks's Bitter; Marston's Pedigree; guest beers. H
Originally a farmhouse, this attractive, whitewashed village inn nestles in pleasant

countryside overlooking the church.
🏚 Q ☙ ❀ ◖ ⛁ ▲ ♣ P

Brinsley

Robin Hood
Hall Lane (off A608)
☎ (01773) 713604
12–2 (3 summer), 7–11; 12–3, 7–10.30 Sun
Hardys & Hansons Best Mild, Best Bitter H
Quiet village local in DH Lawrence country. Piano nights and singers Sat. Two skittle alleys. 🏚 Q ❀ ⛁ ♣ P

Bunny

Rancliffe Arms
139 Loughborough Road
☎ (0115) 984 4727
11.30–2.30, 6 (7 Mon)–11; 12–3, 7–10.30 Sun
Mansfield Riding Mild, Riding Bitter, Bitter, Old Baily H
Imposing, 17th-century coaching inn: three bars and a restaurant serving good food (no meals Sun eve). The car park is on a sharp bend.
🏚 Q ❀ 🛏 ◖ ▶ ⛁ P

Chilwell

Chequers Inn
High Road
☎ (0115) 925 4312
11–11; 12–3, 7–10.30 Sun
Shipstone's Mild, Bitter; Worthington Bitter; guest beers (occasional) H
Pub with three distinct drinking areas, popular with the young at weekends, when it can be loud. ❀ ◖ ♣

Costock

Generous Briton
14 Main Street
11.30–2.30, 6.30–11; 12–2.30, 7–10.30 Sun
Mansfield Riding Bitter, Bitter, Old Baily H
Real village local of a type that is increasingly rare. Quiet and convivial atmosphere. A centre for the local community.
🏚 ◖ ⛁ ♣ P

Cropwell Bishop

Wheatsheaf
11 Nottingham Road
☎ (0115) 989 2247
12–3, 6–11; 11–11 Fri & Sat; 12–10.30 Sun
Mansfield Riding Mild, Riding Bitter, Bitter, Old Baily H
Village local, dating back 500 years and reputedly haunted.
🏚 ❀ ⛁ ♣ P

Dunham on Trent

Bridge Inn
Main Street
☎ (01777) 228385
12–3.30, 7–11; 12–10.30 Sun
Brains Dark, Bitter; guest beers H
Roadside pub close to Dunham toll bridge. One beer is keenly priced. Good food.
🏚 ❀ 🛏 ◖ ▶ ▲ P ✂ 🍽

Eastwood

Greasley Castle
1 Castle Street, Hilltop (off B6010)
☎ (01773) 761080
10.30–3, 6 (5 Fri & Sat)–11; 12–4, 7–10.30 Sun
Hardys & Hansons Best Mild, Best Bitter E
Established, relaxed corner pub on a one-way terraced street. Live local artistes Fri and Sun.
❀ ⛁ ♣

Edingley

Old Reindeer
Main Street (off A614)
☎ (01623) 882253
12–3 (not winter), 6–11; 12–11 Sat; 12–4, 7–10.30 Sun
Mansfield Riding Mild, Riding Bitter, Bitter, Old Baily H
Friendly, family-run, 18th-century village pub. The convivial tap room is popular with rugby enthusiasts. Excellent restaurant with a varied menu.
🏚 Q ❀ ▶ ⛁ ▲ ♣ P 🍽

Everton

Sun Inn
Gainborough Road
☎ (01777) 817260
12–11; 12–10.30 Sun
Ruddles County; John Smith's Bitter; Theakston Best Bitter; guest beer H
Busy, multi-roomed pub attracting both village and passing trade. Popular for its good food.
🏚 Q ❀ ◖ ▶ P ✂

Farnsfield

Red Lion
Main Street (off A614)
☎ (01623) 882304
11–3, 6.30–11; 12–3, 7–10.30 Sun
Mansfield Riding Mild, Riding Bitter, Bitter, Old Baily H
Friendly, family-run village local, serving all Mansfield's ales. Live folk music Mon eve. Good varied menu (no meals Sun/Mon eves).
🏚 Q ☙ ❀ ◖ ▶ & ♣ P 🍽

Gringley on the Hill

Blue Bell
High Street
☎ (01777) 817406
6 (12 Sat)–11; 12–10.30 Sun
Marston's Pedigree; Tetley Bitter; guest beer Ⓗ
Quiet village pub. Weekend lunches served.
🏨 🌣 🌓 ▶ ♣

Hucknall

Lord Byron
6A Annesley Road
☎ (0115) 963 0193
7–11; 12–3, 7–11 Sat; 12–4.30, 7–10.30 Sun
Beer range varies Ⓗ
1960s-oriented local with an upstairs disco. The bar is decorated with pictures of old Hucknall and Lord Byron.
♣

Nabb Inn
Nabbs Lane
☎ (0115) 963 0297
11–2.30 (3 Sat), 6–11; 12–3, 7–10.30 Sun
Hardys & Hansons Best Mild, Best Bitter, seasonal beers Ⓗ
Friendly local, close to Hucknall Town FC. Although a single room, it retains a two-room feel with Sky TV and pool in the 'bar'. Eve meals end at 8.30; no food Sun eve.
🌣 🌓 ▶ ♣ P

Kegworth

Station Hotel
Station Road
☎ (01509) 672252
11.30–2.30 (may extend summer), 6–11; 12–3, 7–10.30 Sun
Draught Bass; guest beers Ⓗ
Built in 1847 as an hotel for the now closed station; three characterful rooms with an upstairs restaurant serving excellent home-cooked food. The large garden affords fine views.
🏨 Q 🌣 🛏 🌓 ▶ ▲ ♣ P

Kimberley

Nelson & Railway
Station Road
☎ (0115) 938 2177
11–3, 5–11; 11–11 Thu–Sat; 12–10.30 Sun
Hardys & Hansons Best Mild Ⓔ**, Best Bitter** Ⓗ/Ⓔ**, Classic, seasonal beers** Ⓗ
Excellent village local, 100 yards from the brewery: a wood-panelled bar, plus a restored, beamed lounge and a dining area. Good value food (wide-ranging menu). Sun meals served 12–6.
🌣 🛏 🌓 🍺 ♣ P

Kirkby in Ashfield

Countryman
Park Lane (B6018, S of town)
☎ (01623) 752314
12–3 (4 Fri & Sat), 7–11; 12–3, 7–10.30 Sun
Draught Bass; Theakston Mild, Best Bitter, XB; Townes GMT; guest beers Ⓗ
Friendly, 18th-century roadside inn with a cosy lounge bar and beamed alcoves. Live music Fri eve. No food Sun eve. 🌣 🌓 ▶ ♣ P

Langar

Unicorn's Head
Main Street ☎ (01949) 860460
11–3, 6–11; 11–11 Sat; 12–3, 7–10.30 Sun
Home Mild, Bitter; Mansfield Riding Bitter; guest beer Ⓗ
Comfortable, two-room village local in the Vale of Belvoir. Live jazz Fri.
🏨 🛳 🌣 🌓 ▶ 🍺 ♣ P

Linby

Horse & Groom
Main Street ☎ (0115) 963 2219
12–11; 12–10.30 Sun
Home Mild, Bitter; Marston's Pedigree; guest beers Ⓗ
Popular, four-roomed village pub with a restaurant. Each room has its own log/coal fires in winter. Extensive children's play area and garden.
🏨 Q 🌣 🌓 🍺 ♣ P

Lowdham

World's End
Plough Lane
☎ (0115) 966 3857
12–3, 5.30 (6 Sat)–11; 12–3.30, 7–10.30 Sun
Banks's Mild; Marston's Bitter, Pedigree Ⓗ
White-painted, single-room village pub, decked out with flowers in summer. Good value food (not served Sun eve). 🏨 Q 🌣 🌓 ▲ 🍺 P

Lower Bagthorpe

Dixies Arms
School Road (off B600 at Underwood) ☎ (01773) 810505
1.30–4.30, 7–11; 12–11 Sat; 12–3.30, 7–10.30 Sun
Home Mild, Bitter; guest beer Ⓗ
250-year-old, beamed country pub with a tap room, snug and lounge. 🏨 🌣 🌓 ▲ ♣ P

Lower Blidworth

Fox & Hounds
Calverton Road, Blidworth Bottoms (1 mile off A614)
☎ (01623) 792383
12–3.30, 6–11; 12–3, 7–10.30 Sun
Hardys & Hansons Best Mild, Best Bitter, seasonal beers Ⓗ
Traditional, welcoming, three-room village pub serving excellent, home-cooked food, a mile south of Blidworth. Thu folk night.
🏨 Q 🛳 🌣 🌓 ▶ 🍺 ▲ ♣ P 🍴

Mansfield

Bleak House Club
117 Sutton Road (near A38)
☎ (01623) 659850
12–4 (not Tue–Thu), 7–11; 12–3, 7–10.30 Sun
Draught Bass; guest beers Ⓗ
Established in 1926 as a men-only club, now much more accommodating. A homely lounge and a games room with a TV. 🏨 ♣ 🍴

Boothy's Club
2 Westhill Drive (ring road, opp. cinema) ☎ (01623) 23729
11–11; 12–3, 7–10.30 Sun
Adnams Bitter; Mansfield Riding Bitter, Bitter, seasonal beer; Wells Bombardier Ⓗ
Large, private club with a lounge and a concert room, regularly used. Black Bess Mild is supplied by Mansfield. Wheelchair WC. 🌓 ⇌ ♣ P

Ling Forest
Eakring Road (1½ miles E of centre) ☎ (01623) 23202
11.30 (11 Sat)–11; 12–3, 7–10.30 Sun
Mansfield Riding Mild, Riding Bitter, Bitter Ⓗ
Friendly, two-roomed pub; a jukebox-free lounge and a busy tap room. Q ♣ P

Plough
180 Nottingham Road (A60, ½ mile from centre)
☎ (01623) 23031
11–11; 12–10.30 Sun
Boddingtons Bitter; Flowers Original; Marston's Pedigree; Whitbread Fuggles IPA; guest beers Ⓗ
Large, friendly, one-roomed pub. Always eight ales; good value food (not served Thu eve). 🌣 🌓 ♿ ⇌ P ✂

Reindeer
Southwell Road
☎ (01623) 651180
11–11; 12–10.30 Sun
Mansfield Bitter, Old Baily, seasonal beers Ⓗ
Large, modern pub with a games room, a public bar and a restaurant area.
🌣 🌓 ▶ 🍺 ♣ P

Mansfield Woodhouse

Greyhound Inn
82 High Street
☎ (01623) 643005
12–11; 12–3, 7–10.30 Sun

Home Mild, Bitter; Theakston Best Bitter, XB; guest beers H
Friendly village local: a lounge and a tap room with a pool table and darts, in a central location, close to the Robin Hood Line. Q ❀ 🍺 ⇌ ♣ P

Star Inn

Warsop Road ☎ (01623) 24145
12–3, 6 (7 Sat)–11; 12–10.30 Sun
Vaux Samson, Waggle Dance; Ward's Best Bitter; guest beers H
Old, low-beamed, three-roomed pub. Excellent garden play facilities for children (who are welcome inside for meals). Good food (not served Sat/Sun eves). Q ⛺ ❀ ◑ ▶ ⇌ ♣ P

Moorgreen

Horse & Groom

On B600 ☎ (01773) 713417
11–11; 12–10.30 Sun
Hardys & Hansons Best Mild, Best Bitter, Classic, seasonal beers H
Country pub with a restaurant upstairs. An unspoilt inn with a single, L-shaped room, and a large well-equipped garden.
🏚 ❀ ◑ ▶ P

Nether Langwith

Jug & Glass

Queens Walk (A632)
☎ (01623) 742283
11.30–4, 7–11; 12–4, 7–10.30 Sun
Hardys & Hansons Best Bitter E, Classic, seasonal beers H
Unpretentious stone pub dating from the 15th century, beside the village stream. No eve meals Wed or Sun.
🏚 🛏 ◑ ▶ 🍺 & ♣ P

Newark-on-Trent

Mailcoach

13 London Road
☎ (01636) 605164
11.30–2.30 (3 Wed & Fri), 5.30–11; 11–4, 7–11 Sat; 12–3, 7–10.30 Sun
Bateman XB; Boddingtons Mild, Bitter; Flowers IPA; Marston's Pedigree; Wadworth 6X; guest beers H
Inviting, busy, town pub offering varied home-cooked food (not Sun). Live music Sat eve (jazz/blues). Cider in summer. 🏚 ❀ 🛏 ◑ ⇌ (Castle) ♣ ⌂ P

Newcastle Arms

34 George Street
12–2.30 (3 Fri & Sat), 7–11; 12–3, 7–10.30 Sun
Home Mild, Bitter; Theakston XB; Wells Bombardier; Younger Scotch; guest beer H
Traditional Victorian local with a basic public bar and a comfortable lounge.
Q ❀ 🍺 & ⇌ (Northgate) ♣

Old Malt Shovel

25 Northgate
☎ (01636) 702036
11.30–3, 7 (6 Wed–Sat)–11; 12–4, 7–10.30 Sun
Taylor Landlord; Theakston XB; Ward's Best Bitter; guest beers H
A pub for all ages, originally a bakery in the 16th century. The garden room restaurant (no food Mon/Tue eves) specialises in Portuguese and Mexican dishes. The house beer is from Rugdate.
🏚 ⛺ ❀ ◑ ▶ & ⇌ (Castle/Northgate) ♣ ✄

Wheatsheaf

Slaughterhouse Lane
☎ (01636) 702709
11–3, 7–11; 11–11 Fri & Sat; 12–10.30 Sun
Mansfield Riding Mild, Riding Bitter, Bitter, Old Baily H
Unpretentious, 'niche' pub, frequented by students and motorcyclists, where the atmosphere is cordial.
❀ ⇌ (Northgate/Castle) ♣

Wing Tavern

13 Bridge Street, Market Place
☎ (01636) 702689
11–3, 7–11; 12–3, 7–10.30 Sun
Theakston Black Bull, Best Bitter, XB, Old Peculier H
Well-hidden, in the corner of the market place, this unpretentious local dates back to the 18th century and is one of the last unspoilt pubs in the town. ⛺ ❀ 🍺 & ⇌ (Castle/Northgate) ♣

Newthorpe

Ram Inn

Beauvale Road (B6010)
☎ (01773) 713312
11–4, 5.30–11; 11–11 Sat; 12–3.45, 7–10.30 (12–10.30 summer) Sun
Hardys & Hansons Best Mild, Best Bitter E, Classic, seasonal beers H
1960s roadside community pub; popular for darts and quizzes. Good food.
🏚 Q ❀ ◑ ▶ 🍺 ♣ P

North Muskham

Lord Nelson

Great North Road (on roundabout off A1 slip road, exit B6325)
☎ (01636) 704010
12–3, 7–11; 12–3, 7–10.30 Sun
Draught Bass; John Smith's Bitter; Tetley Bitter; guest beers H
Attractive, two-bar, late-17th-century village pub, popular with anglers. International menu (not served Mon eve). 🏚 Q ⛺ ❀ ◑ ▶ 🍺 & ♠ ♣ P ✄ 🚭

Nottingham

Bell Inn

18 Angel Row, Old Market Square
☎ (0115) 947 5241
10.30–11; 10.30–3, 6–11 Sat; 12–3, 7–10.30 Sun
Draught Bass; Black Sheep Special; Jennings Mild, Bitter; Mansfield Bitter; Ruddles County; guest beers H
Popular, timber-framed, 15th-century inn, with original beams in the entrance. A regular live jazz venue. Guest beers are in the back room.
Q ❀ ◑ ⌂

Coopers Arms

3 Porchester Road, Thorneywood
☎ (0115) 950 2433
12–3 (not Wed), 6 (5.30 Fri, 7 Sat)–11; 12–3, 7–10.30 Sun
Home Mild, Bitter E; Theakston Mild H
Large Victorian local with a lounge, a bar, a darts room, a tiny family room, plus a covered skittle alley outside.
⛺ 🍺 ♣ P ⌂

Hole in the Wall

63 North Sherwood Street (near Victoria Centre)
☎ (0115) 947 3162
11–11; 12–3, 7–10.30 Sun
Mansfield Riding Bitter, Old Baily; guest beers H
Well-refurbished pub, popular with students: one room with a long bar. Originally, the pub was extremely small – literally just a hole in the wall! Eve meals till 7; no food Sun eve. Wheelchair WC. ❀ ◑ ▶ &

Langtry's

4 South Sherwood Street (opp. Royal Concert Hall)
☎ (0115) 947 2124
10.30–11; 12–10.30 Sun
Boddingtons Bitter; Castle Eden Ale; Chester's Mild; Flowers IPA; Whitbread Trophy H; guest beers H/G
One-roomed, corner pub serving ten beers, with guests (including a mild) from micros. Good selection of cheap food till 6pm (3pm Sun). Typical Hogshead floorboards and bare brick decor. ◑ ▶ ⌂

Limelight Bar

Wellington Circus (Nottingham Playhouse complex)
☎ (0115) 941 8467
11–11; 12–10.30 Sun
Adnams Bitter; Bateman Mild, XB; Courage Directors; Marston's Pedigree; Theakston XB; guest beers H
Traditionally-styled bar in a listed 1960s theatre complex, extended to create three rooms. Six changing guest beers; good

meals (no food Sun lunch). The outdoor area is a delight. Live music some nights.
Q 🐱 🍴 ◖ ⌣ ⍭

Lincolnshire Poacher
161–163 Mansfield Road (A60, near Victoria Centre)
☎ (0115) 941 1584
11–11; 12–10.30 Sun
Draught Bass; Bateman Mild, XB, Valiant, XXXB; Marston's Pedigree; guest beers H
The city's leading alehouse with two rooms, a conservatory and a no-smoking area for diners, serving a varied menu (no food Sun eve). At least ten beers, plus over 80 whiskies. Regular 'brewery nights' are held.
Q 🐱 🍴 ◗ ⌣

Lord Nelson
Thurgarton Street, Sneinton
☎ (0115) 911 0069
11–3 (4 Sat), 5.30–11; 12–4, 7–10.30 Sun
Hardys & Hansons Best Bitter, Classic, seasonal beers H
Two farm cottages until c1800, now surrounded by Victorian housing; four immaculate rooms around a small bar. No-smoking area lunchtime. No meals Sun.
🐜 🐱 ◗ 🍴 ♣ ⍭

Magpies
Meadow Lane
☎ (0115) 911 8877
11–2.30, 5–11; 11–11 Fri & Sat; 12–3, 7–10.30 Sun
Home Mild, Bitter E; **Marston's Pedigree; Theakston XB** H
Pub close to both football grounds, the cricket club and Colwick racecourse. A drinkers' bar has Sky TV and pool; comfortable L-shaped lounge. Eve meals (not Sat) are served till 8.30.
🐱 ◗ 🍴 ♣ P

March Hare
243 Carlton Road
☎ (0115) 950 4320
11.30–2.30, 5–11; 11.30–11 Fri & Sat; 12–3, 7–10.30 Sun
Courage Directors; John Smith's Bitter H
Typical 1950s two-roomer, where nothing has changed. Great value lunches; eve meals are available 6–8.
◗ 🍴 ♣ P

Navigation Inn
6 Wilford Street
☎ (0115) 941 7139
11.30–2.30, 5–11; 11.30–11 Fri & Sat; 12–3, 7–10.30 Sun
Banks's Mild, Bitter, seasonal beers; Camerons Strongarm; guest beers H
Pub next to locks on the canal, displaying much canal memorabilia in one, split-level bar. 🐱 ◖ ⍭ 🏺

Olde Trip to Jerusalem ☆
1 Brewhouse Yard, Castle Road
☎ (0115) 947 3171
11–11; 12–10.30 Sun
Hardys & Hansons Best Mild, Best Bitter, Classic, seasonal beers; Marston's Pedigree H
One of England's oldest pubs, dating back to 1189. The back rooms are cut out of a cliff below Nottingham Castle. Restoration has revealed further caves and a cosy snug. Food available 11–6.
🐜 Q 🐱 ◗ ⍭ ♣

Red Lion
21 Alfreton Road (A610)
☎ (0115) 952 0309
11–11; 12–10.30 Sun
Boddingtons Bitter; Flowers Original; Greene King Abbot; Marston's Pedigree; Wadworth 6X; guest beers H
Enterprising pub, just north of the centre: one room with well-defined areas; unusual roof garden. Open 11 Sun for brunch. 🐱 ◗ ♣

Nuthall

Three Ponds
Nottingham Road (follow Kimberley signs off M1 jct 26)
☎ (0115) 938 3170
11–11; 12–10.30 Sun
Hardys & Hansons Best Mild, Best Bitter, Classic, seasonal beers H
Village local close to the M1: a 1930s pub, with a skittle alley, large garden and a children's play area. Eve meals 6–8 Mon–Fri. 🐱 ◗ 🍴 ♣ P

Ollerton

Snooty Fox
Main Street
☎ (01623) 823073
12–2 (4 Sat), 5 (6 Sat)–11; 12–4, 7–10.30 Sun
Theakston Mild, XB; guest beers H
Pub in modernised old buildings with several small rooms. The large garden backs on to a river. Children's certificate. 🐜 🐱 ◗ ♣ P

Orston

Durham Ox
Church Street
☎ (01949) 850059
12 (11 Sat)–3, 6–11; 12–3, 7–10.30 Sun
Home Bitter; Marston's Pedigree; John Smith's Bitter; Theakston Best Bitter; Wadworth 6X; guest beer H
Pleasant, split-room country pub with a large garden and pavement café areas. Table and long alley skittles played.
🐜 Q 🐦 🐱 ♣ P ⍭

Pleasley

Olde Plough
Chesterfield Road, North
☎ (01623) 810386
11–3, 5.30–11; 11–11 Sat; 12–3, 7–10.30 Sun
Marston's Bitter, Pedigree, Owd Rodger, HBC H
Old, beamed, stone pub, well-renovated, with one large, open-plan area and alcoves. Wide range of home-produced food (no meals Sun eve).
Q 🐱 ◗ P ⍭

Retford

Clinton Arms
24 Albert Road
☎ (01777) 702703
11–11; 12–10.30 Sun
Courage Directors; John Smith's Bitter; Theakston Best Bitter; Webster's Green Label; guest beers H
Popular, three-roomed pub attracting all ages; especially busy for live music nights (rock/blues). Occasional cider in summer. Independents' guest beers. Q 🐦 🐱 ◗ 🍴 ⍭ ♣ ⌣ P 🏺

Market Hotel
West Carr Road (by station)
☎ (01777) 703278
11–3, 6 (5 Fri)–11; 11–11 Sat; 12–4, 7–10.30 Sun
Boddingtons Bitter; Courage Directors; Marston's Pedigree; Theakston Black Bull, Best Bitter; guest beers H
Old, traditional family pub and restaurant offering excellent food and good service.
Q 🐱 ◗ ⍭ P

Turk's Head
Grove Street ☎ (01777) 702742
11–3.30, 7–11; 12–3.30, 7–10.30 Sun
Vaux Samson; Ward's Best Bitter; guest beers H
Very attractive, cosy, town pub with an oak-panelled interior. Good value food (not served Sun). The guest beers come from the Ward's list.
🐜 🍴 ♣ P

Ruddington

Red Lion
1 Easthorpe Street
☎ (0115) 984 4654
11–11; 12–10.30 Sun
Home Mild, Bitter; Theakston XB; guest beers H
Excellent village local with a cosy, mock-beamed lounge.
Q 🐱 🍴 ♣ P

South Leverton

Plough Inn
Town Street ☎ (01427) 880323
2 (12 Sat)–11; 12–4, 7–10.30 Sun

Adnams Bitter; Ansells Bitter; guest beers [H]
Little gem which doubles as a post office. No-frills: old wooden trestle tables and benches provide furnishings.
⌂ Q ❀ ♣ P ☐

Strelley

Broad Oak Inn
Main Street
☎ (0115) 929 3340
11–11; 12–10.30 Sun
Hardys & Hansons Best Mild, Best Bitter, Classic, seasonal beers [H]
Attractive, 17th-century, listed building with a drinking area and two eating areas (one for non-smokers).
❀ ◖ ◗ ⊟ P ⚡

Tollerton

Air Hostess
Stansfield Avenue
☎ (0115) 937 2485
11.30–2.30 (3 Sat), 5.30 (6.30 Sat)–11; 12–2.30, 7–10.30 Sun
Home Mild, Bitter; Marston's Pedigree; Theakston XB; guest beers [H]
Comfortable modern village pub, with a lounge and a bar. No food Sun.
Q ❀ ◖ ⊟ ♿ ♣ P

Underwood

Red Lion
Church Lane (off B600)
☎ (01773) 810482
12–3, 6–11; 12–11 Sat; 12–10.30 Sun
Boddingtons Bitter; Flowers Original; Marston's Pedigree; guest beers [H]
300-year-old, beamed, friendly village pub with an eating area where children are welcome, plus a large garden and play area. Barbecues are held in summer.
❀ ◖ ◗ P

Upton

Cross Keys
Main Street
☎ (01636) 813269
11.30–2.30, 5.30 (6 Sat)–11; 12–3, 7–10.30 Sun
Boddingtons Bitter; Marston's Pedigree; Springhead Bitter; Taylor Landlord; guest beers [H]
17th-century pub with a split-level bar and a restaurant upstairs (open Fri and Sat eve).
⌂ Q ❀ ◖ ◗ ♣ P

Walkeringham

Three Horseshoes
High Street
☎ (01427) 890959
11.30–3, 7–11; 12–4, 7–10.30 Sun
Draught Bass; Stones Bitter; Worthington Bitter; guest beers [H]
Village pub and restaurant, renowned for its home-cooked food (not served Mon) and flower displays.
Q ❀ ◖ ◗ ♿ ▲ ♣ P ☐

Watnall

Queen's Head
Main Road
☎ (0115) 938 3148
11–11; 12–10.30 Sun
Home Mild, Bitter; Theakston XB, Old Peculier; guest beers [H]
17th-century village inn, sensitively renovated, keeping the small, intimate snug. Generous rear garden. Eve meals 6–8; no food is served Sat eve or Sun. ⌂ Q ❀ ◖ ◗ ♣ P

Royal Oak
Main Road
☎ (0115) 938 3110
11–3.30, 5–11 (11–11 summer); 12–10.30 Sun
Hardys & Hansons Best Mild, Best Bitter [H]/[E], **Classic, seasonal beers** [H]
Friendly, unusual, village local with a lounge bar upstairs.
❀ ⊟ ♣ P

Wellow

Olde Red Lion
Eakring Road
☎ (01623) 861000
11–2.30, 6–11; 12–2, 7–10.30 Sun
Courage Directors; Ruddles Best Bitter [H]
Comfortable old village pub, popular for food. The house beer comes from Maypole Brewery. Q ❀ ◖ ◗ P ⚡

West Bridgford

Willow Tree
Rufford Way
☎ (0115) 923 4976
11–11; 12–10.30 Sun
Draught Bass; M&B Mild; Worthington Bitter; guest beers [H]
Suburban, 1960s community pub offering up to six guest beers. Q ♘ ❀ ◖ ◗ ⊟ ♣ P ⚡

West Leake

Star Inn (Pit House)
Melton Lane
☎ (01509) 852233
11–3, 6–11; 12–3, 7–10.30 Sun
Draught Bass; Gibbs Mew Salisbury; Theakston XB; guest beers [H]
Former coaching inn where alterations have increased the space without altering its traditional character. No eve meals Sun or Mon.
⌂ Q ❀ ◖ ◗ ⊟ ♣ P

West Stockwith

Waterfront Inn
The Marina, Canal Lane (off A161 at Misterton)
☎ (01427) 891223
12–3, 5–11; 12–11 Sat & summer; 12–10.30 Sun
Fuller's London Pride; Marston's Bitter, Pedigree; John Smith's Bitter; guest beers [H]
Welcoming, family-run pub overlooking Stockwith Marina on the River Trent. Excellent bar meals (the carvery is recommended).
⌂ Q ❀ ◖ ◗ ⊟ ▲ ♣ P

Worksop

Greendale Oak
Norfolk Street
☎ (01909) 489680
12–11; 12–4.30, 7–11 Sat; 12–3, 7–10.30 Sun
Stones Bitter; Tetley Bitter; guest beer [H]
Cosy, gas-lit mid-terrace pub, built in 1790, fielding darts and dominoes teams. Good food.
Q ❀ ◖ ◗ ▲ ♣ P ☐

Mallard
Station Approach, Carlton Road
☎ (01909) 530757
12 (11 Fri & Sat)–11; 12–3, 7–10.30 Sun
Beer range varies [H]
Friendly free house offering changing beers from small breweries, in Grade II-listed station buildings.
Q ❀ ⇌ ♣ ⌓ P ☐

Manor Lodge
Mansfield Road (signed from A60)
☎ (01909) 474177
12–2, 5–11; 12–11 Sat; 12–5, 7–10.30 Sun
Theakston Old Peculier; guest beers [H]
Grade I-listed Elizabethan manor house, built in 1593, set in its own grounds and maintaining original character. Good, varied food.
⌂ Q ♘ ❀ ⊨ ◖ ◗ ♣ P

Oxfordshire

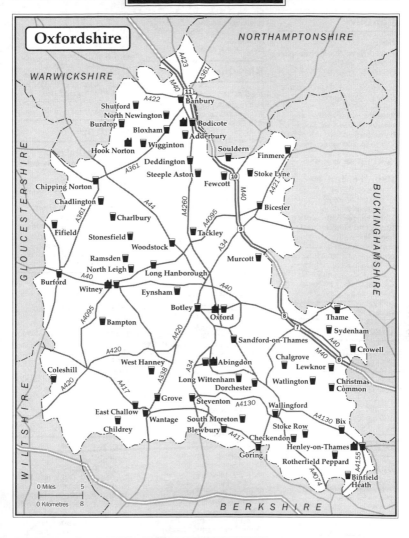

Oxfordshire

NORTHAMPTONSHIRE

WARWICKSHIRE

Banbury
Shutford
North Newington
Burdrop
Bloxham
Bodicote
Hook Norton
Wigginton
Adderbury
Souldern
Finmere
Deddington
Stoke Lyne
Steeple Aston
Fewcott
Chipping Norton
Chadlington
Bicester
Charlbury
Fifield
Stonesfield
Tackley
Woodstock
Ramsden
Murcott
North Leigh
Long Hanborough
Burford
Witney
Eynsham
Botley
Bampton
Oxford
Thame
Sydenham
Sandford-on-Thames
Crowell
Chalgrove
Coleshill
West Hanney
Abingdon
Lewknor
Long Wittenham
Watlington
Christmas Common
Dorchester
Grove
Steventon
Wallingford
Bix
East Challow
Wantage
South Moreton
Stoke Row
Childrey
Blewbury
Checkendon
Henley-on-Thames
Goring
Rotherfield Peppard
Binfield Heath

GLOUCESTERSHIRE

BUCKINGHAMSHIRE

WILTSHIRE

BERKSHIRE

0 Miles 5
0 Kilometres 8

Abingdon

Broad Face
30 Bridge Street
☎ (01235) 524516
11–3, 6–11; 12–3, 7–10.30 Sun
Morland IPA, Original, Old Speckled Hen, seasonal beers *or* **guest beers** H
Large single-bar, corner town pub, built pre-1694, near the historic abbey and the Thames. Its name refers to the bloated face of a man hanged at the old gaol opposite. Home-cooked food, including Sun roasts. Use the public car park over the bridges. Q ❀ ◑ ♣ ♣

> JOIN CAMRA! – see the back of the book for details.

Adderbury

White Hart
Tanners Lane, West Adderbury (off Horn Hill Rd)
☎ (01295) 810406
11–2.30, 5–11; 12–3, 7–10.30 Sun
Boddingtons Bitter; guest beers H
Idyllic, unassuming, 17th-century, back-of-village local, small, quiet and friendly.
🏚 Q ❀ 🚲 ♣ P

Bampton

Morris Clown
17 High Street
☎ (01993) 850217
12–3, 6–11; 12–4, 7–10.30 Sun
Courage Best Bitter; Wadworth 6X; guest beers H

800-year-old pub which welcomes all ages, though its long-term future is uncertain. The name relates to the village history of morris dancing.
🏚 ❀ 🚲 ◑ ▶ ♣ P

🍺 INDEPENDENT BREWERIES

Brakspear:
Henley-on-Thames

Hook Norton:
Hook Norton

Morland: Abingdon

Morrells: Oxford

Plough Inn: Bodicote

Wychwood: Witney

Banbury

Bell

12 Middleton Road, Grimsbury
☎ (01295) 253169
11–3, 7–11; 11–11 Sat; 12–3, 7–10.30 Sun
Highgate Dark; Worthington Bitter; guest beers
(weekend) Ⓗ
Pleasant and friendly, two-roomed pub serving good, home-cooked food (Mon–Fri). The steak and kidney pie is a speciality.
🏚 🏠 ◑ 🍴 🚋 ♣ P

Reindeer Inn

47 Parsons Street
☎ (01295) 264031
11–11; closed Sun
Hook Norton Mild, Best Bitter, Old Hooky; guest beers Ⓗ
Superbly restored, 15th-century former coaching inn with a relaxed atmosphere (tidy dress – no under-21s). See the outstanding Jacobean, panelled back room. Quiet background music is played.
🏚 🏠 ◑ 🚋 ♣ P

Bicester

Hobgoblin

84 Sheep Street
☎ (01869) 252220
11.30–11; 12–10.30 Sun
Beer range varies Ⓗ
Pleasant and friendly, two-roomed, town-centre pub. Live music occasionally.
🏚 🏠 ◑ 🍴 🚋 (North) ♣

Binfield Heath

Bottle & Glass

Harpsden Road (off A4155, ½ mile NE of centre)
☎ (01491) 575755
11–4, 6–11; 12–4, 7–10.30 Sun
Brakspear Bitter, Old, Special Ⓗ
Chocolate box, thatched, beamed, 17th-century, country pub with a flagstoned floor in its larger bar. Home-cooked food includes vegetarian options (no meals Sun eve). Large garden. Gas-assisted pumps (no gas in contact with the beer) activated by handpumps may be used.
Q 🏠 ◑ ▶ P

Bix

Fox at Bix

Oxford Road (A4130)
☎ (01491) 574134
11–3, 7–11; 12–3, 7–10.30 Sun
Brakspear Bitter, Special Ⓗ
Large, solidly-built, creeper-covered roadside pub, with 53 doors. The two wood-panelled bars each have a log fire. Good, home-cooked food (not served

Mon eve); game dishes a speciality in season. The large garden boasts a hitching rail for horses.
🏚 Q 🏠 ◑ ▶ 🍴 ♣ P

Blewbury

Red Lion

Nottingham Fee (300 yds N of A417 in village centre)
☎ (01235) 850403
11–2.30, 6–11; 12–3, 7–10.30 Sun
Brakspear Bitter, Old, Special Ⓗ
Unspoilt, picturesque pub, dating from 1785. Cosy and comfortable, it has beams, brasses, two old clocks and a large inglenook. There is an emphasis on excellent value food, with daily specials and vegetarian choices, plus a separate restaurant with a no-smoking area. No bar meals Sun eve.
🏚 Q 🏠 🏡 ◑ ▶ ♿ ♣ P

Bloxham

Red Lion Inn

High Street (A361)
☎ (01295) 720352
11.30–2.30, 7–11; 12–3, 7–10.30 Sun
Adnams Bitter; Wadworth 6X; guest beers Ⓗ
Welcoming, two-bar pub with a large garden. Extended lounge/dining area – food is served seven days. Good mix of customers.
🏚 Q 🏠 ◑ ▶ 🚋 🍴 ♣ P

Bodicote

Plough

9 High Street
☎ (01295) 262327
11–3, 6.45–11; 12–3, 7–10.30 Sun
Bodicote Bitter, Three Goslings, No. 9, Porter, Triple X Ⓗ
Pleasant, welcoming, two-roomed brew pub. Good, home-cooked food is served in the lounge/dining room (meals cooked to order Sun). A beer festival is held first week of Aug.
🏚 🏠 ◑ ▶ 🚋 ♣

Botley

Fair Rosamund

Chestnut Road
☎ (01865) 243376
12–2.30, 7–11; 12–3, 7–10.30 Sun
Marston's Bitter Ⓗ
1950s pub on the pleasant Elms Rise estate with a large, L-shaped bar and a very comfortable lounge. Winner of the 1996 Marston's cellarmanship award. Beer prices are very reasonable for the area.
Q 🏠 🚋 ♣ P

Wine Shop (off-licence)

8 The Square, West Way Shopping Centre
☎ (01865) 243393
10 (9.30 Sat)–8.30; 6.30–8 Sun
Excellent off-licence with an extensive range of bottled and bottle-conditioned ales, including Belgian, Dutch and German beers.

Burdrop

Bishops Blaize

Between Sibford Ferris and Sibford Gower
☎ (01295) 780323
12–2.30 (not Mon), 6–11; 12–3, 7–10.30 Sun
Hook Norton Best Bitter; Theakston XB; guest beers Ⓗ
Friendly, 17th-century village inn. The large garden offers stunning views. Regular quizzes; darts and crib played.
🏚 🏠 ◑ ▶ ♣ P

Burford

Lamb

19 Sheep Street
☎ (01993) 823155
11–2.30, 6 (7 Sat)–11; 12–2.30, 7–10.30 Sun
Hook Norton Best Bitter; Wadworth IPA, 6X, Old Timer Ⓗ
Cosy, flagstone-floored locals' bar in a very smart hotel: comfortable and homely. A gem. 🏚 Q 🏡 ◑ ▶ 🚋

Chadlington

Tite Inn

Mill End (near A361)
☎ (01608) 676475
12–2.30, 6.30–11; 12–3, 7–10.30 Sun; closed Mon except bank hols
Archers Village; guest beers Ⓗ
Cotswold stone free house on the edge of the village with fine open views, an extensive garden, and a no-smoking garden room in summer. Children welcome. Separate restaurant – all food is freshly prepared and cooked. Three guest beers.
🏚 Q 🏠 ◑ ▶ ♡ P ⚥

Chalgrove

Red Lion

High Street (off B480)
☎ (01865) 890625
12–3, 6–11; 12–3, 7–10.30 Sun
Brakspear Bitter; Fuller's London Pride; guest beers Ⓗ
Popular, 350-year-old, attractive village pub, Grade II-listed, with several drinking areas. Families welcome. A wide range of good-value, home-cooked food includes vegetarian (no eve meals Sun). Separate no-smoking dining

room. Wheelchair WC. Two guest beers. 🏠 🏵 ◐ ▶ ⅊ ♣ P

Charlbury

Rose & Crown
Market Street
☎ (01608) 810103
12–11; 12–10.30 Sun
Archers Village, Best Bitter; Morrells Varsity; guest beers Ⓗ
Popular, town-centre pub appealing to all ages, with a patio-courtyard. Excellent rotation of guest beers. Walkers very welcome. Live music Sun eve. 🏠 🏵 Å ⇌

Checkendon

Black Horse ☆
Burncote Lane (off A4074 towards Stoke Row; left up narrow lane) OS667841
☎ (01491) 680418
12–2.30, 7–11; 12–3, 7–10.30 Sun
Brakspear Bitter; Old Luxters Barn Ale Special; Rebellion IPA; West Berkshire Good Old Boy Ⓖ
Known locally as the 'Pub in the Woods', this pub is hidden away next to a farm. In the same family for over 90 years, it remains unaltered and has been used for film/TV location work. 🏠 Q ⏁ 🏵 Å ♣ P

Childrey

Hatchet
High Street ☎ (01235) 751213
11.30–2.30, 7–11; 12–3, 7–10.30 Sun
Brains Dark; Flowers Original; Morland Original; guest beers Ⓗ
Very friendly, family-run village local with an impressive range of beers. 🏵 ◐ ▶ Å ♣ P

Chipping Norton

Chequers
Goddards Lane
☎ (01608) 644717
11–2.30, 5.30–11; 11–11 Sat; 12–3, 7–10.30 Sun
Fuller's Chiswick, London Pride, ESB, seasonal beers Ⓗ
Friendly, traditional pub next to the theatre. Good mix of clientele. Good food, but no meals Sun eve. 🏠 Q 🏵 ◐ ▶ ♣

Christmas Common

Fox & Hounds
Off B480/B481 and B4009
OS715932 ☎ (01491) 612599
11.30–2.30, 6–11; 12–2.30, 7–10.30 Sun
Brakspear Bitter, Special Ⓖ
Delightful, unspoilt, traditional Chilterns pub at the top of Watlington Hill; popular with hikers and cyclists. The small

public bar has a tiled floor and a large inglenook. The family room is reached through the public bar.
🏠 Q ⏁ 🏵 🖼 ♣ P

Coleshill

Radnor Arms
32 Coleshill (B4019)
☎ (01793) 762366
11–2.30 (3 Sat), 7–11; 12–3, 7–10.30 Sun
Flowers Original; guest beers Ⓖ
Former village smithy, now a friendly and popular local serving beers from casks behind the bar. Its split-level rooms include a dining room (good food).
🏠 ⏁ 🏵 ◐ ▶ ♣ P

Crowell

Shepherd's Crook
The Green (B4009)
☎ (01844) 351431
11.30–3, 5–11; 11–11 Sat; 12–3, 7–10.30 Sun
Bateman XB; Batham Best Bitter; Hook Norton Best Bitter; guest beers Ⓗ
Tastefully refurbished pub situated under the Chiltern ridge and off the main road, near a point to point course. Interesting choice of beers; good value food (several fish dishes). Cider in summer. Dominoes and cribbage are played. 🏠 Q 🏵 ◐ ▶ ♣ ⌂ P

Deddington

Crown & Tuns
New Street (main road)
☎ (01869) 337371
11–11; 12–10.30 Sun
Hook Norton Mild, Best Bitter, Old Hooky, seasonal beers Ⓗ
16th-century inn, tastefully re-designed and catering for all ages. In every book of this guide. 🏠 Q 🏵 ◐ ♣

Dorchester

Chequers
20 Bridge End (off High St off A4074; from S turn sharp left after bridge)
☎ (01865) 340015
12–2 (3 Sat & summer; not Mon), 7–11; 12–3, 7–10.30 Sun
Courage Best Bitter; Hook Norton Best Bitter; Wadworth IPA Ⓖ
Genuine, 17th-century local in an attractive village which has an historic abbey. Its many games include Aunt Sally on summer Fri. Handy for walkers and the Rivers Thames and Thame. A large, no-smoking family room is available.
🏠 Q ⏁ 🏵 🖼 ♣ P ⅋

East Challow

Coach & Horses
Coach Row, Main Street
☎ (01235) 762251
12–11; 12–10.30 Sun
Draught Bass; Morland Original; guest beers Ⓗ
Friendly, attractive, one-bar village pub with a split-level back room/restaurant. The excellent menu includes exotic dishes. Small car park, but the village hall car park is nearby. Children welcome.
🏠 🏵 ◐ ▶ ♣ P

Eynsham

Queen's Head
Queen Street
☎ (01865) 881229
12–2.30, 6–11; 12–2.30, 7–10.30 Sun
Morland IPA, Original; guest beers Ⓗ
Very friendly, 18th-century local comprised of two bars: a quiet public bar and a more vibrant lounge with a pool table. Railway memorabilia adorns both. Ask which guest beers are available.
🏠 Q 🏵 🖼 ◐ ⅊ ♣

Fewcott

White Lion
Fritwell Road (off A43 at Ardley)
☎ (01869) 346639
7 (11 Sat)–11; 12–4, 7–10.30 Sun
Beer range varies Ⓗ
Friendly, 18th-century, one-bar village local serving an excellent, varied range of guest beers. 🏠 🏵 ⅊ ♣ P

Fifield

Merrymouth Inn
Stow Road (A424)
☎ (01993) 831652
11–3, 6–11; 12–3, 7–10.30 Sun
Banks's Bitter; Donnington BB, SBA; guest beers Ⓗ
13th-century inn with a beamed bar and a stone floor, mentioned in the *Domesday Book*. Good home cooking and accommodation.
🏠 Q ⏁ 🏵 🖼 ◐ ▶ Å ♣ P

Finmere

King's Head
Main Road (B4031)
☎ (01280) 848285
11–3, 5.30–11; 12–4, 7–10.30 Sun
Mansfield Bitter; guest beers Ⓗ
Unpretentious roadhouse noted for its value food and guest beers, just the Oxon side of the Bucks border.
🏵 ◐ ▶ 🖼 ♣ ⅋

Goring

Catherine Wheel

Station Road (off B4009, High
St) ☎ (01491) 872379
11.30–2.30 (11–3 Sat), 6–11; 12–3,
7–10.30 Sun
**Brakspear Mild, Bitter, Old,
Special, OBJ** Ⓗ
The oldest pub in this popular
riverside village. Extended into
the old blacksmith's shop, it
has low beams and an
inglenook. Children are
welcome in the 'Forge Bar' and
large, safe garden. Good value,
home-cooked food (no meals
Sun eve).
🏠 Q ✿ ◖ ▶ ⇌ ♣

Grove

Volunteer

Station Road
☎ (01235) 769557
11–11; 12–10.30 Sun
**Hook Norton Mild, Best
Bitter, Old Hooky, Double
Stout, seasonal beers; guest
beers** Ⓗ
Although half a mile north of
the village itself, this is truly a
locals' pub, with a genuinely
friendly atmosphere. A wide
range of value for money meals
is served (no food Sun eve or
Mon). ✿ 🍴 ◖ ▶ ♣ ▭ P

Henley-on-Thames

Bird in Hand

61 Greys Road (off A4155, near
Greys Rd car park)
☎ (01491) 575775
11.30–3, 5–11; 11.30–11 (may close 3–5
in winter) Sat; 12–10.30 Sun
**Brakspear Mild *or* Bitter;
Fuller's London Pride; guest
beers** Ⓗ
Comfortable, welcoming,
one-bar, town local: the only
real ale free house in Henley.
Its surprisingly large garden
has a pond and pets, and is safe
for children. No meals Sun.
Two guest beers.
Q ✿ ◖ ▲ ⇌ (summer only
Sun) ♣

Lewknor

Olde Leathern Bottel

1 High Street (off B4009, near
M40 jct 6)
☎ (01844) 351482
11–2.30, 6–11; 12–3, 7–10.30 Sun
**Brakspear Bitter, Old,
Special** Ⓗ
Comfortable, inviting, family-
run village pub with a large
inglenook, low beams and a
large, well-kept garden.
Excellent and extensive range
of home-cooked food,
reasonably priced, catering for
all tastes.
🏠 🚲 🍴 ◖ ▶ 🍽 ⅋ ♣ P ✄

Long Hanborough

Swan

Millwood End (off A4095 –
turn towards Coombe, 400 yds)
☎ (01993) 881347
11–2 (not Mon), 6–11; 12–3, 7–10.30
Sun
**Morrells Bitter, Varsity; guest
beers** Ⓗ
Traditional, unspoilt pub in an
old part of the village, with a
welcoming atmosphere. Good
mix of ages. ✿ ◖ ▶ ⇌ ♣ P

Long Wittenham

Machine Man Inn

Fieldside (1 mile off A415 at
Clifton Hampden, follow
signs) ☎ (01865) 407835
11–3, 6–11; 12–4, 6–10.30 Sun
**Adnams Bitter; Hop Back
Summer Lightning; West
Berkshire Skiff, Good Old
Boy; guest beers** Ⓗ
Hospitable, unpretentious
village pub with a good mix of
clients. Good value, home-
made food, including
vegetarian (book Sun eve
meals). ETB-approved
accommodation. Families
welcome. Three changing
guest beers.
🏠 ✿ 🍴 ◖ ▶ ♣ P

Murcott

Nut Tree Inn

Main Street ☎ (01865) 331253
11–3.30, 6–11; 12–3, 7–10.30 Sun
Morrells Bitter; guest beers Ⓗ
Very attractive, welcoming
village pub offering five or six
ever-changing, well-chosen
ales and a superb menu.
Although food plays an
important role, the drinker is
not overlooked.
🏠 Q ✿ ◖ ▶ ⅋ P

North Leigh

Woodman Inn

New Yatt Road (off A4095)
☎ (01993) 881790
12–2.30 (4 summer Sat), 6–11;
12–10.30 Sun
**Hook Norton Best Bitter;
Wadworth 6X; guest beers** Ⓗ
Small, friendly village pub
serving freshly-cooked, home-
made food (no eve meals Mon).
The large terrace and garden
host beer festivals Easter and
Aug Bank Hols.
🏠 ✿ 🍴 ◖ ▶ ♣ P

North Newington

Roebuck Inn

Banbury Road (B4035 from
Banbury Cross; 1st right after
town) ☎ (01295) 730444
12–3 (not Mon), 7–11; 12–3, 7–10.30
Sun

**Fuller's London Pride;
Morrells Original, Old
Speckled Hen; guest beers**
(occasional) Ⓗ
Welcoming, 17th-century inn
with an emphasis on freshly
prepared food and a relaxed,
bistro atmosphere (no food Sun
eve). Well-behaved children
welcome. 🏠 ✿ ◖ ▶ ⅋ P

Oxford

Angel & Greyhound

30 St Clement's Street
☎ (01865) 242660
11–11; 12–10.30 Sun
**Young's Bitter, Special, Ram
Rod, seasonal beers** Ⓗ
Popular, relaxed and friendly
pub with a public car park
behind; just across Magdalen
Bridge, east of the centre. No
meals Sun eve. Small patios to
the front and rear.
🏠 Q ✿ ◖ ▶ ♣

Butcher's Arms

5 Wilberforce Street,
Headington (off New High St)
☎ (01865) 61252
11.30–2.30 (3 Sat), 5.30 (4.30 Fri, 6
Sat)–11; 12–3, 7–10.30 Sun
**Fuller's Chiswick, London
Pride, ESB, seasonal beers** Ⓗ
Enlarged, friendly backstreet
local with a single bar and a
mixed clientele. Interesting
collections of beer bottles,
tankards and football match
tickets. No food Sat and Sun.
🏠 ✿ ◖ ▶ ♣

Duke of Monmouth

Abingdon Road
☎ (01865) 721612
11.30–2.30 (3.30 Sat), 6.30–11; 12–3,
7–10.30 Sun
**Marston's Bitter, Pedigree;
guest beers** Ⓗ
Large, open-plan pub,
comfortably refurbished.
✿ ◖ ▶ P

Fir Tree Tavern

163 Iffley Road (A4158)
☎ (01865) 247373
12–3, 5.30–11; 12–11 Sat; 12–10.30 Sun
**Morrells Bitter, Mild, Varsity,
Graduate, College; guest
beer** Ⓗ
Small, split-level, Victorian
pub, sympathetically
refurbished. Regular live
music, including Sat eve;
popular folk session Tue eve.
Food is available all day
weekends; freshly-made pizzas
a speciality. Traditional perry
in summer. ✿ ◖ ▶ ♣ ▭

Folly Bridge Inn

38 Abingdon Road
☎ (01865) 790106
11–11; 12–3, 7–10.30 Sun
**Badger Tanglefoot; Wadworth
IPA, 6X, Farmers Glory, Old
Timer; guest beers** Ⓗ
Open-plan, single-bar pub
with a very good range of

beers. Monthly mini-beer festivals are held in the upstairs function room. Good food. Ten mins' walk south from the centre (Carfax tower).
❀ ◖ ♣ P

Jude the Obscure

54 Walton Street
☎ (01865) 557309
12–3, 5–11; 12–11 Sat; 12–10.30 Sun
Morrells Bitter, Mild, Varsity, Graduate; guest beers Ⓗ
Performance arts-based pub – poetry reading is popular with the Jericho locals. Live folk music Sun. It can get busy (and smoky). Eve meals end at 8.
❀ ◖ ♣ ➪ ♣

Marsh Harrier

40 Marsh Road (off Cowley Rd, B480) ☎ (01865) 775937
12–2.30, 6–11; 12–11 Fri & Sat; 12–10.30 Sun
Fuller's London Pride, ESB, seasonal beers Ⓗ
Neat, friendly, two-bar pub with an attractive, cosy lounge. Recently extended, it serves all the local community. An award-winning garden ensures plenty of space for families in summer. ⚏ ❀ ◖ ♣ ➪ ♣

Philosopher & Firkin

288 Cowley Road (opp. bingo hall) ☎ (01865) 244386
12–11; 12–10.30 Sun
Firkin Thesis, Philosopher, Stout, Nostradamus, Dogbolter Ⓗ
Formerly the University & City Arms: one large, open-plan, friendly bar with lots of seating. Brewery tours on request. Wheelchair WC.
❀ ◖ ♿ ♡ P

Prince of Wales

73 Church Way, Iffley
☎ (01865) 778543
11–2.30, 6–11; 12–3, 7–10.30 Sun
Adnams Extra; Badger Tanglefoot; Wadworth IPA, 6X, Farmers Glory, seasonal beers; guest beers Ⓗ
Friendly pub in a pleasant riverside area, two miles from the centre and a short walk from Iffley Lock on the Thames. Good range of home-cooked food; usually eight beers. No food Sun eves.
❀ ◖ ♣ P

Rose & Crown

14 North Parade Avenue
☎ (01865) 510551
10–3, 5 (6 Sat)–11; 12–3, 6–10.30 Sun
ABC Best Bitter; Ind Coope Burton Ale Ⓗ
Popular, unspoilt pub, purpose-built in the 1870s, with an unusual corridor drinking area and small bars front and rear. The courtyard drinking area at the rear is covered and heated in winter.
Q ❀ ◖ ♣

Wharf House

14 Butterwyke Place, St Ebbes
☎ (01865) 246752
11–3, 5.30–11; 11–11 Sat; 12–4, 7–10.30 Sun
Brakspear Special; Hook Norton Best Bitter; guest beers Ⓗ
Oxford's only true free house, offering changing guest beers, a superb range of Belgian beers and real cider and perry. A mixed clientele enjoys this down to earth, friendly boozer, where the ambience may vary according to the time of day.
Q ❀ ♿ ➪ ♡ P

Ramsden

Royal Oak

High Street (off B4022)
☎ (01993) 868213
11.30–2.30, 6.30–11; 12–3, 7–10.30 Sun
Archers Golden; Hook Norton Best Bitter; Morrells Graduate; guest beers Ⓗ
17th-century former coaching inn with a courtyard. High quality, local produce food is served in the restaurant and bar. Long-serving staff create a friendly atmosphere. Noted accommodation.
⚏ Q ❀ ⇔ ◖ ♿ ♣ P

Rotherfield Peppard

Red Lion

Peppard Common (B481)
☎ (01491) 628329
11–3, 5.30–11; 11–11 Sat & summer; 12–10.30 Sun
Brakspear Mild, Bitter, Old, Special, OBJ Ⓗ
Friendly village pub refurbished in keeping with its 18th-century origins, nicely situated overlooking a large common. A good value, extensive menu caters for all tastes. Large enclosed garden and play area.
⚏ ⛺ ❀ ◖ ♣ ♿ A P ⚟

Sandford-on-Thames

Fox

25 Henley Road
☎ (01865) 777803
12–3, 6–11; 12–3, 7–10.30 Sun
Morrells Bitter, Mild (winter), **Graduate** *or* **guest beer** Ⓗ
Locals' pub on the old Reading road, serving the best and cheapest Morrells beer around.
⚏ Q ❀ ♣ ♣ P

Shutford

George & Dragon

Church Lane ☎ (01295) 780320
7 (11 Sat)–11; 12–10.30 Sun

Adnams Bitter; Fuller's London Pride; Hook Norton Best Bitter Ⓗ
Traditional village pub partly dating back to the 11th century. Interesting mix of clientele – locals, the farming community and tourists. No lunches weekdays.
⚏ Q ❀ ⇔ ◖ ♣ ♿ ♣

Souldern

Fox

Fox Lane ☎ (01869) 345284
11–3, 5 (6 Sat)–11; 12–2.30, 7–10.30 Sun
Draught Bass; Fuller's London Pride; Hook Norton Old Hooky; Worthington Bitter; guest beers Ⓗ
Cotswold stone pub in the village centre. Award-winning food is served in the bar and restaurant.
⚏ Q ❀ ⇔ ◖ ♣ P

South Moreton

Crown

High Street (off A4130, 1 mile E of Didcot) ☎ (01235) 812262
11–3, 5.30–11; 12–3, 7–10.30 Sun
Adnams Bitter; Badger Tanglefoot; Wadworth IPA Ⓗ, **6X; guest beer** Ⓖ
Enthusiastically-run village local, deservedly popular for meals, including vegetarian. Water coolers are used on the casks behind the bar. Families welcome throughout the pub.
⚏ ❀ ◖ ♣ P

Steeple Aston

Red Lion

South Side (SW corner of village) ☎ (01869) 340225
11–3, 6–11; 12–3, 7–10.30 Sun
Badger Tanglefoot; Hook Norton Best Bitter; Wadworth 6X Ⓗ
Friendly adult retreat with a collection of reference books to settle arguments. A classic. No food Sun. ⚏ Q ❀ ◖ P

Steventon

Cherry Tree

33 High Street
☎ (01235) 831222
11.30–2.30, 5.30 (6.30 Sat)–11; 12–2.30, 7–10.30 Sun
Wadworth IPA, 6X, Farmers Glory, Old Timer Ⓗ
Comfortable roadside pub. Very popular lunchtime and early eve (plenty of space).
⚏ Q ❀ ◖ P ⚟

Stoke Lyne

Peyton Arms ☆

Off B4100 ☎ (01869) 345285
11.30–3 (not Mon), 6–11; 11–11 Sat; 12–10.30 Sun

Hook Norton Mild, Best
Bitter, Old Hooky; guest beers
(occasional) G
Small, basic, two-bar village
pub unchanged by time. A
rural gem. Aunt Sally played.
No hot food served.
🏚 Q ✿ ◑ ♣ P

Stoke Row

Cherry Tree
Off B481 at Highmoor
☎ (01491) 680430
11–3, 6–11; 12–3, 7–10.30 Sun
Brakspear Mild, Bitter,
Special, OBJ G
Low-beamed, attractive village
local close to the famous
Maharajah's Well. Families are
welcome in the lounge and the
games room; the garden has
swings and a slide. Snacks
available (rolls only Mon).
🏚 Q ✿ 🍴 ◑ ♣ P

Stonesfield

Black Head
Church Street
☎ (01993) 891616
10.30–2.30, 5.30–11; 12–3, 7–10.30 Sun
Courage Best Bitter; guest
beers
Pleasant and welcoming, two-
roomed village pub. Two guest
beers. 🏚 ✿ 🍴 ♣ P

Sydenham

Crown
Sydenham Road
☎ (01844) 351634
12–2, 6–11; 12–3, 7–10.30 (12–10.30
summer) Sun
Morrells Bitter, Varsity; guest
beer
Cosy, black and white, low-
beamed country pub dating
from 1680, located in a quiet
farming village off the beaten
track. No food Sun eve;
interesting and varied menu at
other times. 🏚 Q ✿ ◑ ♣ P

Tackley

Gardiners Arms
95 Medcroft Road (main street)
☎ (01869) 331266
11–3, 6.30–11; 12–4, 6.30–10.30
(12–10.30 summer) Sun
Morrells Bitter, Varsity,
Graduate; guest beers H
Comfortable and welcoming,
17th-century village pub with
two bars and a skittle alley.
Barbecues on summer Sun.
🏚 ✿ ◑ ▶ �# ♣ P

Thame

Swan Hotel
9 Upper High Street (by public
car park)
☎ (01844) 261211

11–11; 12–10.30 Sun
Brakspear Bitter; Hook
Norton Best Bitter; guest
beers H
Popular, 15th-century coaching
inn overlooking the market
place, with many unusual
fittings (spot the boar's head).
Excellent restaurant and bar
meals, including vegetarian
and children's options.
🏚 Q ✿ 🍴 ◑ ▶ &

Wallingford

Coachmakers Arms
St Mary's Street (A329)
☎ (01491) 839382
12–2.30, 5.30–11; 12–3, 7–10.30 Sun
Brakspear Bitter, Special H
Comfortable and friendly town
pub – known locally as 'the
Cat'. No food Sun.
Q ✿ 🍴 ◑ ♣

King's Head
2 St Martin's Street (A329, near
A4130 jct)
☎ (01491) 838309
11–11; 12–10.30 Sun
Brakspear Bitter H
Popular, one bar, modern,
town-centre pub, recently
refurbished. Families welcome
until 4pm. & ♣ P

Wantage

Royal Oak
Newbury Street
☎ (01235) 763129
5.30–11; 12–2.30, 5.30–11 Fri; 12–2.30,
7–11 Sat; 12–3, 7–10.30 Sun
Draught Bass; Wadworth 6X;
guest beers G/H
Thriving corner local near the
civic hall car park. Up to ten
changing guest beers, plus a
house beer from West
Berkshire. Lunches Fri and Sat.
🍴 ◑ 🍴 ♣

Watlington

Fox & Hounds
Shirburn Street (B4009)
☎ (01491) 612142
11–2.30 (3 Sat), 6 (5 Fri & Sat)–11;
12–3, 7–10.30 Sun
Brakspear Bitter, Old (winter),
Special H
15th/16th-century inn, recently
extended to incorporate the
butcher's shop next door.
Three drinking areas; families
welcome. The dining room is
no-smoking. Large selection
(40–45) of chili dips. No
lunches Sun.
🏚 ✿ 🍴 ◑ ▶ ⚑ ♣ P

West Hanney

Lamb Inn
School Road (off A338)
☎ (01235) 868917
11.30–3, 6–11; 12–3, 7–10.30 Sun

Draught Bass; Flowers
Original; Morland Original;
Shepherd Neame Spitfire;
guest beers H
Very friendly free house
serving good food. Beer
festival Aug Bank Hol.
✿ ◑ ▶ P

Wigginton

White Swan Inn
Pretty Bush Lane (off A361,
follow signs for Waterfowl
Sanctuary)
☎ (01608) 737669
12–11; 12–3, 7–10.30 Sun
Hook Norton Mild, Best
Bitter, Old Hooky, seasonal
beers H; guest beers G/H
Early 17th-century stone pub,
elm-beamed, with an
inglenook and a quarry-tiled
bar area. O'Hagan sausage
menu; game stews available at
weekends. Pets and muddy
boots welcome.
🏚 Q ✿ ◑ ▶ ♣ ⌂ P

Witney

House of Windsor
31 West End
☎ (01993) 704277
6–11; 12–3, 6–11 Sat; 12–10.30 Sun
Hook Norton Best Bitter;
Marston's Pedigree;
Wadworth 6X; guest beers H
Popular free house with a
varied and well-chosen beer
list. Comfortable and homely
front bar with a roaring open
fire; small eating area at the
rear. Aunt Sally and shove-
ha'penny are played.
🏚 Q ✿ ♣ ♣

Three Horseshoes
78 Corn Street
☎ (01993) 703086
11.30–2.30 (3 Sat), 6.30–11; 12–3,
7–10.30 Sun
Draught Bass; Morland
Original; Wells Bombardier H
16th-century inn, five mins'
walk from the centre. A
flagstone floor and a profusion
of antique furniture combine to
give comfort. Good food.
🏚 Q ✿ ✿ ◑ ▶

Woodstock

Queen's Own
59 Oxford Street
☎ (01993) 813582
11–3, 5–11 (11–11 summer); 12–10.30
Sun
Hampshire Lionheart; Hook
Norton Best Bitter, Old
Hooky; guest beers H
Pub with a single long bar with
a thoroughly traditional feel:
bare floorboards, beams and
stone walls bedecked with
hopbines. Two guests from
microbreweries. Winter eve
meals Tue–Thu only.
🏚 ◑ ▶

Shropshire

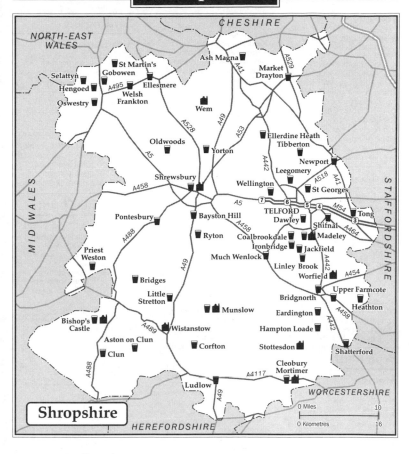

Ash Magna

White Lion
E off A525 bypass
☎ (01948) 663153
12–2 (3 Sat; not Mon), 6–11; 12–3,
7–10.30 Sun
**Draught Bass; Highgate
Dark** E; **guest beers** E/H
Unchanged, two-roomed pub.
The public bar features real ale
mementoes; the lounge
displays hickory-handled golf
clubs. Bar billiards and skittles
played; bowling green.
🏨 Q 🏠 ◑ ▶ ⊞ ♣ ⊟

Aston on Clun

Kangaroo
☎ (01588) 660263
12–3, 7–11; hours vary weekends and
summer
**Draught Bass; Highgate Dark;
guest beers** H
Pub with a large public bar and
a smaller, no-smoking lounge,
with Australian mementoes for
decor. Large garden (camping
in own grounds). Guest beers
at busy times. 🏨 ◑ ▶ ▲ ♣ ✄

Bayston Hill

Compasses
Hereford Road
☎ (01743) 722921
5 (12 Fri & Sat)–11 (varies winter);
12–10.30 Sun
**Draught Bass; Highgate
Dark; M&B Brew XI; guest
beers** H
Traditional pub retaining a
separate snug and bar. Many
shipping mementoes reflect the
pub's name but the eye-
catching display is the
collection of carved elephants.
Wheelchair access at the rear.
Q ◑ ▶ ♿ ♣

Bishop's Castle

Castle Hotel
Market Square
☎ (01588) 638403
12–2.30, 5.30–11; 12–3, 7–10.30 Sun
**Worthington Bitter; guest
beers** H
Fine country town hotel. The
front entrance leads to a snug
with much original woodwork.

There is a larger room off and a
public bar at the rear. Excellent
food; good games selection;
large garden.
🏨 Q 🏠 🛏 ◑ ▶ ♣ P

🏭 INDEPENDENT
BREWERIES

All Nations: Madeley

Crown Inn: Munslow

Davenports Arms:
Worfield

Fox & Hounds: Stottesdon

Hanby: Wem

Hobsons:
Cleobury Mortimer

Salopian: Shrewsbury

Six Bells: Bishop's Castle

Three Tuns:
Bishop's Castle

Wood: Wistanstow

Six Bells

Church Street
☎ (01588) 630144
12–3, 6 (5.30 Thu–Sat)–11; 12–3,
7–10.30 Sun
Fox & Hounds Wust; Six Bells
Big Nev's, Little Jem; Wood
Shropshire Lad; Worthington
Bitter; Wye Valley Bitter Ⓗ
Pub owned by a trust formed
to save it from re-development.
The site also incorporates the
separately-owned Six Bells
Brewery. Friendly public bar;
attractive, café-style lounge.
🏚 Q ✤ ◑ ♣ P

Bridges

Horseshoe Inn

OS394964
☎ (01588) 650260
12–3 (not Mon or winter Tue–Thu),
6–11; 12–3, 7–10.30 Sun
Adnams Bitter, Extra;
Shepherd Neame Spitfire;
guest beers Ⓗ
Attractively situated pub in a
quiet valley by the River Onny,
between Long Mynd and
Stiperstones: an excellent local
expertly run by the 'next
generation' of the Muller
family. Two guest beers.
🏚 Q ☎ ✤ ◑ ♣ ♠ ◗ P ✂

Bridgnorth

Bear Inn

Northgate
☎ (01746) 763250
11–2.30 (10.30–3 Fri & Sat), 5.15 (6
Sat)–11; 12–2.30, 7.30–10.30 Sun
Batham Mild, Best Bitter;
Boddingtons Bitter; Ruddles
Best Bitter; guest beer Ⓗ
Comfortable and friendly,
two-roomed, former brew pub
off the high street of this
historic market town. A locals'
pub with a daily changing
guest beer. Exceptional food;
gourmet eve Thu (book).
Above average
accommodation.
❀ ✤ ◑ ♠ ♣

Bell & Talbot

Salop Street ☎ (01746) 763233
12–3 (not Mon–Wed), 7–11; 12–3,
7–10.30 Sun
Banks's Mild, Bitter;
Camerons Strongarm;
Marston's Pedigree; Morrells
Varsity Ⓗ
250-year-old coaching inn with
three attractive bars, two with
log fires. The old brewhouse is
visible from the rear patio.
Irish live music Sun eve. Good
food (no meals Sun). 🏚 Q ❀
✤ ◑ ♠ ≠ (SVR) ♣

Black Horse
(Bentley's)

4 Bridge Street, Lowtown
☎ (01746) 762415
11–11 (12–3, 6–11 winter); 12–10.30
Sun

Banks's Mild, Bitter; Morrells
Varsity, Graduate; guest
beer Ⓗ
Refurbished pub consisting of
a front bar, lounge and
separate restaurant. The
landlord is a winner of many
CAMRA awards. Varsity and
Graduate are served as 'Black
Horse Best Bitter' and 'Shire
Bitter'. No meals Sun eve.
Q ❀ ✤ ◑ ♦ ♠ ♣ ≠ (SVR)
♣ P ⛁

Railwayman's Arms

Platform 1, Severn Valley
Railway Station (off Holyhead
Rd) ☎ (01746) 764361
12–2 (11–4 summer), 7–11; 11–11 Sat;
12–10.30 Sun
Batham Best Bitter; guest
beers Ⓗ
Railway memorabilia adorns
this former waiting room
which serves a good selection
of mainly independents' beers
and some hot snacks.
🏚 ❀ ♠ ≠ (SVR) ♣ ◗ P

Cleobury Mortimer

King's Arms Hotel

Church Street
☎ (01299) 270252
11.30–11; 12–10.30 Sun
Hobsons Best Bitter; guest
beers Ⓗ
16th-century coaching inn
where a log fire is a central
feature of the main room;
separate dining area. Classical
music is played during the day.
Country/folk music eves. Only
fresh food is used for the meals
(not served Sun eve).
🏚 ✤ ◑ ♦ ♠

Clun

White Horse

The Square ☎ (01588) 640305
11.30–3, 6.30–11; 11–11 Sat; 12–3,
7–10.30 Sun
Draught Bass; guest beers Ⓗ
Set in the centre of this timeless
village, a pub with one,
L-shaped bar which provides
spaces for customers of all
ages. One of the two guests is
always a local beer. Eve meals
end at 8.30. 🏚 ✤ ◑ ♦ ♠ ♣

Corfton

Sun Inn

On B4368 ☎ (01584) 861239
11–2.30, 6–11; 12–3, 7 (6
summer)–10.30 Sun
Boddingtons Mild, Bitter;
Flowers IPA; guest beers Ⓗ
Featuring a well in the
restaurant, this family-run,
17th-century inn has excellent
facilities for guests with
disabilities and children. Good
value meals. Good views of
Clee Hill from the garden. Wye
Valley beers are also sold.
🏚 Q ❀ ◑ ♦ ♦ ♠ ♦ ♣ ◗ P ⛁

Eardington

Swan Inn

Knowle Sands (1 mile from
Bridgnorth on B4555)
☎ (01746) 763424
12–2.30 (not winter Mon–Fri), 5 (6
Sat)–11; 12–3, 7–10.30 Sun
Matthew Clark Twelve Bore;
Hobsons Town Crier; guest
beers Ⓗ
Family-owned, 18th-century
inn with four rooms around a
central bar area. Up to four
changing real ales are served in
summer. Quality food at all
times. Families welcome.
🏚 Q ❀ ✤ ◑ ♦ ♠ P

Ellerdine Heath

Royal Oak

Midway between A53 and
A442 ☎ (01939) 250300
11–3, 5–11; 11–11 Sat; 12–3, 7–10.30
Sun
Brains Dark, SA; Hanby
Drawwell; Hobsons Best
Bitter; Wood Parish; guest
beer Ⓗ
Rural pub nicknamed 'the
Tiddly', with a fairly small,
one-room bar, an adjoining
games room and a large
outside area. Good food; very
reasonably-priced beer.
Children's certificate. No food
Tue. 🏚 Q ❀ ◑ ♦ ♣ ◗ P

Ellesmere

White Hart Inn

Birch Road ☎ (01691) 622333
7–11; 11–6, 7–11 Sat; 7–10.30 Sun
Bateman Mild; Marston's
Bitter, Pedigree Ⓗ
17th-century, listed local in a
quiet backstreet, with a cosy
bar and a quiet lounge. Near
the Llangollen Canal and in
Shropshire's 'lake' (mere)
district. Q ❀ ◑ ♠ ♣ P

Gobowen

Cross Foxes

By railway station
☎ (01691) 670827
11–11; 12–10.30 Sun
Banks's Mild; Marston's
Pedigree Ⓗ
Real local with a lively
atmosphere, recently
refurbished. ❀ ♠ ≠ ♣ P

Hampton Loade

Lion Inn

Off A442 ☎ (01746) 780263
12–2.30 (not winter Mon–Fri), 7–11;
12–2.30 (3 summer), 7–10.30 Sun
Boddingtons Bitter; Hook
Norton Old Hooky; guest
beer Ⓗ
Splendid country pub close to
the River Severn, offering
characterful bars and a local

guest beer. Good, home-cooked food; large garden.
🏨 ❀ ◖ ▶ 🍴 🅰 ⇌ (SVR) ♣ P

Heathton

Old Gate
From Claverley Village follow signs to Bobbington OS813924
☎ (01746) 710431
12–2.30, 6.30–11; 12–3, 7–10.30 Sun
Draught Bass; Enville Ale; Tetley Bitter; guest beers Ⓗ
Bustling country pub off the beaten track: two rooms with exposed beams and log fires, first licensed in 1784. Families welcome (play equipment and barbecue in the rear garden). Exceptional food. Cider in summer. 🏨 ❀ ◖ ▶ 🅰 ◡ ♣ P

Hengoed

Last Inn
☎ (01691) 659747
7–11; 12–3, 7–10.30 Sun
Draught Bass; Boddingtons Bitter; guest beers Ⓗ
Welcoming rural pub in the attractive Welsh borderland, offering a varied selection of guest beers. Families well provided for. Sun lunches served; no meals Tue eve.
🏨 Q 🍴 ◖ ▶ ♣ ◡ P

Linley Brook

Pheasant Inn
Britons Lane (400 yds off B4373) ☎ (01746) 762260
12–2.30, 7 (6.30 summer)–11; 12–3, 7 (6.30 summer)–10.30 Sun
Beer range varies Ⓗ
Pleasantly situated, two-roomed pub on a quiet country lane. Three low- to mid-gravity beers include micros' beers. Strictly 'no children'.
🏨 Q ❀ ◖ ▶ ♣ P

Little Stretton

Ragleth
Ludlow Road
☎ (01694) 722711
12–2.30, 6–11 (extends bank hols); 12–10.30 Sun
Bateman Mild; Marston's Bitter, Pedigree; guest beers Ⓗ
17th-century inn close to the Long Mynd. Its public bar, with inglenook, woodwork and brick and tiled floor, maintains an unspoilt air; separate lounge and restaurant. Children's certificate.
🏨 ❀ 🚗 ◖ ▶ 🍴 🅰 ♣ P

Ludlow

Church Inn
Buttercross ☎ (01584) 872174
11–11; 12–10.30 (12–3, 7–10.30 winter) Sun

Courage Directors; Ruddles County; Theakston XB; guest beers (summer) Ⓗ
Tucked away pub in the original pedestrian sidestreets, on an ancient site. This upmarket inn acquired its name in 1979 and stands near the church of St Lawrence, the largest in Shropshire.
Q 🚗 ◖ ▶ ⇌

Old Bull Ring Tavern
44 Bull Ring ☎ (01584) 872311
11–11; 12–10.30 Sun
Ansells Mild, Bitter; Tetley Bitter; guest beer Ⓗ
Cosy, two-roomed pub and restaurant dating back 650 years, though not always a pub. Very popular with all ages. No eve meals Sun.
🏨 ◖ ▶ ⇌ ♣

Market Drayton

Stag's Head
Great Hales Street
☎ (01630) 657012
10.30–4, 6–11; 10.30–11 Wed, Fri & Sat; 12–3, 7–10.30 Sun
Marston's Bitter Ⓗ
Friendly, three-roomed market town pub, close to the Shropshire Union Canal.
Q 🍴 ❀ 🍴 🅰 ♣ P

Much Wenlock

George & Dragon ☆
2 High Street ☎ (01952) 727312
11–2.30, 6–11; 12–10.30 Sun
Hook Norton Best Bitter; guest beers Ⓗ
A plain frontage belies the rare and unspoilt interior of this classic pub. Good food; three, changing guest beers (a cask-conditioned stout is always available). Local CAMRA 1997 *Pub of the Year*. 🏨 Q ◖ ▶ ♣

Munslow

Crown
On B4368 ☎ (01584) 841205
12–2.30, 7–11; 12–3, 7–10.30 Sun
Banks's Mild; Crown Boy's Pale Ale, Munslow Ale; Marston's Pedigree Ⓗ
Roadside brew pub with a Georgian facade disguising an original Tudor interior. The menu includes French and Thai specials. Donkey in the garden. Children's certificate.
🏨 Q ❀ ◖ ▶ ♣ ◡ P

Newport

New Inn
Stafford Road (town end)
☎ (01952) 814729
11.30–3.30, 7–11; 12–4, 7–10.30 Sun
Banks's Mild, Bitter; Draught Bass; Highgate Dark Ⓗ
Quaint, three-room pub with a cosy atmosphere and a strong games following. Mostly older

clientele. Public car park nearby. Q ❀ ♣

Shakespeare
Upper Bar (high street)
☎ (01952) 811924
11–11; 12–10.30 Sun
Banks's Mild; Draught Bass; Theakston Best Bitter, XB; guest beer Ⓗ
Lively, one-room pub with an adjoining pool room. Frequented by all ages, it can be crowded weekend eves. A constant winner of the town's floral display contest.
❀ ♿ P

Oldwoods

Romping Cat
☎ (01939) 290273
12–3, 7–11; 12–2.30, 7–10.30 Sun
Boddingtons Bitter; Castle Eden Ale; guest beers Ⓗ
No-frills country pub where beers have top priority: no food, loud music or TV. Guests include an occasional selection from Shropshire breweries.
🏨 Q ❀ ♣ P 🍴

Oswestry

Bell
Church Street
☎ (01691) 657068
11–11; 12–10.30 Sun
Draught Bass; M&B Brew XI; guest beers Ⓗ
Busy town local opposite the parish church. Although much altered internally, parts remain to remind people that the pub is, reputedly, the oldest in town. Q ❀ ♣ P

Pontesbury

Horseshoes Inn
Minsterley Road (A488)
☎ (01743) 790278
12–3, 5–11; 12–4, 7–10.30 Sun
Castle Eden Ale; Flowers Original; guest beers Ⓗ
Busy local in a large village, handy for walking in the South Shropshire hills. Friendly service; several games teams. One or two guest beers.
❀ 🚗 ◖ ▶ ♣ P

Priest Weston

Miners Arms
OS293973 ☎ (01938) 561352
11–4, 7–11; 7–10.30 Sun
Draught Bass; Worthington Bitter Ⓗ
Remote, classic country pub, still largely unspoilt. It draws walkers visiting the nearby stone circle. The well can be viewed en route to the toilet. Folk singing first Wed of the month.
🏨 ❀ ◖ ▶ ♿ 🅰 ♣ ◡ P

Ryton

Fox

E of A49 at Dorrington
☎ (01743) 718499
12–3, 7–11; 12–3, 7–10.30 Sun
Draught Bass; guest beers H
Slightly elevated pub and
restaurant with views toward
the South Shropshire hills. One
guest beer in winter, two in
summer; imaginative, home-
prepared food. Boules played.
❀ ◑ ▶ P

St Martin's

Greyhound Inn

Overton Road (B5069, 1 mile
from village) ☎ (01691) 774307
12–11; 12–10.30 Sun
**Banks's Mild; Webster's
Yorkshire Bitter; guest
beers** H
Refurbished, rural pub with an
extensive outdoor area with
play facilities. The bar has a
collection of artefacts from the
closed Ifton colliery. Steak and
kidney pie is a special (all food
is home-made).
🏚 ❀ ◑ ▶ 🕭 ▲ ♣ P

Selattyn

Cross Keys ☆

On B4579 ☎ (01691) 774307
6–11 (phone for lunchtime hours);
12–3 (may vary), 7–10.30 Sun
Banks's Mild E, **Bitter** H
Superb example of a village
pub of 17th century origin with
an unspoiled interior of
various rooms, including a
skittle alley. Close to Offa's
Dyke Walk. Holiday flat to let.
🏚 Q ☎ ❀ 🛏 ♣ P

Shatterford

Red Lion

Bridgnorth Road (A442)
☎ (01299) 861221
11.30–2.30, 6–11; 12–3, 7–10.30 Sun
Banks's Mild, Bitter E;
**Batham Best Bitter; guest
beers** H
Family-owned, roadside free
house with smoking and no-
smoking bars and a barn-style
restaurant. Exceptional food,
with fresh fish and daily chef's
specials. Guest beers change
frequently.
🏚 ❀ ◑ ▶ 🕭 ▲ P ⊁ 🕮

Shifnal

White Hart

4 High Street ☎ (01952) 461161
12–3, 6–11; 12–11 Fri & Sat; 12–3,
7–10.30 Sun
**Ansells Bitter; Enville Mild,
Simpkiss Bitter, Ale; Ind
Coope Burton Ale; guest
beers** H

Popular, friendly, 16th-century
free house which has served
over 500 guest beers in three
years. Much prized is Albert's
Bench, a long seat in the
lounge. Local CAMRA *Pub of
the Year* 1996. No food Sun.
Q ❀ ◑ 🛏 ≋ ♣ P

Shrewsbury

Boat House

New Street, Port Hill (A488)
☎ (01743) 362965
11–11; 12–10.30 Sun
**Boddingtons Bitter; Flowers
IPA; Fuller's London Pride;
Whitbread Abroad Cooper,
Fuggles IPA; guest beers** H
Hogshead Ale House
overlooking Quarry Park.
Tables in the terraced garden
overlook the river; bouncy
castle in summer. Occasional
guest beers from Shropshire
breweries. The pub can be
approached from the park by a
footbridge.
🏚 Q ❀ ◑ ▶ 🛏 ♣ ⌂ P

Castle Vaults

16 Castle Gates
☎ (01743) 358807
11.30–3, 6–11; 7–10.30 Sun
**Hobsons Best Bitter;
Marston's Pedigree; guest
beers** H
Free house with a roof garden
in the shadow of the castle. The
specialist Mexican food is
served in a no-smoking area off
the bar. Six ales.
🏚 Q ❀ 🛏 ◑ ▶ ≋ ⌂ ⊁ 🕮

Coach & Horses

Swan Hill ☎ (01743) 365661
11–11; 12–10.30 Sun
Draught Bass; guest beers H
Unspoilt Victorian pub in a
quiet part of town. The wood-
panelled bar has a partitioned
area; the lounge has been
magnificently extended using
old wood. Goodalls Gold is the
house beer from Salopian. Ring
to check if eve meals are being
served. 🏚 Q ◑ ▶

Dolphin

48 St Michaels Street
☎ (01743) 350419
5 (3 Fri & Sat)–11; 12–3, 7–10.30 Sun
Beer range varies H
Early Victorian, gas-lit
drinking house with a
porticoed entrance and its
original layout. Up to six ales
but no lager – not even bottled.
Q 🛏 ≋

Loggerheads
(Tap House) ☆

Church Street
☎ (01743) 355457
10.30–11; 12–3 (10.30 summer) Sun
**Draught Bass; Banks's Mild,
Bitter, seasonal beers;
Camerons Strongarm; guest
beers** H

Sensitively refurbished in 1996,
following a change of
ownership, this town pub
retains its cosy atmosphere.
Don't miss the room to the left
of the entrance, with its
scrubbed-top tables and high-
backed settles.
Q ◑ ▶ 🛏 ৬ ♣ 🕮

Nag's Head

22 Wyle Cop ☎ (01743) 362455
11–11; 12–10.30 Sun
Beer range varies H
Often lively, reputedly
haunted, historic house of
considerable architectural
interest. Three or four
Carlsberg-Tetley beers are on
sale. ❀ ≋ ♣

Peacock

42 Wenlock Road (A458, 300
yds from Shire Hall)
☎ (01743) 355215
11–3, 6–11; 7–10.30 Sun
**Bateman Mild; Marston's
Bitter, Pedigree, Owd Rodger,
HBC** H
Spacious, open-plan pub near
Lord Hill's column (Britain's
tallest Doric column). Note the
ornate peacock on the wall by
the lounge entrance.
❀ ◑ ▶ ♣ P

Proud Salopian

Smithfield Road
☎ (01743) 236887
11–11; 12–10.30 Sun
**Castle Eden Ale; John Smith's
Bitter; Tetley Imperial;
Whitbread Fuggles IPA; guest
beers** H
Busy pub just off the town
centre, occasionally under
threat from the River Severn.
Guest beers include Shropshire
ales. Thomas Southam, the
Shrewsbury brewer, was the
Proud Salopian. ◑ ▶ ৬ ≋ ♣

Telford:
Coalbrookdale

Coalbrookdale Inn

12 Wellington Road (opp.
Museum of Iron)
☎ (01952) 433953
12–3, 6–11; 12–3, 7–10.30 Sun
**Courage Directors; Enville
Bitter, Ale; guest beers** H
Cosy pub with a wood-
panelled central bar where a
warm welcome is always given
by the fun-loving landlord.
CAMRA national *Pub of the
Year* 1995. Eve meals till 8 (no
eve meals Sun).
🏚 Q ❀ ◑ ▶ ♣ ⌂ P

Dawley

Three Crowns Inn

Hinksay Road (off B4373 at
Finger Rd Garage)
☎ (01952) 590868
11.30–3 (11–4 Sat), 6.30–11; 12–3.30,
7–10.30 Sun

Marston's Bitter, Pedigree, HBC Ⓗ
Small town pub, part of which is given over to pool and darts. No food Sun.
❀ ◗ ♣ P

Ironbridge

Golden Ball
1 Newbridge Road (off B4373 at Jockey Bank, Madeley Hill)
☎ (01952) 432179
12–3, 6–11; 12–3, 7–10.30 Sun
Courage Directors; Marston's Pedigree; Ruddles Best Bitter; guest beers Ⓗ
First licensed in 1728, this inn retains a sense of the past whilst addressing the needs of the modern consumer. Excellent food from an international menu (no-smoking dining room). Guest beers from established independents.
⛼ Q ❀ 🛏 ◗ ◖ ♣ P 🛇

Jackfield

Boat
Ferry Road (across river footbridge at foot of incline)
☎ (01952) 882178
11 (5.30 winter)–11; 12–10.30 Sun
Banks's Mild Ⓔ**, Bitter; Morrells Varsity** Ⓗ
Welcoming, 18th-century riverside pub with traditional values. Children welcome until 8.30 in a no-smoking family room. The large garden gives a fine view of the Severn gorge. Note the flood level markers on the door.
⛼ Q ⛾ ❀ ◗ ♿ ♣ ⌓ ⚟ 🛇

Leegomery

Malt Shovel Inn
Hadley Park Road (off A442 at Leegomery roundabout)
☎ (01952) 242963
12–2.30 (3 Sat), 5–11; 12–3, 7.30–10.30 Sun
Banks's Mild; Marston's Pedigree, HBC Ⓗ
Friendly, two-roomed pub where horse brasses and rugby memorabilia festoon the walls. Real home-made chips and specials every day.
⛼ ❀ ◗ ⊞ ♣ P

Madeley

All Nations
20 Coalport Road (opp. Blists Hill Museum)
☎ (01952) 585747
12–3, 7–11; 12–3, 7–10.30 Sun
All Nations Pale Ale Ⓗ
Unique brew pub set amidst the heritage of the Industrial Revolution. The garden overlooks Blists Hill and the valley leading down to Ironbridge gorge.
Q ❀ ♣ P

Royal Oak
High Street
☎ (01952) 585598
12–3, 7–11; 12–3, 7–10.30 Sun
Burtonwood Mild, Bitter; Flowers Original; guest beers Ⓗ
Friendly pub within easy reach of Blists Hill Museum. The small, intimate lounge is separate from the larger bar area in this Grade II-listed building. Up to ten ales.
⛼ Q ❀ ⊞ ▲ ♣ P

St Georges

Albion Inn
Station Hill
☎ (01952) 614193
12–2.30 (4 Sat), 5 (7 Sat)–11; 12–3, 7–10.30 Sun
Marston's Bitter, Pedigree, HBC Ⓗ
Small, one-bar local which serves good, home-cooked meals. The large, award-winning garden overlooks the North Shropshire plain.
❀ 🛏 ◗ ◖ ♣ P

Wellington

Cock Hotel
Holyhead Road
☎ (01952) 244954
12–3, 7 (5 Thu–Sat)–11; 12–3, 7–10.30 Sun
Beer range varies Ⓗ
18th-century coaching inn refurbished to produce the Old Wrekin Tap on one side, complete with settles. Dark wood panelling around the bar links through to the no-smoking front room with its impressive bow window.
Q ❀ 🛏 ⊞ ♣ P ⚟ 🛇

Tibberton

Sutherland Arms
☎ (01952) 550533
12–2.30, 6–11; 12–11 Sat; 12–10.30 Sun
Banks's Mild; Marston's Bitter, Pedigree, Owd Rodger (winter)**, HBC** Ⓗ
Village community pub with several open, but distinctive drinking areas, a selection of 40 whiskies and various games. Eve meals Tue–Sat till 8.30.
⛼ Q ❀ ◗ ◖ ⊞ ♣ P

Tong

Bell Inn
Newport Road (A41)
☎ (01952) 850210
11.30–3, 5–11; 11.30–11 Sat; 12–10.30 Sun
Banks's Mild, Bitter Ⓔ**; Camerons Bitter; Marston's Pedigree** Ⓗ
Busy, 17th-century roadside pub, one of Banks's Milestone Taverns, catering for all ages. Good food at very reasonable prices. Large, attractive garden with play area. Popular in summer months.
⛼ ⛾ ❀ ◗ ◖ ♿ ♣ P ⚟ 🛇

Upper Farmcote

Lion O'Morfe
Off Bridgnorth–Stourbridge road, follow Claverley sign
☎ (01746) 710678
11.30–3 (5 Sat), 7–11; 12–4, 7–10.30 Sun
Banks's Mild, Bitter Ⓔ**; Draught Bass; guest beer** Ⓗ
Georgian farmhouse with a modern feel; a quality country pub which welcomes families and functions. Live jazz, folk or comedy second Thu of the month. Games room; floodlit boules pitch. Good selection of food.
⛼ Q ❀ ◗ ◖ ⊞ ▲ ♣ P ⚟ 🛇

Welsh Frankton

Narrow Boat Inn
Ellesmere Road (A495), Whittington
☎ (01691) 661051
11–3, 7–11; 12–3, 7–10.30 Sun
Tetley Bitter; guest beers Ⓗ
Comfortable pub alongside the Shropshire Union (Llangollen) Canal with an appropriate canal theme. Formerly the office of a canal carrying company.
⛼ Q ⛾ ❀ ◗ ◖ ▲ P ⚟

Yorton

Railway Inn
By station
☎ (01939) 220240
11.30–3, 6–11; 12–3.30, 7–10.30 Sun
Wadworth 6X; Wood Parish, Special, Shropshire Lad Ⓗ**; guest beers** Ⓗ/Ⓖ
Friendly pub in the same family for 60 years, with a simple bar and a well-appointed lounge adorned with fishing trophies. Regional CAMRA *Pub of the Year*. Many visitors arrive by train.
⛼ Q ❀ ⇌ P

Join CAMRA – with big discounts on books, products and entrance fees to beer festivals, it's the best £14 you'll ever spend!

Somerset

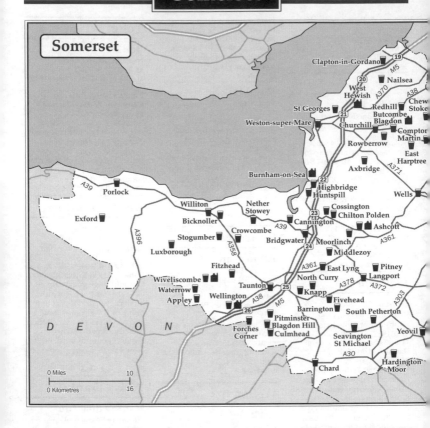

Somerset

Clapton-in-Gordano
Nailsea
West Hewish
St Georges
Redhill
Chew Stoke
Butcombe
Weston-super-Mare
Churchill
Blagdon
Compton Martin
Rowberrow
East Harptree
Axbridge
Burnham-on-Sea
Wells
Highbridge
Huntspill
Porlock
Williton
Nether Stowey
Cossington
Chilton Polden
Exford
Bicknoller
Cannington
Ashcott
Crowcombe
Stogumber
Bridgwater
Moorlinch
Luxborough
Middlezoy
Fitzhead
East Lyng
Pitney
Wiveliscombe
North Curry
Langport
Waterrow
Taunton
Knapp
Fivehead
Appley
Wellington
Barrington
South Petherton
Pitminster
Blagdon Hill
Forches Corner
Culmhead
Seavington St Michael
Yeovil
Chard
Hardington Moor

D E V O N

0 Miles 10
0 Kilometres 16

Appley

Globe Inn ☆
2½ miles N of A38 at White Ball
Hill OS071215
☎ (01823) 672327
11–3 (not Mon), 6.30–11; 12–3, 7–10.30
Sun
Cotleigh Tawny; guest beer H
Wonderful old village inn
hidden deep in the
countryside. The bar is just a
hatchway in a flagstone
corridor with several cosy
rooms leading off. The garden
has some play equipment.
Good food; cider in summer.

Ashcott

Ring O' Bells
High Street (off A39)
☎ (01458) 210232
12–2.30, 7–11; 12–2.30, 7–10.30 Sun
**Moor Withy Cutter; guest
beers** H
Popular, multi-level village
pub with a cosy bar area.
Superb, award-winning, home-
made food.

Axbridge

Lamb Inn
The Square
☎ (01934) 732253
12–2.30 (11.30–3 Sat), 6.30–11; 12–3,
7–10.30 Sun
**Butcombe Bitter, Wilmot's;
Wadworth 6X; guest beer** H
Rambling old pub, now owned
by Butcombe, opposite King
John's hunting lodge, with a
large, terraced garden. The
unusual bar is made of bottles.

Barrington

Royal Oak
☎ (01460) 53455
12–3, 6.30 (6 Fri)–11; 12–11 Sat; 12–4,
7–10.30 Sun
**Theakston Best Bitter; guest
beers** H
17th-century village pub where
families are made welcome: a
quiet lounge and a busy public
bar. At least six ales from all
over the country are sold, plus
a house beer from Juwards.
Good value food.

Bath

Bell Inn
103 Walcot Street
☎ (01225) 460426
11.30–11; 12–3, 7–10.30 Sun
**Bath Barnstormer; Courage
Best Bitter, Directors; Fuller's
London Pride; Smiles Best** H
Open-plan bar renowned for
its music. ❀ ♣

Bladud Arms
Gloucester Road, Lower
Swainswick (A46)
☎ (01225) 420152
11–3, 5.30–11; 12–3, 7–10.30 Sun
**Draught Bass; Butcombe
Bitter; Wickwar BOB; guest
beer** H
Very popular local on the city
outskirts, one of few genuine
free houses in Bath. Eve meals
until 8. ❀ ◖ ♪ ♣ P

Cross Keys Inn
Midford Road, Combe Down
(B3110) ☎ (01225) 832002
11–2.30 (3 Sat), 6–11; 12–3, 7–10.30
Sun
**Courage Best Bitter; Ushers
Best Bitter, Founders, seasonal
beers** H

252

Attractive, Bath stone 'roadhouse'-type pub on the southern edge of the city, with two traditional bars. An aviary is a feature of the large, walled garden. Good value food.
🏺 ❀ ◗ ♠ P ▯

Foresters Arms

Bradford Road, Combe Down
☎ (01225) 837671
11.30–3.30, 5–11; 11.30–11 Sat; 12–3.30, 7.30–10.30 Sun
Draught Bass; Courage Best Bitter; Otter Bitter, Head; guest beer Ⓗ
Pub with a comfortable, friendly main bar and an adjacent skittle alley. One wall is dominated by a vast mirror-like mural of the room. No food Sat. ◗ ♠ P

Golden Fleece

1–3 Avon Buildings, Lower Bristol Road
☎ (01225) 429572
11–2.30 (3 Sat), 5.30 (4.30 Fri, 6 Sat)–11; 12–2.30, 7–10.30 Sun
Courage Georges BA, Best Bitter; guest beers Ⓗ
Popular, street-corner local convenient for Twerton Park football ground. The two guest beers change daily. Weekday lunches. ◗ ♠ P

Hobgoblin

St James Parade
☎ (01225) 460785
11–11; 12–10.30 Sun
Wychwood Special, DB, Hobgoblin Ⓗ
Large, noisy, busy, city-centre pub, very popular with students from the college across the road. Three floors, with a pool table upstairs. Occasional cider. ◗ ⇌ ⌂

Larkhall Inn

St Saviours Road, Larkhall (400 yds off A4/A46 jct)
☎ (01225) 425710
11–2 (2.30 Fri), 6–10.30 (11 Fri & Sat); 12–2, 7–10.30 Sun
Courage Best Bitter, Directors Ⓗ
Distinctive local on the outskirts of the city. The garden is very popular in summer. 🏺 Q ❀ ◗ ♠

Old Crown Inn

1 Crown Hill, Weston
☎ (01225) 423371
11–2.30, 5–11; 11–11 Fri & Sat; 12–10.30 Sun
Draught Bass; Courage Best Bitter; Greene King Abbot; Smiles Best; Webster's Green Label; guest beer Ⓗ
Large, justly popular, 16th-century pub in Weston village, on the edge of Bath. The garden is recommended for summer family outings. No food Sun eve.
🏺 ☜ ❀ ◗ ◖ ♠ ✄

Old Farmhouse

1 Lansdown Road
☎ (01225) 316162
12–11; 12–10.30 Sun
Badger Tanglefoot; Draught Bass; Butcombe Bitter; Wadworth 6X Ⓗ
Lively local of great character. The unusual pub sign is a caricature of its landlord. Limited parking.
🏺 ❀ ♠ ⌂ P

Old Green Tree ☆

12 Green Street
11–11 (10 Sat); 7–10.30 (closed lunch) Sun
RCH Pitchfork; Wickwar BOB; guest beers Ⓗ
Cosy, welcoming, three-roomed, city-centre local. A house beer is brewed by Uley, and a porter is also usually available. After 10 on Sat ring the bell for entry.
Q ◗ ⇌ ♠ ✄

Pig & Fiddle

2 Saracen Street
☎ (01225) 460868
11.30–11; 12–10.30 Sun
Ash Vine Bitter, Challenger, Black Bess Porter, Hop & Glory; guest beers Ⓗ
Very lively, city-centre local. The place to go on a balmy summer eve. ❀ ◗ ◖ ⇌ ⌂

Porter Butt

York Place, London Road
☎ (01225) 425084
12–3, 5.30–11; 12–11 Sat; 12–10.30 Sun
Butcombe Wilmot's; Courage Georges BA, Best Bitter; Marston's Pedigree; guest beer Ⓗ
Two-bar local staging regular live music in the 'Walcot Palais' downstairs. Next to the bus depot. Q ❀ ◗ ◖ ⑄ & ♠ P

Ram

Widcombe Parade
☎ (01225) 421938
11–2.30, 5–11; 11–11 Fri & Sat; 12–7 Sun
Draught Bass; Smiles Best; Ushers Best Bitter; Wadworth 6X Ⓗ
Newly refurbished, large local, very convenient for the station. Wood panelling gives the single bar a warm atmosphere. Weekday lunches.
Q ◗ & ⇌ ◖

Richmond Arms

7 Richmond Place, Beacon Hill
☎ (01225) 316725
12–3 (not Mon), 6–11; 12–3, 7–10.30 Sun
Ushers Best Bitter, Founders, seasonal beers Ⓗ
Work up an appetite by walking up to this fine pub set in a Georgian terrace. The genuine home-cooked food is much appreciated by the locals and rightly so. Q ❀ ◗ ◖

Bicknoller

Bicknoller Inn

32 Church Lane
☎ (01984) 656234
11–3, 5.30–11; 12–3, 7–10.30 Sun
Draught Bass; Worthington Bitter; guest beers Ⓗ
Olde-worlde thatched inn in a picturesque village at the foot of the Quantocks, an ideal base for hillwalking: a flagstoned public bar with an inglenook, a

large, child-friendly garden, and a skittle alley. Comprehensive menu.
🏾 Q 🏵 🟂 ◑ ▶ 🍴 ♣ P

Blagdon

New Inn
Church Street
☎ (01761) 462475
11.30–2.30, 7–11; 12–3, 7–10.30 Sun
Butcombe Bitter; Wadworth IPA, 6X; guest beers Ⓗ
Attractive, three-roomed country pub with extensive views over lake and the Mendips. Popular, particularly at Sun lunchtime.
🏾 🏵 ◑ ▶ ♣ P ✕

Blagdon Hill

Lamb & Flag
On unclassified road, 3 miles S of Taunton OS212181
☎ (01823) 421736
12 (11.30 summer)–2.30, 6.30–11; 12–2.30, 7–10.30 Sun
Boddingtons Bitter; Flowers Original; Otter Bitter; Wadworth 6X Ⓗ
17th-century, friendly country pub with exposed beams, a restaurant, a large garden and a skittle alley. Children welcome. 🏾 Q 🏵 ◑ ▶ ♣ P

Bridgwater

Crowpill Inn
91 Chilton Street
☎ (01278) 422129
11–3, 7–11; 12–3, 7–10.30 Sun
RCH PG Steam; guest beers Ⓗ
Friendly corner local near the former Bridgwater docks. Once a seafarers' haunt, the pub is named after an old local ship. Good choice of guest beers. Families welcome in the skittle alley. 🏾 🟂 🏵 🟂 ♣ ♣

Fountain Inn
1 West Quay (near town bridge) ☎ (01278) 424115
11.30 (11 Fri & Sat)–3, 6.30–11; 12–3, 7–10.30 Sun
Badger Tanglefoot; Butcombe Bitter; Wadworth IPA, 6X; guest beer Ⓗ
One-room, riverside pub, a friendly, town-centre local. The guest beers come from Wadworth's list. Q ← 🚲 ♣

Cannington

Malt Shovel Inn
Blackmoor Lane, Bradley Green (off A39, E of Cannington) ☎ (01278) 653432
11.30–3, 6.30 (7 winter)–11; 12–3, 7–10.30 Sun
Butcombe Bitter; Morland Old Speckled Hen; John Smith's Bitter; guest beer Ⓗ
Family-run free house overlooking the Quantocks, boasting a large garden and a

---

skittle alley. No meals Sun eve in winter.
🏾 Q 🏵 🟂 🟂 ◑ ▶ 🍴 🛒 P

Castle Cary

George Hotel
Market Place
☎ (01963) 350761
10.30–3, 6–11; 12–2.30, 7–10.30 Sun
Butcombe Bitter, Wilmot's Ⓗ
Thatched Grade II-coaching inn (1470) in a handsome old town. Walkers are welcome at this privately-owned hotel with a good reputation for food. 🏾 Q 🟂 ◑ ▶ 🍴 ⇌ P

Chard

Bell & Crown
Combe Street, Crimchard
☎ (01460) 62470
11–2.30, 7–11; 12–3, 7–10.30 Sun
Shepherd Neame Best Bitter; guest beers Ⓗ
Ten mins' walk from the town centre, this popular local still has gas lighting. Good value food (not served Sun/Mon eves). 🏵 ◑ ▶ ♣ P

Chelynch

Poacher's Pocket
1 mile N of A361 at Doulting OS648438
☎ (01749) 880220
11.30 (12 Mon & Tue)–2.30, 6–11; 12–3, 7–10.30 Sun
Butcombe Bitter; Oakhill Bitter; Wadworth 6X; guest beer Ⓗ
Part-14th-century pub in a small village. Although mostly given over to food, it remains popular as a locals' drinking pub. The large garden is well patronised summer weekends.
🏾 Q 🏵 ◑ ▶ ♣ 🛒 P

Chew Magna

Bear & Swan
South Parade
☎ (01275) 332577
12–3, 6–11; 12–11 Sat; 12–3, 7–10.30 Sun (may vary)
Courage Georges BA, Best Bitter; Mole's Tap; guest beer Ⓗ
Friendly, stone-built local with two main bars; deservedly popular for food (book Sun lunch). Live music most Sat eves. No-smoking area Sun–Fri. 🏾 ◑ ▶ 🅰 ♣ P ✕

Pony & Trap
Newtown
☎ (01275) 332627
12–3, 7–11; 12–3, 7–10.30 Sun
Ushers Best Bitter, Founders, seasonal beers Ⓗ
Converted, cosy, multi-roomed cottage displaying old adverts and the pub's original sign.
Q 🟂 🏵 ◑ ▶ 🛒 P

Chew Stoke

Stoke Inn
Old Bristol Road
☎ (01275) 332120
11.30–2.30, 6–11; 11–11 Sat; 12–10.30 Sun
Draught Bass; Butcombe Bitter; Courage Best Bitter; guest beers Ⓗ
Large, stone pub near Chew Valley lake: a lounge bar and 'Stables', popular with diners. It fields several teams for skittles, table skittles, shove-ha'penny, and darts.
🏾 🏾 ◑ ▶ 🛒 ♣ 🛒 P

Chilton Polden

Toby Jug Inn
On A39 ☎ (01278) 722202
12–3, 6–11; 12–3, 7–10.30 Sun
Exmoor Ale; Moor Withy Cutter Ⓗ
Welcoming wayside pub boasting outside floral displays, good value, home-cooked food and monthly jazz sessions. Q 🏵 ◑ ▶ 🛒 🅰 ♣ P

Churchill

Crown Inn
The Batch, Skinners Lane (small lane off A38 S of A368 jct) ☎ (01934) 852995
11–3.30, 5.30–11; 12–10.30 Sun
Draught Bass; Butcombe Bitter; Palmers IPA; RCH PG Steam; guest beers Ⓖ
Characterful old stone free house, with various indoor and outdoor drinking areas, which supports local independent brewers. Cotleigh Harrier is sold as Batch Bitter. It can get busy, especially in summer. Good lunches, but eve meals only by arrangement.
🏾 Q 🏵 ◑ 🅰 P

Clapton-in-Gordano

Black Horse
Clevedon Lane
☎ (01275) 842105
11–3, 6–11; 11–11 Fri & Sat; 12–3, 7–10.30 Sun
Courage Georges BA, Best Bitter; Smiles Best; Wickwar Olde Merryford Ⓖ
Delightful, 14th-century pub. Built at the same time as the village church, it was once used as a lock up. Flagstone floors and wooden beams help make it a popular local. No meals Sun. 🏾 Q 🟂 🏵 ◑ 🛒 P

Compton Martin

Ring O' Bells
Bath Road (A368, W of W Harptree) ☎ (01761) 221284

SOMERSET

11.30–3, 7–11; 12–3, 7–10.30 Sun
**Butcombe Bitter, Wilmot's;
Wadworth 6X; guest beer** H
Welcoming, 200-year-old,
two-bar pub with excellent
food, a superb family room
and a large, safe garden. A pub
for everyone!
🏭 Q ⚞ ⊛ ◑ 𝄞 🍴 🐕 ▲ ♣ P ⚥

Corton Denham

Queens Arms Inn
3 miles S of A303
☎ (01963) 220317
12–2.30, 6.30–11; 11.30–2.30, 6–11 Fri,
Sat & summer; 12–2.30, 7–10.30 Sun
**Archers Best Bitter; Cotleigh
Tawny; guest beers** H
Superb country inn set in a
valley with excellent hillside
walks. Guest ales of the month
are featured on a chalkboard. A
wide choice of freshly
prepared food is served in both
bars. Kingston Golden Rutter
cider.
🏭 Q ⊛ 🛏 ◑ 𝄞 🍴 ⚓ ○ P

Cossington

Red Tile
On A39
☎ (01278) 722333
11–3, 6–11; 12–3, 7–10.30 Sun
**Draught Bass; Butcombe
Bitter; Exmoor Ale; Moor
Withy Cutter** H
Friendly village pub with a
flagstoned public bar, a small,
no-smoking restaurant with
good value food and a pleasant
garden. Families welcome.
🏭 Q ⊛ ◑ 𝄞 ♣ P

Crowcombe

Carew Arms ☆
On A358
☎ (01984) 618631
11–3, 6–11; 12–3, 7–10.30 Sun
**Butcombe Wilmot's; Exmoor
Ale** H
Unspoilt village inn at the base
of the Quantocks: a real gem.
Good quality food and
accommodation. Lanes cider.
🏭 Q ⚞ ⊛ 🛏 ◑ 𝄞 🐕 ▲ ♣ ○
P

Culmhead

Holman Clavel
Top of Blackdown Hills, just
off B3170 OS222162
☎ (01823) 421432
11–3 (not Tue), 7–11; 12–3, 7–10.30
Sun
**Butcombe Bitter, Wilmot's;
Cotleigh Tawny; guest beer** H
Reputedly 14th-century inn
which is haunted by a ghost
named Charlie (a de-frocked
monk). Beamed ceilings and
log fires feature; families
welcome. Good food includes a
traditional Sun lunch (no food
Sun eve). 🏭 ⊛ ◑ 𝄞 ▲ ♣ P

East Harptree

Castle of Comfort
On B3143, ½ mile N of B3135
☎ (01761) 221321
12–2.30, 7–11; 12–2.30, 7–10.30 Sun
**Draught Bass; Butcombe
Bitter; guest beers** H
Stone coaching inn on the old
Roman road. Two bars serve
up to four ales, including wide-
ranging guest beers. Good food
(book Sun lunch). Large
garden play area.
🏭 ⊛ ◑ 𝄞 ♣ P

East Lyng

Rose & Crown
☎ (01823) 698235
11–2.30, 6–11; 12–3, 7–10.30 Sun
**Butcombe Bitter, Wilmot's;
Eldridge Pope Royal Oak** H
Comfortable, civilised village
local serving good food.
Antique furniture, exposed
beams and a large stone
fireplace give the one bar a
timeless feel. A small
restaurant area leads off.
🏭 Q ⊛ 🛏 ◑ 𝄞 ♣ P

East Woodlands

Horse & Groom
1 mile SE of A361/B3092 jct
OS792445 ☎ (01373) 462802
11.30 (12 Mon)–2.30, 6.30–11; 12–3,
7–10.30 Sun
**Bateman XB; Butcombe Bitter;
Wadworth 6X; guest beer** G
17th-century inn on the
western edge of Longleat
estate: a cosy bar with an open
fireplace and flagstone floor,
plus a small dining room. A
new extension has been
completed for a family room.
Seafood is a speciality (no
meals Sun eve or Mon).
🏭 Q ⚞ ⊛ ◑ 𝄞 ♣ P

Evercreech

Bell Inn
Bruton Road (B3081) OS652387
☎ (01749) 830287
11.30–3, 6.30–11; 11.30–11 Sat; 12–3,
7–10.30 Sun
**Butcombe Bitter; Cottage Our
Ken; guest beer** H
17th-century inn with roaring
fires: one bar with a restaurant
area, plus a games room.
🏭 Q ◑ 𝄞 ♣ P

Exford

White Horse
☎ (01643) 831229
11–11; 12–10.30 Sun
**Dartmoor Best Bitter; Eldridge
Pope Royal Oak; Tetley Bitter;
guest beers** (summer) H
Traditional country hotel with
a welcoming public bar,

flagstones and benches, well-
placed for country sports,
including fishing in the
adjacent River Exe. Cider in
summer. 🏭 Q ⊛ 🛏 ◑ 𝄞 🐕 &
▲ ♣ ○ P ⚥

Faulkland

Tuckers Grave Inn ☆
On A366, 1 mile E of village
OS752552
☎ (01373) 834230
11–3, 6–11; 12–3, 7–10.30 Sun
**Draught Bass; Butcombe
Bitter** G
The burial site of a suicide in
1747, a former cottage that has
been an inn for over 200 years.
Three old-fashioned rooms; no
bar counter – the stillage is set
in a small bay window. The
story of the unfortunate
Edward Tucker can be found
above the parlour.
🏭 Q ⚞ ⊛ ▲ ♣ ○ P

Fitzhead

Fitzhead Inn
Off B3187 at Milverton
OS285124
☎ (01823) 400667
12–3, 7–11; 12–3, 7–10.30 Sun
**Cotleigh Tawny; guest
beers** H
Cosy village pub used by
regulars as well as those
attracted by the excellent food
(booking recommended).
Three guest beers, plus
Bollhayes cider.
🏭 Q ⊛ ◑ 𝄞 & ▲ ♣ ○

Fivehead

Crown Inn
Off A378, Taunton–Curry
Rival road
☎ (01460) 281312
12–3, 6.30–11; 12–3, 7–10.30 Sun
**Flowers Original; guest
beers** H
16th-century village pub with
several drinking areas and a
skittle alley. Good value food
(not served Sun eve); four
guest beers.
🏭 ⚞ ⊛ 🛏 ◑ 𝄞 ♣ ○ P

Forches Corner

Merry Harriers
3 miles SE of Wellington
OS183171
☎ (01823) 421270
11–2.30, 6.30–11; 12–3, 7–10.30 Sun;
closed Mon
**Badger Tanglefoot;
Boddingtons Bitter; Exmoor
Gold; Wadworth 6X** H
Isolated, but friendly, old inn
on the Devon border, on top of
the Blackdown Hills. The large
garden has a children's play
area. Live music Fri and Sat.
🏭 ⚞ ⊛ ◑ 𝄞 ♣ P

Frome

Packhorse
13–14 Christchurch Street West
☎ (01373) 467161
11–2.30 (not Mon), 6.30–11 (7–10.30 Mon); 12–2.30, 7–10.30 Sun
Ushers Best Bitter, Founders, seasonal beers ⒣
Friendly town local with a warm, sociable atmosphere.
◑ 🍴 ♣

Hallatrow

Old Station Inn
Wells Road (A39, 400 yds from A37 jct) ☎ (01761) 452228
11–3, 5 (6 Sat)–11; 12–3, 7–10.30 Sun
Draught Bass; Mole's Best Bitter; Oakhill Best Bitter; Otter Ale; guest beer ⒣
Friendly village free house, where bric-a-brac covers every wall and ceiling. It has a railway carriage dining room and good motel-type accommodation. Good food.
🏚 ❀ 🛏 ◑ ▶ ♣ P ⍽

Hardington Moor

Royal Oak
Moor Lane (off A30)
☎ (01935) 862354
12–3 (not Mon), 7–11; 12–3, 7–10.30 Sun
Butcombe Bitter; Hook Norton Old Hooky; guest beers ⒣
Former farmhouse offering a warm, friendly atmosphere and a good choice of snacks and meals (not served Mon). Three ciders are usually available. Skittle alley for functions.
🏚 Q ❀ ◑ ▶ ▲ ♣ ⌂ P

Highbridge

Coopers Arms
Market Street
☎ (01278) 783562
11–3, 5–11 Fri & Sat; 12–3, 7.30–10.30 Sun
Fuller's London Pride; Ringwood Fortyniner; guest beers ⒠
Large pub with two lounges and a bar with a skittle alley. Beers are listed on a blackboard – usually six, including two house ales supplied by big brewers.
❀ 🍴 ▲ ⇌ ♣ P

Hinton Blewitt

Ring of Bells
☎ (01761) 452239
11–3.30, 5 (6 Sat)–11; 12–3.30, 7–10.30 Sun
Wadworth 6X; guest beers ⒣
Small, friendly village local, tucked away behind the parish church. Up to three guest beers. 🏚 ◑ ◑ ♣ ▶ P

Huntspill

Crossways Inn
West Huntspill (A38, S of Highbridge) ☎ (01278) 783756
10.30–3, 5.30–11; 12–3, 7–10.30 Sun
Eldridge Pope Royal Oak; Flowers IPA, Original; guest beers ⒣
Comfortable, 17th-century coaching inn with three frequently changing guest ales, an extensive home-cooked food menu, and a skittle alley. The large bar is cosy thanks to dividing walls. 🏚 Q ⛺ ❀ 🏚 ◑ ▶ ▲ ♣ ⌂ P ⍽

Kelston

Old Crown Inn
Bath Road ☎ (01225) 423032
11.30–2.30 (3 Sat), 5–11; 12–3, 7–10.30 Sun
Draught Bass; Butcombe Bitter; Smiles Best; Wadworth 6X ⒣
Traditional, 18th-century coaching inn with a flagstone floor and cosy drinking areas. Note the original bank of unusual beer engines. Large garden at the rear. Children under 14 are not allowed in. No food Sun; eve meals Thu–Sat (restaurant).
🏚 Q ⛺ ◑ ♣ P

Keynsham

Ship Inn
Temple Street
☎ (0117) 986 9841
11.30–2.30 (3 Fri), 6–11; 11.30–11 Sat; 12–4, 7–10.30 Sun
Draught Bass; Butcombe Bitter; Courage Georges BA, Best Bitter; Smiles Best; Wickwar BOB; guest beer ⒣
Two-bar pub, just off the high street with a large main bar and a recently refurbished and extended lounge. Other Wickwar beers may replace BOB. Pleasant garden. The car park is very small and street parking is awkward. Eve meals Thu–Sat. ❀ ◑ ⇌ ♣ P

Knapp

Rising Sun Inn
Off A358 to Langport, left towards N Curry OS301254
☎ (01823) 490436
11.30–2.30, 6.30–11; 12–3, 7–10.30 Sun
Draught Bass; Boddingtons Bitter; Exmoor Ale ⒣
15th-century inn: a fine example of a Somerset longhouse with many original features, including two inglenooks. Winner of many national awards for its extensive fish menu, it has a busy weekend food trade. Local farm cider in summer.
🏚 Q ⛺ ❀ 🏚 ◑ ▶ ▲ ⌂ P

Langport

Black Swan
North Street ☎ (01458) 250355
11–3, 6–11; 12–4, 7–10.30 Sun
Smiles Golden Brew; Wadworth 6X; guest beers ⒣
Attractive, 19th-century converted coaching inn, popular with locals. It stages various annual events including a sponsored bike ride. Bingo Sun eve. Freshly home-cooked food in the restaurant. ⛺ ❀ ◑ ▶ ▲ P

Leigh upon Mendip

Bell
High Street OS692473
☎ (01373) 812316
12–3, 7–11; 12–3, 7–10.30 Sun
Draught Bass; Butcombe Bitter; Wadworth IPA, 6X ⒣
Much altered and extended village inn, now comfortably furnished, with an emphasis on the food trade – it has a restaurant but food is served throughout the pub. Friendly, local atmosphere at the bar.
❀ ◑ ♣ P

Luxborough

Royal Oak
☎ (01984) 640319
11–3, 6–11; 12–2.30, 7–10.30 Sun
Cotleigh Tawny; Exmoor Gold; Flowers IPA ⒣; **guest beers** ⒢
Unspoilt rural pub at the heart of the Brendon Hills (superb walks): flagstone floors, open log fires, beamed ceilings and noted, home-cooked food are features. Guest beers come mainly from local brewers. Folk club Fri. Rich's and Cheddar Valley cider. Good B&B.
🏚 Q ⛺ ❀ 🏚 ◑ ▲ ♣ ⌂ P

Middlezoy

George Inn
42 Main Road
☎ (01823) 698215
12–3 (not Mon or Tue), 7–11; 12–3, 7–10.30 Sun
Butcombe Bitter; Courage Best Bitter; guest beers ⒣
Thriving village pub, now owned by a local couple. Old beams and a flagged floor enhance the main bar. There is also a dining room and a large skittle alley with a bar. Good value food (not served Sun eve). Lanes cider in summer.
🏚 ⛺ ❀ 🏚 ◑ ▶ 🍴 ▲ ♣ ⌂ P

Milborne Port

Queen's Head
High Street (A30)
☎ (01963) 250314
11–11; 12–10.30 Sun
Butcombe Bitter; Flowers IPA, Original; Ringwood Fortyniner; guest beers H
Busy, multi-room village pub with a restaurant and a skittle alley/function room, plus a pleasant all-weather courtyard drinking area and a garden. Good food (especially the curries). A mystery beer is featured each week.
Q ☎ ✿ ⊨ ◑ ▶ ⊞ ♣ ⌒ P ✄

Moorlinch

Ring O' Bells
Pit Hill Lane ☎ (01458) 210358
12–3 (not Mon), 7–11; 12–3, 7–10.30 Sun
Draught Bass; guest beers H
Traditional village local with a welcoming atmosphere, near Moorlinch Vineyard: a friendly lounge and a lively bar with games. Three guest beers, mostly from local micros, plus Wilkins cider.
▲ Q ✿ ◑ ▶ ♣ ⌒ P

Nailsea

Blue Flame
West End (2 miles from Nailsea) OS449690
☎ (01275) 856910
12–3.30 (4.30 Sat), 6–11; 12–4.30, 7–10.30 Sun
Draught Bass H; **Smiles Best, Heritage** G; **guest beers** H/G
Well worth seeking out, this excellent, 19th-century pub has a large garden and a small public bar drawing a mixed clientele. Usually two guest beers are sold, dispensed from casks behind the bar.
▲ Q ☎ ✿ ▲ ♣ ⌒ P

Nether Stowey

Rose & Crown
St Mary Street
☎ (01278) 732265
12–11; 12–4, 7–10.30 Sun
Cotleigh Barn Owl; Moor Withy Cutter; Oakhill Mendip Gold H
16th-century coaching inn at the village centre: a popular, multi-roomed pub with a public bar and a strong local following. Good food; Lanes cider. Q ✿ ⊨ ◑ ▶ ♣ ⌒

Nettlebridge

Nettlebridge Inn
On A367, 1 mile N of Oakhill
☎ (01749) 841360
11.30–2.30, 5–11; 12–11 Sat; 12–10.30 Sun

Oakhill Best Bitter, Black Magic, Mendip Gold, Yeoman; guest beer H
Big roadside pub in a pretty valley on the edge of the Mendips. Priority is given to diners in the large main bar; snacks only in the smaller Bridges Bar which has been given a sophisticated city pub decor. ✿ ⊨ ◑ ▶ ⊞ P

North Brewham

Old Red Lion
On Maiden Bradley–Bruton road OS722368
☎ (01749) 850287
11–3, 6–11; 12–3, 7–10.30 Sun
Butcombe Bitter; guest beer H
Stone built former farmhouse in an isolated rural setting. The bar is an old dairy with flagged floors. Two regular guest beers, one usually a mild in summer.
▲ Q ✿ ⊨ ◑ ▶ ▲ ♣ ⌒ P

North Curry

Bird in Hand
Queen Square
☎ (01823) 490248
12–3, 7–11; 12–3, 7–10.30 Sun
Badger Tanglefoot; Butcombe Bitter; Otter Ale; guest beers H
Superbly renovated village local with low beams and ever-changing guest ales. The pub runs many special eves and produces a 'What's On' newsletter for the village. Good quality food. Rich's Farmhouse cider.
▲ Q ☎ ✿ ◑ ▶ ♿ ▲ ♣ ⌒

Norton St Philip

Fleur de Lys
High Street (B3110)
☎ (01373) 834333
11–3, 5–11; 11–11 Sat; 12–3, 7–10.30 Sun
Draught Bass; Oakhill Best Bitter; Wadworth 6X; Worthington Bitter H
Ancient stone building, partly dating from the 13th century, enjoying recent extensive, but mainly sympathetic, refurbishment. Unfortunately, the re-sited bar now blocks the old passageway through which the pub ghost was said to pass on his way to the gallows.
▲ Q ☎ ◑ ▶ ♣ P

Pitminster

Queen's Arms
3 miles S of Taunton, off B3170 at Corfe OS220191
☎ (01823) 421529
11–3, 5–11; 12–3, 7–10.30 Sun
Boddingtons Bitter; Cotleigh Tawny; Exmoor Gold; Juwards Premium; guest beers H

Cosy, popular village pub; the main bar is divided by a black iron, wood-burning stove. Usually six beers are sold, mainly from small local brewers. Interesting bar meals, plus an excellent no-smoking restaurant. Cider in summer.
▲ Q ✿ ⊨ ◑ ▶ P

Pitney

Halfway House
On main road
☎ (01458) 252513
11.30–2.30, 5.30–11; 12–3, 7–10.30 Sun
Berrow Topsy Turvy; Butcombe Bitter; Cotleigh Tawny; Oakhill Best Bitter; Teignworthy Reel Ale; guest beers G
Old village pub featuring flagstone floors and rudimentary wooden furniture. It always stocks six–nine beers, mostly from South-West micros. Try the superb home-cooked curries (no food Sun). CAMRA national *Pub of the Year* 1996, and Somerset *Pub of the Year* 1997. ▲ Q ☎ ✿ ◑ ▶ ▲ ♣

Porlock

Ship Inn
High Street (foot of Porlock Hill, A39) ☎ (01643) 862507
10.30–3.30, 5.30–11; 12–3.30, 6.30–10.30 Sun
Draught Bass; Cotleigh Barn Owl (summer)**; Old Buzzard; Courage Best Bitter; guest beer** (summer) H
13th-century thatched inn mentioned in *Lorna Doone*, within walking distance of both sea and moor: an historic old bar with a stone floor, plus a modern games room. A pub for conversation. ▲ Q ☎ ✿ ⊨ ◑ ▶ ▲ ♣ ⌒ P ⊟

Redhill

Bungalow Inn
Winford Lane (½ mile off A38) OS513640 ☎ (01275) 472386
12–3 (4 Sat), 7–11 (12–11 Fri & Sat in summer); 12–4, 7–10.30 (12–10.30 summer) Sun
Draught Bass E; **Wadworth IPA, 6X; guest beer** H
Pub with two cosy bars, and a well-equipped children's room; handy for Bristol Airport. 'Sing-alongs' Wed; live music Sat eve. No food Sun–Thu eves in winter.
▲ ☎ ✿ ◑ ▶ ▲ ♣ P

Rowberrow

Swan Inn
Signed off A38, S of Churchill
☎ (01934) 852371
12–3, 6–11; 12–3, 7–10.30 Sun

Draught Bass; Butcombe Bitter, Wilmot's; Wadworth 6X H
Butcombe-owned house, converted from three stone cottages: two bars with fake beams, one with a large fireplace. Good food trade, but no meals Sun eve.
🏚 Q ❀ ◁ ▶ P

Rudge

Full Moon
1 mile N of A36 bypass at Standerwick OS829518
☎ (01373) 830936
12–3, 6–11; 12–3, 7–10.30 Sun
Draught Bass; Butcombe Bitter; Wadworth 6X H
Splendid, 300-year-old building, greatly extended in 1991 but retaining most of the original features, including stone floors. The emphasis is on the food trade, the skittle alley, families and accommodation. No meals Sun eve. 🏚 Q ❀ 🛏 ◁ ▶ ⊟ ఉ ▲ ♣ ◔ P ⊟

St Georges

Woolpack Inn
Shepherds Way (off M5 jct 21)
☎ (01934) 521670
12–2.30 (3 Sat), 6–11; 12–3, 7–10.30 Sun
Courage Best Bitter; guest beers H
Warm, friendly, former 17th-century coaching house and wool-packing station, well patronised by locals. Two bars and a restaurant serve good quality food. The skittle alley doubles as a function room. Three guest beers. 🏚 ☺ ❀ ◁ ▶ ⊟ ▲ 🚆 (Worle) ♣ P

Saltford

Bird in Hand
High Street ☎ (01225) 873335
11–3, 6.30 (6 Fri & Sat)–11; 12–3 or 4, 7–10.30 Sun
Draught Bass; Courage Best Bitter; guest beers H
Food-oriented pub with access from the Bristol–Bath cycle track. The no-smoking conservatory for diners offers good views over the Avon Valley and an excellent value, extensive menu. Children allowed in a small raised area at one end of the U-shaped bar.
Q ❀ ◁ ▶ ♣ ◔

Seavington St Michael

Volunteer
On old A303 ☎ (01460) 240126
12–2.30 (not Mon), 5.30–11; 12–11 Sat; 12–3, 7–10.30 Sun
Badger Dorset Best; Cottage S&D; guest beers H

Friendly, family-run, roadside pub with two bars. The lounge has low beams and a central fireplace. Good food includes Sun lunch and Fri eve curries (no food Sun/Mon eves).
🏚 Q ◁ ▶ ⊟ ▲ ♣ P ⊟

Shepton Montague

Montague Inn
Off A359 ☎ (01749) 813213
12–2 (2.30 Sat; not Mon), 6–11; 12–3, 7–10.30 Sun
Butcombe Bitter; Greene King IPA; Moor Withy Cutter G
Delightful pub in a rural setting. Meals served Tue–Sat. It also stocks a house beer.
🏚 Q ❀ 🛏 ◁ ▶ ♣ ◔ P

Shoscombe

Apple Tree
1 mile S of A367 at Peasedown OS712565 ☎ (01761) 432263
7–11; 12–3, 7–11 Sat; 12–3, 7–10.30 Sun
Draught Bass; Oakhill Best Bitter; Otter Bitter; guest beer G
Friendly village local nestling in a hidden valley, worth seeking out for the welcome. Sun lunch served; eve meals on request. 🏚 ❀ ▲ ♣ ◔ P

South Petherton

Brewers Arms
18 St James Street
☎ (01460) 241887
11.30–2.30, 6–11; 12–3, 7–10.30 Sun
Oakhill Best Bitter; Worthington Bitter; guest beers H
17th-century coaching inn run by two brothers: a single-bar pub, popular with a wide cross-section of customers. Pleasant rear courtyard; skittle alley. Good value, extensive home-cooked food menu.
🏚 ❀ ◁ ▶ ▲ ♣ ◔

Sparkford

Sparkford Inn
Off A303 ☎ (01963) 440218
11–2.30, 6.30–11; 12–3, 7–10.30 Sun
Draught Bass; Worthington Bitter; guest beers H
15th-century coaching inn retaining many original features, including several rooms and corridors. Catering for all the family, it has indoor and outdoor children's play areas. Inch's cider in summer. Regular music eves. 🏚 Q ☺ ❀ 🛏 ◁ ▶ ⊟ ఉ ▲ ♣ ◔ P ⊬

Stogumber

White Horse Inn
The Square ☎ (01984) 656277
11–2.30, 6–11; 12–2.30, 6–10.30 Sun
Cotleigh Tawny; Otter Bitter; guest beers H

Traditional local opposite the 12th-century church, serving excellent value, good, wholesome country cooking in the bar and restaurant. Lanes cider is sold in summer. Handy for the West Somerset Railway.
🏚 ❀ 🛏 ◁ ▶ ⊟ ◔ P

Taunton

Hankridge Arms
Hankridge Way, Riverside (business/shopping park, off M5 jct 25)
☎ (01823) 444405
11–11; 12–10.30 Sun
Badger Dorset Best, Tanglefoot H
Converted 16th-century farmhouse which has won commendation for architectural conservation. The house beer is brewed by Badger. Quiet bar; pleasant surroundings. Wide range of meals in both the bar and the restaurant.
🏚 Q ◁ ▶ ఉ P

Masons Arms
Magdalene Street (from centre follow Hammett St for 500 yds)
☎ (01823) 288916
11.30 (10.30 Sat)–3, 5 (6 Sat)–11; 12–3, 7–10.30 Sun
Exe Valley Bitter; Ind Coope Burton Ale; guest beers H
Comfortable, one-bar pub with a relaxing atmosphere, away from the main streets. Fresh food is always available, including grillstone steaks. Self-catering flat to let.
Q 🛏 ◁ ▶ 🚆

Wood Street Inn
Wood Street
☎ (01823) 333011
11–11; 12–10.30 Sun
Juwards Premium; guest beers H
Friendly, backstreet pub serving three, usually locally produced, beers. Large public car park opposite. Reasonably priced accommodation.
❀ 🛏 ఉ 🚆 ♣ ⊟

Try also: **Minstrels**, Castle Green (Free)

Trudoxhill

White Hart
1 mile S of A361 at Nunney Catch OS749438
☎ (01373) 836324
12–3, 7 (6.30 Fri & Sat)–11; 12–3, 7–10.30 Sun
Ash Vine Bitter, Challenger, Hop & Glory; Courage Directors H
Comfortable, food-oriented, open-plan village pub with exposed beams and a large fireplace. Ash Vine brewery is situated at the rear.
🏚 ❀ ◁ ▶ ◔ P

Waterrow

Rock Inn
On B3227 ☎ (01984) 623293
11–3, 6–11; 12–3, 7–10.30 Sun
Cotleigh Tawny; Exmoor Gold; John Smith's Bitter Ⓗ
Interesting old inn set against a rockface, which forms the rear wall of part of the bar area (public style at one end with a lounge and restaurant at the other). Inch's cider served.
🏨 Q 🛏 ◖▶ ▲ ♣ ⌂ P

Wellington

Cottage Inn
31 Champford Lane
☎ (01823) 664650
11–3, 6–11; 12–3, 7–10.30 Sun
Juwards Bitter; John Smith's Bitter; guest beers Ⓗ
Friendly local, a short walk from the town centre and handy for the cinema. A wide range of games are played; Sun night quiz. Usually three guest beers on, mainly from local independent breweries. Good value basic bar lunches, Mon–Sat. ❀ ◖▶ ♣ P

Try also: Ship Inn, Mantle St (Gibbs Mew)

Wellow

Fox & Badger
Railway Lane (2 miles W of B3110 at Hinton Charterhouse)
☎ (01225) 832293
11–3, 6–11; 11–11 Fri & Sat; 12–10.30 Sun
Draught Bass; Butcombe Bitter; Wadworth 6X; guest beer Ⓗ
Pretty Wellow's only pub, a two-bar local where, unusually, the public bar is carpeted and the lounge bar is flagstoned. It can be difficult to park. 🏨 ❀ ◖▶ 🍽 ♣ ⌂

Wells

Britannia Inn
Bath Road (B3139)
☎ (01749) 672033
11–2.30, 5–11; 11–11 Sat; 12–3, 7–10.30 Sun
Butcombe Bitter; Courage Best Bitter; Ushers Best Bitter; guest beer Ⓗ
Comfortable, two-bar local serving housing estates at the north end of the city. Eve meals Fri–Sun.
❀ ◖▶ 🍽 ⅋ ♣ ⌂ P

Weston-super-Mare

Dragon Inn
15 Meadow Street
☎ (01934) 621304
11–11; 12–10.30 Sun
Butcombe Bitter; Courage Directors; Theakston Best Bitter; Younger Scotch; guest beer Ⓗ
Wetherspoons conversion, opened in 1996, a most welcome addition in a notorious beer desert. Not as big as most of the chain but still spacious, with a good-sized no-smoking area and proper wheelchair facilities. It can get very busy.
Q ❀ ◖▶ ♿ ⇌ ⌂ ⅋

Williton

Foresters Arms
55 Long Street (A39)
☎ (01984) 632508
11–11; 12–3, 7–10.30 Sun
Cotleigh Tawny; Exmoor Gold; Theakston Best Bitter; guest beers Ⓗ
17th-century coaching inn near the West Somerset Railway station; an ideal base for walking the Quantocks. Reputed to be haunted by the ghost of a girl from the

neighbouring old workhouse. Usually up to six ales available, plus Rich's cider. 🏨 🐎 ❀ 🛏 ◖ ▶ ♿ ⇌ (WSR) ♣ ⌂ P

Witham Friary

Seymour Arms ☆
On minor road off B3092, by old station OS745410
☎ (01749) 850742
11–3, 6–11; 12–3, 7–10.30 Sun
Ushers Best Bitter Ⓗ
Old village local unspoilt by progress, with a central serving hatch and a fine garden. Rich's cider on gravity.
🏨 Q ❀ 🍽 ▲ ♣ ⌂

Wiveliscombe

Bear Inn
10 North Street
☎ (01984) 623537
11–3, 5–11; 11–11 Fri, Sat & summer; 12–10.30 Sun
Cotleigh Barn Owl; Exmoor Gold; guest beers Ⓗ
Former 17th-century coaching inn, near the town centre: a friendly bar and a dining room serving good, home-cooked food. It organises beer-lovers' weekends in conjunction with local breweries. Local farm cider in summer. Skittles, darts and quizzes feature.
🏨 🐎 ❀ 🛏 ◖▶ ♣ ⌂ P

Yeovil

Armoury
1 The Park ☎ (01935) 71047
12–2.30, 6 (6.30 Mon & Tue)–11; 11–11 Fri & Sat; 12–3, 7–10.30 Sun
Adnams Broadside; Butcombe Bitter; Wadworth 6X; guest beers Ⓗ
Lively, simply-furnished town pub, formerly an armoury. Snacks and salads available lunchtimes (not Sun). Live bands play alternate Sat eves.
Q ❀ ♿ ♣ ⌂ P

THE REAL ALTERNATIVE

Companion to the *Good Beer Guide*, *The CAMRA Guide to Real Cider*, has been a huge success. This invaluable book for lovers of traditional scrumpy has been snapped up by drinkers in well-known cider areas like Somerset, but has also captured the imagination of cider fans across the country. Compiled by Ted Bruning, editor of *Cider Press*, the quarterly cider supplement to CAMRA's national newspaper, *What's Brewing*, it lists more than 2,000 pubs where real cider – and, occasionally, its sister drink, real perry – can be found. It also features a directory of the country's cidermakers and the ciders they produce. Copies are available from all good bookshops, or direct (and post-free) at £7.99 from CAMRA, 230 Hatfield Road, St Albans, Hertfordshire AL1 4LW.

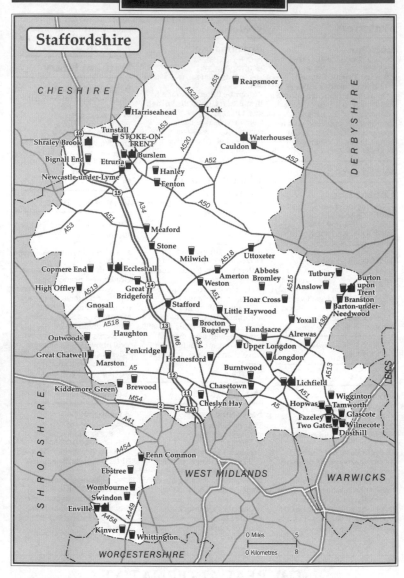

Staffordshire

Abbots Bromley

Bagot Arms

Bagot Street ☎ (01283) 840371
11–2.30, 5.30–11; 12–3, 7–10.30 Sun
Marston's Pedigree, HBC Ⓗ
18th-century coaching inn,
specialising in good food, close
to Blithfield Reservoir.
Q ✿ ◑ ▶ ♣ P

Alrewas

Crown

7 Post Office Road
☎ (01283) 790328
11–3, 5–11; 12–3, 7–10.30 Sun
**Draught Bass; Marston's
Pedigree; guest beer** Ⓗ
Traditional, 500-year-old
village local with log fires, 300
yards from the Trent & Mersey
Canal: a public bar and lounge
with an adjacent snug. Good
value bar meals. Tapster's
Choice guest beer.
🏠 Q ☎ ❀ ◑ ▶ 🍴 ♣ P

Try also: George & Dragon,
Main St (Marston's)

🍺 INDEPENDENT BREWERIES

Burton Bridge: Burton upon Trent	**Marston's:** Burton upon Trent
Eccleshall: Eccleshall	**Rising Sun:** Shraley Brook
Enville: Enville	**Stony Rock:** Waterhouses
Lichfield: Lichfield	**Titanic:** Burslem

Amerton

Plough
On A518 ☎ (01889) 270308
11–3, 6–11 (11–11 summer); 12–10.30
Sun
**Marston's Bitter, Pedigree;
Morland Old Speckled Hen;
guest beer** H
Agreeable country inn
opposite Amerton working
farm, craft and garden centre.
All meals are served in the
dining room. The large garden
has a children's play area.
🚪 🛏 🏠 ◑ ▶ 🍴 Å ♣ P

Anslow

Bell Inn
Main Road OS212252
☎ (01283) 812101
11–11; 12–4, 7–10.30 Sun
**Marston's Pedigree, Owd
Rodger, HBC** H
Two-roomed, friendly, village
inn, displaying local
photographs in the lounge.
Reasonably priced meals.
🚪 🏠 ◑ ▶ 🍴 ♿ ♣ P

Barton-under-Needwood

Shoulder of Mutton
16 Main Street
☎ (01283) 712568
11–3, 5–11; 11–11 Fri & Sat; 12–10.30
Sun
**Draught Bass; Worthington
Bitter; guest beer** H
Quiet village local in the midst
of a small community, just off
the village green.
Accommodation and
wheelchair access planned.
🚪 Q 🏠 ◑ ▶ Å P

Branston

Bridge Inn
Tatenhill Lane (off A38 island,
by canal bridge)
☎ (01283) 564177
11–11; 12–10.30 Sun
Marston's Pedigree, HBC G
Snug, canalside inn with a
single bar, popular with locals
and bargees. The beer is served
by gravity from the adjacent
cellar (the handpump on the
bar is ornamental). Excellent
food, including home-made
dishes; eve main meals contain
at least 12 different vegetables!
🚪 🏠 ◑ ▶ ♣ P

Brewood

Swan
15 Market Square
☎ (01902) 850330
12–2.30 (3 Sat), 7–11; 12–3, 7–10.30 Sun
**Draught Bass; Mansfield
Riding Bitter; Theakston XB;
guest beer** H

Comfortable village pub with
low-beamed ceilings and two
cosy snugs, offering a good
range of beers. Skittle alley at
the back. 🚪 ◑ ♣ P

Brocton

Chetwynd Arms
Cannock Road (A34)
☎ (01785) 661087
11.30–3, 5.45–11; 11–11 Sat; 12–10.30
Sun
Banks's Mild, Bitter E;
**Camerons Strongarm;
Marston's Pedigree** H
Bustling main road pub at the
north-western boundary of
Cannock Chase, with a
genuine, unspoilt bar. The
garden has a children's play
area. No food Sat eve.
🏠 ◑ ▶ 🍴 ♿ ♣ P

Burntwood

Drill
Springle Styche Lane
☎ (01543) 674092
12–11; 12–10.30 Sun
**Everards Tiger; Tetley Bitter;
guest beers** H
Comfortable, friendly pub and
restaurant in a rural setting.
🏠 ◑ ▶ ♣ P

Burton upon Trent

Bass Museum - Burton Bar
Horninglow Street
☎ (01283) 511000 ext 3504
11–7 (5 Sat); 12–5 Sun
**Draught Bass; Museum No. 6
Mild, Offilers Bitter, P2, 'E';
guest beers** H
Comfortable bar within the
Bass Museum of Brewing,
selling beers from the
Museum's own microbrewery
(the oldest in England).
Regular displays of shire
horses, steam engines, etc. Free
entry for CAMRA members –
show current membership
card. 🛏 🏠 ◑ ♿ ♣ P

Boat House
The Dingle, Stapenhill (off
Ferry St) ☎ (01283) 538831
12–3 (not Mon or Tue), 7–11; 12–3,
7–10.30 Sun
**Draught Bass; Greene King
Abbot; Marston's Pedigree;
Morland Old Speckled Hen;
Taylor Landlord; Theakston
Old Peculier** H
Set on a bank of the Trent,
beside the ferry bridge, this
pub features a garden play
area for children, and an
upstairs restaurant. Live jazz
Thu eve. Q 🏠 ◑ ▶ P

Burton Bridge Inn
24 Bridge Street (A50, by Trent
bridge) ☎ (01283) 536596
11.30–2.15, 5.30–11; 12–2, 7–10.30 Sun

**Burton Bridge XL, Bridge
Bitter, Porter, Festival Ale,
Old Expensive, seasonal
beers** H
Welcoming brewery tap with
wooden pews and award-
covered walls. It stocks an
excellent range of whiskies and
country wines and hosts an
Easter beer festival. Skittle
alley. Q 🏠 ◑ ♣

Coopers Tavern
43 Cross Street (off Station St)
☎ (01283) 532551
12–2.30, 5 (7 Sat)–11; 12–3, 7–10.30
Sun
**Draught Bass; Hardys &
Hansons Best Mild** G, **Best
Bitter** H, **Classic, seasonal
beers** G; **Marston's
Pedigree** H
Truly traditional alehouse with
a renowned tap room; note the
stillaged casks (cooled in
summer) and 'top bench' seat.
Simple, good value food (not
served Sun). Friendly
welcome, including for coach
parties. 🚪 Q ◑ 🚲

Derby Inn
17 Derby Road
☎ (01283) 564460
11–3, 5.30–11; 10.30–3, 4–11 Sat; 12–3,
7–10.30 Sun
Marston's Pedigree H
Small, down-to-earth local: a
bustling and a cosy lounge
serving arguably the best
Pedigree in Marston's home
town. Read the newspaper
cuttings decorating the bar
front and buy local vegetables!
🍴 ♣ P

Roebuck
Station Street ☎ (01283) 568660
11–11; 11–3, 6–11 Sat; 12–3, 7–10.30
Sun
**Ansells Bitter; Greene King
Abbot; Ind Coope Burton Ale;
Marston's Pedigree; Morland
Old Speckled Hen; Tetley
Bitter** H
Pub opposite the brewery,
known locally as 'Ale House',
selling a good selection of
Carlsberg-Tetley and Tapster's
Choice beers. A very well-
presented pub.
🏠 🛏 ◑ ▶ 🚲 ♣ ⌂

Thomas Sykes
Anglesey Road (off Moor St)
☎ (01283) 510246
11.30–3, 5 (7 Sat)–11; 11.30–11 Fri;
12–3, 7–10.30 Sun
**Draught Bass; Marston's
Pedigree** H, **Owd Rodger** G;
guest beers H
Classic simple alehouse
formed from stables and sheds
of a former brewery. Stone
floors and breweriana support
a friendly atmosphere.
Q 🛏 🏠 ♣ P

Try also: Alfred, Derby St
(Burton Bridge)

Cauldon

Yew Tree
Off A52/A53 ☎ (01538) 308348
11–3, 6–11; 12–3, 7–10.30 Sun
Draught Bass; Burton Bridge Bridge Bitter; M&B Mild [H]
17th-century inn of great character, amongst the finest in the country. Objects of a bygone age abound including working polyphons, pianolas and grandfather clocks. Snacks available at most times. Family area. A visit is a must; no expensive drinks sold.
Q ❀ ♿ ▲ ♣ P

Chasetown

Uxbridge Arms
2 Church Street
☎ (01543) 674853
12–3, 6–11; 12–11 Sat; 12–10.30 Sun
Draught Bass; Highgate Dark; Worthington Bitter; guest beers [H]
Popular, comfortable local, dating from the 1830s. The two guest beers change regularly and are usually from smaller breweries. ❀ ◑ ◗ ⊞ ♣ P

Cheslyn Hay

Woodman Inn
Littlewood Lane (off A34)
☎ (01922) 413686
12–3, 6.30–11; 11–11 Sat; 12.30–3.30, 7–10.30 Sun
Marston's Pedigree; Theakston Best Bitter, XB; guest beers [H]
Welcoming village pub and restaurant, offering a relaxed atmosphere in comfortable surroundings.
ᵹ ❀ ◑ ◗ ⊞ ♿ ⇌ (Landywood) ♣ P ⊁

Copmere End

Star
1½ miles W of Eccleshall OS803294 ☎ (01785) 850279
12–3, 6–11; 12–11 Sat; 12–3, 7–10.30 Sun
Draught Bass; Boddingtons Bitter; Marston's Pedigree; guest beer (occasional) [H]
Cosy, traditional country pub, popular with walkers and a meeting place for a cycling club. Occasionally auctions are held for summer produce. Situated opposite Cop Mere pool.
♨ Q ᵹ ❀ ◑ ◗ ⊞ ▲ ♣ P

Dosthill

Fox
105 High Street (A51)
☎ (01827) 280847
12–3, 5–11; 12–3, 7–10.30 Sun
Ansells Mild; Tetley Bitter; guest beers [H]
Welcoming local serving an excellent selection of regularly changing guest beers from a wide range of breweries – typically up to six guests on sale. Good selection of food (not served during Sun eve quiz).
♨ Q ❀ ◑ ◗ ⊞ ♣ P

Ebstree

Hollybush Inn
OS854959
☎ (01902) 895587
11.30–3, 6–11; 12–3, 7–10.30 Sun
Ansells Bitter; Ind Coope Burton Ale; Tetley Bitter; guest beers [H]
Pleasant country inn, half a mile west of the Staffs & Worcs Canal: a large lounge area (children allowed), plus a more traditional public bar with pub games and a piano. No food served Sun.
♨ ❀ ◑ ◗ ♣ P

Eccleshall

George Hotel
Castle Street
☎ (01785) 850300
11–11; 12–10.30 Sun
Eccleshall Slaters Bitter, Original, Premium, Supreme, seasonal beers; guest beers [H]
Originally a coaching inn, this town-centre hotel now has ten luxurious bedrooms and a bistro. Eccleshall's first brewery for over a century opened behind the hotel in 1995. Eight cask beers usually on sale. Midnight supper licence.
♨ ᵹ ❀ ⛺ ◑ ◗ ▲ P

Enville

Cat Inn
Bridgnorth Road (A458)
☎ (01384) 872209
12–3 (may close earlier), 7–11; closed Sun
Enville Ale, seasonal beers; Theakston XB; guest beers [H]
Four-roomed, part-16th-century inn, popular with walkers on the Staffordshire Way.
♨ Q ❀ ◑ ◗ ⊞ ♿ ♣ P

Fazeley

Three Horseshoes
New Street (off A4091)
☎ (01827) 289754
12–3, 7–11; 12–3, 7–10.30 Sun
Draught Bass; M&B Brew XI [E]**; Marston's Pedigree** [H]
Small, cosy, traditional pub, popular with locals: an old coaching inn near Drayton Manor Park and the junction of the Birmingham/Fazeley and Coventry Canals. No food Sun.
ᵹ ❀ ◑ ♣

Glascote

Dolphin Inn
New Street ☎ (01827) 64386
12–3, 5.30–11; 12–11 Fri & Sat; 12–10.30 Sun
Draught Bass [H]
Three-roomed roadside pub with a small snug. ⊞ ♣

Gnosall

Navigation
Newport Road (A518, by Bridge 35 of Shropshire Union Canal) ☎ (01785) 822327
12–3, 6–11; 12–3, 7–10.30 Sun
Vaux Samson; Ward's Best Bitter [H]
Large canalside pub with a restaurant, garden and a children's play area. A third cask beer is available in summer. No lunches winter Mon or Tue.
❀ ◑ ◗ ⊞ ♿ ▲ ♣ P

Great Bridgeford

Mill at Worston
1 mile off A5013 OS878278
☎ (01785) 282170
12–3, 5.30–11; 11–11 Sat & summer; 12–10.30 Sun
Marston's Bitter, Pedigree, HBC [H]
Renovated mill set in extensive gardens around a lake. A family pub, it has a large restaurant, a well laid-out children's play area and a Billy Bear's indoor fun fair; also a working water wheel (tours of the mill museum often available on request).
ᵹ ❀ ◑ ◗ ♿ ▲ P

Great Chatwell

Red Lion
2 miles E of A41, near Newport OS792143 ☎ (01952) 691366
6 (12 Sat)–11; 12–10.30 Sun
Draught Bass; Everards Tiger; Worthington Bitter; guest beers [H]
Friendly, family-run country pub with a range of guest beers. Excellent children's play area in the garden. Good value food in the bar and restaurant.
♨ ᵹ ❀ ◑ ◗ ⊞ ▲ ♣ P ⊓

Handsacre

Crown Inn
24 The Green (A513, by canal)
☎ (01543) 490239
12–3, 6–11; 12–3, 7–10.30 Sun
Draught Bass; Worthington Bitter [H]
Characterful, canalside, two-roomed local, incorporating a games room where children are welcome.
Q ᵹ ❀ ◑ ⊞ ♣ P

Haughton

Bell
Newport Road (A518)
☎ (01785) 780301
11.30–3, 6–11; 12–3.30, 7–10.30 Sun
Banks's Mild; Marston's Bitter, Pedigree; guest beer H
Homely village free house with an L-shaped room split into two distinct bar areas. Collections of book matches, jugs and foreign currency notes are displayed. 🏠 🌸 ◁ ▷ ♣ P

Hednesford

Queen's Arms
37 Hill Street
☎ (01543) 878437
12–4, 6.30–11; 12–11 Sat; 12–3, 7–10.30 Sun
Draught Bass; Highgate Dark E
Two-roomed local with a welcoming atmosphere.
Q ◁ ⊕ ♣ P

High Offley

Anchor ☆
Old Lea (by Bridge 42 of Shropshire Union Canal) OS775256
☎ (01785) 284569
12–3, 6 (7 winter Sat)–11 (closed Mon–Fri in winter); 12–3, 7–10.30 (closed winter eve) Sun
Wadworth 6X H/G
Once called the Sebastopol Inn, this classic, basic, two-bar canalside pub is not easily found by road. Behind the pub is a gift shop for canalware. A second cask beer is usually available in summer.
🏠 Q 🌸 ⊕ ▲ ♣ ▷ P

Hoar Cross

Meynell Ingram Arms
1 mile W of A515 at Newchurch OS133234
☎ (01283) 575202
12–3, 6–11; 12–11 Sat; 12–5, 7–10.30 Sun
Marston's Pedigree; guest beers H
16th-century former estate pub in a small village: two unspoilt bars and a restaurant (no food Sun eve). 🏠 Q 🌸 ◁ ▷ ♣ P

Hopwas

Red Lion
Lichfield Road (2 miles N of Tamworth)
☎ (01827) 62514
11.30–2.30 (3 Sat), 6–11 (11.30–11 summer Sat); 12–3, 7–10.30 Sun
Ansells Bitter; guest beers H
Friendly, canalside pub with a large waterside garden. Beware of the hump-backed bridge. 🌸 ◁ ▷ P

Kiddemore Green

New Inns
Between Brewood and Bishops Wood OS858089
☎ (01902) 850614
12–3 (not winter Mon–Wed), 6–11; 12–3, 7–10.30 Sun
Burtonwood Mild, Bitter, Forshaw's, Buccaneer H
Small, cosy country inn with a comfortable, L-shaped lounge and two real fires in winter.
🏠 🌸 ◁ P

Kinver

Plough & Harrow
High Street ☎ (01384) 872659
7–11;12–4.30, 7–11 Sat; 12–4.30, 7–10.30 Sun
Batham Mild, Best Bitter, XXX H
Popular pub known locally as 'the Steps' – its rooms are on different levels. Film star pictures decorate the lounge. Cider in summer.
🌸 ◁ ▷ ⊕ ♣ ▷ P

Whittington Inn
Whittington (A449, S of A458 jct) ☎ (01384) 872110
11–2.30 (3 Sat), 5.30–11; 12–3, 7–10.30 Sun
Banks's Mild, Bitter E; **Marston's Pedigree; Morrells Graduate** H
Converted, 14th-century manor house visited by Charles II after the Battle of Worcester. It boasts panelled walls, ornate moulded ceilings with low beams, and a walled Tudor garden.
🏠 Q 🌸 ◁ ▷ P ⊡

Leek

Blue Mugge
17 Osbourne Street (off A53)
☎ (01538) 384450
11–2.30, 6–11; 11–11 Sat; 12–10.30 Sun
Draught Bass; Worthington Bitter; guest beer H
Popular local on a street corner, consisting of several different rooms off a central island bar; a lot larger inside than the outside suggests.
🌸 ◁ ⊕ ♣

Den Engel
Saint Edward Street (links A53/A523) ☎ (01538) 373751
11–3 (4 Wed; not Mon & Tue), 7–11; 12–2.30, 7–10.30 Sun
Beer range varies H
Belgian-style café-bar where a constantly changing beer menu combines the best of British independents with the classic beers and genevers of the Low Countries. Relaxed atmosphere; waiter service; classical music. Light lunches and Sun eve meals.
Q ◁ ⊡

Swan
2 St Edward Street
☎ (01538) 382081
11–3, 7–11; 12–3, 7–10.30 Sun
Draught Bass; Highgate Dark; Worthington Bitter; guest beer H
Three-roomed former coaching inn opposite St Edward's church. The lounge is mainly given over to non-smoking diners at lunchtime. The function room hosts the Cuckoo's Nest folk club. Diverse, ever-changing guest beers. 🌸 ◁ ▷ ♣

Wilkes Head
16 St Edward Street
☎ (01538) 383616
11–11; 12–10.30 Sun
Whim Magic Mushroom Mild, Hartington Bitter, IPA, Old Izaak, Black Christmas; guest beers H
Whim Brewery's only tied outlet increases choice in the best drinking town in North Staffs: a basic, lively, three-roomer where robust conversation is the norm.
🌸 ♣

Lichfield

Earl of Lichfield Arms
10 Conduit Street
☎ (01543) 251020
11–11; 11–4, 7–11 Sat; 12–3, 7–10.30 Sun
Banks's Mild; Marston's Bitter, Pedigree, HBC H
Popular, no-frills, city-centre bar in the corner of the market square, known locally as 'the Drum'. No food Sun.
🌸 ◁ ⇌ (City)

Greyhound
121 Upper St John Street
☎ (01543) 262303
12–3, 5–11; 12–11 Fri & Sat; 12–3, 7–10.30 Sun
Ansells Bitter; Draught Bass; guest beer H
Friendly local within easy reach of the centre, enjoying an excellent reputation for its good value bar meals. Regularly changing premium guest beer.
🛏 🌸 ◁ ▷ ⊕ ⇌ (City) ♣ P

Queen's Head
14 Queen Street (near Beacon Park) ☎ (01543) 410932
12–11; 12–3, 7–10.30 Sun
Adnams Bitter; Marston's Pedigree; guest beers H
A Marston's Ale House with at least two guest ales available, this one-roomed pub is often frequented by sports fans. Known for its very original food choice, especially cheeses and sausages. Q ⇌ (City) ▷

Scales
24 Market Street (near cathedral) ☎ (01543) 410653

STAFFORDSHIRE

11–11; 12–10.30 Sun
**Draught Bass; Lichfield
Steeplejack; Worthington
Bitter; guest beers** H
Bustling, city-centre pub with a
long bar and a choice of five or
six ales attracting clientele of
all ages; very busy at
weekends.
🌞 ◖ & ⇌ (City) ♣

Little Haywood

Red Lion
Main Road
☎ (01889) 881314
12 (4 winter)–11; 12–4, 7–10.30 Sun
**Marston's Bitter, Pedigree,
HBC** H
Lively village pub, very much
a community-based local with
an award-winning garden.
🏚 🌞 ⊟ ▲ ♣ P

Longdon

Swan With Two Necks
40 Brook End (100 yds off A51)
☎ (01543) 490251
12–2.30 (3 Sat), 7–11; 12–3, 7–10.30
Sun
**Ansells Bitter; Ind Coope
Burton Ale; Marston's HBC;
guest beers** H
400-year-old, beamed village
pub with a stone-flagged bar, a
comfortable lounge and a
restaurant serving a good
choice of home-cooked food.
🏚 Q 🌞 ◖ ▶ P

Marston

Fox
1 mile NW of Wheaton Aston
OS835140
☎ (01785) 840729
12–2 (3 Sat; not Mon–Fri in winter),
7–11; 12–3, 7–10.30 Sun
**Draught Bass; Bateman XB;
Shepherd Neame Spitfire;
Wells Eagle; guest beers** H
Remote country free house
with a relaxed, homely
atmosphere. The garden has a
children's play area.
Restaurant meals Tue–Sat eve
and Sun lunch.
🏚 Q 🌞 ◖ ▶ ▲ ♣ ⌂ P

Meaford

George & Dragon
The Highway (100 yds S of
A34/A51 jct)
☎ (01785) 818497
11–11; 12–10.30 Sun
**Burtonwood Bitter, Forshaw's,
Top Hat** H
Main road inn with a spacious,
wood-panelled lounge bar. The
first-floor restaurant is large
enough to cater for wedding
parties, etc. Lunches served
downstairs Mon–Sat (Sun
lunch and eve meals upstairs).
🌞 ◖ ▶ & ▲ ♣ P

Milwich

Green Man
Sandon Lane (B5027)
☎ (01889) 505310
12–2 (not Mon or Tue), 5–11; 12–11
Sat; 12–4, 7–10.30 Sun
**Draught Bass; Highgate Dark;
Worthington Bitter; guest
beers** H
Welcoming village pub, well
situated for hikers. A list of
landlords since 1792 is
displayed in the bar.
🏚 🌞 ◖ ▲ ♣ P

Newcastle-under-Lyme

Albion
99 High Street
☎ (01782) 719784
11–11; 12–10.30 Sun
**Marston's Bitter, Pedigree,
HBC; guest beers** H
Recently refurbished town-
centre pub, attracting a varied
clientele. It can get very busy
Fri and Sat nights. No food
Sun. There is a patio for
outside drinking. 🌞 ◖

Cricketers Arms
Alexandra Road, May Bank
☎ (01782) 619169
6 (11 Sat)–11; 12–5, 7–10.30 Sun
**Courage Directors; John
Smith's Bitter; guest beers** H
Unspoilt, 1930s-style pub
retaining the original Parkers
Burslem Brewery fittings. The
cosy lounge features wood-
panelled walls and the larger
public bar gives clues to the
landlord – five times and
reigning world darts
champion, Phil Taylor.
🏚 🌞 ⊟ & ♣ P

Crossways
Nelson Place
☎ (01782) 616953
11–11; 11–4, 7–11 Sat; 12–3, 7–10.30
Sun
**Vaux Samson; Ward's Best
Bitter; guest beers** H
Popular, large, town-centre
pub: a bar with a small games
area off. The house beer, Bear
Cross, is brewed by Coach
House. ◖ ♣

Dunkirk Tavern
Dunkirk
☎ (01782) 618735
12–3.30, 7–11; 12–3, 7–10.30 Sun
**Burtonwood Bitter, Top Hat,
Buccaneer, seasonal beers** H
Popular, community local just
outside the town centre: a
traditional bar area and a large
lounge area with live music on
Sat eve (when no food is
served). (Book meals other
eves.) The games room is
available for meetings.
🌞 ◖ ▶ ♣

Outwoods

Village Tavern
Signed from A518 OS787182
☎ (01952) 691216
6 (7.30 winter)–11; 12–3, 6 (7.30
winter)–11 Sat & bank hols; 12–3,
7–10.30 Sun
**Boddingtons Bitter;
Hobsons Best Bitter; guest
beers** H
Friendly country inn in a small
village, frequented by walkers
and cyclists. Good value food
(full curry menu available);
families are made welcome.
Wildman's, the house beer, is
brewed by Enville.
🏚 Q 🌞 ◖ ▶ ▲ P

Penkridge

Boat
Cannock Road (by Bridge 86 of
Staffs & Worcs Canal)
☎ (01785) 714178
12–3, 6.30–11; 12–3, 7–10.30 Sun
**Ansells Bitter; Ind Coope
Burton Ale; Marston's
Pedigree; Tetley Bitter** H
Comfortable, homely,
canalside pub with plenty of
brass on display. Bar skittles in
the corridor. No Sun eve meals
in winter.
🌞 ◖ ▶ ♣ P

Penn Common

Barley Mow
Pennwood Lane (off Wakeley
Hill) OS949902
☎ (01902) 333510
12–3, 6.30–11; 11.30–11 Sat; 12–10.30
Sun
**Ansells Mild; Ind Coope
Burton Ale; guest beer** H
Hidden gem, circa 1630, with a
warm welcome. Popular
children's playground in
summer. Bar food is served in
the small bar every day. One
guest beer from Ind Coope and
one Holden's beer are
available, along with various
guest ciders.
🏚 Q 🌞 ◖ ▶ ⌂ P ▯

Reapsmoor

Butcher's Arms
Off B5053 OS082614
☎ (01298) 84477
12–3, 7–11; 12–3, 7–10.30 Sun
**Marston's Pedigree; guest
beer** H
Gem of a pub with several
drinking areas, surrounded by
moorland. Continuing
improvements add character
and atmosphere; this is no
identikit pub. Superb value
food; Sun lunches served.
Camping for tents only (free to
customers). It can be isolated
during severe weather.
🏚 Q 🚲 🌞 ▲ ♣ P

264

Rugeley

Red Lion
Market Street
☎ (01889) 570328
11–11; 12–10.30 Sun
Banks's Mild, Bitter Ⓔ
Small, three-roomed pub with
bags of atmosphere in a pool
and darts room and a cosy bar.
✿ ≢ ♣ P

Stafford

Bird in Hand
Mill Street (near Victoria Park)
☎ (01785) 252198
11–11; 12–10.30 Sun
**Courage Best Bitter, Directors;
John Smith's Bitter;
Worthington Bitter; guest
beer** Ⓗ
Justifiably popular, this
enterprising town-centre pub
has a bar, snug, games room
and a lounge. No meals Sun.
No-smoking dining area
lunchtime.
🏘 🐾 ✿ ◖ ≢ ♣

Forester & Firkin
3 Eastgate Street (opp. Borough
Hall)
☎ (01785) 223742
11–11; 12–10.30 Sun
**Firkin Forester, Golden Glory,
Dogbolter; guest beer** Ⓗ
Pub furbished in a similar style
to other Firkin pubs, with basic
decor. Live music some
sessions; many student
customers. Snacks all day.
Behind the pub is Stafford's
first brewery since 1952.
✿ ◖ ♣ P

Railway
23 Castle Street
☎ (01785) 604221
12–3, 6–11; 12–3, 6–10.30 Sun
**Ind Coope Burton Ale; Tetley
Bitter; guest beers** Ⓗ
Welcoming, Victorian, street-
corner local with a large
selection of whiskies. A
refurbished meeting room is
available.
🏘 Q ✿ ◖ ▶ 🍴 ≢ ♣

Stafford Arms
Railway Street (opp. station)
☎ (01785) 253313
12–11; 12–3, 7–10.30 Sun
**Titanic Best Bitter, Lifeboat,
Premium, Stout, Captain
Smith's, White Star,
Wreckage; guest beers** Ⓗ
Local CAMRA *Pub of the Year*
and runner up in the county
1996. Titanic Inns' second pub
sells the brewery's full range,
plus four guests from
independent brewers (cider in
summer). Two beer festivals
are held a year. Games include
bar billiards and corridor
skittles. Eve meals 5–8.
✿ ◖ ▶ ≢ ♣ 🍴 ✂

Tap & Spile
59 Peel Terrace (off B5066, 1
mile from centre)
☎ (01785) 223563
12–2.30, 6.30–11; 12–11 Fri & Sat;
12–10.30 Sun
Beer range varies Ⓗ
This 1994 sympathetic
conversion to a Tap & Spile has
greatly increased beer choice in
northern Stafford: eight
continually changing guest
beers; 200 cask ales sold each
year. Regular quizzes; free bar
billiards. Staffordshire
CAMRA *Pub of the Year* 1995.
🏘 ✿ ◖ ▶ 🍴 ♣ 🍴 ✂

Telegraph
Wolverhampton Road (by
railway bridge)
☎ (01785) 258858
11–11; 12–10.30 Sun
**Draught Bass; Highgate Dark;
Worthington Bitter; guest
beer** Ⓗ
Good, honest local with a bar
and lounge, not far from the
town centre. Good value
meals. Large function room.
◖ ▶ 🍴 ♣ P

*Try also: Picture House,
Bridge St (Wetherspoons)*

Stoke on Trent: Bignall End

Plough
Ravens Lane (½ mile E of
Audley on B5500)
☎ (01782) 720469
12–3, 7–11; 12–11 Fri & Sat; 12–10.30
Sun
**Banks's Bitter; Marston's
Pedigree; guest beers** Ⓗ
Popular roadside hostelry,
with constantly changing guest
beers – at least five available.
Two rooms: a pleasant lounge
and a traditional bar. Good
value food (not served Sun
eve). CAMRA Potteries *Pub of
the Year* 1995. ✿ ◖ ▶ ♣ P 🍴

Burslem

George Hotel
Swan Square ☎ (01782) 577544
11.30–2, 7–11; 12–2, 7–10.30 Sun
**Marston's Bitter, Pedigree;
Morland Old Speckled Hen** Ⓗ
Fine, pseudo-Georgian
building on the site of Arnold
Bennett's 'Dragon'. The bar is
ideal for a quiet drink, but
smart casual dress is required.
Special accommodation rates
for CAMRA members. Highly
recommended restaurant.
Q 🛏 ◖ ▶

White Swan
107 Newport Lane, Middleport
☎ (01782) 813639
11–11; 11–4, 7–11 Sat; 12–3, 7–10.30
Sun
**Vaux Mild, Bitter, Samson;
guest beers** Ⓗ

Friendly, popular community
local with an imaginative guest
beer policy.
🏘 ≢ (Longport) ♣

Etruria

Plough
147 Etruria Road (250 yds from
Festival Park roundabout,
towards Hanley)
☎ (01782) 269445
12–3, 6 (5 Fri, 7 Sat)–11; 7–10.30
(closed lunch) Sun
**Robinson's Old Stockport,
Hartleys XB, Best Bitter,
Frederics, Old Tom** Ⓗ
The only Robinson's pub in the
city. Excellent, varied home-
made meals. Old Tom is only
served in half-pints. Friendly
welcome. 🏘 Q ✿ P

Fenton

Malt 'n' Hops
295 King Street
☎ (01782) 313406
12–3, 7–11; 12–3, 7–10.30 Sun
**Burtonwood Mild; guest
beers** Ⓗ
Ever-popular house, where
beer is the main feature – at
least 15 guest ales per week,
plus two house beers. A typical
town pub, situated on a busy
main road, it is comprised of
an L-shaped, split-level bar.
Former Potteries CAMRA *Pub
of the Year*. ≢ (Longton) 🍴

Hanley

Golden Cup
65 Old Town Road
☎ (01782) 212405
11.30–11; 12–3, 7.30–10.30 Sun
**Draught Bass; Ruddles
County** Ⓗ
Friendly local, with an
imposing Edwardian frontage
proudly proclaiming 'Bass
only'. The interior boasts
splendid bar fittings and can be
crowded at weekends. A
typical former beer house – the
last in Hanley to obtain a liquor
licence. Pleasant garden.
✿ ◖ ♿ ♣

Harriseahead

Royal Oak
42 High Street
☎ (01782) 513362
7–11; 12–3, 7–11 Sat; 12–3, 7–10.30
Sun
**Courage Directors; John
Smith's Bitter; guest beers** Ⓗ
Busy, genuine, free house in a
semi-rural location on the
Kidsgrove side of Mow Cop
Folly (NT). A smallish bar and
a larger lounge offer the best
choice of guest beers in the
area. Popular with all ages.
✿ 🍴 ♣ P 🍴

Tunstall

Paradise Inn
42 Paradise Street (off Tower Sq) ☎ (01782) 833266
12–11; 12–4, 7.30–11 Sat; 12–4, 7.30–10.30 Sun
Vaux Double Maxim; Ward's Thorne BB Ⓗ
Cosy, town-centre inn with a single U-shaped room.
♣ ♅

Stone

Pheasant
Old Road ☎ (01785) 814603
11.30–11; 12–10.30 Sun
Banks's Mild, Bitter; Bateman Mild; Greene King Abbot; Marston's Bitter, Pedigree Ⓗ
Busy, friendly local where darts, crib and football are well supported. Fine selection of home-cooked meals at sensible prices (eve meals Fri and Sat; no lunches Sun). ❀ ◖▶ ⊞ ≠ ♣

Star Inn
21 Stafford Street (by Trent & Mersey Canal)
☎ (01785) 813096
11–11; 12–10.30 Sun
Banks's Mild, Bitter; Camerons Strongarm; Marston's Pedigree; guest beers Ⓗ
Dating from 1568, this canalside pub is located on 13 different floor levels. Very busy in summer.
🚌 Q ❀ ◖▶ ⊞ ♣ P ♅

Swindon

Old Bush
High Street ☎ (01384) 279235
12–3, 6–11; 11–11 Sat; 12–3, 7–10.30 Sun
Banks's Hanson's Mild, Bitter Ⓔ**; Marston's Pedigree** (occasional) Ⓗ
Comfortable, friendly, one-roomed village local, 100 yards from the Staffs & Worcs Canal. Weekday happy hour 6–7.30. No food Sun. ♉ ❀ ◖▶ ♣ P

Tamworth

Boot Inn
Lichfield Street
☎ (01827) 68024
11–11; 12–10.30 Sun
Marston's Pedigree, HBC Ⓗ
Busy, town-centre pub, popular with young pub-goers; very busy at weekends.
❀ ◖≠

Market Vaults
7 Market Street
☎ (01827) 69653
11–3, 6–11; 11–11 Fri, Sat & summer; 12–3, 7–10.30 Sun
Banks's Mild, Bitter Ⓔ**; Camerons Strongarm** Ⓗ

Two-roomed, town-centre pub accessed via a narrow alleyway. It can be busy at weekends and fields a pub football team.
Q ◖≠ ♅

Three Tuns
Lichfield Street
☎ (01827) 66029
11–11; 12–3, 7–10.30 Sun
Draught Bass; M&B Mild, Brew XI; Ruddles County Ⓗ
Popular, two-roomed, town-centre pub with a comfortable lounge. Very busy weekend eves with young drinkers.
❀ ⊞ ≠ P

White Lion
Aldergate
☎ (01827) 64630
11–11; 12–10.30 Sun
Banks's Mild, Bitter; Marston's Pedigree Ⓗ
Basic, three-roomed, corner pub with a no-smoking restaurant area. There are plans to extend the pub which can be busy at weekends. No food Sun. ◖≠ P

Tutbury

Cross Keys
Burton Street (A50)
☎ (01283) 813677
10.30–3, 5.30–11; 12–3, 7–10.30 Sun
Ind Coope Burton Ale; Tetley Bitter; guest beer Ⓗ
Village pub and restaurant with a friendly atmosphere. Home-cooking a speciality.
Q ❀ ◖▶ ⊞ ♿ ≠ ♣ P

Two Gates

Bull's Head
Watling Street (A51/B5404 jct)
☎ (01827) 287820
12–2.30 (3 Sat), 6.30–11; 12–2.30, 7–10.30 Sun
Banks's Mild; Marston's Pedigree, HBC Ⓗ
Popular, friendly, comfortable local, tastefully modernised, with a golf society and a keen racing following. No food Sun.
Q ❀ ◖≠ (Wilnecote) P

Upper Longdon

Chetwynd Arms
57 Upper Way (400 yds off A51)
☎ (01543) 490266
5 (12 Sat)–11; 12–10.30 Sun
Lichfield Steeplejack; Marston's Pedigree; Tetley Bitter; guest beer Ⓗ
Friendly, one-roomed pub on the edge of Cannock Chase, popular with locals and walkers alike. The guest beer is from the Tapster's Choice list. No food Mon eve.
🚌 ❀ ◖▶ ▲ ♣ P

Uttoxeter

Black Swan
Market Street
☎ (01889) 564657
11–3, 5–11; 11–11 Wed, Fri & Sat; 12–3.30, 7–10.30 Sun
Draught Bass Ⓗ
17th-century listed building of great character. Visitors are made welcome by locals and the Scottish landlord.
⊞ ≠ ♣ P

Roebuck
Dove Bank (A518)
☎ (01889) 565563
11–2, 5–11; 11–11 Fri & Sat; 12–3, 7–10.30 Sun
Courage Directors; Theakston Best Bitter, XB; guest beers Ⓗ
Characterful, 17th-century inn, once a beer retailing premises which only became a pub at the turn of this century. It comprises a bar with a pool area, two lounge areas and a room where children are allowed in for meals (ring to check meal availability).
🛏 ◖▶ ▲ ≠ ♣ P

Smithfield Hotel
Smithfield Road
☎ (01889) 562682
11–3, 7–11; 12–3, 7–10.30 Sun
Burtonwood Forshaw's, Top Hat, Buccaneer Ⓗ
Named the Plume of Feathers in 1627, the Smithfield was renamed circa 1900 and run by the Jagger family for much of this century. The 'men-only' bar was changed only by Act of Parliament, but is to be restored to its former architectural condition by the present landlord. No food Wed eve (other eves till 8.30).
🛏 ◖▶ ⊞ ≠ ♣

Vaults
Market Place ☎ (01889) 562997
11–3 (3.30, 4 Sat), 5.30 (5 Fri, 7 Sat)–11; 12–3.30, 7–10.30 Sun
Draught Bass; Worthington Bitter Ⓗ
Friendly, unspoilt three-roomer with a large bottle collection.
⊞ ≠ ♣

Weston

Saracen's Head
Stafford Road (A518)
☎ (01889) 270286
11.30–11; 12–3, 7–10.30 Sun
Draught Bass; Worthington Bitter Ⓔ**; guest beer** Ⓗ
Situated below Weston Bank, this country pub has a new conservatory for meals and provides a courtesy bus for regulars and parties of at least six diners.
🚌 ❀ ◖▶ ⊞ ♣ P ♅

Woolpack

The Green ☎ (01889) 270238
11.30–3, 5.30–11; 11.30–11 Fri & Sat;
12–3, 7–10.30 Sun
**Marston's Bitter, Pedigree;
guest beer** H
This 17th-century 'inn on the green' has been carefully extended, retaining separate drinking and dining areas. Good selection of quality, home-cooked food at sensible prices (no food Sun eve).
🍴 ⊛ ◑ ▶ 🏠 ♣ P

Whittington

Bell

27 Main Street
☎ (01543) 432377
12–3, 7–11; 12–11 Fri & Sat; 12–10.30 Sun
**Draught Bass; Everards Tiger;
Morland Old Speckled Hen;
Tetley Bitter** H
Traditional village pub featuring an oak-beamed lounge. No food Mon. Small outside drinking area at the front, larger one behind.
🍴 Q ⊛ ◑ ▶ 🏠 P

Wigginton

Old Crown

1½ miles N of Tamworth
12–3, 6–11; 12–11 Sat; 12–10.30 Sun
**Banks's Mild; Marston's
Pedigree, HBC** H

Comfortable, two-roomed village pub with country views. The garden is popular in summer.
Q ⊛ ◑ ▶ 🏠 P ⊬

Wilnecote

Globe

Watling Street
☎ (01827) 280885
1–3.30, 7–11; 12–3, 7–10.30 Sun
**Banks's Mild; Marston's
Pedigree, HBC** H
Basic, one-roomed local on the former A5. ⊛ ⇌ ♣

Prince of Wales

70 Hockley Road
☎ (01827) 280013
12–3, 7–11; 12–3, 7–10.30 Sun
**Marston's Pedigree; Ruddles
County; Theakston Mild, Best
Bitter, XB; guest beers** H
Roadside, two-roomed local with a comfortable lounge, offering a selection of single-malt whiskies. It fields a ladies darts team and a football team. Winner of the 1996 William Younger *Best Kept Ale* award.
Q ⊛ 🏠 ⇌ P

Wombourne

New Inn

1 Station Road (½ mile from A459/A463 jct)
☎ (01902) 892037

11–3.30, 5.30–11; 11–11 Fri & Sat;
12–4, 7–10.30 Sun
Banks's Mild, Bitter E; **guest
beer** H
Friendly pub near the village centre, with a plain bar and a large, comfortable lounge. Book eve meals.
⊛ ◑ ▶ 🏠 ♣ P 🍴

Old Bush

High Street (off A449)
☎ (01902) 893509
11.30–3, 5.30–11; 11–11 Sat; 12–3,
7–10.30 Sun
Banks's Mild, Bitter E
Pleasant, friendly pub on the edge of the village, noted for its family atmosphere and good home-cooked food (not served Sun eve; other eves till 8.30). Roast dinners are always available.
⊛ ◑ ▶ 🏠 ♣ P 🍴

Yoxall

Crown Inn

Main Street
☎ (01543) 472551
11.30–3, 5.30–11; 11.30–11 Sat;
12–10.30 Sun
**Marston's Pedigree, Owd
Rodger** H
Attractive village pub with a no-smoking conservatory, suitable for families. Live music Thu eve. Darts and dominoes are played.
Q 🐶 ⊛ ◑ ▶ 🏠 ♣ P ⊬

Mine's a full pint! Midlands drinkers are guaranteed a full pint in a Banks's pub, as the brewery's Richard Westwood (right) proves to CAMRA director Bob Jones.

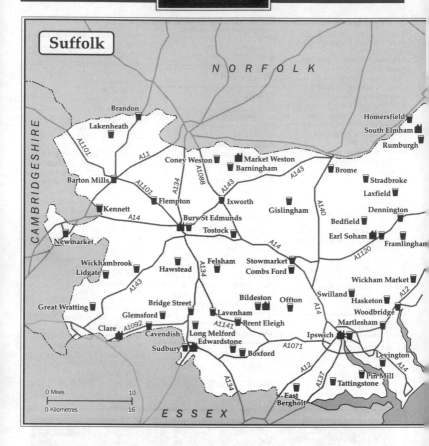

Aldeburgh

Mill Inn
Market Cross Place (opp. Moot Hall)
☎ (01728) 452563
11–3, 6–11 (11–11 summer); 12–10.30 Sun
Adnams Mild (summer), **Bitter, Old, Broadside** Ⓗ
Warm, welcoming pub, overlooking the sea and beach. Local fish is a good food speciality. Q ⊨ ◑ ▶ ▲ ♣

White Hart Inn
222 High Street
☎ (01728) 453205
11.30–3, 6–11; 11–11 Fri, Sat & summer; 12–3, 7–10.30 Sun
Adnams Bitter, Old *or* **Mild, Extra, Broadside, seasonal beers** Ⓗ
Lively, one-bar pub prominently positioned in this popular coastal town. Wood panelling and mainly nautical pictures cover the walls. A cheery welcome is guaranteed, but it can be busy weekends. Eve meals in summer.
🏚 ⊛ ⊨ ◑ ▶ ▲ ♣ ◔

Barningham

Royal George
Church Road
☎ (01359) 221246
11–3, 6–11; 11–11 Fri & Sat; 12–10.30 Sun
Greene King XX Mild, IPA, Abbot, seasonal beers Ⓗ
Beautifully situated pub in the village centre, quite spacious inside with many old beams and a huge inglenook, but no real fires due to the thatched roof! The new dining room welcomes families; pleasant outside drinking in summer.
⚘ ⊛ ◑ ▶ ⊞ ♣ P 🍽

Barton Mills

Bull Inn
The Street
☎ (01638) 713230
11–11; 12–3, 7–10.30 Sun
Draught Bass Ⓗ; **Greene King IPA** Ⓖ; **guest beers** Ⓗ/Ⓖ
Classic coaching inn, just off the A11, family-run with full hotel facilities. A modern gravity dispense system is used in the beer-oriented bar.
🏚 ⊛ ⊨ ◑ ▶ P

Bedfield

Crown
Church Lane (leave A1120 at Earl Soham)
☎ (01728) 628431
11.30–3, 6–11; 11–11 Sat; 12–10.30 Sun (may vary)
Greene King IPA; guest beer Ⓗ
Friendly village local with many pub games, including shove-ha'penny and bar billiards. No food Tue.
🏚 ⊛ ◑ ▶ ▲ ♣ P

Bildeston

Kings Head
132 High Street
☎ (01449) 741434
12–3, 5–11; 11–11 Sat; 12–10.30 Sun
Brettvale Bitter; Greene King IPA; Mauldons Best Bitter; Old Chimneys Military Mild; guest beer Ⓗ
Now brewing on the premises, this lively village-centre pub continues to cater for all ages

park 200 yards away. No food Mon; eve meals from 8pm.
🏠 ◑ ▶ ⇌ ♣

Brent Eleigh

Cock ☆
Lavenham Road
☎ (01787) 247371
12–3, 6–11; 12–3, 7–10.30 Sun
Adnams Mild Ⓖ, Bitter; Greene King IPA Ⓗ, Abbot Ⓖ
An absolute gem! Thatched, unspoilt and at peace with the world. 🏠 Q ⑱ ⊞ ♣ ⌂ P

Bridge Street

Rose & Crown
On A134 ☎ (01787) 247022
12–3, 6 (6.30 Sat)–11; 12–3, 7–10.30 Sun
Greene King IPA, Abbot Ⓖ
Homely, village pub with an abundance of exposed beams and a friendly atmosphere. The ales are drawn straight from the cask and there is a wide selection of home-made food. Near Long Melford and Kentwell Halls.
Q ⑱ ◑ ▶ ⊞ ♣ P

Brome

Cornwallis Arms
By A140/B1077 jct
☎ (01379) 870326
11–3, 6–11; 12–3, 6–10.30 Sun
St Peter's Mild, Wheat, Best Bitter, Extra, Honey Porter, Strong Bitter Ⓗ
16th-century dower house and rectory, now a country house hotel, approached via a tree-lined avenue, boasting outstanding examples of topiary. It offers at least six of the owners' own beers and stylish food. 🏠 ⑱ 🛏 ◑ ▶ P

Bungay

Green Dragon
29 Broad Street
☎ (01986) 892681
11–3, 5–11; 11–11 Fri & Sat; 12–4, 7–10.30 Sun
Adnams Bitter; Green Dragon Chaucer, Bridge Street, Dragon, seasonal beers Ⓗ
Basic bar and lounge with a dining room that doubles as a

family room. The beers are brewed behind the pub.
🏠 🛏 ⑱ ◑ ▶ ♿ ☕ ♣ P

Bury St Edmunds

Falcon
58 Risbygate Street
☎ (01284) 754128
11–11; 12–10.30 Sun
Greene King IPA, Abbot, seasonal beers Ⓔ
Friendly, edge of town local established in 1859. Mostly unmodernised, it does have an extension to the rear. No meals Sun eve. ⑱ ◑ ▶ ⊞ ♣ P

Ipswich Arms
1 Tayfen Road (200 yds from station) ☎ (01284) 703623
11–2 (2.30 Fri), 6.30–11; 11–11 Sat; 12–10.30 Sun
Greene King XX Mild, IPA, Abbot, seasonal beers Ⓗ
Interesting, semi-circular, 19th-century, light brick pub named to celebrate the railway link with Ipswich in 1864. Good value food.
⑱ ◑ ▶ ⇌ P

Nutshell ☆
The Traverse ☎ (01284) 705387
11–11; closed Sun
Greene King IPA, Abbot Ⓗ
The smallest pub in Britain; a quiet, friendly local, full of character. Q

Queens Head
39 Churchgate Street
☎ (01284) 761554
11–11; 12–10.30 Sun
Adnams Bitter, Broadside; Courage Directors; Nethergate IPA; Shepherd Neame Spitfire; guest beers Ⓗ
White brick, 18th-century coaching inn with plenty of history beneath a Victorian-style refurbishment. The courtyard conservatory is a recent addition. Young trade at weekends. Beer festivals Easter and Aug Bank Hol. ◑ ▶ ⇌

Rose & Crown
48 Whiting Street
☎ (01284) 755934
11–11; 11–3, 7–11 Sat; 12–2.30, 7–10.30 Sun
Greene King XX Mild, IPA, Abbot, seasonal beers Ⓗ

and tastes. Live music at weekends; beer festival Whitsun Bank Hol. Cider in summer.
🛏 ⑱ 🛏 ◑ ▶ ♣ ⌂ P

Boxford

White Hart
Broad Street ☎ (01787) 211071
12–3, 6 (6.30 Mon–Fri in winter)–11; 12–3, 7–10.30 Sun
Adnams Extra or Broadside; Greene King IPA; guest beers Ⓗ
Timber-framed building in the village centre with a good menu and interesting guest beers. 🏠 ⑱ ◑ ▶ ♣ P

Brandon

Duke of Wellington
35 Thetford Road
☎ (01842) 810219
11–11; 11–3.30, 6.30–11 Mon; 12–10.30 Sun
Greene King XX Mild, IPA, Abbot Ⓗ
Handsome, 250-year-old flint building, typical of the town: a busy community pub with a lively atmosphere. Public car

🏠 INDEPENDENT BREWERIES

Adnams: Southwold	**Mauldons**: Sudbury
Brettvale: Bildeston	**Nethergate**: Clare
Earl Soham: Earl Soham	**Old Chimneys**: Market Weston
Green Dragon: Bungay	
Greene King: Bury St Edmunds	**St Peter's**: South Elmham
	Scott's: Lowestoft
Green Jack: Oulton Broad	**Tolly Cobbold**: Ipswich

Characterful, unspoilt, family-run, town local in sight of the brewery and frequented by its staff. Mild outsells the bitter.
Q ◁ 🏠 ♣

Butley

Oyster
☎ (01394) 450790
11.30–3, 6 (5 summer)–11; 11–11 Fri & Sat; 12–3, 7–10.30 Sun
Adnams Mild, Bitter, Old, Broadside, seasonal beers Ⓗ
Prominent, characterful pub whose bar areas provide a cosy, traditional environment for drinking, talking, eating and singing. Regular folk singing Sun eve. Excellent!
🏠 Q ⅃ 🌲 ◁ ▶ ▲ ♣ P

Cavendish

Bull
High Street ☎ (01787) 280245
11–3, 6–11; 12–3, 7–10.30 Sun
Adnams Bitter, Broadside Ⓗ
Friendly, High Street pub with a large garden and a wide selection of food. Q 🌲 ◁ ▶ P

Chillesford

Froize Inn
Orford Road ☎ (01394) 450282
12 (11 summer)–2.30 (3 Sat & summer), 6.30 (6 summer)–11 (12–11 summer Sat); 12–3, 6–10.30 (12–10.30 summer) Sun; closed Mon
Adnams Bitter, seasonal beers; guest beers Ⓗ
15th-century country inn built on the site of a friary, set in two acres of land with a camping and caravan site. The single, comfortable bar with exposed beams is known for its extensive menu (seafood a speciality). The 'Nuns' house beers are brewed by Mauldons. Wheelchair WC.
🏠 Q 🌲 🚐 ◁ ▶ ♿ ▲ ♣ P

Combs Ford

Gladstone Arms
2 Combs Ford (1 mile from Stowmarket centre, on Needham road)
☎ (01449) 612339
11–2.30, 5 (6 Sat)–11; 12–3, 7–10.30 Sun
Adnams Bitter, Old, Broadside Ⓗ
Adnams tied house on the southern outskirts of Stowmarket. Cross a bridge to the garden. 🌲 ♣ P

Coney Weston

Swan Inn
Thetford Road
☎ (01359) 221295
12–3, 5 (6 Sat)–11; 12–3, 7–10.30 Sun
Greene King XX Mild, IPA, Abbot Ⓗ

Victorian local, run on most traditional lines – no food, no jukebox, no noisy machines. Early eve trade is from locals. Bowling green.
🏠 Q 🌲 🏠 ♣ P

Dennington

Queens Head
The Square
☎ (01728) 638241
11.30–2.30, 5.30–11; 12–3, 6.30–10.30 Sun
Adnams Bitter, seasonal beers Ⓗ
In the shadow of the church, this 17th-century, two-roomed pub is set back from the road. Timber framed, it has exposed beams. Children are welcome in the family area of the bar, but not in the dining area. Breakfast available from 9am. Note: Broadside and Old Speckled Hen are kept using a cask breather.
🏠 Q 🌲 ◁ ▶ P

Earl Soham

Victoria
By A1120
☎ (01728) 685758
11.30–3.30, 5.30–11; 12–3, 7–10.30 Sun
Earl Soham Gannet Mild, Victoria, Albert Ⓗ, **Jolabrugg** Ⓖ; **guest beers** Ⓗ
Simple country pub with its own brewery. Excellent, home-cooked, inexpensive meals are always available. Local musicians Tue eve.
🏠 Q 🌲 ◁ ▶ ♣ P

East Bergholt

Hare & Hounds
Neath Road
☎ (01206) 298438
11.30–2.30, 5–11; 11–11 Sat; 12–2.30, 6–10.30 Sun
Adnams Mild, Bitter, Broadside; guest beer Ⓗ
Grade II-listed, traditional old inn retaining two bars. The lounge has an impressive pargetted ceiling dating from 1590. Interesting and changing guest ales; good food.
Q 🌲 🚐 ◁ ▶ ♿ ▲ ♣ P

Edwardstone

White Horse
Mill Green
☎ (01787) 211211
12–2, 6.30–11; 12–3, 7–10.30 Sun
Greene King XX Mild, IPA, Abbot Ⓗ
Characterful, two-bar rural pub with a large car park and garden. Popular for darts, dominoes and cards in winter. It can be difficult to find in this dispersed village.
🏠 Q 🌲 ◁ ▶ 🏠 ▲ ♣ ⏸ P

Felsham

Six Bells
Church Road
☎ (01449) 736268
12–2.30 (3 Sat; not Mon), 6 (7 Sat)–11; 12–3, 7–10.30 Sun
Greene King XX Mild Ⓖ, **IPA** Ⓗ, **Abbot** Ⓖ
Pretty, flint-faced village pub opposite the church, parts dating from the 16th century. No-smoking restaurant.
🌲 ◁ ▶ ♣ P

Flempton

Greyhound
The Green ☎ (01284) 728400
11.30–2.30, 5–11; 11.30–11 Sat; 12–4, 7–10.30 Sun
Greene King XX Mild, IPA, Abbot Ⓗ, **seasonal beers** Ⓖ
Easy to miss pub when passing through on the A1101, tucked away behind the church, overlooking a village green which has attractive thatched cottages. Good food – vegetarians are well catered for. 🏠 Q 🌲 ◁ ▶ 🏠 ♣ P

Framlingham

Railway Inn
Station Road ☎ (01728) 723693
12–3, 5.30–11; 12–3, 7–10.30 Sun
Adnams Mild, Bitter, Old, Broadside Ⓗ
Fine, small, market town pub where the lounge bar, with its Victorian fireplace, ensures a warm atmosphere. A new 'Dive' bar has games; prize-winning garden.
🏠 Q 🌲 ◁ 🏠 ♣ P

Gislingham

Six Bells
High Street ☎ (01379) 783349
12–3, 7 (5.30 Fri)–11; 12–3, 7–10.30 Sun
Beer range varies Ⓗ
Spacious village-centre pub which supports local microbreweries (three house beers are brewed by Old Chimneys). Excellent home-made food from an interesting menu (not served Mon). Annual Dwile Flonk for charity. 🌲 ◁ ▶ ▲ ♣ P

Glemsford

Angel
Egremont Street
☎ (01787) 281671
12–2.30, 5–11; 12–4, 7–10.30 Sun
Greene King IPA, Abbot (winter) Ⓗ
Quiet, traditional pub at one end of a large village where it's reputed to be the oldest house – once home to Cardinal Wolsey's secretary, John

Cavendish, whose ghost is said to appear. Q ❀ ♣ P

Great Wratting

Red Lion
School Road ☎ (01440) 783237
11–2.30, 5–11; 11–11 Fri & Sat; 12–3, 7–10.30 Sun
Adnams Mild (summer), **Bitter, Old, Extra, Broadside; Boddingtons Bitter** Ⓗ
Village local with a whalebone arch door. The large garden features birds, goats and a children's play tree. No food Tue or Sun eves.
🏠 Q ❀ ◖ ▶ ⊟ P

Haskerton

Turks Head
Low Road ☎ (01394) 382584
12–3 (not Mon), 6–11; 12–4, 7–10.30 Sun
Tolly Cobbold Mild, Original, IPA, Old Strong; guest beers Ⓗ
Subtle alterations have connected the two bars but preserved the character and intimacy of this lively community pub's various tables and alcoves. No food Sun or Mon eve.
🏠 Q ❀ ◖ ▶ ▲ ♣ P

Hawstead

Metcalfe Arms
Lawshall Road (¼ mile S of village green)
☎ (01284) 386321
12–3, 5–11; 12–11 Sat; 12–10.30 Sun
Greene King IPA Ⓗ, **Abbot** Ⓖ
Friendly rural pub offering a warm welcome from a landlord who is ex-USAF. Two bars, a prize-winning garden, camping and good food.
🏠 Q ❀ ◖ ▶ ⊟ ▲ ♣ P

Homersfield

Black Swan
Off A143, by B1062 turn
☎ (01986) 788204
11.30–3, 6–11; 12–3.30, 6–10.30 Sun
Adnams Mild, Bitter, Old; guest beers Ⓗ
Victorian village pub in the Waveney Valley, retaining separate drinking and eating areas, including a flagstone-floored and wood-panelled saloon. Note the first concrete and iron bridge ever built, nearby.
🏠 Q ❀ 🏠 ◖ ▶ ⊟ ▲ ♣ P

Ipswich

Brewery Tap
Cliff Road ☎ (01473) 281508
11–11; 12–10.30 Sun
Tolly Cobbold Mild, Bitter, Original, Tollyshooter, seasonal beers Ⓗ

Waterfront pub at the foot of Tolly's old brewery, much of which is now a museum/visitor centre (closed Sun 3–7 mid-winter). Ask to have the sparkler removed, as all ales are served using swan necks. No food Sun or Mon eves.
🏠 ⛟ ❀ ◖ ▶ ⅙ ♣ P ⸙

Dales
Dales Road ☎ (01473) 250024
11–3, 5–11; 12–3, 7–10.30 Sun
Adnams Bitter; Draught Bass; Tolly Cobbold Mild, Bitter; guest beers Ⓗ
Modern, two-bar pub, now a free house, in a quiet housing estate. Patio access is via the comfortable lounge or car park. No food Sun; eve meals Wed–Fri. Q ❀ ◖ ▶ ⊟ ⅙ ♣ P

Greyhound
9 Henley Road
☎ (01473) 252105
11–2.30, 5–11; 11–11 Sat; 12–10.30 Sun
Adnams Mild, Bitter, Old, Extra, Broadside; guest beers Ⓗ
Attractive, busy, two-room pub popular for food.
❀ ◖ ▶ ⊟ ♣ P

Lord Nelson
81 Fore Street
☎ (01473) 254072
11–11; 12–4, 7–10.30 Sun
Adnams Bitter, Old, Extra, Broadside Ⓗ, **seasonal beers** Ⓖ
Dating back to 1652, this attractive pub was renovated in 1991; many original features have been exposed and new alcoves and intimate areas created. Novel beer dispense system – ask the landlord! No food Sun eve.
❀ 🏠 ◖ ▶ ⅙ ⇌ ♣ ⅙

Ixworth

Greyhound
High Street ☎ (01359) 230887
11–3, 6–11; 12–3, 7–10.30 Sun
Greene King XX Mild, IPA, Abbot, seasonal beers Ⓗ
Fine, large pub which retains two spacious bars with a super little snug in between. The lively public bar fields games teams; pool played. No food Sun. ❀ ◖ ▲ ♣ P

Kennett

Bell Inn
Bury Road ☎ (01638) 750286
11–2.30, 6.30–11; 12–3, 7–10.30 Sun
Greene King IPA, Abbot; Marston's Pedigree; guest beers Ⓗ
Circa 15th century, this inn draws large numbers, including plenty of locals. Food available at all times.
🏠 🏠 ◖ ▶ ⊟ ⇌ P ⍟

Lakenheath

Half Moon
4 High Street ☎ (01842) 861484
11–2.30 (3 Sat), 6–11; 12–3, 7–10.30 Sun
Greene King XX Mild, IPA Ⓗ
Fine local on the outskirts of the village; a handsome flint building retaining an old-fashioned off-sales window between its two bars. Excellent, home-made food at reasonable prices (book at weekend). Note: Abbot Ale is kept using a cask breather.
🏠 ❀ ◖ ▶ ⊟ ♣ P

Plough
Mill Road ☎ (01842) 860285
11–2.30, 6–11; 11–11 Sat; 12–4, 6–10.30 Sun
Greene King IPA, Abbot Ⓗ
Popular pub in the centre of a busy village. A fine 19th-century flint exterior conceals spacious bars.
❀ ⊟ ♣ P

Lavenham

Angel
Market Place ☎ (01787) 247388
11–11; 12–10.30 Sun
Adnams Bitter; Greene King IPA; Mauldons White Adder; Nethergate Bitter Ⓗ
Award-winning, 15th-century inn overlooking the Guildhall. The restaurant and bar have a pleasant, relaxed atmosphere and serve good food from local ingredients. Accommodation is of a high standard.
🏠 Q ⛟ ❀ 🏠 ◖ ▶ ♣ P

Cock Inn
Church Street
☎ (01787) 247407
11–11; 12–10.30 (12–4, 7–10.30 winter) Sun
Greene King XX Mild, IPA; guest beer Ⓗ
Traditional three-roomer opposite an impressive church: a beamed bar with a stone floor, a lounge and a garden room which is no-smoking and licensed for families. The large, safe gardens have a play area. The house beer, O'Sullivans, comes from Mauldons.
🏠 Q ⛟ ❀ ◖ ▶ ⊟ ♣ ⌂ P ⅙

Laxfield

Kings Head/Low House ☆
Gorams Mill Lane (off B1117)
☎ (01986) 798395
11–3, 6–11; 11–11 Tue; 12–3, 7–10.30 Sun
Adnams Mild (summer), **Bitter, Old, Extra, Broadside, seasonal beers; Greene King IPA** Ⓖ
Classic, timeless pub – not to be missed: a tap room with no

bar; high-backed settles and a range in the front room. Many customers arrive by horse and trap. Noted, home-cooked food (try a pudding).
🏚 Q 🍺 ❀ ◑ ▲ ⌣ P

Levington

Ship Inn
Gun Hill ☎ (01473) 659573
11–3, 6–11; 12–3, 7–10.30 Sun
Flowers IPA; Greene King IPA, Abbot; Ind Coope Burton Ale Ⓖ; Tetley Bitter Ⓗ; guest beers Ⓖ
14th-century, Grade II-listed, thatched building in an area of outstanding natural beauty: a warm, friendly local that caters for walkers, birdwatchers and sailors from Levington Marina. Eve meals Wed–Sat.
🏚 Q ❀ ◑ ❀ P ⌿

Lidgate

Star
The Street ☎ (01638) 500275
11–3, 5 (6 Sat)–11; 12–3, 6–10.30 Sun
Greene King XX Mild, IPA, Abbot Ⓗ
Busy local known for its lively conversation in the bar. Look out for the unusual, below-bar level handpumps. Food has a Mediterranean flavour.
🏚 Q ❀ ❀ P ☖

Long Melford

George & Dragon
Hall Street ☎ (01787) 371285
11.30–11; 12–10.30 Sun
Greene King IPA, Abbot Ⓗ
Family-run, former coaching inn with a lounge-style, single bar and a restaurant with an interesting menu. Still a good drinking pub with live music (folk & blues) Wed eve. The overnight accommodation caters for guests with disabilities. 🏚 ❀ 🛏 ◑ ⏃ P

Lowestoft

Blues & Bloater
6 Mill Road ☎ (01502) 561160
11–11; 12–3, 7–10.30 Sun
Scott's Golden Best, Blues & Bloater, East Point, Strong Mild, Hopleaf, William French Ⓗ
Surprisingly roomy backstreet pub, simply furnished and decorated. ⇌ ❀

Factory Arms
214 Raglan Street (off inner ring road) ☎ (01502) 574523
10.30–11; 12–10.30 Sun
Boddingtons Bitter; Courage Directors; Woodforde's Wherry; guest beers Ⓗ
Small, community-based pub appealing to young folk with

darts, pool, pinball, etc. – bustling at weekends.
⏃ ⇌ ❀ ⌣

Triangle Tavern
29 St Peters Street (opp. Triangle market)
☎ (01502) 582711
11–11; 12–10.30 Sun
Green Jack Bitter, Grasshopper, Golden Sickle, Wolf Porter, Lurcher, seasonal beers; guest beers Ⓗ
Straightforward, town-centre pub: a front bar with a large open fire and a back bar with a pool table; one of Green Jack's houses. Sun lunch available. Regular live music. 🍺 ⇌ ❀

Welcome
182 London Road North
☎ (01502) 585500
10.30–4, 7.30–11; 12–4, 7.30–10.30 Sun
Adnams Bitter, Old, Broadside; Greene King Abbot; Worthington Bitter; guest beer Ⓗ
This small, friendly, busy pub contrasts well with the more trendy pubs in the area. Live music Fri eve. ⇌ ❀

Martlesham

Black Tiles
Main Road (off A12 Kesgrave roundabout)
☎ (01473) 610298
11–11; 12–10.30 Sun
Adnams Bitter, Broadside; guest beers Ⓗ
Busy pub with a lounge bar, a 'locals' bar and a no-smoking conservatory. Originally a 1930s tea room, it has a pleasant garden.
🏚 Q 🍺 ❀ ◑ ▶ ⏃ ▲ ❀ P ⌿

Middleton

Bell
The Street
☎ (01728) 648286
11–3.30, 6.30–11; 12–3, 7–10.30 Sun
Adnams Mild, Bitter, Old, Broadside Ⓖ
Part-thatched village local with a traditional bar and a large garden. Regular folk music.
🏚 Q ❀ ◑ ▶ ⏃ ▲ ❀ P

Newmarket

Bushel
Market Street
☎ (01638) 663967
10–2.30 (4.30 Sat), 6 (7 Sat)–11; 12–3, 7–10.30 Sun
Greene King IPA, Abbot Ⓗ
Town-centre pub, reputed to be the oldest in Newmarket, situated in Rookery shopping arcade (so-called because this area of narrow lanes was supposedly a thieves' den). No food Sun eve.
Q ◑ ▶ ⇌ ❀ ☖

Offton

Limeburners
Willisham Road
☎ (01473) 658318
12–2.30 (not Mon), 5–11; 12–11 Sat; 12–3, 7–10.30 Sun
Adnams Bitter; Wells Eagle; guest beers Ⓗ
Two-bar local with a large garden; named after a local limekiln. No food Mon eve.
❀ ◑ ▶ P

Pin Mill

Butt & Oyster ☆
Signed from Chelmondiston on B1456, SE of Ipswich
☎ (01473) 780764
11–3, 7–11; 11–11 Sat & summer; 12–10.30 Sun
Tolly Cobbold Mild, Bitter, Original, IPA, Tollyshooter, Old Strong Ⓗ/Ⓖ; guest beers Ⓗ
Genuine, old bargees' pub at the edge of the River Orwell, boasting some wood panelling, a tiled floor and fine old settles. Very busy in summer; popular with yachtsmen.
🏚 Q 🍺 ❀ ◑ ▶ ❀ P

Rumburgh

Buck ☆
Mill Road ☎ (01986) 785257
11–11 (may vary); 12–3, 7–10.30 Sun
Adnams Bitter, Old; guest beer (summer) Ⓗ
The core of this old building is splendid, and extensions have been tastefully done. It is believed to have been the guest house for a priory that once stood nearby. Good value food.
❀ ◑ ▶ 🍺 ▲ ❀ P

Sibton

White Horse
Halesworth Road
☎ (01728) 660337
11.30–2.30, 7–11; 12–3, 7–10.30 Sun
Adnams Bitter, Old, Broadside; guest beer (occasional) Ⓗ
Single-bar local. The separate dining room has a raised gallery where well-behaved children are welcome; there's also a large garden with play area. No food Sun eve or winter Mon.
🏚 ❀ 🛏 ◑ ▶ ⏃ ❀ P

Snape

Golden Key
Priory Road ☎ (01728) 688510
11–3, 6–11; 12–3, 7–10.30 Sun
Adnams Bitter, Old, Broadside (summer) Ⓗ
Handy for the Maltings. The small bar area offers cosy

settles near the fireplace and excellent food.
🏚 Q ❀ 🍴 ◖ ▶ & ♣ P

Southwold

Lord Nelson
East Street
☎ (01502) 722079
10.30–11; 12–10.30 Sun
Adnams Mild, Bitter, Old, Extra (summer)**, Broadside, seasonal beers** H
Popular town pub, very busy in summer. Note the Nelson memorabilia.
🏚 Q ⛄ ❀ ◖ ▶ A ♣

Red Lion
East Green ☎ (01502) 722385
11–11; 12–10.30 Sun
Adnams Mild, Bitter, Old, Extra, Broadside, seasonal beers H
Bar with a flagstone floor, and a dining room; popular with locals and tourists.
⛄ ❀ 🍴 ◖ ▶ & ♣

Sole Bay
7 East Green ☎ (01502) 723736
11–11; 12–10.30 Sun
Adnams Mild, Bitter, Old, Broadside H
Small, one-room pub opposite the brewery and next to the lighthouse. Q ❀ 🍴 A ♣

Stowmarket

Royal William
Union Street (from station, up Stowupland St, then 2nd right)
☎ (01449) 674553
11–3, 6–11; 12–3, 7–10.30 Sun
Greene King XX Mild, IPA, Abbot, seasonal beers G
Still a good example of a small, market town, backstreet local, serving all its cask ales from a room behind the bar. ◖ ⇌ ♣

Stradbroke

Queens Head
Queen Street (B1118)
☎ (01379) 384384
11.30–3, 6.30–11; 12–3.30, 7–10.30 Sun
Adnams Bitter, Broadside; John Smith's Bitter; guest beers (weekends) H
17th-century pub fronted with Victorian brick. This friendly village local offers good value food, including cheap weekday lunches. 🏚 ❀ ◖ ▶ P

Sudbury

Waggon & Horses
Acton Square
☎ (01787) 312147
11–3, 6.30 (5 Fri)–11; 12–3, 7.30–10.30 Sun
Greene King IPA H
Revitalised, backstreet pub retaining an interesting layout: the public bar has a games

room; a small restaurant leads through to a cosy snug.
🏚 ⛄ ❀ ◖ ▶ ⇌ ♣

Swilland

Moon & Mushroom
High Road
☎ (01473) 785320
11–2.30 (not Mon), 6–11; 12–3, 7–10.30 Sun
Adnams Bitter; Friary Meux BB; Nethergate Bitter, Umbel Magna; guest beers G
Friendly local, formerly the Half Moon, now a single-bar free house, with a low ceiling, exposed beams and a small eating area. Meals Tue–Sat.
🏚 Q ❀ ◖ ▶ & A ♣ P

Tattingstone

Orange Box
Church Road (opp. school)
☎ (01473) 328330
12–3.30, 7.30–11; 12–3.30, 7.30–10.30 Sun
Adnams Bitter; guest beer (summer) H
Tiny, one-roomed bar in a pub which gets its name from its exterior appearance. Can you tell who brews Box Bitter?
Q ❀ ♣ P

Theberton

Lion Inn
☎ (01728) 830185
11–3, 6–11; 12–3, 7–10.30 Sun
Adnams Bitter; guest beers H
Popular village local serving three guest beers – normally from East Anglia. Pool room.
🏚 ❀ ◖ ▶ & A ♣ P

Tostock

Gardeners Arms
Church Road
☎ (01359) 270460
11.30–3, 7–11; 12–3, 7–10.30 Sun
Greene King IPA, Abbot, seasonal beers H
Fine old building, boasting beams and a large fire in the lounge. The good, basic public bar has church pews and a tiled floor. Good value food (no lunches Sun or eve meals Mon–Tue). Pool played.
🏚 ❀ ◖ ▶ 🍴 ♣ P

Walberswick

Bell Inn ☆
Bell Green ☎ (01502) 723109
11–3 (may extend summer Sat), 6–11; 12–3.30 (may extend summer), 7–10.30 Sun
Adnams Mild, Bitter, Old, Extra, Broadside, seasonal beers H
Fine old inn, close by the sea, featuring high-backed settles, flagstone floors, and a large

garden. Well-behaved children welcome.
🏚 Q ❀ 🍴 ◖ ▶ 🍴 A ♣ P

Wenhaston

Star
Hall Road
☎ (01502) 478240
11–3, 6–11; 12–3, 7–10.30 Sun
Adnams Bitter, Old, Extra G
Three-roomed village local displaying local art. Large garden.
🏚 Q ⛄ ❀ ◖ ▶ & A ♣ P

Wickhambrook

Greyhound
Meeting Green
☎ (01440) 820548
11–3, 5.30–11; 11–11 Sat; 12–3, 5.30–10.30 Sun
Greene King XX Mild, IPA H
Good village pub with a great social atmosphere – very easy to get into conversation.
Q ❀ ◖ ▶ 🍴 ♣ P 🍴

Wickham Market

George
95 The High Street
☎ (01728) 746306
11–3, 6–11; 12–3, 7–10.30 Sun
Tolly Cobbold Mild, Original, Old Strong, seasonal beers; guest beer H
Homely local with two main drinking areas and a new extension to the rear. It is now able to cater for all tastes with its lively pool room, friendly main bar and quieter lounge. Ramblers/cyclists welcome.
🏚 Q ❀ ◖ 🍴 & A ♣ P

Woodbridge

Bell & Steelyard
103 New Street
☎ (01394) 382933
11.30–3, 5.30–11; 12–3 Sun
Greene King IPA, Abbot, seasonal beers; guest beers H
Verified the 'twelfth oldest pub in England', with a wealth of exposed beams, this is home to the finest example of a steelyard in the country. Home-cooked fresh food.
🏚 Q ⛄ ❀ ◖ ▶ 🍴 ⇌ ♣ ⚥

Kings Head
17 Market Hill
☎ (01394) 387750
11.30–3, 5 (6 Sat)–11; 12–3, 7–10.30 Sun
Adnams Mild, Bitter, Old, Extra, Broadside; Boddingtons Bitter H
Well-situated pub of great character: the main bar is spacious with high beams and a large open fire; the back bar (Barrack Room) is also used as a restaurant (excellent food).
🏚 Q ❀ ◖ ▶ & ⇌ ♣ P

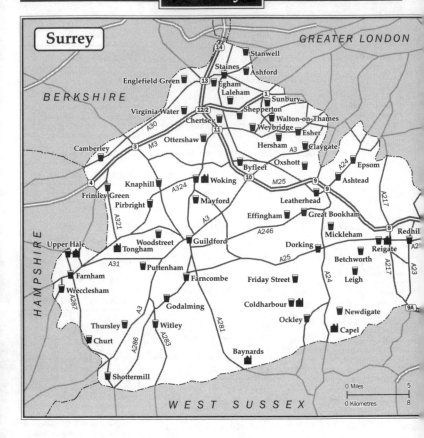

Surrey

BERKSHIRE

GREATER LONDON

Stanwell
Staines
Ashford
Englefield Green
Egham
Laleham
Virginia Water
Shepperton
Sunbury
Chertsey
Walton-on-Thames
Weybridge
Esher
Ottershaw
Hersham
Claygate
Camberley
Byfleet
Oxshott
Epsom
Knaphill
Woking
Ashtead
Frimley Green
Mayford
Leatherhead
Pirbright
Effingham
Great Bookham
Woodstreet
Guildford
Mickleham
Redhill
Upper Hale
Tongham
Dorking
Reigate
Farnham
Puttenham
Betchworth
Wrecclesham
Farncombe
Friday Street
Leigh
Godalming
Coldharbour
Newdigate
Thursley
Witley
Ockley
Capel
Churt
Baynards
Shottermill

WEST SUSSEX

HAMPSHIRE

0 Miles 5
0 Kilometres 8

Ashford

District Arms
180 Woodthorpe Road
☎ (01784) 252160
11–11; 12–10.30 Sun
**Courage Best Bitter, Directors;
John Smith's Bitter; guest
beer** H
Local pub with a friendly
welcome. Excellent home-
cooked lunches Mon–Fri.
🏨 ❀ ◑ ⇌ P

Ashtead

Brewery Inn
15 The Street (A24)
☎ (01372) 272405
11–11; 12–10.30 Sun
**Eldridge Pope Royal Oak;
Friary Meux BB; Ind Coope
Burton Ale; King & Barnes
Sussex; Marston's Pedigree;
Tetley Bitter** H
Large, Victorian pub on the site
of a former brewery, with a
raised lounge and dining area.
It can get crowded at
weekends. ⛴ ❀ ◑ ▶ ♣ P

Betchworth

Dolphin Inn
The Street (off A25)
☎ (01737) 842288
11–3, 5.30–11; 12–3, 7–10.30 Sun
**Young's Bitter, Special,
Winter Warmer, seasonal
beers** H
Friendly, 16th-century village
pub with a flagstone floor and
two wood-burning inglenooks,
in a very attractive spot,
opposite the village church and
blacksmith's.
🏨 Q ❀ ◑ ▶ ♣ P

Bletchingley

William IV
Little Common Lane (off A25,
W of village)
☎ (01883) 743278
11–3, 6–11; 12–3, 7–10.30 Sun
**Draught Bass; Fuller's London
Pride; Harveys BB; Morland
Old Speckled Hen; Pilgrim
Progress; Shepherd Neame
Master Brew Bitter** H

Victorian country inn: two
small bars at the front, a good
restaurant at the rear, and a
secluded garden.
Q ❀ ◑ ▶ 🏠 P

Byfleet

King's Head
59 Chertsey Road (off A245)
☎ (01932) 342671
11–11; 12–10.30 Sun
**Greene King IPA; Tetley
Bitter; guest beer** H
Comfortable, traditional-style
family pub with a strong darts
following; pool table. Dogs
welcome. 🏨 ❀ ◑ ← ♣ P

Plough
104 High Road (off A245)
☎ (01932) 353257
11–3, 5–11; 12–3, 7–10.30 Sun
**Courage Best Bitter; Fuller's
London Pride; guest beers** H
Popular with all ages, a true
village gem with seven guest
beers from micros and
independents. No meals
weekends.
🏨 Q ❀ ◑ ♣ P

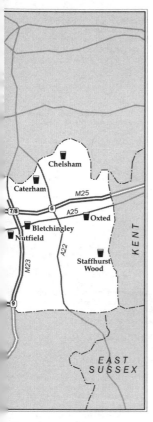

Camberley

William IV
19 Frimley Road (A321)
☎ (01276) 677654
11–11; 12–10.30 Sun
Greene King IPA, Abbot, seasonal beers H
Since refurbishment in 1995 this has become one of the best pubs in the area: a small, single-bar local with a busy office trade at lunchtime; quiet most eves. Q ❀ ◖ ▶ P

Caterham

Clifton Arms
110 Chaldon Road (B2031)
☎ (01883) 343525
11–2.30 (3 Sat), 5.30 (6 Sat)–11; 12–10.30 Sun
Draught Bass; Fuller's London Pride; Greene King IPA; guest beers H
Pub where entertainment is provided by music videos and, on Sun afternoons, live music. There's also a quieter back bar. One guest beer in winter, two

in summer; occasional cider. No food Sun. ❀ ◖ ♣ ⌂ P

King & Queen
34 High Street (B2030)
☎ (01883) 345438
11–11; 12–10.30 Sun
Fuller's Chiswick, London Pride, ESB, seasonal beers H
400-year-old building: a room with a dartboard, a central area with a large fire and a small no-smoking area off, plus a front bar. The menu has an oriental flavour (no food Sun eve). ♨ ❀ ◖ ▶ ♣ P ✠

Chelsham

Bull Inn
Chelsham Common (½ mile N of B269 at Warlingham Sainsbury's) OS372590
☎ (01883) 622970
11–11; 12–10.30 Sun
Draught Bass; Fuller's London Pride; Worthington Bitter; guest beer H
One-bar pub on the common with a large garden and children's play area. The guest beer is usually from an independent. ❀ ◖ ▶ ♣ P

Chertsey

Coach & Horses
14 St Anns Road (B375)
☎ (01932) 563085
11 (12 Sat)–11; 12–3, 7–10.30 Sun
Fuller's Chiswick, London Pride, ESB, seasonal beers H
Welcoming pub, dating from around 1860, with a tile-hung frontage.
♨ Q ❀ ⏚ ◖ ▶ ▲ ⇌ ♣ P

Churt

Crossways
Churt Road (A287)
☎ (01428) 714323
11–3.30, 5–11; 11–11 Sat; 12–4, 7–10.30 Sun
Cheriton Best Bitter; Courage Best Bitter; Ringwood Fortyniner, Old Thumper H**; guest beers** G
Well-run, friendly village local with an excellent range of ales.
Q ❀ ◖ ⏚ ▲ ♣ P

Claygate

Foley Arms
Foley Road
☎ (01372) 463431
11–2.30, 5.30–11; 11–11 Fri & Sat; 12–4, 7–10.30 (12–10.30 summer) Sun
Young's Bitter, Special, seasonal beers H
Comfortable, two-bar Victorian village pub. The large garden has a children's play area. Eve meals summer only; no food Sun. ♨ Q ❀ ◖ ▶ ⏚ ⇌ P

Griffin
58 Common Road
☎ (01372) 463799
11–11; 12–10.30 Sun
Badger Dorset Best; Fuller's London Pride; Pilgrim Surrey Bitter; guest beer H
Popular, backstreet local offering good lunches (not served Sun), a lively public bar and a comfortable lounge. Note the Mann, Crossman and Paulin windows. ♨ Q ❀ ◖ P

Coldharbour

Plough
Coldharbour Lane (Leith Hill–Dorking road) OS152441
☎ (01306) 711793
11.30–3, 6 (6.30 winter)–11; 11.30–11 Sat; 12–10.30 Sun
Adnams Broadside; Badger Dorset Best; Leith Hill Crooked Furrow, Tallywhacker; Ringwood Best Bitter; guest beers H
Up to nine ales are on sale here, including some brewed on the premises. Three bar areas provide for games, drinking and eating. The pub is set on Leith Hill in walking country.
♨ ❀ ⇐ ◖ ♣ ⌂

Dorking

Bush
10 Horsham Road (A2003)
☎ (01306) 889830
12–2.30 (3 Sat), 6–11; 12–3, 7–10.30 Sun
Beards Best Bitter; Brakspear Bitter; Fuller's London Pride; Thwaites Bitter; guest beer H
Locals' pub whose house championships include marbles and conkers. There is a covered patio and a garden. The guest beer is usually from an independent. Eve meals Tue–Sat. ❀ ◖ ▶ ♣

Cricketers
81 South Street (A25 westbound) ☎ (01306) 889938
12–11; 12–3, 7–10.30 Sun
Fuller's Chiswick, London Pride, ESB, seasonal beers H
Well-run pub whose bare brick walls have a large mirror and

■ INDEPENDENT BREWERIES

Baynards: Baynards

Hale & Hearty: Upper Hale

Hogs Back: Tongham

Leith Hill: Coldharbour

Pilgrim: Reigate

Planets: Woking

Weltons: Capel

several pictures illustrating the cricketing theme. Sheltered patio garden. No food Sun.
🏠 ◑ ♣

King's Arms
45 West Street (A25 eastbound)
☎ (01306) 883361
11–11; 12–3, 7–10.30 Sun
Eldridge Pope Royal Oak; King & Barnes Sussex; Ringwood Best Bitter; Tetley Bitter; Wadworth 6X; guest beer Ⓗ
Popular, 400-year-old town pub. The back area has a no-smoking area at lunchtimes and becomes a restaurant eves, except Sun (music night) and Mon (quiz night). The guest beer is from an independent.
🏠 ◑ ▶ ≢ (West) P ✗

Effingham

Plough
Orestan Lane
☎ (01372) 458121
11–2.45 (3 Sat), 6–11; 12–3, 7–10.30 Sun
Young's Bitter, Special, seasonal beers Ⓗ
A long-standing landlord provides a warm welcome at this pub which is famed for its food. Q 🏠 ◑ ▶ P ✗

Egham

Crown
38 High Street (off A30)
☎ (01784) 432608
11–3, 5.30 (6 Sat)–11; 12–3, 7–10.30 Sun
Fuller's London Pride; guest beers Ⓗ
Well-run, 1930s pub with a pretty, secluded garden to the rear, and benches at the front. A lively public bar is rather dominated by a pool table. No food Sun. 🏠 ◑ ⊞ ≢ ♣ P

Englefield Green

Beehive
34 Middle Hill (off A30)
☎ (01784) 431621
12–11; 12–10.30 Sun
Gale's Best Bitter, IPA, HSB; guest beers Ⓗ
Friendly, popular village pub with one, L-shaped bar in a quiet road in a residential area. Sun roast; three independent guest beers; cider in summer.
🏠 🏠 ◑ ♣ ▭ P

Epsom

Barley Mow
12 Pikes Hill (off A2022)
☎ (01372) 721044
11–3, 5.30–11; 12–3, 7–10.30 Sun
Fuller's London Pride, ESB, seasonal beers Ⓗ
Civilised, backstreet local. The original pub was sited on the opposite side of the road; the

present building is a conversion from two cottages. No food Sun eve.
Q 🏠 ◑ ▶ ♣ ♣

Olde King's Head
26 Church Street (B284)
☎ (01372) 729125
11–3, 5.30–11; 12–3, 7–10.30 Sun
Friary Meux BB; Fuller's London Pride; Marston's Pedigree; Young's Bitter Ⓗ
This cosy, friendly pub with two real fires, is Epsom's oldest. Home-cooked specials at very reasonable prices (no food Sun). Mixed clientele.
🏠 Q 🏠 ◑ ≢

Esher

Albert Arms
82 High Street (A307)
☎ (01372) 465290
10.30–11; 12–10.30 Sun
Draught Bass; Boddingtons Bitter; Brakspear Special; Fuller's London Pride; Young's Bitter; guest beer Ⓗ
Popular, two-bar local hosting occasional live piano or guitar music. Bar and bistro meals are all home-cooked (no food Sun eve). ◑ ♣

Farncombe

Cricketers
37 Nightingale Road
☎ (01483) 420273
12–3, 5.30–11; 12–11 Fri & Sat; 12–10.30 Sun
Fuller's Chiswick, London Pride, ESB, seasonal beers Ⓗ
Large amounts of beer are consumed in this busy local, consisting of several drinking areas around a central bar.
🏠 🏠 ◑ ▶ ≢ ✗

Farnham

Lamb
43 Abbey Street (off A287)
☎ (01252) 714133
11–2.30, 5–11; 11–11 Fri & Sat; 12–10.30 Sun
Shepherd Neame Master Brew Bitter, Best Bitter, Spitfire, Bishops Finger, seasonal beers Ⓗ/Ⓖ
Very friendly, traditional town local with unusual beers for the area. Good value food (Mon–Sat). Two pleasant patios behind. 🏠 🏠 ◑ ▶ ≢ ♣

Queen's Head
9 The Borough (A325)
☎ (01252) 726524
11–11; 12–10.30 Sun
Gale's Butser, Best Bitter, HSB, seasonal beers; guest beer Ⓗ
Recently enhanced by a first rate refurbishment, this busy, friendly pub, at the centre of

the town, attracts a wide range of customers. No food Sun.
🏠 🏠 ◑ ⊞ ≢ ♣

Shepherd & Flock
22 Moor Park Lane (off A31, N of Farnham)
☎ (01252) 716675
11–3, 5.30–11; 11–11 Fri & Sat; 12–10.30 Sun
Courage Best Bitter; Gale's HSB; Hampshire 1066; King & Barnes Sussex; guest beers Ⓗ
Large pub on an island roundabout, off the Farnham bypass. A narrow bar area leads to cosy nooks either side. Up to eight beers; fine selection of snacks and main meals; Sun curry night. Q 🏠 ◑ ▶ P

Six Bells
55 Hale Road (B3007 1 mile from town)
☎ (01252) 716697
11–3, 5–11; 12–3, 7–10.30 Sun
Morland IPA, Original, Old Masters, Old Speckled Hen, seasonal beers; guest beers Ⓗ
Big pub with an island bar splitting it into two areas. Its cellars were created from a Roman aqueduct. Excellent food. 🏠 Q 🏠 ◑ ▶ P

William Cobbett
4 Bridge Square, Abbey Street (A287)
☎ (01252) 726281
11–11; 12–10.30 Sun
Courage Best Bitter, Directors; Theakston Old Peculier; guest beer Ⓗ
This 16th-century pub, the birthplace of the 18th-century radical whose name it bears, is now a lively venue for a mostly young clientele. Interesting guest beers. The jukebox is loud, but good. 🏠 ◑ ≢ ♣ P

Friday Street

Stephan Langton
OS128456
☎ (01306) 730775
11–3 (11.30–2.30 winter), 6–11; 11–11 Sat; 12–10.30 (7 winter) Sun
Fuller's London Pride; Harveys BB; guest beers Ⓗ
Pub in a valley in good walking country: a bar area, an eating area, and a small enclosed balcony at the back for non-smokers. One guest is supplied by Bass, the other by an independent. Eve meals Tue–Sat. 🏠 🏠 ◑ ▶ ♣ P ✗

Frimley Green

Old Wheatsheaf
205 Frimley Green Road (A321)
☎ (01252) 835074
11–3, 5.30–11; 11–11 Sat; 12–4, 7–10.30 Sun
Morland IPA, Original, Old Masters, Old Speckled Hen; guest beer Ⓗ

Beautifully kept, large, single-bar pub by the main road, offering excellent food. Skittle alley-cum-family room at the rear. ♨ Q ⛄ ✿ ◖ ▶ ♣ P

Godalming

Anchor
110 Ockford Road (A3100)
☎ (01483) 417085
12–2.30 (3 Sat), 5.30 (6 Sat)–11; 12–3, 7–10.30 Sun
Badger Tanglefoot; Brakspear Bitter; Flowers Original; Gale's HSB; Hop Back Summer Lightning; guest beers H
Busy, L-shaped bar offering two, changing guest beers. Bar billiards. ✿ ◖ ⇌ ♣

Inn on the Lake
Ockford Road (A3100)
☎ (01483) 425575
11–11; 12–10.30 Sun
Boddingtons Bitter; Flowers IPA; Hogs Back TEA; Wadworth 6X H
Hotel with a popular restaurant and a two-roomed bar. ♨ Q ⛄ ✿ 🛏 ◖ ▶ ⇌ P

Old Wharf
5 Wharf Street (off A3100)
☎ (01483) 419543
11–11; 12–10.30 Sun
Boddingtons Bitter; Flowers Original; Fuller's London Pride; Marston's Pedigree; Young's Special H**; guest beers** G/H
Barn-style Hogshead beer emporium where many guest beers overshadow a dull basic range. Free tasters! Friendly attentive service. Two ciders, one changing. Meals served 12–6pm. ♨ Q ◖ ⇌ ♣ ♨

Red Lion
1 Mill Lane ☎ (01483) 415207
11–11; 11–3, 6.30–11 Sat; 12–3, 7–10.30 Sun
Courage Best Bitter, Directors; guest beers H
Town-centre local, featuring a large, games-oriented public and a smaller lounge. Imaginative guest beers; lined glasses on request. No food Sun eve.
Q ✿ ◖ ▶ 🍴 ⇌ ♣ 🍺

Great Bookham

Anchor ✂
161 Lower Road (off A246, via Eastwick Rd) ☎ (01372) 452429
11–2.30, 5.30–11; 12–3, 7–10.30 Sun
Courage Best Bitter, Directors; guest beer H
500-year-old local with exposed brickwork, beams, inglenook and a pleasant patio. It enjoys a rustic feel despite the surrounding suburbia. No food Sun.
♨ Q ✿ ◖ ♣ P

Guildford

King's Head
27 Kings Road (A320)
☎ (01483) 568957
11–3, 5–11; 11–11 Fri & Sat; 12–10.30 Sun
Fuller's Chiswick, London Pride, ESB, seasonal beers H
Popular, multi-roomed pub on the edge of the town centre, featuring bare board flooring, an outdoor patio and an illuminated well. Good value food. ♨ ✿ ◖ ▶ ♿ ⇌ (London Rd) ♣ P ✂

Sanford Arms
58 Epsom Road (A246)
☎ (01483) 572551
11 (11.45 Mon)–3, 5.30–11; 11.30–3.30, 6–11 Sat; 12–3, 7–10.30 Sun
Courage Best Bitter; Theakston XB; guest beer H
Quiet, friendly local: two wood-panelled bars and a small conservatory. The pleasant garden features an aviary and swings. No food Thu and Sun eves. Independent guest ale.
Q ✿ ◖ ▶ ⇌ (London Rd) ♣

Hersham

Royal George
130 Hersham Road (off A244)
☎ (01932) 220910
11–3, 5–11; 11–11 Sat; 12–10.30 Sun
Young's Bitter, Special, seasonal beers H
Family-oriented, spacious, two-bar pub with a nautical theme. The post-war building includes a friendly public bar.
♨ ✿ 🛏 ◖ ▶ 🍴 ♣ P

Knaphill

Garibaldi
136 High Street (off A322)
☎ (01483) 473374
11–11; 12–10.30 Sun
Fuller's London Pride; guest beers H
Bastion of real ale where the usual question is 'What's on tonight?': a small, L-shaped bar with two identities: the public bar area dominated by a 1930s OS map, contrasts with the cosier lounge. Excellent garden for children. Q ✿ ◖ ▶ P

Laleham

Feathers
The Broadway (B377)
☎ (01784) 453561
11–11; 12–10.30 Sun
Courage Best Bitter; Fuller's London Pride; Morland Old Speckled Hen; guest beers H
Friendly, popular, village pub, offering an adventurous guest beer range. ♨ ✿ ◖ ▶ ♿ ♣ P

Leatherhead

Running Horse
38 Bridge Street
☎ (01372) 372081
11–11; 12–3, 7–10.30 Sun
Ansells Mild, Bitter; Friary Meux BB; Ind Coope Burton Ale; Young's Special; guest beer H
Tudor-framed, Grade II-listed building, a genuine community local. ◖ 🍴 ⇌ ♣ P

Leigh

Plough
Church Road
☎ (01306) 611348
11–2.30, 5–11; 11–11 Sat; 12–10.30 Sun
King & Barnes Sussex, Broadwood, Old, Festive, seasonal beers H
Two-bar, country village inn. The public bar, dating from Victorian times, is popular for games. The lounge is 15th century and is used by diners.
Q ✿ ◖ ▶ 🍴 ♣ P

Mayford

Mayford Arms
Guildford Road (off A320)
☎ (01483) 761018
11–3, 5–11; 12–3, 7–10.30 Sun
Greene King IPA, Abbot, seasonal beers H
Comfortable pub where the lounge serves excellent, home-cooked food. There are also several drinking areas and a pool room. No food Sun eve.
✿ ◖ ▶ ♣ P

Mickleham ✂

William IV
Byttom Hill (off A24 southbound) OS174538
☎ (01372) 372590
11–3, 6–11; 12–3, 7–10.30 Sun
Adnams Bitter; Badger Dorset Best; Hogs Back TEA, Hop Garden Gold (summer); **guest beer** H
Charming free house, perched on a hillside, with stunning views. Excellent food. No meals Mon eve.
♨ Q ⛄ ✿ ◖ ▶

Newdigate

Surrey Oaks
Parkgate Road, Parkgate OS205436 ☎ (01306) 631200
11.30–2.30 (3 Sat), 5.30 (6 Sat)–11; 12–3, 7–10.30 Sun
Young's Bitter; guest beer H
Excellent old country inn, Surrey CAMRA *Pub of the Year* 1995–97. Beers from micros across the country (plus a Tapster's Choice beer); excellent menu, often with an Asian bias. No food Sun eve.
♨ Q ✿ ◖ ▶ ♣ ♨ P

Nutfield

Crown Inn
1 High Street (A25)
☎ (01737) 823240
12–3, 5–11; 11–11 Sat; 12–4, 7–10.30 Sun
Greene King IPA, Abbot H
Family-run, community-minded pub and restaurant, 400 years old.
❀ ◑ ▶ ♣ P

Ockley

Cricketers Arms
Stane Street (A29)
☎ (01306) 627205
11–3, 6–11; 12–3, 7–10.30 Sun
Draught Bass; Fuller's London Pride; Ringwood Best Bitter; guest beer (occasional) H
16th-century, family-run pub with an inglenook. Horsham flagstones are used on the roof as well as the floor. Patio at the front; garden at the side. Good value food.
❀ ❀ ◑ ▶ ♣ P

Ottershaw

Castle
222 Brox Road
☎ (01932) 872373
11–2.30, 5.30–11; 12–2.30, 7–10.30 Sun
Fuller's London Pride; Tetley Bitter; Wadworth 6X; Young's Special; guest beers H
Comfortable, two-bar, beamed pub with exposed brick walls and all manner of old country tools. ❀ Q ❀ ◑ ▶ P ✂

Oxshott

Bear
Leatherhead Road (A244)
☎ (01372) 842747
11–3, 5.30–11; 11–11 Sat; 12–10.30 Sun
Young's Bitter, Special, seasonal beers H
Very pleasant pub on the main road just out of the village: one bar with a seating area divided by an arched wall, and a conservatory restaurant.
❀ Q ☺ ❀ ◑ ▶ & ♣ P

Oxted

George Inn
52 High Street, Old Oxted (off A25)
☎ (01883) 713453
11–11; 12–10.30 Sun
Adnams Bitter; Fuller's London Pride; Harveys BB; Morland Old Speckled Hen; Wadworth 6X; Young's Bitter H
Very comfortable, and often very busy, 500-year-old pub well known for its quality and value food.
❀ Q ❀ ◑ ▶ P

Pirbright

Royal Oak
Aldershot Road (A324)
☎ (01483) 232466
11–11; 12–10.30 Sun
Boddingtons Bitter; Flowers Original; Marston's Pedigree; guest beers H
Picture book pub and location – a low-beamed, olde-worlde building set in gardens leading down to a stream. Three distinct bar areas, one dedicated to food and families. Regular brewery and price promotions.
❀ Q ☺ ❀ ◑ ▶ P ✂

Puttenham

Good Intent
The Street ☎ (01483) 810387
11–3, 6–11; 11–11 Sat; 12–3, 7–10.30 Sun
Courage Best Bitter; Wadworth 6X; guest beers H
Deservedly popular, old village local with three distinct drinking areas. An independent guest beer complements Inch's cider and almost 50 whiskies. Eve meals Tue–Sat. ❀ Q ❀ ◑ ▶ ♣ ☺ P

Redhill

Home Cottage
3 Redstone Hill (behind station) ☎ (01737) 762771
10.30–11; 12–3, 7–10.30 Sun
Young's Bitter, Special, Winter Warmer, seasonal beers H
Large, lively, pub with an impressive set of handpumps in the front bar. Note also the etched-glass windows.
❀ ❀ ◑ ▶ ⇌ ♣ P

Reigate

Nutley Hall
8 Nutley Lane (behind car park on one-way road at W end of town) ☎ (01737) 241741
11–11; 12–3, 7–10.30 Sun
King & Barnes Sussex, Broadwood, Old, Festive, seasonal beers H
Busy drinkers' pub with a quieter rear bar.
❀ Q ☺ ❀ ◑ ▶ ⊟ ⇌ ♣ ☺ P

Tap & Spile
96 High Street (A25)
☎ (01737) 243955
11–3, 5.30–11; 11–11 Fri & Sat; 1–4, 7–10.30 Sun
Beer range varies H
Old pub whose bare brick walls are covered with bric-a-brac. Eight handpumps serve a changing range of beers and cider, with usually at least one from the Pilgrim Brewery

across the road. Weekday lunches. ❀ Q ◑ ⇌ ♣ ☺

Yew Tree
99 Reigate Hill (A217, N of town) ☎ (01737) 244944
11–11; 12–10.30 Sun
Courage Best Bitter; Morland Old Speckled Hen; Wadworth 6X; Young's Bitter H
Local landmark with one comfortable, wood-panelled bar. Food all day; good steaks.
❀ ◑ ▶ P ⊟

Shepperton

Barley Mow
67 Watersplash Road, Shepperton Green (off B376)
☎ (01932) 225580
11–11; 12–10.30 Sun
Courage Best Bitter, Directors; Young's Bitter, Winter Warmer; guest beer H
Popular, single-bar pub with several drinking areas, close to Shepperton Studios.
Q ❀ ◑ & ♣ P

Shottermill

Mill Tavern
Liphook Road (B2131)
☎ (01428) 643183
11–3, 5–11; 11–11 Sat; 12–3, 7–10.30 Sun
Beer range varies H
Traditional-style, convivial pub with bare boards, rugs and low beams in a single bar with an adjoining restaurant. Excellent, changing beer selection. Roaring log fire in the inglenook. ❀ Q ❀ ◑ ▶ P

Staffhurst Wood

Royal Oak
Caterfield Lane (2½ miles S of A25 at Limpsfield) OS407485
☎ (01883) 722207
11–3, 5.30–11; 12–3, 7–10.30 Sun
Adnams Bitter; Larkins Traditional Ale; M&B Brew XI; guest beer (occasional) H
French food is featured here both in the bar and in the large restaurant. The garden boasts good countryside views. No eve meals Sun or Mon.
❀ ❀ ◑ ▶ ♣ P

Staines

Angel Hotel
24 High Street (A308)
☎ (01784) 452509
11–11; 12–10.30 Sun
Courage Best Bitter; John Smith's; guest beers H
Deservedly popular inn. The extensive range of guest beers changes daily, and a 'budget' beer is always available. The home-cooked food is first-rate.
Q ❀ ☒ ◑ ▶ & ⇌ P ✂

George

2 High Street (A308)
☎ (01784) 462181
11–11; 12–10.30 Sun
Courage Directors; Fuller's London Pride; Theakston Best Bitter; Younger Scotch; guest beers H
Welcome addition to the local pub scene, newly built on the site of a previous George Inn, closed 200 years ago. All ages are catered for in comfortable surroundings. Four guest beers. Q ❀ ◖ ▶ & ⇌ ♻ ⚹

Hobgoblin

14 Church Street (off A308)
☎ (01784) 452012
11.30–11; 12–10.30 Sun
Wychwood Special, Old Devil, DB, Hobgoblin; guest beers H
Lively, wooden-floored town-centre pub. The eve custom is usually young, and they enjoy a few decibels with their drinks. Lunches Mon–Fri.
🏚 ❀ ◖ & ⇌

Stanwell

Wheatsheaf

Town Lane (B378)
☎ (01784) 253372
11–11; 11–4, 7–11 Sat; 12–4, 7–10.30 Sun
Courage Best Bitter, Directors; Marston's Pedigree; guest beer H
Popular corner pub in a part of Stanwell that retains its village atmosphere, despite the nearby airport. Two distinct drinking areas. No eve meals weekends, nor Sun lunch.
Q ❀ ◖ ▶ ♣ P

Sunbury

Magpie

64 Thames Street
☎ (01932) 782024
11–11; 12–10.30 Sun
Draught Bass; Gibbs Mew Wiltshire, Salisbury, Wake Ale, Bishop's Tipple; guest beer H
Two-bar riverside pub with a patio and landing stage. Food is served in an upstairs conservatory area. Children are allowed in several areas. Wheelchair WC.
Q ❀ ◖ ▶ &

Thursley

Three Horseshoes

Dye House Road (off A3)
☎ (01252) 703268
12–3, 6–11; 12–4 (12–4, 7–10.30 summer) Sun
Gale's Butser, HSB H
A Victorian facade hides the Tudor cottage behind the main bar of this privately-owned pub which has traditional

values and a fine, home-made menu. Panoramic views.
🏚 Q ❀ 🐾 ◖ ▶ & P ⊟

Upper Hale

Ball & Wicket

104 Upper Hale Road (A3106)
☎ (01252) 735278
4 (12 Sat)–11; 12–3, 7–10.30 Sun
B&T Dragonslayer; Hale & Hearty Wicket Bitter; guest beers H
Lovely brew pub opposite the green. Watch the cricket in summer. Note the unusual opening hours. 🏚 ❀ ♣ ♻ P

Virginia Water

Rose & Olive Branch

Callow Hill OS993689
☎ (01344) 843713
11–3, 5.30–11; 12–3, 7–10.30 Sun
Morland IPA, Old Speckled Hen, seasonal beers; Wells Bombardier H
Small, slightly up-market pub in an out of the way situation. The heavily beamed bar features horse brasses, lamps and the occasional clock. Its name refers to a Civil War treaty: the Cavaliers gave a rose and the Roundheads an olive branch. Q ❀ 🐾 ◖ ▶ P

Walton-on-Thames

Regent

19 Church Street (A3050)
☎ (01932) 243980
11–11; 12–10.30 Sun
Courage Directors; Fuller's London Pride; Theakston Best Bitter; Younger Scotch; guest beer H
Refurbished former cinema, decorated with film memorabilia reflecting the town's long connection with the industry. Popular with students. ◖ ▶ & ♣ ♻ ⚹

Weybridge

Jolly Farmer

41 Princes Road (off B373)
☎ (01932) 856873
10.30–3, 5–11; 11–11 Sat; 12–3, 7–10.30 Sun
Courage Best Bitter; Fuller's London Pride; Hop Back GFB, Thunderstorm, Summer Lightning, seasonal beers H
Comfortable, friendly, backstreet local with a low, beamed ceiling. The family room is a tent behind the pub. The prices reflect the local affluence. 🐂 ❀ ◖ P

Prince of Wales

11 Cross Road, Oatlands (off A3050, via Anderson Rd)
☎ (01932) 852082
12 (11 Sat)–11; 12–10.30 Sun

Adnams Bitter; Boddingtons Bitter; Tetley Bitter; guest beer H
Backstreet pub, popular with locals. Good food. ❀ ◖ ▶ P

Witley

White Hart

Petworth Road (A283)
☎ (01428) 683695
11–2.30, 5.30–11; 11–11 Sat; 12–3, 7–10.30 (12–10.30 summer) Sun
Shepherd Neame Master Brew Bitter, Spitfire, Bishops Finger, seasonal beers H
Haunted 14th-century pub: a public bar, lounge and a restaurant. Garden play area (children also welcome in the restaurant which has wheelchair access).
🏚 ❀ ◖ ⊟ ♣ P

Woking

Wetherspoons

Chertsey Road
☎ (01483) 722818
11–11; 12–10.30 Sun
Courage Directors; Hogs Back TEA; Theakston Best Bitter; Younger Scotch; guest beers H
An excellent addition to the revitalised town centre, with up to four guest beers. Often crowded at weekends.
Q ◖ ▶ & ⇌ ♻ ⚹

Woodstreet

Royal Oak

89 Oak Hill ☎ (01483) 235137
11–2.30 (3 Fri, 3.30 Sat), 5–11; 12–3.30, 7–10.30 Sun
Courage Best Bitter; Hogs Back TEA; guest beers H
Superb free house. Four often rare guest beers. ❀ ◖ ♣ P

Wrecclesham

Bat & Ball

Bat & Ball Lane, Boundstone (off Upper Bourne Lane, off Sandrock) OS833445
☎ (01252) 794564
11–11; 12–10.30 Sun
Boddingtons Bitter; Brakspear Bitter; Fuller's London Pride; Young's Special; guest beer H
Hard to find free house, popular with diners and families. Three interesting guest beers. No food Sun eve.
Q 🐂 ❀ ◖ ▶ ♣ P

Sandrock

Sandrock Hill OS830445
☎ (01252) 715865
11–11; 12–10.30 Sun
Batham Best Bitter; Boddingtons Bitter; Enville Ale; guest beers H
First-rate ale pub with an emphasis on Black Country beers (eight beers in all). Very friendly – not to be missed. No food Sun. 🏚 Q ❀ ♣ P

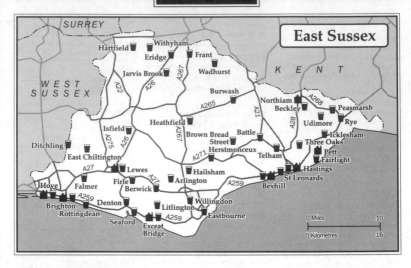

East Sussex

East Sussex

Arlington

Old Oak
Cane Heath (Hailsham–Arlington/Wilmington road)
OS558078 ☎ (01323) 482072
11–3, 6–11; 12–3, 7–10.30 Sun
Badger Dorset Best; Harveys BB; guest beers G
Imposing country pub situated out in the sticks, by Abbotts Wood nature reserve: a comfy lounge and restaurant, not far from the speedway but quiet nonetheless. ♨ Q ☸ ◗ ❍ ♣ P

Battle

King's Head
37 Mount Street (off High St)
☎ (01424) 772317
10.30–3, 5.30–11; 10.30–11 Sat; 12–3, 7–10.30 Sun
Courage Best Bitter, Directors; Harveys BB; John Smith's Bitter H
15th-century inn boasting award-winning floral displays. The inglenook and low beams make it the sort of pub you would expect in this ancient town. No food Sun eve in winter ♨ ☸ ⇥ ◗ ♣ ♠

Try also: **1066**, High St (Whitbread)

Beckley

Rose & Crown
Northiam Road (B2188/B2165 jct) ☎ (01797) 252161
11–3, 6–11; 12–4.30, 7–10.30 Sun
Adnams Bitter; Harveys BB; Greene King Abbot; guest beers H

Spacious, welcoming family pub with fine views from the garden. Beers from distant breweries are frequently available. ♨ Q ☸ ◗ ❍ ♣ P

Berwick

Cricketers Arms ☆
Berwick Village (S of A27, just off Drusilla's roundabout)
☎ (01323) 870469
11–3, 6–11 (11–11 summer Sat); 12–3, 6.30–10.30 Sun
Harveys BB, seasonal beers G
Always a fine pub, but a change of landlord here some time ago has extended the range of beer and food (reasonable prices for the area). A fine old house (once two cottages) where time has stood still, winner of Harveys *Cellar of the Year* 1997.
♨ Q ☸ ◗ ❍ ♠ P

Bexhill

Rose & Crown
Turkey Road (outskirts of town, near Sidley)
☎ (01424) 214625
11–3.30, 5.30–11; 11–11 Sat; 12–3, 7–10.30 Sun
Beards Best Bitter; Harveys BB; guest beers H
1930s Beards house, spacious, comfortable and well worth finding. There are always four guest ales on offer; the range changes monthly.
☸ ◗ ❍ ♿ ♣ P ✄

Brighton

Basketmakers Arms
12 Gloucester Road
☎ (01273) 689006
11–3, 5.30 (5 Wed & Thu)–11; 11–11 Fri & Sat; 12–10.30 Sun

Gale's Butser, Best Bitter, IPA, HSB, Festival Mild; guest beers H
Popular, backstreet local with an interesting collection of tins. Excellent menu, with Sunday roasts including a vegetarian option. Winner of many Gale's cellar awards. One guest beer comes from the Gale's Beer Club. Eve meals Mon–Fri until 8.30. ◗ ❍

Cobbler's Thumb
10 New England Road (100 yds W of A23/A270 jct)
☎ (01273) 605636
11–11; 12–10.30 Sun
Badger Tanglefoot; Harveys BB, seasonal beers; guest beers H
Unspoilt, two-bar corner local, popular with all ages. One bar is used for pool. Following a threat of closure, there have been no internal changes and the original fittings remain. Note the recreation of the

---

original cobbler's workshop in the main bar.
🏛 🌑 🌗 ⇌ ♣ ♨

Constant Service

96 Islingword Road
☎ (01273) 607058
12 (11 Sat)–11; 12–10.30 Sun
Harveys XX Mild, BB, Armada, seasonal beers 🄷
Single-bar pub of unusual shape that gained it name from the adjacent reservoir, which, being on a hillside, offered a constant service. 🏛 🌑 ♣

Dover Castle

43 Southover Street
☎ (01273) 889808
11–11; 12–3, 7–10.30 Sun
Shepherd Neame Best Bitter, Spitfire 🄷
Basic, welcoming, family local where games are much in evidence. The TV is only in use for sporting events.
♣ 🍺

Evening Star

55–56 Surrey Street (200 yds S of station)
☎ (01273) 328931
12 (11 Sat)–11; 12–10.30 Sun
Dark Star Skinner's Pale Ale, Skinner's Golden Gate Bitter, Skinner's Penguin Stout, Dark Star; guest beers 🄷
Home of the Dark Star brewery. Brighton's permanent real ale festival features 11 pumps dispensing an ever-changing range of in-house and rare guest beers; over 2,100 since March 1992. Occasional theme nights with live music.
🌑 ⇌ ♣ ♨

Greys

105 Southover Street
☎ (01273) 680734
11–3, 5.30–11; 11–11 Sat; 12–10.30 Sun
Brewery on Sea Spinnaker Classic; Flowers Original; Fuller's Chiswick 🄷
Corner pub with a good reputation for food, stocking a range of Belgian bottled beers. It can become crowded eves when live music is often to be heard. Lunches Mon–Sat, eve meals Tue–Thu. 🌑 🌗 🌕

Hand in Hand

33 Upper St James Street
☎ (01273) 602521
11–11; 12–10.30 Sun
Badger Dorset Best, Tanglefoot; Kemptown Brighton Bitter, Bitter, Olde Trout, SID, Old Grumpy; guest beers 🄷
Compact home of Kemptown Brewery, with very unusual decor: the walls are covered with extracts from old newspapers, and historic local pictures, whilst ties adorn the ceiling. 🌑

Park Crescent

39 Park Crescent Terrace
☎ (01273) 645997
12–11; 12–10.30 Sun
King & Barnes Sussex, Broadwood, Festive, seasonal beers 🄷
Historic pictures of the local area are displayed in this town pub, recently opened by King & Barnes (one of only three in the area). Coffee and a newspaper rack add to the café atmosphere. No eve meals Sun. Popular with students.
🌑 🌕

Prince Arthur

38 Dean Street (off Western Rd)
☎ (01273) 203472
12–11; 12–10.30 Sun
Draught Bass; Flowers Original; Fuller's London Pride; Greene King Abbot; Harveys BB; Morland Old Speckled Hen 🄷
One of the few unspoilt pubs in the main shopping area. The main bar is wood panelled and there is a small conservatory-like bar at the rear. A strong local trade ensures regular turnover of ales. No food Sun.
🛏 🌑 🌕

Sir Charles Napier

50 Southover Street
☎ (01273) 601413
12–3, 6–11; 12–11 Sat; 12–4, 7–10.30 Sun
Gale's Butser, IPA, HSB 🄷; **guest beer** 🄶/🄷
Victorian corner local adorned with some fascinating memorabilia. The sheltered garden, with an abundance of flowers, features a George V post box. Food is home-made, including vegetarian options.
🌑 🌕 🌗

Sir Loyne of Beefe

63 Sussex Street
☎ (01273) 380580
11.30–11; 12–5, 7.30–10.30 Sun
Draught Bass; Ringwood True Glory; guest beers 🄷
Sympathetically renovated corner local, one of a growing chain stretching from Hampshire to Sussex. Fine panoramic view of the town from the rear patio. SLOB Ale is usually John Smith's Bitter.
Q 🌑

Sudeley Arms

33 Sudeley Street (near Royal Sussex County Hospital)
☎ (01273) 682991
11–3, 5–11; 11–11 Fri & Sat; 12–10.30 Sun
Harveys BB; Marston's Pedigree; Morland Old Speckled Hen 🄷
Corner pub with two distinct bars and many other nice touches: note the chocolate box collection in the saloon bar and various old enamel advertising

signs. Theme and party nights are popular. 🌑 🌕 🌗 🍴 ♣

Sussex Yeoman

7 Guildford Road (100 yds W of station) ☎ (01273) 327985
11–3, 5–11; 11–11 Sat; 12–10.30 Sun
Bateman XB; Harveys BB, seasonal beers; Hop Back Summer Lightning; guest beers 🄷
Friendly, comfortable, popular, single-bar corner pub. A selection of eight ales is served, plus 40 speciality sausages, including six vegetarian varieties; monthly curry nights. No food Sun eve. Occasional cider. 🌕 ⇌ ♣ ♨

Tap & Spile

67A Upper Gloucester Road
☎ (01273) 327075
11–11; 12–10.30 Sun
Tap & Spile Premium; guest beers 🄷
Opened as a Tap & Spile in 1995 (previously the Edinburgh). Up to eight constantly changing beers plus a range of bottled Belgian beers are available, plus cider in summer. Q ⇌ ♣ ♨

Brown Bread Street

Ash Tree Inn

On by-road off lane signed Ashburnham from A271
OS675149 ☎ (01424) 892104
12–3, 7–11; 12–4, 7–10.30 Sun
Harveys BB; Morland Old Speckled Hen; guest beer 🄷
Cosy, 400-year-old building with three areas, replete with beams; an ale house for 200 years. The public bar was originally the village hall. Two family rooms. Quality food.
🏛 Q 🛏 🌑 🌕 🌗 🍴 ♣ P

Burwash

Rose & Crown

Ham Lane (off A265)
☎ (01485) 882600
11–11; 12–10.30 Sun
Greene King IPA; guest beers 🄷
Old country inn at the village centre with low, beamed ceilings, large inglenook and a restaurant area. No food Sun eve. 🏛 Q 🌑 🍴 🌕 ♣

Denton

Flying Fish

42 Denton Road (off A26)
☎ (01273) 515440
11–3, 6 (5 Fri)–11; 12–3, 7–10.30 Sun
Shepherd Neame Best Bitter, Spitfire, Bishops Finger 🄷
Recently acquired by Shepherd Neame: originally a 16th-century barn, but now a pub of many years' standing, with two bars and a pool room. An interesting stillage is built into

the bar. Check tide tables before visiting, as it can flood at high water! No food Mon eve or Sun. ♨ ❀ ◖ ▶ ⬭ ♣ P

Ditchling

White Horse
16 West Street
☎ (01273) 842006
11–11; 12–10.30 Sun
Harveys BB; guest beers H
Friendly, single-bar village pub near Anne of Cleves's house. A wide range of food includes vegetarian options. The cellar is said to be haunted.
♨ ❀ ◖ ▶

Eastbourne

Alexandra Arms
453 Seaside (2 miles E of centre on A259) ☎ (01323) 720913
11.30–3, 5–11; 12–3, 7–10.30 Sun
Beards Best Bitter; Fuller's London Pride; Harveys BB; Theakston Old Peculier; guest beers H
Recently extended, post-war pub with two contrasting bars, but a friendly welcome in both. Annual beer festival – July.
❀ ◖ ▶ ♣ P ✏

Hurst Arms
76 Willingdon Road (1 mile N of centre on A22)
☎ (01323) 721762
11–11; 12–10.30 Sun
Harveys BB, Old, Armada H, **seasonal beers** H/G
A *Guide* regular since 1978: an imposing Victorian local housing a large public bar and a smaller saloon. It was probably named after the Hurst mill, which was situated nearby. Barbecues in the back garden in summer.
Q ❀ ♣

Lamb
High Street, Old Town (A259 W of centre) ☎ (01323) 720545
10–3, 5.30–11; 10.30–11 Fri & Sat; 12–4, 7–10.30 Sun
Harveys XX Mild, Pale Ale, BB, Armada, seasonal beers H
Possibly the premier house in the Harveys estate, with three bars, each on a slightly different level, and each distinctly different. Part of the pub dates from 1290. Limited parking. Recommended food.
Q ❀ ◖ ▶ ⇌ P

Try also: Victoria, Latimer Rd (Harveys)

East Chiltington

Jolly Sportsman
Chapel Lane ☎ (01273) 890400
11–3 (not Mon), 6–11; 12–3, 7–10.30 Sun
Courage Best Bitter; King & Barnes Sussex; John Smith's Bitter; guest beer H

Rural pub popular with walkers enjoying excellent views of the downs. Bar billiards, pool and dining areas are away from the bar area. Lunches Wed–Mon; no Sun eve meals. ❀ ◖ ▶ ♣ P

Eridge

Huntsman
Just off A26, Tunbridge Wells–Crowborough road
☎ (01892) 864258
11.30–3, 6–11; 12–3, 7–10.30 Sun
King & Barnes Mild, Sussex, Broadwood, Festive, seasonal beer H
Friendly, well-run, two-bar pub in a rural location, popular with walkers and climbers, offering a good wine selection and traditional English food. Riverside garden.
Q ❀ ◖ ▶ ♨ ⇌ ♣ ◔ P

Exceat Bridge

Golden Galleon
On A259, 2 miles E of Seaford
☎ (01323) 892247
11–11; 12–10.30 Sun (4 winter Sun)
Cuckmere Haven Best Bitter, Saxon King, Guv'nor, Golden Peace; Greene King IPA; Harveys Armada; guest beers H
Scenic home of Cuckmere Haven Brewery, boasting fine views of the estuary, channel and Seven Sisters Country Park. Strong emphasis on food; the River Room eases congestion for beer drinkers. Up to 14 beers available.
♨ ⬭ ❀ ♨ ♣ ◔

Fairlight

Fairlight Lodge
Martineau Lane OS851117
☎ (01424) 812104
11–3, 7–11; 12–3, 6–10.30 Sun
Greene King Abbot; Old Forge Pett Progress; guest beers H
Recently refurbished hotel bar set in the idyllic country park. Local micros' beers are usually sold. No food Wed eve.
♨ ❀ ⬭ ◖ ▶ ♨ ♣ P

Falmer

Swan
Middle Street, North Falmer (near Sussex University, off A27) ☎ (01273) 681842
11–3, 6–11; 12–3, 7–10.30 Sun
Palmers IPA, 200; guest beers H/G
Village local run by the landlord's family since 1903. Three bars: one no-smoking, one games-oriented. The decor features breweriana and local pictures. A children's certificate allows under 14s in until 9pm. ♨ ❀ ◖ ▶ ⇌ P ✏

Firle

Ram
Off A27 ☎ (01273) 858222
11.30–3, 7–11; 12–3, 7–10.30 Sun
Harveys BB; Otter Bitter; guest beers H
Popular village local; a centre for local ramblers. It features pictures of historic village life, plus a Georgian court room. Excellent pub food and generally four ales on offer.
♨ Q ❀ ◖ ▶

Frant

Abergavenny Arms
Frant Road (A267)
☎ (01892) 750233
11–3, 6–11; 12–3, 7–10.30 Sun
Harveys BB H; **Rother Valley Level Best; guest beers** G
Large country free house on two levels; the pub dates back to 1450. Constantly changing guest beers from Sussex brewers and distant micros. Good food. ♨ Q ❀ ◖ ▶ ♣ P

Hailsham

Grenadier
High Street ☎ (01323) 842152
11–11; 12–3, 7–10.30 Sun
Harveys XX Mild, BB, Old, Armada, seasonal beers H
Popular, two-bar town pub, in the same family for over 40 years. An imposing building with a well renovated interior – particularly the public and private bars. Spot the original gas lamp fittings. Close to the Cuckoo Trail foot and cycle way. ❀ ◖ ▶ ⬭ & ♣

Hartfield

Anchor
Church Street
☎ (01892) 770424
11–11; 12–10.30 Sun
Boddingtons Bitter; Flowers Original; Harveys BB; Marston's Pedigree; Wadworth 6X; guest beers H
A pleasant welcome rewards the search for this slightly hidden hostelry, now enjoying a well-deserved second year in the *Guide*.
♨ Q ❀ ◖ ▶ & ♣ P ⊟

Hastings

Carlisle
24 Pelham Place (seafront)
☎ (01424) 420193
11–11; 12–10.30 Sun
Tetley Bitter; guest beers H
Busy, loud, bikers'-type pub with three bars; the largest has live bands. Quieter bars are at the rear. Music and beer festival in summer.
Q & ⇌ ♣

First In, Last Out

14 High Street, Old Town
☎ (01424) 425079
11–11; 12–10.30 Sun
FILO Crofter, Cardinal; guest beers ℍ
Home of the FILO brewery, featuring alcove seating and central heating with a difference – an open central fireplace complete with flue. Busy eves and weekends; frequent mini-beer festivals. Lunches Tue–Sat.
🏚 Q ❀ ◖ ⌂

Royal George

Devonshire Road
☎ (01424) 443685
11–11; 12–3, 7–10.30 Sun
Harveys BB; guest beer ℍ
Lively town-centre pub near the station and shopping centre. ◖ ⇌ ♣

Stag

All Saints Street, Old Town (off the Bourne) ☎ (01424) 425734
12–3, 6–11; 11–11 Sat; 12–10.30 Sun
Shepherd Neame Master Brew Bitter, Best Bitter, Spitfire, Bishops Finger ℍ
Ancient smugglers' pub in the old town, hosting folk music Wed eve. The pub's own game of Loggits is played. Known for its whiskies.
🏚 ❄ ♒ ◖ ▶ ♠ ♣

Heathfield

Prince of Wales

Station Road ☎ (01435) 862919
11–3, 5–11; 11–11 Sat; 12–10.30 Sun
Greene King Abbot; Harveys BB; guest beers ℍ
Popular local, often crowded, featuring a good value carvery restaurant as well as a public bar. Close to the Cuckoo Trail foot and cycle way.
🏚 ❀ ◖ ▶ ♿ ♣ P

Herstmonceux

Brewer's Arms

Gardner Street (A271)
☎ (01323) 832226
11–2.30, 6–11; 12–2, 7–10.30 Sun
Adnams Broadside; Beards Best Bitter; Harveys BB; guest beers ℍ
Traditional country village pub with an olde-worlde atmosphere and many antiques. Beers from distant breweries are frequently available. No eve meals Tue.
🏚 Q ❀ ◖ ▶ P ⊬

Welcome Stranger

Chapel Row (100 yds S of A271) ☎ (01323) 832119
7–11; 12–2.30, 7–11 Sat; 12–3, 7–10.30 Sun
Harveys BB, Old; guest beers (occasional) ℍ
Fine example of an unspoilt country ale house, the last in

Sussex to obtain a full licence: known locally as the 'Kicking Donkey' and in same family for 90 years. Beer is served through a hatch into a simple bar room. Worth finding – but open eves only Mon–Fri.
🏚 Q ❀ ♣ P ⌷

Hove

Eclipse

33 Montgomery Street
☎ (01273) 272212
11–3, 6–11; 11–11 Sat; 12–4, 7–10.30 Sun
Harveys XX Mild, Pale Ale, BB, seasonal beers ℍ
Formerly a Charrington house, this pub has been well restored into a comfortable local. Note the painted mouldings on the exterior – the pub has a connection with the turf. Eve meals Tue–Sat.
🏚 Q ❀ ◖ ▶ ♿ ⇌ ♣

Farm Tavern

13 Farm Road (off Western Rd)
☎ (01273) 325902
11–11; 12–3, 7–10.30 Sun
Bateman XB; Beards Best Bitter; Harveys BB; guest beers ℍ
True backstreet local – small, cosy, and well worth finding. Note the impressive coat of arms above the fireplace. Good food. Q ❀ ◖ ♣

Icklesham

Queen's Head

Parsonage Lane (E of village, off A259) ☎ (01424) 814552
11–11; 12–5, 7–10.30 Sun
Beer range varies ℍ
Tile-hung country pub in a rural setting, with a magnificent mahogany bar, superb views from the garden and a warm, friendly atmosphere. Usually four or five beers and excellent food are served. Boules played.
🏚 Q ❀ ◖ ▶ ♿ ♠ ♣ ⌷ P

Isfield

Laughing Fish

Station Road (W of A26)
☎ (01825) 750349
11.30–3, 6–11; 12–3, 7–10.30 Sun
Harveys Pale Ale, BB; guest beers ℍ
Traditional village local next to the Lavender Line railway. Its porch was built by the Canadian army during World War II. Small snug at the back. No eve meals Mon.
🏚 ♒ ❀ ◖ ▶ ♣ P

Jarvis Brook

Wheatsheaf

Mount Pleasant Road (100 yds from bridge over railway)
OS530294 ☎ (01892) 663756

12–2.30 (4 Sat), 5.30 (6 Sat)–11; 12–11 Fri; 12–3, 7–10.30 Sun
Fuller's ESB; Harveys BB, Old; guest beers ℍ
Old country inn that has survived unspoilt as the town of Crowborough has grown around it. Its cosy interior has three rooms on two different levels. It can be hard to find, but is worth the effort.
🏚 Q ❀ ◖ ▶ ⊞ ⇌ ♣

Lewes

Black Horse

55 Western Road
☎ (01273) 473653
11–2.30, 5.30 (6 Sat)–11; 12–2.30, 7–10.30 Sun
Archers Golden; Beards Best Bitter; Brakspear Special; Harveys BB, seasonal beers; guest beers ℍ
Originally a coaching inn, this Beards pub now features two bars, one with a fascinating collection of photos of old Lewes pubs. No food Sun.
Q ❀ ♒ ◖ ⊞ ♣

Brewers Arms

91 High Street
☎ (01273) 479475
10.30–11; 12–10.30 Sun
Draught Bass; Harveys BB, seasonal beers; guest beers ℍ
Comfortable, plush, friendly local, well refurbished, with a games bar at the rear. There has been a pub on this site since 1540; see the list of landlords since 1744. Food is available all sessions. Children's certificate. Cider in summer.
Q ♒ ◖ ▶ ⇌ ♣ ⌷

Dorset Arms

22 Malling Street (400 yds E of Harveys Brewery)
☎ (01273) 477110
11–3, 6–11; 12–4, 7–10.30 Sun
Harveys XX Mild, Pale Ale, BB, Armada, seasonal beers ℍ
The Harveys brewery tap: a large, plush, two-bar pub with a restaurant and a no-smoking family room. No eve meals Sun or Mon.
🏚 Q ♒ ❀ ◖ ▶ ⇌ P ⊬

Elephant & Castle

White Hill (A2029)
☎ (01273) 473797
11.30–11; 12–10.30 Sun
Harveys BB, seasonal beers; Morland Old Speckled Hen; guest beers ℍ
Large, unspoilt, friendly, two-bar local featuring a large collection of ornaments, a real fire in each bar and a room for table football. The pub has its own rugby club. The menu includes home-made burgers called 'Eleburgers'.
🏚 ♒ ◖ ⇌ ♣

Gardeners Arms
46 Cliffe High Street (almost
opp. Harveys Brewery)
☎ (01273) 474808
11–3, 5.30–11; 11–11 Fri & Sat; 12–3,
7–10.30 Sun
**Harveys BB, seasonal beers;
guest beers** H
Friendly, two-bar free house, a
sister pub of Brighton's
Evening Star, featuring
Skinner's and Dark Star beers
in the range. Bar snacks.
Q ◖ ≈ ♻

Royal Oak
3 Station Street
☎ (01273) 474803
11–3, 5 (6.30 Sat)–11; 12–3, 7–10.30
Sun
**Beards Best Bitter; Courage
Directors; Harveys BB; guest
beers** H
In business since 1812, this pub
(like others) takes its name
from the tree in which Charles
II hid after the Battle of
Worcester – an early landlord
was descended from the family
that saved the King. A
comfortable pub with an
extensive menu.
🏚 Q ❀ ◖ ◗ ≈

Snowdrop
119 South Street
☎ (01273) 471018
11–11; 12–10.30 Sun
**Fuller's London Pride;
Harveys BB, seasonal beers;
Hop Back Summer Lightning;
guest beers** H
Popular, two-storey pub with a
cosmopolitan clientele.
Interesting wall murals; pool
table. Brewery on Sea's
Avalanche is a house beer.
Good selection of organic,
vegetarian and seafood meals.
Occasional cider.
❀ ◖ ◗ ≈ ♻ P

Litlington

Plough & Harrow
On Exceat by-road to
Wilmington OS523018
☎ (01323) 870632
11–3, 6.30–11; 12–3, 7–10.30 Sun
**Badger IPA, Dorset Best,
Tanglefoot; Harveys BB; guest
beers** H
A rare outlet for Badger beers
in the area. A Southern
Railway theme dominates the
main bar and small snug. The
bar billiards table dates from
1935. Q ❀ ◖ ◗ ♣ P

Peasmarsh

Cock Horse Inn
Main Street (A268, N of village)
☎ (01797) 230281
11–3, 6–11; 12–3, 7–10.30 Sun
Harveys BB; guest beers H
Spacious, pleasant, 17th-
century country inn with a
dining area. Boules played.

Camping facilities for caravans
only. Large patio.
🏚 Q ♜ ❀ ◖ ◗ ⊞ ♣ P

Rottingdean

Black Horse
65 High Street
☎ (01273) 302581
10.30–2.30, 6–11; 12–3, 7–10.30 Sun
**Adnams Broadside; Beards
Best Bitter; Harveys BB;
Mansfield Old Baily; guest
beers** H
Popular village local with two
bars plus a snug (where
children are welcome). It is
believed to date back to 1531.
No-smoking area lunchtime.
🏚 Q ◖ ⊞ ♣ ✂

Rye

Ypres Castle
Gun Gardens (behind Ypres
Tower) ☎ (01797) 223248
12–11; 12–10.30 Sun
**Harveys XX Mild; Hook
Norton Best Bitter; Old
Hooky; guest beers** H
Not immediately obvious, this
unspoilt pub is well worth
seeking out. Access is on foot
only. With a superb view of the
harbour, it stands near Rye's
most picturesque parts. Fresh
fish, local game and poultry are
specialities. Safe garden.
Accommodation planned.
🏚 Q ♜ ❀ ◖ ◗ ≈ ♣ ♻

St Leonards

Dripping Spring
34 Tower Road (off A2100, 1
mile from seafront)
☎ (01424) 434055
11–3, 5–11; 11–11 Fri & Sat; 12–3,
7–10.30 Sun
**Fuller's London Pride;
Harveys BB; Tetley Bitter;
guest beers** H
Friendly, backstreet local, well
worth finding. 300 guest beers
have been served to date: a
good outlet for the rare and
unusual.
❀ ♿ ≈ (Warrior Sq) ♣ ♻

Duke
48 Duke Road
☎ (01424) 436241
11–3 (not Mon–Tue), 6–11; 11–11 Fri &
Sat; 12–10.30 Sun
**Bateman XB; Beards Best
Bitter; Harveys BB; Taylor
Landlord; guest beers** H
Cosy two-bar local, in the
Silverhill area of St Leonards,
taken over by Beards in 1996.
🏚 Q ❀ ⊞ ♣

Seaford

Wellington
Steyne Road ☎ (01323) 890032
11–11; 12–10.30 Sun

**Beards Best Bitter; Greene
King IPA; Harveys BB;
Wadworth 6X** H
Popular, two-bar, dog-friendly
local, aimed at a cross-section
of clientele. Generally eight
beers are available. Note the
day's motto on the blackboard.
No food Sun. ◖ ≈

White Lion
74 Claremont Road
☎ (01323) 892473
11–2.30, 6–11; 11–11 Sat; 12–10.30 Sun
**Harveys BB; Fuller's London
Pride; Harveys BB; guest beers** H
Hotel bar where music is
played to a tolerable level. A
pool table and TV are to one
side of the bar. Generally four
ales are on offer. ❀ 🛏 ◖ ◗

Telham

Black Horse
Hastings Road (A2100)
☎ (01424) 773109
11–3, 5–11; 12–3, 7–10.30 Sun
**Shepherd Neame Master
Brew Bitter, Best Bitter,
Spitfire, Bishops Finger** H
Weatherboarded pub between
Battle and Hastings. It has a
games room on the first floor
and a skittle alley in the attic;
boules played in summer. A
music festival is held in a
marquee every Spring Bank
Hol. Occasional folk music.
🏚 Q ❀ ◖ ◗ ♠ ♣ P

Three Oaks

Three Oaks
Butchers Lane (by station)
☎ (01424) 813303
11–3, 6–11; 12–3, 7–10.30 Sun
**Harveys BB; Rother Valley
Level Best; guest beers** H
Pleasant country pub with
plenty of atmosphere, serving
home-cooked food. A good
base for walking.
🏚 Q ❀ ◖ ◗ ♠ ≈ P ⛴

Udimore

King's Head
Udimore Road (B2089, W of
village) ☎ (01424) 882349
11–4, 5.30–11; 12–4, 7–10.30 Sun
Harveys BB; guest beers H
Built in 1535, this traditional
village ale house, boasts
beams, open fires, wood floors,
a no-smoking dining room and
home-cooked food. Scenic
walks nearby.
🏚 Q ❀ ◖ ◗ ♿ ♠ ♣ P

Wadhurst

Greyhound
St James Square
☎ (01892) 783224
11–2.30, 6–11; 11–11 Sat; 12–3, 7–10.30
Sun

Draught Bass; Harveys BB; Rother Valley Level Best; Young's Bitter; guest beer H
Fine old inn, built in 1502, set in a busy Wealden village. Large inglenook; separate eating area.
🏚 Q ✿ ◑ ▶ ♣ P

Willingdon

Red Lion
99 Wish Hill ☎ (01323) 502062
11–2.30, 5.30–11; 12–2.30, 7–10.30 Sun
King & Barnes Sussex, Broadwood, Festive, seasonal beers H
Comfortable, modernised local in a small downland village near Eastbourne. An ideal place to start (or finish) a walk on the downs. A rare East Sussex outlet for King & Barnes beers. ✿ ◑ ▶ ♣ P

Withyham

Dorset Arms
On B2110 ☎ (01892) 770278
11–3, 5.30 (6 Sat)–11; 12–3, 7–10.30 Sun
Harveys XX Mild, Pale Ale, BB, seasonal beers H
16th-century building with interesting architectural features, including a cosy, Wealden oak floored bar with a log fire. Spot the Wealden iron fireback plate, evidence of when this area was the centre of the English iron industry. Characterful, quality restaurant.
🏚 Q ✿ ◑ ▶ ⌿ ♣ P

West Sussex

Arundel

King's Arms
36 Tarrant Street
☎ (01903) 882312
11–3, 5.30–11; 11–11 Sat; 12–10.30 Sun
Fuller's London Pride; Young's Special; guest beers H
Small and cosy, two-bar friendly local in a pleasant sidestreet, just below the RC cathedral and the castle, seat of the Dukes of Norfolk. Lunches served Sat. ✿ ⌿ A ⇌ ♣

Swan Hotel
27–29 High Street
☎ (01903) 882314
11–11; 12–10.30 Sun
Arundel Best Bitter, Gold, ASB, Stronghold, seasonal beers; guest beers H
Upmarket corner house in the shadow of Arundel castle, selling the full range of its brewery's beers. Food is available in the bar or the more

expensive à la carte restaurant. Parking for residents.
🛏 ◑ ▶ ⇌

Balcombe

Cowdray Arms
London Road (B2036/B2110 jct) ☎ (01444) 811280
11–3, 5.30–11; 12–3, 7–10.30 Sun
Adnams Extra; Beards Best Bitter; Harveys BB H**, seasonal beers; guest beers** H/G
Popular roadside pub with a good selection of guest ales. Balcombe Best Bitter is a renamed Adnams brew. The large no-smoking eating area in the conservatory offers a wide range of good food. Children's certificate.
Q ⌂ ✿ ◑ ▶ ♣ P

Binsted

Black Horse Inn
Off A27/B2132 OS980064
☎ (01243) 551213
11–3, 6–11; 12–3, 7–10.30 Sun
Arundel Best Bitter; Gale's HSB; Harveys BB; Wadworth 6X; guest beers H
Pub hidden off the beaten track, amidst lovely countryside. Excellent food in the bar or conservatory/restaurant. Note the 22 different sweets sold by the ounce or quarter alongside the more usual products.
🏚 Q ✿ ◑ ▶ ⌂ ♣ P

Bognor Regis

Hatters
2–10 Queensway (W end of High St) ☎ (01243) 840406
11–11; 12–10.30 Sun
Courage Directors; Theakston Best Bitter; Younger Scotch; guest beers H
Large single bar selling guest beers at very reasonable prices. The games machines are soundless. Twice yearly beer festivals are held at this former Sainsbury's supermarket, converted in 1995 by Wetherspoons.
Q ✿ ◑ ▶ ⇌ ⌂ ⌿

Try also: **Ship**, Aldwick St (Free)

Chichester

Coach & Horses
125B St Pancras (250 yds E of Eastgate Sq) ☎ (01243) 782313
11–3, 7–11; 12–3, 7–10.30 Sun
King & Barnes Mild, Sussex, Festive, seasonal beers H
Welcoming, comfortable, spacious local recently acquired and refurbished by King & Barnes (their only pub in the city). Summer barbecues

at weekends in the enclosed large rear garden. Pool played.
🏚 ✿ 🛏 ◑ ▶ ⇌ ♣

Christ's Hospital

Bax Castle
Two Mile Ash (Southwater–Christ's Hospital road)
OS148273 ☎ (01403) 730369
11.30 (11 Fri & Sat)–2.30 (3 Sat), 6–11; 12–3, 7–10.30 Sun
Draught Bass; Brakspear Bitter; Fuller's London Pride; John Smith's Bitter; guest beer H
Pub situated behind a former railway bridge at a T-junction on the Southwater–Barns Green road. Popular with walkers on the Downs Link. Large, safe garden for children.
🏚 Q ⌂ ✿ ◑ ▶ ♣ P ⌿

Colgate

Dragon
Off A264, Forest road
☎ (01293) 851206
11–2.30, 5.30–11; 12–2.30, 7–10.30 Sun
King & Barnes Sussex, Old, Festive, seasonal beers H
Peaceful, two-roomed pub in an idyllic setting in St Leonards Forest, with a large, well-planned garden. No food Sun.
🏚 Q ✿ ◑ ⌿ P

Compton

Coach & Horses
On B2146 ☎ (01705) 631228
11–3, 6–11; 12–3, 7–10.30 Sun
Fuller's ESB; guest beers H
16th-century pub in a charming downland village, surrounded by excellent walking country. The large front bar has two open fires. There is also a smaller rear bar, a restaurant and a skittle alley.
🏚 ✿ ◑ ▶ ⌿ ♣

Cowfold

Hare & Hounds
Henfield Road (A281)
☎ (01403) 865354
11.30–3, 6–11; 12–3, 7–10.30 Sun
Friary Meux BB; Harveys BB; King & Barnes Sussex; guest beer H
Victorian village local, refurbished in 1995. Timber from gale-damaged trees from nearby Leonardslee Gardens was used in the bar. No eve meals winter Mon.
🏚 ✿ ◑ ▶ ♣ P

Crawley

Snooty Fox
Haslett Avenue, Three Bridges (opp. station)
☎ (01293) 619759
11–11; 12–10.30 Sun

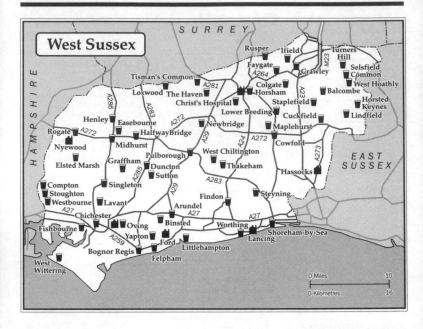

Friary Meux BB; Ind Coope
Burton Ale; Tetley Bitter;
guest beers H
Large, purpose-built pub with
plenty of character in modern
surroundings. Pictures of
Three Bridges, dating back to
1906, are displayed. The pub
has a strong regular following.
Children's certificate. ✿ ◖ ▶ &
⇌ (Three Bridges) P ⚭

Swan

1 Horsham Road, West Green
(off Ifield Rd)
☎ (01293) 531466
11–11; 12–10.30 Sun
Beer range varies H/G
Country-style pub offering
good food. Live music at
weekends.
🏠 ☕ ✿ ◖ ♣

White Hart

High Street
☎ (01293) 520033
10–11; 12–10.30 Sun
Harveys Pale Ale, BB,
Armada, seasonal beers H
Popular, two-bar, town-centre
pub occasionally hosting live
music. Weekday lunches.
🏠 ✿ ◖ ⊟ ⇌ ♣ P

Cuckfield

White Harte

South Street
☎ (01444) 413454
11–3, 6–11; 12–3, 7–10.30 Sun
King & Barnes Sussex,
Broadwood, Old, Festive,
seasonal beers H
Two-bar village pub situated
on a double bend. The saloon
bar has genuine beams and an

inglenook, in contrast to the
more spartan public bar. The
family room opens in summer
months.
🏠 Q ✿ ☕ ◖ ⊟ ♣ P

Duncton

Cricketers

Main road (A285)
☎ (01798) 342473
11–2.30, 6–11; 12–3, 7–10.30 (not
winter eves) Sun
Archers Golden; Friary Meux
BB; Ind Coope Burton Ale;
Young's Bitter; guest beer
(summer) H
A large inglenook in a cosy bar
adds to the welcome of this
fine hostelry, which is steeped
in history. Separate, split-level
dining areas, attractive gardens
(summer barbecues) and a
skittle alley are other features.
Darts is played. Cider in
summer.
🏠 Q ✿ ◖ ▶ ▲ ♣ ⌂ P

Easebourne

White Horse

Easebourne Street (near A272
jct) ☎ (01730) 813521
11–11; 12–10.30 Sun
Greene King IPA, Abbot,
seasonal beers H
Welcoming, two-bar village
inn handy for Cowdray Park
polo. Challenging monthly pub
quiz. Varied fresh seafood
features on an interesting
menu which changes daily.
Large garden.
🏠 Q ✿ ◖ ▶ ⊟ & ♣ P

Elsted Marsh

Elsted Inn

Off A272 near disused railway
bridge OS834207
☎ (01730) 813662
11–3, 5.30–11; 12–3, 7–10.30 Sun
Ballards Trotton, Best Bitter,
Wild, Wassail; Bunces Old
Smokey; Fuller's London
Pride H; guest beers G
Popular country pub in a rural
setting, next to the disused
railway from Petersfield to
Midhurst. Unchanged
Victorian decor; note the
unusual window shutters.
Excellent home-cooked food in
the cosy bars and restaurant.
🏠 Q ✿ 🛏 ◖ ▶ ♣ P

Faygate

Cherry Tree

Crawley Road (A264 Horsham
road) ☎ (01293) 851305
11–3 (3.30 Sat), 6–11; 12–3, 7–10.30
Sun
King & Barnes Sussex,
Broadwood, seasonal beers H

Formerly two cottages dating back to 1660, converted in 1870; two open fires, an inglenook and original beams are features. Warm atmosphere; good value meals.
🏠 Q ✿ ◑ ▶ ♣ P

Felpham

Old Barn

42 Felpham Road
☎ (01243) 821564
11–11; 12–10.30 Sun
Arundel Best Bitter; Fuller's ESB; Gale's Best Bitter; Ringwood Best Bitter; guest beers H
One-bar pub divided into three distinct areas: the front part is cosy; the main area has bare boards with two TVs and a dartboard; the rear part is the pool area. Food is served from 11–7: grills, burgers, etc. The TV is always switched on for live football matches.
✿ ◑ ♣ P

Findon

Village House Hotel

The Square, Old Horsham Road ☎ (01903) 873350
10.30–11; 12–10.30 Sun
Courage Directors; Harveys BB; King & Barnes Sussex; Webster's Yorkshire Bitter; Young's Special H
Attractive, 16th-century village inn with a bar-cum-restaurant. Racing silks from local stables adorn the walls. The choice and quality of the food are exceptional. Children's certificate.
🏠 Q ✿ 🛏 ◑ ▶ ▲ P

Fishbourne

Bull's Head

99 Fishbourne Road (A259)
☎ (01243) 785707
11–11; 12–10.30 Sun
Fuller's London Pride; Gale's Butser, IPA, HSB; guest beers H
Large, comfortable local with guest beers from small independent breweries. The restaurant serves home-cooked food from fresh local ingredients (no food Sun eve). Skittles/function room. Cider in summer. Car park access is off Mill Lane.
🏠 Q ⛺ ✿ ◑ ▶ ≈ ♣ ○ P ⚲

Graffham

Forester's Arms

☎ (01798) 867202
11–2.30, 5.30–11; 12–3, 7.30–10.30 Sun
Courage Directors; guest beers H
Heavily-beamed, 17th-century inn in good walking country, close to the South Downs Way. The restaurant and bar menus

feature English farmhouse fare. Three guest beers from regional brewers.
🏠 Q ✿ ◑ ▶ ▲ P

Halfway Bridge

Halfway Bridge Inn

On A272, near Lodsworth
☎ (01798) 861281
11–3, 6–11; 12–3, 7–10.30 (not winter eves) Sun
Cheriton Pots Ale; Fuller's London Pride; Gale's HSB; guest beers H
Rambling, 18th-century former coaching inn. Children are allowed in the restaurant area and the front garden. The rear patio is a suntrap. Guest beers come from independent small breweries. Food is all home cooked; local fish and game dishes are a speciality (book restaurant at weekends).
🏠 ✿ ◑ ▶ ♣ ○ P ⚲

The Haven

Blue Ship

500 yds down a lane W of A281 at Bucks Green OS084306
☎ (01403) 822709
11–3, 6–11; 12–3, 7–10.30 Sun
King & Barnes Sussex, Broadwood, seasonal beers G
Classic, four-room country pub without a bar – the gravity beers are served through a 'stable' door. Good value food is mostly home produced (no food Sun or Mon).
Q ✿ ◑ ▶ ▤ ♣ P

Henley

Duke of Cumberland

Off A286, 3 miles N of Midhurst OS894258
☎ (01428) 652280
11–3, 5–11; 12–3, 7–10.30 Sun
Adnams Broadside; Brakspear Special; Flowers Original; Gale's Butser, HSB; Theakston Old Peculier G
Pub worth seeking out for its early 17th-century origins: red tiled floor, scrubbed tables, gas lighting, back cellar, gravity-served beer and a trout pond in the garden. No meals Sun.
🏠 Q ✿ ◑ ▶ ○ P

Horsham

Dog & Bacon

North Parade (B2237, 800 yds from A24 jct) ☎ (01403) 252176
11–3, 6–11; 12–3, 7–10.30 Sun
King & Barnes Sussex, Broadwood, Old, Festive, seasonal beers H
Popular pub in the suburbs, attracting a good cross-section of local people, with a strong darts, golf and dominoes following. Regular theme food nights are held; eve meals

Tue–Sat. No-smoking family room.
👶 ✿ ◑ ▶ ▤ ♣ P ⚲

Foresters Arms

43 St Leonards Road (off Brighton road, A281)
☎ (01403) 254458
11–3, 6–11; 11–11 Sat; 12–10.30 Sun
Shepherd Neame Master Brew Bitter, Spitfire, Bishops Finger H
Small, one-bar pub with a flagged floor and open fireplace; popular with locals.
🏠 Q ✿ ≈ ♣

Malt Shovel

15 Springfield Road
☎ (01403) 254543
11–11; 12–10.30 Sun
Boddingtons Bitter; Flowers Original; Marston's Pedigree; Young's Special H **; guest beers** H/G
Pub in the Hogshead style: boarded floor and scatter rugs. Food is available 12–7 daily. Wide selection of beers from six handpumps, as well as three on gravity; foreign bottled beers. Crib available. The best pub in Horsham for atmosphere.
🏠 ✿ ◑ ▶ ≈ ♣ ○ P

Norfolk Arms

Crawley Road, Roffey
☎ (01403) 264913
11.30–3, 6–11; 12–3, 7–10.30 Sun
King & Barnes Sussex, Festive, seasonal beers H
Main road, two-bar pub, recently refurbished, with a comfortable lounge. Darts and games in the public bar. Varied food menu.
🏠 Q ✿ ◑ ▶ ▤ ♿ ♣ P

Stout House

29 Carfax (opp. bandstand)
☎ (01403) 252176
10–4, 7.30–11 (not Tue eve); 12–4, 7–10.30 Sun
King & Barnes Mild, Sussex, Festive, seasonal beers H
Very popular, town-centre pub which concentrates on beer – food is limited to snacks; recently refurbished in traditional style. Sussex CAMRA *Pub of the Year* 1997.
≈ ♣

Horsted Keynes

Green Man

The Green ☎ (01825) 790656
11–3, 5.30–11 (11–11 summer); 12–3, 7–10.30 Sun
Adnams Bitter; Beards Best Bitter; Harveys BB; guest beers H
Pub on the edge of the village green: two bars and a lounge area for food. The bare-floored bar features a hop-laden beam. No food Mon eve in winter.
🏠 Q ◑ ▶ ▤ ♣ P

Ifield

Plough
☎ (01293) 525404
11–3 (4 Fri & Sat), 6–11; 12–4, 6–10.30 Sun

King & Barnes Sussex, Broadwood, Festive, seasonal beers Ⓗ
Traditional village local which now finds itself on the edge of Crawley, near Ifield Barn Theatre. Popular with both locals and customers from further afield. No food Sun.
◑ ▶ ⊞ ⇌ ♣ P

Lavant

Earl of March
Lavant Road (A286, 2 miles N of Chichester)
☎ (01243) 774751
10.30–3, 6–11; 12–3, 7–10.30 Sun

Ballard's Best Bitter; Ringwood Fortyniner, Old Thumper; Woodforde's Wherry; guest beers Ⓗ
Spacious, wood-panelled pub, popular and often lively. Fine views of the downs are afforded by the garden. Good food (large, home-cooked portions), with local game prominent. Still the best value pub in the area, offering three guest beers. Dogs welcome.
❀ ◑ ▶ ♣ ◔ P

Lindfield

Linden Tree
47 High Street (B2028)
☎ (01444) 482995
11–3, 6–11; 12–3, 7–10.30 Sun

Arundel Best Bitter; Marston's Pedigree; Ringwood Old Thumper; Wadworth 6X; guest beers Ⓗ
Small, friendly, free house in an attractive village. The remains of an old brewery may be seen at the rear. Usually two guest beers available. No food Sun. 🏚 Q ❀ ◑

Littlehampton

Locomotive
74 Lyminster Road, Wick (S of railway gates)
☎ (01903) 716658
11–2.30, 6–11; 12–3, 7–10.30 (12–10.30 summer) Sun

Ansells Mild; Greene King Abbot; King & Barnes Sussex; Ringwood Best Bitter; guest beers Ⓗ
Friendly, one-bar local offering food at all sessions, with a family room and a large garden with a play area, patio and boules pistes. Popular quiz Wed and Sun.
🏚 ♜ ❀ ◑ ▶ Å P

Try also: Dew Drop, Wick St (Gale's)

Lower Beeding

Plough
Leech Pond Hill (A279, 500 yds N of Leonardslee Gardens)
☎ (01403) 891277
11–3, 5.30–11; 11–11 Fri & Sat; 12–4, 7–10.30 Sun

King & Barnes Sussex Ⓗ, **Old** Ⓖ, **Festive** Ⓗ, **seasonal beers** Ⓖ
Basic, two-bar pub with the cheapest beer in the area. Its position on the outside of a sweeping bend has meant a few lorries have dropped in over the years.
🏚 Q ❀ ⊞ ♣ P

Loxwood

Sir Roger Tichbourne
Billingshurst Road, Alfold Bars (N end of Loxwood on B2133)
☎ (01403) 752377
12–2, 6–11; 12–3, 7–10.30 (not winter eves) Sun

King & Barnes Sussex, seasonal beers Ⓗ
Typical, rural, low-beamed pub with a quiet saloon on the right and a busier stone-floored bar on the left with an inglenook. Set back from the main road, it can easily be missed on dark eves. Eve meals Fri and Sat only. Camping by arrangement.
🏚 Q ❀ ◑ ▶ ⊞ Å ♣ P

Maplehurst

White Horse
Park Lane (between A281 and A272, S of Nuthurst)
☎ (01403) 891208
12–2.30 (3 Sat), 6–11; 12–3, 7–10.30 Sun

Brakspear Bitter; Harveys BB; King & Barnes Sussex; guest beers Ⓗ
Friendly country pub with an ever-changing selection of ales – well over 200 in the last 12 years of inclusion in the *Guide*. The landlord is a classic car fanatic. The pub has a children's certificate; no-smoking area available at lunchtime. Note the extra wide bar.
🏚 Q ❀ ◑ ▶ ♣ ◔ P ⊬

Midhurst

Bricklayers Arms
Wool Lane
☎ (01730) 812084
11–3, 6–11; 11–11 Sat; 12–10.30 Sun

Greene King IPA, Abbot Ⓗ, **seasonal beers** Ⓖ
Two-bar, town pub, 400 years old and close to the shops and car park. The public bar is wooden-floored with wall panels, while the main bar has bare brick walls. Polo is the theme of many photographs. Good value food. It can be busy weekends.
🏚 ❀ ◑ ▶ ⊞ ♣ P

Crown
Edinburgh Square
☎ (01730) 813462
11–11; 12–10.30 Sun

Beer range varies Ⓗ/Ⓖ
Popular town pub, close to the shops, with a large, ever-changing beer range. Justifiably busy at weekends and Tue eve (live band session). Gravity beer comes from a cooled bar-level cellar room. Indoor lamb spit-roast on the first Sun each month. Cider in summer. Good B&B.
🏚 ❀ 🛏 ◑ ▶ ♣ ◔

Newbridge

Limeburners
On B2133, 200 yds S of A272 jct
12–3, 6–11 (11–11 summer Sat); 12–3, 7–10.30 (12–10.30 summer) Sun

Gale's Best Bitter, Winter Brew, HSB Ⓗ
Originally three limeburners' cottages dating back to the 16th century, this low, beamed pub has stone floors and an inglenook. Popular in summer when the pub's caravan park is busy. Children's certificate.
🏚 ❀ ◑ ▶ Å ♣ ◔ P

Oving

Gribble Inn
☎ (01243) 786893
11–3, 6–11 (11–11 summer); 12–3, 7–10.30 (12–10.30 summer) Sun

Badger Dorset Best; Gribble Ewe Brew, Ale, Reg's Tipple, Plucking Pheasant, Pig's Ear Ⓗ
Picturesque 16th-century thatched village local with a fine garden. The popular home-brewed ales are produced in a compact brewhouse adjoining the skittle alley (view the process). Deceptively spacious; mind the low beams. Good bar food.
🏚 Q ♜ ❀ ◑ ▶ ♣ ◔ P ⊬

Pulborough

White Horse
Marehill (½ mile E of village, on A283)
☎ (01798) 872189
11.30–3, 5–11; 12–10.30 Sun

Draught Bass; Fuller's London Pride; Harveys BB; Hogs Back TEA; guest beers Ⓗ
Comfortable village inn with a brick and stone wall bar and snug, both with open log fires; also a cosy lounge/TV room with a fire, a children's area, and a restaurant. No food Sun eve.
🏚 Q ♜ ❀ ◑ ▶ ♣ P

Rogate

Wyndham Arms
☎ (01730) 821315
11.30–3 (2.30 winter Mon–Fri), 6–11;
12–3, 7–10.30 (12–10.30 summer) Sun
**Ballard's Wassail; Bunces Old
Smokey; Cheriton Pots Ale;
Harveys BB; Hop Back
Summer Lightning; guest
beers** G
Cosy, friendly, 16th-century
inn opposite the church and
reputedly haunted. The beer
stillages can be viewed via a
glass panel from the bar. The
bar area and accommodation
have been recently extended.
Annual midsummer beer
festival. CAMRA Sussex *Pub of
the Year* 1995. Cobbled patio for
outside drinking to the front
and the side. Good,
imaginative food.
🛏 Q ✿ 🚪 ◖▮ ♿ ♣ 👜 P

Rusper

Plough
High Street
☎ (01293) 871215
11–2.30 (3 Sat), 6–11; 12–3, 7–10.30
Sun
**Courage Directors; Fuller's
London Pride, ESB; King &
Barnes Sussex; guest beers** H
Popular village pub with a
reinstated stone floor in front
of the bar and low beams; parts
date back to the 15th century.
Good food. Large garden at the
rear. Function room upstairs.
🛏 Q ✿ ◖▮ ♣ P

Royal Oak
Friday Street (left fork N of
church)
☎ (01293) 871393
11–3, 6–11, 12–3, 7–10.30 Sun
**King & Barnes Sussex,
Broadwood, Festive, seasonal
beers** H
15th-century rural local, a mile
west of the village. The bar is
long and narrow, with two
smaller rooms either side at
each end, featuring split
levels and low beams. No eve
meals Sun.
🛏 Q ✿ ◖▮ ♣ P

Selsfield Common

White Hart Inn
Ardingly Road, West Hoathly
(1 mile N of South of England
Showground)
☎ (01342) 715217
11–3, 5–11; 12–4, 6–10.30 Sun
Beer range varies H
Olde-worlde building with oak
beams and an inglenook. A
large, converted tithe barn is
used as a restaurant Tue–Sat
eves; lunchtime food in the bar.
Two real ales in winter, four in
summer, plus cider.
🛏 Q ☕ ✿ ◖▮ 👜 P

Shoreham-by-Sea

Buckingham Arms
(Sir Loyne of Beefe)
35–39 Brunswick Road
☎ (01273) 453660
11–11; 12–4, 7.30–10.30 Sun
**Courage Best Bitter, Directors;
Ringwood True Glory; guest
beers** H
Former coaching inn, now part
of the chain of 'Sir Loyne of
Beefe' real free houses, serving
up to six guest beers per week
at realistic prices.
✿ ◖ ⇌ ♣ 👜 P

Marlipins
38 High Street
☎ (01273) 453359
10–11; 12–3.30, 7–10.30 Sun
**Draught Bass; Fuller's London
Pride; Harveys BB** H
16th-century, one-bar pub with
low beams, a conservatory and
a patio at the rear. Good food
from a full menu of home-
made meals and sandwiches
(no food Sun eve).
Q ✿ ◖▮ ⇌

Red Lion Inn
Old Shoreham Road
☎ (01273) 453171
11.30–3, 6–11; 12–4, 7–10.30 Sun
**Courage Best Bitter, Directors;
Theakston XB; guest beers** H
16th-century inn overlooking
the old toll bridge. Good food
is always available. Four guest
beers per week mainly come
from microbrewers. Home to
the Adur beer festival, held at
Easter. 🛏 Q ✿ ◖▮ P ⚥

Royal Sovereign
6 Middle Street
☎ (01273) 453518
11–11; 12–4.30, 7–10.30 Sun
**Brakspear Special; Castle
Eden Ale; Fuller's London
Pride; Greene King Abbot;
King & Barnes Sussex;
Young's Ram Rod** H
Splendid example of a local.
The original United Brewery
windows are still a feature.
Fairly busy; no food Sun.
🛏 ◖ ⇌

Singleton

Horse & Groom
On A286 ☎ (01243) 811455
11–3, 6–11; 12–10.30 Sun
**Ballard's Best Bitter; Cheriton
Pots Ale; Gale's HSB; guest
beer** H
Convivial village free house
close to Goodwood and the
Downland Museum. The
enclosed rear garden has
swingboats and a trampoline.
All food is home-made for the
cosy restaurant which holds
special food nights Thu and
Fri. New en suite

accommodation in another
building. Bar billiards.
🛏 Q ✿ 🚪 ◖▮ ♿ 👜 P

Try also: **Fox & Hounds**,
Singleton Lane (Gibbs Mew)

Staplefield

Jolly Tanners
Handcross Road
☎ (01444) 400335
11–3, 5.30–11; 11–11 Sat; 12–3, 7–10.30
Sun
**Fuller's Chiswick, London
Pride; Wadworth 6X; guest
beer** H
Busy and popular local pub
opposite the cricket field,
serving a good selection of
meals. Pleasant, large garden
with good facilities for
children. Guest beers often
include a mild.
🛏 Q ✿ ◖▮ 🍴 ♣ P

Steyning

Chequers Inn
41 High Street
☎ (01903) 814437
10–2.30, 5–11; 10–11 Fri & Sat;
12–10.30 Sun
**Flowers Original; Fuller's
London Pride; King & Barnes
Sussex; guest beers** H
Wonderful old market town
pub with a variety of drinking
areas creating a warm
atmosphere. The
comprehensive food menu
includes a wide vegetarian
choice.
🛏 Q ✿ ◖▮ 🍴 ♣ P ⚥

Star
130 High Street
☎ (01903) 813078
10.30–2.30 (3 Fri), 5.30–11; 10.30–11
Sat; 12–3.30, 7–10.30 Sun
**Castle Eden Ale; Flowers
Original; Fuller's London
Pride; King & Barnes Sussex;
Wadworth 6X** H
300-year-old village pub with a
warm welcome. Full of
interesting features: flagstone
floors, low beams, open fires
and a full range of facilities for
the family.
🛏 ☕ ✿ ◖▮ ♿ ♣ P ⚥

Stoughton

Hare & Hounds
Off B2146, through Walderton
OS791107 ☎ (01705) 631433
11–3, 6–11; 12–10.30 Sun
**Boddingtons Bitter; Gale's
HSB; Gibbs Mew Bishop's
Tipple; Taylor Landlord;
guest beers** H
Fine example of a Sussex flint-
faced building in a secluded
South Downs setting; 23 years
in the *Guide*. Popular and
lively, it enjoys a good local
trade. Humorous posters
advertise the guest beers. Good
value, home-made food, with

fresh local seafood and game specialities. 🏚 Q ✿ ◖ ♣ P

Sutton

White Horse Inn

The Street ☎ (01798) 869221
11–2.30, 6–11; 12–3, 7–10.30 Sun
Arundel Best Bitter; Courage Best Bitter; Young's Bitter; guest beers H
18th-century Georgian inn, set in a peaceful downland village, close to Bignor Roman villa. Excellent restaurant and accommodation. Popular with both locals and walkers.
🏚 Q ✿ 🛏 ◖ ◗ 🚲 ♣ P

Thakeham

White Lion

The Street (off B2139)
☎ (01798) 813141
11–11; 12–10.30 Sun
Arundel ASB; Brewery on Sea Golden Lite; Flowers Original; Harveys BB H
Former assize inn, 500 years old, with a welcoming landlord and friendly regulars.
🏚 Q 🛏 ✿ ◖ ◗ 🚲 ♣ P ⚲

Tisman's Common

Mucky Duck

1 mile from A281/B2133 jct
OS067322 ☎ (01403) 822300
11–11; 12–10.30 Sun
Draught Bass; Fuller's London Pride; Greene King IPA; guest beers H
Basic, friendly, village pub with a pool room. Good value meals. 🏚 ✿ ◖ ◗ ⌂ P

Turners Hill

Red Lion

Lion Lane (off B2028)
☎ (01342) 715416
11–3, 6–11; 12–10.30 Sun
Harveys XX Mild, Pale Ale, BB, Old, seasonal beers H
Unchanging village pub with a collection of bottled beers; its 23rd entry in the *Guide*. Pool room upstairs. Folk club Sat eve. No food Sun.
🏚 Q ✿ ◖ ♣ P

Westbourne

Good Intent

North Street ☎ (01243) 372656
10.30–2.30 (3 Sat), 5 (6 Sat)–11; 12–3, 7–10.30 Sun
Ansells Mild; Dartmoor Best Bitter; Friary Meux BB; Ind Coope Burton Ale; guest beer H
Two-bar, 16th-century pub in a large village. Open fires burn in winter in the very welcoming wood-panelled bars. The lounge bar used to be a bakery. No food Sun, or Wed eve. 🏚 ✿ ◖ ◗ 🚲 ♣ P

West Chiltington

Five Bells

Smock Alley ☎ (01798) 812143
11–3, 6–11; 12–3, 7–10.30 Sun
King & Barnes Sussex; guest beers H
Attractive, one-bar pub with a log fire at one end and a conservatory restaurant with a stove at the other. Always an inspired choice of guest beers. No food Sun eve.
🏚 Q ✿ ◖ ◗ 🚲 ♣ ⌂ P

West Hoathly

Vinols Cross Inn

Hammingdean Lane
☎ (01342) 810644
12–3, 6–11; 12–3, 7–10.30 Sun
Harveys BB, Old; Wadworth 6X; guest beers H
Old village pub, now popular with both villagers and diners. Converted from three cottages, it is named after John Vinol, a local character about whom little is known. The pub is said to be haunted by a former landlord. 🏚 ✿ ◖ ◗ ▲ P

West Wittering

Lamb Inn

Chichester Road (B2179, 2 miles NE of village)
☎ (01243) 511105
11–2.30, 6–11; 12–3, 7–10.30 Sun
Badger Dorset Best, Tanglefoot; Ballard's Best Bitter; Bunces Benchmark; Hop Back Summer Lightning; Ringwood XXXX Porter H
Popular, old, convivial roadside inn, handy for sailing centres and beaches, with a wide range of good, home-cooked food and still room for drinkers in the eve. No meals Sun eve in winter. May open all day summer weekends.
🏚 Q ✿ ◖ ◗ ⚅ ▲ P ⚲

Worthing

Alexandra Arms

28 Lyndhurst Road (E of hospital) ☎ (01903) 234833
11–11; 12–10.30 Sun
Draught Bass; Fuller's London Pride; Harveys BB; guest beers H
Unspoilt, friendly town local with three bars, including a games room. Consistently high standards of service.
🏚 Q ✿ 🚲 ♣

Cricketers

66 Broadwater Street West (A24) ☎ (01903) 233369
11–3, 6–11; 11–11 Fri & Sat; 12–10.30 Sun
Draught Bass; Fuller's London Pride; Greene King IPA; Harveys BB; guest beers H

Popular, one-bar pub a mile north of the town centre. The large saloon dining area incorporates a snug corner, whilst the other end of the bar manages to retain a traditional public bar appearance. No eve meals Sun or Mon.
Q ✿ ◖ ◗ ♣ 🍴

George & Dragon

1 High Street, Tarring
☎ (01903) 202497
11–3, 6–11; 12–10.30 Sun
King & Barnes Festive; Morland Old Speckled Hen; Ruddles Best Bitter; John Smith's Bitter; guest beers H
Cosy, welcoming, 18th-century, low-beamed local in a well preserved street, retaining the feel of a traditional, multi-roomed pub.
Q ✿ ◖ ⇌ (West) ♣ P

Hogshead

25 Warwick Street
☎ (01903) 206088
10.30–11; 12–10.30 Sun
Boddingtons Bitter; Flowers Original; King & Barnes Sussex; Marston's Pedigree; Morland Old Speckled Hen; Wadworth 6X H**; guest beers** H/G
Busy, family-run town-centre pub in a pedestrian precinct, appealing to all ages. Friendly atmosphere. ◖ ◗ ⇌ ♣ ⌂

Old House at Home

77 Broadwater Street East (off A24, one-way system)
☎ (01903) 232661
11.30–2.30, 6–11; 12–3, 7–10.30 Sun
Arundel Gold G**; Draught Bass; Fuller's London Pride** H**; guest beers** H/G
Popular, two-bar, wood-panelled pub in traditional Sussex style. Gravity beer is served using a professional cooling system. Large garden, patio and play area.
Q ✿ ◖ ◗ ♣ P

Richard Cobden

2 Cobden Road
☎ (01903) 236856
11–3, 5.30–11; 11–11 Sat; 12–3, 7–10.30 Sun
Draught Bass; Flowers Original; guest beers H
Friendly, town local; a *Guide* regular for many years.
◖ ⇌ ♣

Yapton

Lamb Inn

Bilsham Road (B2132, S of village) ☎ (01243) 551232
11–3, 5.30 (5 Fri, 6 Sat)–11; 12–4.30, 6.30–10.30 Sun
Fuller's London Pride; Harveys BB; Marston's Pedigree; guest beer (occasional) H
Friendly, roadside pub on the edge of the village. The large

rustic public bar is busy; the smaller lounge (with a family room off) is more relaxed. The large garden with play equipment (bouncy castle in summer) is fenced from the road and has boules courts. Wheelchair WC.

🏚 🛏 ☺ ◖ 🌔 🛨 ⅄ 🍴 P ☷

Maypole Inn
Maypole Lane (off B2132, ½ mile N of village)
☎ (01243) 551417
11–2.30, 5.30–11; 12–3, 7–10.30 Sun
Courage Best Bitter; Flowers

Original; Ringwood Best Bitter; guest beers Ⓗ
Family-run pub with a rural atmosphere, tucked away down a lane away from the village centre, boasting a cosy lounge with two log fires, a large public bar (children's certificate) and a skittle alley (available for functions). Bank hol beer festivals (Easter and summer). Up to four guest beers change regularly. No eve meals Tue or Sun. Very good value, traditional pub food.

🏚 Q ☺ ◖ 🌔 🛨 ⅄ 🍴 P

Joint venture! Brewers Andy Hepworth (left) of King & Barnes and Martin Barry of Salopian swap secrets to bring production of Salopian's bottle-conditioned beer range to K&B's new high tech bottling plant. The range includes a ginger wheat beer, a black wheat beer, a spice beer and an oat beer with raspberries!

Tyne & Wear

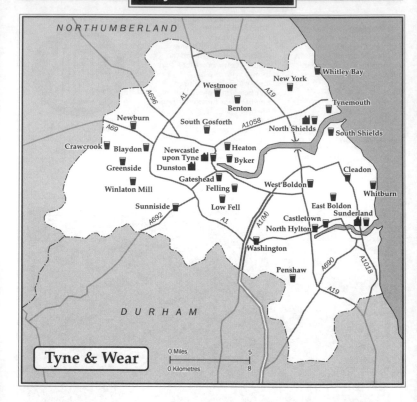

Tyne & Wear

0 Miles 5
0 Kilometres 8

Benton

Benton Ale House
Front Street
☎ (0191) 266 1512
11–11; 12–10.30 Sun
Banks's Bitter; Camerons Bitter, Strongarm; guest beers Ⓗ
Large, well refurbished pub selling a good selection of guest beers. Popular with civil servants at lunchtime and utilised by students in the eve.
◖ ⊖ (Four Lane Ends) P ⊟

Blaydon

Black Bull
Bridge Street
☎ (0191) 414 2486
4–11; 12–3, 6–11 Sat; 12–3, 7–10.30 Sun
Camerons Bitter, Strongarm; Castle Eden Ale; Ind Coope Burton Ale; guest beers Ⓗ
Friendly, well-run pub, popular with locals. The bar has fine displays of photographs depicting the decline of Blaydon.
🏚 Q ❀ ⊕ ⇌ (limited service) ♣ P

Byker

Free Trade Inn
St Lawrence Road
☎ (0191) 265 5764
11–11; 12–10.30 Sun
McEwan 80/-; Mordue Five Bridge Bitter, Workie Ticket, Radgie Gadgie; Theakston Best Bitter, XB; guest beers Ⓗ
Wonderfully basic pub overlooking the River Tyne. Large windows face the ever-changing quayside development. 🏚 ❀

Tyne
1 Maling Street
☎ (0191) 265 2550
11–11; 12–10.30 Sun
Boddingtons Bitter; Castle Eden Ale; Four Rivers Gladiator; Marston's Pedigree Ⓗ
Standing on the east bank of the Ouseburn, near its mouth, this single room pub is hard to find. The reward is in the beer quality, an interesting, free jukebox and an unusual garden. ❀

Try also: Tap & Spile, Shields Rd (range varies)

Castletown

Wessington
Wessington Way
☎ (0191) 548 9384
11–11; 12–10.30 Sun
Boddingtons Bitter; Castle Eden Ale; Flowers Original; guest beer Ⓗ
Large, purpose-built, modern pub/motel. The interior is open-plan, with the restaurant separated from the bar by an entrance hall. Very family-oriented, with excellent children's facilities, it can get

INDEPENDENT BREWERIES

Big Lamp: Newcastle upon Tyne

Darwin: Sunderland

Federation: Dunston

Four Rivers: Newcastle upon Tyne

Mordue: North Shields

Riverside: Sunderland

Vaux: Sunderland

very busy at weekends. Meals served all day Sun.
🍽 ❀ 🛏 ◐ ◗ ♿ P ⚡

Cleadon

Cottage Tavern
North Street (A1018)
☎ (0191) 536 7883
12–11; 12–10.30 Sun
Vaux Samson; guest beer Ⓗ
Well-established, roadside village pub with a long, semi-circular bar. A cosy atmosphere, created by subdued lighting and typical Vaux decor, makes this a comfortable, popular pub.
❀ ♣

Crawcrook

Rising Sun Inn
Bank Top (off A695 at Crawcrook, W of lights)
☎ (0191) 413 3316
11.30–11; 12–10.30 Sun
Boddingtons Bitter; Castle Eden Ale; Marston's Pedigree; guest beers Ⓗ
Comfortable pub with a pleasant atmosphere, a good selection of beers and a range of home-cooked snacks and meals. One of the few establishments that combine food catering with consideration for ale drinkers.
❀ ◐ ◗ ♣ P

East Boldon

Grey Horse
14 Front Street
☎ (0191) 536 4186
11–11; 12–10.30 Sun
Vaux Samson, Waggle Dance; guest beer Ⓗ
Impressive, 17th-century village pub with friendly staff. A compact bar and a large lounge, with various small corners, make it a classic pub. No food Sun eve.
Q ❀ ◐ ◗ ⊞ ♿ ⇌ ♣ P

Try also: Beaumont Wines (off-licence), Station Rd

Felling

Old Fox
Carlisle Street
☎ (0191) 420 0357
12–4, 6–11; 11–11 Sat; 12–10.30 Sun
Bateman XB; Fuller's London Pride; guest beers Ⓗ
Friendly, comfortable pub, attracting a mixed clientele for its musical events and fast turnover of guest ales (sparklers removed on request). 🏠 ❀ 🛏 ◐ ⊖ ♣

Wheatsheaf
26 Carlisle Street
☎ (0191) 420 0659
12–3, 6–11; 12–11 Sat; 12–3, 7–10.30 Sun
Big Lamp Bitter, Prince Bishop, Premium, Summerhill Stout Ⓗ
Good, honest, street-corner boozer with a loyal following. Good value beers. Cheerful and welcoming. 🏠 ⊖

Gateshead

Borough Arms
80–82 Bensham Road (near metro) ☎ (0191) 478 1323
12–3, 6–11; 12–11 Sat; 12–3, 7–10.30 Sun
Draught Bass; Stones Bitter; guest beers Ⓗ
Welcoming, two-roomed pub offering a varied range of guest ales. Popular with locals, but visitors are made welcome.
🏠 ❀ ◐ ⊖ P

Greenside

White Swan
Main Street ☎ (0191) 413 4255
4 (12 Sat)–11; 12–10.30 Sun
Banks's Bitter; Camerons Bitter, Strongarm Ⓗ
Many-roomed, friendly village pub with a comfortable lounge.
🏠 Q 🍽 ❀ ⊞ P

Heaton

Chillingham
Chillingham Road
☎ (0191) 265 5915
11–11 (lounge closed 2–5); 12–10.30 (lounge closed 3–7) Sun
Draught Bass; Courage Directors; Theakston Best Bitter, XB; guest beers Ⓗ
Large, two-roomed pub, very popular with students and sometimes very busy in term time. High standards of fittings; children's certificate for the lounge. Eve meals (not served Sun) finish at 8pm.
◐ ◗ ⊞ ♿ ⊖ (Chillingham Rd)

Low Fell

Aletaster
706 Durham Road
☎ (0191) 487 0770
11–11; 12–10.30 Sun
Courage Directors; Marston's Pedigree; Mordue Workie Ticket, Radgie Gadgie; Theakston Old Peculier; guest beers Ⓗ
Popular local – T&J Bernard's flagship pub which has 16 handpumps. Mini-beer festivals held. ❀ ⌓ P

Newburn

Keelman
Grange Road
☎ (0191) 267 0772
11–11; 12–10.30 Sun
Big Lamp Bitter, Premium, Prince Bishop, Summerhill Stout, Winter Warmer Ⓗ
Big Lamp's second tied house, now effectively the brewery tap. A sensitively converted, former water pumping station now houses the brewery and pub, and is attractively situated next to Riverside Country Park and leisure centre. ❀ 🛏 ◐ ◗ P

Newcastle upon Tyne

Bacchus
High Bridge
☎ (0191) 232 6451
11.30–11; 7–10.30 Sun
Draught Bass; Stones Bitter; Tetley Bitter; Theakston XB; guest beers Ⓗ
Comfortable, city-centre pub offering welcome relief from the hurly-burly of life: pleasant surroundings and excellent lunchtime food.
◐ ⇌ (Central) ⊖

Bodega
125 Westgate Road
☎ (0191) 221 1552
11–11; 12–10.30 Sun
Butterknowle Conciliation Ale; Theakston Best Bitter; guest beers Ⓗ
Impressive pub next to Tyne Theatre, retaining two majestic stained-glass domes. Three guest and three regular beers include ales from local small breweries; No. 9 is Mordue's Geordie Pride. The food's good, too (not served Sat).
◐ ⇌ (Central) ⊖

Bridge Hotel
Castle Garth
☎ (0191) 232 6400
11–11; 12–10.30 Sun
Draught Bass; Boddingtons Bitter; Butterknowle Conciliation Ale; Theakston XB; guest beers Ⓗ
Recently refurbished to a high standard, the Bridge offers a number of intimate seating areas within a single room. The garden overlooks Newcastle's historic city walls, bridges and river. Folk nights. ❀ ◐ ⇌ (Central) ⊖ (Monument)

Crown Posada ☆
33 Side
☎ (0191) 232 1269
11 (12 Sat)–11; 12–3, 7–10.30 Sun
Draught Bass; Boddingtons Bitter; Butterknowle Conciliation Ale; Jennings Bitter; Theakston Best Bitter; guest beer Ⓗ
One of the few unspoilt pubs in the area with original stained-glass windows and a great bunch of regulars. Everything you could wish for and no jukebox or TV – just good conversation.
⇌ (Central) ⊖ (Monument)

Duke of Wellington
High Bridge ☎ (0191) 261 8852
11–11; 7–10.30 Sun
Ind Coope Burton Ale; Marston's Pedigree; Taylor Landlord; Tetley Bitter; guest beers H
Thriving, city-centre pub, selling a good selection of beer. At quiet times, examine the photographs on display. Handy for the fashion shops.
⊖ (Monument)

Fitzgerald's
60 Grey Street
☎ (0191) 261 5038
11–11; 7–10.30 Sun
Draught Bass; Butterknowle Conciliation Ale; guest beers H
A narrow frontage on one of the finest streets in the city leads into a huge pub which is quite often packed. Fine woodwork, fittings and features. ◖ ⇌ (Central) ⊖ (Monument)

Newcastle Arms
57 St Andrews Street
☎ (0191) 232 3567
11–11; 7–10.30 Sun
Ind Coope Burton Ale; Marston's Pedigree; Tetley Bitter; guest beers H
Popular, single-room pub near the home of Newcastle Utd. Frequently changing guest ales and friendly staff encourage a good atmosphere.
⊖ (St James/Monument)

Tap & Spile
Nun Street ☎ (0191) 232 0026
11–11; 7–10.30 Sun
Beer range varies H
Occupying a corner site, adjoining the Grainger covered market, this pub offers a rapid rotation of beers. Frequent live music. No food Sun. ◖ ⇌ (Central) ⊖ (Monument) ⊖

Tut 'n' Shive
52 Clayton Street West
☎ (0191) 261 8778
11–11; 12–10.30 Sun
Boddingtons Bitter; Castle Eden Ale; Flowers Original; Marston's Pedigree; guest beers H
Up to ten cask beers greet the visitor to this lively and busy pub. The upstairs room (entrance outside) is one of Newcastle's major live music venues, presenting bands five nights a week. No cask upstairs, but jugs of beer available in the main bar.
⇌ (Central) ⊖

New York

Shiremoor Farm
Middle Engine Lane
☎ (0191) 257 6302
11–11; 12–10.30 Sun

Stones Bitter; Taylor Landlord; Theakston Old Peculier; guest beers H
Award-winning Fitzgerald's outlet, well known for its excellent food (meals 12–9 daily). Close to a steam railway. Q ✿ ◖ ▶ 🚌 P

North Hylton

Shipwrights
Ferryboat Lane
☎ (0191) 549 5139
11–4, 5–11 (11–11 summer); 12–3, 7–10.30 Sun
Vaux Samson, Waggle Dance; Ward's Best Bitter; guest beer H
350-year-old pub on the banks of the River Wear, close to the A19, celebrating 21 consecutive years in the *Guide*. The interior is full of brass fittings and wooden beams. Various commendations are on show. Excellent, home-cooked food and popular accommodation.
🚌 ⛺ ◖ ▶ P

North Shields

Bell & Bucket
37 Norfolk Street
☎ (0191) 257 4634
11–11; 12–10.30 Sun
Banks's Bitter; Camerons Bitter, Strongarm; Marston's Pedigree; guest beers H
Interesting conversion from a redundant fire station – a 'warm' welcome awaits!
◖ ⊖ 🚻

Magnesia Bank
1 Camden Street
☎ (0191) 257 4831
11–11; 12–10.30 Sun
Vaux Waggle Dance; Ward's Thorne BB, Best Bitter; guest beers H
Large, friendly pub featuring beers from local microbrewers and guests from further afield. The house beer is called Maggie Mayhem. The function room upstairs doubles as restaurant on Sun – good food. The pub overlooks the River Tyne. Children's certificate. Weekly music nights are held.
✿ ◖ ▶ ⊖ 🚻

Tap & Spile
184 Tynemouth Road
☎ (0191) 257 2523
11–11; 12–10.30 Sun
Beer range varies H
A popular member of the Tap & Spile chain, this pub offers the usual wide variety of cask beer in a simple, uncluttered, long bar which opens out at one end to a comfortable sitting area and, at the other, to a more basic area used for live music and chat.
◖ ⊖

Penshaw

Grey Horse
Village Green, Old Penshaw
☎ (0191) 584 4882
11–3.30 (4 Sat), 6–11; 12–4, 7–10.30 Sun
Tetley Bitter H
Pleasant, friendly village pub, with a cosy atmosphere, near the 'Penshaw Monument', a local landmark. A *Guide* regular for 17 years. No food Sun. Tiny car park.
✿ ◖ 🍴 ♣ P

Prospect
Victoria Terrace, Old Penshaw
☎ (0191) 584 4001
12–3, 7–11; 12–11 Sat; 12–10.30 Sun
Vaux Samson; guest beer H
Refurbished, two-roomed roadside pub comprised of a large public bar with a pool area, and a plush lounge with a raised dining area. Baby changing facilities available. The car park is across a very busy road. ◖ ▶ 🍴 ♣ P

South Gosforth

Victory
Killingworth Road
☎ (0191) 285 1254
12 (11.30 Fri)–11; 12–10.30 Sun
Marston's Pedigree; McEwan 80/-; Theakston Best Bitter, XB; guest beers H
T&J Bernard pub: a tasteful conversion with a friendly atmosphere and a good range of beers. ◖ ▶ ⊖ P

South Shields

Alum Ale House
River Drive (by ferry landing)
☎ (0191) 427 7245
11–11; 12–3, 7–10.30 Sun
Banks's Bitter; Camerons Strongarm; Marston's Pedigree; guest beer H
Quiet, cosy, yet popular pub, decorated in traditional style with bare wood floors and panelled walls. The bar boasts an unusual copper top and cast iron hearth. Regular live folk music and rock/blues.
🚌 Q ⊖ 🚻

Bamburgh
175 Bamburgh Avenue
☎ (0191) 454 1899
11–11; 12–10.30 Sun
Boddingtons Bitter; Castle Eden Ale; Jennings Cumberland Ale; Morland Old Speckled Hen; guest beer H
This open-plan 'Berni Inn' overlooks the Leas. The main bar has raised games/seating areas, whilst a secluded restaurant caters for diners; both offer excellent views of

the spectacular coast. No-smoking area in summer.
Q ☙ ⊛ ◖ ♦ ⅋ ♣ P ⅊

Dolly Peel

137 Commercial Road
☎ (0191) 427 1441
11–11; 12–3, 7–10.30 Sun
Courage Directors; Taylor Landlord; Theakston XB; Younger No. 3; guest beer Ⓗ
First-rate pub with a fine selection of ales. This popular, friendly, award-winning house is a must for all lovers of real ales and malt whiskies.
Q ♣ P

Holborn Rose & Crown

East Holborn (opp. Middle Dock gate)
☎ (0191) 455 2379
11–11; 12–10.30 Sun
Courage Directors; Theakston XB; guest beers Ⓗ
Dockside pub off the main track, with an old-fashioned atmosphere and shipyard/riverside memorabilia. Changing guest beers.
Q ⊛ ♣ ⅊

Riverside

3 Commercial Road
☎ (0191) 455 2328
12–11; 12–3, 7–10.30 Sun
Courage Directors; Taylor Landlord; Theakston Best Bitter, XB; guest beer Ⓗ
Compact, street-corner free house, near the Customs House, offering an outlet for independent/micros' guest ales. Well-trained, pleasant staff. Q ⊛ ⊖ ⌕

Steamboat

51 Coronation Street
☎ (0191) 454 0134
12–11; 12–10.30 Sun
Vaux Samson, Double Maxim, Waggle Dance; guest beer Ⓗ
One of the town's oldest pubs, boasting a preserved shop window exterior and a split-level interior with wood-panelled walls and a ceiling decorated with maritime flags. Very busy at weekends; popular with students.
⊕ ⊖

Sunderland: *North*

Harbour View

Harbour View
☎ (0191) 567 1402
11–11; 12–10.30 Sun
Draught Bass; Worthington Bitter; guest beer Ⓗ
Modern, traditional-style ale house with excellent views over the harbour and marina. Always busy at weekends; the outside seating is popular in summer. Close to Roker Park and the beach. ⊛

Smugglers

Marine Walk
☎ (0191) 514 3844
11.30–3, 5–11; 11–11 Sat; 12–10.30 Sun
Theakston Best Bitter; Younger No. 3; guest beer Ⓗ
Popular pub at the edge of Roker Park, tucked away on the lower promenade by the beach, extending a warm welcome to families. Nautical artefacts decorate a small dining area, and a good range of meals ensures its popularity.
⋈ ⊛ ◖ ▶

Sunderland: *South*

Borough

1 Vine Place
☎ (0191) 567 7909
11–11; 7–10.30 Sun
Vaux Lorimer's Best Scotch, Samson, Double Maxim, Waggle Dance; guest beer Ⓗ
Busy, street-corner, city-centre pub with real ales available only in the basic ground-floor bar, served from a circular bar counter with offset seating areas. ⊕ ≩

Brewery Tap

9 Dunning Street
☎ (0191) 567 7472
11–11; 12–10.30 Sun
Vaux Samson Ⓗ
Traditional pub adjoining the brewery: a quiet, basic, small bar linked to a cosy back room by a wood-panelled corridor. Framed prints of old Sunderland are on show. A rotating Vaux ale complements the Samson. Car park eves/weekends only.
⊛ ⊕ ≩ ♣ P

Chesters

Chester Road
☎ (0191) 565 9952
11–11; 12–10.30 Sun
Vaux Samson; Ward's Best Bitter; guest beer Ⓗ
Impressive, white-washed building set back from the road and once a vicarage. The open-plan interior is cleverly disguised by partitions, creating an impression of several rooms. There is also an upstairs function room.
⊛ ◖ ⊕ ⅋ ♣ P ⅊

Fitzgerald's

10–12 Green Terrace
☎ (0191) 567 0852
11–11; 12–10.30 Sun
Boddingtons Bitter; Theakston Best Bitter, XB; guest beer Ⓗ
Large 'circuit' pub near the University, popular with the young and always packed eves and weekends. A large bar area and small 'Chart Room' serve the hordes that pass through daily. The Sunday night quiz attracts students. ⊛ ◖ ⊕ ≩

Lansdowne

32 Deptford Road
☎ (0191) 567 1886
11–11; 12–10.30 Sun
Vaux Lorimer's Best Scotch, Samson; guest beer Ⓗ
Comfortable local in a quiet area, offering a friendly and relaxed atmosphere in a one-room bar and a partitioned pool area. ♣

Saltgrass

36 Ayres Quay
☎ (0191) 565 7229
11–3, 6–11; 11–11 Fri & Sat; 12–3, 7–10.30 Sun
Vaux Samson, Waggle Dance; Ward's Best Bitter; guest beer Ⓗ
Well-established pub, offering free transport at weekends to other local pubs.
⋈ ⊛ ◖ ♣ ♣

Tap & Spile

Salem Street, Hendon
☎ (0191) 514 2810
12–3, 5.30–11; 12–3, 7–10.30 Sun
Beer range varies Ⓗ
Award-winning, traditional alehouse offering the largest choice of beers and cider in the area. Local CAMRA *Pub of the Year* 1993–1997; *Regional Pub* 1996. Annual beer festivals and an ever-changing array of guest ales help draw a mixed clientele.
⋈ ◖ ≩ ♣ ⌕

Sunniside

Potters Wheel

Sun Street
☎ (0191) 488 3628
11.30–11; 11–3, 5.30–11 Mon; 12–3, 7–10.30 Sun
Courage Directors; Theakston Best Bitter; guest beers Ⓗ
Fine pub within a mile of Tanfield Steam Railway and six miles from Beamish Open Air Museum. The use of light-coloured wood creates a spacious feel throughout the various, separate areas. Children's certificate. No meals Sun eve.
⊛ ◖ ▶ ⅋ P

Tynemouth

Fitzpatrick's

29 Front Street
☎ (0191) 257 8956
11–11; 12–10.30 Sun
Theakston Best Bitter, XB; guest beers Ⓗ
Long, beautifully furnished pub with a raised seating area and a small, cosy snug. Good food means the pub is well used at lunchtimes (eve meals in summer). Close to Tynemouth Priory and beach.
Q ◖ ▶ ⊖

Tynemouth Lodge Hotel

Correction House Bank
☎ (0191) 257 7565
11–11; 12–10.30 Sun
Draught Bass; Belhaven 80/-; Black Sheep Best Bitter Ⓗ
Welcoming, lively 18th-century free house; the only permanent outlet for Belhaven in the North of England. No children, no dogs, no hot food, no music and no games, but excellent beer! ⚌ Q ⊛ ⊖ P

Washington

Sandpiper

Easby Road, Biddick (follow signs for District 7)
☎ (0191) 416 0038
11–11; 12–10.30 Sun
Boddingtons Bitter; Castle Eden Ale; Morland Old Speckled Hen; guest beer Ⓗ
Modern pub, featuring a large lounge with a stone-flagged floor, surrounded by carpeted seating areas, plus a modern games room-cum-bar area. Seven real ales. ⊛ ◑ ▶ ♣ P

Three Horse Shoes

Washington Road, Usworth (opp. Nissan factory)
☎ (0191) 536 4183
12–3, 6.30–11; 11–11 Fri & Sat; 12–3, 7–10.30 Sun
Vaux Lorimer's Best Scotch, Samson, Double Maxim; guest beer Ⓗ
Isolated, former coaching inn with a reputation for good value meals in its large modern lounge (no food Sun eve). There's also a bar and pool room. Q ⊛ ◑ ▶ ⊕ ♣ P

West Boldon

Black Horse

Rectory Bank
☎ (0191) 536 1814
11–3, 7–11; 12–3, 7–10.30 Sun
Boddingtons Bitter; Castle Eden Ale; Flowers Original; Fuller's ESB; Mordue Radgie Gadgie; guest beer Ⓗ
Smartly decorated, food-oriented pub by the ancient parish church at the top of Boldon Bank. A wide selection of ales is available in the compact, L-shaped bar, with quality meals in the restaurant area (no food Sun). Small car park. Q ⊛ ◑ ▶ ♣ P

Westmoor

George Stephenson

Great Line Road
☎ (0191) 268 1073
12–3, 5–11; 12–11 Fri & Sat; 12–4, 7–10.30 Sun
Beer range varies Ⓗ
Two-roomed pub by a railway bridge. Lunches Mon–Fri. The range of three beers includes S&N and usually local Mordue ales. ◑ ♣ P ⛴

Whitburn

Jolly Sailor

1 East Street ☎ (0191) 529 3221
11–11; 12–10.30 Sun
Draught Bass; Stones Bitter; Worthington Bitter Ⓗ
18th-century coaching inn in the centre of a scenic village. Popular with tourists and locals, it is comprised of a small bar and two small rooms. The upstairs bar is open in summer. No food Sun
⚌ Q ⊛ ◑ ⊕ ♣

Whitley Bay

Briar Dene

The Links ☎ (0191) 252 0926
11–11; 12–10.30 Sun
Stones Bitter; Theakston Best Bitter, XB; guest beers Ⓗ
Large, attractive Fitzgerald's house with several drinking areas. The bar boasts seaviews over the links and St Mary's Lighthouse.
Q ⛄ ⊛ ◑ ▶ ◐ ♣ P

Fitzgerald's

2 South Parade
☎ (0191) 251 1255
11–11; 12–10.30 Sun
Draught Bass; Newcastle Exhibition; Theakston Best Bitter; guest beers Ⓗ
Lovely pub with a large main bar area and a cosy, quieter snug. Popular with diners at lunchtime, it gets more lively in the eve, with regular music. Children's certificate. Eve meals till 7pm. ◑ ⊖ P

Tap & Spile

278 Whitley Road
☎ (0191) 251 3852
12 (11 Sat)–11; 12–10.30 Sun
Beer range varies Ⓗ
Large, corner pub split into a number of standing and sitting sections. Even when busy, it never seems to get overcrowded. ◑ ◐ ◌

Winlaton Mill

Golden Lion

Shotley Bridge Road (A694)
☎ (0191) 414 5840
12–3, 6–11; 12–10.30 Sun
Courage Directors; Theakston Best Bitter; guest beers Ⓗ
Lively, friendly pub with a strong local following. Highly regarded restaurant on the lower floor. ⊛ ◑ ▶ ⊕ ♣ P

Huntley Well

Shotley Bridge Road
☎ (0191) 414 2731
12–4, 6–11; 12–11 Fri & Sat; 12–10.30 Sun
Ind Coope Burton Ale; Tetley Bitter; guest beers Ⓗ
Friendly pub that was once a club; very popular with local residents, but visitors can expect a warm welcome. ◑ ▶ ♣ P

Ted Blaze of Vaux and friend spar over a pint of 'Boxing Hare'.

Warwickshire

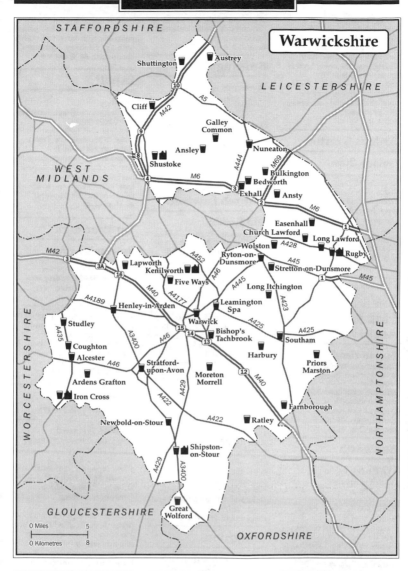

Alcester

Three Tuns
34 High Street
11–11; 12–10.30 Sun
**Goff's Jouster; Highgate Fox's
Nob; Hobsons Best Bitter;
guest beers** Ⓗ
Clear, small-paned windows
make it look more like a
teashop from the outside, but
inside this is a proper pub. Up
to eight ales at most times;
mini-festivals are a frequent
attraction. Q ⅙ ▲ ♣

Ansley

Lord Nelson Inn
Birmingham Road (B4112)
☎ (01203) 392305
12–2.30, 5.30–11; 12–10.30 Sun
**Draught Bass; Tetley Bitter;
guest beer** Ⓗ
Welcoming pub with a nautical
theme. Two guest beers are
available during busy holiday
periods, for special events and
in winter. The restaurant is
very popular.
🍴 🏠 ◑ ▯ ⅙ ♣ P

Ansty

Rose & Castle Inn
Main Road (B4065, off M6 jct 2)
☎ (01203) 612822
11–3, 6 (5.30 Fri)–11; 11–11 Sat; 12–
10.30 Sun

🏭 INDEPENDENT BREWERIES
Church End: Shustoke

Feldon: Shipston-on-Stour

Judges: Rugby

Queen's Head: Iron Cross

Warwickshire: Kenilworth

Join CAMRA – 50,000 members can't all be wrong!

Draught Bass; Marston's Pedigree; Morland Old Speckled Hen; Tetley Bitter ⒽＨ Extremely popular roadside pub with a split-level bar/dining area (the lower level is for non-smokers). The canalside garden has mooring facilities plus a safe activity area for children. Food served all day Sat and Sun.
✿ ◖▶ P

Ardens Grafton

Golden Cross
Wixford Road OS114538
☎ (01789) 772420
11–2.30, 6–11; 12–2.30, 7–10.30 Sun
Draught Bass; Goff's Jouster; guest beers Ⓗ
Old stone pub commanding views over the Vale of Evesham to the Cotswolds. Note the fine collections of teddy bears and dolls. Always six ales, many from independent brewers. Home to a plethora of societies. Good and copious food – a trencherman's paradise.
✿ ◖▶ ▲ ♣ P ⌫

Austrey

Bird in Hand
Church Lane ☎ (01827) 830260
12–3.30 (not Mon–Thu), 6.30–11; 12–5, 7–10.30 Sun
Marston's Pedigree, HBC Ⓗ
Popular village local with a thatched roof and a restaurant. Thrice local CAMRA *Pub of the Year*. ♨ Q ✿ ⊞ P

Bedworth

White Swan
All Saints Square
☎ (01203) 312164
11–11; 12–10.30 Sun
Banks's Mild; Wells Eagle, Bombardier Ⓗ
Situated in the heart of town, near the Civic Hall, this large mature pub is busy with locals and shoppers at the nearby market. ◖⊞ ⇌ ♣

Bishop's Tachbrook

Leopard Inn
Oakley Wood Road (B4087)
☎ (01926) 426466
11.30–2.30, 7 (5 Thu & Fri)–11; 11–11 Sat; 12–3, 7–10.30 Sun
Draught Bass; Boddingtons Bitter; Flowers Original; Marston's Pedigree; Whitbread seasonal beers; guest beers Ⓗ
Grade II-listed building: a much improved old village pub with a friendly atmosphere and a good selection of beers. Families welcome – children's play area

in the garden. Beer festivals Feb and July. Book Sun lunch as food is popular.
♨ ✿ ◖▶ ⅃ P

Bulkington

Weavers Arms
12 Long Street, Ryton
☎ (01203) 314415
12–3.30, 6–11; 12–3.30, 7–10.30 Sun
Draught Bass; M&B Mild, Brew XI; guest beers Ⓗ
Popular, two-room, traditional village free house: a friendly locals' bar and a small cosy lounge; well worth a visit. No food Sun. ♨ Q ✿ ◖⊞ ♣

Church Lawford

Old Smithy
1 Green Lane ☎ (01203) 542333
11–3, 5–11; 11–11 Sat; 12–10.30 Sun
Ansells Mild; Judges Old Gavel Bender; Marston's Pedigree; Shipstone's Bitter; Tetley Bitter; guest beers Ⓗ
Very friendly, improved village inn, twice local CAMRA *Pub of the Year*, with a quality restaurant. Two regularly changing guest beers, plus one or two beers from the local Judges Brewery.
♨ ✿ ◖▶ ⅃ ♣ P

Cliff

Malt House
Tamworth Road (A51 Kingsbury road)
☎ (01827) 874747
11.30–2.30, 5.30–11; 12–10.30 Sun
Ansells Mild Ⓔ; Marston's Pedigree Ⓗ
Old malt works, now converted into a comfortable pub serving excellent food in a relaxed atmosphere. Families welcome, although no separate room. Smart casual dress required. Q ✿ ◖▶ ⅃ P

Coughton

Throckmorton Arms
On A435 ☎ (01789) 762879
11–3, 5 (6 Sat)–11; 12–3, 7–10.30 Sun
Banks's Bitter; Draught Bass; M&B Brew XI Ⓗ
Large pub/diner with three open-plan rooms and a no-smoking restaurant serving a wide range of dishes; bar meals also available.
♨ Q ✿ ☎ ◖▶ ⅃ ♣ P

Easenhall

Golden Lion
Main Street ☎ (01788) 832265
11–11; 12–10.30 Sun
Flowers Original; guest beer Ⓗ
16th-century village pub in rural Warwickshire, with original wooden beams,

narrow doors and uneven floors. The large garden has a patio and a children's play area with a pet donkey. Barbecues in summer. ♨ ✿ ☎ ◖▶ P

Exhall

Boat
188 Blackhorse Road, Longford
☎ (01203) 361438
12–3, 7–11; 12–3, 7–10.30 Sun
Ansells Mild, Bitter; Tetley Bitter; guest beers Ⓗ
18th-century, characterful pub near the canal (Sutton stop). It has been run by the same family since 1840 and in the *Guide* for the last 21 years.
♨ Q ✿ ⊞ ♣ P

Farnborough

Butcher's Arms
Off A423 ☎ (01295) 690615
12–3, 7–11; 12–5, 7–10.30 Sun
Draught Bass; Boddingtons Bitter; Hook Norton Best Bitter; guest beers Ⓗ
Traditional, stone village pub, with two bars, stone-flagged floors, roaring log fires and a large garden. The well-regarded restaurant is open every day except Sun eve. Live music Fri eve.
♨ Q ✿ ◖▶ ⊞ ▲ ♣ P

Fiveways (Haseley Knob)

Case is Altered   ☆
Case Lane (off A4177/A4141 island) OS225701
☎ (01926) 484206
11.30–2.30, 6–11; 12–2, 7–10.30 Sun
Ansells Mild, Bitter; Flowers Original Ⓖ; Samuel Smith OBB Ⓗ; guest beer (weekend) Ⓖ
Unspoilt, rural pub with a low, beamed ceiling, tiled floor and a log fire. One room has bar billiards which still needs old sixpences. The lounge is open Fri and Sat eves and Sun lunch. The gravity beers are served through unusual cask pumps. Warwickshire CAMRA *Pub of the Year* 1996. ♨ Q ✿ ♣ P

Galley Common

Plough Inn
Plough Hill Road (½ mile off B4114) ☎ (01203) 392425
12–3 (4 Sat), 6–11; 12–3, 7–10.30 Sun
Draught Bass; Home Mild; M&B Brew XI; guest beer Ⓗ
Roadside inn, popular with locals. Dogs regularly patrol the tiled bar and side room. The cosy lounge at the rear provides access to the large garden with its crown bowling green. ♨ ✿ ⊞ ♣ P

Great Wolford

Fox & Hounds
☎ (01608) 674220
12–3, 7–11; 12–3, 7–10.30 Sun
Hook Norton Best Bitter; Shepherd Neame Spitfire; guest beers H
Excellently-run, atmospheric old pub offering a superb range of beers, an extensive choice of malt whiskies and good lunch food. Try your hand at Aunt Sally.
🚪 Q ❀ 🍴 ◖ ▶ ᴅ ▲ ♣ ᴼ P

Harbury

Crown
Crown Street ☎ (01926) 612283
12–3, 5–11; 12–11 Fri & Sat; 12–5, 7–10.30 Sun
Flowers IPA; Theakston Best Bitter; Whitbread seasonal beers; guest beer H
Friendly pub believed to be the oldest in the village. The lounge has a large TV, which draws a crowd for sport. Late night supper menu (curries and baltis). No meals Thu or Sun eve. 🚪 ❀ ◖ ▶ ♣ ᴼ P

Dog Inn
The Bull Ring
☎ (01926) 612599
11.30–3, 6.30–11; 11.30–11 Sat; 12–3.30, 6.30–10.30 (12–10.30 summer) Sun
Ansells Bitter; Draught Bass; guest beers H
Brick pub dating from early this century, the only purpose-built pub in the village, featuring a good, traditional bar, a cosy lounge and a large restaurant. Steady following for the recently introduced guest beers and the high quality food.
🚪 ◖ ▶ 🍴 ᴅ ♣ P

Henley-in-Arden

White Swan
100 High Street
☎ (01564) 792623
11–11; 12–10.30 Sun
Ansells Bitter; HP&D Mild; Marston's Pedigree; Tetley Bitter; guest beer H
Large, busy, coaching house, partly dating back to the 14th century, serving good value food in the restaurant. Reputedly haunted by a housemaid hanged at the gallows for murder, it is a rare local outlet for the mild.
Q ❀ 📠 ◖ ▶ ⇌ ♣ P

Iron Cross

Queen's Head
On B4088 (old A435)
☎ (01386) 871012
11–11; 12–10.30 Sun

Fat God's Best Bitter; Theakston XB, Old Peculier; guest beers H
Excellent food, but this is definitely a pub with food, not the other way round. Usually up to seven ales, including beer from its own brewery. Beer festival June. Wheelchair WC.
🚪 ❀ ◖ ▶ 🍴 ᴅ ▲ ♣ ᴼ P

Kenilworth

Clarendon House Hotel
High Street (A429/A452 jct)
☎ (01926) 857668
11.30–2.30 (3 Sat), 6–11; 12–3, 7–10.30 Sun
Boddingtons Bitter; Flowers IPA, Original; Hook Norton Best Bitter; guest beers H
Well-appointed hotel which maintains a friendly atmosphere. Restaurant and bar meals (not served Sun eve).
Q 📠 ◖ ▶ P

Virgins & Castle
7 High Street (A429/A452 jct)
☎ (01926) 853737
12–11; 12–10.30 Sun
Draught Bass; Davenports Bitter; Greenalls Original; guest beers H
Extended medieval pub with low, exposed beams and many rooms served by a central bar. Cosmopolitan clientele; especially popular with students. No food Sun eve.
🚪 Q ❀ ◖ ▶

Lapworth

Navigation
Old Warwick Road (B4439)
☎ (01564) 783337
11–2.30, 5.30–11; 11–11 Sat; 12–10.30 Sun
Draught Bass; Highgate Dark; M&B Brew XI; guest beers H
Very popular traditional pub on the Grand Union Canal: a stone-flagged bar with an open fire, a small lounge and a sympathetic extension at the rear. Local CAMRA *Pub of the Year* 1996.
🚪 Q ❀ ◖ ▶ ▲ ⇌ ♣ ᴼ P

Leamington Spa

Hope & Anchor
41 Hill Street
☎ (01926) 423031
11–11; 12–10.30 Sun
Ansells Mild, Bitter; guest beer H
Thriving, Victorian street-corner local near the town centre, with always a warm welcome. Games include dominoes, darts and cribbage; satellite TV for live events. The guest beer may come from a small independent. ♣

Red House
113 Radford Road
☎ (01926) 881725
11.30–2.30, 5–11; 11–11 Fri & Sat; 12–3, 7–10.30 Sun
Adnams Extra; Draught Bass; Worthington Bitter H
Victorian pub which has Irish connections. The relaxed atmosphere is conducive to conversation. The only regular local outlet for Adnams Extra and a regular *Guide* entry.
Q ❀ ♣

Somerville Arms
4 Campion Terrace (take Leicester St from town centre, right at island)
☎ (01926) 426746
11–2.30 (3 Fri), 5.30–11; 11–11 Sat; 12.30–3, 7–10.30 Sun
Ansells Mild, Bitter; Marston's Pedigree; Tetley Bitter; guest beer H
Traditional town pub tucked away and well worth seeking out. Popular with discerning locals (thriving domino team), it has a friendly, relaxed atmosphere and thoroughly deserves its 21 consecutive years in the *Guide*. ᴅ ♣

Long Itchington

Harvester
6 Church Road
☎ (01926) 812698
11–3, 6–11; 12–3, 7–10.30 Sun
Hook Norton Best Bitter, Old Hooky; guest beer H
Unchanging country pub consisting of a bar, a lounge with a large fish tank and a popular restaurant. A frequent *Guide* entry.
◖ ▶ ᴅ ▲ ♣ P

Long Lawford

Country Inn
29 Main Street
☎ (01788) 565188
12–2.30, 7 (6 summer)–11; 12–11 Fri & Sat; 12–2.30, 7–10.30 Sun
Ansells Bitter; M&B Mild, Brew XI; guest beers H
Friendly, single-bar village local boasting genuine oak beams, a flagstoned floor and a log fire. It has a games room and a good restaurant (eve meals Tue–Sat).
🚪 ⛺ ❀ ◖ ▶ ♣ P

Sheaf & Sickle
Coventry Road (A428)
☎ (01788) 544622
12–2.30, 6–11; 12–11 Sat; 12–10.30 Sun
Ansells Mild, Bitter; Tetley Bitter; guest beers H
Very friendly pub, with a good choice of guest beers. The quality restaurant is very popular. A good local with a quiet snug and a busy bar.
Q ❀ ◖ ▶ ᴅ ♣ P

Moreton Morrell

Black Horse
☎ (01926) 651231
11.30–2.30 (3 Sat), 7–11; 12–3, 7–10.30 Sun
Hook Norton Best Bitter; guest beer H
Unpretentious village pub with a games area at the back; popular with locals and students from the nearby agricultural college. A pleasant garden offers views of countryside. The rolls are good value and recommended. ❀

Newbold-on-Stour

Bird in Hand
☎ (01789) 450253
12–2.30, 6–11; 12–3, 7–10.30 Sun
Hook Norton Best Bitter, Old Hooky, seasonal beers; guest beer H
Busy, friendly local comprised of a main bar and an adjacent games room. Excellent food includes seasonal game dishes. Aunt Sally league champions again in 1996. Weston's Old Rosie cider.
🏚 ❀ 🛏 🌓 ▶ ♣ ⌂ P

Nuneaton

Chase Hotel
Higham Lane
☎ (01203) 341013
11–11; 12–10.30 Sun
Ind Coope Burton Ale; Marston's Pedigree; Tetley Bitter H
Large, modernised pub with an emphasis on food (served all day). The spacious bar is popular with drinkers and can get busy at weekends. Children are welcome in the restaurant; there is also a safe play area.
🏇 ❀ 🛏 🌓 ▶ & ⇄ P

Priors Marston

Holly Bush Inn
Holly Bush Lane
☎ (01327) 260934
12–3, 5.30 (6 Sat)–11; 12–10.30 Sun
Draught Bass; Hook Norton Best Bitter; Marston's Pedigree; guest beers H
Traditional country pub with several drinking areas, a games room and a restaurant. Two guest beers are usually available. The friendly atmosphere attracts locals and visitors. Skittles played.
🏚 Q ❀ 🛏 🌓 ♣ P ✂

Ratley

Rose & Crown
Church Lane ☎ (01295) 678148
12–2.30 (3 Sat), 6–11; 12–3, 7–10.30 Sun

Badger Tanglefoot; Everards Tiger; Morland Old Speckled Hen; Wells Eagle, Bombardier H
Gem of a pub in a small, secluded village. A friendly, family-run local, it attracts people from a wide area and is reputedly haunted by a Roundhead ghost from the nearby Battle of Edgehill. Families welcome in a cosy, well-restored children's room, which is also the no-smoking area.
🏚 Q 🛏 ❀ 🌓 ▶ & ♠ ✂

Rugby

Half Moon
28–30 Lawford Road
☎ (01788) 574420
4 (12 Fri & Sat)–11; 12–10.30 Sun
Ansells Mild, Bitter; Ind Coope Burton Ale; guest beers H
Basic, mid-terrace boozer. No frills, but its character is enhanced by 19th-century pictures of Rugby on the walls. Popular with locals.
🏚 Q ♣

Raglan Arms
50 Dunchurch Road (opp. Rugby School playing field)
☎ (01788) 544441
12 (11 Sat)–3, 7–11; 12–3, 7–10.30 Sun
Fuller's London Pride; Greene King Abbot; Marston's Bitter, Pedigree; guest beers H
Friendly local with a strong darts and dominoes following. No noisy machines, just a good atmosphere and a good selection of beers.
Q 🍺 ♣ P

Three Horse Shoes Hotel
Sheep Street
☎ (01788) 544585
11–3, 5.30–11; 11–11 Sat; 12–3, 7–10.30 Sun
Boddingtons Bitter; Flowers Original; guest beer H
Plush old coaching inn providing a quiet haven from noisy neighbours. An outlet for local independent guest beers. Thirty-six rooms for overnight accommodation.
🏚 🛏 🌓 ✂

Victoria
1 Lower Hillmorton Road
☎ (01788) 544374
12–2.30 (4 Sat), 6 (7 Sat)–11; 12–3, 7–10.30 Sun
Draught Bass; M&B Brew XI; guest beers H
Victorian corner pub with original fittings, close to the town centre. An excellent, basic bar is complemented by an impressively refurbished lounge. Trad jazz Mon eve. Weekday lunches.
🌓 🍺 ⇄

Ryton-on-Dunsmore

Old Bull & Butcher
Oxford Road (A423)
☎ (01203) 507400
11–11; 12–10.30 Sun
Ansells Mild; Ind Coope Burton Ale; Tetley Bitter H
Old coaching inn, now a good, community-spirited pub with superb steak meals at cheap prices. A last bastion of Burton Ale in the Coventry area.
🏚 ❀ 🌓 ▶ & P

Shipston-on-Stour

Black Horse
Station Road (100 yds from A3400) ☎ (01608) 661617
12–3, 7–11; 12–3, 7–10.30 Sun
Courage Directors; Home Bitter; Ruddles Best Bitter; Webster's Yorkshire Bitter; guest beer H
Thatched pub dating back 800 years; originally a row of cottages for Cotswold sheep farmers. Note the lovely inglenook. Across the garden is a large, decorated children's room. Special offer meals for pensioners Mon–Thu. Dogs welcome.
🏚 🛏 ❀ 🌓 ▶ 🍺 ♣ P

Coach & Horses
16 New Street (A3400)
☎ (01608) 661335
11–11; 12–10.30 Sun
Feldon seasonal beers; Hook Norton Best Bitter, seasonal beers; guest beers H
Friendly, cosy single-room pub, dating back to the 18th century, with a small brewery in the back yard. Aunt Sally played. Popular with locals. The guest beer usually comes from a small independent brewer. Dogs welcome.
🏚 ❀ & ♣

Shustoke

Griffin Inn
Church End (B4116 on a sharp bend) ☎ (01675) 481205
12–2.30, 7–11; 12–2.30, 7–10.30 Sun
Marston's Pedigree; guest beers H
Old country village inn full of charm, with a low, beamed ceiling and log fires. It sells beers from Church End Brewery next door, plus wide-ranging guests. No food Sun.
🏚 Q 🛏 ❀ 🌓 & ♠ P

Shuttington

Wolferstan Arms
Main Road ☎ (01827) 892238
11–2.30 (3 Sat), 6–11; 12–10.30 Sun
Banks's Mild; Marston's Pedigree, HBC H

Large hillside pub with a popular restaurant (excellent food; try the beef sizzlers). The spacious outdoor drinking area affords views across the valley. Very busy during Sun lunchtimes.
Q ❀ ◖ ▶ ⊟ P

Southam

Olde Mint
Coventry Street
☎ (01926) 812339
11.30–3, 5.30–11; 11.30–11 Sat; 12–10.30 Sun
Adnams Broadside; Boddingtons Bitter; Wadworth 6X; guest beers H
This fine old stone pub in the town centre dates back to the time of the English Civil War. It has recently undergone significant, successful modifications; stone, timber, weapons and ancient torch-like lamps create an impression of a medieval manor house. Bar billiards is played.
🏺 ❀ ◖ ▶ ♣ P

Stratford-upon-Avon

Queen's Head
54 Ely Street
☎ (01789) 204914
11.30–11; 12–10.30 Sun
Draught Bass; Fuller's London Pride; Highgate Saddlers; M&B Brew XI; guest beers H
Popular, 18th-century, town-centre pub featuring exposed beams, two real fires and a stone-flagged floor. A wide range of guest ales comes mostly from small breweries. Eve meals Fri and Sat only; summer barbecues. Weston's cider is available. Outdoor skittles played.
🏺 ❀ ◖ ▶ ≽ ♣ ⏁

Stretton-on-Dunsmore

Shoulder of Mutton
Brookside
12–3 (not Mon–Thu), 8–11; 8–10.30 Sun
Draught Bass; M&B Mild, Brew XI H
Wonderfully unspoilt pub caught in two time zones, with an original 19th-century snug and a 'modern', early 1950s extension where period records to suit the surroundings are played. No food, but you are welcome to bring your own sandwiches.
🏺 Q ⪫ ⊟ ♿ ♣ P

Studley

Railway Inn
64 Station Road (B4092, ½ mile from centre) ☎ (01527) 857715
12–3, 5–11; 12–11 Fri & Sat; 12–4, 7–10.30 Sun
Ansells Mild, Bitter; Everards Tiger; Tetley Bitter H
Pub with a large, single room, punctuated by nooks, corners and a darts area. Large, well-organised garden at the back. Friendly, chatty, local atmosphere. Eve meals end at 8; no food Sun.
🏺 ❀ ◖ ▶ ♣ P

Try also: **Little Lark**, Alcester Rd (Carlsberg-Tetley)

Warwick

Cape of Good Hope
66 Lower Cape
☎ (01926) 498138
12–3, 6–11; 12–3, 7–10.30 Sun
Boddingtons Bitter H; **Judges Old Gavel Bender** G; **guest beer** H
Victorian canalside pub, just feet from the water's edge, next to Cape top lock; a popular local with a warm welcome for all. Good food seven days a week; fish is a speciality. Limited parking; it is easier to reach by boat. ❀ ◖ ▶ ♿ ♣ P

Old Fourpenny Shop
27–29 Crompton Street
☎ (01926) 491360
12–2.30 (3 Fri & Sat), 5.30 (5 Fri, 6 Sat)–11; 12–2.30, 7–10.30 Sun
M&B Brew XI; guest beers H
Busy, one-room free house near the racecourse, with a restaurant. Five guest ales, regularly changed, are always available, many from local breweries. A regular *Guide* entry. No food Sun.
❀ ⊨ ◖ ▶ P

Rose & Crown
30 Market Place
☎ (01926) 492876
11–11; 12–10.30 Sun
Draught Bass; Highgate Dark; M&B Brew XI; guest beer H
National winner of the 1996 Bass Brewing *Most Improved Pub* award, proof that extensive redecoration *can* add character: a busy front bar, a small snug and a back room for meals and functions. On request, beer is served without sparklers. Cider varies.
🏺 ◖ ⏁

Wolston

Red Lion
23 Main Street (off A428)
☎ (01203) 542519
12–3, 6–11; 12–11 Fri & Sat; 12–3, 6–10.30 Sun
Boddingtons Bitter; Marston's Pedigree; Warwickshire Kingmaker; guest beer H
Old pub at the village centre, very popular with locals. The guest beer is usually a local brew, changing every two or three days. 🏺 ❀ ◖ ▶ ♿ ♣ P

BATH TUBS, BUCKETS AND BOOKS

If you're one of those beer lovers who dabbles in home-brewing, CAMRA has just the books to help you along. *The CAMRA Guide to Home Brewing* (priced £6.99), by Graham Wheeler, provides all the information you need to make a start, plus tips for more experienced home-producers. *Brew Your Own Real Ale at Home* (also priced £6.99), by Graham Wheeler and Roger Protz, takes readers a step further and reveals how they can recreate over 100 famous British commercial brands. And for fans of Continental beers like wheat beers, Guezes, Pilsners and Trappist ales, *Brew Classic European Beers at Home*, at £8.99, by the same authors, is a must. Copies are available from all good bookshops, or direct (and post-free) from CAMRA, 230 Hatfield Road, St Albans, Hertfordshire AL1 4LW. Discounts are available for CAMRA members.

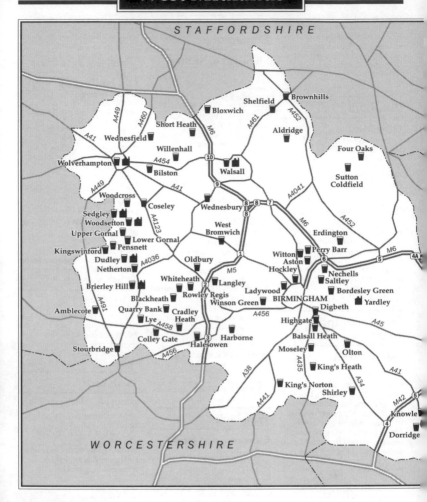

Aldridge

Lazy Hill
196 Walsall Wood Road (1 mile from centre) ☎ (01922) 52040
12–2.30 (3 Sat), 6–11; 12–2.30, 7–10.30 Sun
Ansells Mild, Bitter; Ind Coope Burton Ale; Marston's Pedigree; Tetley Bitter; guest beer Ⓗ
16th-century farmhouse and later manor house, now one large room split into four areas, plus a function room. Walsall CAMRA 1996 *Pub of the Year*. Tapster's Choice guest beers.
🏠 P

Amblecote

Moorings Tavern
78 Lower High Street (A491)
☎ (01384) 374124
12–3, 5–11; 12–11 Fri & Sat; 12–10.30 Sun

Draught Bass; Marston's Pedigree; Tetley Bitter; guest beers Ⓗ
Ideally placed to explore the canal history of Stourbridge, this one-roomed pub has plenty of linked areas and space for both drinkers and diners. Lunches Fri.
🌢 🛏 ▶ ≇ (Stourbridge) P

Starving Rascal
Brettell Lane ☎ (01384) 834040
12–3.30 (not Mon or Tue), 7–11; 12–3.30, 7–10.30 Sun
Theakston Mild, Best Bitter; guest beers Ⓗ
Welcoming three-bar pub with a cellar bar and restaurant. Regular folk music.
🏠 🛏 ◀ ▶ 🍴 ♣ P

Barston

Bull's Head
Barston Lane
☎ (01675) 442830

11 (12 Sat)–2.30, 5.30 (6 Sat)–11; 12–10.30 Sun
Draught Bass; M&B Brew XI; Tetley Bitter; guest beers Ⓗ
Beamed country pub and restaurant, the centre of village life, partly dating back to 1490. No meals Sun. There are real fires in both rooms.
🏠 Q 🌢 ◀ ▶ P

Bilston

Trumpet
58 High Street (A4039)
☎ (01902) 493723
12–3 (3.30 Sat), 7–11; 12–3, 7–10.30 Sun
Holden's Mild, Bitter, Special Ⓗ
Popular town-centre pub known for its jazz (eves and Sun lunch). Local caricatures and celebrity photographs adorn the walls.
🌢

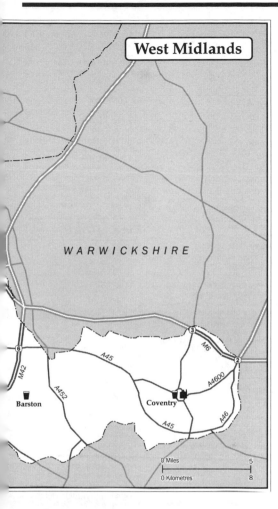

West Midlands

WARWICKSHIRE

Barston

Coventry

0 Miles 5

0 Kilometres 8

M6

M42

M42

A45

A452

A4600

A45

A46

City Centre

City Tavern

38 Bishopgate Street (off Broad St, by Five Ways island)
☎ (0121) 643 4394
12–11; 12–10.30 Sun
Ansells Mild; Ind Coope Burton Ale; Marston's Pedigree; Tetley Bitter Ⓗ
Two-roomed, backstreet local boasting live music most of the week and a theatre group upstairs Sun eve. Much different to nearby Broad St pubs (prices reflect this).
◖ ⇌ (Five Ways) ♣

Flapper & Firkin

Kingston Row/Cambrian Wharf (off Cambridge St)
☎ (0121) 236 2421
12–11; 12–10.30 Sun
Firkin Flapper, Dogbolter; guest beers Ⓗ
Canalside pub in the city centre, with upstairs and downstairs bars, the latter mainly used for live music. Popular with students; standing room only weekend nights. Tapster's Choice guest beers. ✿ ◖ ▶ ♣

Old Contemptibles

176 Edmund Street (right from Snow Hill station then 1st right) ☎ (0121) 236 5264
12–11; 12–3.30, 7–11 Sat; closed Sun
Draught Bass; Highgate Dark; M&B Brew XI; guest beers Ⓗ
OC's was built in the 1800s and is now a Grade II-listed building. Inside the walls boast World War I memorabilia. A separate lounge is sometimes set aside for functions.
Q ◖ ▶ ⇌ (Snow Hill/New St)

Wellington

37 Bennetts Hill
☎ (0121) 233 2439
11–11; closed Sun
Banks's Bitter; Camerons Strongarm; Marston's Bitter, Pedigree; Morrells Varsity, Graduate Ⓗ

Birmingham: *Aston*

Manor Tavern

6 Portland Street (near HP Sauce factory)
☎ (0121) 326 8780
12–2.30, 5.30 (7 Sat)–11; 12–3, 7–10.30 Sun
Ansells Mild, Bitter; Tetley Bitter Ⓗ
Two-roomed local, popular with factory workers lunchtimes. Very full when the local team plays at home, but it still maintains a friendly atmosphere. Photographs of old Birmingham adorn the walls. ◖ ⊞ ⇌

Balsall Heath

Old Moseley Arms

53 Tindal Street
☎ (0121) 440 1954
3 (1 Fri & Sat)–11; 1–10.30 Sun

Ansells Bitter; Highgate Dark; HP&D Entire; Marston's Pedigree; guest beer Ⓗ
Small, two-roomed pub with a 1930s, oak-panelled interior. Clients range from students to local workers and environmentalists. Panoramic view of the city centre. Tapster's Choice guest beer. ✿ ⊞ ♣

Bordesley Green

Tipsy Gent

157 Cherrywood Road (just off B4128 ☎ (0121) 772 1858
11–11; 12–10.30 Sun
Beer range varies Ⓗ
Football memorabilia fills the walls of the lounge in this two-roomed pub which gets very full before home games. A list indicates forthcoming beers. No lunches Sat/Sun.
✿ ◖ ⇌ (Adderley Pk) ♣

Popular pub with students and
business people.
🐌 ◖ ≽ (Snow Hill/New St) ♣

Digbeth

Adam & Eve
701 Bradford Street
☎ (0121) 693 1500
11–11; 7–10.30 (closed lunch) Sun
**Ansells Mild; HP&D Entire;
Marston's Pedigree** Ⓗ
Pub with a large lounge (live
music every night except Tue)
and a small bar, housing a pool
table. ◖ ⊟ ♣

Anchor
308 Bradford Street (rear of
coach station)
☎ (0121) 622 4516
11–11; 12–10.30 Sun
**Ansells Mild; Tetley Bitter;
guest beers** Ⓗ
Victorian corner pub boasting
three rooms, all served from
one bar. Friendly atmosphere;
varied clientele. Regular beer
festivals; changing range of
guest beers. Local CAMRA *Pub
of the Year 1996.* 🐌 ◖
≽ (New St/Moor St) ♣

White Swan
276 Bradford Street
☎ (0121) 622 2586
11–3, 5.30–11; 12–3, 7–10.30 Sun
Ansells Mild; Tetley Bitter Ⓗ
Two-roomed, tiled, Victorian
gem set amidst more modern
warehouses. It has won awards
for the quality of the mild.
◖ ≽ (New St/Moor St)

Woodman
106 Albert Street
☎ (0121) 643 1959
11–11; 12–4 (closed eve) Sun
**Ansells Mild; Tetley Bitter;
guest beer** Ⓗ
Victorian pub with a
beautifully tiled interior.
Unchanged since 1897, it has a
public bar and a smoke room.
Popular with factory workers.
Q ◖ ▶ ⊟

Erdington

Lad in the Lane
22 Bromford Lane (400 yds N
of A38) ☎ (0121) 377 7471
11–11; 11–2.30, 5.30–11 Tue; 11–2.30,
5–11 Wed; 11–3, 6–11 Sat; 12–3,
7–10.30 Sun
**Ansells Mild; Marston's
Pedigree; Tetley Bitter** Ⓗ
Part-14th-century, listed
building: a large, rambling
lounge on different levels and a
public bar. Good food. Large
garden. 🐌 ◖ ▶ ⊟ P

Harborne

Bell
Old Church Road (by St Peter's
church) ☎ (0121) 427 3477

12–11; 12–10.30 Sun
M&B Mild Ⓔ; **guest beer** Ⓗ
300-year-old survivor in a
developing area. The bar is
situated within the
passageway. Changing guest
beer. No eve meals Sun.
🐌 ◖ ♣ P

Junction
212 High Street
☎ (0121) 426 1838
11–11; 12–3, 7–10.30 Sun
**Draught Bass; Highgate Dark;
M&B Brew XI; guest beers** Ⓗ
One- (very big) roomed pub
served by an island bar, with
up to seven ales. Some of the
fixtures are originals from the
Bass Museum. Guest beers are
from the Cask Master range.
No meals Sun eve.
🐌 ◖ ▶ & ♣

New Inn
74 Vivian Road
☎ (0121) 427 5062
11–3.30, 5.30–11; 12–3, 7–10.30 Sun
**Banks's Mild, Bitter;
Camerons Strongarm** Ⓗ
Popular, friendly, village-style
pub in a busy suburb. The
landlord is a Banks's
cellarmanship award-winner.
Wheelchair WC. No meals Sun
eve. Q 🐌 ◖ ⊟ & ♣ ⊟

Highgate

Lamp Tavern
157 Barford Street
☎ (0121) 622 2599
12–11; 12–3, 7–10.30 Sun
**Bateman Mild; Boddingtons
Bitter; Marston's Pedigree;
Stanway Stanney Bitter;
Wadworth 6X; guest beer**
(weekend) Ⓗ
Popular pub with a wide-
ranging clientele and an
excellent choice of ales, still the
only regular local outlet for
Stanway beer. Regular live
music in the back room. Past
local CAMRA *Pub of the Year.*
◖ ≽ (New St/Moor St)

Hockley

Black Eagle
16 Factory Road (near Soho
House Museum)
☎ (0121) 523 4008
11.30 (12 Sat)–3, 5.30 (7 Sat)–11; 12–3,
7–10.30 Sun
**Ansells Mild, Bitter; HP&D
Entire; Marston's Pedigree;
guest beer** Ⓗ
Friendly pub built on the
foundations of Birmingham's
first warehouse. Excellent food
(not served Sun eve). Past local
CAMRA *Pub of the Year.*
🐌 ◖ ⊟

Church Inn
22 Great Hampton Street
☎ (0121) 515 1851
11–11; 12–3, 6–11 Sat; 12–3 (closed
eve) Sun

**Ansells Mild; Batham Best
Bitter; Marston's Pedigree; Morland
Old Speckled Hen** Ⓗ
Excellent, out-of-town pub
with good food (excellent
portions). No meals are served
Sun eve. The room off the bar is
a real gem.
◖ ▶ ⊟ ≽ ♣

White House
Unett Street
☎ (0121) 523 0782
11–11; 12–4.30, 7.30–10.30 Sun
**M&B Mild, Brew XI; guest
beer** Ⓗ
Popular pub serving good
food. Live music is staged at
weekends.
⊠ 🐌 ◖ ⊟ & ≽ ♣ P

King's Heath

Pavilion
229 Alcester Road South
☎ (0121) 441 3286
12–3, 5–11; 12–3.30, 7–10.30 Sun
**Banks's Mild; Camerons
Strongarm; Marston's
Pedigree; Morrells Varsity** Ⓗ
Modern, two-room pub inside
an 1860 building. The interior
has been designed with style
and its traditional ambience
does not feel contrived.
Popular with a wide age
group. If all modern pubs were
like this, there would be few
complaints.
⊠ Q ◖ ▶ ⊟ & P ⊟

King's Norton

Navigation Inn
Wharf Road (off Redditch Rd)
☎ (0121) 458 1652
11–11; 12–3, 7–10.30 Sun
**Banks's Mild; Draught Bass;
Greenall's Original; Tetley
Bitter; guest beer** Ⓗ
Over 100-year-old pub which
adopted its name from the Irish
workers who worked on the
local canal: a very large lounge
and, in comparison, a small
bar. All food is home-made.
Popular with students from the
nearby college.
🐌 ◖ ▶ ⊟ & ≽ ♣ P

Ladywood

Vine Inn
Rawlins Street (rear of Five
Ways Tesco)
☎ (0121) 454 7943
11–3, 5.30 (7 Sat)–11; 12–3, 7–10.30
Sun
**Ansells Mild; Ind Coope
Burton Ale; Marston's
Pedigree; Tetley Bitter** Ⓗ
One-roomed pub in a
residential area, wooden-
floored and boasting dominoes
and darts teams. No food at
weekends.
◖ ≽ (Five Ways) ♣

Moseley

Prince of Wales
118 Alcester Road
☎ (0121) 449 4198
11–3 (3.30 Sat), 5.30 (6 Sat)–11; 12–3,
7–10.30 Sun
**Ansells Mild; Ind Coope
Burton Ale** Ⓗ
Community pub whose
traditional interior has
changed little since 1900. It
contains a public bar and two
smoke rooms and oozes
cosiness. Q ❀ ⊞

Nechells

Villa Tavern
307 Nechells Park Road
☎ (0121) 328 9831
11–2.30, 5.30–11; 11–11 Fri & Sat;
12–3, 7–10.30 Sun
**Ansells Mild, Bitter; Greene
King Abbot; Marston's
Pedigree; Tetley Bitter** Ⓗ
Busy, three-roomed, terracotta-
tiled pub which recently
celebrated its one hundredth
anniversary.
Q ◖ ⊞ ⇌ (Aston) ♣ P

Perry Barr

Seventh Trap
81 Regina Drive (A34, next to
One Stop shopping centre)
☎ (0121) 356 2092
11–11; 12–3, 7–10.30 Sun
Banks's Mild, Bitter Ⓔ
Attractive, two-roomed
Banks's pub holding regular
quiz nights. An entertainment
night is held every quarter; fun
day once a year. No food Sun.
❀ ◖ ⊞ & ⇌ ♣ P 🏠

Saltley

Havelock Tavern
28 Havelock Road
☎ (0121) 327 0054
11–11; 12–3, 7–10.30 Sun
M&B Mild Ⓗ**, Brew XI** Ⓔ
Real Irish pub with a china-
decorated lounge and a
function room available for
hire. ⊞ ♣

Winson Green

Bellefield ☆
36 Winson Street
☎ (0121) 558 0647
1 (12 Sat)–11; 12–10.30 Sun
Banks's Bitter; guest beers Ⓗ
Beautifully unspoilt pub with
an ornate bar ceiling. The
lounge has tile-framed
pictures. Function room
upstairs. Three or more guest
beers are available; regular
mini-beer festivals.
Q ⊞ & ♣ P

Queen's Head
286 Heath Street, Smethwick
☎ (0121) 558 4577
12–11; 12–10.30 Sun
**Blackbeard Stairway to
Heaven; guest beer**
(occasional) Ⓗ
Pub with a tiled exterior, a
relaxed interior and a partly
paved outdoor drinking area.
❀ 🛏 ⊞ ♣

Witton

Safe Harbour
Moor Lane (between A4040
and A453) ☎ (0121) 356 4527
11–2.30 (3 Fri & Sat), 5 (6 Sat)–11;
12–3, 7–10.30 Sun
Ansells Mild; Tetley Bitter Ⓗ
Pub locally known as the
'Gravediggers', situated
between the cemetery and
canal: a basic, but comfortable
bar and a cosy lounge. Very
friendly. ☞ ❀ ◖ ⊞ ♣ P

Blackheath

Hawthorns
162 Ross (off A4100)
☎ (0121) 561 2276
12–2.30 (3 Fri & Sat), 7–11; 12–3,
7–10.30 Sun
**Ansells Mild; Tetley Bitter;
guest beer** Ⓗ
Popular, friendly pub with a
small bar and comfortable
lounge, which houses the beer
pumps. No food Sun. 🛏 ❀ ◖
⊞ ⇌ (Rowley Regis) ♣ P

Waterfall
132 Waterfall Lane
☎ (0121) 561 3499
12–3, 5–11; 12–11 Fri & Sat; 12–10.30
Sun
**Batham Best Bitter; Enville
Ale; Freeminer Celestial
Steam Gale; Holden's Special;
Hook Norton Old Hooky;
Marston's Pedigree; guest
beers** Ⓗ
Busy, two-roomed pub on a
steep hill, worth the ten mins'
walk down from the town.
Regular music eves; good food.
Cider in summer.
❀ ◖ ▶ ⇌ (Old Hill) ♣ ⌂ P

Bloxwich

Romping Cat
97 Elmore Green Road
☎ (01922) 475041
12–11; 12–3, 7–10.30 Sun
Banks's Mild, Bitter Ⓔ
Traditional, late-Victorian,
street-corner local, recently
refurbished but retaining its
original three-room layout.
Q ⊞ ⇌ ♣

Royal Exchange
24 Stafford Road
☎ (01922) 479618
12–3, 5–11; 12–11 Sat; 12–3, 7–10.30
Sun

**Banks's Mild; Marston's
Bitter, Pedigree, HBC** Ⓗ
Pleasant, 270-year-old local
with a Grade II-listed former
brewery at the rear. The small
bar has sporting memorabilia;
the lounge has a quiet corner
nook. Live music Wed eve.
❀ ◖ ⊞ ♣ P

Brierley Hill

Black Horse
52 Delph Road (B4172 near
A4100 jct) ☎ (01384) 350633
12–11; 12–3, 7–10.30 Sun
**Enville Ale; Ruddles
County** Ⓗ
Cosy, one-roomed pub in the
middle of the famous Delph
Run, handy for Merry Hill
shopping centre. Good food all
day (not served Sun).
❀ ◖ ▶ P

Blue Brick Tap House
153 Dudley Road (A461)
☎ (01384) 78448
11–11; 12–4, 7–10.30 Sun
**Banks's Mild, Bitter;
Camerons Strongarm;
Marston's Pedigree; Morrells
Graduate; guest beers** Ⓗ
Large pub with one room
divided into a number of gaslit
areas. Hanson's Mild and
Camerons Bitter are sold as
house beers. Handy for Merry
Hill shopping centre.
🛏 ❀ ◖ ♣ P 🏠

Vine (Bull & Bladder)
10 Delph Road (B4172 near
A4100 jct) ☎ (01384) 78293
12–11; 12–4, 7–10.30 Sun
**Batham Mild, Best Bitter,
XXX** Ⓗ
Famous, multi-roomed
brewery tap at the top of the
Delph Run. The sensitive
extension into the old brewery
office won CAMRA's *Joe
Goodwin Award* for the least
obtrusive refurbishment.
Dudley CAMRA *Pub of the Year*
1996. 🛏 Q ☞ ❀ ◖ ⊞ ♣ P

Brownhills

Prince of Wales
98 Watling Street
☎ (01543) 372551
7.30–11; 12–3, 7.30–11 Sat; 12–2.30
(closed eve) Sun
Ansells Bitter Ⓗ
Warm, cosy, small, one-room
pub with 1920s/'30s decor.
Coal fire in winter. 🛏 Q ♣

Colley Gate

Why Not?
Whynot Street (½ mile S from
bottom of Windmill Hill, A458)
☎ (01384) 561019
12–3, 6–11; 12–11 Sat; 12–3, 7–10.30
Sun
**Batham Best Bitter; guest
beers** Ⓗ

Rambling, one-room pub close to countryside. A central bar serves several zones, including a small dining area. How many different beer bottles can you spot in the wall cabinets? Two guest beers are usually sold. Occasional quizzes.
🏮 🕭 ◖ ▶ ♣ ⌂ 🍽

Coseley

Gate Hangs Well ⊞
127 Hurst Road
☎ (01902) 884868
11.30–3, 6–11; 11–11 Sat; 12–3, 7–10.30 Sun
Banks's Hanson's Mild, Bitter Ⓔ
Locals' pub with separate bar, lounge and children's room.
🏵 P 🍽

Hurst Hill Tavern
Caddick Street, Hurst Hill (off A463) ☎ (01902) 880318
1 (12 Sat)–5, 7–11; 12–4, 7–10.30 Sun
Banks's Hanson's Mild, Mild, Bitter Ⓔ
Excellent, two-roomed drinkers' local. Eve opening times are not strictly followed.
🏮 Q 🏵 ♣ P 🍽

Old Bush
23 Skidmore Road (off B4163)
☎ (01902) 492776
12–3.30, 7–11; 12–3.30, 7–10.30 Sun
Holden's Mild, Bitter Ⓔ
Quiet, backstreet local with a down-to-earth bar, a peaceful lounge and a function room.
Q 🏵 ⊟ ⇌ ♣ P 🍽

Painter's Arms
Avenue Road (off A4123/B4483) ☎ (01902) 883095
12–11; 12–4, 7–10.30 Sun
Holden's Mild, Bitter Ⓔ, Special ⊞
Two-roomed pub popular with all ages. Handy for the Birmingham Canal (near Coseley tunnel). No food Sun.
🏀 🏵 ◖ ⇌ ♣ P 🍽

White House
1 Daisy Street (B4163)
☎ (01902) 402703
11–3, 6–11; 12–3, 7–10.30 Sun
Ansells Mild; HP&D Entire; Tetley Bitter; guest beers ⊞
Comfortable free house offering two guest beers from independents; popular for food (no meals Sun). Quizzes Wed and Sun eves.
🏮 🏵 ◖ ▶ ⇌ ♣

Coventry

Biggin Hall Hotel
214 Binley Road, Copsewood
(A428, 3 miles E of centre)
☎ (01203) 451046
10.30–11; 10.30–3.30, 6–11 Sat; 12–10.30 Sun

Banks's Mild; Marston's Bitter, Pedigree, Owd Rodger, HBC ⊞
Large, distinctive roadside pub built in mock-Tudor style: a smart bar and a plush lounge with a renowned, central oak table. A games room doubles as a family room. Friendly, cosmopolitan clientele.
Q 🏀 🏵 ◖ ⊟ ♣ P

Black Horse
Spon End (B4010, near inner ring road jct 7)
☎ (01203) 677360
10–11; 12–3, 7–10.30 Sun
Draught Bass; M&B Mild, Brew XI; guest beer ⊞
Traditional drinking establishment on a busy road, saved from a road widening scheme. Separate rooms, with attractive panelling in the lounge. 🏮 Q 🏀 🏵 ⊟ ♿ ♣ P

Boat
31 Shilton Lane (N of centre, between Wood End and Shilton) ☎ (01203) 613572
12–3, 7–11; 12–11 Sat; 12–3, 7–10.30 Sun
Draught Bass; M&B Brew XI; guest beer ⊞
Country pub in town, near the canal, with three small rooms. Not a swan neck in sight. Sawdust on the bar floor. The restaurant closes at 8.30.
🏵 ◖ ▶ ⊟ ♣ P

Chestnut Tree
113 Craven Street, Chapelfields (1 mile W of centre, off Allesley Old Rd) ☎ (01203) 675830
12 (11 Sat)–11; 12–4, 7–10.30 Sun
Ansells Mild; Courage Directors; Marston's Pedigree; John Smith's Bitter; Webster's Yorkshire Bitter; guest beers ⊞
Two-room pub in a former watch-making area, with over 70 whiskies. No eve meals Sun; the restaurant closes at 8 other eves. 🏵 ◖ ▶ ⊟ ♣

Fowl & Firkin
1–2 The Butts (near Technical College, off Albany Rd)
☎ (01203) 221622
11 (12 Sat)–11; 12–10.30 Sun
Firkin Pullet, Fowl, Golden Glory, Dogbolter, seasonal beers ⊞
Spacious, one-roomed brew pub, with the brewery visible through a window. Young, friendly clientele.
🏵 ◖ ♿ ⇌ ♣

Gatehouse Tavern
Hill Street (near Belgrade Theatre) ☎ (01203) 256769
11–3, 5–11; 11–11 Fri; 12–4, 7–10.30 Sun
Draught Bass; Judges M'lud; M&B Brew XI; guest beers ⊞
Small, busy, one-roomed pub, converted by the landlord from the gatehouse of a long gone

mill. A garden added in 1997 may be covered and heated in winter. No meals Sat eve or Sun. Q 🏵 ◖ ▶

Greyhound
Much Park Street (near university) ☎ (01203) 221274
12–11; 12–3, 7–10.30 Sun
Mansfield Riding Mild; Wells Eagle, Bombardier, Fargo; guest beers ⊞
Pub close to the law courts, with a daytime clientele of students and legal folk. No food Sun. 🏵 ◖ ♣

Malt Shovel
93 Spon End (¼ mile from inner ring road jct 7)
☎ (01203) 220204
12–3.30, 7–11; 12–11 Fri & Sat; 12–10.30 Sun
Ansells Bitter; Tetley Bitter; guest beers ⊞
Popular, three-roomed pub served by a central bar. Weekday lunches. The guest beers often feature local breweries. 🏮 🏀 🏵 ◖ P

Nursery Tavern
38–39 Lord Street, Chapelfields
☎ (01203) 674530
11–11; 12–10.30 Sun
Courage Best Bitter; John Smith's Bitter; guest beers ⊞
Busy pub with a changing range of guest beers, always including one special value mild. Social events include beer festivals. Good value Sun roasts; barbecues summer weekend eves.
Q 🏀 🏵 ◖ ⊟ ♣ ⌂

Old Windmill
22 Spon Street (½ mile W of centre, inside ring road)
☎ (01203) 252183
11–3, 6 (6.30 Sat)–11; 12–3, 7–10.30 Sun
Courage Directors; Marston's Pedigree; Morland Old Speckled Hen; Webster's Yorkshire Bitter; guest beers ⊞
Medieval pub in a restored 16th-century street, extended in more recent times to provide a number of rooms, including the original brewhouse. It can get a little noisy, particularly at weekends. Popular for lunch.
🏮 ◖ ♿ ⇌ ⌂

Rainbow Inn
73 Birmingham Road, Allesley (old Birmingham road, off A45) ☎ (01203) 402888
11–11; 12–3, 6–10.30 Sun
Courage Best Bitter, Directors; Rainbow Piddlebrook, Firecracker; guest beer ⊞
Village pub with a brewery, to the west of Coventry. Old as the hills and part of village life. No eve meals Sun/Mon.
Q 🏵 ◖ ▶ ⊟ P

Royal Oak
28 Earlsdon Street, Earlsdon
☎ (01203) 674140
5–11; 12–3, 7–10.30 Sun
ABC Best Bitter; Ansells Mild; Draught Bass; Tetley Bitter; guest beers Ⓗ
Popular pub with both sexes, offering table service throughout. Interesting painting of old Earlsdon in the back room – do not stare too long at the tramlines. ⏚ Q ✿

Cradley Heath

Little Sausage & Porter
78 St Anne's Road (off A4100 near Five Ways)
☎ (01384) 635494
11.30–3, 6–11; 12–3, 7–10.30 Sun
Little Lumphammer; guest beers Ⓗ
Large 'Little Pub Company' pub with the usual bizarre decor. Sausages a speciality. Live folk music Thu.
⏚ ✿ ◁ ▶ ≠ ♣

Plough & Harrow
82 Corngreaves Road (S off High St) ☎ (01384) 560377
11–3, 7–11; 11–11 Fri & Sat (may vary); 12–3, 7–10.30 Sun
Banks's Mild, Bitter Ⓔ
Typical backstreet hostelry welcoming local industry at lunchtime and local residents eves. One bar serves several rooms, including a pool room.
✿ ≠ ♣ P ⍾

Waggon & Horses
100 Reddall Hill Road (A4100)
☎ (01384) 350130
11.30–3.30, 7.30–11; 12–3, 7–10.30 Sun
Banks's Mild, Bitter Ⓔ
Boisterous local with various artefacts and sporting prints in the bar (beware of the darts oche on entering). Comfortable lounge. ♨ ✿ ⊞ ≠ ♣ P

Dorridge

Forest Hotel
Station Approach
☎ (01564) 772120
11–2.30, 5.30–11; 12–3, 7–10.30 Sun
Draught Bass; guest beer Ⓗ
Large, friendly free house with three separate drinking areas, directly opposite the rail station. Guest beers are normally from a small independent. No food Sun eve. No-smoking area lunchtime.
Q ⏚ ◁ ▶ ⊞ ≠ ♣ P ⍾

Railway
Grange Road ☎ (01564) 773531
11–3, 4.30–11; 11–11 Fri & Sat; 12–10.30 Sun
Draught Bass; M&B Brew XI; guest beers Ⓗ
Family-run pub, popular with locals.
⏚ Q ✿ ◁ ▶ ⊞ ⅃ ♣ P

Dudley

Full Moon
58–60 High Street
☎ (01384) 212294
11–11; 12–10.30 Sun
Banks's Mild; Courage Directors; Theakston Best Bitter; Younger Scotch; guest beers Ⓗ
Vast Wetherspoons emporium in the centre of town. Photographs of old Dudley and art works depicting local industry provide decor.
Q ◁ ▶ ⅃ ⌂ ⍾

Four Oaks

Halfway House
226 Lichfield Road (between Mere Green and station)
☎ (0121) 308 1311
11–11; 12–10.30 Sun
Draught Bass; Highgate Dark Ⓗ**; M&B Brew XI** Ⓔ
Suburban pub with typical '90s refurbishment: pleasant and comfortable, with a local clientele. No food Sun eve.
Q ✿ ◁ ▶ ⊞ ⅃ ≠ ♣ P ⍾

Halesowen

Fairfield
Fairfield Road, Hurst Green
☎ (0121) 422 8289
11–3 (3.30 Sat), 5.30–11; 12–3, 7–10.30 Sun
Banks's Hanson's Mild Ⓔ**, Mild** Ⓗ**, Bitter** Ⓔ**; Marston's Pedigree** Ⓗ
Popular roadhouse with two large rooms – a lively bar and a smart, busy lounge. No food Sun. ✿ ◁ ▶ ⊞ ⅃ ≠ ♣ P ⍾

King Edward VII
88 Stourbridge Road, Hawne (A458 ½ mile from centre)
☎ (0121) 550 4493
12–2.30, 5.30–11; 12–3, 7–10.30 Sun
Ansells Mild; Tetley Bitter; guest beers Ⓗ
Popular pub next to the 'Yeltz' football ground. Good value food. A central bar serves both a comfortable lounge and a back bar.
◁ ▶ ⊞ ♣ P

Waggon & Horses
21 Stourbridge Road (A458 just out of centre)
☎ (0121) 550 4989
12–11; 12–10.30 Sun
Batham Best Bitter; Enville Ale; guest beers Ⓗ
Friendly hostelry with a clientele from far and near, enjoying changing ales from 14 pumps. Recent refurbishment hasn't altered the character.
♣ ⌂

Try also: Rose & Crown, Hagley Rd (HP&D)

Kingswinford

Park Tavern
182 Cot Lane (500 yds from A4101) ☎ (01384) 287178
12–11; 12–3, 7–10.30 Sun
Ansells Bitter; Batham Best Bitter; Tetley Bitter; guest beer Ⓗ
Comfortable, friendly and popular pub close to Broadfield House Glass Museum. ✿ ⊞ ♣ P

Union
Water Street (off A4101)
☎ (01384) 830668
12–2.30 (3 Fri, 4 Sat), 6 (7 Sat)–11; 12–3.30, 7–10.30 Sun
Banks's Mild, Bitter Ⓔ
Small, traditional local hidden in a sidestreet. The present licensee has run the pub since 1962. It still bears a Rolinson's Brewery etched window.
✿ ♣ P ⍾

Knowle

Vaults
St John's Close
☎ (01564) 773656
12–2.30, 5 (6 Sat)–11; 12–3, 7–10.30 Sun
Ansells Mild; HP&D Bitter; Ind Coope Burton Ale; Tetley Bitter; guest beers Ⓗ
Popular pub in a picturesque village; a former local CAMRA *Pub of the Year.* ◁ ⌂

Langley

New Navigation
Titford Road (A4123 near M5 jct 2) ☎ (0121) 552 2525
11.30–3 (3.30 Sat), 6 (7 Sat)–11; 12–3, 7 10.30 Sun
Ansells Mild; HP&D Entire; Marston's Pedigree; Tetley Bitter Ⓗ
Friendly pub near the end of the Titford Canal. The single, U-shaped room is welcoming. Good value lunches (not served Sun). ⏚ ◁ ♣

Lower Gornal

Fountain Real Ale Bar
8 Temple Street (B4175 between centre and Five Ways)
☎ (01384) 242777
7–11; 12–3, 7–11 Sat; 12–3, 7–10.30 Sun
Adnams Broadside; Everards Tiger; RCH Pitchfork; guest beers Ⓗ
Popular, one-roomed free house which was the best known brewhouse in Lower Gornal. Seasonal beer festivals. The house beers are brewed by Wye Valley. Skittle alley in 'the Pen'. Up to six guest beers.
✿ ⅃ ♣ ⌂

Lye

Fox

8 Green Lane (off A4036 near
A458 jct)
☎ (01384) 827808
11–11; 12–3, 7–10.30 Sun
Banks's Mild, Bitter E
Friendly, two-roomed hostelry
that epitomises a Black
Country backstreet local. A
quiet, cosy lounge offers a
chance for a talk, whilst the
busier bar caters for sporting
clientele.
✿ ⌂ ⇌ ♣ P ▯

Netherton

Elephant & Castle

250 Cradley Road (B4173)
☎ (01384) 636849
12–3, 5.30–11; 12–11 Sat; 12–3.30,
7–10.30 Sun
**Ansells Bitter; Tetley Dark
Mild, Bitter; guest beers** H
Small, comfortable, welcoming
hostelry accommodating locals
and visitors seeking out the
good value, traditional, home-
cooked food (served till 8.30).
✿ ◑ ▶ ♣

Oldbury

Fountain

Albion Street (off A457)
☎ (0121) 544 6892
12–11; 12–5, 6.30–11 Sat; 12–4, 7–10.30
Sun
Banks's Mild, Bitter E**; guest
beer** H
Small, cosy, friendly pub in a
sidestreet. Well worth finding.
⌂ ♣ P ▯

Olton

Harvester

Tanhouse Farm Road
☎ (0121) 742 0770
12–2.30 (3 Thu–Sat), 6–11; 12–3,
7–10.30 Sun
**Courage Directors; John
Smith's Bitter; guest beer** H
Two-roomed, friendly
drinkers' pub, one of the first in
the area to support guest beers
from independents. Regular
quizzes and live music. Pool,
darts and board games are
played.
✿ ⌂ ♣ P

Pensnett

Holly Bush Inn

Bell Street (off A4101)
☎ (01384) 78711
1–4 (12–4.30 Sat), 7–11; 12–3, 7–10.30
Sun
**Batham Mild, Best Bitter,
XXX** H
One-roomed estate pub with a
strong local following; famous
for the quality of its mild.
Q ♣ P

Quarry Bank

Three Shovels

36 High Street (A4100)
☎ (01384) 568757
11–11; 12–10.30 Sun
Banks's Mild, Bitter E**; Brains
Bitter, SA** H
Formerly known as the Church
Tavern, this is the best West
Midlands acquisition by Brains
to date: a cheerful and popular,
two-roomed pub, handy for
Merry Hill shoppers. 🚍 ⌂ ⇌
(Cradley Heath) ♣ P ▯

Rowley Regis

Sir Robert Peel

1 Rowley Village (B4171)
☎ (0121) 559 2835
12–4, 7–11; 12–3.30, 7–10.30 Sun
**Ansells Mild, Bitter; Tetley
Bitter; guest beers** H
The oldest building in Rowley
village, a former police station
licensed since 1840: two cosy
rooms, plus a games room and
an entrance passage where
beer is served. 🚍 Q ⇌ ♣

Sedgley

Beacon Hotel   ☆

129 Bilston Street (A463 ½ mile
from A459 jct)
☎ (01902) 883380
12–2.30, 5.30–10.45 (11 Fri & Sat);
12–3, 7–10.30 Sun
**Hook Norton Best Bitter;
Hughes Sedgley Surprise,
Ruby Mild; guest beer** H
Authentic Victorian brewery
tap with four rooms around an
island bar with snob screens.
No jukebox or bandits.
Q ▱ ✿ ♠ ♣ P

Shelfield

Four Crosses

1 Green Lane (just off A461)
☎ (01922) 682518
12–11; 12–3, 7–10.30 Sun
Banks's Mild E**; Marston's
Bitter, Pedigree; guest beers** H
Large, 18th-century building
with surprisingly small
drinking areas: a saloon bar
and a cottage-style lounge.
'Passage' seating area for
children. Sun lunches in the
restaurant upstairs. ✿ ⌂ ♣ P

Shirley

Bernie's Real Ale
Off-Licence

266 Cranmore Boulevard (off
A34) ☎ (0121) 744 2827
12–2 (not Mon), 5.30–10; 12–2, 7–9.45
Sun
Beer range varies H/E
Enterprising off-licence selling
up to seven real ales which
change regularly (sampling
cups for the indecisive). Good

selection of bottled beers from
around the world. ♿

Red Lion

Stratford Road
☎ (0121) 744 1030
11–2.30 (3 Sat), 5.30 (6.30 Sat)–11;
12–3, 7–10.30 Sun
**ABC Best Bitter; Ansells Mild;
Friary Meux BB; Marston's
Pedigree; Morland Old
Speckled Hen; Tetley Bitter;
guest beer** H
Don't be put off by the facade
of this pub which has a front
room divided into three
distinct areas, one no-smoking,
plus a pool room at the back.
Guest beers can come from
local breweries. No food Sun.
◑ ✂

Short Heath

Duke of Cambridge

82 Coltham Road
☎ (01922) 408895
12–3, 7.30–11; 12–3, 7.30–10.30 Sun
Draught Bass H**; Highgate
Dark** E**; Saddlers** H**;
Worthington Bitter** E**; guest
beer** H
17th-century farmhouse
converted in the 1820s; a cosy,
friendly local with a small
Dinky/Corgi toy collection in
the bar. Varied guest beer.
🚍 Q ✿ ⌂ ♣ P

Stourbridge

Crown

208 Hagley Road, Oldswinford
(A491) ☎ (01384) 394777
11–3, 5.30–11; 11–11 Fri & Sat; 12–3,
7–10.30 Sun
**Ansells Mild, Bitter; Batham
Best Bitter; Tetley Bitter** H
Friendly, one-roomed pub
with a large, U-shaped bar,
popular early eve with
homeward-bound workers.
The car park is at the rear on
the B4187. No meals Sun.
🚍 ✿ ◑ ⇌ (Junction) P

Hogshead

21–26 Foster Street (just off ring
road between high street and
bus station) ☎ (01384) 370140
11–11; 12–10.30 Sun
**Enville White; Marston's
Pedigree; Whitbread Abroad
Cooper, Fuggles IPA** H**; guest
beers** H/G
Large, one-room pub with a
long bar. Various seating areas
on two levels and bare
floorboards add character.
There's a TV, but no piped
music. Meals served 12–8.
◑ ▶ ♿ ⇌ (Town) ⌂ ✂

Old White Horse

South Road, Norton
(A451/B4186 jct)
☎ (01384) 394258
11–3, 5–11; 11–11 Fri & Sat; 12–10.30
Sun

M&B Mild, Brew XI; Stones Bitter; guest beer (occasional) H
Popular pub with families (garden play equipment). The large lounge has various areas served from one bar. Varied bar food; Harvester restaurant. Wheelchair WC. ❀ ◁ ▶ ♿ P

Plough

154 Bridgnorth Road, Wollaston ☎ (01384) 393414
12–2.30 (3 Sat), 6–11; 12–3, 7–10.30 Sun
Draught Bass; M&B Mild; Stones Bitter; guest beers H
Well-decorated old coaching house with original windows. A keen sporting pub, it has a petanque piste at the rear. The lounge is busy lunch and early eve (till 7.30) for excellent quality and value meals. No food Sun eve.
❀ ◁ ▶ ⌂ ♿ ♣ P

Seven Stars

Brook Road, Oldswinford (B4186) ☎ (01384) 394483
11–11; 12–10.30 Sun
Batham Best Bitter; Courage Directors; Theakston Best Bitter, XB; guest beers H
Bustling pub full of character in two large rooms plus a restaurant. Look for the ornate tiling and the beautiful carved-wood back bar fitting. Good food. ❀ ◁ ▶ ≉ (Junction) P

Shrubbery Cottage

28 Heath Lane, Oldswinford ☎ (01384) 377598
12–2.30, 6–11; 12–3, 7–10.30 Sun
Holden's Mild, Bitter, Special, seasonal beers; guest beer H
Small, one-room local, a popular drinkers' pub with a regular lunchtime trade and a lively, friendly eve crowd.
♨ ❀ ◁ ♿ ≉ (Junction) P

Unicorn

145 Bridgnorth Road, Wollaston ☎ (01384) 394833
11–3, 6–11; 11–11 Fri & Sat; 12–4, 7–10.30 Sun
Batham Mild, Best Bitter, seasonal beers H
Batham's ninth pub, a basic drinking house, popular with all ages, and unspoilt by progress. The original brewhouse still stands.
Q ❀ ⌂ ♿ P

Sutton Coldfield

Duke Inn

12 Duke Street (off Birmingham Rd)
☎ (0121) 355 1767
11.30–3, 5.30–11; 12–3, 7–10.30 Sun
Ansells Mild, Bitter; Ind Coope Burton Ale; Tetley Bitter H
Excellent, traditional pub full of character; the only unspoilt pub left in the area. One of the

two rooms features ornate mahogany, the other is a cosy back room. Q ❀ ♣ P

Falstaff & Firkin

19 High Street
☎ (0121) 355 2996
12–11; 12–10.30 Sun
Firkin Mild, Fal Ale, Golden Glory, Dogbolter; guest beer H
Listed coaching inn famous for its ghost and a cobbled passage separating two bars. Occasional beer festivals.
♨ Q ◁ ⌂ ≉ ♣ P

Laurel Wines

63 Westwood Road (off A452 opp. Sutton Park)
☎ (0121) 353 0399
12–2 (4 Sat), 5.30–10.30; 12–3, 7–10.30 Sun
Adnams Extra; Batham Best Bitter; Cottage Golden Arrow; guest beers G
Friendly off-licence with a good choice of beers from independents around the country. ⌂

White Horse

Whitehouse Common Rd (¾ mile W of Tamworth Rd junction) ☎ (0121) 378 0149
11–11; 12–10.30 Sun
Draught Bass; Davenports Bitter; Greenalls Mild, Original; guest beers H
Large suburban pub oriented towards the food trade (food served throughout opening hours). Families welcome when eating (children's menu); safe, enclosed play area.
❀ ◁ ▶ ⌂ ♿ ♣ P

Upper Gornal

Crown

16 Holloway Street (off A459)
☎ (01902) 665177
5–11; 12–4, 7–11 Sat; 12–3, 7–10.30 Sun
Banks's Hanson's Mild, Bitter E
Genuine Black Country local with an L-shaped bar and a tiny snug.
♨ ❀ ⇇ ⌂ ⌂ P 🍴

Good Intent

21 Vale Street (off A459)
☎ (01902) 673414
6–11; 12–3, 7–10.30 Sun
Banks's Hanson's Mild, Bitter E; Marston's Pedigree; Morrells Graduate H
Comfortable, old-fashioned, two-roomed pub with a separate dining room. Regular themed food eves. Sun lunches served. ♨ Q ❀ ▶ ♿ P 🍴

Old Mill

Windmill Street (off A459)
☎ (01902) 887707
12–3, 6–11; 12–11 Sat; 12–3.30, 7–10.30 Sun

Holden's Mild, Bitter E, Special, seasonal beers; guest beers H
Pleasant pub in a quiet residential area, with two rooms and a first-floor restaurant. No food Sun.
❀ ◁ ▶ ♿ ♣ ⌂ P

Walsall

Fountain

49 Lower Forster Street
☎ (01922) 29741
12–11; 12–3, 7–10.30 Sun
Draught Bass; Highgate Dark; guest beer H
Small, traditional, two-roomed backstreet pub; very friendly. Weekday lunches.
Q ◁ ⇇ ≉ ♣

Katz

23 Lower Rushall Street
☎ (01922) 725848
12–3, 5.30 (7 Sat)–11; closed Sun
Greene King Abbot; HP&D Entire; Marston's Pedigree; Tetley Bitter; guest beers H
Friendly, two-roomed pub with a varied clientele. Good value food till 8pm (no eve meals Sat). ♨ ❀ ◁ ▶ ≉

King Arthur

Liskeard Road (by Park Hall shopping precinct)
☎ (01922) 31400
12–3, 5.30–11; 12–11 Fri & Sat; 12–10.30 Sun
Courage Best Bitter, Directors; Highgate Dark; Ruddles Best Bitter, County; John Smith's Bitter H
Friendly pub with two substantial rooms. Good 'pub grub', especially curry, served in the lounge (not Sun).
❀ ◁ ▶ ⇇ P

Lyndon House Hotel

9–10 Upper Rushall Street (top of market) ☎ (01922) 612511
11–11; 12–10.30 Sun
Ansells Mild; Boddingtons Bitter; HP&D Bitter, Entire; guest beer H
Recently modernised, luxurious, one-roomed local which retains a cosy atmosphere: a conversation not a music pub. Popular with local businessmen (dress restrictions). Indian food a speciality.
Q ❀ ⇇ ◁ ▶ ♿ ≉ P

Oak

336 Green Lane
☎ (01922) 645758
12–2.30 (3 Sat), 7–11; 8–10.30 (closed lunch) Sun
Flowers IPA; guest beers H
Popular pub close to the town centre, with an island bar and a collection of china mugs. No eve meals Sun, Tue or Sat. Four or five guest beers.
♨ ❀ ◁ ▶ ≉ P 🍴

Rose & Crown

Old Birchills, Birchills (1 mile from centre off Green Lane, A34) ☎ (01922) 720533
11–11; 12–5.30, 7–10.30 Sun
Highgate Dark, Saddlers, Old H
Fine Victorian pub. Highgate memorabilia and an etched mirror, depicting the pub's name, adorn the bar. Children allowed in the lounge.
🏠 ❀ 🕭 ♣

Tap & Spile

John Street ☎ (01922) 27660
12–3, 5–11; 12–11 Fri & Sat; 12–3, 7–10.30 Sun
Highgate Dark; Wells Eagle; guest beers H
Formerly the 'Pretty Bricks': a friendly, two-bar pub near the town centre with changing guest ales. No eve food Sun or Mon. 🏠 ❀ 🕭 ▶ 🍴 ♣

White Lion

150 Sandwell Street (Little London jct) ☎ (01922) 28542
12–3.30, 6–11; 12–11 Sat; 12–3.30, 7–10.30 Sun
Ansells Mild, Bitter; HP&D Bitter, Entire; Ind Coope Burton Ale; guest beers H
Classic Victorian pub where the lounge is popular with students and the bar, featuring a high ceiling and a sloping floor, caters more for locals. Q ❀ 🕭 ▶ 🍴 ♣

Wednesbury

Old Blue Ball

19 Hall End ☎ (0121) 556 0197
12–3, 5–11; 11.15–4.15, 7–11 Sat; 12–3, 7–10.30 Sun
Draught Bass H**; Highgate Dark; Stones Bitter** E**; guest beers** H
Popular backstreet local with a small bar, smoke room and a lounge, plus a large garden at the rear. Two guest beers.
Q ⛺ ❀ 🍴 ♣ 🍽

Star

Wood Green Road (A461, 300 yds from M6 jct 9)
☎ (0121) 502 2218
12–3 (not Sat), 5–11; 12–4, 7–10.30 Sun
Banks's Mild, Bitter E**; Marston's Pedigree; guest beer** H
Smart roadside food pub with a restaurant. Varied menu (no meals Sun eve). Good conversation is the main activity. Q 🕭 ▶ P

Wednesfield

Pyle Cock

Rookery Street (A4124)
☎ (01902) 732125
10.30–11; 12–4, 7–10.30 Sun
Banks's Mild, Bitter H
Excellent locals' boozer with lovely etched windows

depicting a pyle cock. The family room is quite basic; the traditional bar is always busy.
⛺ 🍴 ♣ P

Vine

35 Lichfield Road
☎ (01902) 733529
11–3 (4 Fri, 5 Sat), 6 (7 Sat)–11; 12–3, 7–10.30 Sun
Boddingtons Bitter; Thwaites Bitter; guest beers H
Revitalised, friendly multi-roomed local. Wide range of guest beers, including a mild; Blackbeard beers often feature. Good value food (eves till 8.30).
🏠 ❀ 🕭 ▶ ♣ 🍽 P

West Bromwich

Churchfield Tavern

12 Little Lane (by Sandwell General Hospital)
☎ (0121) 558 5468
11–11; 12–10.30 Sun
Banks's Hanson's Mild, Bitter; Camerons Bitter E**, Strongarm** H
Friendly, flourishing boozer. The bowling green and garden, with children's play area, have added to its popularity. Eve meals 6–8. ⛺ 🕭 ▶ 🍴 ♣ P 🍽

Old Crown

56 Sandwell Road (near A41/A4031 jct)
☎ (0121) 525 4600
12–4, 5 (6 Sat)–11; 12–4, 7–10.30 Sun
M&B Mild, Brew XI E**; guest beers** H
Popular one-roomed pub in a quiet sidestreet. The mainly Indian menu has proved a hit with locals. Two rapidly changing guests – micros and independents featuring strongly. 🕭 ▶ 🍽

Vine

Roebuck Street (near M5 jct 1)
☎ (0121) 553 2866
11.30–2.30 (3 summer), 5–11; 11–11 Fri & Sat; 12–10.30 Sun
M&B Mild, Brew XI E**; guest beer** H
Extended corner house famous for its spectacular indoor Indian barbecue (weekday eves and all day Sat/Sun). One changing independent guest beer.
❀ 🕭 ▶ ⇌ (Galton Bridge) 🍽

Wheatsheaf

379 High Street, Carter's Green (200 yds from A41/Black Country Spine road jct)
☎ (0121) 553 4221
11–11; 12–2.30, 7–10.30 Sun
Holden's Mild E**, Bitter** H/E**, Special, seasonal beer** H
Busy pub with a basic bar and a comfortable lounge, both recently renovated. Holden's XB is sold as Baggies Bitter. Good food. ❀ 🕭 ▶ ♣ 🍽

Whiteheath

Whiteheath Tavern

400 Birchfield Lane, Oldbury (A4034 near M5 jct 2)
☎ (0121) 552 3603
8–11; 12–3, 8–11 Mon, Fri & Sat; 12–3.30, 8–10.30 Sun
Ansell's Mild, Bitter H**; Banks's Mild** E
Friendly local with a games-oriented bar and a comfortable lounge. The licensees have been here for 15 years.
🍴 ⇌ (Rowley Regis) ♣ 🍽

Willenhall

Brewers Droop

44 Wolverhampton Street (behind Lock Museum)
☎ (01902) 607827
12–3 (4 Sat), 8–11; 12–3, 7–10.30 Sun
Batham Best Bitter; Enville Ale; Hook Norton Old Hooky; guest beers H
Former coaching inn, now famous for having three old racing motorbikes parked halfway up a wall (inside). Two or three beer festivals per year. No food Sun.
🏠 🕭 ♦ ♣

Falcon

Gomer Street West (behind Lock Museum)
☎ (01902) 633378
12–11; 12–10.30 Sun
Banks's Mild; Greene King Abbot; Highgate Dark; Marston's Bitter; Samuel Smith OBB; guest beers H
Friendly, two-roomed, backstreet local, serving three changing guest beers. Cellar tours when quiet. ❀ 🍴 ♣ 🍽

Wolverhampton

Chindit

113 Merridale Road (½ mile from Chapel Ash towards Bantock Park) ☎ (01902) 25582
12–3, 5–11; 11–11 Sat; 12–3, 7–10.30 Sun
Highgate Dark; Worthington Bitter; guest beers H
Basic corner local with a bar and a lounge, named after soldiers of 1st South Staffs Regiment who fought in Burma in 1944. Whitbread guest beers. 🍴 ♣

Clarendon Hotel

Chapel Ash (A41 near ring road island) ☎ (01902) 20587
11–11; 12–3, 7–10.30 Sun
Banks's Mild, Bitter E**; Camerons Strongarm; Marston's Pedigree** H
Popular brewery tap with a large, split-level lounge. The smaller smoke room has its own bar and can be quieter. Breakfast available from 8am; eve meals end at 8pm (no eve

meals Sat/Sun); good
sandwich bar. ◑ ▶ P ⑪

Great Western

Sun Street (behind rail station)
☎ (01902) 351090
11–11; 12–3, 7–10.30 Sun
**Batham Best Bitter; Holden's
Mild, Bitter, Special** H
Pub where a new conservatory
has added space and GWR
memorabilia is featured. Good
value food. W Midlands
CAMRA *Pub of the Year.*
⚒ ✿ ◑ ▶ ⇌ ♣ P

Homestead

Lodge Road, Oxley (off A449 at
Goodyear roundabout)
☎ (01902) 787357
12–3, 6–11; 12–3, 7–10.30 Sun
**Ansells Bitter; Banks's Mild;
Marston's Pedigree; guest
beers** H
Large, two-bar suburban pub
where children are welcome
(large outdoor play area).
Good, home-cooked food.
✿ ⚒ ◑ ▶ ⊟ ♣ P

Mitre Inn

Lower Green, Tettenhall (near
A41/Lower St jct)
☎ (01902) 753487
12–2.30 (3 Sat), 6–11 (12–11 summer
Sat); 12–3, 7–10.30 (12–10.30 summer)
Sun
**Draught Bass; Stones Bitter;
Worthington Bitter; guest
beer** H
Surprisingly spacious, two-
room local in a pleasant
location opposite the Lower
Green. Small patio at the front.
✿ ◑ ▶ ⊟ ♣

Moon Under Water

Lichfield Street (opp. Grand
Theatre) ☎ (01902) 22447
10–11; 12–10.30 Sun
**Banks's Mild; Courage
Directors; Marston's Pedigree;
Theakston Best Bitter, XB;
Younger Scotch; guest beers** H
Large, open-plan
Wetherspoons pub with a
U-shaped bar. Heritage

information and local art are
featured on the wood-panelled
walls – note the tree sculpture.
Q ◑ ▶ ⅋ ⇌ ♣ ✂

Newhampton Inn

Riches Street, Whitmore Reans
(off A41) ☎ (01902) 745773
11–11; 12–10.30 Sun
**Courage Best Bitter, Directors;
Marston's Pedigree; Ruddles
County; John Smith's Bitter;
guest beers** H
Busy, corner local attracting a
wide clientele to four distinctly
different rooms and a large
garden with a bowling green.
The function room is used as a
music venue. No-smoking area
lunchtime. Mini-beer festival
Bonfire Night.
⚒ Q ✿ ◑ ▶ ♣ ⟳ ✂ ⑪

Old Stag's Head

Pennwood Lane, Penn
Common ☎ (01902) 341023
11.30–2.30, 6–11; 11.30–11 Sat; 12–3,
7–10.30 Sun
Banks's Mild, Bitter E
Rustic pub on the edge of Penn
Common, with a small bar
frequented by locals and a
large lounge where children
are welcome if eating.
✿ ◑ ▶ ⊟ ♣ P ⑪

Red Lion

252 Bilston Road, Monmore
Green ☎ (01902) 454511
12–3, 5–11; 12–11 Fri & Sat; 12–4,
7–10.30 Sun
Banks's Mild, Bitter E
Basic pub on the outskirts of
town with a bar, snug and pool
room. Asian bar snacks;
barbecues in summer. ⚶ P

Royal Oak

70 Compton Road
☎ (01902) 22845
11–11; 1–3.30, 7–10.30 Sun
**Banks's Mild, Bitter;
Camerons Strongarm** H
Pleasant local, also popular
with students. Good value
lunches in the conservatory.
Small outside area. ✿ ◑ P ⑪

Stamford Arms

Lime Street, Penn Fields (off
Lea Rd) ☎ (01902) 24172
12–3.30, 7–11; 12–11 Sat; 12–5, 7–10.30
Sun
Banks's Mild, Bitter E
Welcoming corner local with
notable exterior tiling. The
three unspoilt rooms are
served by a single bar with a
hatch. A hidden gem in an old
residential area. Q ✿ ⊟ ♣

Swan

Bridgnorth Road, Compton
☎ (01902) 754736
11–3, 5–11; 11–11 Sat; 12–10.30 Sun
Banks's Mild, Bitter E
A newly refurbished lounge
improves this Victorian pub
with its small public bar and
snug with real fire.
⚒ Q ✿ ⊟ ♣ P ⑪

Woodcross

Horse & Jockey

Robert Wynd
☎ (01902) 659666
11–3, 6–11; 11–11 Sat; 12–3, 7–10.30
Sun
Banks's Mild E; **Marston's
Bitter; Morland Old Speckled
Hen; Tetley Bitter; guest
beer** H
Popular local being extended
to include a larger lounge as a
dining area. Keen darts and
dominoes club. ◑ ▶ P

Woodsetton

Park Inn

George Street (off A457, ¼ mile
from A4123) ☎ (01902) 882843
11–11; 12–3.30, 7–10.30 Sun
**Holden's Mild, Bitter, Lucy B,
Special, seasonal beers** H
Friendly brewery tap, popular
with all ages. It has a U-shaped
bar, small dining or function
room and a conservatory
where families are welcome.
Barbecues in summer.
⚒ ⚶ ✿ ◑ ▶ ⅋ ♣ P ✂

FIRKIN UP THE BLACK COUNTRY

The relentless march of the Firkin chain has seen plenty of
traditional pubs destroyed. In the West Midlands, however,
Firkin has gone a step further and killed off an active brewing
company. The Holt, Plant & Deakin division of Allied was set up in
1984 to provide genuinely local competition for other Black Country
brewers. HP&D operated from two breweries: the first in Oldbury,
the other in Wolverhampton, and enjoyed good local patronage.
Now the two HP&D breweries have been turned into Firkins and
production of the HP&D beers has been switched elsewhere in the
Allied/Carlsberg-Tetley empire. Sadly, one fine initiative by a
national brewer has given way to the formula-driven universality
one expects from a giant company.

Wiltshire

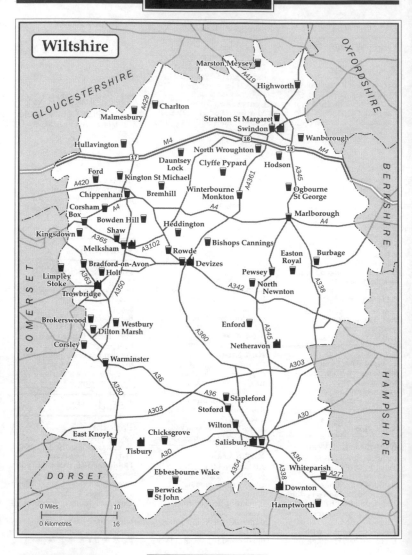

Wiltshire

(Map showing locations in Wiltshire including:)

Marston Meysey, Highworth, Charlton, Malmesbury, Stratton St Margaret, Swindon, Wanborough, Hullavington, North Wroughton, Hodson, Dauntsey Lock, Clyffe Pypard, Ford, Kington St Michael, Winterbourne Monkton, Ogbourne St George, Chippenham, Bremhill, Corsham, Box, Bowden Hill, Heddington, Marlborough, Shaw, Kingsdown, Bishops Cannings, Melksham, Rowde, Easton Royal, Burbage, Bradford-on-Avon, Holt, Devizes, Pewsey, Limpley Stoke, North Newnton, Trowbridge, Brokerswood, Westbury, Dilton Marsh, Enford, Corsley, Netheravon, Warminster, Stapleford, Stoford, Wilton, East Knoyle, Chicksgrove, Salisbury, Tisbury, Ebbesbourne Wake, Whiteparish, Berwick St John, Downton, Hamptworth

GLOUCESTERSHIRE, OXFORDSHIRE, BERKSHIRE, HAMPSHIRE, DORSET, SOMERSET

0 Miles 10
0 Kilometres 16

INDEPENDENT BREWERIES

Archers: Swindon

Arkell's: Swindon

Bunces: Netheravon

Gibbs Mew: Salisbury

Hop Back: Downton

Mole's: Melksham

Tisbury: Tisbury

Ushers: Trowbridge

Wadworth: Devizes

Berwick St John

Talbot

The Cross OS947224
☎ (01747) 828222
11.30–2.30, 7 (6.30 Fri & Sat)–11 (10.30 Mon); 12–2.30 (closed eve) Sun
Adnams Bitter, Broadside; Draught Bass; Wadworth 6X Ⓗ, Old Timer Ⓖ
Unspoilt village pub, 400 years old, with a beamed ceiling and an inglenook. Good food (not served Sun).
🏚 Q ❀ ◑ ▶ ▲ P

Bishops Cannings

Crown

Chandlers Lane
☎ (01380) 860218
11–3, 7–11; 12–3, 7–10.30 Sun

Wadworth IPA, 6X Ⓗ
Well-appointed village pub that boasts its own crazy golf course. It stands next to the impressive parish church.
🏚 Q ❀ ◑ ▶ ⊞ ▲ P

Bowden Hill

Bell

1 mile E of Lacock
☎ (01249) 730308
11–2.30, 7 (6 Sat & summer)–11; 12–3, 7–10.30 Sun
Smiles Best; Wadworth 6X; Wickwar Coopers' WPA; guest beer Ⓗ
Pleasant pub with a large garden featuring livestock. Near the NT village of Laycock. Good food.
🐕 ❀ 🛏 ◑ ▶ ᕑ P

312

Rising Sun
32 Bowden Hill (1 mile E of Lacock) ☎ (01249) 730363
11–3, 6–11; 12–3, 7–10.30 Sun
Mole's Tap, Best Bitter, Barley Mole, Brew 97 H
Attractive, single-bar, 17th-century stone inn, high above the Avon Valley with spectacular views. No food Sun eve or Mon lunch.
🏰 Q ❀ ◐ ▶ ♣ P

Box

Quarryman's Arms
Box Hill (300 yds S of A4)
OS834693 ☎ (01225) 743569
11–11; 12–10.30 Sun
Butcombe Bitter; Wadworth 6X; Wickwar BOB H**; guest beers** G
Open-plan pub with views over the valley, well hidden in a maze of lanes (phone for directions!).
🏰 ⛵ ❀ 🍴 ◐ ▶ ▲ ♣ P ⅙

Bradford-on-Avon

Beehive
263 Trowbridge Road
☎ (01225) 863620
11.30–2.30, 7–11; 12–3, 7–10.30 Sun
Butcombe Bitter; guest beers G/H
Friendly, canalside pub with seven changing ales, plus Belgian bottled beers. No food Sun eve.
🏰 Q ❀ ◐ ▶ ▲ ♣ P

Masons Arms
52 Newtown
☎ (01225) 863435
11–11; 12–3.30, 7–10.30 Sun
Ushers Best Bitter, Founders, seasonal beers H
Old-fashioned, unpretentious local above the main town.
❀ 🍴 ⇌ ♣ 🍷

Bremhill

Dumb Post
Dumb Post Hill (off A4 W of Calne) OS975727
☎ (01249) 813192
11.30–2.30 (not Wed), 7–11; 12–3, 7–10.30 Sun
Archers Best Bitter; Wadworth 6X H
Pub with fine views, outside the village. The new restaurant has a varied menu (Wed–Sat eves) and also serves Sun lunch.
🏰 Q ❀ ◐ ▶ 🍴 ▲ ♣ P

Brokerswood

Kicking Donkey
Follow signs to Woodland Park from A36/A350 OS833520
☎ (01373) 823250
11.30–2.30, 6 (6.30 Sat)–11; 12–10.30 Sun

Burbage

Three Horseshoes
Stibb Green (off A346)
☎ (01672) 810324
12–2 (2.30 Sat), 6–11; 12–2.30, 7–10.30 Sun
Wadworth IPA, 6X, seasonal beers H
Small, cosy, thatched pub on the edge of Savernake Forest. Good food (not served Sun eve). 🏰 ❀ ◐ ▶ 🍴 P

Charlton

Horse & Groom
The Street (B4040)
☎ (01666) 823904
12–3, 7–11 (11–3, 6–11 summer; 11–11 summer Sat); 12–3, 7–10.30 (12–10.30 summer) Sun
Archers Village; Wadworth 6X; guest beers H
Attractive country inn in Cotswold stone, fronted by a lawn. Roomy public bar; the smaller bar serves the restaurant (good food). Children welcome.
🏰 Q ❀ 🍴 ◐ ▶ ♣ P

Chicksgrove

Compasses Inn
Signed off A30 OS973294
☎ (01722) 714318
11–3, 6.30–11; 12–3, 7–10.30 Sun; closed Mon
Adnams Best Bitter; Draught Bass; Tisbury Old Wardour; Wadworth 6X H
14th-century inn in a superb setting, boasting beams and a quarry-tiled floor. Q ❀ ◐ ▶ P

Chippenham

Little George
29 New Road
☎ (01249) 652136
11–2.30, 6–11; 7–10.30 (closed lunch) Sun
Courage Best Bitter; Marston's Pedigree; Morland Old Speckled Hen; guest beers H
Busy town-centre pub with gas lights in the lounge.
❀ 🍴 ◐ 🍺 ⇌ ♣ P

Clyffe Pypard

Goddard Arms
Wood Street OS074769
☎ (01793) 731386
12–2.30, 7–11; 12–3, 7–10.30 Sun
Flowers IPA; Greene King Abbot; Wadworth 6X; guest beers H

Well-hidden, lively village local: a small bar and a split-level lounge. Thai food, sculpture, painting and drama events feature.
🏰 Q ⛵ ❀ ◐ ▶ 🍺 ⛄ P ⅙

Corsham

Two Pigs
38 Pickwick (A4)
☎ (01249) 712515
7–11; 12–2.30, 7–10.30 Sun
Bunces Pigswill; guest beers H
Lovely pub with a strong commitment to real ale. Over-21s only. Regular local CAMRA *Pub of the Year*. Live blues Mon. 🏰 ❀

Corsley

Cross Keys
Lye's Green (1 mile N of A362 at Royal Oak jct) OS821462
☎ (01373) 832406
12–3 (not Mon, Tue, Thu or Fri), 6.30 (7 Sat & Mon)–11; 12–3, 7–10.30 Sun
Draught Bass; Butcombe Bitter; guest beer (occasional) H
Welcoming, spacious free house of character, with a splendid fireplace. Lunches Wed and Sat.
🏰 ❀ ◐ ▶ ♣ ⛄ P

Dauntsey Lock

Peterborough Arms
B4069 Lyneham–Sutton Benger road
☎ (01249) 890409
11.30–2.30 (3 Sat), 6–11; 12–3, 7–10.30 Sun
Archers Best Bitter; Federation Buchanan's Best Bitter; Wadworth 6X; guest beer H
Friendly free house with a cosy lounge. Children welcome in the skittle alley and large garden. Good range of food.
🏰 ❀ ◐ ▶ ♣ P

Devizes

British Lion
9 Estcourt Street
☎ (01380) 720665
11–11; 12–10.30 Sun
Beer range varies H
A *Guide* regular; the house beer comes from Ash Vine.
❀ ♣ ⛄ P 🍷

Hare & Hounds
Hare & Hounds Street
☎ (01380) 723231
11–2.30, 7–11; 12–3, 7–10.30 Sun
Wadworth IPA, 6X, seasonal beers H
Pub with a small, friendly, split-level bar.
🏰 ❀ ◐ ♣ P

Queen's Head
Dunkirk Hill (A342)
☎ (01380) 723726
11–3, 7–11; 12–3, 7–10.30 Sun
Mole's Tap, Best Bitter, seasonal beers Ⓗ
Friendly roadside pub serving good food. ❀ ◖ ◗ ▲ ♣ P ⍉

White Bear
Monday Market Street
☎ (01380) 722583
11–2.30 (3 Sat), 7–11; 12–3, 7–10.30 Sun
Wadworth IPA, 6X, Old Timer Ⓗ
Improved pub selling some of the best Wadworth beer around. ⛰ Q 🛏 ◖ ◗

Dilton Marsh

Prince of Wales
High Street ☎ (01373) 865487
12–2.30, 7–11; 12–11 Sat; 12–10.30 Sun
Federation Buchanan's Best Bitter, Original; Fuller's London Pride; Shepherd Neame Spitfire; Worthington Bitter; guest beer (occasional) Ⓗ
Simple, friendly, well-run, open-plan local.
Q ❀ ◖ ◗ ⇌ ♣ P

East Knoyle

Fox & Hounds
The Green (½ mile S of A303 at Willoughby Hedge)
☎ (01747) 830573
11–2.30 (3 Sat), 6–11; 12–3.30, 7–10.30 Sun
Fuller's London Pride; Marston's Pedigree; Smiles Golden Brew; guest beers Ⓗ
Remote, 14th-century, thatched inn in a hamlet at the top of a hill, with panoramic views. Three bars and a skittle alley; good food.
⛰ Q 🐎 ❀ ◖ ◗ ⊟ ♣ P

Easton Royal

Bruce Arms ☆
On B3087 ☎ (01672) 810216
11–2.30 (3 Sat), 6–11; 12–3, 7–10.30 Sun
Ringwood Best Bitter; Wadworth 6X Ⓗ
Fine basic bar with a brick floor and scrubbed pine tables. The games room/skittle alley extension does not spoil the atmosphere.
⛰ Q ❀ ⊟ ▲ ♣ ⌒ P

Ebbesbourne Wake

Horseshoe
Hanley Street
☎ (01722) 780474
11.30–3, 6.30–11; 12–4, 7–10.30 Sun
Adnams Broadside; Ringwood Best Bitter; Wadworth 6X; guest beer Ⓖ
This true village pub has a cracking atmosphere. Its bars are adorned with old farm tools. No eve food Sun/Mon.
⛰ Q 🐎 ❀ 🛏 ◖ ◗ ▲ ♣ P

Enford

Swan
Long Street (off A345)
☎ (01980) 670338
12–3, 7–11; 12–3, 7–10.30 Sun
Hop Back Crop Circle; guest beers Ⓗ
Friendly village pub with cosy nooks and crannies and a good family room. The gantry sign straddles the road. Good menu (excellent curries). Three guest beers are available.
⛰ 🐎 ❀ ◖ ◗ ♣ P

Ford

White Hart
☎ (01249) 782213
11–2.45, 5–11; 12–3, 7–10.30 Sun
Beer range varies Ⓗ/Ⓖ
Superb 16th-century inn, with an award-winning restaurant, in a picturesque setting beside a trout stream. Up to ten ales.
⛰ Q ❀ 🛏 ◖ ◗ ⌒ P

Hamptworth

Cuckoo
Hamptworth Road (1 mile off A36 at Landford turn)
☎ (01794) 390302
11.30–2.30, 6–11; 11.30–11 Sat; 12–10.30 Sun
Badger Tanglefoot; Cheriton Pots Ale; Hop Back GFB, Summer Lightning; Wadworth 6X Ⓖ
Well-run, friendly, unspoilt, country pub on the edge of the New Forest. The large garden has a play area and petanque.
⛰ Q 🐎 ❀ ♿ ▲ ♣ ⌒ P

Heddington

Ivy
Stockley Lane (off A3102/A4)
☎ (01380) 850276
12–3, 6.30–11; 12–11 Sat; 12–10.30 Sun
Wadworth IPA, 6X, seasonal beers Ⓖ
Popular, 15th-century village local. Good, home-cooked food (not served eves Sun–Wed).
⛰ Q ❀ ◖ ◗ ▲ ♣ P

Highworth

Wine Cellar
High Street
☎ (01793) 763828
7 (11 Fri & Sat)–11; 12–10.30 Sun
Archers Village, Best Bitter; guest beer Ⓖ
A stairway between shop fronts leads down to a stone-walled cellar which serves a good choice of wines and whiskies. Live music is staged on the second Sun of the month. Q ⌒

Hodson

Calley Arms
Off B4005
☎ (01793) 740350
12–2.30 (11.30–3 Sat), 6.30–11; 12–3, 7–10.30 Sun
Wadworth IPA, 6X, seasonal beers; guest beer Ⓗ
Modern pub with an open-plan bar with a raised dining area (eve meals Tue–Sat). Above average pub food.
⛰ ❀ ◖ ◗ ♣ ⌒ P

Holt

Old Ham Tree
Ham Green (B3107)
☎ (01225) 782581
11.15–3, 6–11; 12–3.30, 7–10.30 Sun
Draught Bass; Marston's Pedigree; Robinson's Best Bitter; Wadworth IPA, 6X; guest beers Ⓗ
18th-century coaching inn of character with a comfortable lounge/restaurant which contrasts with the simple, friendly locals' bar. Good variety of meals (generous portions).
Q ❀ 🛏 ◖ ◗ ⊟ ♣ ⌒ P

Hullavington

Queen's Head
The Street
☎ (01666) 837221
12–3, 7–11; 12–3, 7–10.30 Sun
Archers Village; Wadworth 6X; guest beers Ⓗ
Homely local with open coal fires and a skittle alley.
⛰ Q 🛏 ♿ ♣ P

Kingsdown

Swan
☎ (01225) 742269
11–3, 7–11; 11–11 Sat; 12–10.30 Sun
Draught Bass; Gibbs Mew Salisbury, Wake Ale, Deacon Ⓗ
Friendly, three-roomed pub with a stone-flagged main bar and an open fire. Spectacular views. No food Sun.
⛰ Q ❀ ◖ ◗ ♣ P

Kington St Michael

Jolly Huntsman Inn
High Street
☎ (01249) 750305
11.30–3, 6.30 (5.30 Fri)–11 (may vary summer); 12–3, 7–10.30 Sun
Badger Dorset Best, Tanglefoot; Draught Bass; Matthew Clark Twelve Bore; Wadworth 6X; guest beers Ⓗ
Friendly village local: a comfortable L-shaped lounge with a dining area, offering up to seven ales. Excellent meals. Quiz Mon; live music Wed.
⛰ 🛏 ◖ ◗ ♣ P

Limpley Stoke

Hop Pole Inn
Woods Hill (off A36)
☎ (01225) 723134
11–2.30 (3 Sat), 6–11; 12–3, 7–10.30 Sun

Draught Bass; Butcombe Bitter; Courage Best Bitter; guest beer H
Comfortable, authentic village pub with a beautiful, dark-panelled public bar. A large garden overlooks the Avon Valley. ♔ Q ☞ ❀ ◖ ▶ ⬠ ⬱ (Freshford) ♣ P ✠

Malmesbury

Red Bull
Sherston Road (B4040, 1½ miles W of town) ☎ (01666) 822108
11–2.30 (not Tue; 11.30–3 Sat), 6.30–11; 12–3, 7–10.30 Sun
Draught Bass; Boddingtons Bitter; Flowers IPA; guest beer H
Popular family pub with a garden play area and children's room/skittle alley.
♔ ☎ ❀ ⬥ ♣ P

Marlborough

Lamb
The Parade ☎ (01672) 512668
11–11; 12–10.30 Sun
Wadworth IPA, 6X; guest beer G
Down-to-earth town local with an L-shaped bar. ❀ ☞ ◖ ♣

Marston Meysey

Old Spotted Cow
2½ miles from A419 OS129969
☎ (01285) 810264
11–3, 5.30–11; 12–3, 12–10.30 Sun
Draught Bass; Hook Norton Best Bitter; Wadworth 6X; guest beer H
Cotswold stone building, a former farmhouse, now a popular local.
♔ Q ❀ ◖ ▶ ⬠ P

Melksham

Red Lion
3 The City ☎ (01225) 702960
11–2.30 (3 Sat), 5–11 (midnight Thu & Sat); 11–midnight Fri; 12–2.50, 7–10.30 Sun
Draught Bass; Crown Buckley Dark; Oakhill Best Bitter; guest beer H
Unspoilt pub, dating back to 1220, with a prize-winning floral display. A rare outlet for mild/dark ales. Q ❀ ◖ ♣ P

North Newnton

Woodbridge Inn
On A345 ☎ (01980) 630266
11–11; 12–3, 7–10.30 Sun

Wadworth IPA, 6X, Farmers Glory; guest beer H
Smart foody pub with an interesting collection of old signs and china. Riverside garden. ❀ ☞ ◖ ▶ ⬠ P

North Wroughton

Check Inn
Woodland View (off A4361)
☎ (01793) 845382
11–2.30, 6.30–11; 11–11 Fri & Sat; 12–10.30 Sun
Beer range varies H
True free house; a country pub in an urban area. The single bar has a children's area; garden bar in summer. Five real ales and an extensive range of Czech bottled beers.
♔ ❀ ☞ ◖ ⬥ ♣ ⬡ P ✠

Ogbourne St George

Old Crown
Marlborough Road (off A346)
☎ (01672) 841445
11.30–3, 6–11; 12–3, 7–10.30 Sun
Wadworth 6X; guest beer H
Food-oriented local serving cider in summer. Wheelchair ramp on request.
♔ ❀ ☞ ◖ ▶ ⬠ ♣ ⬡ P

Pewsey

Coopers Arms
Ball Road (off B3087)
☎ (01672) 562495
12–2, 7–11; 12–4, 7–10.30 Sun
Gale's HSB; Marston's Pedigree; Wadworth 6X; guest beer H
Bar of character in a thatched building, hidden down a side road. ♔ ☞ ❀ ◖ ▶ ⬱ ♣ ⬡ P

Rowde

George & Dragon
High Street ☎ (01380) 723053
12–3 (not Mon), 7.30–11; 12–3, 7.30–10.30 Sun
Butcombe Bitter; Wadworth 6X; guest beers H
Recently freed from the Wadworth tie, this comfortable pub has established an excellent reputation for quality food (meals Tue–Sat).
♔ Q ❀ ◖ ▶ ⬠ ♣ P

Salisbury

Blackbird Inn
30 Churchfields
☎ (01722) 502828
12–3, 6–11; 11–11 Fri & Sat; 12–10.30 Sun
Courage Best Bitter; guest beers H
Cosy, one-room, friendly local offering a changing range of ales. Limited selection of good value lunches Mon–Fri.
❀ ◖ ⬱ ♣

Deacons Alms
118 Fisherton Street
☎ (01722) 336409
11–3, 6–11; 12–3, 7–10.30 Sun
Bunces Danish Dynamite; Hop Back GFB; Summer Lightning; Ringwood Old Thumper; Wadworth 6X; guest beers H
Excellent town pub with interesting split-level drinking areas. Good food.
♔ ☞ ◖ ▶ ⬠ ⬱

Royal George
17 Bedwin Street
☎ (01722) 327782
11–3 (4 Sat), 6 (5.30 Sat)–11; 12–3, 7–10.30 Sun
Gibbs Mew Salisbury, Wake Ale, Deacon (summer), Bishop's Tipple H
Grade II-listed pub near the arts centre; one of its beams is from the old *Royal George* ship.
❀ ☞ ◖ ♣ P

Star
69 Brown Street
☎ (01722) 327137
11–11; 12–10.30 Sun
Bunces Danish Dynamite; Hop Back GFB; Wadworth 6X; guest beers H
14th-century, city-centre pub. Unpretentious and loud, but very friendly. ♔ ⬡

Wyndham Arms
27 Estcourt Road
☎ (01722) 331026
4.30 (3 Fri, 12 Sat)–11; 12–10.30 Sun
Hop Back GFB, Crop Circle, Entire Stout, Thunderstorm, Summer Lightning, seasonal beers H
No frills, welcoming boozer, the first home of Hop Back Brewery. Not to be missed.
♔ ☞ ♣

Try also: Village, Wilton Rd (Free)

Shaw

Golden Fleece
☎ (01225) 702050
11.30–2.30, 6–11; 12–3, 6–10.30 Sun
Butcombe Bitter, Wilmot's; Marston's Pedigree; Wickwar BOB H
Handsome old pub in a small hamlet. Good garden next to the cricket green.
❀ ◖ ▶ ⬥ ♣ P

Stapleford

Pelican
Warminster Road
☎ (01722) 790291
11–2.30 (3 Sat), 6–11; 12–2.30, 7 (6 summer)–10.30 Sun
Otter Bitter; Ringwood Best Bitter, Fortyniner; guest beers H
Extended, 18th-century coaching inn; one large bar but also a cosy restaurant serving

excellent food at reasonable prices. Large garden.
🏨 ❀ ◖ ▶ P

Stoford

Swan Inn
On A36
☎ (01722) 790236
11–3, 6–11; 11–11 Sat; 12–3.30, 7–10.30 Sun
Hampshire Ironside; Ringwood Best Bitter; guest beers Ⓗ
Friendly, 400-year-old pub with a good atmosphere, excellent food, a skittle alley and good facilities for families and guests with disabilities.
🏨 Q ⛲ ❀ 🛏 ◖ ▶ ⊟ ♿ ♣ P ⚲ ⊟

Stratton St Margaret

Wheatsheaf
167 Ermin Street
☎ (01793) 823149
11–3, 6–11; 12–2, 7–10.30 Sun
Arkell's Bitter, 3B Ⓗ
Busy, popular community pub. No food Sun.
❀ ◖ ▶ ⊟ ♣ P

Swindon

Clifton
Clifton Street, Old Town
☎ (01793) 523162
11–2.30, 6–11; 12–2, 7–10.30 Sun
Arkell's Bitter, 3B, seasonal beers Ⓗ
Backstreet local run by a popular landlord, serving some of the best Arkell's in Swindon. Hard to find.
P

Glue Pot
5 Emlin Square
☎ (01793) 523935
11–11; 12–3, 7–10.30 Sun
Archers Village, Best Bitter, Golden; guest beer Ⓗ
Busy one-bar, no-nonsense pub built in the mid-19th-century as part of Brunel's Railway Village. Patio area for outside drinking. Q ❀ ◖ ⇌ ⊟

King's Arms
20 Wood Street, Old Town
☎ (01793) 522156
11–3, 6–11; 12–3, 7–10.30 Sun
Arkell's Bitter, 3B, Kingsdown, seasonal beers Ⓗ
Busy Old Town pub, popular at weekends, with a large, open-plan drinking area on two levels, the lower level being quiet. 🛏 ◖ ▶ ♿ P

Nine Elms
Old Shaw Lane
☎ (01793) 770442
12–3, 6–11; 12–11 Fri & Sat; 12–10.30 Sun

Ushers Best Bitter, Founders, seasonal beers Ⓗ
Refurbished redbrick village pub, surrounded by new housing. Hard to find down a cul-de-sac. Eve meals Wed–Sun. 🏨 ❀ ▶ ⊟ ♿ P

Rising Sun
6 Albert Street, Old Town
☎ (01793) 529916
11–11; 12–10.30 Sun
Ushers Best Bitter, Founders, seasonal beers Ⓗ
Local CAMRA award-winning, backstreet pub in the Old Town area; known as the 'Roaring Donkey'. Q

Savoy
38–40 Regent Street (near town hall)
☎ (01793) 533970
11–11; 12–10.30 Sun
Archers Best Bitter; Arkell's 3B; Courage Directors; Theakston Best Bitter; Younger Scotch; guest beers Ⓗ
Large, air-conditioned, popular converted cinema with a single bar. Built in 1937, it features cinema stills and old books.
Q ◖ ▶ ♿ ⇌ ⊙ ⚲

Wheatsheaf
32 Newport Street
☎ (01793) 523188
11–2.30, 5.30–11; 12–11 Sun
Adnams Bitter; Badger Tanglefoot; Wadworth IPA, 6X, Farmers Glory, Old Timer or seasonal beer Ⓗ
Popular, two-bar pub; the larger back bar is busy Fri and Sat eves; quieter front bar and a small courtyard. No food Sat, or Sun eve.
❀ ◖ ▶ ⊟

Wanborough

Plough
High Street
☎ (01793) 790523
12–2.30, 5–11; 11–11 Fri & Sat; 12–2.30, 7–10.30 Sun
Archers Village; Draught Bass; Boddingtons Bitter; Fuller's London Pride; Wadworth 6X; guest beer Ⓗ
Listed, thatched pub with beams, exposed stone walls, log fires and a cosy atmosphere. The Harrow (100 yards away), under the same management, is also recommended. Good food (weekday lunches; eve meals Mon–Sat). 🏨 Q ❀ ◖ ▶ ♣ P

Warminster

Yew Tree
174 Boreham Road
☎ (01985) 212335
12–2 (4 Sat), 6.30–11; 12–4, 7–10.30 Sun

Ringwood Best Bitter, XXXX Porter; guest beers Ⓗ
18th-century former coaching inn on the outskirts, catering mainly for the local trade.
❀ 🛏 ◖ ▶ ♣ P

Westbury

Crown Inn
Market Place
☎ (01373) 822828
11–2.30, 5.30 (6 Sat)–11; 12–2.30, 7–10.30 Sun
Wadworth 6X, seasonal beers Ⓗ
Welcoming, well-appointed local. Eve meals Fri and Sat; no food Sun.
❀ ◖ ▶ ⊟ ⊙ P

Whiteparish

King's Head
The Street
☎ (01794) 884287
12–3.30, 6–11; 12–11 Sat; 12–3.30, 7–10.30 Sun
Brains SA; Brakspear Bitter; Whitbread Best Bitter; guest beer Ⓗ
Traditional village pub and restaurant, the hub of local activities. Large play area; well-stocked duck pond.
🏨 ❀ ◖ ▶ ♣ P

Parish Lantern
Romsey Road
☎ (01794) 884392
11.30–3, 6.30–11; 12–3, 7–10.30 Sun
Courage Best Bitter; Ringwood Best Bitter; guest beers Ⓗ
Large, friendly, one-bar pub, just out of the main village, with many drinking areas. The spacious, but secure garden is equipped for children.
🏨 ❀ ◖ ▶ ♿ ▲ ♣ P

Wilton

Bear
12 West Street
☎ (01722) 742398
11–3.30 (3 Sat), 6 (5 Sat)–11; 12–3, 7–10.30 Sun
Badger Dorset Best Ⓗ
16th-century inn near the market square. 🏨 ❀ ♣

Winterbourne Monkton

New Inn
Signed off A4369 N of Avebury
☎ (01672) 539240
11–3, 6–11; 12–3, 7–10.30 Sun
Adnams Bitter; Wadworth 6X; guest beer Ⓗ
Friendly local with a cosy bar and a restaurant (good, home-cooked food in large portions). Cider in summer. En suite accommodation is available.
🏨 Q ❀ 🛏 ◖ ▶ ▲ ♣ ⊙ P

Worcestershire

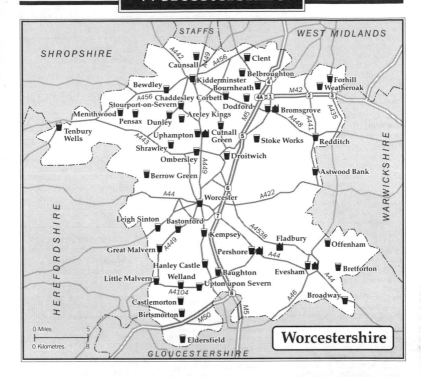

Worcestershire

Areley Kings

King's Arms
19 Redhouse Road (off B4196)
☎ (01299) 827132
12–3, 6–11; 11–11 Fri & Sat; 12–3,
7–10.30 Sun
Banks's Mild H/E, Bitter E;
guest beer H
Locals' pub with a single bar in
an L-shaped room, plus a
dining room. Outside there is a
garden and bowling green. Eve
food until 9.30 (not Sun eve).
🏠 ⓓ ▶ ♣ P ⏱

Astwood Bank

Red Lion
31 Church Road
☎ (01527) 892848
11–3, 6–11; 12–3, 7–10.30 Sun
Banks's Mild, Bitter; guest
beer H
Lively village local catering for
diners and drinkers in an old-
style bar, a games room, a
children's play area and a
garden. 🏠 ⛱ ⓓ ▶ ♣ P

Why Not?
The Ridgeway (A441, 1 mile S
of village) ☎ (01527) 893566
11–2.30, 6–11; 12–3, 7–10.30 Sun
Boddingtons Mild, Bitter;
Wadworth 6X H
Comfortable, friendly roadside
pub, popular with locals and
tourists. Excellent good value

food (daily specials available)
in a no-smoking dining area;
pleasant public bar.
🏠 ⊛ ⓓ ▶ ♣ P ⏱

Bastonford

Halfway House
On A449
☎ (01905) 831098
11–3, 6–11; 12–2.30, 7–10.30 Sun
Marston's Bitter; Taylor
Landlord; guest beer H
Pub halfway between Malvern
and Worcester, catering for
local and passing trades. Two
food-oriented bars with dining
tables and 'muzak' create a
bistro-style atmosphere. The
guest beer is usually from an
independent brewer.
⊛ ⓓ ▶ P

Baughton

Jockey Inn
On A4104
☎ (01684) 592153
11.30–3, 6.30–11; 12–3, 7–10.30 Sun;
closed Mon, except bank hols
Adnams Bitter H; Banks's
Bitter E; Hook Norton Best
Bitter; Wood Parish H; guest
beers G
Busy village pub with a good
atmosphere, popular for its
excellent range of food. Skittle
alley. There is a small garden at
the front.
🏠 ⊛ ⓓ ▶ ♣ ⏏ P ⏱

Belbroughton

Queens
Queens Hill (B4188)
☎ (01562) 730276
11.30–3, 5.30 (6 Sat)–11; 12–3.30,
7–10.30 Sun
Marston's Bitter, Pedigree,
HBC H
Popular, smart village inn:
three lounge areas served by
one main bar. Good quality
food (not served Sun eve).
⊛ ⓓ ▶ ♿ P

Try also: Robin Hood,
Drayton (Carlsberg-Tetley)

Berrow Green

Admiral Rodney
On B4197 ☎ (01886) 821375
12–3 (not winter Mon), 7–11; 12–3,
7–10.30 Sun
Hook Norton Best Bitter;
guest beers H

INDEPENDENT BREWERIES
Brandy Cask: Pershore

Cannon Royall:
Uphampton

Evesham: Evesham

Red Cross: Bromsgrove

Wyre Piddle: Fladbury

317

Friendly pub set in rolling countryside with bar, lounge and pool areas. Check availability of meals. It has a registered tourist campsite with basic washing facilities. Up to three guest beers, plus a cider in summer. There is also a skittle alley.

🏚 Q ✿ ◑ ▷ ▲ ♣ ○ P

Bewdley

Black Boy

50 Wyre Hill (off B4194 at Welch Gate)
☎ (01299) 403523
12–3, 7–11; 12–3, 7–10.30 Sun
Banks's Mild Ⓔ, **Bitter** Ⓔ/Ⓗ;
Marston's Pedigree; guest beer Ⓗ
A short, steep climb from the town centre, this 400-year-old pub is not to be confused with the Black Boy Hotel. Regularly featured in Banks's *Best Kept Cellar* awards. Children may be allowed in the games room if it is not in use.

🏚 Q ✿ ⊞ ♣ 🍺

Cock & Magpie

Severnside North
☎ (01299) 403748
11–4, 6–11; 11–11 Sat & summer; 12–4, 7–10.30 (12–10.30 summer) Sun
Banks's Mild, Bitter Ⓔ
Small, traditional, two-roomed pub on the former quayside by the River Severn, near Thomas Telford's bridge. Popular with both locals and visitors. Access is occasionally hampered by winter floods.

⊞ ⇌ (SVR) ♣ 🍺

George Hotel

Load Street
☎ (01299) 402117
11–3, 5.30–11; 11–11 Sat; 12–4, 6.30–10.30 Sun
Ind Coope Burton Ale; Tetley Bitter; guest beer Ⓗ
Town-centre hotel with a small popular bar, accessed via a side passage, and a lounge to the front. Some 300 different guest beers have been offered over the past few years. 🏚 Q ⏰ ✿
🏠 ◑ ▷ & ⇌ (SVR) P

Rising Sun

139 Kidderminster Road
☎ (01299) 404177
1 (12 Fri & Sat)–11; 12–4.30, 7–10.30 Sun
Banks's Mild, Bitter Ⓔ;
Marston's Pedigree Ⓗ
Sympathetically renovated, friendly local with a small, comfortable family room. An L-shaped main bar room retains the effect of two distinct drinking areas. Rich's traditional cider.

Q ⏰ ✿ ⇌ (SVR) ♣ ○

Try also: Woodcolliers Arms, Welch Gate (Free)

Birtsmorton

Farmer's Arms

Birts Street (signed off B4208)
OS792363 ☎ (01684) 833308
11–2.30, 6–11 (11–11 summer Sat); 12–2.30, 7–10.30 (12–10.30 summer) Sun
Hook Norton Best Bitter, Old Hooky; guest beer
(weekends) Ⓗ
Black and white country pub, tucked away down a lane: a small lounge with a very low beamed ceiling, plus a larger, more basic bar with darts and games. The large garden with swings has a fine view of the Malvern Hills. Guest beers come from local breweries.

🏚 Q ✿ ◑ ♣ P

Bournheath

Gate Inn

Dodford Road
☎ (01527) 878169
11–2.30, 6–10.30 (11 Fri & Sat); 12–3, 7–10.30 Sun
Boddingtons Bitter; Smiles Best, Heritage; guest beer Ⓗ
Busy village pub with an emphasis on food, specialising in Mexican and Cajun dishes, plus up to 20 vegetarian options. A rare outlet for Smiles. Families welcome though facilities are minimal.

🏚 ✿ ◑ ▷ & P

Bretforton

Fleece ☆

The Cross (signed off B4035)
☎ (01386) 831173
11–2.30, 6–11; 12–2.30, 7–10.30 Sun
Highgate Fox's Nob; M&B Brew XI; Uley Old Spot; guest beers Ⓗ
Famous old pub owned by the NT. The interior (including a no-smoking room) has been untouched for many years, boasting inglenooks, antique furniture and a world-famous pewter collection. The large garden is popular with families.

🏚 Q ⏰ ✿ ◑ ▷ ⊞ ♣ ○ ✗

Broadway

Crown & Trumpet

Church Street
☎ (01386) 853202
11–2.30 (3.30 summer), 4.45–11; 11–11 Sat; 12–3.30, 6–10.30 Sun
Boddingtons Bitter; Flowers IPA; Morland Old Speckled Hen; Stanway Stanney Bitter; Wadworth 6X Ⓗ
Fine, 17th-century Cotswold stone inn, complete with oak beams and log fires. Deservedly popular with locals, tourists and walkers. Unusual range of pub games.

🏚 ✿ 🏠 ◑ ▷ ▲ ♣ P

Bromsgrove

Hop Pole

78 Birmingham Road
☎ (01527) 870100
12–2.30, 5.30–11; 12–3, 7–11 Sat; 12–3, 7–10.30 Sun
Draught Bass; M&B Brew XI; Red Cross Nailers OBJ, OKJ (occasional) Ⓗ
Excellent, no-frills, street-corner local near the Rovers football ground. A small, L-shaped bar serves two lounges with a good, bustling atmosphere. The main outlet for Red Cross beers. Good value food (not served Sun). The upstairs function room is used by many societies.

✿ ◑

Castlemorton

Plume of Feathers

Feathers Pitch (B4208)
☎ (01684) 833554
11–11; 12–10.30 Sun
Draught Bass Ⓖ; **Brandy Cask Whistling Joe; Hobsons Best Bitter; Marston's Bitter** Ⓗ;
guest beers Ⓗ/Ⓖ
Classic country pub with fine views of the Malvern Hills from the front garden and Bredon Hill from the back garden. The bar is heavily beamed; separate dining area. The beer range can vary, but never disappoints! Good food (home-made dishes and grills).

🏚 Q ⏰ ✿ ◑ ▷ ▲ ♣ ○ P

Caunsall

Anchor Inn

600 yds from A449
☎ (01562) 850254
12–4, 7–11; 12–3, 7–10.30 Sun
Draught Bass; Highgate Dark; Stones Bitter Ⓗ
Pleasant, two-roomed pub in a small village, a short walk from the Staffs & Worcs Canal. Filled rolls are available.

Q ⏰ ✿ & ▲ ♣ P

Chaddesley Corbett

Swan

☎ (01562) 777302
11–3, 6–11; 11–11 Fri & Sat; 12–3, 7–10.30 Sun
Batham Mild, Best Bitter, XXX (Christmas) Ⓗ
Friendly old village pub with a bar, large lounge and a restaurant, all serving a good range of good value food (not Sun eve). Jazz Thu eve; barbecues in summer. Weston's Old Rosie Cider.

🏚 ✿ ◑ ▷ ⊞ ♣ ○ P

Try also: Fox, Bromsgrove Rd (Theakston)

Clent

Bell & Cross

Holy Cross (off A491, signed Clent)
☎ (01562) 730319
12–3, 6–11; 12–4, 7–10.30 Sun
Banks's Mild, Bitter; Marston's Pedigree Ⓗ
Unspoilt gem based on traditional values; three cosy rooms each with a real fire. Families welcome. Morris dancers perform in summer. A guest beer appears at Christmas. Eve meals Tue–Sat.
🏚 Q ♿ ☀ ◖ ▶ ⊟ ♣

Cutnall Green

New Inn

Kidderminster Road (A442)
☎ (01299) 851202
12–3, 5.30 (6 Sat)–11; 12–3, 7–10.30 Sun
Banks's Mild; Marston's Pedigree, HBC Ⓗ
Welcoming village local serving good, home-cooked bar food and a full restaurant menu with an international flavour. Cider is sometimes available in summer.
🏚 ☀ ◖ ▶ ♣ P

Dodford

Dodford Inn

Whinfield Road (off A448, near Bournheath) OS939726
☎ (01527) 832470
12–3, 7 (5.30 summer)–11; 12–3 (4 summer), 7–10.30 Sun
Greenalls Bitter, Original; guest beers Ⓗ
Superb, basic, single-bar country pub set amidst eight acres of rolling countryside. Ideal for walkers/cyclists, it serves good value, home-cooked food. Children's certificate. Listed camping/Caravan Club site. Local CAMRA *Pub of the Year* 1996.
🏚 ☀ ◖ ▶ Å ♣ ⌂ P ⚲

Droitwich

Railway Inn

Kidderminster Road
☎ (01905) 770056
12–3, 5.30–11 (11–11 summer); 11.30–11 Sat; 12–3, 7–10.30 Sun
Banks's Mild; Marston's Bitter, Pedigree, HBC Ⓗ
Small, basic, two-roomed canalside pub with a good atmosphere in bars adorned with steam railway memorabilia; the friendly landlord is a railway enthusiast. Good value bar meals, all freshly prepared (no food Sun). A large roof-top patio overlooks the restored canal basin.
☀ ◖ ⊟ ⇌ ♣ P

Dunley

Dog Inn

On A451 ☎ (01299) 822833
12–3, 5.30–11; 12–11 Sat; 12–4, 7–10.30 (12–10.30 summer) Sun
Hobsons Best Bitter; Theakston Best Bitter; guest beers Ⓗ
Traditional, wisteria-clad country pub with a lounge, public bar and a games room. Outside there is a garden, play area and crown green bowls.
🏚 ☀ ◖ ▶ ⊟ Å ♣ ⌂ P

Eldersfield

Greyhound Inn

Lime Street (off B4211) OS815304 ☎ (01452) 840381
11.30–3.30, 7–11; 12–3, 7–10.30 Sun
Butcombe Bitter; Wadworth 6X; guest beers Ⓖ
Very traditional, isolated country pub, comprising a lounge and adjoining bar, plus a skittle alley-cum-function room. An archetypal rural boozer with a warm welcome. Note the dovecote in the garden where quoits are played. No food Mon.
🏚 Q ☀ ◖ ▶ Å ♣ P

Evesham

Green Dragon

17 Oat Street ☎ (01386) 446337
11–2.30, 7–11; 11–11 Fri & Sat; 12–2.30, 7–10.30 Sun
Courage Directors; Evesham Asum Ale, Asum Gold; guest beers Ⓗ
Busy, town-centre pub with its own brewery: a large modern bar in a 16th-century building, plus a small lounge and dining area (no food Sun eve).
Q ☀ ◖ ▶ ⊟ ⇌ ♣

Trumpet Inn

13 Merstow Green
☎ (01386) 446227
11–11; 12–10.30 Sun
Banks's Bitter; guest beer Ⓗ
Popular pub where the large lounge area is elegantly decorated with risqué 1950s prints. 🏚 ☀ ◖ ⇌

Forhill

Peacock Inn

Icknield Street (2 miles from A441) OS054755
☎ (01564) 823232
12–11; 12–10.30 Sun
Banks's Mild, Bitter; Enville Bitter; Judges Old Gavel Bender, Solicitor's Ruin; guest beers Ⓗ
Although recently extended to include a restaurant, this pub's chatty atmosphere has not been affected. Open fires contribute to the ambience. Bar billiards and bagatelle are played. 🏚 ☀ ◖ ▶ ⊟ Å ♣ P ⚲

Great Malvern

Foley Arms Hotel

14 Worcester Road
☎ (01684) 573397
12–3, 5.30–11; 12–11 Sat; 12–3.30, 7–10.30 Sun
Draught Bass; guest beers Ⓗ
Popular bar in an enlarged 1810 coaching inn affording splendid views across the Severn Valley from the bar and terrace. Three imaginative guest beers offer a choice of strengths. Busy at weekends, but solace can be sought in the lounge areas.
☀ ⛵ ◖ ▶ ⇌ ♣ P ⚲

Hanley Castle

Three Kings ☆

Church End (off B4211) OS838420
☎ (01684) 592686
12–3 (may vary), 7–11; 12–3, 7–10.30 Sun
Butcombe Bitter; Thwaites Bitter; guest beers Ⓗ
Marvellous, unspoilt village pub, over 80 years in the same family: a tiny bar with an inglenook, plus a larger 'Nells Bar'. Occasional live music; great atmosphere and welcome. CAMRA national *Pub of the Year* 1993. No eve meals Sun.
🏚 Q ☀ ☀ ⛵ ◖ ▶ ⊟ ♣ ⌂

Kempsey

Walter de Cantelupe Inn

Main Road (A38)
☎ (01905) 820572
12–2.30 (not Mon), 6 (7 Mon)–11; 12–2.30, 7–10.30 Sun
Marston's Bitter; Taylor Landlord; guest beers Ⓗ
Cosy, welcoming pub offering a beer price discount for card-carrying CAMRA members. The small restaurant area serves good food (no meals Sun/Mon eves).
🏚 ☀ ◖ ▶ Å P

Kidderminster

Boar's Head

Worcester Street
☎ (01562) 862450
11–11; 12–3, 7–10.30 Sun
Banks's Mild, Bitter; Camerons Strongarm; Marston's Pedigree; guest beers Ⓗ
Lively town-centre pub with two bars and a covered yard to the rear with further seating. Real fires and bar billiards feature. No food Sun.
🏚 ☀ ◖ ⇌ ♣ ⊟

319

King & Castle
SVR Station, Comberton Hill
(opp. mainline station)
☎ (01562) 747505
11–3, 5–11; 11–11 Sat; 12–10.30 Sun
Beer range varies Ⓗ
Friendly, single-bar pub, part
of the Severn Valley Railway's
southern terminus, an
authentic recreation of a 1930s
station bar/buffet. Children
allowed in until 9. Full station
facilities (e.g. wheelchair WC)
available when trains are
operating. Eve meals served
Thu–Sun. One mild is always
on tap.
🏚 Q ❀ ◑ ▷ ᕼ ⇌ ♣ P

Station Inn
7 Farfield (off Comberton Hill)
☎ (01562) 822764
12–3, 6–11; 12–11 Fri & Sat; 12–3,
7–10.30 Sun
**Banks's Mild; Davenports
Bitter; Greenalls Original;
Tetley Bitter** Ⓗ
Hidden in a quiet street, just
above the stations, this
welcoming pub has a public
bar, a comfortable lounge and
a pleasant, safe garden.
Weekday lunches; filled rolls
served eves and weekends.
Q ❀ ◑ ᕼ ᕼ ⇌ ♣ P

Try also: Red Man, Blackwell
St (Carlsberg-Tetley)

Leigh Sinton

Royal Oak
Malvern Road (A4103/B4503
jct)
☎ (01886) 832664
11–3, 6–11; 12–3, 7–10.30 Sun
Marston's Bitter, Pedigree Ⓗ
Friendly, two-roomed, cosy
village local with lots of low
beams and an impressive
collection of implements,
brasses and knick-knacks. The
genial Irish host ensures a
lively flow of conversation. A
good range of food is available
lunchtimes.
🏚 Q ❀ ◑ ᕼ ♣ P

Little Malvern

Malvern Hills Hotel
Wynds Point (A449/B4232 jct)
☎ (01684) 540237
11–3, 7–11 (11–11 summer); 12–3,
7–10.30 (12–10.30 summer) Sun
**Draught Bass; Hobsons Best
Bitter; guest beer** Ⓗ
Comfortable hotel lounge bar
in an upmarket weekend
retreat, ideally placed on the
ridge of the Malvern Hills.
Walkers are welcomed but are
asked to remove their boots
before entering. The restaurant
offers a full à la carte menu –
but no chips. The guest beer is
often from Otter or Wood
breweries.
🏚 Q ❀ ᕼ ◑ ▷ P

Menithwood

Cross Keys Inn
1 mile off B4202 OS709690
☎ (01584) 881425
11–3, 6–11; 11–11 Thu–Sat; 12–3,
7–10.30 Sun
**Marston's Bitter, Pedigree;
guest beer** Ⓗ
Comfortable country local with
a friendly atmosphere in a
number of drinking areas
around a single bar. Well
worth seeking out. Sandwiches
available.
🏚 Q ᕼ ❀ ᕼ ᕼ ▲ ♣ P

Offenham

Bridge Inn
Boat Lane (follow signs for
river or ferry)
☎ (01386) 446565
11–11; 12–10.30 Sun
**Banks's Bitter; Theakston
Best Bitter, XB; guest beers** Ⓗ
Ancient riverside inn with its
own moorings (but no bridge).
Thriving local trade; warm
welcome for visitors. Guest
beers are usually from local
independents. Well worth a
try. 🏚 Q ❀ ◑ ▷ ♣ P

Ombersley

Crown & Sandys Arms
Main Street (off A449)
☎ (01905) 620252
11–3, 5.30–11; 12–3, 7–10.30 Sun
**Hook Norton Best Bitter, Old
Hooky; guest beers** Ⓗ
Hotel in a pretty village, with a
delightful historic interior and
a wonderful open fireplace.
The guest beers usually feature
local ales. Excellent, home-
made food is served, with at
least three vegetarian dishes.
🏚 Q ❀ ᕼ ◑ ▷ P

Pensax

Bell
On B4202 ☎ (01299) 896677
12–2.30, 6–11; 12–11 Sat; 12–10.30 Sun
**Hook Norton Best Bitter;
guest beers** Ⓗ
Popular country pub where a
varied beer list has an
emphasis on microbrewers.
The bar is surrounded by
different drinking areas; the
dining room serves good value
meals. 🏚 Q ❀ ◑ ▷ ◔ P

Pershore

Brandy Cask
25 Bridge Street
☎ (01386) 552602
11.30–2.30 (3 Sat), 7–11; 12–3, 7–10.30
Sun
**Brandy Cask Whistling Joe,
Brandy Snapper, John Baker's
Original; Ruddles Best Bitter,
County** Ⓗ

Popular, town-centre brew pub
with a riverside garden and a
brasserie. The beer is brewed at
the rear. Beer festival Aug
Bank Hol. Q ❀ ◑ ▷ ▲ ♣

Try also: Millers Arms, Bridge
St (Wadworth)

Redditch

Brodie's Bar
(Crazy Eddie's)
163 Evesham Road, Headless
Cross
☎ (01527) 550448
5.30 (3 Fri, 12 Sat)–11; 12–3.30, 7–10.30
Sun
**Boddingtons Bitter; guest
beers** Ⓗ
Fun pub with interesting decor
and a young clientele. The
guest beer changes every
couple of days. Beer
promotion every Sun lunch.
Over 50 bottled beers
from around the world.
❀ ♣

Seven Stars
75 Birchfield Road, Headless
Cross
☎ (01527) 402138
12–11; 12–4, 7–10.30 Sun
**Marston's Pedigree;
Theakston Best Bitter;
Webster's Yorkshire Bitter** Ⓗ
Very much a drinkers' pub –
small, with a good atmosphere.
The walls are covered with
snatches of conversations
overheard in the bar. Limited
on-street parking.
❀ ᕼ ♣ ◔

Shrawley

New Inn
New Inn Lane OS798663
☎ (01299) 822701
12–2.30, 6–11 (12–11 summer); 12–
10.30 Sun
**Banks's Mild; Marston's
Bitter, Pedigree, HBC** Ⓗ
Cosy, welcoming pub in a
quiet hamlet with a small
lounge and a dining room
(families welcome). No food
winter Sun eve.
🏚 Q ❀ ◑ ▷ ᕼ ♣ P

Stoke Works

Boat & Railway
Shaw Lane (1 mile from B4091
jct) OS943663
☎ (01527) 831065
11.30–3, 6–11; 12–3, 7–10.30 Sun
**Banks's Hanson's Mild,
Bitter** Ⓔ**; Morrells Graduate** Ⓗ
Busy, canalside village local: a
small lounge and a tidy public
bar, plus a skittle alley. Popular
with boat people (moorings
available); canalside patio. No
food Sun eve.
🏚 ᕼ ❀ ◑ ▷ ᕼ ♣ 🍴

Stourport-on-Severn

Holly Bush
54 Mitton Street
☎ (01299) 822569
12–3, 7–11; 11–11 Sat; 12–10.30 Sun
Enville Ale; Hobsons Best Bitter; guest beers H
Small, friendly pub close to the town centre and canal with a single bar and three drinking areas. Guest beers come from independent breweries. The pub operates an over-21 rule. Bar food served 12–8 Sun.
🏠 ❀ ◑ ▶ Å ♣

Old Crown
9 Bridge Street
☎ (01299) 822187
11–11; 12–10.30 Sun
Banks's Mild; Bass Toby Cask, Draught Bass; Greene King Abbot H
Town-centre pub with a large single room incorporating a dining area and a long bar. Close to the river, it gets busy at weekends. Food served 12–9.
◑ ▶ Å P ⊁

Wheatsheaf
39 High Street
☎ (01299) 822613
10.30–11; 12–10.30 Sun
Banks's Hanson's Mild, Mild, Bitter E; **Marston's Pedigree** H
Pleasant town-centre pub a few mins' walk from the river and canal, with lounge and public bars. Children's certificate.
❀ ◑ ▶ Å ♣ P ⛾

Try also: Rising Sun, Lombard St (Banks's)

Tenbury Wells

Ship Inn
Teme Street ☎ (01584) 810269
11–2.30, 7–11; 12–3, 7–10.30 Sun
Ansells Bitter; guest beers H
Well-furnished, market town pub with some character. It features a restaurant and a large garden. The emphasis is on quality rather than quantity, hence only two ales.
❀ 🛏 ◑ ▶

Uphampton

Fruiterer's Arms
Uphampton Lane (off A449 at Reindeer pub) OS839649
☎ (01905) 620305
12.30–3, 7–11; 12–3, 7–10.30 Sun
Cannon Royall Fruiterer's Mild, Arrowhead, Buckshot, Old Merrie (winter)**; John Smith's Bitter** H
Award-winning country pub run by the same family for 150 years: a friendly place to enjoy

a very reasonably-priced pint. The cosy lounge features a wood-burning stove; the bar is larger. Good value lunches (not served Sun). Home of Cannon Royall brewery.
🏠 Q ❀ ◑ 🛏 Å ♣ ⛬ P

Upton upon Severn

Old Anchor Inn
High Street ☎ (01684) 592146
11–11; 12–3, 7–10.30 (varies summer) Sun
Theakston Best Bitter, XB H
Popular, listed, town-centre inn built in 1601. Narrow doors add character. Popular with locals, especially during Festival events in the town.
🏠 Q ❀ ◑ Å ♣

Weatheroak

Coach & Horses
Weatheroak Hill (Alvechurch–Wythall road)
☎ (01564) 823386
11.30–2.30, 5.30 (6 Sat)–11 (may open 11–11); 12–3, 7–10.30 Sun
Boddingtons Bitter; Flowers Original; Hook Norton Old Hooky; Marston's Pedigree; Wood Special; guest beers H
Set in rolling hills, this pub's beer is racked behind the bar on the flagged floor. A number of rooms at different levels, from bar to restaurant, give character. A patio enhances the pleasures of alfresco drinking.
🏠 ❀ ◑ ▶ 🛏 Å ♣ ⛬ P

Welland

Anchor Inn
Drake Street (200 yds off A4104) OS813403
☎ (01684) 592317
12–3, 7–11; 12–3, 7–10.30 Sun (closed winter Sun eve)
Draught Bass; Black Sheep Best Bitter; guest beers H
Comfortable, beamed country pub with an extensive bar food board and a cosy restaurant. Children are welcome in the large garden, but check before taking under-14s into the bar. Camping is in the field next to the pub. Anchor house ale comes from a small independent brewer.
🏠 Q ❀ ◑ ▶ Å ♣ P

Worcester

Bell Inn
35 St Johns ☎ (01905) 424570
11–3 (4 Sat), 7–11; 12–3, 7–10.30 Sun
M&B Mild, Brew XI; guest beer H
Popular local, west of the River Severn and ten mins' walk from the county cricket ground: a bar with TV and a jukebox, plus two quiet, characterful side rooms. Skittle alley. 🛏 ❀ ♣

Cardinal's Hat
Friar Street ☎ (01905) 22222
11–11; 12–10.30 Sun
Banks's Mild, Bitter; Marston's Pedigree; guest beers H
Worcester's oldest pub was established in 1482 and almost perished with the demise of the Jolly Roger Brewery. Its three rooms have been well restored by the new owners, Banks's. Three guest beers. ❀ ◑ ▶ 🛏

Dragon Inn
51 The Tything
☎ (01905) 25845
11–11; 4–10.30 (closed lunch) Sun
Marston's Bitter; Taylor Landlord; guest beers H
A *Guide* regular, near the cinema: a one-roomed bar, popular with musicians for folk sessions Wed eves and blues Sun. A rare outlet in the city for real cider. Parking is tricky. ❀ ⇌ (Foregate St) ⛬

Lamb & Flag
The Tything ☎ (01905) 26894
10.30–2.30, 5.30–11; 12–2, 7–10.30 Sun
Marston's Bitter, Pedigree H
Small, two-roomed local just outside the city centre. Jukebox in the public bar; the lounge bar is quieter. The tables and chairs are basic in this no-frills, drinking pub with a strong Irish flavour. It can get smoky.
Q ❀ ⇌ (Foregate St) ♣

Olde Talbot Hotel
Friar Street ☎ (01905) 23573
11–11; 12–10.30 Sun
Banks's Bitter; Greene King Abbot H**; guest beers** H/G
Relaxed, oak-beamed, city-centre bar/lounge – part of a two-star hotel. Six ales on handpump in winter, with possibly two more on gravity.
❀ 🛏 ◑ ▶ P

Sebright Arms
158 London Road
☎ (01905) 355142
11–11; 12–10.30 Sun
Banks's Mild; Marston's Bitter, Pedigree, HBC H
Refurbished, suburban pub with a lively, welcoming atmosphere and an attractive patio and children's play area at the rear. No food Sun.
❀ ◑ ▶ P

Virgin Tavern
Tolladine Road (opp. golf course) ☎ (01905) 23988
11–3, 5–11; 11–11 Sat; 12–4, 7–10.30 Sun
Marston's Bitter, Pedigree, Owd Roger (winter)**, HBC** H
Spacious, modernised, one-roomer with a large drinking area on three sides of the bar. Good value bar snacks; children's menu (and play equipment in the garden).
❀ ◑ ♣ P

Yorkshire

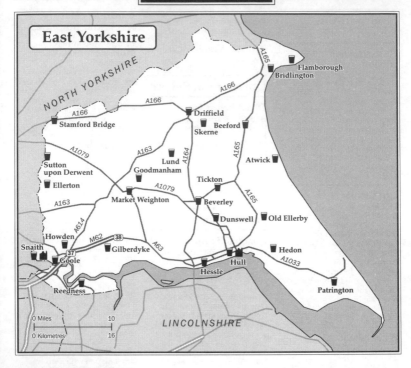

East Yorkshire

Atwick

Black Horse
☎ (01964) 532691
11–4, 7–11; 11–11 Sat; 12–10.30 Sun
John Smith's Bitter; guest beers H
Superb village pub dated circa 1750, overlooking the village green. The bar serves three rooms, one of which doubles as a restaurant, although food is served in all areas of the pub. Look out for Whale and Chips among the good value, mainly home-cooked dishes. Guest ales change almost daily.
❀ ◑ ♿ ♣ P

Beeford

Tiger
Main Street (A165/B1249 jct)
☎ (01262) 488733
11.30–3, 6–11 (11–11 Apr–Oct); 12–3, 6–10.30 Sun
John Smith's Bitter; guest beers H
Old coaching house with its original horse mounting steps outside: a traditional bar and a comfortable lounge with a restaurant; real fires in all three areas. Extensive garden with a play area. Barbecues are held in summer months.
🏨 ❀ ◑ ♿ ♣ P

Beverley

Grovehill
183 Holme Church Lane (1 mile E of centre)
☎ (01482) 867409
11.30–2, 7–11; 11–11 Sat; 12–10.30 Sun
Marston's Bitter, Pedigree H
Pub built in the 1920s by Moors & Robson: a plain bar and a well-furnished lounge. Popular with pigeon fanciers, model enthusiasts and motorcyclists. A rare local outlet for Marston's. ♿ ❀ ♿ ♣ P

Oddfellows Arms
15 Eastgate ☎ (01482) 868139
11–11; 12–10.30 Sun
Mansfield Riding Mild, Riding Bitter, Old Baily H
Unspoilt, street-corner local near the Minster, Masonic Lodge and the station. A tiled entrance lobby leads to a public bar (with original windows and bench seating) and to a front parlour (with a listed, cast iron fireplace). Games room. 🏨 ♿ ⇌ ♣

Queen's Head
Wednesday Market
☎ (01482) 867363
11–11; 12–10.30 Sun
Vaux Mild, Waggle Dance; Ward's Thorne BB; guest beer H
Pub with an attractive brewer's Tudor exterior overlooking the town's smaller market place. Well-refurbished in 1996, it was opened out into a modern extension which forms a lounge and games area. Eve meals end at 8. ◑ ♿ ⇌

Rose & Crown
North Bar Without
☎ (01482) 862532
11–3, 5–11; 12–10.30 Sun
Vaux Double Maxim, Waggle Dance; Ward's Thorne BB, Best Bitter; guest beer H
Substantial brewer's Tudor pub next to the historic North Bar, Westwood and racecourse. Popular for home-made food in the comfortable lounge and smoke room. Q ❀ ◑ ♿ ♣ P

Royal Standard Inn
30 North Bar Within
☎ (01482) 882434
12–4, 6.30–11; 12–6.30, 7–10.30 Sun
Vaux Double Maxim; Ward's Thorne BB H
Two-roomed town local in a white-painted terrace between North Bar and St Mary's church. The front bar features 1920s bentwood seating and an etched Darley's window; well-furnished lounge to the rear.
❀ ◑

🍺 **INDEPENDENT BREWERIES**

Hull: Hull

Old Mill: Snaith

Tap & Spile (Sun Inn)
1 Flemingate ☎ (01482) 881547
12 (11 Sat)–11; 12–10.30 Sun
Beer range varies H
Sympathetic restoration of a
medieval, timber-framed
building; Beverley's oldest
pub, set opposite the Minster.
The eight guest beers have
transformed the local drinking
scene. Bar billiards.
🏠 ◖ ⇌ ♣ ◠ ⊁

Bridlington

Bull & Sun
11 Baylegate ☎ (01262) 676105
11–11; 12–3,30, 7–10.30 Sun
**Vaux Mild, Double Maxim;
Ward's Thorne BB; guest
beer** H
Former millinery shop near the
historic Baylegate and priory: a
large, one-roomer with two
distinct drinking areas. Eve
meals served Easter–
Christmas. ◖ ▶

New Crown
158 Quay Road
☎ (01262) 604370
11–11; 12–10.30 Sun
**Vaux Waggle Dance; Ward's
Best Bitter** H
Substantial Victorian pub
between the old town and the
harbour. The large bar/games
room, with its wooden floor, is
popular with all ages; the
lounge is spacious and
comfortable. 🏠 ⇌ ♣

Old Ship Inn
90 St John Street
☎ (01262) 670466
11–11; 12–10.30 Sun
**Vaux Mild, Samson, Double
Maxim; Ward's Thorne BB;
guest beer** H
Thriving local by the old town,
with a traditional atmosphere,
comfortable drinking areas and
a pool table in the large bar.
Outdoor play area for children.
Q ☺ 🏠 ◖ ♣

Pack Horse Inn
7 Market Place
☎ (01262) 675701
11–3 (may extend summer), 7–11;
12–3, 7–10.30 Sun
Burtonwood Bitter, Top Hat H
Listed old building, thought to
be 300 years old. The upper
windows give the impression
of three storeys but the pub is
in fact only two (a relic from
the Daylight Tax days). Inside
there is an open-plan lounge
and a pool room. 🏠 ◖ ♣

Seabirds
6 Fortyfoot (1 mile N of centre)
☎ (01262) 674174
11–11; 12–10.30 Sun
**Camerons Bitter, Strongarm;
guest beer** H
Large, attractively extended
pub: a comfortable bar with a
pool table and a well-furnished

lounge decorated with sailing
items. 🏠 ◖ ▶ ♣ P ⊟

Driffield

Bell Hotel
Market Place
☎ (01377) 256661
10–2.30, 6–11; 10–11 Thu; 12–3,
7–10.30 Sun
Stones Bitter; guest beer H
Historic coaching inn and
restaurant, with a wood-
panelled bar serving 250
whiskies. Leather seating,
substantial fireplaces and
antiques lend a quality feel.
Hotel accommodation.
Q 🏠 ◖ ▶ 🏠 ◖ P

Mariner's Arms
47 Eastgate (near cattle market)
☎ (01377) 253708
3–11 (11.45 Sat); 12–10.30 Sun
**Burtonwood Mild, Bitter,
seasonal beers** H
Traditional, market town,
street-corner local that has
retained its two rooms.
Friendly atmosphere.
🏠 🏠 ⇌ ♣ P

Dunswell

Ship Inn
Beverley Road (A1174, Hull
road)
☎ (01482) 859160
11–11; 12–10.30 Sun
**Hull Mild; Ind Coope Burton
Ale; Tetley Bitter** H
Welcoming pub, part of which
is a dining area with church
pew seating. Tasty, home-
cooked food served 11–7 (12–3
Sun). 🏠 🏠 ◖ ▶ ♣ P

Ellerton

Boot & Shoe
Main Street (off B1228)
☎ (01757) 288346
6–11; 12–3, 7–10.30 Sun
**Old Mill Bitter; John Smith's
Bitter** H
Cosy gem in a quiet village.
Dating back 400 years, it has
authentic low beams. Excellent
choice of food.
🏠 Q 🏠 ◖ ▶ ♣ P

Flamborough

Rose & Crown
High Street
☎ (01262) 850455
11–3, 7–11; 12–3, 7–10.30 Sun
**Camerons Bitter; Tetley
Bitter** H
Small pub, frequented by local
fishermen. The L-shaped room
has a beamed ceiling and walls
decorated with local scenes.
The pool table is nicely tucked
away. Meals in summer.
◖ ▲ ♣ P

Gilberdyke

Cross Keys Inn
Main Road (B1230, W edge of
village) ☎ (01430) 440310
12–11; 12–10.30 Sun
**Boddingtons Bitter; John
Smith's Bitter; Tetley Bitter;
guest beers** H
Welcoming pub on the old
A63, with a strong local
following of all ages who
appreciate the emphasis on
traditional beer and games.
Three rotating guest beers.
🏠 🏠 ♣ P

Goodmanham

Goodmanham Arms
Main Street ☎ (01430) 873849
7 (12 Sat)–11; 12–3, 7–10.30 Sun
**Black Sheep Best Bitter;
Theakston Best Bitter; guest
beer** H
Superb country pub offering a
warm welcome. Popular with
walkers (the Wolds Way runs
past the door). The gents' WC
is in the car park. A rural gem.
🏠 Q 🏠 🏠 🏠 ▲ ♣ P

Goole

Old George
Market Square
☎ (01405) 763147
11–3, 7–11; 7–11 (closed lunch) Sun
**John Smith's Bitter; Stones
Bitter** H
Oddly-shaped old building
with one room divided into
three distinct sections. Good
value lunches (not served Sun)
draw a varied clientele.
🏠 ◖ ⇌ P

Macintosh Arms
13 Aire Street
☎ (01405) 763850
11–11; 12–10.30 Sun
**John Smith's Bitter; Tetley
Dark Mild, Bitter; guest
beer** H
Historic building alongside the
docks. Note the original
ceilings, visible through
skylights in the modern
suspended ceilings. Very busy
weekend eves, but the front bar
remains relatively calm.
🏠 🏠 ⇌ P

Hedon

Shakespeare Inn
9 Baxtergate ☎ (01482) 898371
11–11; 12–10.30 Sun
**Vaux Mild, Samson; Ward's
Thorne BB, Best Bitter; guest
beer** H
Popular one-roomer noted for
its food, range of whiskies,
brewery memorabilia and
interesting photos of old
Hedon, with modern
comparison shots. Eve meals

end at 7.30; no eve meals Sat/
Sun. 🏮 ⚶ ◁ ▶ ♣ P

Hessle

Darley's

Boothferry Road (A1105, near
Humber Bridge)
☎ (01482) 643121
11–3, 5.30–11; 11–11 Sat; 12–10.30 Sun
**Vaux Samson; Ward's Thorne
BB, Best Bitter** Ⓗ
Substantial brewer's Tudor
roadhouse on the old western
approach to Hull. Built in 1939,
and named after the brewery
closed in 1986, it retains its
public bar, comfortable lounge
and carvery restaurant (open
eves and Sun lunch).
Q ❀ ⚶ ◁ ▶ 🔲 ♣ P

Howden

Barnes Wallis

Station Road (B1228, 1 mile N
of town) ☎ (01430) 430639
5 (7 Mon, 12 Sat)–11; 12–10.30 Sun
**Boddingtons Bitter; Flowers
IPA; guest beers** Ⓗ
Friendly, open-plan pub next
to the station, always stocking
two interesting guest beers.
Snacks at weekends.
🏮 ⚶ ⅋ ⇌ P

Hull

Anlaby Ale House

283–285 Anlaby Road
☎ (01482) 328971
11–11; 12–10 30 Sun
**Banks's Bitter; Camerons
Bitter; Marston's Pedigree;
guest beers** Ⓗ
Refurbished Camerons ale
house with a split room
consisting of a bar area with
pool and darts, plus a lounge
area. Another quiet lounge is to
the rear. A house beer,
Kingston Mild, is Hanson's
Mild; three guest beers.
Q ⚶ ♣ 🍺

Bay Horse

113 Wincolmlee (400 yds N of
N Bridge on W bank of River
Hull) ☎ (01482) 329227
11–11; 12–4.30, 7–10.30 Sun
**Bateman Mild, XB, XXXB,
Victory; guest beer** Ⓗ
Cosy, street-corner local,
Bateman's only tied pub north
of the Humber. The public bar
contrasts with the spectacular,
lofty, stable lounge. Home-
cooked food is a speciality.
🏮 Q ◁ ▶ 🔲 ⅋ ♣ P

Duke of Wellington

104 Peel Street (N of Spring
Bank) ☎ (01482) 329603
12–3, 6–11; 12–11 Sat; 12–10.30 Sun
**Taylor Landlord; Tetley Bitter;
guest beers** Ⓗ
Good, re-styled, backstreet,
Victorian corner pub, popular
with locals and students; big

screen TV for sports. Home-
cooked food until 8.
⚶ ◁ ▶ ⅋ ♣ 🍺

Gardeners Arms

35 Cottingham Road
☎ (01482) 342396
11–11; 12–10.30 Sun
**Marston's Pedigree; Tetley
Bitter; guest beers** Ⓗ
Tetley Festival Ale House near
the university. The front room
is popular with locals and
students, with its dark wood,
bare brick walls and original
matchboard ceiling. Mr Q's
games room at the rear. Up to
five guest beers. ⚶ ◁ ▶ ⅋ P

King William

41 Market Place, Old Town
☎ (01482) 227013
11–11; 12–10.30 Sun
**Draught Bass; Courage
Directors; Cropton King Billy;
John Smith's Bitter; guest
beers** Ⓗ
Large, recently-built pub on
the site of the old King William
Hotel. It features a wood-
panelled lounge and a local
sporting heroes hall of fame.
Regular live music during the
week; very busy at weekends.
Eve meals weekdays 5–7.
⚶ ◁ ▶ ♣ P

Mission

11–13 Posterngate, Old Town
(By Princes Quay shopping
centre) ☎ (01482) 221187
11–11; 12–10.30 Sun
**Old Mill Mild, Nellie Dene,
Bitter, Old Curiosity, Bullion,
seasonal beers** Ⓗ
Old Mill's first Hull pub is a
converted seaman's mission.
Very large, somewhat like a
baronial hall, it includes a
minstrel's gallery and a
deconsecrated chapel. Very
busy at weekends; children's
certificate. Eve meals Fri and
Sat. ◁ ▶ ⅋ ⇌ (Paragon) ♣

New Clarence

77 Charles Street
☎ (01482) 320327
11–11; 12–10.30 Sun
**Marston's Pedigree; Tetley
Mild, Bitter; guest beers** Ⓗ
Tetley Festival Ale House off
Kingston Square, near the New
Theatre. It caters for all in a
relaxed atmosphere. Belgian
bottled beers stocked. Eve
meals until 7.30 (not Sun).
◁ ▶ ⇌ (Paragon) ♣ 🍺

Oberon

Queen Street ☎ (01482) 324886
11–3, 5.30–11; 11–11 Fri & Sat; 12–3,
7–10.30 Sun
**Bass Mild, Draught Bass;
Stones Bitter** Ⓗ
Traditional, basic, two-roomer,
near the pier and marina,
decorated with nautical
memorabilia and frequented
by Humber pilots. Games,

including bar billiards and
pool, in the back room.
Q 🔲 ♣

Old Blue Bell

Market Place, Old Town
☎ (01482) 324382
11–11; 7–10.30 Sun
Samuel Smith OBB Ⓗ
Interesting old town pub with
a narrow bar, snug, lounge and
a corridor. A courtyard
connects to the adjoining
market. Pool room upstairs.
⚶ ◁ ▶ ⅋ ♣

Olde Black Boy

150 High Street, Old Town
☎ (01482) 326516
12–3, 5–11; 12–3, 7–10.30 Sun
Beer range varies Ⓗ
Pub situated in Hull's historic
old town and sympathetically
refurbished as an unbadged
Tap & Spile. It retains a bar, a
wood-panelled front room,
where the pub's history is
displayed, an upstairs bar and
a dining room. The interior
warrants official protection.
Q ◁ ▶ ♣ 🍺

Red Lion

Clarence Street (400 yds E of
Drypool Bridge)
☎ (01482) 324773
12–11; 12–5, 7–11 Sat; 12–4, 7–10.30
Sun
**Hull Mild, Bitter, Amber Ale,
Northern Pride** Ⓗ
Pub built in 1939 for Moors &
Robsons, now the first tied
house for the present Hull
Brewery. It retains two rooms,
hosting weekend concerts in
the wood-panelled lounge.
🔲 ♣

Rugby Tavern

5 Dock Street ☎ (01482) 324759
11–4, 7–11; 11–11 Thu–Sat; closed Sun
Samuel Smith OBB Ⓗ
U-shaped, one-roomer with
comfortable seating and a nice
wooden facade; popular for
lunchtime food. It once stood
on Queens Dock, which was
filled in to form Queens
Gardens. Popular with
motorcyclists Fri and Sat
nights. ◁ ⇌ (Paragon) ♣

St John's Hotel

10 Queens Road (off Beverley
Rd) ☎ (01482) 343669
12–11; 12–10.30 Sun
**Mansfield Riding Mild,
Riding Bitter, Old Baily,
seasonal beers** Ⓗ
Victorian pub, the epitome of a
street-corner local, well-loved
by regulars and friendly to
visitors; 'Johnnies' is an
unpretentious multi-roomer.
The front corner bar retains its
original gaslight pipes across
the windows. Family room till
8.30. Q ❀ ⚶ 🔲 ⅋ ♣ P

Spring Bank Tavern

29 Spring Bank
☎ (01482) 581879
11–11; 12–3, 7–10.30 Sun
**Mansfield Riding Mild,
Riding Bitter, Bitter, Old
Baily, seasonal beers; guest
beers** H
Mansfield's first cask ale
house, sympathetically
refurbished as a street-corner
local. Usually three guest
beers. ◖ ⇌ (Paragon) ♣

Tap & Spile (Eagle)

169–171 Spring Bank
☎ (01482) 323518
12–11; 12–10.30 Sun
Beer range varies H
Conversion of a street-corner
local into a large, friendly ale
house constantly
changing beers and two ciders.
It can be very busy, but the
atmosphere is always
welcoming. Local CAMRA *Pub
of the Year* 1996. Sun lunch
served. ዿ ♣ ⌂ P ⊁

Varsity

10 Bowlalley Lane, Lowgate
Old Town ☎ (01482) 226543
11–11; 12–10.30 Sun
**Banks's Mild; Camerons
Bitter, Strongarm; Morrells
Varsity** H
A recent conversion of the Law
Society's Hall, in the heart of
the old town on the Land of
Green Ginger. A loud circuit
pub at weekends, its decor and
lighting could have been more
sympathetic to the building's
origins. A welcome addition to
the Old Town beer scene.
◖ ዿ ⊟

Wellington Inn

55 Russell Street
☎ (01482) 329486
11.30–3 (4.30 Thu), 7–11; 11.30–11 Fri
& Sat; 12–10.30 Sun
**Mansfield Riding Mild,
Riding Bitter, Old Baily,
seasonal beers** H
Rejuvenated, street-corner
one-roomer with a central bar
and a games area. Live music
Fri and Sat. Good value food.
❀ ◖ ⇌ (Paragon) P

Lund

Wellington Inn

19 The Green ☎ (01377) 217294
12–3 (not Mon), 7–11; 12–3, 7–10.30
Sun
**Bateman Mild; Black Sheep
Best Bitter; Taylor Landlord;
guest beer** (summer) H
Attractive inn overlooking the
village green, next to the
church. Completely renovated
in 1995, it has Yorkshire
flagstones, open fires and
quality seating. The restaurant
is open Tue–Sat eve and Sun
lunch. ⋈ ❀ ◖ ▶ ዿ ♣ P

Market Weighton

Carpenter's Arms

56 Southgate (A1034)
☎ (01430) 873446
11 (12 Sat)–11; 12–3, 7–10.30 Sun
**Vaux Samson; Ward's Thorne
BB** H
Extensive modernisation has
left one large room at this listed
building which now caters for
a young clientele. Strong darts
following. ♣ P

Half Moon Inn

39 High Street
☎ (01430) 872247
11–11; 12–10.30 Sun
**Burtonwood Bitter, Top Hat,
Buccaneer** H
Single-room, market town pub
which is friendly and popular
with locals. Note the 'original'
Hull Brewery wrought iron
gates to the car park.
❀ ♣ P

Old Ellerby

Blue Bell Inn

☎ (01964) 562364
7–11; 12–5; 7–11 Sat; 12–5, 7–10.30
(12–10.30 summer) Sun
**Tetley Dark Mild, Bitter;
guest beers** H
Cosy, characterful, village local
boasting lots of dark oak,
copper and brass. New games
room for darts and pool; large
outside area for families.
Barbecues are held in summer,
otherwise no food is served.
⋈ ❀ ዿ ♣ P

Patrington

Hildyard Arms

1 Market Place
☎ (01964) 630234
12–11; 12–10.30 Sun
**Tetley Dark Mild, Bitter;
guest beers** H
Four-roomed former coaching
inn which once served as a
corn exchange for local
farmers. Well-refurbished, it
has a variety of rooms. Eve
meals end at 8.30 (not served
Sun).
⋈ Q ❀ ◖ ▶ ⊞ ♣ P

Reedness

Half Moon

Main Street
☎ (01405) 704484
12–3 (not winter Mon–Fri), 7–11;
12–10.30 (12–4, 7–10.30 winter) Sun
Beer range varies H
Traditional, polished local with
a caravan and campsite
behind, on the bank of the
River Ouse, with Blacktoft
Sands RSPB reserve nearby.
Excellent food; popular
Sunday lunches are served.
⋈ ❀ ◖ ▶ ▲ ♣ P

Skerne

Eagle Inn ☆

Wansford Road
☎ (01377) 252178
7–11; 12–2, 7–11 Sat; 12–3, 7–10.30
Sun
Camerons Bitter H
Classic, unspoilt, village local
with a basic bar and a front
parlour. Drinks are served to
your table from a small cellar
off the entrance corridor. Beer
is dispensed from a Victorian
cash register beer engine.
Outside toilets.
⋈ Q ❀ ⊞ ♣ P

Snaith

Brewers Arms

10 Pontefract Road (A645)
☎ (01405) 862404
11–3, 6–11; 12–3, 7–10.30 Sun
**Old Mill Mild, Nellie Dene,
Bitter, Old Curiosity, Bullion,
Black Jack** H
Grade II-listed building: a
single large room with alcoves
and beams. A good selection of
food is served by friendly staff.
Don't forget to look down the
well. ❀ ⋈ ◖ ▶ ⇌ (limited
service) P

Downe Arms

15 Market Place
☎ (01405) 860544
11.30–2.30, 5–11; 11.30–11 Sat; 12–
10.30 Sun
Mansfield Riding Bitter H
Friendly, listed building
serving real food. Function
rooms available. ⋈ ❀ ◖ ⇌
(limited service) ♣ P

Stamford Bridge

Swordsman

Front Street (A166)
☎ (01759) 371307
12–11; 12–3, 7–10 Sun
Samuel Smith OBB H
Tiled floors and a view of the
river make this a popular pub
with visitors. A central bar
keeps the lounge separate.
Ϩ ❀ ◖ ▲ P

Sutton upon Derwent

St Vincent Arms

Main Street (B1228)
☎ (01904) 608349
11.30–3, 6–11; 12–3, 7–10.30 Sun
**Fuller's London Pride; Taylor
Landlord; Wells Bombardier;
guest beers** H
Popular, friendly country pub
known for its wide choice of
ales at very keen prices. Good,
wholesome food is also
reasonably priced. Only oversized glasses are used.
⋈ Q ❀ ◖ ▶ ♣ P ⊟

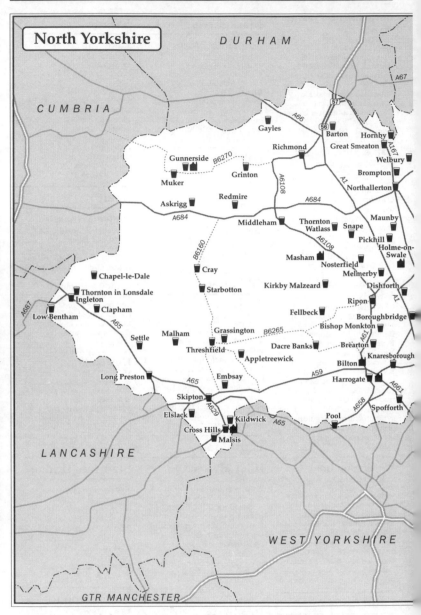

North Yorkshire

DURHAM

CUMBRIA

Gayles

Barton

Hornby

Richmond

Great Smeaton

Welbury

Gunnerside

Brompton

Grinton

Muker

Northallerton

Askrigg

Redmire

Maunby

Middleham

Thornton Watlass

Snape

Pickhill

Holme-on-Swale

Masham

Nosterfield

Melmerby

Dishforth

Chapel-le-Dale

Cray

Kirkby Malzeard

Thornton in Lonsdale

Starbotton

Fellbeck

Ripon

Boroughbridge

Ingleton

Clapham

Bishop Monkton

Low Bentham

Grassington

Brearton

Settle

Malham

Dacre Banks

Knaresborough

Threshfield

Appletreewick

Bilton

Long Preston

Embsay

Harrogate

Skipton

Spofforth

Elslack

Kildwick

Pool

Cross Hills

Malsis

LANCASHIRE

WEST YORKSHIRE

GTR MANCHESTER

Tickton

Tickton Arms
Main Street
☎ (01964) 542371
12–3, 6.30–11; 12–11 Sat; 12–3, 6.30–10.30 Sun
Banks's Mild; Camerons Bitter; Marston's Pedigree Ⓗ
Attractive, gabled pub in a suburbanised village east of Beverley. The etched tap room and smoke room doors lead into two drinking areas served by a central bar. Photos of rural scenes are displayed.
❀ ◑ ▶ 🍴 ♣ P

North Yorkshire

Acklam

Coronation at Acklam
Acklam Road (A1032/A1130 jct) ☎ (01642) 817599
11.30–11; 12–3, 7–10.30 Sun
Camerons Strongarm Ⓗ

Inter-war, brick-built pub, recently refurbished as a W&D house, with a bar, lounge and function room. Q ◑ 🍴 ♣ P 🍴

Aldborough

Ship Inn
Low Road ☎ (01423) 322749
11–3, 5.30–11; 12–3, 7–10.30 Sun
John Smith's Bitter; Tetley Bitter; Theakston Best Bitter Ⓗ
14th-century inn in an excellent setting in an historic village.

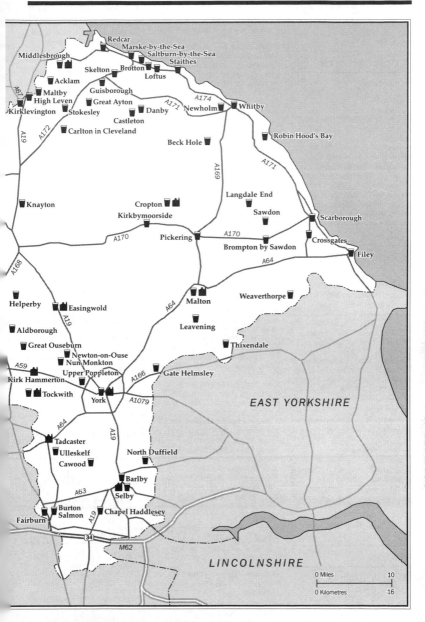

INDEPENDENT BREWERIES

Black Sheep: Masham

Cropton: Cropton

Daleside: Harrogate

Easingwold: Easingwold

Franklin's: Bilton

Hambleton: Holme-on-Swale

Malton: Malton

Marston Moor: Kirk Hammerton

North Yorkshire: Middlesbrough

Old Bear: Cross Hills

Rooster's: Harrogate

Rudgate: Tockwith

Selby: Selby

Samuel Smith: Tadcaster

Swaled Ale: Gunnerside

York: York

Known for its food, it can get busy mealtimes.
🏨 🌣 🚬 🄳 ♣ P 🖃

Appletreewick

New Inn

Main Street ☎ (01756) 720252
12–3 (not Mon, except bank hols), 7–11; 12–3, 7–10.30 Sun
Daleside Nightjar; John Smith's Bitter; Theakston XB Ⓗ
Friendly Dales hostelry whose owners specialise in outdoor activities. The main bar is L-shaped with another room across the hall. Extensive range of foreign bottled beers, and some on tap. Cider in summer.
🏨 🛏 🌣 🚬 🄳 ▲ ♣ ⏴ P

Askrigg

King's Arms Hotel

Main Street ☎ (01969) 650258
11–3, 6.30–11; 12–3, 7–10.30 Sun
Dent Bitter; John Smith's Bitter; Theakston XB; Younger No. 3; guest beer (occasional) Ⓗ
Classic Dales pub, an 18th-century coaching inn which appeared as the 'Drovers Arms' in TV's *All Creatures Great and Small*. Each room is full of character. Excellent bar food; sophisticated restaurant.
🏨 Q 🛏 🌣 🚬 🄳 🄳 ♿ ♣ P

Barlby

Bay Horse

York Road (off A19)
☎ (01257) 703878
3.30 (11 Sat)–11; 12–3, 7–10.30 Sun
Morland Old Speckled Hen; John Smith's Bitter Ⓗ
Small, friendly village pub with knocked through bars but still separate rooms. Keen darts team; various entertainments eves. Pizzas available.
Q 🌣 ♣ P

Barton

King William IV

1 Silver Street
☎ (01325) 377256
12–3 (not Mon or Tue; 11.30–4 Sat), 6.30 (5 Thu & Fri)–11; 12–3, 7–10.30 Sun
John Smith's Bitter, Magnet Ⓗ
Enlarged roadside local with a number of drinking spaces clustered around a single serving area. Excellent garden with play equipment. Thai meals are a speciality (no food Mon). 🏨 🄳 🄳 ♣ P

Beck Hole

Birch Hall Inn ☆

1 mile N of Goathland
OS822022 ☎ (01947) 896245

11–3, 7.30–11 (closed winter Mon eve; 11–11 summer); 12 (7.30 winter)–10.30 Sun
Black Sheep Best Bitter; Theakston Mild (summer), **Best Bitter, XB; guest beer** Ⓗ
Tiny, two-room, time-warp pub in a charming village in *Heartbeat* country. It also houses a small shop and serves teas. Popular with walkers, it is near N York Moors railway. Not to be missed.
🏨 Q 🌣 🄳 ♣

Bishop Monkton

Lamb & Flag

Boroughbridge Road
☎ (01765) 677322
12–3, 5.30–11; 12–3, 7–10.30 Sun
Black Sheep Best Bitter; Tetley Bitter; Theakston Best Bitter Ⓗ
Very friendly and welcoming country inn in an attractive village. 🏨 Q 🛏 🌣 🄳 ♣ P

Boroughbridge

Black Bull

6 St James Square
☎ (01423) 322413
11–11; 12–10.30 Sun
Black Sheep Best Bitter; John Smith's Bitter; guest beer Ⓗ
Friendly, historic, 13th-century free house with a large bar and a cosy snug. The spacious restaurant is popular for its quality meals. 🏨 Q 🚬 🄳 ▲

Three Horseshoes ☆

Bridge Street ☎ (01423) 322314
11–3, 5–11; 12–10.30 Sun
Black Sheep Best Bitter; Vaux Samson Ⓔ
Welcoming, friendly, genuinely unspoilt 1930s hotel: a true classic of its style.
🏨 Q 🛏 🌣 🚬 🄳 🄳 🄳 ▲ ♣ P

Brearton

Malt Shovel

Off B6165 ☎ (01423) 862929
12–3, 6.30–11; 12–3, 7–10.30 Sun; closed Mon
Daleside Nightjar; Old Mill Bitter; Theakston Best Bitter; guest beer Ⓗ
Welcoming, unspoilt, 16th-century village pub with exposed stone and beams. Good, home-cooked food (not served Sun eve). Cider in summer.
🏨 Q 🛏 🌣 🄳 🄳 ♣ ⏴ P

Brompton (Northallerton)

Crown Inn

Station Road ☎ (01609) 772547
12–3 (not Tue), 7–11; 11–11 Fri & Sat; 12–10.30 Sun
John Smith's Bitter, Magnet; guest beers Ⓗ

Plain village local opened out into a single long bar, stocking a wide range of guest beers.
🏨 🌣 ♣ P

Brompton by Sawdon

Cayley Arms

On A170 ☎ (01723) 859372
11.30–2.30 (not Mon), 5.30–11; 12–3, 7–10.30 Sun
Tetley Bitter; Theakston Best Bitter, XB; guest beer Ⓗ
Prominent roadside pub with a children's play area. The excellent food includes local specialities. The guest beer is usually from the Tapster's Choice list.
🏨 Q 🛏 🌣 🄳 ▲ ♣ P ⚥

Brotton

Green Tree Inn

90 High Street
☎ (01287) 676377
12–2.30, 7–11; 12–3, 7–10.30 Sun
Camerons Strongarm Ⓗ
Old mining community pub, popular with locals, friendly and comfortable. Sat is music night. 🏨 Q 🛏 🄳 🄳 ♿ ♣

Burton Salmon

Plough

Main Street (½ mile E of A162)
☎ (01977) 672422
12–3 (not Mon or Tue), 6–11; 12–11 Sat; 12–4, 7–10.30 Sun
Black Sheep Best Bitter; Boddingtons Bitter; John Smith's Bitter; guest beers Ⓗ
Friendly village pub with a spacious bar and a large garden; a free house with an excellent guest beer policy. The dining room serves superb home-made food.
🏨 Q 🌣 🄳 🄳 ♿ ♣ P

Carlton in Cleveland

Blackwell Ox

Off A172 ☎ (01642) 712287
11.30–3, 6.30 (5.30 summer)–11; 11–11 Sat; 12–10.30 Sun
John Smith's Bitter; Theakston XB; guest beers Ⓗ
The only pub in the village. Nicely refurbished, it has a central bar with seating areas at different levels. Thai cooking is a speciality. Popular with walkers, campers and locals.
🏨 Q 🛏 🌣 🚬 🄳 🄳 ▲ ♣ P ⚥

Castleton

Downe Arms

3 High Street OS688080
☎ (01287) 660223
7–11; 12–3, 7–11 Sat; 12–3, 7–10.30 Sun
John Smith's Bitter, Magnet; Theakston Black Bull Ⓗ

Early 19th-century traditional, country village pub featuring an exposed stone, beamed interior. Sun lunch served. 🏚 Q 🍴 ⚫ & ⇌ ♣ P

Cawood

Anchor
4 Market Place
☎ (01757) 268358
11–11; 12–10.30 Sun
John Smith's Bitter; Tetley Bitter Ⓗ
300-year-old pub; its narrow back bar leads on to a vine-covered terrace for outside drinking. The restaurant has a late licence. 🏚 Q 🍴 ⚫ ◐ ▶ ⚫ & ▲ (Cawood Pk) ♣ P

Ferry
King Street ☎ (01757) 268515
12–4, 6.30–11 (11–11 summer Sat);
12–4, 7–10.30 Sun
Adnams Broadside; Mansfield Riding Mild, Riding Bitter, Bitter, seasonal beers; Marston's Pedigree; guest beer Ⓗ
Quiet pub on the bank of the River Ouse boasting historic connections with Cardinal Wolsey, who lived at Cawood Castle. Low, timbered ceilings and a wood-burning stove lend atmosphere. 🏚 Q 🍴 ⚫ ◐ ▶ ▲ ♣ P

Chapel Haddlesey

Jug
Main Street ☎ (01757) 270307
12–3, 7–11; 11–11 Sat; 12–10.30 Sun
Marston's Pedigree; Taylor Landlord; guest beers Ⓗ
250-year-old, small village pub, once a blacksmith's shop, on the north bank of the River Aire, with a welcoming atmosphere and a friendly ghost. Renowned for its Desperate Dan cow pies. 🏚 Q ⚫ ◐ ▶ ⊟ ▲ ♣ P

Chapel-le-Dale

Hill Inn
On B6255 ☎ (0152 42) 41256
12–3 (may extend summer), 7–11;
11.30–11 Sat; 12–3, 7–10.30 Sun
Black Sheep Best Bitter; Dent Bitter; Tetley Bitter; Theakston Best Bitter, XB, Old Peculier; guest beers Ⓗ
Well-known, isolated pub on the Three Peaks Walk, with bare floorboards and exposed stonework, a pool room and a food bar (children welcome). Music Sat night; folk Sun lunch. 🏚 ⚫ ◐ ▶ ♣ P

Clapham

New Inn
☎ (0152 42) 51203
11.30–3, 7–11; 11.30–11 Sat; 12–10.30 Sun

Black Sheep Best Bitter; Dent Bitter; Tetley Bitter; Theakston XB; guest beer Ⓗ
Large coaching inn, dated 1776: two lounge bars with oak panelling (1990 vintage). Cycling and caving pictures are displayed. Children are welcome in the no-smoking restaurant. 🏚 ⚫ 🍴 ◐ ▶ ▲ ♣ P

Cray

White Lion Inn
☎ (01756) 760262
11–2.30, 6–11; 11–11 Sat & summer;
12–3, 7–10.30 (12–10.30 summer) Sun
Moorhouse's Premier, Pendle Witches Brew; Tetley Bitter; guest beer (summer) Ⓗ
Traditional Dales inn, nestling beneath Buckden Pike: a two-roomed pub with original beams, an open log fire and an old Ring the Bull game. The highest pub in Wharfedale. 🏚 Q ⚫ 🍴 ◐ ▶ ▲ ♣ P ⌿

Cropton

New Inn
☎ (01751) 417310
12–3, 7–11; 12–10.30 Sun
Cropton King Billy, Two Pints, Scoresby Stout, Backwoods Bitter, seasonal beer; Tetley Mild Ⓗ
Whatever the weather be sure of a warm welcome here, and look around the brewery, too. 🏚 Q ⚫ 🍴 ◐ ▶ & ▲ ♣ P ⌿ ⊟

Crossgates

Byways
Station Road (off A64)
☎ (01723) 863254
11–11; 12–10.30 Sun
Boddingtons Bitter; Castle Eden Ale; Whitbread Trophy; guest beer Ⓗ
Refurbished, prominent pub which caters for all ages and is family-oriented (large indoor and outdoor children's play area). Guest beers are from the Whitbread Cask Collection. All food is home-cooked (steaks are specialities). ⚫ 🍴 ◐ ▶ & ▲ ⇌ (Seamer) P ⌿

Cross Hills

Old White Bear
6 Keighley Road
☎ (01535) 632115
11.30 (6 Mon, 11 Fri & Sat)–11;
12–10.30 Sun
Boddingtons Bitter; Old Bear Bitter Ⓗ
Popular, olde-worlde, 18th-century coach house with a brewery in the attached former stables. 🏚 Q ⚫ ◐ ▶ & ♣ P

Dacre Banks

Royal Oak
☎ (01423) 780200
12–3, 6–11; 12–3, 7–10.30 Sun
Black Sheep Best Bitter; Daleside Old Legover; Theakston Best Bitter Ⓗ
18th-century coaching inn featuring beams and oak panelling, with pleasant views over Nidderdale. 🏚 Q ⚫ 🍴 ◐ ▶ ♣ P

Danby

Duke of Wellington
2 West Lane
☎ (01287) 660351
11–3, 7–11 (11–11 summer); 12–3, 7–10.30 (12–10.30 summer) Sun
Camerons Strongarm; Ruddles Best Bitter; John Smith's Magnet; guest beer Ⓗ
Coaching inn, dating from 1732, popular with locals, families and walkers. Good for bar meals, it also has a restaurant. 🏚 Q ⚫ 🍴 ◐ ▶ ▲ ♣

Dishforth

Crown
Main Street
☎ (01845) 577398
12–3, 6.30–11; 12–3, 7–10.30 Sun
Hambleton Bitter; Robinson's Best Bitter; guest beers Ⓗ
Friendly, welcoming village local, keen to promote guest beers. Local CAMRA *Pub of the Year* 1996. Occasional Pipkin cider. 🏚 ⚫ ♣ ⊙ P

Easingwold

Station Hotel
Knott Lane, Raskel Road
☎ (01347) 822635
12–3, 5–11; 12–3, 7–10.30 Sun
Easingwold Tender Mild, Steamcock; Marston's Pedigree; John Smith's Bitter Ⓗ
Pleasant, friendly pub with a new brewery at the rear. 🏚 Q ⚫ 🍴 ▶ & ⊟

Elslack

Tempest Arms
On A56
☎ (01282) 842450
11–11; 12–10.30 Sun
Black Sheep Best Bitter, Special; Jennings Mild, Bitter, Cumberland Ale, Sneck Lifter Ⓗ
Large, 18th-century, rambling country inn. Purchased by Jennings in 1996, it offers a high standard of food and accommodation (ETB three crowns). 🏚 Q ⚫ 🍴 ◐ ▶ & ♣ P

Embsay

Elm Tree
Elm Tree Square
☎ (01756) 790717
11.30–3, 5.30–11; 12–3, 7–10.30 Sun
Bateman XB; Castle Eden Ale;
Fuller's London Pride; Greene
King Abbot; guest beers Ⓗ
Very popular pub for both ale
and food. The main entrance
leads to a large bar with a
smaller bar to the side, mainly
for diners. Good views of
Embsay Crag and the
surrounding moorland from
the garden.
Q ❀ 🚲 🌙 🕭 ♣ P

Fairburn

Waggon & Horses
Old Great North Road (by A1)
☎ (01977) 675459
12–3, 5.30 (7 Tue)–11; 12–3, 7–10.30
Sun
Samuel Smith OBB Ⓗ
Friendly local where the long
bar room has comfortable wall
seating as well as chairs and
tables. Darts in the public bar
area but the pool table is in a
separate room.
Q ❀ 🌙 🕭 ♣ P

Fellbeck

Half Moon
☎ (01423) 711560
12–3, 6.30–11; 12–10.30 Sun
Black Sheep Best Bitter;
Taylor Landlord; Theakston
Best Bitter; Younger Scotch Ⓗ
Good roadside pub close to
Brimham Rocks: a large sunny
lounge and a small back bar. A
self-catering cottage is
available to let.
🚲 Q ➴ 🚲 🌙 🕭 ♠ P

Filey

Imperial
20–22 Hope Street
☎ (01723) 512185
12–11; 12–10.30 Sun
Boddingtons Bitter; John
Smith's Bitter; Whitbread
Trophy; guest beers Ⓗ
Refurbished, friendly, two-
roomed, town-centre pub.
Meals available until early eve
in summer.
🚲 🌙 🕭 ➴ ♣

Gate Helmsley

Duke of York
☎ (01759) 372429
11–11; 12–10.30 Sun
John Smith's Bitter; Tetley
Bitter Ⓗ
Busy, but well-run pub, known
for good food (booking
advisable).
🚲 ❀ 🌙 🕭 P

Gayles

Bay Horse Inn
Off A66
☎ (01833) 621468
6–11; 12–3, 6–11 Sat; 12–3, 6–10.30
Sun
Butterknowle Conciliation
Ale; Younger Scotch; guest
beers (occasional) Ⓗ
Spick and span country village
pub in a farming community.
Good meals.
Q ❀ 🌙 🕭 ♣ P 🍴

Grassington

Black Horse
Garrs Lane
☎ (01756) 752770
11–11; 12–10.30 Sun
Black Sheep Best Bitter,
Riggwelter; Tetley Mild,
Bitter; Theakston Best Bitter,
XB Ⓗ
Coaching inn, dating from the
17th century, in the village
centre, serving excellent meals
in the restaurant and bar food
in the open lounge.
🚲 Q ❀ 🚲 🌙 🕭 ♣

Great Ayton

Buck
1 West Terrace (A173, near
bridge)
☎ (01642) 722242
11–11; 12–10.30 Sun
Boddingtons Bitter; Flowers
Original; Whitbread Trophy;
guest beers Ⓗ
Friendly, riverside coaching
inn dating from the 1700s, in
Captain Cook's village. Strong
local patronage; good bar
meals. Q ➴ ❀ 🌙 ♣ P

Great Ouseburn

Crown
Main Street
☎ (01423) 330430
5 (11 Sat)–11; 12–10.30 Sun
Black Sheep Best Bitter; John
Smith's Bitter; Theakston Best
Bitter; guest beers Ⓗ
Attractive village inn with
many old features and a
reputation for good food.
🚲 Q ❀ 🌙 🕭 P ✕

Great Smeaton

Bay Horse
On A167 ☎ (01609) 881466
12–3, 6.30–11; 12–3, 7–10.30 Sun
Ruddles County; John Smith's
Bitter; guest beer Ⓗ
Small, 18th-century free house
in the middle of a row of
roadside cottages, with two
linked rooms: a soft-furnished
lounge and a bustling little bar.
Food is always available.
🚲 ❀ 🌙 🕭 ♣ 🍴

Grinton

Bridge Inn
☎ (01748) 884224
11–11; 12–10.30 Sun
Black Sheep Best Bitter,
Special, Riggwelter; Tetley
Bitter; Theakston Best Bitter,
Old Peculier Ⓗ
Comfortable, hospitable pub in
an idyllic setting in Swaledale,
popular with both locals and
visitors. Very good bar and
restaurant meals; excellent
accommodation.
🚲 Q ➴ ❀ 🌙 🕭 ♣ P

Guisborough

Anchor Inn
16 Belmangate
☎ (01287) 632715
11.30–11; 12–10.30 Sun
Samuel Smith OBB Ⓗ
18th-century cottage pub,
refurbished in 1996.
🚲 Q ➴ ❀ 🌙 🕭

Globe
Northgate (next to hospital)
☎ (01287) 632778
12–3.30, 6.30–11; 12–10.30 Sun
Camerons Bitter, Strongarm;
guest beer Ⓗ
Friendly, busy, street-corner
pub with a bustling public bar
and a large lounge.
➴ ❀ 🚲 🕭 ♣ P 🍴

Ship Inn
145 Westgate (A171)
☎ (01287) 632233
11.30–11; 12–10.30 Sun
Draught Bass Ⓗ
Busy town-centre pub, a
former coaching inn with an
authentic, unaltered interior.
🚲 ❀ ♣

Gunnerside

King's Head
☎ (01748) 886261
12 (11.30 summer)–2 (3 Sat &
summer), 7–11; 12–3, 7–10.30 Sun
Beer range varies Ⓗ
Stone pub opened into a single
bar, selling beer from Swaled
Ale microbrewery in
Gunnerside. Popular walking
area. 🚲 ❀ 🌙 🕭 ♣ 🍴

Harrogate

Gardener's Arms ☆
Bilton Lane ☎ (01423) 506051
12–3 (not Wed), 6 (7 Sat)–11; 12–4,
7–10.30 Sun
Samuel Smith OBB Ⓗ
Very old pub (circa 1709),
popular with locals. It boasts a
large stone fireplace in one of
the rooms; its thick stone walls
are wood panelled in some
areas. Eve meals in winter.
Franklin's brewery is adjacent.
🚲 Q ❀ 🌙 🕭 P

Prince of Wales
49 High Street, Starbeck
☎ (01423) 884235
11–11; 12–10.30 Sun
John Smith's Bitter H
Very strong community pub with a large children's play area. ❧ ❀ ◖ ❑ ♿ ⇌ (Starbeck) ♣ P

Slip Inn
30 Cold Bath Road
☎ (01423) 560437
12 (11 Sat)–11; 12–10.30 Sun
John Smith's Bitter; Theakston XB; Wilson's Mild; guest beers H
Basic, but comfortable, single-roomed local, a short distance from the town centre. Various entertainments Wed–Sat. ♣

Tap & Spile
Tower Street (off West Park Stray) ☎ (01423) 526785
11–11; 12–10.30 Sun
Beer range varies H
Town-centre pub with exposed stone and wood panelling in three rooms with a central bar. No meals Sun eve.
Q ◖ ▶ ⇌ ▭

Helperby

Golden Lion
☎ (01423) 360870
6 (12 Sat)–11; 12–3, 5–10.30 Sun
Taylor Best Bitter; guest beers H
A fabulous range of guest beers is guaranteed at this pub which has stone-flagged floors, a real fire at each end and a great atmosphere. Note the painted wall in the gents. ❧ Q ❀ ♣

High Leven

Fox Covert
Low Lane (A1044)
☎ (01642) 760033
11.30–3, 5–11; 12–3, 7–10.30 Sun
Vaux Samson, Double Maxim H
Once the Half Moon, this uniquely named former farmhouse dominates its rural crossroads location. Warm and welcoming, open-plan interior. ❧ Q ❀ ◖ ▶ ♣ P

Hornby

Grange Arms
☎ (01609) 881249
12–3 (not Mon or Tue), 7–11; 12–3, 7–10.30 Sun
Theakston XB, Old Peculier; guest beer H
Pleasant, whitewashed and red-pantiled village pub with a snug little bar and a dining room. Friendly atmosphere. The home-cooked food is very popular.
❧ ❀ ⌂ ◖ ▶ ❑ ♣ P ⊟

Ingleton

Bridge
New Road (A65)
☎ (0152 42) 41183
11–11 (11–3, 6–11 winter); 12–3, 7–10.30 Sun
Black Sheep Best Bitter; Theakston Best Bitter; guest beers H
Main road hotel with a spacious pub/restaurant. Children's play area outside. Guest beers are often from Black Sheep or are national brands.
❧ ❀ ⌂ ◖ ▶ ♿ ▲ ♣ P

Wheatsheaf
High Street ☎ (0152 42) 41275
11 (12 winter)–11; 12–10.30 Sun
Black Sheep Best Bitter, Special (summer), Riggwelter; Moorhouse's Pendle Witches Brew; Theakston Mild, Best Bitter; guest beers H
Pub with a single long, cosy bar, handy for the finish of the Waterfalls Walk. No-smoking dining room. ❀ ⌂ ◖ ▶ ▲ P

Kildwick

White Lion
Priest Bank Road (off A629 at Crosshills roundabout)
☎ (01535) 632225
11–11 (may vary); 12–10.30 Sun
Greene King Abbot; Marston's Pedigree; Tetley Mild, Bitter; guest beers H
Centuries-old, two-roomed, traditional pub, providing home cooking and a warm welcome in an historic village. It won a local CAMRA award in 1996 for improving beer choice in the area. Lion Brew is a house beer from Carlsberg-Tetley. ❧ Q ❀ ◖ ▶ ❑ ▲ ♣ P

Kirkby Malzeard

Henry Jenkins
Main Street ☎ (01765) 658557
11–3, 5.30–11; 12–3, 7–10.30 Sun
Black Sheep Best Bitter; John Smith's Bitter; Theakston Best Bitter; guest beers H
Two-room local with a lounge bar having open access to the restaurant. A house beer is produced by Daleside Brewery. Pool room.
❀ ◖ ▶ ❑ ⌂ P

Kirkbymoorside

George & Dragon
Market Place ☎ (01751) 433334
11–3, 6–11; 12–3, 7–10.30 Sun
Black Sheep Best Bitter; Taylor Landlord; Theakston Best Bitter H
17th-century coaching inn at the town centre. The large, comfortable lounge is divided into distinct areas.
❧ ❀ ⌂ ◖ ▶ P

White Swan
4 Church Street
☎ (01751) 431041
12–11; 12–10.30 Sun
Black Sheep Best Bitter; Tetley Bitter; guest beers H
Fine, basic pub, opposite the market place: a bar with an adjoining pool room. ❧ ❀ ♣

Kirklevington

Crown
Thirsk Road ☎ (01642) 780044
5 (12 Sat; may extend summer)–11; 12–10.30 Sun
Boddingtons Bitter; Castle Eden Ale; John Smith's Magnet H
Friendly, welcoming, old village inn with two rooms, both with open fires. Sun lunch is served, but no Sun eve meals. ❧ Q ▶ ♣ P

Knaresborough

Beer-Ritz
17 Market Place
☎ (01423) 862850
10 (9 Sat)–10; 12–10 Sun
Beer range varies G
Enterprising off-licence selling cask ales and over 300 bottled beers from around the world. The house beer is brewed by Daleside. Discount on draught beers to card-carrying CAMRA members. ⇌ ⌂

Blind Jacks
19 Market Place
☎ (01423) 869148
12 (5.30 Mon, 4 Tue & Wed, 11.30 Sat)–11; 12–10.30 Sun
Beer range varies H
CAMRA's *Best New Pub* in 1992; a regular outlet for Village Brewery's beers, this gem exudes warmth with decor and atmosphere belonging to a past era.
Q ⇌ ⌂

Half Moon
Abbey Road (off Briggate)
☎ (01423) 862663
5.30 (11 Sat)–11; 12–10.30 Sun
Mansfield Riding Bitter H
Small, comfortable, one-roomed pub overlooking the River Nidd, renowned for its Boxing Day tug-of-war with a rival pub across the river. ▲ ♣

Marquis of Granby
York Place (A59)
☎ (01423) 862207
11.30–3, 5.30–11; 11.30–11 Wed & Sat; 12–10.30 Sun
Samuel Smith OBB H
Smartly furnished, twin-roomed, Victorian-style pub, displaying prints of old

Knaresborough in the lounge.
No meals winter Sun.
Q ◑ ⊕ P

Knayton

Dog & Gun
Off A19 ☎ (01845) 537368
12–3, 6.30–11; 12–11 Sat; 12–3, 7–10.30
Sun
**Camerons Bitter; Marston's
Pedigree; Tetley Bitter** H
Nice village pub with a
restaurant, open log fire and
country magazines.
ﬕ Q ✿ ﬔ ◑ ▶ ♣ P

Langdale End

Moorcock Inn
OS938913 ☎ (01723) 882268
7 (11 summer)–11 (closed winter Mon
& Tue); 11–3, 7–11 (11–11 summer)
Sat; 12–3, 7–10.30 (12–10.30 summer)
Sun
**Daleside Old Legover,
Monkey Wrench; Malton
Double Chance; guest beers** H
Remote, stone pub,
sympathetically renovated,
near a forest drive. Busy in
summer.
ﬕ Q ✿ ◑ ▶ ▲ ♣ P ✗

Leavening

Jolly Farmers
Main Street ☎ (01653) 658276
12–3, 7–11; 12–3, 7–10.30 Sun
**Hambleton Stallion; John
Smith's Bitter; Tetley Bitter;
guest beer** H
Friendly, 17th-century village
local. Excellent, reasonably-
priced food includes locally
caught game. Local CAMRA
Pub of the Year 1997.
ﬕ ✿ ◑ ▶ ♣ P

Loftus

Murphy's Bar
65 High Street
☎ (01287) 640612
12–11; 12–10.30 Sun
**John Smith's Bitter; guest
beer** H
Small pub with a strong local
patronage. ✿ ♣ P ⊟

Long Preston

Maypole Inn
☎ (01729) 840219
11–3, 6–11; 11–11 Sat; 12–10.30 Sun
**Boddingtons Bitter; Castle
Eden Ale; Taylor Landlord;
Worth Alesman; guest beer** H
Large pub with two bars,
popular with locals and
passers-by. It faces the village
green and maypole. Food in
the bar or dining room (high
standards but reasonable
prices). ﬕ Q ✿ ﬔ ◑ ▶ ⅙ ▲
⇌ ♣ ○ P

Low Bentham

Punch Bowl
☎ (0152 42) 61344
12–3 (not Mon), 6.30–11; 12–10.30 Sun
Mitchell's Original H
Small country pub run by
locals for locals: a cosy bar,
plus a room down steps with
games and extra seats. The
restaurant (no-smoking) is
open Fri and Sat eves and Sun
lunch.
ﬕ ✿ ﬔ ◑ ▲ ♣ P

Malham

Lister Arms
☎ (01729) 830330
12–3, 7–11; 12–3, 7–10.30 Sun
**Ind Coope Burton Ale;
Younger Scotch; guest beers** H
Popular, three-roomed pub
dating from 1702, featuring an
original inglenook and a large,
sheltered garden. Wide range
of foreign (mainly Belgian)
bottled beers. Cider in
summer.
ﬕ ✿ ﬔ ◑ ▲ ♣ ○ P

Malsis

Dog & Gun
Colne Road (A6068)
☎ (01535) 633855
12.30–3, 5.30–11; 12–10.30 Sun
Taylor Golden Best H, **Mild** E,
**Best Bitter, Landlord; Tetley
Bitter** H
200-year-old pub with a
shooting lodge theme to reflect
its name: a single main room
with a no-smoking dining
room (good food served in
either room). ﬕ ✿ ◑ ▶ P

Maltby

Pathfinders
High Lane
☎ (01642) 590300
11–11; 12–10.30 Sun
**Boddingtons Bitter; Castle
Eden Ale; Flowers Original;
Morland Old Speckled Hen;
guest beers** H
Pub with a large, L-shaped bar
on split levels, plus a dining
area, named in honour of the
WWII Pathfinder squadrons.
Q ✿ ◑ ▶ ♣ P

Yorkshire Dragoon
High Lane (A1044)
☎ (01642) 760341
11–11; 12–10.30 Sun
**Theakston Black Bull, XB;
guest beer** H
Large, modern, multi-roomed
pub with a new outdoor
children's play area. Wide
range of meals. Large upstairs
function room. Wheelchair
WC.
✿ ◑ ▶ ⅙ ▲ ♣ P

Malton

Crown Hotel
(Suddaby's)
12 Wheelgate
☎ (01653) 692038
11–11; 12–4, 7–10.30 Sun
**Malton Double Chance,
Crown Bitter, Owd Bob; guest
beer** H
Busy, town-centre pub with a
conservatory eating area.
Malton Brewery is situated in
the rear courtyard. Eve meals
must be booked.
ﬕ Q ⅚ ﬔ ◑ ▲ ⇌ P

King's Head
5 Market Place
☎ (01653) 692289
10.30–2.30 (later in summer), 7–11;
12–3, 7–10.30 Sun
**Marston's Bitter, Pedigree;
guest beers** H
Ivy-clad pub, popular with
locals and visitors and busy on
market days. Excellent, good
value food. Up to three guest
beers.
Q ﬔ ◑ ▶ ▲ ⇌ ♣ P ✗ ⊟

Marske-by-the-Sea

Zetland
9 High Street ☎ (01642) 483973
12–11; 12–4, 7–10.30 Sun
Vaux Samson; guest beers H
Old, established hotel with a
bar, lounge and games room.
Various entertainments; hot
snacks. ﬔ ⊕ ⇌ ♣ P

Maunby

Buck Inn
1½ miles from A167 OS352865
☎ (01845) 587236
7 (11.30 Fri, Sat & summer)–11;
12–10.30 Sun
**Courage Directors; Black
Sheep Best Bitter; Hambleton
Bitter; John Smith's Bitter** H
Deservedly popular local in an
isolated village by the River
Swale. Excellent food.
ﬕ ﬔ ◑ ▶ ▲ ♣ P

Melmerby

George & Dragon
Main Street ☎ (01765) 640303
11–3, 5–11 (11–11 summer); 12–3,
7–10.30 Sun
**Franklin's Bitter; Theakston
Best Bitter; guest beers** H
Traditional, three-roomed
village inn with log fires in
each room. A rare outlet for
Franklin's beers (when
available). ﬕ ◑ ▶ ♣ P ✗

Middleham

White Swan Hotel
Market Place ☎ (01969) 622093
12–2 (not winter Mon or Tue), 7–11
(11–11 summer); 12–10.30 Sun

Black Sheep Special;
Hambleton Bitter; John
Smith's Bitter H
Stone-flagged bar of character,
with hop-laden beams. Good
food. 🚶 ✿ 🛏 ◁ ▶ ♿ ▲ P

Middlesbrough

Star & Garter
14 Southfield Road
☎ (01642) 245307
11–11; 12–10.30 Sun
Draught Bass; Boddingtons
Bitter; Theakston XB;
Worthington Bitter; guest
beers H
Winner of CAMRA's *Pub
Preservation* award for its
conversion from a club,
boasting a fine, Victorian-style
bar. The large lounge has a
quiet eating area. Popular with
students. ✿ ◁ ▶ 🚃 ♣ P

Tavern
228 Linthorpe Road
☎ (01642) 242589
11–11; 12–10.30 Sun
Boddingtons Bitter; Castle
Eden Ale; guest beers H
Large pub with up to 14 guest
beers from the Whitbread
portfolio. Games room and Sky
TV. ✿ 🛏 ◁ ♿ ♣

Muker

Farmers Arms
☎ (01748) 886297
11–3, 7–11; 12–3, 7–10.30 Sun
Butterknowle Bitter; John
Smith's Bitter; Theakston Best
Bitter, XB, Old Peculier H
Dales village local opened out
into a single room but retaining
its old character, with massive
stone flags and an open fire.
🚶 Q 🐕 ✿ ◁ ▶ ▲ ♣ P

Newholm

Old Beehive Inn
Off A171, 2 miles from Whitby
☎ (01947) 602703
11.30–3, 7–11; 12–3, 7–10.30 Sun
John Smith's Magnet;
Theakston Best Bitter; Old
Peculier; guest beers H
Ancient village pub, full of
character, with oak beams and
a pub sign written in verse.
Family run.
🚶 Q ✿ 🛏 ◁ ▶ ▲ ♣ P 🖵

Newton-on-Ouse

Blacksmith's Arms
Cherry Tree Avenue
☎ (01347) 848249
12–3, 6–11; 12–3, 7–10.30 Sun
Banks's Bitter; Camerons
Bitter, Strongarm H
Popular community pub at the
heart of the village. Recently
extended, it offers good value
meals. ✿ ◁ ▶ P 🖵

Northallerton

Tanner Hop
2A Friarage Street (off High St)
☎ (01609) 778482
7–11 (midnight Tue, 1am Fri); 12–1am
Sat; 12–10.30 Sun
Black Sheep Best Bitter; John
Smith's Bitter; guest beers H
Very busy town-centre
conversion of a former dance
hall. There's always a local
beer plus one from Hambleton.
Popular beer festivals.
Occasional cider.
🐕 ▶ ♿ 🚃 ♣ ◔

North Duffield

King's Arms
Main Street (off A163)
☎ (01757) 288492
4 (11 Sat)–11; 12–10.30 Sun
Black Sheep Best Bitter; John
Smith's Bitter; guest beers H
Welcoming pub next to an
attractive village green and
duck pond. Constantly
changing guest beers; cider in
summer. No food Sun–Tue
eve. 🚶 ✿ ◁ ▶ ♣ ◔ P

Nosterfield

Freemasons
On B6267
12–3 (not Mon), 6 (7 Mon)–11; 12–3,
7–10.30 Sun
Black Sheep Best Bitter;
Taylor Landlord; Theakston
Best Bitter; guest beer
(occasional) H
Friendly country inn, on the
main road through the village,
with a flagstoned bar area.
Excellent meals make it often
very busy. Cider in summer.
🚶 Q ◁ ▶ ◔ P

Nun Monkton

Alice Hawthorn
Signed from A59 at Skipbridge
☎ (01423) 330303
12–2, 6.30–11; 12–10.30 Sun
Camerons Bitter; Castle Eden
Ale; Tetley Bitter H
Off the beaten track, this pub
overlooks the picturesque
village maypole and duck
pond. The food is good and
home cooked. A regular award
winner.
🚶 ✿ ◁ ▶ 🍴 ♿ ▲ ♣ P

Pickering

White Swan Hotel
Market Place ☎ (01751) 472288
11–3, 6–11; 11–11 Sat; 12–3, 7–10.30
Sun
Black Sheep Best Bitter; guest
beers H
Former coaching inn with a
small, cosy bar offering
welcoming Yorkshire
hospitality. The excellent bar

menu is based on local
produce. Guest beers only
from Yorkshire.
🚶 Q 🐕 ✿ 🛏 ◁ ▶ ▲ 🚃 (N
Yk Moors Railway) P ✂ 🖵

Pickhill

Nag's Head Country
Inn
1¼ miles E of A1
☎ (01845) 567391
11–11; 12–10.30 Sun
Black Sheep Best Bitter;
Hambleton Bitter; John
Smith's Bitter, Magnet;
Theakston Black Bull, Old
Peculier H
Comfortable village pub with
lots of character, enjoying a
reputation for excellent food.
🚶 Q ✿ 🛏 ◁ ▶ 🍴 ▲ ♣ P

Pool

Hunters Inn
On A658, ½ mile N of Pool
☎ (0113) 284 1090
11–11; 12–10.30 Sun
Theakston Best Bitter; Tetley
Bitter; guest beer H
Popular pub, particularly at
weekends, with a pool table
and a jukebox. Cooked Sun
lunch, otherwise no food. ✿ P

Redcar

Pig & Whistle
West Dyke Road (next to
station) ☎ (01642) 482697
11–11; 12–10.30 Sun
Courage Directors; Marston's
Pedigree; Morland Old
Speckled Hen; John Smith's
Magnet; Theakston XB H
Traditional pub, over 100 years
old, in the town centre,
displaying a collection of over
2,500 pigs. A games room,
public bar and several snug
rooms are complemented by a
new upstairs function room
and restaurant.
🐕 ◁ ▲ 🚃 (Central) ♣ 🖵

Yorkshire Coble
West Dyke Road (by
racecourse) ☎ (01642) 482071
11–3, 6–11; 11–11 Fri & Sat; 12–10.30
Sun
Samuel Smith OBB H
Large Samuel Smith estate
pub, with a strong regular
clientele: a comfortable lounge,
large functional bar and a
games room. Big screen TV in
the bar.
✿ ◁ ▶ 🍴 🚃 (Central) ♣ P 🖵

Redmire

King's Arms
☎ (01969) 622316
11–3, 6–11; 12–3, 7–10.30 Sun
Black Sheep Special; John
Smith's Bitter; Theakston Best
Bitter, XB; guest beers H

Busy, but cosy bar, popular for home-cooked food. The patio affords views across the dale. 🍴 Q ❀ 🛏 ◖ ▶ ♨ ♣ P

Richmond

Black Lion Hotel

Finkle Street ☎ (01748) 823121
10.30–11; 12–10.30 Sun
Camerons Strongarm; Flowers Original; Tetley Bitter, Imperial Ⓗ
Traditional, family-run hotel, an old coaching inn with a well established traditional bar and cosy lounge bars with open fires. Noted locally for food. 🍴 Q ➳ 🛏 ◖ ▶ ♨ ♿ ♣ P ⚓

Ripon

Golden Lion

69 Allhallowgate
☎ (01765) 602598
11–3, 7–11; 12–3, 7–10.30 Sun
Black Sheep Best Bitter; Hambleton Goldfield; John Smith's Bitter; Theakston Best Bitter Ⓗ
Friendly pub displaying naval memorabilia. Excellent quality, good value meals (eve meals Fri and Sat). ◖ ▶ ♣

One Eyed Rat

51 Allhallowgate
☎ (01765) 607704
12–2 (not Mon–Wed), 6–11; 12–3, 7–10.30 Sun
Black Sheep Best Bitter; Tetley Bitter; guest beers Ⓗ
Popular terraced pub close to the town centre offering excellent guest beers. Meals in summer. 🍴 Q ❀ ◖ ♿ ♣ ♨

Wheatsheaf

Harrogate Road
☎ (01765) 602410
12–3, 6–11; 12–3, 7–10.30 Sun
Vaux Samson; Ward's Best Bitter; guest beer Ⓗ
Friendly old inn on the edge of the city, with a sunken garden at the rear. 🍴 Q ➳ ❀ ♣ P

Robin Hood's Bay

Bay Hotel

The Dock ☎ (01947) 880278
11–11; 12–10.30 Sun
Courage Directors; Ruddles County; John Smith's Bitter; Theakston Black Bull Ⓗ
Old, multi-roomed pub in a superb position overlooking the bay; popular with locals and visitors. 🍴 Q ➳ ❀ 🛏 ◖ ▶ ♣

Victoria Hotel

Station Road ☎ (01947) 880205
11–3, 6.30–11; 11–11 Fri, Sat & summer; 12–3, 7–10.30 (12–10.30 summer) Sun
Camerons Bitter, Strongarm; guest beers Ⓗ
Large hotel built in 1897 on the clifftop, overlooking the bay

and village where all pubs sell real ale. 🍴 Q ➳ ❀ 🛏 ◖ ▶ ♣

Saltburn-by-the-Sea

Queens Public House

Windsor Road
☎ (01287) 622222
11–11; 12–10.30 Sun
Marston's Pedigree; John Smith's Bitter; Theakston XB; guest beer (occasional) Ⓗ
Two-roomed pub with a traditional bar and lounge atmosphere. ❀ 🍴 ♿ ▲ ♨ ☐

Saltburn Cricket, Bowls & Tennis Club

Marske Mill Lane (opp. sports centre)
☎ (01287) 622761
8 (6 Sat & Sun in summer)–11; all day on cricket match days
Tetley Bitter; guest beers Ⓗ
Club consisting of a lounge and a games room with a bar spanning both areas. Bar snacks at all times. Casual visitors welcome.
❀ ▲ ⇌ ♣ P ☐

Sawdon

Anvil Inn

Main Street (off A170)
☎ (01723) 859896
11–11; 12–10.30 Sun
Theakston Best Bitter; Younger Scotch; guest beers Ⓗ
Friendly, restored blacksmith's shop with a recently extended dining area (excellent value meals). Scarborough CAMRA *Rural Pub of the Year* 1996.
🍴 Q ➳ ❀ 🛏 ◖ ▲ ♣ P ☐

Scarborough

Alma Inn

1 Alma Parade
☎ (01723) 375587
11.30–2.30 (3 Thu), 7–11; 11.30–11 Fri & Sat; 12–3, 7–10.30 Sun
Tetley Bitter; Theakston Best Bitter, XB; Younger Scotch, No. 3; guest beers Ⓗ
Busy, two-roomed pub, just off the main shopping precinct. Good value meals (no food Sun). ❀ ◖ ♿ ⇌ ♣

Highlander

Esplanade
☎ (01723) 365627
11–11; 12–10.30 Sun
Tetley Bitter; Younger IPA; guest beers Ⓗ
Busy, one-roomed pub with a patio at the front overlooking South Bay. It boasts an extensive range of malt whiskies, plus a showman's steam engine. The Thistle Mild house beer is contract brewed.
🍴 ❀ 🛏 ◖ ♿ ▲ ⇌

Hole in the Wall

26–32 Vernon Road
☎ (01723) 373746
11.30–2.30 (3 Sat), 7–11; 12–3, 7–10.30 Sun
Brakspear Bitter; Fuller's ESB; Malton Double Chance; guest beers Ⓗ
Busy, but friendly, conversational pub near the town centre and the Spa complex. Varied lunchtime meals (vegetarian selection). Q ◖ ▲ ⇌ ♣ ○

Leeds Arms

26 St Mary's Street
☎ (01723) 361699
11.30–3.30, 7–11; 11.30–11 Fri & Sat; 12–10.30 Sun
Draught Bass; Highgate Dark; Worthington Bitter; guest beer Ⓗ
Unspoilt, one-roomed pub where fishing and lifeboat memorabilia adorn the walls. Pleasant atmosphere.
🍴 Q ▲ ⇌ ♣

Old Scalby Mills Hotel

Scalby Mills Road (by Sea Life Centre) ☎ (01723) 500449
11–11; 12–10.30 Sun
Daleside Dales Delight; Highwood Tom Wood Harvest; Tetley Bitter; guest beers Ⓗ
Historic, 500-year-old building (formerly a watermill) on the Cleveland Way, with views across the bay. Busy in summer; children's certificate. Q ❀ ◖ ♿ ▲ ♣

Scarborough Arms

1 North Terrace
☎ (01723) 373575
11–11; 12–10.30 Sun
Banks's Mild; Camerons Bitter; Marston's Pedigree; guest beer Ⓗ
Popular pub just off the town centre, offering a welcoming atmosphere and excellent value meals (eve meals end at 8). ❀ ◖ ▲ ♣ P ☐

Talbot Inn

13 Queen Street
☎ (01723) 364723
11.30–11; 12–10.30 Sun
Theakston Best Bitter, XB; guest beers Ⓗ
17th-century coaching inn, a Grade II-listed building incorporating three bars: a concert room, a large airy lounge and a period snug with a Yorkshire range. Belgian beer on draught. No eve meals weekends.
🍴 ❀ ◖ ▶ ⇌ ♣ P

Tap & Spile

28 Falsgrave Road
☎ (01723) 363837
11–11; 12–10.30 Sun
Big Lamp Bitter; Tap & Spile Premium; Theakston XB, Old Peculier; guest beers Ⓗ

Sympathetically renovated, busy old coaching inn displaying local memorabilia: three rooms and a large patio. Excellent value, home-cooked lunches.
Q ❀ ◁ ▲ ⇌ ⌂ P ✗

Selby

Albion Vaults

New Street
☎ (01757) 213817
12–11; 12–10.30 Sun
Old Mill Mild, Bitter, Bullion, seasonal beers H
Reputed to be the oldest pub in Selby, with comfortable, traditional Edwardian furnishings. The rear bar has darts and a pool table.
Q ❀ ◁ 🕁 ⇌ ♣

Cricketers

Market Place
☎ (01757) 202120
11–11; 11–3.30, 5.30–11 Tue & Wed; 12–10.30 Sun
Samuel Smith OBB H
Pub with partitioned seating alcoves and the cheapest beer in town. Wheelchair access is from the rear.
❀ ◁ 🕁 ⇌

Unicorn

15 Bondgate (Wistow road, outskirts of town)
☎ (01757) 202254
2 (7 Tue, 1 Sat)–11; 12–4, 7–10.30 Sun
John Smith's Bitter; Theakston Mild; guest beers H
Reputedly a 17th-century building, but now a modernised pub with one room and a central bar.
Q ❀ 🕁 🕁 ⇌ ♣ P 🍺

Settle

Royal Oak

Market Place
☎ (01729) 822561
11–11; 12–10.30 Sun
Boddingtons Bitter; Flowers IPA; Taylor Best Bitter, Landlord H
Town-centre hostelry with a pleasant olde-worlde feel; its high-ceilinged, wood-panelled bar is split into two main areas. Open 8am for coffee.
❀ 🛏 ◁ ▶ 🕁 ⇌ ♣ P

Skelton

Royal George

North Terrace (A173)
☎ (01287) 650326
2 (12.30 Sat)–11; 12–3, 7–10.30 Sun
John Smith's Magnet; guest beers H
Pub with a strong local patronage: a small front bar with a larger bar at the rear. Guest beers come from the Whitbread range. ❀ 🕁 🕁 ♣

Skipton

Cock & Bottle

30 Swadford Street
☎ (01756) 794734
11–11; 12–10.30 Sun
Boddingtons Bitter; Castle Eden Ale; Whitbread Abroad Cooper; guest beers H
18th-century coaching inn converted into a single-bar Hogshead Ale House, but retaining many original features.
🛏 ❀ ◁ ⇌ ♣ ⌂

Railway

13–15 Carleton Street (opp. Tesco)
☎ (01756) 793186
11–11; 12–10.30 Sun
Tap & Spile Premium; Tetley Mild, Bitter; guest beer H
Friendly, traditional, two-roomed, street-corner local, popular with domino players. The guest beer is from the Tapster's Choice range.
🕁 🕁 ⇌ ♣

Snape

Castle Arms Inn

☎ (01677) 470270
12–3, 7 (6 Fri & Sat)–11; 12–3, 7–10.30 Sun
Black Sheep Best Bitter; Hambleton Bitter; John Smith's Bitter; guest beers H
Cosy, Grade II-listed building, a 14th-century inn with its own caravan and camping facilities. The function room doubles as a family room.
🛏 Q ❀ 🛏 ◁ ▶ 🕁 ▲ ♣ P

Spofforth

King William IV

Church Hill
☎ (01937) 590293
12–3 (not Mon), 5.30–11; 12–11 Sat; 12–10.30 Sun
John Smith's Bitter; guest beers H
Small, friendly village pub, tucked away from the main road. Above average food is prepared by a Belgian chef. No food Mon.
🛏 Q ❀ ◁ ▶ 🕁 ♣ P

Staithes

Black Lion

High Street (off A174)
☎ (01947) 841132
12 (6 winter Mon–Thu)–11; 12–10.30 Sun
Draught Bass; John Smith's Magnet; Theakston Best Bitter; guest beer H
Georgian coaching inn: a cosy bar and a lounge, each with open fires. A cottage and bunk accommodation are available.
🛏 🐚 🛏 ◁ ▶ 🕁 ▲ ♣

Royal George

High Street
☎ (01947) 841432
12–4, 7–11 (11–11 summer); 12 (11 summer)–11 Fri; 12–4, 7–10.30 (12–10.30 summer) Sun
Camerons Strongarm; guest beer (summer) H
Three-roomed, terraced local in a charming fishing village: a small atmospheric bar and a comfortable lounge in Victorian style displaying local scenes. Real food includes local fish. 🛏 Q 🛏 ◁ ▶ 🕁 ▲ ♣

Starbotton

Fox & Hounds

☎ (01756) 760269
11.30–3, 6.30–11 (not Mon eve); 12–3, 7–10.30 Sun
Black Sheep Best Bitter; Theakston Best Bitter, Old Peculier; guest beers H
Stone building dating back to the 17th century, with a large stone fireplace and a flagstone floor. The varied menu includes vegetarian meals (small no-smoking dining room); no meals winter Mon.
🛏 Q ❀ 🛏 ◁ ▶ P

Stokesley

Spread Eagle

39 High Street
☎ (01642) 710278
11–11; 12–10.30 Sun
Camerons Strongarm; Marston's Pedigree H
Old town-centre pub with a long back room and extensive gardens. The food is excellent value: try the rabbit pie.
🛏 ❀ ◁ ▶ 🕁 ♣ 🍺

White Swan

1 West End
☎ (01642) 710263
11.30–3, 5.30 (7 Sat)–11; 12–3, 7–10.30 Sun
Castle Eden Ale; guest beers H
Cosy, traditional pub: the oak-panelled bar displays agricultural memorabilia. Lots of unusual pub games. Ploughman's meals come with a wide selection of cheeses and patés. Up to seven ales.
🛏 Q ♣ ⌂ 🍺

Thixendale

Cross Keys

☎ (01377) 288272
12–3 (not winter Mon), 6–11; 12–3, 7–10.30 Sun
Jennings Bitter; Tetley Bitter; guest beer H
Traditional, one-roomed village gem in a beautiful setting in the Yorkshire Wolds; unspoilt and welcoming. No meals between Christmas and New Year. 🛏 ❀ ◁ ▶ ▲ ♣

Thornton in Lonsdale

Marton Arms
Off 'Waterfalls' road, ½ mile from Ingleton
☎ (0152 42) 41281
12–3 (not winter Mon–Fri), 6 (7 winter)–11; 11–11 Sat; 12–10.30 Sun
Black Sheep Best Bitter; Dent Bitter; Theakston Best Bitter; guest beers H
Pre-turnpike coaching inn, dated 1679: a large, comfortable, oak-beamed lounge and a restaurant (food all day Sun). Up to 15 beers, one always from Taylor. A ten-min walk from the start of the Waterfalls Walk.
🏚 ❀ ⛭ ◖ ▶ ♣ ➫ P

Thornton Watlass

Buck
☎ (01677) 422461
11–3, 6–11; 11–11 Sat; 12–3, 6.30–10.30 Sun
Black Sheep Best Bitter; John Smith's Bitter; Tetley Bitter; Theakston Best Bitter; guest beer H
Pub beside a peaceful village green: a cosy public bar and a popular restaurant. Quoits is played.
🏚 Q ➺ ❀ ⛭ ◖ ▶ ♣ P

Threshfield

Old Hall Inn
☎ (01756) 752441
11–3 (not Mon), 6 (6.30 Mon)–11; 12–3, 7–10.30 Sun
Taylor Best Bitter, Landlord; Theakston Best Bitter; guest beer (summer) H
Well-extended country inn with several distinct seating areas, plus a conservatory which leads to a side garden. It boasts a Yorkshire range and two open fires. Good quality food (not served Mon or winter Sun eve). The 'old hall' itself is a listed building at the rear.
🏚 Q ➺ ❀ ⛭ ◖ ▶ ♿ ▲ ♣ P

Tockwith

Spotted Ox
Westfield Road (off B1224)
☎ (01423) 358387
11–3, 6–11; 11–11 Fri & Sat; 12–10.30 Sun
Tetley Bitter; guest beers H
Village local with open areas which can be separated for special activities. It has an indoor barbecue in a converted blacksmith's forge and serves an extensive menu of almost entirely home-cooked food, including ever-changing daily specials (meals all day Sun until 7.30). Occasional cider.
🏚 Q ❀ ◖ ▶ ⛁ ♣ ➫

Ulleskelf

Ulleskelf Arms
Church Fenton Lane
☎ (01937) 832136
6–11; 12–3, 6.30–11 Sat; 12–3, 7–10.30 Sun
Black Sheep Best Bitter; John Smith's Bitter; guest beers H
One-room pub where the garden entrance leads to the station. Entertainment most eves. Good value B&B.
Q ❀ ⛭ ◖ ▶ ▲ ➤ ♣ P

Upper Poppleton

Lord Collingwood
The Green
11.30–3, 5.30–11; 12–3, 7.30–10.30 Sun
Mansfield Riding Bitter, Old Baily H
Friendly pub in a pleasant village, a stone's throw from York's outer ring road.
🏚 ◖ ▶ P

Weaverthorpe

Star Inn
Off A64 ☎ (01944) 738273
7–11; 12–4, 7–11 Sat; 12–3.30, 7–10.30 Sun
Malton Double Chance; John Smith's Bitter; Tetley Bitter; guest beer H
Traditional, popular, welcoming village pub serving an extensive menu of home-made food, including game.
🏚 Q ❀ ⛭ ◖ ▶ ▲ ♣ P ✂

Welbury

Duke of Wellington
☎ (01609) 882464
12–3 (not Mon or Tue), 7 (6.30 Sat)–11; 12–10.30 Sun
John Smith's Bitter, Magnet; guest beer H
Large, pleasant village pub with a friendly atmosphere and an excellent menu.
🏚 ➺ ❀ ⛭ ◖ ▶ ♣ P

Whitby

Duke of York
Church Street (foot of abbey steps) ☎ (01947) 600324
11–11; 12–10.30 Sun
Black Sheep Best Bitter; Courage Directors; John Smith's Magnet; guest beer H
Busy, unspoilt pub with traditional decor and fine views of the harbour. Popular in folk week. Meals served 12–10 daily. ⛭ ◖ ▶ ➤ ♣

Tap & Spile
New Quay Road (opp. bus and rail stations) ☎ (01947) 603937
12 (11 summer)–11; 12–4.30, 7–10.30 (12–10.30 summer) Sun
Tap & Spile Premium; guest beers H
Large, multi-roomed, red-brick pub, formerly the Cutty Sark. Six guest beers and three ciders. Meals end at 7pm (4 Sun). Q ➺ ◖ ▶ ➤ ♣ ➫ ✂

York

Blue Bell ☆
Fossgate ☎ (01904) 654904
12–11; 12–3, 7–10.30 (may vary) Sun
Vaux Bitter, Samson, Waggle Dance; Ward's Best Bitter; guest beers H
Civilised and welcoming pub with two small rooms off a corridor and Edwardian decor.
⛁ ♣

Golden Lion
9 Church Street
☎ (01904) 620942
11–11; 12–10.30 Sun
John Smith's Bitter; Theakston Best Bitter, XB, Old Peculier; guest beers H
Open-plan, themed ale house (S&N), sympathetically refurbished in 1995 and now offering a much improved selection of beers. Old brewery and city prints feature.
◖ ➤

Lendal Cellars
26 Lendal ☎ (01904) 623121
11–11; 12–10.30 Sun
Boddingtons Bitter; Castle Eden Ale; Flowers Original; Whitbread Abroad Cooper; guest beers H
Whitbread Hogshead Ale House in York's oldest pub building. It attracts young drinkers and can get quite noisy at weekends.
◖ ▶ ➤ ➫

Lighthorseman
124 Fulford Road
☎ (01904) 624818
11.30–2.30, 5.30–11; 12–3, 7–10.30 Sun
Thwaites Bitter, Chairman's, seasonal beers H
Airy, Victorian pub with attractive bar fittings, and an ornate lightshade. ❀ ⛭ ◖ P

Maltings
Tanners Moat (below Lendal bridge) ☎ (01904) 655387
11–11; 12–10.30 Sun
Black Sheep Best Bitter; guest beers H
A beer-spotter's shrine: soak up your ale with the marvellous value victuals. Popular, regular beer festivals.
◖ ➤ ♣ ➫

Masons Arms
6 Fishergate ☎ (01904) 646046
11–11; 12–10.30 Sun
Fuller's London Pride; John Smith's Bitter; guest beers H
Large pub opposite the city wall, offering an attractive range of food and drink. Enhanced by recent, sympathetic refurbishment of

the bar, the lounge contains oak-panelling from the former York Castle gatehouse.
🏠 ◁ ▶ ⌗ P

Minster

24 Marygate, Bootham
☎ (01904) 624499
11.30–11; 12–10.30 Sun
Draught Bass; John Smith's Bitter; guest beers ⒣
Pub with its original passage entrance and three rooms, with a bar in a fourth room.
Q 🏠 ⌗ & ⇌ ⚲

Royal Oak

18 Goodramgate
☎ (01904) 635850
11–11; 12–10.30 Sun
Ind Coope Burton Ale; Tetley Bitter; guest beers ⒣
Stylish town pub with three rooms. ♨ Q ◁ ▶ ⌗ ⚲

Saddle Inn

Main Street, Fulford
☎ (01904) 633317
12–3, 6.30–11; 12–11 Sat; 12–3, 7–10.30 Sun
Banks's Bitter; Camerons Bitter, Strongarm; guest beers ⒣
Attractive, suburban local, selling beers now rare in this area: one L-shaped bar and a dining room. Guest beers are supplied by Banks's.
♨ 🏠 🛏 ◁ ▶ P ⎕

Spread Eagle

98 Walmgate ☎ (01904) 635868
11–11; 12–10.30 Sun
Adnams Broadside; Mansfield Riding Bitter, Bitter, Old Baily; York Stonewall; Yorkshire Terrier; guest beers ⒣
Now a Mansfield house, but offering a generous range of beers (usually 12). Note the large collection of photos of customers. Fish dishes are a speciality in the upstairs restaurant; live music Sun lunch. 🏠 ◁ ▶ P

Sun Inn

The Green, Acomb
☎ (01904) 798500
12–11; 12–10.30 Sun
John Smith's Bitter, Magnet; guest beers ⒣
Very much a village local, though Acomb is now just a large suburb. Note the ornate mirror in the small bar; even smaller, comfortable lounge.
🏠 ♣ P

Swan Inn

Clementhorpe
☎ (01904) 634968
12–3, 5–11; 12–11 Thu–Sat; 12–10.30 Sun
Flowers Original; Marston's Pedigree; Tetley Bitter ⒣
Classic, street-corner local. One of few pubs in this area with the 'West Riding' layout – a drinking corridor/lobby with

rooms off: fine enough to be an original Tetley Heritage Inn.
🏠 ⇌ ♣

Wellington

47 Alma Terrace
☎ (01904) 654642
11–3, 6–11; 12–3, 7–10.30 Sun
Samuel Smith OBB ⒣
Splendid terraced local, blending into the weathered streetscape: three rooms, one bar, a serving hatch and a central corridor. The best value ale in town. ♨ Q 🏠 ⌗

York Beer Shop

Sandringham Street (off A19/Fishergate)
☎ (01904) 647136
11 (4 Mon, 10 Sat)–10; 12–2, 6–10 Sun
Taylor Landlord; guest beers ⒣
Off-licence selling draught beer and cider in any quantity, plus an astonishing range of British and foreign bottle-conditioned beers. Fine cheeses, too. ⌂

South Yorkshire

Barnby Dun

Gateway Inn

Station Road ☎ (01302) 882849
12–3 (not Mon), 6–11.30; 12–3, 7–10.30 Sun
Barnsley Bitter; Glentworth Dizzy Blonde; John Smith's Bitter ⒣
Hotel and restaurant which cultivates a warm, friendly pub atmosphere in its bar. 🛏 ◁ ▶ P

Barnsley

Miners Rest

Palm Street, Old Town
☎ (01226) 282339
12–3 (4 Sat), 6 (7 Sat)–11; 12–3, 7–10.30 Sun
John Smith's Bitter; Theakston Best Bitter ⒣
Victorian local with three comfortable and contrasting rooms, and its own bowling green. 🏠 ⌗ ♣ P

Shaw Inn

Racecommon Road
☎ (01226) 294021
11 (12 Fri & Sat)–11; 12–4, 7–10.30 Sun
John Smith's Bitter; Whitbread seasonal beers; guest beers ⒣
Pub just off the 'Bunny Run' and so avoiding the weekend excesses of the town centre. Pizzas always available.
🌀 🏠 ⌗ ⇌ ♣ P

Bawtry

Turnpike

High Street
☎ (01302) 711960
11–11; 12–10.30 Sun

Barnsley Bitter; John Smith's Bitter; Worthington Bitter; guest beer ⒣
Welcoming pub opposite the market place, with lots of wood panelling and a flagstone floor around the bar. CAMRA awards adorn the walls. Eve meals Tue–Fri. 🏠 ◁ ▶

Birdwell

Cock Inn

Pilley Hill (off A61)
☎ (01226) 742155
12–3, 7–11; 12–3, 7–10.30 Sun
Draught Bass; John Smith's Bitter ⒣
Popular, 200-year-old village local in Yorkshire stone, with a slate floor, a superb fireplace and much brass. The extensive garden has a quality play area. No food Sun eve.
♨ Q 🌀 🏠 ◁ ▶ ♣ P

Blackburn

Sportsman Inn

Blackburn Road
☎ (01709) 551124
11–5, 7–11; 12–3, 7–10.30 Sun
Barnsley Bitter; Tetley Bitter; guest beers ⒣
Multi-roomed, friendly traditional pub near the Meadowhall complex. Competitive prices.
Q ⌗ ♣ P

Bradfield

Strines Inn

Bradfield Dale OS223907
☎ (0114) 285 1247
10.30–3 (not Mon), 6.30–11; 10.30–11 Sat & summer; 12–10.30 Sun
Beer range varies ⒣
Country free house, parts of which date back to the 13th century; popular with walkers and bikers.
♨ Q 🏠 🛏 ◁ ▶ & ♣ P ⚲

Bramley

Master Brewer

Main Street ☎ (01709) 541103
11–11; 12–10.30 Sun
Mansfield Riding Mild, Riding Bitter, Old Baily ⒣
Modern, two-roomed, brick-built pub. The beamed lounge is quiet and softly lit; the bar caters mainly for the young (pool, pinball, TV). Varied home-made meals (the pies are a must). 🏠 ◁ ▶ ⌗ P

Brookhouse

Traveller's Rest

☎ (01909) 562661
12–3, 6–11; 11–11 Fri, Sat & summer; 12–4, 7–10.30 (12–10.30 summer) Sun
Hardys & Hansons Best Bitter, seasonal beers; Stones Bitter ⒣

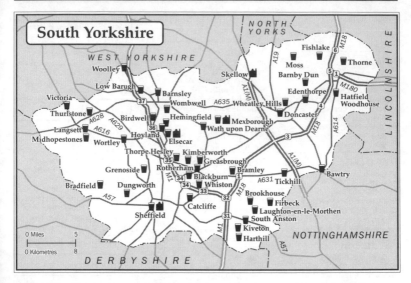

South Yorkshire

Stone pub in a picturesque village: a tap room and a lounge/dining room. The garden, with children's play area, overlooks a stream.
🍴 ❀ ◖ ◗ 🍺 ♣ P

Catcliffe

Waverley
Brinsworth Road (B6067)
☎ (01709) 360906
12–3.30 (11.30–4.30 Sat), 6–11; 12–3.30, 7–10.30 Sun
Beer range varies Ⓗ
Modern, three-roomed genuine free house with four guest beers, featuring independent local breweries. Large, comfortable family room; garden with children's entertainment provided on Fri and Sat eves.
🛏 ❀ ◖ ◗ 🍺 ♣ P 🍽

Doncaster

Greyfriars Inn
Greyfriars Road
☎ (01302) 360096
12–3 (not Mon or Wed in winter); 11–4 Sat), 7–11; 12–3, 7–10.30 Sun
Barnsley Bitter; Stones Bitter; guest beer Ⓗ
Welcoming pub, close to secure moorings on the Sheffield & S Yorks Navigation: a refurbished lounge, a comfortable bar and a garden with fine views of the church. Supportive of local breweries. Eve meals Mon–Fri.
❀ 🍴 ◖ ◗ 🍺 ♣ P 🍽

Leopard
West Street
☎ (01302) 363054
11–11; 12–10.30 Sun
Marston's Pedigree; John Smith's Bitter; guest beer Ⓗ

Lively, street-corner pub with a superb tiled frontage.
◖ 🍺 ♣ P

Masons Arms
Market Place
☎ (01302) 3464391
11–3 (4 Tue & Fri), 7.30–11; 12–3, 7.30–10.30 Sun
Tetley Bitter Ⓗ
Tetley Heritage pub over 200 years old, displaying original pub documents and bills of sale. The rear courtyard is ablaze with flowers in summer. A tranquil oasis.
Q ❀ 🍺 🍺 ♣

Plough
8 West Laith Gate
☎ (01302) 738310
11–4, 6.30–11; 11–11 Tue, Fri & Sat; 12–3, 7–10.30 Sun
Barnsley Bitter; Draught Bass; guest beer (occasional) Ⓗ
Warm, traditional, two-room pub, a popular escape from the bustle of the shopping area and the 'fun pub' circuit: a basic, bright bar with a comfortable and unusual lounge. Possibly the world's smallest beer 'garden'. Q ❀ 🍺 🍺 ♣

Railway
West Street ☎ (01302) 349700
11–11; 12–3, 7–10.30 Sun
Barnsley Bitter; John Smith's Bitter, Magnet Ⓗ
Popular street-corner local, just away from the centre, near the station: a small snug and a large comfortable bar with a pool area. No food Sun.
◖ 🍺 ♣ 🍽

Salutation
14 South Parade
☎ (01302) 368464
11.30–3, 5–11; 11.30–11 Thu–Sat; 12–3, 7–10.30 Sun

Ind Coope Burton Ale; Marston's Pedigree; Tetley Bitter; guest beers Ⓗ
The oldest pub in the centre, a coaching inn since 1745 with decoration to match, now a Tetley Festival Ale House. No food after 7, or on Sun.
🍴 ❀ ◖ ◗ ♣ P

White Swan
34A Frenchgate
☎ (01302) 366573
11–11; 12–10.30 Sun
Vaux Waggle Dance; Ward's Best Bitter; guest beer Ⓗ
Friendly town-centre pub with the highest bar in Britain (the tap room and rear lounge are on different levels). Popular with shoppers. Ramped access; next to an 'orange badge' holders' car park. Good value lunches (no food Sun).
❀ ◖ ◗ ♿ 🍺

Dungworth

Royal Hotel
Main Road (B6076)
☎ (0114) 285 1213
12–3 (not Mon), 7–11; 12–4, 7–10.30 Sun
Stones Bitter; John Smith's Magnet; Tetley Bitter; guest beer Ⓗ

 INDEPENDENT BREWERIES

Abbeydale: Sheffield

Barnsley: Elsecar

Concertina: Mexborough

Glentworth: Skellow

Kelham Island: Sheffield

Ward's: Sheffield

Friendly, village local, popular with walkers. Book eve meals.
🛏 Q ❀ ◑ ➧ ❅ ♣ P ✼

Edenthorpe

Beverley Inn

117 Thorne Road (off A18, near Tesco) ☎ (01302) 882724
11.45–3, 5 (6.30 Sat)–11; 12–3, 7–10.30 Sun
John Smith's Bitter; Theakston XB; guest beers Ⓗ
Busy, friendly local which serves a mature clientele, specialising in good, reasonably priced food and beer. Background music is played at most times. No food Sun eve. ❀ 🛏 ◑ ➧ ❅ P ✼

Elsecar

Fitzwilliam Arms

42 Hill Street ☎ (01226) 742461
12–3.30 (not Mon), 7–11; 12–3, 7–10.30 Sun
Vaux Samson; Ward's Thorne BB, Best Bitter; guest beer (occasional) Ⓗ
Friendly, two-roomed local with a central bar, serving excellent value lunches.
Q ❀ ◑ ❅ ♣ ➧ P ＼

Firbeck

Black Lion

9 New Road ☎ (01709) 812575
12–3, 5.30–11; 12–3, 5.30–10.30 Sun
Barnsley Bitter; Ruddles County; John Smith's Bitter; Stones Bitter Ⓗ
17th-century, reputedly haunted pub, popular with local societies.
🛏 ❀ 🛏 ◑ ➧ ♣ P 🍴

Fishlake

Hare & Hounds

Church Street
☎ (01302) 841208
12–4, 7–11; 12–3, 7–10.30 Sun
Mansfield Riding Bitter, Old Baily Ⓗ
Traditional local: a spacious but cosy lounge, decorated with brasses and old village photographs, plus a small public bar, popular for dominoes. No food, but customers are welcome to bring sandwiches. ❀ ♣ P

Greasbrough

Prince of Wales

9 Potter Hill (B6089)
☎ (01709) 551358
11–4, 7–11; 12–3, 7–10.30 Sun
John Smith's Bitter Ⓔ**; guest beer** Ⓗ
Popular, friendly, two-bar village local with a traditional tap room and a comfortable lounge. The continuously-changing independent guest beer is sold at a below-average price. ❀ 🍴 ♣ 🍴

Grenoside

Cow & Calf

88 Skew Hill Lane (½ mile off A61) ☎ (0114) 246 8191
11.30–3, 6–11; 11.30–11 Sun; 12–10.30 Sun
Samuel Smith OBB Ⓗ
Converted farmhouse with several drinking areas and a family room. Welcoming atmosphere; plenty of rural charm. No eve meals Sun.
Q 🛏 ❀ ◑ ➧ ♣ P ✼

Harthill

Beehive

16 Union Street
☎ (01909) 770205
12–3 (not Mon), 6 (7 Sat)–11; 12–3, 7–10.30 Sun
Marston's Pedigree; Tetley Bitter Ⓗ
Typical, three-roomed country pub with a function room upstairs (folk club monthly; quiz every Tue). ❀ ◑ ➧ P

Hatfield Woodhouse

Green Tree

Bearswood Green (A18/A614 jct) ☎ (01302) 840305
11–11; 12–10.30 Sun
Vaux Samson; Ward's Thorne BB; guest beers Ⓗ
Welcoming roadside inn, popular for its excellent, home-cooked food.
Q 🛏 ❀ 🛏 ◑ ➧ P ✼

Hemingfield

Lundhill Tavern

Beech House Road (off A633)
☎ (01226) 752283
12–11; 12–10.30 Sun
Barnsley Bitter, IPA; John Smith's Bitter; Samuel Smith OBB; guest beers Ⓗ
Pub off the beaten track, steeped in local coal mining history. It stages charity open-air rock festivals on bank hols. Good value meals (not served Sun eve). ◑ ➧ ❅ P

Hoyland

Beggar & Gentleman (Beer Engine)

Market Street
☎ (01226) 742364
11–11; 12–10.30 Sun
Barnsley Bitter; Boddingtons Bitter; Whitbread Trophy; guest beers Ⓗ
Spacious, town-centre alehouse catering for all ages. Good value lunches (not served Sun). Free pie and peas Tue pm.
❀ ◑ ➧ ➷ (Elsecar) ♣ P

Furnace Inn

163 Milton Road (B6097)
☎ (01226) 742000
12–3, 6.30–11; 12–3, 7–10.30 Sun
Vaux Double Maxim; Ward's Thorne BB Ⓔ**, Best Bitter** Ⓗ/Ⓔ**; guest beers** Ⓗ
Award-winning, friendly village local alongside a pond.
Q ❀ ➷ (Elsecar) ♣ P

Kimberworth

Green Dragon

High Street ☎ (01709) 566910
12–11; 12–3, 7–10.30 Sun
Draught Bass; Stones Bitter; guest beers Ⓗ
Comfortable, friendly two-roomed local, featuring a large garden with a children's play area. Eve meals 5–7.30.
❀ ◑ ➧ ♣ P

Kiveton

Station Hotel

Dog Kennel Hill, Kiveton Park (opp. station)
☎ (01909) 773201
12–4, 7–11; 12–3, 7–10.30 Sun
John Smith's Bitter; Marston's Pedigree; Stones Bitter; guest beers Ⓗ
Next to a recently restored waterway, this pub is full of railway memorabilia; note the unusual carpet. A central bar serves two rooms; families welcome. 🛏 Q ❀ ◑ ➧ ➷ (Kiveton Pk) ♣ P

Langsett

Waggon & Horses

On A616 ☎ (01226) 763259
12–2.30, 5.30–11; 11.30–11 Fri & Sat; 12–3, 7–10.30 Sun
Theakston Best Bitter, XB; Younger No. 3 Ⓗ
Cosy, friendly roadside pub with an excellent reputation for its food. 🛏 Q ❀ 🛏 ◑ ➧ P

Laughton-en-le-Morthen

St Leger

4 High Street ☎ (01909) 562940
12–11; 12–10.30 Sun
Barnsley Bitter; Boddingtons Bitter; Whitbread Trophy Ⓗ
Friendly village local serving excellent, home-cooked meals (carvery all day Sun). Popular with ramblers. Live entertainment Fri eve.
❀ ◑ ➧ ♣ P 🍴

Low Barugh

Millers Inn

Dearne Hall Road (B6428)
11.30–2.30, 5.30–11; 11.30–11 Fri & Sat; 12–3, 7–10.30 Sun
Barnsley Bitter; Taylor Landlord; guest beers Ⓗ

Free house backing on to the River Dearne; a meeting place for various clubs. No eve meals Sat–Thu. Q ❀ ◖ ▶ ⛧ ♣ P

Mexborough

Concertina Band Club

9A Dolcliffe Road
☎ (01709) 580841
12–4, 7–11; 12–2, 7–10.30 Sun
**Concertina Best Bitter;
Mansfield Bitter; John Smith's
Bitter; guest beers** Ⓗ
Visitors are welcome at this small, friendly club which is steeped in local history. The choice of Concertina beers (brewed here) continues to grow. A frequent award winner. ⇌ ♣ 🗗

Falcon

12 Main Street
☎ (01709) 571170
11.30–5, 7–11; 11–11 Fri & Sat; 12–2, 7–10.30 Sun
Old Mill Bitter Ⓗ
Lively pub: a smart lounge with raised seating areas and a games-oriented tap room. Other beers from the Old Mill range are sometimes available.
❀ ⌂ & ⇌ ♣

George & Dragon

81 Church Street (off A6023, near river and canal)
☎ (01709) 584375
12–11; 12–10.30 Sun
**Vaux Samson, Double Maxim;
Ward's Best Bitter; guest
beers** Ⓗ
Welcoming, cosy pub with a central bar. The pleasant garden at the rear is popular with families. No meals Sat eve or Sun. ❀ ◖ ▶ & ♣ P 🗗

Midhopestones

Midhopestones Arms

Mortimer Road (400 yds from A616) ☎ (01226) 762305
12–3, 6–11; 12–10.30 Sun
**Badger Tanglefoot; Barnsley
Bitter; Boddingtons Bitter;
Courage Directors; Ruddles
County; Taylor Landlord;
guest beer** Ⓗ
300-year-old village inn, popular with walkers: a stone-flagged floor, original beams and four real fires are features. One room is dedicated to an antiques and craft shop.
🏨 Q ❀ ◖ ▶ & ♠ ♣ P ⚮

Moss

Star Inn

Moss Road ☎ (01302) 700497
5.30 (7 Sat)–11; 12–3, 9 (7 summer)–10.30 Sun
**Ward's Thorne BB; guest
beer** Ⓗ
White-walled country pub with an interesting layout and an aeronautical theme. The

garden has a children's playground. The licensee has won a brewery cellar award. Good value, home-cooked food. 🏨 Q ❀ 🐕 ❀ ◖ ▶ ♠ P

Rotherham

Charter Arms

Eastwood Lane
☎ (01709) 373066
10.30–11; 12–10.30 Sun
**Mansfield Riding Bitter,
Bitter, Old Baily; guest beer** Ⓗ
Friendly, modern, refurbished pub offering excellent food: a comfortable, large lounge, and a games room. Very popular with shoppers and musicians.
◖ 🍴 ⇌ ♣

Effingham Arms

Effingham Street (opp. bus station) ☎ (01709) 539030
11–11; 12–3, 7–10.30 Sun
**Fuller's London Pride; Stones
Bitter** Ⓗ
Friendly, multi-roomed, town-centre, wood-panelled Victorian pub, with 1930s original stained-glass windows depicting Captain Effingham's exploits. Games room. ⇌

Moulders Rest

110–112 Masbrough Street (near Rotherham FC)
12–3, 6 (7.30 Sat)–11; 12–3, 7–10.30 Sun
Stones Bitter; guest beer Ⓗ
Large, main road corner pub: a busy tap room, a snug and a through lounge, popular for games. Good value food (not served weekends).
🍴 ◖ 🍴 ⇌ (Central) ♣ P

Woodman

Midland Road, Masbrough (off A629, by bus depot)
☎ (01709) 512128
12–3, 7–11; 12–2, 7–10.30 Sun
Stones Bitter; guest beer Ⓗ
Friendly, former Bentley's pub with a traditional tap room, a snooker room upstairs and a snug lounge. It was built as a corner local in 1853 but the housing's now gone. Guest beer prices are competitive.
Q ❀ 🍴 ♣

Sheffield: *Central*

Banker's Draft

1–3 Market Place
☎ (0114) 275 6609
11–11; 12–10.30 Sun
**Courage Directors; Taylor
Landlord; Theakston Best
Bitter; Younger Scotch; guest
beers** Ⓗ
Typical Wetherspoons conversion of a former bank with spacious bars on two floors. A busy pub with low prices, adjacent to a tram stop.
Q ◖ ▶ & ⇌ (Midland) ⊖
(Castle Sq) ⚮

Fat Cat

23 Alma Street
☎ (0114) 249 4801
12–3, 5.30–11; 12–3, 7–10.30 Sun
**Kelham Island Bitter;
Marston's Pedigree; Taylor
Landlord; guest beers** Ⓗ
Sheffield's first real ale free house, opened in 1981. Two comfortable rooms (one no-smoking), a corridor drinking area and an upstairs function room used for overspill. Kelham Island Brewery is situated in the grounds and two of its beers are always on sale.
🏨 Q ❀ ◖ ♣ ⌂ ⚮

Harlequin

26 Johnson Street
☎ (0114) 249 3069
12–4, 7 (8 Sat)–11; 12–5, 8–10.30 Sun
Ward's Best Bitter Ⓔ
Traditional, street-corner local noted for the pot-bellied stove in the tap room, which leads through to the pool area. A room off the corridor drinking area is used for live music Thu–Sat eves and Sun–Mon lunch. A function room is available upstairs.
🏨 Q ❀ 🍴 ⇌ (Midland) ♣

Lord Nelson

166 Arundel Street
☎ (0114) 272 2650
12–11; 12–6, 7.30–11 Sat; 12–5, 7.30–10.30 Sun
**Hardys & Hansons Best Bitter,
seasonal beers; Stones
Bitter** Ⓗ
Comfortable, street-corner local in an area of small workshops near the edge of the city centre. Upstairs games/function room.
◖ ⇌ (Midland) ♣

Morrissey's Riverside

1 Mowbray Street
☎ (0114) 275 7306
12–3, 5 (7 Sat)–11; 12–3, 7–10.30 Sun
**Adnams Bitter; Archers
Golden; Highwood Tom
Wood Best Bitter; Taylor
Landlord; guest beers** Ⓗ
Three-roomed, street-corner pub with an upstairs function room for entertainment, including comedy and poetry nights. A pleasant garden overlooks the River Don.
Q ❀ ◖ ⇌ (Midland) ♣ ⚮

Moseley's Arms

81–85 West Bar
☎ (0114) 249 1656
11–11; 12–3, 7–11 Sat; 7–10.30 (closed lunch) Sun
Stones Bitter; guest beer Ⓗ
Superbly renovated pub just off the city centre; three comfortably furnished rooms, with a friendly atmosphere. Function room with a snooker table upstairs.
◖ 🍴 ⇌ (Midland) ♣

Red House

168 Solly Street
☎ (0114) 272 7926
12–3 (4 Sat), 5.30 (7.30 Sat)–11; 12–3,
7–10.30 Sun
**Ward's Best Bitter; guest
beers** Ⓗ
Renovated traditional local,
retaining three drinking areas,
one with a pool table. Regular
live music and quizzes.
Weekday lunches. Q ◗ ♣

Rutland Arms

86 Brown Street
☎ (0114) 272 9003
11.30–3, 5–11; 11.30–11 Wed–Fri; 12–4,
7.30–11 Sat; 12–3, 8–10.30 Sun
**Greene King Abbot; Ind
Coope Burton Ale; Marston's
Pedigree; Tetley Bitter;
Younger No. 3** Ⓗ
Cosmopolitan pub in the city-
centre's cultural quarter. A
comfortable lounge lies behind
the impressive Gilmours
frontage. No eve meals
weekends.
❀ ⌂ ◗ ▶ ⇌ (Midland) P

Ship Inn

312 Shalesmoor
☎ (0114) 281 2204
12–3, 6 (5 Fri, 7.30 Sat)–11; 12–3,
7.30–10.30 Sun
**Hardys & Hansons Best Bitter;
guest beers** Ⓗ
Community pub with an
impressive Tomlinson's
frontage. The comfortable,
L-shaped lounge has a pool
area at the rear.
⊖ (Shalesmoor) ♣ P ⊟

Tap & Spile

42 Waingate ☎ (0114) 272 7042
11.30–3, 5.30 (7 Sat)–11; 7–10.30
(closed lunch) Sun
Beer range varies Ⓗ
Street-corner pub where the
large bar has exposed
brickwork and bare boards. A
smaller side room (no-smoking
lunchtime) has a raised area for
darts and pool. Folk sessions
Wed. Usually at least six beers
available. ◗ ⇌ (Midland) ⊖
(Fitzalan Sq) ♣ ⌂ ✂

Sheffield: *East*

Alma

76 South Street, Mosborough
(behind Eckington Hall)
☎ (0114) 248 4781
11.30–3.30, 7–11; 12–4, 7–10.30 Sun
**Vaux Samson; Ward's Best
Bitter** Ⓗ/Ⓔ
Traditional, two-roomed local
at the quieter end of the village.
The low-beamed lounge
provides a cosy drinking
atmosphere. Well worth
seeking out. Q ❀ ▣ ♣ P

Carbrook Hall

537 Attercliffe Common,
Carbrook ☎ (0114) 244 0117
12–3, 5 (6 Sat)–11; 12–11 Fri; 12–3,
7–10.30 Sun

**John Smith's Magnet; Stones
Bitter; guest beer**
(occasional) Ⓗ
Sheffield's most haunted pub:
three contrasting rooms
include a fine oak-panelled
parlour with its original ornate
ceiling and intricate carving
around the fireplace. Decor is
on a Civil War theme. No food
Sat. A no-smoking area is
available when food is being
served.
⌖ Q ❀ ◗ ⊖ (Carbrook) P

Cocked Hat

75 Worksop Road, Attercliffe
☎ (0114) 244 8332
11–11; 11–3, 7–11 Sat & bank hols;
12–2, 7–10.30 Sun
**Marston's Bitter, Pedigree,
HBC** Ⓗ
Ever-popular, small,
150-year-old pub by Don
Valley Stadium, displaying
photos of old Attercliffe. A
well-used bar billiards table
and a good collection of bottled
beers are features. No food
weekends. On-street parking is
available.
❀ ◗ ⊖ (Attercliffe) ♣

Milestone

12 Peaks Mount, Waterthorpe
☎ (0114) 247 1614
11–11; 12–3, 7–10.30 Sun
Banks's Bitter Ⓔ**; Camerons
Strongarm; Marston's
Pedigree** Ⓗ
Modern, but appealing, pub
serving Crystal Peaks
shopping centre; a local
meeting place with a large
lounge with a conservatory,
but there's cheaper beer in the
public bar. Children welcome
if dining (eve meals Mon–Thu
till 8). ◗ ▶ ▣ ⅊ ⊖ (Crystal
Peaks) ♣ P ✂

Red Lion

145 Duke Street
☎ (0114) 272 8296
11–11; 12–10.30 Sun
Burtonwood Bitter Ⓗ
Largely unspoilt, heritage pub,
a traditional local with a
central bar and drinking area,
plus three other rooms, one a
pool room. Pictures and maps
illustrate local history back to
1797. ⌖ Q ⌂ ❀ ⇌
(Midland) ⊖ (Hallam
University) ♣ P

Sheffield: *North*

Cask & Cutler

1 Henry Street, Shalesmoor
☎ (0114) 249 2295
12–2, 5.30–11; 12–11 Fri & Sat; 12–3,
7–10.30 Sun
Beer range varies Ⓗ
Shrine to real ale, serving some
of the lowest priced beers in
the city (six ales). Eve meals
end at 6.30.
⌖ Q ❀ ◗ ▶ ⅊ ⊖
(Shalesmoor) ♣ ⌂ P ✂ ⊟

Morrissey's East House

18 Spital Hill
☎ (0114) 272 6916
12–3 (not Mon–Thu), 5 (4.30 Fri)–11;
12–3, 7–10.30 Sun
**Barnsley Bitter; Flowers IPA;
Fuller's London Pride; Taylor
Landlord; guest beer** Ⓗ
Long, narrow pub with a single
bar, displaying local history
and maps. Some 18 Irish
whiskeys in stock. Lunches
served Fri and Sat.
Q ◗ ♣ P

New Barrack Tavern

601 Penistone Road
☎ (0114) 234 9148
12–3, 5–11; 12–11 Fri & Sat; 12–10.30
Sun
**Abbeydale Moonshine;
Barnsley Bitter; John Smith's
Magnet; Stones Bitter; guest
beers** Ⓗ
Lively, three-roomed local
close to Hillsborough barracks,
serving up to six guest beers,
plus imported Czech and
Belgian draught lagers.
Regular live music. Eve meals
weekdays 5.30–7.30.
Q ❀ ◗ ▶ ▣ ⊖ (Bamforth St) ♣
⌂ P

Robin Hood

Little Matlock, Stannington
☎ (0114) 234 4565
12–2.30 (3 summer), 7–11; 12–3,
7–10.30 Sun
Stones Bitter Ⓗ/Ⓔ
Relaxing, 200-year-old former
coaching inn, in beautiful
countryside near the River
Loxley. Q ❀ ◗ ▶ ♣ P

Staffordshire Arms

40 Sorby Street, Burngreave
☎ (0114) 272 1381
11–11; 12–3, 7–10.30 Sun
Stones Bitter Ⓔ
Unspoilt, two-roomed,
backstreet local with a central
bar – a rare survivor. ♣ ⊟

Sheffield: *South*

Archer Road Beer Stop

57 Archer Road
☎ (0114) 255 1356
11–10; 10.30–10 Sat; 12–2, 6–10 Sun
**Taylor Landlord; guest
beers** Ⓗ
Small, corner-shop off-licence
stocking a wide range of
British, bottle-conditioned and
overseas beers. ⌂ ⊟

Broadfield

452 Abbeydale Road
☎ (0114) 255 0200
11–11; 12–10.30 Sun
**Boddingtons Bitter; Castle
Eden Ale; Whitbread Trophy;
guest beers** Ⓗ
Large tavern with a games
room and a traditional bar; a
popular local. Good food is
available all week (until 6.30)
but only breakfasts (10–12.30)

at weekends. Two big screens are used for sport. Up to nine beers on sale.
❀ ◖ ▶ ♣ P

Cremorne

185 London Road
☎ (0114) 255 0126
12–11; 11–3.30, 7.30–11 Sat; 12–3, 7–10.30 Sun
Marston's Pedigree; Tetley Bitter; guest beers ⊞
Tetley Festival Ale House in the stone and bare-boards tradition: a large, L-shaped drinking area, plus a lower level games area with a pool table. One of the better places to drink in an area awash with pubs. ♣

Old Mother Redcap

Prospect Road, Bradway
☎ (0114) 236 0179
11.30–3, 5.30–11; 11.30–11 Sat; 12–10.30 Sun
Samuel Smith OBB ⊞
Modern, farmhouse-style building at Bradway bus terminus, with a single L-shaped lounge. Eve meals Thu and Fri.
❀ ◖ ▶ ≠ (Dore) ♣ P ⏚

Shakespeare

106 Well Road
☎ (0114) 255 3995
12–3.30 (4 Sat), 5.30 (7 Sat)–11; 12–3, 7–10.30 Sun
Stones Bitter; Tetley Bitter, Imperial; guest beers ⊞
Welcoming, community pub very near Heeley City Farm. One bar serves several drinking areas.
❀ ♣ P

White Swan

57 Greenhill Main Road
☎ (0114) 237 7851
11–11; 12–10.30 Sun
Boddingtons Bitter; Castle Eden Ale; Marston's Pedigree; Whitbread Trophy; guest beer ⊞
Fine village community pub with four distinct drinking areas served from a central bar. Good, home-cooked food daily, except Sun eve (book Sun lunch). Guest beers are from the Whitbread range. Pianist Sun eve.
Q ❀ ◖ ▶ ⊟ ♣ P

Sheffield: *West*

Banner Cross

971 Ecclesall Road
☎ (0114) 266 1479
11.30–11; 12–10.30 Sun
Ind Coope Burton Ale; Marston's Pedigree; Tetley Bitter ⊞
Traditional suburban local with an upstairs games room, a large, panelled lounge and a tap room. ❀ ♣ ♣

Devonshire Arms

118 Ecclesall Road
☎ (0114) 277 7202
11–11; 12–10.30 Sun
Ward's Best Bitter ⊞/Ⓔ**; guest beers** ⊞
Extensively renovated local with several partitioned seating areas and a conservatory: the Ward's brewery tap.
❀ ◖ ▶ ≈ ♣ P

Lescar

303 Sharrowvale Road
☎ (0114) 266 3857
12–11; 12–10.30 Sun
Draught Bass; Stones Bitter; Taylor Landlord; guest beer ⊞
Friendly, corner pub, popular with locals and students, comprised of a tap room, a lounge and a function room used for live bands and the comedy club (Thu eve). Eve meals end at 7.
❀ ◖ ▶ ⊟ ♣ P

Old Grindstone

3 Crookes
☎ (0114) 266 0322
11–11; 12–10.30 Sun
Taylor Landlord; Vaux Waggle Dance ⊞**; Ward's Best Bitter** ⊞/Ⓔ**; guest beer** ⊞
Spacious, busy pub. Tiered levels lead to a games area which retains oak-panelled walls. Eve meals finish at 7.30.
◖ ▶ ♿ ♣

Old Heavygate

114 Matlock Road
☎ (0114) 234 0003
2 (12 Sat)–4, 7–11; 12–3, 7–10.30 Sun
Hardys & Hansons Best Bitter; guest beer ⊞
Pub dating from 1696, previously a cottage and toll house. ❀ ♣ P ⏚

Sportsman

569 Redmires Road
☎ (0114) 230 1935
11.30–4, 6–11; 11.30–11 Sat; 12–3, 7–10.30 (12–10.30 summer) Sun
Courage Directors; Ruddles Best Bitter; John Smith's Bitter; Theakston XB ⊞
Country pub within the city boundary, family-run with genuine friendliness. Note the curious corner mirrored cabinets. Q ❀ ◖ ▲ ♣ P

South Anston

Loyal Trooper

34 Sheffield Road (off A57)
☎ (01909) 562203
12–3, 7–11; 12–11 Sat; 12–3, 7–10.30 Sun
Tetley Bitter, Imperial ⊞
Traditional, three-roomed local, thought to be sited on an old staging post. Children's certificate. ❀ ◖ ♿ ♣ P

Thorne

Canal Tavern

South Parade (by canal bridge)
☎ (01405) 813688
11.30–3, 5.30–11; 11.30–11 Sat; 12–4, 7–10.30 Sun
Barnsley Bitter; Boddingtons Bitter; John Smith's Bitter; Tetley Bitter; guest beers ⊞
Canalside hostelry, popular with boaters, offering a wide range of beers and an extensive menu (roasts a speciality).
⌂ ❀ ◖ ▶ ≈ (South) ♣ P

John Bull

Waterside (by M18 jct 6)
☎ (01405) 814677
12–2 (not Mon), 7 (6 summer)–11; 12–3, 7–10.30 Sun
Old Mill Bitter; John Smith's Bitter; guest beers ⊞
Pleasant, popular tavern with a restaurant.
Q ◖ ▶ ♿ ≈ (North) P

Thorpe Hesley

Masons Arms

Thorpe Street
☎ (0114) 246 8079
11.30–3, 7–11; 12–3, 7–10.30 Sun
John Smith's Bitter; Theakston Best Bitter, Old Peculier; Younger IPA ⊞
Welcoming, early 19th-century pub with one bar and three rooms on a split level. No food Sun. ❀ ◖ ▶ P

Thurlstone

Huntsman

136 Manchester Road (A628, 1½ miles W of Penistone)
☎ (01226) 762278
12–3 (4 Sat), 5–11; 12–4, 5–10.30 Sun
Boddingtons Bitter; Clark's Bitter; John Smith's Bitter; Taylor Landlord; guest beers ⊞
Charming, old terraced pub. A working Yorkshire range at one end provides respite from the Pennine winters. Stunning views from the garden.
⌂ ❀ ♣

Tickhill

Royal Oak

Northgate
☎ (01302) 742351
11.30–3, 5.30–11; 11.30–11 Sat; 12–4.30, 7–10.30 Sun
Boddingtons Bitter; Castle Eden Ale; Morland Old Speckled Hen; John Smith's Bitter; Taylor Landlord; guest beers ⊞
Refurbished village local with a good range of cask beers and a growing reputation for its food. ❀ ◖ ▶ ♣ P

Scarbrough Arms

Sunderland Street
☎ (01302) 742977
11–3, 6–11; 12–3, 7–10.30 Sun
Courage Directors; Newcastle Exhibition; Ruddles County; John Smith's Bitter, Magnet; guest beers H
Popular local with three rooms of differing character. Home-made lunches (not served Sun) include imaginative vegetarian dishes. ♨ Q ❀ ◖ ♣ P ☖

Victoria

Victoria Inn

Hepworth (A616, near pipe works) ☎ (01484) 682785
12–2 (not Mon–Thu), 7–11; 12–2, 7–10.30 Sun
Tetley Bitter H
Barnsley area's longest standing *Guide* entry, with possibly the longest serving licensees (since 1956) offering a good welcome. ♨ Q ⊞ P

Wath upon Dearne

Staithes

Doncaster Road (off A6023)
☎ (01709) 873546
12–11; 12–10.30 Sun
John Smith's Bitter; Stones Bitter; Theakston Old Peculier; guest beer H
Spacious comfortable, well-appointed, free house surrounded by a huge, exciting regeneration project. Multi-roomed, with nooks and crannies, it offers an extensive home-cooked menu. Family atmosphere; outside children's play area. ♨ ❀ ◖ ▶ P

Wheatley Hills

Wheatley Hotel

Thorne Road ☎ (01302) 364092
11–11; 12–10.30 Sun
John Smith's Bitter, Magnet; guest beer H
Large, friendly hotel with a comfortable lounge, divided by impressive wood/leaded glass sliding doors. Well-equipped children's play area. The restaurant (closed Sun eve) serves excellent value, home-cooked meals. ☎ ❀ ⌂ ◖ ▶ P

Whiston

Golden Ball

Turner Lane ☎ (01709) 378200
11.45–11; 12–10 Sun
Greene King Abbot; Ind Coope Burton Ale; Taylor Landlord; Tetley Bitter; guest beer H
Picture postcard pub offering a pleasant outside drinking area. Full of olde-worlde charm, it boasts an extensive menu. ♨ ❀ ◖ ▶ P ✗

Wombwell

Royal Oak

13 Church Street
☎ (01226) 210900
11–11; 12–10.30 Sun
Boddingtons Bitter; guest beers H
The last surviving pub bearing Clarkson's old brewery windows. It caters for all tastes, providing anything from chess to loud live music at weekends. Restaurant upstairs.
⌂ ◖ ▶ ⇌ ♣

Woolley

Woolley

Woolley Colliery Road
☎ (01226) 382847
11.30–3, 7–11 (11.30–11 summer); 12–4, 7–10.30 Sun
Barnsley Bitter; John Smith's Bitter; Tetley Bitter; guest beer H
Built in the 1920s as the Woolley Miners' Welfare Club, this very large pub has a number of drinking areas, plus a sun room and a bowling green.
♨ ☎ ❀ ◖ ⊞ ⇌ (Darton) P

Wortley

Wortley Arms

Halifax Road
☎ (0114) 288 2245
11–3, 5–11; 12–3, 7–10.30 Sun
Beer range varies H
16th-century coaching house in a picturesque village, ideally placed for walkers. Note the very large feature fireplace in the lounge.
♨ Q ☎ ⌂ ◖ ▶ ♣ P ✗

West Yorkshire

Bardsey

Bingley Arms

37 Church Lane
☎ (01937) 572462
12–3, 5.30–11; 12–10.30 Sun
Black Sheep Best Bitter, Special; Tetley Bitter H
With parts dating back to the 10th century, this inn boasts two priest holes, a Dutch oven, and exposed timbers in the upstairs restaurant.
♨ ❀ ◖ ▶ ⊞ ♣ P

Bradford

Blue Pig

Fagley Road, Lower Fagley
☎ (0113) 256 2738
3 (12 Fri & Sat)–11; 12–10.30 Sun
Tetley Bitter; Theakston Best Bitter; guest beers H
Split-level pub on the Leeds Country Way with a good atmosphere and an excellent family room.
☎ ❀ ◖ ♣ P

Castle

20 Grattan Road (off Westgate)
☎ (01274) 393166
11.30–11; closed Sun
Mansfield Riding Mild, Riding Bitter, Bitter; guest beers H
Popular city-centre house, built in 1898. The single room has been partitioned to provide a drinking area away from the main bar. Free food Fri lunchtime. Car park open eves and weekends.
Q ⇌ (Exchange/Forster Sq) P

Corn Dolly

110 Bolton Road (near cathedral) ☎ (01274) 720219
11.30–11; 12–3.30, 7–10.30 Sun
Black Sheep Best Bitter; Moorhouse's Premier; Theakston Best Bitter; guest beers H
Comfortable and friendly pub, built as the Wharf Hotel in 1834; busy at lunchtimes. Up to five guest beers (over 1,000 pumpclips on display).
♨ ◖ ⇌ (Forster Sq) ♣ P

Fighting Cock

21–23 Preston Street
☎ (01274) 726907
11.30–11; 12–10.30 Sun
Black Sheep Special; Glentworth Buttercross; Old Mill Bitter; Taylor Landlord; Theakston Old Peculier; guest beers H
Down-to-earth, bare-boarded drinker's haven in an industrial area, with at least 11 beers. The menu (not served Sun) consists of chilli and 'docker's wedge' sandwiches.
♨ ❀ ◖ ⅋ ⌂

Goldsborough

1 Captain Street (off Bolton Rd)
☎ (01274) 740138
11.30–11; 12–10.30 Sun
Boddingtons Bitter; Fuller's London Pride; Greene King Abbot; Old Mill Bitter; Tetley Dark Mild, Bitter; guest beers H
Friendly, open-plan ale house, now re-opened under the control of the legendary Jim Wright.
◖ ⊖ (Forster Sq) ⌂ P

Haigy's

31 Lumb Lane
☎ (01274) 731644
5 (12 Fri & Sat)–1am; 12–5 Sun
Black Sheep Best Bitter; Tetley Bitter; guest beers H
Lively pub with a late licence, offering a friendly welcome, five guest beers and good value meals. Pool room at the rear. Meals served till late.
❀ ◖ ▶ ♣ P

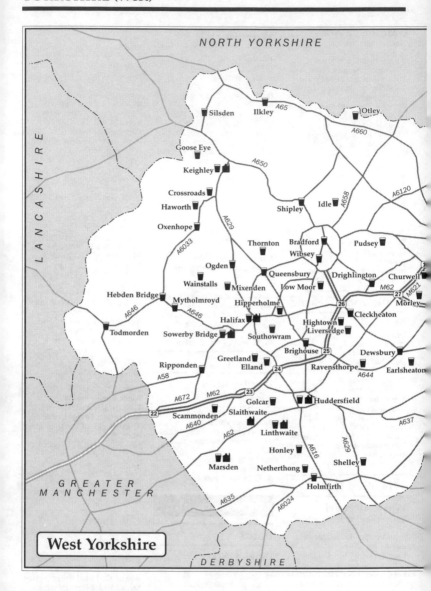

West Yorkshire

 INDEPENDENT BREWERIES

Barnfield: Slaithwaite

Black Horse: Halifax

Clark's: Wakefield

Eastwood's: Huddersfield

Fernandes: Wakefield

Goose Eye: Keighley

Kitchen: Huddersfield

Linfit: Linthwaite

Merrimans: Leeds

Rat & Ratchet: Huddersfield

Riverhead: Marsden

Ryburn: Sowerby Bridge

Steam Packet: Knottingley

Taylor: Keighley

Tigertops: Wakefield

Tomlinson's: Pontefract

Worth: Keighley

Melborn Hotel
104 White Abbey Road (road to infirmary)
☎ (01274) 726867
12–11; 12–10.30 Sun
Moorhouse's Premier; Old Mill Bitter; Tetley Bitter; guest beers Ⓗ
Multi-roomed, friendly, down-to-earth pub with a large tap room and lounge. Regular live music; the pub is adorned with musical instruments and breweriana. Home of the Topic folk club (the beer of the same name is brewed by Moorhouse's).
❀ 🛏 🍴 ♣ P

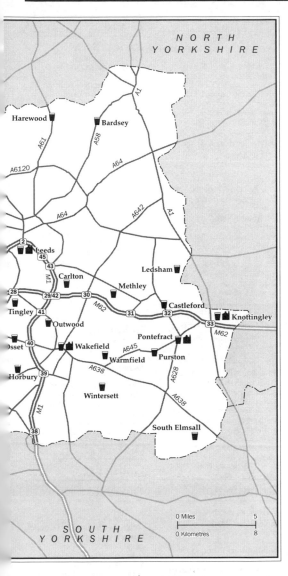

Victorian building affording extensive views of Bradford. Organ music and sing-alongs at weekends. Curries are recommended (take-aways available). 🏠 ♣ P

Steve Biko Bar

D Floor, Bradford University, Richmond Building, Richmond Road ☎ (01274) 383257
11 (5.30 Sat)–11; 6–10.30 Sun
Boddingtons Bitter; Castle Eden Ale; Courage Directors; John Smith's Bitter; Theakston Best Bitter; guest beers Ⓗ
Thriving, lively, open-plan bar run by the Students' Union. With regular cheap beer promotions, it can get very busy. Eve meals Mon–Fri. Car park open eves. ◐ ▶ ♣ ⇨ P

Tap & Spile

26 Sackville Street
☎ (01274) 725003
12–11; 12–3, 7–10.30 Sun
Beer range varies Ⓗ
18th-century former coach house, inn and stables with three friendly drinking areas, including a tap room. No food Sun. ⚘ ◐ 🍴 ⇌ (Interchange/ Forster Sq) ♣ ⇨

Brighouse

Red Rooster

123 Elland Road, Brookfoot (A6025) ☎ (01484) 713737
12–2, 5–11; 12–11 Sat; 12–3, 7–10.30 Sun
Black Sheep Best Bitter; Moorhouse's Pendle Witches Brew; Old Mill Bitter; Rooster's Yankee; Theakston Best Bitter, XB; guest beers Ⓗ
Compact and friendly roadside local stocking four guest beers, often from microbreweries.
🏠 ⚘ ◐ ♣ ⇨ P

Carlton

Carlton WMC

Main Street ☎ (0113) 282 2293
7 (4 Fri)–11; 12–4, 7–11 Sat; 12–4, 7–10.30 Sun
Robinson's Best Bitter Ⓗ
Club in the heart of Carlton village with many affiliations, including RAOB and Royal British Legion. Show the *Guide* or a CAMRA membership card at the bar to be signed in.
Q ⚘ 🍴 ♿ ♣ P

Castleford

Garden House Inn

Wheldon Road (near River Aire bridge) ☎ (01977) 552934
11.30–3.30, 5–11; 12–3, 5–10.30 Sun
Vaux Samson; Ward's Thorne BB; guest beers Ⓗ
Attractive, two-roomed pub away from the hustle and bustle of the town centre. Good

New Beehive ☆

171 Westgate
☎ (01274) 721784
12–11 (1am Sat); 7–10.30 (closed lunch) Sun
Goose Eye Bitter; Old Mill Bitter; Taylor Landlord; Worth Alesman; guest beers Ⓗ
Built by the local council in 1901 to replace pubs lost to road widening, and bought by an ancestor of the current licensee, this gas-lit, multi-roomed pub has a splendid atmosphere. Inch's cider is available. Live bands perform regularly in the cellar bar.
🏠 ⚘ 🛏 ◐ ▶ 🍴 ⇌ (Forster Sq) ♣ ⇨ P

Oakleigh

4 Oak Avenue, Manningham
☎ (01274) 544307
12–11; 12–10.30 Sun
Mansfield Riding Bitter, Bitter; guest beers Ⓗ
Free house which has recently been renovated and seems more spacious than ever, with a large garden and patio. Near Lister Park. No food Sat.
⚘ 🛏 ◐ P

Prospect of Bradford

527 Bolton Road
☎ (01274) 727018
7–11; 3–5, 7–11 Sat; 12–4, 7–10.30 Sun
Tetley Bitter; Theakston Best Bitter Ⓗ

value meals. Many prints of
old Castleford and its rugby
team by a local artist are
displayed.
Q ❀ ◁▶ ⊟ ᴧ ♣ P

Churwell

Commercial
Elland Road
☎ (0113) 253 2776
12–3, 7–11; 12–3, 7–10.30 Sun
**Tetley Mild, Bitter; guest
beer** 🄷
Split-roomed local known as
'Top 'Ole'. Children welcome
in the back room until 8.
ᴤ ❀ P

Cleckheaton

Marsh
28 Bradford Road (near bus
station)
☎ (01274) 872104
11.45–3, 7–11; 12–5, 7–10.30 Sun
**Old Mill Mild, Bitter, Bullion,
seasonal beers** 🄷
Good local with a friendly
welcome. The layout includes a
quiet dais and a games area.
♣ P

Crossroads

Quarry House Inn
Bingley Road, Lees Moor
(½ mile from A629/A6033 jct)
☎ (01535) 642239
12–3, 7–11; 12–3, 7–10.30 Sun
**Taylor Golden Best, Landlord;
Tetley Bitter** 🄷
Family-run, converted
farmhouse set in open
countryside with extensive
views. The bar is a former
church pulpit set in a small
cosy area. Excellent food (late
supper licence).
🏭 ᴤ ❀ ◁▶ ᴧ P

Dewsbury

Beer Street
Nowells Yard, Boothroyd Lane
☎ (01924) 466207
5 (12 Thu–Sat)–11; 12–10.30 Sun
Bateman XB; guest beers 🄷
Four rooms and a games room
in a traditional, 19th-century
village pub. Bare floor boards
add character to this popular,
lively hostelry. Q ❀ ⇶

Gate
50 Thornhill Road
☎ (01924) 461897
4 (12 Fri & Sat)–11; 12–10.30 Sun
**Black Sheep Best Bitter; Old
Mill Bitter; Tetley Bitter; guest
beers** 🄷
Stone-built Victorian pub, with
its original layout; a traditional
local fielding football teams
and a fishing club.
ᴤ ❀ ⊟ ♣ P

Saville Arms
Church Lane, Thornhill
☎ (01924) 463738
5–11; 12–3, 7.30–11 Sat; 12–3, 8–10.30
Sun
**Black Sheep Best Bitter;
Tetley Bitter; guest beers** 🄷
14th-century pub, built on
consecrated ground, boasting
an authentic tap room. A good
atmosphere prevails.
Q ᴤ ❀ P

'Sir' Geoffrey Boycott
125 High Street
☎ (01924) 457610
11–2 (3 Fri; not Tue), 5–11; 11–11 Sat;
12–10.30 Sun
**Courage Directors; Ruddles
County; Theakston Best
Bitter; guest beers** 🄷
Community pub, renovated
with a rustic feel, and designed
with visitors with disabilities
in mind. Families are
welcomed but this is not a
children's pub. Real
commitment to cider (two
festivals a year).
🏭 ❀ ◁▶ ᴧ ♣ ⌂ P

West Riding Licensed Refreshment Rooms
Dewsbury Railway Station,
Wellington Road
☎ (01924) 459193
11–11; 12–10.30 Sun
**Bateman Mild, XB, XXXB;
Linfit English Guineas
(winter); guest beers** 🄷
Victorian building in the
station (celebrating its 150th
anniversary), drawing a
cosmopolitan clientele. Noted
for its weekday lunches. The
no-smoking area is available
until 6.
🏭 ❀ ◁▶ ᴧ ⇶ ⌂ P ✂

Drighlington

Painters Arms
35 Bradford Road
☎ (0113) 285 2557
11–11; 12–10.30 Sun
**Boddingtons Bitter; guest
beers** 🄷
Pub with two distinct halves:
the front is all stripped wood
and bare boards for young
drinkers, the back is comfy,
cosy and carpeted for the older
generation. Up to four guest
beers sold. ❀ ◁ P

Earlsheaton

Spangled Bull
6 Town Street
☎ (01924) 462949
11–11; 12–10.30 Sun
Tetley Mild, Bitter 🄷
Village local; the front used to
be the back and the building is
held together with an iron rod.
Food served Mon, Tue and Fri.
❀ ◁ ♣ P

Elland

Barge & Barrel
Park Road (A6025)
☎ (01422) 373623
11–11; 12–10.30 Sun
**Black Sheep Best Bitter,
Special; Taylor Landlord;
Tetley Bitter; guest beers** 🄷
Large, popular pub near Elland
Bridge, overlooking the canal
basin. Up to five guest beers,
plus a house beer from Coach
House. Eve meals 5–7.
🏭 ᴤ ◁▶ ᴧ ♣ ⌂ P

Golden Fleece
Lindley Road, Blackley (1 mile
S of Elland, near M62 jct 24)
☎ (01422) 372704
12–2.30 (2 Tue; not Sat); 7–11; 12–3,
7–10.30 Sun
**Vaux Samson; Ward's Thorne
BB; guest beer** 🄷
Pub where a cosy lounge, with
brassware and pictures, is
complemented by a dining
area (business lunches a
speciality). ❀ ◁ ♣ P

Golcar

Golcar Lily
101 Slades Road (follow signs
to Heath House Mill) OS087158
☎ (01484) 659277
12–3 (not Mon), 5.30–11; 12–11 Fri &
Sat; 12–3, 7–10.30 Sun
**Mansfield Riding Bitter,
Bitter, Old Baily; guest beer** 🄷
Former Co-op, converted into a
pub and restaurant, with
panoramic views over the
surrounding countryside. Well
noted for its food (not served
Mon). ❀ ◁▶ P

Goose Eye

Turkey Inn
☎ (01535) 681339
12–3 (5 Sat; not Mon), 5.30 (7 Sat)–11;
12–3, 7–10.30 Sun
**Goose Eye Bronte; Ind Coope
Burton Ale; Tetley Bitter;
guest beers** 🄷
Steep, twisting roads lead to
this 200-year-old inn in an
attractive village. Three
drinking areas ba the bar; two
boast open fires. Steaks are a
speciality in the dining area.
Children welcome till 8.
🏭 ❀ ◁▶ ᴧ ♣ P

Greetland

Duke of York
Stainland Road, Stainland
☎ (01422) 370217
12–3, 6–11; 12–11 Sat; 12–10.30 Sun
**Taylor Landlord, Ram Tam;
Tetley Bitter; guest beer** 🄷
Recently re-opened after a
two-year closure; a welcoming
and friendly village local.
Well-behaved children
welcome. ❀ ◁▶ ᴧ ♣ P

Greetland Community & Sporting Association

Rochdale Road (B6113)
☎ (01422) 370140
7–11; 12–3, 7–11 Wed; 12–11 Sat;
12–10.30 Sun
Beer range varies [H]
Club which caters for all ages
in a single, friendly bar serving
six cask beers (normally one
from Taylor and one from
Black Sheep). CAMRA
members admitted. ❀ ♣ P

Star

1 Lindwell (off B6113)
☎ (01422) 373164
12–4 (not Tue), 7–11; 12–3, 7–10.30
Sun
Ward's Thorne BB, Best Bitter,
guest beer (occasional) [H]
Friendly village local: a busy
tap room and a cosy lounge
with subdued lighting. The
start of the Calderdale Way is
nearby. ❀ ♣

Halifax

Brown Cow Inn

569 Gibbet Street, Highroad
Well (1½ miles W of centre)
☎ (01422) 361640
11.30–11; 12–10.30 Sun
Castle Eden Ale; Taylor
Landlord; Whitbread Trophy;
guest beer [H]
Unpretentious and deservedly
popular pub with strong
sporting interests. Lunches
Mon–Fri; meals 4–7 Sun.
❀ ◁ ▶ ♣

Shears Inn

Paris Gates, Boys Lane
☎ (01422) 362936
11.45–11; 12–10.30 Sun
Taylor Golden Best, Best
Bitter, Landlord; Younger
Scotch, No. 3; guest beers [H]
Hidden in a wooded valley
bottom and overshadowed by
Holdsworth's Mill, this small,
one-roomed pub is popular
with all ages. The Hebble Trail
footpath passes close by. No
food Sun.
⚰ ❀ ◁ ♣ P

Three Pigeons Ale House

1 Sun Fold, South Parade (near
station)
☎ (01422) 347001
12–3, 5–11; 12–11 Sat; 12–3, 7–10.30
Sun
Beer range varies [H]
Friendly, hospitable alehouse
with an octagonal drinking
area (note the mural overhead)
and three rooms radiating off.
The house beer is by Coach
House; regular beers are from
Black Sheep, Old Mill and
Taylor, plus three guests. Small
car park.
⚰ ❀ ◁ ➤ ♣ P

Harewood

Harewood Arms

Harrogate Road (A61)
☎ (0113) 288 6566
11–11; 12–10.30 Sun
Samuel Smith OBB [H]
Large, roadside inn catering for
diners, conference delegates,
overnight guests and serious
beer drinkers. Friendly and
efficient staff. Q ❀ ⚱ ◁ ▶ P

Haworth

Fleece Inn

67 Main Street
☎ (01535) 642772
12–11; 12–10.30 Sun
Taylor Golden Best, Mild,
Best Bitter, Porter, Landlord,
Ram Tam [H]
Former coaching inn with a
small stone-flagged bar area
and three downstairs drinking
areas, plus an upstairs games
room; comfortable decor
throughout. Warm welcome
for visitors.
🛏 ➤ (KWVLR) ♣

King's Arms

2 Church Street
☎ (01535) 643146
11–11; 12–10.30 Sun
Greene King Abbot; Ind
Coope Burton Ale; Tetley
Bitter; guest beer [H]
Popular village pub, once a
manor/toll house, dating back
to 1600. The main bar is
L-shaped; an area on the lower
level at the rear is normally for
diners. No meals Sun eve
(quiz). Tapster's Choice guest
beer. ❀ ◁ ▶ ▲ ➤ (KWVLR)

Royal Oak Inn

2 Mill Hey (opp. station)
☎ (01535) 643257
12–3, 7–11; 12–11 Sat & summer Fri;
12–10.30 Sun
Black Sheep Best Bitter;
Courage Directors; John
Smith's Bitter; Webster's
Yorkshire Bitter [H]
Pub with a comfortable, open
lounge area, decorated with
brass and copper, and a small
family room, with railway
memorabilia and a stone-faced
open fire. It was used as the
village mortuary during the
plague. Children welcome
until 8. ⚰ 🛏 ❀ ◁ ▶ ▲ ➤
(KWVLR) ♣ P

Hebden Bridge

Fox & Goose

9 Heptonstall Road
☎ (01422) 842649
11.30–3, 7–11; 12–3, 7–10.30 Sun
Goose Eye Bitter; guest
beers [H]
A haven for sociable people –
no jukebox or bandit. Three
changing guest beers from

independent breweries. The
only local pub using lined
glasses. Q ❀ ➤ ♣ ◠ 🍺

Hare & Hounds

Billy Lane, Chiserley, Old
Town OS005280
☎ (01422) 842671
12–3 (4 Sat; not Mon or Tue except
bank hols), 7–11; 12–10.30 Sun
Taylor Golden Best, Best
Bitter, Landlord, Ram Tam [H]
Hillside pub above Hebden
Bridge, known locally as 'Lane
Ends'. Families with well-
behaved children welcome. No
eve meals Mon.
⚰ Q ❀ ◁ ▶ ♣ P

White Lion Hotel

Bridge Gate ☎ (01422) 842197
11–11; 12–10.30 Sun
Boddingtons Bitter; Castle
Eden Ale; Flowers Original;
Taylor Landlord; guest
beers [H]
Pleasant, opened-out former
coaching inn, offering a mix of
styles to a wide-ranging
clientele. Riverside garden.
Wheelchair WC.
⚰ 🛏 ❀ ⚱ ◁ ▶ ♿ ➤ P ⚥

Hightown

Cross Keys

283 Halifax Road (A649)
☎ (01274) 873294
12–2.30 (not Mon–Wed), 5.30–11;
12–11 Sat; 12–10.30 Sun
Bateman Mild; Marston's
Bitter, Pedigree, HBC [H]
Friendly, well-laid-out local
with a conservatory eating area
(no food Mon). ❀ ◁ ▶ ♿ P

Hipperholme

Brown Horse Inn

Denholme Gate Road, Coley
(A644) ☎ (01422) 202112
11–11; 12–3, 7–10.30 Sun
Ruddles Best Bitter; John
Smith's Bitter; Taylor
Landlord; Webster's
Yorkshire Bitter [H]
Yorkshire's only Brown Horse
pub on the site of an inn since
the late 18th century. The
interior is comfortably
spacious. Food is cooked to
order (eve meals Mon–Fri).
❀ ◁ ▶ P

Holmfirth

Farmers Arms

2–4 Liphill Road, Burnlee (off
A635) ☎ (01484) 683713
6 (12 Sat)–11; 12–10.30 Sun
Black Sheep Best Bitter;
Taylor Best Bitter; Tetley
Dark Mild, Bitter; guest
beers [H]
Cosy, friendly pub tucked
away down a sidestreet near
Compo's Café. The bar opens
on to three rooms with low
ceilings. A rare outlet for

Porter Brewery beers; cider in summer. Car parking is limited. Q ❀ ⌺ ᴴ ♣ ⌂ P

Rose & Crown (Nook)

Victoria Square (off Hollowgate) ☎ (01484) 683960
11.30–11; 12–10.30 Sun
Samuel Smith OBB; Stones Bitter; Taylor Best Bitter, Landlord; Tetley Mild; Younger No. 3; guest beers Ⓗ
Legendary, basic, traditional boozer, which has had the same landlord for longer than its 23 year stint in the *Guide*. Strong local following.
▥ Q ♨ ❀ ◖ ♣

Honley

Jacobs Well Inn

16 Woodhead Road (A6024)
☎ (01484) 666135
11–2.30, 5–11; 11–11 Sat; 12–4, 7–10.30 Sun
Black Sheep Best Bitter; Ind Coope Burton Ale; Tetley Mild, Bitter; guest beers Ⓗ
Roadside pub of open-plan design, but retaining a feel of individual rooms. Good reputation for food (eve meals Mon and Wed; no food Sun).
◖ ▮ ≷

Horbury

Caldervale Hotel

Millroyd Road (400 yds from A642) ☎ (01924) 275351
12 (11.30 Fri)–4, 6.15–11; 12–3.30, 7–10.30 Sun
John Smith's Bitter; guest beers Ⓗ
Three-roomed pub built in 1884 for Fernandes Brewery, now a friendly local. Meals planned. Q ❀ ▮ & ♣ P

Huddersfield

Rat & Ratchet

40 Chapel Hill (A616, near ring road) ☎ (01484) 516734
3.30 (12 Wed–Sat)–11; 12–10.30 Sun
Adnams Bitter; Bateman Mild; Marston's Bitter, Pedigree; Taylor Best Bitter, Landlord; guest beers Ⓗ
No-nonsense, bareboarded alehouse offering 14 different beers, normally including one brewed on the premises. Foreign bottled beers are also stocked. A popular meeting place. Eve meals Tue (chilli) and Wed (curry).
❀ ◖ ▮ ≷ ♣ ⌂ P

Shoulder of Mutton

11 Neale Road, Lockwood (off B6108, near A616 jct)
☎ (01484) 424835
7 (3 Sat)–11; 12–3.30, 7–10.30 Sun
Boddingtons Bitter; Taylor Best Bitter, Landlord; Tetley Mild, Bitter; guest beers Ⓗ

Tucked away at the head of a cobbled street, this genuine free house has charm, a cosy atmosphere and a legendary jukebox. ❀ ≷ (Lockwood) ♣

Zeneca Recreation Club

509 Leeds Road (A62, 1½ miles NE of town) ☎ (01484) 514367
11–11; 12–10.30 Sun
Taylor Best Bitter; Tetley Mild, Bitter; guest beer Ⓗ
Twice winner of CAMRA's national *Club of the Year* award: a large club with two bars, three lounges and extensive sports facilities. Show the *Guide* or CAMRA membership to be signed in. ❀ ◖ ♣ P ⅙

Try also: **Head of Steam**, St George's Sq (Free)

Idle

Brewery Tap

51 Albion Road
☎ (01274) 613936
11.30–3, 6.30–11; 12–3, 7–10.30 Sun
Castle Eden Ale; Flowers IPA; Tetley Bitter Ⓗ
Ex-Trough Brewery pub with old Trough memorabilia and a large central bar. Live blues bands play Tue and Sat eves.
♣ P

Idle Workingmen's Club

23 High Street
☎ (01274) 613602
12–3 (4 Sat; not Tue–Thu), 7.30 (7 Fri & Sat)–11; 12–3, 7–10.30 Sun
Tetley Mild, Bitter; guest beers Ⓗ
Very friendly social club where visitors can be signed in if showing a CAMRA card or the *Guide*. Live entertainment Sat and Sun eve. ♨ & ♣

Springfield

179 Bradford Road
☎ (01274) 612710
12–11; 12–10.30 Sun
Vaux Samson Ⓗ
Roadside local on the edge of a large housing estate, featuring two small rooms: a lounge with pool and a tap room popular with darts players. Like the car park, it is often not big enough.
❀ ⌺ ♣ P

Ilkley

Ilkley Moor Vaults

Stockeld Road
☎ (01943) 607012
12–11; 12–10.30 Sun
Taylor Best Bitter, Landlord; Tetley Bitter; guest beers Ⓗ
Tetley Festival Ale House by the River Wharfe. Its stone floors and wood attract a wide range of customers. The small,

snug-like room is warm and welcoming.
▥ Q ❀ ◖ ⌺ ≷ ♣ P

Midland

Station Road ☎ (01943) 607433
11–11; 12–10.30 Sun
Marston's Pedigree; John Smith's Bitter; Theakston XB; guest beer Ⓗ
Convenient for bus and train stations; a pub with two rooms, both with fine wooden barbacks and glasswork. Lots of pictures of old Ilkley and railway history.
▥ Q ◖ ⌺ ≷ ♣ ⌂ P

Keighley

Boltmakers Arms

117 East Parade
☎ (01535) 661936
11.30–11; 11–4, 7–11 Sat; 12–4, 7–10.30 Sun
Taylor Golden Best, Best Bitter, Landlord; Tetley Bitter Ⓗ
Split-level, one-roomed, popular town-centre gem, not to be missed. ≷ ♣

Brewery Arms

Longcroft/Sun Street
☎ (01535) 603102
11–11; 12–10.30 Sun
Worth Alesman, Neary's Stout, Best Bitter, seasonal beers; guest beers Ⓗ
Refurbished, relaxed and friendly town pub offering up to four guests. Near Worth Brewery. ❀ ≷ ♣ ⌂ P

Globe

2 Parkwood Street
☎ (01535) 610802
11.30–11; 12–10.30 Sun
Taylor Golden Best, Best Bitter, Landlord; Tetley Bitter Ⓗ
Friendly, refurbished local. Worth Valley Railway passes by the window.
▥ Q ♨ ◖ ≷ ♣ P

Red Pig

Church Street
☎ (01535) 604383
12–11; 12–10.30 Sun
Taylor Golden Best, Landlord; Worth Neary's Stout; guest beers Ⓗ
Lively, one-roomed, town-centre pub, with up to three guest beers. Works by local artists are on show.
▥ ≷ ♣

Volunteer Arms

Lawkholme Lane
☎ (01535) 600173
11–11; 12–10.30 Sun
Taylor Golden Best, Best Bitter Ⓗ
Compact, town-centre local, with two rooms; the smaller one is used mainly for games.
≷ ♣

Keighley to Oxenhope and Back

Keighley & Worth Valley Railway Buffet Car

Stations at Keighley, Ingrow West, Oakworth, Haworth and Oxenhope ☎ (01535) 645214; talking timetable 647777
Sat, Sun & bank hols, March–Oct
Beer range varies H
Volunteer-run railway buffet car giving changing views of the Worth Valley.
Q ▲ (Marsh/Oxenhope) ⇌ (Keighley) P (Keighley/Ingrow W/Oxenhope) ⚲ ⊟

Knottingley

Steam Packet Inn

The Bendles, 2 Racca Green (A645) ☎ (01977) 674176
11–11; 12–10.30 Sun
Beer range varies H
Large, three-roomed pub on the canal bank, with a brewery behind. ▥ ❀ ⊞ ▲ ♣ P ⊟

Ledsham

Chequers

Claypit Lane (off Selby fork of A1) ☎ (01977) 683135
11–3, 5.30–11; closed Sun
John Smith's Bitter; Theakston Best Bitter; Younger Scotch, No. 3 H
Unspoilt and untouched, this village inn is deservedly popular. Amiable staff guarantee a warm welcome.
▥ Q ❀ ◖ P

Leeds: *City*

Duck & Drake

48 Kirkgate ☎ (0113) 246 5806
11–11; 12–10.30 Sun
Old Mill Bitter; John Smith's Bitter; Taylor Landlord; Theakston Best Bitter, XB, Old Peculier; Younger No. 3; guest beers H
Tucked behind the market and next to the railway bridge, this place had bare boards and beermats on the walls before the word 'alehouse' was invented. A central bar serves two rooms, one of which houses a rare Yorkshire doubles dartboard.
▥ ◖ ⇌ ♣ ◠

Felon & Firkin

26 Great George Street (behind Town Hall) ☎ (0113) 244 6263
11–11; 12–10.30 Sun
Firkin Fuzz Bitter, Felon Bitter, Bobby's Bitter, Dogbolter; guest beer (occasional) H

Converted in 1995 from a derelict courtroom, featuring a balcony drinking area. The beers are supplied by the on-site brewery. Busy Fri and Sat nights. Parking is difficult.
◖ ♿ ⇌ ♣

Horse & Trumpet

The Headrow ☎ (0113) 245 5961
11–11; 12–10.30 Sun
Marston's Pedigree; Tetley Bitter; guest beers H
Popular Tetley Festival Ale House where a late-Victorian facade gives way to an opened-out interior. Doormen weekend eves. Four independent guests are available. No food Sun. ◖ ⇌

Londoner

Lovell Park Road, Little London ☎ (0113) 245 3666
11–11; 12–3, 7–10.30 Sun
Ind Coope Burton Ale; Marston's Pedigree; Tetley Bitter; guest beers H
Open-plan Tetley Festival Ale House featuring bare boards and partitioned areas. Four guest beers per week. No food Sun. ❀ ◖ ♣ P ⚲

Palace

Kirkgate ☎ (0113) 244 5882
11–11; 12–10.30 Sun
Ind Coope Burton Ale; Marston's Pedigree; Tetley Mild, Bitter, Imperial; guest beers H
Tetley Festival Ale House boasting the city's most extensive choice of ale (up to 12 beers). The reservation of one handpump for a stout or a porter has proved a resounding success.
❀ ◖ ♣ ⚲

Prince of Wales

Mill Hill ☎ (0113) 245 2434
11–11; 12–10.30 Sun
Black Sheep Best Bitter, Riggwelter; John Smith's Bitter; guest beers H
One of the last untouched city-centre pubs, displaying knick-knacks acquired over many years. Comfortable front room; pool table and TV in the rear room. ◖ ⇌ ♣

Tap & Spile

Georgian Arcade, Merrion Centre ☎ (0113) 244 5355
11–11; closed Sun & bank hols
Beer range varies H
Extremely popular, back-to-basics ale house selling up to eight guest beers (mostly from independents), and an occasional perry. Amiable and approachable staff.
◖ ♣ ◠

Viaduct

11 Lower Briggate ☎ (0113) 246 9178
11–11; 12–3, 7–10.30 Sun
Ind Coope Burton Ale; Marston's Pedigree; Tetley Dark Mild, Mild, Bitter, Imperial; guest beer H
Refurbishment has transformed this basic boozer, which now offers a warm welcome in pleasant surroundings.
❀ ◖ ♿ ⇌ ♣ ⚲

Whip

Bowers Yard, Duncan Street ☎ (0113) 245 7571
11–11; 12–3, 8–10.30 Sun
Tetley Mild, Bitter, Imperial H
Down-to-earth, split-level, wooden-floorboarded boozer where only real ale is served on the bar. Snacks served.
⇌ ♣

Whitelocks ☆

Turk's Head Yard (off Briggate) ☎ (0113) 245 3950
11–11; 12–10.30 Sun
Theakston Best Bitter; Younger Scotch, IPA, No. 3; guest beer H
Very attractive, award-winning pub, boasting an array of brass and glass. Boisterous and loud, but only with lively conversation! The restaurant closes at 8. Q ❀ ◖ ▮ ⇌

Wrens

61A New Briggate (opp. Grand Theatre) ☎ (0113) 245 8888
11–11; 12–3, 7–10.30 Sun
Ind Coope Burton Ale; Marston's Pedigree; Tetley Mild, Bitter; guest beer H
Compact, three-roomed pub; the no-smoking room has a theatre theme. No meals Sun.
◖ ⊞ ♣ ⚲

Leeds: *East*

Cross Green

Cross Green Lane ☎ (0113) 248 0338
12–11; 12–10.30 Sun
John Smith's Bitter; Tetley Mild, Bitter H
Unusual, wedge-shaped local with notable etched glass, at a busy junction. Good views of the rebuilding project around the Armouries Museum.
❀ ⊞ ♣

Leeds: *North*

Chemic Tavern

9 Johnston Street, Woodhouse ☎ (0113) 244 0092
11–3, 5.30–11; 11.30–11 Sat; 12–10.30 Sun
Marston's Pedigree; Taylor Landlord; Tetley Bitter; guest beer H

YORKSHIRE (West)

Two-roomed local with a rural village feel, among old terraced houses, featuring low beams, mirrors and wall plates. Tapster's Choice guest beer. Q 🍺 ♣ P

City of Mabgate
45 Mabgate (near bus station)
☎ (0113) 245 7789
11–11; 12–3, 7–10.30 Sun
Black Sheep Special; Boddingtons Bitter; Marston's Pedigree; Whitbread Trophy; guest beers Ⓗ
Friendly pub with a comfortable lounge, a basic tap room and always one beer from Rooster's brewery. Weekday lunches.
🏮 🍺 ◖ 🍺 ♣

Feast & Firkin
229 Woodhouse Lane (A660, by Leeds University)
☎ (0113) 245 3669
11–11; 12–10.30 Sun
Firkin Fuzz Bitter, Feast Bitter, Morning Glory, Dogbolter, guest beer (occasional) Ⓗ
Firkin converted in 1994 from a derelict fire and police station and a library, the character of which comes through in the pub. Comedy and quiz nights.
◖ & ♣ P

New Roscoe
Bristol Street, Sheepscar
☎ (0113) 246 0778
11.30–11; 12–10.30 Sun
Marston's Pedigree; Tetley Bitter; guest beers Ⓗ
Enormous and slightly eccentric pub with reminders of its namesake (demolished for the nearby road system), including a mural outside. Regular live music. The house beer is brewed by Moorhouse's; a mild and a Rooster's beer are usually available. 🍺 ◖ 🍺 P

Leeds: South

Blooming Rose
19 Burton Row, Hunslet (off Dewsbury Rd)
☎ (0113) 270 0426
11–11; 12–3, 7–10.30 Sun
Tetley Mild, Bitter; guest beer Ⓗ
Welcoming local next to Hunslet Moor, attracting business clients at lunchtime. A pool room is an extension off the tap room. No food Sun. Tapster's Choice guest beer.
🍺 ◖ 🍺 P ✞

Grove Inn
Back Row, Holbeck
☎ (0113) 243 9254
12–11; 12–10.30 Sun
Ruddles County; John Smith's Bitter; Theakston XB; Younger No. 3; guest beer Ⓗ

Classic inter-war pub: two small rooms and a tap room, plus a drinking corridor leading to a large concert room at the rear (live music most eves and Sun lunch). No food Sat. Q 🍺 ◖ 🍺 ⇒ ♣

Leeds: West

Cardigan Arms ☆
364 Kirkstall Road, Burley
☎ (0113) 274 2000
12–11; 12–10.30 Sun
Marston's Pedigree; Tetley Mild, Bitter; guest beer Ⓗ
Pub with a central bar and a large corridor drinking area leading to four rooms and a traditional tap room. Tapster's Choice guest beers.
◖ 🍺 ♣ P

Highland
Cavendish Street, Burley
☎ (0113) 242 8592
11–11; 12–10.30 Sun
Tetley Mild, Bitter Ⓗ
Friendly, untouched pub in the student accommodation area. Good selection of sandwiches always available. 🍺 ♣

Old Unicorn
165 Stocks Hill, Bramley
☎ (0113) 256 4465
11.30–3 (4 Fri & Sat), 5.30 (7 Sat)–11; 12–3, 7–10.30 Sun
Black Sheep Best Bitter; Tetley Mild, Bitter; Younger No. 3 Ⓗ
200-year-old free house overlooking Bramley centre. Once a brewhouse, it is now extended into adjacent cottages, and the open interior is busy with a mixed local clientele. Weekday meals (eves till 7.30). 🏮 🍺 ◖ ▶ & P

Old Vic
17 Whitecote Hill, Bramley
☎ (0113) 256 1207
4 (2 Fri, 11 Sat)–11; 12–3, 7–10.30 Sun
Black Sheep Best Bitter; Taylor Landlord; Tetley Bitter; guest beers Ⓗ
In an area where real ale choice is fast diminishing, this former vicarage is a haven for beer lovers. Set back from the road, in its own grounds, it has two cosy lounges and a tap/games room, served from a central bar. 🏮 Q 🍺 🍺 P

Owl
1 Rodley Lane
☎ (0113) 256 5242
11.30–3 (5 Sat), 5 (7 Sat)–11; 12–3, 7–10.30 Sun
Morland Old Speckled Hen; Ruddles County; John Smith's Bitter; Taylor Mild; Theakston Old Peculier Ⓗ
Comfortable, two-roomed pub where the large rear lounge doubles as a restaurant, serving hearty meals (eves until 7 or 8). The smaller public

bar displays pictures of old Rodley. 🍺 ◖ ▶ 🍺 ♣ P

Linthwaite

Sair Inn
139 Lane Top, Hoyle Ing (off A62) OS100143
☎ (01484) 842370
7 (4 Fri, 12 Sat)–11; 12–10.30 Sun
Linfit Mild, Swift, Special, Old Eli, English Guineas, Enoch's Hammer Ⓗ
Multi-roomed, brew pub steeped in history, perched on the preposterously steep Hoyle Ing. Stone-flagged floors and real fires in each room. National CAMRA *Pub of the Year 1997.* 🏮 Q 🛏 ♣ ✞

Liversedge

Black Bull
37 Halifax Road (A649, 400 yds N of A62) ☎ (01924) 403779
12–4 (5 Sat), 5.30 (7 Sat)–11; 12–5, 7–10.30 Sun
Stones Bitter; Tetley Bitter; guest beers Ⓗ
Good local which caters for all ages: a pool room with music, plus quieter rooms leading off, selling a good range of changing guest beers. Limited parking. P

Low Moor

Black Horse
2 Lockwood Street (A638)
☎ (01274) 671357
11.30–3, 5.30–11; 11–11 Fri & Sat, 12–10.30 Sun
Samuel Smith OBB Ⓗ
Well-modernised local on the site of a former station, near Transperience Transport Museum (open spring–autumn). 🏮 🍺 ◖ 🍺 P

Marsden

Riverhead Brewery Tap
2 Peel Street (off A62)
☎ (01484) 841270
5 (11 Sat)–11; 12–10.30 Sun
Riverhead Sparth Mild, Butterley Bitter, Deer Hill Porter, Cupwith Light, Black Moss Stout, March Haigh Ⓗ
Pub fashioned out of a Co-op building next to the River Colne, with a brewery in the cellar. The beers are named after local reservoirs.
Q & ⇒ ⏏

Tunnel End
Reddisher Road OS041211
☎ (01484) 844636
7.30–11; 12–3, 7.30–11 Sat; 12–3.30, 7.30–10.30 Sun
Barnsley IPA; Tetley Mild, Bitter; guest beer Ⓗ
Pub close to the Standedge Tunnel entrance and picnic area, with always a friendly

350

welcome. The front and pool rooms are away from the piano; various board games and a library. Accommodation should be available soon.
🏠 ⛄ 🕮 ⇌ ♣

Methley

New Bay Horse
Main Street, Mickletown
☎ (01977) 553557
12–4, 6–11; 12–3, 7–10.30 Sun
Tetley Bitter; Theakston XB; guest beers Ⓗ
Improving and expanding pub with an emphasis now on food (huge portions) and an increased guest beer range (up to five). Families welcome in the restaurant (no-smoking area) which is open eves till 8.30 pm, Mon–Thu (9 Fri, Sat and Sun), plus Sun lunch.
⛄ 🕮 ◖▶ 🍴 ♣ P

Mixenden

Hebble Brook
2 Mill Lane (⅔ mile off A629)
☎ (01422) 242059
12–3, 5.15–11; 12–11 Sat; 12–10.30 Sun
Taylor Golden Best; guest beers Ⓗ
Proudly independent pub serving five often very rare guests. Regular, themed beer festivals; some weekends feature a range of one brewer's products. Draught Liefmans Kriek plus another Belgian/German beer, plus over 40 international bottled beers. Eve meals Mon (steaks) and Wed (curries). Biddenden cider. Bar billiards played.
🏠 🕮 ◖▶ 🍴 A ♣ ◔ P

Morley

Stump Cross
Britannia Road
☎ (0113) 253 4655
11.30–11; 12–10.30 Sun
Tetley Mild, Bitter Ⓗ
Stone pub on the main road, with a simple public bar. The larger, oddly-shaped lounge is very comfortable. Cracking photos of old Morley. No-smoking area 12–8 weekdays.
🕮 ◖ 🍴 P ✂

Mytholmroyd

Shoulder of Mutton
38 New Road (B6138)
☎ (01422) 883165
11.30–3, 7–11; 11.30–11 Fri & Sat; 12–10.30 Sun
Black Sheep Best Bitter; Boddingtons Bitter; Flowers IPA; Castle Eden Ale; guest beer Ⓗ
Popular roadside local with a fine display of Toby jugs and china. No food Tue eve.
◖▶ ⇌ ♣ P

Netherthong

Clothiers' Arms
106 School Street (off A6024)
☎ (01484) 683480
12–4 (not Mon), 7–11; 12–11 Fri & Sat; 12–10.30 Sun
Black Sheep Best Bitter; Old Mill Bitter; Taylor Best Bitter; Tetley Mild, Bitter; guest beers Ⓗ
Genuine free house serving the village community well. Brewery memorabilia is a feature. No food Mon.
◖ ♣ ◔

Ogden

Moorlands Inn
Keighley Road (A629)
☎ (01422) 248943
11–11; 12–10.30 Sun
Black Sheep Special; Taylor Landlord; Tetley Bitter; Theakston Best Bitter; guest beers Ⓗ
Large roadside free house on the edge of town. Food is served all day until 9. Big money quiz nights a speciality. Menagerie outside.
🕮 🏨 ◖▶ A P

Ossett

Brewers Pride
Low Mill Road
☎ (01924) 273865
12–3, 5.30–11; 12–11 Fri & Sat; 12–10.30 Sun
Taylor Landlord; guest beers Ⓗ
Popular, true free house, well frequented despite its out of the way location. Five guest beers include a mild; range of Belgian beers. Unspoilt decor makes this pub a must. Good choice of meals Mon–Sat.
🏠 Q 🕮 ◖ ♣ ◔

Red Lion
73 Dewsbury Road (A638, 1 mile from M1 jct 40)
☎ (01924) 273487
12–11; 12–4, 7–10.30 Sun
John Smith's Bitter; Tetley Bitter; guest beers Ⓗ
18th-century inn with a low, oak-beamed ceiling and a small central bar. Popular for good value, home-cooked meals; the landlord invites guest chefs to produce special menus (no food Mon eve). One guest beer is from a Yorkshire brewery.
◖▶ P

Otley

Bay Horse
20 Market Place
☎ (01943) 461122
11–11; 12–10.30 Sun
Tetley Mild, Bitter; guest beers Ⓗ

Smashing little pub. The public bar is at the front; to the rear is an opened-out, yet cosy lounge. The guest beers are from small, usually local, independents. Suntrap beer yard. Outdoor gents.
🕮 🍴 ♣

Dyneley Arms
Otley Road (Leeds road, 2 miles from centre)
☎ (0113) 284 2887
11.30–2.30, 5.30–11; 12–2.30, 5.30–10.30 Sun
Samuel Smith OBB Ⓗ
Large roadhouse with an open-plan interior which caters for drinkers and diners alike (no eve meals Fri–Mon). Spectacular views over the Wharfe Valley.
🕮 ◖▶ P

Junction
44 Bondgate ☎ (01943) 463233
11–11; 12–10.30 Sun
Taylor Best Bitter, Landlord; Tetley Bitter; Theakston XB, Old Peculier; guest beer Ⓗ
One-roomed, but nevertheless cosy, pub with exposed stone-work, a tiled floor and wooden pew seats. The pinball is tucked away. 🏠 ◖ ♣

Outwood

Kirklands Hotel
605 Leeds Road
☎ (01924) 826666
11–11; 12–3, 7–10.30 Sun
Old Mill Mild, Bitter, Bullion, seasonal beers Ⓗ
Three rooms in an hotel tied to Old Mill Brewery, with a busy local trade. Reasonable prices. Children welcome until 9. No food Sun eve.
Q 🕮 🏨 ◖▶ ⇌ P

Oxenhope

Lamb Inn
Denholme Road (B6141)
☎ (01535) 643061
12–3, 7–11; 12–11 Sat; 12–10.30 Sun
Vaux Waggle Dance; Ward's Thorne BB, Best Bitter; guest beers Ⓗ
Comfortable, traditional country inn with two rooms, one a warm, cosy lounge decorated with pictures, the other a family room displaying railway memorabilia. Folk band Thu eve. Children welcome until 8.30. Eve meals till 8.30. 🏠 Q ⛄ 🕮 ◖▶ A ⇌ (KWVLR) ♣ P

Pontefract

Greyhound
13 Front Street
☎ (01977) 791571
12–4, 7–11; 12–11 Sat; 12–5, 7–10.30 Sun

Ruddles Best Bitter; John
Smith's Bitter; Tomlinson's
Sessions H; Webster's
Yorkshire Bitter E
Two-roomed, town-centre pub
with a busy bar area and a
comfortable lounge. Live
music Fri.
🏚 ⊟ ≋ (Tanshelf) ♣

Tap & Spile

28 Horsefair (opp. bus station)
☎ (01977) 793468
12–11; 12–3, 7–10.30 Sun
Bateman XB, Valiant; Cropton
King Billy; Daleside Nightjar;
Hull Ellwood's; Tomlinson's
Deceitful Rose; York
Stonewall; guest beers H
Chain alehouse with bare
floorboards and brickwork,
split into three drinking areas,
offering eight regularly
changing guest beers and
quality, home-cooked lunches
(not served Mon).
⊄ ≋ (Baghill/Monkhill) ♣ ⌂
P

Pudsey

Butchers Arms

Church Lane
☎ (0113) 256 4313
11–11; 12–10.30 Sun
Samuel Smith OBB H
Stone pub on the main street; a
friendly local with homely
decor. No food Sun. Benches at
the front for outside drinking.
🏚 ❀ ⊄ ♣

Royal

30 Station Street
☎ (0113) 256 4085
11–11; 12–10.30 Sun
Thwaites Best Mild, Bitter H
Imposing stone pub, a much
appreciated Thwaites outlet,
comprising a basic bar room, a
hidden pool room and a fine
example of twin lounges. There
are benches outside.
❀ ⊟ ♣ P

Purston

White House

257 Pontefract Road
☎ (01977) 791878
11–4, 7–11; 12–3, 7–10.30 Sun
Samuel Smith OBB H
Busy roadside local, open-plan
with a central bar, displaying
pictures of local rugby league
and football teams.
Q ❀ ⊄ P

Queensbury

New Dolphin

Ambler Thorn Ford (A647)
☎ (01274) 882053
12–11; 12–10.30 Sun
Tetley Bitter; Webster's
Yorkshire Bitter; guest
beers H
Three-room local; warm and
friendly. ❀ ♣ P

Ravensthorpe

Royal

616 Huddersfield Road
☎ (01924) 463726
11.30–11; 11.30–5, 7–11 Sat; 12–10.30
Sun
Tetley Mild, Bitter H
Traditional, three-room local.
Look out for the memorial
plaques to former customers
on the tap room long saddle.
Q ❀ ⊟ ≋ ♣ P

Ripponden

Alma Inn

Cottonstones, Mill Bank,
Sowerby Bridge (1¼ miles off
A58 at Triangle pub) OS028215
☎ (01422) 823334
6–11; 12–2, 6–11 Wed; 11–11 Sat;
12–10.30 Sun
Phoenix Tyke; Taylor Golden
Best; Tetley Bitter; guest
beer H
Traditional village inn with a
stone-flagged floor and fine
views over the lower Ryburn
Valley to Norland Moor. Over
65 bottled Belgian beers and
two draught foreign beers;
varied menu.
🏚 Q ⌂ ❀ ⊄ ▲ ♣ P

Blue Ball Inn

Blue Ball Road, Soyland (off
A58, near Baitings Reservoir)
OS011192 ☎ (01422) 823603
12–3 (not Tue), 7 (5.30 Fri)–11; 12–3,
7–10.30 Sun
Taylor Golden Best, Landlord;
Theakston Old Peculier;
Worthington Bitter; guest
beers H
Reputedly haunted, cosy
moorland inn, dating from the
17th century, enjoying
extensive views over the upper
Ryburn Valley. Pianist every
other Fri. The house beer is
brewed by Phoenix. Restaurant
open Thu–Sat eves.
🏚 Q ❀ ⊄ ⊳ P

Old Bridge Inn

Priest Lane (off A58, near
B6113 jct) ☎ (01422) 822595
11.30–3, 5.30–11; 12–11.30 Sat;
12–10.30 Sun
Black Sheep Special; Ryburn
Best Bitter; Taylor Golden
Best, Best Bitter; guest beer H
Possibly Yorkshire's oldest pub
(recorded as early as 1307), in a
picturesque setting by a
packhorse bridge. Only the
guest beer pumps are labelled.
🏚 Q ❀ ⊄ ⊳ P

Scammonden

Brown Cow

Saddleworth Road (B6114,
2½ miles S of Barkisland)
OS045165 ☎ (01422) 822227
12–3 (not Mon–Thu), 7–11; 12–3,
7–10.30 Sun

Mansfield Riding Bitter,
Bitter; guest beers H
Old coaching inn in an
elevated moorland setting
above Scammonden Water, yet
only 500 ft from the M62 (no
access). A central lounge bar,
with collections of brass fire
extinguishers, gauges and
walking sticks, serves three
other rooms. No food Mon.
🏚 Q ❀ ⊄ ♣ P

Shelley

Three Acres Inn

Roydhouse (off B6116 near
Emley Moor TV mast)
OS214124
☎ (01484) 602606
12–3 (not Sat), 7–11; 12–3, 7–10.30 Sun
Adnams Extra; Mansfield
Bitter; Morland Old Speckled
Hen; Taylor Landlord; guest
beers H
Welcoming, turn of the century
coaching inn, set in the rolling,
Pennine countryside. Well-
deserved reputation for
excellent food. Resident
pianist. 🏚 ❀ 🛏 ⊄ ⊳ P

Shipley

Shipley Pride

1 Saltaire Road (A657 Keighley
road)
☎ (01274) 585341
11.30 (11 Sat)–11; 12–3, 7–10.30 Sun
Tetley Bitter; guest beers H
Friendly, traditional, two-
roomed local; originally
Hammonds Old Beehive Hotel.
Home-made lunches
weekdays. ❀ ⊄ ≋ ♣ P

Victoria Hotel

192 Saltaire Road
☎ (01274) 585642
11.30–11; 12–10.30 Sun
Boddingtons Bitter; Taylor
Landlord; Whitbread Trophy;
guest beers H
Friendly local with Victorian-
style decor (stained-glass and
wood); the nearest pub to the
historic village of Saltaire. Eve
meals end at 8 (no food Sat or
Sun).
⊄ ⊳ ⊟ ≋ (Saltaire) ♣ P

Silsden

Bridge Inn

Keighley Road
☎ (01535) 653144
11–11; 12–10.30 Sun
Black Sheep Best Bitter; John
Smith's Bitter; Theakston XB;
guest beer H
Canalside pub which predates
the canal, being first recorded
in 1660. The original drinking
rooms are now the cellar and
toilets. Parking for boats only.
Meals served 12–7.
Q ⌂ ❀ 🛏 ⊄ ⊳ ♣

South Elmsall

Barnsley Oak
Mill Lane (½ mile from
A628/B6428 roundabout)
☎ (01977) 643427
12–3.30 (5 Sat), 7–11; 12–3, 7–10.30
Sun

John Smith's Bitter H
1960s estate pub on the edge of
an ex-mining village, offering
panoramic views of the Elms
Valley from the conservatory.
⌂ ⊛ ◗ ⊟ & ⇌ ♣ P

Southowram

Shoulder of Mutton
14 Cain Lane ☎ (01422) 361101
11.30 (4 Wed)–11; 12–10.30 Sun
**Marston's Pedigree; Ruddles
County; John Smith's Bitter;
guest beers** H
Village local with changing
guest beers from non-
Yorkshire breweries. Regular
activities include charity quiz
nights and slideshows.
Occasional cider. ⌸ ♣ ⌂

Sowerby Bridge

Ram's Head
26 Wakefield Road (A6026,
¼ mile from centre)
☎ (01422) 835876
12–3, 7–11; 12–11 Sat; 12–3, 7–10.30
Sun

**Ryburn Mild, Best Bitter,
Rydale, Luddite, Stabbers,
Coiners** H
Cottage-style pub which has
been gradually extended into
adjoining property. Exposed
stonework and four open
fireplaces complete interior
features. Home to Ryburn
Brewery.
⌸ ⊛ ◗ ⇌ ♣ P

Thornton

Blue Boar
354 Thornton Road
☎ (01274) 833298
4 (12 Fri & Sat)–11; 12–10.30 Sun
**Taylor Golden Best, Best
Bitter** H
Open-plan, comfortable village
pub with a pool and darts
room. ⊛ ♣

Tingley

British Oak
407 Westerton Road
☎ (0113) 253 4792
12–3, 6 (7 Sat)–11; 12–3, 7–10.30 Sun
**Boddingtons Bitter; Castle
Eden Ale; Flowers Original;
guest beers** H
Excellent local – Leeds
CAMRA *Pub of the Year* 1996 –
staging live music and quiz
nights. Ever-changing guest
beers usually come from small

independents; cider in
summer. ⊛ ♣ ⌂ P

Todmorden

Cross Keys
649 Rochdale Road, Walsden
☎ (01706) 815185
12–11; 12–10.30 Sun
**Black Sheep Best Bitter;
Tetley Bitter; guest beers** H
Busy, traditional pub, with a
conservatory overlooking the
canal and a cosy tap room. Up
to five guest beers. Meals end
at 8. ⌸ ⌷ ◗ ▶ & ⇌
(Walsden) ♣

White Hart
White Hart Fold
☎ (01706) 812198
11.30–3.30, 7–11; 11–11 Fri & Sat;
12–10.30 Sun
**Tetley Mild, Bitter; guest
beers** H
Imposing brewers' Tudor pub,
near the station. Popular,
especially at weekends.
⊛ ◗ ▲ ⇌ ♣ P

Woodpecker
224 Rochdale Road (A6033,
½ mile W of centre)
☎ (01706) 816088
12–2.30, 5–11; 11–11 Sat; 12–10.30 Sun
Lees GB Mild, Bitter H
Friendly, L-shaped local,
popular with games players.
Lees' only Yorkshire pub.
⇌ ♣

Wainstalls

Cat i'th'well Inn
Wainstalls Lane, Lower
Saltonstall (¼ mile W of
Wainstalls) OS042285
☎ (01422) 244841
7 (6 summer)–11; 12–3, 7 (6
summer)–11 Sat; 12–3, 7 (6
summer)–10.30 Sun
Boddingtons Bitter (summer);
**Castle Eden Ale; Taylor
Golden Best, Best Bitter,
Landlord** H
Olde-worlde free house in a
picturesque wooded valley,
boasting lots of brass and oak
panelling which came from a
demolished Victorian 'castle'.
Popular with walkers.
Weekend lunches. Q ⊛ ◗ P

Wakefield

Flanshaw Hotel
Flanshaw Lane (off A638)
☎ (01924) 290830
11 (1 Tue)–11; 12–3, 7–10.30 Sun
**John Smith's Bitter; Tetley
Bitter** H
Large, friendly, community
pub with cheap guest beers. A
good family pub with a social
club. ⊛ ◗ ▶ & ♣ P ⊟

Primrose Tavern
Monk Street (near Kirkgate
station) ☎ (01924) 375847

11–11; 12–3, 7–10.30 Sun
**Mansfield Riding Bitter, Old
Baily** H
Friendly, old, two-bar local; a
very sporty pub.
Q ⊛ & ⇌ (Kirkgate) ♣ P

Redoubt ☆
28 Horbury Road
☎ (01924) 377085
11–11; 12–4, 7–10.30 Sun
**Taylor Landlord; Tetley Mild,
Bitter** H
Four-roomed Tetley Heritage
pub with strong rugby league
connections; very cosy.
⊛ & ⇌ (Westgate) ♣ P

Smiths Arms
7 Westgate End (near Westgate
station)
☎ (01924) 376657
11–11; 12–10.30 Sun
**John Smith's Bitter; guest
beers** H
Very popular, traditional local;
a two-room, semi-open-plan
pub with a warm welcome. Q
⌷ ◗ ▶ & ⇌ (Westgate) ♣ P

Talbot & Falcon
56 Northgate (near bus station)
☎ (01924) 201693
11–11; 12–10.30 Sun
**Marston's Pedigree; Taylor
Landlord; Tetley Bitter; guest
beers** H
Long, narrow, Tetley Festival
Ale House with sepia-coloured
walls, bare floorboards, and a
single central bar. Five guest
beers. ◗

Tap & Spile
77 Westgate End
☎ (01924) 375887
12–11; 12–10.30 Sun
Beer range varies H
Pub with a varied clientele and
a changing beer range. Good
value meals (no food Sun).
⌸ ⊛ ◗ & ⇌ (Westgate) ♣ ⌂

Tut'n'Shive
38 Teall Street (opp. market
hall)
☎ (01924) 374191
11–11; 12–10.30 Sun
**Boddingtons Bitter; Castle
Eden Ale; Morland Old
Speckled Hen; Taylor
Landlord; guest beers** H
Refurbished pub attracting a
young crowd. ⊛ ◗ ▶ & ⇌
(Kirkgate/Westgate) ♣ P

Wagon
45 Westgate End (right from
station)
☎ (01924) 372478
11–11; 12–10.30 Sun
**Black Sheep Best Bitter,
Special; Hop Back Summer
Lightning; Rooster's Yankee;
Tetley Bitter; guest beer** H
Out-of-town-centre pub with a
friendly atmosphere, open fires
and good lunchtime snacks.
⌸ Q ⊛ ◗ ⇌ (Westgate) ♣ P

Wakefield Labour Club

18 Vicarage Street (near market hall)
☎ (01924) 215626
7–11; 12–3, 7–11 Sat; 12–3 (closed eve) Sun
Townes Sunshine; guest beers [H]
Welcoming club that offers beers from small breweries at reasonable prices and a large range of bottled Belgian beers. Visitors must be signed in; CAMRA members admitted. Occasional real cider. CAMRA 1997 *Club of the Year* finalist.
Q ❀ ♿ ⇌ (Westgate/Kirkgate) ♣ ⌓ P

York Street Hotel

76 Lower York Street (next to sports centre)
☎ (01924) 371297
11–4, 7–11; 11–11 Thu–Sat (may vary); 12–10.30 Sun
Stones Bitter; Taylor Landlord; guest beer [H]
Edge-of-town pub, popular with locals, displaying prints of old Wakefield. No food Sun. Quiz night Wed. ❀ ◐ ♿ ♣ P

Warmfield

Plough Inn

45 Warmfield Lane (400 yds from A655) ☎ (01924) 892007
12–2, 7–11 (12–11 summer); 12–10.30 Sun
Barnsley Bitter; Theakston XB, Old Peculier; guest beer [H]
Unspoilt, 18th-century inn overlooking the lower Calder Valley, with low, beamed ceilings and a small corner bar. Good bar meals.
Q ❀ ⛟ ◐ ◑ ⊟ P

Wibsey

Gaping Goose

5–6 Slack Bottom Road (off Buttershaw Lane)
☎ (01274) 601701
2–5, 7–11; 12–10.30 Sun
Black Sheep Best Bitter; Taylor Landlord; Tetley Bitter; Theakston Old Peculier (winter); **Whitbread Trophy** [H]
Intimate and friendly, true village local with much brassware in the lounge. There is a beer garden to the rear.
❀ ♿ ♣ P

Wintersett

Angler's Retreat

Ferry Top Lane OS382157
☎ (01924) 862370
12–3, 7–11; 12–3, 7–10.30 Sun
Tetley Bitter; Theakston Best Bitter, XB; guest beer [H]
Cosy rural pub, situated between the villages of Ryhill and Crofton, handy for anglers and birdwatchers visiting Wintersett Reservoir. Biker friendly.
♨ Q ❀ ♿ ♣ P

National **Pub of the Year!** *Ron Crabtree and Hilary Cooper, licensees of Linthwaite's Sair Inn, receive the 1997 award from CAMRA director Neil Leeson (right).*

CAMRA's CHAMPION BEERS

Every year, at the Great British Beer Festival, CAMRA selects its *Champion Beer of Britain*. Judging is in the hands of trained tasters, industry experts and celebrity guests who, without knowing the identity of any of the finalists, choose the winning beer from a selection of beers which have already won their category (Bitter, Best Bitter, Mild, etc.) for that year. This is a full list of *Champion Beers of Britain* to date.

1978	Thwaites Best Mild/Fuller's ESB (tied)
1979	Fuller's London Pride
1980	Thwaites Best Mild
1981	Fuller's ESB
1982	Taylor Landlord
1983	Taylor Landlord
1984	No event
1985	Fuller's ESB
1986	Bateman XXXB
1987	Pitfield Dark Star
1988	Ringwood Old Thumper
1989	Fuller's Chiswick Bitter
1990	Ind Coope Burton Ale
1991	Mauldons Black Adder
1992	Woodforde's Norfolk Nog
1993	Adnams Extra
1994	Taylor Landlord
1995	Cottage Norman's Conquest
1996	Woodforde's Wherry Best Bitter
1997	Mordue Workie Ticket

Special mention should also be made of Hambleton Nightmare, CAMRA's *Champion Winter Beer of Britain* at the inaugural contest in 1997.

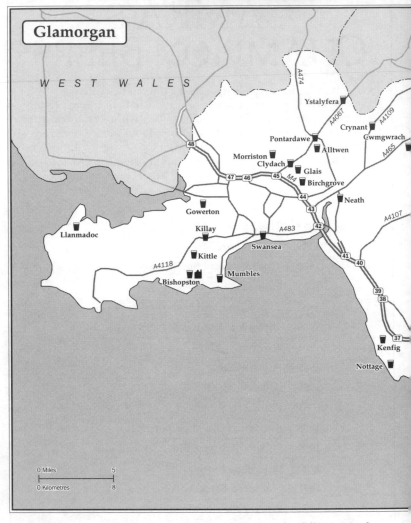

Glamorgan

WEST WALES

Ystalyfera
Pontardawe
Crynant
Cwmgwrach
Alltwen
Morriston
Clydach
Glais
Birchgrove
Neath
Gowerton
Killay
Llanmadoc
Kittle
Swansea
Mumbles
Bishopston
Kenfig
Nottage

0 Miles 5
0 Kilometres 8

Authority areas covered: Bridgend UA, Caerphilly UA, Cardiff UA, Merthyr Tydfil UA, Neath & Port Talbot UA, Rhondda, Cynon, Taff UA, Swansea UA, Vale of Glamorgan UA

Aberaman

Blaengwawr Inn
Cardiff Road ☎ (01685) 871706
12–11; 12–10.30 Sun
Brains Bitter; Cains Bitter; Worthington Bitter; guest beer Ⓗ
Pleasant, single-bar pub with a good community atmosphere. Quiz Thu. ♣

Temple Bar
Cardiff Road ☎ (01685) 876137
12–4, 6.30–11; 12–4, 7–10.30 Sun
Bullmastiff Best Bitter; Wye Valley Supreme; guest beer (occasional) Ⓗ

Small, friendly, single-bar pub where time seems to have stopped: in the same family for over 100 years.
🏚 Q ♣ P

Aberthin

Hare & Hounds
On A4222
☎ (01446) 774892
11.30–11; 12–10.30 Sun
Draught Bass Ⓖ**; Hancock's HB** Ⓗ**; Worthington Bitter** Ⓖ
Small community local with a tiny car park, a good family room and a garden. Meals in summer. Fortunately, some

things don't change.
🏚 Q 🥾 🏠 🍽 ♣ P

Alltwen

Butcher's Arms
Alltwen Hill
☎ (01792) 863100
12–3, 6.30–11; 12–3, 6.30–10.30 Sun
Courage Directors; Everards Old Original; John Smith's Bitter; Wadworth 6X; guest beer Ⓗ
Hillside local where the atmosphere is ideal for talking, drinking and eating (meals are generous). No food Sun eve.
🏚 🏠 🍽 ♪ P

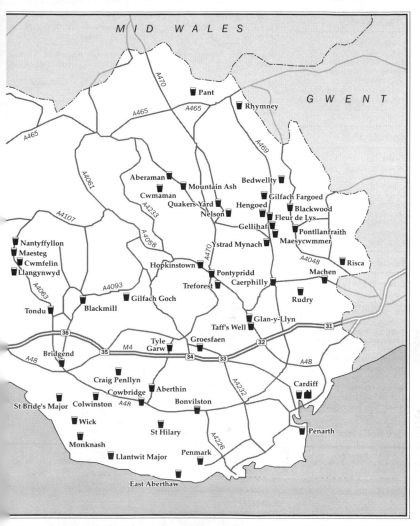

Bedwellty

New Inn
Near church
☎ (01443) 831625
12–3.30, 7–11; 12–3 (closed eve) Sun
**Crown Buckley Rev. James;
Felinfoel Double Dragon;
Hancock's HB; guest beers** H
Welcoming, pleasantly
furnished free house with a
comfortable drinking area and
a separate restaurant. No meals
Mon eve or Sun.
🏾 ❀ ◑ ▶ P

Birchgrove

Bridgend Inn
265 Birchgrove Road (off M4 jct
44) ☎ (01792) 321878
11–11; 12–10.30 Sun
**Crown Buckley Best Bitter;
Theakston Mild** *or* **Brains
Dark; guest beers** H
Local with a bar, a pool room
and a large, comfortable
lounge (families welcome).
Live music Thu and Fri.
Q ❀ ◑ ▶ & ♣ P

Bishopston

Joiners Arms
50 Bishopston Road
☎ (01792) 232658
11–11; 12–10.30 Sun
**Courage Best Bitter; Felinfoel
Double Dragon; John Smith's
Bitter; Swansea Bishops
Wood Bitter; guest beers** H
Comfortable village local, a
free house with good value
food and a wide variety of
guest ales. Home of Swansea

Brewery. Occasional beer
festivals. 🏾 Q ❀ ◑ ▶ ♣ P

Blackmill

Ogmore Junction
Hotel
On A4061 ☎ (01656) 840371
11.30–11; 12–10.30 Sun
**Draught Bass; Worthington
Bitter; guest beers** H
Attractive, old, friendly, well-
run pub. Exceptional beer
variety for the area.
Q ❀ ◑ ▶ 🗄 & ♣

**INDEPENDENT
BREWERIES**

Brains: Cardiff

Bullmastiff: Cardiff

Swansea: Bishopston

Blackwood

Masons Arms
Bridge Street ☎ (01495) 227979
12–4, 7–11; 11–11 Sat; 12–10.30 Sun
Hancock's HB; guest beer
(occasional) H
Spacious, busy town pub,
popular with all ages. Events
every day of the week.
❀ ◖ ▶ P

Bonvilston

Red Lion
On A48 ☎ (01446) 781208
11.30–3, 5–11; 11.30–11 Sat; 12–3,
7–10.30 Sun
Brains Dark, Bitter, SA H
Well-known village pub with a
reputation for good food.
Winner of recent cellarmanship
awards. No meals Sun or Mon.
❀ ◖ ▶ ♣ P

Bridgend

Famous Penybont Inn
Derwen Road
☎ (01656) 652266
11.30–11; 12–10.30 Sun
Brains SA; Marston's
Pedigree; Wadworth 6X;
Worthington Bitter; guest
beers H
Friendly town-centre pub with
much railway memorabilia,
reasonably priced meals and
up to six cask beers; close to
rail and bus stations. Eve meals
end at 8 Fri/Sat; no eve meals
Sun. Q ◖ ▶ ≢

Five Bells Inn
Ewenny Road
☎ (01656) 668188
11.30–4, 6–11; 11.30–11 Thu–Sat;
12–10.30 Sun
Draught Bass; Worthington
Bitter H
Cosy pub on a busy junction
(A4063/B4265/A4061): a
spacious, comfortable bar with
an adjoining games area, plus a
quiet lounge on an upper level.
Limited parking.
◖ ⊟ ♿ ≢ ♣ P

Haywain
Coychurch Road, Brackla
☎ (01656) 669945
11–11; 12–10.30 Sun
Courage Best Bitter, Directors;
Ruddles County; Worthington
Bitter; guest beers H
Large, bustling estate pub,
popular for lunches. No eve
meals Sun. Q ❀ ◖ ▶ ♿ P

Princess of Wales
17 Market Street
☎ (01656) 654107
11–11; 12–10.30 Sun
Brains SA; Worthington
Bitter; guest beers H
Basic pub near the bus station.
Cask beer prices are notably
low for the area. ♿ ≢

Red Dragon
Litchard Hill (A4061)
☎ (01656) 654753
11–11; 12–10.30 Sun
Courage Best Bitter; guest
beers H
Popular, large pub on the
outskirts, near M4 jct 36.
❀ ◖ ⊟ ♣ P

Victoria Hotel
7 Adare Street
☎ (01656) 659802
11–11; 12–10.30 Sun
John Smith's Bitter; Ushers
Best Bitter, seasonal beers H
Traditional, pleasant, town-
centre pub, busy at lunchtimes.
Live music several eves a
week. Roof garden.
♿ ❀ ◖ ≢

Caerphilly

Courthouse
Cardiff Road ☎ (01222) 888120
11–11; 12–10.30 Sun
Courage Best Bitter;
Federation Buchanan's
Original; guest beers H
Traditional, 14th-century long-
house with original features.
Its conservatory overlooks the
castle, the second largest in the
UK. Q ❀ ◖ ▶ ≢

Green Lady
Pontygwindy Road
☎ (01222) 851510
11–11; 12–3, 7–10.30 Sun
Banks's Bitter, seasonal beers;
Camerons Strongarm H
Newly-built, traditionally
furnished pub with a good
atmosphere and warm
welcome. Good facilities for
visitors with disabilities. No
eve meals Fri or Sun.
❀ ◖ ▶ ♿ P ⊟

Cardiff

Black Lion
Cardiff Road, Llandaff
(A4119/High St jct)
11–11; 12–10.30 Sun
Brains Dark, Bitter, SA; guest
beer H
Traditional Brains house on a
busy road near Llandaff
cathedral. Spacious lounge. A
Brains cellarmanship award-
winner. Good food.
Q ◖ ⊟ ≢ (Fairwater) ♣

City Arms
Quay Street (off High St)
☎ (01222) 225258
11–11; 12–10.30 Sun
Brains Dark, Bitter, SA H
Deservedly popular with all
ages: a welcoming oasis,
contrasting with other city-
centre leisure experiences.
Recently extended. Live bands
Thu.
Q ◖ ⊟ ♿ ≢ (Central) ♣

Cottage
25 St Mary Street
☎ (01222) 230600
11–11; 12–10.30 Sun
Brains Dark, Bitter, SA H
19th-century, city-centre pub,
featuring handsome
woodwork and glass. Popular
with a wide range of
customers. Home-cooked
lunches are available.
◖ ≢ (Central)

Discovery
Celyn Avenue, Lakeside
☎ (01222) 755015
11–3, 5.30–11; 11–11 Fri & Sat; 12–
10.30 Sun
Courage Best Bitter, Directors;
Hancock's HB; Marston's
Pedigree; Ruddles County;
John Smith's Bitter H
Comfortable, two-lounge,
1960s pub in a pleasant North
Cardiff location, near Roath
Park lake. The younger crowd
takes over one bar (large-
screen TV for sports). Neat
dress preferred. Good Sun
lunches are served.
Q ❀ ◖ ♿ P

Full Moon
(off-licence)
88 Ty'n y Parc Road, Rhiwbina
☎ (01222) 623303
12–9.15; 5–9.15 Sun
Beer range varies G
Off-licence stocking a good
range of bottled-conditioned
ales, Trappist beers and rare
Lambics, plus two
independent cask beers.
Seasonal cider/perry.
♿ ≢ (Rhiwbina) ⌂

Hogshead at the
Owain Glyndwr
St John Square
☎ (01222) 221980
11–11 (midnight Fri & Sat); 12–10.30
Sun
Beer range varies H
Hogshead pub with typical
wooden furnishings in its
split-level drinking area with
wheelchair access to the lower.
Live music some Tue/Wed
eves. Imaginative beers (up to
six available). Meals are served
12–6. Daytime family area
upstairs.
♿ ◖ ♿ ≢ (Central) ⌂

Horse & Groom
Womanby Street (off Castle St)
☎ (01222) 344691
12–11; 12–3 Sun
Draught Bass; Hancock's
HB H
One of the few surviving
traditional pubs in the city
centre, this backstreet local is
well worth a visit. Good value
food; friendly, lively
atmosphere. A little gem.
Darts, cribbage and board
games are played.
◖ ▶ ≢ (Central) ♣

Insole Arms

16 Harvey Street, Canton
☎ (01222) 390485
12–11; 12–10.30 Sun
Brains Dark, Bitter Ⓗ
Large, Edwardian pub
refurbished in typical Brains
style. Music night Fri.
◑ ◲ ♣

Packet

96 Bute Street
☎ (01222) 465513
11–11; 12–10.30 Sun
Brains Dark, Bitter, SA Ⓗ
Opposite the Welsh Maritime
and Industrial Museum: a
one-bar pub with a few cosy
corners. No food Sun.
✿ ◑ ▶ ⇌ (Bay) ♣

Three Horse Shoes

Merthyr Road, Gabalfa
☎ (01222) 625703
11–11; 12–10.30 Sun
Brains Dark, Bitter, SA Ⓗ
Pub of unremarkable
appearance but with a friendly
atmosphere and good food
(Mon–Fri); built in 1968 to
replace the original pub which
was demolished to make way
for the A470. Q ✿ ◑ ◲ ♣ P

Vulcan

10 Adam Street (A4160 behind
prison) ☎ (01222) 461580
11–8 (11 Fri & Sat; may vary); 12–6 Sun
Brains Dark, Bitter Ⓗ
Down-to-earth pub just outside
the city centre. Good value
lunches in the lounge.
◑ ◲ ⇌ (Queen St)

White Hart

James Street, Cardiff Bay
☎ (01222) 472561
11–11; 12–5 Sun
Brains Dark, Bitter Ⓗ
Well-kept, single-bar, mainly
locals' pub, winner of best-kept
cellar awards. Lunches on
request. ◑ ⇌ (Bay)

Clydach

New Inn

Lone Road ☎ (01792) 842839
11–4, 6–11; 11–11 Fri & Sat; 12–3,
7–10.30 Sun
**Draught Bass; Brains SA;
Greene King Abbot; Morland
Old Speckled Hen; Wadworth
6X; guest beers** Ⓗ
Friendly pub with a good
atmosphere and an excellent,
varied food menu. Children's
play area. Set in a valley with a
river alongside; close to an
RSPB site. ✿ Q ✿ ◑ ▶ ◲ P

Colwinston

Sycamore Tree

Off A48 ☎ (01656) 652827
12–3 (not Mon or Tue in winter), 6
(6.30 winter)–11; 12–3, 7–10.30 Sun
**Draught Bass; Hancock's HB;
guest beer** (occasional) Ⓗ

Totally unspoilt, friendly pub,
always a joy to visit. Excellent,
home-produced fare (no-
smoking dining room); no
meals Mon or Tue in winter.
Families welcome in the
lounge.
✿ Q ✿ ◑ ▶ ◲ ♠ ♣ P

Cowbridge

Edmondes Arms

High Street (A4222 jct)
☎ (01446) 773192
3 (12 Sat)–11; 12–10.30 Sun
Hancock's HB Ⓗ
Lively local on the east side of
town: a great street-corner
boozer. ✿ ◲ ♣

Craig Penllyn

Barley Mow

1½ miles N of A48 OS978773
☎ (01446) 772558
12–3 (not Mon), 6–11; 12–3, 7–10.30
Sun
Hancock's HB; guest beers Ⓗ
Popular village pub attracting
many visitors to the area;
former local CAMRA *Pub of the
Year*. The landlord has a great
sense of humour. No eve meals
Sun. ✿ Q ✿ ◑ ▶ ◲ ♣ P

Crynant

Kingfisher

☎ (01639) 750040
11–3.30, 5.30–11; 11–11 Fri & Sat;
12–10.30 Sun
**Courage Best Bitter; Ushers
Founders** Ⓗ
Friendly village pub with two
attractive bars.
✿ Q ✿ ◑ ▶ ♠ ♣ ◓ P ⊬

Cwmaman

Falcon Inn

1 Incline Row (off B4275)
OS008998 ☎ (01685) 873758
11–11; 12–10.30 Sun
Beer range varies Ⓗ
Small, friendly pub offering at
least three beers. Hard to find,
but worth the effort.
✿ ◑ ▶ P

Cwmfelin

Cross Inn

Maesteg Road
☎ (01656) 732476
11.45–11; 12–10.30 Sun
**Brains Bitter, SA; Morland
Old Speckled Hen** Ⓗ
Friendly local on a busy road: a
traditional, benched public bar
and a smart lounge. Limited
parking. ◲ ⇌ (Garth) P

Cwmgwrach

Star Inn

17 Glannant Place (off A465 at
Glyn Neath) ☎ (01639) 720365
12–3, 7–11; 12–11 Fri & Sat; 12–3,
7–10.30 Sun

**Crown Buckley CPA, Dark,
Best Bitter** Ⓗ
Small, friendly local with a bar,
a bar-lounge and a small
children's area; built over 100
years ago. ✿ ♣ P

East Aberthaw

Blue Anchor Inn

☎ (01446) 750329
11–11; 12–10.30 Sun
**Crown Buckley Best Bitter;
Flowers IPA; Marston's
Pedigree; Theakston Old
Peculier; Wadworth 6X; guest
beer** Ⓗ
Beautiful, thatched inn dating
from 1385. With its low
doorways, beamed ceilings
and six inter-connecting
rooms, it is the archetypal
historic pub. The food is good,
too (upstairs restaurant).
✿ Q ⚲ ✿ ◑ ▶ ◲ ♣ P

Fleur de Lys

Toby Jug

Ivor Street (off High St, behind
post office) ☎ (01443) 832777
12–5, 6.30–11; 12–5, 6.30–10.30 Sun
**Crown Buckley Best Bitter,
Rev. James; guest beers** Ⓗ
Cosy village pub and
restaurant, converted from
three 300-year-old cottages and
retaining some original
features. ✿ ◑ ▶ P ⊬

Gellihaf

Coal Hole

Bryn Road ☎ (01443) 830280
12–3, 6.30–11; 12–4, 7–10.30 Sun
Hancock's HB; guest beer Ⓗ
Popular, one-bar pub with a
separate dining area, offering
good value food (no eve meals
Sun). ✿ ◑ ▶ P

Gilfach Fargoed

Capel

Park Place ☎ (01443) 830272
12–4 (5 Wed), 7–11; 12–11 Fri & Sat;
12–10.30 Sun
**Courage Best Bitter; John
Smith's Bitter; guest beer** Ⓗ
Large, friendly, traditional
valleys pub with lots of
original features. Lunches
served Sat and Sun.
⇌ ◑ ▶ ◲ ⇌

Gilfach Goch

Griffin Inn

Hendreforgan OS988875
☎ (01443) 672247
7 (12 Sat)–11; 12–4, 7–10.30 Sun
Brains SA; guest beer
(occasional) Ⓗ
Traditional local, nestled at the
bottom of a small valley.
Interesting bric-a-brac and
hunting trophies abound.
Q ✿ ◲ ♣ P

Glais

Old Glais Inn
Birchgrove Road
☎ (01792) 843316
12–11; 12–10.30 Sun
Ruddles Best Bitter; Wells Bombardier; guest beers Ⓗ
Popular, two-bar pub and restaurant close to the river, boasting a fine display of cheese dishes and plates. Good meals. ⏣ ◖ ♿ ♣ P

Glan-y-Llyn

Fagin's Ale & Chop House
8 Cardiff Road
☎ (01222) 811800
12–11; 12–10.30 Sun
Brains Bitter; Hancock's HB; Morland Old Speckled Hen; guest beers Ⓖ/Ⓗ
Popular, vibrant alehouse offering an ever-changing selection of beers. Note the stone floor and wooden beams displaying 'Wenglish' sayings.
⏣ ◖ ▶ ⇌ (Taff's Well)

Gowerton

Welcome to Gower
2 Mount Street
☎ (01792) 872611
11.30–3, 7–11; 12–3, 7–10.30 Sun
Crown Buckley Best Bitter, Rev. James, seasonal beers Ⓗ
Charming, wood-panelled pub with a very relaxing atmosphere. It caters for all, with a good selection of food on offer.
Q ⏣ ◖ ▶ ⇌ P

Groesfaen

Dynevor Arms
Llantrisant Road
☎ (01222) 890530
11–11; 12–3, 7–10.30 Sun
Draught Bass; Hancock's HB; guest beer Ⓗ
Large, cosy, open-plan, comfortably furnished roadside pub with a separate dining area. No meals Sun eve or Mon.
⏣ ◖ ▶ ⌂ P

Hengoed

Junction
9 Kings Hill (by station)
☎ (01443) 812192
12–4 (4.30 Fri & Sat), 7–11; 12–3, 7–10.30 Sun
Hancock's HB; Worthington Bitter Ⓗ
Immaculately appointed local featuring railway memorabilia, on the western side of the Hengoed viaduct.
◖ ▶ ⊞ ⇌ ♣

Hopkinstown

Hollybush
Tŷ Mawr Road (main road from Pontypridd to the Rhondda) ☎ (01443) 402325
11.30–11; 12–10.30 Sun
Hancock's HB; Worthington Bitter; guest beer Ⓗ
Terraced house catering for all tastes. The bar is a haven for sports enthusiasts, both armchair and intellectual. The comfortable lounge doubles as an eating area (no food Sun eve). The guest beer is always keenly priced.
◖ ▶ ⊞ ♿ ♣ P ⊟

Kenfig

Prince of Wales
Maudlam OS804818
☎ (01656) 740356
11.30–4, 6–11; 12–10.30 (varies) Sun
Draught Bass Ⓖ; **Worthington Bitter** Ⓗ
Historic pub with exposed stone walls and a large, open fireplace: the former town hall of the lost city of Kenfig. Renowned for Bass on gravity.
♨ Q ⏣ ◖ ▶ ♿ ♣ P

Killay

Railway Inn
555 Gower Road, Upper Killay (500 yds from Killay shops, towards Gower)
☎ (01792) 203946
12–11; 12–10.30 Sun
Crown Buckley Best Bitter, Rev. James Ⓗ
Former station waiting rooms with three small rooms, situated on the old Clyne railway line. It could possibly do with updating, though it does have a cosy atmosphere. Interesting railway memorabilia.
⏣ ⊞ ♣ P

Try also: Village Inn, Killay Sq (Bass)

Kittle

Beaufort Arms
18 Pennard Road
☎ (01792) 234521
11–11; 12–10.30 Sun
Crown Buckley Best Bitter, Rev. James, seasonal beers Ⓗ
Village pub with an adjoining restaurant and a large outside play area. ⏣ ◖ ▶ ♣ P

Llangynwyd

Old House (Yr Hen Dŷ)
W of A4063 OS858889
☎ (01656) 733310
11–11; 12–10.30 Sun
Flowers IPA; guest beers Ⓗ

One of Wales's oldest pubs (1147 AD): a thatched house, full of atmosphere, with an extremely popular restaurant (booking advised eves and Sun). The favoured local of Wil Hopcyn, who courted the Maid of Cefn Ydfa.
♿ ⏣ ◖ ▶ ⊞ P ⌿

Llanmadoc

Britannia
Cheriton
☎ (01792) 386624
11.30–3, 7–11 (11–11 summer); 12–10.30 Sun
Marston's Pedigree Ⓗ
17th-century country inn with a small menagerie. Good views to the coast from the rear garden; handy for good walks. More beers are sold in summer.
♨ ⏣ ⊨ ◖ ▶ ⊞ ▲ ♣ P

Llantwit Major

Llantwit Major Social Club
The Hayes, Colhugh Street (main beach road)
☎ (01446) 792266
11.30–3.30 (not Wed), 6.30–11; 12–2, 7–10.30 Sun
Hancock's HB; guest beer Ⓗ
Imposing building behind the town hall car park; recently refurbished. Non-members must be signed in (normal CIU rules apply). Snooker played.
Q ♿ ▲ ♣ P

Machen

White Hart Inn
Nant y Ceisiad (100 yds N off A468 under railway bridge) OS203892
☎ (01633) 441005
11.30–3.30, 6.30–11; 11–11 Sat & summer; 12–10.30 Sun
Hancock's HB; guest beers Ⓗ
Rambling pub with extensive wood panelling, some salvaged from a luxury liner. Enterprising range of beers (three guests); one or two mini-beer festivals yearly. The present licensee is carrying on the tradition set by his predecessor.
♨ Q ⏣ ⊨ ◖ ▶ P

Maesteg

Sawyer's Arms
4 Commercial Street
☎ (01656) 734500
11–11; 12–3, 7–10.30 Sun
Brains Bitter, SA Ⓗ
An oasis: a popular, traditional public bar and a smart lounge offering quizzes and live music at times. No lunches Sun; eve meals by arrangement. Wheelchair WC.
◖ ▶ ⊞ ♿ ⇌

Maesycwmmer

Maesycwmmer Inn
Main Road ☎ (01443) 814385
12–4, 7–11; 12–3, 7–10.30 Sun
Brains Bitter; Hancock's HB Ⓗ
Small bar and a comfortable
lounge in a pub on the eastern
side of the Hengoed viaduct.
Q ❀ ⊕ ⅋ ⇌

Monknash

Plough & Harrow
Off B4265 between Llantwit
Major and Wick
☎ (01656) 890209
12–11; 12–10.30 Sun
Draught Bass Ⓖ**; Hancock's
HB; Worthington Bitter** Ⓗ**;
guest beers** Ⓖ
CAMRA S Wales *Pub of the
Year*, offering an excellent
range of guest beers and cider.
Live music Sun eve. Lively
locals; livelier licensee.
🏠 ❀ ⓓ ⊕ ♣ ⌂ P

Morriston

Masons Arms
Rhydypandy Road,
Rhydypandy OS667020
☎ (01792) 842535
12–11; 12–10.30 Sun
**Brains SA; Theakston Old
Peculier; Wadworth 6X; guest
beers** Ⓗ
17th-century inn set in the
country, close to a trout farm.
Friendly atmosphere; log fires;
good food. Various groups
play in the bar.
🏠 Q ❀ ⓓ ▶ ⊕ ♣ ⌂ P 🛏

Mountain Ash

Jeffreys Arms
Jeffrey Street ☎ (01443) 472976
7 (12 Fri & Sat)–11; 12–10.30 Sun
**Worthington Bitter; guest
beer** Ⓗ
Large, friendly village pub
with a good atmosphere.
⊕ ♣

Mumbles

Park Inn
23 Park Street (turn opp. Boots,
then 1st left) ☎ (01792) 366738
12–3 (not Mon), 5.30–11; 12–10.30 Sun
**Marston's Pedigree; Ruddles
County; Worthington Bitter;
guest beers** Ⓗ
Popular, 19th-century local, a
free house with a wide range of
guest beers and good, home-
cooked food. Beer festival Nov.
🏠 Q ⌷ ⓓ ♣

Nantyffyllon

General Picton
3 Picton Place
☎ (01656) 732474
11–11; 12–10.30 Sun

**Brains Bitter; Courage
Directors; John Smith's Bitter;
guest beer** (occasional) Ⓗ
A delightful surprise in an area
where possible *Guide* qualifiers
are sparse: a very highly
regarded pub and restaurant
for catering, beer and
company. A courtesy bus gets
you home afterwards. Note the
pig theme in the public bar.
Wheelchair WC planned.
🐕 ❀ ⓓ ▶ ⊕ ⅋ ♣ P 🛏

Neath

Highlander
2 Lewis Road
☎ (01639) 633586
12–2.30, 6–11; 12–11 Sat; 12–3, 7–10.30
Sun
**Worthington Bitter; guest
beers** Ⓗ
Very popular local, catering for
a wide age range. It has a
restaurant upstairs and one
large, split-level room
downstairs, plus a well-
deserved reputation for good
value food (no meals Sun eve).
ⓓ ▶ ⇌

Star Inn
83 Penydre
☎ (01639) 637745
12.30–4.30, 6–11; 12.30–11 Fri & Sat;
12–2.30, 7–10.30 Sun
**Draught Bass; Hancock's HB;
Worthington Dark; guest
beer** Ⓗ
Thoughtfully refurbished,
two-roomed pub and
restaurant close to Neath RFC
and busy on match days.
Altogether pleasant.
Q ❀ ⓓ ▶ ⇌ ♣ P

Nelson

Dynevor Arms
Commercial Street (village
square)
☎ (01443) 450295
11–11; 12–10.30 Sun
**Brains Bitter; Hancock's HB;
Worthington Bitter** Ⓗ
Former brew pub (and
mortuary), over 200 years old,
with a busy public bar. Live
music Sat eve. ⊕ ♣ P

Nottage

Rose & Crown
Heol-y-Capel (village centre)
☎ (01656) 784850
11.30–11; 12–10.30 Sun
**Courage Best Bitter, Directors;
Theakston Best Bitter, XB;
Younger IPA** Ⓗ
Smartly-kept old pub with a
rustic ambience; pleasantly
modernised and 'Dickensian'
in the best sense of the word.
Other beers from Scottish
Courage may replace those
listed. ❀ ⌷ ⓓ ▶ ▲ P

Seagull
Sandpiper Road (in shopping
precinct off West Park Drive)
☎ (01656) 785420
11.30–11; 12–5, 7–10.30 Sun
**Crown Buckley Best Bitter,
Rev. James** Ⓗ
Pleasant estate pub, popular
for meals; a rare Crown
Buckley outlet for this area. No
eve meals Sun. Q ❀ ⓓ ▶ ⅋ P

Swan
West Road (village centre)
☎ (01656) 782568
11.30–11; 12–10.30 Sun
**Draught Bass; Courage Best
Bitter, Directors; John Smith's
Bitter; guest beer** Ⓗ
Popular pub frequented
especially by locals and rugby
notables. Interesting collection
of rugby memorabilia. No food
Sun. ❀ ⓓ ▲ P

Pant

Pant Cad Ifor Inn
By mountain railway
☎ (01685) 723688
11–11; 12–10.30 Sun
**Draught Bass; Hancock's HB;
Worthington Bitter; guest
beers** Ⓗ
Bustling, welcoming pub
serving a good range of beers.
No eve meals Sun.
🏠 ❀ ⌷ ⓓ ▶ P

Penarth

Golden Lion
69 Glebe Street
☎ (01222) 701574
12.30–11; 12–10.30 Sun
**Cains Bitter; Fuller's London
Pride; Hancock's HB** Ⓗ
Traditional, street-corner local
in old Penarth.
❀ ⇌ (Dingle Rd) ♣

Royal Hotel
1 Queens Road
☎ (01222) 708048
11–11; 12–10.30 Sun
**Bullmastiff Gold Brew,
Brindle, Son of a Bitch,
seasonal beer; Hancock's
HB** Ⓗ
Former Victorian hotel
overshadowing the River Ely
estuary and Penarth marina; a
rare regular outlet for
Bullmastiff beers, with a
mainly local clientele.
❀ ⌷ ⇌ (Dingle Rd)

Penmark

Six Bells
☎ (01446) 710229
12–11; 12–10.30 Sun
Hancock's HB Ⓗ
Wonderfully contrasting bar
and lounge/restaurant rooms
offer something for everyone
in this rural gem, close to
Cardiff Airport. Q ❀ ▶ ⊕ P

Pontardawe

Pontardawe Inn
Herbert Street
☎ (01792) 830791
12–11; 12–10.30 Sun
Crown Buckley CPA, Best Bitter, Rev. James; guest beer H
Riverside coaching inn that is home to Pontardawe international music festival. New boules court at the rear. Wheelchair WC. ❀ ◑ ₺ ♣ P

Pontllanfraith

Crown
The Bryn ☎ (01495) 223404
12–3, 5–11; 12–11 Fri & Sat; 12–3, 7–10.30 Sun
Courage Best Bitter; Felinfoel Double Dragon; John Smith's Bitter; guest beer H
Two-roomed pub with a basic public bar and a spacious lounge; a haven for golfers and locals alike. ❀ ◑ ▶ ⊞ ♣ P ⊬

Pontypridd

Llanover Arms
Bridge Street (beneath A470)
☎ (01443) 403215
11–11; 12–3, 7–10.30 Sun
Brains Dark, Bitter, SA; Worthington Bitter; guest beer H
Bustling town pub brimming with character(s).
Q ❀ ⊞ ⇌ ♣ P

Market Tavern
Market Square
☎ (01443) 485331
11–11; 12–3, 7–10.30 Sun
Courage Directors; Hancock's HB; John Smith's Bitter; Theakston XB; Wadworth 6X; Worthington Bitter H
Town-centre local with a cellar bar for younger clientele, plus a restaurant and comfortable accommodation. ⋈ ◑ ▶ ⇌

Quakers Yard

Glantaff Inn
Cardiff Road ☎ (01443) 410822
12–4, 7–11; 12–4, 7–10.30 Sun
Brains SA; Courage Best Bitter, Directors; John Smith's Bitter; guest beer H
Comfortable inn with a good collection of water jugs and a warm atmosphere. Upstairs restaurant; no eve meals Sun. Good food. Q ❀ ◑ ▶ P

Rhymney

Farmers Arms
Brewery Row
☎ (01685) 840257
12–11; 12–3, 7–10.30 Sun
Boddingtons Bitter; Brains Bitter; guest beers H

Friendly, spacious and comfortable pub with a separate restaurant; traditionally furnished with interesting bric-a-brac, including Rhymney Brewery memorabilia. No eve meals Sun. ◑ ▶ ⇌ ♣

Risca

Exchange Inn
52 St Mary Street
☎ (01633) 612716
12–11; 12–3, 7–10.30 Sun
Crown Buckley Best Bitter, SBB; Wye Valley Stout; guest beer (occasional) H
Small, but lively pub on the main road. The public bar has many trophy cabinets and old Hancock's prints. ❀ ◑ ⊞ ♣

Rudry

Maenllwyd Inn
☎ (01222) 888505
11.30–3.30, 6–11; 12–10.30 Sun
Theakston Best Bitter, XB H
Characterful old country inn with stone walls, low ceilings and discrete eating and drinking areas. Forestry walks nearby. ⋒ Q ❀ ◑ P

St Bride's Major

Farmers Arms
Wick Road (B4265)
☎ (01656) 880224
12–3, 6–11; 12–10.30 Sun
Courage Best Bitter; John Smith's Bitter; Ushers Best Bitter, Founders, seasonal beers H
Cosy bar and restaurant across the road from the village pond (inhabited by swans). Busy and popular. Good meals.
⋒ Q ⇖ ◑ P

Fox & Hounds
Ewenny Road (B4265)
☎ (01656) 880285
5.30 (2 Fri, 12 Sat)–11; 12–10.30 Sun
Brains Bitter; Wadworth 6X; guest beer H
The village local, popular with all ages; families welcome. Excellent food in the lounge (not served Sun eve). A gem.
Q ❀ ◑ ▶ ₺ ♣ P

St Hilary

Bush Inn
¾ mile S of A48
☎ (01446) 772745
11–11; 12–10.30 Sun
Draught Bass G**; Hancock's HB** H**; Morland Old Speckled Hen** G
Superb, old, thatched inn in a quiet part of the Vale. The food is excellent (no meals Sun eve). Families welcome. Weston's Old Rosie Cider is now available all year.
⋒ Q ❀ ⋈ ◑ ▶ ⊞ ♣ ⇔ P

Swansea

Bryn-y-Mor Hotel
17 Bryn-y-Mor Road
☎ (01792) 466650
11–11; 12–10.30 Sun
Ansells Bitter; Ind Coope Burton Ale; Tetley Bitter; guest beer H
Friendly local with a bar and a lounge, handy for rugby and cricket at St Helens. Live music Wed and Sun; quiz Mon. Eve meals end at 7.30. ❀ ◑ ▶ ♣

Eli Jenkins Alehouse
24 Oxford Street (near Quadrant bus station)
☎ (01792) 465289
11–11; 7–10.30 (closed lunch) Sun
Draught Bass; Worthington Bitter; guest beers H
Pub enlarged and renamed in 1995 (after the reverend in Dylan Thomas's *Under Milk Wood*). Decorative wooden alcoves, nooks and prints of old Swansea are features. Two guest beers. ◑ ▶ ₺ ⊬

O'Brian's Exchange Bar
Green Dragon Lane (near castle) ☎ (01792) 645345
11–11; closed Sun
Brains SA H
A superb collection of jazz photographs and unique wooden decor make this friendly pub well worth visiting. ◑ ▶ ⇌

Queens Hotel
Gloucester Place
☎ (01792) 643460
11–11; 12–10.30 Sun
Crown Buckley Best Bitter; Theakston Mild, Best Bitter, Old Peculier; guest beers H
One-roomed lounge bar on the edge of the marina. Its numerous pictures reveal the maritime history of the area. Excellent lunches. Quiz nights Wed and Sun. ❀ ◑ ₺ ⇌

St George
30 Walter Road
☎ (01792) 469317
11.30–11; 12–10.30 Sun
Felinfoel Double Dragon; Hancock's HB; Worthington Bitter H
Large, one-roomed pub on the edge of the city centre. Live music Sun eve; quiz Tue. The only outlet in the city for Felinfoel (unavailable in high summer). ◑ ₺

Singleton
1–2 Dillwyn Street (opp. Grand Theatre) ☎ (01792) 655987
11–11; 12–10.30 Sun
Brains SA; Courage Best Bitter; Swansea Bishops Wood Bitter; guest beers (occasional) H

Red-brick, late-Victorian building: one single, comfortable bar within a two-room set-up. Q ⬥ ◖ ◗ ⚲ ♣

Vivian Arms

1 Vivian Road, Sketty (100 yds W of A4118/A4126 jct)
☎ (01792) 203015
12–11; 12–10.30 Sun
Brains Dark, Bitter, SA, seasonal beers Ⓗ
Well-maintained suburban pub on a busy crossroads, with a split-level bar, a large lounge and an enclosed garden. Excellent food – try a curry. Q ⚘ ◖ ♣

Westbourne Hotel

1 Bryn-y-Mor Road
☎ (01792) 459054
12–11; 12–10.30 Sun
Draught Bass; Hancock's HB; Worthington Dark; guest beers Ⓗ
Striking corner pub, near the Guildhall. The imposing slate plaque in the bar is of uncertain age. Mind the steps in the bar. Eve meals end at 8; no-smoking lounge till 9. ⚘ ◖ ◗ ⛉ ✗

Taff's Well

Anchor Hotel

Cardiff Road ☎ (01222) 810104
11–11; 12–3, 7–10.30 Sun
Brains Bitter; Marston's Pedigree; Wadworth 6X Ⓗ
Comfortable pub with a nautical theme. A separate restaurant offers Mongolian cuisine. ◖ ◗ ⛉ ⇌ ♣ P

Taff's Well Inn

Cardiff Road ☎ (01222) 810324
12–11; 12–10.30 Sun
Draught Bass; Tetley Bitter Ⓗ
Comfortable roadside inn adjacent to a bowling green and an ancient well. No eve meals Sat or Sun. ⚘ ◖ ◗ ⇌ P

Tondu

Llynfi Arms

Maesteg Road
☎ (01656) 720010
1 (12 Fri & Sat)–4, 6.30–11; 12–3, 6.30–10.30 Sun
Hancock's HB; Worthington Bitter Ⓗ**; guest beers** Ⓖ
Roadside pub with a lively bar and a comfortable lounge. Guest beers come from the Bass Caskmaster range. Lunches Fri–Sun; eve meals Thu–Sat. Q ◖ ◗ ⛉ ⛉ ⇌

Treforest

Otley Arms

Forest Road
☎ (01443) 402033
11–11; 12–10.30 Sun
Brains SA; Bullmastiff Gold Brew; Crown Buckley SBB; Worthington Bitter; guest beer Ⓗ
Pub known as 'O Block' by students of the nearby university; less frenetic outside term time. A rare outlet for Bullmastiff beer. Limited parking. ◖ ⇌ ♣ P

Tyle Garw

Boar's Head

Coed Cae Lane
☎ (01443) 225400
12–4, 7–11; 12–2.30, 7–10.30 Sun
Beer range varies Ⓗ
Small, welcoming pub set near forest walks: a totally unspoilt local. Q ⚘ ♣

Wick

Lamb & Flag

St Bride's Road (B4265)
☎ (01656) 890278
11.30–5, 7–11; 11.30–11 Sat; 12–4, 7–10.30 Sun

Draught Bass; Hancock's HB; Worthington Bitter Ⓗ
Wonderfully unchanged village inn, almost like stepping back in time. Friendly staff and locals. Meals are served Tue–Fri. ≋ Q ☎ ⚘ ◖ ◗ ⛉ ♣ P

Star Inn

Ewenny Road (B4265)
☎ (01656) 890519
12–3, 5–11 (11–11 summer); 12–5.30, 7–10.30 Sun
Hancock's HB; Worthington Bitter; guest beer Ⓗ
A real bonus to the area since re-opening in 1994; popular with locals and visitors alike. Fortunately the piano doesn't work, so it can't drown out the sound of laughter and chat. ≋ Q ⚘ ◖ ◗ ⛉ ♣ P ⛿

Ystalyfera

Wern Fawr

Wern Road (main street)
7–11; 12–3, 7–10.30 Sun
Beer range varies Ⓗ
Small village pub with a comfortable lounge. The bar has a collection of old tools on display. Well worth a visit if you like 60s music. Enjoy the friendly atmosphere. ≋ Q ♣ ⛿

Ystrad Mynach

Royal Oak

Commercial Street
☎ (01443) 814196
12–3, 5.30–11; 12–11 Sat; 12–3, 7–10.30 Sun
Draught Bass; Hancock's HB; Worthington Bitter Ⓗ
Unmistakable brewers' Tudor pub with interesting acid-etched-glass windows. Busy public bar. Good food available. ⚘ ◖ ◗ ⛉ ⛉ ⇌ ♣ P

BUCKLING UNDER

Whilst the brewing world was preoccupied with the proposed Bass-Carlsberg-Tetley merger, a more modest meeting of minds was taking place in Wales.

In March 1997 it was announced that Brains and Crown Buckley breweries were to merge, the marriage described by insiders as a perfect match, joining the Brains tied estate in South-East Wales to the strong free trade presence in South-West Wales and the clubs trade enjoyed by Crown Buckley. Sadly, although the beer brands appear safe for the moment, thirty jobs are to go when the old Buckley's brewery in Llanelli brews its last in 1998.

It's a disappointing end to a brewing tradition which stretches back some 230 years.

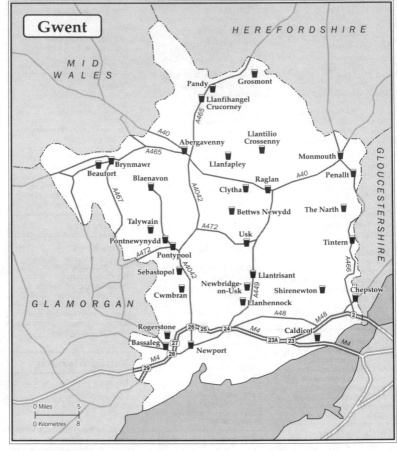

Gwent

H E R E F O R D S H I R E

MID WALES

Pandy
Grosmont
Llanfihangel Crucorney
A40
A465
Abergavenny
Llantilio Crossenny
Monmouth
Brynmawr
Beaufort
Blaenavon
Llanfapley
Raglan
A40
Penallt
GLOUCESTERSHIRE
A467
A465
Clytha
The Narth
A4042
Bettws Newydd
Talywain
A472
Usk
Pontnewynydd
Tintern
A472
Pontypool
A4042
Sebastopol
Llantrisant
A466
Newbridge-on-Usk
Shirenewton
A449
Cwmbran
Llanhennock
Chepstow
GLAMORGAN
A48
M48
Rogerstone
26 25
24
M4
Caldicot
2
Bassaleg
27
23A 23
28
Newport
M4
M4
29

0 Miles   5
0 Kilometres   8

Authority areas covered: Blaenau Gwent UA, Monmouthshire UA, Newport UA, Torfaen UA

Abergavenny

Coach & Horses
41 Cross Street
11–11; 12–10.30 Sun
Draught Bass; Brains SA; Flowers IPA; Wadworth 6X Ⓗ
Basic, one-bar pub near the bus station, a favourite of many locals. One of the few pubs in the area to open all afternoon, all week. ❀ ♣

Station
37 Brecon Road
☎ (01873) 854759
12–11; 12–3, 7–10.30 Sun
Draught Bass; Freeminer Bitter; Tetley Bitter; guest beer Ⓗ
Rare Freeminer beer and good value, adventurous guest beers are only two of the reasons for this pub's success. In addition, the chemistry, the cross-section of people, the basic bars and

the sheer vitality make it a vibrant pub. Limited parking.
🏰 ⊞ ♣ P

Try also: King's Arms, Neville St (Free)

Bassaleg

Tredegar Arms
4 Caerphilly Road (off M4 jct 28) ☎ (01633) 893247
11–11; 12–10.30 Sun
Badger Tanglefoot; Boddingtons Bitter; Brains Bitter; Flowers Original Ⓗ**; Greene King Abbot** Ⓖ**; guest beers** Ⓗ/Ⓖ
Gwent CAMRA *Pub of the Year* 1996, serving up to 13 beers, six on gravity, in a very comfortable bar with a log fire and armchairs. Large dining areas lead off a small drinking space. Huge menu of mostly home-cooked food. Beer festivals May Day and Aug

Bank Hol weekends. Cider in spring and summer. A garden with playthings leads off the family dining area.
🏰 ⊱ ❀ ◑ ◗ ⊞ ᗢ P ⊱

Beaufort

Rhyd y Blew
Rassau Road, Carmeltown (near A4046/A4047 jct)
☎ (01495) 308935
12–3 (11.30–3.30 Sat), 6 (6.30 Mon, Tue & Thu)–11; 12–3, 7–10.30 Sun
Flowers IPA, Original; guest beers Ⓗ
Real ale flagship which has done much to promote cask beers in the area. Its split-level interior has several adjoining areas. The name means Ford of the Hairs, from the days when horses were washed in a nearby stream – note the pub sign. No lunches Sat/Sun.
🏰 ❀ ◑ ♣ P

Bettws Newydd

Black Bear
Off B4598 OS361062
☎ (01873) 880701
11–3 (not Mon), 6–11; 12–10.30 Sun
Beer range varies Ⓖ
Village pub featuring two
constantly changing beers,
usually from small breweries.
The food selection includes an
exciting 'Whatever comes out
of the Kitchen' option – three
courses at a reduced price;
half-price portions for children.
🏨 ✹ ◖ ▶ ꝸ P

Blaenavon

Cambrian Inn
Llanover Road
☎ (01495) 790327
6 (1 Fri, 12 Sat)–11; 12–3, 7–10.30 Sun
**Brains Bitter, SA; Hancock's
HB; guest beers** Ⓗ
Friendly corner local where the
bar is the focal point and
features local photos of
yesteryear, sporting pictures
and comic sayings. Leading off
is a cosy lounge and a games
room. Q ⊞ ♣

Castle Hotel
Broad Street ☎ (01495) 792477
11.30–11; 12–3, 7–10.30 Sun
Tetley Bitter; guest beer Ⓗ
Old pub offering two kinds of
friendly welcome – human and
canine! Its open-plan interior
includes a dining area;
separate games room. Good
value accommodation makes
this a handy base for exploring
local industrial heritage sites.
🛏 ◖ ▶ ♣

Brynmawr

Gwesty Bach
Clarence Street
☎ (01495) 310245
11–11; 12–3.30, 7–10.30 Sun
Brains Bitter, SA Ⓗ
The 'Little Inn' is a smart pub
featuring much stone within.
Both the bar and spacious
lounge are comfortably
furnished. Very popular at
weekends. Close to the bus
station and shopping precinct.
✹ ◖ ⊞ P

Caldicot

Cross Inn
1 Newport Road
☎ (01291) 420692
11–4, 7–11; 11–11 Sat; 12–3, 7–10.30
Sun
**Brains Dark; Courage Best
Bitter; Ruddles County; John
Smith's Bitter; Wadworth 6X;
guest beer** Ⓗ
Popular pub at one end of the
pedestrian shopping precinct,
overlooking the town cross.

Home-cooked lunchtime food
(no meals Sun); regularly
changing guest beer. About a
mile from the railway station
(adjacent to main road bus
stops). ✹ ◖ ⊞ ♣ ꝸ P

Chepstow

Five Alls
Hocker Hill Street
☎ (01291) 622528
11–5, 7–11; 12–4.30, 7–10.30 Sun
**John Smith's Bitter; Ushers
Best Bitter, Founders, seasonal
beers** Ⓗ
Traditional pub on a cobbled
street near the castle. The
superb sign depicts the Five
Alls. ⇌ ♣

Clytha

Clytha Arms
☎ (01873) 840206
12–3.30 (not Mon), 6–11; 11–11 Sat;
12–3.30, 7–10.30 Sun
**Banks's Mild; Draught Bass;
Brains Bitter; guest beers** Ⓗ
CAMRA award-winning,
converted former dower house
with an enviable reputation for
its food (no lunches Sun/Mon;
no eve meals Sat/Sun). The
varied clientele reveals the
warm welcome extended to all.
🏨 Q ✹ 🛏 ◖ ▶ ♣ ꝸ P ⊟

Cwmbran

Commodore Hotel
Mill Lane, Llanyravon (off
A4042 and Llanfrechfa Way)
☎ (01633) 484091
11–11; 12–10.30 Sun
**Crown Buckley Best Bitter;
guest beers** Ⓗ
Very comfortable, family-run
hotel with a reputation for
friendliness. Real ales and
good value bar meals can be
enjoyed in the relaxing
'Pilliners Lounge'; seasonal à la
carte dining is offered in
'Willows Restaurant'.
✹ 🛏 ◖ ▶ P ⊟

Mount Pleasant Inn
Wesley Street, Cwmbran
Village ☎ (01633) 484289
12–3, 7–11; 12–3, 7–10.30 Sun
**Ushers Best Bitter,
Founders** Ⓗ
Homely locals' pub with a bar
and split-level lounge which
are both comfortably furnished
and tastefully decorated. A
good place for a quiet drink
and a meal (no lunches Sun).
Q ✹ ◖ ▶ ⊞ ♣ P ⊟

Grosmont

Angel
Main Street (off A465)
☎ (01981) 240646
12–2.30, 7–11; 12–3, 7–10.30 (may vary
in summer) Sun

**Crown Buckley Best Bitter,
Rev. James** Ⓗ
Small and charming village
pub at the heart of a
community with a Norman
castle, an impressive church
and a tiny town hall, all
reflecting their former
importance.
🏨 Q ✹ 🛏 ◖ ▶ ♣

Llanfapley

Red Hart Inn
On B4233 ☎ (01600) 780227
12–3 (not Tue), 6–11; 12–3, 7–10.30
Sun (closed Sun Oct–Feb)
Beer range varies Ⓗ
Three changing guest beers are
available at this village pub
where a large log fire inspires a
welcoming atmosphere in
winter. Good range of food.
🏨 Q ✹ ◖ ▶ ♣ P

Llanfihangel
Crucorney

Skirrid Inn
Hereford Road (A465, 4 miles
N of Abergavenny)
☎ (01873) 890258
11–3, 6–11 (11–11 summer); 12–3,
6–10.30 (12–10.30 summer) Sun
**Ushers Best Bitter, Founders,
seasonal beers** Ⓗ
Award-winning food is served
at this ancient and venerable
pub, once a court for Judge
Jefferies at which men were
hanged. Massive walls and
flagstone floors support the
claim that this is the oldest pub
in Wales.
🏨 Q ✹ 🛏 ◖ ▶ ⊞ ♣ P

Llanhennock

Wheatsheaf Inn
OS353929 ☎ (01633) 420468
11–3, 5.30–11; 11–11 Sat; 12–3, 7–10.30
Sun
**Draught Bass; Worthington
Bitter; guest beer** Ⓗ
Quaint, old-fashioned village
pub with original 1950s decor.
Boules is popular, as are home-
made lunches. A favourite in
summer thanks to its excellent
countryside views.
🏨 Q ✹ ◖ ⊞ ♣ P

Llantilio Crossenny

Hostry Inn
On B4233 ☎ (01600) 780278
12–3 (not winter Mon–Fri), 6.30–11;
12–3, 7–10.30 Sun
Wye Valley Bitter, Supreme Ⓗ
Rural pub presided over by a
chatty licensee. The food choice
includes vegetarian options
and Sun lunch. A hall and a
vintage Rolls Royce are
available for functions.
Resident ghost (subject to
availability)! Skittles played.
✹ ◖ ▶ Å ♣ P ⅄

Llantrisant

Greyhound Inn
3 miles S of Usk by A449 (no access) ☎ (01291) 672505
11–3, 6–11; 12–3, 6–10.30 Sun
Flowers Original; Marston's Pedigree; Morland Old Speckled Hen; guest beer ⊞
Charming country pub, originally a 17th-century farmhouse, close to Wentwood Forest. An excellent range of home-cooked food (book early Sat eve/Sun lunch) can be enjoyed in cosy surroundings. Pine furniture shop on site.
🏚 Q ➷ 🌣 ⛺ ◁ ▶ 🍴 ఉ P

Monmouth

Green Dragon
St Thomas Square
☎ (01600) 712561
11–11; 12–3, 7–10.30 Sun
Hancock's HB; Marston's Bitter, Pedigree, HBC; guest beers ⊞
Pub offering up to three guest beers, comfortably furnished throughout. Extensive menu. The gents features a cartoon gallery. Q 🌣 ◁ ▶ 🅰

Old Nag's Head
St James' Square (Dixton Gate)
☎ (01600) 713782
12–2, 7–11; 11–11 Sat; 12–3, 7–10.30 Sun
Brains Bitter, SA; Fuller's London Pride ⊞
Corner pub incorporating a medieval tower from the town gate. Popular at weekends.
Q 🌣 ◁ 🅱 🍴 🅰

Try also: **Mayhill Hotel**, Mayhill (Marston's)

The Narth

Trekkers
OS525064 ☎ (01600) 860367
11–3.30, 6–11; 12–10.30 Sun
Felinfoel Bitter; Freeminer Bitter; guest beers ⊞
Former pony trekking centre, converted into a pub and post office, in the style of a log cabin. A central open fire divides the drinking and dining (no-smoking) areas. Fine views; an excellent base for country walks. A separate skittle alley doubles as a family room.
🏚 Q ➷ 🌣 ◁ ▶ ఉ 🅰 🍴 P

Newbridge-on-Usk

Newbridge Inn
3rd right off Caerleon–Usk road through village OS384948
☎ (01633) 450227
11.30–3, 6.30 (7 winter)–11; 12–10.30 Sun
Draught Bass; Fuller's London Pride; guest beer ⊞

Large country pub nestling by the Usk river, with views across the valley. It runs a gourmet club and has a function room doubling as a skittle alley. Families welcome.
🏚 🌣 ◁ ▶ 🍴 P

Newport

George Hotel
157 Chepstow Road, Maindee
☎ (01633) 255528
11–11; 12–10.30 Sun
John Smith's Bitter; guest beer ⊞
Refurbished, large local on a busy road junction, in the heart of the local shopping area. Attractively priced guest beers. Live music some eves.
🌣 🅱 🍴

Olde Murenger House
53 High Street
☎ (01633) 263977
11–11; 12–10.30 Sun
Samuel Smith OBB ⊞
Popular, town-centre pub close to the railway station. The building dates from the 16th century and is Sam Smith's only pub in Wales. Home-cooked bar meals served until 8pm (4pm Sun). Very busy Fri/Sat eves. ◁ ▶ 🍺 🍴

Red Lion
47 Stow Hill ☎ (01633) 264398
11–11; 12–10.30 Sun
John Smith's Bitter; Ushers Best Bitter, seasonal beers ⊞
Corner pub offering a few surprises, including home-made pickled eggs. The menu is proudly non-vegetarian (no meals Sun). Live music Fri. The welcoming fire is an attractive focal point in winter.
🏚 🌣 ◁ ▶ 🍺 🍴 🍴

St Julian Inn
Caerleon Road
☎ (01633) 258663
11.30–11; 12–10.30 Sun
Courage Best Bitter; John Smith's Bitter; guest beers ⊞
Still deservedly popular pub, beautifully situated on the River Usk. Distinctly different drinking areas cater for all tastes and ages. Guest beers are often unusual. Eve meals end at 8.30; no meals Sun. Occasional cider. Not to be missed if visiting the area.
🌣 ◁ ▶ 🍴 🍴 P

Wetherspoons
Units 10–12, Cambrian Centre, Cambrian Road
☎ (01633) 251752
11–11; 12–10.30 Sun
Courage Directors; Felinfoel Double Dragon; Theakston Best Bitter, XB; Younger Scotch; guest beers ⊞
Large open-plan pub serving two guest beers. Photos of old Newport decorate the walls.

Popular at weekends. Good value bar meals.
Q ◁ ▶ ఉ 🍺 🍴 🍴

Pandy

Lancaster Arms
Old Hereford Road (A465, N of Abergavenny)
☎ (01873) 890699
11.30–2.30 (not Mon), 7–11; 12–3, 7–10.30 Sun
Ushers Best Bitter; guest beer ⊞
Adjacent to Offa's Dyke Path and but a short climb up to some outstanding Black Mountains scenery, this roadside free house provides welcome refreshment for the walker and for the less energetic. Daily special meals.
🏚 🌣 ⛺ ◁ ▶ 🍴 P

Penallt

Boat Inn
Lone Lane (across footbridge from A466 at Redbrook)
☎ (01600) 712615
11 (11.30 winter)–3, 6–11; 11–11 Sat; 12–4, 6.15–10.30 Sun
Crown Buckley Rev. James; Freeminer Bitter; Fuller's London Pride; Theakston Old Peculier; Wadworth 6X; guest beers ⑤
Riverside pub with two small rooms. Stone built, it is overshadowed by an old railway bridge. The car park is in England! Good riverside walks along the Wye. Cider in summer. Popular home cooking. 🏚 Q 🌣 ◁ ▶ 🍴 🍺 P

Pontnewynydd

Horseshoe Inn
Hill Street ☎ (01495) 762188
12–11; 12–3, 7–10.30 Sun
John Smith's Bitter; Ushers Best Bitter, Founders ⊞
Pleasant former coaching inn which operates on two levels: a small public bar and a cosy lounge downstairs, a games room and the 'Hayloft Restaurant' upstairs. The enclosed garden has children's play apparatus. A children's certificate applies to the lounge (12–3, 7–9). No meals Mon/ Tue; book Sun lunch.
➷ 🌣 ◁ ▶ 🍴

Pontypool

George
Commercial Street
☎ (01495) 764734
11.30–11; 12–3, 7–10.30 Sun
Brains SA; John Smith's Bitter ⊞
Edwardian-style bar which gets very busy at weekends. Pictures related to the pub's name adorn the walls and also of interest are the coloured

lamp stand tables. Close to the local heritage centre (start of the Cordell Trail) and Pontypool Park. Sun lunches are served in the restaurant (book). ◖

Raglan

Ship Inn

High Street ☎ (01291) 690635
11.30 (12 Mon)–11; 12–10.30 Sun
Draught Bass; Hancock's HB; guest beers Ⓗ
16th-century coaching inn with an attractive cobbled forecourt and water pump. The low-beamed interior is comprised of adjoining bars and a separate dining room. Within 15 mins' walk of Raglan Castle.
♒ ❀ ◖ ▶ ⌷ ♣

Rogerstone

Old Globe

1 St John's Crescent
☎ (01633) 668918
12–3, 5.30–11; 12–2.30, 7–10.30 Sun
Hancock's HB; guest beers Ⓗ
Friendly and comfortable pub, popular with locals. The open lounge includes a pool table. Small meeting room available.
❀ ♣ P

Tredegar Arms

Cefn Road ☎ (01633) 893417
12–3, 5.30–11; 12–11 Fri & Sat; 12–3, 7–10.30 Sun
Courage Best Bitter; Ruddles County; guest beers Ⓗ
Well-appointed traditional pub on the former main valleys road. Good reputation for quality food. ❀ ◖ ▶ ⌷ ♣ P

Sebastopol

Open Hearth

Wern Road (off South St)
☎ (01495) 763752
11.30 (11 Sat)–3, 6–11; 12–4, 7–10.30 Sun
Archers Golden; Boddingtons Bitter; Greene King Abbot; Hancock's HB; guest beers Ⓗ
Superb canalside pub with a cosy interior. A beer menu is posted on blackboards. Good bar meals can be selected from

a varied menu plus daily specials. The outside towpath is popular in fine weather (feed the ducks). ❀ ◖ ▶ ⌷ ♣ P

Shirenewton

Carpenters Arms

Usk Road ☎ (01291) 641231
12–2.30, 6–11; 12–3, 7–10.30 Sun
Boddingtons Bitter; Flowers IPA; Fuller's London Pride; Marston's Owd Rodger; Wadworth 6X; guest beer Ⓗ
Very popular, 400-year-old country pub on the outskirts of the village. The warm, cosy atmosphere, friendly staff and excellent choice of good food and cask ales combine to make this well worth a detour. No lunches Sun.
♒ Q ❀ ◖ ▶ ♣ P

Tredegar Arms

The Square ☎ (01291) 641274
12–3, 6–11; 12–11 Sat; 12–4, 7–10.30 Sun
Draught Bass; Hancock's HB; Hook Norton Best Bitter; guest beers Ⓗ
Ever popular pub at the heart of the village. The bar is the haunt of locals while the cosy lounge is an excellent place to sample the fine selection of food.
♒ Q ❀ ⇔ ◖ ▶ ⌷ ♣ P

Talywain

Globe Inn

Commercial Road (B4246)
☎ (01495) 772053
6.30 (11 Sat)–11; 12–4, 7–10.30 Sun
Brains Bitter; Hancock's HB; guest beers Ⓗ
Roadside inn with a distinctive, weather-beaten sign. The small public bar has a real fire in winter. A pool room leads off the comfortable lounge. Live weekend entertainment. Cider in summer. ♒ ⌷ ♣ ⌂

Tintern

Cherry Tree

Devauden Road (off A466)
OS526001 ☎ (01291) 689292

11.30–2.30 (not winter Mon), 6 (6.30 winter)–11; 12–3, 7–10.30 Sun
Hancock's HB Ⓖ
Single-roomed village pub with beer brought up from the cellar and a rare Hancock's 'toastmaster' sign outside. Bulmers cider is sold. It has appeared in every edition of this guide – use it or lose it!
♒ Q ❀ ♣ ⌂ P

Usk

Greyhound Inn

Old Chepstow Road
☎ (01291) 672074
12–3, 6–11; 12–3, 7–10.30 Sun
Draught Bass; Hancock's HB; guest beers Ⓗ
Comfortable, quiet, single-roomed local, a short stroll from Twyn Sq. Interesting guest ales for the area.
❀ ◖ ▶ P

King's Head Hotel

18 Old Market Street
☎ (01291) 672963
11–11; 12–10.30 Sun
Badger Tanglefoot; Flowers Original; Fuller's London Pride; Marston's Pedigree Ⓗ
Hotel where the attractively furnished lounge has a large fireplace and fishing mementoes. No real ale in the public bar. A small dining area sometimes exhibits local artists' work. Good food is available. All accommodation is en suite.
♒ ⇔ ◖ ▶ ⌷ ♣ P

New Court Hotel

62 Maryport Street
☎ (01291) 673364
11–11; 12–10.30 Sun
Draught Bass; Brains SA; Marston's Pedigree; Tetley Bitter; guest beer Ⓗ
Situated opposite the original court and the prison, this deceptively large hotel bar has a collection of ties (donations welcome). There is a dining area at the rear and a cosy snug at the front.
♒ ❀ ⇔ ◖ ▶ ♣

Try also: **Nag's Head**, Twyn Sq (Free)

A SILVER STAR

The Cherry Tree at Tintern in Gwent is one of the select few pubs which have appeared in every edition of the *Good Beer Guide*.

As each pub in the *Guide* is chosen annually on its merits at the time, to feature in all 25 editions is a remarkable achievement, revealing admirable consistency in beer keeping standards.

For a full list of 25-year pubs, see the front of the book.

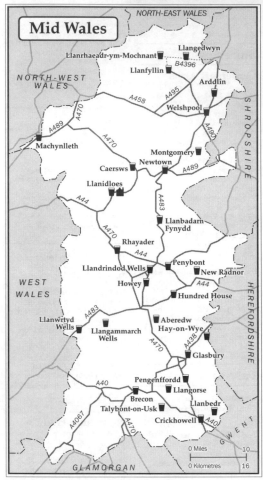

Mid Wales

Authority area covered: Powys UA

Aberedw

Seven Stars Inn
Off B4567
☎ (01982) 560494
11.30–2.30, 6.30–11 (closed winter Tue); 12–2.30, 7–10.30 Sun
Watkin BB; Wood Shropshire Lad H
Set amid fine hill-walking country, this low-beamed pub has been rescued from dereliction: cosy atmosphere, good food at keen prices and a warm welcome.
🏨 Q ◑ ▶ ♣ ⊟

Arddlîn

Horseshoe
☎ (01938) 590318
12–3, 5.30–11; 12–4, 6–10.30 Sun
Marston's Pedigree; Worthington Bitter H

Welcoming village pub: a public bar and a lounge/restaurant, serving a wide range of well-priced food. Children's play area in the garden. Weston's ciders.
🏨 ❀ ◑ ▶ ⊟ ♣ ⌂ P

Brecon

Old Boar's Head
14 Ship Street
☎ (01874) 622856
11–3, 5.30–11; 11–11 Fri, Sat & summer Tue; 12–4, 7–10.30 (12–10.30 summer) Sun
Brains SA; Everards Tiger; Fuller's London Pride, ESB; Thwaites Bitter; guest beer H
Ancient town pub, a haven for cask ale lovers in the dark days of the 1970s and still serving a wide choice. Modern public bar for drinkers; spacious rear bar for the younger element.

Limited parking.
🏨 ❀ ◑ ⊟ P

Caersws

Red Lion
3–4 Main Street (off A470)
☎ (01686) 688023
11–11; 12–5, 7–10.30 Sun
Banks's Mild; Marston's Pedigree H
Pleasant, welcoming village local, now offering a variety of take-away meals.
◑ ▶ ⊟ ⇄ ♣

Crickhowell

Bear Hotel
On A40 ☎ (01873) 810408
11–3, 6–11; 12–3, 7–10.30 Sun
Draught Bass; Ruddles Best Bitter, County; John Smith's Bitter; guest beers (occasional) H
Fine coaching inn dating back to the 15th century, continuing to win awards for its bar and cuisine. Deservedly popular. Parking is limited.
🏨 Q ⛟ ❀ 🛏 ◑ ▶ P

White Hart Inn
Brecon Road (A40)
☎ (01873) 810473
12–3, 6–11; 12–11 Sat; 12–3, 7–10.30 Sun (may extend in summer)
Brains Bitter; Hancock's HB; Theakston XB; guest beer H
Small, but very friendly, old inn, formerly a toll house (tolls are still displayed outside). Don't miss the landlord's collection of old photographs in the restaurant, which serves a good range of pub food, Welsh dishes a speciality.
Q ❀ ◑ ▶ ▲ ♣ P

Glasbury

Harp Inn
On B4350, near A438 jct
☎ (01497) 847373
11–3, 6 (6.30 winter)–11; 12–3, 7–10.30 Sun
Boddingtons Bitter; Robinson's Best Bitter; Watkin BB; guest beer H
Friendly village inn, on the River Wye, formerly an 18th-century cider house; a good base for outdoor activities and, for bookhounds, Hay-on-Wye is close by. Good range of bar meals at keen prices.
🏨 Q ❀ 🛏 ◑ ▶ ⊟ ♣ P

Hay-on-Wye

Blue Boar
Castle Street ☎ (01497) 820884
11–11; 12–10.30 Sun

Draught Bass; Flowers IPA, Original; Wadworth 6X; Whitbread Fuggles IPA Ⓗ
Old town pub with lots of character, near the castle, frequented by locals and visitors to the 'town of books'. Good, home-cooked bar food (eve meals in summer). Busy on market days and in summer. 🏨 Q ◖ ▶

Howey

Drovers Arms
Off A483, 1½ miles S of Llandrindod Wells
☎ (01597) 822508
12–2.30 (not Tue), 7–11; 12–3, 7–10.30 Sun
Brains SA Ⓗ
Picturesque, two-bar village inn on the original drovers' route, with a 13th-century cellar. An attractive patio garden overlooks a brook. The varied home-cooked food uses local produce. House beer sold.
🏨 Q ❀ 🛏 ◖ ▶ 🍴 ♣ P

Hundred House

Hundred House Inn
On A481 ☎ (01982) 570231
12 (11 summer)–3, 6.30 (6 summer)–11; 12–3, 7–10.30 Sun
Hancock's HB; Worthington Bitter; guest beers (summer) Ⓗ
Welcoming pub, formerly a drovers' inn, set amid fine upland scenery. Bars include a pool room and a garden bar.
🏨 Q 🐾 ❀ 🛏 ◖ ▶ 🍴 P

Llanbadarn Fynydd

New Inn
On A483 ☎ (01597) 840378
12 (11 summer)–3, 7 (6.30 summer)–11 (11–11 midsummer); 12–4, 6.30–10.30 Sun
Wood Shropshire Lad; guest beer Ⓗ
Refurbished inn with a public bar and a games room, a superbly furnished lounge-cum-restaurant and a comfortable conservatory overlooking a large, well-tended garden with a stream. Midnight supper licence.
🏨 🐾 ❀ 🛏 ◖ ▶ 🍴 & ▲ ♣ P

Llanbedr

Red Lion
☎ (01873) 810754
12–2.30 (not winter Mon & Tue), 7–11; 12–11 Sat; 12–3, 7–10.30 Sun (may extend)
Felinfoel Double Dragon; Hook Norton Old Hooky; Worthington Bitter Ⓗ
Cosy, old pub next to the church in a small village in the foothills of the Black Mountains. Good food (wide choice of vegetarian dishes). Limited parking.
🏨 Q 🐾 ❀ ◖ ▶ ▲ ♣ P ⚥

Llandrindod Wells

Conservative Club
South Crescent
☎ (01597) 822126
11–2, 5.30 (4.30 Fri)–11; 11–11 Sat; 12–2, 7–10.30 Sun
Worthington Bitter; guest beer Ⓗ
Quiet, comfortable club, not as political as its name implies. Non-members must be signed in. Q ◖ & ⇌ ♣

Llanerch Inn
Llanerch Lane
☎ (01597) 822086
11.30–2.30 (3 Sat), 6–11; 12–3, 7–10.30 Sun
Hancock's HB; guest beers Ⓗ
16th-century coaching inn, substantially rebuilt. The main bar has a low, beamed ceiling and a large stone hearth; cosy lounge. No-smoking area until 8. Q ❀ 🛏 ◖ ▶ 🍴 ⇌ ♣ P ⚥

Royal British Legion Club
Tremont Road (A483)
☎ (01597) 822558
7.30–11; 12–3, 7.30–11 Fri; 11–11 Sat; 12–3, 7–10.30 Sun
Hancock's HB; guest beers Ⓗ
Small, gabled, timber building extended at the rear. Non-members must be signed in.
& ⇌ ♣ P

Llanfyllin

Cain Valley Hotel
High Street (A490)
☎ (01691) 648366
11–11; 12–10.30 Sun
Ansells Bitter; Draught Bass; Worthington Bitter Ⓗ
Excellent, 17th-century coaching inn: a plush wood-panelled lounge, a small, basic public bar and a refurbished, large back bar.
❀ 🛏 ◖ ▶ 🍴 ♣ P

Llangammarch Wells

Aberceiros Inn
OS934469 ☎ (01591) 620227
12–3 (not Mon–Wed), 6.30–11; 12–3, 7–10.30 Sun
Hancock's HB; Worthington Bitter; guest beer Ⓗ
Although recently modernised, this remains a quiet and traditional pub in an attractive rural location at the edge of the village. In the same family for over 150 years.
🏨 Q ❀ ◖ ▶ ▲ ⇌ ♣ P 🍴

Llangedwyn

Green Inn
On B4396 ☎ (01691) 828234
11–3, 6–11; 12–3.30, 7–10.30 Sun

Boddingtons Bitter; guest beers Ⓗ
Out of the way pub in the picturesque Tanat Valley; popular with walkers and families. Four guest ales; excellent bar and restaurant meals. 🏨 ❀ ◖ ▶ 🍴 ♣ P

Llangorse

Castle Inn
☎ (01874) 658225
12–2.30 (later summer), 6–11; 12–3, 7–10.30 Sun
Brains Bitter, SA; Watkin OSB; guest beer Ⓗ
Friendly, old village pub in the heart of the Brecon Beacons National Park, close to Llangorse lake (popular for water sports and other activities). Very busy in summer; parking limited. Good food at reasonable prices.
🏨 Q ❀ ◖ ▶ ▲ ♣ P

Llanidloes

Red Lion Hotel
Longbridge Street
☎ (01686) 412270
11–3 (5 Sat), 7–11; 12–5, 7–10.30 Sun
Banks's Bitter; Flowers Original; Red Lion Cobbler's Thumb; guest beer Ⓗ
Old building converted to open-plan, popular with all and offering the widest choice of real ales for miles, including its own brews.
❀ 🛏 ◖ ▶ ♣ P

Llanrhaeadr-ym-Mochnant

Hand Inn
☎ (01691) 780413
11–11 (1am Fri, midnight Sat); 12–3, 7–10.30 Sun
Banks's Mild; Greene King Abbot Ⓗ
Excellent, friendly, timbered town pub with impressive stone inglenooks and real fires in all bars; tiled public bar and a back room with a games area.
🏨 ❀ 🛏 ◖ ▶ 🍴 ♣

Llanwrtyd Wells

Neuadd Arms Hotel
The Square ☎ (01591) 610236
11.30–11; 12–3, 7–10.30 Sun
Draught Bass; Felinfoel Double Dragon; Hancock's HB; guest beer Ⓗ
Georgian hotel, enlarged in the 1860s; an excellent centre for activities in the surrounding mountains and forests. A venue for the Mid Wales Beer Festival (Nov) and Saturnalia (winter ales) Festival (Jan). Eve meals end at 8.30. Afternoon hours may vary. 🏨 Q ❀ 🛏 ◖ ▶ 🍴 ▲ ⇌ ♣ P ⚥

Stonecroft Inn
Dolecoed Road
☎ (01591) 610332
12–3 (not Mon–Thu), 5–11 (12–11 summer); 12–3, 7–10.30 Sun
Brains SA; guest beers Ⓗ
Friendly Victorian pub in Britain's smallest town, amid beautiful scenery, on the spectacular Heart of Wales railway line. The large riverside garden has a barbecue patio. Regular events and live music. Children welcome.
🏦 ❀ 🛏 ◑ ▶ ▲ ≈ ♣ P

Machynlleth

Red Lion
Maengwyn Street
☎ (01654) 702675
11–11; 12–10.30 Sun
Banks's Bitter Ⓔ; **Marston's Pedigree** Ⓗ
Friendly, basic local, popular with a wide range of clientele. Games area. ❀ ≈ P

White Horse
Maengwyn Street
☎ (01654) 702247
11–3, 6–11; 11–11 Sat; 12–10.30 Sun
Hancock's HB Ⓗ
Popular public and lounge bars in an old coaching inn.
❀ 🛏 ◑ ▶ ≈ P

Wynnstay Arms Hotel
Maengwyn Street
☎ (01654) 702941
11–11; 12–10.30 Sun
Boddingtons Bitter; guest beers Ⓗ
Small bar serving a number of rooms in a comfortable town-centre hotel.
🏦 Q ❀ 🛏 ◑ ▶ ≈ P

Montgomery

Dragon Hotel
Off B4385
☎ (01686) 668359
11–11; 12–2, 7–10.30 Sun
Wood Special; guest beers Ⓗ
Excellent, comfortable bar in a 17th-century coaching inn. The stone and timber behind the bar are reputed to have come from the local castle. The hotel has an indoor swimming pool.
Q 🛏 ◑ ▶ ♣

New Radnor

Eagle Hotel
Broad Street (off A44)
☎ (01544) 350208
11–6, 7–11; 12–6, 7–10.30 Sun

Draught Bass; Hook Norton Best Bitter; guest beer Ⓗ
Old coaching inn with beamed bars and lounge; handy for local outdoor activities. It doubles as a newsagent on Sun. Supper licence to 1.30am Fri. 🏦 Q ❀ 🛏 ◑ ▶ 🍴 ▲ ♣ ♺ P ✄ ♺ P ✄

Newtown

Cross Guns
32 Park Street (off A483)
☎ (01686) 625546
11–11; 12–10.30 Sun
Theakston Best Bitter; guest beer Ⓗ
Many-roomed, beamed inn, offering guest beers from independents not usually found in the area.
🛏 ◑ ▶ 🍴 ≈ P

Railway Tavern
Old Kerry Road (off A483)
☎ (01686) 626151
11–2.30 (4.30 Tue, Fri & Sat), 6.30–11; 12–4, 7–10.30 Sun
Draught Bass; Worthington Bitter; guest beer Ⓗ
Small, friendly, one-bar local near the station. ≈ ♣

Sportsman
Severn Street (off A483)
☎ (01686) 625885
11–2.30, 5.30–11; 11–11 Fri & Sat; 12–3, 7–10.30 Sun
Ind Coope Burton Ale; Tetley Bitter; guest beer Ⓗ
Friendly, town-centre local, popular with a wide range of customers. Folk music jam sessions. Q ❀ ◑ ▶ ≈ ♣

Pengenffordd

Castle Inn
On A479, 3 miles S of Talgarth
☎ (01874) 711353
11–3, 7–11; 11–11 Sat, summer & bank hols; 12–3, 7–10.30 Sun
Ruddles County; Wadworth 6X; guest beer (summer) Ⓗ
Friendly old pub popular with hill-walkers and pony-trekkers, situated at the summit of the A479. Castell Dinas, the highest hillfort in Wales, and the Black Mountains form a dramatic backdrop.
🏦 ❀ 🛏 ◑ ▶ 🍴 ▲ ♣ P

Penybont

Severn Arms Hotel
At A44/A488 jct
☎ (01597) 851224
11–2.30, 6–11; 12–3, 7–10.30 Sun

Draught Bass; Worthington Bitter; guest beer Ⓗ
Roadside inn with an extensive garden sloping down to the River Ithon (fishing rights): a large public bar with an open fire, a games room, a lounge and a restaurant. Wheelchair WC (ask for key at the bar).
🏦 Q ❀ 🛏 ◑ ▶ 🍴 ⅍ ▲ ♣ P

Rhayader

Cornhill Inn
West Street
☎ (01597) 810869
11–3, 7 (earlier summer)–11; 11–11 Sat; 12–10.30 Sun
Hancock's HB; Watkin OSB; guest beer Ⓗ
Friendly, low-beamed, 400-year-old pub, reputedly haunted, with a single, L-shaped bar.
🏦 Q 🛏 ◑ ▶ ▲ ♣

Triangle Inn
Off Bridge Street (B4518)
☎ (01597) 810537
12–3, 6.30–11; 11–11 Fri & Sat; 12–3, 7–10.30 Sun
Draught Bass; Hancock's HB Ⓗ
Beautiful little weatherboarded pub, overlooking the River Wye. The ceilings are so low that customers have to stand in a hole to play darts. Eve meals end at 8.30 (9 Sat).
Q ❀ ◑ ▶ ▲ ♣ P

Talybont-on-Usk

Star Inn
On B4558 ☎ (01874) 676635
11–3, 6–11; 11–11 Sat; 12–10.30 Sun
Beer range varies Ⓗ
Canalside pub extensively renovated in 1995 after a major flood, but retaining its old atmosphere. It enjoys a loyal following among the locals. Excellent choice of up to 12 ales; good food. Cider varies.
🏦 ❀ 🛏 ◑ ▶ ▲ ♺

Welshpool

Royal Oak Hotel
Severn Street (off A483)
☎ (01938) 552217
11–3, 5.30–11; 11–11 Mon; 12–3, 7–10.30 Sun
Worthington Bitter; guest beers Ⓗ
Plush, 350-year-old, coaching inn, formerly the manor house of the Earls of Powis, now an hotel which has been in the same family for 60 years.
🏦 Q 🛏 ◑ ▶ ≈ P

For an at-a-glance guide to the Welsh regions used in this book, check the Key Map on the inside back cover.

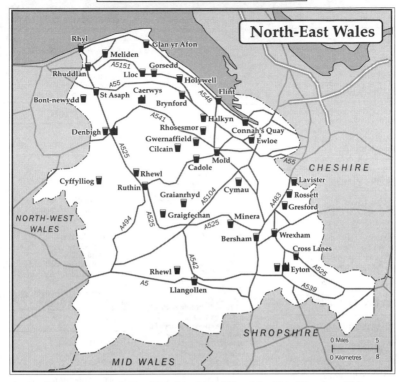

North-East Wales

Rhyl
Meliden
Glan yr Afon
A5151
Gorsedd
Rhuddlan
Lloc
Holywell
A55
Caerwys
Flint
Bont-newydd
St Asaph
Brynford
A548
Denbigh
A541
Halkyn
Rhosesmor
Connah's Quay
Gwernaffield
Ewloe
Cilcain
Mold
A55
CHESHIRE
Rhewl
Cadole
Cyffylliog
Lavister
Ruthin
Graianrhyd
Cymau
Rossett
A483
Gresford
Graigfechan
Minera
NORTH-WEST
WALES
A525
Bersham
Wrexham
Rhewl
A542
Cross Lanes
Eyton
A525
Llangollen
A539
A5
SHROPSHIRE
0 Miles 5
0 Kilometres 8
MID WALES

Authority areas covered: Denbighshire UA, Flintshire UA, Wrexham UA

Bersham

Black Lion Inn
Yddol (off B5099) OS313492
☎ (01978) 365588
12–4 (4.30 Fri & Sat), 7–11 (12–11
summer Sat); 12–4.30, 7–10.30 (12–
10.30 summer) Sun
**Hydes' Anvil, Billy
Westwood's** Ⓔ, **Dark Mild** Ⓗ,
Bitter Ⓔ
Friendly, three-roomed pub on
the Clywedog Valley Industrial
Trail and close to Bersham
Heritage Centre. Popular with
locals and ramblers and well
worth the effort to find.
🏚 ✿ ⬔ ♣ P ⏚

Bont-newydd

Dolben Arms
3 miles SW of St Asaph
OS013708
☎ (01745) 582207
7–11; 12–10.30 Sun
Theakston XB; guest beer Ⓗ
16th-century, remote country
inn in a picturesque valley, on
the River Elwy, accessible only
by narrow lanes. One single
bar separates into restaurant,
lounge and games areas. Sun
lunch served.
✿ ▶ ♣ P

Brynford

Llyn y Mawn
Brynford Hill (B5121)
☎ (01352) 714367
5.30–11; 12–3, 6–11 Sat; 12–3, 7–10.30
Sun
**Brains SA; Crown Buckley
Best Bitter; guest beers** Ⓗ
Award-winning, family-run
former coaching inn, with the
emphasis on quality
throughout. Ever-changing
guest beers from independent
breweries; Ales of Wales beer
festival in March annually.
Booking advisable for meals
(lunches served Sat; no meals
Mon).
🏚 Q ✿ ▶ ⅙ ▲ ♣ ⏛ P ⏚

Cadole

Colomendy Arms
100 yds off A494, Ruthin road
☎ (01352) 810217
7 (12 Fri & Sat)–11; 12–10.30 Sun
**Marston's Bitter; guest
beers** Ⓗ
Welcoming, two-roomed
village local, near Loggerheads
Country Park. Potholers are
regular visitors after exploring
local mines, pictures of which
adorn the walls. 🏚 ✿ ▲ ♣ P

Cilcain

White Horse
On B5122 ☎ (01352) 740142
12–3, 5.30, 7–10.30, 3–7–10.30
Sun
Beer range varies Ⓗ
Attractive village pub, close to
Moel Fammau Country Park.
The split-level lounge serves
meals; the public bar has a
museum-piece beer engine.
🏚 Q ⏙ ▶ ♣ P

Connah's Quay

Sir Gawain & The
Green Knight
Golftyn Lane ☎ (01244) 812623
12–3, 5.30–11; 12–11 Sat; 12–10.30 Sun
Samuel Smith OBB Ⓗ
Comfortable pub near a leisure
centre. Lunches Thu–Tue, eve
meals Mon–Fri. ✿ ⏙ ▶ ♣ P

**INDEPENDENT
BREWERIES**
Dyffryn Clwyd: Denbigh

Plassey: Eyton

Travellers Inn: Caerwys

Cross Lanes

Kiln
Off A525 at crossroads to Cock
Bank ☎ (01978) 780429
12–3, 7–11 (may vary winter); 12–3,
7–10.30 Sun
Plassey Bitter, Stout H
Malt kiln converted to a pub
around 1800, and attractively
expanded: two bright lounge
areas and a pool room,
surrounding a central servery.
A Hanby beer is also sold. Eve
meals till 8.30.
🏠 ☀ ◖ ▶ ▲ ♣ P ⊟

Cyffylliog

Red Lion
Off B5105 at Llanfwrog
☎ (01824) 710664
7–11; 11–3, 6–11 Sat; 12–3, 7–10.30
Sun
Lees GB Mild, Bitter H
Fine village pub in a semi-rural
setting. Its unspoilt interior
includes a lounge comprised of
three rooms with beams and
old furniture. Good food.
🏠 Q ☀ ◖ ▶ ⊞ ▲ P

Cymau

Talbot
Cymau Road (off A541)
☎ (01978) 761410
12–4 (not Mon–Thu), 7–11; 12–10.30
(12–4, 7–10.30 winter) Sun
Hydes' Anvil Mild, Bitter E
Hilltop pub with two distinct
rooms: a locals' bar with Sky
TV and games and a more
convivial lounge. Close to
Hope Mountain Country Park.
Q ☀ ⊞ ♣ P ⊟

Denbigh

Plough
Bridge Street ☎ (01745) 812961
11–11; 12–10.30 Sun
Marston's Bitter, Pedigree H
Traditional, friendly, two-bar,
town pub. ☀ ◖ ▲ ♣ P

Ewloe

Crown & Liver
The Highway (B5125)
☎ (01244) 531182
11–11; 12–10.30 Sun
**Burtonwood Bitter; guest
beers** H
Pub with a bar (Sky Sports)
and a comfortable, L-shaped
lounge. No weekend meals.
☀ ◖ ⊞ ♿ ⇌ (Hawarden) ♣ P

Eyton

Plassey Leisure Park
Off B5426; signed from A483
11–11 (Treetops closed Nov–March;
Hay Bank Inn may close early winter
eves); 12–10.30 Sun
**Plassey Bitter, Cwrw Tudno,
Stout, Dragon's Breath** H
Diversified farm craft centre.
The Treetops bar is on the
caravan park; Hay Bank Inn is
in the golf clubhouse. The
bistro sells Plassey, too.
Q ⛺ ◖ ▶ P

Flint

Three Pigeons
Coleshill Street
☎ (01352) 735068
11–11; 12–10.30 Sun
Banks's Bitter H
Attractive, one-bar town pub
close to the leisure centre,
shops and industrial estates.
🏠 ◖ ▶ ⇌ ♣ P ⊟

Glan yr Afon

White Lion
Glan yr Afon Road (W of A548
at Ffynnongroew) OS118817
☎ (01745) 560280
12–2 (not winter or Mon & Tue in
summer), 6–11; 12–3, 7–10.30 Sun
**Ruddles Best Bitter; guest
beer** H
Pub of real character with a
bar, a dining area, no-smoking
snug, and a conservatory. The
former home of actor/writer
Emlyn Williams. Extensive
outdoor drinking area.
🏠 ☀ ◖ ▶ ⊞ P ✓

Gorsedd

Druid Inn
The Village ☎ (01352) 710944
7–11; 12–3, 7–10.30 Sun
**Boddingtons Bitter; Taylor
Landlord; guest beers**
(summer) H
400-year-old pub with many
rooms to suit all tastes and a
conservatory restaurant (no
meals Sun or Mon).
🏠 ☀ ▶ ⊞ ▲ ♣ P

Graianrhyd

Rose & Crown
Llanarmon Road (B5430)
☎ (01824) 780727
12–11; 12–10.30 Sun
**Boddingtons Bitter; Flowers
IPA; guest beer** H
Popular country pub boasting
a teapot collection. Good value
food. Children welcome in the
dining room. 🏠 ☀ ◖ ▶ ⊞ ♣ P

Graigfechan

Three Pigeons
On B5429 ☎ (01824) 703178
6.30–11; 12–3, 7–10.30 Sun
Draught Bass; guest beers G
Enterprising country pub
offering ale from the jug and
fine views from the patio.
Walkers welcome. Eve meals
Thu–Sat; Sun lunch served. 🏠
Q ⛺ ☀ 🛏 ▶ ⊞ ♿ ▲ ♣ P ✓

Gresford

Griffin Inn
The Green ☎ (01978) 852231
1 (12.15 Sat)–4.30, 7–11; 1–4, 7–10.30
Sun
Greenalls Mild, Bitter H
Unspoilt village local, strong
on conversation. Q ☀ ♣ P

Gwernaffield

Hand Inn
Church Lane ☎ (01352) 740283
12–3 (not Mon), 6–11; 11–11 Sat;
12–10.30 Sun
Tetley Bitter; guest beer H
Modernised, whitewashed,
17th-century pub with a cosy
lounge, basic bar and a pool
room. Welsh guest beer.
🏠 ☀ ◖ ▶ ⊞ ▲ ♣ P

Miners Arms
Church Lane ☎ (01352) 740803
11–11; 12–10.30 Sun
**Marston's Bitter, Pedigree,
HBC; Thwaites Bitter; guest
beer** H
Unpretentious, friendly local of
simple decor. ☀ ⊞ ▲ ♣ P

Halkyn

Britannia Inn
Pentre Road (off A55)
☎ (01352) 780272
11–11; 12–10.30 Sun
**Lees GB Mild, Bitter,
Moonraker** H
500-year-old stone pub
boasting wonderful views over
the Dee estuary from the
conservatory restaurant.
🏠 Q ☀ ◖ ▶ ♿ ▲ ♣ P

Holywell

Glan yr Afon
Glan yr Afon Road (signed
from A5026) OS196739
☎ (01352) 710052
12–3, 7–11; 12–3, 7–10.30 Sun
**Courage Directors; Ruddles
Best Bitter; Webster's
Yorkshire Bitter** H
Traditional Welsh longhouse
with many additions, well
known for its food.
🏠 Q ⛺ ☀ ◖ ▶ ♣ P ✓

Red Lion
28 High Street
☎ (01352) 710097
11–4, 7–11; 11–11 Sat; 12–4, 7–10.30
Sun
Tetley Bitter H
Basic, busy, town local: a no-
frills pub. Carlsberg-Tetley
house beer. ♣

Lavister

Nag's Head
Chester Road (B5445)
☎ (01244) 570486
12–3, 5–11; 12–11 Thu–Sat; 12–10.30
Sun

Boddingtons Mild, Bitter;
Plassey Bitter; Thwaites
Bitter; guest beers ⌂
Large, busy, welcoming village
pub near the Welsh border.
Whitbread-supplied guests.
🏠 ⚘ ▲ P

Llangollen

Wynnstay Arms Hotel
Bridge Street
☎ (01978) 860710
12–3, 7–11 (11–11 summer); 12–3,
7–10.30 Sun
Cambrian Original; Ind
Coope Burton Ale; Morland
Old Speckled Hen; Tetley
Bitter; guest beers ⌂
Welcoming hotel near the
River Dee, with a cosy bar, a
restaurant and a large garden.
Home-cooked food.
🏠 Q ⚘ 🛏 ◖ ▮ ⊞ ▲ ♣

Lloc

Rock Inn
St Asaph Road (A5151)
☎ (01352) 710049
11–11; 12–10.30 Sun
Burtonwood Mild, Bitter ⌂
Friendly, beamed inn on the
old A55. Food always
available; families welcome.
🏠 ⚘ ◖ ▮ ▲ ♣ P

Meliden

Red Lion Inn
4 Ffordd Talargoch (off A547)
☎ (01745) 852565
11–11; 12–10.30 Sun
Draught Bass; Stones Bitter;
Tetley Bitter; Theakston Best
Bitter; guest beers ⌂
Sympathetically renovated,
cosy, village local featuring
military decor. ◖ ▮ ▲ ♣ P

Minera

Tyn-y-Capel
Church Road (off A525)
☎ (01978) 757502
7–11; 12–4, 7–11 Sat; 12–4, 7–10.30
Sun
Tetley Bitter; Thwaites Bitter;
guest beer ⌂
Cosy village local: a basic bar
with pool and a plush lounge.
The outdoor drinking area
(with play area) offers fine
views. Welsh guest beer.
🏠 ⚘ ⊞ ♣ P

Mold

Y Pentan
New Street ☎ (01352) 753772
11–3, 6.30–11; 11–11 Fri & Sat; 12–
10.30 Sun
Bateman Mild; Marston's
Bitter, Pedigree, HBC ⌂
Pub with a games bar and a
comfortable, L-shaped lounge
with large windows on to the
street. The Daniel Owen theme

relates to a nearby museum.
Good food. ⚘ ◖ ▮ ♿ ♣

Rhewl (Llangollen)

Sun
Off B5103 OS178448
☎ (01978) 861043
12–3, 6–11; 12–3, 7–10.30 Sun
Worthington Bitter; guest
beer ⌂
Rural gem: a 14th-century
drovers' pub with stone floors
and low ceilings; a centre for
walking and fell running.
Welsh guest beers.
🏠 Q ⚘ ◖ ▮ ⊞ ▲ ♣ P

Rhewl (Ruthin)

Drovers Arms
On A525
☎ (01824) 703163
12–3 (not Mon), 6–11; 12–10.30 Sun
Dyffryn Clwyd Dr Johnson's,
Four Thumbs; Ruddles Best
Bitter ⌂
Village pub with several rooms
and a restaurant, at the foot of
Moel Fammau mountain. A
rare local outlet for Dyffryn
Clwyd. ⚘ ◖ ▮ ▲ ♣ P

Rhosesmor

Red Lion Inn
Rhosesmor Road (B5123)
☎ (01352) 780570
12–2 (not Mon), 7–11; 12–4, 7–10.30
Sun
Burtonwood Bitter, seasonal
beers ⌂
Unspoilt pub in the hills, with a
cosy lounge. 🏠 ⚘ ⊞ ♣ P

Rhuddlan

New Inn
High Street ☎ (01745) 591305
12–3, 5.30–11; 12–11 Fri & Sat; 12–
10.30 Sun
Theakston Best Bitter, XB;
guest beer ⌂
Multi-roomed, popular, village
pub with a restaurant, near the
castle; a single bar with several
serving areas. ⚘ 🛏 ◖ ▮ ▲ P

Rhyl

White Horse
Bedford Street
☎ (01745) 334927
11–11; 12–10.30 Sun
Theakston Best Bitter; guest
beers ⌂
Much appreciated and
improved pub, near the town
hall, offering up to five beers.
Busy at weekends, but
friendly. 🏠 ▲ ⇌ ♣

Rossett

Butchers Arms
Chester Road (B5445)
☎ (01244) 570233
12–3, 5–11; 12–11 Fri, Sat & summer;
12–10.30 Sun

Burtonwood Bitter, Top Hat,
seasonal beers ⌂
Friendly pub with a loyal local
clientele. ⚘ ◖ ▮ ⊞ ♣ P

Ruthin

Wine Vaults
St Peter's Square
1.30 (12 Sat)–11; 12–10.30 Sun
Robinson's Best Bitter ⌂
Unchanging, gimmick-free pub
opposite the historic court
house. ⚘ ⊞ ▲ ♣ P

St Asaph

Kentigern Arms
High Street
☎ (01745) 584157
12–3, 7–11; 12–3, 7–10.30 Sun
Marston's Bitter, Pedigree;
guest beers ⌂
Cosy, multi-roomed local with
an area for meals (book eves),
and two main serving areas.
Near River Elwy.
🏠 ⛴ 🛏 ◖ ▮ ▲ P

Wrexham

Albion Hotel
1 Pen-y-Bryn ☎ (01978) 364969
12.30 (12 Sat)–4, 7–11; 12–3, 7–10.30
Sun
Lees Bitter ⌂
Cosy Victorian corner house,
pleasantly refurbished, but
retaining its original etched
windows. The only town outlet
for Lees. 🛏 ⊞ ⇌ (Central) ♣

Black Horse
Yorke Street (near church and
old Border Brewery tower)
☎ (01978) 352474
11.30 (11 Fri & Sat)–4 (3 Tue & Wed),
7–11 (midnight Thu–Sat); 12–4,
7–10.30 Sun
Marston's Bitter, Pedigree,
HBC ⌂
Lively pub, popular with
youngsters. ⇌ (Central) P

Horse & Jockey
Hope Street (pedestrianised
area) ☎ (01978) 351081
11–11; 12–10.30 Sun
Tetley Dark Mild, Bitter;
guest beer ⌂
Distinctive, thatched pub,
largely unaltered. Carlsberg-
Tetley house beer.
⊞ ⇌ (Central/General)

Nag's Head
Mount Street (by old Border
Brewery tower)
☎ (01978) 261177
11–3.30, 5 (7 Sat)–11; 12–2, 7–10.30
Sun
Banks's Mild; Marston's
Bitter, Pedigree, HBC ⌂
Popular pub, busy at
weekends at the former Border
Brewery tap.
⚘ ◖ ▮ ⇌ (Central) P ⚲

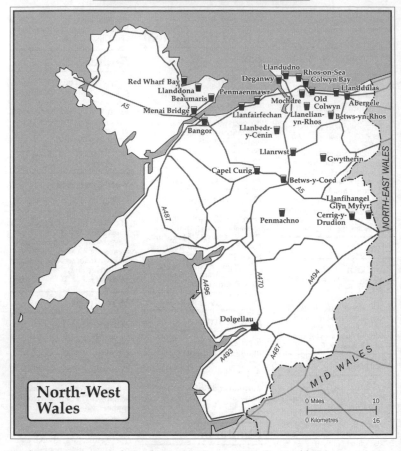

North-West Wales

Authority areas covered: Anglesey UA, Conwy UA, Gwynedd UA

Abergele

Bull Hotel
Chapel Street
☎ (01745) 832115
11–3, 6–11; 12–3, 7–10.30 Sun
Lees GB Mild, Bitter Ⓗ
Two-roomed pub, with a large, homely lounge and restaurant, popular with locals. One of the oldest buildings in town. The walls display transport theme charts.
🏨 Q ♣ ⇔ ◗ ▶ ⇌ ♣ P

George & Dragon
Market Street
☎ (01745) 824094
11–3, 5.30–11; 12–3, 7–10.30 Sun
Ansells Mild; Tetley Bitter; guest beer Ⓗ
Friendly pub with a horseshoe-shaped bar, boasting a collection of military hats. The 'billiard room' has a pool table. The guest beer changes every fortnight. Courtyard for outside drinking.
❀ ◗ ⇌ ♣

Bangor

Castle
Off High Street (opp. cathedral) ☎ (01248) 355866
11–11; 12–10.30 Sun
Boddingtons Bitter; Whitbread Abroad Cooper; guest beers Ⓗ
Large, single-bar chain pub with stone floors and wooden seating. It offers the largest selection of handpumped beer in Bangor. Popular with locals and students. Wheelchair WC. No no-smoking area eves.
◗ ▶ ぐ ⇌ ⅄

Tap & Spile
Garth Road (next to pier)
☎ (01248) 370835
11–11; 12–10.30 Sun
Beer range varies Ⓗ
Popular, multi-level pub, with a changing range of eight beers. Varied, reasonably-priced food menu with daily specials. Eight rooms for overnight accommodation.
❀ ⇔ ◗ ▶ ぐ ⇌ ♣ ♡

Union Hotel
Garth Road (near pier)
☎ (01248) 362462
11–11; 12–10.30 Sun
Burtonwood Bitter, Top Hat; guest beer Ⓗ
With a garden overlooking the Menai Straits, this friendly, multi-roomed pub, filled with brasses and plates, has a maritime atmosphere. No lunches Tue or Thu.
Q ♣ ❀ ⇔ ◗ ▶ ぐ P

Beaumaris

Olde Bull's Head
Castle Street ☎ (01248) 810329
11–11; 12–10.30 Sun
Draught Bass; Worthington Bitter; guest beers Ⓗ
Historic Grade II-listed building, 360 years old. Dr Johnson and Dickens stayed

▮ **INDEPENDENT BREWERIES**
Cambrian: Dolgellau

374

here. The two bars, heavily beamed, are full of antique weaponry and china. Enjoy the log fire and the food (booking advisable). ♨ Q ☜ 🏠 🌜 🍺 ♦ P

Sailor's Return
Church Street
☎ (01248) 811314
11.30–3, 6–11; 12–3, 7–10.30 Sun
Boddingtons Bitter; Flowers IPA; Morland Old Speckled Hen; guest beers H
1800s pub, modernised, but retaining its character. Fine selection of beers and food; great welcome. 🏠 🌜 ♦ ৬

Try also: Liverpool Arms, High St (Free)

Betws-y-Coed

Glan Aber Hotel
Holyhead Road
☎ (01690) 710325
11–11; 12–10.30 Sun
Dyffryn Clwyd Four Thumbs; Morland Old Speckled Hen; Tetley Mild, Bitter H
Popular, family-run hotel in the middle of the village. Three rooms for non-residents, in which all tastes are catered for. Three-star en suite accommodation. The food is highly recommended.
Q ☜ ❀ 🏠 🌜 ♦ ▲ ≋ ♣ P

Pont-y-Pair
Holyhead Road
☎ (01690) 710407
11–11; 12–10.30 (11 summer) Sun
Cambrian Original; Dyffryn Clwyd Four Thumbs; Greene King Abbot; Tetley Bitter H
Comfortable, family-run hotel opposite the Pont-y-Pair river bridge. A good selection of freshly-cooked meals is served in the bar. ♨ Q 🏠 🌜 ♦ ▲ ≋

Betws-yn-Rhos

Wheatsheaf
On B5381, 2 miles from A548
☎ (01492) 680218
12–3, 6–11; 12–3, 6–10.30 Sun
Banks's Mild; Marston's Bitter, Pedigree, HBC; Wadworth 6X H
Old village pub, extended to the rear, on split levels, but retaining a pleasant bar area at the front. Good food is served in the lounge, the bar and the restaurant. The best choice of real ale for miles. Children welcome in the lounge.
Q ❀ 🏠 🌜 ♦ ৬ ▲ ♣ P

Capel Curig

Bryn Tyrch Hotel
Holyhead Road (A5)
☎ (01690) 720223
11–11; 12–10.30 Sun
Castle Eden Ale; Flowers IPA; Marston's Pedigree H

Old pub with a quiet room and a TV room, situated in a walker's paradise. Extensive food menu.
♨ Q 🏠 🌜 ♦ 🍺 ▲ P

Cerrig-y-Drudion

White Lion
Off A5 ☎ (01490) 420202
12–4, 7–11 (11–11 summer); 12–4, 6–10.30 Sun
Lees GB Mild, Bitter, Moonraker (winter) H
Rural pub with a camping and caravan site in the grounds; popular with fishermen and walkers. Winner of Lees *Best Kept Cellar* award (Welsh region). Good value accommodation and food. Lloyd George really did stay here. Children's play area outside.
♨ Q ☜ ❀ 🏠 🌜 ♦ 🍺 ▲ P

Colwyn Bay

Wings Club
Station Square (above Imperial Hotel) ☎ (01492) 530682
12–3, 6.30–11; 11–11 Sat; 12–3, 7–10.30 Sun
Lees GB Mild, Bitter H
Ex-RAFA Club, now a social club open to all visitors (families welcome): a large lounge, a billiard room, a room for pool and darts, plus a snug with a TV. ≋ ♣

Deganwy

Deganwy Castle Hotel
Station Road ☎ (01492) 583555
12–11; 12–10.30 Sun
Courage Directors; John Smith's Bitter; Tetley Bitter H
17th-century listed building, originally a farmhouse, extended over the years. 100 yards from the beach, and adjacent to the railway station, it has many different rooms, to suit all tastes; good, olde-worlde atmosphere. No-smoking front room. ♨ Q ☜ ❀ 🏠 🌜 ♦ ৬ ≋ ♣ P ⊬

Gwytherin

Lion Inn
On B5384 ☎ (01745) 860244
12–2.30 (not Mon), 6–11 (12–11 summer); 12–3.30, 7–10.30 Sun
Marston's Bitter, Pedigree; guest beer H
Traditional village local reputed to be over 300 years old. The present building is a mixture of old and new, with beamed ceilings. A tourist board two crown commended inn, with en suite accommodation, well off the beaten track. A wide range of good meals is served.
♨ Q ❀ 🏠 🌜 ♦ 🍺 ▲ ♣ P

Llanbedr-y-Cenin

Olde Bull Inn
Off B5106 ☎ (01492) 660508
12–4, 6.30–11; 12–4, 7.30–10.30 (11 summer) Sun
Lees GB Mild, Bitter H
Small pub on the side of a hill, enjoying splendid views over the Conwy Valley. Excellent food (booking recommended).
♨ Q ❀ 🌜 ♦ P

Llanddona

Owain Glyndwr
Off B5109 ☎ (01248) 810655
12–3, 6–11 (11–11 summer); 12–4, 6–10.30 (12–10.30 summer) Sun
Tetley Bitter; guest beers H
18th-century village pub overlooking the picturesque Red Wharf Bay. Wonderful atmosphere; roaring log fire in winter. Renowned for its good food. ♨ ❀ 🌜 ♦ ৬ ▲ ♣ P

Llanddulas

Dulas Arms Hotel
Abergele Road (A547)
☎ (01492) 515747
12–11; 12–10.30 Sun (winter hours vary)
Lees GB Mild, Bitter H
Six-roomed pub: a lounge, snug, games room, quiet front room, family room and a restaurant. Clearly visible from the A55 expressway, it is easily recognised from the dinosaur in the large garden overlooking the sea. Children's certificate.
Q ☜ ❀ 🏠 🌜 ♦ ৬ ▲ ♣ P ⊬

Llandudno

Cross Keys
Madoc Street ☎ (01492) 876132
11–11; 12–10.30 Sun
Boddingtons Bitter; Castle Eden Ale; Flowers Original; guest beers H
Spacious, open-plan town-centre, family-run pub. Quiz nights Mon and Tue.
♨ ☜ ❀ 🌜 ৬ ≋ ⊙

Fat Cat Café Bar
149 Upper Mostyn Street
☎ (01492) 871844
11–11; 12–10.30 Sun
Boddingtons Bitter; Theakston XB; guest beers H
Traditional café-bar featuring wooden floors and furniture, popular with drinkers and diners of all ages.
♨ Q 🌜 ≋

Links Hotel
Conwy Road ☎ (01492) 879180
11–11; 12–10.30 Sun
Lees GB Mild, Bitter H
Friendly, family-run pub with ample room. It enjoys a consistent local trade, and is well patronised by

holidaymakers. Near two golf courses. Children welcome in the large conservatory; spacious outdoor play area. Good value meals.
🛏 ❀ ⋈ ◗ 🕮 ⚓ & ⩙ ♣ P

Olde Victoria

4 Church Walks
☎ (01492) 860949
11–11; 12–10.30 Sun
Banks's Mild, Bitter; Camerons Strongarm; Marston's Pedigree; Morrells Graduate Ⓗ
The 'Old Vic' is a popular, traditional, Victorian pub with a family atmosphere. Good value, home-made food includes daily specials and a Sunday roast lunch. Quiz Mon and Wed; folk club Sun eve.
Q 🛏 ❀ ◗ 🕮 ♣

Llanelian-yn-Rhos

White Lion Inn

1½ miles from A547, S of Old Colwyn
☎ (01492) 515807
11–3, 6–11; 12–3, 6–10.30 Sun
Marston's Pedigree; Tetley Bitter; guest beer Ⓗ
'Olde-worlde', traditional Welsh village inn, with a pleasant extension for diners. The slate-floored bar, tiny snug and lounge suit all visitors. The oldest part dates back to the 16th century. A true free house, with (often Welsh) guest beers. Very wide choice of well-presented meals, including daily specials. Tastefully converted hayloft accommodation.
⋈ Q ❀ ⋈ ◗ 🕮 ⚓ & ⚓ ♣ P

Llanfairfechan

Virginia Inn

Mill Road (off A55)
☎ (01248) 680584
11–11; 12–2, 7–10.30 Sun
Boddingtons Mild Ⓗ
Busy, basic, terraced pub at the centre of an old village. The hallway, boasting a quarry-tiled floor, leads to a small bar with basic period furniture.
Q ⇌ ♣

Llanfihangel Glyn Myfyr

Crown Inn

Near B5105, 3 miles E of Cerrig-y-Drudion
☎ (01490) 420209
7 (12 Sat)–11; 12–10.30 Sun; closed Mon
Draught Bass; guest beer Ⓗ
A front bar, pool room, and another room at the rear, in a lovely old inn on the road from Ruthin to Cerrig-y-Drudion. A warm welcome awaits (including for children).
⋈ Q ❀ ⋈ ◗ & ⚓ ♣ P

Llanrwst

New Inn

1 Denbigh Street
☎ (01492) 640476
11–11; 12–10.30 (11 summer) Sun
Bateman Mild; Marston's Bitter, Pedigree, HBC Ⓗ
Popular, traditional, town pub with a single bar, a snug, a general seating area and a rear games area. Hospitable tenants and friendly clientele.
⋈ ❀ ⚓ ⇌ ♣

Menai Bridge

Liverpool Arms

St George's Pier
☎ (01248) 713335
11–4, 5.30–11; 12–3, 7–10.30 Sun
Greenalls Bitter, Original, seasonal beers; guest beers Ⓗ
150-year-old pub with two bars, various nooks and crannies and a conservatory. Popular with the sailing fraternity (close to the slipway and pier) and students. Note the old nautical artefacts. Very good food and accommodation.
Q 🛏 ❀ ⋈ ◗ 🕮 ⚓ &

Victoria Hotel

Telford Road
☎ (01248) 712309
11–11; 12–10.30 Sun
Bass Mild Ⓖ**, Draught Bass** Ⓗ**; Stones Bitter** Ⓖ**; guest beers** Ⓗ
Popular, comfortable, residential hotel near the Menai suspension bridge, offering excellent views from the conservatory and garden. An ideal base for island exploration.
⋈ 🛏 ❀ ⋈ ◗ & ♣ P ⅏

Try also: **Auckland**, St George's Rd (Greenalls)

Mochdre

Mountain View

Old Conwy Road (A547)
☎ (01492) 544724
11.30–3, 5–11; 11–11 Sat; 12–4, 7–10.30 Sun
Burtonwood Bitter, Forshaw's, Top Hat; guest beer Ⓗ
The village local: a large lounge with a raised dining area and a bar with a pool table and TV; pleasant atmosphere. The no-smoking area for drinkers (and diners) was recently reinstated.
❀ ◗ 🕮 & ⚓ ♣ P ⅏

Old Colwyn

Red Lion

385 Abergele Road
☎ (01492) 515042
5–11; 12–10.30 Sun
Boddingtons Bitter; Everards Tiger; Greene King IPA;

Higsons Bitter; M&B Mild; guest beer Ⓗ
Popular, traditional pub, with a quiet lounge, and music in the bar. A popular meeting place for locals, where all are made welcome. Local CAMRA *Pub of the Year* 1996.
⋈ Q 🛏 & ⇌ ♣

Penmachno

Machno Inn

On B4406, 3 miles S of A5 jct
☎ (01690) 760317
12–3, 6–11; 12–11 Sat; 12–10.30 Sun
Tetley Bitter; Theakston Best Bitter; guest beer Ⓗ
Village pub: a modern building, in a remote valley, comfortably catering for all tastes, with an extensive menu. Outside, benches are beside a small stream.
⋈ ❀ ⋈ ◗ 🕮 & ♣ P

Penmaenmawr

Mountain View Hotel

Off A55
☎ (01492) 623446
11–11; 12–10.30 Sun
Ansells Mild; Tetley Bitter; guest beers Ⓗ
Large, comfortable, well-furnished, village pub, with a TV/pool room. A busy local.
◗ ⇌ ♣ P

Red Wharf Bay

Ship Inn

☎ (01248) 852568
12–3.30, 7–11 (11–11 summer); 12–10.30 Sun
ABC Best Bitter; Benskins BB; Friary Meux BB; Ind Coope Burton Ale; Tetley Dark Mild; guest beer Ⓗ
Nautically themed, beautifully situated pub on the beach with wonderful views over Red Wharf Bay. Award-winning food (restaurant open eves), lovely log fires, stone walls and wooden beams complement the setting.
⋈ Q 🛏 ❀ ◗ 🕮 & P ⅏

Rhos-on-Sea

Rhos Fynach

Rhos Promenade
☎ (01492) 548185
11–11; 12–10.30 Sun
Banks's Bitter; Marston's Pedigree; Morrells Graduate Ⓗ
Pub reconstructed on the ruins of an old monastery. The bar area leads to a lounge and a cosy snug-cum-disco area on rave eves.
⋈ ❀ ◗ 🕮 & P ⅏

> Protect your pleasure – join CAMRA today!

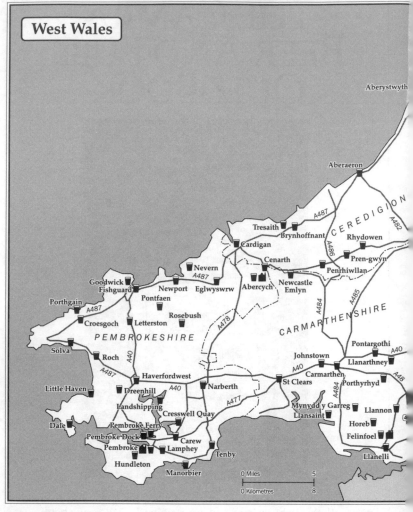

West Wales

Authority areas covered: Carmarthenshire UA, Ceredigion UA, Pembrokeshire UA

Carmarthenshire

Caio

Brunant Arms
Church Street (1 mile NE of A482)
☎ (01558) 650483
12–3, 6.30–11; 11–11 Sat; 12–3, 7–10.30 Sun
Boddingtons Mild, Bitter; Flowers IPA; guest beers Ⓗ
Friendly pub, full of character, in the centre of the UK's largest parish, close to the Dolaucothi gold mines. Many pub games.
🏰 🟊 🚪 🔾 ▶ ♿ Å ♣ P

Carmarthen

Mansel Arms
1 Mansel Street
☎ (01267) 236385
11–11; 12–3, 7–10.30 Sun
Draught Bass; Worthington Dark, Bitter; guest beers Ⓗ
Lively town pub, popular with shoppers and locals.
🟊 🔾 ♿ ⇄

Queens Hotel
Queens Street
☎ (01267) 231800
11–11; 12–10.30 Sun
Draught Bass; Worthington Bitter; guest beers Ⓗ
Convivial town-centre pub, popular with all ages. Snacks lunchtime. 🟊 🖳 ⇄

Try also: Boar's Head,
Lammas St (Felinfoel)

Cenarth

Three Horseshoes
On A484
☎ (01239) 710119
11–11; 12–10.30 (closed winter Sun eve)
Draught Bass Ⓖ**; Crown Buckley Dark, Best Bitter** Ⓗ**, Rev. James** Ⓖ
Cosy, traditional inn with a thatched former brewhouse at

Hours vary – phone
Crown Buckley Best Bitter *or* **Worthington Bitter** G
Family-run pub where a tiny public bar leads to a large restaurant. Very friendly.
🏚 Q ▶ P

Felinfoel

Royal Oak
33 Farmers Row (opp. brewery)
☎ (01554) 751140
11–11; 12–4, 7–10.30 Sun
Felinfoel Bitter, Dark, Double Dragon H
Very friendly pub, especially if you are Scottish! Excellent food (served Wed–Sun).
◑ ▶ &

Ffairfach

Torbay Inn
Heol Cennen (A483 near level crossing)
☎ (01558) 822029
11–11; 12–10.30 Sun
Crown Buckley Best Bitter; guest beers H
Friendly pub catering for the more mature person.
🏚 ❀ ◑ ▶ ⇌ P

Horeb

Waunwyllt Inn
Horeb Road (off B4309 at Fiveroads)
☎ (01269) 860209
12–3, 6.30–11; 12–3, 7–10.30 Sun
Felinfoel Bitter; guest beers H
Very friendly pub where children are welcome. Extensive bar and restaurant menus; supper licence to midnight. Large garden. The house beer is from Wye Valley.
Q ❀ 🛏 ◑ ▶ ⊟ & ▲ P

Johnstown

Friends Arms
St Clears Road
☎ (01267) 234073
11–11; 12–10.30 Sun
Ansells Mild; Ind Coope Burton Ale; Tetley Bitter H
Friendly, old village tavern.
❀

Try also: Poplars, Pondside (Watkin)

Llanarthney

Golden Grove
On B4300, edge of village
☎ (01558) 668551
12–2.30, 6–11; 12–3, 7–10.30 Sun
Crown Buckley Dark, Best Bitter, Rev. James H
Former coaching inn with congenial staff and an excellent menu.
🏚 Q 🛏 ❀ 🛏 ◑ ▶ ♣ P

Llandeilo

Castle Hotel
113 Rhosmaen Street (main street) ☎ (01558) 823446
12–11; 12–3, 7–10.30 Sun
Watkin BB, OSB; guest beer H
Once derelict pub which has been restored and reopened. Tomos Watkin's beer is brewed at the rear and visitors are welcome. Eve meals in summer only.
🏚 ❀ 🛏 ◑ ▶ ⇌ P ⅄

White Horse Inn
125 Rhosmaen Street (through archway at top of main street)
☎ (01558) 822424
12–11; 12–3.30, 7–10.30 Sun
Wadworth 6X; Worthington Bitter; Wells Bombardier; guest beers H
17th-century coaching inn with a courtyard; friendly atmosphere.
🏚 ⊠ ❀ ◑ ▲ ⇌ ⟳ P

Llandovery

Castle Hotel
Kings Road (A40)
☎ (01550) 720343
11–10; 12–3 Sun
Flowers Original; Watkin OSB; Worthington Bitter H
Large, town-centre hotel with a good reputation for its food. Newly refurbished lounge bar.
Q ⊠ 🛏 ◑ ▶ ⊟ & ▲ ⇌ P ⅄

White Swan
High Street (A40)
☎ (01550) 720816
12–3.30, 7–11; 12–3, 7–10.30 Sun
Wadworth 6X (summer); **Watkin BB** H
Comfortable, small town pub with a warm welcome for visitors. 🏚 ❀ ▲ ⇌ ✦

Try also: Red Lion☆, Market Sq (Crown Buckley)

Llandybie

Ivy Bush
18 Church Street
☎ (01269) 850272
12–4, 6–11; 12–2 (closed eve) Sun; closed Mon

the rear. The garden overlooks Cenarth Falls.
🏚 Q ❀ ◑ ▶ ♣ P

Cwmann

Ram Inn
On A482 1 mile from Lampeter
☎ (01570) 422556
11–11; 12–10.30 Sun
Draught Bass; Fuller's London Pride; guest beers H
Dating from the 16th century: a traditional pub with a superb display of Welsh love spoons. Imaginative range of guest beers. CAMRA regional *Pub of the Year* 1996. 🏚 Q ◑ ▶ ♣ P

Dryslwyn

New Cross Inn
Off A40 at Dryslwyn crossroads ☎ (01558) 668276

INDEPENDENT BREWERIES
Felinfoel: Felinfoel

Flannery's: Aberystwyth

Nag's Head: Abercych

Pembroke: Pembroke

Tynllidiart Arms: Capel Bangor

Watkin: Llandeilo

Draught Bass; Crown Buckley
Best Bitter; Ind Coope Burton
Ale; Worthington Bitter Ⓗ
Friendly village pub,
welcoming children.
Gymnasium and sauna at the
back. 🍴 ≋ ♣ 🍴

Try also: Red Lion, Llandeilo
Rd (Whitbread)

Llanelli

Apple Tree Inn
Station Road ☎ (01554) 774562
11–11; 12–10.30 Sun
Draught Bass; Worthington
Bitter Ⓗ
Basic pub, full of local
character. ≋ P

Half Moon
71A Wern Road
☎ (01554) 772626
11.30–3, 5–11; 11–11 Fri & Sat; 12–
10.30 Sun
Crown Buckley Best Bitter,
seasonal beers Ⓗ
Pub of two halves: younger
and noisy on one side, older
and quieter on the other.
🌸 ◖ ▮ 🍴 P

Lemon Tree
2 Prospect Place (behind
Crown Buckley brewery)
☎ (01554) 775121
12–11; 12–10.30 Sun
Crown Buckley CPA, Best
Bitter; guest beer Ⓗ
Friendly pub convenient for
the shopping centre. Bowling
green at the back. 🌸 ♣

Try also: Island House, Island
Place (Bass)

Llangadog

Plough & Stars
Dyrfal Road (A4069)
☎ (01550) 777913
11–11; 12–10.30 Sun
Draught Bass; guest beers Ⓖ
Friendly, lively village local,
popular with all ages.
Originally two cottages, it has
been a pub for a century.
Reputed to be haunted and a
site of murders. Try the pizzas.
🏚 🌸 ◖ ▲ ≋ ♣ P

Llannon

Red Lion
3 Heol y Plas ☎ (01269) 841276
5 (12 Sat)–11; 12–3, 7–10.30 Sun
Felinfoel Dark, Bitter, Double
Dragon Ⓗ
Pub with a long history, a well
and a secret tunnel.
🏚 Q 🛏 ▮ P

Llansaint

Kings Arms
13 Maes yr Eglwys
☎ (01267) 267487
12–2, 6–11; 12–10.30 (12–3, 7–10.30
winter) Sun

Beer range varies Ⓗ
Traditional style pub serving
good food; hidden behind the
church.
🏚 Q 🌸 🛏 ◖ ▮ & ▲ ♣ P

Llansawel

Black Lion Hotel
☎ (01558) 685263
5 (11 Sat)–11; 12–4, 7–10.30 Sun
Ansells Mild; Worthington
Bitter; guest beer Ⓗ
Unspoiled village pub which
also serves as HQ for the local
rugby club. 🏚 🛏 ◖ ♣

Mynydd y Garreg

Prince of Wales Inn
Heol Meinciau
☎ (01554) 890522
5–11; 12–3, 7–10.30 Sun
Beer range varies Ⓗ
Cosy, atmospheric village inn
displaying interesting cinema
memorabilia. Six ever-
changing ales; excellent food
for every taste, including
vegetarian. Sun lunch is served
(closed other lunchtimes).
No-smoking restaurant. No
under-14s. 🏚 Q 🌸 ▮ ▲ P

Newcastle Emlyn

Coopers Arms
Station Road (A484 E of centre)
☎ (01239) 710323
12–3.30, 5.30–11; 12–3, 7–10.30 Sun
Draught Bass; Worthington
Bitter Ⓗ
Friendly pub, known for its
excellent food and extensive
wine list. Spotlessly clean in all
aspects. 🌸 ◖ ▮ ♣ P 🗶

Try also: Ivy Bush, Emlyn Sq
(Bass)

Pontargothi

Cresselly Arms
On A40 ☎ (01267) 290221
12–3, 6.30–11; 12–3, 7–10.30 Sun
Flowers Original; Marston's
Pedigree; guest beers Ⓗ
Pleasant pub and restaurant
with a garden overlooking the
River Cothi. Good food.
🏚 Q 🌸 ◖ ▮ P

Porthyrhyd

Mansel Arms
Banc y Mansel (off A48)
☎ (01267) 275305
6–11; 12–3, 6–11 Sat; 12–3, 7–10 Sun
Beer varies Ⓗ
Comfortable and inviting
country pub a couple of miles
off the busy A48. Welcoming
fires in both the bar and
lounge. Eve meals Fri and Sat.
The one beer is usually
Marston's Pedigree.
🏚 ▮ ▲ ♣ P

Rhandirmwyn

Royal Oak Inn
☎ (01550) 760201
11–11 (may vary in winter); 12–2,
7–10.30 (may vary) Sun
Ind Coope Burton Ale; Tetley
Imperial; guest beers Ⓗ
Friendly, family-owned
establishment, popular with
locals and visitors. Excellent
views; a good centre for
walkers, campers, cyclists and
ornithologists (RSPB reserve
close by). En suite rooms.
🏚 🌸 🛏 ◖ ▲ P

St Clears

Corvus
Station Road ☎ (01994) 230965
11–11; 12–10.30 Sun
Courage Best Bitter;
Worthington Bitter; guest
beers Ⓗ
Comfortable pub in a large
village. Beers vary according to
the taste of regulars.
◖ ▮ 🍴 ♣

Ceredigion

Aberaeron

Royal Oak
North Road ☎ (01545) 570233
11–11 (may close afternoons); 12–
10.30 (may close afternoons) Sun
Ind Coope Burton Ale; Tetley
Bitter Ⓗ
Pub with a lounge bar and a
large public bar/games room
behind, both of great character
and furnished to a very high
standard. Fine porcelain
collection in the lounge.
🏚 Q 🛏 ◖ ▮ 🍴 & ▲ ♣

Aberystwyth

Cambrian Hotel
Alexandra Road
☎ (01970) 612446
11–11; 12–3, 7–10.30 Sun
Draught Bass; Hancock's HB;
guest beer Ⓗ
Elegant, though slightly jaded,
hotel opposite the railway and
bus termini: a lounge bar and a
cocktail lounge, popular with
locals, students and visitors.
🛏 ◖ ▮ ▲ ≋ ♣

Coopers
Northgate Street
☎ (01970) 624050
11–11; 12–10.30 (may close
afternoons) Sun
Felinfoel Bitter, Double
Dragon Ⓗ
The coopers, or Y Cŵps, is a
strongly Welsh pub with a
basic, long, narrow public bar,
bedecked with posters and
'maps Cymraeg', and a small
snug. Chess and other

interesting board games played. Self-catering summer accommodation.
🏠 🛈 🍴 🅰 ➹ ♣

Flannery's

High Street
☎ (01970) 612334
12–11; 12–10.30 Sun
Camerons Strongarm; Crown Buckley Best Bitter; Flannery's Granny Flan's, Celtic Ale; guest beer Ⓗ
Popular pub with several, basically furnished drinking areas. Photos on the walls depict the town's maritime heritage. 🅰 ➹ ♣

Fountain Inn

Trefechan (100 yds over river bridge from centre)
☎ (01970) 612430
12–11; 12–10.30 Sun
Banks's Mild; Hancock's HB; guest beer Ⓗ
Characterful, edge-of-town local with a warm welcome. The wide spectrum of clientele makes for a fascinating atmosphere.
🏵 🛈 🍴 🅰 ➹ ♣

Borth

Friendship Inn

High Street
☎ (01970) 871213
12–3 (may extend Aug & Sept), 7–11;
12–4, 7–10.30 Sun
Ansells Bitter; Benskins BB Ⓗ
Cottage-style pub in a seaside village, featuring an art gallery to the rear which also serves as a no-smoking family room; a free house run by the same family since 1921.
🏠 🏵 🍴 🅰 ➹ ♣ ✠

Brynhoffnant

Brynhoffnant Inn

On A487
☎ (01239) 654413
12 (6 winter)–11; 12 (6 winter)–10.30
Sun
Ruddles Best Bitter; Webster's Yorkshire Bitter; guest beer Ⓗ
Large, one-room bar with a games room attached, popular with locals and tourists. Huge log fire. 🏠 🏵 🛈 🍴 🅰 ♣ P

Capel Bangor

Tynllidiart Arms

On A44 5 miles E of
Aberystwyth ☎ (01970) 880248
11–2.30, 6–11; closed Sun except bank
hol weekends
Boddingtons Bitter; Tynllidiart Arms Rheidol Reserve; guest beers Ⓗ
19th-century, stone-built cottage pub housing Britain's smallest brewery. One guest beer from an independent plus one from the Whitbread range.
🏵 🛈 🍴 ♣ 🖵

Cardigan

Eagle Inn

Castle Street (across river from centre)
☎ (01239) 612046
11.30–3.30, 5.30–11; 11–11 Mon & Sat;
closed Sun
Crown Buckley Best Bitter; Worthington; guest beer (occasional) Ⓗ
Beautiful little pub with a tiled floor and impeccably polished furniture. The main bar leads into a quiet area and a lounge bar-cum-dining room. Sun-trap garden. Q ➳ 🏵 🛈 🍴 🅰 ♿ ♣

Ffair-Rhos

Teifi Inn

On B4343 6 miles N of Tregaron
☎ (01974) 831608
11–11 (may close afternoons); 12–
10.30 (may close afternoons) Sun
Brains SA; Hancock's HB; Worthington Bitter Ⓗ
Single, comfortable bar with a dartboard at one end, a pool table at the other and a lounge area in the middle. A useful base for exploring the Cambrian Mountains. The beer range may vary.
🏠 🏵 🛈 🅰 ♣ P

Goginan

Druid Inn

On A44 7 miles E of
Aberystwyth ☎ (01970) 880650
6–11; closed Sun
Banks's Bitter; guest beers Ⓗ
Free house on the hillside in a former lead mining village, offering two changing guest beers. Families welcome.
🏵 🍴 ♣

Llanbadarn Fawr

Black Lion

Off A44 ☎ (01970) 623448
11–11; 12–10.30 Sun
Banks's Mild, Bitter Ⓔ; **guest beers** Ⓗ
Friendly pub, frequented by locals and students. Function room at the rear; garden at the side. Live music most Fris.
🏵 🛈 🅰 ♣ P 🖵

Penrhiwllan

Penrhiwllan Inn

On A475 ☎ (01559) 370394
11–11; 12–10.30 Sun
Draught Bass; Hancock's HB; Worthington Bitter Ⓖ
Country pub and restaurant with very reasonable beer prices, a transport service for customers within a five-mile radius and a nine-hole pitch and putt golf course.
🏠 ➳ 🏵 🛈 🍴 ♣ P

Pren-gwyn

Gwarcefel Arms

On A475 ☎ (01559) 362720
12–11; 12–3 (closed eve) Sun
Crown Buckley Best Bitter; guest beer Ⓗ
Pub popular for meals. Children are welcome.
🏠 🛈 🍴 ♣ P

Rhydowen

Allt yr Odyn Arms

At A475/B4459 jct
☎ (01545) 590319
12–11; 12–10.30 (4 winter) Sun
Badger Tanglefoot; Crown Buckley Best Bitter; guest beers Ⓗ
Friendly village pub dating back to Queen Elizabeth I. Exceptional collection of mugs and jugs. Excellent food.
🏠 Q ➳ 🏵 🏠 🛈 🍴 ♣ P

Tresaith

Ship Inn

Tresaith Beach
☎ (01239) 810380
12–3 (2.30 winter; closed winter Mon
lunch), 6–11; 12–3, 6–10.30 Sun
Crown Buckley Best Bitter; guest beers Ⓗ
Stylish lounge bar with a no-smoking conservatory looking out over the beach and the coast beyond. Games room at the rear; large patio in front. Imaginative menu.
Q ➳ 🏵 🏠 🛈 🍴 🅰 ♿ ♣ P ✠

Pembrokeshire

Abercych

Nag's Head

☎ (01239) 841200
11–3, 5.30–11; 11–11 Sat; 12–10.30 Sun
Flowers Original; Nag's Head Old Emrys; Worthington Bitter; guest beers Ⓗ
Well-restored old smithy with a beamed bar, riverside gardens and a microbrewery. Local CAMRA *Pub of the Year* 1996. 🏠 Q ➳ 🏵 ♿ P

Carew

Carew Inn

☎ (01646) 651267
12–2.30, 4.30–11; 11–11 Sat &
summer; 12–3 (may extend), 7–10.30
Sun
Crown Buckley Rev. James; Worthington Bitter; guest beer Ⓗ
Unspoilt, traditional pub and restaurant with friendly locals. Why not explore the castle at the same time? 🏠 🏵 🛈 🍴 🅰 P

Try also: Plough Inn, Sageston (Free)

Cresswell Quay

Cresselly Arms
☎ (01646) 621210
11–3, 5–11 (11–11 summer); 12–3,
7–10.30 Sun
Flowers IPA; guest beer
(Monday) G
Waterside pub unaltered since
1900. Beer is served in jugs.
Popular with all ages. ♨ ❀ P

Croesgoch

Artramont Arms
On A487 ☎ (01348) 831309
7–11 (12–3, 6–11 summer); 12–3,
6–10.30 (11 summer) Fri & Sat; 12–3,
7–10.30 Sun
Brains SA; guest beers H
Friendly local with a large bar
and a separate dining room.
Interesting menu.
♨ ❀ ◖▶ ▲ ⌂ P ✄

Dale

Griffin
☎ (01646) 636227
12–3, 7–11 (12–11 summer); 11–11 Sat;
12–4.30, 7–10.30 (12–10.30 summer)
Sun
**Worthington Bitter; guest
beers** H
Harbour pub with outside
seating on the sea wall. Public
car park. Good food.
♨ ❀ ◖▶ ▲ ⌂

Dreenhill

Denant Mill Inn
Off B4327 OS924136
☎ (01437) 766569
11 (5.30 winter)–11; 11–11 Sat; 12–
10.30 Sun
Beer range varies H
Bar featuring a waterwheel
and the sound of running
water. Flagstone floor. Cider in
summer.
Q ❀ ⛵ ◖▶ ⌂ P

Eglwyswrw

Butchers Arms
On A487 between Newport
and Cardigan
☎ (01239) 891630
11–3, 7–11; 11–11 Sat; 12–3, 7–10.30
Sun
**Crown Buckley Rev. James;
Tetley Bitter; Worthington
Bitter** H
Pub with a cosy bar, offering
meals in summer (also
weekends in winter). No-
smoking restaurant.
Q ❀ ⛵ ◖▶ ♿

Fishguard

Fishguard Arms
Main Street
☎ (01348) 872763
11–3, 6.30–11; 12–3, 7–10.30 Sun
**Worthington Bitter; guest
beer** G

Step back in time at this
unspoilt two-roomer – an
essential visit. ♨ Q ◖⊟ ▲

Royal Oak Inn
Market Square
☎ (01348) 872514
11–11; 12–10.30 Sun
**Draught Bass; Hancock's HB;
guest beer** H
Charming, popular, friendly
pub of historic importance. The
treaty following the last
invasion of Britain was signed
here in 1797. Home-cooking is
a speciality, with a large,
comfortable restaurant and
very reasonable prices.
❀ ◖▶ ⊟ ▲ ♣

Try also: Ship Inn, Lower
Fishguard (Free)

Goodwick

Rose & Crown
☎ (01348) 874449
11–11; 12–3, 7–10.30 Sun
**James Williams IPA;
Worthington Bitter; guest
beer** H
Very picturesque pub with
harbour views and a friendly
welcome. Small, but cosy,
no-smoking restaurant.
(reasonably priced menu).
❀ ◖▶ ▲ ⇌ (Fishguard
Harbour) ♣ P

Haverfordwest

King's Arms
Dew Street ☎ (01437) 763726
11–11; 12–10.30 Sun
**Theakston Best Bitter; guest
beers** H
Pub at the top of town with a
large selection of ales enjoyed
by a local following. ♨ ♣

Pembroke Yeoman
Hill Street (off St Thomas
Green, top of town)
☎ (01437) 762500
11–11; 12–3, 7–10.30 Sun
**Flowers IPA; Greene King
Abbot; Worthington Bitter** H;
guest beers H/G
Comfortable local attracting all
ages. Good food. ♨ ◖ ♣

Hundleton

Speculation Inn
☎ (01646) 661306
12–3 (2 winter), 6–11; 12–3, 7–10.30
Sun
**Felinfoel Bitter, Double
Dragon; Worthington Bitter;
guest beer** (summer) H
Built in 1730 as a local for
farmers, this pub has been in
the Nelson family since 1915.
Totally unspoilt, it offers a step
back in time. Very reasonable,
but basic, menu (snacks only
eves). Children's certificate.
♨ Q ⛟ ❀ ◖▶ ⊟ ▲ ♣ P

Lamphey

Dial Inn
☎ (01646) 672426
11–3 (may extend in summer), 6–11;
11–11 Sat; 12–10.30 Sun
**Draught Bass; Hancock's HB;
Worthington Bitter; guest
beer** H
Delightful village pub serving
excellent food (separate
restaurant). Families are made
very welcome. ♨ Q ⛟ ❀ ◖▶
⊟ ▲ ⇌ ♣ P ✄

Landshipping

Stanley Arms
OS011118 ☎ (01834) 891227
12–3, 6–11; 12–3, 7–10.30 Sun
**Worthington Bitter; guest
beers** H
Attractive pub near the
estuary, in a quiet location.
Excellent choice of beers and
food. ♨ Q ❀ ⊟ ▲ ♣ P

Letterston

Harp Inn
31 Haverfordwest Road (A40)
☎ (01348) 840061
11–11 (11–3, 6–11 winter Mon–Fri);
12–10.30 Sun
Flowers IPA; Wadworth 6X H
Pub with a tastefully
modernised public bar, with
TV, pool and darts. The lounge
leads to a restaurant.
Attractive, creeper-covered
exterior.
Q ◖▶ ⊟ ♣ P

Little Haven

Swan
☎ (01437) 781256
11–3, 7–11; 12–3, 7–10.30 Sun
**Wadworth 6X; Watkin OSB;
Worthington Bitter** H
Waterside pub with a seafaring
flavour in its own haven.
Popular for food (book).
♨ Q ❀ ◖▶ ▲

Manorbier

Castle Inn
☎ (01834) 871268
11–11; 12–10.30 Sun
**Theakston Best Bitter, Old
Peculier; Wadworth 6X; guest
beer** (summer) H
Welcoming pub near the castle
and beach. Excellent restaurant
and menu. Families welcome.
❀ ◖▶ ▲ ♣

Narberth

Kirkland Arms
East Gate, St James Street
☎ (01834) 860423
11–11; 12–3, 7–10.30 Sun
**Felinfoel Bitter, Double
Dragon; guest beer** H

Pub with an unspoilt, traditional bar and original fittings. ❀ ⊞ ▲ ♣ P

Nevern

Trewern Arms
☎ (01239) 820395
11–3 (may vary), 6–11; 12–3, 7–10.30 Sun

Castle Eden Ale; Flowers Original; guest beer Ⓗ
Ivy-clad, 16th-century inn, popular with visitors to the coast. The beer range may vary. The restaurant overlooks the river. ♨ ☙ ❀ ⋈ ⊲ ▶ P

Newport

Castle Hotel
Bridge Street ☎ (01239) 820742
11–11; 12–10.30 Sun

Wadworth 6X; Worthington Bitter; guest beer Ⓗ
Friendly, popular local. The attractive bar has a real fire. Extensive dining area.
♨ ☙ ❀ ⋈ ⊲ ▶ ▲ P

Pembroke

Castle Inn
Main Street ☎ (01646) 682883
11–11; 12–10.30 Sun

Greene King Abbot; Wadworth 6X; Worthington Bitter; guest beer Ⓗ
Old pub, full of character and characters of various nationalities and backgrounds. Very busy at weekends with young people. ❀ ▲ ⋈ ♣ P

Old Cross Saws Inn
Main Street ☎ (01646) 682475
11–11; 12–10.30 Sun

Crown Buckley Best Bitter, Rev. James; guest beer Ⓗ
Friendly, rugby followers' pub. With a very reasonably-priced menu and accommodation, this makes an excellent base for sightseeing. Live music Sat night. ❀ ⋈ ⊲ ▶ ▲ ⋈ ♣ P

Pembroke Dock

First & Last
London Road
☎ (01646) 682687
11–11; 12–10.30 Sun

Worthington Bitter; guest beer Ⓗ
Lively, friendly local where the guest beer changes regularly; one of the cheapest places to drink in the area. Live music Sat night. Very cheap special meals and snacks.
❀ ⊲ ▶ ▲ ⋈ ♣ P

Station Inn
Dimond Street
☎ (01646) 621255
12–2 (not Mon–Wed; may extend summer), 7–11; 12–2, 7–10.30 Sun

Pembroke Darklin, Dimond Lager, Main Street Bitter, Old Nobbie, Off the Rails; guest beer Ⓗ
Redundant station building at the end of the line, brought back to life as the tap for Pembroke Brewery. The beer range may vary. Live music Sat eve. ♨ Q ▲ ⋈ P

Pembroke Ferry

Ferry Inn
☎ (01646) 682947
11–2.45, 6.30 (7 Mon)–11; 12–2.45, 7–10.30 Sun

Draught Bass; Hancock's HB Ⓗ
Charming waterside pub with a nautical theme. The excellent menu specialises in fresh seafood. ♨ Q ❀ ⊲ ▶ ▲ P

Pontfaen

Dyffryn Arms ☆
Off B4313 ☎ (01348) 881305
Hours vary

Draught Bass or Ind Coope Burton Ale Ⓖ
Heritage pub set in a 1920s front room. Beer is served in jugged form through a serving hatch. A rare treat and an insight into the pubs of yesteryear. ♨ Q ❀ ▲ ♣

Porthgain

Sloop Inn
☎ (01348) 831449
11.30–3, 6–11 (11–11 summer); 12–4, 6–10.30 Sun

Brains SA; Felinfoel Double Dragon; Worthington Bitter Ⓗ

Old fishing pub featuring quarrying and shipping ephemera. ♨ ❀ ⊲ ▶ ♣ P

Roch

Victoria Inn
On A487
☎ (01437) 710426
12–3, 7–11; 12–6 Sun

Draught Bass; Worthington Bitter; guest beer Ⓗ
Small, family-run pub, popular with locals. Families are welcome both in and out. Active in the local darts and pool leagues. ♨ Q ❀ ▲ ♣ P

Rosebush

New Inn
On B4329
☎ (01437) 532542
11–11; 12–3, 6–10.30 Sun

Crown Buckley Best Bitter, Rev. James; guest beers Ⓗ
Pub close to the spa village of Rosebush, specialising in continental bottled beers. Two guest ales in summer, one in winter. Q ❀ ⊲ ▶ ▲ ⌣

Solva

Ship Inn
15 Main Street
☎ (01437) 721247
12–11; 12–10.30 Sun

Draught Bass; Brains SA; Worthington Bitter; guest beer Ⓗ
Genuine, 300-year-old, family-run pub in an attractive riverside setting. The garden is well-tended and, like the spacious restaurant, is family friendly. Steaks are a speciality.
♨ Q ❀ ⊲ ▶ ▲ ♣

Tenby

Hope & Anchor
St Julian Street
☎ (01834) 842131
11–3, 7–11 (11–11 summer); 12–10.30 (closed winter afternoons) Sun

Crown Buckley Rev. James; Worthington Bitter; guest beers Ⓗ
Friendly local close to the harbour. Q ▲ ⋈ ♣

WET WALES

Good news! Beer lovers can now enjoy their favourite tipple seven days a week in all parts of Wales. 'Dry Sunday' polls in 1996 confirmed that the vast majority of Welsh people wanted Sunday pub opening – not before time! The change benefits all pub users, publicans and everyone involved in the Welsh tourist industry. There should be no more costly polls – keep Welsh pubs open on Sunday!

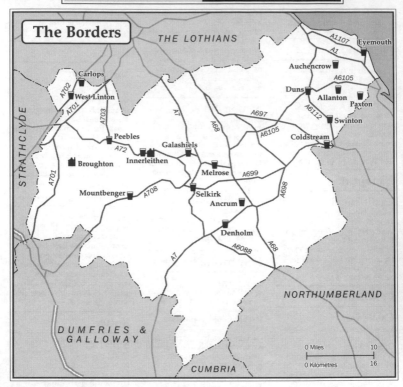

Authority area covered: The Borders UA

Allanton

Allanton Inn
On B6437
☎ (01890) 818260
12–2.30, 6–11 (midnight Thu & Fri);
12–11.30 Sat; 12.30–11.30 Sun
Beer range varies Ⓗ
Old coaching house with a
restaurant, in a village
surrounded by rolling
farmland. The unchanged
exterior still boasts hitching
rings for horses. Stone flags
surround the bar in the
comfortable, functional
interior. 🏚 ❀ 🚪 ◖▮ ♣ P

Ancrum

Cross Keys Inn ☆
The Green (B6400, off A68)
☎ (01835) 830344
12–2.30, 6–11 including Sun
**Caledonian Deuchars IPA,
80/-; guest beer** Ⓗ
Wonderfully unspoilt village
boozer, virtually unaltered
since it was built in 1908. The
lounge used to be the cellar
and retains the overhead tram
lines used for moving the
casks. Play on the Scalextric
track upstairs.
🏚 Q ⛴ ❀ 🕇 ♣ P

Auchencrow

Craw Inn
On B6438 ☎ (01890) 761253
12–2, 6–11.30; 12–11.30 Sat & Sun
Beer range varies Ⓗ
Attractive village local possibly
dating from 1680, with a
putting green opposite. A cosy,
wooden-beamed bar is
decorated with equestrian
trophies and warmed by a log
fire. Two rooms, one no-
smoking, serve as a restaurant.
A small snug serves as a family
room. Two guest beers.
🏚 Q ⛴ ❀ 🚪 ◖▮ 🕇 & ♣ P

Carlops

Allan Ramsay Hotel
Main Street (A702)
☎ (01968) 660258
11–midnight
**Belhaven Sandy Hunter's Ale,
80/-; guest beer** Ⓗ
Pub set in a small village under
the Pentland Hills. Originally a
flax mill, the building bears the
date 1792. It has been knocked
through into a single eating/
drinking area but retains
atmosphere through the use of
dark panelling. Children
welcome. 🏚 ❀ 🚪 ◖▮ P

Coldstream

Crown Hotel
23 Market Square (off A697)
☎ (01890) 882558
11–midnight; 11–11.30 Sat; 12.30–
11.30 Sun
Caledonian 80/- Ⓗ
Pub in a quiet residential
square. A labyrinthine
passageway leads to a snug bar
with an angling theme and an
impressive collection of
whisky miniatures. Children's
certificate. ❀ 🚪 ◖▮ ▲ ♣

Denholm

Auld Cross Keys Inn
Main Street (A698)
☎ (01450) 870305
11–2.30 (not Mon), 5–11 (midnight
Thu, 1am Fri); 11–midnight Sat;
12.30–11 Sun
**Broughton Greenmantle Ale;
guest beer** Ⓗ
Picturesque, 18th-century inn
overlooking the village green.

🍺 **INDEPENDENT
BREWERIES**

Broughton: Broughton

Traquair: Innerleithen

384

A low ceiling and a blazing fire add to the cosy conviviality of the bar. The cheesy eggs in the bar and high teas in the comfortable restaurant are highly recommended (no food Mon). Children welcome in the lounge. 🏚 ❀ ◑ ▶ ⊟ ♣ P

Fox & Hounds Inn

Main Street (A698)
☎ (01450) 870247
11–midnight (1am Fri & Sat) including Sun
Belhaven 80/-; guest beers Ⓗ
Cluttered local facing the village green. The cosy bar is festooned with tin cigarette adverts, breweriana and horsey pictures. Note the characterful courtyard round the back.
🏚 Q ❀ 🛏 ◑ ▶ ⊟ ▲ ♣ P

Duns

Whip & Saddle

Market Square
☎ (01361) 883215
11–11 (midnight Fri, 11.30 Sat); 12.30–11.30 Sun
Belhaven St Andrew's Ale; Caledonian Deuchars IPA; Theakston XB Ⓗ
Town-centre bar, dating from 1790; the modern and airy interior features wooden floors, leaded windows and views across the town square. The dining room upstairs is also a family room (no food Sun). River Whiteadder angling permits are available.
Q ⛱ ◑ ♣

Eyemouth

Ship Hotel

Harbour Road
☎ (01890) 750224
11 (12.30 Sun)–midnight (11.30 Sat)
Beer range varies Ⓗ
A real fisherman's haunt, with more trawlers than cars parked outside, a point to bear in mind if you leave after a few too many. A warm fire, a vast selection of rums and a wide range of maritime memorabilia add character to this family-run hotel. 🏚 ❀ 🛏 ◑ ▶ ▲ P

Galashiels

Ladhope Inn

33 High Buckholmside (A7, ½ mile N of centre)
☎ (01896) 752446
11–3, 5–11; 11–11 Wed; 11–midnight Thu–Sat; 12.30–11 Sun
Caledonian Deuchars IPA; Tetley Imperial; guest beer Ⓗ
Well-appointed locals' bar built into the hillside and dating from 1792, although much altered since. Vibrant Borders atmosphere. ❀ ♣

Innerleithen

Traquair Arms Hotel

Traquair Road (B709, off A72 close to centre)
☎ (01896) 830229
11–11 (midnight Fri & Sat); 12–midnight Sun
Broughton Greenmantle Ale; Traquair Bear Ale Ⓗ
Family-run hotel in an elegant 18th-century building. The plush lounge is warmed by a log fire. Both it and the adjacent dining room offer good food, home-cooked from local produce (served 12–9). Try the draught Traquair, as this is the only regular outlet in Scotland. Children welcome.
🏚 ❀ 🛏 ◑ ▶ ▲ ♣ ♺ P

Melrose

Burt's Hotel

Market Square
☎ (01896) 822285
11–2, 5–11; 12–2, 6–11 Sun
Belhaven 80/-; Courage Directors; guest beers Ⓗ
Elegant, well-appointed hotel bar in the town square. The interior decor reflects a huntin', shootin', fishin', theme, echoed by most of the clientele. Children's certificate.
🏚 ❀ 🛏 ◑ ▶ P

Mountbenger

Gordon Arms Hotel

At A708/B709 crossroads
☎ (01750) 82232
11 (12.30 Sun)–11 (midnight Fri & Sat; closed weekday lunch in winter)
Broughton Greenmantle Ale, Oatmeal Stout Ⓗ
Dating from 1828, this is a welcoming hotel of considerable historic interest, situated at an isolated cross-roads. A converted hayloft accommodates walkers on the Southern Upland way, which passes close by. Children welcome in the lounge and dining room (children's certificate). High teas served.
🏚 Q ❀ 🛏 ◑ ▶ ▲ ♣ P

Paxton

Hoolit's Nest

Off B6460 ☎ (01289) 386267
11–2.30 (not Mon), 6.30–midnight; 12.30–2.30, 6.30–midnight Sun
Beer range varies Ⓗ
Comfortable village bar and dining room themed on hoolits (owls) – stuffed, wooden, brass, painted, porcelain, pottery, they survey the bar from every nook and cranny. Paxton House, a stately home, is nearby. Children's certificate in the dining room.
❀ ◑ ▶ & ▲ ♣ P

Peebles

Green Tree Hotel

41 Eastgate (A72)
☎ (01721) 720582
11 (12 Sun)–midnight
Caledonian 80/-; guest beers Ⓗ
Hotel featuring a bustling, friendly locals' bar at the front with interesting leaded windows. A comfortable lounge and no-smoking dining room to the rear, in which children are welcome, are much more relaxed. Two guest beers. Eve meals 5–7.30.
🏚 ❀ 🛏 ◑ ▶ ⊟ & ▲ ♣ P

Selkirk

Cross Keys Inn

Market Place (A7)
☎ (01750) 21283
11 (12.30 Sun)–11 (midnight Fri & Sat)
Caledonian 80/-; Tetley Bitter Ⓗ
Next to the town cross, handy for the Bannock shop and buses, and often very busy, this pub has a vibrant, wee, wood-panelled public bar, with steps leading up to a comfortable lounge. Awards on the wall are for its excellent food (not served Sat eve). The no-smoking family room is upstairs. ⛱ ◑ ▶ ▲ ♣ ½

Swinton

Wheatsheaf Hotel

Main Street ☎ (01890) 860257
11–2, 6–11 (11.30 Fri & Sat); 11.30–3.30, 6–11 (not winter eve) Sun; closed Mon
Broughton Greenmantle Ale; guest beer Ⓗ
Multi-roomed pub-cum-restaurant. A small, dimly-lit snug bar is adorned with pictures of local legend Jim Clark, whilst a comfortable, well-furnished lounge has pictures of country pursuits. A wood-panelled conservatory/dining room offers an extensive quality menu.
🏚 Q ❀ 🛏 ◑ ▶ ⊟ P

West Linton

Gordon Arms Hotel

Dolphinton Road (A702)
☎ (01968) 660208
11 (12 Sun)–midnight
Alloa Arrol's 80/-; guest beers Ⓐ
Hotel boasting an excellent public bar with a blazing fire and settles, and an assortment of old phones, bottles and motoring paraphernalia. An attractive, wooden-floored restaurant serves excellent food and has a children's certificate. Two guest beers.
🏚 Q ❀ 🛏 ◑ ▶ ⊟ ♣ P

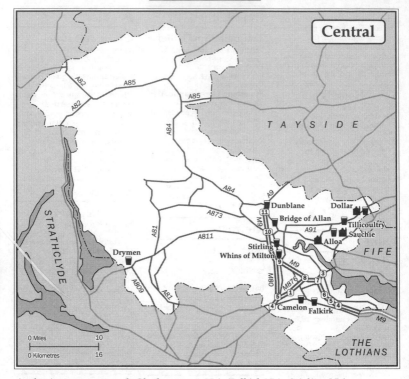

Authority areas covered: Clackmannan UA, Falkirk UA, Stirling UA

Bridge of Allan

Queens Hotel
24 Henderson Street
☎ (01786) 833268
12–midnight (1am Fri & Sat); 12–midnight Sun
Alloa Arrol's 80/-; Tetley Bitter; Younger IPA; guest beers H
Popular alehouse which has been granted permission to start brewing.
🛏 ◑ ▸ ⇌ ♣ P

Camelon

Rosebank
Main Street
☎ (01324) 611842
11–11 (midnight Fri & Sat); 12.30–11 Sun
Boddingtons Bitter; Marston's Pedigree; Wadworth 6X; guest beers (summer) H
Beefeater restaurant and bar housed in the former Rosebank distillery bonded warehouse, situated opposite the distillery on the Forth & Clyde Canal. Its unusual architecture and size dominate the crossroads on which it stands. ❀ ◑ ▸ P

Dollar

Castle Campbell Hotel
11 Bridge Street
☎ (01259) 742519
11–11.30 (1am Fri & Sat); 12.30–midnight Sun
Harviestoun 80/-; guest beers H
Coaching inn dating back to 1822, with good facilities. It is named after the nearby National Trust property. Sloe Gin competition every Feb. Wheelchair access to the public bar.
🏨 ❀ 🛏 ◑ ▸ ⊞ ♿ ▲ ♣ P

King's Seat Hotel
19 Bridge Street
☎ (01259) 742515
11–midnight (1am Fri & Sat); 12.30–midnight Sun
Harviestoun 80/-; guest beers H
Comfortable pub on the main street, with an ever-changing range of guest beers and a wide choice of home-cooked food, which includes daily specials and vegetarian meals.
◑ ▸ ⊞ ▲

Lorne Tavern
17 Argyll Street
☎ (01259) 743423
11–2.30, 5–11 Mon; 5–11 Tue; 3–11 Wed & Thu; 11–1am Fri & Sat; 12.30–11 Sun
Greene King IPA; Harviestoun Ptarmigan; guest beers H
Pub with the oldest licence in Dollar (1850), handy for the Ochil Hills. Q ❀ ⊞ ▲ ♣ P

Drymen

Clachan
2 Main Street ☎ (01360) 660824
11–midnight; 12–midnight Sun
Caledonian Deuchars IPA; guest beer (summer) H
Friendly village local dating from 1734. The lounge is now used as a restaurant and is very busy for meals at weekends (children allowed in for meals).

INDEPENDENT BREWERIES

Devon: Sauchie

Harviestoun: Dollar

Maclay: Alloa

Beer prices are a bit on the high side. 🍺 🍶 🍷

Winnock Hotel

The Square ☎ (01360) 660245
10.30–midnight (1am Fri & Sat);
12–midnight Sun

Alloa Arrol's 80/-; Broughton Merlin's Ale; Tetley Bitter; Wadworth 6X; guest beer Ⓗ
Pleasant hotel in a tourist area which stages regular Murder Mystery weekends: a large main bar with a restaurant leading off. Well-known for food and accommodation.
🏨 Q ⊛ 🛏 🍶 🍷 🍷 P

Dunblane

Tappit Hen

Kirk Street ☎ (01786) 825226
11–midnight (1am Fri & Sat); 12.30–
midnight Sun

Harviestoun 80/-; Maclay Kane's Amber Ale, Wallace; guest beers Ⓗ
Traditional, one-room local opposite the cathedral. Seven handpumps serve an extensive range of guest beers. ⇌

Falkirk

Eglesbrech at Behind the Wall

14 Melville Street
☎ (01324) 633338
12–11.30 (1am Thu–Sat); 12.30–
midnight Sun

Belhaven 80/-; Broughton Merlin's Ale; Courage Directors; Harviestoun Ptarmigan; Theakston Best Bitter Ⓗ

Alehouse on the upper floor of a former Playtex bra factory. Food is served in all areas, except the alehouse on Sat. Mexican food is a speciality. Local CAMRA *Pub of the Year* 1997. ⊛ ⇌ (Grahamston)

Sauchie

Mansfield Arms

7 Main Street ☎ (01259) 722020
11–11 (12.30am Fri & Sat); 11–11 Sun

Devon Original, Thick Black, Pride Ⓐ
Devon pub-brewery: a family-run local with a workingmen's bar and a warm, friendly lounge. Good, inexpensive meals every day till 9pm. Separate restaurant. Local CAMRA *Pub of the Year* 1996.
⊛ 🍶 🍷 🍷 P

Stirling

Birds & Bees

Easter Cornton Road, Causewayhead (off Causewayhead Road)
☎ (01786) 473663
11–3, 5–11.45; 11–12.45am Fri & Sat;
11–11.45 Sun

Caledonian 80/-; Fuller's London Pride; Harviestoun 70/-; guest beers Ⓗ
Former farm on the edge of a housing scheme on the outskirts of Stirling. The old stalls have been converted to pub seating, as have tractor seats and milk churns. Look out for the sheep (which are also seats). Petanque played.
⊛ 🍶 🍷 ♣ P

Hogshead

2 Baker Street (top of Friar St)
☎ (01786) 448722
11–midnight (1am Fri & Sat); 12.30–
midnight Sun

Boddingtons Bitter; Castle Eden Ale; Flowers Original; guest beers Ⓗ
Friendly, city-centre local, modernised to look old. Meals until 5pm. 🍶 ⇌ 🍴

Tillicoultry

Woolpack

1 Glassford Square (W end of town) ☎ (01259) 750332
11–midnight (1am Fri & Sat); 12.30–11
Sun

Fuller's London Pride; Orkney Dark Island; Taylor Landlord; guest beers Ⓗ
Traditional old drovers' inn with five ales on tap; a friendly pub with a strong local trade and occasional business from walkers from the Ochil Hills. Eve meals Fri–Sun. 🍶 🍷 ♣

Whins of Milton

Pirnhall Inn

Glasgow Road
☎ (01786) 811256
11.30–11; 12.30–11 Sun

Boddingtons Bitter; Caledonian Deuchars IPA; Marston's Pedigree; guest beers Ⓗ
Brewer's Fayre pub which has been converted from the original pub. Friendly; food- and family-oriented.
🛏 ⊛ 🛏 🍶 🍷 ⅃ A P ⅄

Nick Stafford of Hambleton Ales celebrates winning CAMRA's **Champion Winter Beer of Britain** *contest, held in Glasgow in February 1997, with his Nightmare porter.*

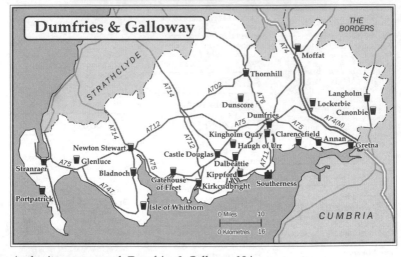

Dumfries & Galloway

Authority area covered: Dumfries & Galloway UA

Annan

Blue Bell Inn
10 High Street
☎ (01461) 202385
11 (12.30 Sun)–11 (12.30am Thu–Sat)
Theakston Best Bitter; guest beers H
Top class border alehouse offering an excellent variety of guest beers. An extremely popular and friendly pub; a consistent CAMRA award-winner. ❀ ▲ ⇌ ♣

Bladnoch

Bladnoch Inn
On A714, 6 miles S of Newton Stewart ☎ (01988) 402200
11 (12.30 Sun)–11 (midnight Fri & Sat)
Beer range varies H
A gem of a village local, decorated with a country sports theme; opposite the Bladnoch Distillery Museum.
🏚 Q ⌖ ❀ 🚗 ◖ ▶ P

Canonbie

Riverside Inn
☎ (0138 73) 71512
12–2.30, 6.30–11 (midnight Fri & Sat) including Sun (closed Sun eve in winter)
Yates Bitter; guest beer H
Charming, comfortable, country inn on the River Esk. Good quality food.
🏚 Q ❀ 🚗 ◖ ▶ ⌂ P 🍴

Castle Douglas

Royal Hotel
17 King Street
☎ (01556) 502040
11 (12.30 Sun)–midnight

Alloa Arrol's 80/-; Tetley Bitter; guest beers H
Edge-of-town-centre hotel with a front bar, a games room and a larger rear lounge. Food is available all day. Children's certificate. 🚗 ◖ ▶ ♣

Clarencefield

Farmers Arms
Main Street ☎ (01387) 870675
11–2.30, 6–11.30 (12.30am Fri); 11–12.30am Sat; 12.30–11.30 Sun
Maclay 80/-; Theakston Best Bitter; guest beer H
Welcoming, 18th-century inn, once a Temperance hotel. Reputedly used by Burns.
🏚 Q ⌖ ❀ 🚗 ◖ ▶ ♿ ▲ ♣ P

Dalbeattie

Pheasant Hotel
1 Maxwell Street (A711)
☎ (01556) 610345
10.30 (12.30 Sun)–midnight
Beer range varies H
Open-plan bar with a jukebox, and a pool table to the rear; very popular with locals. Children's certificate.
⌖ 🚗 ◖ ▶ 🍺 ♣

Dumfries

New Bazaar
39 Whitesands
☎ (01387) 268776
11–11 (midnight Thu–Sat) including Sun
Belhaven St Andrew's Ale; Broughton Greenmantle Ale; McEwan 80/-; Moorhouse's Pendle Witches Brew; guest beers H
Traditional bar with wonderful Victorian fittings and good

views over the River Nith. Good choice of guest beers.
🏚 Q ⇌ ♣

Ship Inn
97 St Michael Street
☎ (01387) 255189
11–2.30, 5–11; 12.30–2.30, 6.30–11 Sun
Caledonian Double Amber Ale, Merman XXX H; **McEwan 70/-, 80/-** A; **Marston's Pedigree; guest beers** H
Superb, award-winning pub, keeping to traditional opening hours. Large selection of guest beers. Q ⇌ ♣

Tam O'Shanter
113 Queensberry Street
☎ (01387) 254055
11–midnight (11 Mon & Tue); 12.30–11 Sun
Caledonian Deuchars IPA A; **Flowers IPA** H; **guest beers** A/H
Excellent bar with several small rooms and an upstairs restaurant, Pierre Victoire, which does not serve real ale (customers may take beer up from the bar). Q ⇌ ♣

Dunscore

George Hotel
Main Street ☎ (01387) 820250
12 (12.30 Sun)–11 (midnight Mon & Fri, 1am Sat)
Broughton Greenmantle Ale; guest beer H
Traditional village hotel with a cosy public bar and a larger function room staging monthly live entertainment. Bar meals

INDEPENDENT BREWERIES
Sulwath: Southerness

and snacks are served; more extensive eve menu.
🛏 🌑 🍴 P

Gatehouse of Fleet

Masonic Arms
Ann Street (side street opp. Bank of Scotland)
☎ (01557) 814335
11–2.30, 5–midnight; 12–3, 6.30–midnight Sun
Theakston XB H
Comfortable lounge bar with exposed beams and timber screens. A large conservatory is used as a no-smoking eating area. Children's certificate.
🌑 🍴 🍽 ♿ ♣

Glenluce

Kelvin House Hotel
53 Main Street (off A75)
☎ (01581) 300303
11–11 (midnight Fri & Sat); 12–11.30 Sun
Orkney Red MacGregor; guest beers H
Small, friendly hotel near Luce Bay in a bypassed village. Excellent home-cooked meals, specialising in local game. Children's certificate.
🛏 🌑 🍴 🍽 ♿ ♣

Gretna

Solway Lodge Hotel
Annan Road ☎ (01461) 338266
12–11 (midnight Fri & Sat, 3 winter Mon)
Tetley Bitter; guest beer H
Welcoming, comfortable hotel serving good value food. The guest beer is from Broughton and varies each week.
🛏 🌑 🍴 🍽 ♿ ⇌ P

Haugh of Urr

Laurie Arms Hotel
On B794, 1 mile S of A75
☎ (01556) 660246
11.45–2.30, 5.30–midnight; 11.45–3.30, 6–midnight Sun
Beer range varies H
Attractive country inn, off the beaten track; a good local which gives a welcome to all in its wood-panelled bar with a fireplace of local stone. Up to three guest beers and a wide selection of bar meals. Local CAMRA *Pub of the Year* 1996. Children's certificate.
🛏 🌑 🍴 🍴 P

Isle of Whithorn

Steam Packet Hotel
Harbour Row (A750)
☎ (01988) 500334
11 (12.30 Sun)–11
Theakston XB; guest beer (summer) H
Quaint harbourside inn in a popular sailing centre. The

Kingholm Quay

Swan Hotel
On B726, 1½ miles S of Dumfries ☎ (01387) 253756
12–2.30, 5–11 (11.30 Thu, midnight Fri & Sat); 11.30–3, 5–11.30 Sun
Theakston Best Bitter H
Attractive, friendly hotel overlooking the river. Excellent bar meals. Regular bus service from Dumfries centre.
🛏 🌑 🍴 🍽 ♣ P

Kippford

Anchor Hotel
Main Street ☎ (01556) 620205
11–midnight; 12.30–11 Sun
Boddingtons Bitter; Theakston Best Bitter; guest beers H
Traditional village inn in a popular sailing centre. It has a wood-panelled bar and a larger lounge with original stone walls. Fine views over the estuary to the hills. Children's certificate. 🛏 🛏 🌑 🍴 🍽 ♿ P

Kirkcudbright

Masonic Arms
19 Castle Street
☎ (01557) 330517
11–2.30, 5–midnight; 11–midnight Sat; 12.30–5, 6–midnight Sun
Draught Bass; guest beers H
Pub with a small lounge, plus a lively, friendly bar with some old mirrors, and barrel tables and stools. 🛏 🍽 ♿ ♣

Selkirk Arms Hotel
High Street ☎ (01557) 330402
11 (12 Sun)–11
Draught Bass; guest beers H
Comfortable and plush, upmarket lounge bar in the hotel where Robert Burns wrote his *Selkirk Grace*. No real ale in the public bar, but it is brought through on request.
Q 🌑 🛏 🌑 🍴 🍽 ♿

Langholm

Crown Hotel
High Street ☎ (0138 73) 80247
11 (12 Sun)–11 (midnight Thu–Sat)
Beer range varies H
Comfortable, 18th-century inn with Langholm Common riding connections. High teas served. 🛏 🛏 🍴 🌑 ♿ ♣

Lockerbie

Somerton House Hotel
35 Carlisle Road
☎ (01576) 202583
11–11 (midnight Thu–Sat)
Broughton Greenmantle Ale; guest beer (summer) H

Deservedly popular, well-appointed hotel. Excellent meals and first class service.
🍴 🌑 🍴 ♿ ♣ ⇌ P ✄

Moffat

Black Bull Hotel
Church Gate ☎ (01683) 220206
11 (12 Sun)–11 (midnight Thu–Sat)
McEwan 80/-; Theakston Best Bitter; guest beers (summer) H
Historic, 16th-century hotel with a comfortable lounge and a traditional bar.
🛏 🍴 🛏 🌑 🍴 ♿ ♣

Newton Stewart

Creebridge House Hotel
On old main road, E of river
☎ (01671) 402121
11–2.30, 6–11 (11.30 Sat); 12.30–2.30, 7–11 Sun
Orkney Dark Island; Theakston XB; guest beers H
Beautiful country house hotel in spacious grounds on the outskirts of Minigaff. Excellent, home-cooked meals.
🛏 Q 🛏 🌑 🛏 🌑 ♿ ♣ ⌂ P

Portpatrick

Downshire Arms Hotel
Main Street (A77, near harbour) ☎ (01776) 810300
11 (12.30 Sun)–11.30 (midnight Sat, rear lounge 1am Fri & Sat)
Marston's Pedigree; guest beer (summer) H
Traditional coaching inn with three bars. An extensive menu features local seafood and game. Children's certificate.
🛏 🛏 🌑 🍴 🍽 ♿ ♣

Stranraer

George Hotel
49 George Street
☎ (01776) 702487
12–3, 6–11 including Sun (12–11 summer)
Theakston Best Bitter; guest beer H
Old coaching inn dating from 1731. Two lounges share one bar; one is quiet, the other has music. 🍴 🛏 🌑 ♿ ⇌ (Harbour) ♣ P

Thornhill

Buccleugh & Queensbury Hotel
112 Drumlanrig Street (A76)
☎ (01848) 330215
11–1am (midnight Sun)
Beer range varies H
Hotel with a comfortable lounge where meals are served all day (breakfast as early as required in the fishing season). Two real ales in the lounge and one in the public bar.
🛏 Q 🛏 🛏 🌑 🍴 🍽 ♿ ♣ P

389

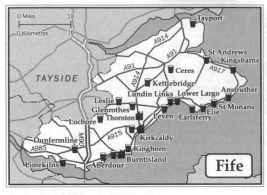

Authority area covered: Fife UA

Aberdour

Aberdour Hotel
38 High Street
☎ (01383) 860325
4–11; 12–midnight Sat (11–11 Mon–
Sat summer); 12–midnight Sun
Draught Bass; guest beers Ⓗ
Old coaching inn with stables
across a cobbled yard which
are used for the annual beer
festival. Approved
accommodation for guests
with disabilities.
🏮 Q 🕭 ⋈ ◑ 🌶 ▲ ⇌ ♣ P

Anstruther

Dreel Tavern
16 High Street
☎ (01333) 310727
11–midnight; 12.30–11 Sun
**Alloa Arrol's 80/-; Orkney
Dark Island;** **guest beers** Ⓗ
Stone-built pub at the site of an
old ford over Dreel Burn.
James V may have enjoyed a
pint here before being carried
over the burn. Popular with
locals and visitors for its good
atmosphere and excellent bar
meals. 🏮 Q 🌶 ◑ 🌶 ♣

Burntisland

Crown Tavern
19 Links Place (off High St)
☎ (01592) 873697
4 (12 Fri & Sat, 12.30 Sun)–11
**Belhaven Sandy Hunter's Ale;
guest beer** Ⓗ
Two-roomed lounge bar
opposite the links, site of the
permanent fun fair. Excellent
pies (Pillan's). 🎇 ⇌ ♣

Ceres

Ceres Inn
The Cross (B939)
☎ (01334) 828305)
11–2.30, 5 (6 Tue)–11 (1am Thu & Fri,
midnight Sat & Mon); 12.30–2.30, 5–11
Sun
Beer range varies Ⓗ
Attractive village pub catering
for locals and visitors alike.
Good value, home-cooked
meals (not served Tue, or
Mon–Wed in winter); Sun high
teas. Two real ales available, as
well as board games and a pool
table in an alcove.
Q 🌶 ◑ 🌶 P

Dunfermline

City Hotel
18 Bridge Street
☎ (01383) 722538
11 (12.30 Sun)–11 (midnight Fri & Sat)
Maclay 80/-; guest beers Ⓗ
Town-centre hotel, near the
famous abbey and ruins. The
Cask Bar, where ales are
served, is small and quiet; food
is served in a separate bar.
Friendly staff.
Q ⋈ ◑ 🌶 ⇌ P

Coady's
16 Pilmuir Street (by bus
station)
☎ (01383) 723865
11 (12.30 Sun)–11.30
Theakston Best Bitter Ⓗ
Busy, street-corner bar with
bare wooden floorboards, a
back sitting room and a pool
room upstairs. Pictures of old
Irish pubs cover the walls.
⇌ ♣

Commercial Inn
Douglas Street (by Kingsgate
shopping centre)
☎ (01383) 733876
11 (12.30 Sun)–11 (midnight Fri & Sat)
**Theakston Best Bitter, Old
Peculier; guest beers** Ⓗ
Busy, town-centre pub with
wooden floorboards and walls
covered with pictures of
brewing and breweries.
Friendly staff. Food is served
all day; excellent range of ales.
◑ 🌶 ⇌ 🍽

Earlsferry

Golf Tavern, 19th Hole
Links Road ☎ (01333) 330610
11–midnight (1am Fri) (11–2.30,
5–midnight winter); 12.30–11 Sun
**Caledonian Deuchars IPA;
Maclay 80/-; guest beers** Ⓗ
Good, traditional bar and
lounge overlooking the golf
course, popular with locals and
visitors, and providing good
quality, well-priced food,
served by friendly staff.
Children welcome until 8pm.
🏮 Q 🌶 ◑ 🌶 ⚑ ▲ ♣

Elie

Ship Inn
The Toft (by Elie harbour)
☎ (01333) 330246
11–midnight; 12.30–11 Sun
Belhaven 80/- Ⓗ
Old pub, renovated in
traditional style, with stone-
flag floors and beams. The inn
dates back to 1838 and has
three dining areas with fine
views over the harbour. The
garden (across the road) is
tented over in summer to host
live jazz. Cricket or rugby
matches at low tide.
🏮 Q 🌶 ⚑ ◑ 🌶 ⚑ ▲ ♣

Glenrothes

Glenrothes Snooker Centre
Plot 7, Caskieberran Road (off
A92) ☎ (01592) 642083
11 (12.30 Sun)–11 (midnight Thu–Sat)
**Alloa Arrol's 80/-; Ind Coope
Burton Ale; guest beer** Ⓗ
Plush lounge bar with
comfortable leather armchairs
and sofas. Seventeen snooker
tables are housed in various
private rooms. No entry
restrictions. 🌶 P

Kettlebridge

Kettlebridge Inn
9 Cupar Road (A92, Glenrothes
road) ☎ (01337) 830232
11.30–2.30, 5–11 (4.30–midnight Fri &
Sat); 12.30–11 Sun
**Belhaven Sandy Hunter's Ale,
80/-, St Andrew's Ale; guest
beers** Ⓗ
Neat little bar displaying old
photographs of the area.
Former local CAMRA *Pub of
the Year*. Separate restaurant
(no bar food Mon; restaurant
closed Mon eve). 🏮 Q ⚑ ◑ 🌶

**📕 INDEPENDENT
BREWERIES**

Backdykes: Thornton

Burntisland: Burntisland

Fyfe: Kirkcaldy

Kinghorn

Auld Hoose

8 Nethergate (off A921)
☎ (01592) 891074
12 (12.30 Sun)–midnight
**Broughton Greenmantle
Ale** Ⓐ; **guest beers** Ⓗ/Ⓐ
Busy sidestreet pub with a pool
table; cosy during winter with
its blazing coal fire. It stages an
annual run along the beach.
🏨 Q ⊟ & ⇌ ♣

Kingsbarns

Cambo Arms Hotel

5 Main Street ☎ (01334) 880226
11 (12.30 Sun)–11 (midnight Fri & Sat)
**Belhaven 80/-, St Andrew's
Ale; guest beer** Ⓗ
Village-centre hotel with a
traditional, cosy bar and a
comfy sitting room. Good food.
🏨 Q ☎ ❀ 🛏 ◖ ▶ & ♣ P

Kirkcaldy

Harbour Bar

471–473 High Street (opp.
harbour and flour mill)
☎ (01592) 264270
11–2.30, 5–11; 11–midnight Fri & Sat;
12.30–midnight Sun
**Belhaven St Andrew's Ale;
Fyfe Rope of Sand, Auld
Alliance, Fyre; guest beers** Ⓗ
Traditional, unspoilt local,
home of the Fyfe Brewery. The
walls display murals of the
town's whaling history. Beers
from small breweries;
excellent, home-made pies.
Q ☎ ⊟ & ♣

Leslie

Burns Tavern

184 High Street (A911)
☎ (01592) 741345
12–11; 11–midnight Wed–Sat; 12.30–
midnight Sun
**Boddingtons Bitter;
Wadworth 6X** Ⓗ
Busy local with a narrow bar
leading on to a games room;
Fife's only pub offering lined
glasses. No food Sun.
🏨 🛏 ◖ ⊟ ♣ 🖻

Leven

Hawkshill Hotel

Hawkslaw Street
☎ (01333) 426056
11–2.30, 6–midnight; 11–1am Fri &
Sat; 12.30–midnight Sun

**Ind Coope Burton Ale; Tetley
Bitter; guest beer** Ⓗ
Comfortable, friendly hotel
which hosts an annual beer
festival. Excellent bar food is
available.
🏨 ❀ 🛏 ◖ ▶ & P

Limekilns

Ship Inn

Halketts Hall (off A985)
☎ (01383) 872247
11 (12.30 Sun)–11 (midnight Thu–Sat)
**Belhaven Sandy Hunter's Ale,
80/-, St Andrew's Ale; guest
beer** Ⓗ
Small, friendly village local
where the walls feature
nautical and rugby
memorabilia. Wonderful views
over the Firth of Forth.
◖ & ♣

Lochore

Lochore Miners'
Welfare Society &
Social Club

1 Lochleven Road (B920)
☎ (01592) 860358
12–3.30, 6.30–11; 11.30–midnight Fri &
Sat; 12.30–11.30 Sun
Maclay 70/- Ⓐ
Large club with a public bar, a
lounge and two dance halls, in
what was once part of the
thriving Fife coalfields. Non-
members will be signed in on
production of a CAMRA
membership card or this guide.
Q ⊟ & ♣ P

Lower Largo

Railway Inn

1 Station Wynd
☎ (01333) 320239
11–midnight; 12.30–11 Sun
Beer range varies Ⓗ
Village local set in what will
soon become a 'Robinson
Crusoe' tourist paradise.
🏨 ❀ ◖ & ♣

Lundin Links

Coachman's
(Old Manor Hotel)

Leven Road
☎ (01333) 320368
11–3, 5–11; 12–3, 5–11 Sun
Beer range varies Ⓗ
The only three-star hotel in
Fife, serving beers from near
and far, and a superb menu
featuring grills and local
seafood as specialities.
Q 🛏 ◖ ▶ & P

St Andrews

Aikman's (Cellar Bar)

32 Bell Street ☎ (01334) 477425
11–3 (not winter), 5–midnight; 11–
11.45 Sat (all year); 6.30–midnight Sun
Belhaven 80/-; guest beers Ⓗ
Over ten years in the *Guide*: a
basement lounge below a
bistro (food may be brought
downstairs). ◖ ▶

Lafferty's

99 South Street
☎ (01334) 474543
11 (12.30 Sun)–midnight (11.30 Sat)
**Alloa Arrol's 80/-; Taylor
Landlord; guest beer** Ⓗ
New Irish theme pub – but
don't be put off: the beer and
'crack' are still as good as when
it was 'Bert's Bar'. Food is
available all day. ◖ ♣

Whey Pat Tavern

1 Bridge Street
☎ (01334) 477740
11–midnight; 12–11.30 Sun
Theakston XB; guest beers Ⓗ
Great mix of town and gown in
a pleasant, L-shaped bar.
Excellent service, but pots of
whey are no longer served!
◖ ♣

St Monans

Cabin Bar

16 West End ☎ (01333) 730327
11–midnight (1am Fri); 12.30–11 Sun
**Belhaven 80/-, St Andrew's
Ale; guest beer** Ⓗ
Traditional village local, with
an outdoor area overlooking
the harbour. Carefully
refurbished by the present
owners, it reflects the local
fishing tradition. Meals are
excellent, with fish and seafood
a speciality. Possible seasonal
variations in opening hours.
Q ❀ ◖ ▶ ⊟ & ▲ ♣ 🖻

Tayport

Bell Rock Tavern

4–6 Dalgliesh Street (by
harbour) ☎ (01382) 552388
11 (12.30 Sun)–midnight (1am Thu &
Fri)
Beer range varies Ⓗ
Great local with a busy social
life, adorned with nautical
memorabilia and pictures. Two
ales in the bar, one in the
lounge/function room
upstairs. Children's certificate.
Q ☎ ◖ ▲ ♣

KEY MAP

For a quick guide to the geographical areas used in the *Good Beer
Guide*, see the Key Map on the inside back cover.

Grampian

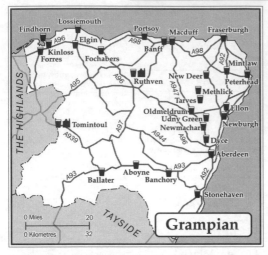

Authority areas covered: Aberdeenshire UA, City of Aberdeen UA, Moray UA

Aberdeen

Blue Lamp
121 Gallowgate
☎ (01224) 647472
11–midnight (lounge 1am Fri & Sat);
12.30–2.30, 7–11 Sun
**Caledonian Deuchars IPA,
80/-; Theakston Best Bitter** H**;
Younger No. 3** A**; guest beers**
Small, intimate public bar and
a large, modern lounge which
hosts live bands (mainly at
weekends); free jukeboxes.
Note for 1am drinking you
must be in by midnight.
Different beers are available in
each bar. Wheelchair access to
the lounge only. ⊕ &

Carriages
101 Crown Street (below
Brentwood Hotel)
☎ (01224) 595440
11–2.30, 5–midnight; 6–11.30 (closed
lunch) Sun
**Boddingtons Bitter;
Caledonian Deuchars IPA;
Castle Eden Ale; Courage
Directors; Flowers Original;
guest beers** H
Welcoming, busy, city-centre
bar with an excellent choice of
ten beers, also bottled Belgian
and German Weisse beers.
Excellent food in both bar and
restaurant.
🍴 ◖ ▶ ⇌ P

Donview
2 Ellon Road, Bridge of Don
(A92, 2½ miles N of centre)
☎ (01224) 703239
11–midnight; 12.30–11 Sun
**Ind Coope Burton Ale; guest
beers** H

Pub set in a scenic spot, handy
for river walks. Meals Thu–Sat.
◖ ▶ P

MacAndrews
6 Crown Street
☎ (01224) 583724
11–midnight; 12.30–11 Sun
Beer range varies H
Former local CAMRA *Pub of
the Year*, stocking a wide range
of beers from independent
Scottish breweries. No food
Sun. ◖ ⇌

Moorings
2 Trinity Quay (on harbour)
☎ (01224) 587602
11–midnight; 12.30–11 Sun
**Isle of Skye Red Cuillin; guest
beers** H
Five guest beers (Scottish
independents a speciality) are
sold in this sometimes noisy
haven for rock 'n' real ale fans.
Live music most weekends.
◖ ⇌ ♣

Prince of Wales
7 St Nicholas Lane
☎ (01224) 640597
11–11.45; 12.30–10.45 Sun
**Draught Bass; Caledonian
80/-; Theakston Old Peculier;
Younger No. 3; guest beers** H
Friendly, unspoilt, city-centre
pub where a long, traditional
bar boasts two fine gantries.
Occasional live (unamplified)
music at the back of the pub.
Good, wholesome lunches are
served Mon–Sat.
Q ◖ ⇌ ♣

Tilted Wig
55 Castle Street (opp. Court
House) ☎ (01224) 583248
12–midnight; 7–11 (closed lunch) Sun

**Alloa Arrol's 80/-; Caledonian
80/-; Ind Coope Burton Ale;
Tetley Bitter; guest beers** H
Bar brimming with legal eagles
and fallen angels and offering
regular price promotions. Food
is served until late. Tue is quiz
night. ◖ ▶ & ⇌ ♣ ○

Under the Hammer
11 North Silver Street
☎ (01224) 640253
5 (2 Sat)–midnight; 6.30–11 Sun
Beer range varies H
Pleasant, one-room wine bar in
the basement of auction rooms.
Table candles give an intimate
atmosphere. Q ▶ ⇌

Aboyne

Boat Inn
Charleston Road (N bank of
River Dee, by road bridge)
☎ (0133 98) 86137
11–2.30, 5–11 (midnight Fri);
11–midnight Sat; 12.30–11 Sun
Draught Bass; guest beers H
Old-style, riverside inn with an
emphasis on food in the
lounge. Popular with walkers
and holidaymakers; children
welcome – ask to see the train
set. 🚌 Q ⊛ ◖ ▶ ⊞ ▲ P

Ballater

Prince of Wales
2 Church Square
☎ (0133 97) 55877
11 (12.30 Sun)–midnight
Beer range varies H
Welcoming lounge in the
centre of a tourist village. Good
value food (adjacent
restaurant). ◖ ▶ ♣

Banchory

Ravenswood Club,
Royal British Legion
25 Ramsay Road (right off
Mount St from centre)
☎ (01330) 322347
11–2.30, 5–11; 11–midnight Sat; 12–11
Sun
Beer range varies H
Friendly club offering value for
money. Members are always
on hand to welcome passing
guests bearing this book.
⊛ 🚌 ◖ ▶ ▲ ♣ P

Scott Skinner's
North Deeside Road (A93 E
side of town) ☎ (01330) 824393
11–2.30, 5–11 (midnight Thu & Fri);
11–midnight Sat; 12.30–11 Sun
Beer range varies H
Converted Victorian house
with a restaurant and snug bar,
a play area and games room.

🏭 **INDEPENDENT
BREWERIES**

Borve: Ruthven

Tomintoul: Tomintoul

Varied choice of ales (three guests). Children welcome in the restaurant.
⛫ ❀ ◖ ◗ ▲ ♣ P

Banff

Castle Inn
47 Castle Street
☎ (01261) 815068
11–midnight, including Sun
Courage Directors; guest beer [H]
Pub with a refurbished lounge and a public bar offering pool and darts. Very popular with younger drinkers.
◖ ⊞ ▲

Dyce

Tap & Spile
Aberdeen Airport Terminal (off A96, 6 miles from Aberdeen centre)
☎ (01224) 722331
8am–10pm (7 winter Sat); 12.30–10 Sun
Beer range varies [H]
Pleasant, if expensive, lounge bar in which to kill time if your flight is delayed or if in need of a decent pint after a trip abroad. The luggage carousel is visible from your bar stool.
♿ ♣ P ⚡

Elgin

Flanagan's Bar
Shepherds Close, High Street
☎ (01343) 549737
11.30–2.30, 5–11 (11.45 Wed & Thu); 11.30–12.30am Fri & Sat; 12.30–11 Sun
Beer range varies [H]
Lively, friendly, Irish-themed pub with live music at weekends.
◖ ◗ ⇌

Sunninghill Hotel
Hay Street (near station)
☎ (01343) 547799
11–2.30, 5–11 including Sun
Boddingtons Bitter; Ind Coope Burton Ale; guest beer [H]
Small, pleasant, friendly lounge in a family-run hotel. Limited, but varied, menu and a good choice of snacks. Front lawn for outside drinking.
❀ 🛏 ◖ ◗ ▲ ⇌ P ⊓

Ellon

Tolbooth
21–23 Station Road
☎ (01358) 721308
11–2.30, 5–11 (midnight Thu & Fri); 11–11.45 Sat; 6.30–11 (closed lunch) Sun
Draught Bass; guest beers [H]
Pub converted from a pair of semi-detached houses, with a large conservatory, on a split-level. Function room in the attic; patio outside.
❀ ♿ ♣

Findhorn

Crown & Anchor Inn
Off A96, 4 miles from Forres
☎ (01309) 690243
11–11 (11.45 Thu, 12.30am Fri & Sat); 12–11.45 Sun
Draught Bass; Boddingtons Bitter; guest beers [H]
Situated on the picturesque Findhorn Bay: a beamed, two-bar pub serving up to four guest beers and a wide variety of good food. Children welcome until 9pm.
⛫ ❀ 🛏 ◖ ◗ ⊞ ♿ ▲ ♣ P

Kimberley Inn
Off A96, 4 miles from Forres
☎ (01309) 690492
11–11 (11.45 Thu, 12.30am Sat); 12.30–11.45 Sun
Beer range varies [H]
Very popular, friendly, one-bar pub with a pool room, boasting bay views from the front patio. Good food at reasonable prices; try the chicken tikka. Children's certificate until 8pm. ⛫ ❀ ◖ ◗ ▲ ♣

Fochabers

Gordon Arms Hotel
80 High Street
☎ (01343) 820508
11.30–2.30, 5–11 (12.30am Fri & Sat); 12.30–11 Sun
Caledonian Deuchars IPA; guest beers [H]
200-year-old coaching inn, popular with fishing guests. A good range of malt whiskies is available.
Q ❀ 🛏 ◖ ◗ ⊞ ♿ ▲ P

Forres

Carisbrooke Hotel
Drumduan Rd (½ mile off A96, E end of Forres)
☎ (01309) 672582
11–11 (11.45 Tue & Thu, 12.30am Fri & Sat)
Boddingtons Bitter; Marston's Pedigree; guest beer [H]
Cosy, two-bar, extended small hotel on the outskirts of town. Families welcome. Regular barbecues. Three-crown accommodation.
⛫ ❀ 🛏 ◖ ◗ ♿ ♣ P

Fraserburgh

Crown Bar
125 Shore Street (alley off Broad St)
☎ (01346) 518452
11–11.30 (12.30am Fri, midnight Sat); 12.30–11.30 Sun
Beer range varies [H]
Unspoilt, cosy bar overlooking the harbour: a gem in a real ale desert, enjoying its 19th consecutive entry in the *Guide*. The lounge opens at weekends.
⊞ ♣

Kinloss

Abbey Inn
☎ (01309) 690475
11–11 (11.45 Thu, 12.30am Fri & Sat); 12.30–11.45 Sun
Beer range varies [H]
Busy, two-bar pub in a row of listed stone cottages. Pool table in the rear bar.
⛫ ❀ ⊞ ♿ ▲ ♣ P

Lossiemouth

Clifton Bar
4 Clifton Road
☎ (01343) 812100
11–2.30, 5–11 (11.45 Wed & Thu); 11–12.30am Fri & Sat; 12.30–11 Sun
Boddingtons Bitter; McEwan 80/-; Theakston Old Peculier; guest beer [H]
Very popular free house on the east side of the village, overlooking the river and East Beach. The two large bars sell the cheapest real ale in the area. ⛫ ◖ ⊞ ▲ ♣ P

Skerry Brae Hotel
Stotfield Road
☎ (01343) 812040
11–11 (11.45 Wed, 12.30am Thu–Sat)
Boddingtons Bitter; guest beer [H]
Very popular hotel bar on the outskirts of the village, with views over the sea and golf course: an extended one-room bar with a pool table, no-smoking conservatory and an outdoor balcony. Very good food. The accommodation is three-crown rated.
⛫ ❀ 🛏 ◖ ◗ ♿ ▲ ♣ P ⚡

Macduff

Knowes Hotel
78 Market Street
☎ (01261) 832229
11–midnight; 12.30–11 Sun
Draught Bass; guest beer [H]
Small, family-run hotel enjoying panoramic views of the Moray Firth. Get in early for the comfy chairs!
❀ 🛏 ◖ ◗ ▲ ♣ P

Methlick

Gight House Hotel
Sunnybrae (B9170, ½ mile N of river)
☎ (01651) 806389
12–2.30, 5–midnight (1am Fri, 11.45 Sat); 12–11 Sun
Beer range varies [H]
Attractive lounge bar in a former church manse, with two conservatories. The home-cooked meals incorporate local produce. The two regularly changing beers are usually Scottish. Petanque played
🐴 ❀ 🛏 ◖ ◗ ♿ ♣ P

Mintlaw

Country Park Inn
Station Road (A950, ½ mile W
of Mintlaw) ☎ (01771) 622622
11–11.30; 12.30–11 Sun
Beer range varies H
Welcoming country inn with a
children's certificate. It offers a
varied food selection and two
regularly changing beers.
Handy for Aden Country Park
and Heritage Centre.
🛏 🍴 🚐 🌙 ♿ P

Newburgh

Udny Arms Hotel
Main Street ☎ (01358) 789444
12–2.30, 5–11.30; 11–11.30 Sat;
11–11.30 Sun
Flowers Original; guest beer
(summer) H
Imposing hotel in an attractive
coastal village, near a golf
course and nature reserve.
Children's certificate.
🛏 Q 🍴 🌂 🚐 🌙 🌆 P

New Deer

Earl of Aberdeen Arms
Hotel
Auchreddie Road East (A948/
B9107 jct) ☎ (01771) 644242
11 (12.30 Sun)–midnight
Beer range varies H
Two-roomed howff on the
southern side of the village.
🛏 🚐 🌙 🌆 ♣ P

Newmachar

Newmachar Hotel
(Tilley Lounge)
Oldmeldrum Road (N side of
village, A947)
☎ (01651) 862636
11–1am (11.45 Sat); 12.30–11 Sun
**Courage Directors; guest
beers** (summer) H
Open views of a rural
landscape are afforded by the
smart lounge bar and
restaurant here, which feature
an extensive range of Tilley
lamps. Only the public bar is
open all day. Children's
certificate. 🛏 🍴 🌙 🌆 ♣ P

Oldmeldrum

Redgarth
Kirk Brae (off A947)
☎ (01651) 872353
11–2.30, 5–11 (11.45 Fri & Sat);
12.30–2.30, 5.30–11 Sun
Beer range varies H/G
A good variety of guest ales are
served by a cheery host in this
comfortable lounge bar. Fine
views from the garden. Good
value menu. The house beer is
rebadged Caledonian 80/-.
Q 🌂 🌆 🚐 🌙 ♣ P

Peterhead

Grange Inn
West Road (1 mile W of centre,
on A950) ☎ (01779) 473472
11–2.30, 5–11.30; 11–12.30am Fri–Sun
Beer range varies H
A public bar and a lounge with
jukeboxes, in an area not noted
for a surplus of real ale; a
pleasant and friendly pub.
🌆 ♿ ⚓ ♣ P

Portsoy

Shore Inn
Church Street (on old harbour
front) ☎ (01261) 842831
11 (12 Sun)–11 (12.30am Fri & Sat)
Beer range varies H
18th-century seafaring inn
featuring traditional music Fri
and Sat; Mon is games night.
The beers are always from
Scottish breweries. Meals in
summer. 🛏 🌙 ⚓ ♣

Ruthven

Borve Brew House
Off A96, Huntly–Keith road
OS506469 ☎ (01466) 760343
12.30–11 (11.45 Fri & Sat) including
Sun
Borve Ale, Tall Ships IPA H
One-bar brew pub in a
converted primary school, with
a coal stove. The visitors' book
makes interesting reading.
Bottled beers are available, as
are occasional one-off brews. If
shut call at the school house
next door.
🛏 Q ♿ ♣ P

Stonehaven

Marine Hotel
Shorehead (harbour front)
☎ (01569) 762155
11–midnight; 12–11 Sun
**Draught Bass; Taylor
Landlord; guest beers** H
Wood-panelled bar which
always stocks unusual guest
beers. The picturesque harbour
makes this a must in summer;
outside seating is on the
harbour wall. The family room
is upstairs.
🛏 🌂 🌆 🚐 🌙 ♿ ⚓ 🛏

Tarves

Aberdeen Arms Hotel
The Square ☎ (01651) 851214
11–2.30, 5–midnight (1am Fri);
11–11.45 Sat; 12.30–11 Sun
**Flowers Original; guest
beer** H
Small, family-run hotel with a
dining room, in the village
conservation area. Children's
certificate until 8pm.
🛏 🌂 🚐 🌙 🌆 ♣ P

Tomintoul

Glen Avon Hotel
1 The Square ☎ (01807) 580218
11 (12.30 Sun)–11 (11.45 Fri & Sat)
Beer range varies H
Cosy and welcoming village
pub set on the edge of the
Cairngorms, used by walkers,
climbers and skiers. Try the
Drambuie haggis starter on the
good value menu.
🛏 🚐 🌙 ⚓ ♣ P

Udny Green

Udny Green Hotel
OS881262 ☎ (01651) 842337
12–3 (not Mon), 6 (5.30 Sun)–11 (1am
Fri); 12–3, 5.30–11.45 Sat
Beer range varies H
200-year-old, Grade II-listed
building in a conservation
village. Cask beers (two in
summer, one in winter) are
served in the modern lounge.
Children's certificate; garden
play area.
🌂 🌆 🌙 🌆 ♣ P

SCOTLAND'S SCORE

Although Grampian has lost one of its breweries in the past year
(Aberdeenshire Ales), Scotland as a whole still reflects the
national growth in microbreweries. There are now 20 independent
breweries North of the Border, many of them producing award-
winning beers. With so many local pubs tied to Scottish Courage,
and keg products still dominant, small brewery beers take some
finding, particularly outside the main centres. But make the effort
and enjoy the Scottish ale revival!

The Highlands & Islands

Authority areas covered: Highland UA, Orkney Islands UA, Shetland Islands UA, Western Isles UA

Aultbea

Drumchork Lodge Hotel
400 yds above A832, southern edge of village
☎ (01445) 731242
11–11 (1am Fri, 11.30 Sat); 12.30–11 Sun
Bateman XXXB; guest beers Ⓗ
Popular, family-run holiday hotel with splendid views over Loch Ewe and of west coast sunsets. This old shooting lodge stands in a peaceful walking area.
🏚 🛏 🍴 🕭 🐕 ♣ P

Aviemore

Old Bridge Inn
Dalfaber Road (S end of village along Ski Rd then left, 300 yds)
☎ (01479) 811137
11–11 (midnight Thu–Sat); 12.30–11 Sun
Caledonian 60/-; guest beers Ⓗ
Converted cottage popular with walkers, skiers and other outdoor enthusiasts. On the road to the Strathspey steam railway.
🏚 Q 🕭 🍴 🕭 🛏 🐕 ♣ P

Winking Owl
Grampian Road (main street)
☎ (01479) 810646
11–midnight; 12.30–11 Sun
Alloa Arrol's 80/-; Marston's Pedigree; Ind Coope Burton

Ale; Orkney Dark Island; guest beers Ⓗ
Well-established pub converted from a farm building years ago; popular with walkers, climbers and skiers as well as locals. One guest is from Tomintoul Brewery. 🏚 🕭 🍴 🕭 🐕 P

Avoch

Station Hotel
Bridge Street ☎ (01381) 620246
11–2.30, 5–11 (midnight Fri); 11–11.30 Sat (11–11 summer Mon–Fri); 12.30–11.30 Sun
Beer varies Ⓗ
Busy local in a pleasant Black Isle fishing village with a friendly atmosphere. Popular at weekends for good value food, served all day. Good variety of guest beers.
🕭 🍴 ♣ P

Carrbridge

Cairn Hotel
Main Road ☎ (01479) 841212
11.30–midnight (1am Fri & Sat); 11.30–11 Sun
Beer range varies Ⓗ
This converted cottage, attached to an hotel, also serves as a locals' bar. Popular with bird watchers, walkers and skiers. Children's certificate. Beers come from Tomintoul Brewery. 🏚 🕭 🛏 🍴 🐕 P

Dingwall

National Hotel
High Street ☎ (01349) 862166
11–midnight (1am Thu & Fri, 11.30 Sat); 12.30–11 Sun
Caledonian 80/-; Tetley Bitter; guest beers Ⓗ
One of the principal hotels in town, with real ale served in the bar in a modern, comfortable extension. Up to six guest ales in summer.
🕭 🛏 🍴 🐕 P ✠

Fort William

Alexandra Hotel
The Parade ☎ (01397) 702241
11–11; 12.30–11 Sun
Draught Bass; Caledonian Deuchars IPA, 80/- Ⓗ
Bright, friendly, lounge bar in the town's main hotel, modern looking and tastefully decorated, although built last century. Popular with coach parties and walkers. Live music most nights. Good value food in the restaurant.
🚌 🕭 🛏 🍴 🐕 A P

Grog & Gruel
66 High Street
☎ (01397) 705078
11–11.45 (12.45am Thu–Sat); 5–11 Sun
Beer range varies Ⓗ
Refurbished pub, bought by the owners of the prize-winning Clachaig Inn. Meals are served most of the day in the restaurant upstairs (Tex-Mex a speciality). Popular in the tourist season when some guest beers sell out in hours.
🕭 🍴 A 🐕

Gairloch

Old Inn
The Harbour ☎ (01445) 712006
11–11 (11.30)–midnight; 12.30–11 Sun
Beer range varies Ⓗ
Small highland hotel in a picturesque setting by a burn and an old bridge. Popular all year round with sailors, walkers and climbers. Safe garden for children.
Q 🕭 🛏 🍴 🐕 A ♣ P

Glencoe

Clachaig Inn
On old riverside road, at rear of NT centre ☎ (01855) 811252
11–11 (midnight Fri, 11.30 Sat); 12.30–11 Sun
Alloa Arrol's 80/-; Ind Coope Burton Ale; guest beers Ⓗ
Vibrant public bar surrounded by some of Britain's highest

INDEPENDENT BREWERIES
Isle of Skye: Uig

Orkney: Quoyloo

mountains, attracting walkers and climbers from afar. Live folk music.
🛏 ❄ 🛌 ◑ ▶ ♿ ▲ P

Inverie

Old Forge
By ferry from Mallaig, Mon/Wed/Fri; no road access OS766000
☎ (01687) 462267
11–midnight including Sun
Draught Bass; guest beers (summer) Ⓗ
The most remote pub in Britain, reached by ferry (one hour) or by foot (16 miles from Kinloch Hourn). Used by walkers and yachtsmen but also by daytrippers and the small local community. Lovely views. 🛏 Q ❄ ◑ ▶ ▲ ♣

Inverness

Blackfriars
93–95 Academy Street (right from station, 400 yds)
☎ (01463) 233881
11–11 (12.30am Thu & Fri, 11.45 Sat); 11–11 Sun
Marston's Pedigree; McEwan 80/-; Theakston Best Bitter, Old Peculier; guest beers Ⓗ
Beer drinkers' pub with a good selection of foreign bottled beers: one large bar with snug alcoves. Speciality pies available most of the day. Live music Wed and Thu eve.
◑ ▶ ⇌ ⌂

Clachnaharry Inn
17–19 High Street (Beauly road, western outskirts of town) ☎ (01463) 239806
11–11 (midnight Thu & Fri, 11.45 Sat); 12.30–11 Sun
McEwan 80/- Ⓗ**; Tomintoul Culloden, Wildcat** Ⓖ**; guest beers** Ⓗ
300-year-old coaching inn overlooking the railway, the Beauly Firth and the sea lock of the Caledonian Canal. The garden was once the platform of the old station. The lounge bar has a snug area with a coal fire. A house beer is also sold.
🛏 ৯ ❄ ◑ ▶ 🍴 ♣ P

Phoenix
108 Academy Street
☎ (01463) 233685
11–11 (12.30am Thu & Fri, 11.30 Sat); 12.30–11 Sun
Draught Bass; Maclay Wallace; Worthington Bitter; guest beers Ⓗ

Busy, town-centre pub; the traditional public bar has a rare example of an island bar. The lounge has been transformed into 'Jock Tamson's' Scottish theme pub. Children's certificate. The house beers are brewed by Tomintoul and Caledonian. Food all day.
◑ ▶ 🍴 ⇌ ♣

Kingussie

Royal Hotel
High Street Ⓗ ☎ (01540) 661898
11–midnight (1am Thu–Sat); 12.30–midnight Sun
Alloa Arrol's 80/-; Ind Coope Burton Ale; Tetley Bitter; guest beers Ⓗ
Large, extended, old coaching inn, still popular with coach parties. The large lounge bar serves good value food, accompanied by music at weekends.
৯ ❄ 🛌 ◑ ▶ ♿ ▲ ⇌ ♣ P ⧉

Nairn

Claymore House Hotel
Seabank Road (off A96)
☎ (01667) 453731
12–11.30 (12.30am Fri & Sat); 12–11.30 Sun
Beer varies Ⓗ
Popular bar with a cosy fireside dining area, also a restaurant in a new conservatory. Situated on the road to the golf course and West Beach, it has a children's certificate. Good bar meals.
🛏 Q 🛌 ◑ ▶ P

Invernairne Hotel
Thurlow Road (off A96, down Seabank Rd, 3rd right)
☎ (01667) 452039
11–11.30 (12.30am Fri, midnight Sat); 11–11.30 Sun
Isle of Skye Red Cuillin; guest beer Ⓗ
Friendly, Victorian seaside hotel with a lovely wood-panelled bar, complete with a large fireplace. Panoramic views of the Moray Firth. The garden path leads to West Beach. Popular for high teas. Children's certificate.
🛏 Q ❄ 🛌 ◑ ▶ ♿ P

Newtonmore

Glen Hotel
Main Street ☎ (01540) 673203
11–midnight including Sun
Boddingtons Bitter; guest beer Ⓗ

Family-owned hotel, popular with outdoor enthusiasts, skiers and golfers.
🛏 ❄ 🛌 ◑ ▶ ▲ ⇌ P

Onich

Nether Lochaber
By south terminal of Corran ferry, 200 yds off A82
☎ (01855) 821235
11–2.30, 5–11; 12.30–2.30, 6.30–11 Sun
Draught Bass Ⓗ
Delightful, wee, family-run bar, tucked behind the hotel, on the slipway to the ferry.
Q ❄ 🛌 ◑ ▲ ♣ P

Strathcarron

Strathcarron Hotel
On A890 by the station at the head of Loch Carron
☎ (01520) 722227
11–11 including Sun
Theakston Best Bitter; guest beers Ⓗ
Typical hillwalkers' pub, allowing free use of the hotel facilities for campers. Meals served all day. It enjoys a spectacular position overlooking Loch Carron on the road to Skye.
🛏 ❄ 🛌 ◑ ▶ ▲ ⇌ ♣ P

Tain

Mansfield House Hotel
Scotsburn Road (between the bypass and town centre)
☎ (01862) 892052
11–11 (11.30 Fri & Sat); 12.30–11 Sun
Tomintoul Stillman's 80/-; guest beer Ⓗ
Victorian, baronial-style mansion house, once the home of the provost of Tain, now a high-standard hotel, family-run and welcoming. Ornate plasterwork ceilings and pitch pine panelling feature throughout. A *Taste of Scotland* award-winner.
Q ৯ ❄ 🛌 ◑ ▶ ⇌ P

Ullapool

Ferryboat Inn
Shore Street
☎ (01854) 612366
11–11; 12.30–11 Sun
Beer range varies Ⓗ
Small, comfortable, lounge bar on the village waterfront with open views inland over Loch Broom. 🛏 Q ৯ 🛌 ◑ ▶ ▲

SYMBOLISM

A full explanation of all the symbols used in the *Good Beer Guide* can be found on the inside front cover.

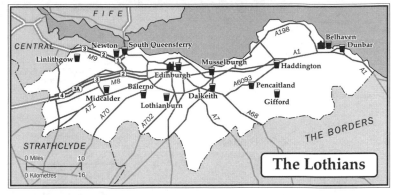

The Lothians

Authority areas covered: City of Edinburgh UA, East Lothian UA, Midlothian UA, West Lothian UA

Balerno

Grey Horse
18–22 Main Street (off A70; on pedestrianised street)
☎ (0131) 449 3092
11 (12.30 Sun)–11 (midnight Thu–Sat)
Belhaven Sandy Hunter's Ale, 80/-; Boddingtons Bitter; Caledonian Deuchars IPA H
200-year-old, traditional, stone-built village-centre pub. The public bar is unspoilt and there is a comfortable small lounge. Dominoes and cards are played.
Q ⌂ ♣

Johnsburn House
64 Johnsburn Road (off A70)
☎ (0131) 449 3847
12.30–2.30, 6.30–midnight; 12–midnight Sat & Sun; closed Mon
Caledonian Deuchars IPA; guest beers H
Baronial mansion dating from 1760 and now Grade B listed, with a well deserved reputation for meals. The cosy bar has a convivial atmosphere and a real fire. Four guest beers. Children made welcome.
♨ Q ☀ ◑ ▶ ♣ P

Belhaven

Masons Arms
8 High Street (A1087, ½ mile W of Dunbar)
☎ (01368) 863700
11–2.30 (4 Fri; not Wed), 5–11 (1am Fri); 11–midnight Sat; 12.30–5 Sun
Beer varies H
Friendly local close to the brewery, with fine views to the Lammermuir Hills. The beer is usually from Belhaven. Eve meals Fri and Sat in the comfortable lounge. Lovely beaches nearby. There is an aviary in the back yard.
☀ ▶ ⌂ ▲ ♣

Dalkeith

Black Bull
1 Lothian Street (behind Jarnac Court shopping precinct)
☎ (0131) 663 2095
11 (12.30 Sun)–midnight
Caledonian Deuchars IPA, 80/-; guest beers H
Good example of a 'Gothenburg'; a busy traditional bar with fine arched windows, cornice work and a well-crafted gantry. Large TV for sport. The quieter lounge (with children's certificate) is modern in contrast. Good facilities for customers with disabilities. Two guest beers.
☀ ◑ ⌂ ♿ ♣

Dunbar

Volunteer Arms
17 Victoria Street (between harbour and swimming pool)
☎ (01368) 862278
11–11 (1am Thu–Sat); 12.30–midnight Sun
Belhaven 80/-, St Andrew's Ale; Marston's Pedigree H
The history of the local lifeboat and the area adorn the walls of this oak-beamed, friendly, boisterous bar near the harbour. Meals served in the upstairs lounge. ☀ ◑ ▶ ▲ ⇌ ♣

Edinburgh

Bellevue Bar
49–51 London Street
☎ (0131) 556 2945
11 (12.30 Sun)–1am
Caledonian Deuchars IPA, 80/-; guest beers H
Long, thin pub with a collection of old books and golfing artefacts. There is an upstairs room. Addlestones cider is not kept under CO$_2$.
♣ ♁

Bow Bar
80 West Bow (between Royal Mile and Grassmarket)
☎ (0131) 226 7667
11–11.30; 7–11 Sun
Caledonian Deuchars IPA, 80/-; Courage Directors; Flying Firkin Aviator; Village White Boar; guest beers A
Traditional, one-room, stand-up bar with efficient, friendly service. Several extinct brewery mirrors and old cigarette ephemera cover the walls. Large selection of malts; quality hot snacks. Q

Cambridge
20 Young Street
☎ (0131) 225 4266
11–1am; closed Sun
Harviestoun Schiehallion; guest beers H
Bare-floored bar adorned with knick-knacks; the building fabric dates from 1775. Five guest beers, one is from a rotation of Maclay's 80/-, Caledonian IPA or 80/-, and Village White Boar.
◑ ▶ ♣ ♁

Canons' Gait
232 Canongate
☎ (0131) 556 4481
11–midnight (1am Thu–Sat); 12.30–1am Sun
Caledonian Deuchars IPA, 80/-; Isle of Skye Red Cuillin; Orkney Dark Island; guest beers H
Refurbished bar/restaurant on two levels on the historic Royal Mile. The ground-floor bar is reserved for diners at weekends, but the basement is

INDEPENDENT BREWERIES

Belhaven: Belhaven

Caledonian: Edinburgh

open for drinkers. Four guest
ales downstairs.
◑ ▶ ≷ (Waverley)

Cloisters Bar

26 Brougham Street (between
Tollcross and the Meadows)
☎ (0131) 221 9997
11 (12.30 Sun)–midnight (12.30am Fri
& Sat)
**Caledonian Deuchars IPA,
80/-; Courage Directors; Flying
Firkin Aviator; Village White
Boar Ⓐ; guest beers** Ⓗ
Alehouse which reflects its
previous use as a parsonage,
with bare boards, church pews
and a bar and gantry built from
wood reclaimed from a
redundant church. The walls
are decorated with rare, old
brewery mirrors. Imaginative
meals; four guest beers. Q ◑

Cumberland Bar

1–3 Cumberland Street (off
Dundas St, New Town)
☎ (0131) 558 3134
12–11.30 (midnight Fri & Sat); closed
Sun
**Draught Bass; Caledonian
Murrays Summer Ale,
Deuchars IPA, 80/-** Ⓐ**; guest
beers** Ⓐ/Ⓗ
Elegant New Town pub with
half-wood-panelling, exquisite,
large ornate brewery mirrors,
framed, decorative posters,
and dark green leather seating.
Eight guest beers.
Q ✿ ◑

Golden Rule

30 Yeaman Place (off Dundee
St near Scottish Courage
factory)
☎ (0131) 229 3413
11–11.30; 12.30–11 Sun
**Draught Bass; Caledonian
Deuchars IPA, 80/-;
Harviestoun Schiehallion;
Orkney Dark Island; guest
beers** Ⓗ
Friendly, street-corner local in
a Victorian tenement, with a
comfortable, split-level lounge
bar. Spicy snacks are served all
day. Five guest beers. ⊞

Guildford Arms

1 West Register Street (behind
Burger King at E end of
Princes St)
☎ (0131) 556 4312
11.30 (12.30 Sun)–11 (midnight Fri &
Sat)
**Draught Bass; Belhaven 60/-;
Caledonian Deuchars IPA,
80/-; Harviestoun 70/-; Orkney
Dark Island; guest beers** Ⓗ
Busy, city-centre pub with
ornate plasterwork and
ceilings, spectacular cornices
and friezes, window arches
and screens, and an unusual
wood-panelled gallery bar
above the main bar. Five guest
beers often include Traquair
Bear Ale. No food Sun.
Q ◑ ≷ (Waverley)

Halfway House

24 Fleshmarket Close (between
Cockburn St and Waverley
station rear entrance)
☎ (0131) 225 7101
11–11.30 (midnight Thu, 1am Fri &
Sat); 12.30–11.30 Sun
Beer range varies Ⓗ
Cosy, wee, L-shaped howff
down an Old Town close.
Often crowded and smoky, it
features railway memorabilia.
Three guest beers.
≷ (Waverley) ♣

Homes Bar

102 Constitution Street, Leith
(between foot of Leith Walk
and the shore)
☎ (0131) 553 7710
12 (12.30 Sun)–11 (midnight Thu, 1am
Fri & Sat)
Beer range varies Ⓗ
Fine, traditional, one-roomed
public bar with no frills. The
decor includes antique tin
boxes, pump clips and a new
bank of five custom
handpumps. Friendly staff and
clientele. Toasties available
lunchtime. Folk music Fri and
Sat eves. ♣

Leslie's

45 Ratcliffe Terrace (between
Newington and The Grange)
☎ (0131) 667 5957
11–11 (12.30am Thu–Sat) including Sun
**Draught Bass; Belhaven 80/-;
Caledonian Deuchars IPA,
80/-; guest beer** Ⓗ
Superb, busy, Victorian pub
with one of the finest interiors
in the city. A snob screen
separates the saloon and snug
from the public bar. Snacks
served. ▦ Q ⊞ ♣

Royal Ettrick Hotel

13 Ettrick Road (behind
Merchiston Tennis and
Bowling Club)
☎ (0131) 228 6413
11–midnight, including Sun
**Draught Bass; Caledonian
80/-; Maclay Kane's Amber
Ale; guest beers** Ⓗ
Built as a town house in 1875;
now a splendid, family-run
hotel, set in leafy suburbs. The
lounge bar is comfortably
appointed and the two
conservatories are bright and
airy (one is no-smoking).
Excellent meals; five guest
beers. Q ✿ ⋈ ◑ ▶ P ⊬

Starbank Inn

64 Laverockbank Road
(between Leith and Granton)
☎ (0131) 552 4141
11 (12.30 Sun)–11 (midnight Thu–Sat)
**Belhaven Sandy Hunter's Ale,
80/-, St Andrew's Ale; Taylor
Landlord; guest beers** Ⓗ
Bright and airy, bare-boarded
ale house with three separate
areas. The decor includes rare
brewery mirrors. Five guest
beers. Children welcome until
8.30pm. Q ◑ ▶ ♿ ♣

Winston's

20 Kirk Loan, Corstorphine (off
St Johns Road, A8)
☎ (0131) 539 7077
11–11.30 (midnight Fri & Sat);
12.30–11 Sun
**Alloa Arrol's 80/-; Caledonian
70/-, Deuchars IPA; Ind Coope
Burton Ale; guest beers** Ⓗ
Not far from Edinburgh Zoo,
this is a smart suburban lounge
bar well favoured by locals.
Golfing and rugby themes play
their part in the decor. Two
guest beers. The home-made
pies are recommended.
Q ◑ ♿

Gifford

Goblin'ha Hotel

Main Street
☎ (01620) 810244
11–2.30, 4.30–11; 11–midnight Fri &
Sat; 11–11 Sun
**Caledonian Deuchars IPA;
Fuller's London Pride;
Marston's Pedigree; guest
beer** Ⓗ
Village hotel with a light,
warm, functional public bar,
which has an oak-panelled
counter and a busy local events
board. The lounge/cocktail bar
has a comfortable seating area,
and a conservatory looks out
over the extensive garden with
its play area. Children's
certificate.
▦ ✿ ⋈ ◑ ▶ ⊞ ♣

Tweeddale Arms Hotel

High Street (off B6355)
☎ (01620) 810240
11–11 (midnight Fri & Sat) including
Sun
**Broughton Greenmantle Ale;
Ind Coope Burton Ale; guest
beers** Ⓗ
Referred to in a 1687 deed as
the 'Great Inn of Gifford', this
attractive, whitewashed hotel
looks across the village green
to a 300-year-old avenue of
lime trees. The public bar, with
its large collection of
miniatures, attracts a loyal
local following. Two guest
beers. Children welcome.
▦ ⋈ ◑ ▶ ⊞ ♣

Haddington

Pheasant

72 Market Street
☎ (01620) 824428
11–11 (midnight Thu–Sun)
**Alloa Arrol's 80/-; Ind Coope
Burton Ale; Tetley Bitter;
guest beers** Ⓗ
Vibrant and sometimes noisy
pub attracting younger folk.
Past the pool table, a long thin
bar snakes through to a lounge
area where Basil the African
Grey oversees, and joins in, the
proceedings. Two guest beers.
▦ ♣

Linlithgow

Black Bitch
14A West Port (25 yds from
A803/A706 jct)
☎ (01506) 842147
11 (12.30 Sun)–midnight
Caledonian Deuchars IPA;
guest beer Ⓗ
Traditional pub whose name is
derived from the town crest.
The oldest pub in Linlithgow.
🕭 🍺 ⇌ ♣

Lothianburn

Steading
118–120 Biggar Road (A702,
near dry ski slope)
☎ (0131) 445 1128
11–midnight; 12.30–11 Sun
Belhaven 70/-, 80/-;
Caledonian Deuchars IPA;
Ind Coope Burton Ale;
Orkney Dark Island; Taylor
Landlord Ⓗ
Stone cottages converted into
an attractive bar and
restaurant, with a conservatory
extension. Although it's a
popular eating establishment,
there is still a sizeable bar area
where only snacks are served.
🛏 Q 🕭 🍺 ◗ ♿ P

Midcalder

Torphichen Arms
36 Bank Street (main street)
☎ (01506) 880020
11–11 (11.45 Thu–Sun)
Caledonian Deuchars IPA,
80/-; Ind Coope Burton Ale;
Orkney Dark Island; Taylor
Landlord; guest beers Ⓗ

Village local, originally an
hotel dating back to 1778.
Several rooms have become
one L-shaped bar with public
and lounge areas. Live music at
weekends. Children's
certificate. Good choice of
lunches. Patio for outside
drinking.
🕭 ◗ ♣ P

Musselburgh

Levenhall Arms
10 Ravensheugh Road (B1348,
near Racecourse roundabout)
☎ (0131) 665 3220
11 (12.30 Sun)–11 (1am Thu–Sat)
Caledonian Deuchars IPA,
80/-; Ind Coope Burton Ale;
guest beers Ⓔ
Busy public bar, popular with
locals and racegoers. The
building dates from 1830 and
houses a functional three-room
pub. A tram terminus once
stood outside.
🍺 ♿ ⇌ (Wallyford) ♣ P

Volunteer Arms (Stagg's)
78–81 North High Street
(behind Brunton Hall)
☎ (0131) 665 9654
11–2.30, 5–11; 11–11 Mon; 11–11.30
Thu; 11–midnight Fri & Sat; closed
Sun
Caledonian 60/-, Deuchars
IPA, 80/-; guest beers Ⓗ
Run by the same family since
1858, this is a busy, traditional
bar with dark wood panelling,
defunct brewery mirrors and a
superb gantry topped with old
casks. A comfortable lounge to
the rear has no real ale.
🕭 🍺 ♿ ♣ P

Newton

Duddingston Arms
13–14 Main Street (A904)
☎ (0131) 331 1948
11–2.30, 5–11; 11–11 Sat; 12.30–4, 7–11
Sun
Maclay 80/-; guest beers Ⓗ
Friendly village local which
extends a warm welcome to
visitors. Snacks only at
weekends. ◗ 🍺 ♿

Pencaitland

Old Smiddy Inn
Main Street (A6093)
☎ (01875) 340368
11.30 (12 Sun)–11 (1am Fri & Sat)
Caledonian 80/-; guest beers Ⓗ
Previously the village smithy
and now a friendly country
inn, with a large, comfortable
lounge bar and a noted
restaurant. High teas are
popular Sat/Sun. Well worth
seeking out. Glenkinchie
distillery is nearby. 🕭 ◗ ▶ ♣

South Queensferry

Ferry Tap
36 High Street
☎ (0131) 331 2000
11.30 (12.30 Sun)–11.30 (midnight
Thu, 12.30am Fri & Sat)
Caledonian Deuchars IPA,
80/-; Orkney Dark Island;
Taylor Landlord; guest beer Ⓗ
Well-appointed, one-roomed,
L-shaped bar with an unusual
barrel-vaulted ceiling, brewery
artefacts and ephemera.
Popular with a younger
clientele. ◗ ⇌ (Dalmeny) ♣

CAMRA's Great British Beer Festival at London's Olympia attracts over 40,000 visitors every August and offers a selection of over 500 beers from all over the world. Be there!

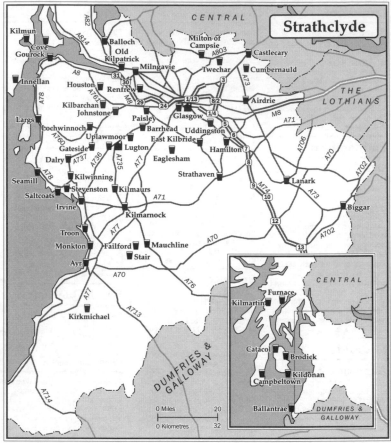

Strathclyde

Authority areas covered: Argyll & Bute UA, City of Glasgow UA, Dumbarton & Clydebank UA, East Ayrshire UA, East Dunbartonshire UA, East Renfrewshire UA, Inverclyde UA, North Ayrshire UA, North Lanarkshire UA, Renfrewshire UA, South Ayrshire UA, South Lanarkshire UA

Note: Licensing laws permit no entry after 11pm to pubs in the following locations: Barrhead, Gourock, Houston, Johnstone, Kilbarchan, Lochwinnoch, Paisley, Renfrew and Uplawmoor

Airdrie

Cellar Bar
79 Stirling Street
11–midnight; 12.30–5, 8–midnight Sun
Beer range varies H
Single bar on several levels. In addition to the ever-changing guest beers (two or three ales), it offers a wide range of whiskies (it was *Malt Whisky Pub of the Year 1997*). Folk music is performed on Mon eve.
🕮 ≷

Ayr

Burrowfields
13 Beresford Terrace
☎ (01292) 269152
11–12.30am; 12.30–midnight Sun
Beer range varies H
Pleasant, wood-panelled café/bar in a corner location in the town centre. Formerly an insurance office, it has been well converted in Art Deco style and is particularly handy for the station.
◖ 🕭 ≷

Chapman Billie's Bothy
13 Dalblair Road (near Gaiety Theatre) ☎ (01292) 618161
11–12.30am; 12.30–midnight Sun
Caledonian Deuchars IPA; guest beer H
Modern lounge bar behind the shopping centre. It features

INDEPENDENT BREWERIES

Heather: Glasgow

Lugton: Lugton

rough stone walls, a central bar, a Burns theme and some unusual artefacts.
🍴 🛏 ◖ ▶ ૐ ≈ ♣ P ✔

Geordie's Byre

103 Main Street (over river towards Prestwick)
☎ (01292) 264925
11 (12.30 Sun)–11 (midnight Thu–Sat)
Belhaven 80/-; Caledonian Deuchars IPA; guest beers Ⓐ
Warm, friendly, traditional pub. The back lounge (open weekends) features a collection of Victoriana and bric-a-brac. Three guest beers come from anywhere between Orkney and Cornwall. 1996 Scottish CAMRA *Pub of the Year*.
Ⓐ

Tam o' Shanter

230 High Street
☎ (01292) 611684
11–12.30am; 12.30–midnight Sun
Beer range varies Ⓗ
Small, town-centre bar which has returned to its original use after years as a Burns museum. Note the flagstoned floor and thatched roof. The music can be loud. ♿ ≈

Wellington's

17 Wellington Square (behind seafront) ☎ (01292) 262794
11–12.30am; 12.30–midnight Sun
Beer range varies Ⓗ
Basement lounge bar in a Georgian square near the beach. Folk music Sun and Tue eves; quiz Wed eve. Student discount; good bar meals (12–7; 12.30–6.30 Sun). ◖ ▶ ♣

Ballantrae

King's Arms Hotel

40 Main Street (A77, coast road) ☎ (01465) 831202
11–12.30am; 12–midnight Sun
Beer range varies Ⓗ
Comfortable village hotel on the main route between Central Scotland and Northern Ireland. The bar is decorated with old local photos. Two or three guest beers in summer, less in winter. Children's certificate.
🛏 ⊛ 🍴 ◖ ▶ Å P

Balloch

Balloch Hotel

Balloch Road ☎ (01389) 752579
11 (12.30 Sun)–11 (midnight Fri, 11.45 Sat)
Alloa Arrol's 80/-; Ind Coope Burton Ale; guest beer Ⓗ
Attractive hotel by the source of the River Leven, at the southern end of Loch Lomond. Beer is on tap in the lounge bar only, but is supplied to the public bar as required.
⊛ 🍴 ◖ ▶ 🍴 ♿ Å ≈ P

Barrhead

Hurlet

Hurlet Crossroads
☎ (0141) 876 1637
11–11 including Sun
Boddingtons Bitter; Flowers Original; Marston's Pedigree; Whitbread Fuggles IPA; guest beers Ⓗ
Brewer's Fayre pub/restaurant providing food and drink with good provision for children. The beer range comes primarily from the Whitbread stable. ⊛ ♿ P

Biggar

Crown Hotel

109 High Street
☎ (01899) 220116
11.30 (12.30 Sun)–11 (midnight Thu, 1am Fri); 11–midnight Sat
Beer range varies Ⓗ
Busy lounge bar in a small hotel opposite a thimble museum in an attractive Borders village. Two beers are supplied by Belhaven.
⊛ 🍴 ◖ ▶ Å

Brodick

Duncan's Bar

Kingsley Hotel, Shore Road
☎ (01770) 302531
11–1am (winter hours: 11–2.30, closed eves Mon–Thu; 11–2.30, 7–midnight Fri & Sat; closed Sun)
Boddingtons Bitter; Theakston XB; guest beer Ⓗ
Large, comfortable bar to the side of a shorefront hotel. It is sometimes busy in summer with students staying nearby, but beware of limited opening hours in winter. Excellent views from the garden across the bay to Goat Fell. Eve meals summer only; accommodation April–Sept.
🏨 Q 🛏 ⊛ 🍴 ◖ ▶ ♿ Å P

Campbeltown

Commercial Inn

Cross Street ☎ (01586) 553703
11 (12.30 Sun)–1am
Caledonian Deuchars IPA; guest beers Ⓗ
Superb, friendly, family-run pub in the town centre. Good guest beer range. Ⓐ

Castlecary

Castlecary House Hotel

Main Street (off A80)
☎ (01324) 840233
11 (12.30 Sun)–11 (11.30 Thu–Sat)
Draught Bass; Broughton IPA; Caledonian Deuchars IPA; guest beers Ⓗ
Small private hotel with three drinking areas. Most beers are

found in the Castle Lounge. The recommended restaurant serves high teas. The village is on the site of one of the major forts along the Antonine Wall.
Q 🛏 ◖ ▶ 🍴 P

Catacol

Catacol Bay Hotel

☎ (01770) 830231
11–midnight (1am Thu–Sat) including Sun
Boddingtons Bitter; guest beers Ⓗ
Small hotel on the north coast of Arran, facing across the Firth to Kintyre. The cosy bar is a centre for the community. Children welcome until 8pm.
🏨 Q 🐾 ⊛ 🛏 ◖ ▶ Å P

Cove

Knockderry Hotel

204 Shore Road (B833)
☎ (01436) 842283
11–midnight; 12–11 Sun
Maclay Broadsword, Wallace, seasonal beers; guest beer Ⓗ
Splendid Victorian mansion on the Rosneath Peninsula. The large, comfortable lounge boasts fine wood panelling and views across Loch Long. Good food at all times. Snooker room. 🏨 Q ⊛ 🛏 ◖ ▶ ♣ P

Cumbernauld

Broadwood Farm

Craiglinn ☎ (01236) 737556
11 (12 Sun)–11
Boddingtons Bitter; Castle Eden Ale; Flowers IPA; Marston's Pedigree; guest beer Ⓗ
Typical Brewer's Fayre pub with the usual menu. Excellent facilities for children, including large indoor and outdoor play areas. The guest beer is from Caledonian. Very busy at weekends. 🐾 ⊛ ◖ ▶ ♿ P

Dalry

Greenbank Inn

97 New Street (A737, E of centre) ☎ (01294) 835522
11–2.30, 5–midnight; 11–1am Fri & Sat; 12.30–3.30, 6–midnight Sun
Beer range varies Ⓗ
Friendly, comfortable bar and lounge. The guest beers tend to be from Maclay. Meals served Thu–Sat. ◖ ▶ 🍴 ≈ ♣

Eaglesham

Cross Keys

1 Montgomery Street
☎ (0135 53) 2002
11–11 (11.30 Thu, midnight Fri, 11.45 Sat); 12.30–11 Sun
Broughton Greenmantle Ale; Stones Bitter Ⓐ
Traditional public bar and a quieter, comfortable lounge

which gives access to the award-winning Pepper Pot restaurant. ⊞

East Kilbride

East Kilbride Sports Club

Torrance House, Strathaven Road (along A726 to Strathaven; follow sign for country park)
☎ (01355) 249720
12 (11 Sat, 12.30 Sun)–11
Maclay Kane's Amber Ale; guest beers Ⓗ
Club with a compact bar with a comfortable seating area. Not open to the general public, but by members' invitation only (CAMRA members admitted on showing membership card).
⚒ ✿ ◁ ⊞ P

New Farm

Strathaven Road
☎ (01355) 267177
11 (12.30 Sun)–11 (midnight Fri & Sat)
Boddingtons Bitter; Flowers Original; guest beers Ⓗ
Typical Brewer's Fayre bar and restaurant but with a special reputation for its choice of ales. Two annual beer festivals – the summer one in a marquee.
✿ ◁ ▶ & P

Failford

Failford Inn

On B743 ☎ (01292) 541674
11–midnight; 11–5 Sun
Belhaven 80/- Ⓗ
Rural gem on the banks of the River Ayr, featuring a low-ceilinged bar with an old tiled range. The restaurant (booking advised) and the garden overlook the river. A popular river walk starts nearby. Limited parking. Children's certificate. ⚒ ✿ ◁ ▶ P

Furnace

Furnace Inn

☎ (01499) 500200
12 (5 winter weekdays)–1am; 12.30–11 Sun
Beer range varies Ⓗ
Friendly, stone-walled local selling two cask beers. Originally a private house and post office, built around 1860, it was tastefully converted into a pub in 1987. Iron-smelting once took place in this Loch Fyne village, hence the name. No meals in winter. Self-catering accommodation.
⚒ ✿ ⛴ ◁ ▶ P

Gateside

Gateside Inn

39 Main Road (B777, 1 mile E of Beith) ☎ (01505) 503362
11–2.30, 5–11; 11–midnight Sat; 12.30–11 Sun

Broughton Greenmantle Ale Ⓗ
Cosy country inn with a modernised interior, in a small village near Beith. Eve meals are served Thu–Sun.
✿ ◁ ▶ P ⏠

Glasgow

Athena Taverna

780 Pollokshaws Road (next to Queen's Park)
☎ (0141) 424 0858
11–2.30, 5–11; closed Sun
Beer range varies Ⓗ
Modern-style café-bar selling an excellent, changing range of six guest beers, a large selection of German bottled beers, Czech and Belgian beers on draught and a fine choice of wines. Arrive early on weekend eves as it is usually extremely busy. Superb!
Q ◁ ▶ & ≢ (Queen's Pk/ Pollockshields W)

Babbity Bowster

16–18 Blackfriars Street, Merchant City
☎ (0141) 552 5055
11 (12.30 Sun)–midnight
Maclay 70/-, 80/-, Kane's Amber Ale; guest beers Ⓐ
Classic café-style pub whose interior features give it a distinctive Scottish character. Diverse clientele, including folk musicians. Food available 8am–11pm. Petanque is played. ♨ ◁ ▶ ⛴ ◁ ▶ ≢ (High St) ♠ ⏠ ⏢

Blackfriars

36 Bell Street, Merchant City
☎ (0141) 552 5924
11.30 (12.30 Sun)–midnight
Alloa Arrol's 80/-; Belhaven 60/-; Ind Coope Burton Ale; Tetley Bitter; guest beers Ⓗ
First-class pub in the heart of the Merchant City, catering for business people during the day and a younger clientele eves. Live bands four times a week; club night weekly in the downstairs lounge. Good food is served.
◁ ▶ ≢ (Argyle St/High St) ⏠

Brewery Tap

1055 Sauchiehall Street
☎ (0141) 339 8866
11 (12.30 Sun)–11 (midnight Fri & Sat)
Alloa Arrol's 80/-; Belhaven 60/-; Caledonian Deuchars IPA Ⓔ; **Tetley Bitter; guest beers** Ⓗ
Modernised, dark-painted pub enlightened by a myriad of posters and entertaining chalk boards. Overlooked by the university, it is well frequented by students. Some interesting foreign bottled beers; one Belgian ale is available on draught.
◁ ⊖ (Kelvinhall) ⏠

Hogshead

1397 Argyle Street
☎ (0141) 334 1831
11 (12.30 Sun)–11 (midnight Fri & Sat)
Boddingtons Bitter; Whitbread Abroad Cooper; guest beers Ⓗ
Traditional alehouse, part of the Whitbread chain, decorated with old brewery artefacts and serving up to six guest beers. Occasional beer festivals.
◁ ⊖ (Kelvinhall) ⏠

State Bar

148 Holland Street
☎ (0141) 332 2159
11 (12.30 Sun)–midnight
Courage Directors; Orkney Dark Island; Theakston Best Bitter; guest beers Ⓗ
Popular, city-centre bar which attracts office staff during the day and a trendier group eves and weekends. Live music twice weekly; occasional beer festivals. Excellent bar food weekday lunchtimes.
◁ & ≢ (Charing Cross)

Station Bar

55 Port Dundas Road (opp. Scotrail HQ)
☎ (0141) 332 3117
11 (12.30 Sun)–midnight
Caledonian Deuchars IPA; guest beers Ⓗ
Popular, street-corner local serving both office workers and the local community. The bar boasts a fine McEwan's mirror. A gem not to be missed. ≢ (Queen St) ⊖ (Cowcaddens)

Stoat & Ferret

1534 Pollokshaws Road (Haggs Rd jct)
☎ (0141) 632 0161
11 (12.30 Sun)–11 (midnight Fri & Sat)
Alloa Arrol's 80/- Ⓗ; **Belhaven 60/-** Ⓔ; **Caledonian Deuchars IPA; guest beers** Ⓗ
Corner pub where a large, wooden-floored bar area offers ample seating and standing room. Four guest ales, plus a guest draught Belgian beer, a small, but good, foreign bottled beer selection, and a fine choice of wines and malts. Well worth a visit.
◁ ▶ & ≢ (Shawlands/ Pollokshaws W) ♠ ⏠

Three Judges

141 Dumbarton Road
☎ (0141) 337 3055
11 (12.30 Sun)–11 (midnight Fri & Sat)
Maclay Broadsword, 80/-, seasonal beers; guest beers Ⓗ
Busy, West End tenement pub, serving over 1,400 guest ales in five years. It monopolises the local CAMRA *Landlord of the Year* and *Glasgow Pub of the Year* awards. Fast, efficient service. A must! ≢ (Partick) ⊖ (Kelvinhall) ⏠

Gourock

Spinnaker Hotel
121 Albert Road
☎ (01475) 633107
11–11.30 (midnight Sat); 12.30–11 Sun
Belhaven 80/-; guest beer Ⓐ
Family-owned, small hotel on the Clyde coast affording delightful sea views. The local yachting club has many small craft moored nearby. Comfortable lounge bar, small but cosy; the excellent restaurant is used for extra seating (after meals). ❀ 🛏

Hamilton

George
18 Campbell Street
☎ (01698) 424225
11 (12.30 Sun)–11.45
Maclay 80/-; guest beers Ⓗ
Small, friendly, family-run pub in the town centre. A frequent winner of Lanarkshire CAMRA *Pub of the Year*, but surprisingly difficult to find for such a central pub. No food Sun. The family room closes 8pm Mon.
🛏 ◖ 🛉 🚋 (Central)

Houston

Fox & Hounds
South Street ☎ (01505) 612448
11–midnight (1am Fri, 12.45am Sat)
Isle of Skye Red Cuillin; guest beers Ⓗ
Popular pub in a rural setting with today's comforts, but the atmosphere of a bygone age. A hunting theme permeates three olde-English style bars. Four real ales in the Fox & Vixen lounge, with plans to sell in the other bars when the pub brewery opens (late 1997). Bar and restaurant meals.
Q ◖ ▶ P ✂

Innellan

Braemar Hotel
Shore Road (A815, 4 miles S of Dunoon) ☎ (01369) 830792
12 (12.30 Sun)–midnight
Beer range varies Ⓗ
Hotel built in the 19th century as the superb seaside home of textile magnate JP Coates, with a splendid view over the Firth of Clyde from the large outdoor seating area. Children's play area. Practice cricket nets available.
🛏 ❀ 🛏 ◖ 🛉 ♣ P

Irvine

Marina Inn
110 Harbour Street
☎ (01294) 274079
11–3, 6–midnight (11–midnight summer); 11–1am Fri & Sat; 12.30–midnight Sun
Belhaven St Andrew's Ale Ⓗ
Attractive harbourside lounge bar next to the Magnum Centre and the Scottish Maritime Museum. The emphasis is on food at lunchtime and early eve, with an extensive menu. The beer price is higher than average for the area. Folk session Tue eve. Children's certificate. ❀ ◖ 🛉 🚋

Ship Inn
120–122 Harbour Street (by Magnum Leisure Centre)
☎ (01294) 279722
11–2.30, 5–midnight (1am Fri); 11–1am Sat; 12.30–11 Sun
Theakston Best Bitter Ⓗ
Harbourside pub, the oldest licensed premises in town, renowned for its well-cooked and good value meals. A quiet atmosphere prevails lunchtime and early eve, but it gets rather lively later on. See the local scenes drawn on the vaulted ceiling. Children's certificate.
Q ❀ ◖ 🛉 🚋

Turf Hotel
32–34 Eglinton Street
☎ (01294) 275836
11–midnight (1am Fri & Sat); 12.30–11 Sun
Theakston Best Bitter; guest beers Ⓗ
Totally unspoilt, traditional Scottish bar, with a lounge to the rear which has its own character (but more restricted hours). Quite cosmopolitan at lunchtime, when quality lunches of amazing value are served; more of a local at night.
🛏 ◖ 🍴 ♣

Johnstone

Coanes
26 High Street
☎ (01505) 322925
11 (12.30 Sun)–11.30 (1am Fri, 11.45 Sat)
Boddingtons Bitter; Caledonian Deuchars IPA, 80/-; Orkney Red MacGregor, Dark Island; guest beers Ⓗ
Friendly, town-centre local. The cosy bar features fake beams and bric-a-brac, while a comfortable, open-plan lounge offers a full à la carte menu of excellent food at competitive prices (eve meals Wed–Sun)
◖ ▶ 🍴 🛉 🚋

Kilbarchan

Trust Inn
8 Low Barholm
☎ (01505) 702401
11.30–11.30 (midnight Thu & Sat, 12.30am Fri); 12.30–11 Sun
Ind Coope Burton Ale; Tetley Bitter; guest beer Ⓗ
Cosy pub in a conservation village, within easy walking distance of the Glasgow–Irvine cycle path; nearby is the Weaver's Cottage. This warm, friendly pub is decorated with brasses and has several nooks. No food Sun unless advertised.
◖ ▶ 🚋 (Milliken Park)

Kildonan

Breadalbane Hotel
W end of the front, on the loop road ☎ (01770) 820284
11–midnight (1am Thu–Sat) including Sun
Draught Bass Ⓗ
Long, whitewashed building set back from the road in the south-east corner of the Isle of Arran: a large bar with a fine stone fireplace and an enclosed verandah offering views to Ailsa Craig (seals on rocks in the foreground). Self-catering accommodation.
🛏 🛏 ❀ 🛏 ◖ 🛉 🛉 A P

Kilmarnock

Hunting Lodge
14–16 Glencairn Square (opp. Safeway) ☎ (01563) 522920
11–3, 5–midnight; 11–12.30am Fri & Sat; 12.30–midnight Sun
Beer range varies Ⓗ
Pub where seven handpumps dispense a changing range of beers in the Malty Hop lounge. An additional ten handpumps are used for mini-festivals. The venue for the local folk club (Thu), quizzes (Mon) and occasional ceilidhs. Children's certificate. ❀ ◖ 🛉 ✂

Kilmartin

Kilmartin Hotel
☎ (01546) 510250
11 (12.30 Sun)–1am
Caledonian Deuchars IPA; guest beer Ⓗ
Small country hotel in the centre of a small village between Oban and Kintyre. Old brewery mirrors and a large key collection adorn the bar. 🛏 🛏 ◖ ▶ P

Kilmaurs

Weston Tavern
27 Main Street (A735, at the cross) ☎ (01563) 538805
11 (12.30 Sun)–midnight
Beer range varies Ⓗ
Originally a manse, school and a smithy, in an historic area next to the 'Jougs', this pub dates back to circa 1500. The partly tiled floor is a listed feature; note, too, the craggy stoneworked bar and panelled games area. The rear lounge is for families and meetings. Eve meals by request.
Q 🛏 ◖ 🍴 🛉 🚋 ♣ P

Kilmun

Coylet Inn
Loch Eck (A815, 9 miles N of
Dunoon) ☎ (01369) 840426
11–2, 5–midnight; 12–2.30, 6.30–11
Sun
**Caledonian Deuchars IPA;
McEwan 80/-; Younger No.3** Ⓗ
Attractive and inviting
lochside bar where you can
relax around the open fire after
a day's fishing, touring or
walking in the hills. The setting
for the film *The Blue Boy*. Good
bar food. ⚲ ❀ ⇔ ◖ ▶ Å P

Kilwinning

Claremont Hotel
67 Byres Road (A738)
☎ (01294) 558445
12–2.30, 5–midnight; 12–1am Fri &
Sat; 12–midnight Sun
Beer range varies Ⓗ
Attractive, comfortable lounge
in a small hotel, right next to
the station. The range of beers
is less extensive than
previously and is pricey,
except during 'happy hour'.
The traditional Scottish bar has
longer opening hours but no
real ale. Children's certificate.
⇔ ◖ ▶ ⊟ & ⇔ P

Kirkmichael

Kirkmichael Arms
3 Straiton Road (B7045, 3 miles
E of Maybole)
☎ (01655) 750375
11–2.30, 5–11; 11–11 Fri, Sat &
summer; 12.30–11 Sun
Beer range varies Ⓗ
Pub with a small, friendly
public bar, with a real fire and
low ceiling, set in the heart of
rural Ayrshire. There's also a
comfortable lounge and a
restaurant serving good value
food. Children's certificate.
⚲ Q ⟊ ◖ ▶ ⊟

Lanark

UK Real Ale Co.
38 Bannatyne Street (opp.
station) ☎ (01555) 661919
12.30 (9 Sat)–9; 12.30–5 Sun; closed
Mon
Beer range varies Ⓗ
Off-licence in a beer desert,
offering an excellent range of
draught ales, cider and British
and foreign bottled beers.
⇔ ⌀

Largs

Clachan
14 Bath Street (B7025)
☎ (01475) 672224
11–midnight (1am Thu–Sat); 12.30–11
Sun
Belhaven 70/-, 80/- Ⓐ;
Boddingtons Bitter Ⓗ

Refurbished, single-bar pub
with a games room, just off the
main street, near the seafront
and ferry. & ⇔ ♠

Lochwinnoch

Brown Bull
33 Main Street (Largs road, off
A737) ☎ (01505) 843250
11 (12.30 Sun)–11 (midnight Fri & Sat)
**Belhaven Sandy Hunter's Ale;
Orkney Dark Island; guest
beer** Ⓗ
Very friendly country pub in a
small village, featuring a low
ceiling and pictures by local
artists. Folk music Fri. Handy
for the Glasgow–Irvine cycle
track. ⚲ ❀ ⇔

Mossend Hotel
Largs Road (200 yds from
A737) ☎ (01505) 842672
11 (12.30 Sun)–11
**Boddingtons Bitter; guest
beers** Ⓗ
Brewer's Fayre pub, with a
'Charlie Chalk Fun Factory'
attached, in an excellent
situation, next to the station
and the RSPB Nature Centre.
The Watersports Centre is also
nearby. No dogs except guide
dogs. ❀ ◖ ▶ & ⇔ P ⅄

Lugton

Paraffin Lamp
1 Beith Road (A736/B777 jct)
☎ (01505) 850510
11 (12.30 Sun)–11
Beer range varies Ⓗ
Brewer's Fayre country eatery
with a separate bar. Food is
available all day. Guest beers
are mostly from the Whitbread
range. Popular with families
(children's certificate). Handy
for the Lugton Inn Brewery.
Q ❀ ◖ ▶ & ♠ P

Mauchline

Loudoun Arms
12–14 Loudoun Street (B743)
☎ (01290) 551011
11 (12 Sun)–midnight
**Belhaven Sandy Hunter's
Ale** Ⓗ
Popular, comfortable village
bar with strong Robert Burns
connections: a comfortable
lounge, a function room and a
restaurant. ⚲ ◖ ▶ ⊟ ♠

Milngavie

Talbot Arms
30 Main Street
☎ (0141) 956 3989
11 (12 Sun)–11 (midnight Thu–Sat)
**Alloa Arrol's 80/-; Marston's
Pedigree; Morland Old
Speckled Hen; Tetley Bitter;
guest beers** Ⓗ
100-year-old pub named after a
now extinct breed of hunting

dog. A strong local clientele
mixes with walkers setting off
on the West Highland Way. No
food Sun.
◖ Å ⇔ P

Milton of Campsie

Kincaid House Hotel
Birdston Road
☎ (0141) 776 2226
12–midnight (1am Fri)
Beer range varies Ⓗ
Attractive hotel set in large
grounds, with a large
conservatory where children
are welcome for meals, and a
public bar. Popular for food.
Regular happy hours.
Wheelchair WC.
⚲ ❀ ⇔ ◖ ▶ ⊟ & P

Monkton

Monkton Lodge
Kilmarnock Road (A77/A78
roundabout)
☎ (01292) 678262
11–11 (midnight Sat) including Sun
Beer range varies Ⓗ
Purpose built Brewer's Fayre
pub close to Prestwick airport.
Food is available all day. The
guest beers are mostly from the
Whitbread range. Popular with
families (children's certificate).
Accommodation is at the
adjacent Travel Inn motel.
❀ ⇔ ◖ ▶ & Å P

Old Kilpatrick

Ettrick
159 Dumbarton Road
☎ (01389) 872821
11 (12.30 Sun)–11.30 (midnight
Thu–Sat)
**Caledonian Deuchars IPA;
Orkney Dark Island; guest
beer** Ⓗ
Traditional, late Victorian
village local with a horseshoe-
shaped public bar, named after
the Ettrick Shepherd, James
Hogg, a friend of Sir Walter
Scott and a famed poet in his
own right. Handy for the Forth
and Clyde Canal.
❀ ◖ ▶ ⊟ & ⇔ (Kilpatrick) P
⅄

Paisley

RH Finlay
33 Causeyside Street
☎ (0141) 889 9036
11–midnight (12.45am Fri & Sat);
12.30–11 Sun
**Draught Bass; Caledonian
Deuchars IPA** Ⓗ
Traditional-style, town-centre
pub with two lounge bars,
where care is taken to give
good service. The first pub in
Britain to open all day,
appealing to all over 21.
◖ ⇔ (Gilmour St/Canal St)

Wee Howff
53 High Street
☎ (0141) 889 2095
11–11 (1am Fri, 11.30 Sat); closed Sun
**Caledonian 70/-; Ind Coope
Burton Ale; guest beer** H
Small, but perfectly formed,
local near the university. The
interior has Tudor-style beams
and panelling. It can get busy,
so go early! The only regular
outlet for Caley 70/- in town.
⇌ (Gilmour St)

Renfrew

Ferry Inn
2 Clyde Street (at Yoker ferry
slipway) ☎ (0141) 886 2104
11 (12.30 Sun)–11 (11.45 Fri & Sat)
Beer range varies H
Listed building housing a
two-roomed pub: a friendly
local, unchanged in years, with
a strong shipbuilding influence
in the decor. ♨ Q

Tap & Spile
Terminal Building, Glasgow
Airport ☎ (0141) 848 4869
8am–11 (1am Fri, 11.45 Sat; may vary);
12.30–11 Sun
Beer range varies H
Refurbished public bar making
use of wood and stained-glass
to good effect. Sadly prices
have soared. Eight beers in
summer; four in winter.
& ✔

Saltcoats

Hip Flask
13 Winton Street (near
seafront) ☎ (01294) 465222
11–midnight (1am Thu–Sat) including
Sun
**Belhaven St Andrew's Ale;
guest beer** H
Small, friendly café-bar, well-
placed for both the town centre
and the beach. The raised
seating area can double as a
stage; music and quizzes some
eves. Good value food.
Newspapers are supplied.
Children's certificate. ♨ ◖

Sawney Bean's Howff
84 Dockhead Street
☎ (01294) 603342
11–midnight (1am Thu–Sat) including
Sun
Beer range varies H
Busy, town-centre bar with a
Scottish theme, named after a
legendary Scottish cannibal!
Up to two guest beers, usually
Scottish and very reasonably
priced. ⭘ ⊞ ⇌

Seamill

Waterside Inn
Ardrossan Road (A78, S of
village) ☎ (01294) 823238
11–midnight (1am Fri & Sat); 12.30–11
Sun

Beer range varies H
Brewer's Fayre house with a
bar that has more of a pub feel
than others. It sits right on the
beach and has wonderful sea
views from the restaurant and
garden. Food is available all
day. Guest beers mostly come
from the Whitbread range.
Children's certificate.
♨ ◖ ▶ & ♣ P

Stair

Stair Inn
On B730, between A70 and
B743
☎ (01292) 591650
11 (12.30 Sun)–11 (1am Fri & Sat)
**Belhaven Sandy Hunter's
Ale** H
Open-plan lounge and
restaurant, set in the heart of
rural Ayrshire in an extremely
picturesque location. Very
popular for meals at weekends.
Beware of the adjacent narrow
bridge. ♨ ♨ ◖ ▶ & P

Stevenston

Champion Shell Inn
5 Schoolwell Street (just off
A738)
☎ (01294) 463055
11 (12.30 Sun)–midnight (1am Thu–
Sat)
Beer range varies H
Refurbished bar/lounge in a
listed building – the oldest
inhabited building in the
'Three Towns'. Its name comes
from an 18th-century
competition for drinking mead
from a shell. Two guest beers
come from a variety of sources.
Public car park opposite. Quiz
Tue eve. Q ◖ ▶ & ♣

Strathaven

Waterside
31 Waterside Street (near main
square)
☎ (01357) 522588
11 (12.30 Sun)–midnight
**Alloa Arrol's 80/-; Morland
Old Speckled Hen; guest
beers** H
Pub and restaurant set in this
historic town, adjacent to the
green. Excellent food is served
all day. Music is a touch loud,
but this is a warm and
welcoming pub. ♨ ◖ ▶ &

Troon

Harbour Bar
169 Templehill (B749 to
harbour) ☎ (01292) 312668
11 (12.30 Sun)–midnight
**Broughton Greenmantle Ale;
guest beer** (occasional) H
Friendly harbourside lounge
bar with a games room. Both
bars have been refurbished
recently. Q ♣ P

McKay's
69 Portland Street (A759)
☎ (01292) 311079
11–12.30am; 12.30–midnight Sun
Boddingtons Bitter H**; Maclay
80/-; guest beers** E
Popular, town-centre bar with
up to three guest beers. Four
ales are dispensed by electric
'handpumps' which use air
pressure. The bar can be loud
weekend eves. ♨ ◖ ▶ ⇌

Piersland House Hotel
15 Craigend Road (B749, S of
centre) ☎ (01292) 314747
12–3, 6–midnight; 11–midnight Sun
**Courage Directors; guest
beer** H
Popular, three-star hotel,
overlooking Royal Troon Golf
Course. The hotel has a good
reputation for its food and
drinking space can be limited
at meal times. The beer prices
reflect the quality of the hotel.
Children's certificate.
♨ Q ♨ ⋈ ◖ ▶ & P

Twechar

Quarry Inn
Main Street ☎ (01236) 821496
11 (12.30 Sun)–11 (1am Fri)
**Maclay 70/-, Broadsword;
Tetley Bitter; guest beer** H
Traditional village pub with a
selection of brewery mirrors.
The locals are very friendly.
Beer festival Oct. ♨ ⊞ ♣ P

Uddingston

Rowan Tree ☆
60 Old Mill Road
☎ (01698) 812678
11–11.45; 12.30–11 Sun
**Maclay 80/-, Wallace; guest
beers** H
CAMRA Scottish *Pub of the
Year* 1997: a vibrant
community pub with an
unspoilt wooden interior, two
fireplaces and splendid
brewery mirrors. The pub
ghost is a stable lad who died
after being kicked by a horse.
♨ ◖ ⇌ P

Uplawmoor

Uplawmoor Hotel
66 Neilston Road (off A736
Barrhead–Irvine road)
☎ (01505) 850565
12–2.30, 5–11 (midnight Fri); 12–
midnight Sat; 12.30–11 Sun
Beer range varies H
Hotel nestling in a hamlet, but
worth the trek: an open fire is a
feature in the lounge.
Refurbished bedrooms make it
a good stop for a weekend
break amid rolling hilly
countryside. Friendly, efficient
staff; good value meals.
♨ ⭘ ♨ ⋈ ◖ ▶ & P

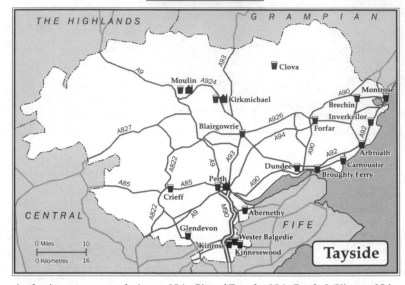

Authority areas covered: Angus UA, City of Dundee UA, Perth & Kinross UA

Abernethy

Crees Inn
Main Street
☎ (01738) 850714
11–2.30, 5–11; 11–11 Sat; 12.30–11 Sun
Beer range varies H
Comfortable, inviting village pub with a lounge area and a snug. Three beers are usually available – two Scottish.
🏚 ◑ P ✂

Arbroath

Lochlands
14–16 Lochlands Street
☎ (01241) 873286
11 (12.30 Sun)–11
Beer range varies H
Loud, lively local with a friendly atmosphere.
🍺 Å 🚌 ♣

Newgate Inn
31 West Newgate
☎ (01241) 872616
11 (12.30 Sun)–midnight
Beer range varies H
100-year-old, two-roomed pub in an area of traditional fisherman's houses near the harbour. Only one beer, but this changes frequently. Comfortable lounge.
🍺 ♣ 🍴

Blairgowrie

Stormont Arms
101 Perth Street
☎ (01250) 873142
11–2.45, 5–11; 11–11 Fri & Sat; 12.30–2.30, 6.30–11 Sun
Beer range varies H

Traditional bar in a busy town local with a comfortable lounge. Up to three beers.
🍺 ♣

Brechin

Dalhousie
1 Market Street
☎ (01356) 622096
11 (12.30 Sun)–11
Beer varies H
Pleasant, street-corner local with a high ceiling, horseshoe bar and wood-panelled walls. One real ale. 🍺 ♣

Broughty Ferry

Fisherman's Tavern
10–12 Fort Street (by lifeboat station) ☎ (01382) 775941
11 (12.30 Sun)–midnight (1am Thu–Sat)
Belhaven St Andrew's Ale; Boddingtons Bitter; Maclay 80/-; guest beers H
Former national CAMRA *Pub of the Year* and in every *Guide* since Scotland first appeared in 1975. A new extension has not affected the atmosphere: very busy, cosy, low-ceilinged and welcoming. Good food.
Q 🛏 🏚 ◑ 🚌 (limited service) ♣

Old Anchor
48 Gray Street
☎ (01382) 737899
11–midnight; 12.30–11 Sun
Courage Directors; Theakston Best Bitter; guest beers H
Comfortable one-room bar with nautical memorabilia. Partitions provide cosy nooks. Very busy late eve and

weekends. Family/no-smoking area lunchtime only.
🛏 ◑ 🚌 (limited service) ✂

Carnoustie

Stag's Head
61 Dundee Street
☎ (01241) 852265
11 (12.30 Sun)–midnight (1am Fri)
Ind Coope Burton Ale; Marston's Pedigree; guest beers H
Wide, refurbished bar in a busy local with a lounge and games room. Meals served May–September. Ales requested by locals are stocked.
🛏 🍺 ◑ 🚌 (Burnside Halt, limited service) ♣

Clova

Clova Hotel
Glen Clova (B955, 15 miles N of Kirriemuir) ☎ (01575) 550222
11–midnight; 12.30–11 Sun
Beer range varies H
Welcome watering hole for walkers, climbers, fishers and tourists, hosting a real ale festival at Easter and a lively summer social programme. Roast pig barbecues, ceilidhs, and occasional helicopter flights. Three beers: one each from Alloa, Broughton and Orkney. 🏚 🛏 🏚 ◑ Å P

INDEPENDENT BREWERIES

Aldchlappie: Kirkmichael

Inveralmond: Perth

Moulin: Moulin

Crieff

Oakbank Inn
Turret Bridge (off A85)
☎ (01764) 652420
12–3 (not Mon & Tue in winter), 5–11 (11.45 Fri & Sat) including Sun
Beer varies H
Modern pub in a pleasant setting, near a camping/caravan site approximately one mile from Glenturret Distillery. The beer is supplied by Belhaven. No eve meals winter weekdays.
❀ ◐ ◑ ▲ ♣

Dundee

Drouthy Neebors
142 Perth Road
☎ (01382) 202187
11–midnight; 12–11 Sun
Belhaven 80/-; Boddingtons Bitter; Flowers Original; Orkney Dark Island; guest beers H
Cosy bar, popular with students from the nearby art college, featuring bare floorboards and stone floors.
◐ ≉

Frew's
117 Strathmartine Road
☎ (01382) 810975
11–11.45; 12.30–11 Sun
Draught Bass H
Pub with a tastefully enhanced Victorian interior in the bar, and two lounges, one Art Deco, modelled on the first class lounge of the *Queen Mary*; splendid fireplace. Stained-glass panels depict a plough – the pub's former name. Worthington White Shield is stocked. 🜂 ⊟

Hogshead
7–9 Union Street (opp. city churches)
☎ (01382) 205037
11–midnight; 12.30–11 Sun
Boddingtons Bitter; Whitbread Abroad Cooper; guest beers H
Popular, town-centre bar; a bank converted into a Hogshead bar with the customary bare floorboards and paraphernalia. Friendly service; six guest beers.
Q ◐ ◑ ♿ ≉ ⌀

Mickey Coyle's
21–23 Old Hawkhill
☎ (01382) 225871
11–11.30 (midnight Fri & Sat); 7–11 Sun
Boddingtons Bitter; Broughton Greenmantle Ale; guest beers H
Friendly bar, popular with locals and students alike. Along with the fine selection of ales (four guests) is a good choice of rums.
◐ ◑ ♿ ≉ P

Speedwell Bar ☆
165–167 Perth Road
☎ (01382) 667783
11–midnight; 12.30–11 Sun
Beer range varies A/H
InverPub with a quality, listed interior (circa 1903), boasting mahogany and glass fittings and excellent Art Nouveau etched windows.
Q ⊟ ♿ ≉ ♣ ⊁

Forfar

O'Hara's
41 West High Street, Angus
☎ (01307) 464350
11–2.30, 5.30–11 (midnight Fri & Sat); 12.30–2, 6.30–11 Sun
Beer varies H
Upstairs bar-bistro with a real welcome, friendly service and excellent food. Occasional live music; one, varying, beer.
🜂 ◐ ◑

Glendevon

Tormaukin Hotel
On A823 ☎ (01259) 781252
11 (12 Sun)–11
Harviestoun Original; Ind Coope Burton Ale; guest beer H
The 'Hotel of the Hill of the Mountain Hare', once a drovers' inn, is now a cosy refuge with good food. Handy for Gleneagles.
🜂 Q ⚲ 🛏 ◐ ◑ ▲ P

Inverkeilor

Chance Inn
Main Street, Angus (off A92, coast road) ☎ (01241) 830308
12–2.30, 5–11; 12–11 Sat; 12.30–11 Sun
Beer range varies H
18th-century coaching inn, now popular for meals: a lively bar with an adjoining lounge/dining room where handpumps are installed. Eve meals end at 8.30 (7.30 Sun).
🛏 ◐ ◑ ⊟ ♿ ♣ P

Kinnesswood

Lomond Country Inn
Main Street ☎ (01592) 840253
11–11 (midnight Fri & Sat) including Sun
Draught Bass; Jennings Bitter; guest beer H
Pub in a quiet corner of rural Perthshire, with commanding views over Loch Leven from an open plan bar/restaurant.
🜂 Q ⚲ ❀ 🛏 ◐ ◑ ♿ P ⊁

Kinross

Kirklands Hotel
High Street ☎ (01577) 863313
11–2.30, 5–11 (11.45 Sat); 12.30–11 Sun
Maclay 80/-; guest beers H
Traditional, small hotel with a basic bar and a comfortable lounge area.
Q 🛏 ◐ ◑ ⊟ ♿ P ⊁

Muirs Inn
49 The Muirs (Milnathort road, N of town) ☎ (01577) 862270
11–2.30, 5–11 (11.45 Fri); 11–11.45 Sat; 12.30–11 Sun
Beer range varies H
Inn with a small, panelled bar, complete with eight handpumps and rare brewery mirrors behind the gantry, plus a comfortable lounge and a restaurant. The house beer comes from Belhaven.
Q ❀ 🛏 ◐ ◑ ⊟ ♿ ▲ ♣ P

Kirkmichael

Aldchlappie Hotel
At A924/B950 jct
☎ (01250) 881224
11–3 (not Mon), 5.30–11.45; 12–3, 6.30–11 Sun
Beer range varies H
Old country inn promoting real ale with its own microbrewery. A haven for walkers and skiers. Eve meals end at 8.45.
🜂 ⚲ ❀ 🛏 ◐ ◑ ⊟ ♿ ▲ P

Montrose

George Hotel
22 George Street
☎ (01674) 675050
11–2, 4.30–11; 11–11 Sat; 12–11 Sun
Beer range varies H
Long, cheerfully decorated lounge-cum-restaurant serving four beers. 🛏 ◐ ◑ ≉ P ⊁

Market Arms
95 High Street
☎ (01674) 673384
11–midnight; 12.30–2.30, 6.30–11 Sun
Caledonian 80/-; Theakston XB; guest beer H
Large, town-centre bar/lounge, lively eves.
≉ ♣

Moulin

Moulin Inn
11–13 Kirkmichael Road (¾ mile NE of Pitlochry)
☎ (01796) 472196
11 (12 Sun)–11 (11.45 Fri & Sat)
Moulin Light, Braveheart, Ale of Atholl, Old Remedial H
300-year-old inn, extended into an hotel but retaining its original character. Adjacent brewhouse.
🜂 ⚲ 🛏 ◐ ◑ ⊟ ♿ ▲ P

Perth

King's Arms
5 George Street
☎ (01738) 629914
11 (12.30 Sun)–11
Maclay 80/-, Kane's Amber Ale; guest beer H

Busy, town-centre pub with an upstairs lounge. Five hand-pumps. ◖ ▶ ⌣

Old Ship Inn

Skinnergate ☎ (01738) 624929
11–2.30, 5–11; 11–11.45 Fri & Sat, closed Sun
Caledonian Deuchars IPA; guest beers Ⓗ
Perth's historic pub (established 1665) – a welcome retreat in the heart of the city. Eve meals available Sat.
Q ◖ ⌱ ♣

Wester Balgedie

Balgedie Toll Tavern
At B919/A911 jct near Kinross
☎ (01592) 840212
11 (12.30 Sun)–11
Ind Coope Burton Ale Ⓗ
Comfortable, cosy tavern, with wooden beams, home-cooking and a friendly atmosphere. A private dining room is available.
🐾 Q ✿ ◖ ▶ ᚦ P

Peter Moneghan and Chris Tomlinson of Moulin Brewery, one of Scotland's growing band of independent real ale producers. There are now 20 'indies' in Scotland.

Northern Ireland

0 Miles 10
0 Kilometres 16

Limavady
Crosskeys
Jordanstown
Bangor
Glengormley
Belfast
Ballydorn
Lisburn
Saintfield
Hillsborough
Downpatrick
IRELAND
Kilkeel

Ballydorn

Daft Eddy's
Take Killinchy road from Comber; follow signs to Whiterock
☎ (01238) 541615
11.30–11.30 (1.30am Fri & Sat); 12.30–10 Sun
Draught Bass; Theakston Best Bitter H
Modern two-bar building where the public bar has a tiled floor, an open range fire, a beamed ceiling and a quiet atmosphere. The lounge features an open fire and driftwood, and the restaurant and patio offer scenic views of the lough. Children welcome; handy for the boating marina and club.
🏨 Q 🕿 ⊛ ◖ ▶ ⊞ ㋡ P

Bangor

Jenny Watts
41 High Street (marina end)
☎ (01247) 270401
11–11; 12–10.30 Sun
Theakston Best Bitter H
Open-plan seaside bar dating from 1740. It features a stone floor and displays local memorabilia. Famous for its jazz brunch on Sundays. Children are welcome.
🏨 ⊛ ◖ ▶

Belfast

Beaten Docket
48–52 Great Victoria Street (opp. Europa Hotel)
☎ (01232) 242986
8am–11.30pm (1am Fri); 11.30am–1am Sat; 12.30–10 Sun
Draught Bass; Cains Bitter *or* **Theakston Best Bitter; Caledonian Deuchars IPA; guest beers** H
Decorative, modern-looking alehouse, comprised of a public bar downstairs and a lounge upstairs; notable for its collection of cigarette sports cards, music sessions and occasional ale festivals. Children's certificate applied for.
🏨 ◖ ▶ ㋡ (Gt Victoria St)

Bittles Bar
70 Upper Church Lane
☎ (01232) 311088
11.30–11.30 (10.30 Sun)
Draught Bass H
Small, triangular-shaped bar built on a corner, very tastefully decorated and comfortable. Its walls are adorned with various watercolours depicting Belfast and famous characters. Well worth a visit; a very relaxing bar. Worthington White Shield sold.
◖ ㋡ (Central/Gt Victoria St)

Botanic Inn
23–27 Malone Road
☎ (01232) 660460
11.30–midnight (1am Wed–Sat); 12.30–10 Sun
Cains Bitter, FA; guest beers H
Recently rebuilt, this is a large, pub in the university area of the city. Tue nights feature traditional music and the 'Real Ale Club'. Tapas served 5–11pm. A very busy pub.
🏨 ◖ ㋡ ㋡ (Botanic)

Crown Liquor Saloon ☆
44 Great Victoria Street (opp. Europa Hotel)
☎ (01232) 249426
11.30–midnight (1am Fri & Sat); 12.30–10.30 Sun
Draught Bass H
Unique bar, remarkable not only for its decor, but for being jointly run by the NT and Bass. As Belfast's most famous bar, a large crowd and a good atmosphere are ensured. Arrive early for one of the snugs. ◖ ㋡ (Gt Victoria St)

Crow's Nest
22 Skipper Street
☎ (01232) 325491
11.30–1am; 12.30–11.30 Sun
Large, comfortable, open-plan bar offering good food at reasonable prices and very good portions. Popular with Belfast's gay community eves. Entertainment at weekends. Worthington White Shield is sold. ◖ ㋡ ㋡ (Central)

Errigle
320 Ormeau Road (by Curzon cinema) ☎ (01232) 641410
11.30–1am (10 Sun)
Beer range varies H
Pub boasting five bars with modern decor, one without TV. Children are allowed in the restaurant. Q ⊛ ◖ ▶ ⊞ ㋡ ♣

Lavery's Gin Palace
12–16 Bradbury Place
☎ (01232) 328205
11.30–1am; 12.30–midnight Sun
Beer range varies H
Large, open-plan pub with real ale in the public bar only. The back bar has a small snug and there are two floors above, one housing a disco. Near Queens University, it is popular with students. Entertainment nightly. Entrance queues at weekends. ⊞ ㋡ (Gt Victoria St/ Botanic)

INDEPENDENT BREWERIES
Hilden: Lisburn
Whitewater: Kilkeel

409

Monico Bars

17 Lombard Street
☎ (01232) 323211
10.30am–11pm; closed Sun
Beer range varies Ⓗ
Comfortable public bar with a very small snug; popular with horse racing punters. The back bar is a lot larger and quieter drawing a varied clientele; its wood and bare brick decor features a range of mirrors and prints on wood, plus several enclosed cubicles.
🏠 ◖▶ & (Gt Victoria St)

Nick's Warehouse

35–43 Hill Street
☎ (01232) 439690
12–11; closed Sun
Busy bar and an excellent restaurant, currently serving bottled wheat beer but looking to take on cask ales. Although situated in a Belfast daytime backwater, it bustles at night.
◖▶ &

Try also: Portside Inn, Dargan Rd (range varies)

Crosskeys

Crosskeys

Grange Road, Toomebridge (left turn 7 miles from Randalstown on Portglenone road) ☎ (01648) 50694
7.30 (3 Fri)–11; 12–11 Sat, Sun & summer
Absolutely classic, listed pub with a thatched roof and whitewashed stone walls. Relax to the aroma of a turf fire and the quiet talk of country matters. Folk music at night. Miss it and weep, but ring to check opening hours. Worthington White Shield sold. 🏠 Q ❀ ♣ ♠ P

Downpatrick

Denvirs Hotel

14–16 English Street (near Down cathedral)
☎ (01396) 612012
11 (12.30 Sun)–11
Hilden Ale Ⓗ
17th-century coaching inn undergoing renovations to

return to its original form of three bars, featuring three discovered fireplaces. Food every day.
🏠 Q ➳ 🏠 ◖▶ ♣ & P

Glengormley

Crown & Shamrock

540 Antrim Road (A6, 1½ miles W of town)
☎ (01232) 832889
11.30–11.30; 7–10.30 Sun
Traditional, old, one-bar pub, family-run, with a warm welcome and a snug lounge. Occasional folk music nights. Light snacks are normally available and Worthington White Shield is sold.
🏠 Q ❀ P

Whittley's

401 Ballyclare Road, Kings Moss (B56, 2½ miles NW of town) ☎ (01232) 832438
11.30–11; 5.30–10.30 Sun
Welcoming, two-bar pub with a large lounge and a quiet public bar, featuring wood and stone floors and real fires. A games room keeps poker machines separate; the bar has an adjoining railway-themed restaurant. Meals 12–2.30 (5 Sat); not served Sun. Worthington White Shield is sold. 🏠 Q ❀ ◖♣ P

Hillsborough

Hillside

21 Main Street
☎ (01846) 682765
12–11 (10 Sun)
Cains Bitter; Whitewater Mountain Ale; guest beers Ⓗ
Long, narrow bar with a stone floor, dating back to the 1800s. A new extension to the rear serves excellent pub food – popular at weekends – and there's a quality restaurant upstairs (booking advised).
🏠 Q ❀ ◖▶

Plough

3 The Square
☎ (01846) 682985
11.30–11; 12.30–10 Sun

Theakston Best Bitter; Whitewater Mountain Ale Ⓗ
Traditional village pub, first established in 1758, with wood-panelled walls and ceiling beams. The comfortable, spacious, U-shaped layout boasts much memorabilia. Good pub food; excellent restaurant.
🏠 Q ❀ ◖▶ P

Jordanstown

Woody's

607 Shore Road, Whiteabbey
☎ (01232) 863206
11.30–11; 1–10 Sun
Beer range varies Ⓗ
Comfortable upstairs bar regularly staging quiz or wine-tasting nights. The off-licence beneath also stocks bottled ales. Lunches weekdays only.
Q ◖ P

Limavady

Owen's Bar

50 Main Street
☎ (01504) 722328
11–11; closed Sun
Old, traditional, family-run pub attracting a wide-ranging clientele. Barbecues during summer months. Worthington White Shield is sold. 🏠 Q

Saintfield

White Horse

49 Main Street
☎ (01238) 510417
10–11; closed Sun
Theakston Best Bitter; Cains FA; Mill Ale, Glen Ale; Whitewater Mountain Ale; guest beers Ⓗ
Very popular, friendly, family-run pub with a comfortable atmosphere. A wide range of excellent food is served in the bar and downstairs restaurant (no wheelchair access). Two changing guest beers and an annual beer festival (Nov). Local CAMRA *Pub of the Year* 1996. Home of Mill Ale Brewery whose beers are brewed by Whitewater under contract. 🏠 Q ◖▶ &

SUNDAY BEST

The biggest event to affect drinkers in Northern Ireland in 1997 came in February. The long-awaited shake up in licensing laws means that pubs can now stay open all day on Sundays. Pubs which serve Sunday lunch, and especially those which are investigating the children's certificate, have welcomed this legislation. The full effect is yet to be seen however, as trade may not warrant full-day opening in some areas. Until the situation stabilises, it would be advisable to contact each pub before setting out for a Sunday drink.

Channel Islands

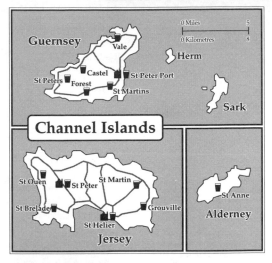

Beer range varies Ⓗ
Small, often busy pub with two bars. Occasional live music and quiz eves. Well worth the stagger uphill from the town. You can't miss the garish exterior. ◁ ▯ ♣

Ship & Crown
North Pier Steps, North Esplanade ☎ (01481) 721368
10–11.45; 12–3.30, 6–11 Sun
Guernsey Braye (summer), **Sunbeam, Winter Warmer; Jersey Ann's Treat** Ⓗ
Busy single-bar town pub opposite the marina. The walls are covered with pictures of ships and local shipwrecks. Popular with bankers at lunchtime and young people eves. Eve meals May–Sept, 5.30–8. ◁ ▯

Try also: **Prince of Wales**, Manor Place (Randalls)

Alderney

St Anne

Nellie's Garden Bistro
Victoria Street
☎ (01481) 824000
10–12.30am; 10–midnight Sun
Tipsy Toad Jimmy's Bitter, Horny Toad Ⓗ
Bistro-style bar and restaurant set back from the main shopping street, overlooking a large lawn. The ale is collected from Jersey by plane.
❀ ◁ ▯ P

Try also: **Moorings Hotel**, Braye St (Free)

Guernsey

Note: Sunday drinking on Guernsey is only available to customers purchasing a meal to the value of £3 or more.

Castel

Fleur du Jardin
Kings Mill
☎ (01481) 57996
11–3, 6–11.45; 12–2, 7–10.30 Sun
Guernsey Sunbeam, seasonal beers Ⓗ
Comfortable, attractive hotel in a pleasant setting, renovated in keeping with its farmhouse origins. The public bar does not open winter lunchtimes. Excellent, home-cooked food using fresh local produce is served (the restaurant is open all week).
▟▙ Q ❀ ▱ ◁ ▯ ▯ P

Forest

Venture Inn
Rue de la Villiaze (New Road)
☎ (01481) 63211
10–11.45; closed Sun
Randalls Patois Ale Ⓗ
Established local not too far from the airport. The functional, sports-oriented bar contrasts with a comfortable lounge. Handy for the cinema (next door).
▟▙ Q ❀ ◁ ▯ ▯ ♣ P

St Martins

Captain's Hotel
La Fosse ☎ (01481) 38990
10–11.45; 12–3.30, 6.30–11 (closed winter) Sun
Guernsey Sunbeam Ⓗ
Near Moulin Huet Bay and Pottery: a single lounge bar with a genuine pub feel, and an adjoining bistro-style restaurant. Note the impressive handpump. ❀ ▱ ◁ ▯ P

L'Auberge Divette
Jerbourg Road
☎ (01481) 38485
10.30–11.45; 12–3 Sun
Guernsey Braye, Sunbeam Ⓗ
Comfortable pub with two bars (magnificent views from the lounge), close to cliff path walks. The garden area is very busy in summer with locals and visitors. Al fresco dining available. ▟▙ ❀ ◁ ▯ ▯ P

St Peter Port

Drunken Duck
Le Charroterie
☎ (01481) 725045
11–11.45; closed Sun

St Peters

Longfrie Inn
Route de Longfrie
☎ (01481) 63107
11–2.30, 5.30–11.45; 6.30–9.30 Sun
Guernsey Sunbeam, seasonal beers Ⓗ
Food and family-oriented hostelry, sometimes very busy. A well-equipped children's play room, a large garden and a good, varied menu are features. ☂ ❀ ◁ ▯ P

Vale

Chandlers Hotel
Braye Road ☎ (01481) 44280
11–11.45; closed Sun
Randalls Patois Ale Ⓗ
Local CAMRA *Pub of the Year* 1996, where a lively locals' bar contrasts with a cosy lounge. Frequent live music in the upstairs function room. Good value food includes Thai specials. Q ❀ ▱ ◁ ▯ ▯ ♣ P

Houmet Tavern
Grande Havre ☎ (01481) 43037
10.30–11.45; closed Sun
Guernsey Braye Ⓗ
Very popular pub with a pleasant outlook over a picturesque bay. Well-deserved reputation for bar meals (no eve meals Mon or Thu). Q ❀ ◁ ▯ ▯ ▲ ♣ P

🏭 INDEPENDENT BREWERIES

Guernsey: St Peter Port

Jersey: St Helier

Randalls: St Peter Port

Tipsy Toad: St Peter

CHANNEL ISLANDS

Jersey

Grouville

Pembroke
Coast Road ☎ (01534) 855756
9am–11.30pm; 11–11.30 Sun
Draught Bass; Boddingtons Bitter; Theakston XB (summer); **guest beers** H
Large, popular, welcoming pub with a family atmosphere. Book for Sun lunch or large parties as the food is excellent (outside patio eating area). Games in the public bar; outside play area for children.
🏨 Q 🛏 ☀ ◖ 🌙 ⊟ ♣ ♣ P

Seymour Inn
La Rocque ☎ (01534) 854558
10–11.30 including Sun
Guernsey Sunbeam; Jersey Old Jersey Ale, Ann's Treat, Winter Ale H
Friendly coastal pub offering a choice of bars, including a real ale bar. Good, no-nonsense food at very reasonable prices; large range of games. Across the road from the beach.
🏨 Q 🛏 ☀ ◖ 🌙 ⊟ ♣ P

St Brelade

La Pulente Hotel
La Route de la Pulente
☎ (01534) 41760
9.30am–11.30pm; 11–11.30 Sun
Draught Bass; Boddingtons Bitter; guest beer H
Pleasant rendezvous during all seasons, set at the end of St Ouen's Bay with splendid views of the beach from the lounge bay window. Popular with locals; coach parties by arrangement only. No food Sun eve.
🏨 Q 🛏 ☀ ◖ 🌙 ⊟ ♣ P ⊁

Old Smugglers Inn
Ouaisne Bay ☎ (01534) 41510
11–11.30 including Sun
Boddingtons Bitter; guest beers H
17th-century granite pub with regularly varied guest ales, in a romantic setting next to the beach. Live music Sun eve. The

food is excellent and diners are well catered for.
🏨 Q 🛏 ◖ 🌙 ♣

St Helier

Dog & Sausage
Hilary Street ☎ (01534) 30982
9.30am–11.30pm including Sun
Draught Bass H
Small pub in a pedestrian shopping area, fashioned like the inside of a pre-war railway carriage. A welcome stop in a busy town. Note: Boddingtons Bitter is kept under a cask breather. ☀ ◖

Lamplighter
Mulcaster Street (near bus station) ☎ (01534) 23119
10–11.30; 11–11.30 Sun
Draught Bass; Boddingtons Bitter; Marston's Pedigree; guest beers H
The only gas-lit pub on Jersey. It serves a wide range of beers, Bulmers Traditional cider and good value, no-nonsense food. No TV or music: this is a lively conversational pub with a dark, panelled interior.
Q ◖ ♣ ○

St Martin

Anne Port Bay Hotel
Anne Port Bay
☎ (01534) 852058
11–2.30, 5–11; 11–11 Sat & Sun
Draught Bass; Marston's Pedigree; Tipsy Toad Ale H
Small, quiet, hotel bar tucked away in the east of the island, enjoying a strong local following. Guest beers may be hidden, so check the blackboard. Good B&B and a local craft centre have been recently incorporated into the hotel. 🛏 ☀ 🚪 P

Royal Hotel
La Grande Route de Faldouet
☎ (01534) 856289
9.30am–11.30pm; 11–11.30 Sun
Boddingtons Bitter; guest beer H
Large pub next to St Martin's church: a quiet lounge area and busy public bar. The upstairs restaurant serves excellent food and is popular with

locals. Real ale can be provided in the restaurant on request. Large children's play area; families welcome.
🏨 Q 🛏 ◖ 🌙 ⊟ ♣ ♣ P

Try also: Prince of Wales Tavern, Hilgrove St (Randalls)

St Ouen

Moulin de Lecq
Grève de Lecq
☎ (01534) 482818
11–11.30 including Sun
Guernsey Sunbeam; Jersey Old Jersey Ale, Winter Ale H
Converted, working 12th-century watermill displaying the moving drive wheel behind the bar. A large outdoor barbecue area, a landscaped garden, a full children's play area and excellent food add to its attraction. Situated in a pleasant valley leading to the beach.
🏨 Q 🛏 ☀ ◖ 🌙 P ⊁

St Peter

Goose on the Green
La Route de la Haule
☎ (01534) 888273
11–11.30 including Sun
Boddingtons Bitter; guest beer H
Recently refurbished, friendly, family pub serving good food in a large restaurant and an outdoor dining area. Children's play area; live music in summer (can be loud).
🏨 ☀ ◖ 🌙 P

Star & Tipsy Toad
La Route de Beaumont
☎ (01534) 485556
10–11.30; 11–11.30 Sun
Tipsy Toad Ale, Jimmy's Bitter, Horny Toad; guest beer H
Tipsy Toad brew pub: a spacious and tasteful renovation which includes indoor and outdoor children's play areas. Good food, live music and brewery tours are features of this popular and busy pub which caters well for families. New brews are regularly introduced.
🏨 🛏 ☀ ◖ 🌙 ♣ ○ P

ALE-LESS ABROAD?

Travelling abroad? Take a *Good Beer Guide* with you! CAMRA publishes a small series of overseas beer books which are invaluable items for your journey. Choose from *Good Beer Guides* to Belgium and Holland (£9.99), Munich and Bavaria (£8.99) and Prague and the Czech Republic (£7.99). Copies are available from all good bookshops, or direct (and post-free) from CAMRA, 230 Hatfield Road, St Albans, Hertfordshire AL1 4LW.

Isle of Man

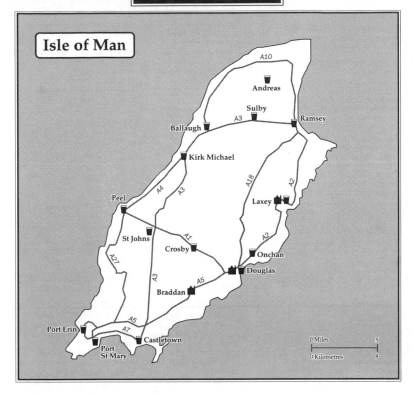

Andreas

Grosvenor
☎ (01624) 880227
12–11 (midnight Fri & Sat); 12–3,
7–10.30 Sun
Cains Bitter; Okells Bitter H
Country pub with bar and
restaurant areas. Good home
cooking.
Q ❀ ◑ 🍴 & ♣ P

Ballaugh

Raven
☎ (01624) 897272
12–11 (midnight Fri & Sat); 12–3,
7–10.30 Sun
**Boddingtons Bitter; Bushy's
Best Bitter; Marston's
Pedigree; guest beers** H
Country pub on the TT course.
Friendly natives; good food.
❀ ◑ ♣ P

Castletown

Castle Arms (Gluepot)
Quayside ☎ (01624) 824673
12–11 (midnight Fri & Sat); 12–3,
7–10.30 Sun
**Boddingtons Bitter; Cains
Mild; Tetley Bitter** H
One of the oldest pubs on the
island: a comfortable pub with
a nautical theme, on the
harbourside. Good food.
🏨 Q ❀ ◑ ▶ & ▲ ≷ (IMR) ♣

Sidings
Victoria Road (by station)
☎ (01624) 823282
12–11 (midnight Fri & Sat); 12–3,
7–10.30 Sun
**Boddingtons Bitter; Bushy's
Best Bitter; Marston's
Pedigree; guest beers** H
Cosy pub with an excellent
range of beers (six guests);
popular with locals and
visitors. Large garden.
❀ ◑ & ▲ ≷ (IMR) ♣ P

Viking Hotel
Victoria Road
12–11 (midnight Fri & Sat); 12–3,
7–10.30 Sun
**Courage Directors; Okells
Mild; John Smith's Bitter;
Tetley Bitter** H
Very popular, family-run pub
serving good food (barbecues
in the garden). Q ☂ ❀ ◑ ▶ 🍴
& ▲ ≷ (IMR) ♣ P

Crosby

Crosby Hotel
Peel Road ☎ (01624) 851293
12–11 (midnight Fri & Sat); 12–3,
7–10.30 Sun
Okells Mild, Bitter H
Large pub on the TT course in
the village. Popular with locals
and busy at TT time. Good
food; friendly staff.
🏨 Q ❀ ◑ 🍴 & ♣ P

Douglas

Albert
Church Row (between bus
station and market hall)
☎ (01624) 673632
12–11 (midnight Fri & Sat); 12–3,
7–10.30 Sun
Okells Bitter H
Very popular, busy town-
centre drinkers' pub.
🍴 ≷ (IMR) ⊖ ♣

Foresters Arms
St Georges Street (50 yds from
Circular Rd)
☎ (01624) 676509
12–11 (midnight Fri & Sat); 12–3,
7–10.30 Sun
Okells Mild, Bitter H
Traditional, sociable, Manx
local, popular with business
people. Baps and toasties
served all day.
🏨 🍴 ≷ (IMR) ⊖ ♣

413

Old Market Inn

Church Row (near bus station)
☎ (01624) 675202
12–11 (midnight Fri & Sat); 12–3,
7–10.30 Sun
**Bushy's Best Bitter; Okells
Bitter** Ⓗ
Genuine Manx pub close to the
shops and harbour, with a
good atmosphere.
🏨 🕮 ⇌ (IMR) ⊖ ♣

Rovers Return

Church Road (rear of Town
Hall) ☎ (01624) 676459
12–11 (midnight Fri & Sat); 12–3,
7–10.30 Sun
**Bushy's Mild, Best Bitter,
seasonal beers** Ⓗ
Central pub, very popular with
locals, displaying pictures of
old fire engines (it was once
known as the Fireman's). One
room is a shrine to Blackburn
Rovers. Good meals.
🏨 🕮 ◖ ⇌ (IMR) ⊖ ♣

Samuel Webbs

Marina Road ☎ (01624) 625595
12–11 (midnight Fri & Sat); 12–3,
7–10.30 Sun
**Courage Directors; Marston's
Pedigree; Okells Bitter;
Ruddles County; John Smith's
Bitter; guest beers** Ⓗ
Town-centre pub, very popular
with all ages. Excellent food.
Local CAMRA *Pub of the Year*
1995.
Q 🕮 ◖ ♨ ♿

Terminus Tavern

Strathalan Crescent
☎ (01624) 624312
12–11 (midnight Fri & Sat); 12–3,
7–10.30 Sun
Okells Mild, Bitter Ⓗ
Pub at the end of the
promenade, opposite the
electric tram and horse tram
termini. Very good selection of
home-cooked food. 🏨 Q ▱ 🕮
◖ ▶ ⇌ (MER) ♣ P

Kirk Michael

Mitre Hotel

Main Road ☎ (01624) 878244
12–11 (midnight Fri & Sat); 12–3,
7–10.30 Sun
Okells Bitter Ⓗ
Reputed to be the oldest pub
on the island, popular with
locals and visitors. Very
friendly hosts offer excellent
food. Live music, karaoke
nights and folk music.
🏨 Q ▱ 🕮 ◖ ▶ ◖ ♣ P

Laxey

Mines Tavern

Captain's Hill (at tram station)
☎ (01624) 861484
12–11 (midnight Fri & Sat); 12–3,
7–10.30 Sun
**Bushy's Best Bitter,
Manannan's Cloak; Okells
Bitter** Ⓗ

Pub popular with tram buffs
and locals. Note the tram
memorabilia and the bar
decked out in the style of
tramcar No.9, but this is still a
traditional pub, not a theme
pub. The track runs alongside.
🏨 🕮 ◖ ▶ ◖ ⊖ P

Queens Hotel

New Road ☎ (01624) 861195
12–11 (midnight Fri & Sat); 12–3,
7–10.30 Sun
**Bushy's Best Bitter; Okells
Bitter; guest beers** Ⓗ
Traditional, one-roomed
village pub, run for the benefit
of its customers. No food but
good barbecues in summer.
The trams run at the bottom of
the garden. Well patronised by
bikers during the TT races.
Good range of guest ales.
🏨 🕮 ▲ ◖ ⇌ (MER) P

Shore Hotel

Old Laxey ☎ (01624) 861509
12–11 (midnight Fri & Sat); 12–3,
7–10.30 Sun
**Okells Bitter; Old Laxey
Bosun Bitter** Ⓗ
A quasi-nautical theme
features in this traditional pub
with an excellent selection of
whiskies, set in a very pleasant
location, half a mile from the
shore, by the river. Old Laxey
Brewery is behind the pub. Eve
meals finish early.
🏨 🕮 ◖ ▶ ▲ ⊖ P

Onchan

Manx Arms

Main Road ☎ (01624) 675484
12–11 (midnight Fri & Sat); 12–3,
7–10.30 Sun
Okells Mild, Bitter Ⓗ
Large, busy pub in the village
centre, on the corner of the
former car racing course (see
the old photos). Family room
lunchtime. Good value food.
Q ▱ ◖ ◖ ♣ P

Peel

Whitehouse

2 Tynwald Road (near bus
station) ☎ (01624) 842252
12–11 (midnight Fri & Sat); 12–3,
7–10.30 Sun
**Draught Bass; Bushy's Best
Bitter; Flowers Original;
Okells Mild, Bitter; Old Laxey
Bosun Bitter; guest beers** Ⓗ
Comfortable, friendly pub with
a cosy snug (Captain's Cabin),
and a games and music room.
Past local CAMRA *Pub of the
Year.* 🏨 Q ▲ ♣ P

Port Erin

Falcon's Nest Hotel

Station Road ☎ (01624) 834072
12–11 (midnight Fri & Sat); 12–3,
7–10.30 Sun

**Boddingtons Bitter; Castle
Eden Ale; Flowers Original;
Okells Bitter; Tetley Bitter;
guest beers** Ⓗ
Friendly hotel by the beach,
with original features and
comfortable bars.
🏨 Q 🛏 ◖ ▶ ◖ ⇌ (IMR) ♣ P

Port St Mary

Albert

Athol Street ☎ (01624) 832118
12–11 (midnight Fri & Sat); 12–3,
7–10.30 Sun
**Bushy's Best Bitter; Cains
Mild; Flowers Original;
Okells Bitter; guest beers** Ⓗ
Friendly pub near the harbour,
popular with fishermen and
yacht crews. Wide range of
ales. 🏨 ◖ ◖ ♣

Ramsey

Swan

Parliament Square
☎ (01624) 814236
12–11 (midnight Fri & Sat); 12–3,
7–10.30 Sun
Okells Mild, Bitter Ⓗ
Situated on the TT course: a
popular pub with large lounge
and bar areas, and a garden at
the rear.
🕮 ◖ ◖ ▲ ⇌ (MER) ♣

Trafalgar

West Quay ☎ (01624) 814601
12–11 (midnight Fri & Sat); 12–3,
7–10.30 Sun
**Bushy's Best Bitter; Cains
Mild; guest beers** Ⓗ
Harbourside pub, popular
with harbour workers. Food is
served in the upstairs dining
room; the cosy bar is accessible
from one of the many lanes of
the shopping street.
◖ ▲ ⇌ (MER) ♣

St Johns

Farmers Arms

In front of St Johns cattle
market ☎ (01624) 801372
12–11 (midnight Fri & Sat); 12–3,
7–10.30 Sun
**Ind Coope Burton Ale; Okells
Bitter; guest beers** Ⓗ
Friendly village pub, busy on
market days with farmers.
Genial hosts; good food.
🏨 Q ◖ ◖ ♣ P

Sulby

Sulby Glen Hotel

☎ (01624) 897240
12–11 (midnight Fri & Sat); 12–3,
7–10.30 Sun
**Bushy's Best Bitter; Okells
Mild, Bitter** Ⓗ
Typical, friendly Manx pub on
the TT course (the Sulby
Straight). Local history and TT
memorabilia are displayed.
🏨 🕮 🛏 ◖ ▶ ◖ ◖ ▲ ♣ P

THE BREWERIES

THE BREWERIES

AFTER THE EUPHORIA of the past few years, when hundreds of new small breweries arrived to take advantage of the guest beer scene, the past year has brought many would-be producers down to earth with a bump. It looks as if we are reaching market saturation point, as numerous breweries have sadly departed in the last 12 months. Goodbye, but hopefully only au revoir, to the likes of Foxley, Hardington, Mill, New Ale and Whitby's. All is not doom and gloom, however – far from it. There are still more breweries opening up than closing down. No less than 48 new breweries have arrived this year and as we went to press several others were well advanced and looking to be on the bar in the near future. So look out for these names and others: Abbey Ales in Bath, The Abbey Arms in Blaenau Ffestiniog, Brecknock in Glamorgan, Tripple F in Hampshire, Teme Valley in Worcestershire and Frome Valley in Herefordshire.

OUT OF SEASON

It seems as if the trend towards seasonal and special ales may be drying up. One or two breweries have either exhausted their repertoire or have decided to concentrate once again on their core brews. Perhaps there has simply been too much choice in our pubs of late. Certainly the pressure on brewers to come up with new beer after new beer has been enormous, particularly from pubs keen to stock something different every week and drinkers who are always looking for an unusual pint.

NATIONAL TRENDS

Amongst the Nationals, it seems Whitbread is losing some of its enthusiasm for cask beer, having phased out most of its regional beers, ended its run of special brews and put more money into nitrokeg and other beer styles. At least the company's Hogshead Ale House concept is still buoyant. Also buoyant is the Firkin chain which continues to expand, upsetting many pub lovers in places where traditional pubs have been converted in Firkin style. However, the big event in the past year was the rejection of the merger of Bass and Carlsberg-Tetley by new President of the Board of Trade, Margaret Beckett. The merger would have created Britain's largest brewer, with 40 per cent of all beer production and would have had serious consequences for jobs, beer brands and beer prices.

However, rejection of the merger does not mean all is well. Carlsberg-Tetley faces an uncertain future, with Allied Domecq known to be keen to dispose of its share of the company, to concentrate on pub retailing. We could still see brewery closures (management buyouts would be clearly preferable) and brand rationalisation – Ind Coope Burton Ale, *Champion Beer of Britain* 1990, is believed to be heading for extinction.

The fact that, 25 years on from the first edition of the *Good Beer Guide*, big breweries are still seeking to concentrate beer production into fewer hands and dictate what people drink and in which sort of places they can drink it, proves once again that the *Guide* is as relevant as ever to anyone who appreciates good beer and good pubs.

KEY TO THE BREWERIES SECTION

Breweries are listed in alphabetical order. The Independents (including brew pubs) are listed first, followed by The Nationals. The major Pub Groups (non-brewing pub owning chains) complete the section. Within each brewery listing, beers are listed in increasing order of strength. Beers which are available for less than three months of the year are listed in the main brewery description as 'occasional' or 'seasonal' beers. Bottle-conditioned beers are also mentioned. These are bottled beers which have not been pasteurised and still contain yeast, allowing them to continue to ferment in the bottle just like draught real ale ferments in the cask. For more information about bottle-conditioned beers see the new *CAMRA Guide to Real Ale in a Bottle* (available from bookshops or direct from CAMRA at £7.99).

Symbols:

A brew pub: a pub which produces beer on the premises.

◆ CAMRA tasting notes (supplied by a trained CAMRA tasting panel). Beer descriptions not preceded by this symbol are based on limited tastings only or have been obtained from other sources. Tasting notes are not provided for brew pub beers which are available in less than five outlets, nor for other breweries' beers which are available for less than three months of the year.

🖫 A *Good Beer Guide Beer of the Year* in the last three years.

◼ One of the year's *Good Beer Guide Beers of the Year*, finalist in the *Champion Beer of Britain* contest held during the Great British Beer Festival at Olympia in August 1997 or in the *Champion Winter Beer of Britain* contest held in Glasgow in February 1997.

Abbreviations:

OG stands for Original Gravity, the reading taken before fermentation of the amount of fermentable material in the brew. It is a rough indicator of strength. More reliable is the ABV (Alcohol by Volume) rating, which gives the percentage of alcohol in the finished beer. Many breweries now only declare ABV figures, but where OGs are available these have been included.

ABC See Nationals, Carlsberg-Tetley.

ABBEYDALE
Abbeydale Brewery, Unit 8, Aizlewood Road, Sheffield, S. Yorkshire S8 0YX.
☎ (0114) 281 2712
FAX (0114) 281 2713

When it opened in September 1996, this brewery won immediate acclaim at the Sheffield Beer Festival with one of the first brews of its best bitter, Moonshine. Future plans include brewing special beers and experimenting with different flavourings.

Matins (OG 1035, ABV 3.5%)

Moonshine (OG 1041, ABV 4.3%)

Absolution (OG 1051, ABV 5.3%)

Black Mass (OG 1065, ABV 6.7%)

Last Rites (OG 1100, ABV 10.5%)

ABERDEENSHIRE
Aberdeenshire Ales Ltd., Ellon, Aberdeenshire.

Brewery closed.

ABINGTON PARK
See Nationals, Scottish Courage.

ADNAMS
Adnams and Company PLC, Sole Bay Brewery, East Green, Southwold, Suffolk IP18 6JW. ☎ (01502) 727200
FAX (01502) 727201

ADNAMS

East Anglia's seaside brewery, established in 1890, whose local deliveries are still made by horse drays. Real ale is available in all its 102 pubs, and it also supplies some 650 other outlets direct, with the beers available nationwide via agents. Gradual expansion is planned for the tied estate. Brewery shop open 10–6 Mon–Fri. Tours available for trade customers only. Seasonal beers: Oyster Stout (OG 1046, ABV 4.3%, October), Mayday (OG 1049, ABV 5%, mid-April–May), Barley Mow (OG 1050, ABV 5%), Tally Ho (OG 1075, ABV 6.5%, Christmas).

Mild (OG 1035, ABV 3.2%) ◈ In this fine black/red mild, the aroma is a subtle blend of fruit and malt with a hint of roast. A good balance of malt, roast and hops on a bittersweet base precedes a dry, faintly malty finish.

Bitter (OG 1036, ABV 3.7%) ▤ ◈ An excellent drinking beer, with the characteristic Adnams aroma of hops, citrus fruits and sulphur. The flavour is dry and hoppy, with some fruit. The finish is long, dry and hoppy.

Old Ale (OG 1041, ABV 4.1%) ▯ ▤ ◈ A rich, dark brown winter beer, a well-balanced blend of grain, roast malt and raisin, on a bittersweet base. The rich fruit aroma has faint roast and grain elements. Dry, faintly fruity aftertaste.

Extra (OG 1043, ABV 4.3%) ▯ ◈ An aroma of hops and citrus fruit leads through to bitter orange and hops on the palate, before a long dry, finish with some hops and fruit. *Champion Beer of Britain 1993.*

Regatta (OG 1044, ABV 4.3%) A summer beer, brewed July–September.

Broadside (OG 1049, ABV 4.7%) ◈ A mid-brown beer with a well-balanced flavour of fruit, malt and hops on a bittersweet base. The aroma is fruity, with some underlying malt and hops. Bitter fruit finish.

ALDCHLAPPIE

Aldchlappie Hotel, Kirkmichael, Perthshire & Kinross, PH10 7NS.
☎ (01250) 881224
FAX (01250) 881373

🍺 A microbrewery opened alongside this pub in 1996, initially as an experiment to produce two beers (a combination of full mash and malt extract) for its clientele of walkers and skiers. It has been so successful that plans are in hand to enlarge the plant to provide enough beer for all the hotel's needs, plus two beers for sale as guests. The beer names follow a Scottish/English history theme. Beers: 1707 (OG 1044, ABV 4.4%), 1314 (OG 1050, ABV 4.6%).

ALFORD ARMS
See Nationals, Whitbread.

ALL NATIONS
All Nations, Coalport Road, Madeley, Telford, Shropshire TF7 5DP.
☎ (01952) 585747

🍺 One of the very few brew pubs left before the new wave, All Nations has, in fact, been brewing for 200 years. Still known

as Mrs Lewis's, the inn has been in the same family since 1934. Beer: Pale Ale (OG 1032, ABV 3%).

ALLIED BREWERIES
See Nationals, Carlsberg-Tetley.

ALLOA See Nationals, Carlsberg-Tetley.

ANCIENT DRUIDS
Ancient Druids, Napier Street, Cambridge CB1 1HR. ☎ (01223) 576324
FAX (01223) 576323

🍺 Brew pub set up in 1984 by Charles Wells, brewing with malt extract. It occasionally supplies one or two other Wells pubs. Tours by arrangement. Beers: Druids' Mild, Pcella (a honey beer), Elle's SB (the ABVs tend to vary).

ANN STREET See Jersey.

ANSELLS
See Nationals, Carlsberg-Tetley.

ARCHERS

Archers Ales Ltd., Penzance Drive, Churchward, Swindon, Wiltshire SN5 7JL. ☎ (01793) 879929
FAX (01793) 879489

Brewery set up in 1979 in the old Great Western Railway works. Production of Archers' beers was moved in 1996 into the former weighbridge, now converted into a traditional tower brewery. The company supplies three tied houses and another 200 free trade outlets via wholesalers. Shop open 9–5. Tours by arrangement for customers and CAMRA groups.

Village Bitter (OG 1035, ABV 3.6%) ◈ A dry, well-balanced beer, with a full body for its gravity. Malty and fruity in the nose, then a fresh, hoppy flavour with balancing malt and a hoppy, fruity finish.

Best Bitter (OG 1040, ABV 4%) ◈ Slightly sweeter and rounder than Village, with a malty, fruity aroma and a pronounced bitter finish.

Black Jack Porter (OG 1046, ABV 4.6%) ◈ An autumn brew: a black beer with intense roast malt dominant on the tongue. The aroma is fruity and there is some sweetness on the palate, but the finish is pure roast grain.

Golden Bitter (OG 1046, ABV 4.7%) ◈ A full-bodied, hoppy, straw-coloured brew with an underlying fruity sweetness. Very little aroma, but a strong bitter finish.

Headbanger (OG 1065, ABV 6.3%) A sweet, strong beer with a pleasant, dry finish.

ARKELL'S

Arkell's Brewery Ltd.,
Kingsdown, Swindon,
Wiltshire SN2 6RU.
☎ (01793) 823026
FAX (01793) 828864

Established in 1843 and now one of the few remaining breweries whose shares are all held by one family, with its managing director, James Arkell, a great-great-grandson of founder John Arkell. A gradual expansion is taking place in the tied estate, mainly along the M4 corridor, and the brewery is committed to a continual programme of upgrading and refurbishment for its pubs. All 86 tied pubs serve real ale, which is also supplied direct to around 200 free trade accounts. Brewery tours by arrangement. Occasional/seasonal beers: Yeomanry (OG 1045, ABV 4.5%), Peter's Porter (OG 1050, ABV 4.8%), Noel Ale (OG 1055, ABV 5.5%, Christmas) – these may not be available in all Arkell's pubs and may need seeking out.

Bitter (OG 1032, ABV 3.2%) ◥ Formerly 2B: a hoppy, pale beer with a hint of fruit and honey. A most refreshing lunchtime or session ale, with good body for its OG.

3B (OG 1040, ABV 4%) ◥ An unusual and distinctive bitter. The crystal malt gives a nutty taste which persists throughout and combines with bitterness in the aftertaste.

Kingsdown Ale (OG 1052, ABV 5%) ◥ 3B's big brother with which it is parti-gyled (derived from the same mash). A powerful roast malt/fruit flavour is followed by a lingering, dry aftertaste.

ARUNDEL

Arundel Brewery, Unit C7,
Ford Airfield Estate, Ford,
Arundel, W. Sussex
BN18 0BE.
☎ (01903) 733111
FAX (01903) 733381

Set up in 1992, the town's first brewery in 60 years, Arundel produces beers from authentic Sussex recipes, without the use of additives. Its commitment to this tradition has led to steady growth and the brewery now supplies around 100 outlets, plus its single tied house, the Swan in Arundel. Old Knucker was named after a legendary dragon, who terrorised townsfolk before being slain by a local hero. Arundel has increased its range of occasional and seasonal beers and also brews a beer for Beards of Sussex (see Pub Groups). Tours by arrangement. Occasional/seasonal beers: Footslogger (OG 1044, ABV 4.4%), Summer Daze (OG 1047, ABV 4.7%, June), Old Conspirator (OG 1050, ABV 5%, Guy Fawkes Night), Romeo's Rouser (ABV 5.3%, Valentine's Day), Old Scrooge (OG 1060, ABV 6%, Christmas).

Best Bitter (OG 1040, ABV 4%) ◥ A pale tawny beer with fruit and malt noticeable in the aroma. The flavour exhibits a good balance of malt, fruit and hops, with a dry, hoppy finish.

Gold (OG 1042, ABV 4.2%) A light golden ale with a malty, fruity flavour and a little hop in the finish.

ASB (OG 1045, ABV 4.5%) A golden brown beer with roast malt and hop flavour giving way to a fruity, hoppy, bittersweet finish.

Stronghold (OG 1050, ABV 5%) ◥ A good balance of malt, fruit and hops come through in this rich, malty beer.

Old Knucker (OG 1055, ABV 5.5%) ◥ A dark, full-bodied beer. The flavour is a complex blend of sweet fruit and caramel maltiness, which balances a dry roast bitterness. This is mirrored in the aftertaste. Roast malt, fruit, caramel and some hops feature in the aroma. Brewed September–April.

For Beards:

Beards Best Bitter (OG 1040/ABV 4%) ◥ Hints of fruit and hops in the aroma lead into a sweet, malty beer, with a dry, hoppy aftertaste.

ASH VINE

Ash Vine Brewery (South West) Ltd., The White Hart, Trudoxhill, Frome, Somerset BA11 5DP.
☎ /FAX (01373) 836344

Celebrating its tenth anniversary in November 1997, Ash Vine has been brewing at the White Hart pub since 1989. The company acquired its third pub in 1995 when brewing capacity was increased by 50 per cent. Over 50 free trade outlets are supplied with real ale, while bottled Hop & Glory is widely available in supermarkets and may soon be brewed under licence in the USA. Ash Vine also brews two beers for the small wholesaler Quality Cask Ales ☎ (01373) 473591. Tours by arrangement. Bottle-conditioned beers: Penguin Porter (OG 1044, ABV 4.2%), Hop & Glory (OG 1052, ABV 5%).

Bitter (OG 1036, ABV 3.5%) ◥ A light gold bitter with a floral hop aroma. A powerful, bitter hoppiness dominates the taste and leads to a dry, and occasionally astringent, finish. An unusual and distinctive beer.

Challenger (OG 1043, ABV 4.1%) ◥ A mid-brown beer with a solid malt flavour balanced by a good hoppy bitterness and subtle citrus fruits. It can be sulphurous and slightly metallic.

Black Bess Porter (OG 1044, ABV 4.2%) ◥ A dark copper-brown, bitter porter with roast malt, hops and a sweet fruitiness. Roast malt and hop nose; dry, bitter finish. Bottled as Penguin Porter.

Hop & Glory (OG 1052, ABV 5%) ◥ A pale straw-coloured beer with a malt, fruit and hop aroma. The taste is bittersweet, with hops in abundance and some citrus fruits. Similar finish. A complex, rich and warming winter ale.

For Quality Cask Ales:

Munro's Mickey Finn (OG 1047, ABV 4.5%)

Six '5' Special (OG 1068, ABV 6.5%)

ASTON MANOR
Aston Manor Brewery Company Ltd., Birmingham, W. Midlands.

Brewery not in operation. Its PET bottle mild and bitter are now contract brewed.

AYLESBURY (ABC)
See Nationals, Carlsberg-Tetley.

B&T
B&T Brewery Ltd., The Brewery, Shefford, Bedfordshire SG17 5DZ.
☎ (01462) 815080
FAX (01462) 850841

Banks & Taylor, founded in 1981, fell into receivership in 1994 but was quickly rescued under the name of B&T, with key Banks & Taylor personnel retained to produce the same extensive range of beers, including the monthly special brews. The company now supplies around 60 outlets direct, including two pubs of its own. Brewery tours by arrangement. Occasional/seasonal beers: Midsummer Ale (OG 1035, ABV 3.5%), Bedfordshire Clanger (OG 1038, ABV 4%, March), Santa Slayer (OG 1040, ABV, 4%), Madhatter (OG 1042, ABV 4.2%, May), Maiden's Rescue (OG 1042, ABV 4.2%, April), Bodysnatcher (OG 1044, ABV 4.4%, October), Guy Fawkes Bitter (OG 1045, ABV 4.5%, November), Romeo's Ruin (OG 1045, ABV 4.5%, February), Emerald Ale (OG 1050, ABV 5%, March), Juliet's Revenge (OG 1050, ABV 5%, February), Shefford Wheat Beer (OG 1050, ABV 5%, July–August), Frostbite (OG 1055, ABV 5.5%, December–January), Bat out of Hell (OG 1060, ABV 6%, November), Skeleton Special (OG 1060, ABV 6%).

Shefford Bitter (OG 1038, ABV 3.8%) ◆ A pleasant, well-hopped session beer with a balance of malt and fruit aromas and flavours.

Shefford Mild (OG 1038, ABV 3.8%) ◆ A dark beer with a well-balanced taste. Sweetish, roast malt aftertaste.

Dragonslayer (OG 1045, ABV 4.5%) ◆ A straw-coloured beer, dry, malty and lightly hopped.

Edwin Taylor's Extra Stout (OG 1045, ABV 4.5%) ◼◆ A pleasant, bitter beer with a strong roast malt flavour.

Shefford Pale Ale (SPA) (OG 1045, ABV 4.5%) ◆ A well-balanced beer, with hop, fruit and malt flavours. Dry, bitter aftertaste.

Shefford Old Dark (SOD) (OG 1050, ABV 5%) ◆ SOS with caramel added for colour. Often sold under house names.

Shefford Old Strong (SOS) (OG 1050, ABV 5%) ◆ A rich mixture of fruit, hops and malt is present in the taste and aftertaste of this beer. Predominantly hoppy aroma.

Black Bat (OG 1060, ABV 6%) ◆ A powerful, sweet, fruity and malty beer for winter. Fruity, nutty aroma; strong roast malt aftertaste.

2XS (OG 1060, ABV 6%) ◆ A reddish beer with a strong, fruity, hoppy aroma. The taste is full-flavoured and the finish strong and sweetish.

Old Bat (OG 1070, ABV 7%) ◆ A powerful-tasting, sweet winter beer, with bitterness coming through in the aftertaste. Fruit is present in both aroma and taste.

BACKDYKES
Backdykes Brewing Company, Mid Strathore Farm, Strathore Road, Thornton, Fife KY1 4DF. ☎ (01592) 775303

This brewery was set up in a former dairy in 1995 and began production in January 1996. 'Malcolm's Severely Drinkable Ales' (named after the King of Scotland responsible for the death of Macbeth) are supplied to 20–30 free trade outlets. Tours by arrangement.

Malcolm's Ceilidh (ABV 3.7%) Sold South of the Border as Session.

Malcolm's Folly (ABV 4%)

Malcolm's Premier Ale (ABV 4.3%)

Malcolm's Golden Vale (ABV 4.4%)

BADGER
Hall & Woodhouse Ltd., The Badger Brewery, Blandford St Mary, Blandford Forum, Dorset DT11 9LS. ☎ (01258) 452141
FAX (01258) 459953

BADGER BREWERY

When Charles Hall founded the Ansty Brewery in 1777, it prospered by supplying beer to the troops fighting the French. In 1847, Charles's son took George Woodhouse into partnership, to create Hall & Woodhouse, although the company soon became known by its logo, featuring a badger. The Badger name, however, has only recently been adopted as its trading name, with alterations made to the beer range at the same time. Still largely family-run, the brewery, which moved to its present site in the 1890s, continues to broaden its trading area and is always on the lookout for new pubs in the South of England. All 190 of its houses take cask ale (although some use cask breathers) and a further 300 outlets are supplied direct. The brewery also owns the Gribble Inn brew pub in Oving, W. Sussex (qv). Shop open 9–7 Mon–Sat, 10–2 Sun. Tours by arrangement.

IPA (OG 1036, ABV 3.6%) A light, smooth, thin-bodied bitter with a slightly hoppy aftertaste. Always served with a creamy head.

Dorset Best (OG 1041, ABV 4.1%) ◆ A fine best bitter whose taste is strong in hop and bitterness, with underlying malt and fruit. Hoppy finish with a bitter edge.

Tanglefoot (OG 1050, ABV 5.1%) ◆ A pale-coloured beer, with a full fruit character throughout. Some malt and hops are also present in the palate, whilst the finish is bittersweet. Dangerously drinkable.

BALLARD'S

**Ballard's Brewery Ltd.,
Unit C, The Old Sawmill,
Nyewood, Petersfield,
Hampshire GU31 5HA.
☎ (01730) 821301
FAX (01730) 821742**

Founded in 1980 at Cumbers Farm, Trotton, Ballard's has been trading at Nyewood (in W. Sussex, despite the postal address) since 1988 and now supplies around 60 free trade outlets. Shop open 8.30–4.30 Mon–Fri (weekends by arrangement). Tours by arrangement. Occasional/seasonal beers: Golden Bine (OG 1042, ABV 4.2%), plus a Christmas ale with a gravity to match the number of the year. Bottle-conditioned beers: Wassail (OG 1060, ABV 6%), Old Pecker (ABV 9.7%).

Midhurst Mild (OG 1034, ABV 3.5%) A rarely seen, basic dark mild, brewed in autumn and winter.

Trotton Bitter (OG 1035, ABV 3.6%) ◆ Complex for its gravity, this well-balanced beer has an initial maltiness which fades to a hoppy finish.

Best Bitter (OG 1042, ABV 4.2%) ◆ A copper-coloured beer with a malty aroma. A good balance of fruit and malt in the flavour gives way to a dry, hoppy aftertaste.

Wild (ABV 4.7%) ◆ A dark brown beer, produced for autumn and winter, by blending Mild with Wassail. Initial hints of fruit give way to a malty flavour and a dry, hoppy aftertaste.

Nyewood Gold (OG 1050, ABV 5%) A light golden, hoppy beer from the start to the dry finish.

Wassail (OG 1060, ABV 6%) ◆ A strong, full-bodied, fruity beer with a predominance of malt throughout, but also an underlying hoppiness. Tawny/red in colour.

BANKS & TAYLOR See B&T.

BANKS'S

**The Wolverhampton &
Dudley Breweries PLC, PO
Box 26, Park Brewery, Bath
Road, Wolverhampton,
W. Midlands WV1 4NY.
☎ (01902) 711811 FAX (01902) 29136**

Wolverhampton & Dudley Breweries was formed in 1890 by the amalgamation of three local companies. Hanson's was acquired in 1943, but its Dudley brewery was closed in 1991 and its beers are now brewed at Wolverhampton. The 100 Hanson's pubs keep their own livery. In 1992, W&D bought Camerons Brewery and 51 pubs from Brent Walker. The total estate for the whole group now stands at 1,119 houses, virtually all serving traditional ales, mostly through electric, metered dispense. The company also has 20 'Taphouses', cask alehouses which also sell Taphouse Bitter, a general name given to various Banks's brews prepared from different recipes. There is also extensive free trade throughout the country, particularly in clubs. Tours by arrangement.

Hanson's Bitter (OG 1035, ABV 3.3%)

Hanson's Mild (OG 1035, ABV 3.3%) ◆ A mid- to dark brown mild with a malty roast flavour and aftertaste.

Mild (OG 1036, ABV 3.5%) ◆ Also known as Banks's Ale, or simply Banks's. A top-selling, amber-coloured, well-balanced, refreshing light mild.

Bitter (OG 1039, ABV 3.8%) ◆ A pale brown bitter with a pleasant balance of hops and malt. Hops continue from the taste through to a bittersweet aftertaste.

BANK TOP

Bank Top Brewery, Unit 1, Back Lane, off Vernon Street, Bolton, Greater Manchester BL1 2LD. ☎ (01204) 528865

John Feeney learned about the brewing business at Sunderland University and then at Thomas McGuinness Brewery. In 1995, he set up this brewery, originally as a partnership, but now runs it on his own. His award-winning beers are supplied to 40–50 outlets locally, and John has plans to infiltrate Yorkshire. Tours by arrangement. Seasonal beer: Santa's Claws (OG 1048, ABV 5%, Christmas).

Bridge Bitter (OG 1036, ABV 3.8%)

Goldrush (OG 1038, ABV 4%)

Fred's Cap (OG 1039, ABV 4%)

Samuel Crompton's Ale (OG 1040, ABV 4.2%)

Cliffhanger (OG 1044, ABV 4.5%)

Satanic Mills (OG 1048, ABV 5%)

Smokestack Lightnin' (OG 1048, ABV 5%)

BARLEY See Fox & Hounds.

BARNFIELD

Barnfield Brewery, Unit 3F,
Spa Field Industrial Estate,
Slaithwaite, Huddersfield,
W. Yorkshire HD7 5BB.
☎ (01484) 845757

This new brewery was set up in February 1997 in premises formerly occupied by Wild's Brewery (now ceased trading), using equipment purchased from the Wortley Arms brewery in Sheffield, which closed in November 1996. The first beers were brewed using Wortley Arms recipes. The brewery currently supplies ten free trade outlets. Tours by arrangement.

Bitter (ABV 3.8%) A light, malty and hoppy bitter with a gentle, bitter finish.

Earls Ale (ABV 4.3%) A medium-bodied bitter with a malty and fruity character which leaves a clean and dry aftertaste.

Countess Ale (ABV 5.3%) A dark, full-bodied, strong bitter with a pleasant, fruity and hoppy taste; slightly bitter with a sweet finish.

Bloody Hell Fire (ABV 6%) A dark, full-bodied, strong ale with chocolate overtones and a slightly sweet finish.

BARNGATES See Drunken Duck.

BARNSLEY

Barnsley Brewing Co. Ltd.,
Wath Road, Elsecar,
Barnsley, S. Yorkshire
S74 8HJ. ☎ (01226) 741010
FAX (01226) 741009

Established in 1994 as the South Yorkshire Brewing Company, Barnsley changed its name in 1996. It brews with an old yeast culture from the town's long-defunct Oakwell Brewery. Demand continues to grow, and the company has plans to increase production capacity and to start producing keg beer for clubs. Around 200 outlets are supplied with the real thing and a new cask ale was added to the range in March 1997.

Bitter (OG 1037, ABV 3.8%) 🗂 🍺 A smooth ruby/mid-brown-coloured beer which has little aroma, but an even balance of malt and hops in the taste compensates. A distinctive bitter with a lasting aftertaste.

Oakwell (ABV 4%)

IPA (OG 1041, ABV 4.2%) A beer dominated by fruit and hops, leading on to a hoppy finish. Yellowish in colour; flowery aroma.

Black Heart Stout (OG 1044, ABV 4.6%) 🍺 A black stout with a hoppy aroma, and lots of roasted malt flavour throughout. Chocolatey, bitter finish. Hard to find.

BASS See Nationals.

BATEMAN

George Bateman & Son
Ltd., Salem Bridge Brewery,
Wainfleet, Lincolnshire
PE24 4JE. ☎ (01754) 880317
FAX (01754) 880939

A family-owned and -run brewery, established in 1874 by an erstwhile farmer, the grandfather of present chairman George Bateman. In the mid-1980s a family dispute threatened the brewery's future, but, after a three-year battle, George secured the brewery's independence and is now steadily expanding its sales area to cover nearly the whole of the UK. Around 200 outlets are supplied direct and Bateman owns 59 houses which all serve real ale. Shop open 9–5 Mon–Fri. Tours by arrangement. Occasional/seasonal beers: two new seasonal ranges have been introduced, Mr George's Unique Flavours – beers with added vanilla, toffee, etc. – and Mystic Brews – a beer for each sign of the zodiac. Unique Flavours: Flower Power (OG 1038, ABV 3.7%, elderflower, May–June), Jaw Breaker (OG 1041, ABV 4%, toffee, March–April), Yellow Belly Bitter (OG 1041, ABV 4%, vanilla, July–August), Farmers Quencher (OG 1048, ABV 4.6%, wheat and cloves, September–October), Coopers Tipple (OG 1049, ABV 5%, Scotch whisky, November–December). Mystic Brews: Virgo (OG 1037, ABV 3.8%), Pisces (OG 1037, ABV 3.9%), Cancer (OG 1040, ABV 3.9%), Leo (OG 1041, ABV 4%), Sagittarius (OG 1042, ABV 4%), Aries (OG 1041, ABV 4.1%), Libra (OG1043, ABV 4.1%), Capricorn (OG 1043, ABV 4.2%), Aquarius (OG 1043, ABV 4.4%), Gemini (OG 1043, ABV 4.4%), Scorpio (OG 1043, ABV 4.4%), Taurus (OG 1046, ABV 4.5%). Bateman also brews under contract for the non-brewing Sherwood Forest Brewery ☎ (0115) 911 8822.

Dark Mild (OG 1033, ABV 3%) 🗂 🍺 🍺 A complex ruby/black mild, with a roast malt and orchard fruit nose, and a hoppy, bitter finish.

XB (OG 1037, ABV 3.7%) 🍺 A pale brown beer, with a strong hop presence throughout. Malt is always there, playing a fine supporting role, whilst there is orchard fruitiness on the nose. Bitter and refreshing.

Hill Billy Bitter (OG 1043, ABV 4.2%)

Valiant (OG 1043, ABV 4.2%) 🍺 An old-gold-coloured beer featuring hop on the nose with apple fruit. The taste is well-rounded, with malt joining the mixture. Not as bitter as others from the brewery. It can be hard to find in the tied estate.

Salem Porter (OG 1049, ABV 4.7%) 🗂 🍺 🍺 A beautiful, complex, black beer, perhaps best sampled on gravity dispense. The orchard fruit and hop nose are distinctive, leading to a roast malt and liquorice taste and a bitter finish.

XXXB (OG 1050, ABV 4.8%) 🍺 🍺 A powerful, dark amber ale that has an aroma of the orchard, a hoppy bitterness that grows and underlying malt. Very drinkable.

Victory Ale (OG 1059, ABV 5.7%) ◆ Light chestnut in colour, Victory has a dominating banana fruitiness, joined by malt and hops in the finish.

For Sherwood Forest:

Lionheart Ale (ABV 4.2%)

BATH

Bath Ales, c/o Barvick Engineering, Bow Bridge Works, Henstridge, Somerset BA8 0HE.
☎ **(0117) 907 1797**
FAX **(0117) 909 5140**

Brewery founded in 1995 by two former Smiles Brewery employees, using the same brewing plant as Henstridge Brewery (qv). Bath supplies its own pub, plus around 150 other outlets, but not on a regular basis. The company still aims to move into premises in Bath itself at the earliest opportunity. Tours occasionally by arrangement.

SPA (OG 1038, ABV 3.7%) ◆ A refreshing, dry bitter beer, medium-bodied and full-flavoured, with lots of malt and a good apple/citrus fruit/floral hop taste. The aroma is of pale and lager malts and citric hops. Long, pale malty, bitter finish, with some fruit. Golden yellow in colour.

Gem (OG 1042, ABV 4.1%) ■ ◆ A medium-bodied, well-hopped, dry bitter with good malt, hints of chocolate and a little balancing sweetness. The aroma is of malt and fruit (notably blackcurrant) and the good finish has fruit, malt and dryness. Pale brown/amber in colour.

Barnstormer (OG 1046, ABV 4.5%) ◆ A smooth, well-crafted, mid-brown ale. The aroma is a combination of malt, a little roasted malt and chocolate, hops and fruit. On the palate it has a well-balanced mix of malt/roast/chocolate and bittersweet fruits, before a complex malt and bitter finish.

BATHAM

Daniel Batham & Son Ltd., Delph Brewery, Delph Road, Brierley Hill, W. Midlands DY5 2TN.
☎ **(01384) 77229**
FAX **(01384) 482292**

Small brewery established in 1877 and now in its fifth generation of family ownership. Batham's sympathetic programme of upgrading and refurbishment in its tied estate has been rewarded by winning CAMRA's 1996 *Joe Goodwin Award* for pub refurbishment for the Vine (or Bull & Bladder), one of the Black Country's most famous pubs and the site of the brewery. The company has recently acquired a tenth tied house, the historic Britannia in Upper Gornal, which has now ceased brewing in its

own right. A further 20 free trade outlets are supplied. Tours are no longer available. Occasional/seasonal beers: AJ's Mild Ale (OG 1049, ABV 5%), XXX (OG 1063, ABV 6.3%, Christmas).

Mild Ale (OG 1037, ABV 3.5%) ◆ A fruity, dark brown mild with a malty sweetness and a roast malt finish.

Best Bitter (OG 1044, ABV 4.3%) ▯ ◆ A pale yellow, fruity, sweetish bitter, with a dry, hoppy finish. A good, light, refreshing beer when on form.

BATTLE See Rother Valley.

BAYNARDS

Baynards Brewhouse, The Thurlow Arms, Baynards, Rudgwick, W. Sussex RH12 3AD. ☎ **(01403) 822459**
FAX **(01403) 822125**

▯ Brewery established in February 1996 (in Surrey despite the W. Sussex postal address), using equipment transferred from the owner's brother's pub, the Cyder House Inn at Shackleford. Tours by arrangement. Beers: Station House Brew (ABV 4.2%), Old Shunter (ABV 4.8%), Tunnel Vision (ABV 6%).

BEARDS See Arundel and Pub Groups.

BEARTOWN

Beartown Brewery, Unit 9, Varey Road, Eaton Bank Trading Estate, Congleton, Cheshire CW12 1UW.
☎ **(01260) 299964**
FAX **(01260) 274263**

Congleton's links with brewing can be traced back to 1272, when the town received charter status. Two of its most senior officers at the time were Ale Taster and Bear Warden, hence the name of this brewery, set up in 1994 on land which once housed a silk mill. Still run by two partners on a part-time basis, the brewery supplies around 15 free trade outlets. Tours by arrangement. Seasonal/occasional beer: Spirityule Ale (OG 1055, ABV 5.5%, Christmas).

Ambeardextrous (OG 1036, ABV 3.8%) ◆ A mid-brown, well-balanced bitter with coffee and chocolate notes.

Bear Ass (OG 1038, ABV 4%)

Hoppy Rambler (OG 1038, ABV 4%) A summer brew.

Bearskinful (OG 1040, ABV 4.2%) ◆ A tawny, malty beer, with a clean hop finish.

Polar Eclipse Oatmeal Stout (OG 1046, ABV 4.8%) ◆ A smooth and roasty, dark beer with chocolate notes and a dryish finish.

Bruin's Ruin (OG 1048, ABV 5%) ◆ A smooth, darkish and well-balanced beer, with a hint of roast.

BECKETT'S

Beckett's Brewery Ltd.,
8 Enterprise Court,
Basingstoke, Hampshire
RG24 8GE.
☎ (01256) 472986
FAX (01256) 703205

After 16 years working for Fuller's, Richard Swinhoe took the plunge and set up his own brewery in March 1997. The first brewery in Basingstoke for 50 years, Beckett's portfolio is to be based on three mainstream brews, plus seasonal beers to be introduced as the business becomes established.

Best Bitter (OG 1041, ABV 4%)

BEECHAM'S

Beecham's Bar & Brewery,
Westfield Street, St Helens,
Merseyside WA10 1PZ.
☎ (01744) 623420

Full mash brewery opened in 1997 as a training facility for students at St Helens College. The students not only learn to brew but also how to be a successful licensee. The public are welcome to use the bar which is housed beneath the town's famous Beecham's clock tower, in buildings donated by the Beecham's Powders company. Beers: Dark Mild (ABV 4.5%), BBB (ABV 4.7%).

BEER ENGINE

The Beer Engine,
Sweetham, Newton St
Cyres, Exeter, Devon
EX5 5AX. ☎ (01392) 851282

Brew pub set up in 1983, next to the Barnstaple branch railway line (hence the beer names). Two other outlets are supplied regularly and the beers are also distributed via agencies. Tours by arrangement. Occasional/seasonal beers: Return Ticket (OG 1033, ABV 3.4%, a summer mild), Porter (OG 1042, ABV 4.3%), Whistlemas (ABV 6.1%, Christmas).

Rail Ale (OG 1036, ABV 3.8%) ✦ A straw-coloured beer with a fruity aroma and a sweet, fruity finish.

Piston Bitter (OG 1043, ABV 4.3%) ✦ A mid-brown, sweet-tasting beer with a pleasant, bittersweet aftertaste.

Sleeper Heavy (OG 1054, ABV 5.4%) ✦ A red-coloured beer with a fruity, sweet taste and a bitter finish.

BEER SELLER See Hampshire.

BELCHERS See Hedgehog & Hogshead.

ꞎ The pub sign indicates a brew pub: a pub which produces beer on the premises.

BELHAVEN

Belhaven Brewery Co. Ltd.,
Belhaven Brewery Group
PLC, Spott Road, Dunbar,
Lothian EH42 1RS.
☎ (01368) 862734
FAX (01368) 864450

With a tradition of brewing going back almost 800 years, Scotland's oldest brewery has had a chequered recent history. It was bought in 1989 by the London-based Control Securities PLC, but in 1993 its employees successfully engineered a management buyout of the brewery. It continues to produce award-winning beers, supplying all of its 69 houses, and a further 300 outlets, with cask beer. Tours by arrangement. Occasional beer: 90/- (OG 1071, ABV 8%) ❖

60/- Ale (OG 1030, ABV 2.9%) ✦ A fine, but sadly rare, example of a Scottish light: a reddish-brown beer dominated by malt throughout. Roast is evident, with fruit in the aftertaste. Characteristic Belhaven sulphury nose.

70/- Ale (OG 1035, ABV 3.5%) ✦ An underrated malty, bittersweet, pale brown beer in which hops and fruit are increasingly evident in the aftertaste. The Belhaven sulphury nose is noticeable.

Sandy Hunter's Traditional Ale (OG 1038, ABV 3.6%) ✦ A distinctive, medium-bodied beer named after a past chairman and head brewer. An aroma of malt, hops and characteristic sulphur greets the nose. A hint of roast combines with the malt and hops to give a bittersweet taste and finish.

80/- Ale (OG 1041, ABV 4.2%) ✦ An incredibly robust, malty beer with the characteristic sulphury aroma. This classic ale has a burst of complex flavours and a rich, bittersweet finish.

St Andrew's Ale (OG 1046, ABV 4.9%) ✦ A bittersweet beer with plenty of body. There are malt and fruit in the taste, with a developing hop character leading to an increasingly bitter aftertaste. Beware of the nitrokeg beer with the same name.

BELVOIR

Belvoir Brewery Ltd.,
Woodhill, Nottingham
Lane, Old Dalby,
Leicestershire LE14 3LX.
☎ / FAX (01664) 823455

Brewery founded at the edge of the Vale of Belvoir by a former Theakston and Shipstone's brewer in 1995, with equipment largely obtained from the defunct Shipstone's Brewery. Occasional/seasonal beers: Peacock's Glory (OG 1047, ABV 4.7%), Beaver Special (ABV 4.9%), Owd Merry (ABV 6%, Christmas).

Whippling Golden Bitter (OG 1036, ABV 3.6%) Brewed for spring and summer.

Star Bitter (OG 1039, ABV 3.9%) A beer designed to replicate the bitter flavour of the old Shipstone's Bitter.

Beaver Bitter (OG 1043, ABV 4.3%) ◆ A light brown bitter, which starts malty in both aroma and taste, but soon develops a hoppy bitterness. Appreciably fruity.

Old Dalby (OG 1051, ABV 5.1%) A winter brew.

BENSKINS
See Nationals, Carlsberg-Tetley.

BEOWULF
The Beowulf Brewing Company, Waterloo Buildings, 14 Waterloo Road, Yardley, Birmingham, W. Midlands B25 8JR. ☎ (0121) 706 4116 FAX (0121) 706 0735

Five-barrel brewery opened in old shop premises in February 1997 and selling its one beer to the free trade and as a guest beer mostly in the Black Country, Shropshire and Warwickshire.

Heroes Bitter (OG 1046, ABV 4.7%)

BERKELEY
Berkeley Brewing Co., The Brewery, Bucketts Hill Farm, Berkeley, Gloucestershire GL13 9NZ. ☎ (01453) 811895

This small operation was set up in an old farm cider cellar in 1994, but did not start brewing full-time until October 1996 when the beer range was expanded to include seasonal ales. Twenty-five free trade outlets are supplied. Tours by arrangement. Seasonal beers: Late Starter (OG 1047, ABV 4.8%, October–November), Christmas Ale (OG 1048, ABV 4.9%, December), Old (OG 1052, ABV 5.3%, January–February).

Old Friend (OG 1037, ABV 3.8%) ◆ A hoppy aroma introduces this golden, fruity, hoppy beer which has a moderately hoppy, bitter finish.

Dicky Pearce (OG 1042, ABV 4.3%) ◆ A copper-coloured best bitter, with a hoppy aroma. A good balance of hop and malt in the mouth leads to a rich, bittersweet aftertaste.

Early Riser (OG 1047, ABV 4.8%) Available March–June.

Lord's Prayer (OG 1049, ABV 5%) Brewed July–September.

BERROW
Berrow Brewery, Coast Road, Berrow, Somerset TA8 2QU. ☎ (01278) 751345

Brewery founded in 1982 to supply pubs and clubs

locally (about 15 direct free trade outlets). Tours by arrangement.

4Bs (OG 1038, ABV 3.9%) ◆ A pleasant, pale brown session beer, with a fruity aroma, a malty, fruity flavour and bitterness in the palate and finish.

Porter (OG 1045, ABV 4.5%)

Topsy Turvy (TT) (OG 1055, ABV 6%) ◆ A straw-coloured beer with an aroma of malt and hops, which are also evident in the taste, together with sweetness. The aftertaste is malty. Very easy to drink. Beware!

BIG LAMP
Big Lamp Brewers, Big Lamp Brewery, Grange Road, Newburn, Newcastle upon Tyne, Tyne & Wear NE15 8NL. ☎ (0191) 267 1689

Big Lamp was set up in 1982 and changed hands at the end of 1990. Currently undergoing phased development, the brewery has acquired a second tied house, which is effectively the brewery tap at the company's new premises, a converted water pumping station where brewing commenced in February 1997. Tours by arrangement.

Bitter (OG 1038, ABV 3.9%) 🗂 🍴 ◆ Hops dominate this amber ale from aroma to aftertaste. Solid body; some sweetness.

Prince Bishop Ale (OG 1048, ABV 4.8%) ◆ A rich and fruity beer with a complex character and smooth body. Maltiness is strong and lasting, but look for the light, but spiky, bitterness.

Summerhill or Mulligan's Stout (OG 1048, ABV 4.8%) ◆ Another beer with many features, including a rich roast aroma and a malty mouthfeel. Look for a light bitterness and some sweetness.

Premium (OG 1052, ABV 5.2%) ◆ A solid bitter, well flavoured, with a big nose and strong, hoppy impact. Sweetness lasts to give a mellow taste merging into a dry finish.

Winter Warmer (OG 1055, ABV 5.5%) ◆ A strong bitter, fortified with roast malt character and rich maltiness. Try it for its mouthfeel and lasting bitterness.

BIRD IN HAND
Wheal Ale Brewery Ltd., Paradise Park, Hayle, Cornwall TR27 4HY. ☎ (01736) 753974

🍺 Unusual brewery in a bird park, founded in 1980 as Paradise Brewery and now brewing intermittently. Beers: Paradise Bitter (OG 1040, ABV 3.8%), Miller's Ale (OG 1045, ABV 4.3%), Artists Ale (OG 1055, ABV 5.1%), Old Speckled Parrot (ABV 6.3%).

BISHOPS
**Bishops Brewery, 2 Park
Street, Borough Market,
London SE1 9AB.**
☎/[FAX] **(0171) 357 8343**

Small brewery established in 1993 by
the former brewer at the Market Porter brew
pub. The brewery has grown in strength and
reputation and, since switching to full mash
production in 1996, its trade has increased
dramatically, well beyond its South-East
London home. Bishops supplies 20 free
trade outlets in Greater London direct, and
opened its first pub in early summer 1997.
Tours by arrangement (May–August).
Seasonal beer: Holy Grail (ABV 5.2%,
Christmas).

Cathedral Bitter (OG 1037, ABV 3.7%) 🍺 A
light golden brown bitter. Crisp hoppiness is
present from the aroma through to the
finish, with a fruitiness also present.
Astringently bitter.

Thirsty Willies (ABV 3.7%) A straw-
coloured session beer, made from Bramling
Cross and Styrian Goldings. Delightfully
hoppy, it has a delicate, acidic freshness that
makes it refreshing.

Mitre Best Bitter (ABV 4.2%) A richly
hopped, malty beer with a delicate bitter
taste. The late hopping adds to the character
of this complex ale.

Cardinal Winter Ale (OG 1047, ABV 4.7%)
A darkish beer, almost ruby-coloured. Its
full-bodied taste has a strong hop content,
with malt and subtle, fruity undertones to
balance.

Willies Revenge (ABV 4.7%) A golden beer
with a mouthwatering, hoppy aroma and a
delicate, dry finish.

BITTER END
**The Bitter End Brewing Co., 15 Kirkgate,
Cockermouth, Cumbria CA13 9PJ.**
☎ **(01900) 828993**

🍺 Bitter End opened in 1995, housed in a
derelict building which had been used as
a pub until 1974. The one-barrel plant can be
viewed from the bar and lounge. Both the
regular beers and the seasonals which are
produced are only sold in the pub itself.

Cockersnoot (OG 1038, ABV 3.8%)

Skinners Old Strong (OG 1054, ABV 5.5%)

BLACKAWTON
**Blackawton Brewery,
Washbourne, Totnes,
Devon TQ9 7UF.**
☎ **(01803) 732339**
[FAX] **(01803) 732151**

Situated just outside the village of
Washbourne, this small family brewery was
founded in 1977 and is now the oldest in
Devon. It originated in the village of
Blackawton, but moved to its present site in
1981 and, although it changed ownership in

1988, it retains a loyal local following for its
additive-free beers. These are served in
around 50 free trade outlets, but Blackawton
has no pubs of its own. Occasional beer: Dart
Mild (OG 1036, ABV 3.6%). Bottle-
conditioned beer: Devon Gold Export (OG
1045, ABV 5%, occasional).

Bitter (OG 1037, ABV 3.8%) 🍺 Tawny in
colour, with a bitter/fruity taste and a bitter
aftertaste.

Devon Gold (OG 1038, ABV 4.1%) A straw-
coloured summer brew, available April–
October.

Shepherds Delight (OG 1042, ABV 4.6%)
🍺 A wheat beer for springtime: a pale
brown beer with a complex bitter/fruity
taste and finish.

44 Special (OG 1043, ABV 4.5%) 🍺 A tawny,
fruity-flavoured bitter with a slightly sweet
taste and finish.

Winter Fuel (OG 1048, ABV 5%) Available
in winter.

Headstrong (OG 1049, ABV 5.2%) 🍺 A mid-
brown, strong beer, with a pleasant, fruity,
sweet taste and finish.

BLACKBEARD
See Fox & Hounds and Freeminer.

BLACK BULL
**Black Bull Brewery, Ashes
Farm, Ashes Lane, Fenny
Bentley, Ashbourne,
Derbyshire DE6 1LD.**
☎/[FAX] **(01335) 350581**

Brewery opened as a part-time venture by a
keen home brewer in 1994. He moved the
brewery to a larger, converted building on
his farm in summer 1996 to provide greater
capacity to serve a steadily growing trade.
Tours by arrangement.

Dovedale Bitter (OG 1036, ABV 3.6%) A
light straw-coloured summer beer, partly
hopped with American lager hops.

Best Bitter (OG 1040, ABV 4%) A ruby-
coloured, well-hopped bitter.

Anklecracker (OG 1041, ABV 4.2%) A
summer beer.

Raging Bull (OG 1049, ABV 4.9%) A light
copper-coloured beer, similar to the best
bitter but stronger.

Jacobs Ladder (Dovedale Special) (OG
1050, ABV 5%) A stronger version of
Dovedale.

Owd Shrovetide (OG 1060, ABV 5.9%) A
winter warmer, available October–February.

BLACKBURN
**Blackburn Brewing
Company, 39 King Street,
Blackburn, Lancashire
BB2 2DW.** ☎ **(01254) 698111**

🍺 Opened in the autumn of 1996, this pub/
brewery was built on two levels. The

brewery on the ground floor supplies the Cellar Bar downstairs. Up to ten other local outlets also take the beers which are more widely available via wholesalers. Tours by arrangement.

BBC3 (ABV 3.8%) A dark beer, with a well-balanced hop and malt flavour which gives way to a chocolate aftertaste.

BBC2 (ABV 4.1%) A beer that makes the best use of crystal malt, with a good hop flavour.

BBC1 (ABV 4.4%) ◥ A pale amber brew beginning malty on the nose and tongue then developing a delicate but persistent hoppiness before a dry finish. Deceptively drinkable for its strength.

BLACK HORSE
Black Horse Brewery, Victoria Buildings, Burnley Road, Luddenfoot, Halifax, W. Yorkshire HX2 6AR. ☎ (01422) 885930

Brewery founded in 1995 at Walkleys Clogs centre in Hebden Bridge, sharing facilities with Eastwood's Brewery until its relocation to Luddenfoot, when the two breweries parted company. Black Horse Brewery is now located in a former textile mill on the Rochdale Canal, and currently supplies around 20 outlets locally. Tours by arrangement.

Bitter (OG 1040, ABV 4%) A well-balanced, golden beer with a light, hoppy taste and aroma.

Spur (OG 1044, ABV 4.4%) A well-balanced premium bitter, golden in colour, with a hoppy taste and aroma.

Shire (ABV 5%) A single malt beer which is pale in colour, with a smooth, clean taste and light, hoppy aroma.

Black Stallion (OG 1053, ABV 5.3%) A porter with a rich, roasted barley flavour and a distinctive taste.

BLACK HORSE & RAINBOW
See Liverpool.

BLACKMOOR
Blackmoor Brewery, Batley, W. Yorkshire.

Brewery closed.

◥ The tilted glass indicates CAMRA tasting notes (supplied by a trained CAMRA tasting panel). Beer descriptions not preceded by this symbol are based on limited tastings only or have been obtained from other sources.

BLACK SHEEP
The Black Sheep Brewery PLC, Wellgarth, Masham, Ripon, N. Yorkshire HG4 3EN. ☎ (01765) 689227 FAX (01765) 689746

Set up in 1992 by Paul Theakston, a member of Masham's famous brewing family, in the former Wellgarth Maltings, Black Sheep now supplies a free trade of almost 400 outlets, in the Yorkshire Dales and within a 70-mile-radius of Masham, but it owns no pubs. A limited number of wholesalers is also supplied. Most of the output is fermented in Yorkshire slate squares, although some Yorkshire stainless rounds have been added to cope with demand. A second fermenting room, opened in summer 1997, has taken the brewery's capacity up to 1,000 barrels a week. There is a visitor centre, incorporating a shop (open 10–5.30 daily), bar and bistro (open 10–5 Mon, 10am–11pm Tue–Sun). Tours by arrangement.

Best Bitter (OG 1039, ABV 3.8%) ◥ A predominantly bitter beer with an underlying balance of malt, hops and fruit, leading to a long, dry, mainly bitter finish.

Special Bitter (OG 1046, ABV 4.4%) ◥ A warming, very bitter beer with a good helping of hops and fruit in both the taste and aroma. The finish is long and well balanced.

Riggwelter (OG 1056, ABV 5.9%) ◥ A fruity bitter, with complex underlying tastes and hints of liquorice and pear drops leading to a long, dry, bitter finish.

BLEWITTS
Blewitts Brewery, The Ship & Plough, The Promenade, Kingsbridge, Devon TQ7 1JD. ☎ (01548) 852485

Brewery established in 1991 which moved for a while to a business park before returning to its original home, the Ship & Plough. Only brewing for the one pub, its range has been slimmed down in the last year. Tours by arrangement. Beers: Best (OG 1038, ABV 3.8%), Wages (OG 1045, ABV 4.5%), Head Off (OG 1050, ABV 5%).

BLUE ANCHOR
Blue Anchor, 50 Coinagehall Street, Helston, Cornwall TR13 8EX. ☎ (01326) 562821

Historic thatched brew pub, possibly the oldest in the UK, originating as a monks' resting place in the 15th century. It produces powerful ales known locally as 'Spingo' beers. Tours by arrangement. Beers: Middle (OG 1050, ABV 5.1%), Best (OG 1056, ABV 5.7%), Special (OG 1066, ABV 6.6%), Easter and Christmas Special (OG 1076, ABV 7.6%).

BLUE BOAR
Blue Boar Inn, Oulton Village, Lowestoft, Suffolk.

Brewery closed.

BLUE COW
The Blue Cow Inn and Brewery, 29 High Street, South Witham, Grantham, Lincolnshire NG33 5QB.
☎ /FAX **(01572) 768432**

Landlord Dick Thirlwell installed a four-barrel brew plant himself in a converted outbuilding at his pub and started brewing here in March 1997. His full mash beers (stored in both casks and cellar tanks) were immediately appreciated by his customers, not least because of the low prices. Two other local outlets are supplied. Beers: Thirlwell Best Bitter (OG 1039, ABV 3.8%), Templars Tipple (OG 1042, ABV 3.8%), Witham Wobbler (OG 1043, ABV 4.2%).

BLUE MOON
The Blue Moon Brewery, Pearces Farm, Seamere, Hingham, Norfolk NR9 4LP. ☎ **(01953) 851625**

After nearly 20 years in the pub trade, former publican Peter Turner opted for a quieter life as a brewer. He opened the Blue Moon Brewery at his farm in January 1997, with plans to brew 200 gallons a week for the local club trade, free houses and private functions. Tours by arrangement.

Easy Life (OG 1036, ABV 3.8%)

Dark Side (OG 1041, ABV 4%)

Virgin Firkin (OG 1042, ABV 4.2%)

Hingham High (OG 1054, ABV 5.2%)

Milk of Amnesia (OG 1058, ABV 5.5%)

Liquor Mortis (OG 1060, ABV 6.2%)

BODDINGTONS
See Nationals, Whitbread.

BODICOTE See Plough Inn.

BORDER
Border Brewery Company, The Old Kiln, Brewery Lane, Tweedmouth, Berwick-upon-Tweed, Northumberland TD15 2AH. ☎ **(01289) 303303** FAX **(01289) 306115**

Do not confuse with the Wrexham brewery taken over and closed by Marston's; this operation opened in 1992 in an old kiln, on the site of Berwick's original (defunct) Border Brewery, which was established in the 17th century. A change in ownership

took place in 1994, with the company becoming a partnership. The output is slowly increasing, and the brewery supplies roughly 100 outlets. A new cask-conditioned lager has been added to the range. Tours by arrangement.

Special Bitter (OG 1037, ABV 3.8%) ◆ A light and drinkable bitter, with soft hoppiness and spicy character. It ends dry, but is smooth and refreshing.

Farne Island (OG 1039, ABV 4%) A session beer, taking its name from the Northumbrian isle. Hoppy, fruity and malty, it has a fine nose, pleasing taste and a robust aftertaste.

Noggins Nog (OG 1041, ABV 4.2%) ◆ An unusual mix of malt and roast malt leaves an impressive chocolate character in the aftertaste of this solidly made beer.

Rampart (OG 1047, ABV 4.8%) Another drinkable beer, with a combination of hop and malt characteristics. Subtle aftertaste with fruit notes.

SOB (OG 1048, ABV 5%) ◆ A malty ale with a resinous bitterness, finishing with a woody dryness.

BORVE
Borve Brew House, Ruthven, Huntly, Moray AB54 4SG. ☎ **(01466) 760343**

Established in 1983, Borve moved from its original site, on the Isle of Lewis, five years later, taking up residence in a former school on the mainland. The school is now a pub, with the brewhouse adjacent. Tours by arrangement. Beers: Ale (OG 1040, ABV 3.9%), Union Street 200 (OG 1050, ABV 4.9%),Tall Ships (OG 1050, ABV 5%). Bottle-conditioned beers: as cask, plus Extra Strong (OG 1085, ABV 10%).

BRAINS
SA Brain & Co. Ltd., The Old Brewery, 49 St Mary Street, Cardiff CF1 1SP. ☎ **(01222) 399022** FAX **(01222) 383127**

Traditional brewery which has been in the Brain family since Samuel Brain and his uncle Joseph bought the Old Brewery in 1882. In March 1997 the company merged with the other major Welsh brewer, Crown Buckley, to become the largest independent brewery in Wales and fears that the merger would lead to brewery closures have already been realised. Crown Buckley's Llanelli site is to close in early 1998, with the loss of 30 jobs. The beers will be transferred to the Brains brewery in Cardiff (the tasting notes below are based on Llanelli brews), but brand rationalisation seems almost inevitable. Crown Buckley's Pontyclun site will be the company's packaging centre, with all administration based in Cardiff. The new company will run 185 pubs, as well as having a sizeable free trade market, plus interests in hotel and leisure projects in Wales and the West Country. Brewery shop open 9.30–5.45 Mon–Sat. Tours by arrangement.

Buckley's Dark Mild (OG 1035, ABV 3.4%) 🍺 🍂 A very dark, malty mild, fairly sweet with traces of chocolate, followed by a nutty, bitter finish. Very drinkable.

Buckley's IPA (OG 1035, ABV 3.4%)

Crown Pale Ale (CPA) (OG 1035, ABV 3.4%) A pale brown, mildish bitter, but with a hint of hops and a thin taste.

Brains Dark (OG 1035, ABV 3.5%) 🍺 🍂 A dark brown mild with malt, caramel and roast flavours. Bittersweet, it has hints of fruit and a rounded finish.

Brains Mild Ale or MA (OG 1036, 3.6%) A brewery mix of Dark and Bitter

Brains Bitter (OG 1036, ABV 3.7%) 🍂 A distinctively bitter beer, pale and somewhat hoppy, with a hint of malt and fruit and a dry finish. Commonly known as 'Light'.

Buckley's Best Bitter (OG 1036, ABV 3.7%) 🍂 A well-balanced, medium gravity bitter which has a rather sweet, malty flavour and a pleasant, bitter finish.

Special Best Bitter (SBB) (OG 1036, ABV 3.7%) 🍂 Distinctively malty and clean-tasting, with a pronounced bitter flavour and a rather dry aftertaste.

SA Best Bitter (OG 1042, ABV 4.2%) 🍂 A full-bodied, noticeably bitter beer, well-balanced with fruit and hops, ending in a mellow, dry aftertaste.

Reverend James Original Ale (OG 1046, ABV 4.5%) 🍂 A malty, copper-coloured, full-bodied bitter with hops and fruit coming through strongly for a long finish.

BRAKSPEAR
WH Brakspear & Sons PLC, The Brewery, New Street, Henley-on-Thames, Oxfordshire RG9 2BU.
☎ **(01491) 570200**
FAX **(01491) 410254**

Brewing took place before 1700 on this Henley site, but the Brakspear family involvement only began in 1799, when Robert Brakspear formed a partnership with Richard Hayward. It was Robert's son, William Henry, who greatly expanded the brewery and its trade. Investment continues at the site and a new bottling plant for bottle-conditioned beers was about to open as we went to press. More seasonal beers are also in the pipeline. After years of closing small, unprofitable pubs in the Henley area, Brakspear is now displaying a greater determination to enhance its tied estate of 103 pubs, which boasts many excellent, unspoilt hostelries, all serving traditional

ales. Over 300 free trade outlets are supplied direct and trading arrangements with Whitbread and Scottish Courage mean that Brakspear's ales are available throughout southern England. Shop open 9–6 Mon–Sat (closes 7 Fri). Tours by arrangement. Bottle-conditioned beer: Christmas Ale (ABV 6.5%).

XXX Mild (OG 1031, ABV 3%) 🍂 A thin beer with a red/brown colour and a sweet, malty, fruity aroma. The well-balanced taste of malt, hops and caramel have a faint bitterness, complemented by a sweet, fruity flavour. The main characteristics extend through to the bittersweet finish.

Bitter (OG 1035.5, ABV 3.4%) 🍺 🍂 Amber in colour, with a good fruit, hop and malt nose. The initial taste of malt and the dry, well-hopped bitterness quickly dissolves into a predominantly bitter, sweet and fruity aftertaste.

Regatta Gold (OG 1038, ABV 3.8%) A light, crisp, refreshing beer brewed with Czech Saaz hops. Only sold in the Henley area.

Hop Demon (OG 1040, ABV 4.2%) A new spring beer, golden in colour and dry-hopped, giving an intense aroma. Slightly sweet, it has a bite of hops in the aftertaste.

Old Ale (OG 1043, ABV 4.3%) 🍂 Red/brown in colour with good body. The strong, fruity aroma is well complemented by malt, hops and roast caramel. Its pronounced taste of malt, with discernible sweet, roast malt and caramel flavours, gives way to fruitiness. The aftertaste is of bittersweet chocolate, even though chocolate malt is not used.

Special (OG 1043, ABV 4.3%) 🍂 A tawny/amber beer offering a good, well-balanced aroma with a hint of sweetness. The initial taste is moderately sweet and malty, but is quickly overpowered by the dry bitterness of the hops, before a slightly sweet fruitiness. A distinct, dry, malty finish.

OBJ (OG 1050, ABV 5%) Available November–January. Red/brown in colour, with an intensely fruity/hoppy aroma. An initial sweetish taste, strong in fruit and hops, is followed by bitterness with some malt and a lasting hops/bitter aftertaste.

BRAMCOTE
Bramcote Brewing Company, 236 Derby Road, Bramcote, Nottinghamshire NG9 3JN. ☎ **(0115) 939 3930**

Philip Darby and Niven Balfour had been brewing non-commercially for over ten years when they decided to go professional in 1996. Response from the free trade was so good that they were planning a move to new premises in Nottingham in summer 1997. The name Bramcote may be changed to coincide with the move.

Golliards Gold (ABV 3.8%) Brewed for the autumn.

Summer Daze (ABV 3.8%) A seasonal beer.

Hemlock Bitter (OG 1040, ABV 4%) A fruity session ale.

Bendigo Bitter (OG 1045, ABV 4.5%) A robust, hoppy beer.

Elsie Mo (OG 1045, ABV 4.5%) A pale-coloured premium bitter.

Salsa (ABV 4.5%) The spring offering.

Trentsman (OG 1048, ABV 4.8%)

Black Jack Stout (ABV 4.9%) A winter brew.

BRANDY CASK
Brandy Cask Brewing Company, r/o 25 Bridge Street, Pershore, Worcestershire WR10 1AJ. ☎ / FAX (01386) 555338

Brewing started in a refurbished bottle store behind the Brandy Cask pub in 1995, supplying that pub (which is a separate business) and 20 other local outlets, but not all on a regular basis. Tours by arrangement. Occasional beer: Ale Mary (OG 1046, ABV 4.8%).

Whistling Joe (OG 1036, ABV 3.6%) 🍺 A powerful hop aroma and a skilful balance between malt and hop tastes make this a very enjoyable bitter.

Brandy Snapper (OG 1040, ABV 4%) 🍺 Sweet and hoppy flavours make this a very drinkable, straw-coloured beer.

John Baker's Original (OG 1046, ABV 4.8%) 🍺 A warming, tawny drink that has a full array of flavours to attack the palate. Malty, fruity and sweetish.

BRANSCOMBE VALE
The Branscombe Vale Brewery, Great Seaside Farm, Branscombe, Seaton, Devon EX12 3DP. ☎ (01297) 680511

Brewery set up in 1992 in two cowsheds owned by the National Trust, by former dairy workers Paul Dimond and Graham Luxton, who converted the sheds and dug their own well. It currently supplies 40 outlets regularly, but plans to double capacity have been put back a short time. An own label house beer (OG 1044, ABV 4.6%) is produced for several local pubs in East Devon and beer is also brewed for Lock, Stock and Barrel wholesaling company ☎ (01364) 644124. Tours in winter only, by arrangement. Seasonal beers: Anniversary Ale (OG 1044, ABV 4.6%, January), Yo Ho Ho (OG 1065, ABV 6%, Christmas) 🍺.

Branoc (OG 1037, ABV 3.8%) 🍺🍺 A pale brown, well-balanced bitter with a fruity aroma and a hoppy, bitter taste and aftertaste.

Summa That (OG 1048, ABV 5%) Brewed April–October.

Olde Stoker (OG 1053, ABV 5.4%) 🍺 A dark brown, smooth, sweet, roast malt-tasting

beer, with a bitter finish. Available November–March.

For Lock, Stock and Barrel:
Pistol Knight (OG 1043, ABV 4.3%)

BRETTVALE
Brettvale Brewing Company Ltd.., The King's Head, 132 High Street, Bildeston, Ipswich, Suffolk IP7 7ED. Tel: (01449) 741434

This new brewery was set up with a five-barrel plant at the rear of the King's Head in Bildeston. Its first beer having been successfully received, a stronger beer was launched soon afterwards and a mild is also in the pipeline. It supplies two other pubs beside the Kings Head. Tours by arrangement. Beers: Bitter (OG 1039, ABV 3.8%), First Gold (OG 1042, ABV 4.3%).

THE BREWERY See Liverpool.

BREWERY ON SEA
The Brewery on Sea Ltd., Unit 24, Winston Business Centre, Chartwell Road, Lancing, W. Sussex BN15 8TU. ☎ / FAX (01903) 851482

This brewery was established in 1993 and increased its capacity in 1995 to around 55 barrels a week, some of which is taken by wholesalers, although up to 100 outlets are supplied directly. Beers are also brewed for East-West Ales ☎ (01892) 834040, and the brewery often produces beers for special occasions. Seasonal beers: Big Fat Santa (ABV 4.2%, Christmas), Dragon (ABV 4.2%, St George's Day), Spinnaker Shamrock (ABV 4.2%, a green beer for St Patrick's Day), Shell Shock (ABV 4.3%, Easter), Spinnaker Valentine (ABV 4.6%, February), Up in Smoke (ABV 4.8% Guy Fawkes Night), Candyman (ABV 5%, Hallowe'en), Wild Turkey (ABV 5.2%, Christmas).

Spinnaker Bitter (OG 1036, ABV 3.5%) 🍺 A hoppy-tasting, smooth, basic ale.

Spinnaker Mild or Lancing Special Dark (OG 1036, ABV 3.5%) Dark in colour and rich in flavour.

Spinnaker Golden Lite (ABV 3.8%) The popularity of this summer brew now ensures its year-round availability. Golden brown in colour and flavoursome.

Spinnaker Classic (OG 1040, ABV 4%) 🍺 The brewery's first beer: copper-coloured, with hints of malt in the aroma, giving way to a fruity flavour.

Rain Dance (ABV 4.4%) 🍺 Originally a 'one-off' wheat beer, now permanently established. Very pale with a cereal aroma.

Spinnaker Buzz (OG 1045, ABV 4.5%) 🍺 An amber-coloured beer primed with honey, which dominates the aroma. An initial sweetness gives way to an intriguing flavour mix of malt, honey and hops. Hoppy aftertaste.

Black Rock (OG 1050, ABV 5.5%) A dark beer with a good measure of roasted barley.

Special Crew (OG 1050, ABV 5.5%) A full-bodied bitter which gains its flavour and copper colour from a mix of pale and crystal malts.

Spinnaker Ginger (OG 1050, ABV 5.5%) Mid-light brown in colour, this beer contains pure ginger, making it highly aromatic.

Riptide (OG 1060, ABV 6.5%) A premium strong ale, fully fermented.

Tidal Wave (OG 1065, ABV 7%) A dry-tasting, strong, dark beer.

For East-West Ales:

Winter Widget (OG 1043, ABV 4.5%)

Wicked Widget (OG 1045, ABV 4.7%)

BRISTOL BREWHOUSE See Ross.

BRITANNIA See Batham.

BRITISH OAK

British Oak Brewery, Salop Street, Eve Hill, Dudley, W. Midlands DY1 3AX.
☎ **(01384) 236297**

Brew pub which began production in 1988. The brewery's second pub in Bilston has now been sold. Tours by arrangement. Beers: Mild (OG 1038, ABV 3.7%), Eve'ill Bitter (OG 1042, ABV 4%), Colonel Pickering's Porter (OG 1046, ABV 4.6%, occasional), Dungeon Draught (OG 1050, ABV 4.8%, occasional), Old Jones (OG 1062, ABV 6.2%, September–April).

BROOKLANDS See Planets.

BROUGHTON

Broughton Ales Ltd., The Brewery, Broughton, Biggar, The Borders ML12 6HQ.
☎ **(01899) 830345**
FAX **(01899) 830474**

Brewery founded in 1979 by former S&N executive David Younger. The company grew successfully, but went into receivership in 1995. It was taken over by Whim Brewery owner Giles Litchfield who has created six new ales and is steadily expanding the trading area for the cask products and developing the export market for the bottled beers. There is also a single tied house and plans to acquire more. Shop open 9–5 Mon–Fri. Group tours by arrangement (evenings). Seasonal beer: Reeket Yill (OG 1048, ABV 4.8%, a smoked winter ale).

IPA (OG 1036, ABV 3.8%)

Greenmantle Ale (OG 1038, ABV 3.9%) 🍺 A beer with a predominantly malty aroma, a malty taste with hints of fruit and hops, but little aftertaste. Somewhat lacking in character.

Special Bitter (OG 1038, ABV 3.9%) 🍺 A dry-hopped version of Greenmantle Ale. An aroma of hop, with malt and fruit, leads into a pleasingly bitter beer balanced with more malt and fruit. The bitterness and fruit last into the aftertaste. Slightly lacking in body.

Merlin's Ale (OG 1042, ABV 4.2%) 🍺 A much improved golden ale. A well-hopped, fruity flavour is balanced by malt. The finish is bittersweet and light, but dry.

80/- (OG 1042, ABV 4.2%)

Scottish Oatmeal Stout (OG 1045, ABV 4.2%) 🍺 A rare pleasure, this wonderfully dry stout has a bitter aftertaste, dominated by roast malt. A distinctive malt aroma is followed by a prominent roast taste, with fruit evident throughout.

The Ghillie (OG 1043, ABV 4.5%) 🍺 This superb ale assaults the nose with a strong aroma of hop. Hops continue to dominate the palate, with malt and fruit, and it ends in a hop-dominated, dry finish.

Black Douglas (OG 1053, ABV 5.2%) A winter brew, dark ruby in colour.

Old Jock (OG 1070, ABV 6.7%) Strong, sweetish and fruity in the finish. Also sold as River Tweed Festival Ale.

MATTHEW BROWN
See Nationals, Scottish Courage.

ABEL BROWN'S

Abel Brown's Brewery, The Stag, 35 Brook Street, Stotfold, Hitchin, Hertfordshire SG5 4LA.
☎ **(01462) 730261**
FAX **(01462) 483100**

Abel Browns Brewery

This pub (which is in Bedfordshire, despite the postal address), began brewing in the summer of 1995, using the name of its first publican, Abel Brown, on the pump clips. Some of the beers take their names from the village's famous traction engines. In January 1997, the business became a partnership. The brewery is set to double its capacity and currently supplies 12 other outlets. Tours by arrangement. Occasional beers: Lord Douglas Mild (ABV 4%), Ploughmans Pickle (ABV 5%), Poco Loco (ABV 5%).

Saracen (ABV 3.8%) A light ruby-coloured beer. Smooth on the palate and strong in flavour for a beer of this strength.

Jack of Herts (OG 1040, ABV 4%) The flagship brew, named after a local traction engine. A traditional bitter, slightly fruity, with a dryish aftertaste.

Little Billy (OG 1040, ABV 4%) A triple-hopped beer, using Hallertau hops. Dry, with a fresh hop finish.

Lord Douglas Mild (ABV 4%)

First Gold (ABV 4.1%)

Knucklehead (ABV 4.7%) An old-fashioned ale, high in crystal malt; hoppy, with a dry aftertaste.

Kinsale Stout (ABV 4.8%)

Grizzly Bear (ABV 6%) Hops, blackberries and malt feature in the aroma of this beer which has a smoky, fruity aftertaste.

TOM BROWN'S See Goldfinch.

BRUNSWICK
The Brunswick Brewery Co. Ltd., 1 Railway Terrace, Derby DE1 2RU.
☎ **(01332) 290677**
FAX **(01332) 370226**

Purpose-built tower brewery attached to the Brunswick Inn, the first purpose-built railwaymen's hostelry in the world, which was partly restored by the Derbyshire Historic Building Trust and bought by the present owners in 1987. Brewing began in 1991 and a viewing area allows pub-users to watch production. The beers are supplied to the Inn and a few other outlets directly. Numerous one-off beers are also produced. Tours by arrangement. Beers: Recession Ale (OG 1033, ABV 3.3%), First Brew (OG 1036, ABV 3.6%), Second Brew (OG 1042, ABV 4.2%), Railway Porter (OG 1045, ABV 4.3%), Old Accidental (OG 1050, ABV 5%).

BUCHANAN See Federation.

BUCKLEY See Brains.

BUFFY'S
Buffy's Brewery, Mardle Hall, Rectory Road, Tivetshall St Mary, Norfolk NR15 2DD.
☎ **(01379) 676523**

Situated alongside a 15th-century house, Buffy's started life as Mardle Hall Brewery in 1993, but was forced to change its name after a complaint from another brewery. Thirty local free houses are supplied and Buffy's is now looking to expand into Suffolk, but the bulk of the beer is sold through wholesalers. Plans are underway to virtually double the brewery's capacity. Tours by arrangement. Seasonal beers: Festival 8X (OG 1075, ABV 8%), Festival 9X (OG 1080, ABV 9%) both brewed for CAMRA's Norwich Beer Festival.

Bitter (OG 1038, ABV 3.9%) Very well-balanced throughout, this is a flavoursome session beer, not at all bland or cloying, with

more complexity than its gravity may suggest.

Polly's Folly (OG 1041, ABV 4.3%) A well-balanced amber beer with a flowery hop character to its aroma. The palate is clean and bitter, with malt and some citrus notes which die away in the aftertaste to let the hops and bitterness come through.

Mild (OG 1042, ABV 4.2%) A stronger than average dark mild.

Polly's Extra Folly (OG 1046, ABV 4.9%) Much like the bitter, only stronger and fuller-bodied. It is just as well-balanced, but with a rounder, fruitier palate. It is also moreish, with a clean, bitter finish.

Ale (OG 1052, ABV 5.5%) A pale brown beer which is a smooth and malty, strong bitter throughout. Slightly warming and easy to drink.

Strong Ale (OG 1062, ABV 6.5%) A rich, hearty and complex, darkish brown beer which is full of malt and fruit, with some hoppiness. Very drinkable for its strength.

BULLMASTIFF
Bullmastiff Brewery, 14 Bessemer Close, Leckwith, Cardiff CF1 8DL.
☎ **(01222) 665292**

Small brewery set up in the Penarth docklands in 1987 and moved to larger premises in Cardiff in 1992. Bullmastiff now supplies about 30 outlets locally, though much of the production is sold in other parts of the country through wholesalers. Seasonal beers have recently been added to the range.

Gold Brew (OG 1039, ABV 3.8%) A refreshing golden pale ale, predominantly hoppy, but balanced by malt and fruit. A welcome addition to the range.

Best Bitter (OG 1042, ABV 4%) A well-balanced, malty, bitter beer with a hoppy and fruity finish.

Spring Fever (OG 1043, ABV 4.3%) The spring beer.

Summer Moult (OG 1043, ABV 4.3%) The summer beer.

Thoroughbred (OG 1046, ABV 4.5%)

Southpaw (OG 1048, ABV 4.7%) Brewed for the autumn.

Brindle (OG 1050, ABV 5%) A full-bodied beer, well hopped throughout, with malt and fruit coming through in the taste. Rounded, dry finish.

Son of a Bitch (OG 1062, ABV 6%) A powerful premium bitter with a fine blend of hop, malt and fruit flavours, balanced by bitterness. Distinctive, complex, dry finish. A worthy award winner.

BULL'S HEAD

Bull's Head Brewery, The Three Tuns, Alcester, Warwickshire.

Brewery closed.

BUNCES

Bunces Brewery, The Old Mill, Mill Road, Netheravon, Salisbury, Wiltshire SP4 9QB.
☎ / [FAX] (01980) 670631

Tower brewery housed in a listed building on the Wiltshire Avon, established in 1984 and sold to Danish proprietors in summer 1993. Its cask-conditioned beers are delivered to around 50 free trade outlets within a radius of 50 miles, and a number of wholesalers are also supplied. Shop open 8.30–5.30 Mon–Fri, 10–1 Sat. Tours by arrangement. Seasonal beers: Sign of Spring (OG 1044, ABV 4.6%, March–April), Rudolph (OG 1050, ABV 5%, Christmas).

Benchmark (OG 1035, ABV 3.5%) ◆ A pleasant, bitter ale of remarkable character, which maintains one's interest for a long time. The taste is malty, the aroma subtle and the very long finish is quite dry on the palate.

Pigswill (OG 1040, ABV 4%) A beer first brewed for the Two Pigs at Corsham, now more widely available.

Best Bitter (OG 1042, ABV 4.1%) ◆ A first-rate beer. The piquant aroma introduces a complex, malty and bitter taste with a hint of fruit. Long, fresh, bitter aftertaste.

Second to None (ABV 4.6%) A new wheat beer for summer, replacing Vice Beer.

Danish Dynamite (OG 1050, ABV 5%) A light golden, slightly fruity, dry strong ale with hop and bitter balance.

Old Smokey (OG 1050, ABV 5%) ◆ A delightful, warming, dark bitter ale, with a roasted malt taste and a hint of liquorice surrounding a developing bitter flavour. Very appealing to the eye.

Stig Swig (OG 1050, ABV 5%) A golden autumn beer brewed with the herb sweet gale, an old Viking beer ingredient.

BURNTISLAND

Burntisland Brewing Co., Burntisland Brewery, 83 High Street, Burntisland, Fife KY3 9AA.
☎ / [FAX] (01592) 873333

Brewery housed behind a delicatessen/off-licence which began operation in 1996. It was upgraded in March 1997 with the installation of new stainless steel plant, and there are plans to add a bottling line, to produce more bottle-conditioned beers. Some beer has been contract-brewed for Burntisland by Harviestoun. Over 20 outlets are now supplied with the beers and the

shop is open 7–7 (7–2 Wed, 12–3 Sun) May–September; 8–6 in winter. Bottle-conditioned beers: Alexander's Downfall (OG 1045, ABV 4.3%), Dockyard Rivets (OG 1050, ABV 5.1%).

Alexander's Downfall (OG 1045, ABV 4.3%)

Dockyard Rivets (OG 1050, ABV 5.1%) A real pilsner-style lager.

BURTON BRIDGE

Burton Bridge Brewery, 24 Bridge Street, Burton upon Trent, Staffordshire DE14 1SY. ☎ (01283) 510573

Brewery established in 1982, with one tied outlet at the front and another opened in January 1997. Conversion of the adjoining premises, an early 19th-century building, into a new brewhouse was completed later the same year. Guest beers are supplied to around 250 outlets virtually nationwide, and Burton Bridge specialises in commemorative bottled beers to order. Tours by arrangement. Seasonal beers: Spring Ale (OG 1047, ABV 4.7% March–April), Battle Brew (OG 1050, ABV 5%, July–August), Hearty Ale (OG 1050, ABV 5%, December–January). Bottle-conditioned beers: Burton Porter (OG 1045, ABV 4.5%) ⏏, Empire Pale Ale (ABV 7.5%), Tickle Brain (ABV 8%).

Summer Ale (OG 1038, ABV 3.8%) Only available during British Summer Time. A beer with a strong hop aroma and a dry, bitter finish.

XL Bitter (OG 1040, ABV 4%) ◆ A golden, malty, drinking bitter, with a faint, hoppy and fruity aroma. An excellent mix of flavours follows, with fruitiness dominating.

Bridge Bitter (OG 1042, ABV 4.2%) ◆ An amber-coloured, robust and malty beer. The taste is bittersweet, with fruit, and gives way to a dominating hoppy finish.

Burton Porter (OG 1045, ABV 4.5%) ◆ Dark ruby-red, with a faint aroma. The taste combines moderate liquorice flavour with hops and fruit; slightly sweet. Dry, astringent aftertaste.

Staffordshire Knot Brown Ale (OG 1048, ABV 4.8%) An autumn beer.

Top Dog Stout (OG 1050, ABV 5%) ◆ A winter brew with a strong roast malt and fruit mix, developing into a potent malt and roast malt aftertaste.

Festival Ale (OG 1055, ABV 5.5%) ◆ A full-bodied, copper-coloured, strong but sweet beer. The aroma is hoppy, malty and slightly fruity. Malt and hops in the flavour give way to a fruity finish. Tremendous mouthfeel.

Old Expensive (OG 1065, ABV 6.5%) A winter warmer, virtually a barley wine. Its wonderful mix of sweetness and fruit certainly hits the throat.

Thomas Sykes Ale (OG 1100, ABV 11%)

THE INDEPENDENTS

BURTONWOOD

**Burtonwood Brewery PLC,
Bold Lane, Burtonwood,
Warrington, Cheshire
WA5 4PJ. ☎ (01925) 225131
[FAX] (01925) 224562**

Family-run public company established in
1867 by James Forshaw. In the 1980s,
Burtonwood embarked on a £6 million
extension plan and a new brewhouse was
completed in 1990. Burtonwood still has
shares in, and remains a major supplier to,
the Paramount pub group, and in fact
manages the distribution of all products to
the Paramount estate. Its own tied estate of
490 house includes 50 Top Hat Taverns and
100 pubs on a long lease from Allied
Domecq. However, a fifth of Burtonwood's
pubs do not take real ale. Around 100 free
trade outlets are supplied direct. Some
seasonal beers have occasionally been
produced.

Mild (OG 1032, ABV 3%) ◆ A smooth, dark
brown, malty mild with a good roast
flavour, some caramel taste and a hint of
bitterness. Slightly dry finish.

Bitter (OG 1037, ABV 3.7%) ◆ A well-
balanced, refreshing, malty bitter, with good
hoppiness. Fairly dry aftertaste.

James Forshaw's Bitter (OG 1040, ABV 4%)
◆ A malty and hoppy, well-balanced bitter.

Top Hat (OG 1046, ABV 4.8%) ◆ Soft, nutty,
malty and a little sweet. Fairly thin for its
gravity.

Buccaneer (OG 1052, ABV 5.2%) ◆ A pale
golden, sweet and malty bitter, with subtle
hop flavour. Its light taste belies its strength.

For Whitbread:

Oldham Bitter (OB) (OG 1037, ABV 3.8%) ◆
A copper-coloured beer with an aroma of
malt and fruit. The flavour is malty and
bitter, with a bittersweet tinge and a dry,
malty finish. A relic of the Oldham Brewery
closed by Boddingtons.

BURTS

**Burts (Sandown Brewery)
Ltd., Sandown Brewery &
Stillroom, 15 St Johns Road,
Sandown, Isle of Wight
PO36 8EN.
☎ (01983) 408308 [FAX] (01983) 408337**

Brewery originally founded in Newport in
1840, but which went into receivership in
1992. The name and brands were bought by
the Hampshire soft drinks firm Hartridges,
owners of Island Brewery, who now use the
Burts name for all their brewing operations.
The Newport brewery was closed in 1996
and all the brewing was carried out at the
new brew pub, Sandown Brewery &
Stillroom, supplying five tied houses and 16
other outlets. A shop is planned. Tours by
arrangement.

Nipper Bitter (OG 1035, ABV 3.4%) ◆ A
thin, malty and fruity, golden brown session
beer, with some astringency and acidity.

Parkhurst Porter (OG 1038, ABV 3.8%)

Vectis Premium Ale or VPA (OG 1042, ABV
4.2%) ◆ A refreshing, malty, bitter beer with
a fruity nose.

Newport Nobbler (OG 1044, ABV 4.4%)
◆ A malty, fruity, light bitter with a clean
finish and solid body. Pale straw in hue.

Vectis Venom (OG 1049, ABV 5%) ◆ A
heavy, fruity beer with a dominant acidic
quality.

Codswallop (OG 1050, ABV 5%)

Crustache (OG 1052, ABV 5.5%)

BUSHY'S

**The Mount Murray
Brewing Co. Ltd., Mount
Murray, Castletown Road,
Braddan, Isle of Man
IM4 1JE. ☎ (01624) 661244
[FAX] (01624) 611101**

Set up in 1986 as a brew pub, Bushy's moved
to its present site in 1990, when demand
outgrew capacity. The beers, all brewed to
the stipulations of the Manx Brewers' Act of
1874, are supplied to four tied houses and 20
other outlets. Tours by arrangement.
Occasional/seasonal beers: Mild (OG 1035,
ABV 3.5%), Summer Ale (OG 1036, ABV
3.6%, July), Celebration Ale (OG 1040, ABV
4%), Oyster Stout (OG 1042, ABV 4.2%),
Piston Brew (OG 1045, ABV 4.5%, for the TT
races in May–June), Old Bushy Tail (OG
1045, ABV 4.5%), Old Shunter (OG 1045,
ABV 4.5%, August–September), Lovely
Jubbely Christmas Ale (OG 1052, ABV 5.2%).

Bitter (OG 1038, ABV 3.8%) ◆ An aroma full
of pale malt and hops introduces you to a
beautifully hoppy, bitter beer. Despite the
predominant hop character, malt is also
evident. Fresh and clean-tasting.

Manannan's Cloak (OG 1040, ABV 4%)

BUTCOMBE

**Butcombe Brewery Ltd.,
Butcombe, Bristol
BS18 6XQ.
☎ (01275) 472240
[FAX] (01275) 474734**

One of the most successful of the newer
breweries, set up in 1978 by a former
Courage Western MD, Simon Whitmore.
During 1992–93, the brewery virtually
doubled in size (for the third time) and, after
18 years of brewing just a single beer, a
second ale went into production in 1996.
Butcombe currently supplies four tied
houses and 300 free trade outlets, most
within a 50-mile radius of the brewery, but

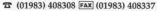

434

others further afield via wholesalers. Tours (for trade only) by arrangement.

Bitter (OG 1039, ABV 4%) An amber-coloured, malty and notably bitter beer, with subtle peardrop and citrus fruit qualities. It has a hoppy, malty, citrus aroma and a long, dry, bitter finish with light fruit notes. Consistent.

Wilmot's Premium Ale (OG 1048, ABV 4.8%) Full-bodied, with good malt, strong hops and some fruit. Pale brown/amber in colour, it has an aroma of hops, malt and citrus/peardrop fruits; long, dry, bitter, resinous finish. A robust premium ale.

BUTTERKNOWLE

Butterknowle Brewery, The Old School House, Lynesack, Butterknowle, Bishop Auckland, Co. Durham DL13 5QF.
☎ (01388) 710109 FAX (01388) 710373

Since its launch in 1990, Butterknowle has continued to prosper and grow by producing award-winning ales. It now supplies almost 200 outlets nationwide on a regular basis. The brewery is situated in Victorian buildings, once home to the Lynesack National School. Occasional/seasonal beers: West Auckland Mild (OG 1034, ABV 3.3%), First Gold (ABV 3.8%). Bottle-conditioned beers: Conciliation Ale (OG 1042, ABV 4.3%), High Force (OG 1060, ABV 6.2%).

Bitter (OG 1036, ABV 3.6%) A light, fruity pale ale with a good balance of flavours. Fruity aroma; slight hoppy aftertaste.

Banner Bitter (OG 1040, ABV 4%) A good, moderately bitter-tasting, pale brown beer. Lingering aftertaste; hoppy aroma with fruity undertones.

Conciliation Ale (OG 1042, ABV 4.2%) Returning to its original form, this classic beer continues to impress. Well-balanced and warming, it is decidedly bitter with a long, fruity aftertaste which finishes dry and bitter.

Black Diamond (OG 1050, ABV 4.8%) A rich malty/toffee/liquorice taste dominates this deep red/brown ale. Fruity aroma; bitterness complements the initial sweetness in the mouth.

Lynesack Porter (OG 1050, ABV 5%) A dark, traditional porter.

High Force (OG 1060, ABV 6.2%) A smooth strong ale, well-hopped, with some fruity sweetness. A good depth of flavour develops in the aftertaste. A multi-dimensional beer.

Old Ebenezer (OG 1080, ABV 8%) A splendid, rich and fruity, seasonal barley wine: liquid Christmas cake with a potent punch. Surprisingly moreish, if only in sips!

BUTTS

Butts Brewery Ltd., Northfield Farm, Great Shefford, Hungerford, Berkshire RG16 7DQ.
☎ (01488) 648133
FAX (01734) 345860

Brewery set up in converted farm buildings in 1994 with plant acquired from Butcombe. New beers have been added to the range in the last twelve months; Barbus Barbus (Latin for the barbel fish) was brewed as a one-off to celebrate the start of the coarse fishing season and proved popular enough to become permanent. Butts now supplies 50 outlets, mainly in Berkshire, but also in Oxfordshire, Hampshire and Wiltshire. Tours by arrangement.

Jester (OG 1035, ABV 3.5%)

Bitter (OG 1040, ABV 4%)

Blackguard (OG 1045, ABV 4.5%) A new winter porter.

Barbus Barbus (OG 1046, ABV 4.6%)

CAINS

Robert Cain & Co. Ltd., The Robert Cain Brewery, Stanhope Street, Liverpool, Merseyside L8 5XJ.
☎ (0151) 709 8734
FAX (0151) 708 8395

Robert Cain's brewery was first established on this site in 1850, but was bought out by Higsons in the 1920s, then by Boddingtons in 1985. Whitbread took control of the Boddingtons breweries in 1990 and closed the site, switching the brewing of Higsons to Sheffield and later Castle Eden. The site was then bought by GB Breweries to brew canned beers, but with enthusiastic staff and CAMRA support, it soon moved on to cask ales. The company is now a division of the Brewery Group Denmark A/S. Cains now has three tied houses and there are plans to expand the estate. An arrangement has been made to badge some of Greenalls' pubs as Cains pubs, and these (two so far) will sell the full range of Cains beers. Around 400 outlets in Merseyside and the North-West also take the beers which include a monthly guest beer. Tours by arrangement. Occasional/seasonal beers: Red Fox (OG 1039 ABV 4%), Golden Summer Ale (OG 1040, ABV 4%), Mayflower Ale (OG 1044, ABV 4.5%), Styrian Gold (OG 1045, ABV 4.5%), Superior Stout (OG 1048, ABV 4.8%), Chocolate Ale (OG 1048, ABV 5%), Brewer's Droop (OG 1049, ABV 5%), Springbok Ale (OG 1049, ABV 5%), Victorian Winter Ale (OG 1049, ABV 5%), Blackout Porter (OG 1056, ABV 5.5%).

Dark Mild (OG 1032, ABV 3.2%) A smooth, dry and roasty, dark mild, with some chocolate and coffee notes.

Brewery Bitter (OG 1036, ABV 3.5%) A new bitter, brewed exclusively for Cains-badged

Greenalls pubs: a malty and smooth, light tan-coloured beer with a fragant nose.

Traditional Bitter (OG 1039, ABV 4%) ◆ A darkish, full-bodied and fruity bitter, with a good, hoppy nose and a dry aftertaste.

Formidable Ale (FA) (OG 1048, ABV 5%) ◆ A bitter and hoppy beer with a good, dry aftertaste. Sharp, clean and dry.

CALEDONIAN

The Caledonian Brewing Company Ltd., 42 Slateford Road, Edinburgh EH11 1PH. ☎ (0131) 337 1286 FAX (0131) 313 2370

Described by Michael Jackson as a 'living, working museum of beer making', Caledonian operates from a Victorian brewhouse, using the last three direct-fired, open coppers in Britain, one of which dates back to 1869, when the brewery was founded by George Lorimer and Robert Clark. The site was taken over by Vaux of Sunderland in 1919, who continued to brew there until 1987, when, under threat of closure, it was acquired by a management buyout team. A disastrous fire in 1994, which destroyed the historic maltings, necessitated a major rebuild and a new visitors' centre was incorporated. Caledonian has no tied estate, but around 400 free trade outlets are supplied directly, and the beers are increasingly available South of the Border. Some occasional beers are produced, including a bottle-conditioned beer in summer 1997 to celebrate the tenth anniversary of the management buyout. Tours by arrangement. Bottle-conditioned beer: Tempus Fugit (ABV 4.4%).

60/- Ale (OG 1032, ABV 3.2%) ◆ A dark beer with plenty of body for a 'light'. A bittersweet balance of malt, hops, roast and fruit gives a complex taste, while the aroma and aftertaste are dominated by malt and hop. Sadly, not widely available.

70/- Ale (OG 1036, ABV 3.5%) ◆ A traditional Scottish session beer, with malt to the fore in the aroma. The subtle, bittersweet taste has a balance of malt, fruit and roast, with hop to the fore. The malt fades in the aftertaste. It can be hard to find and may soon only be a seasonal beer.

Murrays Summer Ale (OG 1036, ABV 3.6%) ◆ A clean-tasting, thirst-quenching, golden session beer, with hop and fruit evident throughout. A bitter beer, balanced by malt in the taste and aftertaste.

Deuchars IPA (OG 1038, ABV 3.8%) 🍷 🍺 ◆ An extremely tasty and refreshing, amber-coloured session beer. Hops and malt are very evident and are balanced by fruit throughout.The lingering aftertaste is delightfully bitter and hoppy.

Edinburgh Real Ale or ERA (OG 1042, ABV 4.1%) ◆ Full-bodied, with hops, malt and fruit, this bittersweet, dark brown beer retains its character in the aftertaste. Fruity aroma.

80/- Ale (OG 1042, ABV 4.1%) ◆ A predominantly malty, copper-coloured beer, well-balanced by hop and fruit; a complex Scottish heavy with the hop characteristics of a best bitter. 1996 *Champion Beer of Scotland*.

Porter (OG 1042, ABV 4.1%) A dry and malty, dark beer, well-balanced with hops. Not easy to find.

Murrays Heavy (OG 1044, ABV 4.3%) An amber-coloured ale brewed in the traditional Scottish style. Clean tasting, with a malty sweetness.

Campbell, Hope & King's Double Amber Ale (OG 1046, ABV 4.6%) ◆ A full-bodied, complex beer. Mid-brown in colour and dominated by malt and fruit throughout, its bittersweet taste is followed by a bitter finish of hop with a hint of roast. This may soon be discontinued.

Golden Promise (OG 1048, ABV 5%) An organic beer, pale in colour, with pronounced hop character. Floral and fruity on the nose.

Merman XXX (OG 1050, ABV 4.8%) ◆ A mid-brown beer, based on a Victorian recipe. This rich, malty, fruity beer has a thick, initially sweetish, taste which becomes increasingly complex, with roast, hops and a hint of caramel.

Edinburgh Strong Ale or ESA (OG 1064, ABV 6.4%) A complex mix of malt and hops without the cloying sweetness that beers of this strength can have. Most commonly available in bottles (not bottle-conditioned).

CAMBRIAN

Cambrian Brewery Co. Ltd., Units 17–18, Marian Mawr Enterprise Park, Dolgellau, Gwynedd LL40 1UU. ☎ (01341) 421000 FAX (01341) 421111

Brewery opened by two brothers in June 1996, deep in the Snowdonia National Park – the first brewery in the Welsh mountains in nearly 90 years. The additive-free beers are supplied direct to 100 outlets, including a pub Cambrian has taken over in Barmouth. Tours by arrangement. Occasional/seasonal beers: Cwrw Sesh (ABV 4%), Cwrw Gwyl Dewi (ABV 4.2%, St David's Day), Turkey's Last (ABV 4.4%, Christmas).

Original (OG 1037, ABV 3.7%) ◆ A smooth, well-balanced and fruity bitter. Very drinkable.

Best Bitter (OG 1042, ABV 4.2%) ◆ A darkish brown bitter in which initial roast and fruit flavours give way to bitterness.

Mountain Ale (OG 1039, ABV 4.1%) Available April–July.

Premium (OG 1048, ABV 4.8%) ◆ A clean and refreshing, well-balanced, strong bitter.

CAMERONS

**Camerons Brewery
Company, Lion Brewery,
Hartlepool TS24 7QS.**
☎ **(01429) 266666**
[FAX] **(01429) 868195**

This major brewer of real ale, established in 1865, went through a period of neglect for some 17 years when it was owned by non-brewers, including the ill-fated Brent Walker group. In 1992 it was bought by Wolverhampton & Dudley Breweries, in a deal that included the brewery, 51 pubs and the brands. With solid investment and a successful re-launch of the beers, Camerons has turned a corner. The company now has 172 tied houses, most of which take real ale, and the beers are also widely available in the free trade. Tours by arrangement.

Bitter (OG 1036, ABV 3.6%) ◈ A light bitter, but well-balanced, with hops and malt.

Strongarm (OG 1042, ABV 4%) ◈ A well-rounded, ruby-red ale with a distinctive, tight creamy head; initially fruity, but with a good balance of malt, hops and moderate bitterness.

CANNON

**Parker & Son Brewers Ltd.,
The Cannon, Cannon Street,
Wellingborough,
Northamptonshire
NN8 4DJ.**
☎ / [FAX] **(01933) 279629**

Brewery founded in 1993, in the old bottle store of the Cannon pub. A family-run business, it supplies the pub and five other free trade outlets, as well as Flying Firkin and other wholesalers. Tours by arrangement.

Light Brigade (OG 1036, ABV 3.6%) A thin-bodied, amber/gold session beer, with a fruity malt aroma and apple fruitiness on the tongue. Faint, dry bitterness in the aftertaste.

Pride (OG 1042, ABV 4.2%) Cascade hops give tart fruitiness to the malt aroma. Hops finally overcome the intense malt of this amber brew in a well-balanced finish.

Florrie Night-in-Ale (OG 1048, ABV 4.8%) Hops and malt battle in an astringent fruitiness for dominance on the tongue. The bitter aftertaste finally wins through with dryness building. Light brown, with medium body.

Vivaldi (ABV 4.7%) A new addition.

Fodder (OG 1055, ABV 5.5%) Mid-brown, very fruity and vinous.

CANNON ROYALL

**Cannon Royall Brewery,
The Fruiterer's Arms,
Uphampton, Ombersley,
Worcestershire WR9 0JW.**
☎ **(01905) 621161**

This five-barrel plant was set up in 1993, in a converted cider house behind the

Fruiterer's Arms pub. Slowly expanding, the brewery plans to acquire its first tied house in 1998. Besides the Fruiterer's Arms, 20 other outlets are supplied, though a new sales rep should boost this figure. Tours by arrangement. Occasional beer: Heart of Oak (OG 1054, ABV 5.4%).

Fruiterer's Mild (OG 1037, ABV 3.7%) ◈ A rich, black mixture of malt, roast and fruit flavours make this a joy to drink.

Arrowhead (OG 1039, ABV 3.9%) ◈ A fruity and hoppy, golden brew that fills the mouth with flavour. Refreshing bitter finish.

Buckshot (OG 1045, ABV 4.5%) ◈ Malt, hops and a juicy, fruity taste battle for prominence in this premium bitter.

Olde Merrie (OG 1060, ABV 6%) ◈ A sweet and fruity old ale with plenty of malt flavour.

CARTMEL

**Cartmel Brewery, Unit 7,
Fell View Trading Park,
Shap Road, Kendal,
Cumbria LA9 6NZ.**
☎ **(01539) 724085**

Set up by Nick Murray, in a disused barn at the Cavendish Arms, Cartmel in 1994, this new brewery took off so successfully that larger premises were soon required and the plant was moved to nearby Kendal. Continuing to develop its trade, Cartmel now supplies around 40 local outlets, plus a few in Scotland.

Pride (OG 1035, ABV 3.5%) ◈ A beer with a full mouthfeel and sweet, complex fruit and roast malt in the taste, with flowery hops in the middle. Unbalanced bitter astringency in the aftertaste. Lots of taste for a beer of this gravity.

Lakeland Gold (OG 1038, ABV 4%) A golden beer with a light, clean taste, a hoppy aroma and a dry finish.

Thoroughbred (OG 1044, ABV 4.5%)

Winter Warmer (OG 1050, ABV 5.2%)

CASTLE EDEN
See Nationals, Whitbread.

CASTLETOWN See Okells.

CHALK HILL

**Chalk Hill Brewery, Rosary
Road, Thorpe Hamlet,
Norwich, Norfolk
NR1 4DA.** ☎ **(01603) 477078**

Run by former Reindeer brew pub owner Bill Thomas and his partners, Chalk Hill began production with a 15-barrel plant in 1993. It now supplies around 20 local free trade outlets and the beers are available nationwide via beer agencies. Tours by arrangement.

Tap Bitter (OG 1036, ABV 3.6%) ❧ A simple and unpretentious session beer, hoppy and quite well-balanced, but not strongly flavoured. A gentle, hoppy bitterness lingers in the aftertaste.

CHB (OG 1042, ABV 4.2%) ❧ A fairly well-balanced, mid-brown beer, not very strongly flavoured.

Dreadnought (OG 1049, ABV 4.9%) ❧ A strong brown bitter which, despite having little aroma, is full-flavoured, well-balanced, rounded and fruity. The aftertaste is similar but short. Easier to drink than its strength may suggest.

Flintknapper's Mild (OG 1050, ABV 5%)

Old Tackle (OG 1056, ABV 5.6%) ❧ A reddish-brown beer with little aroma but a fairly full body and a full palate. The taste is complex, with mainly fruit but even hints of liquorice.

CHARRINGTON See Nationals, Bass.

CHERITON

The Cheriton Brewhouse, Cheriton, Alresford, Hampshire SO24 0QQ.
☎ (01962) 771166

📱 Purpose-built brewery, opened in 1993 by the proprietors of the Flower Pots Inn (next door). With a ten-barrel plant, it supplies around 30 free trade outlets on a regular basis, plus a further 30 with guest beers. Tours by arrangement. Occasional/seasonal beers: Chilli Beer (OG 1041, ABV 4%), Beltane (OG 1045, ABV 4.5%), Turkey's Revenge (OG 1059, ABV 5.9%, Christmas).

Pots Ale (OG 1038, ABV 3.8%) 🍺 🍺 ❧ Pale brown, with a hoppy nose, a well-balanced bitter taste with a little fruit, and a bitter aftertaste.

Best Bitter (OG 1041, ABV 4.2%) ❧ A dark brown beer, with a predominantly malty and fruity taste which continues into the aftertaste. Fruity aroma. Very different to the brewery's other products.

Diggers Gold (OG 1046, ABV 4.6%) 🍺 ❧ A golden beer with a citric, hoppy aroma; bitter and hoppy in all aspects, with some fruit, and a dry aftertaste.

Flower Power (OG 1056, ABV 5.2%) A new addition to the range.

CHESTER'S
See Everards and Nationals, Whitbread.

> 🍺 The empty tankard indicates the beer was a *Good Beer Guide Beer of the Year* in the last three years.

CHILTERN

The Chiltern Brewery, Nash Lee Road, Terrick, Aylesbury, Buckinghamshire HP17 0TQ.
☎ (01296) 613647 [FAX] (01296) 612419

Set up in 1980 on a small farm (and now the oldest working brewery in the county), Chiltern specialises in an unusual range of beer-related products, like beer mustards, Old Ale chutneys, cheeses and even hop cologne. These products are available from the brewery shop (open 9–5.30 Mon–Fri, 11–5.30 Sat–Sun) and also from about 20 other retail outlets. Cask beer is regularly supplied to four free trade outlets and a couple of beers are brewed just for individual outlets. There is a small museum on site and brewery tours are at noon Saturday, or by arrangement. Bottle-conditioned beer: Bodgers Barley Wine (OG 1080, ABV 8%).

Ale (OG 1038, ABV 3.7%) A distinctive, tangy light bitter.

Beechwood Bitter (OG 1043, ABV 4.3%) Full-bodied and nutty.

Three Hundreds Old Ale (OG 1050, ABV 5%) A strong, rich, deep chestnut-coloured beer.

CHURCH END

Church End Brewery Ltd., The Griffin Inn, Church Road, Shustoke, Warwickshire B46 2LB.
☎ (01675) 481567

Brewery founded in 1994 in an old coffin workshop next to the Griffin Inn. Brewing about six barrels a week, it supplies around 150 outlets on a guest beer basis, often with special brews. A beer named after the latest car registration letter is also brewed. Tours by arrangement.

Cuthberts (OG 1038, ABV 3.8%) ❧ A refreshing, hoppy beer, with hints of malt, fruit and caramel taste. Lingering bitter aftertaste.

Gravediggers (OG 1038, ABV 3.8%) A premium mild. Black and red in colour, with a complex mix of chocolate and roast flavours, it is almost a light porter. Available in spring and summer.

Wheat-a-Bix (OG 1042, ABV 4.2%) A wheat beer; clear, malty and very pale, combining German hops and English wheat.

What the Fox's Hat (OG 1043, ABV 4.2%) ❧ A beer with a malty aroma and a hoppy and malty taste with some caramel flavour.

Pooh Beer (OG 1044, ABV 4.3%) ❧ A bright golden beer brewed with honey. Sweet, yet hoppy; moreish.

Vicar's Ruin (OG 1044, ABV 4.4%) A straw-coloured best bitter with an initially hoppy, bitter flavour, softening to a delicate malt finish.

Pews Porter (OG 1045, ABV 4.5%) A moderately hopped, rich chocolate porter with a dry finish. Available in autumn and winter.

Old Pal (OG 1055, ABV 5.5%) A strong, copper-coloured ale, full of rich, malty flavours. Three different types of hops are used; dry finish.

Rest In Peace (RIP) (OG 1070, ABV 7%) A light amber-coloured strong bitter, with a malty mouthfeel and a well-balanced sweet finish.

CITY OF CAMBRIDGE

City of Cambridge Brewery Ltd., 19 Cheddars Lane, Cambridge CB5 8LD.
☎ (01223) 353939

Brewery opened in May 1997 serving outlets within 30 miles of Cambridge. Additional beers, including a mild, are planned.

Hobson's Choice (OG 1042, ABV 4.1%) A golden beer brewed with First Gold hops.

MATTHEW CLARK See Ushers.

WILLIAM CLARK

William Clark Brewing Company, Scarborough, N. Yorkshire.

Brewery closed. Its one beer, Thistle Mild (OG 1040, ABV 4%), is contract brewed by an undeclared brewer.

CLARK'S

HB Clark & Co. (Successors) Ltd., Westgate Brewery, Westgate, Wakefield, W. Yorkshire WF2 9SW.
☎ (01924) 373328
FAX (01924) 372306

Founded in 1905, Clark's ceased brewing during the keg revolution of the 1960s and 1970s, although it continued to operate as a drinks wholesaler. It resumed cask ale production in 1982. It now has six tied houses and Clark's beers are widely available (including in London) either supplied directly from the brewery or via beer agencies. A range of special brews are produced throughout the year for special occasions, the beer name depending on the event. Brewery shop open 8–5 Mon–Fri, 8–1 Sat and Sun. Tours by arrangement.

Traditional Bitter (OG 1038, ABV 3.8%) ♠ A copper-coloured, well-balanced, smooth beer, with a malty and hoppy aroma, leading to a hoppy, fruity taste and a good, clean, strong malt flavour. Bitterness and dryness linger in the taste and aftertaste.

Festival Ale (OG 1042, ABV 4.2%) ♠ A light, fruity, pleasantly hopped premium bitter with a good fruity, hoppy nose. Moderate

bitterness follows, with a dry, fruity finish. Gold in colour.

Burglar Bill (OG 1044, ABV 4.4%) ♠ A good, hoppy, fruity aroma precedes an enjoyable, strongly hoppy and fruity taste, with moderate bitterness and good malt character. A lingering, dry, hoppy finish follows. Dark brown in colour.

Rams Revenge (OG 1046, ABV 4.6%) ♠ A strong, dark brown ale with good body, a strong malt flavour and some caramel, balanced with a fruit and hop taste which does not linger.

Hammerhead (OG 1056, ABV 5.6%) ♠ Rich malt in the mouth, but with hop flavour and bitterness to balance. The malty, hoppy aroma is faint, but the finish is long, malty and dry. A robust, strong bitter.

Winter Warmer (OG 1060, ABV 6%) ♠ A dark brown, powerful strong ale. A strong, mouth-filling blend of roast malt, hop flavour, sweetness and fruit notes concludes with a satisfying finish of bittersweet roast malt.

Old Dreadnought (OG 1080, ABV 9%) A strong, powerful, mid-brown beer, moderately malty with a good hop flavour. Easy to drink for its strength.

COACH HOUSE

The Coach House Brewing Company Ltd., Wharf Street, Howley, Warrington, Cheshire WA1 2DQ.
☎ (01925) 232800
FAX (01925) 232700

Brewery founded in 1991 by four ex-Greenall Whitley employees. In 1995 Coach House increased its brewing capacity to cope with growing demand and it now delivers to outlets throughout England, Wales and Scotland, either direct or via wholesalers. The brewery also produces specially commissioned beers and brews three beers for non-brewing company John Joule of Stone ☎ (01785) 814909. Tours by arrangement. Seasonal beers: Wizards Wonder Halloween Bitter (OG 1042, ABV 4.2% October), Cracker Barrel Bitter (OG 1046, ABV 4.6% November), Dewi Sant Heritage Ale (OG 1047, ABV 4.7% February), Regal Birthday Ale (OG 1047, ABV 4.7% April), St Patrick's Leprechaun Ale (OG 1047, ABV 4.7%, February–March), St George's Heritage Ale (OG 1049, ABV 4.9% April), Bootleg Valentines Ale (OG 1050, ABV 5%, February), Combine Harvester (OG 1052, ABV 5.1%, late summer), Burns Auld Sleekit (OG 1055, ABV 5.5%, January), Anniversary Ale (OG 1060, ABV 6%, January), Cheshire Cat (OG 1060, ABV 6%, June), Three Kings Christmas Ale (OG 1060, ABV 6%).

Coachman's Best Bitter (OG 1037, ABV 3.7%) ♠ A well-hopped, malty bitter, moderately fruity with a hint of sweetness and a peppery nose.

Gunpowder Strong Mild (OG 1037, ABV 3.8%) 🗂 🍺 🥄 A full-bodied and roasty dark mild with hints of pepper, fruit and liquorice, plus chocolate overtones. Malty aroma and full finish.

Ostlers Summer Pale Ale (OG 1038, ABV 3.8%) 🥄 Light, refreshing and very bitter, with a hint of pepper and a very dry finish.

Dick Turpin (ABV 4.2%) Also sold under other names as a pub house beer.

Squires Gold Spring Ale (OG 1042, 4.2%) 🥄 A golden spring beer. New Zealand hops give intense bitterness which is followed by a strong chocolate flavour from amber malt. Uncompromising and characterful.

Innkeeper's Special Reserve (OG 1045, ABV 4.5%) 🥄 A darkish, full-flavoured bitter. Quite fruity, with a strong, bitter aftertaste.

Posthorn Premium Ale (OG 1050, ABV 5%) 🗂 🥄 Well-hopped and very fruity, with bitterness and malt also prominent. Hoppy aroma and fruity aftertaste.

Taverners Autumn Ale (OG 1050, ABV 5%) 🥄 A fruity, bitter, golden ale with a slightly dry aftertaste. A warming, autumnal ale.

Blunderbus Old Porter (OG 1055, ABV 5.5%) 🗂 🥄 A superb winter beer. The intense roast flavour is backed up by coffee, chocolate and liquorice, and hints of spice and smoke. Very well-hopped with massive mouthfeel. An intense, chewy pint which is surprisingly refreshing and moreish.

For Joule:

Old Knotty (OG 1037, ABV 3.7%)

Old Priory (OG 1044, ABV 4.4%)

Victory Brew (OG 1050, ABV 5%)

COBDEN'S
Richard Cobden's Brewery, Peaches, Wellington Street, Stockport, Cheshire SK1 1JE. ☎ **(0161) 480 0842**

🍺 Brewery housed beneath Peaches nightclub, supplying this and another club in Cheadle, plus customers who come to collect the beer (no deliveries). The club is on the site where Richard Cobden and John Bright repealed the Corn Laws in the 19th century. A cask-conditioned lager has been trialled. Beers: Bitter (ABV 3.6%), Premier Bitter (ABV 4.2%), Festival Bitter (ABV 5%).

COCK
The Cock Tavern, Harborough Road, Kingsthorpe, Northamptonshire NN2 7AZ. ☎ **(01604) 715221**

🍺 This brew pub was opened in 1995 as The Hop House Brewery, after the total refurbishment and renaming of the Cock Hotel. In 1996 its parent company, Labatt Retail, sold out to Enterprise Inns, which has since sold the pub on to McManus Taverns, a local pub chain. The full mash brewery is still operational, although only one beer is now produced. This is also sold in some other McManus pubs. At the Cock itself, the beer is kept under blanket pressure. Beer: Bitter (ABV 4%).

COMMERCIAL See Worth.

CONCERTINA
The Concertina Brewery, The Mexborough Concertina Band Club, 9A Dolcliffe Road, Mexborough, S. Yorkshire S64 9AZ. ☎ **(01709) 580841**

🍺 Brewery in the cellar of a club, which began production in 1993, brewing eight barrels a week and supplying about 25 occasional outlets. Occasional beers: Shot Firers Porter (OG 1040, ABV 4.5%), Fitzpatrick's Stout (OG 1043, ABV 4.5%), Bandsman Strong Ale (OG 1048, ABV 5.2%).

Best Bitter (OG 1038, ABV 4%) 🥄 This mid-brown bitter has lots of hops on the nose, a hoppy taste and a dry finish, plus gentle fruitiness throughout.

Old Dark Attic (OG 1038, ABV 4%) A very dark brown beer with a fairly sweet, fruity taste.

One-eyed Jack (OG 1038, ABV 4%) Fairly pale in colour, with plenty of hop bitterness. Brewed with the same malt and hops combination as Bengal Tiger, but more of a session beer. Also known as Mexborough Bitter.

Hackett VC (OG 1040, ABV 4.2%) 🥄 A well-balanced, malty ale with a hop underlay and even coffee tastes, though the finish has a bitter edge. Mid-brown to amber in colour.

KW Special Pride (OG 1042, ABV 4.5%) 🗂 🥄 A smooth, medium-bodied premium bitter with a fine mixture of grain, fruit and hop in the mouth, followed by a balanced, mellow aftertaste. Easy drinking for a beer of its strength.

Bengal Tiger (OG 1043, ABV 4.5%) 🍺 Brewed in the style of an IPA; pale in colour, bitter and very hoppy.

CONISTON
The Coniston Brewing Co. Ltd., Coppermines Road, Coniston, Cumbria LA21 8HL. ☎ **(01539) 441133** FAX **(01539) 441177**

CONISTON BREWING Co.

🍺 Brewery set up in 1995 behind the Black Bull pub. The ten-barrel plant was built by Marston Moor and now supplies 30 other pubs locally, and others nationwide via a wholesaler. Tours by arrangement.

Bluebird Bitter (OG 1036, ABV 3.6%) ◈ A well-regarded beer named after Donald Campbell's *Bluebird*. Its pronounced, complex fruitiness is backed by a lingering, soft sweetness, and balanced by hoppy bitterness.

Opium (OG 1040, ABV 4%)

Old Man Ale (OG 1043, ABV 4.4%) A ruby-red ale.

Blacksmith's Ale (OG 1048, ABV 5%) A winter brew.

COTLEIGH

Cotleigh Brewery, Ford
Road, Wiveliscombe,
Somerset TA4 2RE.
☎ (01984) 624086
FAX (01984) 624365

Continued growth has taken this brewery a long way from its first home, a stable block at Cotleigh Farmhouse in 1979. It is now housed in specially converted premises in Wiveliscombe, capable of producing 140 barrels a week. Cotleigh supplies around 135 outlets direct, within a 40-mile radius of the brewery, and the beers are also available across the country via wholesalers. Two beers are produced exclusively for the Kent wholesalers East-West Ales Ltd. ☎ (01892) 834040. Occasional beers (made available to customers on a monthly rota): Swift (OG 1030, ABV 3.2%), Nutcracker Mild (OG 1036, ABV 3.6%), Harvest Ale (OG 1040, ABV 4%), Hobby Ale (OG 1042, ABV 4.2%), Goshawk (OG 1043, ABV 4.3%), Peregrine Porter (OG 1045, ABV 4.4%), Golden Eagle (OG 1045, ABV 4.5%), Merlin Ale (OG 1049, ABV 4.8%), Osprey (OG 1050, ABV 5%), Monmouth Rebellion (OG 1050, ABV 5%), Snowy Ale (OG 1050, ABV 5%), Red Nose Reinbeer (OG 1060, ABV 5.6%, Christmas).

Harrier SPA (OG 1035, ABV 3.6%) ◈ A straw-coloured beer with a very hoppy aroma and flavour, and a hoppy, bitter finish. Plenty of flavour for a light, low gravity beer.

Tawny Bitter (OG 1039, ABV 3.8%) 🗍 ◈ A mid-brown-coloured, very consistent beer. A hoppy aroma, a hoppy but quite well-balanced flavour, and a hoppy, bitter finish.

Barn Owl Bitter (OG 1045, ABV 4.5%)

Old Buzzard (OG 1047, ABV 4.8%) 🗍 ◈ A winter brew: a dark, ruby beer tasting of roast malt balanced with hops. Roast malt continues in the finish, with bitterness.

For East-West Ales:

Aldercote Ale (OG 1042, ABV 4.2%)

Aldercote Extra (OG 1046, ABV 4.7%)

COTTAGE

Cottage Brewing Company,
The Old Cheese Dairy,
Lovington, Castle Cary,
Somerset BA7 7PS.
☎ (01963) 240551
FAX (01963) 240383

Brewery founded in West Lydford in 1993 and upgraded to a ten-barrel plant in 1994. Owned by an airline pilot, the company got off to a flying start, with Norman's Conquest taking the *Champion Beer of Britain* title at the 1995 Great British Beer Festival. Other awards followed and, on the strength of this success, the brewery moved to larger premises in September 1996, doubling the brewing capacity at the same time. The beer is served in 450 outlets nationally, with local deliveries made by the company's steam lorry and horse-drawn dray. The names mostly follow a railway theme. Goldrush, the latest addition to the range, is an American lager-style cask-conditioned ale. Tours by arrangement. Bottle-conditioned Norman's Conquest (OG 1066, ABV 7%) is brewed under contract by Hardy (qv).

Southern Bitter (OG 1037, ABV 3.7%)

Wheeltappers Ale (OG 1040, ABV 4%)

Somerset & Dorset Ale (S&D) (OG 1043, ABV 4.4%) Named after the Somerset & Dorset Railway: a well-hopped, malty brew, with a deep red colour.

Golden Arrow (OG 1044, ABV 4.5%) ▮ A gold-coloured, hoppy ale.

Our Ken (OG 1044, ABV 4.5%)

Goldrush (OG 1049, ABV 5%) A deep golden beer brewed with American hops.

Great Western Real Ale (GWR) (OG 1053, ABV 5.4%) Similar to S&D but stronger and darker, with a full-bodied maltiness.

Norman's Conquest (OG 1066, ABV 7%) 🗍 ▮ ◈ A dark strong ale, with plenty of fruit flavour and a touch of bitterness.

COURAGE
See Nationals, Scottish Courage.

CRANBORNE
The Cranborne Brewery, Sheaf of Arrows,
4 The Square, Cranborne, Dorset
BH21 5PR. ☎ / FAX (01725) 517456

🗍 This brewery, set up in a stable block behind the Sheaf of Arrows pub, went into production at Easter 1996, initially just to serve just that pub. Its second year has seen beers sold to wholesalers and the development of specific beers for particular pubs; Cranborne now supplies four other local outlets directly. Tours by arrangement.

Quiver (ABV 3.8%)

Porter (ABV 4%) Brewed November–April.

Summer Ale (ABV 4.2%)

CROPTON

**Cropton Brewery Co.,
Woolcroft, Cropton, near
Pickering, N. Yorkshire
YO18 8HH.
☎ /FAX (01751) 417310**

Brewery set up in 1984 in the cellar of the New Inn just to supply the pub. The plant was expanded in 1988, but by 1994 it had outgrown the cellar and a purpose-built brewery was installed behind the pub. Cropton's additive-free beers are now supplied to 50 outlets locally, plus wholesalers. A visitor centre adjoining the pub offers tours, with or without appointment. Shop open 10–4 daily. Bottle-conditioned beers: Two Pints (OG 1042, ABV 4%), Scoresby Stout (OG 1042, ABV 4.2%), Uncle Sams (OG 1044, ABV 4.4%), Backwoods Bitter (ABV 5.1%).

King Billy (OG 1039, ABV 3.6%) ◆ A refreshing, straw-coloured bitter, quite hoppy, with a strong, but pleasant, bitter finish that leaves a clean, dry taste on the palate.

Two Pints (OG 1042, ABV 4%) ◆ A good, full-bodied bitter, perhaps with a more balanced flavour than in previous years. Malt flavours initially dominate, with a touch of caramel, but the balancing hoppiness and residual sweetness come through.

Scoresby Stout (OG 1042, ABV 4.2%) 🍺 ◆ Truly a classic of the genre. A jet-black stout whose roast malt and chocolate flavours contrast with a satisfying bitter finish.

Uncle Sams (OG 1044, ABV 4.4%) A clean-tasting and refreshing premium pale ale. The overriding characteristic is the fruity bouquet yielded by authentic Stateside ingredients.

Backwoods Bitter (OG 1048, ABV 4.7%) ◆ A malty premium bitter, tawny-coloured and full-bodied. A long and satisfying, sweet finish contains an abundance of fruit flavours. Now with a lower ABV.

Monkmans Slaughter (OG 1063, ABV 6%)

CROUCH VALE

**Crouch Vale Brewery Ltd.,
12 Redhills Road, South
Woodham Ferrers,
Chelmsford, Essex
CM3 5UP. ☎ (01245) 322744
FAX (01245) 329082**

Founded in 1981, Crouch Vale's business continues to grow steadily. Growth in the guest beer and wholesale markets has resulted in investment in new brewing plant, the latest development being the installation of four new fermenters in 1997 to increase production by 15 barrels a week. The new occasional brew, First Gold, won first prize in its class at the 1997 National Hop Association Awards. The brewery's single tied house, the Cap & Feathers at Tillingham, was the CAMRA national *Pub of the Year* in 1989. Crouch Vale currently delivers its wares by liveried dray to over 250 free trade outlets in Suffolk, Essex and Greater London. Tours for CAMRA members and customers only, by arrangement. Occasional/seasonal beers: First Gold (OG 1047, ABV 4.7%), Essex Porter (OG 1050, ABV 5.1%), Santa's Revenge (OG 1053, ABV 5.5%, Christmas), Fine Pale Ale (OG 1057, ABV 5.9%), Willie Warmer (OG 1060, ABV 6.4%).

Best Dark Ale (OG 1036, ABV 3.6%) A smooth, malty mild.

Woodham IPA (OG 1036, ABV 3.6%) ◆ An amber beer with a fresh, hoppy nose. A good session bitter with a well-balanced malt and hop taste leading to a fruit and hop finish.

The Golden Duck (OG 1038, ABV 3.8%) A summer beer.

Best Bitter (OG 1040, ABV 4%) ◆ The fruit in the aroma melts into a hoppy, malty taste before dominating the finish.

Millennium Gold (OG 1042, ABV 4.2%) ◆ A golden beer with a notable hop nose. The strong hop/fruit presence makes this a deceptively easy-drinking premium bitter.

The Conkeror (OG 1043, ABV 4.3%) A smooth, chocolate malt-flavoured, autumn ale.

Kursaal Flyer (OG 1045, ABV 4.5%) A seasonal beer for the spring.

Strong Anglian Special or SAS (OG 1050, ABV 5%) ◆ Well-balanced and full-bodied, this is a sharply bitter beer; dry finish.

CROWN BUCKLEY See Brains.

CROWN HOTEL See Scott's.

CROWN INN

**Munslow Brewhouse, The
Crown Inn, Munslow,
Shropshire SY7 9ET.
Tel (01584) 841205**

Pub brewery established in 1994 to supply just the pub itself, using a two-barrel plant and the brewer's own recipes. Some occasional beers are also produced. Beers: Boy's Pale Ale (OG 1034, ABV 3.6%), Munslow Ale (OG 1041, ABV 4.1%).

CUCKMERE HAVEN

**The Cuckmere Haven
Brewery, Exceat Bridge,
Cuckmere Haven, Seaford,
E. Sussex BN25 4AB.
☎ (01323) 892247
FAX (01323) 893728 (ring first)**

This tiny brewhouse went into production in 1994 to serve the Golden

Galleon pub (the brewery's owner), plus five other outlets on an occasional basis. Deliveries are made in the brewery's much publicised, 1957 Ford 10 pickup truck. Plans to expand both the pub and the brewery have been delayed until 1998. Tours by arrangement. Occasional/seasonal beers: Downland Dancer (OG 1043, ABV 4.4%), Fuggl'olmullable (OG 1063, ABV 6.2%, a spicy Christmas ale).

Saxon King Stout (OG 1041, ABV 4.2%)

Best Bitter (OG 1042, ABV 4.1%) ◆ Malty overtones in the aroma are joined by a hoppy bitterness in the flavour. Hop character increases in the aftertaste.

Gentlemen's Gold (OG 1046, ABV 4.5%)

Guv'nor (OG 1046, ABV 4.7%) ◆ A pleasant bitter in which malt in the aroma gives way to a hoppy bitterness in the taste and aftertaste.

Dark Velvet Mild (OG 1048, ABV 4.7%) Brewed Autumn–Easter.

Golden Peace (OG 1054, ABV 5.5%) An amber-coloured, strong beer.

CYDER HOUSE INN
See Baynards.

DALESIDE
Daleside Brewery, Camwal Road, Starbeck, Harrogate, N. Yorkshire HG1 4PT.
☎ / [FAX] (01423) 880041

Formerly Big End brewery, founded in the mid-1980s, this company moved to new premises and changed its name in 1992. It supplies 200 outlets, mainly on the A1 corridor between North London and Northumberland, plus other outlets nationwide via wholesalers. Bottling began in 1995, and there are plans to produce bottle-conditioned beers.

Nightjar (OG 1038, ABV 3.7%) An amber-coloured, medium-hopped beer with some sweetness and a touch of fruitiness.

Old Legover or Country Stile (OG 1042, ABV 4.1%) ◆ A well-balanced, mid-brown, refreshing beer which leaves a lingering hop and bitter aftertaste.

Old Lubrication (OG 1042, ABV 4.1%) A full-bodied beer with a hoppy aroma and a fruity taste.

St George's Ale (OG 1042, ABV 4.1%) Formerly Dales Delight, a full-bodied, light-coloured, hoppy beer.

Monkey Wrench (OG 1056, ABV 5.3%) ◆ A powerful strong ale, mid-brown to ruby in hue. Aromas of fruit, hops, malt and roast malt give way to well-balanced fruit, malt and hoppiness on the tongue, with some sweetness throughout. A very flavoursome beer.

Morocco Ale (OG 1058, ABV 5.5%) A very dark, full-bodied, malty brew with spicy overtones.

DARK HORSE
Dark Horse Brewing Co. (Hertford) Ltd., Adams Yard, off Maidenhead Street, Hertford SG14 1DR.
☎ (01992) 509800
[FAX] (01992) 509801

Brewery set up in the cellar of the White Horse free house in 1994, but moved in summer 1996 to its own premises, in converted Victorian stables in the town centre, giving scope for greatly increased output. The aim initially was to supply its own chain of pubs – the White Horse is the brewery tap, and a second pub has been acquired – but the beer is also sold to 23 other outlets in Hertfordshire, and further afield via wholesalers. Wetherspoons pubs also take the beers. Tours by arrangement. Occasional/seasonal beers: St Elmo's Fire (OG 1046, ABV 4.6%, a wheat beer), Black Widow Stout (OG 1048, ABV 4.6%).

Ale (OG 1038, ABV 3.6%) A tasty light bitter, with a hint of roast grain. Slightly more malty than when first produced.

Sunrunner (OG 1042, ABV 4.1%) A well-balanced, full-flavoured bitter, with fruit notes and a strong, bitter finish.

Fallen Angel (OG 1042, ABV 4.2%)

Death Wish (OG 1053, ABV 5%)

DARK STAR
Dark Star Brewing Co. Ltd. (incorporating Skinner's of Brighton), 55–56 Surrey Street, Brighton, E. Sussex BN1 3PB.
☎ (01273) 701758

🍺 Brewery set up by Peter Skinner and Peter Halliday in 1994 in the cellar of their pub, the Evening Star. In 1995 they formed Dark Star Brewing Co. Ltd. with Rob Jones (formerly of Pitfield Brewery), adding Rob's Dark Star beers alongside the Skinner's range. The two company names are still in use on the beers, but do not confuse the Skinner's beers with those produced by the new Skinner's Cornish Ales (qv). The small brew plant has allowed Rob to experiment with many different brews and styles to supplement the regular beers listed below. The beers are supplied to Peter Skinner's two pubs (the other being the Gardener's Arms in Lewes), and occasionally to a few other outlets. Tours for very small groups by arrangement. Dark Star beers: Dark Side of the Moon (OG 1045, ABV 4.5%), Dark Star (OG 1050, ABV 5%), Black Hole (OG 1060, ABV 6%), Critical Mass (OG 1073, ABV 7.5%). Skinner's beers: Target Practice (ABV 3.4%), BSM (OG 1035, ABV 3.5%), Roast Mild (OG 1035, ABV 3.5%), Summer Ale (OG 1035, ABV 3.6%),

Pale Ale (OG 1037, ABV 3.7%), Brighton Rock (OG 1040, ABV 4.1%), Penguin Stout (OG 1042, ABV 4.2%, winter), Golden Gate Bitter (OG 1043, ABV 4.3%), Old Familiar (OG 1050, ABV 5%), Cliffe Hanger Porter (OG 1055, ABV 5.5%), Pavilion Beast (OG 1060, ABV 6%).

DARKTRIBE
**DarkTribe Brewery,
25 Doncaster Road,
Gunness, Scunthorpe,
Lincolnshire DN15 8TG.
☎ / FAX (01724) 782324**

Dave 'Dixie' Dean caught the brewing bug by helping out at the Iceni Brewery and in June 1996 installed a small plant, made from converted dairy equipment, in his garage. He went into production in November with the first beer named after his dog; the later brews recall his former trade as marine engineer. Currently around 25 pubs take the beer. Tours for small CAMRA groups by arrangement. Occasional beers: Navigator (OG 1045, ABV 4.7%), Dixie's Midnight Runner (OG 1057, ABV 6.5%), both brewed for festivals.

Full Ahead (OG 1037, ABV 3.8%) A well-balanced session bitter with hop and fruit flavours and a dryish, bitter aftertaste.

Terrier (OG 1041, ABV 4.2%) A light, refreshing bitter ale with a gentle, malty, sustained bitter finish.

Galleon (OG 1045, ABV 4.7%) A tasty, golden, smooth, full-bodied ale with a thirst-quenching, fruity aftertaste that lingers.

Twin Screw (OG 1047, ABV 5.1%)

DARLEY See Ward's.

DARTMOOR See St Austell and
Nationals, Carlsberg-Tetley.

DARWIN
**Darwin Brewery, Brewlab,
University of Sunderland,
Darwin Annexe, Chester
Road, Sunderland SR1 3SD.
☎ (0191) 515 2535
FAX (0191) 515 2531**

Brewery founded in 1994 with a tiny half-barrel brewlength, as a research facility for the staff and students at the University of Sunderland. In summer 1997 Darwin took over Hodge's brewery (qv) with the intention of switching its mainstream production to the Hodge's site, but keeping the University's plant for student training and research. The one Hodge's beer will continue to be produced as before.

Dragons Tear (OG 1038, ABV 3.6%)

Evolution Ale (OG 1042, ABV 4%) A dark amber, full-bodied bitter with a malty flavour and a clean, bitter aftertaste.

Double Brown (OG 1048, ABV 4.5%)

Saints Sinner (OG 1052, ABV 5%) A rich, smooth-tasting, ruby-red ale with a fruity aroma and hop character in the taste.

Killer Bee (OG 1054, ABV 6%) A strong beer made with honey.

DAVENPORTS
See Nationals, Carlsberg-Tetley, and Pub Groups, Greenalls.

DAVENPORTS ARMS
**Davenports Arms, Main Street, Worfield,
Bridgnorth, Shropshire WV15 5LF.
☎ (01746) 716320**

Pub brewery established in 1994. The plant was upgraded in 1995 and the range increased, but the beers are still only sold at the pub itself and are not always available. Beers: JLK Pale Ale (OG 1039, ABV 3.8%), Hopstone Bitter (OG 1042, ABV 4%), Reynold's Redneck (OG 1056, ABV 5.5%, a strong mild), Hermitage Barley Wine (OG 1100, ABV 8.8%).

DAVIS'ES See Grainstore.

DEEPING
**Deeping Ales, 12 Peacock Square,
Blenheim Way, Northfields, Market
Deeping, Lincolnshire PE6 8LW.
☎ (01778) 345988.**

This new brewery was set up in January 1997, producing up to 20 barrels a week for the free trade (five regular outlets and another 40 on a guest basis). Its second beer was launched to celebrate St George's Day, and a summer ale is planned. Tours by arrangement.

Sun (ABV 3.7%)

Red (OG 1040, ABV 4.1%) A fruit beer.

Summer Ale (ABV 4.4%) A fairly strong but light summer beer.

St George (OG 1045, ABV 4.5%)

DENT
**Dent Brewery, Hollins,
Cowgill, Dent, Cumbria
LA10 5TQ.
☎ (01539) 625326
FAX (01539) 625033**

Brewery set up in a converted barn in the Yorkshire Dales in 1990, originally to supply just three local pubs. It now has two tied houses and supplies 12 free trade outlets directly. Its own distribution company, Flying Firkin Distribution ☎ (01282) 865923, delivers all over northern England and is making some inroads into the South. All Dent's beers are brewed using the brewery's own spring water. Tours by arrangement (minimum six people). Occasional beer: Sheep Dip (OG 1044, ABV 4.5%).

Bitter (OG 1036, ABV 3.7%) ◆ A clean-tasting, light bitter with hints of grapefruit in the nose and more general fruit flavours, along with some hoppiness and malt, in the taste. The finish is short.

Ramsbottom Strong Ale (OG 1044, ABV 4.5%) ◆ This rich and complex, chestnut-coloured beer has a warming, dry finish to follow its unusual combination of sweet and bitter flavours. A coffee aroma, with hints of fruit, precedes chocolate, malt, dried fruit and hops, which vie for attention in the taste.

T'Owd Tup (OG 1058, ABV 6%) ◆ A rich, full-flavoured, strong stout with a roast coffee aroma. The dominant roast character is balanced by a warming sweetness and a raisiny, fruit-cake taste which linger on into the long aftertaste, making this a very satisfying drink.

For Flying Firkin:

Aviator (OG 1038, ABV 4%) ◆ This medium-bodied amber ale is characterised throughout by strong citrus and hoppy flavours which develop into an enjoyable bitter finish.

Kamikaze (OG 1048, ABV 5%) ■ ◆ Hops and fruit dominate this full-bodied, gold-coloured strong bitter, with a pleasant, dry bitterness growing in the aftertaste. Citrus and honey in the aroma, and a hint of spiciness in the taste.

DERWENT
Derwent Brewery, Unit 1B, Derwent Mills, Cockermouth, Cumbria CA13 0HX.
☎ (01900) 826626

Brewery run by a former head brewer at Jennings. Around 50 customers currently take the beers.

Bitter (ABV 3.6%)

Mutineer (ABV 4.1%)

Old Cocker (ABV 5%)

DEVON
Devon Ales, Mansfield Arms, 7 Main Street, Sauchie, Alloa, Clackmannanshire FK10 3JR. ☎ (01259) 722020
[FAX] (01259) 218409

Brewery founded in 1994 at CAMRA's 1993 *Scottish Pub of the Year*, the Mansfield Arms. It has since been expanded by the addition of two five-barrel fermenters. One other associated pub also takes the beer. Tours by arrangement. Beers: Gold (OG 1037, ABV 3.8%), Original (OG 1037, ABV 3.8%), Thick Black (OG 1040, ABV 4.1%), Pride (OG 1046, ABV 4.6%).

DONNINGTON
Donnington Brewery, Stow-on-the-Wold, Gloucestershire GL54 1EP.
☎ (01451) 830603

Possibly the most attractive brewery in the country, set in a 13th-century watermill in idyllic surroundings. Bought by Thomas Arkell in 1827, it became a brewery in 1865, and is still owned and run by the Arkell family. The millhouse is in excellent condition and the millwheel remains in use to drive small pumps and machinery. Unfortunately, the brewery is not open to the public. Donnington supplies its own 15 tied houses, and 12 free trade outlets, with cask ales.

BB (OG 1036, ABV 3.6%) ◆ A pleasant bitter with a slight hop aroma, a good malt/hops taste balance and a bitter aftertaste.

XXX (OG 1036, ABV 3.6%) ◆ Thin in aroma, but flavoursome. More subtle than others in its class, it has some fruit and traces of chocolate and liquorice in the taste, and a notably malty finish. Rarely seen.

SBA (OG 1040, ABV 3.8%) ◆ Malt dominates over bitterness in the subtle flavour of this premium bitter, which has a hint of fruit and a dry, malty finish. Faint malt aroma.

DRUNKEN DUCK
Barngates Brewery at The Drunken Duck Inn, Barngates, Ambleside, Cumbria LA22 0NG.
☎ (0153 94) 36347
[FAX] (0153 94) 36781

Brewery opened in May 1997 at the famous Drunken Duck Inn, with assistance from Peter Yates of Yates Brewery. The brew plant is small, just one-barrel in length, but there are plans to use it to the full, producing a stronger ale and a stout to complement the single beer, which is only available at the pub at present. Beer: Cracker Ale (OG 1038, ABV 3.9%).

DUFFIELD
The Duffield Brewing Co., The Thorold Arms, High Street, Harmston, Lincolnshire LN5 9SN.
☎ (01522) 720358

Tiny brewery, founded in November 1996 in the cellar of the Thorold Arms. It currently brews just nine gallons at a time to serve the free house itself. Beers: Bitter (OG 1038, ABV 3.6%), Special Bitter (OG 1044, ABV 4.3%), Mulley's Irish Stout (OG 1044, ABV 4.4%), Extra Special Bitter (OG 1047, ABV 4.8%).

DUNN PLOWMAN See Three Tuns.

DURHAM

The Durham Brewery, Units 6D/E, Bowburn North Industrial Estate, Bowburn, Co. Durham DH6 5PF.
☎/FAX **(0191) 377 1991**

Brewery established in 1994 which has doubled its capacity in the last year. The beers are currently supplied to 150 outlets.

Sunstroke (OG 1038, ABV 3.6%) Available April–September.

Magus (OG 1038, ABV 3.8%) ❧ No strong flavours permeate this light session ale, but there is a well-balanced and light bitterness in the aftertaste.

Palatine (OG 1040, ABV 4%)

Celtic (OG 1043, ABV 4.2%) ❧ A mid-brown ale with a slight malty and fruity aroma. The aftertaste is predominantly dry and well-balanced.

Old Hundred (OG 1043, ABV 4.4%)

Invincible (OG 1044, ABV 4.5%)

Black Bishop Stout (OG 1045, ABV 4.5%) ❧ A moderate stout, not too sharp on the palate and not too dry in the aftertaste. Gentle roast aroma; smooth taste.

Canny Lad (OG 1045, ABV 4.5%)

Pagan (OG 1047, ABV 4.8%) ❧ There's a decent balance of malt and hops in this premium ale. Slight sweetness in the mouth and a faint bitter aftertaste are preceded by a hint of fruit in the aroma.

Sanctuary (OG 1057, ABV 6%) An old ale for winter.

DYFFRYN CLWYD

Bragdy Dyffryn Clwyd Brewery, Old Buttermarket, Chapel Street, Denbigh LL16 3TJ. ☎ **(01745) 815007**

Brewery founded by local pub landlord Ioan Evans in 1994. Its trade in North Wales is growing, with around 30 outlets now supplied direct. The beers, which have bilingual pump clips, are also widely available in England via wholesalers. There are plans to open a small public bar in part of the brewery. Tours by arrangement.

Dr Johnson's Draught (OG 1036, ABV 3.6%) ❧ Clean tasting and fruity, with a lasting bitter aftertaste.

Archdruid (OG 1038, ABV 3.9%) ❧ A blend of Dr Johnson and Castell. A smooth, nutty and full-bodied beer, which is well hopped and has a short and very dry aftertaste.

Cwrw Castell or Castle Bitter (OG 1042, ABV 4.2%) ◱ ❧ A darkish, smooth bitter, with good hop character. Fairly fruity, with some roast malt flavour. A complex bitter.

Jolly Jack Tar Porter (OG 1045, ABV 4.5%) ❧ A smooth, dry porter with good roast malt and chocolate flavours; reasonably well hopped.

Pedwar Bawd or Four Thumbs (OG 1048, ABV 4.8%) ◱ ❧ A well-balanced, fruity and sweetish bitter with a hint of caramel. Dryish aftertaste.

EARL SOHAM

Earl Soham Brewery, c/o The Victoria, Earl Soham, Woodbridge, Suffolk IP13 7RL.
☎ **(01728) 685758**

🚪 Brewery set up behind the Victoria in 1984, initially to supply just that pub. It expanded to supply a second tied house (since sold to Everards) and other pubs. The company ceased brewing for a while in 1996, but has now just acquired another tied house and sales to the free trade (ten outlets) are healthy. Seasonal beer: Jolabrugg (OG 1060, ABV 5.5%, Christmas).

Gannet Mild (OG 1033, ABV 3%) An unusual, full-tasting mild with a bitter finish and roast flavours which compete with underlying maltiness.

Victoria Bitter (OG 1037, ABV 3.6%) A characterful, well-hopped, malty beer with a tangy, hoppy aftertaste.

Albert Ale (OG 1045, ABV 4.4%) Hops dominate every aspect of this beer, but especially the finish. A fruity, astringent beer.

EASINGWOLD

Easingwold Brewery, Station Hotel, Knott Lane, Raskelf Road, Easingwold, N. Yorkshire YO6 3NT. ☎ **(01347) 822635**
FAX **(01347) 823491**

🚪 Brewery set up in a stable block behind the Station Hotel in May 1996, supplying the hotel itself and beer festivals. Now a further seven local outlets take the beer. The range has expanded, with new brews following the railway theme. Plans for a brewery shop and bottled beers are in hand. Tours by arrangement.

Tender Mild (OG 1035, ABV 3.4%) A thin, dark brown mild with traces of roast malt and chocolate flavours. A session beer.

Steamcock Bitter (OG 1038, ABV 3.8%) ❧ A sweet, malty bitter. The predominant aroma is of fruit. Maltiness is balanced by a slight bitterness in the aftertaste.

Express (OG 1047, ABV 4.6%) ❧ A full-bodied, well-balanced, amber-coloured premium bitter. Fruit and malt attack the nose and front of the tongue, joined later by a pleasant hoppiness and a strong, fruity, bittersweet aftertaste.

Pullman Porter (OG 1050, ABV 5%) A porter featuring roast malts, with a hint of chocolate in the flavour and aroma, and a clean, dry finish.

EAST-WEST ALES
See Brewery on Sea and Cotleigh.

EASTWOOD'S
Eastwood's Brewery, 11A Parkwood Road, Longwood, Huddersfield, W. Yorkshire HD3 3TL. ☎ (01484) 656024

Originally set up in Huddersfield, Eastwood's moved to the Walkleys Clogs tourist attraction at Hebden Bridge in 1995, sharing facilities with the Black Horse Brewery. In April 1996 it parted company with Black Horse and moved to its present site. Since then the beer range has been expanded and recipes refined. The company sells to 12 local outlets.

Best Bitter (ABV 3.9%) Three types of hop and three different barleys make this fine-tasting beer.

Reserve (ABV 4.3%) A ruby-red bitter from an old recipe.

Nettlethrasher (ABV 4.4%) A distinctively flavoured premium bitter, resulting from a blend of three different hops.

Black Stump (ABV 5.1%) A full-bodied, dark winter brew with a roasted malt and bitter character.

Leveller (ABV 5.7%) A well-hopped, full-tasting strong bitter.

Myrtle's Temper (ABV 7%) A dangerously drinkable extra strong beer. A well-balanced, hoppy and malty brew.

ECCLESHALL

Eccleshall Brewery, George Hotel, Castle Street, Eccleshall, Stafford ST21 6DF. ☎ (01785) 850300 [FAX] (01785) 851452

Brewery opened in outbuildings behind the George Hotel in 1995, and extended two years later. Its 'Slaters Ales' are supplied to around 50 other local outlets and wholesalers. Tours by arrangement.

Slaters Bitter (OG 1036, ABV 3.6%) ❦ Malt and hops combine with a fruity flavour in this light amber beer.

Slaters Original (OG 1040, ABV 4%) A distinctive, creamy amber beer.

HiDuck (OG 1041, ABV 4.1%) Available March–June.

Slaters Premium (OG 1044, ABV 4.4%) A strong, but light and creamy, dry bitter, darker than the other brews.

Slaters Supreme (OG 1047, ABV 4.7%) A well-hopped, dry bitter added to the range in 1997.

All Mighty (OG 1053, ABV 5.3%) Available November–March.

ELDRIDGE POPE
See Hardy and Pub Groups.

ELGOOD'S
Elgood & Sons Ltd., North Brink Brewery, Wisbech, Cambridgeshire PE13 1LN. ☎ (01945) 583160 [FAX] (01945) 587711

Based in Georgian, riverside premises, converted in 1786 from a mill and granary and acquired by the Elgood family in 1877, this brewery is one of the few remaining to use open copper coolers. It supplies real ale to all its 46 tied houses, to a free trade of around 200 outlets, and to other pubs throughout England and Wales via wholesalers. In 1998 the brewery gardens, which are being remodelled as a Georgian garden (complete with maze), will be open to visitors. Brewery tours by arrangement. Seasonal beers: Barleymead (OG 1049, ABV 4.8%, September), North Brink Porter (OG 1056, ABV 5.5%, December–January), Wenceslas Winter Warmer (OG 1076, ABV 7.5%, December).

Black Dog Mild (OG 1035, ABV 3.6%) Malt dominates the aroma of this black/ruby mild. Malt and roast grain on the palate are blended with hops and fruit. Dry, roast grain finish.

Cambridge Bitter (OG 1037, ABV 3.8%) ❦ An amber beer with an aroma of fresh hops and fruit. The flavour is predominately of hops, with some malt and fruit on a dry base. Very dry finish, with faint hops.

Pageant Ale (OG 1043, ABV 4.3%)

Golden Newt (OG 1045, ABV 4.6%) A golden brew. The aroma of malt and caramel leads to an even balance of malt and hops with an underlying sweetness; bitter finish.

Greyhound Strong Bitter or GSB (OG 1052, ABV 5.2%) ❦ Preceded by a fruity and faintly malty aroma, the flavour of this mid-brown beer is a blend of fruit, malt and hops on a dry, but slightly sweet, base. Very dry finish, with some malt and fruit.

MARTIN ELMS See Nethergate.

ENVILLE
Enville Ales, Enville Brewery, Cox Green, Enville, Stourbridge, W. Midlands DY7 5LG. ☎ (01384) 873728 [FAX] (01384) 873770

Brewery on a picturesque Victorian farm complex. Using the same water source as the original village brewery (closed in 1919), the beers also incorporate over three tons of honey annually, using recipes passed down from the proprietor's great-great aunt. Enville's owner had originally intended to go into full-time beekeeping with brewing as a sideline, but the position is now entirely reversed, and the brewery now grows its own barley, too. Enville (in Staffordshire, despite the postal address) also runs the Victoria Pub Co. Tours by arrangement.

Bitter (OG 1038, ABV 3.8%) ✦ A straw-coloured, hoppy and bitter beer which leaves a malty, moreish aftertaste.

Low Gravity Mild (OG 1038, ABV 3.8%)

Simpkiss Bitter (OG 1038, ABV 3.9%) ✦ A medium-bodied, golden bitter. The refreshing, hoppy taste lingers.

White (OG 1042, ABV 4%) ✦ A clean, well-balanced, golden, sweet bitter, light in flavour. An appealing beer.

High Gravity Mild (OG 1042, ABV 4.2%).

Ale (OG 1045, ABV 4.5%) ▉ ✦ A pale gold, medium-bodied bitter. Light hops and sweet fruit in the taste; a hint of honey in the aroma and aftertaste.

Phoenix Indian Ale (ABV 4.8%) A new pale beer using Phoenix hops. Available April–September.

Gothic Ale (OG 1054, ABV 5.2%) ✦ Malt, hops and caramel combine with a strong roast malt taste in this dark, stout-like beer. Well-balanced, with lurking hints of honey. Available October–March.

EVENING STAR See Dark Star.

EVERARDS
**Everards Brewery Ltd.,
Castle Acres, Narborough,
Leicester LE9 5BY.**
☎ **(0116) 201 4100**
[FAX] **(0116) 281 4199**

Small, forward-looking, family-owned brewery, founded in 1849 by William Everard, great-great-grandfather of the current chairman, Richard Everard. Over the years Everards beers were brewed in both Leicester and Burton upon Trent, until all production was transferred to Castle Acres in 1991. Its gradually expanding tied estate of 155 pubs includes many attractive, historic houses and over 90 per cent of them sell cask ale (but with the occasional use of cask breathers). Everards also supplies ale to some 500 free trade accounts, and the beers are increasingly available nationally via wholesalers, retailers and other brewers. Brewery tours for customers and CAMRA groups by arrangement. Seasonal beers: Equinox (OG 1048, ABV 4.8% autumn), Daredevil Winter Warmer (OG 1068, ABV 7.1%, December–January).

Mild (OG 1036, ABV 3.3%) ✦ A smooth, rather thin mild, red-brown in colour and malty throughout, with liquorice and roast flavours also in evidence. Often found on a cask breather.

Beacon Bitter (OG 1036, ABV 3.8%) ⬚ ✦ A refreshing, well-balanced, tawny/brown session beer. A bitter, hoppy taste leads to a long, dry, bitter finish that can be sulphurous in character. Very drinkable.

Tiger Best Bitter (OG 1041, ABV 4.2%) ✦ Mid-brown and smooth, this bitter has a gentle aroma of malt, hops and fruit, leading to a well-balanced palate and dry finish. It can have hints of sulphur on the nose.

Old Original (OG 1050, ABV 5.2%) ✦ A mid-brown beer with a sulphurous, hop/malt aroma and a complex taste dominated by a bitter maltiness. Fruit is also present.

For Whitbread:

Chester's Best Mild (OG 1032, ABV 3.5%)

EVESHAM
**Murphy Associates Ltd.,
The Evesham Brewery,
17 Oat Street, Evesham,
Worcestershire WR11 4PJ.**
☎ / [FAX] **(01386) 443462**

🚪 Brewery set up in 1992 in the old bottle store at the Green Dragon Inn in Evesham. The owner and licensee, Steve Murphy, who also owns another pub, currently supplies a further 20 outlets direct. The lack of local market penetration is compensated for by beer swaps with other small breweries and sales via agents. The brewery has become something of a tourist attraction drawing thousands of visitors each year; tours by arrangement. The 'Asum' in the beer names is the local pronunciation of Evesham. Seasonal beer: Santa's Nightmare (OG 1060, ABV 6%).

Asum Ale (OG 1038, ABV 3.8%) ✦ Lots of character and flavour make this a very enjoyable bitter with a dry finish. Tawny-coloured, and hoppy throughout.

Asum Gold (OG 1050, ABV 5.2%) ✦ A distinctive premium bitter with plenty of flavours to satisfy the palate. Copper-coloured, with balanced hops and malt, it is also sweetish, with fruit developing .

EXE VALLEY
**Exe Valley Brewery, Land
Farm, Silverton, Exeter,
Devon EX5 4HF.**
☎ / [FAX] **(01392) 860406**

Founded as Barron Brewery in 1984 by Richard Barron, this company's name changed in 1991 with the expansion of the brewery, when Guy Sheppard became a partner. It operates from an old barn (using the farm's own spring water), using new plant installed in 1993 which trebled capacity. Seasonal beers, introduced in 1995, have proved very popular. The brewery supplies 40 outlets within a 30-mile radius and other customers nationally via wholesalers. Tours for groups by arrangement.

Bitter (OG 1038, ABV 3.7%) ✦ A pale brown beer, with a fruit and malt aroma and taste, and a bitter finish.

Devon Summer (OG 1039, ABV 3.9%) A seasonal beer.

Dob's Best Bitter (OG 1040, ABV 4.1%) ◆ A mid-brown beer, with a malt/fruit aroma and taste.

Spring Beer (OG 1042, ABV 4.3%) ◆ A straw-coloured beer with a malt and fruit aroma and taste before a bitter finish.

Autumn Glory (OG 1044, ABV 4.5%) ◆ A fresh-tasting, bittersweet beer with a fruity aroma.

Devon Glory (OG 1046, ABV 4.7%) ◆ A light brown beer, with malt and fruit running through the aroma, taste and aftertaste.

Exeter Old Bitter (OG 1047, ABV 4.8%) ◆ A well-balanced beer with a malt/fruit aroma and taste, and a complex, sweet, fruity finish.

Winter Glow (OG 1058, ABV 6%) ◆ A dark brown, malty winter brew with a sweet, fruity taste and aftertaste.

EXMOOR

Exmoor Ales Ltd., Golden Hill Brewery, Wiveliscombe, Somerset TA4 2NY. ☎ (01984) 623798 ‖FAX‖ (01984) 624572

Somerset's largest brewery was founded in 1980 in the old Hancock's brewery, which had been closed since 1959. It quickly won national acclaim, as its Exmoor Ale took the *Best Bitter* award at CAMRA's Great British Beer Festival, the first of over 30 prizes. The brewery has seen many years of continuous expansion and, with steadily increasing demand, growth looks set to continue. Around 250 pubs in the South-West are supplied directly, and others nationwide via wholesalers and pub chains. Tours by arrangement. Occasional/seasonal beers: XV (OG 1043, ABV 4.3%), Exmas (OG 1050, ABV 5%, Christmas).

Ale (OG 1039, ABV 3.8%) ◆ A pale brown beer with a malty aroma, a malty, dry taste and a bitter and malty finish. Very drinkable.

Gold (OG 1045, ABV 4.5%) ◆ Yellow/ golden in colour, with a malty aroma and flavour, and a slight sweetness and hoppiness. Sweet, malty finish.

Hart (OG 1049, ABV 4.8%)

Stag (OG 1050, ABV 5.2%) ◆ A pale brown beer, with a malty taste and aroma, and a bitter finish. Slightly sweet. Very similar to Exmoor Ale and drinks as easily.

Beast (OG 1066, ABV 6.6%) A winter brew, available October–Easter.

FARMERS ARMS

Mayhem's Brewery, Lower Apperley, Gloucestershire GL19 4DR.
☎ (01452) 780172
‖FAX‖ (01452) 780307

Brewery opened in 1992 in a thatched barn in the grounds of the Farmers Arms, which also produces its own cider. In October 1996 it was taken over by Wadworth which is keen to keep the business going as a separate concern. The beers are only available at the pub. Tours by arrangement. Beers: Mayhem's Odda's Light (OG 1038, ABV 3.8%), Mayhem's Sundowner (OG 1044, ABV 4.5%).

FAT GOD'S See Queen's Head.

FEATHERSTONE

Featherstone Brewery, Unit 3, King Street Buildings, King Street, Enderby, Leicestershire LE9 5NT.
☎ / ‖FAX‖ (0116) 275 0952

Small brewery which has moved site several times. It specialises in supplying custom beers to pubs for sale under house names and turnover has grown considerably since it started in 1989. Four local outlets take the beers regularly. Occasional beer: Vulcan (OG 1049, ABV 5.1%, brewed to order).

Hows Howler (OG 1036, ABV 3.6%)

Best Bitter (OG 1042, ABV 4.2%)

Stage Ale (OG 1045, ABV 4.8%)

Kingstone Bitter (ABV 7.2%)

FEDERATION

Federation Brewery Ltd., Lancaster Road, Dunston, Tyne & Wear NE11 9JR.
☎ (0191) 460 9023
‖FAX‖ (0191) 460 1297

Federation was founded as a co-operative by local clubs in 1919, to overcome the post-war beer shortage. It moved to the Oystershell Brewery in 1921, but quickly outgrew that, and moved on to John Buchanan's Brewery in 1930. Expansion some 50 years later led to the company moving out to a green field site at Dunston. The brewery is still owned by local clubs, and their business accounts for the majority of the brewery's trade. Cask beers were reinstated in 1986, but only since the introduction of the Buchanan range in 1991 have sales taken off (90 outlets supplied). However, not all the beers have been successful and the Mild and Special have been withdrawn. Tours for CAMRA groups by arrangement.

Buchanan's Best Bitter (OG 1036, ABV 3.6%) ◆ Very difficult to find, especially on top form, when it has a pleasant aroma, a bitter flavour and a well-balanced aftertaste, with a hint of fruit throughout. Really an ordinary bitter, not a best.

Buchanan's Original (OG 1045, ABV 4.4%)
🍺 A rich, ruby-red bitter with a smooth, creamy taste and lingering mouthfeel. A robust malt character makes this a better than average drinking bitter.

FELDON
Feldon Brewery, Coach & Horses, 16 New Street, Shipston- on-Stour, Warwickshire CV36 4EN. ☎ (01608) 661335

🍺 Brewing was suspended here in 1997 whilst renovation work was in process on a new pub-restaurant extension. There are plans to re-start in the near future.

FELINFOEL
Felinfoel Brewery Co. Ltd., Farmers Row, Felinfoel, Llanelli, Dyfed SA14 8LB. ☎ (01554) 773357 FAX (01554) 752452

This renowned Welsh brewery was built by David John in 1878, when the village brew pub could no longer keep up with demand. Famously, it was the first brewery in Europe to can beer (in the 1930s). Still family owned, Felinfoel now supplies cask ale to most of its 80 houses (though some use top pressure) and to roughly 50 free trade outlets. Shop open 9–4.30 Mon–Thu, 9–3 Fri.

Bitter (OG 1032, ABV 3.2%) 🍺 A pale brown, hoppy, fruity beer with a hint of sulphur and a trace of malt. Balanced hoppy and fruity finish.

Dark (OG 1032, ABV 3.2%) 🍺 A dark brown/red mild, rather thin, with a slightly bitter flavour and aftertaste.

Double Dragon (OG 1042, ABV 4.2%) 🍺 A sulphurous aroma fades to leave apple and malt. A taste of apple weaves around the malt and hops to give a distinctive finish. Very drinkable.

FELLOWS, MORTON & CLAYTON
See Nationals, Whitbread.

FENLAND
The Fenland Brewery, Unit 4, Prospect Way, Chatteris, Cambridgeshire PE16 6TY. ☎ (01354) 696776 FAX (01354) 695852

Research chemist Dr Rob Thomas set up his new brewery in Chatteris early in 1997, so opening the first brewery in the town for 65 years. Tours by arrangement. Occasional beer: Smokestack Lightning (ABV 4.2%).

FBB (OG 1043, ABV 4%)

Sparkling Wit (ABV 4.5%) A wheat beer for spring and summer.

Doctor's Orders (OG 1051, ABV 5%)

Rudolph's Rocket Fuel (ABV 5.5%) A winter brew.

FERNANDES
Fernandes Brewery, The Old Malthouse, Savison Yard, Kirkgate, Wakefield, W. Yorkshire WF1 1VA. ☎ (01924) 291709 FAX (01924) 369547

New brewery, set up in the former malt kiln of the Fernandes & Co. Ale & Porter Brewery which ceased trading in 1919. The names of the beers are taken from lost Wakefield pubs. Shop open 10–6 Mon–Wed, 10–8 Thu–Sat. Tours by arrangement.

Old Bridge Bitter (OG 1040, ABV 3.8%)

Wakefield Pride (OG 1045, ABV 4.5%)

Double Six (OG 1060, ABV 6%)

FIDDLERS
Fiddlers Ales Ltd., The Brewhouse, The Fox & Crown, Church Street, Old Basford, Nottinghamshire NG6 0GA. ☎ (0115) 942 2002

🍺 Using brand new plant originally destined for the USA, this brewery was installed in autumn 1996 and went into service in December. Brewed by Harvey Gould, formerly with Sutton Brewery, the beers are just supplied to the Fox & Crown, but there are plans to expand into the free trade. Tours by arrangement. Beers: Mild (OG 1035, ABV 3.4%), Best Bitter (OG 1037, ABV 3.7%), Finest (OG 1046, ABV 4.5%), Old Fashioned Porter (OG 1066, ABV 6.5%, occasional).

FILO See First In, Last Out.

FIRKIN See Nationals, Carlsberg-Tetley.

FIRST IN, LAST OUT
FILO Brewery, 14–15 High Street, Old Town, Hastings, E. Sussex TN34 3EY. ☎ (01424) 425079 FAX (01424) 447141

The First In, Last Out began brewing in 1985 and changed hands three years later. The new father and son partnership introduced their own yeast in 1995, but further developments have been restricted by space, so they still just brew for their own pub and beer festivals. The ABVs of the beers can vary. Tours by arrangement. Beers: Crofters (OG 1040, ABV 4%), Cardinal (OG 1045, ABV 4.3%).

> 🍺 The full tankard indicates the beer is one of this year's *Good Beer Guide Beers of the Year*.

FLAGSHIP

The Flagship Brewery, Unit 2, Building 64, The Historic Dockyard, Chatham, Kent ME4 4TE.
☎ (01634) 832828

Brewery set up in 1995 in Chatham's preserved Georgian dockyard, now a major tourist site. A new visitor centre at the brewery features an exhibition about beer and the navy, and a display of labels from defunct Medway breweries. Some 40 outlets are supplied direct, and other pubs throughout the UK take the beer via wholesalers. Tours by arrangement. Occasional beer: Nelson's Blood (OG 1056, ABV 6%).

Capstan Ale (OG 1039, ABV 3.8%) A medium-dry beer with a balanced malt and hop flavour and hints of honey.

Spring Pride (OG 1042, ABV 4%) A new seasonal beer.

Ensign Ale (OG 1042, ABV 4.2%) A fruity ale, with a good balance of malt and hops.

Friggin in the Riggin (OG 1045, ABV 4.7%) A premium bitter with a smooth malt flavour and a bittersweet aftertaste.

Crow's Nest Ale (OG 1048, ABV 4.8%) A straw-coloured, sweet and fruity ale with a hoppy aroma.

Futtock Ale (OG 1050, ABV 5.2%) A fruity, ruby-coloured ale, with a roast malt aftertaste.

Gangplank Ale (OG 1055, ABV 5.8%) A dark winter ale, with balanced malt and hops.

FLAMINGO See Hog & Stump.

FLANNERY'S

Flannery's, 1 High Street, Aberystwyth, Ceredigion SY23 1JG. ☎ (01970) 612334

This free house, formerly known as the Ship & Castle, began brewing in May 1997 and just serves the pub itself. Beers: Granny's Flan (ABV 3.8%), Celtic Ale (ABV 4.2%).

FLOWER POTS INN See Cheriton.

FLOWERS See Nationals, Whitbread.

FLYING FIRKIN See Dent.

FOUR RIVERS

Four Rivers Brewing Company Ltd., Unit 10, Hawick Crescent Industrial Estate, Newcastle upon Tyne, Tyne & Wear NE6 1AS. ☎ / FAX (0191) 276 5302

Brewery founded in October 1996 by former Tap & Spile executive Mike Wallbank and former Hadrian brewer Trevor Smith. The first beers were produced using equipment at Hull Brewery but in spring 1997 Four Rivers acquired the assets, site and trading names of the closed Hadrian Brewery. The old Hadrian beers have since been revived and are sold alongside Four Rivers beers in around 40 pubs in the 'four rivers' trading area (bounded by the Rivers Tyne, Wear, Tees and Humber). Tap & Spile also take the beers. Seasonal beer: Yule Fuel (OG 1060, ABV 6.2%, December).

Moondance (ABV 3.8%)

Gladiator Bitter (ABV 4%)

Legion Ale (OG 1042, ABV 4.2%)

Rowan Ale (ABV 4.2%)

Centurion Best Bitter (OG 1045, ABV 4.5%)

Emperor Ale (OG 1050, ABV 5%)

FOX & HOUNDS

Barley Brewery, Barley, Hertfordshire SG8 8HU. ☎ (01763) 848459

An early member of the pub brewing revival, using a 19th-century brewhouse at what used to be the Waggon & Horses before changing its name. Some special brews are occasionally produced. Beers: Nathaniel's Special (OG 1037, ABV 3.3%), Flame Thrower (OG 1048, ABV 4.2%).

FOX & HOUNDS

Woody Woodward's Brewery, c/o The Fox & Hounds, High Street, Stottesdon, Shropshire DY14 8TZ.
☎ (01746) 718222

Brewing commenced at this pub in 1979 and saw two changes of ownership before Glen Woodward took over in 1992 and started selling to the free trade (currently four outlets). He also brews under contract for the Blackbeard Trading Company ☎ (01584) 872908. The brewery can be visited during pub opening hours. The 'wust' and 'bostin' in the beer names are Black Country expressions meaning worst and best. Beers: Wust Bitter (OG 1035, ABV 3.6%), Bostin Bitter (OG 1043, ABV 4.2%), Wild Mild (OG 1043, ABV 4.2%), Gobstopper Bitter (OG 1060, ABV 6%, winter).

For Blackbeard Trading:

Brew 37 (OG 1052, ABV 5.1%).

FOX & NEWT

See Nationals, Whitbread.

FOXLEY

Foxley Brewing Company Ltd., Mildenhall, Marlborough, Wiltshire.

Brewery closed.

FRANKLIN'S

Franklin's Brewery, Bilton Lane, Bilton, Harrogate, N. Yorkshire HG1 4DH.
☎ (01423) 322345

Brewery set up in 1980 and now run by Leeds CAMRA founder-member Tommy Thomas, supplying guest beers to eight pubs in N. Yorkshire, plus beer festivals. Occasional beers: Summer Blotto (OG 1052, ABV 4.7%), Winter Blotto (OG 1052, ABV 4.7%).

Bitter (OG 1038, ABV 3.8%) 🍴 A tremendous hop aroma precedes a flowery hop flavour, combined with malt. Long, hoppy, bitter finish. A fine, unusual amber bitter.

FREEDOM

Freedom Brewing Company Ltd., The Coachworks, 80 Parsons Green Lane, Fulham, London SW6 4HU.
☎ (0171) 731 7372
FAX (0171) 731 1218

Brewery opened in 1995 primarily to produce an unpasteurised premium lager (following the edicts of the German Beer Purity Law). The lager is available in 100 London bars and nationwide in Tescos. The company only brews cask ales occasionally. Tours by arrangement.

FREEMINER

Freeminer Brewery Ltd., The Laurels, Sling, Coleford, Gloucestershire GL16 8JJ.
☎ / FAX (01594) 810408

Established at the edge of the Forest of Dean in 1992, Freeminer is now brewing to full capacity. It has one tied house (the Miners Arms in Sling) and supplies over 50 free trade outlets directly (including several in Manchester), plus others nationwide via wholesalers. Beers are also brewed under contract for wholesalers, including Blackbeard Trading Company ☎ (01584) 872908. Tours by arrangement. Occasional beers: Iron Brew (OG 1044, ABV 4.2%), Hopewell Special (OG 1050, ABV 5%), Trafalgar IPA (OG 1060, ABV 6%). Bottle-conditioned beers: Bitter (OG 1038, ABV 4%), Speculation Ale (OG 1047, ABV 4.7%), Shakemantle Ginger Ale (OG 1050, ABV 5%), Trafalgar IPA (OG 1060, ABV 6%), Deep Shaft Stout (OG 1060, ABV 6.2%).

Bitter (OG 1038, ABV 4%) 🍴 A light, hoppy bitter with a wonderful hop aroma and a very dry, hoppy finish. Very moreish.

Strip and At It (OG 1038, ABV 4%) 🍴 A pale summer bitter with a refreshing, hoppy taste and a smooth, hoppy finish with a hint of bitterness.

Speculation Ale (OG 1047, ABV 4.7%) 🍴 An aromatic, chestnut-brown beer with a smooth, well-balanced mix of malt and hops and a predominantly hoppy aftertaste.

Celestial Steam Gale (OG 1050, ABV 5%) A pale, full-bodied ale. Bitterness is immediately present, with some hoppiness in the mouth and finish.

Shakemantle Ginger Ale (OG 1050, ABV 5%) A refreshing ginger ale brewed for summer. Unfined, with a high wheat content, it is like a European-style wheat beer. Ginger dominates throughout, mingled with a light hoppiness.

Slaughter Porter (OG 1050, ABV 5%) 🍴 A dark, full-bodied ale, mainly produced for spring and autumn. The roast malt flavour is followed by a hoppy finish.

Deep Shaft Stout (OG 1060, ABV 6.2%) 🍴 A black, complex stout. A roast malt and bitter chocolate flavour hits you immediately, followed by dry, bitter aftertaste.

For Blackbeard Trading:

Stairway to Heaven (OG 1050, ABV 5%) Celestial Steam Gale re-badged.

FREETRADERS See Ushers.

FREMLINS See Nationals, Whitbread.

FRIARY MEUX
See Nationals, Carlsberg-Tetley.

FROG & PARROT
See Nationals, Whitbread.

FROG ISLAND

Frog Island Brewery, Westbridge Maltings, St James Road, Northampton NN5 5HS. ☎ (01604) 587772

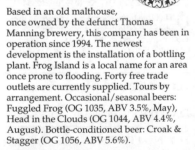

Based in an old malthouse, once owned by the defunct Thomas Manning brewery, this company has been in operation since 1994. The newest development is the installation of a bottling plant. Frog Island is a local name for an area once prone to flooding. Forty free trade outlets are currently supplied. Tours by arrangement. Occasional/seasonal beers: Fuggled Frog (OG 1035, ABV 3.5%, May), Head in the Clouds (OG 1044, ABV 4.4%, August). Bottle-conditioned beer: Croak & Stagger (OG 1056, ABV 5.6%).

Best Bitter (OG 1039, ABV 3.8%) A fairly complex beer, with malt, roast malt and fruit, plus a hint of sulphur, before a powerful kick of hop bitterness and astringency in the aftertaste. Pale brown in colour, and light on the tongue.

Shoemaker (OG 1044, ABV 4.2%) The Cascade hop citrus notes on the tongue are preceded by a huge malty aroma with passion fruit and roast characteristics. The malty aftertaste fades into a dry, nuttiness. Rich, pale brown and complex.

Natterjack (OG 1048, ABV 4.8%) Deceptively robust, golden and smooth. Fruit and hop aromas fight for dominance before the grainy astringency and floral palate give way to a long, strong, dry aftertaste with a hint of lingering malt.

Croak & Stagger (OG 1056, ABV 5.8%) The initial honey/fruit aroma is quickly overpowered by roast malt then bitter chocolate and pale malt sweetness on the tongue. Gentle, bittersweet finish. A winter brew.

FROMES HILL
Fromes Hill Brewery, Wheatsheaf Inn, Fromes Hill, Ledbury, Herefordshire HR8 1HT. ☎/[FAX] (01531) 640888

Brewery founded in 1993, supplying the Wheatsheaf and some other outlets with beers produced with local hops. Tours by arrangement.

Buckswood Dingle (OG 1038, ABV 3.6%) ◆ Sweet to begin, but fruitiness comes through. Pleasant and sweet aftertaste.

Overture (OG 1042, ABV 4.2%) ◆ A distinctive and well-balanced bitter that leaves a dry, hoppy taste in the mouth.

FRUITERER'S ARMS
See Cannon Royall.

FULBECK See O'Gaunt.

FULLER'S
Fuller, Smith and Turner PLC, Griffin Brewery, Chiswick Lane South, Chiswick, London W4 2QB. ☎ (0181) 996 2000 [FAX] (0181) 996 2079

Beer has been brewed on the Fuller's site for over 325 years, John Fuller being joined by Henry Smith and John Turner in 1845. Descendants of the original partners are still on the board today. The brewery recently completed a £1.6 million brewhouse redevelopment to cope with growing demand, and the installation of new mash tuns in 1993 led to an increase in capacity of 50 per cent. Fuller's owns 200 pubs, roughly half of which are managed and half tenanted, and all serve its award-winning real ale. Fuller's also supplies 350 other outlets within a 50-mile radius of Chiswick. Shop open 10–6 Mon–Sat. Tours by arrangement. Occasional/seasonal beers: Honey Dew (OG 1042, ABV 4.3%), Old Winter Ale (OG 1048, ABV 4.8%), London Porter (OG 1053, ABV 5%). Bottle-conditioned beer: 1845 Celebration Ale (OG 1062, ABV 6.3%)■.

Chiswick Bitter (OG 1034, ABV 3.5%) ◆ A distinctively hoppy, refreshing beer, with underlying maltiness and a lasting bitter finish. *Champion Beer of Britain* 1989.

Summer Ale (OG 1037, ABV 3.9%) ◆ A refreshing, golden, hoppy bitter with balancing malt flavour. Available June–September.

London Pride (OG 1040, ABV 4.1%) ⬚ ■ ◆ An award-winning beer with a good, malty base and a rich balance of well-developed hop flavours.

ESB (OG 1054, ABV 5.5%) ⬚ ◆ A strong and aromatic beer of great character. The immediate, full-bodied maltiness gives way to a rich hoppiness in the finish.

FYFE
Fyfe Brewing Company, 469 High Street, Kirkcaldy, Fife KY1 2SN. ☎/[FAX] (01592) 646211

Established in 1995 behind the Harbour Bar, this is Fife's first brew pub this century. Most of the output is taken by the pub, the remainder being available to the free trade via Belhaven Brewery and some wholesalers. The three main ales are due to be produced as bottle-conditioned beers. Tours by arrangement. Seasonal beer: Cauld Turkey (OG 1060, ABV 6%, Christmas).

Rope of Sand (OG 1037, ABV 3.7%) ◆ Named after the legendary local Rope of Sand, this is a quenching bitter. Malt and fruit throughout, with a hoppy, bitter aftertaste.

Auld Alliance (OG 1040, ABV 4%) ◆ A very bitter beer with a lingering, dry, hoppy finish. Malt and fruit are present throughout, fading in the finish.

Fyre (OG 1048, ABV 4.8%) Golden, smooth and well-hopped, with a fruity aftertaste.

GALE'S
George Gale & Co. Ltd., The Hampshire Brewery, London Road, Horndean, Hampshire PO8 0DA. ☎ (01705) 571212 [FAX] (01705) 598641

Hampshire's major brewery, Gale's was founded in 1847. The original building was largely destroyed by fire and a new, enlarged brewery was built on the site in 1869. This was extended to incorporate a new brewhouse in 1983. A new bottling line installed in 1997 is dedicated to packaging bottle-conditioned, corked beers, particularly Prize Old Ale which enjoys a good export trade. Still family owned, the company has grown slowly and steadily and all 122 tied houses (which include some very attractive old inns) serve real ale. Gale's also supplies over 550 free trade outlets directly, and other pubs via the big breweries.

Licensees who join the Gale's Beer Club can take a series of special one-off brews. Shop open 10–5 Mon–Fri. Tours by arrangement. Anniversary Ale (ABV 4.4%), produced in 1997 for the brewery's 150th birthday, may be added to the permanent range. Occasional/seasonal beers: Trafalgar Ale (ABV 4.2%, October), Hampshire Glory (ABV 4.3%, June), Harvest Ale (ABV 4.5%, September), Christmas Ale (ABV 5.5%, December), Force Eight (ABV 5.8%). Bottle-conditioned beer: Prize Old Ale (OG 1095, ABV 9%).

Butser Bitter (OG 1034, ABV 3.4%) A mid-brown chestnut beer. A slightly malty and fruity aroma preludes a sweet taste, with some fruit and malt. The aftertaste is sweet and fruity with a little bitterness.

Best Bitter (OG 1039, ABV 3.8%) A sweet, malty taste with some fruitiness leads to a malty and bitter aftertaste. Delicate, fruity aroma. Chestnut in colour.

IPA (OG 1042, ABV 4.2%) A light amber beer with a hoppy, bitter taste and aftertaste, marked by a hint of citrus. Hoppy aroma.

Winter Brew (OG 1044, ABV 4.2%) A rich winter ale, containing Prize Old Ale. Almost black in colour, it has a roast malt aroma with fruit and caramel, all of which are echoed in the taste and finish. Available November–March.

HSB (OG 1050, ABV 4.8%) A mid-brown beer with a fruity aroma. The full-bodied, sweet and fruity taste, with some maltiness, follows through to the aftertaste. For those with a sweet tooth.

Festival Mild (OG 1052, ABV 4.8%) Black in colour, with a red tinge. The aroma is fruity, with hops and malt. A sweet, fruity and malty taste, with some caramel, carries through to the aftertaste, but with more bitterness.

GIBBS MEW

Gibbs Mew PLC, Anchor Brewery, Gigant Street, Salisbury, Wiltshire SP1 2AR. ☎ (01722) 411911 FAX (01722) 410013

Gibbs Mew was established in 1898 by the amalgamation of Salisbury brewers Bridger Gibbs & Sons and Herbert Mew & Co. Charrington bought a stake in the company in the 1960s, which the Gibbs family bought back in 1972, and, in 1992, with CAMRA support, it saw off new predators Brierly Investments. However, in July 1997 it was announced that the brewery was to close with the potential loss of 21 jobs. Brewing was to transfer to Ushers of Trowbridge in the autumn. The beers have not been tasted since the move. The company's tied estate is still growing: in 1994 it bought the Centric Pub Company (197 pubs) and in 1995 it exchanged the Castle Leisure Complex in Cardiff for the six pubs formerly owned by Harmony Leisure Group. Gibbs Mew now owns 300 pubs, with most of those in the south of England taking real ale, which is also supplied to around 200 other outlets.

Wiltshire Traditional Bitter (OG 1036, ABV 3.6%) A beer with a pleasant enough flavour of malt and hops, and a dry finish.

Salisbury Best Bitter (OG 1042, ABV 4%) A rather chewy, sweet ale, decidedly lacking in bitterness. All the same, a pleasant beer.

Deacon (OG 1050, ABV 4.8%) A pale, golden beer with a faint orange aroma, an initial bitter taste, and a lingering, dry aftertaste.

Wake Ale (OG 1050, ABV 5%) A rich, warming ruby-red winter ale (available October–March). Basically sweet, but with almost herbal hop flavours in the finish.

The Bishop's Tipple (OG 1066, ABV 6.5%) Weaker than the average barley wine, but not lacking in flavour. The full-bodied taste is marvellously malty with a kick that leaves the brain rather less clear than the beer.

GLENTWORTH

Glentworth Brewery, Glentworth House, Crossfield Lane, Skellow, Doncaster, S. Yorkshire DN6 8PL. ☎ (01302) 725555 FAX (01302) 724133

Brewery established in January 1996 in former dairy outbuildings at the owners' home. The beer range has been expanded and almost entirely revised in the last 12 months. Deliveries are made direct to 80 outlets in Yorkshire, Lincolnshire, Derbyshire and Nottinghamshire.

Light Year (OG 1040, ABV 3.9%) Brewed for the spring/summer.

Doncaster Best (OG 1043, ABV 4.2%) An autumn/winter brew.

Buttercross (OG 1044, ABV 4.3%)

Dizzy Blonde (OG 1046, ABV 4.5%)

Old Flame (OG 1046, ABV 4.5%)

Henpecked (OG 1050, ABV 5%)

GOACHER'S

P&DJ Goacher, The Bockingford Brewery, Unit 8, Tovil Green Business Park, Tovil, Maidstone, Kent ME15 6TA. ☎ (01622) 682112

Kent's most successful small independent brewer, set up in 1983 by Phil and Debbie Goacher, producing all-malt ales with Kentish hops for two tied houses and around 30 free trade outlets in the Maidstone area. Special, a 75/25 per cent mix of Light and Dark, is also available to pubs for sale under house names. Tours by arrangement.

Real Mild Ale (OG 1033, ABV 3.4%) A full-flavoured malty ale with a background bitterness.

Fine Light Ale (OG 1036, ABV 3.7%) A pale, golden brown bitter with a strong, hoppy aroma and aftertaste. A very hoppy and moderately malty session beer.

Best Dark Ale (OG 1040, ABV 4.1%) An intensely bitter beer, balanced by a moderate maltiness, with a complex aftertaste. Now back to its original darker colour.

Gold Star (OG 1050, ABV 5.1%) A summer pale ale.

Maidstone Porter (OG 1050, ABV 5.1%) A dark ruby winter beer with a roast malt flavour.

Old 1066 Ale (OG 1066, ABV 6.7%) A black, potent old ale, produced in winter only.

GODDARDS
Goddards Brewery, Barnsley Farm, Bullen Road, Ryde, Isle of Wight PO33 1QF.
☎ (01983) 611011
FAX (01983) 611012

Housed in a picturesque converted 18th-century barn, on a farm near Ryde, this brewery went into production in 1993. Sales of its award-winning beers have been rising steadily and brewery capacity quadrupled in 1997, although this is partly to allow for kegging and the production of a new lager, Bazooka (occasionally available cask-conditioned, ABV 4%). A bottled (not bottle-conditioned) version of Fuggle-Dee-Dum is produced using equipment at King & Barnes.

Special Bitter (OG 1039, ABV 4%) A refreshing, clean, easy-drinking bitter, with a wonderful aroma of freshly-rubbed hops that carries right through to a satisfying aftertaste.

Fuggle-Dee-Dum (ABV 4.8%) An intensely flavoured, malty, hoppy, strong ale that makes your mouth water. Amber/brown in colour and full bodied.

GOFF'S
Goff's Brewery Ltd., 9 Isbourne Way, Winchcombe, Gloucestershire GL54 5NS.
☎ (01242) 603383
FAX (01242) 603959

Family concern which started brewing in 1994, using plant purchased from Nethergate Brewery. Goff's now supplies 50 outlets and there are plans to bottle its main brew, Jouster. Tours by arrangement.

Jouster (OG 1040, ABV 4%) A very drinkable, tawny-coloured ale, with a light hoppiness in the aroma. It has a good balance of malt and bitterness in the mouth, with a clean, hoppy aftertaste.

White Knight (OG 1046, ABV 4.7%) A well-hopped bitter with a light colour and full-bodied taste. Bitter predominates in the mouth and leads to a dry, hoppy aftertaste. Deceptively drinkable for its strength.

Black Knight (OG 1053, ABV 5.3%) A dark, ruby-red-tinted beer with a strong chocolate malt aroma. It has a smooth, dry, malty taste, with a subtle hoppiness, leading to a dry finish. A classic winter porter.

GOLDFINCH
Goldfinch Brewery, 47 High East Street, Dorchester, Dorset DT1 1HU.
☎ (01305) 264020

Brewery established in 1987 at Tom Brown's Public House, whose theme is broadly based on *Tom Brown's Schooldays*. A second tied house in Salisbury is also called Tom Brown's. The brewery supplies these two pubs and 15 other free trade outlets direct, plus others via wholesalers.

Tom Brown's Best Bitter (OG 1039, ABV 4%) A pale-coloured bitter which is fruity in both aroma and taste, with hops and some malt. The bittersweet taste gives way to a predominantly bitter finish.

Flashman's Clout Strong Ale (OG 1043, ABV 4.5%) A tawny/mid-brown beer with an attractive, honeyed aroma, and, again, a bittersweet taste with malt and some hops. Hoppiness continues through to give a bitter edge to the aftertaste.

Midnight Blinder (OG 1050, ABV 5%) A ruby-red-coloured beer with an intense fruit aroma. Malt, hops and fruit combine to give the familiar bittersweet taste of Goldfinch beers, leading into a marvellous hoppy, bitter finish.

DOROTHY GOODBODY
See Wye Valley.

GOOSE EYE
Goose Eye Brewery, Ingrow Bridge, South Street, Keighley, W. Yorkshire BD21 5AX.
☎ (01535) 605807
FAX (01535) 605735

After an absence of four years from the brewing scene, Goose Eye was re-opened in 1991 in a converted carpet warehouse. Around 50 free trade outlets in North and West Yorkshire and Lancashire take the beers, which are also available through national wholesalers and the Tap & Spile pub chain. Tours for small parties by arrangement. Seasonal beer: Xmas Goose (OG 1044, ABV 4.5%).

Bitter (OG 1037, ABV 3.8%) Hoppy fruit flavours and a light bitterness, with some background malt, characterise this refreshing, golden beer. The bitter finish is quite short.

Bronte (OG 1039, ABV 4%) 🍺 A gold-coloured bitter whose malty aroma is followed by a slightly sweet, malty taste, with some hoppy and fruity notes. The aftertaste is short.

Spellbound (OG 1039, ABV 4%)

Summer Jacks (OG 1041, ABV 4.2%)

Wandi Wabbitt (OG 1041, ABV 4.2%)

Wharfedale (OG 1044, ABV 4.5%) A copper-coloured best bitter, becoming increasingly hard to find.

Pommie's Revenge (OG 1051, ABV 5.2%) A light-coloured, full-bodied and fruity, strong bitter.

GRAINSTORE

Davis'es Brewing Company Ltd., The Grainstore Brewery, Station Approach, Oakham, Rutland LE15 6QW.
☎ (01572) 770065 [FAX] (01572) 770068

THE GRAINSTORE BREWERY
DAVISES BREWING Co Ltd.

This new brewery's rather strange company name comes from the fact that it was founded by Tony Davis and Mike Davies. After 30 years in the industry, latterly with Ruddles, Tony decided to set up his own business after finding a derelict Victorian railway building which had the potential of becoming an ideal brewhouse and tap. The tap room was opened first, in 1995, offering guest beers, then a few months later the brewery went into production. It now supplies over 45 other outlets. Bottle-conditioned beers are planned. Tours by arrangement. Seasonal beer: Liberty (OG 1043, ABV 4.5%, Easter).

Cooking (OG 1036, ABV 3.6%) 🍺 A smooth, copper-coloured beer, full-bodied for its gravity. Malt and hops on the nose; malt and fruit to the taste, with a malty aftertaste.

Triple B (OG 1042, ABV 4.2%) 🍺 Initially, hops dominate over malt in both the aroma and taste, but fruit is there, too. All three linger in varying degrees in the sweetish aftertaste of this tawny brew.

Gold (OG 1045, ABV 4.5%) A new summer beer.

Tom Cribb (OG 1047, ABV 4.5%) A winter brew.

Ten Fifty (OG 1050, ABV 5%) 🍺 This full-bodied, tawny beer is very hoppy and fruity right into the aftertaste. A little malt on the nose and in the initial taste, with an undying sweetness and an increasing bitterness.

GRAND METROPOLITAN
See Nationals, Scottish Courage, and Pub Groups, Inntrepreneur.

GRAY'S See Mansfield.

GREENALLS See Smiles, Nationals, Carlsberg-Tetley, and Pub Groups.

GREEN CUCUMBER See Salopian.

GREEN DRAGON
Green Dragon Free House & Brewery, 29 Broad Street, Bungay, Suffolk NR35 1EE.
☎ / [FAX] (01986) 892681

The Green Dragon was purchased from Brent Walker in 1991 and the buildings at the rear converted to a brewery. In 1994 the plant was expanded and moved into a converted barn across the car park. The 100 per cent increase in capacity has allowed the production of a larger range of ales, including seasonal and occasional brews, but the beers are only available at the pub itself and a couple of other outlets. Tours by arrangement. Beers: Mildew (OG 1035, ABV 3.4%), Chaucer Ale (OG 1038, ABV 3.7%), Bridge Street Bitter (OG 1045, ABV 4.5%), Summer Ale (OG 1045, ABV 4.5%), Dragon (OG 1055, ABV 5.4%), Slack Bladder (OG 1065, ABV 6%, winter), Old Forgetful (OG 1080, ABV 7.5%, summer).

GREEN DRAGON See Evesham.

GREENE KING
Greene King PLC, Westgate Brewery, Westgate Street, Bury St Edmunds, Suffolk IP33 1QT. ☎ (01284) 763222
[FAX] (01284) 723803

Greene King is East Anglia's largest brewery and was established in 1799. For years it ran a second brewery at Biggleswade, which produced lager, but this was closed during 1997. Acquisitions of pubs from Allied have extended the company's estate into south-eastern England, whilst an additional 65 pubs acquired from Bass has strengthened its position in London. In 1996 the company bought the Magic Pub Company chain of 277 pubs for £197.5 million. Its total estate now stands at 1,134 houses, 864 of which are tied. All Greene King's tied houses take real ale, but many have a cask breather device fitted in the cellar which, happily, some licensees choose not to use. Greene King also supplies some 2,500 free trade outlets. Group tours by arrangement. Twelve 'King's Court' seasonal beers run through the year: Old Goat (ABV 4%, July), Resolution Breaker (ABV 4%, January), King's Champion (ABV 4.2%, June), Mad Judge (ABV 4.2%, September, brewed with cranberries), Old Horny (ABV 4.2%, February), Black Baron (ABV 4.3%, October), Fantasy Ale (ABV 4.3%, August), March Madness (ABV 4.4%, March), Demon Eyes (ABV 4.5%, May), Sorcerer (ABV 4.5%, April), Captain Christmas (ABV 4.6%, November–December), Winter Ale (ABV 6.4%, December).

XX Dark Mild (OG 1036, ABV 3%)
🔶 Smooth and sweetish, with a bitter, slightly astringent aftertaste. Still under threat, due to low volumes.

IPA (OG 1036, ABV 3.6%) 🔶 A blandish session bitter. Not unpleasant, it has weak hop on the nose, with hop and bitterness in the taste, ending in an astringent, bitter finish.

Abbot Ale (OG 1048, ABV 5%) 🔶 A medium-bodied, distinctive, fruity brew, with a pleasant bittersweet and hoppy aftertaste. A much improved brew since changes were made in 1995; it is now fermented longer and is late hopped with pellets instead of hop oil.

GREEN JACK

Green Jack Brewing Co. Ltd., Oulton Broad Brewery, Harbour Road Industrial Estate, Oulton Broad, Suffolk NR32 3LZ.
☎ (01502) 587905 [FAX] (01502) 582621

Green Jack began production in 1993, on the site of the closed Forbes Brewery. A third tied house was opened recently, and the beers are also supplied to 20 other local outlets and to wholesalers. The brewery tap acts as a shop, open 5–11 summer, 7–11 winter. Tours by arrangement. Occasional/seasonal beers: Mild (OG 1032, ABV 3%), Gobsmacked (OG 1068, ABV 7.5%), Ripper (OG 1080, ABV 8.7%).

Bitter (OG 1039, ABV 3.7%) 🔶 A malty, light bitter with a fresh floral hoppiness.

Bramble Bitter (OG 1040, ABV 4%) An autumn brew.

Honey Bunny (OG 1040, ABV 4%) The spring beer, brewed with honey.

Old Thunderbox (OG 1040, ABV 4%) A winter beer.

Summer Dream (OG 1040, ABV 4%) A summer beer, brewed with elderflowers.

Grasshopper (OG 1043, ABV 4.2%)

Golden Sickle (OG 1047, ABV 4.8%) 🔶 An uncomplicated light bitter, stronger than it tastes.

Norfolk Wolf Porter (OG 1050, ABV 5.2%)
🔶 An excellent, dry, roasty winter porter. Brewed on an alternate basis with Lurcher, so not always available.

Lurcher Strong Ale (OG 1056, ABV 6%) 🔶 A sharp-tasting, fruity, strong bitter, mostly brewed in winter, alternating with Norfolk Wolf.

GREENWOOD'S

Greenwood's Brewery, Wokingham, Berkshire.

Brewery closed and planning to recommence production by sharing the equipment at West Berkshire Brewery (qv).

GREYHOUND

See Nationals, Scottish Courage.

GRIBBLE

The Gribble Inn, Oving, Chichester, W. Sussex PO20 6BP.
☎/[FAX] (01243) 786893

🏠 Brew pub owned by Hall & Woodhouse (Badger, qv). While most of the output is taken by the inn, it also supplies ten other pubs. Black Adder II is not to be confused with the beer from Mauldons, nor Pig's Ear with the brew from Uley. New, experimental beers were trialled during 1997. Tours by arrangement.

Ewe Brew (OG 1042, ABV 3.8%)

Ale (OG 1043, ABV 4.1%)

Reg's Tipple (OG 1051, ABV 5%)

Black Adder II (OG 1060, ABV 5.8%)

Pig's Ear Old Ale (OG 1065, ABV 6%)

Wobbler (OG 1080, ABV 7.2%) 🍺 A winter warmer.

GRIFFIN INN See Church End.

GUERNSEY

The Guernsey Brewery Co. (1920) Ltd., South Esplanade, St Peter Port, Guernsey GY1 1BJ.
☎ (01481) 720143
[FAX] (01481) 710658

One of two breweries on this Channel Isle, serving its stronger than average real ales in 13 of its 33 pubs. Originally opened as the London Brewery in 1856, it became a Guernsey registered company in 1920 upon the introduction of income tax on the mainland. It was acquired in 1978 by Bucktrout Co. Ltd., a Guernsey wine and spirit company with several pubs on the island. In 1988 Bucktrout merged with Ann Street (now Jersey) Brewery and Guernsey real ale is still available in selected Jersey Brewery houses. A new microbrewery produces an ever-changing range of real ales and stouts, and has helped secure the future of Braye Ale. Sadly, more beer is now being sold as keg, dispensed with mixed gas. Six free trade outlets in the Channel Isles are supplied with the real thing. Shop open 8–1 and 2–5 Mon–Fri.

Braye Ale (OG 1038, ABV 3.7%) 🔶 Copper-red in colour, with a complex aroma of malt, hops, fruit and toffee. The rich, mellow flavour combines malt, fruit, hops and butterscotch, whilst the finish has malt and hops. Full-flavoured, surprisingly dry and hoppy.

Sunbeam Bitter (OG 1045, ABV 4.6%)
🔶 Golden in colour, with a fine malt aroma.

Malt and fruit are strong on the palate and the beer is quite dry for its strength. Excellent, dry malt and hop finish.

Summer Ale (OG 1055, ABV 5.5%)

Winter Warmer (OG 1060, ABV 5.8%)

GUINNESS See Nationals.

HP&D See Nationals, Carlsberg-Tetley.

HADRIAN See Four Rivers.

HALE & HEARTY
Hale & Hearty Brewery, 104 Upper Hale Road, Upper Hale, Farnham, Surrey GU9 0PB. ☎ (01252) 735278

Beers with a cricketing theme are produced at this new brewery, which opened in November 1996 at the Ball & Wicket pub. Seasonal beers are also now in production and there are plans to supply other outlets via wholesalers. Beers: Upper Ale (ABV 3.8%), First Maiden Over (ABV 4.3%), Wicket Bitter (ABV 4.3%), Elderflower Spring Ale (ABV 5.2%, seasonal).

HALL & WOODHOUSE
See Badger.

HAMBLETON
**Nick Stafford Hambleton Ales, The Brewery, Holme-on-Swale, Thirsk, N. Yorkshire YO7 4JE.
☎ (01845) 567460
FAX (01845) 567741**

Hambleton was set up in 1991 in a Victorian barn on the banks of the River Swale, but production soon outgrew the original premises. A new brewery was opened on the same site in March 1996 and was soon brewing to its full strength of 50 barrels a week. New plant installed in 1997 should provide a further 50 per cent increase in capacity, and plans are also in hand for bottling. The brewery supplies 200 outlets in Yorkshire and the North-East directly, with other parts of the UK served by wholesalers. Hambleton brews beers under contract for the Village Brewer wholesale company ☎ (01325) 374887. Tours by arrangement.

Bitter (OG 1036, ABV 3.6%) 🍺 A lightly aromatic, but strongly hoppy bitter. Hops dominate, but the aftertaste is smooth and satisfying.

Goldfield (OG 1040, ABV 4.2%) 🍺 A light amber bitter with good hop character and increasing dryness. A fine blend of malts gives a smooth overall impression.

Stallion (OG 1040, ABV 4.2%) 🍺 A premium bitter, moderately hoppy throughout and richly balanced in malt and fruit, developing a sound and robust

bitterness, with earthy hop drying the aftertaste.

Stud (OG 1042, ABV 4.3%) 🍺 A strongly bitter beer, with rich hop and fruit. It ends dry and spicy.

Nightmare (OG 1048, ABV 5%) 🍺 🍺 🍺 Fully deserving its acclaim, this impressively flavoured beer satisfies all parts of the palate. Strong roast malts dominate, but hoppiness rears out of this complex blend. *Champion Winter Beer of Britain 1997*.

For Village Brewer:

White Boar (OG 1036, ABV 3.6%) 🍺 A light, flowery and fruity ale; crisp, clean and refreshing, with a dry-hopped, powerful but not aggressive, bitter finish.

Bull (OG 1039, ABV 4%) 🍺 A fairly thin, but very well-hopped bitter, with a very distinct dryness in the aftertaste. Obviously from the Hambleton stable.

Old Raby (OG 1045, ABV 4.8%) 🍺 A full-bodied, smooth, rich-tasting dark ale. A complex balance of malt, fruit character and creamy caramel sweetness offsets the bitterness nicely. A classic old ale.

HAMPSHIRE
**Hampshire Brewery Ltd., 6–8 Romsey Industrial Estate, Greatbridge Road, Romsey, Hampshire SO51 0HR.
☎ (01794) 830000**

Brewery set up as a partnership in 1992 and now a limited company. Its trade has steadily grown (over 300 outlets take the beer) and this forced a move from its home in Andover to a larger site in Romsey in summer 1997. The new premises will also permit the installation of a bottling plant. The beers have not been tasted since the move. Hampshire also brews for The Beer Seller wholesaler ☎ (01963) 34264. Brewery shop open 10–6. Tours by arrangement. Seasonal beers: Bewitched (ABV 4.6%, Halloween), Good King Wenceslas (ABV 5%, Christmas), Hampshire Hare (ABV 5%, Easter).

King Alfred's (OG 1038, ABV 3.8%) 🍺 A mid-brown beer, featuring some malt and fruit in the aroma, a light malty, hoppy and fruity taste and aftertaste, plus a perfumed character. Inferior to the beer of the early 1990s.

Edmond Ironside (OG 1042, ABV 4.2%) 🍺 A beer with little aroma, but some malt. The taste has solid fruit with lasting hops and malt. The aftertaste is more bitter and malty. Pale brown in colour.

Richard Lionheart (OG 1042, ABV 4.2%) A smooth, golden best bitter.

Arthur Pendragon (OG 1048, ABV 4.8%) A full-bodied and fruity premium ale.

William the Conqueror's 1066 (OG 1062, ABV 6%)

For The Beer Seller:

Hampshire Hog (OG 1039, ABV 3.6%)

HANBY
Hanby Ales Ltd., New Brewery, Aston Park, Soulton Road, Wem, Shropshire SY4 5SD.
☎ / FAX (01939) 232432

Following the closure of Wem Brewery by Greenalls in 1988, the former head brewer, Jack Hanby, set up his own business. Brewing commenced the following spring and by 1990 he had moved into a new, larger brewhouse (which was improved in 1991). Hanby supplies a single tied house, plus some 200 pubs directly and others via wholesalers. In addition to the extensive regular range, a monthly 'special' is brewed. Occasional/seasonal beers: Cherry Bomb (OG 1060, ABV 6%), Joy Bringer (OG 1060, ABV 6%). Bottle-conditioned beer: Premium (OG 1046, ABV 4.6%).

Black Magic Mild (OG 1033, ABV 3.3%) ◆ A dark, reddish-brown mild, which is dry and bitter with a roast malt taste.

Drawwell Bitter (OG 1039, ABV 3.9%) ◆ A hoppy beer with excellent bitterness, both in taste and aftertaste. Beautiful amber colour.

All Seasons Bitter (OG 1042, ABV 4.2%)

Rainbow Chaser (OG 1043, ABV 4.3%)

Shropshire Stout (OG 1044, ABV 4.4%) ◆ A full-bodied, rich ruby stout, with a very distinctive, chocolate malt, dry flavour.

Wem Special (OG 1044, ABV 4.4%)

Cascade (OG 1045, ABV 4.5%)

Scorpio (OG 1045, ABV 4.5%)

Treacleminer Bitter (OG 1046, ABV 4.6%) ◆ A pale brown beer which is sweeter and fruitier than the beers above. Slight malt and hop taste.

Old Wemian Ale (OG 1049, ABV 4.9%)

Taverners Ale (OG 1053, ABV 5.3%)

Nutcracker Bitter (OG 1060, ABV 6%) ◆ A warming, smooth, mid-brown beer, with malt and hops coming through. Definitely more bitter than sweet.

HANCOCK'S See Nationals, Bass.

HAND IN HAND See Kemptown.

HANSON'S See Banks's.

HARDINGTON
Hardington Brewery, Bedminster, Bristol.
Brewery closed.

HARDY
Thomas Hardy Brewing Ltd., Weymouth Avenue, Dorchester, Dorset DT1 1QT. ☎ (01305) 251251
FAX (01305) 258300

Founded by the Eldridge family as the Green Dragon Brewery in 1837, this brewery now operates as the Thomas Hardy Brewery, following a division of the Eldridge Pope company in 1996. Eldridge Pope now concentrates on pub ownership (see Pub Groups). Thomas Hardy brews Eldridge Pope's beers under contract, and also brews and packages for other breweries (mostly bottled beers). Shop open Mon–Sat, 9–5. Tours by arrangement.

For Eldridge Pope:

Pope's Traditional (OG 1039, ABV 3.8%) ◆ Formerly Eldridge Pope Best Bitter. A mixture of malt and hop with a hint of fruit.

Hardy Country Bitter (OG 1041, ABV 4.2%) ◆ A dry, hoppy beer with faint undertones of malt and fruit. The taste is smooth despite a bitter edge which continues into the finish.

Royal Oak (OG 1049, ABV 5%) ◆ A full-bodied beer with a distinctive banana aroma and a mainly sweet, fruity taste. This is balanced by malt and some hops and there is a fruity finish to this smooth, well-rounded brew.

Bottle-conditioned beer: Thomas Hardy's Ale (OG 1250, ABV 12%) ⬚.

For Cottage:

Bottle-conditioned beer: Norman's Conquest (ABV 7%).

HARDYS & HANSONS
Hardys & Hansons PLC, Kimberley Brewery, Nottingham NG16 2NS.
☎ (0115) 938 3611
FAX (0115) 945 9055

Established in 1832 and 1847 respectively, Hardys and Hansons were two competitive breweries until a merger in 1931 produced the present company. The brewery is today controlled by descendants of the original Hardy and Hanson families, with all production taking place on the original Hardy site. The majority of its 257 tied houses take its award-winning real ales, although there is still a tendency to spoil them with top pressure (never used on the strong Kimberley Classic). A range of seasonal ales, with a new beer every two months, introduced in the spring of 1996 under the 'Cellarman's Cask' banner, has proved very successful in the tied estate and has brought new custom from the free trade. Around 100 outlets are now supplied. Tours by arrangement. Occasional/seasonal beers: Crazy Crow (ABV 4.1%), Crowing Cock (ABV 4.2%), Frolicking Farmer (ABV 4.2%),

Guzzling Goose (ABV 4.4%), Rocking Rudolph (ABV 5.5%).

Kimberley Best Mild (OG 1035, ABV 3.1%) 🍺 🔷 A deep ruby mild, deliciously dominated by chocolate malt. The fruitiness and caramel sweetness are well balanced in the taste, with a faintly hoppy finish.

Kimberley Best Bitter (OG 1039, ABV 3.9%) 🔷 A beer with a flowery hoppy and fruity nose, although malt is never far away. Fruity hop is evident in the taste and there is a consistent bitterness.

Kimberley Classic (OG 1047, ABV 4.8%) 🔷 A light golden brown beer with an amber hue. Bitter throughout, it has a fruity hop nose, with malt behind the hops in the taste and aftertaste. It is not always easy to find.

HARPENDEN See Verulam.

HART
Hart Brewery, Cartford Hotel, Cartford Lane, Little Eccleston, Lancashire PR3 0YP. ☎ (01995) 671686

🚪 Brewery founded in 1994, in a small private garage, which moved to premises at the rear of the Cartford Hotel in 1995. With a ten-barrel plant, Hart is supplying a growing number (currently over 70) of local free houses as well as the hotel itself. Tours by arrangement. A monthly beer is available alongside the regular range. Seasonal beers: Liberator (OG 1037, ABV 3.7%, September), Fyle Ale (OG 1040, ABV 4%, April), Criminale Porter (OG 1041, ABV 4%, October), Mayson Premier (OG 1042, ABV 4%, August), High Octane Gold Beach (OG 1043, ABV 4.2%, May), Excalibur (OG 1045, ABV 4.5%, June), Hart of Steel (OG 1045, ABV 4.5%, July), No Balls (OG 1045, ABV 4.5%, Christmas), Andrew's Cobblestone Stout (OG 1050, ABV 5%, February), Old Ram (OG 1050, ABV 5%, March), Amadeus (OG 1055, ABV 5.5%, November), Merrie Hart Stout (OG 1055, ABV 5.5%, January).

Cleo's Asp (OG 1037, ABV 3.7%) 🔷 A smooth golden brew with a light, fruity aroma, a slow burst of fruit and hop flavours and a restrained, dry, hoppy finish. Very drinkable.

Ambassador (OG 1041, ABV 4.2%) This ruby-red beer is a little drier than others in the range. Brewed with crystal and chocolate malts and Kent Fuggles.

Squirrels Hoard (OG 1042, ABV 4%) Brewed for the Cartford Hotel and CAMRA festivals. Pale and crystal malts produce a wonderfully nutty flavour.

Nemesis (OG 1046, ABV 4.5%) A light amber-coloured beer with a refreshing flavour.

Road to Rome (OG 1050, ABV 5%) Originally brewed for CAMRA's 25th anniversary, now a permanent addition to the range. A rich, ruby-red beer with a full malt flavour and a sweet aftertaste.

HARTLEYS See Robinson's.

HARVEYS
Harvey & Son (Lewes) Ltd., The Bridge Wharf Brewery, 6 Cliffe High Street, Lewes, E. Sussex BN7 2AH. ☎ (01273) 480209 FAX (01273) 483706

Established in the late 18th century by John Harvey, on the banks of the River Ouse, this Georgian brewery was rebuilt in 1881. The Victorian Gothic tower and brewhouse remain a very attractive feature. A major development in 1985 doubled brewing capacity and the further addition of fermenters has seen production rise to more than 30,000 barrels per year. Still a family-run company, Harveys supplies real ale to all its 40 pubs and about 600 free trade outlets in Sussex and Kent. One of the first breweries to introduce seasonal ales, it also frequently produces commemorative beers, which are sometimes available on draught. Tours by arrangement (two-year waiting list!). Shop open 9.30–4.45 Mon–Sat. Seasonal beers: Knots of May Light Mild (OG 1030, ABV 3%, May), Southdown Harvest Ale (OG 1050, ABV 5%, September), 1859 Porter (OG 1053, ABV 4.8%, March) 🍺, Tom Paine (OG 1055, ABV 5.5%, July), Firecracker (OG 1066, ABV 5.8%, November), Christmas Ale (OG 1090, ABV 8.1%, December). Bottle-conditioned beer: 1859 Porter (OG 1053, ABV 4.8%, occasional).

Sussex XX Mild Ale (OG 1030, ABV 3%) 🔷 A dark, malty brew with slight malt and hops in the aroma and roasted malt and hops coming through in both the flavour and finish.

Sussex Pale Ale (OG 1033, ABV 3.5%) 🔷 An agreeable, light bitter with malt and hops dominating the aroma, whilst a hoppy bitterness develops throughout the taste to dominate the finish.

Sussex Best Bitter (BB) (OG 1040, ABV 4%) 🔷 A medium-strength bitter with a good balance of malt and strong hops in the flavour, which develops into a bitter, hoppy aftertaste.

Sussex XXXX or Old Ale (OG 1043, ABV 4.3%) 🔷 Brewed October–May: a rich, dark beer with a good malty nose, with undertones of roast malt, hops and fruit. The flavour is a complex blend of roast malt, grain, fruit and hops with some caramel. Malty caramel finish with roast malt.

Armada Ale (OG 1045, ABV 4.5%) 🔷 A full-bodied beer in which hops are dominant throughout. Long, dry finish.

HARVIESTOUN

**Harviestoun Brewery Ltd.,
Devon Road, Dollar,
Clackmannanshire
FK14 7LX. ☎ (01259) 742141
FAX (01259) 743141**

Hand-built in a 200-year-old stone byre, by two home-brew enthusiasts in 1985, this small brewery operates from a former dairy at the foot of the Ochil Hills, near Stirling. A new custom-built brewing plant was installed in 1991 and Harviestoun now serves 70 outlets in central Scotland as well as wholesalers' customers throughout Britain. Tours by arrangement. Occasional beers: Spring Fever (OG 1038, ABV 3.8%, March–April), Freshers (OG 1039, ABV 3.9%, October), Mayfest (OG 1044, ABV 4.4%, a wheat beer, brewed May–June), Good King Legless (OG 1045, ABV 4.5%, December), Nouveau (OG 1098, ABV 9.8%, a barley wine, Christmas/New Year).

Waverley 70/- (OG 1037, ABV 3.7%) ◗ Light in body, with a malt, hop and fruit aroma. Malt, hops, some fruit and roast feature in the taste, before a dry finish.

Original 80/- (OG 1041, ABV 4.1%) ◗ This beer has malt, fruit and hops throughout, with a slight toffeeness in the taste. Faintly sulphurous aroma.

Montrose Ale (OG 1042, ABV 4.2%) ◗ A tawny-coloured beer with a complex aroma of malt, roast, caramel and fruit, which remain in the taste, giving way to a slight bitterness.

Ptarmigan 85/- (OG 1045, ABV 4.5%) ◗ A well-balanced, bittersweet beer in which hops and malt dominate. The blend of malt, hops and fruit produces a clean, hoppy aftertaste.

Schiehallion (OG 1048, ABV 4.8%) ▤ ◗ A Scottish cask lager, brewed using a lager yeast and Hersbrücker hops, and properly lagered. A fruity aroma, with hops and malt, leads to a malty, bitter taste with floral hoppiness and a bittersweet finish.

Old Manor (OG 1050, ABV 5%) A winter brew.

HEATHER

**Heather Ale Ltd., 736
Dumbarton Road, Glasgow
G11 6RD.
☎ / FAX (0141) 337 6298**

Bruce Williams started brewing Fraoch (Gaelic for heather) in 1992 at the now closed West Highland Brewery in Argyll, then moved his production to Maclay's Thistle Brewery in 1993 from where he supplies almost 40 outlets (Bruce brews the beer himself, using Maclay's equipment). Heather Ale is made with flowering heather, following an ancient tradition – hence its seasonal nature. Pictish is brewed in November using the last crop of heather flowers.

Fraoch Heather Ale (OG 1041, ABV 4.1%) ▤ Available May–November; a beer with a floral, peaty aroma, a spicy, herbal, woody flavour and a dry finish.

Fraoch Pictish Ale (OG 1052, ABV 5.3%) Available December–April.

HEDGEHOG & HOGSHEAD

**Belchers Brewery, 100
Goldstone Villas, Hove,
E. Sussex BN3 3RX.
☎ (01273) 324660; 163
University Road, Highfield,
Southampton, Hampshire
SO17 1TS. ☎ (01703) 581124;
Highbury Corner, London N1 1RU.
☎ (0171) 226 4627; 2 High Street, Sutton,
Surrey SM1 1HN. ☎ (0181) 661 7525**

🍺 Brew pub chain established with two outlets (Hove and Southampton) in 1990 by David Bruce (of Firkin fame), who sold them in 1994 to Grosvenor Inns (see Pub Groups) for shares, with Bruce taking a seat on the Grosvenor board. The beers are stored in cellar tanks and a cask breather is used on slower sellers. The range may vary from pub to pub and the products may also be found in some other outlets. Tours by arrangement. Beers: BiBi or Best Bitter (OG 1042, ABV 4.2%), Flamin' Ada (OG 1042, ABV 4.2%, an occasional ginger beer), Old Slug Porter (OG 1042, ABV 4.2%), Bootleg Bitter (OG 1052, ABV 5.2%), Hogbolter (OG 1058, ABV 5.8%, occasional).

HENSTRIDGE

**Henstridge Brewery, c/o
Barvick Engineering, Bow
Bridge Works, Henstridge
Trading Estate, Henstridge,
Somerset BA8 0TH.
☎ (01963) 363150 FAX (01963) 363864**

Brewery founded in 1994 and supplying one beer to outlets locally and pubs further afield via an agent. The brewing plant is also used by Bath Ales (qv).

Vickery's Brew (OG 1040, ABV 4%)

HESKET NEWMARKET

**Hesket Newmarket
Brewery, Old Crown Barn,
Back Green, Hesket
Newmarket, Cumbria
CA7 8JG.
☎ / FAX (0169 74) 78066**

Brewery set up in 1988 in a barn behind the Old Crown pub in an attractive North Lakes village. Its beers are named after local fells, with the notable exception of Doris's 90th Birthday Ale (Doris sadly died in 1995, aged 96). Around 30 pubs take the beers and the brewery also produces house beers for three local pubs, as well as occasional brews, the latest of which is a hop-free, medieval-style ale. Tours by arrangement. Occasional/seasonal beers: Show Ale (OG 1040, ABV

461

3.9%), Medieval Ale (OG 1045, ABV 4.3%), Ayala's Angel (OG 1080, ABV 7%, Christmas).

Great Cockup Porter (OG 1035, ABV 2.8%) A refreshing, chocolate-tasting beer.

Blencathra Bitter (OG 1035, ABV 3.1%) A predominantly bitter beer, from the start to the dry finish. Malty nose.

Skiddaw Special Bitter (OG 1035, ABV 3.7%) A golden session beer, despite its name.

Doris's 90th Birthday Ale (OG 1045, ABV 4.3%) A fruity premium ale.

Catbells Pale Ale (OG 1052, ABV 5.1%) An initially sweet, strongly aromatic beer developing a bitter finish.

Old Carrock Strong Ale (OG 1064, ABV 5.6%) A dark red, powerful ale.

HEXHAMSHIRE
Hexhamshire Brewery, Leafields, Ordley, Hexham, Northumberland NE46 1SX.
☎ **(01434) 673031**

Brewery set up in a redundant farm building in 1992 by the owner of the Dipton Mill Inn with two partners. No adjuncts are used in the beers, which are produced for the Inn and other local outlets. Occasional/seasonal beers: Low Quarter Ale (OG 1035, ABV 3.5%), Blackhall Stout (OG 1043, ABV 4.3%), Old Humbug (OG 1055, ABV 5.5%).

Shire Bitter (OG 1037, ABV 3.8%) ◆ Thicker than expected: a bitter beer with a malty overtone.

Devil's Water (OG 1041, ABV 4.1%) ◆ A beer of mixed character and an unexpected range of flavours. Malt dominates and bitterness gradually declines, giving a strong, sweet finish.

Whapweasel (OG 1048, ABV 4.8%) ◆ This malty bitter has a lasting hoppiness and a smooth mouthfeel.

HIGH FORCE
High Force Hotel Brewery, Forest-in-Teesdale, Barnard Castle, Co. Durham DL12 0XH.
☎ **(01833) 622222**
FAX **(01833) 622264**

🚪 This brew pub went into production in 1995 and claims to be the highest brewery in Britain; at 1,060 feet it is situated by the High Force waterfall, a popular tourist attraction. The brewery has won the *Best Beer in Festival* award at the Durham Beer Festival two years running, and is now bottling one of the prize-winners, Cauldron Snout. Cauldron Snout beer sausages are produced in collaboration with a local butcher. Thirty-five other outlets now take the beers. Tours by arrangement. Bottle-

conditioned beer: Cauldron Snout (OG 1052, ABV 5.6%).

Low Force (OG 1035, ABV 3.3%) A summer beer.

Teesdale Bitter (OG 1037, ABV 3.8%) ◆ A hoppy ale with lingering fruit character and a spicy aftertaste.

Forest XB (OG 1041, ABV 4.2%) ◆ An award-winning, smooth ale with a solid bitterness and almond undertones to a spicy finish.

Cauldron Snout (OG 1052, ABV 5.6%) ◆ A beer with a smooth, roasted taste and a rich, solid body. Deceptively drinkable.

HIGHGATE
The Highgate & Walsall Brewing Company Ltd., Sandymount Road, Walsall, W. Midlands WS1 3AP.
☎ **(01922) 644453**
FAX **(01922) 644471**

Celebrating its centenary in 1998, Highgate was an independent brewery until 1938 when it was taken over by Mitchells & Butlers and subsequently became the smallest brewery in the Bass group. It had been under threat of closure for some years until a management buyout brought it back into the independent sector in 1995. Some of the original equipment in the traditional Victorian tower brewery is still in use, but the cask racking unit has been replaced this year and a fully equipped laboratory has been installed. Highgate has acquired five tied houses and the aim is to buy five a year to build up an estate of 50. All the tied houses take the real ale which is also supplied direct to around 35 outlets. The company also has a major contract to supply Bass pubs. Tours by arrangement. Occasional beer: Fox's Nob (OG 1036, ABV 3.4%).

Dark Mild (OG 1035, ABV 3.2%) 🗒 ◆ A dark brown, Black Country mild with a good balance of malt and hops, and traces of roast flavour following a malty aroma.

IPA (OG 1039, ABV 3.4%)

Bitter (ABV 3.7%)

Saddlers Best Bitter (OG 1043, ABV 4%) A very fruity, pale yellow bitter with a strong hop flavour and a light, refreshing bitter aftertaste.

Macleod's Toddy Ale (OG 1044, ABV 4.7%) A seasonal beer.

Old Ale (OG 1054, ABV 5.1%) ◆ A winter beer (November–January): a dark brown/ ruby-coloured old ale, full-flavoured, fruity and malty, with a complex aftertaste which has hints of malt, roast, hops and fruit.

Bains 535 (OG 1053, ABV 5.35%)

HIGH PEAK See Lloyds.

HIGHWOOD

**Highwood Brewery Ltd.,
Melton Highwood,
Barnetby, Lincolnshire
DN38 6AA.**
☎ **(01652) 680020**
FAX **(01652) 680729**

Located in a converted granary on the edge of the Lincolnshire Wolds, this brewery went into production in 1995 and is currently brewing around 40 barrels a week to supply 60 regular outlets. The range always includes a seasonal beer (4–5% ABV). Tours by arrangement.

Tom Wood Best Bitter (OG 1036, ABV 3.5%) ◆ A pleasant drinking bitter, moderately hopped and bitter. Malt plays a good second fiddle, with a faint fruitiness in the taste.

Tom Wood Shepherd's Delight (OG 1039, ABV 4%) ◆ A hoppy beer with fruit up front. The malt grows in the aftertaste and the bitterness remains constant.

Tom Wood Harvest Bitter (OG 1041, ABV 4.3%) ◆ A straw-coloured beer, quite hoppy on the nose with faint malt throughout. There is a certain fruity sweetness, but the beer dries to a bitter finish.

Tom Wood Old Timber (OG 1043, ABV 4.5%) ◆ Hoppy on the nose, but featuring well-balanced malt and hops otherwise. A slight, lingering roast/coffee flavour develops, but this is generally a bitter, darkish brown beer.

HIGSONS

See Cains and Nationals, Whitbread.

HILDEN

**Hilden Brewery, Hilden
House, Grand Street,
Lisburn, Co. Antrim
BT27 4TY.** ☎ **(01846) 663863**

Mini-brewery beside a Georgian country house, set up in 1981 to counter the local Guinness/Bass duopoly. It presently supplies Hilden Ale to just a handful of pubs in Northern Ireland, with the full range of beers exported to some pubs in England. Occasional beers: Special (OG 1037, ABV 3.6%), Festival Ale (OG 1052, ABV 5.2%).

Great Northern Porter (OG 1039, ABV 4%) ◆ A beer with a rich, tawny colour and a pronounced malty aroma. Crystal malt is dominant in both the flavour and aftertaste.

Hilden Ale (OG 1040, ABV 4%) ◆ An amber-coloured beer with an aroma of malt, hops and fruit. The balanced taste is slightly slanted towards hops, and hops are also prominent in the full, malty finish. Bitter and refreshing.

Special Reserve (OG 1048, ABV 4.6%) ◆ Dark red/brown in colour and superbly aromatic – full of dark malts, producing an aroma of liquorice and toffee. Malt, fruit and

toffee on the palate, with a sweet, malty finish. Mellow and satisfying, but not always available.

HOBSONS

**Hobsons Brewery & Co.,
New House Farm, Tenbury
Road, Cleobury Mortimer,
Kidderminster,
Worcestershire DY14 8RD.**
☎ **(01299) 270837** FAX **(01299) 270846**

Opened at Easter 1993 in a former sawmill, Hobsons (a Shropshire brewery, despite its postal address) is now located in a characterful building which was once a farm granary. The brewery is working close to its capacity of 60 barrels a week and supplying around 120 outlets with cask ale. Tours by arrangement.

Best Bitter (OG 1038, ABV 3.8%) ■ ◆ A pale brown to amber, medium-bodied beer with strong hop character throughout. It is consequently bitter, but with malt discernible in the taste.

Town Crier (OG 1045, ABV 4.5%) A straw-coloured bitter.

Old Henry (OG 1052, ABV 5.2%)

HODGE'S

**Hodge's Brewery, Unit 5A,
Castle Close, Crook,
Co. Durham DL15 8LU.**
☎ **(01388) 763200**
FAX **(01388) 746482**

Hodge's (founded in 1994) was bought by Darwin Brewery (qv) in summer 1997. Darwin intends to switch most of its production here but also to continue with the one Hodge's beer listed below (the tasting notes were prepared before the take-over).

Original (OG 1040, ABV 4%) ◆ An excellent, amber-coloured beer, but its condition varies: good texture, smooth mouthfeel and a subtle hint of roast before a slightly hoppy aftertaste.

HOG & STUMP

**The Hog & Stump Brew Pub, 88 London
Road, Kingston upon Thames, Surrey
KT2 6PX.** ☎ **(0181) 541 3717**
FAX **(0181) 549 0128**

The Flamingo pub brewery was taken over by the Mercury Taverns pub group, along with the rest of the Saxon Inns estate, in February 1996. It was closed for refurbishment in January 1997 and re-opened a month later under this name. The brewery has been upgraded and supplies its beers to eight local outlets. At the pub itself some beers are stored under mixed gas in cellar tanks. The old Flamingo beers have been joined by new brews which have proved very popular. Tours by arrangement, Thu–Mon. Occasional/seasonal beers: Tiffin

THE INDEPENDENTS

Ale (OG 1049, ABV 4.8%), Crucifixion (OG 1065, ABV 6.3%, Easter), Hogsmill (OG 1068, ABV 6.6%), Rudolph's Revenge (OG 1070, ABV 7.2%, Christmas).

Hog's Ale (OG 1035, ABV 3.2%)

Fairfield (OG 1037, ABV 3.5%)

Hog's Best (OG 1044, ABV 4.2%)

Royal Charter (OG 1044, ABV 4.2%)

Wort Hog (OG 1048, ABV 4.6%)

Coronation (OG 1059, ABV 5.7%)

HOGS BACK

Hogs Back Brewery, Manor Farm, The Street, Tongham, Surrey GU10 1DE.
☎ (01252) 783000
FAX (01252) 782328

This purpose-built brewery was set up in a restored farm building (circa 1768) in 1992 and the popularity of its ales – particularly the award-winning TEA – has resulted in a major plant change to double the production capacity. Plans are also in hand for in-house bottling facilities and the company is opening two off-licences, in Woking and Guildford. It now supplies 450 outlets directly and may soon open its first pub. From small beginnings, with just a single beer, Hogs Back now brews nearly 20 beer types on a regular or occasional basis. Shop open 10–8.30 Mon–Fri, 9–6 Sat, 10.30–4 Sun. Tours by arrangement. Occasional/seasonal beers: Dark Mild (OG 1036, ABV 3.4%), Legend (OG 1038, ABV 4%), 41 Special (OG 1044, ABV 4.1%), Easter Teaser (OG 1044, ABV 4.2%), Friday 13th (OG 1044, ABV 4.2%), Blackwater Porter (OG 1046, ABV 4.4%), BSA or Burma Star Ale (OG 1048, ABV 4.5%), Utopia (OG 1053, ABV 5.4%), Fuggles Nouveau (OG 1055, ABV 5%), Goldings Nouveau (OG 1055, ABV 5%), YES or Your Every Success (OG 1055, ABV 5%), OTT or Old Tongham Tasty (OG 1066, ABV 6%), Brewster's Bundle (OG 1077, ABV 7.4%), Santa's Wobble (OG 1077, ABV 7.5%, Christmas), A over T or Aromas over Tongham (OG 1091, ABV 9%). Bottle-conditioned beers: TEA (OG 1044, ABV 4.2%), BSA (OG 1048, ABV 4.5%), Brewster's Bundle (OG 1077, ABV 7.4%), Wobble in a Bottle (OG 1077, ABV 7.5%), A over T (OG 1091, ABV 9%).

APB or A Pinta Bitter (OG 1037, ABV 3.5%) ◈ A thin, but well-balanced bitter.

TEA or Traditional English Ale (OG 1044, ABV 4.2%) ◻ ◈ A pale brown, malty bitter with a developing hop balance. Slightly fruity.

Hop Garden Gold (OG 1048, ABV 4.6%) ◈ A malty, golden beer with a hoppy finish.

Rip Snorter (OG 1052, ABV 5%) ◈ A strong, malty and fruity, reddish-brown bitter with a slight hop flavour.

HOLDEN'S

Holden's Brewery Co. Ltd., Hopden Brewery, George Street, Woodsetton, Dudley, W. Midlands DY1 4LN.
☎ (01902) 880051
FAX (01902) 665473

Family brewery going back four generations. Holden's began life as a brew pub when Edwin and Lucy Holden took over the Park Inn (now the brewery tap) in the 1920s. It produces a good range of real ales for its 20 pubs and around 30 free trade customers. Shop open daily 10.30–2, 4–10 (11–9 Sat and Sun). Tours by arrangement. Occasional/seasonal beers: Stout (OG 1035, ABV 3.5%), Old 'XL' Ale (OG 1072, ABV 6.9%, Christmas).

Mild (OG 1037, ABV 3.7%) ◈ A good, red/brown Black Country mild; a refreshing, light blend of roast malt, hops and fruit, dominated by malt throughout.

Bitter (OG 1039, ABV 3.9%) ◈ A medium-bodied, golden ale; a light, well-balanced bitter with a subtle, dry, hoppy finish.

XB or Lucy B (OG 1041, ABV 4.2%) ◈ Named after founder Lucy Blanche Holden, this is a sweeter, slightly fuller version of the bitter. Sold in different outlets under different names.

Special Bitter (OG 1051, ABV 5.1%) ◈ A sweet, malty, full-bodied amber ale with hops to balance in the taste and in the good, bittersweet finish.

HOLT

Joseph Holt PLC, Derby Brewery, Empire Street, Cheetham, Manchester M3 1JD. ☎ (0161) 834 3285
FAX (0161) 834 6458

Successful family brewery, founded in 1849 – not to be confused with Carlsberg-Tetley's Midlands division Holt, Plant & Deakin. The tied estate has been gradually increased over the last 15 years or so, and now exceeds 120 houses, all serving real ale, with most of the pubs taking hogsheads (54-gallon casks), because the low prices result in a high turnover. The beers are also popular as guests and Holt supplies a free trade of around 60 outlets (plus another 40 or so via an agent).

Mild (OG 1032, ABV 3.2%) ◈ A very dark beer with a complex aroma and taste. Roast malt is prominent, but so are hops and fruit. Strong in bitterness for a mild, with a long-lasting, satisfying aftertaste.

Bitter (OG 1039, ABV 4%) ◈ A tawny beer with a good hop aroma. Although balanced by malt and fruit, the uncompromising bitterness can be a shock to the unwary. It has gained a little sweetness in recent years.

HOLTS See Nationals, Carlsberg-Tetley.

HOME See Mansfield and Nationals, Scottish Courage.

HOOK NORTON
The Hook Norton Brewery Co. Ltd., Hook Norton, Banbury, Oxfordshire OX15 5NZ.
☎ **(01608) 737210**
[FAX] **(01608) 730294**

Built by John Harris in a former farm maltings in 1850, and still controlled by his family, Hook Norton remains one of the most delightful, traditional Victorian tower breweries in Britain. It retains much of its original plant and machinery, the showpiece being a 25-horsepower stationary steam engine which still pumps the Cotswold well water used for brewing. The brewery boasts some fine old country pubs, with all 37 of its tied houses serving real ale, and some 350 free trade outlets also supplied direct. Brewery shop open 9–4.15 Mon–Fri. Tours by arrangement. Seasonal beers: Haymaker (OG 1052, ABV 5%, July–August), Twelve Days (OG 1057, ABV 5.5%, December–January).

Best Mild (OG 1031, ABV 3%) ◆ A dark, red/brown mild with a malty aroma and a malty, sweetish taste, tinged with a faint hoppy balance. Malty in the aftertaste. Highly drinkable.

Best Bitter (OG 1035, ABV 3.4%) ◆ An excellently-balanced, golden bitter. Malty and hoppy on the nose and in the mouth, with a hint of fruitiness. Dry, but with some balancing sweetness. A hoppy bitterness dominates the finish.

Generation (ABV 4%)

Old Hooky (OG 1048, ABV 4.6%) ◆ An unusual, tawny beer with a strong fruity and grainy aroma and palate, balanced by a hint of hops. Full-bodied, with a bitter, fruity and malty aftertaste.

Double Stout (OG 1050, ABV 4.8%)

HOP BACK
Hop Back Brewery PLC, Unit 22–24 Batten Road Industrial Estate, Downton, Salisbury, Wiltshire SP5 3HU. ☎ **(01725) 510986**
[FAX] **(01725) 513116**

Founded as a brew pub, the Wyndham Arms, in 1987, Hop Back switched its production to a new brewery at Downton in 1992. A new 50-barrel plant was installed in 1995 to cope with increased demand, and in the same year a fourth tied house, the Hop Leaf in Reading, was opened (see Reading Lion Brewery). A fifth pub was added to the estate in 1996 and Hop Back also sells directly to well over 100 free trade outlets. A small bottling line was installed in 1997. Bottle-conditioned beers: Thunderstorm

(OG 1048, ABV 5%), Summer Lightning (OG 1049, ABV 5%) ◨.

GFB (OG 1034, ABV 3.5%) ◆ A golden beer, with the sort of light, clean, tasty quality which makes an ideal session ale. A hoppy aroma and taste lead to a good, dry finish. Refreshing.

Crop Circle (OG 1041, ABV 4.2%)

Entire Stout (OG 1043, ABV 4.5%) ◨ ◨ ◆ A rich, dark stout with a strong roasted malt flavour and a long, sweet and malty aftertaste. A vegan beer.

Thunderstorm (OG 1048, ABV 5%) ◨ A softly bitter, easy drinking wheat beer.

Summer Lightning (OG 1049, ABV 5%) ◨ ◨ ◆ A very pleasurable pale bitter with a good, fresh, hoppy aroma and a malty, hoppy flavour. Finely balanced, it has an intense bitterness leading to a long, dry finish. Though strong, it tastes like a session ale.

HOP HOUSE See Cock.

HOP LEAF See Reading Lion.

HORSEBRIDGE See Royal Inn.

HOSKINS
Cherryhawk (Leicester) Ltd., Tom Hoskins Brewery, Beaumanor Brewery, 133 Beaumanor Road, Leicester LE4 5QE. ☎ **(0116) 266 1122**
[FAX] **(0116) 261 0150**

This brewery was set up around a hundred years ago by Jabez Penn, in his own cottage, and became Hoskins Brewery some time after his son-in-law took control in 1901. A traditional tower brewery, it remained in family hands until 1983, when it was acquired and expanded by TRD Estates Ltd. Following the sale of eight pubs to Wolverhampton & Dudley in 1992, the brewery was taken over by Halkin Holdings in 1993, and in 1995 it was subject to a management buyout. It has six tied houses (all serving real ale), and supplies just one other outlet direct, but the beer is also distributed via wholesalers. Tours by arrangement. Seasonal beer: Old Nigel (OG 1060, ABV 5%, winter).

Beaumanor Bitter (OG 1037, ABV 3.7%) ◆ A strange mixture of flavours. Thin-bodied, the fruity sweet taste soon gives way to an astringent bitterness in the finish. Metallic hints.

Churchills Pride (OG 1042, ABV 4.2%)

Penn's Ale (OG 1043, ABV 4.6%) ◆ A sweet beer, occasionally with added caramel. An acidic/metallic aftertaste is also present.

Premium (OG 1047, ABV 4.7%) ◆ A beer with more malt and less sugar than Beaumanor.

HOSKINS & OLDFIELD

**Hoskins & Oldfield
Brewery Ltd., North Mills,
Frog Island, Leicester
LE3 5DH. ☎ (0116) 251 0532**

Brewery set up by two
members of Leicester's famous brewing
family, Philip and Stephen Hoskins, in 1984,
after the sale of the old Hoskins Brewery.
The company supplies over 15 outlets
directly, and others nationwide via
wholesalers. A bottle-conditioned beer has
been re-introduced and more are planned.
Occasional/seasonal beers: 'O4' Ale (OG
1052, ABV 5.2%), Tom Kelly's Christmas
Pudding Porter (OG 1052, ABV 5%,
Christmas), Ginger Tom (OG 1053, ABV
5.2%, a ginger beer), Reckless Raspberry
(ABV 5.5%, a wheat beer with raspberries),
Christmas Noggin (OG 1100, ABV 10%).
Bottle-conditioned beer: 'O4' Ale (ABV
5.2%).

HOB Best Mild (OG 1036, ABV 3.5%) An
almost black-coloured beer, with malt and
hops in the taste. Very difficult to find.

Brigadier Bitter (OG 1036, ABV 3.6%)

HOB Bitter (OG 1041, ABV 4%) 🍴 ◆ A
tawny-coloured best bitter with a hoppy,
malty nose and a more complex, fruity,
bittersweet flavour which becomes more
hoppy and bitter in the finish. It frequently
tastes of pear drops.

Little Matty (OG 1041, ABV 4%) A complex
brown/red beer.

White Dolphin (OG 1041, ABV 4%) A fruity
wheat beer.

Tom Kelly's Stout (OG 1043, ABV 4.2%) A
dark, dry stout.

Supreme (OG 1045, ABV 4.4%) A very light
gold best bitter.

Tom Hoskins Porter (OG 1050, ABV 4.8%)
Brewed using honey and oats.

EXS Bitter (OG 1051, ABV 5%) A malty,
full-bodied premium bitter.

Old Navigation Ale (OG 1071, ABV 7%) A
strong ruby/black beer.

HUGHES

**Sarah Hughes Brewery,
Beacon Hotel, 129 Bilston
Street, Sedgley, Dudley,
W. Midlands DY3 1JE.
☎ (01902) 883380**

Brewery re-opened in 1987 after lying
idle for 30 years, to serve the village pub
and a few other local houses, but now also
supplying beers to 50 outlets in the free
trade. A Victorian-style conservatory acts as
a reception area for brewery tours (by
arrangement). Bottle-conditioned beer: Dark
Ruby Mild (OG 1058, ABV 6%).

Pale Amber (OG 1038, ABV 4%) A well-
balanced beer, initially slightly sweet but
with hops close behind.

Sedgley Surprise (OG 1048, ABV 5%) ◆ A
bittersweet, medium-bodied, hoppy ale with
some malt.

Dark Ruby Mild (OG 1058, ABV 6%) 🍴 🍴
◆ A near-black, strong ale with a good
balance of fruit and hops, leading to a
pleasant, lingering, hops and malt finish.

HULL

**The Hull Brewery Co. Ltd., 144–148 English
Street, Hull, E. Yorkshire HU3 2BT.
☎ (01482) 586364 FAX (01482) 586365**

The name of the closed Hull Brewery was
resurrected after a 15-year absence when
this new brewery opened in 1989. It was
taken over by a new owner in 1994, acquired
its first (and only) tied house in 1995 (from
Bass), and now supplies around 100 other
pubs. Alongside its regular range, a special
beer is brewed every month (except
January), the names and recipes changing
from year to year. Hull has now started
brewing beer formerly produced by the
closed Stocks Brewery, through an
arrangement with Century Inns (Stocks'
new owner), which also enables Hull beers
to be sold in Century Inns' managed houses.
Tours by arrangement.

Mild (OG 1034, ABV 3.3%) A smooth and
malty dark mild with a long lasting
aftertaste and a rich aroma of fruit, hops and
roast malt. Served with a tight, creamy head.

Bitter (OG 1039, ABV 3.8%) A refreshing
copper bitter, with a predominantly hoppy
aroma. The initial bitter aftertaste leads to a
pleasant, lingering maltiness. Complex.

Ellwood's Best Bitter (OG 1038, ABV 3.8%)
A golden straw-coloured session bitter,
smooth and rounded, with subtle hints of
hops and malt, and a refreshing aftertaste.

Amber Ale (OG 1040, ABV 4%) ◆ A light
brown beer with an unusual, dry, malty
taste in which amber malt dominates.
Slightly fruity aroma; dry, bitter finish. Some
tartness can be evident.

Northern Pride (OG 1042, ABV 4.2%) A
distinctive, full-bodied beer, with a malty
aroma.

The Governor (OG 1046, ABV 4.4%) A full-
bodied, amber-coloured premium ale; a
deceptively powerful brew with a malty
taste and a distinctive hop aroma.

Mickey Finn (OG 1050, ABV 5%) A robust
strong, deep copper-coloured ale with a
good hop flavour.

For Century Inns:

Stocks Old Horizontal (OG 1054, ABV
5.4%)

HYDES' ANVIL

**Hydes' Anvil Brewery Ltd.,
46 Moss Lane West,
Manchester M15 5PH.
☎ (0161) 226 1317
FAX (0161) 227 9593**

Family-controlled, traditional brewery, first established at the Crown Brewery, Audenshaw, Manchester in 1863 and on its present site, a former vinegar brewery, since the turn of the century. It is slowly expanding its tied estate, supplying cask ale to all its 61 tied houses and 40 free trade outlets. A successful programme of seasonal beers was introduced in the mid-1990s. Tours by arrangement.

Billy Westwood's Bitter (OG 1030, ABV 3.2%) A budget-priced session beer with more flavour than expected for its gravity.

Dark Mild (OG 1032, ABV 3.5%) 🔶 A mild with a caramel and fruit aroma: quite sweet and fruity, with a pleasant aftertaste. Sold mainly in the company's Welsh pubs, but rare in the Manchester area.

Mild (OG 1032, ABV 3.5%) A darker, more bitter and drier beer than the previous mild, using chocolate malt rather than caramel.

Light (OG 1034, ABV 3.7%) 🗔 🔶 A lightly-hopped session beer, with malt and a refreshing fruitiness dominating before a brief, but dry, finish.

Bitter (OG 1036, ABV 3.8%) 🍴 🔶 A good-flavoured bitter, with a malty and fruity nose, malt and hop in the taste, with a fruity background, and good bitterness through into the aftertaste.

4X Strong (ABV 6.8%) A winter warmer; a full-bodied, smooth, dark beer with a good balance of malt, hops and fruitiness. Not too sweet; dangerously drinkable!

ICENI

**The Iceni Brewery,
3 Foulden Road, Ickburgh,
Mundford, Norfolk
IP26 5BJ. ☎ (01842) 878922
FAX (01842) 811539**

Owner Brendan Moore had a dream one night of opening a brewery. A year later, without any prior experience, but armed with redundancy money and a grant from the Rural Development Commission, he set up a ten-barrel plant and his first brew rolled out in 1995. The beers, which are mostly named after Celtic queens and the Iceni tribe, are supplied direct to 25 outlets. Occasional beers: Curse of Macha (OG 1034, ABV 3.4%), Queen Maev Stout (OG 1045, ABV 4.9%).

Boadicea Chariot Ale (OG 1038, ABV 3.8%) The original brew; a well-balanced session bitter with hop and fruit flavours and a dry aftertaste.

Fine Soft Day (OG 1040, ABV 4%)

Celtic Queen (OG 1042, ABV 4.2%) A light summer ale, packed with flavour.

Deirdre of the Sorrows (OG 1044, ABV 4.4%) A gold-coloured ale, with a distinctively pleasant taste that lingers. Moreish; a firm local favourite.

Roisin Dubh (OG 1044, ABV 4.4%) Roisin Dubh translates as 'dark rose'. The beer is also dark in colour, with a slightly sweet taste. Very smooth.

Gold (OG 1046, ABV 5%) A strong ale, sun gold in colour. Crisp taste; smooth and deceptive for its strength.

IND COOPE

See Nationals, Carlsberg-Tetley.

INVERALMOND

**The Inveralmond Brewery
Ltd., 1 Inveralmond Way,
Inveralmond, Perth
PH1 3UQ.
☎ / FAX (01738) 449448**

The first brewery in Perth for over 30 years, Inveralmond was established in April 1997 by former Ruddles, S&N and Courage brewer Fergus Clark. With his ten-barrel plant he produces two beers which are currently sold in about 30 local pubs.

Independence (OG 1040, ABV 3.8%) An amber-red, sweetish beer with a hint of spiciness in the aroma.

Lia Fail (OG 1049, ABV 4.7%) The name is the Gaelic title of the Stone of Destiny: a malty, full-bodied brew with chocolate notes and a balanced finish.

ISLAND See Burts.

ISLE OF MAN See Okells.

ISLE OF SKYE

**The Isle of Skye Brewing
Company (Leann an Eilein),
The Pier, Uig, Isle of Skye
IV51 9XY. ☎ (01470) 542477
FAX (01470) 542488**

Brewery set up in 1995 on an island which has no tradition of real ale. It is housed in purpose-built premises at the pier terminal for the Outer Hebrides. Trade has grown to 40 outlets served directly (nine on the island itself), and others via wholesalers across Scotland and into England. There are also plans to bottle the beers. Shop open 12–6 daily, May–October. Tours by arrangement.

Young Pretender (OG 1040, ABV 4%)

Red Cuillin (OG 1042, ABV 4.2%) 🍴 🔶 A burst of fruit with hop and malt notes introduces this tawny-coloured beer. These characteristics continue into the wonderful taste. Very dry and fruity finish.

Black Cuillin (OG 1045, ABV 4.5%)

Avalanche (OG 1050, ABV 5%)

ITCHEN VALLEY

Itchen Valley Brewery Ltd., Shelf House, New Farm Road, Alresford, Hampshire SO24 9QE.
☎ (01962) 735111
FAX (01962) 735678

This new brewery was established in July 1997 in an industrial estate unit by local business people. They first discussed the venture whilst acting as godfathers at a christening – hence the name of their first beer.

Godfathers (ABV 3.8%) A golden, sweet and fruity beer.

JENNINGS

Jennings Bros PLC, The Castle Brewery, Cockermouth, Cumbria CA13 9NE.
☎ (01900) 823214
FAX (01900) 827462

Founded in 1828, and moved to its present site in 1874, Jennings has gradually expanded over the years (particularly during the 1920s). Although there is no longer any family involvement, many of the company's shares are owned by local people. Over 300 free trade outlets are supplied from its own Leyland and Newcastle depots, and many more via a network of wholesalers throughout the UK. Real ale is also available at 95 of the 117 tied houses. Shop open 9–4.45 Mon–Fri. Tours by arrangement.

Dark Mild (OG 1031, ABV 3.1%) A dark, mellow, malty, sweet mild.

Bitter (OG 1035, ABV 3.5%) ◆ A distinctive, red/brown brew with a hoppy, malty aroma. A good, strong balance of grain and hops in the taste, with a moderate bitterness, develops into a lingering, dry, malty finish.

Cumberland Ale (OG 1040, ABV 4%) ◆ A light, but hoppy, bitter, with a creamy taste and smooth mouthfeel. The aroma can be sulphury, but the taste ends crisp and dry with a spicy bitterness.

Cocker Hoop (OG 1047, ABV 4.8%) ◆ A full-flavoured, malty beer with a pronounced hop flavour and a complex bitter aftertaste.

Sneck Lifter (OG 1053, ABV 5.1%) A very dark bitter, with a rich, full malt flavour, followed by a smooth and mellow mixture of malt and hop in the aftertaste.

La'al Cockle Warmer (OG 1062, ABV 6.5%) A winter brew.

> ⛉ The pub sign indicates a brew pub: a pub which produces beer on the premises.

JERSEY

Ann Street Brewery Co. Ltd. t/a Jersey Brewery, 57 Ann Street, St Helier, Jersey JE1 1BZ. ☎ (01534) 31561
FAX (01534) 67033

Jersey (formerly known by its parent company's title of Ann Street) began brewing cask beer again in 1990 after a break of 30 years. It has 50 tied houses, of which 12 take real ale, including beers from its sister company, Guernsey Brewery. Tours by arrangement.

Old Jersey Ale (OG 1035, ABV 3.6%) ◆ An attractive tawny/copper colour, this bitter ale packs an immense depth of malt flavours, the crystal malt giving hints of barley sugar. The malty bitterness is quite intense in the aftertaste.

Ann's Treat (OG 1050, ABV 5%)

Winter Ale (OG 1070, ABV 7.5%) ◆ Very dark brown, with hues of copper, this is a complex beer, full of roast barley and malt flavours, giving glimpses of chocolate, coffee and butterscotch. Quite bitter for its strength and very rewarding.

JOHN THOMPSON INN

John Thompson Brewery, Ingleby, Derbyshire DE73 1HW. ☎ (01332) 862469

⛉ This 15th-century farmhouse was converted to a pub in 1969. It has brewed since 1977, with most of the production supplied to the free trade through Lloyds Country Beers (qv), a separate enterprise. Beers (on sale here): Summer Gold (OG 1040, ABV 4%), JTS XXX (OG 1042, ABV 4.1%, sold elsewhere as Lloyds Derby Bitter), JTS Rich Porter (OG 1045, ABV 4.3%, winter).

JOLLYBOAT

The Jollyboat Brewery Ltd., 4 Buttgarden Street, Bideford, Devon EX39 2AU.
☎ (01237) 424343

Brewery established in 1995 and currently supplying over 30 local outlets, plus wholesalers. Tours by arrangement.

Buccaneer (OG 1038, ABV 3.7%) A pale brown summer bitter with a pleasant presence of hops from the nose through to the aftertaste.

Mainbrace Bitter (OG 1041, ABV 4.2%)

Plunder (OG 1048, ABV 4.8%) A heavily malty, reddish-brown beer with a full-bodied malt and fruit taste and a bitter finish.

Contrabrand (OG 1055, ABV 5.8%) A porter available November–March and at other times on demand.

JOLLYS DRINKS See Mildmay.

JONES & MATHER

Jones & Mather Ales Ltd., Unit 2, North Street Trading Estate, Brierley Hill, W. Midlands DY5 3QF. ☎ (01384) 482101

Brewery built single-handedly by Spencer Mather over a period of eight months and opened for business in November 1996. Around 20 pubs locally take the beers, with others served by a wholesaler. Seasonal beer: Mather's Merrie (OG 1064, ABV 6.2%, winter).

Dudley No. 1 (OG 1040, ABV 3.8%) A summer wheat beer.

Brewins Ale (OG 1040, ABV 4%)

Brewins Bostin (OG 1040, ABV 4%) A bronze-coloured, hoppy bitter, with a slight aftertaste of apples.

Telford's Tipple (OG 1045, ABV 4.4%)

Crystal Cut (OG 1045, ABV 4.5%)

Secund Cut (OG 1048, ABV 4.8%) A dark, premium bitter with a hoppy, nutty taste.

Nobby's Goat (OG 1050, ABV 5%) A bock beer.

JOULE See Coach House.

JUDGES

Judges Brewery, Unit 15A, Boughton Road, Rugby, Warwickshire CV21 1BU. ☎ (01788) 535356

Brewery set up in 1992 in a Warwickshire village, but now settled on a larger site in Rugby. Its beers are sold in about 12 local outlets on a regular basis, plus another 60 or so in the Midlands on a guest beer basis. Tours by arrangement. Seasonal beer: Santa's Surprise (OG 1052, ABV 5%, a Christmas porter).

M'lud (OG 1036, ABV 3.3%) A medium dark mild.

Barristers Bitter (OG 1038, ABV 3.5%) 🗂 ◆ A well-balanced, pale-coloured session beer; light and easily drinkable.

Grey Wig (ABV 4%) A blend of Barristers and Old Gavel Bender.

Verdict (OG 1042, ABV 4%) A straw-coloured wheat beer, fresh, tangy and quenching.

Coombe Ale (OG 1042, ABV 4.2%) Primed with local honey.

Magistrate's Delight (OG 1046, ABV 4.6%) A reddish brown, balanced ale.

Old Gavel Bender (OG 1050, ABV 5%) ◆ A beer with a complex hop, fruit and malt aroma, with some caramel. There's a perfect bittersweet balance in the taste, but no significant aftertaste.

Solicitor's Ruin (OG 1056, ABV 5.6%) ◆ Dark, strong and full-tasting: a very well-hopped beer, with a smooth, sweetish, treacly taste, and a bitter finish.

JUWARDS

Juwards Brewery, c/o Fox Brothers & Co. Ltd., Wellington, Somerset TA21 0AW. ☎ (01823) 667909

Juwards, the latest venture of Ted Bishop, former brewer at Cotleigh and Ash Vine, went into production in 1994, based in an old wool mill. It supplies around 30 outlets direct in the West Country, plus others in the Midlands and North of England via agents. One beer is brewed for the Lock, Stock and Barrel wholesaling company ☎ (01364) 644124.

Bitter (OG 1040, ABV 3.9%)

Golden (OG 1044, ABV 4.4%) Also sold by Lock, Stock and Barrel as Newt & Abbot Ale.

Premium (OG 1048, ABV 4.8%)

For Lock, Stock and Barrel:

Pistol Dawn (ABV 5%) An occasional brew.

KELHAM ISLAND

Kelham Island Brewery, 23 Alma Street, Sheffield, S. Yorkshire S3 8SA. ☎ (0114) 249 4804 [FAX] (0114) 249 4803

🚪 Brewery opened at the Fat Cat pub in 1990 with plant from the Oxford Brewery and Bakehouse, serving the Fat Cat and over 30 outlets in Derbyshire, Nottinghamshire and S. Yorkshire. Tours by arrangement.

Fat Cat Pale Ale (OG 1037, ABV 3.6%) ◆ A straw-coloured, clean-tasting beer with a powerful hop and fruit aroma, which is reflected in the taste, along with a lingering, dry and bitter finish. A good session beer.

Bitter (OG 1039, ABV 3.8%) ◆ A clean and crisp, pale brown beer of character. The nose and taste are dominated by refreshing hoppiness and fruitiness which last, along with a good bitter dryness, in the aftertaste.

Golden Eagle (OG 1044, ABV 4.2%) ◆ An excellent hoppy, fruity best bitter. The aroma is strong in hops with a slight fruitiness which gets stronger in the taste and in the finish, which is moderately bitter.

Gatecrasher (OG 1046, ABV 4.4%) A light, golden beer with a well-rounded, clean, fruity palate. It is bittered with English hops, with American hops added for aroma.

Pale Rider (OG 1054, ABV 5.2%) ◆ A well-bodied, straw-pale ale, with a good fruity aroma and a strong fruit and hop taste. Its well-balanced sweetness and bitterness continue in the finish.

THE INDEPENDENTS

Bête Noire (OG 1056, ABV 5.5%) 🍶 🔸 A dark ruby beer with little aroma. Malt and caramel, along with some fruitiness and dryness, are in the taste, which also has plum notes and chocolate, and develops into a dry, but sweet, aftertaste.

Grande Pale (OG 1068, ABV 6.6%) A strong, full-bodied pale ale with a mellow hop aroma.

KELTEK

The Keltek Brewing Company Ltd., Highgate, Lower Allens, Tregony, Cornwall TR2 5RP.
☎ /[FAX] (01872) 530814

Keltek was set up in 1997 as a part-time venture, supplying ales to the Roseland peninsula area of Cornwall. It was taken over by a local fibre optic manufacturing company and expanded in summer 1997 with the introduction of new plant. A move to new, purpose-built premises is planned as the company targets outlets throughout Cornwall, concentrating chiefly on the take-home trade and bottle-conditioned beers. Bottle-conditioned beers: Golden Lance (OG 1036, ABV 3.8%), King (OG 1050, ABV 5.5%), Trelawney's Revenge (OG 1081, ABV 9.1%).

Golden Lance (OG 1036, ABV 3.8%) A pale golden beer.

Magik (OG 1040, ABV 4.1%) A fairly dark, strongly flavoured ale.

King (OG 1050, ABV 5.5%) A pale strong bitter.

Trelawney's Revenge (OG 1068, ABV 7.6%) A very dark, complex, sweetish ale.

KEMPTOWN

The Kemptown Brewery Co. Ltd., 33 Upper St James's Street, Kemptown, Brighton, E. Sussex BN2 1JN. ☎ (01273) 699595

🚽 Brewery established in 1989, built in the 'tower' tradition behind the Hand in Hand, which is possibly the smallest pub in England with its own brewery. It takes its name and logo from the former Charrington's Kemptown Brewery 500 yards away, which closed in 1964. Fifteen free trade outlets are supplied. Tours by arrangement. Occasional beers: Crewsaver (OG 1045, ABV 4.5%), Tipper's Tipple (OG 1045, ABV 4.5%).

Brighton Bitter (OG 1036, ABV 3.5%) 🔸 A refreshing, dry beer, with malt and hops in the flavour and a dry, hoppy finish.

Bitter (OG 1040, ABV 4%) 🔸 Hops in the aroma lead into a soft, malt flavour with bitterness, which fades in the aftertaste.

Ye Olde Trout (OG 1045, ABV 4.5%)

Staggering in the Dark (SID) (OG 1050, ABV 5.2%) 🔸 A dark, almost black, beer with a vinous nose and a complex flavour, with roast and bitterness giving way to a dry finish.

Old Grumpy (OG 1060, ABV 6%) Available November–February.

KING & BARNES

King & Barnes Ltd., The Horsham Brewery, 18 Bishopric, Horsham, W. Sussex RH12 1QP.
☎ (01403) 270470
[FAX] (01403) 270570

Long-established brewery, dating back almost 200 years and in the present premises since 1850. It is run by the King family, which united with the Barnes family brewery in 1906. A continuing programme of investment in brewery plant and machinery has meant its 'Fine Sussex Ales' are always in demand and that brewers like Salopian are entrusting K&B with production of their bottled beers. All 57 tied houses take real ale, which is also supplied direct to a further 250 other outlets. Brewery shop open 11–7 Mon–Sat. Tours by arrangement. Seasonal beers: Summer Ale (ABV 3.8%, June–July), Valentine (ABV 4%, February), Crystal Malt Ale (ABV 4.1%, November), Amber Malt Ale (ABV 4.3%, May), Wheat Mash (ABV 4.3%, August), Harvest Ale (OG 1045, ABV 4.5%, September), Oatmeal Stout (ABV 4.5%, March), Rye Beer (ABV 5.5%, October), Christmas Ale (ABV 6.5%, Corn Beer (ABV 6.5%, April). Bottle-conditioned beers: Wheat Mash (ABV 4.5%), Harvest Ale (OG 1045, ABV 4.7%), Festive (OG 1052, ABV 5.3%) 🍶 🍴, Old Porter (OG 1057, ABV 5.5%), Corn Beer (ABV 6.5%), Christmas Ale (ABV 8%), Millennium Ale (ABV 9.5%).

Mild Ale (OG 1034, ABV 3.5%) 🍶 🔸 A smooth, very dark mild, with hints of malt in the aroma. The bittersweet flavour, with some malt and hops, leads to a late-developing bitterness in the aftertaste.

Sussex (OG 1034, ABV 3.5%) 🔸 Whilst hops are still most apparent in the finish of this mid-brown bitter, they are not as evident throughout the beer as they used to be.

Broadwood (OG 1040, ABV 4.2%) 🔸 A tawny-coloured, well-balanced beer from aroma to finish, with hops winning through in the end.

Old Ale (OG 1045, ABV 4.5%) 🍶 🔸 A classic, black old ale. A slightly fruity, roast malt flavour leads to a bittersweet finish, with fruit joining the roast. Lovely roast malt aroma. Available October–March.

Festive (OG 1050, ABV 5%) 🔸 A red-brown beer, with a fruity aroma. The flavour is also fruity and malty, but with a noticeable hop presence. Malt and fruit dominate the aftertaste.

For Salopian:

Bottle-conditioned beers: Proud Salopian (ABV 4%), Choir Porter (OG 1045, ABV 4.5%), Minsterley Ale (OG 1045, ABV 4.5%), Snapdragon (ABV 4.5%, a spice beer), Gingersnap Wheat Beer (OG 1047, ABV 4.7%, with ginger), Jigsaw (ABV 4.8%, a black wheat beer), Dragonfly (OG 1050, ABV 5%, an oat beer with raspberries), Ironbridge Stout (OG 1050, ABV 5%).

KING'S HEAD
King's Head Ale House and Brewery, Plymouth, Devon.

Brewery closed.

KITCHEN
The Kitchen Brewery, Unit J, Shaw Park Industrial Complex, Ivy Street East, Aspley, Huddersfield, W. Yorkshire HD5 9AF. ☎ (01484) 300028 FAX (01484) 542709

Brewery founded in 1996 by CAMRA member Robert Johnson in the pickling shed at the Shaw Park Industrial Complex, with a five-barrel plant which uses steam as a heat source. The beers, whose names are derived from Robert's first career as a chef, are on sale in local pubs and in pubs in Northamptonshire (Robert's home county). The beer range has expanded considerably in the last 12 months and now includes seasonal brews. Tours by arrangement. Seasonal beer: Plum Duff (ABV 5.2%, Christmas).

Commi (ABV 3.6%) Smooth, with a lightly aromatic character. A citrus beginning and fruity flavour are followed by a dry bitterness.

Aperitif (ABV 4%) A smooth, malty beer with a fruity flavour, mild bitterness and a well-balanced, lightly-hopped sweetness. Light brown in colour.

Syllabub (ABV 4.2%) A summer beer with a highly aromatic, dry-hop nose, a very dry flavour and moderate bitterness. Light amber in colour.

Waitress (ABV 4.2%) A smooth and aromatic beer with a slightly citrus beginning and a fruity flavour, ending with dry bitterness. Very light in colour.

Celebration (ABV 4.5%)

Porter (ABV 4.8%) A dark, winter porter with a very smooth, creamy, malty, liquorice flavour. Lightly hopped, with a subtle spice note.

Potage (ABV 4.7%) A spring beer, straw-coloured, with a rich, malty flavour. Well-hopped nose; deep, fruity aftertaste.

Chef's Cut (ABV 5%) A light amber beer, mild, smooth and malty, with a citric, dry-hop note and some fruity flavour.

LAKELAND
The Lakeland Brewing Company, 1 Sepulchre Lane, Kendal, Cumbria LA9 4NJ. ☎ / FAX (01539) 734528

Brewery formerly based at the Masons Arms pub (see also Strawberry Bank). Lakeland's beers are now brewed on 'borrowed' equipment whilst a new site is found. Brewer Nigel Stevenson hires space at an undisclosed brewery and produces the range of beers below for sale in local outlets. All beers are named after novels by local author Arthur Ransome. Bottle-conditioned beers: Amazon (ABV 4.5%), Great Northern (ABV 5%), Winter Holiday (ABV 5%), Big Six (ABV 6%).

Amazon (ABV 4.5%)

Great Northern (ABV 5%)

Big Six (ABV 6%)

LARKINS

Larkins Brewery Ltd., Larkins Farm, Chiddingstone, Edenbridge, Kent TN8 7BB. ☎ (01892) 870328 FAX (01892) 871141

Larkins Brewery was founded in 1986 by the Dockerty family (who are farmers and hop-growers), with the purchase of the Royal Tunbridge Wells Brewery. Brewing was transferred to a converted barn at the family farm in 1989 and an additional copper and fermenter were acquired in 1991 to keep up with the growing local free trade. The additive-free beers can now be found in around 60 pubs and tourist venues in the South-East. Mostly Kent hops are used, some from the farm itself. Tours by arrangement for groups of 15 or more people on weekend mornings in winter.

Traditional Ale (OG 1035, ABV 3.4%) A tawny-coloured beer.

Chiddingstone Bitter (OG 1040, ABV 4%) A malty and slightly fruity, bitter ale, with a very malty finish. Copper-red in colour.

Best Bitter (OG 1045, ABV 4.4%) ◆ Full-bodied, slightly fruity and unusually bitter for its gravity. Dangerously drinkable!

Porter (OG 1052, ABV 5.2%) ◆ Each taste and smell of this potent black winter beer reveals another facet of its character. An explosion of roasted malt, bitter and fruity flavours leaves a bittersweet aftertaste.

LASS O'GOWRIE
See Nationals, Whitbread.

LEANN AN EILEIN See Isle of Skye.

LEATHERBRITCHES

**Leatherbritches Brewery,
Bently Brook Inn, Fenny
Bentley, Ashbourne,
Derbyshire DE6 1LF.**
☎ (01335) 350278
FAX (01335) 350422

Leatherbritches Brewery is housed
behind the Bently Brook Inn, just north
of Ashbourne, a pub owned by the parents
of brewery proprietor Bill Allingham.
Founded in 1994, it has already outgrown an
initial capacity of five barrels a week, and
new plant has been installed. Around 30
other local outlets take the beer, as do two
pubs owned by the Steamin' Billy company,
of which Bill owns 50 per cent. Bottle-
conditioned beers: Steamin' Billy Bitter
(ABV 4.5%), Scrum Down Mild (ABV 5.3%).

Goldings (ABV 3.6%)

Belt 'n' Braces (ABV 3.8%) A light-coloured,
hoppy session beer, with a dry finish.

Steamin' Billy Mild (ABV 3.8%)

Belter (ABV 4%)

Stout (ABV 4%) A beer with a dominant
chocolate flavour, smooth and fruity, with a
long, satisfying finish.

Ashbourne Ale (ABV 4.5%)

Steamin' Billy Bitter (ABV 4.5%) A dry-
hopped version of Ashbourne Ale.

Hairy Helmet (ABV 4.7%)

Bespoke (ABV 5%) A rich, well-balanced,
fruity, full-bodied premium bitter.

Scrum Down Mild (ABV 5.3%)

Tarebrain (ABV 5.8%)

LEDBURY

**Ledbury Brewing Co. Ltd.,
5 The Southend, Ledbury,
Herefordshire HR8 2EY.**
☎ (01531) 632110
FAX (01531) 634761

This brewery was first established in 1841
and was re-opened in the original building,
some 75 years after its closure in 1921. The
beers are all brewed from single hop strains,
mostly from the local area, and a new brew
is produced each month. More than 50
outlets are now supplied. Tours by
arrangement.

Goldings Best (OG 1036, ABV 3.6%) ◈ Not
much nose, but fruitiness balances bitterness
on the tongue; satisfying, dry aftertaste.

Challenger SB (OG 1038, ABV 3.8%)
◈ Bitterness is evident on the tongue in a
rich, malty taste.

Frogend Gold (ABV 4%)

Pioneer (ABV 4.2%)

Chinook IPA (ABV 4.6%)

Northdown Winter (ABV 5%)

Ledbury XB (ABV 6.5%)

LEES

**JW Lees & Co. (Brewers)
Ltd., Greengate Brewery,
Middleton Junction,
Manchester M24 2AX.**
☎ (0161) 643 2487
FAX (0161) 655 3731

Family-owned brewery, founded in 1828 by
John Willie Lees, a retired cotton
manufacturer, and recently joined by sixth-
generation family members. The existing
brewhouse dates from 1876 but has been
expanded and refitted, doubling the
capacity. In 1995 Lees took on its first full-
time cooper for almost 30 years (half its cask
beer is still delivered in traditional oak
casks). All the brewery's 175 pubs (most in
northern Manchester) serve real ale, which is
also supplied to 150 other outlets directly.
Tours by arrangement.

GB Mild (OG 1033, ABV 3.5%) ◈ Malty and
fruity in aroma. The same flavours are found
in the taste, but do not dominate in a beer
with a rounded and smooth character. Dry,
malty aftertaste.

Bitter (OG 1037, ABV 4%) ◈ A pale beer
with a malty, fruity aroma and a distinctive,
malty, dry and slightly metallic taste. Clean,
dry Lees finish.

Moonraker (OG 1073, ABV 7.5%) ◈ A
reddish-brown beer with a strong, malty,
fruity aroma. The flavour is rich and sweet,
with roast malt, and the finish is fruity yet
dry. Only available in a handful of outlets.

LEITH HILL

**RD & AJ Abrehart, T/A The Leith Hill
Brewery, The Plough Inn, Coldharbour,
Dorking, Surrey RH5 6HD.**
☎ / FAX (01306) 711793

Without any previous brewing
experience, the licensees of the Plough
started brewing at their pub in 1996,
'through necessity, due to increasing
overheads'. Using a 'micro-micro' plant they
have learnt through trial and error to
produce beers that have become very
popular with their customers. Spring water
from Leith Hill (the highest point in South-
East England) is used in production. Tours
by arrangement. Beers: Crooked Furrow
(OG 1040, ABV 4%), Tallywhacker (OG 1056,
ABV 5.6%).

LEYLAND

**Leyland Breweries Ltd., Unit 78, Lawrence
Leyland Industrial Estate, Irthlingborough
Road, Wellingborough, Northamptonshire
NN8 1RT.** ☎ (01933) 275215

Leyland is the name given to the new
company established by the merger of the
former Nene Valley and Nix Wincott
breweries and the beers are still labelled
either 'Nene' or 'Wincott' when on sale. The

vast majority of the output is sold via agencies, but future plans include acquiring a chain of pubs. Occasional beer: Trojan Bitter (OG 1038, ABV 3.8%). Tours by arrangement.

Old Cock Up Mild (OG 1032, ABV 3.5%) A black/red mild.

This Bitter (OG 1034, ABV 3.6%)

Unicorn Bitter (OG 1036, ABV 3.6%) A hoppy bitter also sold under house names.

Two Henrys Bitter (OG 1038, ABV 3.8%)

Griffin (ABV 4.4%) A malty brew with hop balance.

Old Black Bob (OG 1047, ABV 4.7%) A dark, roasty strong mild.

Winky's Winter Warmer (ABV 4.7%)

THAT (OG 1048, ABV 5%) A pale brown, fruity beer.

Rawhide (OG 1050, ABV 5%) A full-flavoured, strong bitter.

Midas (ABV 5.2%) A pale, hoppy strong bitter.

Winky Wobbler (OG 1072, ABV 7.5%) A powerful winter brew.

Medusa Ale (OG 1080, ABV 8%) A full-flavoured barley wine.

LICHFIELD

Lichfield Brewery, 3 Europa Way, Boley Park, Lichfield, Staffordshire WS14 9TZ. ☎ (01543) 419919

Two CAMRA members began brewing at Lichfield in 1992, bringing production back to the city after 60 years. The brewery has since doubled its capacity and increased its beer range. Over a hundred outlets are supplied either directly or via agencies. Seasonal beer: Mincespired (OG 1060, ABV 5.8%, Christmas).

Steeplechase (OG 1037, ABV 3.7%) A summer beer.

Inspired (OG 1040, ABV 4%) 🔻 Dark and malty, with a proper bitter aftertaste.

Sheriff's Ride (OG 1042, ABV 4.2%) A seasonal brew for autumn.

Resurrection Ale (OG 1043, ABV 4.3%) A spring beer.

Steeplejack (OG 1045, ABV 4.5%) 🔻 A refreshing, pale brown, hoppy beer, with a bitter finish.

Xpired (OG 1050, ABV 4.8%) 🔻 A dark winter bitter, with malt and chocolate flavours.

Gargoyle (OG 1050, ABV 5%)

LINFIT

Linfit Brewery, Sair Inn, Lane Top, Linthwaite, Huddersfield, W. Yorkshire HD7 5SG. ☎ (01484) 842370

Nineteenth-century brew pub (CAMRA national *Pub of the Year* 1997) which recommenced brewing in 1982, producing an impressive range of ales for sale here and in the free trade as far away as Manchester (27 regular outlets). New plant installed in 1994 has almost doubled its capacity. Tours by arrangement. Occasional/seasonal beers: Smoke House Ale (OG 1040, ABV 5.3%), Xmas Ale (OG 1082, ABV 8.6%). Bottle-conditioned beer: English Guineas Stout (OG 1050, ABV 5.5%).

Mild (OG 1032, ABV 3%) 🔻 Roast malt dominates this straightforward dark mild which has some hops in the aroma and a slightly dry flavour. Malty finish.

Bitter (OG 1035, ABV 3.7%) 🔻 A session beer. A dry-hopped aroma leads to a clean-tasting, hoppy bitterness, balanced with some maltiness. The finish is well-balanced, too, but sometimes has an intense bitterness.

Ginger Beer (OG 1040, ABV 4.2%)

Swift (OG 1040, ABV 4.2%) Previously Summer Ale.

Special (OG 1041, ABV 4.3%) 🔻 Dry-hopping provides the aroma for this rich and mellow bitter, which has a very soft profile and character: it fills the mouth with texture rather than taste. Clean, rounded finish.

Janet Street Porter (OG 1043, ABV 4.5%) A smooth, dry porter with a bitter, roasted malt character.

Autumn Gold (OG 1050, ABV 4.7%) A straw-coloured beer with a dominant hop character and a slightly fruity finish.

English Guineas Stout (OG 1050, ABV 5.3%) 🔻 A fruity, roast aroma preludes a smooth, roasted malt, chocolatey flavour which is bitter but not too dry. Excellent appearance; good, bitter finish.

Old Eli (OG 1050, ABV 5.3%) A well-balanced premium bitter with a dry-hopped aroma and a fruity, bitter finish.

Springbok Bier (OG 1055, ABV 5.7%) A pale amber beer available in spring, with hops balanced by a subtle maltiness in the taste. Hoppy aroma; bitter finish.

Baht Ale (OG 1053, ABV 5.5%)

Leadboiler (OG 1063, ABV 6.6%) 🔻 Flowery and hoppy in aroma, with a very moreish, strong bitter flavour which is well-balanced by a prominent maltiness. Soft mouthfeel; rounded, bitter finish.

Enoch's Hammer (OG 1080, ABV 8.6%) 🔻 A straw-coloured, vinous bitter with no pretensions about its strength or pedigree. A full, fruity aroma leads on to a smooth, alcoholic-tasting, hoppy, bitter flavour, with an unexpectedly bitter finish.

LITTLE See Trueman's.

LITTLE AVENHAM

The Little Avenham Brewery, Arkwright Mill, Hawkins Street, Preston, Lancashire PR1 7HS.
☎ (01772) 555305

Previously based at the CAMRA award-winning Gaston's Real Ale and Fine Wine Pub, this brewery quickly outgrew its original premises and moved in 1995 to a new brewhouse from where it now serves 70 free trade customers. Tours by arrangement.

Arkwright Ale (OG 1035, ABV 3.5%) 🍺 A mid-brown session beer with a gentle aroma but strong fruit and hop flavours which continue through to the aftertaste. A sourness and wine-like tartness are not unpleasant.

Arkwright Mild (OG 1035, ABV 3.5%) A dark mild with intense fruit flavours and a dry aftertaste.

Chartist Ale (OG 1038, ABV 3.8%) A hoppy bitter with a nice amber colour and a touch of fruit and a long biscuit flavour in the mouth. Quite dry aftertaste.

Clog Dancer (OG 1038, ABV 4%) 🍺 A golden yellow, distinctive bitter. Though well-balanced, complex fruit and hop flavours make it rich and moreish.

Ace of Spades (OG 1040, ABV 4%) A black beer, with a complex fruit and hop flavour. Lots of roasted malt and chocolate in the mouth, a hint of biscuit and liquorice, and a dry aftertaste. A good, well-finished beer.

Porter (OG 1040, ABV 4%) 🍺 An excellent dark beer with hints of ruby-red. Thinner than you would expect from its colour, but very satisfying. Chocolate and roast malt flavours are prominent, with a slight hoppiness and a dry aftertaste.

Pickled Priest (OG 1043, ABV 4.3%) 🍺 A pale, thin and tart bitter in which fruit flavours give way to a lasting dryness in the finish.

Torchlight (OG 1046, ABV 4.8%) 🍺 A dark to mid-brown premium ale. Malt and fruit are prominent in the aroma and flavour. Enjoyable and distinctive, it is mild and complex in the mouth, with some sweetness.

Pierrepoints Last Drop (OG 1061, ABV 7%) 🍺 A pale, strong ale with prominent fruit flavours and a dry aftertaste.

LIVERPOOL

The Liverpool Brewery, 21–23 Berry Street, Liverpool, Merseyside L1 9DF.
☎ (0151) 709 5055

🍺 Brewery with a five-barrel plant, set up in 1990 to brew solely for what was the

Black Horse & Rainbow pub, although this was sold and renamed The Brewery in 1996. The beer is stored in casks and cellar tanks and the brewing equipment can be viewed both from inside the pub and from the street. There has been much experimentation with different grains and hop types, with the result that three new beers have been added to the range. The company supplies its own three pubs, plus two other outlets. Tours by arrangement.

Black Horse (OG 1045, ABV 4.3%)

Golden Saaz (OG 1048, ABV 4.6%)

Celebration (OG 1050, ABV 4.8%).

Festival Ale (OG 1055, ABV 5.2%)

LLOYDS

Lloyds Country Beers Ltd., John Thompson Brewery, Ingleby, Derbyshire DE7 1HW.
☎ (01332) 863426

Lloyds is the separate business set up to sell the beers brewed at the John Thompson Inn (qv) to the free trade. It currently supplies over 100 outlets, mainly in the Midlands. It is also brewing the beers of the High Peak Brewery, until suitable premises are found for that company. Lloyds produces occasional brews throughout the year (generally ABV 4–5%). Tours for groups by arrangement (small fee payable).

Country Gold (OG 1040, ABV 4%) Brewed in summer.

Derby Bitter or JTS XXX (OG 1042, ABV 4.1%) Full and fruity.

Scratching Dog (OG 1045, ABV 4.5%)

Vixen Velvet (OG 1045, ABV 4.5%) A winter porter.

VIP (Very Important Pint) (OG 1048, ABV 4.7%) A heavier, darker version of Derby Bitter.

For High Peak:

Peak Pale (ABV 3.8%)

Bagman's Bitter (OG 1045, ABV 4.5%)

Cracken (ABV 5.5%, Christmas)

LOCK, STOCK AND BARREL
See Branscombe Vale, Juwards and Oakham.

LONDON BEER COMPANY
See Pitfield.

LUGTON

Lugton Inn & Brewery, Lugton, Ayrshire KA3 4DZ.
☎ (01505) 850267
FAX (01505) 850509

🍺 This brew pub is Ayrshire's only brewery, producing additive-free beers, just for the pub itself, from hops grown without the use of pesticide. Shop open 12–10. Tours by arrangement. There are plans to bottle-condition the beers. Beers: Black (OG 1036, ABV 3.4%), Best (OG 1044, ABV 4.4%), Gold (OG 1050, ABV 5%), John Barleycorn (OG 1050, ABV 5%).

LWCC See Mansfield.

M&B See Nationals, Bass.

McEWAN
See Nationals, Scottish Courage.

McGUINNESS

Thomas McGuinness Brewing Company, Cask & Feather, 1 Oldham Road, Rochdale, Greater Manchester OL16 1UA.
☎ /FAX (01706) 711476

Small brewery established in 1991 behind the Cask & Feather pub, by the late Thomas McGuinness and brewer Eric Hoare. It currently supplies real ale to its own pub and more than 70 other outlets around the country. 'Personalised contract brewing' was introduced in 1996, for pubs wishing to use their own brand name on beers of a requested colour and strength. Tours by arrangement. Seasonal beers: Christmas Cheer (ABV 4.6%, winter), Egg Nobbler's Strong Ale (ABV 4.6%, Easter).

Feather Plucker Mild (OG 1034, ABV 4%) A dark brown beer, with roast malt dominant in the aroma and taste. There's a touch of bitterness, too.

Best Bitter (OG 1038, ABV 3.8%) 🍺 Gold in colour with a hoppy aroma: a clean, refreshing beer with hop and fruit tastes and a hint of sweetness. Bitter aftertaste.

Utter Nutter (OG 1038, ABV 3.8%)

Special Reserve Bitter (OG 1040, ABV 4%) 🍺 A tawny beer, sweet and malty, with underlying fruit and bitterness, and a bittersweet aftertaste.

Junction Bitter (OG 1042, ABV 4.2%) 🍺 Mid-brown in colour, with a malty aroma. Maltiness is predominant throughout, with some hops and fruit in the taste and bitterness coming through in the finish.

Autumn Glory (ABV 4.6%) Available mid-September–mid-January.

Summer Tipple (ABV 4.6%) Available May–September.

Winter's Revenge (ABV 4.6%) Available January–March.

Tommy Todd's Porter (OG 1050, ABV 5%) 🍺 A winter warmer, with a fruit and roast aroma, leading to a balance of malt and roast malt flavours, with some fruit. Not too sweet for its gravity.

MACLAY

Maclay Group Ltd., Thistle Brewery, Alloa, Clackmannanshire FK10 1ED.
☎ (01259) 723387
FAX (01259) 761353

Founded in 1830 and moved to the present Victorian tower brewery in 1869, Maclay still uses traditional brewing methods and direct-fired coppers, with the beers produced using solely bore-hole water (the only Scottish brewery to do so) without any adjuncts. Until 1992, the company was run by descendants of the founder, James Maclay, but is now owned by the family of Evelyn Matthews, Maclay's chief executive in recent years who died in 1996. Plant improvements have already led to an upturn in sales and alterations to the beer range. Maclay has 29 tied houses, 21 of which serve real ale, which is also supplied to 120 other outlets. Tours by arrangement for trade customers.

70/- (OG 1036, ABV 3.6%) 🍺 A well-rounded, malty, fruity, clean-tasting beer. There is malt in the nose and a dry, but sweet, finish.

Broadsword (OG 1038, ABV 3.8%) 🍺 A golden-coloured beer, with a lingering dry finish. Malt and fruit are dominant in the aroma, with a hop character developing in the bittersweet taste and becoming dominant in the bitter aftertaste.

80/- (OG 1040, ABV 4%) 🍺 A rich, creamy, bittersweet beer, well worth seeking out; plenty of malt and fruit, balanced with bitterness in a lingering dry finish.

Kane's Amber Ale (OG 1040, ABV 4%) 🍺 Brewed to commemorate the contribution of the late Dan Kane to Scottish brewing: a malty, fruity, bittersweet, amber-coloured beer with a good hop character. Perhaps not as bitter as when first launched.

Oat Malt Stout (OG 1045, ABV 4.5%)

Wallace IPA (OG 1045, ABV 4.5%) 🍺 An aroma of malt, hops and fruit preludes a strong malty, hoppy taste with fruit still in evidence. These flavours linger in a bittersweet, hoppy aftertaste.

Scotch Ale (OG 1050, ABV 5%)

McMULLEN

McMullen & Sons Ltd., The Hertford Brewery, 26 Old Cross, Hertford SG14 1RD.
☎ (01992) 584911
FAX (01992) 500729

Hertfordshire's oldest independent brewery, founded in 1827 by Peter McMullen. The Victorian tower brewery, which houses the original oak and copper-lined fermenters still in use today, was built on the site of three wells. Cask ale is served in all McMullen's 135 pubs in Hertfordshire, Essex and London (though some use cask breathers), and also supplied directly to 180 free trade outlets. Seasonal beers are brewed for a limited period under the banner of McMullen Special Reserve. Tours by arrangement.

Original AK (OG 1033, ABV 3.7%) 🏷 🔖 A pleasant mix of malt and hops leads to a distinctive, dry aftertaste. Well-attenuated.

Country Best Bitter (OG 1041, ABV 4.3%) 🔖 A full-bodied beer with a well-balanced mix of malt and hops throughout and fruit flavours coming through later.

Gladstone (OG 1041, ABV 4.3%) 🏷 🔖 A beer with a hoppy, fruity aroma, a full-bodied, mainly malty flavour and a sweetish, fruity aftertaste.

Stronghart (OG 1070, ABV 7%) 🏷 🔖 A sweetish, rich, dark, winter beer, full of fruit and hop aromas and flavours.

MALLARD

Mallard Brewery,
15 Hartington Avenue,
Carlton, Nottingham
NG4 3NR.
☎ (0115) 952 1289

Phil Mallard still works full-time for BT, so his brewery, set up in 1996 is just a sideline. He built the tiny (two-barrel) plant himself and is now running to full capacity, only just keeping up with demand from his 30 regular outlets. Tours by arrangement. Seasonal beer: Quismas Quacker (OG 1060, ABV 6%, Christmas).

Duck & Dive (OG 1036, ABV 3.7%)

Bitter (OG 1038, ABV 4%) 🔖 Golden brown, fruity and hoppy to the nose, with malt more apparent in the taste than anywhere else. The fruity hop carries through to a bitter, dry finish.

Duckling (OG 1039, ABV 4.2%)

Drake (OG 1043, ABV 4.5%)

Owd Duck (OG 1047, ABV 4.8%) 🔖 Intensely roasty and strongly bitter, this ruby/brown drink has moderate undertones of fruit and faint hops throughout.

Friar Duck (OG 1048, ABV 5%)

DA (OG 1058, ABV 5.8%) A dark, sweetish winter ale.

MALTON

Malton Brewery Company
Ltd., Wheelgate, Malton,
N. Yorkshire YO17 0HP.
☎ (01653) 697580

Malton began brewing in 1985 in a stable block at the rear of the Crown Hotel (which is a separate business). The additive-free beers are supplied to

around 20 free trade outlets directly and pubs further afield via wholesalers. There are plans to start bottling the beers, initially on a seasonal basis. Tours by arrangement.

Dark (OG 1035, ABV 3.5%)

Double Chance Bitter (OG 1038, ABV 3.8%) 🔖 A clean-tasting, amber bitter in which hops predominate. Little malt character, but hop and fruit flavours lead to a smooth, bitter finish.

Pickwick's Porter (OG 1042, ABV 4.2%) 🔖 A dry, nutty porter with an abundance of malt and roast aromas and flavours. The grainy malts combine with autumnal fruit flavours into a dry finish.

Crown Bitter (OG 1045, ABV 4.5%) 🔖 A strong, malty pale ale, well-balanced by hop aromas and fruit flavours.

Owd Bob (OG 1055, ABV 6%) 🏷 🔖 A deep ruddy-brown-coloured ale with a rich, warming feel. Powerful malt, roast, hops and fruit attack the nose and palate. The sweet finish, with malt and roast malt flavours, is balanced by a late trace of bitterness.

MAN IN THE MOON 🏷

The Man in the Moon Brewery, Gilmorton Lodge Farm, Ashby Magna, Lutterworth, Leicestershire LE17 5NA. ☎ (0116) 275 0275

This brewery, which opened in 1996, is closely allied with Featherstone Brewery for the purposes of joint promotion and cost sharing. It currently supplies 16 free trade outlets.

Moon Mild (OG 1034, ABV 3.4%)

Special Bitter (OG 1035, ABV 3.6%)

Ivory Stout (OG 1040, ABV 4.1%)

Moon Bitter (OG 1041, ABV 4.2%)

MANSFIELD

Mansfield Brewery PLC,
Littleworth, Mansfield,
Nottinghamshire
NG18 1AB.
☎ (01623) 25691
FAX (01623) 658620

Founded in 1855, Mansfield has developed into one of the major regional brewers, with a tied estate of some 520 houses (another 20 or so pubs with an emphasis on food and children's facilities are being planned). It returned to cask beer production in 1982, after a break of ten years. The purchase of Hull's North Country Brewery in 1985 and subsequent acquisitions from the Scottish Courage group have helped to bring Mansfield's award-winning ales, all fermented in traditional Yorkshire squares, to a wider audience. Sizeable club and free trades are supplied, too. Mansfield produces a number of contract brews for Scottish Courage and LWCC wholesalers in Manchester ☎ (0161) 707 7878. Tours by

arrangement. With the exception of Wild
Boar, all the 'Deakins' seasonal beers were
dropped in 1997, in favour of a single, new
permanent addition to the range, The
Golden Drop.

Riding Mild (OG 1035, ABV 3.5%)
🍂 Chocolate malt on the nose leads to
blackcurrant fruit in the taste, with hops
finishing. However, the chocolate malt
continues throughout this ruby-black beer.

Riding Bitter (OG 1035, ABV 3.6%) 🍂 A
beer first aimed at Mansfield's Yorkshire
market. Mid-brown and moderately bitter, it
is dominated by an aromatic, fruity hop, but
with malt always present.

Mansfield Bitter (OG 1038, ABV 3.9%)
🍂 This mid-brown bitter is well balanced in
taste but has hops to the fore on the nose and
malt lingering in the aftertaste, although
some bitterness is discernible.

Deakins The Golden Drop (OG 1042, ABV
4.3%) Smooth, golden beer with a hoppy
aroma. Malt comes through in the taste; dry
finish.

Old Baily (OG 1045, ABV 4.8%) 🍺 🍂 Malt
dominates over moderate hop in this
discernibly Scotch-style brew. Generally
more bitter than sweet, it has a pleasant
fruitiness on the nose. Complex and
rewarding when on form.

Deakins Wild Boar (OG 1052, ABV 5.5%,
winter)

For Scottish Courage:

Webster's Yorkshire Bitter (OG 1035, ABV
3.5%) This beer supplements supplies from
Scottish Courage's John Smith's brewery.

Wilson's Original Bitter (OG 1035, ABV
3.5%)

Home Mild (OG 1036, ABV 3.6%)

Home Bitter (OG 1038, ABV 3.8%)

For LWCC:

Gray's Mild (ABV 3.5%)

Gray's Bitter (ABV 3.6%)

MANSFIELD ARMS See Devon.

MARCHES

Marches Ales, Unit 6,
Western Close, Southern
Avenue Industrial Estate,
Leominster, Herefordshire
HR6 0QD. ☎ (01568) 611084

The Solstice brewery of Kington was taken
over by Paul Harris in 1995 and moved to
this new purpose-built brewery, which takes
its name from its location at the edge of the
Marches. Demand for the beers has led to
expansion of the brewery. The beer range
has also been expanded, to include seasonal
brews, and future plans include bottling
some beers. A range of ales is brewed

exclusively for the Black Horse in
Leominster; 11 other local outlets are also
currently supplied. Tours by arrangement
Fri and Sat.

Best Bitter (OG 1036, ABV 3.8%)

Forever Autumn (OG 1040, ABV 4.2%)
🍂 Hop fruitiness predominates in a
complex array of flavours, to give a rich
aftertaste.

Priory Ale (OG 1048, ABV 4.8%)

Jenny Pipes Summer Ale (OG 1050, ABV
5.2%)

Earl Leofric Winter Ale (OG 1072, ABV
7.2%)

MARSTON MOOR

Marston Moor Brewery,
Crown House, Kirk
Hammerton, York,
N. Yorkshire YO5 8DD.
☎ / FAX (01423) 330341

Small, but expanding, brewery, set up in
1983 and moved to the rear of its first tied
house, the Crown, in 1988. This pub was
closed in 1993 after the acquisition of the
Beer Exchange at Woodhouse in Leeds. The
company currently produces 1,000 barrels a
year and supplies around 70 free trade
outlets. It also installs brewing plants and
acts as a consultant to mini-brewers; to date
it has helped set up 20 breweries. Tours by
arrangement.

Cromwell Bitter (OG 1037, ABV 3.6%) 🍂 A
golden beer with an initial burst of fruit
flavours that graduate to a malt and hop
taste. A lingering aftertaste is predominantly
fruity.

Brewers Pride (OG 1040, ABV 4.2%) 🍂 A
light and fruity, amber-coloured beer with a
hoppy, bitter aftertaste.

Porter (OG 1040, ABV 4.2%) A seasonal
brew (October–May), ruby-coloured and
stout-like.

Merrie Maker (OG 1045, ABV 4.5%)

Brewers Droop (OG 1050, ABV 5%) A
potent, straw-coloured ale.

Brewers Reward (OG 1050, ABV 5%) The
latest addition to the range.

ESB (OG 1050, ABV 5%)

Trooper (OG 1050, ABV 5%)

MARSTON'S

Marston, Thompson &
Evershed PLC, Shobnall
Road, Burton upon Trent,
Staffordshire DE14 2BW.
☎ (01283) 531131
FAX (01283) 510378

The only brewery still using the Burton
Union system of fermentation (for its
stronger ales), Marston's reinforced its
commitment to this method in 1992 with a

£1 million investment in a new Union room. Real ale is available in all the company's 868 pubs, which stretch from Yorkshire to Hampshire. Marston's also enjoys an enormous free trade, thanks to trading agreements with Wolverhampton & Dudley and the fact that many national brewers' houses stock Pedigree Bitter. The Head Brewer's Choice scheme (noted as HBC in *Good Beer Guide* pub entries) offers a range of new brews to selected outlets for two weeks at a time. Shop open 10–2. Tours by arrangement. Bottle-conditioned beer: Oyster Stout (OG 1045, ABV 4.5%) 🍾.

Bitter (OG 1037, ABV 3.8%) 🍷 An amber/tawny session beer which can often be markedly sulphury in aroma and taste. At its best, a splendid, subtle balance of malt, hops and fruit follows a faintly hoppy aroma and develops into a balanced, dry aftertaste.

Pedigree (OG 1043, ABV 4.5%) 🍷 A beer with a strong hop and malt taste and finish, a sulphurous aroma and a dry aftertaste.

Owd Rodger (OG 1080, ABV 7.6%) 🍷 🍾 🍷 A dark, ruby-red barley wine, with an intense fruity nose before a deep, winey, heavy fruit flavour, with malt and faint hops. The finish is dry and fruity (strawberries).

For Tesco:

Bottle-conditioned beer: Tesco Select Ales IPA (OG 1048, ABV 5%)

MASH & AIR
Mash & Air, 40 Charlton Street, Manchester M1 3HW. ☎ (0161) 661 6161 FAX (0161) 661 6060

🏠 Innovative and adventurous 'brew restaurant' founded in 1997 in a converted mill, specialising in tutored beer-tasting lunches, with beers brewed to accompany various meals. Tours (with a meal) Sat. All beers are conditioned and stored in cellar tanks using a cask-breather-type CO_2 system. Beers: Peach (ABV 5%), Mash (ABV 5.1%), Mash Wheat (ABV 5%), Blackcurrant Porter (ABV 5.3%), India Pale Ale (ABV 5.3%), Scotch (ABV 6%).

MASONS ARMS
See Lakeland and Strawberry Bank.

MAULDONS
Mauldons Brewery, 7 Addison Road, Chilton Industrial Estate, Sudbury, Suffolk CO10 6YW. ☎ / FAX (01787) 311055

Company set up in 1982 by former Watney's brewer Peter Mauldon, whose family had its own local brewery in the late 18th century. Its extensive beer list changes frequently and is supplied to 150 free trade outlets in East Anglia, as well as pubs further afield via wholesalers. Tours by arrangement. Seasonal beers: Broomstick Bitter (OG 1040, ABV 4%, Hallowe'en), Mother's Ruin (OG 1040, ABV 4%, Mothering Sunday), George's Best (OG 1045, ABV 4.4%, St George's Day), Love Potion No. 9 (OG 1045, ABV 4.5%, St Valentine's Day), Bah Humbug (OG 1049, ABV 4.9%, Christmas), Gunpowder Blast (OG 1063, ABV 6%, Guy Fawkes Night), Christmas Reserve (OG 1066, ABV 6.6%).

May Bee (OG 1037, ABV 3.7%) Softer than the Best Bitter, with added honey. Available in summer.

Best Bitter (OG 1037, ABV 3.8%) 🍷 A well-balanced session beer with a crisp, hoppy bitterness balancing sweet malt.

Original Porter (OG 1042, ABV 3.8%) 🍷 A black beer with malt and roast malt flavours dominating. Some hop in the finish.

Midsummer Gold (OG 1040, ABV 4%) A light-coloured summer beer.

Mid Autumn Gold (OG 1041, ABV 4.2%) A seasonal offering.

Eatanswill Old XXXX (OG 1042, ABV 4%) 🍷 Taking its name from the title given to Sudbury by Dickens in *Pickwick Papers*, this is a winter ale of deep red and brown hue, with well-balanced fruit and malt plus a slight sweetness on the palate, ending in a pleasant roast bitterness.

Special Bitter (OG 1044, ABV 4.2%) 🍷 By far the hoppiest of the Mauldons beers, with a good, bitter finish and some balancing malt.

Squires Bitter (OG 1044, ABV 4.2%) 🍷 A best bitter with a good, malty aroma and a reasonably balanced flavour, which leans towards malt. Hops come through late and crisply into the aftertaste.

Midwinter Gold (OG 1045, ABV 4.5%) A winter beer.

Suffolk Punch (OG 1050, ABV 4.8%) 🍷 A full-bodied, strong bitter. The malt and fruit in the aroma are reflected in the taste and there is some hop character in the finish. Deep tawny/red in colour.

Black Adder (OG 1053, ABV 5.3%) 🍷 A dark stout. Roast malt is very strong in the aroma and taste, but malt, hop and bitterness provide an excellent balance and a lingering finish. *Champion Beer of Britain 1991.*

White Adder (OG 1053, ABV 5.3%) 🍷 A pale brown, almost golden, strong ale. A warming, fruity flavour dominates and lingers into a dry, hoppy finish.

Suffolk Comfort (OG 1065, ABV 6.6%) 🍷 A clean, hoppy nose leads to a predominantly malty flavour in this full-bodied beer. Dry, hoppy aftertaste.

MAYHEM'S See Farmers Arms.

MAYPOLE

**Maypole Brewery, North
Laithes Farm, Wellow Road,
Eakring, Newark,
Nottinghamshire
NG22 0AN.**
☎ **(01623) 871690**

Brewery established in 1995 in an 18th-century converted farm building, with equipment purchased from Springhead Brewery. Its name comes from the permanent giant maypole which is a feature of neighbouring Wellow. One beer, Lion's Pride (OG 1038, ABV 3.9%), is brewed just for the Red Lion opposite the maypole. Aiming to consolidate its local trade, Maypole now supplies around 40 outlets, and also brews one-off beers for festivals and other events. Tours by arrangement. Seasonal beer: Donner and Blitzed (OG 1048, ABV 5.1%, a stronger version of Poleaxed for Christmas).

Celebration (OG 1040, ABV 4%) ◆ A ruddy-brown bitter in which malt dominates. Some fruity hop in the nose and taste, with an initial sweetness that drys into a bitter finish where the fruit and hops meet the malt.

Centenary Ale (OG 1041, ABV 4.2%) A light-coloured bitter with a fruity nose and a dry aftertaste. There are hints of vanilla in this crisp, refreshing, moreish beer. Full-bodied.

Flanagan's Stout (OG 1043, ABV 4.4%) Brewed initially for St Patrick's Day: a full-bodied, rich stout. An initial burnt malt dryness gives way to a smooth, mellow, lingering aftertaste with hints of liquorice, dark chocolate and coffee.

Mayday (OG 1045, ABV 4.5%) ◆ A tawny best bitter, with malt and a hint of dates on the nose. The taste is predominantly fruit and malt again, which becomes more bitter and hoppy in the finish.

Mae West (OG 1044, ABV 4.6%) A blonde, 'Belgian-style' summer beer. Citrus flavours predominate in the nose and taste. A deceptively drinkable beer for its strength.

Poleaxed (OG 1046, ABV 4.8%) A tawny, smooth beer. Damsons come out in the nose and taste and give way to a slightly burnt aftertaste. A full-bodied, warming beer which is easily drinkable.

Old Homewrecker (OG 1047, ABV 4.7%) A smooth porter. Initial maltiness gives way to a bittersweet aftertaste. Black in colour.

MERIVALES

**Merivales Ales Ltd.,
Warden Brewery, Manor
Farm, Chipping Warden,
Banbury, Oxfordshire
OX17 1LH.**
☎ **(01295) 660090**

Company set up in 1994 with a tiny, single-barrel brewplant at Edgcote, and moved early in 1996 to a new brewery, with eight times the capacity, in nearby Chipping Warden (which is in Northamptonshire, despite the postal address). Brewing was temporarily suspended in summer 1996, since when the company has taken on the former brewer from RCH Brewery. Free trade has expanded to 52 outlets. Tours by arrangement.

Haywain (OG 1034, ABV 3.4%) Brewed March–September.

CHB or Choice Hopped Bitter (OG 1039, ABV 3.9%)

Twister (OG 1051, ABV 5.1%) A winter beer.

MERRIMANS

**Merrimans Brewery, Old
Fart Ltd., Westland Square,
Beeston, Leeds,
W. Yorkshire LS11 5SS.**
☎ **(01132) 704542**
FAX **(01132) 700778**

After the demise of Robinwood Brewery, Tim Fritchley set up this new operation in 1994, reviving the 'Old Fart' name for its bottled (not bottle-conditioned) beer. Occasional beer: Old Fart (ABV 5%, brewed on request for festivals, etc.).

MIDDLETON'S

**The Middleton Brewery,
Unit 6, Stainton Grove
Industrial Estate, Barnard
Castle, Co. Durham
DL12 8TH.**
☎ **(01833) 690004**

MIDDLETON'S BREWERY

One of the newest breweries in the North-East, set up in spring 1996. It was launched with a single real ale, adding Stainton Bitter later in the year, and acquired its first pub in 1997.

Leo's (OG 1040, ABV 3.8%)

Stainton Bitter (OG 1044, ABV 4.4%)

MIGHTY OAK

**Mighty Oak Brewing
Company, 9 Prospect Way,
Hutton Industrial Estate,
Hutton, Brentwood, Essex
CM13 1XA.**
☎ / FAX **(01277) 263007**

Brewery launched in August 1996, constructed largely from equipment purchased from the defunct Whitworth Hall Brewery in Co. Durham. Mighty Oak has a potential capacity of around 50 barrels a week. Initially selling to just a few local pubs, its trade has quickly expanded to cover about 80 outlets, still mostly in Essex. Tours by arrangement.

Barrack Wood IPA (OG 1038, ABV 3.6%)

Burntwood Bitter (OG 1041, ABV 4%) A very well-balanced mix of hops, malt and fruit; mid-brown in colour.

Twenty Thirst Bitter (OG 1044, ABV 4.4%)
Initially brewed for South-West Essex
CAMRA's 21st anniversary: an amber-
coloured and fairly fruity beer, yet still with
good bitter content.

Bitter (OG 1047, ABV 4.8%) Red-brown in
colour and fairly full-bodied. Malty, with a
balancing bitterness.

MILDMAY

The Mildmay Brewery,
Holbeton, Plymouth, Devon
PL8 1NA. ☎ (01752) 830302
FAX (01752) 830540

Mildmay started brewing in 1993, for its
tied house, the Mildmay Colours Inn. In
1994, the brewery was expanded to triple its
capacity to around 50 barrels per week. Two
of the beers are now also available bottle-
conditioned and are sold nationally (as are
the cask ales) via wholesalers. The brewery
itself supplies 50 outlets directly. It also
brews a single beer for the wholesaler Jollys
Drinks ☎ (01752) 691282. Tours by
arrangement. Bottle-conditioned beers:
Patrick's Stout (ABV 4.2%), Old Horse Whip
(OG 1057, ABV 5.7%).

Colours Best (OG 1040, ABV 3.8%) ◆ A pale
brown beer with a distinctly hoppy aroma
and a citrus hop flavour. It starts dry, but a
slightly malty sweetness develops.

Patrick's Stout (ABV 4.2%) Very much in
the draught Guinness style, but with more
hops. There is a superb chocolate malt start
and a bitter, dark malt finish.

George Brendon's Best Bitter (OG 1047,
ABV 4.5%)

SP or Starting Price Ale (OG 1047, ABV
4.5%) ◆ A mid-brown bitter with a malty,
fruity aroma and taste, and a sharp, bitter
aftertaste.

50/1 (OG 1052, ABV 5.1%) A porter, brewed
November–April.

Old Horse Whip (OG 1057, ABV 5.7%) A
mid-brown-coloured beer with a hoppy,
fruity aroma and a strong, bitter taste and
aftertaste.

For Jollys Drinks:

JCB (OG 1047, ABV 4.5%) A light brown
beer with a hoppy aroma and a considerably
bitter taste and finish.

MILL

Mill Brewery, Newton Abbot, Devon.

Brewery closed.

MILL ALE See Whitewater.

MILLGATE

The Millgate Brewery, Failsworth,
Manchester.

Brewery closed.

MINERVA

See Nationals, Carlsberg-Tetley.

MITCHELL'S

Mitchell's of Lancaster
(Brewers) Ltd., 11 Moor
Lane, Lancaster, Lancashire
LA1 1QB. ☎ (01524) 63773
FAX (01524) 846071

The only surviving independent brewery in
Lancaster (est. 1880), wholly owned and run
by direct descendants of founder William
Mitchell. In February 1997 it increased its
tied estate dramatically by acquiring 26 new
pubs, bringing the total up to 78; all but one
of them sell real ale. The beers are also
available virtually countrywide in the free
trade. Tours by arrangement. Occasional/
seasonal beers: Lakeland Reserve (OG 1036,
ABV 3.6%, July–August), Tempest (OG 1045,
ABV 4.2%), Spooner (OG 1044, ABV 4.5%),
Conqueror (OG 1049, ABV 5%), Old Faithful
(OG 1052, ABV 5.2%), Christmas Cracker
(OG 1056, ABV 5.5%).

Country Mild (OG 1035, ABV 3.3%)

Original Bitter (OG 1036, ABV 3.8%) A dark
gold beer with a light, hoppy aroma, a
malty, hoppy taste and a dry finish.

Lancaster Bomber (OG 1044, ABV 4.4%) A
straw-coloured bitter with an aromatic nose.
Initially sweet on the palate, followed by
plenty of hop and a dry finish.

MITCHELLS & BUTLERS

See Nationals, Bass.

MOLE'S

Mole's Brewery (Cascade
Drinks Ltd.), 5 Merlin Way,
Bowerhill, Melksham,
Wiltshire SN12 6TJ.
☎ (01225) 704734
FAX (01225) 790770

Brewery established in 1982 and run on very
traditional lines by former Ushers brewer
Roger Catté (the brewery name came from
his nickname). The brewery has been
undergoing expansion during 1997 and
there are plans to increase the tied estate
(currently 16 pubs, all of which take at least
two of the cask ales). Mole's also supplies
around 100 free trade outlets directly and
acts as a distributor for other small brewers.
Shop open 9–5 Mon–Fri, 9–noon Sat. Tours
by arrangement. Seasonal beer: Moél Moél
or XB (OG 1060, ABV 6%, Christmas). Bottle-
conditioned beer: Brew 97 (OG 1050, ABV
5%).

Tap Bitter (OG 1035, ABV 3.5%) ◆ A pale
brown beer with a trace of malt in the aroma.
A gentle, malty, dry flavour with apple and
pear fruits follows, then a bitter finish.

Best Bitter (OG 1040, ABV 4%) ◆ A pale
brown/golden-coloured beer with a light
malt aroma. The taste is clean, dry and

malty, with some bitterness and delicate floral hop. A well-balanced, light and subtle ale.

Barley Mole (OG 1042, ABV 4.2%)

Landlords Choice (OG 1045, ABV 4.5%) A dark bitter, not widely available.

Brew 97 (OG 1050, ABV 5%) ♦ A mid-brown, full-bodied beer with a gentle malt and hop aroma. The rich flavour is malty, with fruit, hop and traces of vanilla. A wonderfully warming, malty ale.

MOOR

Moor Beer Company, Whitley Farm, Ashcott, Somerset TA7 9QW.
☎ / FAX (01458) 210050

Farmer Arthur Frampton and his wife, Annette, set up this brewery in a former workshop on their dairy farm in 1996. The business took off quickly, mainly due to the large number of free houses in the area. The dairy cows were soon replaced by Gloucester Old Spot pigs who happily munch through the used malt. The five-barrel plant has been upgraded to ten barrels, and the beer range has increased. The brewery supplies ten regular local outlets, plus another 40 on a guest beer basis. Tours by arrangement.

Withy Cutter (OG 1041, ABV 3.8%) A lightly malty, pale brown beer with a moderate bitter finish.

Merlin's Magic (OG 1045, ABV 4.3%) Amber-coloured, malty and full-bodied, with fruit notes.

Chandos Gold (OG 1052, ABV 5%) A straw-coloured, hoppy strong ale.

MOORHOUSE'S

Moorhouse's Brewery (Burnley) Ltd., 4 Moorhouse Street, Burnley, Lancashire BB11 5EN.
☎ (01282) 422864
FAX (01282) 838493

Long-established (1865) producer of hop bitters, which in 1978 began brewing cask beer. A succession of owners failed to develop the company until it was taken over in 1985 by Bill Parkinson, since when it has grown considerably, opening the first of six tied houses in 1987. A modern brewhouse was installed in 1988 and more fermenting vessels were added in 1991 to keep up with demand. Moorhouse's supplies real ale to around 150 free trade outlets. Tours by arrangement.

Black Cat (ABV 3.4%)

Premier Bitter (OG 1036, ABV 3.7%) ♦ Pale brown in colour, this characterful brew has a superb hop flower aroma, with some fruit and malt. Dry, hoppy finish.

Yates 1884 Bitter (OG 1040, ABV 4.1%) The latest addition to the range.

Pendle Witches Brew (OG 1050, ABV 5.1%) ⬆ ♦ A good hoppy aroma leads through to a full-bodied, malty sweetness, with a trace of hop bitterness.

Owd Ale (OG 1056, ABV 6%) A winter brew, available November–March.

MORDUE

Mordue Brewery, Unit 22C, Middle Engine Lane, West Chirton North Industrial Estate, Shiremoor, Tyne & Wear NE29 8SF.
☎ / FAX (0191) 296 1879

The Mordue brewery, founded in 1995, takes its name from an original family brewery which operated in Wallsend in the 19th century. The beers are now distributed nationally (20 outlets are supplied directly) and a modest expansion is planned to keep pace with demand. Tours by arrangement. Occasional/seasonal beers: Black Midden Stout (OG 1046, ABV 4.6%), Wallsend Brown Ale (OG 1046, ABV 4.6%), Headmaster's Xmas Sermon (OG 1050, ABV 5%, Christmas).

Five Bridge Bitter (OG 1038, ABV 3.8%) ♦ An excellent balance of malt, hops and fruit which carries through to a long, satisfying finish. A superb session beer.

Geordie Pride (OG 1042, ABV 4.2%) ♦ There's plenty of character in this beautifully hoppy beer. Bitterness is light but lingers long after the last swallow.

Workie Ticket (OG 1045, ABV 4.5%) ⬆ ♦ A strong, flowery hop aroma dominates this pale amber ale. Solid maltiness ends in a smooth bitterness.

Radgie Gadgie (OG 1048, ABV 4.8%) ♦ A strong and drinkable northern ale with fruity hoppiness and lasting malt character. A beer to savour.

MORLAND

Morland PLC, The Brewery, Ock Street, Abingdon, Oxfordshire OX14 5BZ.
☎ (01235) 553377
FAX (01235) 540508

Established in 1711, Morland is the second oldest independent brewer in the UK and has been on its present site since 1861. In 1992 it survived a take-over bid by Greene King and in 1995 it purchased the small pub company Unicorn Inns, owner of the Newt & Cucumber mini-chain. Nearly all Morland's 350-plus pubs serve real ale, but in some cases the licensee uses cask-breathers. The company also supplies around 500 free trade outlets around the Thames Valley and Surrey. Old Speckled Hen is now one of the UK's best-known guest beers – it even has its own Internet web site. Recent £5 million investment in the brewery has improved and expanded production facilities. Tours by arrangement. Seasonal beers: Aunt Sally Summer Ale (OG 1042, ABV 3.8%), Bill's Spring Brew (OG 1042, ABV 4.2%), Beechnut Ale (OG 1045, ABV 4.5%, autumn), Christmas Ale (OG 1063, ABV 6%).

Independent IPA (OG 1036, ABV 3.4%)

Original Bitter (OG 1039, ABV 4%) ◆ A light amber beer with a malty, hoppy nose and a hint of fruitiness. Distinct, but lightish, malt and hops carry over to the flavour and leave a sweet but dry, hoppy aftertaste.

Old Masters (OG 1045, ABV 4.6%) ◆ A well-balanced tawny/amber beer with not outstandingly strong flavours. The initial aroma of malt and hops leads to a moderately malty, but dry and hoppy flavour, with a hint of fruit which can be faintly sulphurous. Dry, bitter finish.

Old Speckled Hen (OG 1052, ABV 5.2%) Morland's most distinctive beer, deep tawny/amber in colour. A well-balanced aroma of malt and hops is followed by an initially sweet, malty, fruity taste which soon allows dry hop flavour through.

For Scottish Courage:

Wilson's Original Mild (OG 1032, ABV 3%)

MORRELLS

Morrells Brewery Ltd., The Lion Brewery, St Thomas' Street, Oxford OX1 1LA.
☎ (01865) 792013
[FAX] (01865) 791868

MORRELLS BREWERY
Oxford

The oldest brewery in Oxford has been owned or managed by the Morrell family since they acquired it in 1782. Of its 130 pubs, over 50 are within the city limits and all serve cask ale, though some employ blanket pressure. Free trade has grown to over 300 outlets, all supplied directly from the brewery. Shop open 9–5 Mon–Fri. Tours by arrangement. Seasonal beer: College Ale (OG 1074, ABV 7.4%, winter).

Oxford Bitter (OG 1038, ABV 3.7%) ◆ Golden in colour and light in body, but not in flavour, with a good aroma of hops complemented by malt and fruitiness. An initial dry hop bitterness is well-balanced by malt, which gives way to a refreshing, slightly sweet fruitiness. Bittersweet, hoppy finish.

Oxford Mild (OG 1039, ABV 3.7%) A full-bodied dark mild.

Varsity (OG 1041, ABV 4.3%) ◆ A tawny/amber beer. Malt, hops and fruit are the main features in both aroma and taste, but are well-balanced. The slightly sweet, malty, fruity start fades away to a distinctive, bittersweet finish.

Graduate (OG 1051, ABV 5.2%) ◆ An intense malt and roast malt aroma carries

through to the taste and is complemented by a moderate hoppiness. Pleasant, bitter finish.

MOULIN

Moulin Hotel & Brewery, Kirkmichael Road, Pitlochry, Perthshire & Kinross PH16 5EW.
☎ (01796) 472196
[FAX] (01796) 474098

This brewery was opened in 1995 at the Moulin Hotel during celebrations for the hotel's 300th anniversary (it had a brewery when it first opened in 1695, so it was deemed fitting to recommence brewing on the site). The operation has since moved next door to the Old Coach House. It currently supplies six outlets, but the turnover fluctuates with the tourist season; the new bottle-conditioned beer makes a good souvenir of the area. Shop open 11–4, Thu-Mon. Tours by arrangement during shop hours. Bottle-conditioned beer: Ale of Atholl (OG 1044, ABV 4.5%).

Light (OG 1035, ABV 3.7%) ◆ A refreshing, straw-coloured session bitter with a soft hoppiness and a smooth, mellow palate.

Braveheart (OG 1039, ABV 4%) ◆ An amber bitter with a delicate balance of malt and fruit and a Scottish-style sweetness.

Ale of Atholl (OG 1043, ABV 4.5%) ◆ A reddish Scottish bitter beginning malty, with a solid body and some fruit developing in the mellow finish.

Old Remedial (OG 1050, ABV 5.2%) ◆ Roast malt is to the fore in this robust, sweetish, dark brown old ale with a satisfying palate.

MUNSLOW See Crown Inn.

NAG'S HEAD
Nags Head, Abercych, Boncath, Pembrokeshire SA37 0JH.
☎ (01239) 841200

🔲 Pub brewery producing just one brew on an occasional basis largely for its own consumption. Beer: Old Emrys (ABV 4.1%).

NENE VALLEY See Leyland.

NETHERGATE
Nethergate Brewery Co. Ltd., 11–13 High Street, Clare, Suffolk CO10 8NY.
☎ (01787) 277244
[FAX] (01787) 277123

Small brewer of award-winning beers, set up in 1986, which continues to use traditional methods and no additives. The Umbel beers are infused with coriander seeds, recalling an ancient brewing style, and other brewers have now followed Nethergate in adding herbs and spices to their beers. A single tied house and 180 free trade outlets are now supplied, most in East Anglia. Tours by arrangement. Two beers are produced for the wholesaler Martin Elms Wines ☎ (01245) 478323. Tours by arrangement. Seasonal/occasional beer: Christmas Ale (OG 1048, ABV 4.8%).

IPA (OG 1036, ABV 3.6%) ✦ An apple crisp, refreshing session beer, hoppy throughout, without fully masking the malt. Lingering, bitter aftertaste.

Umbel Ale (OG 1039, ABV 3.8%) ▮ ✦ Wort is percolated through coriander seeds to give a wonderful, warming, spicy fruit tang to both the taste and aroma. The hops are strong enough to make themselves known and a strong, bitter malt finish hits late.

Bitter (OG 1039, ABV 4%) ▯ ✦ A dark bitter in which delightful malt and hop aromas give way to a well-balanced palate. Rich malts and powerful bitterness dominate the flavour, ending in a strong, bitter finish.

Golden Gate (OG 1045, ABV 4.5%) A golden bitter using three hop varieties, giving it a fresh aroma and a hoppy finish. Malt and hops are balanced in the taste.

Old Growler (OG 1055, ABV 5.5%) ▯ ✦ A complex and satisfying porter, smooth and distinctive. Sweetness, roast malt and fruit feature in the palate, with bitter chocolate lingering. The finish is powerfully hoppy.

Umbel Magna (OG 1055, ABV 5.5%) ▮ ✦ The addition of coriander to the Old Growler wort completes the original 1750s recipe for this very distinctive dark beer. The powerful spiciness only adds to this porter's appeal.

For Martin Elms Wines:

Porters Suffolk Bitter (ABV 3.5%)

Porters Sidewinder (ABV 4.5%)

NEWALE
Newale Brewing Co., Ltd., Andover, Hampshire.

Brewery closed.

NICHOLSON'S
See Nationals, Carlsberg-Tetley.

NIX WINCOTT See Leyland.

NORTH DOWNS See Weltons.

NORTHUMBERLAND
The Northumberland Brewery Ltd., Unit 14A, North Seaton Industrial Estate, Ashington, Northumberland NE63 0YB.
☎ / FAX (01670) 819139

This brewery went into production on an industrial estate in 1996, but the ecology-conscious owners are planning to move to a purpose-built, solar-powered brewery on the 220-acre, environmentally sustainable Earth Balance community site, where all the beers will be totally organically produced. A summer beer (ABV 5%) has also been scheduled. Tours by arrangement. Seasonal beer: Santa's Secret (OG 1047, ABV 4.7%, Christmas).

Castles Bitter (OG 1038, ABV 3.8%) A session bitter.

County (OG 1040, ABV 4%) A smooth, hoppy bitter.

Secret Kingdom (OG 1043, ABV 4.3%) A very dark, malty beer which may also be produced in bottle-conditioned form soon.

Best Bitter (OG 1045, ABV 4.5%) A full-bodied bitter.

Duke of Northumberland Premium Ale (OG 1050, ABV 5%) A dark-malted premium bitter.

NORTH YORKSHIRE
North Yorkshire Brewing Co., 84 North Ormesby Road, Middlesbrough, N. Yorkshire TS4 2AG.
☎ (01642) 226224
FAX (01642) 226225

Brewery founded in 1990 which is planning to move to new premises in listed buildings at Pinchinthorpe Hall, near Guisborough. The traditionally brewed beers are in much demand, although the permanent range has been slimmed down and the beers may be renamed once the brewery move is completed. Over 100 free trade outlets are currently supplied. Tours by arrangement. Seasonal beers: Honey Bunny (OG 1036, ABV 3.8%, an Easter beer with added honey), Love Muscle (OG 1038, ABV 4%, February), Xmas Herbert (OG 1044, ABV 4.4%), Cereal Killer (OG 1044, ABV 4.5%, a wheat beer, August).

Best Bitter (OG 1036, ABV 3.6%) ✦ Light, very refreshing and surprisingly full-flavoured for a pale, low gravity beer, with a complex, bittersweet mixture of malt, hops and fruit carrying through into the aftertaste.

Boro Best (OG 1039, ABV 4%) A full-bodied, northern beer with a malty aroma and a balanced malt and hops taste, with vanilla notes.

Fool's Gold (OG 1046, ABV 4.6%) ✦ A well-hopped, lightly malted, golden premium bitter, using Styrian Golding hops.

Flying Herbert (OG 1047, ABV 4.7%) ✦ A refreshing, red/brown beer with a hoppy aroma. The flavour is a pleasant balance of roast malt and sweetness which predominates over hops. The malty, bitter finish develops slowly.

Dizzy Dick (OG 1080, ABV 7%) ✦ A smooth, strong, dark, aromatic ale with an obvious bite, although too sweet for some. The very full, roast malt and caramel flavour has hints of fruit and toffee. The malty sweetness persists in the aftertaste. Available November–March.

OAKHAM

Oakham Ales, 80 Westgate, Peterborough, Cambridgeshire PE1 1RD.
☎ **(01733) 358300**

Established in 1993 in industrial units on a Rutland trading estate, with a custom-built, ten-barrel plant, Oakham found a new owner in 1995. A move to the above address, a former unemployment office in Peterborough, was planned for autumn 1997, the premises split between the brewery and a brewery tap which will accommodate up to 700 people. The design is based on an American-style brew pub, with the brewery visible from the bar through glass panels. Oakham also supplies two other associated pubs, plus over 60 free houses. A range of seasonal brews has been developed to complement the two permanent beers and one beer is brewed just for the Lock, Stock & Barrel wholesaling company ☎ (01364) 644124. The tasting notes below are based on samples brewed before the brewery move. Tours by arrangement. Seasonal beers: White Dwarf (OG 1043, ABV 4.3%), Hunky Dory (OG 1045, ABV 4.5%), Mompessons Gold (OG 1050, ABV 5%), Old Tosspot (OG 1052, ABV 5.2%), Cold Turkey (OG 1063, ABV 6.3%).

Jeffrey Hudson Bitter or JHB (OG 1038, ABV 3.8%) ⬒ 🍴 ◆ A golden bitter with a slightly fruity hop nose. The taste is mainly hoppy, with some malt and a little fruit that fades into a hoppy, bitter finish.

Bishops Farewell (OG 1046, ABV 4.6%) A golden, refreshing, fruity beer, with wheat and malt in the taste and a bitter, citrus finish.

For Lock, Stock and Barrel:

Pistolways (OG 1043, ABV 4.3%)

OAKHILL

Oakhill Brewery, The Old Maltings, Oakhill, Bath, Somerset BA3 5BX.
☎ **(01749) 840134**
FAX **(01749) 840531**

Situated high in the Mendip Hills in Somerset, this brewery was set up by a farmer in 1984 in an old fermentation room of the original Oakhill Brewery (established in 1767 and burnt down in 1924). By the mid-1990s, the brewery had outgrown its original premises and moved during 1997 to the old maltings building in Oakhill which had been newly renovated. By more than doubling its brewlength, Oakhill should now be able to meet the demand from its

own four tied houses and 100 free trade outlets. There are plans to open a shop and offer tours.

Somer Ale (OG 1033, ABV 3.3%) ◆ An amber, light and refreshing, fruity pale ale, with a pleasant, dry, bitter finish. A summer brew.

Best Bitter (OG 1040, ABV 4%) ◆ A clean-tasting, tangy bitter, with a good hop content and citrus fruit and malt balance. Dry finish; light hop aroma. Very quenching.

Black Magic (OG 1045, ABV 4.5%) ⬒ ◆ A black/brown bitter stout with roast malt and a touch of fruit in the nose. Smooth roast malt and bitterness in the taste, with mellow coffee and chocolate.

Mendip Gold (OG 1045, ABV 4.5%)

Yeoman Strong Ale (OG 1050, ABV 5%) ◆ A strong, pale brown, full-bodied bitter, with a floral hop palate and notable fruitiness. Dry, bitter, lasting finish.

Mendip Tickler (OG 1063, ABV 6.3%) A winter warmer.

OFFILERS See Nationals, Bass.

O'GAUNT

John O'Gaunt Brewing Company Ltd., Unit 4B, Rural Industry Estate, John O'Gaunt, near Twyford, Melton Mowbray, Leicestershire LE14 2RE.
☎ / FAX **(01664) 454777**

Originally set up as Fulbeck Brewery and owned by a haulage contractor who planned to brew at his pub, the Hare & Hounds in Fulbeck, this brewery was acquired in 1997 by Celia Atton who moved it next to the Stag & Hounds pub at nearby Burrough on the Hill in July 1997. The office address remains as above. The one beer is named after a local landmark; two further beers are planned.

Robin a Tiptoe (OG 1042, ABV 3.9%)

O'HANLON'S

O'Hanlon's Brewing Company Ltd., 114 Randall Road, Vauxhall, London SE11 5JR. ☎ **(0171) 793 0803**

Brewery set up in April 1996, initially to supply John O'Hanlon's own pub in Clerkenwell, but now some 25 other outlets take the beers on a regular basis. They are also available through wholesalers East-West Ales. One-off specials are occasionally brewed to supplement the permanent range. Seasonal beers: Spring/Summer/Autumn Gold (OG 1035, ABV 3.6%, brewed basically to the same recipe, with subtle changes for each season). Tours by arrangement.

Maltster's Weiss (OG 1039, ABV 4%) A typically hazy wheat beer. It has an aromatic nose giving way to good malt character and a subtle, dry finish. Available May–September.

Dry Stout (OG 1041, ABV 4.2%) Black malt and roasted barley give this rich stout a dense black colour. Hop bitterness and a smooth, lingering finish are features.

Blakeley's Best No. 1 (OG 1044, ABV 4.2%) A premium ale in which roasted barley helps give a more complex flavour. A late addition of hops in the kettle provides a hoppy nose and finish.

Red Ale (OG 1044, ABV 4.5%) A typical Irish red ale using pale and crystal malts, plus roasted barley for extra complexity. Challenger and Styrian Golding hops add bitterness; good, dry finish.

Blakeley's Best No. 2 (OG 1055, ABV 5.2%) A winter warmer.

OKELLS

Okell & Son Ltd., Falcon Brewery, Kewaigue, Douglas, Isle of Man IM2 1QG. ☎ (01624) 661120 FAX (01624) 625234

Formerly trading as Isle of Man Breweries, this is the main brewery on the island, having taken over and closed the rival Castletown brewery in 1986. Production of Castletown beers ceased completely in 1992 after a period at the old Victorian Falcon Brewery, which itself was closed in 1994, when production moved to a new, purpose-built brewery at Kewaigue. All beers are produced under the unique Manx Brewers' Act 1874 (permitted ingredients: water, malt, sugar and hops only). All the company's 54 pubs sell real ale and over 50 free trade outlets are also supplied directly. Tours by arrangement. Seasonal beers: Spring Ram Ale (OG 1042, ABV 4.2%), Olde Skipper (OG 1045, ABV 4.5%, May), St Nicks (OG 1050, ABV 5%, Christmas).

Mild (OG 1034, ABV 3.4%) 🍺 A genuine, well-brewed mild ale, with a fine aroma of hops and crystal malt. Reddish-brown in colour, this beer has a full malt flavour with surprising bitter hop notes and a hint of blackcurrants and oranges. Full, malty finish.

Bitter (OG 1035, ABV 3.7%) 🍺 A golden beer, malty and superbly hoppy in aroma, with a hint of honey. Rich and malty on the tongue, it has a wonderful, dry, malt and hop finish. A complex but rewarding beer.

OLD BEAR

Old Bear Brewery, 6 Keighley Road, Cross Hills, Keighley, N. Yorkshire BD20 7RN. ☎ (01535) 632115

Brewery founded in 1993 by former Goose Eye Brewery owner Bryan Eastell, next to the pub in which he is a partner,

producing beers brewed with local spring water. Other free trade outlets are also supplied. Tours by arrangement.

Bitter (OG 1038, ABV 3.9%) 🍺 A refreshing, easy-drinking bitter with some background sulphur. The predominantly hoppy flavour gives way to a short bitter finish.

Ursa Minor (OG 1044, ABV 4.6%) A copper-coloured, fruity beer, with a hoppy aroma and dry finish.

Ursa Major (OG 1056, ABV 5.8%) A darker, stronger version of Minor, also with a dry finish and a smooth taste.

OLD CHIMNEYS

Old Chimneys Brewery, The Street, Market Weston, Diss, Norfolk IP22 2NZ. ☎ (01359) 221411

Tiny craft brewery opened in 1995 by former Greene King/Broughton brewer Alan Thomson. The beers are brewed with wild hops gathered from local hedgerows and are mostly named after local endangered species. Despite the postal address, the brewery is in Suffolk. It currently supplies 30 outlets directly and, in addition to the beers listed, a winter warmer (OG 1078, ABV 7.5%) is produced to individual customers' requirements. Tours by arrangement. Occasional/seasonal beers: Bittern Bitter (OG 1039, ABV 4.1%, summer), Great Raft Bitter (OG 1042, ABV 4.2%, winter), Polecat Porter (OG 1042, ABV 4.2%), Black Rat Stout (OG 1046, ABV 4.4%), Natterjack Premium Ale (OG 1050, ABV 5%).

Military Mild (OG 1035, ABV 3.4%) 🍺 A moreish dark mild, with good body for its gravity. Light roast bitterness features, with a crisp, dry, malt and hop aftertaste.

Swallowtail IPA (OG 1036, ABV 3.6%) 🍺 An interesting session bitter, with hop dominating over a toffee, nutty flavour.

OLD COTTAGE

Old Cottage Beer Co., Unit 3, Hall House Industrial Estate, New Hutton, Kendal, Cumbria LA8 0AN. ☎ / FAX (01539) 724444

Brewery founded in March 1996, producing just one cask ale and a few occasional brews. Within a year, the range had extended to six permanent beers, brewed using local spring water, with specials produced on request. Old Cottage now supplies 50 outlets in the southern Lake District.

Red Pyke (ABV 3.6%) 🍺 A gold/amber-coloured session beer with a distinct, overriding caramel aroma and a malty middle, but poor balance. Dry, bitter, astringent aftertaste.

Harvest Light (ABV 3.8%)

Barleycorn (ABV 4%) A dark brew with hops and malt in the taste.

Slate Slitter (ABV 4%)

Cobblers Last (ABV 4.6%)

Cottage Pride (ABV 5.6%) An award-winner.

OLD COURT See Nationals, Whitbread.

OLDERSHAW

Oldershaw Brewery, 12 Harrowby Hall Estate, Grantham, Lincolnshire NG31 9HB. ☎/FAX (01476) 572135

Experienced home-brewer Gary Oldershaw and his wife set up this new brewery at their home in January 1997. Grantham's first brewery for 30 years, Oldershaw now supplies 20 local free houses and plans to market the beers further afield. There may also be seasonal additions to the range. Tours by arrangement. Occasional beer: Caskade (ABV 4.2%).

Newton's Drop (OG 1040, ABV 4.1%)

Ermine Ale (OG 1040, ABV 4.2%) A pleasant session bitter.

Old Boy (OG 1047, ABV 4.8%) A full-bodied beer with a fine bitter taste.

OLDHAM

See Burtonwood and Nationals, Whitbread.

OLD FORGE

Pett Brewing Company, The Old Forge Brewery, c/o The Two Sawyers, Pett, Hastings, E. Sussex TN35 4HB. ☎ (01424) 813030

Brewery established in 1995 in a restored old village forge. Its output is still increasing, with 50 local outlets now supplied, plus a new pub in Hastings, the Priory, which trades under the Old Forge sign and always sells at least two of the beers. Tours by arrangement. Occasional beer: White Christmas (OG 1060, ABV 6%).

Brothers Best (OG 1037, ABV 3.9%) ◆ A hoppy, amber-coloured, session beer.

Pett Progress (OG 1043, ABV 4.6%) ◆ A mid-brown beer marked by its maltiness, which dominates the aroma and taste. Caramel comes through in the aftertaste.

Pett Genius (OG 1043, ABV 4.6%) A new stout.

Summer Eclipse (OG 1048, ABV 5%) Now brewed all year.

Ewe Could Be So Lucky (ABV 6%) Light in colour for a strong bitter, with fruit predominant in the aroma and taste before a hoppy bittersweet finish.

OLD LAXEY

Old Laxey Brewing Co. Ltd., Old Laxey, Isle of Man IM4 7DA. ☎ (01624) 862451

🔲 The island's newest brewery is set behind the Shore Hotel, which sold the first cask of Bosun Bitter in March 1997. Six other local free houses are also supplied with the beer. Tours by arrangement.

Bosun Bitter (OG 1038, ABV 3.8%)

OLD LUXTERS

Old Luxters Vineyard Winery & Brewery, Hambleden, Henley-on-Thames, Oxfordshire RG9 6JW. ☎ (01491) 638330 FAX (01491) 638645

Buckinghamshire brewery (despite the postal address) set up in 1990 in a 17th-century barn by David Ealand, owner of Chiltern Valley Wines. Apart from the brewery and vineyard, the site also houses a fine art gallery and a cellar shop. The brewery supplies a few local free trade outlets and pubs further afield via wholesalers. Occasional brews are produced to order for other independent breweries, and these are often also supplied bottle-conditioned. Shop open daily 9–5.30 Mon–Fri, 11–5.30 Sat–Sun. Tours by arrangement. Bottle-conditioned beers: Vintage Ale (OG 1042, ABV 4.5%), Barn Ale (OG 1048, ABV 5.4%).

Barn Ale Bitter (ABV 4%) A fruity, aromatic, fairly hoppy and bitter beer.

Dark Roast Ale (ABV 4%) A dark, chocolatey, nutty beer.

Barn Ale Special (OG 1043, ABV 4.5%) ◆ The original Barn Ale: predominantly malty, fruity and hoppy in taste and nose, and tawny/amber in colour. Fairly strong in flavour: the initial, sharp, malty and fruity taste leaves a dry, bittersweet, fruity aftertaste. It can be slightly sulphurous.

OLD MILL

Old Mill Brewery Ltd., Mill Street, Snaith, Goole, E. Yorkshire DN14 9HS. ☎ (01405) 861813 FAX (01405) 862789

Small brewery opened in 1983 in a 200-year-old former malt kiln and corn mill. A new brewhouse was installed in 1991 to increase the brewlength to 60 barrels and the brewery is slowly building up the tied estate (currently 14 houses). The innovation of selling some beers in plastic, non-returnable handicasks has meant that the beer can now be found nationwide; around 200 free trade outlets are supplied direct from the brewery. Plans are in hand to install a bottling plant. Tours by arrangement.

Traditional Mild (OG 1035, ABV 3.4%) ◆ A satisfying roast malt flavour dominates this easy-drinking, quality dark mild.

Nellie Dene (OG 1035, ABV 3.5%) Available April–October.

Traditional Bitter (OG 1038, ABV 3.9%) ◆ The Old Mill character has returned to this beer, though bitterness remains at a premium. It has a malty nose and initial flavour, with hops hiding until the lingering finish.

Old Curiosity (OG 1044, ABV 4.5%)

Bullion (OG 1045, ABV 4.7%) ◆ The malty and hoppy aroma is followed by a neat mix of hop and fruit tastes within an enveloping maltiness. Dark brown/amber in colour.

Blackjack (OG 1050, ABV 5%) A winter brew.

OLD PINT POT
Old Pint Pot, Adelphi Street, Salford, Greater Manchester M3 6EM.
☎ (0161) 839 1514

Brewing commenced in summer 1996 at this Salford pub, which is part of the locally-based Honeycomb Leisure group. The one beer has no constant name or strength, but it is a full mash brew and is cask-conditioned. It is sold here and in one other pub.

ORANGE
See Nationals, Scottish Courage.

ORIGINAL See Nationals, Bass.

ORKNEY
**The Orkney Brewery,
Quoyloo, Orkney
KW16 3LT.**
☎ (01856) 841802
FAX (01856) 841754

The island's first brewery in living memory, set up in 1988 by former licensee Roger White. Initially only brewing keg beer for local outlets, Roger's personal commitment to real ale has resulted in cask ales now representing 90 per cent of sales. The beers are available nationwide via wholesalers. Tours by arrangement. Seasonal/occasional beers: Island Pale (OG 1040, ABV 4%), White Christmas (OG 1057, ABV 6%).

Raven Ale (OG 1038, ABV 3.8%) ◆ A pale brown beer in which fruit predominates. Roast is evident in the aroma and taste, and hop in the taste and aftertaste. Initially sweet, but with a satisfying dry, bitter aftertaste.

Dragonhead Stout (OG 1040, ABV 4%) ◆ A strong, dark malt aroma flows into a complex, dry roast and caramel flavour. The roast malt continues to dominate the aftertaste and blends with chocolate and

fruit to develop a strong, dry finish. Hard to find.

The Red MacGregor (OG 1041, ABV 4%)

Dark Island (OG 1045, ABV 4.6%) ☐ ▮ ◆ Dark, beautifully balanced and full of roast malt and fruit. A bittersweet taste leads to a long-lasting, roasted, slightly bitter finish. Full-bodied and deceptively drinkable.

Skull Splitter (OG 1080, ABV 8.5%)

OTTER
**Otter Brewery, Mathayes
Farm, Luppitt, Honiton,
Devon EX14 0SA.**
☎ (01404) 891285
FAX (01404) 891124

Otter began brewing in 1990 and grew steadily for almost a year, then disaster struck in the shape of yeast problems. Persistence in finding the right strain paid off and led to a major expansion of the brewery in 1994. The Head and Bright beers are now being bottled (filtered but not pasteurised). Some 90 pubs take the beers, which are produced using local malt and the brewery's own spring water. The business is very much a family affair. Tours by arrangement.

Bitter (OG 1036, ABV 3.6%) ☐ ◆ A light brown bitter with a hoppy, fruity aroma and taste, and a bitter finish.

Bright (OG 1039, ABV 4.3%) A straw-coloured bitter with a hoppy aroma, fruity taste and bitter aftertaste. A summer beer.

Ale (OG 1043, ABV 4.5%) ☐ ◆ A mid-brown, well-balanced beer with a predominant hop/bitter taste and finish.

Head (OG 1054, ABV 5.8%) ◆ Strong fruit aromas provide the first impression of this dark beer, followed up by a roast malt, bittersweet flavour and a bitter aftertaste.

OUTLAW See Rooster's.

PALMERS
**JC & RH Palmer Ltd., The
Old Brewery, West Bay
Road, Bridport, Dorset
DT6 4JA.** ☎ (01308) 422396
FAX (01308) 421149

Thatched brewery, founded in 1794, situated by the sea in former mill buildings. The company is managed by the great-grandsons of brothers John Cleeves and Robert Henry Palmer, who acquired the brewery in the late 19th century. All its 61 pubs serve real ale, although top pressure and cask breathers are widely in use. A further 60 free trade outlets are supplied directly, but Palmers' beers are reaching a wider audience throughout the South via wholesalers. Shop open 10–6 Mon–Thu, 10–8 Fri–Sat. Tours by arrangement.

THE INDEPENDENTS

Bridport Bitter or BB (OG 1030, ABV 3.2%)
◆ A light beer with a hoppy aroma, a bitter, hoppy taste with some malt, and a bitter aftertaste.

Best Bitter or IPA (OG 1038, ABV 4.2%) ◆ A beer that is hoppy and bitter throughout. Fruit and malt undertones give some balance to the aroma and taste, and there is a lingering bitter aftertaste.

Tally Ho! (OG 1046, ABV 4.7%) ◆ A dark and complex brew with a mainly malty aroma. The nutty taste is dominated by roast malt and the aftertaste is malty and bitter. Limited availability, especially in winter.

200 (OG 1052, ABV 5%) A complex anniversary ale, now a permanent feature.

PARADISE See Bird in Hand.

PARISH
Parish Brewery, The Old Brewery Inn Courtyard, High Street, Somerby, Leicestershire LE14 2PZ.
☎ (01664) 454781

The first brewery to be established in Somerby since the 16th century, Parish started life at the Stag & Hounds, Burrough on the Hill, in 1983. It moved to the Old Brewery Inn in 1991, acquiring a new 20-barrel plant. Parish is listed in the *Guinness Book of Records* as brewer of the strongest beer in the world – Baz's Super Brew (ABV 23%), brewed as a one-off in 1995. A slightly weaker bottled version (not bottle-conditioned) of Baz's Bonce Blower is now brewed by Bateman for London-based beer agency Jacktar Ltd., which has licensed the name from Parish. Shop open during licensing hours. Tours (minimum 12 people) by arrangement. Beers: Mild (OG 1035, ABV 3.5%), Special Bitter or PSB (OG 1038, ABV 3.8%), Farm Gold (OG 1038, ABV 3.8%), Somerby Premium (OG 1040, ABV 4%), Wild John Bitter (OG 1048, ABV 4.7%), Poachers Ale (OG 1058, ABV 6%), Baz's Bonce Blower or BBB (OG 1100, ABV 11%).

PARKER See Cannon.

PASSAGEWAY
Passageway Brewing Company, Unit G8, Queens Dock Commercial Centre, Norfolk Street, Liverpool, Merseyside L1 0BG.
☎ (0151) 708 0730 FAX (0151) 709 0925

Adventurous brewery established in 1994. Its two founders, Steve Dugmore and Phil Burke, who brew on a part-time basis, are not afraid to experiment with continental beer styles. They use yeast from a Belgian monastic brewery, and some water from St Arnold's well in Belgium is added to the copper during each brew of St Arnold. The Rauch (smoked) beer incorporates smoked malts from Bavaria. There are plans to launch a bottle-conditioned version of St Arnold during 1998. Tours by arrangement. Occasional/seasonal beers: Unkel Dunkel (OG 1043, ABV 4.5%), Vrolijke Stad (OG 1043, ABV 4.5%), Rauch (OG 1046, ABV 4.8%), Marley's Ghost (OG 1052, ABV 5.5%, Christmas), Advent (OG 1067, ABV 7%, Christmas).

Docker's Hook (1036, ABV 3.6%) ◆ A mid-brown, full-bodied ale. Banana fruitiness dominates the palate and aftertaste.

Redemption (OG 1038, ABV 4%) ◆ A dry, tart and clean beer brewed with rye.

St Arnold (OG 1048, ABV 5%) 🍾 ◆ Deep ruby in colour, this is a very bitter and fruity beer, yet not sweet. Hop, roast malt, chocolate and liquorice flavours also fight for attention in the taste and dry aftertaste. A complex, heavy beer, reminiscent of a Belgian brown ale. Highly drinkable.

PEMBROKE
Pembroke Brewery Co., Eaton House, 108 Main Street, Pembroke SA71 4HN.
☎ (01646) 682517
FAX (01646) 682008

Brewery founded in 1994 in former stables behind the proprietors' house. The plant was re-designed the following year to allow for smaller runs and greater flexibility. Pembroke supplies a single tied house (a converted railway building at Pembroke Dock) and other outlets via distributors, for whom it produces numerous 'specials'. Tours by arrangement.

The Darklin (OG 1035, ABV 3.5%)

Sound Whistler (OG 1037, ABV 3.8%) A summer beer.

Dimond Lager (OG 1040, ABV 4.1%)

Main Street Bitter (OG 1040, ABV 4.1%)

Golden Hill Ale (OG 1044, ABV 4.5%)

Old Nobbie (OG 1048, ABV 4.8%) A new stout.

Off the Rails (OG 1050, ABV 5.1%)

Signal Failure (OG 1058, ABV 6%) A new winter brew.

PETT See Old Forge.

PHOENIX
Phoenix Brewery Ltd., Phoenix Brewery, Green Lane, Heywood, Greater Manchester OL10 2EP.
☎ (01706) 627009

Company established as Oak Brewery in 1982 in Ellesmere Port. It moved in 1991 to Heywood and changed its name in 1996. Phoenix now supplies over 100 free trade outlets in the North-West and W. Yorkshire. Occasional/seasonal beers: Mild (ABV 4%), Jovian (ABV 4.2%), Shamrock (ABV 4.2%), Dominator (ABV 4.3%), Tyke (ABV 4.3%), March Hare (ABV 4.4%), Mayfly (ABV 4.5%), Massacre (ABV 4.7%), Resurrection (ABV 4.7%), Firecracker (ABV 5%), Spooky Brew (ABV 5%), Sticky Wicket (ABV 5.4%).

Bantam Bitter (ABV 3.5%) Darker and drier than Hopwood Bitter below, with a slight nutty finish.

Hopwood Bitter (OG 1035, ABV 3.5%) A pale, quaffing beer with a light fruit and malt aroma. Citrus fruit and bitter hop feature in the taste with a short bitter finish.

Best Bitter (OG 1038, ABV 3.9%) A tawny, hoppy session beer with some balancing malt in the aroma and taste. Strong, dry and hoppy finish.

Midsummer Madness (OG 1044, ABV 4.4%) A pale, hoppy and refreshing, very drinkable beer, available June–August.

Old Oak Ale (OG 1044, ABV 4.5%) A well-balanced, brown beer with a multitude of mellow fruit flavours. Malt and hops balance the strong fruitiness in the aroma and taste, and the finish is malty, fruity and dry.

Thirsty Moon (ABV 4.6%) A beer with a slight malty character and a full and crisp hop finish.

Bonneville (ABV 4.8%) A very malty beer with a short hop finish.

Double Dagger (OG 1050, ABV 5%) A pale brown, malty brew, more pleasantly dry and light than its gravity would suggest. Moderately fruity throughout; a hoppy bitterness in the mouth balances the strong graininess.

Porter (OG 1050, ABV 5%) The roast malt promised by the aroma is joined in the taste by malt, caramel and hops. Long and pleasant aftertaste. Brewed October–January.

Wobbly Bob (OG 1060, ABV 6%) A red/brown beer with a malty, fruity aroma. Strongly malty and fruity in flavour and quite hoppy, with the sweetness yielding to a dryness in the aftertaste.

Humbug (OG 1071, ABV 7%) A rich, dark brown, hoppy beer, available November–January.

PILGRIM
Pilgrim Ales, The Old Brewery, West Street, Reigate, Surrey RH2 9BL.
☎ (01737) 222651
[FAX] (01737) 225785

Set up in 1982, and moved to Reigate in 1985, Pilgrim has gradually increased its capacity and its beers have won both local and national awards, although sales are mostly concentrated in the Surrey area

(around 60 outlets). Tours are available by arrangement on the last Friday of the month in summer. A shop is planned. Occasional/seasonal beers: Autumnal (OG 1045, ABV 4.5%, September–October), Excalibur (OG 1045, ABV 4.5%, Easter), The Great Crusader (OG 1063, ABV 6.5%, June–July), Conqueror (OG 1065, ABV 6.5%), Pudding (OG 1075, ABV 7.3%, November–December). Bottle-conditioned beers: Progress (ABV 4.3%), Royal Gold (ABV 5%), Springbock (ABV 5.2%), Pudding (ABV 6.8%).

Surrey Bitter (OG 1037, ABV 3.7%) A clean, well-balanced session bitter. Hop flavour comes through in the finish.

Porter (OG 1040, ABV 4%) A dark beer with a pleasant roast malt flavour, balanced by a faint hoppiness which is also there at the finish. Noticeable roast malt aroma.

Progress (OG 1040, ABV 4%) Reddish-brown in colour, with a predominantly malty flavour and aroma, although hops are also evident in the taste.

Saracen (OG 1047, ABV 4.5%) Roast malt dominates the aroma of this black stout, but hops balance the roast malt flavour, leading to a bitter finish. Tasty.

Crusader (OG 1047, ABV 4.9%) A summer brew; a light, golden beer with a good marriage of malt and hops from aroma through to finish. Very drinkable.

Talisman (OG 1050, ABV 5%) A strong ale with a mid-brown colour, a fruity, malt flavour and a faint hoppiness.

Springbock (OG 1050, ABV 5.2%) A Bavarian-style wheat beer for spring.

PIONEER See Rooster's.

PITFIELD
Pitfield Brewery, The Beer Shop, 14 Pitfield Street, Hoxton, London N1 6EY.
☎ (0171) 739 3701

Revived brewery next to The Beer Shop off-licence. Pitfield brands were contract-brewed at Brewery on Sea until Pitfield re-opened with new equipment in new premises in July 1996. Now brewing to full capacity, it supplies 15 outlets direct as well as the shop, open 11–7 Mon–Fri, 10–4 Sat. Tours by arrangement. Bottle-conditioned beers: Bitter (ABV 3.7%), Shoreditch Stout (ABV 4%), Amber Ale (ABV 4.2%), Black Eagle (ABV 5%), Honey Ale (ABV 5%), Liquorice Porter (ABV 5%), The Beer Shop's 15th Anniversary Ale (ABV 6%), Millennium 2000 Ale (ABV 10.5%).

Bitter (OG 1036, ABV 3.5%)

Shoreditch Stout (ABV 4%)

Amber Ale (ABV 4.2%)

Hoxton Heavy (OG 1048, ABV 4.8%)

Black Eagle (ABV 5%)

Liquorice Porter (ABV 5%)

PLANETS

HG Wells Planets Brewery,
Crown Square, Woking,
Surrey GU21 1HR.
☎ (01483) 727100
[FAX] (01483) 712701

🚩 Brewery opened in April 1996 in a
leisure complex, supplying its full mash
beers only to the house bars initially,
although now selling to the free trade under
the name of Brooklands Brewery. At the
leisure complex the beers are kept under a
blanket of gas in cellar tanks. Beers: Bobbies
Bitter (OG 1042, ABV 4.2%), HG's Ale (OG
1052, ABV 5%).

PLASSEY

Plassey Brewery, The
Plassey, Eyton, Wrexham
LL13 0SP. ☎ (01978) 780922
[FAX] (01978) 780019

Brewery founded in 1985 on the
250-acre Plassey Estate, which also
incorporates a touring caravan park, craft
centres, a golf course and three licensed
outlets for Plassey's ales. Twenty free trade
outlets also take the beers. A new brewery
was completed in 1996, incorporating a shop
(open 9–5 Mon–Sat, 11–4 Sun), and plans are
in hand for a new bottling plant. Tours by
arrangement.

Bitter (OG 1041, ABV 4%) 🚩 🍺 ◆ A well-
balanced, hoppy, straw-coloured beer with a
citrus fruitiness.

Welsh Stout (OG 1046, ABV 4.6%) 🍺 ◆ A
dry, roasty stout, sweetish, with a long, dry
finish.

Cwrw Tudno (OG 1048, ABV 5%) ◆ More
fruity than the bitter; well-balanced, with a
good, dry aftertaste.

Dragon's Breath (OG 1060, ABV 6%) ◆ A
fruity, strong bitter, smooth and quite sweet,
though not cloying, with an intense, fruity
aroma. A dangerously drinkable winter
warmer.

PLOUGH INN

Bodicote Brewery, Plough Inn, Bodicote,
Banbury, Oxfordshire OX15 4BZ.
☎ (01295) 262327

🚩 Brewery founded in 1982 at the Plough,
No. 9 High Street (hence the beer name),
which has been in the same hands since
1957. Three other outlets are also supplied
with its full mash beers. Two very popular
week-long beer festivals are held each year
in February and August. Tours by
arrangement. Beers: Bodicote Bitter (OG
1035, ABV 3.3%), Three Goslings (OG 1041,
ABV 4%), No. 9 (OG 1045, ABV 4.4%), Old
English Porter (OG 1047, ABV 4.7%, winter),
Triple X (OG 1059, ABV 6.6%, Christmas).

POOLE

The Brewhouse Brewery,
68 High Street, Poole,
Dorset BH15 1DA.
☎ (01202) 682345

🚩 Brewery established in 1980 by David
Rawlins who opened his first (and so far
only) pub, the Brewhouse in 1983. When an
extension to the Brewhouse was completed
in 1990, the whole brewing operation was
moved there. Additional fermenting vessels
were installed in 1995 and 1996. The brewery
now has a capacity of 75 barrels a week and
serves over 15 outlets direct and a
widespread free trade through wholesalers.
Occasional tours by arrangement.

Best Bitter or Dolphin (OG 1038, ABV 3.8%)
The brewery's original session bitter: amber-
coloured and well balanced.

Bedrock Bitter (OG 1042, ABV 4.2%)

Holes Bay Hog (OG 1044, ABV 4.5%) Light
amber in colour, this beer is brewed from
pale malt and malted wheat, and has a
distinctive, dry-hopped character and a
refreshing aftertaste.

Bosun Bitter (OG 1045, ABV 4.6%) The
brewery's top selling beer. A rich, amber-
coloured beer with a smooth, crisp,
powerful malty flavour and a pronounced
hoppy aftertaste.

Double Barrel (OG 1053, ABV 5.5%) A very
pale straw-coloured IPA, smooth, mellow
and deceptively strong. It looks like a
Pilsener, but tastes like a traditional bitter.

PORTER

Porter Brewing Co. Ltd.,
Rossendale Brewery, The
Griffin Inn, Hud Rake,
Haslingden, Lancashire
BB4 5AF.
☎ / [FAX] (01706) 214021

🚩 The Griffin Inn was refurbished and
re-opened, complete with microbrewery,
by new owner David Porter in 1994. A third
tied house was acquired in 1996 and a fourth
acquisition is planned; all the pubs serve real
ale and several other local outlets also take
the beer. Tours by arrangement. Seasonal
beers: Sleighed (OG 1064, ABV 6.5%,
December–January), Celebration Ale (OG
1068, ABV 7.1%, July–August).

Dark Mild (OG 1033, ABV 3.3%) A true
dark mild, with a slight maltiness and a
good hint of roast in the finish.

Bitter (OG 1037, ABV 3.8%) A dark beer for
a standard bitter, with a good, sharp,
northern bitterness that lingers through to
the back of the throat, and a dry finish.

Rossendale Ale (OG 1041, ABV 4.2%) An
initial slight, malty sweetness leads through
to a deep, fruity taste and a lingering fruity
finish.

Porter (OG 1050, ABV 5%) A rich beer with a
slightly sweet, malty start, counterbalanced

with sharp bitterness and a very noticeable roast barley dominance.

Sunshine (OG 1050, ABV 5.3%) An intensely hoppy and bitter golden ale, full-bodied with some malt, a robust mouthfeel and a lingering bitterness.

PORTERS See Nethergate.

POWELL See Wood.

PRINCETOWN
Princetown Breweries Ltd., The Prince of Wales, The Brewery, Tavistock Road, Princetown, Devon PL20 6QF.
☎ (01822) 890789 FAX (01822) 890719

Brewery established in 1994 by a former Gibbs Mew and Hop Back brewer. It now serves four tied pubs with any surplus beer sold to five local free trade outlets. Princetown also brews under contract for the Westbury Ales wholesaling company ☎ (01458) 850845. Tours by arrangement. Bottle-conditioned beer: Jail Ale (OG 1049, ABV 4.8%).

Dartmoor IPA or Best Bitter (OG 1041, ABV 4%)

Jail Ale (OG 1049, ABV 4.8%) ❧ Hops and fruit predominate in the flavour of this mid-brown beer which has a slightly sweet aftertaste.

Dartmoor Gold (OG 1051, ABV 5%)

For Westbury Ales:

Jordy (OG 1043, ABV 4.3%)

QUALITY CASK ALES
See Ash Vine.

QUAY
The Quay Brewery, Lapin Noir Ltd., Hope Square, Weymouth, Dorset DT4 8TR.
☎ / FAX (01305) 777515

Brewery set up in summer 1996 in the old Devenish and Groves brewery buildings, bringing brewing back to Weymouth after a ten-year absence which followed the closure of Devenish. Although Greenalls owns the complex, the brewery is totally independent and is open to visitors as part of the Timewalk attraction. A Victorian Tastings Bar and shop opened at Easter 1997 (9.30–4.30 Mon–Sun). Occasional/seasonal beers: Nicholson's IPA or Independent Plymouth Ale (OG 1040, ABV 4.2%), Groves Oatmeal Stout (OG 1050, ABV 4.8%), Silent Knight (OG 1054, ABV 5.8%, a dark wheat beer). Bottled-conditioned beers: Groves Oatmeal Stout (OG 1050, ABV 4.8%), Old Rott (OG 1050, ABV 5.4%), Silent Knight (OG 1054, ABV 5.9%).

Weymouth Special Pale Ale (SPA) (OG 1038, ABV 4%)

Weymouth JD 1742 (OG 1040, ABV 4.2%)

Bombshell Bitter (OG 1043, ABV 4.5%)

Old Rott (OG 1050, ABV 5%)

QUEEN'S HEAD
Fat God's Brewery, The Queen's Head, Iron Cross, Evesham, Worcestershire WR11 5SH. ☎ (01386) 871012
FAX (01386) 871362

Pub brewery (in Warwickshire, despite the postal address) opened in summer 1997, its first beer having previously been produced under contract by Cannon Royall. The full mash beers are stored in casks and may soon be sold to wholesalers for wider distribution. A stronger ale and a mild are planned. Beer: Fat God's Best Bitter (ABV 3.6%).

RCH
RCH Brewery, West Hewish, Weston-super-Mare, Somerset BS24 6RR.
☎ (01934) 834447
FAX (01934) 834167

Brewery originally installed in the early 1980s behind the Royal Clarence Hotel at Burnham-on-Sea, but since 1993 brewing has taken place on a commercial basis on a new site. RCH now supplies 25 outlets directly and the beers are available nationwide through its own wholesaling company which also distributes beers from other small independent breweries. Tours by arrangement. Seasonal beer: Santa Fé (OG 1074, ABV 7.3%, Christmas). Bottle-conditioned beers: Pitchfork (OG 1043, ABV 4.3%), Old Slug Porter (OG 1046, ABV 4.5%), Firebox (OG 1060, ABV 6%).

Hewish IPA (ABV 3.6%)

PG Steam (OG 1039, ABV 3.9%)

Pitchfork (OG 1043, ABV 4.3%)

Old Slug Porter (OG 1046, ABV 4.5%) 🍺 ❧ A traditional-style porter with a nutty, woody flavour and a toffee and honey aroma.

East Street Cream (OG 1050, ABV 5%)

Firebox (OG 1060, ABV 6%)

RAINBOW
Rainbow Inn & Brewery, 73 Birmingham Road, Allesley Village, Coventry, W. Midlands CV9 5GT. ☎ (01203) 405530

Pub brewery, housed in former stables, which opened in 1994 just to serve its own customers. The brewery was expanded in March 1997. Tours by arrangement. Beers: Piddlebrook (OG 1040, ABV 3.8%), Firecracker (OG 1052, ABV 5%), Santa's Spice (OG 1056, ABV 5.5%, Christmas).

RANDALLS

RW Randall Ltd.,
Vauxlaurens Brewery, St
Julian's Avenue, St Peter
Port, Guernsey GY1 3JG.
☎ (01481) 720134
FAX (01481) 723233

The smaller of Guernsey's two breweries,
purchased by PH Randall from Joseph
Gullick in 1868. Successive generations have
continued to run the business, except during
the period of the German occupation, when
it ceased brewing until after the war.
Randalls owns 18 pubs, but only three serve
real ale. Do not confuse with Randalls
Vautier of Jersey, which no longer brews.
Shop open 10–5 Mon–Sat. Tours at 2.30 on
Thursdays, May–September. Occasional
beer: Light Mild (OG 1036, ABV 3.6%).

Patois Ale (OG 1046, ABV 5%) ◥ Amber in
colour, with a hoppy aroma. Bitter and
hoppy both in the palate and finish.

RAT & RATCHET

The Rat & Ratchet Brewery,
40 Chapel Hill,
Huddersfield, W. Yorkshire
HD1 3EB. ☎ (01484) 516734

Well-known alehouse which began
brewing in 1994 to supply just itself and
occasional beer festivals. Two years of
experimentation with recipes has resulted in
a regular beer and seasonal specials, the aim
being to have at least one Rat beer available
most of the time. Beers: Golden Hamster
(ABV 4%), Cratchet's Christmas Cracker
(ABV 4.3%, seasonal), Black Rat Porter (ABV
4.6%, autumn), Squiffy Squirrel (ABV 6.8%,
winter).

RAVEN See Winfields.

READING LION

Reading Lion Brewery, The Hop Leaf,
163–165 Southampton Street, Reading,
Berkshire RG1 2QZ. ☎ (0118) 931 4700

Brewery opened by Hop Back Brewery
in 1995 at the Hop Leaf pub, a former
Inntrepreneur house, becoming Reading's
first real ale brewery since Courage closed
the old Simonds site in the late 1970s. The
five-barrel plant came from the Wyndham
Arms in Salisbury and beers are stored in
both casks and cellar tanks (no blanket
pressure). Production has been rather erratic
in the past year and there are no regular
beers. Occasional beers are brewed for other
Hop Back pubs and the free trade. Tours by
arrangement.

🍺 The empty tankard indicates the
beer was a *Good Beer Guide Beer of the
Year* in the last three years.

REBELLION

Rebellion Beer Company,
Unit J, Rose Industrial
Estate, Marlow Bottom
Road, Marlow,
Buckinghamshire SL7 3ND.
☎ / FAX (01628) 476594

Opened in 1993, Rebellion helps to fill the
gap left in Marlow by Whitbread's closure of
the Wethered brewery in 1988. A move to a
larger site locally is imminent, in order to
double the brewing capacity. Around 80
local pubs are supplied directly, with others
served via wholesalers. Shop open 8–6 Mon–
Fri, 9–4 Sat. Tours by arrangement for
CAMRA branches. Two new seasonal beers
are now brewed so that the whole year is
covered. Beers (including a range of
occasional brews) are also brewed for
Scanlon's Brewery ☎ (01895) 256270, which
ceased production in summer 1997. Seasonal
beer: Scrooge (OG 1052, ABV 5%, a
Christmas spice beer). Bottle-conditioned
beer: Mutiny (OG 1052, ABV 5%).

IPA (OG 1039, ABV 3.7%) A very clean,
refreshing pale ale. A sweet malt character
dominates the palate, before a crisp, dry
finish. A good session beer.

Smuggler (OG 1041, ABV 4.1%) Different
hops are added at four stages during the
brewing process, resulting in a bittersweet
beer with a fresh, fruity late hop flavour and
aroma.

Blonde Bombshell (OG 1043, ABV 4.3%) A
new summer brew.

Mutiny (OG 1046, ABV 4.5%) A reddish,
full-bodied beer, with a well-balanced malt
and hop taste. Goldings are added for a late
hop charge to give a lasting aftertaste.

Red Oktober (OG 1048, ABV 4.7%) An
autumn beer in the style of a German altbier.
Brewed using crystal and rye malts and
continental hops, it has a deep reddish hue.

Zebedee (OG 1048, ABV 4.7%) The new
spring offering.

Old Codger (OG 1054, ABV 5%) A heart-
warming winter ale with a full, dark-roasted
malt character. The hops give contrast, but
do not overpower the richness of the malt.

For Scanlon's:

Middlesex Gold (OG 1039, ABV 3.8%)

Colne Valley Bitter (OG 1042, ABV 4.1%)

Spike (OG 1046, ABV 4.5%)

Brunel Premier Ale (OG 1048, ABV 4.8%)

RECTORY

Rectory Ales Ltd., Streat Hill Farm, Streat
Hill, Streat, Hassocks, W. Sussex BN6 8RP.
☎ (01273) 890570

Unusual brewery founded in 1996 by the
Rector of Plumpton, Godfrey Broster, to
generate profits for the maintenance of the

three churches in his parish. Financial help from parishioners purchased the equipment and further capital injection increased brewing capacity by 100 per cent. A move to a larger site took place in spring 1997 and the brewery now supplies 12 local outlets. Tours (maximum ten people) by arrangement. Seasonal beer: Christmas Cheer (OG 1047, ABV 5%, December–January).

Rector's Pleasure (OG 1035, ABV 3.8%)

Parson's Porter (OG 1036, ABV 3.6%) A winter beer.

Light Relief (OG 1042, ABV 4.5%)

Rector's Revenge (OG 1048, ABV 5.4%).

RED CROSS

Red Cross Brewery, Perryfields Lane, Bromsgrove, Worcestershire B61 8QW.
☎ / [FAX] (01527) 871409

Red Cross started brewing in 1993 in the old bull pen of Red Cross Farm, a 17th-century yeoman farmhouse. The beer is available in ten local outlets, including the Hop Pole Inn in Bromsgrove, an M&B pub, formerly run by the Red Cross brewer. Tours by arrangement.

Nailer's Oh Be Joyful or OBJ (OG 1040, ABV 4.2%) 🍂 A light-coloured, sweet bitter which puts plenty of hops in the mouth, to leave a refreshing aftertaste.

Old Knee Jerker or OKJ (OG 1049, ABV 4.9%) A darker, maltier ale than OBJ but with the characteristic intense hop flavours.

RED LION

Red Lion Hotel, Long Bridge Street, Llanidloes, Powys SY18 6EE.
☎ (01686) 412270 [FAX] (01686) 413573

Brewery set up in a garage adjoining the Red Lion in 1995, brewing just for the pub itself and beer festivals. Tours by arrangement. Beers: Cobbler's Thumb (OG 1044, ABV 4.4%), Cobbler's Last (OG 1095, ABV 10%, Christmas).

REDRUTH

Redruth Brewery (1742) Ltd., The Brewery, Redruth, Cornwall TR15 1RB.
☎ (01209) 212244 [FAX] (01209) 313793

This old brewery no longer brews cask ales, concentrating instead on contract brewing and packaging.

REEPHAM

Reepham Brewery, Unit 1, Collers Way, Reepham, Norwich, Norfolk NR10 4SW.
☎ (01603) 871091

Family brewery, founded in 1983 by a former Watney's research engineer, with a purpose-built plant in a small industrial unit. Reepham now supplies its award-winning ales to around 20 local outlets. Recent developments have included the production of a cask-conditioned lager, Reepham Gold, and the taking on of small contract brews. Occasional beers: Strong Ruby Ale (OG 1048, ABV 4.5%), Bittern (OG 1050, ABV 5%).

Granary Bitter (OG 1038, ABV 3.8%) 🍂 An amber beer which is well-balanced and makes easy drinking. The malt and hops are complemented by a pleasing amount of bitterness and hints of fruit.

Summer Velvet (OG 1040, ABV 4%)

Rapier Pale Ale (OG 1042, ABV 4.2%) 🍂 A beer with a flower hop aroma and maltiness in the taste on a fruit and hop background.

Velvet (OG 1043, ABV 4.3%) 🍂 The fruity, malt aroma of this darkish brown winter stout gives way to a sweet, mellow taste explosion of malt, roast malt, fruit and hops. This subsides to a pleasant aftertaste with hints of liquorice.

Norfolk Wheat (OG 1045, ABV 4.5%)

Brewhouse (OG 1055, ABV 5.5%) A strong winter ale.

RIDLEYS

TD Ridley & Sons Ltd., Hartford End Brewery, Felsted, Chelmsford, Essex CM3 1JZ. ☎ (01371) 820316 [FAX] (01371) 821216

Ridleys was established by a miller, Thomas Dixon Ridley, on the banks of the picturesque River Chelmer in 1842, under the influence of his wife who came from a brewing family in Chelmsford. Run today by Thomas's great-great grandson, Nicholas, the company currently supplies 62 tenanted pubs (all in Essex) and 120 local free trade outlets. Ridleys also brews under contract for Tavern Wholesaling ☎ (0161) 864 5000. Shop open 8.30–5 Mon–Fri. Tours by arrangement. Seasonal beer: Winter Ale (OG 1050, ABV 5%, Christmas).

IPA (OG 1035, ABV 3.5%) 🍂 Refreshing and hoppy throughout, well-balanced by a persistent maltiness and delicate fruit in the flavour, with a lingering bitterness.

Mild (OG 1035, ABV 3.5%) 🍺 🍂 A very dark mild, with a light aroma of roast malt and subdued hop. Quite bitter for a mild, with roast malt and fruit in the taste and a balanced, dry finish with hops and roast malt.

ESX Best (OG 1043, ABV 4.3%) 🍂 Harmonious malt and hops dominate the taste of this best bitter, with a hint of fruit. Hops just gain over malt in the finish.

Witchfinder Porter (OG 1045, ABV 4.3%) 🍂 A dark ruby, bittersweet winter beer, with strong roast malt and light hoppiness.

Spectacular (OG 1047, ABV 4.6%) A pale, straw-coloured beer, with a flowery nose. It has a delicate malty flavour and a rather bitter aftertaste.

Rumpus (OG 1049, ABV 4.5%) ◆ A tawny, malty beer with a developing fruitiness and a bittersweet balance, becoming dryer, with hops in the finish.

For Tavern Wholesaling:

Norman's Conquest (ABV 4.6%) Not to be confused with the 1995 *Champion Beer of Britain* from Cottage Brewery.

RINGWOOD

Ringwood Brewery Ltd.,
Christchurch Road,
Ringwood, Hampshire
BH24 3AP.
☎ (01425) 471177
FAX (01425) 480273

Ringwood was set up in 1978 and moved in 1986 to attractive 18th-century buildings, formerly part of the old Tunks brewery. A new brewhouse was commissioned at the end of 1994, and a new fermenting room completed in 1995. The brewery supplies two tied houses and 350 free trade outlets directly. Shop open 10–5 Mon–Fri, 9.30–12 Sat. Tours by arrangement. Bottle-conditioned beer: Fortyniner (OG 1048, ABV 4.8%).

Best Bitter (OG 1038, ABV 3.8%) ◆ A well-balanced golden brown beer. A malty and hoppy aroma leads through to a malty taste with some sweetness. Malty and bitter finish, with some fruit present.

True Glory (OG 1043, ABV 4.3%) ◆ A malty aroma precedes a hoppy taste with malt and fruit, followed by a malty, hoppy and fruity aftertaste. Copper-coloured.

Fortyniner (OG 1048, ABV 4.8%) ◆ Pale brown in colour. A malty and fruity aroma leads to a well-balanced taste of malt and hops. Fruity finish.

XXXX Porter (OG 1048, ABV 4.7%) ◆ An aroma of roasted malt and hops leads to a rich, roasted malt taste with coffee and fruit. The aftertaste is dry with bitter fruit and hops. Almost black in colour. Available October–March.

Old Thumper (OG 1058, ABV 5.8%) ◆ A mid-brown beer. A fruity aroma preludes a sweet, malty taste with some fruit. Surprisingly bitter aftertaste, with malt and fruit.

RISING SUN

The Rising Sun Inn,
Knowle Bank Road, Shraley
Brook, Audley, Stoke-on-
Trent, Staffordshire
ST7 8DS. ☎ (01782) 720600
FAX (01782) 721288

🍺 The brewery at the Rising Sun opened in 1989 and was enlarged in 1994. It

supplies the busy pub and 15 other local outlets. Tours by arrangement.

Rising (OG 1038, ABV 3.5%) ◆ A thin, dry bitter with little flavour.

Setting (OG 1047, ABV 4.6%) ◆ A beer with good body, but little taste or aroma. Some bitter aftertaste.

Porter (OG 1048, ABV 4.6%) ◆ A black, stout-like beer with a strong roast and bitter flavour and a long, dry aftertaste. The best of the range.

Sunstroke (OG 1056, ABV 5.6%) ◆ A dark, red/brown, medium-bodied ale. The aroma has roast malt and some hops, whilst the taste is bittersweet with a dominating maltiness. The aftertaste sees malt, roast malt and hops coming through.

Total Eclipse (OG 1072, ABV 6.8%)

Solar Flare (OG 1100, ABV 11%) A winter beer.

RIVERHEAD

Riverhead Brewery Ltd., 2 Peel Street,
Marsden, Huddersfield, W. Yorkshire
HD7 6BR. ☎ (01484) 841270

🍺 Brew pub which opened in 1995, after two years' work converting an old corn merchant's/grocery store. The pub is on two floors, with a window onto the brewing area. The brewery now also supplies ten other local outlets. Tours by arrangement.

Sparth Mild (OG 1036, ABV 3.6%)

Butterley Bitter (OG 1038, ABV 3.8%)

Deer Hill Porter (OG 1040, ABV 4%)

Cupwith Light Bitter (OG 1042, ABV 4.2%)

Black Moss Stout (OG 1043, ABV 4.3%)

March Haigh Special Bitter (OG 1046, ABV 4.6%)

Redbrook Premium Bitter (OG 1055, ABV 5.5%)

RIVERSIDE

Riverside Brewery, The Gatehouse, Pallion
Shipyard, Pallion, Sunderland, Tyne &
Wear SR4 6LL. ☎ (0191) 514 3212

Brew-it-yourself operation which began commercial brewing in December 1996, specialising in tailor-making brews for pubs. All the beers are made from malt extract. Some occasional beers have been produced and the two beers listed below are also available in bottle-conditioned form.

Publican Bitter (OG 1043, ABV 4.2%)

Anti-Perpendicular (OG 1048, ABV 4.8%)

ROBINSON'S

Frederic Robinson Ltd., Unicorn Brewery, Lower Hillgate, Stockport, Cheshire SK1 1JJ.
☎ **(0161) 480 6571**
FAX **(0161) 476 6011**

Major Greater Manchester family brewery, founded in 1838. Robinson's has grown through various pub and brewery acquisitions over the years, including Hartleys of Ulverston in 1982. The Hartleys brewery was closed in 1991 and only Hartleys XB is still brewed (at Stockport). Robinson's supplies real ale to all its 416 tied houses (most in southern Manchester and Cheshire), and to free trade outlets. Shop open Mon–Sat 9–5.30. Tours by arrangement.

Dark Best Mild (OG 1033, ABV 3.3%) ◆ Toffee/malt-tasting, with a slight bitterness. A very quaffable beer with a fruity, malty aroma and a dry finish. A very rare find.

Hatters Mild (OG 1033, ABV 3.3%) ◆ A light mild with an unpronounced malty aroma and a refreshing dry, malty flavour. Short bitter/malty aftertaste.

Old Stockport Bitter (OG 1035, ABV 3.5%) ◆ A beer with a refreshing taste of malt, hops and citrus fruit, a characteristic fruity aroma, and a short, dry finish.

Hartleys XB (OG 1040, ABV 4%) ◆ Robinson's copy of Hartley's XB is far from the beer once brewed in Ulverston. It is an overtly sweet and malty bitter with a bitter citrus peel fruitiness and a hint of liquorice in the finish.

Best Bitter (OG 1041, ABV 4.2%) ◆ A pale brown beer with a malty, hoppy nose. There are malt, hops and bitterness in the flavour and the aftertaste is short and bitter.

Frederics (OG 1050, ABV 5%) A golden, full-bodied, premium bitter. A hoppy nose leads through to a full, hoppy taste, softened by malt in the finish. Rarely found in the Robinson's estate, it is mainly a free trade beer.

Old Tom (OG 1079, ABV 8.5%) 🍷 🍴 ◆ A full-bodied, dark, fruity beer. The aroma is fruity and mouthwatering; the aftertaste is bittersweet, with an alcoholic kick.

ROOSTER'S

Rooster's Brewery, Unit 20, Claro Court Business Centre, Claro Road, Harrogate, N. Yorkshire HG1 4BA.
☎ / FAX **(01423) 561861**

Brewery set up in 1993 by Sean Franklin, formerly of Franklin's Brewery. The plant was expanded in 1994 to cater for the increased demand for the award-winning beers, and a second development in the last 12 months has taken the capacity up to 32

barrels a week. A subsidiary label, Outlaw (previously known as Pioneer), produces a different, experimental beer every two months for the guest beer market, and those that prove popular are repeated. Some 300 outlets are now supplied. Tours by arrangement. Occasional/seasonal beers: Jak's (OG 1039, ABV 3.9%), Nector (ABV 5.8%, Christmas).

Special (OG 1039, ABV 3.9%) A pale yellow beer with a fruity, floral aroma and citrus hop in the taste.

Scorcher (ABV 4.3%) A pale, aromatic, fruity and hoppy beer with a long, moderately bitter finish.

Yankee (OG 1043, ABV 4.3%) ◆ A straw-coloured beer with a delicate aroma. The flavour is an interesting mix of malt and hops, with a gentle sweetness and a bite of orange peel, leading to a short, pleasant finish.

Rooster's (OG 1047, ABV 4.7%) ◆ A light amber beer with a subtle, sweet, slightly hoppy nose. Intense malt flavours, reminiscent of treacle toffee with chocolate and orange undertones, precede an unexpected hoppy finish.

Cream (OG 1047, ABV 4.7%) A pale beer with fruity aromas and a soft bitterness.

ROSE STREET

See Nationals, Carlsberg-Tetley.

ROSS

Ross Brewing Company, The Bristol Brewhouse, 117–119 Stokes Croft, Bristol BS1 3RW.
☎ **(0117) 942 0306**
FAX **(0117) 942 8746**

🚩 Set up in Hartcliffe in 1989, Ross was the first brewery to brew with organic Soil Association barley, initially producing bottle-conditioned beers only. The brewery later moved to the Bristol Brewhouse pub and now no longer produces bottled beers. Ross brews for only its two tied houses, but the range includes many occasional beers. Tours by arrangement. Brewery shop at Brewers Droop, 36 Gloucester Road, Bishopston, Bristol, open 9–5.30 Mon–Sat. Beers: Hartcliffe Bitter (OG 1045, ABV 4.5%), SPA (OG 1050, ABV 5%), Saxon Ale (OG 1055, ABV 5.5%), Uncle Igor (ABV 21%).

ROSSENDALE See Porter.

ROTHER VALLEY

Rother Valley Brewing Company, Gate Court, Northiam, E. Sussex TN31 6QT.
☎ / FAX **(01797) 252922**

Rother Valley Brewing Company was established in Northiam in 1993 but was set to move at the end of 1997 to Sedlescombe, with a name change planned to Battle Brewery (to reflect its new situation near the site of the Battle of Hastings). The brewery uses locally grown hops and malt in the production of its popular beers, which are taken by around 30 local outlets. A Christmas beer has also been brewed.

Lighterman (OG 1035, ABV 3.5%)

Level Best (OG 1040, ABV 4%)

ROYAL CLARENCE See RCH.

ROYAL INN
Royal Inn & Horsebridge Brewery, Horsebridge, near Tavistock, Devon PL19 8PS. ☎ (01822) 870214

Fifteenth-century pub, once a nunnery, which began brewing in 1981. It recently changed hands, but the brewer, Simon Woods, stayed with the new owners. There are plans to enlarge and refurbish the plant, which currently only supplies the single outlet. Tours by arrangement. Beers: Tamar Ale (OG 1039, ABV 3.9%), Right Royal (OG 1050, ABV 5%), Heller (OG 1060, ABV 6%).

RUDDLES
Ruddles Brewery Ltd., Langham, Oakham, Rutland LE15 7JD. ☎ (01572) 756911 FAX (01572) 756116

Famous real ale brewery, founded in 1858, which lost its identity when it was taken over by Grand Metropolitan in 1986. Ruddles beers subsequently became national brands. Ownership passed to Courage in the 'pubs for breweries' swap, and the company is now owned by Dutch lager giants Grolsch, who acquired the business in 1992. Almost 200 outlets are still supplied directly from the brewery. Tours by arrangement.

Best Bitter (OG 1037, ABV 3.7%) 🍺 ◆ The malty and lightly hoppy nose precedes a complex and well-balanced flavour of malt, fruit and hoppy bitterness in this mid-brown beer. Malt and hops are sustained through the bitter finish.

County (OG 1049, ABV 4.9%) ◆ A mid-brown, strong bitter with a good mix of malt, hops and fruit in the nose. All these elements appear in a full-bodied, well-balanced taste that leads to a long hoppy, bitter ending.

For Scottish Courage:

Webster's Green Label Best (OG 1034, ABV 3.2%)

🍺 The full tankard indicates the beer is one of this year's *Good Beer Guide Beers of the Year*.

RUDGATE
Rudgate Brewery Ltd., 2 Centre Park, Marston Business Park, Rudgate, Tockwith, York, N. Yorkshire YO5 8QF. ☎ (01423) 358382

Brewery founded in 1992 and subsequently purchased by two former Bass executives. Operating from an old armoury building on a disused airfield, it supplies 180 outlets from Tyneside to Nottingham. The beers are themed around the York Viking connection and are brewed in open square fermenters. A number of house beers are also produced. Tours for small groups by arrangement. Seasonal beer: Rudolf's Ruin (OG 1060, ABV 5.4%, Christmas).

Viking (OG 1038, ABV 3.8%) ◆ A well-hopped beer with a malty, full-bodied taste of hops and fruit which lingers well into the aftertaste.

Battleaxe (OG 1043, ABV 4.2%) ◆ A smooth beer, with malt and bitterness predominant throughout. Slightly sweet.

Ruby Mild (OG 1041, ABV 4.4%)

Pillage Porter (OG 1045, ABV 4.5%)

Thunderflash (ABV 4.8%) A very pale summer ale.

Thor's Hammer (OG 1055, ABV 5.5%)

RYBURN
Ryburn Brewery, c/o Ram's Head, Wakefield Road, Sowerby Bridge, Halifax, W. Yorkshire HX6 2AZ. ☎ (01422) 835413 FAX (01422) 836488

Founded in 1990 in a former dye works, this brewery moved in 1994 to larger premises beside the re-opened Rochdale Canal. The equipment has since been relocated again and is now housed beneath the brewery's one tied house. Fifteen local free trade outlets are supplied with the beers. Seasonal beer: Porter (OG 1044, ABV 4.2%, Christmas).

Best Mild (OG 1033, ABV 3.3%) ◆ More akin to a thin stout than a dark mild, this dark brown beer has a liquorice aroma, a slightly fruity, burnt flavour and a short, dry finish.

Best Bitter (OG 1038, ABV 3.8%) ◆ A thin beer, initially sweet, with some bitterness in the aftertaste. Some background sulphur throughout.

Rydale Bitter (OG 1044, ABV 4.2%) ◆ A lightly-hopped, sweet, malty bitter with a short, dry, bitter finish.

Luddite (OG 1048, ABV 5%) ◆ This black stout has rich coffee and chocolate flavours, set against a background maltiness. The long aftertaste is dry and quite bitter. Cappuccino-like aroma.

Stabbers Bitter (OG 1052, ABV 5.2%) 🍺 A malty aroma leads to rich maltiness in the mouth, with bittersweet, fruity elements; malty and bitter finish. A mid-brown, powerful strong ale.

Coiners (OG 1060, ABV 6%) 🍺 Hoppy fruitiness and a high gravity sweetness vie for attention in this light-bodied, strong bitter, with sweetness giving way to malty bitterness in the short aftertaste.

SADDLEWORTH
Saddleworth Brewery, Church Inn, Uppermill, Saddleworth, Greater Manchester OL3 6LW. ☎ (01457) 820902

🏠 Pub brewery opened in January 1997 and presently only supplying the pub itself and some beer festivals. The full mash beers are kept in casks. Beers: More (ABV 3.8%), Bert Corner Bitter (ABV 4%), Shaft Bender (ABV 5.4%).

S&N See Nationals, Scottish Courage.

ST AUSTELL
St Austell Brewery Co. Ltd., 63 Trevarthian Road, St Austell, Cornwall PL25 4BY. ☎ (01726) 74444 FAX (01726) 68965

St Austell was set up in 1851 by maltster and wine merchant Walter Hicks. During its boom years, the business grew quickly and by 1893 was forced to move to larger premises, which it still occupies. It remains a family business, selling real ale to all its 160 pubs. A further 600 free trade outlets are supplied directly from the brewery. St Austell brews under contract for Carlsberg-Tetley, re-creating a beer from the closed Furgusons Plympton brewery. Shop open 9.30–4.30 Mon–Fri in the visitors' centre; tours by arrangement.

Bosun's Bitter (OG 1032, ABV 3.1%) 🍺 A refreshing session beer, sweetish in aroma and bittersweet in flavour. Lingering, hoppy finish.

XXXX Mild (OG 1039, ABV 3.6%) 🍺 Little aroma, but a strong, malty character. A caramel-sweetish flavour is followed by a good, lingering aftertaste which is sweet, but with a fruity dryness. Very drinkable.

Tinners Ale (OG 1039, ABV 3.7%) 🍺 A deservedly popular, golden beer with an appetising malt aroma and a good balance of malt and hops in the flavour. Lasting finish.

Trelawny's Pride (OG 1045, ABV 4.4%) 🍺 A beer served through a swan neck and sparkler which robs it of aroma and taste and keeps aftertaste to a minimum.

Hicks Special Draught or HSD (OG 1051, ABV 5%) 🍺 An aromatic, fruity, hoppy bitter which is initially sweet and has an aftertaste of pronounced bitterness, but

whose flavour is fully-rounded. A good premium beer.

Winter Warmer (OG 1060, ABV 6%) 🍺 A red/brown beer, available November–February. Full-bodied, it has a pronounced malty aroma which leads into a palate featuring strong malt and hop flavours.

For Carlsberg-Tetley:
Dartmoor Best Bitter (OG 1038, ABV 3.9%)

ST PETER'S
St Peter's Brewery Co. Ltd., St Peter's Hall, St Peter, South Elmham, Bungay, Suffolk NR35 1NQ. ☎ (01986) 782322 FAX (01986) 782505

This brewery, which opened on midsummer's day 1996, enjoys an enviable, albeit unusual, setting, in the outbuildings of a beautiful 13th-century hall, and is owned by an equally unusual husband and wife team of a businessman and a psychiatry professor. The beers are produced using a pure source of water, pumped from 200 feet below the brewery, to supply five tied houses in the Waveney Valley, plus 70 other outlets direct. The beer range has expanded to eight cask ales, including speciality fruit and wheat beers, and plans are in hand to further develop the bottled (not bottle-conditioned) beers. Tours by arrangement.

Fruit Beer (OG 1035, ABV 3.6%)
Mild (OG 1035, ABV 3.6%)
Wheat Beer (OG 1035, ABV 3.6%)
Best Bitter (OG 1037, ABV 3.7%)
Extra (OG 1043, ABV 4.4%)
Golden Ale (OG 1044, ABV 4.7%)
Honey Porter (OG 1049, ABV 5.1%)
Strong (OG 1049, ABV 5.1%)

SALOPIAN
The Salopian Brewing Company Ltd., The Brewery, 67 Mytton Oak Road, Shrewsbury, Shropshire SY3 8UQ. ☎ /FAX (01743) 248414

This, the first brewery in Shrewsbury in 30 years, began production in 1995 in a former dairy in Copthorne on the outskirts of the town. Brewer Martin Barry, formerly of the Snowdonia Brewery, produces a wide range of beers and is never afraid to experiment. Some are for individual outlets and some for sale by Green Cucumber Wholesale ☎ (01584) 872908. Twenty outlets are supplied directly with the regular beers. Shop open 10–4 Sat, 2–4 Sun, or by arrangement. Tours also by arrangement. Occasional beers: Manchester Festival Beer (OG 1043, ABV 4.3%), Parsons Progress (OG

THE INDEPENDENTS

1045, ABV 4.5%), Lemon Bitter (OG 1045, ABV 4.5%), White Wheat Beer (ABV 4.7%). Salopian's bottle-conditioned beers are all brewed at King & Barnes (qv).

Bitter (OG 1035, ABV 3.5%) A hoppy, fruity bitter.

Monkmoor Bitter (OG 1040, ABV 4%) A dark, malty beer utilising four hop strains.

Choir Porter (OG 1045, ABV 4.5%) A smooth, traditional porter.

Minsterley Ale (OG 1045, ABV 4.5%) A premium bitter using three kinds of hops.

Ironbridge Stout (OG 1050, ABV 5%) A rich, complex beer.

Shropshire Spires Strong Bitter (OG 1050, ABV 5%) A red-coloured, very malty strong ale.

Hollybush Winter Ale (OG 1060, ABV 6%) A deeply malty winter warmer.

For Green Cucumber Wholesale:

Dark Wheat Beer (OG 1037, ABV 3.7%, occasional) A dark, fruity wheat beer.

Pale White (OG 1050, ABV 5%, occasional) A pale bitter with little hop.

SCANLON'S
Scanlon's Fine Ales, Yiewsley, Greater London.

Scanlon's ceased brewing in summer 1997, being unable to keep up with demand for its beers, transferring all its beer production to Rebellion Brewery (qv) and leaving it free to concentrate on selling the beer to pubs.

SCOTTISH & NEWCASTLE
See Nationals, Scottish Courage.

SCOTT'S
Scott's Brewing Co., Crown Street East, Lowestoft, Suffolk NR32 1SH.
☎ (01502) 537237

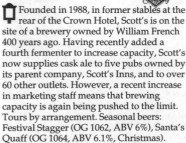

🏠 Founded in 1988, in former stables at the rear of the Crown Hotel, Scott's is on the site of a brewery owned by William French 400 years ago. Having recently added a fourth fermenter to increase capacity, Scott's now supplies cask ale to five pubs owned by its parent company, Scott's Inns, and to over 60 other outlets. However, a recent increase in marketing staff means that brewing capacity is again being pushed to the limit. Tours by arrangement. Seasonal beers: Festival Stagger (OG 1062, ABV 6%), Santa's Quaff (OG 1064, ABV 6.1%, Christmas).

Golden Best Bitter (OG 1033, ABV 3.4%) 🍂 A golden beer with a reasonable balance of malt and (pungent) hop, the latter dominating the aftertaste.

Blues & Bloater (OG 1036, ABV 3.7%) 🍂 This pleasant, malty, fruity beer has some hop bitterness in the aftertaste.

East Point Ale or EPA (OG 1040, ABV 4%) A mid-strength, best bitter of medium colour; dry to the palate throughout, with a hoppy flavour.

Strong Mild (OG 1043, ABV 4.4%) A dark, ruby mild ale, smooth and full-bodied, with medium chocolate flavours.

Hopleaf (OG 1045, ABV 4.5%) A light and dry bitter, dry-hopped, with Challenger hops imparting an aromatic, lasting dry finish.

Bitter Grudge (OG 1047, ABV 4.6%) Well-hopped, darkish premium bitter, brewed in support of the campaign to retain the real ale guest beer.

William French (OG 1048, ABV 5%) 🍂 A full and beautifully-balanced beer. A faint, malty aroma leads into strong malt and hop flavours, with considerable fruitiness. Full and balanced aftertaste, too.

Dark Oast (OG 1048, ABV 5%) 🍂 Red/brown in colour, with less body than its gravity would suggest. The taste has roast malt as its main characteristic, with hoppiness prominent in the aftertaste.

SELBY
Selby (Middlebrough) Brewery Ltd., 131 Millgate, Selby, N. Yorkshire YO8 0LL. ☎ (01757) 702826

Old family brewery which resumed brewing in 1972 after a gap of 18 years but which is now mostly involved in wholesaling. Its beers, which are brewed on an occasional basis, are available, while stocks last, through its Brewery Tap off-licence in Selby (open 10–2, 6–10, Mon–Sat) and not at the company's single pub. They are also sold as guest beers into the local free trade. Occasional beers: No. 1 (OG 1040, ABV 4%), No. 3 (OG 1040, ABV 4%), Old Tom (OG 1065, ABV 6.5%).

SHARDLOW

Shardlow Brewery Ltd., British Waterways Yard, Cavendish Bridge, Leicestershire DE72 2HL. ☎ (01332) 799188

This brewery opened in 1993 in the old kiln house of the original Cavendish Bridge Brewery (closed in the 1920s), and moved in December 1996 to new premises, at the same site on the River Trent, opposite Shardlow Marina. The new brewery is situated on two floors of former stables which retain some original features. Tours by arrangement. Shardlow supplies 30 free trade outlets.

Chancellor's Revenge (OG 1036, ABV 3.6%)

Avon Ale (ABV 3.8%)

Bitter (ABV 4%) A pleasingly dry bitter.

Abu Derby (OG 1042, ABV 4.1%)

New Brewery Bitter (OG 1042, ABV 4.1%)

498

Reverend Eaton's Ale (OG 1046, ABV 4.5%) A medium strong beer with a sweet aftertaste.

Whistle Stop (OG 1050, ABV 5%) A strong and malty beer.

SHARP'S

Sharp's Brewery, Pityme Industrial Estate, Rock, Wadebridge, Cornwall PL27 6NU.
☎ **(01208) 862121**
FAX **(01208) 863727**

Established in 1994, Bill Sharp's brewery currently supplies 300 outlets and there are plans for expansion. Tours by arrangement.

Cornish Coaster (OG 1038, ABV 3.6%) 🍺 A smooth, easy-drinking beer, golden in colour, with a fresh hop aroma and dry malt and hops in the mouth. The finish starts malty but becomes dry and hoppy.

Doom Bar Bitter (OG 1040, ABV 4%) 🍺 A rich, golden brown beer with a hint of barley. Dry malt and hops in the mouth. The malty finish becomes dry and hoppy. Fresh hop aroma.

Own (OG 1044, ABV 4.4%) 🍺 A deep golden brown beer with a delicate hops and malt aroma, and dry malt and hops in the mouth. Like the other beers, its finish starts malty but turns dry and hoppy.

Special Ale (OG 1053, ABV 5.2%) 🍺 Deep golden brown with a fresh hop aroma. Dry malt and hops in the mouth; again, the finish is malty but becomes dry and hoppy.

SHEPHERD NEAME

Shepherd Neame Ltd., 17 Court Street, Faversham, Kent ME13 7AX.
☎ **(01795) 532206**
FAX **(01795) 538907**

Kent's major independent brewery is believed to be the oldest continuous brewer in the country (since 1698), but records show brewing commenced as far back as the 12th century. The same water source is still used today, steam engines are employed and the mash is produced in two teak tuns which date from 1910. A visitors' reception hall is housed in a restored medieval hall (tours by arrangement). The company has 390 tied houses in the South-East, all selling cask ale, but tenants are encouraged to keep beers under blanket pressure if the cask is likely to be on sale for more than three days. Over 500 other outlets are also supplied directly. One bottled beer is brewed under licence for the Bavarian Kaltenberg brewery. Shop open 9–5. Seasonal beer: Goldings Harvest Ale (OG 1050, ABV 5%, September). Bottle-conditioned beer: Spitfire (OG 1047, ABV 4.7%) 🍺🍺.

Master Brew Bitter (OG 1037, ABV 3.7%) 🍺 A very distinctive bitter, mid-brown in colour, with a very hoppy aroma. Well-balanced, with a nicely aggressive bitter taste from its hops, it leaves a hoppy/bitter finish, tinged with sweetness.

Best Bitter (OG 1041, ABV 4.1%) 🍺 Mid-brown, with less marked characteristics than the bitter. However, the nose is very well-balanced and the taste enjoys a malty, bitter smokiness. Malty, well-rounded finish.

Spitfire Premium Ale (OG 1047, ABV 4.7%) A commemorative brew (Battle of Britain) for the RAF Benevolent Fund's appeal, now a permanent feature.

Bishops Finger (OG 1052, ABV 5.2%) A well-known bottled beer, introduced in cask-conditioned form in 1989.

Original Porter (OG 1052, ABV 5.2%) 🍺 A rich, black, full-bodied winter brew. The good malt and roast malt aroma also has a fine fruit edge. The complex blend of flavours is dominated by roast malt, which is also present in a very dry aftertaste.

For Kaltenberg:

Bottle-conditioned beer: Prinzregent Luitpold Weissbier (ABV 5%).

SHERWOOD FOREST See Bateman.

SHIP & PLOUGH See Blewitts.

SHIPSTONE'S
See Nationals, Carlsberg-Tetley, and Pub Groups, Greenalls.

SHOES

Shoes Brewery, Three Horse Shoes Inn, Norton Canon, Hereford HR4 7BH.
☎ **(01544) 318375**

Landlord Frank Goodwin had long been a home-brewer, but decided in 1994 to brew on a commercial basis for his pub. The beers are brewed from malt extract and stored in casks under mixed gas. Beers: Norton Ale (OG 1039, ABV 3.5%), Canon Bitter (OG 1042, ABV 4.2%).

SIX BELLS

Six Bells Brewery, Church Street, Bishop's Castle, Shropshire SY9 5AA.
☎ **(01588) 638930**
FAX **(01588) 630132**

Brewery based in a trust-owned building at the Six Bells pub, but run as a separate business. Production began in January 1997 and now around 25 pubs within a 30-mile radius take the beers. Wholesalers are also supplied.

Big Nev's (OG 1037, ABV 3.8%) A pale, fairly hoppy bitter.

Little Jem (OG 1043, ABV 4.2%) A quite dark, lightly hopped beer, maltier than Big Nev's.

Spring Forward (OG 1045, ABV 4.6%)
Originally a spring beer but now permanent:
dry, hoppy and darkish in colour.

SKINNER'S

**Skinner's Fine Cornish
Ales, Riverside View,
Newham, Truro, Cornwall
TR1 2SU. ☎ (01872) 271885
FAX (01872) 271886**

Brewery founded in July 1997 by Steve and
Sarah Skinner, formerly of the Tipsy Toad
brewery in Jersey. The beer names are
mostly based on characters from Cornish
folklore. Do not confuse the brewery with
Skinner's of Brighton (see Dark Star).

Best Bitter (ABV 3.7%)

Betty Stogs Bitter (ABV 4%)

Cornish Knocker Ale (ABV 4.5%)

SKINNER'S OF BRIGHTON
See Dark Star.

SLATERS See Eccleshall.

SMILES

**Smiles Brewing Co. Ltd.,
Colston Yard, Colston
Street, Bristol BS1 5BD.
☎ (0117) 929 7350
FAX (0117) 925 8235**

Established in 1977 to supply a local
restaurant, Smiles commenced full-scale
brewing a year later. Under the ownership
of Ian Williams, who acquired the company
in 1991, the tied estate has since increased to
15 houses, all selling real ale, and there are
plans to add more. Noted for its good,
traditional pubs (winners of three CAMRA
Pub Design awards), the brewery also
supplies over 250 other outlets. Tours by
arrangement. Seasonal beers: March Hare
(OG 1041, ABV 4%, March–April), Indian
Summer (OG 1046, ABV 4.4%, September–
October), Holly Hops (OG 1052, ABV 5%,
Christmas).

Golden Brew (OG 1039, ABV 3.8%)
🍂 Replacing Brewery Bitter in 1996, this
light to medium-bodied, yellow/gold ale
has a floral, hoppy taste. It is slightly sweet,
with contrasting malt and medium dry
bitterness. Pale malt and citrus hop aroma;
pale malt finish, with hops and a bitter
dryness.

Best Bitter (OG 1040, ABV 4.1%)
🍂 Unexceptional, light-bodied, pale brown
bitter with slight malt and strawberry notes
in both nose and taste, and some
bittersweetness. Brief finish of malt, fruit
and hops.

Mayfly (OG 1046, ABV 4.5%) A light golden
summer ale (May–September), with a
delicate balance of malt and hops.

Bristol Stout (OG 1048, ABV 4.7%) 🍂 A
dark, red/brown stout with a roast malt and
coffee aroma. The predominantly rich roast
malt taste features some hops and fruit.
Roast, bitter, dry finish. Available
September–March.

Heritage (OG 1051, ABV 5.2%) 🍂 Replacing
Exhibition, this dark copper-brown beer has
a brief malt, hop and fruit aroma. The taste is
similar, with a little chocolate malt and fruit
in a thinnish body. Short, dry, roast malt and
bitter finish. A premium beer which doesn't
deliver.

For Greenalls:

Cheshire Cat (OG 1046, ABV 4.5%,
occasional)

JOHN SMITH'S
See Nationals, Scottish Courage.

SAMUEL SMITH

**Samuel Smith Old Brewery
(Tadcaster), High Street,
Tadcaster, N. Yorkshire
LS24 9SB. ☎ (01937) 832225
FAX (01937) 834673**

Small company operating from the oldest
brewery in Yorkshire, dating from 1758 and
once owned by John Smith. Unlike John
Smith's, however, Sam's is still family
owned and fiercely independent. The beer is
brewed from well water without the use of
adjuncts and all cask beer is fermented in
Yorkshire stone squares before being racked
into wooden casks made by the brewery's
own cooper. Real ale is sold in most of its
100-plus tied houses, but, sadly, many of
Sam's London pubs no longer stock cask
beer. Tours by arrangement.

Old Brewery Bitter (OBB) (OG 1040, ABV
4%) 🍂 Malt dominates the aroma, with an
initial burst of malt, hops and fruit in the
taste which is sustained in the aftertaste.

SOLVA
**The Solva Brewing Co. Ltd., Panteg, Solva,
Carmarthenshire.**

Brewery not currently in operation.

SP SPORTING ALES
**SP Sporting Ales Ltd.,
Cantilever Lodge, Stoke
Prior, Leominster,
Herefordshire HR6 0LG.
☎ / FAX (01568) 760226**

Small brewery opened in April 1996 and
now supplying over 65 outlets. Its main
beer, Dove's Delight, is sold under various
names. The brewery is due to be expanded
after which tours will be available by
arrangement.

Winners (ABV 3.5%)

Dove's Delight (OG 1040, ABV 4%)

SPIKES

Spikes Brewery, The Wine Vaults, 43–47 Albert Road, Southsea, Portsmouth, Hampshire PO5 2SF.
☎ **(01705) 864712**

Brewery installed above the Wine Vaults pub in 1994 with a four-barrel plant, but this was changed to a two-and-a-half-barrel plant in September 1996. It currently only supplies the Wine Vaults (which is not a tied house), but there are plans to bottle beer for the American market. Beers: Anorak Ale (OG 1033, ABV 3.3%), Impaled Ale (OG 1036, ABV 3.6%), Stinger (OG 1045, ABV 4.5%), Southsea Bitter (OG 1045, ABV 4.6%), Golden (OG 1052, ABV 5.2%).

SPRINGHEAD
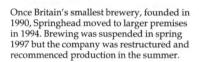

Springhead Fine Ales Ltd., Unit 3, Sutton Workshops, Old Great North Road, Sutton-on-Trent, Nottinghamshire NG23 6QS. Tel (01636) 821000
FAX **(01636) 821150**

Once Britain's smallest brewery, founded in 1990, Springhead moved to larger premises in 1994. Brewing was suspended in spring 1997 but the company was restructured and recommenced production in the summer.

Hersbrucker Weizenbier (OG 1035, ABV 3.6%) A wheat beer available March–September.

Bitter (OG 1038, ABV 4%) ◆ A well-balanced blend of malt and hops with a dry finish. Initially fruity, with malt lingering. Copper-coloured.

Hole-in-Spire (OG 1038, ABV 4%) A dark but not too heavy porter.

Roundhead's Gold (OG 1042, ABV 4.2%) A light, golden beer made with wild flower honey, but not sweet. Saaz hop aroma.

Goodrich Castle (OG 1044, ABV 4.4%) A pale ale from a 17th-century recipe which include rosemary.

Leveller (OG 1046, ABV 4.8%) ⬚ ◆ A fine example of the use of amber malt combined with a fruity aroma hop, this mid-brown beer is dominated by a beautiful coffee roast aroma and taste, and a lingering bitter finish.

Roaring Meg (OG 1052, ABV 5.5%) ⬚ ◆ A strong bitter in the blonde style. Hops and orange fruitiness dominate the aroma and taste, whilst malt takes equal billing in the dry, lasting finish. Dangerously drinkable.

Cromwell's Hat (OG 1060, ABV 6%) A smooth but robust beer with a hint of juniper and cinnamon. Available October–March.

STAG See Abel Brown's and Nationals, Scottish Courage.

STAG & GRIFFIN See Viking.

STANWAY

Stanway Brewery, Stanway, Cheltenham, Gloucestershire GL54 5PQ.
☎ **(01386) 584320**

Small brewery founded in 1993 with a five-barrel plant, which confines its sales to the Cotswolds area (around 25 outlets). Seasonal beer: Lords-a-Leaping (OG 1045, ABV 4.5%, winter).

Stanney Bitter (OG 1042, ABV 4.5%) ◆ A light, refreshing, amber-coloured beer, dominated by hops in the aroma, with a bitter taste and a hoppy, bitter finish.

STEAMIN' BILLY
See Leatherbritches.

STEAM PACKET

The Steam Packet Brewery, The Bendles, Racca Green, Knottingley, W. Yorkshire WF11 8AT.
☎ / FAX **(01977) 674176**

Pub brewery which began producing beers for its own bar in 1990 but which has expanded to supply 50 outlets regularly (and more on an occasional basis), mainly in the North-West. New brews (including fruit beers) are regularly added to the range.

Gamekeeper Bitter (OG 1036, ABV 3.6%) ◆ A bitter and dry, light brown beer, with little aroma. Good, malty taste, but an unbalanced, weak aftertaste. Little hop content.

Blow Job or Bitter Blow (OG 1038, ABV 3.8%) ◆ A gold-coloured beer with a harsh, bitter, strongly fruity taste which echoes the aroma. The moderately malty flavour doesn't last and there is an underlying sourness throughout.

Ginger Minge (OG 1039, ABV 4%) ◆ A wonderfully refreshing and clean-tasting ginger beer with a good hop and fruit taste and well-balanced ginger flavour. The bittersweet aftertaste doesn't linger and gives way to gingerness.

Porter (OG 1040, ABV 4%) A dark porter with a strong malt content and a lingering woody flavour.

Brown Ale (OG 1045, ABV 4.5%) ◆ A malty brown ale, with a hoppy, fruity nose and a good balance of caramel, malt, hops, sweetness and bitterness in the taste, which fades slightly in the finish.

Poacher's Swag (OG 1050, ABV 5%) ◆ A full-bodied, sweetish mid-brown beer, with a moderately fruity aroma, leading to a bitter, slightly fruity and malty taste, and a very dry astringency which dominates the aftertaste. Some yeastiness.

Craam Stout (OG 1050, ABV 5%) ◈ A strong blend of roast malt and malt abounds in this beer, with a moderate hoppiness and some fruit, leading to a lingering, dry, bitterness. Black in colour. Note: the OG varies.

STOCKS
See Hull and Pub Groups, Century Inns.

STONES See Nationals, Bass.

STONY ROCK
Stony Rock Brewery, Leek Road, Waterhouses, Stoke-on-Trent, Staffordshire ST10 3LH. ☎ (01538) 308352

This new brewery opened in March 1997, operating on a very small scale at the owners' farm and selling to around 20 outlets on a fairly regular basis. Plans include the acquisition of a pub or brewery tap. Tours by arrangement. Occasional beer: Old Fossil (OG 1065, ABV 6.7%, brewed to a medieval recipe).

Cavern (OG 1042, ABV 4.2%) A full-flavoured, dry bitter.

STRAWBERRY BANK
Strawberry Bank Brewery, Masons Arms, Cartmel Fell, Grange-over-Sands, Cumbria LA11 6NW. ☎ (0153 95) 68486 [FAX] (0153 95) 68780

▯ Strawberry Bank is the new name of the brewery at the famous Masons Arms, the Lakeland brewery (qv) having moved out. The beer range has also been revised. Tours by arrangement. Beers: Ned's Tipple (OG 1040, ABV 4%), Blackbeck (OG 1045, ABV 4.5%), Damson Ale (OG 1060, ABV 6%), Rulbuts (OG 1060, ABV 6%).

STRONG See Nationals, Whitbread.

SULWATH
Sulwath Brewers Ltd., Gillfoot Brewery, Southerness, Kirkbean, Dumfries & Galloway DG2 8AY. ☎ / [FAX] (01387) 255849

Work started on this new brewery at Gillfoot farm at the end of 1995. Owned by a retired banker and a former dairy farmer, it supplies three regular outlets, plus ten others in South-West Scotland on an occasional basis. Tours by arrangement. Occasional beer: JPJ Special (ABV 5%, originally brewed to commemorate the 250th anniversary of the birth of John Paul Jones in a cottage near the brewery).

Knockendoch (OG 1045, ABV 3.8%)

Criffel (OG 1047, ABV 4.6%)

SUMMERSKILLS
Summerskills Brewery, Unit 15, Pomphlett Farm Industrial Estate, Broxton Drive, Billacombe, Plymouth, Devon PL9 7BG. ☎ / [FAX] (01752) 481283

SEMPER FIDELIS AD BACCUM

Originally set up in a vineyard in 1983, but closed after two years, Summerskills was re-launched by new owners in 1990 with plant from the old Penrhos brewery. Production of its award-winning beers continues to grow at a steady rate, with 35 free trade outlets supplied directly and others nationally via wholesalers. Tours by arrangement. Occasional/seasonal beers: Menacing Dennis (OG 1044, ABV 4.5%), Turkey's Delight (OG 1050, ABV 5.1%, Christmas). Bottle-conditioned beers: Best Bitter (OG 1042, ABV 4.3%), Indiana's Bones (OG 1056, ABV 5.6%).

BBB (OG 1037, ABV 3.7%)

Best Bitter (OG 1042, ABV 4.3%) ◈ A mid-brown beer, with plenty of malt and hops through the aroma, taste and finish.

Tamar Best Bitter (OG 1042, ABV 4.3%) ◈ A tawny-coloured bitter with a fruity aroma and a hop taste and finish.

Whistle Belly Vengeance (OG 1046, ABV 4.7%) ◈ A red/brown beer with a beautiful malt and fruit taste and a pleasant, malty aftertaste.

Ninjabeer (OG 1049, ABV 5%) ◈ A dark gold beer, with a strong, fruity aroma and a predominantly fruity taste and aftertaste. Very drinkable. Brewed October–April.

Indiana's Bones (OG 1056, ABV 5.6%) ⬚ ◈ A mid-brown beer with a good balance of fruit and malt in the aroma and taste, and a sweet, malty finish.

SUTTON
Sutton Brewing Company, 31 Commercial Road, Coxside, Plymouth, Devon PL4 0LE. ☎ / [FAX] (01752) 255335.

SUTTON BREWING COMPANY
Life is too short to drink cheap beer
UNPRIMED REAL ALES

This brewery was built alongside the Thistle Park Tavern, near Plymouth's Sutton Harbour, in 1993. It went into production the following year to supply that pub and one other. It now sells to over 50 outlets in and around Plymouth, and a bigger plant and additional fermenters have been installed to cope with demand. Tours by arrangement. Occasional/seasonal beers: Hopnosis (OG 1045, ABV 4.5%), Weetablitz (OG 1050, ABV 5%, summer), Sleigh'd (OG 1058, ABV 5.8%, Christmas).

Dartmoor Pride (OG 1038, ABV 3.8%)

XSB (OG 1042, ABV 4.2%) ◈ Amber nectar with a fruity nose and a bitter finish.

Gold (OG 1044, ABV 4.4%) Predictably gold-coloured, this is an extremely bitter-tasting beer, right through to the aftertaste.

Jinja (OG 1045, ABV 4.5%)

Eddystone Light (OG 1050, ABV 5%)

Old Pedantic (OG 1050, ABV 5%)

Knickadroppa Glory (OG 1055, ABV 5.5%)

Plymouth Porter (OG 1056, ABV 5.5%)
🍺 Brewed November–February; a dark brown beer with a distinct roast malt aroma, taste and finish.

Winter Warmer (OG 1059, ABV 6%)

SWALE

The Swale Brewery Co.,
Unit 1, D2 Trading Estate,
Castle Road, Eurolink,
Sittingbourne, Kent
ME10 3RH.
🕿 (01795) 426871 [FAX] (01795) 410808

Swale was opened in 1995 in the village of Milton Regis by experienced home-brewer John Davidson. It moved to a new home in Sittingbourne in 1997. The cask ales, including seasonal and special beers, are now supplied to around 50 free trade outlets and the bottle-conditioned ales are proving equally successful. Tours by arrangement. Bottle-conditioned beers: Gold & Amber (OG 1050, ABV 5%), Old Dick (OG 1052, ABV 5.2%).

Kentish Pride (OG 1039, ABV 3.8%) A clean-tasting, light brown-coloured ale, dry-hopped with East Kent Goldings.

Copperwinkle (OG 1040, ABV 4%) A copper-coloured bitter, predominantly hoppy through to the finish.

Gold & Amber (OG 1050, ABV 5%) A pale golden bitter, with a floral, citrus hop finish.

Old Dick (OG 1052, ABV 5.2%) A strong, dark winter bitter, with a smooth taste. Brewed around Christmas.

SWALED ALE

Swaled Ale, West View, Gunnerside,
Richmond, N. Yorkshire DL11 6LD.
🕿 (01748) 886441

Founded in 1995 as a part-time venture, Swaled Ale, churning out just two barrels a week, serves a couple of outlets in N. Yorkshire plus a few others on request. The beers are named after local mines.

Priscilla (OG 1038, ABV 3.8%) Also sold under pub house names.

Old Gang Bitter (OG 1043, ABV 4.4%)

SWANSEA

Swansea Brewing
Company, Joiners Arms,
Bishopston, Swansea
SA3 3EJ. 🕿 (01792) 290197

🍺 Founded in April 1996, this is the first commercial brewery in the Swansea area for almost 30 years. It doubled its capacity within the first year and now produces one

regular beer and four others on an occasional basis for a small number of free trade outlets in Swansea and South Wales. Occasional beers: Three Cliffs Gold (ABV 4.7%), Pwlldu XXXX (ABV 4.9%), The Original Wood (ABV 5.2%), St Teilo's Tipple (ABV 5.5%).

Bishopswood Bitter (ABV 4.3%) A mid-brown beer with a fine balance of malt and fruit leading to a bitter finish.

TALLY HO!

Tally Ho! Country Inn and
Brewery, 14 Market Street,
Hatherleigh, Devon
EX20 3JN. 🕿 (01837) 810306

🍺 The Tally Ho! recommenced brewing at Easter 1990, reviving the tradition of the former New Inn brewery on the same site. New owners took over in December 1994. Its beers are produced from a full mash, with no additives, and, as well as sales at the pub itself, beer agencies now take the beers. Tours by arrangement. Beers: Potboiler's Brew (OG 1036, ABV 3.5%), Master Jack's Mild (OG 1039, ABV 3.5%, summer), Tarka's Tipple (OG 1042, ABV 4%), Nutters Ale (OG 1048, ABV 4.6%), Thurgia (OG 1060, ABV 6%), Jollop (OG 1066, ABV 6.8%, winter). Bottle-conditioned beers: Hunter's Ale (OG 1048, ABV 4.6%), Tarka's Tipple (OG 1048, ABV 4.6%), Thurgia (OG 1060, ABV 6%).

TAVERN

See Ridleys and Pub Groups, Greenalls.

TAYLOR

Timothy Taylor & Co. Ltd.,
Knowle Spring Brewery,
Keighley, W. Yorkshire
BD21 1AW.
🕿 (01535) 603139
[FAX] (01535) 691167

Timothy Taylor began brewing in Keighley in 1858 and moved to the site of the Knowle Spring in 1863. The business was continued by his sons and remains an independent family-owned company to this day. Its prize-winning ales are served in all 27 of the brewery's pubs as well as a wide free trade. The company also owns an ale shop in Raglan Road, Leeds.

Golden Best (OG 1033, ABV 3.5%) 🍺 A clean-tasting and refreshing, amber mild with fruit in the nose, light hoppiness in the taste and a hoppy, bitter finish. A good session beer.

Dark Mild (OG 1034, ABV 3.5%) 🍺 The hops of the underlying Golden Best combine with a caramel sweetness in this thin, dark brown beer with a bitter aftertaste.

Porter (OG 1041, ABV 3.8%) 🍺 Sweetness and caramel can dominate this beer if it is served too young. However, when it's mature, the sweetness is balanced by fruity flavours and bitterness in the finish.

Best Bitter (OG 1037, ABV 4%) 🍺 ✦ Hops and a citrus fruitiness are the key characteristics of this well-balanced and very drinkable amber bitter. Bitterness increases down the glass and lingers in the aftertaste.

Landlord (OG 1042, ABV 4.3%) 🍺 ✦ An increasingly dry, bitter finish complements the combination of hops and complex fruitiness in the aroma and taste of this full-flavoured and well-balanced beer. Some malt and a hint of sulphur are evident in the background. *Champion Beer of Britain 1994.*

Ram Tam (XXXX) (OG 1043, ABV 4.3%) ✦ A dark brown winter beer with red hints. Caramel dominates the aroma and leads to sweetish toffee and chocolate flavours in the taste, well-balanced by the hoppy fruitiness of the underlying Landlord. Increasingly dry and bitter finish.

TAYLOR WALKER
See Nationals, Carlsberg-Tetley.

TEIGNWORTHY
Teignworthy Brewery, The Maltings, Teign Road, Newton Abbot, Devon TQ12 4AA.
☎ **(01626) 332066**

Brewery founded in 1994 with a 15-barrel plant by former Oakhill and Ringwood brewer John Lawton, using part of the historic Victorian malthouse of Edward Tucker & Sons. A new bottling plant has been installed. About 60 outlets take the beer. Brewery (Tucker's Maltings) shop open 10–5, April–October. Maltings and brewery tours available. Seasonal beers: Christmas Cracker (OG 1060, ABV 6%, Christmas), ET's Special Ale (OG 1080, ABV 8%, Christmas). Bottle-conditioned beers: as cask beers (ET's Special Ale is sold as Edwin Tucker's Devonshire Strong Ale).

Reel Ale (OG 1039.5, ABV 4%) ✦ A well-balanced, pale bitter with a dry finish.

Spring Tide (OG 1043.5, ABV 4.3%) ✦ A tawny-coloured beer with a malty nose and a hoppy, bitter taste and finish.

Beachcomber (OG 1045.5, ABV 4.5%) ✦ Available in summer: a pale brown beer with a fruity, malty taste and a bitter finish.

Maltster's Ale (OG 1049.5, ABV 5%) ✦ Available in winter: a mid brown, full-flavoured beer with a hint of chocolate turning to vanilla. Strong malt aftertaste.

TETLEY See Nationals, Carlsberg-Tetley.

🍺 The pub sign indicates a brew pub: a pub which produces beer on the premises.

THEAKSTON
See Nationals, Scottish Courage.

THOMPSON'S
Thompson's Brewery, London Hotel, 11 West Street, Ashburton, Devon TQ13 7DT.
☎ **(01364) 652478**
FAX **(01364) 653095**

Brewery which began operation in 1981 in the function suite of the London Inn in Ashburton. By 1992, demand from other outlets in the South-West had increased and a new brewhouse with a 5,000-barrel capacity was commissioned, housed in the pub's converted stables. Around a dozen other outlets now take the beers. Tours by arrangement.

Best Bitter (OG 1040, ABV 4.2%) ✦ A pale brown beer with a hoppy aroma and taste. Bitter finish.

IPA (OG 1044, ABV 4.6%) ✦ A mid-brown-coloured ale with a distinct hoppy aroma and a bitter taste and finish.

Figurehead (OG 1050, ABV 5%) ✦ A dark brown, full-bodied winter beer with a malty nose and a roasty, bitter taste and finish. Not always available.

Man 'o' War (OG 1050, ABV 5%) ✦ A golden, summer beer with a fruity sweet taste and aftertaste.

Celebration Porter (OG 1058, ABV 6%) A rich porter with a strong malt aroma. It has a fruity, malty flavour and a bitter finish. Available October–March.

THREE HORSESHOES See Shoes.

THREE TUNS
The Three Tuns Brewing Co. Ltd., Salop Street, Bishop's Castle, Shropshire SY9 5BW.
☎ / FAX **(01588) 638797**

🍺 Historic brew pub, with a Victorian tower brewhouse, which first obtained a brewing licence in 1642. It ceased brewing in 1996 but new owners took over in the summer of that year and re-opened the brewery. Only the pub itself currently takes the beer but there are plans to expand the trade. Beers: Dark Mild (OG 1034, ABV 3.4%), Steamer (OG 1041, ABV 4.3%), XXX Bitter (OG 1041.5, ABV 4.3%), Robert's Summer Special (OG 1044, ABV 4.7%), Old Scrooge (OG 1055, ABV 5.5%, Christmas), Robert's Winter Special (OG 1057, ABV 5.8%). Bottle-conditioned beer: Clerics' Cure (OG 1046, ABV 5%).

THWAITES

Daniel Thwaites Brewery PLC, PO Box 50, Star Brewery, Blackburn, Lancashire BB1 5BU.
☎ (01254) 54431
FAX (01254) 681439

Lancashire brewery, founded by excise officer Daniel Thwaites in 1807 and still run by his family. It still uses shire horse drays and about 80 per cent of its 440 pubs serve real ale. A substantial free trade (about 450 outlets) is also supplied. For all Thwaites's tradition, however, investment in technology has now produced a very modern brewhouse. Tours by arrangement. The Connoisseur Cask Ale Collection of limited edition, monthly brews was superseded in 1997 by a new range of seasonal beers, beginning with Bloomin' Ale (ABV 4%, spring).

Best Mild (OG 1034, ABV 3.3%) ◥ A rich, dark mild presenting a smooth, malty flavour and a pleasant, slightly bitter finish.

Bitter (OG 1036, ABV 3.6%) ◥ A gently-flavoured, clean-tasting bitter. Malt and hops lead into a full, lingering, bitter finish.

Chairman's (OG 1042, ABV 4.2%)

Daniels Hammer (OG 1048, ABV 5%)

TIGERTOPS

Tigertops Brewery, 22 Oakes Street, Flanshaw Lane, Flanshaw, Wakefield, W. Yorkshire WF2 9LN.
☎ (01924) 378538

Microbrewery established in September 1995 by two CAMRA enthusiasts. The one-barrel plant is housed in a garden outhouse and is used only intermittently. Several local free houses take the beer, but owners Lynda and Stuart Johnson have now bought their own pub, the Prince of Wales in Foxfield, Cumbria, and hope to site a brewery on the premises. Occasional beer: Internettle (OG 1034, ABV 3.3%, a nettle beer).

Fleur-de-Lys (OG 1039, ABV 3.8%) A refreshing, amber-coloured session bitter with good hop character and a balancing sweetness.

Bullring Best (OG 1040, ABV 4%)

LMS (OG 1045, ABV 4.5%)

Pot Black (OG 1050, ABV 4.8%) A stout with plenty of roast malt and malt in the taste, complemented by a liquorice flavour which lasts.

Flanshaw Flyer (OG 1049, ABV 5%) An amber/golden best bitter with a sweet start, plenty of hop taste and good body.

Kinghorn (OG 1051, ABV 5%) A wheat beer with a yellow hue and a full, wheaty mouthfeel and aftertaste.

TIPSY TOAD

The Tipsy Toad Brewery, St Peter, Jersey JE3 7AA.
☎ (01534) 484944
FAX (01534) 485559

⬛ Following refurbishment of the Star pub, brewing began on these premises in spring 1992. A couple of other outlets are now supplied on a regular basis with the full mash brews and the new management hopes to expand trade to the mainland. Tours by arrangement. Beers: Tipsy Toad Ale (OG 1038, ABV 3.8%), Jimmy's Bitter (OG 1042, ABV 4.2%), Horny Toad (OG 1050, ABV 5%), Festive Toad (OG 1077, ABV 8%).

TISBURY

Tisbury Brewery Ltd., Church Street, Tisbury, Wiltshire SP3 6NH.
☎ (01747) 870986
FAX (01747) 871540

Housed in the old village workhouse, converted by maltster Archibald Beckett in 1868 but rebuilt after a fire in 1885, this brewery ceased production in 1914. It re-opened as Tisbury Brewery in 1980 but this foundered, leaving the premises to be taken over by Wiltshire Brewery, which brewed here until closing the site in 1992. This new Tisbury Brewery took over the building and began production in April 1995. It now provides beer for over 50 outlets, using the slogan 'The small brewery with the big taste'. Tours by arrangement.

Best Bitter (OG 1038, ABV 3.8%) A golden/amber-coloured beer with a malty nose. The malty taste has hints of fruit and hop. Full-bodied for its strength.

Austin Ale (OG 1040, ABV 4%) A pale golden beer with light malt flavours and a clean, light, hoppy finish.

Archibald Beckett (OG 1043, ABV 4.3%) A very malty, full-bodied, dark amber bitter with some caramel on the nose. Strong hop flavours come through in the taste.

Nadderjack Ale (OG 1043, ABV 4.3%) A golden, full-bodied, well-balanced bitter with a spicy hop finish.

Old Wardour (OG 1048, ABV 4.8%) A full-bodied, mahogany-hued beer with a faintly burnt nose. Malty and slightly sweet, it has a delicate fruitiness and a final hop bite.

TITANIC

The Titanic Brewery, Unit G, Harvey Works, Lingard Street, Burslem, Stoke-on-Trent, Staffordshire ST6 1ED. ☎ (01782) 823447
FAX (01782) 812349

This brewery, named in honour of the Titanic's Captain Smith, who hailed from Stoke, was founded in 1985 but fell into difficulties until rescued by the present owners. A move to larger premises took place in 1991 and new brewing plant was installed in 1995. In 1996 Titanic began brewing for demonstration purposes on the log-fired Victorian microbrewery in the Staffordshire County Museum at Shugborough Hall. The company now supplies over 200 free trade outlets, as well as two pubs of its own (which also sell other independents' guest beers). Tours by arrangement. Bottle-conditioned beers: Stout (OG 1046, ABV 4.5%), Captain Smith's (OG 1054, ABV 5.2%), Christmas Ale (OG 1080, ABV 7.8%).

Best Bitter (OG 1036, ABV 3.5%) ◆ A crisp, clean, refreshing bitter with a good balance of fruit, malt and hops. Bitter finish.

Lifeboat Ale (OG 1040, ABV 3.9%) ◆ A fruity and malty, dark red/brown beer, with a fruity finish.

Premium (OG 1042, ABV 4.1%) ⬚ ◆ An impressive, well-balanced pale brown bitter with hops and fruit in the aroma which develop into a full flavour and a dry, hoppy finish.

Red Cap (ABV 4.3%) Available June–August.

Horse Power (ABV 4.5%) Available March–May.

Stout (OG 1046, ABV 4.5%) ◆ A dark combination of malt and roast with some hops. Strongly flavoured and well-balanced.

White Star (OG 1050, ABV 4.8%) ◆ A bittersweet amber ale with a very fruity taste and a long fruit aftertaste.

Saddleback (ABV 5%) Available September–November.

Captain Smith's (OG 1054, ABV 5.2%) ◆ A full-bodied, dark red/brown beer, hoppy and bitter with malt and roast malt flavours, and a long, bittersweet finish.

Longhorn (ABV 5.5%) Available December–February.

Wreckage (OG 1080, ABV 7.8%) ◆ A dark brew, full-flavoured, with a rich bittersweet finish. Available October–January.

TOLLY COBBOLD
Tollemache & Cobbold Brewery Ltd., Cliff Road, Ipswich, Suffolk IP3 0AZ.
☎ (01473) 231723
FAX (01473) 280045

TOLLY COBBOLD

One of the oldest breweries in the country, founded by Thomas Cobbold in 1723 at Harwich, Tolly Cobbold moved to Ipswich in 1746. In 1989 Brent Walker took over the company, closed the Cliff Brewery and transferred production to Camerons in Hartlepool. However, a management buyout saved the day and Tolly Cobbold Ipswich-brewed ales were back on sale in 1990. The new company acquired no pubs

from Brent Walker, but secured a long-term trading agreement with Pubmaster (the company which runs former Brent Walker pubs), and now supplies around 430 outlets. It opened a brewery tap, the only tied house, in 1992. Brewery tours for groups (daily) have become a major attraction and another feature is the Bottlers Room, containing a display of 1,800 commemorative bottled beers. Brewery shop open lunchtimes in the tourist season. Some seasonal beers have been produced.

Mild (OG 1032, ABV 3.2%) ⬚ ◆ A tasty mild with fruit, malt and roast malt characters. Pleasing aftertaste. It tends to lose complexity when forced through a sparkler.

Bitter (OG 1035, ABV 3.5%) ◆ A light, mid-brown-coloured malty beer lacking bitterness.

Original Best Bitter (OG 1038, ABV 3.8%) ◆ A slightly stronger bitter with assertive hop character throughout. The finish is bitter, but with a good balancing maltiness. Disappointingly hard to find.

IPA (OG 1040, ABV 4.2%) A best bitter, full of citrus fruit flavours and flowery hoppiness.

Old Strong Winter Ale (OG 1050, ABV 5%) ◆ Available November–February. A dark winter ale with plenty of roast character throughout. Lingering and complex aftertaste.

Tollyshooter (OG 1050, ABV 5%) ◆ A reddish premium bitter with a full, fruity flavour and a long, bittersweet aftertaste. Good hop character, too. Named after the Sir John Harvey-Jones TV series, *Troubleshooter*, in which Tolly featured.

Conquest (OG 1051, ABV 5%)

TOMINTOUL
Tomintoul Brewery Co. Ltd., Mill of Auchriachan, Tomintoul, Ballindalloch, Banffshire AB37 9EQ.
☎ (01807) 580333
FAX (01807) 580358

Brewery opened in November 1993 in an old watermill, in an area better known for malt whisky and snow-blocked roads. Around 80 outlets are currently supplied and wholesalers take the beer into England and Northern Ireland. Production capacity has been increased to meet demand. Some seasonal ales are produced from time to time and bottle-conditioned beers are planned.

Laird's Ale (OG 1038, ABV 3.8%)

Stag (OG 1039.5, ABV 4.1%)

Stillman's 80/- (OG 1040, ABV 4.2%)

Nessie's Monster Mash (OG 1044, ABV 4.4%)

Black Gold (OG 1048.5, ABV 4.4%)

Culloden (OG 1046, ABV 4.6%)

Wild Cat (OG 1049.5, ABV 5.1%)

TOMLINSON'S

Tomlinson's Old Castle Brewery, Unit 5, Britannia Works, Skinner Lane, Pontefract, W. Yorkshire WF8 1NA. ☎ (01977) 780866 FAX (01977) 690788

Marking a return to brewing in Pontefract after over 60 years, Tomlinson's was built in 1993 and is run by a former pipe fitter and fabricator. The award-winning brews take their names from various local historical connections. Over 40 outlets are now supplied. Tours by arrangement. Shop open 10–3 Mon–Fri. Occasional beers: Femme Fatale (OG 1043, ABV 4.5%), Fractus XB (OG 1045, ABV 4.5%), Double Helix (OG 1055, ABV 5.5%). Bottle-conditioned beer: Three Sieges (OG 1058, ABV 6%).

Hermitage Mild (OG 1036, ABV 3.7%)

Sessions (OG 1038, ABV 4%) ❦ A dry, bitter beer with a light, hoppy, smoky aroma leading to a well-hopped and slightly fruity taste and aftertaste, which is also dry. Light brown/copper in colour.

De Lacy (OG 1044, ABV 4.6%) ❦ An enjoyable amber, bitter, dry beer with a good, hoppy, fruity nose and a well-balanced strong hop and fruit taste with some sweetness. Dry, slightly yeasty aftertaste.

Deceitful Rose (OG 1048, ABV 5%) ❦ Superbly dry, hoppy, straw-coloured beer in the style of an India Pale Ale. Very bitter and dry in the taste and finish, with a clean, hoppy and slightly fruity flavour which lingers.

Richard's Defeat (OG 1050, ABV 5%) ❦ A black, strong porter in which roast flavour dominates throughout along with a moderate fruitiness and some hoppiness, with a good bitter/sweet balance leading to a bitter finish. Available in winter.

Three Sieges (OG 1058, ABV 6%) A liquorice beer, brewed in winter.

TOWNES

Townes Brewery, Bay 9, Suon Buildings, Lockoford Lane, Chesterfield, Derbyshire S41 7JJ. ☎ (01246) 277994

Brewery established in an old bakery in May 1994 by photographer Alan Wood, bringing brewing back to Chesterfield after nearly 40 years. Now some 40 outlets are supplied (most within 25 miles of the brewery) and brewing capacity has been increased accordingly. Now the brewery is planning to move site and set up a brew pub in Staveley, near Chesterfield. One-off brews feature regularly and a series of six, bimonthly 'Blue

Note' beers (all at 4.5% ABV and all named after jazz music titles) has also been produced.

Sunshine (OG 1036, ABV 3.6%) A light-coloured session beer with a full finish.

Best Lockoford Bitter (OG 1040, ABV 4%) A golden-coloured bitter with hop character. This may soon be re-named.

Colliers (OG 1040, ABV 4%) A new brown ale.

GMT (OG 1042, ABV 4.2%) A pale, spicy ale with a malty base and a hoppy finish. Available in summer.

TRAQUAIR

Traquair House Brewery, Traquair Estate, Innerleithen, Peeblesshire EH44 6PW. ☎ (01896) 830323 FAX (01896) 830639

This 18th-century brewhouse is situated in one of the wings of Traquair House (over 1,000 years old) and was rediscovered by the 20th Laird, the late Peter Maxwell Stuart, in 1965. He began brewing again using all the original equipment (which remained intact, despite having lain idle for over 100 years). The brewery has been run by Peter's daughter, Catherine Maxwell Stuart, since his death in 1990. All the beers are oak-fermented and 60 per cent of production is exported (mostly bottled Traquair House Ale and Jacobite Ale). About five outlets take the cask beer. Tours by arrangement, April–September. Shop open daily April–October, 10.30–5.30. Occasional/seasonal beers: Festival Ale (OG 1045, ABV 4%), Fair Ale (OG 1055, ABV 6%).

Bear Ale (OG 1050, ABV 5%) ❦ A powerful, malt/fruit aroma precedes a deep, rich taste bursting with fruit, which lingers and subtly changes into a long-lasting, dry finish.

TRAVELLERS INN

Travellers Inn, Tremeirchion Road, Caerwys, Mold CH7 5BL. ☎ (01352) 720251

Pub brewery which opened in April 1997, producing full mash beers only for sale within the pub itself. Beers: Roy Morgan's Original Ale (OG 1042, ABV 4.2%), Old Elias Strong Pale Ale (OG 1052, ABV 5%).

TRING

The Tring Brewery Company Ltd., 81–82 Akeman Street, Tring, Hertfordshire HP23 6AF. ☎ (01442) 890721 FAX (01442) 890740

Established in 1992, bringing brewing back to this Hertfordshire town after over 50 years, Tring now supplies around 80 outlets. Tours by arrangement on weekday

evenings. In addition to the occasional brews listed below, an Easter beer is also produced each year. Seasonal beer: Death or Glory Ale (OG 1070, ABV 7.2%, brewed October 25 to commemorate the Charge of the Light Brigade in 1854 and sold December–January). Bottle-conditioned beer: Death or Glory Ale (OG 1070, ABV 7.2%).

Finest Summer Ale (OG 1037, ABV 3.7%) Available June–September; a refreshing summer ale with a proportion of wheat malt in the mash.

The Ridgeway Bitter (OG 1039, ABV 4%) ◨ ◈ A beer with a pleasant mix of flowery hops, malt and fruit flavours before a dryish aftertaste.

Old Cantankerous (OG 1048.5, ABV 4.8%) A winter porter, available October–December.

Old Icknield Ale (OG 1049, ABV 5%) ◈ A beer with a distinct, hoppy flavour and a dry, bitter aftertaste.

TRUEMAN'S

Sam Trueman's Brewery, The Little Brewery Co. Ltd., Henley House, School Lane, Medmenham, Buckinghamshire SL7 2HJ.
☎ (01491) 576100 [FAX] (01491) 571764

Henley House is a business training centre set in an idyllic spot near Marlow. Its brewery was set up in 1995 to produce real ale for delegates attending courses. The tiny plant (producing one barrel a week) has now been replaced by five-barrel equipment, in response to demand from other outlets. Bottle-conditioned beers: Northdown Bitter (ABV 4.7%), True Gold Lager (ABV 6%).

Best (OG 1036, ABV 3.5%)

Tipple (OG 1041, ABV 4.2%)

Gold (OG 1050, ABV 5%)

Ice Maiden (ABV 5%) A real lager, sold in summer.

Springloaded (OG 1064, ABV 6.5%)

Percy's Downfall (OG 1084, ABV 8.2%)

TYNLLIDIART ARMS

Tynllidiart Arms, Capel Bangor, Aberystwyth, Ceredigion SY23 3LR.
☎ (01970) 880248

🛑 Pub brewery set up in July 1996, supplying just the pub itself from what the *Guinness Book of Records* acknowledges to be the smallest commercial brewing plant (one firkin capacity). Visitors are advised to ring in advance to make sure the beer will be on sale, as it only lasts a couple of days each week. Beer: Rheidol Reserve (ABV 4.1%).

ULEY

Uley Brewery Ltd., The Old Brewery, Uley, Dursley, Gloucestershire GL11 5TB.
☎ (01453) 860120

Brewing at Uley began in 1833, but Price's Brewery, as it was then, remained inactive for most of this century. Work commenced on restoring the premises in 1984 and Uley Brewery was reborn in 1985. The brewery has no pubs of its own but now serves over 40 free trade outlets in the Cotswolds area. Seasonal beers: Pigor Mortis (OG 1062, ABV 6%, October–November), Severn Boar (OG 1062, ABV 6%, December–January).

Hogshead Bitter (OG 1036, ABV 3.5%) ◈ A pale-coloured, hoppy session bitter with a good hop aroma and a full flavour for its strength, ending in a bittersweet aftertaste.

Bitter (OG 1042, ABV 4%) ◈ A copper-coloured beer with hops and fruit in the aroma and a malty, fruity taste, underscored by a hoppy bitterness. The finish is dry, with a balance of hops and malt.

Old Ric (OG 1046, ABV 4.5%) ◈ A full-flavoured, hoppy bitter with some fruitiness and a smooth, balanced finish. Distinctively copper-coloured.

Old Spot Prize Ale (OG 1050, ABV 5%) ◈ A distinctive full-bodied, red/brown ale with a fruity aroma, a malty, fruity taste, with a hoppy bitterness, and a strong, balanced aftertaste.

Pig's Ear Strong Beer (OG 1050, ABV 5%) ◈ A pale-coloured beer, deceptively strong. Notably bitter in flavour, with a hoppy, fruity aroma and a bitter finish.

USHERS

Ushers of Trowbridge PLC, Directors House, 68 Fore Street, Trowbridge, Wiltshire BA14 8JF.
☎ (01225) 763171
[FAX] (01225) 753661

This famous West Country brewery was founded in 1824, but lost its identity after being swallowed up by Watney (later Grand Met) in 1960. A successful management buyout, purchasing the brewery and 433 pubs from Courage in 1991, gave Ushers back its independence. It has since invested in pubs and plant, with over £6 million spent on the brewery, and a new Cellar Master Award scheme has been introduced to promote good beer care. Ushers was launched on the Stock Exchange in 1997. It now supplies real ale to nearly all its 541 houses (most tenanted and all in the South, South-West and South Wales) and also to Inntrepreneur pubs. Keg and bottled products are brewed for Scottish Courage and other international breweries. Beer is also produced for the Matthew Clark (formerly Freetraders) wholesaling company and Ushers was due to take over production of Gibbs Mew beers following the closure of the Salisbury brewery in autumn 1997. Tours by arrangement Mon–Thu evenings for groups. Seasonal beers: January'Sale (OG 1031, ABV 3%, January), Winter Storm (OG 1041, ABV 4%, December–January), 1824 Particular (OG 1062.5, ABV 6%, December).

Best Bitter (OG 1037.5, ABV 3.8%) 🍺 An amber/pale brown, light bitter with malt and hoppy bitterness in the flavour followed by a dry, bitter finish.

Spring Fever (OG 1040, ABV 4%) Available February–June.

Summer Madness (OG 1040, ABV 4%) Available June–September.

Autumn Frenzy (OG 1041, ABV 4%) Available September–December.

Founders Ale (OG 1046, ABV 4.5%) 🍺 A pale brown beer with a bitter hop taste, balanced by sweet maltiness and faint citrus fruit. Predominantly bitter finish.

For Matthew Clark (Freetraders):

Twelve Bore Bitter (OG 1035, ABV 3.7%)

Chadwick's Finest (OG 1037, ABV 3.7%)

VALE

Vale Brewery Company, Thame Road, Haddenham, Buckinghamshire HP17 8BY.
☎ **(01844) 290008**
[FAX] **(01844) 292505**

After many years working for large regional breweries and allied industries, brothers Mark and Phil Stevens combined their experience and opened a small, purpose-built brewery in Haddenham. This revived brewing in a village where the last brewery closed at the end of World War II. The plant was expanded in November 1996 and now has a capacity of 40 barrels. Around 200 local outlets now take the beers. Tours by arrangement.

Notley Ale (ABV 3.3%) A well-hopped session beer.

Wychert Ale (OG 1040, ABV 3.9%) A full-flavoured beer with nutty fruit undertones.

Hadda's Summer Glory (ABV 4%) A seasonal beer.

Edgar's Golden Ale (ABV 4.3%) 🍺 A full-bodied golden ale made with Fuggle and Golding hops.

Hadda's Autumn Ale (ABV 4.5%) A seasonal beer.

Hadda's Spring Gold (ABV 5%) A seasonal beer.

Hadda's Head Banger (ABV 5.5%) A seasonal (winter) beer.

VAUX

Vaux Breweries Ltd., The Brewery, Sunderland, Tyne & Wear SR1 3AN.
☎ **(0191) 567 6277**
[FAX] **(0191) 514 0422**

First established in 1806 and now one of the country's largest regional brewers, Vaux remains firmly independent. It owns Ward's of Sheffield, but sold off Lorimer & Clark in Edinburgh to Caledonian in 1987. Real ale is sold in over 500 of its 888 houses (which include those run by Ward's and Vaux Inns Ltd.) and is also provided to its 400 free trade customers. Tours by arrangement. Vaux Waggle Dance (OG 1047, ABV 5%) is produced at Ward's (qv), whilst Vaux Mild is Ward's Mild rebadged. Seasonal beer: St Nicholas's Christmas Ale (ABV 5%).

Lorimer's Best Scotch (OG 1036, ABV 3.6%) 🍺 A replica of the original Scottish Scotch. Aroma is often lacking, but, when fresh, there can be a subtle hop character to balance a sweet and malty taste.

Bitter (OG 1038, ABV 3.9%) 🍺 A light and drinkable bitter with low bitterness and some fruit evident. Aroma is easily lost, but can be hoppy.

Samson (OG 1041, ABV 4.2%) 🍺 A very light bitter with a grainy aftertaste, and a sulphury aroma when fresh. Bitterness is moderate and sweetness may persist in the taste.

How's Your Father (ABV 4.3%) A summer ale.

Boxing Hare (ABV 4.7%) A spring beer.

Double Maxim (OG 1048, ABV 4.7%) 🍺 A smooth brown ale, rich and well-balanced, with lasting fruit and good body.

Moonlight Mouse Autumn Ale (ABV 4.7%) A seasonal beer.

VENTNOR

Ventnor Brewery Ltd., 119 High Street, Ventnor, Isle of Wight PO38 1LY.
☎ **(01983) 856161**
[FAX] **(01983) 856404**

The original site of Burts Brewery is now home to Ventnor Brewery. Its new ownership has resurrected brewing here and now serves around 110 pubs, including one tied house. Tours by arrangement. Bottle-conditioned beer: St Boniface Golden Spring Ale (ABV 6%, a limited edition soon to be produced in greater quantity at King & Barnes).

Dark Mild (OG 1033, ABV 3.3%)

Golden Bitter (OG 1040, ABV 4%) 🍺 A truly well-balanced, straw-coloured bitter with an excellent rich and creamy mouthfeel and lasting maltiness.

XAV (OG 1050, ABV 5%) 🍺 Primarily a winter beer, strong, dark and bursting with roast flavour. Roast malt and hops feature in the aroma. Good, solid body.

VERULAM

Verulam Brewery, 134 London Road, St Albans, Hertfordshire AL1 1PQ.
☎ (01727) 766702

Brewery housed behind the Farmers Boy pub in St Albans, having been moved here in 1997 from the Red Cow in Harpenden, where it traded as Harpenden Brewery. Both these pubs take the beer and more ales are planned. Beers: Special (OG 1037, ABV 3.8%), IPA (OG 1040, ABV 4%), Farmers Joy (OG 1043, ABV 4.5%).

VIKING

Viking Ales Ltd., t/a Viking Brewery, 5 Blenheim Close, Pysons Road, Broadstairs, Kent CT10 2YF.
☎ (01843) 865211
FAX (01843) 603933

Brewery founded in August 1995 with the help of a Government grant, and sold to the owners of the Stag & Griffin brew pub in Buckinghamshire in May 1996. The brew pub has since ceased production and its plant has been moved here to supplement the existing equipment and to brew Stiffin Ale (ABV 3.8%) for the pub. Some seasonal beers are brewed and Viking also turns out the Scoopers Collection of very limited-run ales for local consumption. The brewers hope you 'Take a liking to a Viking'. Bottle-conditioned beer: Kentish Ale (ABV 5.4%).

Island Dark Mild (OG 1035, ABV 3.5%) A smooth, dark mild with a hoppy aftertaste.

Summer Solstice (OG 1035, ABV 3.5%) A straw-coloured session beer. Sold all year.

Viking Ale (OG 1039, ABV 3.9%) A strong blend of fruit and hops on the nose is followed by hoppy bitterness at all stages, ending in a dry aftertaste.

Parkin's Pride (OG 1042, ABV 4.2%) Formerly the spring ale called Iduna; now an all-year beer.

Thor's Thunder (OG 1044, ABV 4.4%) A full-bodied, ruby bitter with a dry, hoppy finish.

VILLAGE See Hambleton.

WADWORTH

Wadworth & Co. Ltd., Northgate Brewery, Devizes, Wiltshire SN10 1JW.
☎ (01380) 723361
FAX (01380) 724342

Delightful market town tower brewery set up in 1885 by Henry Wadworth. Though solidly traditional (with its own dray horses), it continues to invest in the future

and to expand, producing up to 2,000 barrels a week to supply a wide-ranging free trade in the South of England, as well as its own 225 tied houses. All the pubs serve real ale and 6X remains one of the South's most famous beers, with national distribution now achieved via the Whitbread guest ale portfolio. Shop (reception) open in office hours. Public tours by arrangement in September. Wadworth also owns the Farmers Arms brew pub (qv). Seasonal beers: Valentine's Oat Malt Ale (OG 1043, ABV 4.5% February), Easter Ale (OG 1043, ABV 4.5%), Malt & Hops (OG 1043, ABV 4.5%, September).

Henry's Original IPA (OG 1035, ABV 3.8%) ♦ A golden brown-coloured beer with a gentle, malty and slightly hoppy aroma, a good balance of flavours, with maltiness gradually dominating, and then a long-lasting aftertaste to match, eventually becoming biscuity. A good session beer.

6X (OG 1040, ABV 4.3%) ♦ Mid-brown in colour, with a malty and fruity nose and some balancing hop character. The flavour is similar, with some bitterness and a lingering malty, but bitter finish. Full-bodied and distinctive.

SummerSault (OG 1043, ABV 4.5%) The summer beer, now available April–September; a pale, refreshing beer made with Saaz lager hops.

Farmers Glory (OG 1046, ABV 4.5%) ♦ This dark beer can be delightfully hoppy and fruity, but varies in flavour and conditioning. The aroma is of malt and it should have a dryish, hoppy aftertaste.

Old Timer (OG 1055, ABV 5.8%)
♦ Available from October–March only: a rich, copper-brown beer with a strong, fruity, malty aroma. The flavour is full-bodied and complete, with hints of butterscotch and peaches, beautifully balanced by a lasting, malty, dry finish.

WALKER
See Nationals, Carlsberg-Tetley.

WARDEN See Merivales.

WARD'S

Ward's Brewery, Ecclesall Road, Sheffield, S. Yorkshire S11 8HZ.
☎ (0114) 275 5155
FAX (0114) 275 1816

Established in 1840 by Josiah Kirby, Ward's has been a subsidiary of Vaux of Sunderland since 1972. Since the closure of the neighbouring Thorne brewery in 1986, it has also produced Darley's (Darley's). Real ale is available in 160 of the brewery's 220 tied houses and around 300 free trade outlets are supplied directly. Tours by arrangement.

THE INDEPENDENTS

Mild or Darley's Dark Mild (OG 1034, ABV 3.4%) ◆ Also sold as Vaux Mild. This beer's rich dark brown and red hue promises more than is delivered. A strong malt nose precedes a roast malt taste, with hints of chocolate. The dry finish can be tinged with sweetness, if it lasts long enough.

Thorne Best Bitter (OG 1038, ABV 3.8%) ◆ Recently improved, this malty-nosed, mid-brown beer has a hoppy bitterness but is well-balanced throughout, including well into the finish.

Best Bitter (OG 1040, ABV 4%) ◆ The rich, malty aroma of this pale brown bitter has been toned down, but it still has a malty base and a bittersweet aftertaste.

For Vaux:

Waggle Dance (OG 1049, ABV 5%) ◆ A beer brewed with honey, gold in colour. A malty drink with a gentle bitterness and a dry, malty finish. Better for not being as sweet as before.

WARWICKSHIRE
The Warwickshire Brewery Ltd., Princes Drive, Kenilworth, Warwickshire CV8 2EG. ☎ (01926) 863346

Brewery established in December 1995, bringing brewing back to the locality after a break of nearly 30 years. Around 40 pubs and clubs now take the beer. Bottling is planned. Tours by arrangement.

Best Bitter (OG 1037, ABV 3.9%)

King's Progress (ABV 4.2%) A pleasant beer, slightly on the sweet side of dry.

King's Champion (OG 1046, ABV 4.6%)

Kingmaker Ale (OG 1049, ABV 5.5%) A premium beer with good balance and some fruity notes.

King's Ruin (OG 1055, ABV 6%)

WATKIN
Tomos Watkin & Sons Ltd., The Castle Brewery, 113 Rhosmaen Street, Llandeilo, Carmarthenshire SA19 6EN. ☎ /FAX (01558) 824140

Brewery established by Simon Buckley (formerly of Buckley and Ushers breweries), adopting the name of a Llandovery brewery which ceased production in 1928. Brewing commenced in December 1995 and the beers were officially launched on St Valentine's Day 1996. The brewery now owns four pubs and an attached craft centre opened in spring 1996. Tours by arrangement. Seasonal beers are occasionally produced for the brewery's own pubs.

BB (OG 1040, ABV 4%) ◆ An amber-coloured beer with a short-lived hoppy and malty aroma. Hops, malt and a hint of fruit in the mouth lead to a building bitterness which overpowers sweetness in the aftertaste.

Cwrw Caio (OG 1040, ABV 4%)

OSB (Old Style Bitter) (OG 1045, ABV 4.5%) ◆ An amber ale with fruit and hops in the aroma and taste, leading on to a malty, dryish finish.

WEBSTER'S See Mansfield, Ruddles and Nationals, Scottish Courage.

WEETWOOD
Weetwood Ales Ltd., Weetwood Grange, Weetwood, Tarporley, Cheshire CW6 0NQ. ☎ (01829) 752377

Brewery set up at an equestrian centre in 1993, with the first brew on sale in March of that year. Around 40 regular customers are now supplied.

Best Bitter (OG 1038.5, ABV 3.8%) ◆ A clean, dry and malty bitter with little aroma. Bitterness dominates the finish.

Old Dog Bitter (OG 1045, ABV 4.5%) ◆ A fuller-bodied version of the bitter: fruitier, with a hint of sweetness.

Oasthouse Gold (OG 1050, ABV 5%) ◆ A golden, sweetish, fruity bitter which lacks body for its strength.

WELLS
Charles Wells Ltd., The Eagle Brewery, Havelock Street, Bedford MK40 4LU. ☎ (01234) 272766 FAX (01234) 279000

Successful, family-owned brewery, established in 1876 and still run by descendants of the founder. The brewery has been on this site since 1976 and most of its 300 or so pubs serve cask ale, though about 50 per cent apply cask breathers. Wells also supplies around 600 other outlets direct and owns the Ancient Druids brew pub in Cambridge (qv). A bottling line was added in 1996. Tours by arrangement.

Eagle IPA (OG 1035, ABV 3.6%) ◆ A refreshing session beer that too often has its hoppy aroma knocked out by the use of a tight sparkler. Citrus fruit hop character dominates throughout, with some sulphur. Dry finish.

Bombardier Premium Bitter (OG 1042, ABV 4.3%) ◆ Citrus fruits are again present but malt balances this beer, making it more rounded than Eagle. Long, dry finish.

Fargo (OG 1050, ABV 5%) ◆ A winter beer to search for. Hops, fruit and sulphur are prominent on the nose, followed by a bitter, citrus fruit flavour with a little malt to add a slight sweetness. Hops and fruit in the long, dry finish.

WELSH BREWERS
See Nationals, Bass.

WELTONS

Weltons North Downs Brewery Ltd., The Brewhouse, Rugge Farm, Wigmore Lane, Capel, Dorking, Surrey RH5 4LF.
☎ (01306) 711300

Brewery founded in 1995 in a farm building near Dorking. It is now planning to expand, following success in the free trade (about 40 outlets supplied directly). The brewery also has one pub of its own. Occasional/seasonal beers: Easter Special (ABV 4.1%, March–April), May Gold (ABV 4.1%, May, a wheat beer), Tam O'Shanter (ABV 4.1%, January), Coronation Ale (ABV 4.4%, May), Lion Brew (ABV 4.5%, August), Guy Fawkes Revenge (ABV 4.6%, October–November), St George's Special (ABV 4.6%, April), Summer Special (ABV 4.8%, July–August), Tower Power (ABV 5%, April and other times), Ups & Downs (ABV 5%, March), Wenceslegless (ABV 5%, December), Wellington's Cannon (ABV 5.4%, June), Dr French's Old Remedy (ABV 6.1%, November).

North Downs Bitter (OG 1038, ABV 3.8%) 🍃 An amber to pale brown bitter with a hoppy flavour balanced by underlying malt.

Predator (OG 1040, ABV 4%) An amber bitter with a malty character, plus hops in the aftertaste.

Old Cocky (OG 1043, ABV 4.3%) 🍃 A beer with a malty and fruity aroma, with hops developing in the flavour and dominating the aftertaste.

Passion Ale or Midsummer Passion (ABV 4.5%) Available in February and June–July: a light beer with subtle spice flavours.

Old Harry (OG 1051, ABV 5.2%) Available September–March: a reddish-coloured beer with a fine Golding hop aroma. Light, but fairly complex.

WEST BERKSHIRE

The West Berkshire Brewery Company, Pot Kiln Lane, Frilsham, Yattendon, Berkshire RG18 0XX.
☎ / FAX (01635) 202638

Brewery established in 1995 in converted farm buildings in the grounds of the Pot Kiln pub, although the businesses are separate. Over 20 outlets take the beers regularly and they guest in other pubs. A small bottling plant may soon be added. Visits by arrangement (phone first). Brick Kiln Bitter (OG 1042, ABV 4%) is only available at the Pot Kiln and Dr Hexter's Healer (OG 1051, ABV 5%) is only sold at the Royal Oak in Wantage. Occasional beers: Hartslock No. 1 (OG 1045, ABV 4.2%), Longdog (ABV 4.3%), Berkshire Dark (OG 1046, ABV 4.4%).

Skiff (OG 1037.5, ABV 3.6%) A beer with a flowery, almost herbal, aroma, and rounded bitter flavours which are more pronounced than expected for its gravity.

Good Old Boy or Old Tyler (OG 1042, ABV 4%) A well-balanced, fruity and hoppy beer with some sweetness in the finish.

Talon (OG 1047, ABV 4.5%) A ruby-coloured bitter full of hop aromas. Chocolate hints balance the bitter finish.

WESTBURY ALES See Princetown.

WETHERED See Nationals, Whitbread.

WHEAL ALE See Bird in Hand.

WHEATSHEAF INN See Fromes Hill.

WHIM

Whim Ales, Whim Farm, Hartington, Buxton, Derbyshire SK17 0AX.
☎ (01298) 84991
FAX (01298) 84702

Brewery opened in 1993 in redundant outbuildings at Whim Farm by Giles Litchfield who, in 1995, purchased Broughton Brewery (qv). There are plans for the two breweries to distribute each other's beers in their local areas. Whim's beers, meanwhile, are available in about 50 outlets. Occasional beers: Arbor Light (OG 1036, ABV 3.6%), High Peak Pale Ale (OG 1041, ABV 4.3%), Schnee Weiss or Snow White (OG 1043, ABV 4.5% a wheat beer), Old Izaak (OG 1048, ABV 4.8%). Bottle-conditioned beer: Black Bear Stout (OG 1062, ABV 6.5%).

Magic Mushroom Mild (OG 1042, ABV 3.8%) A well-balanced mild with a complex mix of flavours. Black/ruby in colour.

Hartington Bitter (OG 1039, ABV 4%) A light, golden, hoppy bitter with a dry finish.

Black Bear Stout (OG 1062, ABV 6.5%)

Black Christmas (OG 1062, ABV 7%)

WHITBREAD See Nationals.

WHITBY'S

Whitby's Own Brewery, Whitby, N. Yorkshire.

Brewery closed.

WHITE

White Brewing Company, The 1066 Country Brewery, Pebsham Farm Industrial Estate, Pebsham Lane, Bexhill, E. Sussex TN40 2RZ. ☎ (01424) 731066

Brewery founded in May 1995 by husband and wife David and Lesley White to serve local free trade outlets and some wholesalers. Visits by appointment only.

1066 Country Bitter (OG 1040, ABV 4%)

WHITEWATER

Whitewater Brewing Co.,
40 Tullyframe Road,
Kilkeel, Newry, Co. Down
BT34 4RZ.
☎ / FAX (0139 67) 26370

Brewery founded in May 1996 on a farm outside Kilkeel. It now supplies around ten outlets in Northern Ireland, and other outlets throughout the British Isles via wholesalers, with beers which have already won beer festival prizes. Beer is also brewed for the non-productive Mill Ale brewery in Killinchy ☎ (01238) 510417.

Mountain Ale (OG 1043, ABV 4.2%).

Eireann Stout (OG 1043, ABV 4.3%)

Bee's Endeavour (OG 1048, ABV 4.8%)

For Mill Ale:

Mill Ale (ABV 3.7%)

Glen Ale (ABV 4.2%)

WICKWAR

The Wickwar Brewing Co.,
Arnolds Cooperage, The
Old Cider Mill, Station
Road, Wickwar,   **WICKWAR**
Gloucestershire GL12 8NB. **BREWING CO**
☎ / FAX (01454) 294168

Brewery launched on the 'Glorious First of May 1990' (guest beer law day) by two Courage tenants with the aim of providing guest ales for their three tenancies. The business proved so successful that they dropped the pubs to concentrate on supplying their other regular outlets (now totalling around 150). The brewery operates from the cooper's shop of the old Arnold, Perret & Co. Ltd. brewery. Tours by arrangement.

Coopers' WPA (OG 1036.5, ABV 3.5%) ♠ A yellow/gold, well-balanced, light, refreshing brew with hops, citrus fruit, peardrop flavour and notable malt character. Bitter, dry finish.

Brand Oak Bitter (BOB) (OG 1038.5, ABV 4%) ♠ A distinctive blend of hops, malt and citrus fruits. The slightly sweet taste turns into a fine, dry bitterness with a similar lasting finish. Amber-coloured.

Olde Merryford Ale (OG 1048, ABV 4.8%) ♠ A pale brown, full-flavoured, well-balanced beer, with malt, hops and fruit elements throughout. Slightly sweet, with a long lasting, malty, dry finish. A fine, complex ale.

Station Porter (OG 1059.5, ABV 6.1%) 🍺 ♠ A smooth, dark brown ale with an aroma of roast malt, coffee and rich fruit. It has a similar, complex and spicy, rich, bittersweet taste and a long, smooth, warming roast finish. Available October–December.

WILD'S

Wild's Brewery, Slaithwaite, Huddersfield, W. Yorkshire.

Brewery closed.

JAMES WILLIAMS See Pub Groups.

WILLY'S

Willy's Brewery Ltd.,
17 High Cliff Road,
Cleethorpes, Lincolnshire
DN35 8RQ.
☎ (01472) 602145
FAX (01472) 603578

🍺 Seafront pub brewery opened in 1989, also supplying a second local outlet and some free trade. A third pub may be added soon. Old Groyne is popular as a guest beer through wholesalers. Tours by arrangement.

Original Bitter (OG 1038, ABV 3.8%) ♠ A tawny beer with a fruity hop nose, and malt coming through in the taste and balanced finish as the moderate bitterness subsides.

Burcom Bitter (OG 1044, ABV 4.2%)

Weiss Buoy (OG 1045, ABV 4.5%) A cloudy wheat beer.

Coxswains Special Bitter (OG 1050, ABV 4.9%)

Old Groyne (OG 1060, ABV 6.2%) ♠ An initial sweet banana fruitiness blends with malt to give a vanilla quality to the taste and slightly bitter aftertaste. A copper-coloured beer with some almost Trappist ale qualities.

WILSON'S See Mansfield, Morland, and Nationals, Scottish Courage.

WINFIELDS

Winfields Brewery, The Raven, Bedford Street, Portsmouth, Hampshire PO5 4BT.
☎ (01705) 829079

🍺 Very small pub brewery set up in 1995, just serving the pub itself and only brewing occasionally. Beers: Mild (ABV 3.5%), Bitter (ABV 3.7%), Stout (ABV 3.8%), Winter Brew (ABV 4.5%).

WOLF

The Wolf Brewery Ltd.,
10 Maurice Gaymer Road,
Attleborough, Norfolk
NR17 2QZ.
☎ (01953) 457775
FAX (01953) 457776

Brewery founded by the former owner of the Reindeer Brewery in 1996, using a 20-barrel plant housed on the site of the old Gaymers cider orchard. Tours by arrangement. About 90 customers take the beer.

Best Bitter (OG 1040, ABV 3.9%)

Coyote (OG 1042, ABV 4.3%)

Granny Wouldn't Like It (OG 1049, ABV 4.8%)

WOLVERHAMPTON & DUDLEY See Banks's and Camerons.

WOOD

**The Wood Brewery Ltd.,
Wistanstow, Craven Arms,
Shropshire SY7 8DG.
☎ (01588) 672523
[FAX] (01588) 673939**

A village brewery, founded by the Wood family in 1980, in buildings adjacent to the Plough Inn. The brewery has enjoyed steady growth in recent years and now supplies around 200 other outlets (locally, and further afield via wholesalers). Sam Powell beers have been brewed here since the Powell brewery in Newtown went into receivership in 1991. One pub is owned at present, but more may be acquired. Tours by arrangement. Seasonal beers: Saturnalia (OG 1040, ABV 4.2%, January), Get Knotted (OG 1047, ABV 4.7%, February), Hopping Mad (OG 1048, ABV 4.7%, March–April), Anniversary Ale (OG 1051, ABV 5%, April), Christmas Cracker (OG 1061, ABV 6%, November–December). Bottle-conditioned beers: Shropshire Lad (OG 1051, ABV 5%), Christmas Cracker (OG 1061, ABV 6%, November–December).

Wallop (OG 1032, ABV 3.4%)

Sam Powell Best Bitter (OG 1033, ABV 3.4%)

Sam Powell Original Bitter (OG 1036, ABV 3.7%)

Summer That (OG 1038, ABV 3.9%) Available May–September.

Parish Bitter (OG 1040, ABV 4%) ◥ A blend of malt and hops with a bitter aftertaste. Pale brown in colour.

Woodcutter (OG 1040, ABV 4.2%) Available October–December.

Special Bitter (OG 1041, ABV 4.2%) ◥ A tawny brown bitter with malt, hops and some fruitiness.

Shropshire Lad (OG 1045, ABV 4.5%)

Sam Powell Old Sam (OG 1047, ABV 4.6%)

Wonderful (OG 1047, ABV 4.8%) ◥ A mid-brown, fruity beer, with a roast and malt taste.

WOODFORDE'S

**Woodforde's Norfolk Ales
(Woodforde's Ltd.),
Broadland Brewery,
Woodbastwick, Norwich,
Norfolk NR13 6SW.
☎ (01603) 720353 [FAX] (01603) 721806**

Founded in late 1980 in Norwich, Woodforde's moved to a converted farm complex, with greatly increased production capacity, in the picturesque Broadland village of Woodbastwick in 1989. It brews an extensive range of beers and runs three tied

houses, with some 250 other outlets supplied on a regular basis. The company launched its own range of home brew kits in 1996, allowing drinkers to brew Wherry, Norfolk Nog and Headcracker at home. Tours for groups by arrangement on Tue and Thu evenings. Visitor centre and shop open 10.30–5 Mon–Fri, 10.30–3 Sat and some Suns. Occasional/seasonal beers: Old Bram (OG 1043, ABV 4.1%), John Browne's Ale (OG 1043, ABV 4.3%), Mother-in-Law's Tongue (ABV 4.3%, for Mother's Day), Phoenix XXX (ABV 4.8%). Bottle-conditioned beers: Wherry Best Bitter (OG 1038, ABV 3.8%), Great Eastern Ale (OG 1043, ABV 4.3%), Nelson's Revenge (OG 1045, ABV 4.5%), Norfolk Nog (OG 1049, ABV 4.6%), Baldric (OG 1052, ABV 5.6%), Headcracker (OG 1069, ABV 7%), Norfolk Nips (OG 1085, ABV 8.6%). With the exception of Norfolk Nips, these are bottled independently of Woodforde's and are only sold at the Woodforde's Visitor Centre.

Broadsman Bitter (OG 1035, ABV 3.5%) ◥ A session beer which is a straightforward combination of malt and hops, with hints of sweetness and fruit. Hops and bitterness dominate the aftertaste.

Mardler's Mild (OG 1035, ABV 3.5%) ◥ A red/brown mild which is fairly dry (for a mild), smooth and malty. Well-balanced, with some subtle fruitiness. The aftertaste is pleasant but short.

Wherry Best Bitter (OG 1038, ABV 3.8%) ▤ ◥ This award-winning, amber beer has a distinctly hoppy nose and a well-balanced palate with pronounced bitterness and, usually, a flowery hop character. Long-lasting, satisfying, bitter aftertaste. *Champion Beer of Britain 1996.*

Norfolk Stout or Emerald Ale (OG 1042, ABV 4.2%) A traditional black Norfolk ale with a milk chocolate-coloured head.

Great Eastern Ale (OG 1043, ABV 4.3%) A refreshing, light straw-coloured bitter with a slightly sweetish, malty taste.

Nelson's Revenge (OG 1045, ABV 4.5%) ◥ This premium bitter has quite a strong, pleasant, malty, fruity, hoppy aroma which the rounded and complex, malty palate doesn't quite live up to. The hoppiness and bitterness come through more distinctly at the end to give a good, lasting aftertaste.

Norfolk Nog (OG 1049, ABV 4.6%) ◥ A full-bodied red/brown beer with plenty of flavour and aroma. Roast malt balances the sweeter components of the palate. A very good, dark winter brew. *Champion Beer of Britain 1992.*

Baldric (OG 1052, ABV 5.6%) ◥ An amber/golden, light beer, with almost delicate hopping. A pleasing combination of malt, hops and fruit, with some sweetness in the palate and bitterness in the finish.

Headcracker (OG 1069, ABV 7%) 🍷 🍴
🔸 This fairly pale brown barley wine is full-bodied and fruity throughout. The sweetness in the palate is balanced by the hoppiness and bitterness, and the aftertaste is warming.

WOODHAMPTON
The Woodhampton Brewing Company, Aymestrey, Herefordshire HR6 9ST.
☎/FAX (01568) 770503

Brewery founded in May 1997 at Woodhampton Farm, brewing 15 barrels a week and selling its beers principally through the local Riverside Inn but also through some other pubs. All beers are produced from locally-grown hops and spring water. Shop open 10–4.30.

Dipper Bitter (ABV 3.6%)

Kingfisher Ale (ABV 4.4%)

WOODY WOODWARD'S
See Fox & Hounds.

WORLDHAM
Worldham Brewery, Smith's Farm, East Worldham, Alton, Hampshire GU34 3AT.
☎ (01420) 83383
FAX (01420) 83600

It took 18 months for experienced brewer Hugo Sharpe to convert a hop kiln into a ten-barrel brewery, using plant acquired from a number of different breweries. Worldham eventually launched its first beer at the 1991 CAMRA Farnham Beerex and now serves around 30 free trade outlets. Tours by arrangement.

Old Dray Bitter (OG 1044, ABV 4.4%) 🔸 A mid- to deep brown beer, low in aroma and with a dry flavour with some grain. Strong on hops in the slightly cloying finish.

Golden Summer Bitter (OG 1046, ABV 4.6%)

Barbarian Bitter (OG 1052, ABV 5.2%) A well-hopped premium bitter.

WORTH
Worth Brewery, Greenbottle Ltd., Worth Way, Keighley, W. Yorkshire BD21 5LP.
☎ (01535) 611914 FAX (01535) 691883

Formerly Commercial Brewing Company, set up in a former garage, this brewery's first beer was produced in 1992. Its direct free trade now covers around 30 outlets in the M62/M1 corridor. A new visitor centre opened at the beginning of 1996, offering tours to groups by arrangement. Shop open during normal office hours. Occasional/seasonal beers: Extra (OG 1049, ABV 4.9%), Gold (OG 1050, ABV 5%), Santa's Toss (OG 1080, ABV 8%, December). Bottle-conditioned beers: Extra (OG 1049, ABV

4.9%), Neary's Extra Stout (OG 1050, ABV 5%), Santa's Toss (OG 1080, ABV 8%).

Alesman (OG 1036, ABV 3.7%) 🔸 Hoppy and bitter throughout, this clean-tasting and well-balanced, amber beer provides an excellent example of a standard quaffing bitter.

Wild Boar (OG 1040, ABV 4%) Malt, hops and bitterness combine to provide a quite refreshing and well-balanced drink with a bitter aftertaste. Brewed to the original Trough Brewery (now defunct) recipe.

Neary's Stout (OG 1042, ABV 4.1%) 🔸 A rich and complex black stout with mellow coffee, chocolate and liquorice flavours balanced by a pleasant fruitiness and some hops. The aftertaste is long, dry and quite bitter. Look for a hint of banana in the predominantly burnt aroma.

Train Fayre (OG 1042, ABV 4.2%) 🔸 A copper-coloured bitter with a powerful dry, hoppy taste and some background roast and malt, turning intensely bitter in the finish. The nose is hoppy with some malt.

Best Bitter (OG 1045, ABV 4.5%) 🔸 A long, dry bitter finish rounds off this satisfyingly hoppy, pale brown bitter. Citrus flavours dominate the aroma, balancing the generally hoppy and quite bitter taste.

Porter (OG 1045, ABV 4.5%) 🔸 This full-bodied and well-rounded, dark brown porter offers a satisfying combination of dark chocolate, roast and fruit flavours in the aroma and taste, followed by an increasingly dry finish. Smooth and very moreish. Available October–March.

Knöbwilter (OG 1049, ABV 5.2%) A pale, dry wheat beer with fruit and hop flavours in the taste and finish, becoming more and more bitter. Available April–September.

Old Toss (OG 1065, ABV 6.5%) A full-bodied and warming, dark old ale. Roast and fruit flavours dominate over background sweetness, malt and hops. Burnt aroma; long, bitter finish.

WORTHINGTON
See Nationals, Bass.

WORTLEY See Barnfield.

WYCHWOOD
Wychwood Brewery Company Ltd., The Eagle Maltings, The Crofts, Corn Street, Witney, Oxfordshire OX8 7AZ ☎ (01993) 702574
FAX (01993) 772553

Set up as Glenny Brewery in 1983, in the old maltings of the extinct Clinch's brewery, this brewery moved to a new site in 1987 and was radically revamped during 1992, when nine pubs were acquired (leased from Allied or Inntrepreneur) by its sister company

THE INDEPENDENTS

Hobgoblinns Ltd. The company now runs 30 managed pubs (ten free, the rest tied to Scottish Courage), in various towns across the South and South-West, all restyled in the bare boards and breweriana idiom, most renamed Hobgoblin and all taking real ale. Wychwood also supplies about 80 other outlets. As a consequence of the extra demand, the brewery moved back to the old Clinch's site in 1994. Tours by arrangement. Shop open 9–5 Mon–Fri. Seasonal beer: Black Wych Stout (OG 1050, ABV 5%, Christmas).

Fiddlers Elbow (OG 1040, ABV 4%) Brewed May–September: a straw-coloured beer containing barley and wheat malts.

Special (OG 1042, ABV 4.2%) ◆ Formerly Wychwood Best: a mid-brown, full-flavoured premium bitter. Moderately strong in hop and malt flavours, with pleasing, fruity overtones which last through to the aftertaste.

Old Devil (OG 1047, ABV 4.7%) A bitter beer featuring honey, with a dry, fruity finish.

The Dog's Bollocks (DB) (OG 1052, ABV 5.2%) A full-bodied, hoppy, golden brew, incorporating Styrian hops and wheat.

Hobgoblin (OG 1055, ABV 5.5%) ◆ Powerful, full-bodied, copper-red, well-balanced brew. Strong in roasted malt, with a moderate, hoppy bitterness and a slight fruity character.

WYE VALLEY
Wye Valley Brewery, 69 St Owen Street, Hereford HR1 2JQ. ☎ (01432) 342546 FAX (01432) 266553

Brewery which began production in 1985 and moved to its present address a year later. New plant was installed in 1992 to increase capacity and cater for a rapidly growing free trade (currently 180 outlets). Tours by arrangement. The company also has three pubs of its own and produces seasonal beers under the Dorothy Goodbody name. Bottle-conditioned beers: Brew 69 (OG 1055, ABV 5.6%), Dorothy Goodbody's Father Christmas Ale (OG 1086, ABV 8.6%, December, also available on draught at Christmas).

Bitter (OG 1036, ABV 3.5%) ◆ A beer whose aroma gives little hint of the bitter hoppiness which follows right through to the aftertaste.

Dorothy Goodbody's Wonderful Springtime Bitter (OG 1040, ABV 4%) Available March–May; a full, malt-flavoured beer with bitterness and a hop aroma.

Hereford Pale Ale or HPA (OG 1040, ABV 4%) ◆ A pale, hoppy, malty brew with a hint of sweetness before a dry finish.

Dorothy Goodbody's Golden Summertime Ale (OG 1042, ABV 4.2%). Available June–August; a golden ale with a light malt flavour.

Supreme (OG 1044, ABV 4.3%) ◆ A rich, fruity, malt aroma leads to a sweet, malt and fruit taste which lingers to the finish.

Dorothy Goodbody's Glowing Autumn Ale (OG 1045, ABV 4.5%). Available September–November; a dry, full-flavoured beer with a deep colour.

Classic (OG 1045, ABV 4.5%) Not sold at the Barrels, the brewery tap.

Dorothy Goodbody's Wholesome Stout (OG 1046, ABV 4.6%) ◆ Available November–April. A very smooth and satisfying stout without a bitter edge to its roast flavours. The finish combines roast grain and malt.

Dorothy Goodbody's Warming Wintertime Ale (OG 1049, ABV 4.9%) ◆ Available December–February. A sweet winter ale with a fruity, hoppy taste and a rich, fruity aftertaste.

Brew 69 (OG 1055, ABV 5.6%) ◆ A pale premium beer named after the brewery's street number. Its hoppy taste has a hint of malt; slightly bitter aftertaste.

WYLYE VALLEY
Wylye Valley Brewery, Corton, Wiltshire.

Brewery closed.

WYRE PIDDLE
Wyre Piddle Brewery, Unit 21, Craycombe Farm, Fladbury, Evesham, Worcestershire WR10 2QS. ☎ (01386) 860473

Brewery established by a former publican and master builder in a converted stable in autumn 1994. Around 120 outlets now take the beer from time to time, in locations throughout the southern Midlands, and a brewery move may be scheduled in the near future to cater for the increased business. Tours by arrangement. Seasonal beer: Piddle in the Snow (OG 1050, ABV 5.2%, December–January).

Piddle in the Hole (OG 1039, ABV 3.9%) ◆ A beer dominated by strong malty tastes throughout.

Piddle in the Wind (OG 1045, ABV 4.5%) ◆ Malt tastes dominate this tawny, full-bodied, sweetish bitter.

Piddle in the Sun (ABV 5.2%) ◆ A strong, copper-coloured summer brew, malty in the mouth with hops on the nose.

YATES
Yates Brewery, Ghyll Farm, Westnewton, Aspatria, Cumbria CA5 3NX. ☎ (0169 73) 21081

Small, traditional brewery set up in 1986 by Peter and Carole Yates in an old farm building on their smallholding, where a herd of pedigree goats makes good use of the brewery's by-products. Brewing award-winning beers to their capacity of 34 barrels a week during summer and other peak times, they serve around 20 free trade outlets and own one pub. House beers are produced for a couple of other pubs. Seasonal beer: Best Cellar (OG 1052, ABV 5.5%, Christmas).

Bitter (OG 1035, ABV 3.7%) ◥ A pale straw, golden bitter with a fresh natural malt taste and a complex hoppy bitterness, rising in the aftertaste with lactic overtones. It is best served through a tight sparkler. Exemplary balance. Very highly regarded.

Premium (OG 1048, ABV 5.2%) ◥ Available at Christmas and a few other times of the year. Straw-coloured, with a strong aroma of malt and hops, and full-flavoured, with a slight toffee taste. The malty aftertaste becomes strongly bitter.

YORK

The York Brewery Co. Ltd., 12 Toft Green, Micklegate, York, N. Yorkshire YO1 1JT.
☎ (01904) 621162
FAX (01904) 621216

Brewery which began production in June 1996, the first brewery in the city for over 40 years. The plant came from the closed Lion's brewery in Burnley and was installed in a former carpet (and later motorbike) showroom on the York Tourist Trail, within the city walls. The brewery was planned with the visitor very much in mind (daily tours); shop open every day (except weekends in winter). Already some 250 pubs take the beer. Occasional beer: M'lud (ABV 4%).

Stonewall (ABV 3.7%) ◥ A light amber bitter with little maltiness but strong hop and fruit aromas and flavours. Clean-tasting, its hoppiness leads to a dry, bitter finish.

Yorkshire Terrier (ABV 4.2%) ◥ A golden premium bitter with a balance of malt and hops to the fore, giving way to an assault of fruit, hops and, finally, an astonishingly dry, bitter finish.

YORK TAVERN
York Brewing Company, York Tavern, 1 Leicester Street, Norwich, Norfolk NR2 2AS. ☎ (01603) 620918

Full mash pub brewery founded in spring 1996 and supplying only itself in the main. Beers: Old Duke (OG 1038, ABV 4%), Old Nick (OG 1047, ABV 4.7%).

YORKSHIRE GREY
See Nationals, Scottish Courage.

YOUNGER
See Nationals, Scottish Courage.

YOUNG'S
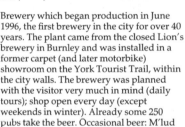
Young & Co.'s Brewery PLC, The Ram Brewery, High Street, Wandsworth, London SW18 4JD.
☎ (0181) 875 7000
FAX (0181) 875 7100

Brewery founded in 1675 by the Draper family, and bought by Charles Young and Anthony Bainbridge in 1831. Their partnership was dissolved in 1884 and the business was continued by the Young family. Though a public company since 1898, Young's is still very much a family affair and was the only London brewer not to join the keg revolution in the 1970s. It still brews award-winning beers in the traditional manner and produces seasonal beers which are well worth trying. However, the company recommends the use of cask breathers on slow-moving nine-gallon casks. Around 500 free trade outlets are supplied, mostly within the M25 ring, though the brewery's presence is extending westward, and the brewery's tied estate now stands at 180 houses. The Bill Bentley's wine bar chain is also part of the business. Paying tours of the brewery were introduced in April 1997. Brewery shop open 10–5 Mon–Fri, 11–3 weekends. Bottle-conditioned beer: Special London Ale (ABV 6.4%).

Bitter (OG 1036, ABV 3.7%) ◥ A distinctive amber beer. A strong, hoppy bitterness is followed by a delightfully astringent and hoppy, bitter aftertaste. An underlying malt balance is present throughout.

Special (OG 1046, ABV 4.6%) ⛶ ◥ A strong, full-flavoured, bitter beer with a powerful hoppiness and a balancing malt flavour. Hops persist in the aftertaste.

Ram Rod (OG 1050, ABV 5%) ◥ A mid-brown beer with a malty aroma which leads to a strong malt flavour and a slightly sweet, malty aftertaste. Only a faint hint of hops throughout.

Winter Warmer (OG 1055, ABV 5%) ⛶ ◥ A dark reddish-brown ale with a malty, fruity aroma, a sweet, malty flavour and a sweet, fruity finish, plus a hint of caramel throughout. Available October–March.

◥ The tilted glass indicates CAMRA tasting notes (supplied by a trained CAMRA tasting panel). Beer descriptions not preceded by this symbol are based on limited tastings only or have been obtained from other sources.

NOTES ON NEW BREWERIES AND BEERS

BASS

Bass

Bass Brewers Ltd., 137 High Street, Burton upon Trent, Staffordshire DE14 1JZ ☎ (01283) 511000 FAX (01283) 513326

Founded in 1777, Bass is Britain's second largest brewer, with some 23 per cent of all beer production. It had hoped to reclaim its former position as the biggest British brewer through a merger with Carlsberg-Tetley, but this was blocked by the new Labour Government in June 1997. Bass produces the country's biggest selling beer brand, Carling Black Label lager, and two of its ale brands (Stones Bitter and Worthington Bitter) feature amongst the top five sellers. Draught Bass, promoted as its flagship brand, is still the biggest-selling premium cask ale, although volumes are thought to be in decline, thanks partly to the company's major innovation of the last decade, Caffrey's Ale. The first of the new breed of nitrokeg beers (brewery-conditioned, pasteurised beers which are served under a mixture of CO_2 and nitrogen), Caffrey's has also had an impact on Bass's regional ales.

Following the closures of the breweries in Edinburgh (Heriot), Sheffield (Hope) and Wolverhampton (Springfield), and the sale of Highgate Brewery in Walsall to a management buyout team (see Independents), Bass now brews at just eight sites, with those at Alton, Belfast and Tadcaster producing only keg beer. There is a cask ale facility at Glasgow and this has attempted a few brews in recent years, though with little success. Bass also has interests in China and in the Czech Republic (through Staropramen, which Bass imports into the UK, and Ostrova).

Over half of Bass's production goes into the free trade. On its pub side, the company runs around 4,200 houses, of which about two-thirds are managed and the balance tenanted or leased. Many pubs still bear the liveries of former Bass trading divisions like Charrington, M&B (Mitchells & Butlers) and Welsh Brewers, but increasingly are being branded under such names as Harvester, Vintage Inns and O'Neills. The company is also investing heavily in large, city-centre pubs like those in the All Bar One and Edwards chains.

BIRMINGHAM

Cape Hill Brewery, PO Box 27, Smethwick, Birmingham, W. Midlands B16 0PQ.
☎ (0121) 558 1481

One of the largest cask beer production centres in the country, subject of a £61 million investment programme in recent years. Bottle-conditioned beer: Worthington White Shield (OG 1050.5, ABV 5.6%).

M&B Mild (OG 1034.5, ABV 3.2%) A dark brown quaffing mild with roast and malt flavours. Dry, slightly bitter finish.

M&B Brew XI (OG 1039.5, ABV 3.8%) A sweet, malty beer with a hoppy, bitter aftertaste.

BURTON

Burton Brewery, Station Street, Burton upon Trent, Staffordshire DE14 1JZ.
☎ (01283) 513578

The original home of Bass, producing one of Britain's most famous ales.

Draught Bass (OG 1043, ABV 4.4%) A malty beer with underlying hops and a dry finish. The classic taste is still occasionally found but modern dispense methods diminish the aroma, taste and finish.

CARDIFF

The Brewery, Crawshay Street, Cardiff CF1 1TR. ☎ (01222) 233071
FAX (01222) 372668

The Hancock's brewery (founded in 1884) which was taken over by Bass Charrington in 1968. Tours by arrangement. Occasional beer: Hancock's IPA (OG 1038, ABV 3.6%).

Worthington Dark Mild (OG 1034.5, ABV 3%) A dark brown, creamy mild with a somewhat malty flavour, followed by a sweet finish. Mainly found in the Swansea area.

Hancock's HB (OG 1038, ABV 3.6%) A pale brown, slightly malty beer. The initial sweetness is balanced by bitterness but it

519

lacks a noticeable finish. A consistent, if inoffensive, regional brand.

Worthington Draught Bitter (OG 1038, ABV 3.6%) ◆ A light brown, slightly malty, bittersweet beer of thin and unremarkable character.

MUSEUM

Museum Brewing Company, The Bass Museum, PO Box 220, Horninglow Street, Burton upon Trent, Staffordshire DE14 1YQ. ☎ (01283) 511000 [FAX] (01283) 513509

Active brewery housed within Bass's popular museum, producing around 50 barrels a week of beers for sale on site and in other outlets. The beer recipes are taken from the Bass archives but the brewery enjoys a substantial degree of independence within the Bass empire. A range of IPAs in the ABV range of 4.9–5.4% is also produced for sale as pub house beers. Museum open 10–5 (last entries 4); shop open 10–6, all week. The bar on site is open until 7 for visitors already inside. Occasional beers: Quaffing Ale (OG 1038, ABV 4%), No. 6 Mild (OG 1037, ABV 3.9%), Offilers Mild (OG 1037, ABV 3.9%), Offilers Bitter (OG 1038, ABV 4%), Joules Bitter (OG 1039, ABV 4.1%), 'E' (OG 1044, ABV 4.8%), Masterpiece IPA (OG 1048, ABV 5.4%). Bottle-conditioned beers: Masterpiece IPA (OG 1048, ABV 5.4%), P2 (OG 1072, ABV 8%), No. 1 Barley Wine (OG 1105, ABV 10.5%).

P2 Imperial Stout (OG 1072, ABV 8%) A black, sweetish, complex stout.

No.1 Barley Wine (OG 1105, ABV 10.5%) A dark ruby beer brewed in summer and fermented in casks for six months, before being sold in the winter.

SHEFFIELD

Cannon Brewery, 43 Rutland Road, Sheffield, S. Yorkshire S3 8BE. ☎ (0114) 272 0323 [FAX] (0114) 272 6442

The original home of William Stones Ltd., dating from at least 1860. It was taken over by Bass in 1968 and, following much investment in recent years, is now the company's specialist cask beer brewery. Tours by arrangement.

Mild (OG 1032, ABV 3.1%) ◆ A pleasant, smooth, dark mild with a faint aroma of caramel, which leads to a caramel and roast, rich taste, with complementing sweetness and bitterness. Good, long, satisfying, roast malt and caramel-sweet finish.

Toby Cask (OG 1032, ABV 3.2%) ◆ An amber-coloured mild: a lightly-flavoured blend of malt, sweetness and bitterness. At its best, it has a delicate, pleasing, flowery taste, but can too often be bland. Disappointing, short, sweetish finish and little aroma.

Worthington Draught Bitter (OG 1038, ABV 3.6%) This supplements supplies from the Cardiff brewery.

Stones Bitter (OG 1039, ABV 3.9%) ◆ Although generally more hoppy than recently, this golden straw-coloured brew retains a careful balance of malt, hop and fruit on the nose, mellow tastes in the mouth and a clean and bitter finish.

Bass Brew Pubs:

ORIGINAL

Original Brewing Company, Bass Leisure Entertainments Ltd., New Castle House, Castle Boulevard, Nottingham NG7 1FT. ☎ (0115) 924 0333 [FAX] (0115) 924 0657

🍺 Chain of microbreweries housed in ten-pin bowling alleys. The first opened in Leicester in 1995, with a brewery visible to the public on the first floor. The company has since opened three further breweries at bowling centres with a fifth planned for Cardiff and another ten or so outlets targeted for the end of 1998. The full mash beers are kept under CO_2 in casks and cellar tanks. Beers: Xmas Cask Lager (OG 1043, ABV 4%), VSP (OG 1045, ABV 4.4%), Disciples' Brew (OG 1049, ABV 5%), 4 Xmas (OG 1061, ABV 6.2%, Christmas).

Current breweries:

Hollywood Bowl, Meridian Leisure Park, Braunstone, Leicester LE3 2WX. ☎ (0116) 263 1234 [FAX] (0116) 263 1102

Hollywood Bowl, Woodside Leisure Park, Kingsway, Garston, Watford, Hertfordshire WD2 6NB. ☎ (01923) 682929 [FAX] (01923) 682442

Hollywood Bowl, Finchley Leisure Park, Finchley High Road, North Finchley, London N12 0GL. ☎ (0181) 446 1958 [FAX] (0181) 446 0292.

Hollywood Bowl, Unit 5, Stevenage Leisure Centre, Six Hills Way, Stevenage, Hertfordshire SG1 2NY. ☎ (01438) 747777

> ◆ The tilted glass indicates CAMRA tasting notes (supplied by a trained CAMRA tasting panel). Beer descriptions not preceded by this symbol are based on limited tastings only or have been obtained from other sources.

CARLSBERG-TETLEY

Carlsberg-Tetley Brewing Ltd., 107 Station Street, Burton upon Trent, Staffordshire DE14 1BZ. ☎ (01283) 512222 FAX (01283) 502357

Britain's third largest brewing concern, Carlsberg-Tetley's story can be traced back to 1961 when Ansells, Tetley Walker and Ind Coope joined forces to become Allied Breweries. In 1992 Allied merged with Danish lager giant Carlsberg and Carlsberg-Tetley was born. Brewing trade analysts immediately predicted brewery closures and brand rationalisation as Carlsberg's modern Northampton brewery was added to Allied's already under-capacity sites. These predictions were realised in 1996, when the closures of Tetley Walker's Warrington brewery and the Plympton brewery in Plymouth were announced. The Warrington brews have been dispersed throughout the Carlsberg-Tetley empire and the one surviving Plympton beer is now brewed under contract by St Austell (see Independents). Also in 1996, the Holt, Plant & Deakin brewery in the Black Country brewed its last. The beers are now produced at Burton and Leeds and the Holts Oldbury and Wolverhampton breweries are now known as the Finings & Firkin and the Fermenter & Firkin, respectively (see Firkin). It is unlikely that this will be the end of the rationalisation and the historic lager plant at Wrexham still looks vulnerable, although the refusal of the Government to allow Carlsberg-Tetley to merge with Bass may boost its chances of survival.

Carlsberg-Tetley is effectively only a brewing company. The former Allied pubs, which are mostly still tied to Carlsberg-Tetley beers, are held by Allied Domecq. Local brewery liveries still decorate many of the pubs, with the old brewing names of Tetley, Peter Walker, Friary Meux, Benskins, ABC, Halls and Ansells still in evidence. In London, the Taylor Walker division is complemented by the small Nicholson's chain of upmarket pubs. The Firkin chain of brew pubs was acquired from Stakis Leisure in 1991 and has been rapidly expanded. There have also been many pub disposals, with hundreds of Allied pubs sold or leased to regional breweries and pub chains, some with the Carlsberg-Tetley beer tie still in place. The current Allied stock stands at around 4,100 pubs.

ALLOA

Carlsberg-Tetley Alloa Ltd., Alloa Brewery, Whins Road, Alloa, Clackmannanshire FK10 3RB. ☎ (01259) 723539

The company's Scottish arm, established in 1819, which was taken over by Archibald Arrol in 1866. It fell to Ind Coope & Allsopp's in 1951, becoming part of Allied in the 1961 merger. Over £2.5 million has been invested in the site in recent years, but less than half of Alloa's 310 pubs sell real ale. Tours by arrangement. Occasional beer: Arrol's 90/- (ABV 4.9%).

Arrol's 80/- (OG 1041, ABV 4.4%) ◆ A fruity Scottish heavy, dominated by malt, fruit and hops, with increasing hoppiness in the aftertaste. Well worth seeking out when in top form.

ALLSOPP

Samuel Allsopp Brewery Company, 107 Station Street, Burton upon Trent, Staffordshire DE14 1BZ. ☎ (01283) 502284 FAX (01283) 502209

Specialist cask ale brewery on the site of the main Burton complex. Reviving the old Allsopp's name, the brewery was re-opened in 1994 to produce limited edition, mid–high strength beers for Carlsberg-Tetley's Tapster's Choice 'guest' beer scheme (each available for about six weeks). These have included Single Malt Ale (ABV 4.1%), Harvest Ale (ABV 4.2%, summer), Sam's Stout (OG 1040, ABV 4.2%), IPA (OG 1041, ABV 4.2%), Old Ruby (OG 1041, ABV 4.2%), Double Diamond Cask (OG 1041.5, ABV 4.3%), Summer Golden Ale (ABV 4.4%), Treason Ale (OG 1046, ABV 4.7%), Devil's Kiss (OG 1050.5, ABV 5.2%), Sam's Porter (ABV 5.2%), Triple Diamond (ABV 5.3%) and Winter Warmer (OG 1052, ABV 5.5%).

For HP&D:

HP&D Mild (OG 1036, ABV 3.7%)

Entire (OG 1043, ABV 4.4%)

> 🍺 The empty tankard indicates the beer was a *Good Beer Guide Beer of the Year* in the last three years.

BURTON

**Carlsberg-Tetley Burton Brewery Ltd.,
107 Station Street, Burton upon Trent,
Staffordshire DE14 1BZ.** ☎ **(01283) 531111**

Brewery established by the merger of the
adjoining Allsopp's and Ind Coope
breweries in 1934. It currently has a capacity
of two and a half million barrels a year and
primarily brews real ales for the South and
the Midlands, providing beer for the
Ansells, Ind Coope Retail and Nicholson's
trading divisions of Allied Domecq. These
'local' beers are largely derived from two
mashes: ABC and Friary from one, Benskins
and Nicholson's from the other. Despite
being voted *Champion Beer of Britain* in 1990,
Ind Coope Burton Ale, a pioneer amongst
big brewery real ales, now looks in danger of
being discontinued. Tours by arrangement.

Ansells Mild (OG 1033, ABV 3.4%) ◥ A
dark red/brown beer with a smooth
mouthfeel. Good caramel and liquorice
aroma and taste.

ABC Best Bitter (OG 1035, ABV 3.7%) A
light, refreshing bitter, owing much of its
character to dry hopping but with malt and
fruit on the tongue.

Ansells Bitter (OG 1035, ABV 3.7%) ◥ A
pale brown, clean and sharp bitter with a
good hop bite. Hop and fruit aroma; dry
finish.

Benskins Best Bitter (OG 1035, ABV 3.7%)
◥ A predominantly hoppy beer with fruit
and malt flavours. It can be a very suppable
pint but sometimes suffers from an
astringent aftertaste.

Friary Meux Best Bitter (OG 1035, ABV
3.7%) ◥ Malt just dominates over hops in
the aroma and flavour of this beer, and a
strange, fruity taste lurks in the background.

Nicholson's Best Bitter (OG 1035, ABV
3.7%)

Ind Coope Burton Ale (OG 1047, ABV 4.8%)
🍾 ◥ A full-tasting hoppy beer with a rich
mixture of malt and fruit in the aroma and
flavour.

For Greenalls:

Greenalls Mild (OG 1032, ABV 3.3%) ◥ A
thin and undemanding dark mild with a
hint of liquorice. More fruity than its
Warrington predecessor.

◥ The tilted glass indicates CAMRA
tasting notes (supplied by a trained
CAMRA tasting panel). Beer
descriptions not preceded by this
symbol are based on limited tastings
only or have been obtained from
other sources.

Shipstone's Mild (OG 1034, ABV 3.4%)

Davenports Traditional Bitter (OG 1037,
ABV 3.7%)

Greenalls Bitter (OG 1036, ABV 3.8%) ◥ A
thin, dry bitter which lacks balance. As with
the mild, fruitiness has increased.

Shipstone's Bitter (OG 1037, ABV 3.9%)

Thomas Greenall's Original Bitter (OG
1045, ABV 4.6%) ◥ Now just a higher
gravity version of Greenalls Bitter. A fruity
bitter with a hint of sweetness.

For Little Pub Company:

Little Lumphammer (OG 1039, ABV 3.5%)

TETLEY

**Carlsberg-Tetley Brewing Ltd., Joshua
Tetley & Son, PO Box 142, The Brewery,
Leeds, W. Yorkshire LS1 1QG.**
☎ **(0113) 259 4594**

Yorkshire's best-known brewery, purchased
in 1822 by maltster Joshua Tetley. The
brewery site covers 20 acres and includes a
brewhouse opened in 1989 to handle the
increased demand for Tetley Bitter
(Carlsberg-Tetley's biggest cask ale brand).
Nineteen new Yorkshire square fermenting
vessels were commissioned in 1996, making
the brewery the largest cask ale site in the
group. A £6 million visitor centre and
museum, Tetley's Brewery Wharf, opened in
1994. Seasonal beers: Autumn Ale (ABV
4.7%), Walker Winter Warmer (OG 1060,
ABV 6.2%).

Tetley Dark Mild or Walker Mild (OG
1032, ABV 3.2%) ◥ A fruity, dark mild with
some hop and a dry finish. A reasonable
match to the former Warrington brew.

Tetley Mild (OG 1032, ABV 3.3%) ◥ A mid-
brown, smooth beer with a light malt and
caramel aroma. A well-balanced taste of
malt and caramel follows, with good
bitterness and a dry, satisfying finish.

Walker Bitter (OG 1033, ABV 3.6%) ◥ A
nutty and fruity light bitter with a dry
aftertaste. Now fuller-flavoured than
previously.

Walker Best Bitter (OG 1036, ABV 3.7%)
◥ A fruity and dry beer with an aggressive
bitterness. As with the Walker Bitter, fuller-
flavoured than before.

Tetley Bitter (OG 1035.5, ABV 3.7%) ◥ A
variable, light, malty beer with a slight malt
and hop aroma leading to a moderate
bitterness and a dry finish. Pale brown in
colour.

Imperial (OG 1042, ABV 4.3%) ◥ A
complex, creamy, copper-coloured beer. A
light malt and fruit nose is followed by a
well-rounded taste of malt, hops and fruit,
leading to a short-lived dry, bitter finish.

For HP&D:

HP&D Bitter (OG 1036, ABV 3.7%)

Allied Domecq Brew Pubs:

FIRKIN

The Firkin Brewery, Allied Domecq House, 2 Waterloo Street, Leeds, W. Yorkshire LS10 1JL. ☎ (0113) 200 2000
FAX (0113) 200 2041

This famous pub brewery chain was founded by David Bruce in 1979, re-launching the brew pub concept in what used to be run-down national brewers' houses. The pubs were refurbished in a back-to-basics fashion and were given in-house breweries, tucked away behind viewing windows. The Bruce's Brewery chain rapidly grew in number until 1988, when he sold all the pubs to Midsummer Leisure (later European Leisure), which, in turn, sold them to Stakis Leisure in 1990. Since 1991, the chain has been owned by Allied Domecq. Much expansion has taken place, with new sites opened in university towns but the callous destruction of some classic pubs to create new Firkins has raised the hackles of many drinkers. The estate currently runs to over 70 pubs, but only 49 of them brew. The remainder are supplied by the brew pubs, so only the actual brew pubs are listed here. Four basic brews are available, usually sold under house names, a 1034 OG/3.4% ABV mild, 1036 OG/3.5% ABV bitter, a stronger bitter at 1043/4.3%, and Dogbolter (OG 1057, ABV 5.6%). Some pubs offer extra one-off brews, including summer and winter ales, and also seen are Stout (OG 1047, ABV 4.6%) and Golden Glory (OG 1051, ABV 5%). All the brews are full mash and most pubs now offer some cask-conditioned beer with no additional gas applied. However, cellar tanks with mixed gas breathers are still used in some outlets.

Current brew pubs:

Faculty & Firkin, Holt Street, Aston University Campus, Gosta Green, Birmingham, W. Midlands B7 4BD.
☎ (0121) 359 6597

Fahrenheit & Firkin, Chobham Road, Woking, Surrey GU2 1HR.
☎ (01483) 714484

Falcon & Firkin, 360 Victoria Park Road, Hackney, London E9 7BT. ☎ (0181) 986 0102

Fathom & Firkin, 20 Chapel Road, Worthing, W. Sussex BN11 1BJ. ☎ (01903) 204431

Feast & Firkin, 229 Woodhouse Lane, Leeds, W. Yorkshire LS2 3AP. ☎ (0113) 244 5076

Fedora & Firkin, Chapel Street, Luton, Bedfordshire LU1 2SE. ☎ (01582) 452130

Felon & Firkin, 26–30 Great George Street, Leeds, W. Yorkshire LS1 3DL
☎ (0113) 245 3198

Fermenter & Firkin, 480 Dudley Road, Wolverhampton, W. Midlands WV2 3AF.
☎ (01902) 454834

Ferret & Firkin, 114 Lots Road, Chelsea, London SW10 0RJ. ☎ (0171) 352 6645

Fiddler & Firkin, 14 South End, Croydon, Surrey CR0 1DL. ☎ (0181) 680 9728

Fielder & Firkin, 346 High Street, Sutton, Surrey SM1 1PR. ☎ (0181) 642 9018

Fieldmouse & Firkin at the Fighting Cocks, St Mary's Row, Moseley, Birmingham, W. Midlands B13 0HW. ☎ (0121) 449 0811

Finch & Firkin, 467 Smithdown Road, Liverpool, Merseyside L15 5AE.
☎ (0151) 733 5267

Finings & Firkin, 91 Station Road, Langley, Oldbury, Warley, W. Midlands B69 4LU.
☎ (0121) 552 5386

Finnesko & Firkin, 10 Dereham Road, Norwich, Norfolk NR2 4AY.
☎ (01603) 617465

Firecracker & Firkin, 2–4 Brighton Road, Southgate, Crawley, W. Sussex RH10 3JT.
☎ (01923) 553196

Firefly & Firkin, 38 Holdenhurst Road, Bournemouth, Dorset BH8 8AD.
☎ (01202) 293576

Fish & Firkin, 53 Alexandra Street, Southend-on-Sea, Essex SS2 6ES.
☎ (01702) 392174

Fizgig & Firkin, St Anne's Well, Lower North Street, Exeter, Devon EX4 9DU.
☎ (01392) 437667

Flag & Firkin, Station Road, Watford, Hertfordshire WD1 1ET. ☎ (01923) 242184

Flamingo & Firkin, 1–7 Beckett Street, Derby DE1 1HT. ☎ (01332) 297598

Flare & Firkin, 225 Holburn Street, Aberdeen AB10 1BP. ☎ (01224) 585836

Fledgling & Firkin, Parliament Square, Hertford SG14 1EX. ☎ (01992) 509287

Flicker & Firkin, 1 Dukes Street, Richmond, Surrey TW9 1HP. ☎ (0181) 332 7807

Flounder & Firkin, 54 Holloway Road, Holloway, London N7 8HP.
☎ (0171) 609 9574

Fly & Firkin, 18 Southfield Road, Middlesbrough, N. Yorkshire TS1 3BZ.
☎ (01642) 253093

Flyer & Firkin, 54 Blagrave Street, Reading, Berkshire RG1 1PZ. ☎ (01734) 569151

Flyman & Firkin, 166–170 Shaftesbury Avenue, London WC2H 8JB.
☎ (0171) 240 7109

Font & Firkin, Union Street, Brighton, E. Sussex BN1 1HB. ☎ (01273) 747727

Footage & Firkin, 137 Grosvenor Street, Manchester M1 7BZ. ☎ (0161) 273 7053

Forger & Firkin, 55–56 Woodridge Road, Guildford, Surrey GU1 4RF. ☎ (01483) 578999

Forester & Firkin, 3 Eastgate Street, Stafford, ST16 2NQ. ☎ (01785) 250755

Fort & Firkin, The Promenade, Windsor, Berkshire SL4 1QX. ☎ (01753) 622273

Foundry & Firkin, 240 West Street, Sheffield, S. Yorkshire S1 4EU. ☎ (0114) 279 5257

Fowl & Firkin, 1–2 The Butts, Coventry, W. Midlands CV1 3GR. ☎ (01203) 231457

Fox & Firkin, 316 Lewisham High Street, Lewisham, London SE13 3HL. ☎ (0181) 690 8343

Fresher & Firkin, 16 Chesterton Road, Cambridge CB4 3AX. ☎ (01223) 324325

Friar & Firkin, 120 Euston Road, Euston, London NW1 2AL. ☎ (0171) 388 0235

Friesian & Firkin, 87 Rectory Grove, Clapham, London SW4 0DR. ☎ (0171) 622 4666

Fringe & Firkin, 2 Goldhawk Road, Shepherd's Bush, London W12 8QD. ☎ (0181) 749 0229

Fuggle & Firkin, 14 Gloucester Street, Gloucester Green, Oxford OX1 2BN. ☎ (01865) 248959

Fuzz & Firkin, 2 Albert Road, Southsea, Portsmouth, Hampshire PO5 2SH. ☎ (01705) 827137

Phantom & Firkin, Leicester Road, Loughborough, Leicestershire LE11 2AG. ☎ (01509) 262051

Pharoah & Firkin, 88–90 High Street, Fulham, London SW6 3LF. ☎ (0171) 731 0732

Philanthropist & Firkin, 11–13 Victoria Street, St Albans, Hertfordshire AL1 3JJ. ☎ (01727) 847021

Philatelist & Firkin, Drill Hall, East Street, Bromley, Kent BR1 1QQ. ☎ (0181) 464 6022

Philosopher & Firkin, 288 Cowley Road, Oxford OX4 1UR. ☎ (01865) 244386

Phoenix & Firkin, 5 Windsor Walk, Camberwell, London SE5 8BB. ☎ (0171) 701 8282

Photographer & Firkin, 23–25 Ealing High Street, London W3 6ND. ☎ (0181) 567 1140

Physician & Firkin, 58 Dalkeith Road, Edinburgh EH16 5AD. ☎ (0131) 662 4746

MINERVA
Minerva Hotel (Allied Domecq Leisure), Nelson Street, Hull, E. Yorkshire HU1 1XE. ☎ (01482) 326909

Full mash operation, set up in 1985 and refurbished in 1995. The pub's own beer is stored under a nitrogen gas blanket in cellar tanks (although the other ales on sale are cask-conditioned). Special brews are produced for special occasions. Tours by arrangement. Beers: Sea Fever Ale (OG 1040, ABV 4%, August–September), Pilots Pride (OG 1042, ABV 4.2%), Midnight Owl (OG 1045, ABV 4.5%, December–February).

REINDEER
See Firkin (re-named Finnesko & Firkin).

ROSE STREET
Rose Street Brewery, 55 Rose Street, Edinburgh EH2 2NH. ☎ (0131) 220 1227

Founded in 1983 and run by Alloa Brewery, supplying a handful of other Alloa outlets with beers produced from malt extract. Beers: Auld Reekie 80/- (OG 1042, ABV 4.1%), Auld Reekie 90/- (OG 1054, ABV 5.3%).

GUINNESS
Guinness Brewing GB, Park Royal Brewery, London NW10 7RR. ☎ (0181) 965 7700 [FAX] (0181) 963 5120

Guinness, for a few years, was the only national brewery which did not produce real ale. There had been no cask beer for decades when, in 1993, at a time when interest in bottle-conditioned beers was reviving, the company decided to axe its naturally-conditioned, bottled stout, Guinness Original. (Guinness Original is still on sale, but only in a brewery-conditioned, pasteurised version, which lacks the complexity and freshness of the bottle-conditioned beer.) However, in 1996, the company launched a new cask-conditioned porter, named after the father of London porter, Ralph Harwood. Brewed at Park Royal, it was distributed by Carlsberg-Tetley and was on sale in around 100 pubs. The beer was withdrawn later that year whilst a new brewing partner to rack the beer into casks was sought (Guinness has no racking facilities), but Guinness confirms that it is committed to this beer and it should soon be on sale once more. The porter apart, all Draught Guinness sold in the UK is keg. In Ireland, Draught Guinness (OG 1038, brewed at Arthur Guinness, St James's Gate, Dublin 8) is not pasteurised but is served with gas pressure. In 1997 it was announced that Guinness was to merge with Grand Metropolitan, although this was being closely studied by the European Commission, who may block the move, as we went to press.

Harwood's Porter Ale (OG 1046, ABV 4.8%)

SCOTTISH COURAGE

Scottish & Newcastle PLC, 111 Holyrood Road, Edinburgh, Lothian EH8 8YS. ☎ (0131) 556 2591 ꜰᴀx (0131) 558 1165

Scottish & Newcastle was formed in 1960, as a merger between Scottish Brewers Ltd. (the former Younger and McEwan breweries) and Newcastle Breweries Ltd. In 1995, it was announced that S&N had agreed to purchase Courage from its Australian owner, Foster's. Courage had been a brewer with no pubs since 1991, following the sale of its pub estate to Inntrepreneur Estates (see Pub Groups), a company Foster's jointly owns with Grand Metropolitan. The Government allowed the S&N takeover to go through without reference to the Monopolies and Mergers Commission, despite the fact that it created Britain's largest brewing company, with nearly 30 per cent of the market in beer production. The consequences for the UK industry were obvious. Brewery rationalisation has already taken place, with the loss of hundreds of jobs and fears for the future of many beer brands. Home Brewery in Nottingham was top of the closures list, along with the Fountain Head brewery at Halifax. This leaves the company with five major UK cask ale breweries, plus keg beer plants in Manchester, Reading and Mortlake (a joint venture with American giant Anheuser-Busch known as The Stag Brewing Company and producing Budweiser). The company also owns the Beamish & Crawford brewery in Cork, Ireland.

Scottish & Newcastle (Retail) at present operates over 2,600 pubs nationwide, around 1,900 being managed houses and some 80 per cent selling cask beer. The pubs are controlled by five regional divisions: Scottish, Tyne, Pennine, Trent and Southern Inns. Themed outlets include, for example, the T&J Bernard and Barras & Co. ale houses and the Rat & Parrot chain. Scottish Courage also continues to have a massive presence in the free trade (particularly through McEwan and Theakston brands and Newcastle Brown Ale), and also dominates many free houses through the loan-tie system of offering financial loans in return for beer sales.

BRISTOL

Scottish Courage Brewing Ltd., The Courage Bristol Brewery, Counterslip, Victoria Street, Bristol BS1 6BX.
☎ (0117) 929 7222 ꜰᴀx (0117) 927 6150

Established in 1702, this brewery was owned and run by the George family from 1788 until 1961, when it was acquired by Courage. Now Scottish Courage's only real ale brewery in the South, it lays claim to being the world's largest dedicated real ale brewery. Though its main beers, Courage

Best and Directors, are very well promoted nationally, Georges Bitter Ale sales are confined mostly to the West Country and South-East Wales. New pumpclips indicate that the beers are brewed only at Bristol, in contrast with the deceptive Theakston (qv) pumpclips. These three beers are all diluted versions of the same original high-gravity brew. A new range of occasional beers has been introduced, based on recipes from the Courage archives and there are plans to focus on the heritage of the brewery by opening a visitor's centre. Occasional/seasonal beers: Old Chopper (OG 1040, ABV 4.1%), Navigator (OG 1043, ABV 4.4%), Rocketeer (OG 1046, ABV 4.5%), Directors Winter Warmer (OG 1055, ABV 5.5%).

Georges Bitter Ale (OG 1032, ABV 3.3%) ◆ An amber, light-bodied session bitter, with a slight malt grain taste, a hoppy aroma and a lasting, dry, bitter finish with some malt, grain and hops. Light, tasty and refreshing.

Matthew Brown Lion Bitter (OG 1034, ABV 3.5%)

Courage Best Bitter (OG 1038, ABV 4%) ◆ A pale brown, medium-bodied, dry and bitter beer with good malt, moderate hops and a balancing sweetness. Dry, bitter finish with malt and a hint of fruit; malt and hop aroma.

Courage Directors (OG 1045, ABV 4.8%) ◲ ◆ A well-balanced, full-bodied, mid-brown malty ale, with grain, hops, malt and fruit in the nose. In the mouth it is dry and bitter with malt, grain, fruits and hops/hop oil, plus a touch of balancing sweetness. Similar, lengthy finish, if less sweet.

FOUNTAIN
Fountain Brewery, 159 Fountainbridge, Edinburgh EH3 9YY. Tel (0131) 229 9377 FAX **(0131) 229 1282**

The Scottish production centre, formerly the home of William McEwan & Co. Ltd., founded in 1856. Its beers are sold under two separate names – McEwan and Younger, depending on the trading area. Occasional beers: Gillespie's Malt Stout (OG 1042, ABV 4.2%), McEwan Export (OG 1043, ABV 4.5%), Raeburn's Edinburgh Ale (OG 1042, ABV 4.7%), McEwan 90/- (OG 1052, ABV 5.5%).

McEwan 70/- or Younger Scotch Bitter (OG 1036, ABV 3.7%) A well-balanced, sweetish brew, becoming more and more rare. Often competitively priced in Wetherspoon pubs.

McEwan 80/- or Younger IPA (OG 1042, ABV 4.5%) ◆ A thin-bodied beer with a cloying metallic aftertaste. Once a classic, now bland and sweet with some maltiness.

Younger No. 3 (OG 1042, ABV 4.5%) ◆ A malty and thin-bodied beer, like McEwan 80/- with added caramel.

JOHN SMITH'S
Scottish Courage Brewing Ltd., John Smith's Brewery, Tadcaster, N. Yorkshire LS24 9SA. ☎ **(01937) 832091** FAX **(01937) 833766**

A business founded at the Old Brewery in 1758 and taken over by John Smith (brother of Samuel Smith – see Independents) in 1847. The present brewery was built in 1879 and became part of the Courage empire in 1970. Major expansion has taken place since the formation of Scottish Courage, with 11 new fermentation vessels installed. Tours by arrangement. Bottle-conditioned beer:

Imperial Russian Stout (OG 1102, ABV 10%, occasional) ◲.

Webster's Green Label Best (OG 1032, ABV 3.2%)

Webster's Yorkshire Bitter (OG 1035, ABV 3.5%)

Bitter (OG 1036, ABV 3.8%) A copper-coloured beer with a mix of hops and malt in the nose. Malt dominates the taste but hops take over in the finish.

Magnet (OG 1040, ABV 4%) An almost ruby-coloured beer. Hops, malt and citrus fruit can be identified in the nose and there are complex flavours of nuts, hops and fruit, giving way to a long, malty finish.

THEAKSTON
T&R Theakston Ltd., Wellgarth, Masham, Ripon, N. Yorkshire HG4 4YD. ☎ **(01765) 689544** FAX **(01765) 689769**

Company formed in 1827 and based at this brewery since 1875. Theakston became part of S&N in 1987 when its parent company, Matthew Brown, was swallowed up. More than £1 million has been spent on this brewery in the 1990s, reflecting the 'national' status its brews have been given by Scottish Courage, yet most of Theakston's production now takes place in Newcastle. The same pump clips are used for Masham and Newcastle beers, so the consumer is not told whether the beer actually comes from Theakston's brewery. There is a brewery shop (ring for opening hours) and tours can be taken by arrangement. Occasional beers: Hogshead Bitter (OG 1040, ABV 4.1%), Masham Ale (OG 1065, ABV 6.6%).

Mild Ale (OG 1035, ABV 3.5%) ◲ ◆ A rich and smooth mild ale with a creamy body and a rounded liquorice taste. Dark ruby/amber in colour, with a mix of malt and fruit in the nose and a dry, hoppy aftertaste.

Black Bull Bitter (OG 1037, ABV 3.9%) ◆ Unique to the Masham brewery, this malty bitter can end dry and refreshing with lasting fruit.

Best Bitter (OG 1038, ABV 3.9%) ◆ A light beer which is easily faulted if old but can show delicate hop character. Look out for regional variations.

XB (OG 1044, ABV 4.6%) ◆ Often found with little character, this can be a drinkable beer when fresh, with its smooth finish and rounded fruitiness.

Old Peculier (OG 1057, ABV 5.7%) ◲ ◧ ◆ A rich and complex ale with a sweet liquorice aroma, a smooth mouthfeel and malty, roast character. It ends memorably spicy and dry.

TYNE
Tyne Brewery, Gallowgate, Newcastle upon Tyne, Tyne & Wear NE99 1RA. ☎ **(0191) 232 5091** FAX **(0191) 261 6297**

The home of Newcastle Breweries Ltd., formed in 1890 as an amalgamation of five local breweries. In recent years it brewed no real ale, until most of Theakston's production was transferred here, but no indication is given at the point of sale or in advertising that Theakston beers are brewed in Newcastle (for tasting notes, see Theakston).

Theakston Mild Ale (OG 1035, ABV 3.5%)
Theakston Best Bitter (OG 1039, ABV 3.8%)
Newcastle Exhibition (OG 1040, ABV 4.4%)
Theakston XB (OG 1045, ABV 4.6%)
Theakston Old Peculier (OG 1057, ABV 5.7%)

Scottish Courage Brew Pubs:

ABINGTON PARK
Abington Park Brewery Co., Wellingborough Road, Northampton NN1 4EY. ☎ (01604) 31240

Victorian-styled brew pub, opened in 1984 by Chef & Brewer and now owned by S&N Retail (Trent Inns Ltd.) Equipped with a five-barrel plant, the pub stores its beer in cellar tanks under mixed nitrogen/CO_2 at atmospheric pressure. Beers: Cobblers Ale (OG 1037, ABV 3.3%), Becket (brewed with malt, wheat and maize, OG 1042, ABV 3.6%), Extra (OG 1047, ABV 4.3%).

GREYHOUND
Greyhound Brewery Company Ltd., 151 Greyhound Lane, Streatham Common, London SW16 5NJ. ☎ (0181) 677 9962

Set up in 1984, the Greyhound brew pub was acquired by Scottish & Newcastle in 1993. Improvements to the plant began in 1994. Cellar tanks, with a blanket of CO_2, are used at the pub. Beers: Special (OG 1037, ABV 3.6%), Streatham Strong (OG 1047, ABV 4.3%), Dynamite (OG 1055, ABV 4.9%).

ORANGE
The Orange Brewery, 37–39 Pimlico Road, Pimlico, London SW1W 8NE. ☎ (0171) 824 8002

Brewery opened in 1983 and refurbished in 1995. The full mash brews are stored in cellar tanks and are kept under blanket pressure. Tours by arrangement. Beers: SW1 (OG 1039, ABV 3.8%), Porter (OG 1045, ABV 4.3%), SW2 (OG 1049, ABV 4.8%), Victoria Lager (OG 1049, ABV 5.5%), Spiritual Reunion (OG 1058, ABV 6.1%, winter).

YORKSHIRE GREY
The Yorkshire Grey Brewery, 26 Theobalds Road, Holborn, London WC1X 8PN. ☎ (0171) 405 8287 FAX (0171) 831 2359

Brew pub extensively refurbished in 1995. The beers are now produced from full mashes but a CO_2 blanket is applied to the cellar tanks. Beers: Barristers Best (OG 1040, ABV 3.8%), Summer Horne Wheat Beer (ABV 4.1%, occasional), QC Best Bitter (OG 1046, ABV 4.5%), Birthday Bevvy Porter (ABV 4.6%, occasional), Patently Oblivious (ABV 4.6%, occasional), Harvest Festival Ale (ABV 4.7%, occasional), Lordship Supreme Old Ale (OG 1050, ABV 5%).

WHITBREAD
The Whitbread Beer Company, Whitbread PLC, Porter Tun House, Capability Green, Luton, Bedfordshire LU1 3LS. ☎ (01582) 391166 FAX (01582) 397397

The smallest of the national brewers, Whitbread has been the most pro-active in the real ale market in the 1990s. This has represented something of a conversion because, for many drinkers, the company's name suggests only one thing – brewery closures. In the 1970s and 1980s, Whitbread wielded a sharp axe and numerous small breweries felt its cruel edge. The likes of Strong's of Romsey, Wethered of Marlow, Fremlins of Faversham, Chester's of Salford and Higsons of Liverpool were all shut down, without a thought for local tradition or customers' preferences. The most recent closure was the Exchange Brewery in Sheffield in 1993. After that Whitbread seemed to have re-discovered cask-conditioned beer and invested heavily in its real ale portfolio. The retail side of the company turned dozens of pubs into Tut 'n' Shive and Hogshead alehouses to support this initiative and there were also some noteworthy special brew promotions, involving limited edition beers brewed in Cheltenham and Castle Eden. However, the company seems now to be switching its emphasis back towards keg products. Many of the various regional beers which survived brewery closures by transferring to other breweries have now been discontinued altogether, and the only cask beer enjoying substantial financial support is Boddingtons Bitter. Trading agreements with regional brewers like Wadworth and Marston's now help fill out Whitbread's cask portfolio. In addition to the cask ale breweries, the company operates keg beer factories in Magor in South Wales and Samlesbury in Lancashire.

Whitbread's 3,850 pubs are controlled by two divisions: Whitbread Inns (managed houses) and Whitbread Pub Partnerships (pubs leased out, usually on 20-year terms).

BODDINGTONS
Strangeways Brewery, PO Box 23, Strangeways, Manchester M60 3WB.
☎ (0161) 828 2000 FAX (0161) 828 2213

Brewery established in 1778 and acquired by Whitbread when the Boddingtons company, which had already taken-over and closed Oldham Brewery, retreated to pub owning and other leisure enterprises. Now Whitbread is pushing Boddingtons Bitter relentlessly nationwide and the beer takes up 90 per cent of the brewery's already expanded production capacity. To create room, Oldham Best (OB) Bitter (OG 1037.5, ABV 3.8%) has been transferred to Burtonwood Brewery (see Independents). Tours by arrangement (charge).

Boddingtons Mild (OG 1032, ABV 3.1%) ◆ A thin, dark mild with a sweet caramel and malt flavour, and a short aftertaste. It has now disappeared from many tied houses.

OB Mild (OG 1032, ABV 3%) ◆ A reddish-brown beer with a malty aroma. A smooth roast malt and fruit flavour follows, then a malty and surprisingly bitter aftertaste.

Boddingtons Bitter (OG 1034.5, ABV 3.8%) ◆ A pale beer in which the grainy malt, hop and bitter character can be spoiled by a rather cloying sweetness.

CASTLE EDEN
Castle Eden Brewery, PO Box 13, Castle Eden, Co. Durham TS27 4SX.
☎ (01429) 836007

Originally attached to a 17th-century coaching inn, the old Nimmo's brewery (established in 1826) was purchased by Whitbread in 1963. It has found a niche within the Whitbread group and now produces some of the company's better quality beers.

Higsons Mild (OG 1034, ABV 3.4%) ◆ A fruity, dark mild with some roast malt and caramel. Fairly bitter and dry.

Higsons Bitter (OG 1038, ABV 3.8%) ◆ A hoppy and fruity bitter with some sweetness and vanilla notes. Thin, inoffensive and bland.

Castle Eden Ale (OG 1042, ABV 4.2%) 🍺 ◆ A light, creamy, malty, sweet ale with fruit and a mellow, dry bitterness to finish. Easily marred by poor cellarmanship.

Fuggles Imperial IPA (OG 1055, ABV 5.5%) A pale but robust beer which oozes hops and has a citrus flavour.

FLOWERS
The Flowers Brewery, Monson Avenue, Cheltenham, Gloucestershire GL50 4EL.
☎ (01242) 265415 FAX (01242) 265404

Brewery established in 1760 by banker John Gardner, which became the Cheltenham Original Brewery when rebuilt in 1898. It merged in 1958 with Stroud Brewery to form West Country Breweries Ltd. and was acquired by Whitbread in 1963. The Flowers brewing operation and title were transferred from Stratford-upon-Avon in 1968 and the brewery became the centre for Whitbread cask ale in the South when it absorbed production from other breweries as they closed. Most of these beers have since moved on or have been phased out and the emphasis now is on improving the quality of the two Flowers beers, plus Trophy and the two Abroad Cooper beers (the last brewed for Whitbread's Hogshead chain of pubs).

Flowers IPA (OG 1036, ABV 3.6%) A light, spicy, floral hop aroma precedes malty bitterness in the taste. Citrus hop finish.

Trophy Bitter (OG 1036, ABV 3.8%) A mellow balance of hop, malt and grain flavours follows a malty and light, floral hop aroma. Dry hop finish.

Whitbread Best Bitter (OG 1036, ABV 3.6%) A beer with light malt and nut aromas, with a hint of hops. Some malt in the mouth, before a malt, nuts and light fruit finish.

Summer Abroad Cooper (ABV 4.1%)

Flowers Original (OG 1044, ABV 4.4%) A fresh lemon/blackcurrant dry hop aroma leads to a distinctive, balanced taste of malt, fruit and hops, before a long, hoppy bitter finish.

The Abroad Cooper (OG 1049, ABV 5.1%) ◆ A dark red/copper-coloured beer with a fruity aroma. A sweet malt taste is followed by a slight bitter aftertaste.

Whitbread Brew Pubs:

ALFORD ARMS
Alford Arms Brewhouse, Frithsden, Hertfordshire.

Brewery closed.

FELLOWS, MORTON & CLAYTON
Fellows, Morton & Clayton Brewhouse Company, 54 Canal Street, Nottingham NG1 7EH. ☎ (0115) 950 6795 . (0115) 955 1412

This pub began brewing in 1980 and still uses malt extract. Some strong seasonal beers are also produced (6%+). Beers: Fellows Bitter (OG 1041, ABV 3.9%), Clayton's Strong Ale (OG 1052, ABV 5%).

FOX & NEWT
Fox & Newt, Leeds, W. Yorkshire.

Brewery closed.

FROG & PARROT
Frog & Parrot, 64 Division Street, Sheffield, S. Yorkshire S1 4SG. ☎ (0114) 272 1280

Malt extract brew pub which began production in 1982. Beers are kept in casks and are sometimes available in a handful of other pubs. Paying tours available. Beers: Do's Brew (ABV 3.9%), Reckless (OG 1045, ABV 4.6%), Conqueror (OG 1066, ABV 6.2%), Armageddon (ABV

6.9%), Roger & Out (OG 1125, ABV 12.5%). Bottle-conditioned beer: Roger & Out (OG 1125, ABV 12.5%).

LASS O'GOWRIE
Lass O'Gowrie Brewhouse, 36 Charles Street, Manchester M1 7DB. ☎ (0161) 273 6932

Victorian pub, revamped and re-opened as a malt extract brew pub in 1983 and now part of the Hogshead division. The brewery in the cellar is visible from the bar and the beer is now stored in casks. Tours by arrangement. Beers: LOG 35 (OG 1035, ABV 3.8%), LOG 42 (OG 1042, ABV 4.7%), Centurion (ABV 5%, occasional), Graduation (ABV 5.1%, occasional).

OLD COURT
The Old Court Brewhouse, Queen Street, Huddersfield, W. Yorkshire HD1 2SL. ☎ (01484) 454035

Malt extract brew pub opened in 1994 in Huddersfield's former County Court. The building's character has been retained and the brewing copper, protruding from the lower ground floor into the ground floor public bar, provides an unusual talking point. Beers: Coppers' Ale (ABV 3.4%), M'Lud (ABV 4%), 1825 (ABV 4.5%), Maximum Sentence (ABV 6%).

Another National brewery lost: The HP&D Brewery Tap in Wolverhampton, now just a Firkin.

NOTES ON NATIONAL BREWERS AND BEERS

Pub Groups

ALLIED DOMECQ
See Nationals, Carlsberg-Tetley.

ASCOT ESTATES
See Mayfair Taverns.

BEARDS
Beards of Sussex Ltd., West End, Herstmonceux, E. Sussex BN27 4NN.
☎ (01323) 832777 [FAX] (01323) 832833
Former brewing company (founded in 1797) which opted out of production in 1959. After contracting out its beers to Harveys from 1960 to 1986, Beards then abandoned brewing altogether and became a cask ale wholesaler as well as a pub company. The wholesaling division was sold off in 1994 and Beards currently runs 46 traditional pubs in Sussex (11 managed, 34 tenanted and one joint venture with Whitbread/ Beefeater), which can sell any beers from the wide list offered by The Beer Seller wholesaler and from Scottish Courage. A new beer, Beards Best Bitter, is now brewed for the company by Arundel Brewery (see Independents).

CAFE INNS
Café Inns PLC, 3 St Thomas's Road, Chorley, Lancashire PR7 1HP.
☎ (01257) 262424 [FAX] (01257) 260497
Company established in 1987 and now running 85 outlets (73 tenanted, 12 managed) in the North-West. The figure includes one restaurant and two coffee shops. Pubs sell beers from Bass and Scottish Courage (Matthew Brown).

CENTURY INNS
Century Inns PLC, Belasis Business Centre, Coxwold Way, Billingham TS23 4EA.
☎ (01642) 343426 [FAX] (01642) 345603
Company formed in 1991 by Camerons employees with the purchase of 185 pubs from Bass. The intention was to establish a pub estate for a buyout of the Camerons brewery, but this was scuppered by Brent Walker. The number of pubs now stands at 422, 22 managed and the rest traditionally tenanted (three-year agreements), with pubs located down the north-eastern side of the country, from Tyneside to Lincolnshire. Four of the pubs are branded 'Dr Brown's' and feature a strong food emphasis and live music. Beer sales in the tenanted houses are still confined to Bass, Scottish Courage and Carlsberg-Tetley products (plus the guest ales these companies supply), though the managed pubs also take some beers from smaller breweries. In summer 1996, Century took over and closed Stocks Brewery in Doncaster. Some Stocks beer is now produced under contract by Hull (see Independents). In summer 1997 Century agreed to buy 78 managed pubs from Pubmaster, including the Tap & Spile branded pubs.

CM GROUP
See Commer Inns.

TOM COBLEIGH
Tom Cobleigh PLC, Phoenix House, Oak Tree Lane, Mansfield, Nottinghamshire NG18 4LF.
☎ (01623) 638800 [FAX] (01623) 638820
Company established in 1992 with two pubs. Since then the estate has grown to 71, 17 tenanted, the remainder managed. The company was taken over by Rank in October 1996 but the direction of the business appears unaltered. The pubs, which aim to conform to the company's slogan of 'unspoilt pubs for nice people', are located mainly in the East Midlands. The tenanted ones were acquired from Whitbread in 1994, though these are signed as belonging to The Nice Pub Company. Licensees choose beers from a head office range of national and regional ales, with Bass and Scottish Courage the main suppliers. A list of rotating guest beers is also offered.

COMMER INNS
CM Group Ltd., Magnet House, Station Road, Tadcaster, N. Yorkshire LS24 9JF.
☎ (01937) 833311 [FAX] (01937) 834236
Thirty-five-strong pub chain in North-East England. The pubs were initially leased, then acquired, from Whitbread, and are all traditionally tenanted. No guest beers are available to tenants, with supplies coming from Whitbread, Scottish Courage, Bass and Carlsberg-Tetley. Parent company CM Group also runs Magnet Management Services (MMS), which holds and operates pubs for brewers (currently 45).

CONQUEST INNS
Conquest Inns Ltd., The Old Vicarage, 10 Church Street, Rickmansworth, Hertfordshire WD3 1BS.
☎ (01923) 711118 [FAX] (01923) 711128
Company set up to obtain 57 pubs from Bass in 1994, backed by Jersey's Ann Street

brewery. Most of the current total of 54 pubs (11 managed, 41 three-year tenanted, two on 15-year leases) are in the South-East. Beers come solely from Bass and Scottish Courage, and tenants have no guest beer rights.

JT DAVIES

JT Davies & Sons Ltd., 7 Aberdeen Road, Croydon, Surrey CR0 1EQ.
☎ (0181) 681 3222 FAX (0181) 760 0390

Wine merchants now controlling 35 tenancies and eight managed houses in the South-East. Its main suppliers are Bass and Scottish Courage, with some beers taken from Fuller's and Harveys.

DAVYS

The Davy Group, 59–63 Bermondsey Street, London SE1 3XF.
☎ (0171) 407 9670 FAX (0171) 407 5844

Long established (1870) wine merchants which has been opening wine bars and ale and port houses in the London since 1965, taking previously unlicensed properties (largely basements) and creating a Dickensian, sawdust, nooks and crannies type of establishment. Two beers are sold: Davy's Ordinary Bitter (ABV 4%) and Davy's Old Wallop (ABV 4.8%), both re-badged brews of undeclared origin (though Courage Best and Directors fit the bill). These are usually served in pewter or copper tankards. The company currently runs around 50 outlets, including the White Hart Hotel in Exeter.

DISCOVERY INNS

See Enterprise Inns.

ELDRIDGE POPE

Eldridge, Pope & Co. PLC, Weymouth Avenue, Dorchester, Dorset ST1 1QT.
☎ (01305) 251251 FAX (01305) 258300

Founded as the Green Dragon Brewery in 1837, Eldridge Pope finally divorced itself from brewing in 1996 when it split into two wings, the brewing side becoming known as Thomas Hardy Brewery (see Independents). The company now runs 200 pubs, 124 managed, the rest tenanted.

ENTERPRISE INNS

Enterprise Inns Ltd., Friars Gate, Stratford Road, Solihull, W. Midlands B90 4BN.
☎ (0121) 733 7700 FAX (0121) 733 6447

Midlands-based company founded in 1991 with the purchase of 372 pubs from Bass. The total now stands at around 1,150, following the acquisition of John Labatt Retail in 1996 and Discovery Inns in May 1997. About half the pubs are run on a 21-year lease basis and the remainder are tenanted, with beers provided by Bass, Whitbread, Carlsberg-Tetley, Scottish Courage and Wolverhampton & Dudley.

Licensees are not allowed to buy beers outside the company. The pubs are situated across the country, with the exception of Scotland. The Hop House brew pub in Kingsthorpe, Northamptonshire (see Independents, Cock) has now been sold.

FAMOUS PUB COMPANY

Famous Pub Company PLC, 510 Hertford Road, Enfield, Greater London EN3 5SS.
☎ (0181) 805 4055 FAX (0181) 805 0115

Expanding pub company established with the purchase of 37 pubs from Whitbread in February 1996 and floated on the stock market the same day. The estate now totals some 45 pubs, all traditionally tenanted (one-year contracts) and supplied with beer by Whitbread. Some tenants are allowed a guest beer.

FITZGERALD'S

Sir John Fitzgerald Ltd., Café Royal Buildings, 8 Nelson Street, Newcastle upon Tyne, Tyne & Wear NE1 5AW.
☎ (0191) 232 0664 FAX (0191) 222 1764

Long-established, family-owned, property and pubs company, dating from the end of the last century. Its pubs convey a 'free house' image, most offering a decent choice of cask beers, including guest ales. All 27 pubs (26 managed, one tenanted) are located in the North-East.

GRAY

Gray & Sons (Chelmsford) Ltd., Rignals Lane, Galley Wood, Chelmsford, Essex CM2 8RE.
☎ (01245) 475181 FAX (01245) 475182

A brewery which ceased production at its Chelmsford brewery in 1974 and which now supplies its 49 tied, tenanted pubs in Essex with beers from Greene King (chiefly IPA and Abbot Ale) and Shepherd Neame (Master Brew Bitter or Spitfire), as well as various guest ales.

GREENALLS

Greenalls Group PLC, PO Box 2, Greenalls Avenue, Warrington, Cheshire WA4 6RH.
☎ (01925) 651234 FAX (01925) 444734

Former brewing giant which destroyed many fine independent breweries before turning its back on brewing in 1991. On a 1980s rampage, Greenalls stormed the Midlands, taking over and closing the Wem, Davenports, Simpkiss and Shipstone's breweries. Since the closure of its own Warrington brewery, Greenalls brands have been brewed by Carlsberg-Tetley, and are now produced at Burton upon Trent. The company further demonstrated its contempt for brewing and pub traditions by bulldozing the famous Tommy Ducks pub in Manchester under the cover of night in 1993, ignoring local planning legislation.

Following its acquisition of Devenish in the same year, and the takeover of The Boddington Pub Company in 1995, the company now operates around 2,500 pubs, about 1,200 of which are tenanted. The Boddingtons acquisition included the Liquid Assets wholesaling arm and this, together with Greenalls own Tavern distribution company, has made Greenalls the country's largest beer wholesaler. Pubwise, Whitbread beers can be found in the former Devenish estate, and these are also sold in the former Boddingtons pubs. Some Liverpool pubs have been re-branded as Cains pubs and sell Cains beers. A new scheme, giving licensees the option of four guest beer programmes (some including unusual microbreweries' beers), was initiated in summer 1997. Various theme outlets have been established, including Irish pubs, Jungle Bungles, Ale & Hearty food pubs and Porters Ale Houses.

GROSVENOR INNS

Grosvenor Inns PLC, The Old Schoolhouse, London Road, Shenley, Hertfordshire WD7 9DX.
☎ (01923) 855837 ᴙ (01923) 857992

Group running 48 (43 managed, five tenanted) pubs in the South-East, many of which are leased from Inntrepreneur or other companies and are tied to Scottish Courage beers. The other pubs take beers from Whitbread, Fuller's and Wadworth, as well as Scottish Courage. Certain licensees are now able to purchase guest beers from a list of approved wholesalers. Grosvenor plans to develop its estate, establishing more of its Slug & Lettuces (currently 17 pubs, but aiming to add another 20 in the next two years). The three Bar Central houses have now been sold. David 'Firkin' Bruce is a director of the company and his Hedgehog & Hogshead brew pubs (see Independents) are also part of the Grosvenor empire.

HEAVITREE

Heavitree Brewery PLC, Trood Lane, Matford, Exeter, Devon EX2 8YP.
☎ (01392) 258406 ᴙ (01392) 411697

West Country brewery (established 1790) which gave up production in 1970 to concentrate on running pubs. The current estate (largely in Devon) stands at 116 – 11 managed, and the rest tenanted or leased out (on ten- or 21-year contracts). The pubs are tied to taking beers from The Whitbread Cask Collection, with some products from Bass and Eldridge Pope.

INN BUSINESS

Inn Business Group PLC, Tingewick Road, Buckingham MK18 1GD.
☎ (01280) 822663 ᴙ (01280) 823728

Inn Business currently runs 518 pubs in southern England (some in the Midlands and the North-East), following the

acquisition of Marr Taverns and Sycamore Taverns in 1996. Only 23 pubs are managed, the rest are leased out (most on three-year agreements). Beers come from Whitbread, Bass, Carlsberg-Tetley and Scottish Courage, and include the guest beers these supply.

INN KENT GROUP

Inn Kent Group Ltd., Victoria Hotel, 141 Week Street, Maidstone, Kent ME14 1RE.
☎ (01622) 661782 ᴙ (01622) 661717

Pub group formed in 1991 as Inn Kent Leisure, with an enterprising guest beer and price promotion policy in some of its 40 or so Kent pubs. Otherwise beers come from Scottish Courage.

INNTREPRENEUR

Inntrepreneur Pub Company Ltd., Mill House, Aylesbury Road, Thame, Oxfordshire OX9 3AT.
☎ (01844) 262000 ᴙ (01844) 261332

The pub-owning company formed by Courage (Foster's) and Grand Metropolitan as part of a pubs-for-breweries swap in 1991. In the deal, Courage bought up all Grand Met.'s (Watney's) breweries, with most of Courage's pubs taken over by Inntrepreneur. Inntrepreneur has led the way with the long lease (20 years) as a replacement for the traditional tenancy, a move which has sadly seen many valued former Courage tenants leave the trade. In 1995, the company belatedly changed tack and installed a new management team to switch the emphasis from property investment to pub operating. Following the sale of 1,410 pubs to a holding company, Spring Inns (qv), in 1996, Inntrepreneur currently operates 2,906 pubs (228 tenanted, 18 managed and the rest on long leases). Scottish Courage remains the sole supplier until March 1998, although the pubs have the right to stock a guest beer of their own choosing. Beyond March 1998, the pubs will still be tied to products approved by Inntrepreneur, although the company is looking to broaden its portfolio of beers. Existing publicans will retain their guest beer rights, but new publicans signing leases after this date will have no guest beer entitlement.

MAYFAIR TAVERNS

Mayfair Taverns Ltd., The Old Malt House, St John's Road, Banbury, Oxfordshire OX16 8HX.
☎ (01295) 275012 ᴙ (01295) 278677

Company established with a management buyout from Ascot Estates and the purchase of 251 Ascot pubs in April 1996 (Ascot's remaining pubs are being gradually disposed of as the company winds down). The pubs are spread throughout most of the UK, as far north as Bradford and Manchester, and are either three-year tenanted or leased out on 20-year contracts. Beers are supplied entirely by Scottish Courage and Carlsberg-Tetley.

MERCURY TAVERNS

Mercury Taverns PLC, Mercury House, Amber Business Village, Amington, Tamworth, Staffordshire B77 4RP.
☎ (01827) 310000 [FAX] (01827) 310530

Company running 160 pubs (31 managed, the rest tenanted), scattered from Cumbria and the North-East to South Wales and into London and the South-East. Brewers Marston's and Wolverhampton & Dudley jointly acquired two-thirds of the company in 1996 and their beers are now supplied to the pubs. Part of the group is the Irish-themed Dublin Pub Company (three outlets and more planned) and the Hog & Stump (formerly Flamingo) brew pub (see Independents).

OLD ENGLISH

The Old English Pub Company PLC, 3 Reliant House, Oakmere Mews, Oakmere Land, Potters Bar, Hertfordshire EN6 5DT.
☎ (01707) 665175 [FAX] (01707) 664767

Five-year-old company now running 88 pubs and looking for 120 by the turn of the century. All the pubs are managed and are largely centred in southern England and the Midlands, from East Anglia and the northern Home Counties across to Gloucestershire. Typically olde-worlde in style, they all have restaurants and about half offer accommodation. All sell cask ale, the main range coming from Scottish Courage, with guests supplied by The Beer Seller wholesaler. Old English has had a full stock market listing since May 1997.

PARAMOUNT

Paramount PLC, Suite H3, Steam Mill Business Centre, Steam Mill Street, Chester CH3 5AN.
☎ (01244) 321171 [FAX] (01244) 317665

Business founded in 1987 as Silver Bear, a games manufacturing company, becoming Paramount in 1988 when it began acquiring pubs. The company is part-owned by Greenalls, Burtonwood and Bass, and now runs 211 pubs, which are centred within 80 miles of Chester. Twenty-two are leased out on long contracts. Licensees are generally restricted to the Burtonwood, Bass, Whitbread and Scottish Courage lists, though some Cains beers are also sold. Two pubs acquired from The Boddington Pub Company continue as 'ale houses', with a greater choice. In 1996 a new chief executive was appointed and a £2.6 million rights issue was made.

PHOENIX INNS

Phoenix Inns Ltd., Units 1 & 2, Thame Business Park, Wenman Road, Thame, Oxfordshire OX9 3XA.
☎ (01844) 262200 [FAX] (01844) 262237

Company running around 1,300 former Inntrepreneur Estates pubs in England and Wales, of which just under 800 are leased out, the rest being tenanted. All the pubs are officially free of tie, with the choice of beers left to the licensees, although favourable terms are available from Whitbread via the PINT (Phoenix Inns Negotiated Terms) scheme. As we went to press, Phoenix looked set to acquire the Spring Inns estate of 1,400 pubs.

PUB ESTATE COMPANY

The Pub Estate Company Ltd., 3–5 Ashfield Road, Chorley, Lancashire PR7 1LH.
☎ (01257) 266299 [FAX] (01257) 233918

Company established with the purchase of 230 pubs from S&N and now consolidated by taking its sister companies, The Second and Third Pub Estate Companies, under its wing. It currently has 335 pubs (28 managed, the rest tenanted or leased) which are based in the North of England and Scotland. According to their existing contracts, the pubs variously sell beers from Scottish Courage, Carlsberg-Tetley, Bass or Whitbread, but some do have guest beer rights. The company's aim is to convert all pubs to its own three-year lease which would offer no guest beer entitlement and would mean all pubs being served by a favoured supplier, probably Scottish Courage.

PUBMASTER

Pubmaster Ltd., Greenbank, Hartlepool TS24 7QS.
☎ (01429) 266699 [FAX] (01429) 278457

Company formed in 1991 to take over the pub estate of Brent Walker (ex-Camerons and Tolly Cobbold pubs). In 1992, 734 houses were leased from Allied, and other acquisitions have been made from Whitbread and Bass. Pubmaster currently runs about 1,500 pubs across the country, 1,400 of which are tenanted (three-year contracts). Its Tap & Spile chain of traditional alehouses which offer an excellent choice of beers, including a house brew, Tap & Spile Premium (ABV 4.3%, from Mansfield Brewery), was sold (along with the BieRRex European-style bars and other pubs) to Century Inns in summer 1997. Pubmaster pubs stock beers from Bass, Carlsberg-Tetley, Whitbread and some regional independents.

RANDALLS VAUTIER
Randalls Vautier Ltd., PO Box 43, Clare Street, St Helier, Jersey JE4 8NZ.
☎ (01534) 887788 [FAX] (01534) 888350

Brewery which ceased production in 1992. It now runs 30 pubs (14 managed, the rest tenanted with three-year agreements) on Jersey which sell beers from Bass, Whitbread, Scottish Courage and Marston's. Not to be confused with Randalls of Guernsey (see Independents).

REGENT INNS
Regent Inns PLC, 10 Ely Place, London EC1N 6RY.
☎ (0171) 405 8855 [FAX] (0171) 242 3103

Company founded in 1980 and now owning 75 managed pubs in London and the Home Counties. Further acquisitions are continually sought and expansion into the Midlands and the North is taking place. The pubs are generally allowed to preserve their individual identities, but some are branded Walkabout Inns, Harvey Floorbangers, Jongleurs or Spoofers. A wide range of beers is sold (the company has contracts with Bass, Scottish Courage and Whitbread, plus half a dozen regional breweries, but licensees can also take beer from The Beer Seller wholesaler). Regent Inns also owns over six per cent of shares in Surrey Free Inns (qv).

RYAN
Ryan Elizabeth Holdings PLC, Ryan Precinct, 33 Fore Street, Ipswich, Suffolk IP4 1JL.
☎ (01473) 217458 [FAX] (01473) 258237

This company's 54 pubs in East Anglia (many bought from national brewers) are mostly leased to individual operators on 35-year contracts, although eight are managed. The pubs are generally free, but some have a tie to Bass. A subsidiary company, Elizabeth Hotels, currently runs six pubs.

SCORPIO INNS
Scorpio Inns Ltd., Commerce House, Abbey Road, Torquay, Devon TQ2 5PJ.
☎ (01803) 296111 [FAX] (01803) 296202

Pub group formed in 1991 and now running 100 pubs leased from Whitbread (nearly all tenanted). These stock beers from Whitbread and Bass and are located in South Wales, the Bristol and Hereford areas and along the M4 corridor to Swindon.

SPRING INNS
Spring Inns Management Ltd., Mill House, Aylesbury Road, Thame, Oxfordshire OX9 3AT.
☎ (01844) 262000 [FAX] (01844) 261332

Holding company set up in May 1996 to purchase 1,410 pubs from Inntrepreneur, allowing Inntrepreneur to target its resources on a smaller estate. These pubs looked set to be sold to Phoenix Inns (qv) as we went to press.

SURREY FREE INNS
Surrey Free Inns PLC, Headley House, Headley Road, Grayshott, Hindhead, Surrey GU26 6TU.
☎ (01428) 602300 [FAX] (01428) 602301

Established in 1986, Surrey Free Inns is now AIM listed and runs around 40 pubs and café bars in London and the South of England. The number is set to increase, with further acquisitions planned for the first part of 1998.

SYCAMORE TAVERNS
See Inn Business.

TRENT TAVERNS
Trent Taverns Ltd., PO Box 1061, Gringley on the Hill, Doncaster, S. Yorkshire DN10 4ED.
☎ (01777) 817408 [FAX] (01777) 817247

Company set up by a former S&N employee. Its 83 tenanted pubs in the Midlands and the South are mostly leased from Whitbread, with some freehold acquisitions. They sell only beers from the Whitbread and Scottish Courage lists.

WETHERSPOONS
JD Wetherspoon PLC, Wetherspoon House, Central Park, Reeds Crescent, Watford, Hertfordshire WD1 1QH.
☎ (01923) 477777 [FAX] (01923) 219810

Expanding national pub group, founded by Tim Martin, which opened its first pub in 1979 and went public in 1992. It currently owns over 170 managed pubs, most in and around London but with others scattered across England, Scotland and Wales. Many of the pubs are conversions from shops, featuring standard wood and granite decor and common names like JJ Moon's and other 'Moon' titles. No music is played in any of the pubs, all offer no-smoking areas and food is served all day. There are three standard beers from Scottish Courage available to managers: Theakston Best Bitter, Younger Scotch and Courage Directors. Regional variants come from the likes of Fuller's, Banks's, Cains and Wadworth. Additional beers from microbreweries are chosen by managers from a central list.

WHARFEDALE TAVERNS

Wharfedale Taverns Ltd., Croft House, Audby Lane, Wetherby, W. Yorkshire LS22 4DN.

☎ (01937) 580805 [FAX] (01937) 580806

Company set up in 1993 by former Tetley employees to lease 90 pubs from Allied. The estate total currently stands at 60 pubs, ten of which are traditionally tenanted (three-year agreements), the remainder managed. Some are managed for banks, receivers, etc. The pubs are situated in Yorkshire, the North-West and the northern Midlands, and the main beers come from Carlsberg-Tetley and Scottish Courage.

WHITE ROSE INNS

White Rose Inns PLC, Chantrell House, 1 Chantrell Court, The Calls, Leeds, W. Yorkshire LS2 7HA.

☎ (0113) 246 1332 [FAX] (0113) 246 1350

Group with 30 tenancies and six managed houses in Yorkshire. The main supplier is Carlsberg-Tetley.

WILLIAMS

James Williams (Narberth), 7 Spring Gardens, Narberth, Pembrokeshire SA67 7BP.

☎ (01834) 860318 [FAX] (01834) 862202

Privately-owned concern, founded in 1830 and operating 50 pubs in Pembrokeshire and Carmarthenshire (all tenanted). Tenants are chiefly supplied by Brains, Crown Buckley, Tomos Watkin, Bass, Carlsberg-Tetley and Whitbread. Worthington Bitter is a permanent feature in all pubs and a house ale, James Williams IPA, brewed by Crown Buckley, is also available.

YATES'S

Yates's Wine Lodges Ltd., Peter Yates House, Manchester Road, Bolton, Greater Manchester BL3 2PY.

☎ (01204) 373737 [FAX] (01204) 388383

Company founded in Oldham in 1884 by wine merchant Peter Yates. It now runs 71 managed pubs, in locations from Scotland to London, and is keen to acquire more outlets. Most are branded, styled in Victorian fashion and feature bold, vivid colours in their decor. Beers are mainly from Scottish Courage and Bass, with some regional ales also featured.

Other notable chains (operated by, or divisions of, brewing companies or pub groups):

All Bar One (Bass)
Artist's Fare (Morland)
Barras & Co. (Scottish Courage)
Beefeater (Whitbread)
Bert's Bars (Alloa)
BieRRex (Century Inns)
Big Steak (Allied Domecq)
Bill Bentley's Wine Bars (Young's)
Bootsy Brogan's (Glendola Leisure)
Brewer's Fayre (Whitbread)
Café Rouge (Whitbread)
Calendars (Allied Domecq)
Countryside Hotels (Greene King)
Dave & Busters (Bass)
Dr Brown's (Century Inns)
Dublin Pub Company (Mercury Taverns)
Edwards (Bass)
Exchanges (Taylor Walker)
Firkin (Allied Domecq)
Fork & Pitcher (Bass)
Harvester (Bass)
Harvey Floorbangers (Regent Inns)
Hedgehog & Hogshead (Grosvenor Inns)
Henry's Café Bars (Greenalls)
Henry's Tables (Greenalls)
High Street Taverns (Grosvenor Inns)
Hobgoblinns (Wychwood)
Hogshead Ale Houses (Whitbread)
Hudsons (Greenalls)
Hungry Horse (Greene King)
It's a Scream (Bass)
JJ Moon's (Wetherspoon)
Jongleurs (Regent Inns)
Jungle Bungle (Greenalls)
King's Fayre (Greene King)
Lacon Inns (Adnams)
Landlord's Table (Mansfield)
Maxwells (Allied Domecq)
Milestone Restaurants and Taverns (Wolverhampton & Dudley)
Millers Kitchen (Greenalls)
Mr Q's (Allied Domecq)
Newt & Cucumber (Morland)
Nice Pub Company (Tom Cobleigh)
O'Neills (Bass)
Pickled Newt (Greene King)
Pitcher & Piano (Marston's)
Pizza Hut (Whitbread)
PJ Pepper (Whitbread)
Porters Ale Houses (Greenalls)
Quincey's (Greenalls)
Rat & Carrot (Greene King)
Rat & Parrot (Scottish Courage)
Roast Inns (Greenalls)
Scruffy Murphy's (Allied Domecq)
Shamus O'Donnell's (Enterprise Inns)
Slug & Lettuce (Grosvenor Inns)
Spoofers (Regent Inns)
T&J Bernard's (Scottish Courage)
Tap & Spile (Century Inns)
TGI Friday (Whitbread)
Toby Restaurants (Bass)
Top Hat Taverns (Burtonwood)
Tut 'n' Shive (Whitbread)
Vintage Inns (Bass)
Walkabout Inns (Regent Inns)
Wayside Inns (Whitbread)
Wig & Pen (Morland)
Wirral Taverns (Enterprise Inns)

Keep up to date with events in the brewery world. Join CAMRA and read *What's Brewing* every month.

The Beers Index

The Beers Index is your quick guide to the real ales of the United Kingdom. Over 2,000 brews are highlighted in the following pages, from Abbot Ale to Zebedee, together with page references to The Breweries, where you can find out more about each beer.

A

B

THE BEERS INDEX

P

P2 Imperial Stout *Museum (Bass)* 520
Pagan *Durham* 446
Pageant Ale *Elgood's* 447
Palatine *Durham* 446
Pale Amber *Hughes* 466
Pale Rider *Kelham Island* 469
Pale White *Green Cucumber (Salopian)* 498
Paradise Bitter *Bird In Hand* 425
Parish Bitter *Wood* 514
Parkhurst Porter *Burts* 434
Parkin's Pride *Viking* 510
Parson's Porter *Rectory* 493
Parsons Progress *Salopian* 497
Passion Ale *Weltons* 512
Patently Oblivious *Yorkshire Grey (Scottish Courage)* 527
Patois Ale *Randalls* 492
Patrick's Stout *Mildmay* 480
Pavilion Beast *Skinner's* 444
Pcella *Ancient Druids* 418
Peach *Mash & Air* 478
Peacock's Glory *Belvoir* 424
Peak Pale *High Peak (Lloyds)* 474
Pedigree *Marston's* 478
Pedwar Bawd *Dyffryn Clwyd* 446
Pendle Witches Brew *Moorhouse's* 481
Penguin Porter *Ash Vine* 419
Penguin Stout *Skinner's* 444
Penn's Ale *Hoskins* 465
Percy's Downfall *Trueman's* 508
Peregrine Porter *Cotleigh* 441
Peter's Porter *Arkell's* 419
Pett Genius *Old Forge* 486
Pett Progress *Old Forge* 486
Pews Porter *Church End* 439
PG Steam *RCH* 491
Phoenix Indian Ale *Enville* 448
Phoenix XXX *Woodforde's* 514
Pickled Priest *Little Avenham* 474
Pickwick's Porter *Malton* 476
Piddlebrook *Rainbow* 491
Piddle in the Hole *Wyre Piddle* 516
Piddle in the Snow *Wyre Piddle* 516
Piddle in the Sun *Wyre Piddle* 516
Piddle in the Wind *Wyre Piddle* 516
Pierrepoints Last Drop *Little Avenham* 474
Pigor Mortis *Uley* 508
Pig's Ear Old Ale *Gribble* 457
Pig's Ear Strong Beer *Uley* 508
Pigswill *Bunces* 433
Pillage Porter *Rudgate* 496
Pilots Pride *Minerva (Carlsberg-Tetley)* 524
Pioneer *Ledbury* 472
Pisces *Bateman* 422
Pistol Dawn *Lock, Stock and Barrel (Juwards)* 469
Pistol Knight *Lock, Stock and Barrel (Branscombe Vale)* 430
Pistolways *Lock, Stock and Barrel (Oakham)* 484
Piston Bitter *Beer Engine* 424
Piston Brew *Bushy's* 434
Pitchfork *RCH* 491
Ploughmans Pickle *Abel Brown's* 431
Plum Duff *Kitchen* 471
Plunder *Jollyboat* 468
Plymouth Porter *Sutton* 503
Poachers Ale *Parish* 488
Poacher's Swag *Steam Packet* 501

Poco Loco *Abel Brown's* 431
Polar Eclipse Oatmeal Stout *Beartown* 423
Poleaxed *Maypole* 479
Polecat Porter *Old Chimneys* 485
Polly's Extra Folly *Buffy's* 432
Polly's Folly *Buffy's* 432
Pommie's Revenge *Goose Eye* 456
Pooh Beer *Church End* 438
Pope's Traditional *Eldridge Pope (Hardy)* 459
Porters Sidewinder *Martin Elms Wines (Nethergate)* 483
Porters Suffolk Bitter *Martin Elms Wines (Nethergate)* 483
Posthorn Premium Ale *Coach House* 440
Potage *Kitchen* 471
Pot Black *Tigertops* 505
Potboiler's Brew *Tally Ho!* 503
Pots Ale *Cheriton* 438
Predator *Weltons* 512
Premier Bitter *Cobden's* 440
      Moorhouse's 481
Pride *Cannon* 437
      Cartmel 437
      Devon 445
Prince Bishop Ale *Big Lamp* 425
Priory Ale *Marches* 477
Priscilla *Swaled Ale* 503
Prize Old Ale *Gale's* 454
Progress *Pilgrim* 489
Proud Salopian *Salopian (King & Barnes)* 471
Ptarmigan 85/- *Harviestoun* 461
Publican Bitter *Riverside* 494
Pudding *Pilgrim* 489
Pullman Porter *Easingwold* 446
Pwlldu XXXX *Swansea* 503

Q

QC Best Bitter *Yorkshire Grey (Scottish Courage)* 527
Quaffing Ale *Museum (Bass)* 520
Queen Maev Stout *Iceni* 467
Quismas Quacker *Mallard* 476
Quiver *Cranborne* 441

R

Radgie Gadgie *Mordue* 481
Raeburn's Edinburgh Ale *Scottish Courage* 526
Raging Bull *Black Bull* 426
Rail Ale *Beer Engine* 424
Railway Porter *Brunswick* 432
Rainbow Chaser *Hanby* 459
Rain Dance *Brewery on Sea* 430
Rampart *Border* 428
Ram Rod *Young's* 517
Ramsbottom Strong Ale *Dent* 445
Rams Revenge *Clark's* 439
Ram Tam *Taylor* 504
Rapier Pale Ale *Reepham* 493
Rauch *Passageway* 488
Raven Ale *Orkney* 487
Rawhide *Leyland* 473
Recession Ale *Brunswick* 432
Reckless *Frog & Parrot (Whitbread)* 528
Reckless Raspberry *Hoskins & Oldfield* 466

S

T

X

Y

Z

BEERS OF THE YEAR

Chosen by CAMRA tasting panels, by votes from the general public at beer festivals and by a poll of CAMRA members, these are the *Good Beer Guide Beers of the Year*. Each was found to be consistently outstanding in its category and took its place in the *Champion Beer of Britain* contest at the Great British Beer Festival at Olympia in August 1997, or in the *Champion Winter Beer of Britain* contest held in Glasgow in February 1997. These beers have also been awarded a 'full tankard' symbol in The Breweries section of this book.

DARK AND LIGHT MILDS

Bateman Dark Mild

Brains Dark

Cains Dark Mild

Coach House Gunpowder Mild

Hardys & Hansons Best Mild

McMullen AK

Taylor Golden Best

BITTERS

Adnams Bitter

Big Lamp Bitter

Brakspear Bitter

Branscombe Vale Branoc

Caledonian Deuchars IPA

Cheriton Pots Ale

Goddards Special Bitter

Hobsons Best Bitter

Hydes' Anvil Bitter

Oakham JHB

Ruddles Best Bitter

Taylor Best Bitter

Tring Ridgeway Bitter

Woodforde's Wherry Best Bitter

BEST BITTERS

Bath Gem

Castle Eden Ale

Concertina Bengal Tiger

Cottage Golden Arrow

Fuller's London Pride

Goff's Jouster

Hoskins & Oldfield HOB Bitter

Isle of Skye Red Cuillin

McMullen Gladstone

Mansfield Old Baily

Mordue Workie Ticket

Plassey Bitter

Vale Edgar's Golden Ale

STRONG BITTERS

Bateman XXXB

Bullmastiff Son of a Bitch

Cheriton Diggers Gold

Flying Firkin (Dent) Kamikaze

Hop Back Summer Lightning

Ind Coope Burton Ale

Phoenix Wobbly Bob

OLD ALES AND STRONG MILDS

Adnams Old

Branscombe Vale Yo Ho Ho

Gribble Wobbler

Hughes Dark Ruby Mild

Kelham Island Bête Noire

Orkney Dark Island

Theakston Old Peculier

PORTERS AND STOUTS

B&T Edwin Taylor's Extra Stout

Bateman Salem Porter

Hambleton Nightmare

Hop Back Entire Stout

Pilgrim Saracen

Plassey Stout

Wickwar Station Porter

BARLEY WINES

Belhaven 90/-

Cottage Norman's Conquest

Gibbs Mew Bishop's Tipple

McMullen Stronghart

Marston's Owd Rodger

Robinson's Old Tom

Woodforde's Headcracker

SPECIALITY BEERS

Enville Ale

Harviestoun Schiehallion

Heather Fraoch Heather Ale

Hop Back Thunderstorm

Nethergate Umbel Ale

Nethergate Umbel Magna

Passageway St Arnold

BOTTLE-CONDITIONED BEERS

Bass Worthington White Shield

Fuller's 1845

Gale's Prize Old Ale

Hop Back Summer Lightning

King & Barnes Festive

Marston's Oyster Stout

Shepherd Neame Spitfire

An Offer For
CAMRA Members
Good Beer Guide
Annual Subscription

BEING A CAMRA member brings many benefits, not least the big discount on the *Good Beer Guide*. Now you can take advantage of an even bigger discount on the *Guide* by taking out an annual subscription.

Simply fill in the form below and the Direct Debit form on page 558 (photocopies will do if you don't want to spoil your book), and send them to CAMRA at the usual St Albans address. You will then receive the *Good Beer Guide* automatically every year. It will be posted to you before the official publication date and before any other postal sales are processed. You won't have to bother with filling in cheques every year and you will receive the book at a lower price than other CAMRA members (the 1998 paperback edition, for instance, is sold to annual subscribers at only £7).

So sign up now and be sure of receiving your copy early every year.

Note: This offer is only open to CAMRA members and is only available through using a Direct Debit instruction to a UK bank. It is limited to one copy per member per year. Additional copies can be ordered separately at the CAMRA members' usual price.

Name _____

CAMRA Membership No. _____

Address and Post Code _____

_____

_____

_____

I wish to purchase the *Good Beer Guide* annually by Direct Debit and I have completed the Direct Debit instructions to my bank which are here enclosed.

Signature _____ Date _____

JOIN CAMRA FREE
FOR THREE MONTHS

HAS A PUB near you been closed or ruined? Has your local brewery been taken over or its beers lost their flavour? Are you concerned about the price of a pint? If you can answer 'yes' to any or all of these questions you are sure to benefit by becoming a member of CAMRA.

The Campaign for Real Ale is a voluntary organisation consisting of over 50,000 ordinary drinkers, run by an unpaid, elected National Executive and backed by a small core of professional executives. It speaks for drinkers everywhere in fighting to save pubs and breweries from closure, and in attempting to improve quality and to ensure pub standards are raised.

■ As a member you can have your say about the issues which affect you. You can stand for election to office, attend the annual conference to speak and vote, and help organise local campaigns.

■ You can help select pubs for the *Good Beer Guide,* help out at beer festivals and enjoy some excellent social activities.

■ You can receive big discounts on the *Good Beer Guide* and other CAMRA books and products, free or reduced price admission to CAMRA beer festivals, plus the *What's Brewing* newspaper, delivered to your door each month. All new members receive the *Members' Handbook* as soon as they are registered.

All this is available at the bargain price of just £14 per year (£17 per year for two people living at the same address). What's more you can even join for three months at no cost and see if you think it's worthwhile being a member. Fill in the application form below (or a photocopy of it) and the Direct Debit form overleaf and if after three months you decide not to continue just write to CAMRA, cancel your membership and you will owe nothing.

If you do not wish to take up the trial offer, but wish to join CAMRA anyway, fill in the application form and return it to us with a cheque for your first year's subscription. Do not fill in the Direct Debit form. To pay by credit card, contact the Membership Secretary on (01727) 867201.

- -

■ Full annual membership £14 ■ Joint annual membership (two people at the same address) £17 ■ Life membership £168 (single)/£204 (joint)

Please delete as appropriate:

☐ I/We wish to take advantage of the trial membership, and have completed the instructions overleaf.

☐ I/We wish to become members of CAMRA.

☐ I/We agree to abide by the memorandum and articles of association of the company.

☐ I/We enclose a cheque/p.o. for £   (payable to CAMRA)

Name(s) _____

Address and Post Code _____

_____

Signature(s) _____

To: CAMRA, 230 Hatfield Road, St Albans, Hertfordshire AL1 4LW

Instructions to your Bank or Building Society to pay Direct Debits

Originator's identification number

9	2	6	1	2	9

Please fill in the whole form and return to CAMRA

1 Name(s) of account holder(s)

2 Branch sort code
(From the top right corner of your cheque)

3 Name and full postal address of your bank or building society

To the Manager

Bank or Building Society

Address

Post Code

4 Bank or Building Society account number

5 CAMRA membership number
(if known)

6 Instructions to your Bank or Building Society
Please pay CAMRA Direct Debits from the account detailed on this instruction subject to the safeguards assured by The Direct Debit Guarantee

Signature(s)

Date

Banks and Building Societies may not accept Direct Debit Instructions for some types of account

CAMRA BOOKS AND GIFTS

CAMRA produces a wide range of books and other items to complement the *Good Beer Guide*. The major items are listed below, but a full catalogue of CAMRA products (including local guides) is available on request. Tear out or copy this form for ease of ordering. All prices include UK postage and packing.

	Quantity	Price each	Amount
CAMRA BOOKS			
Real Ale in a Bottle (The CAMRA guide to bottle-conditioned beer)		£7.99	
Brewery Breaks (The CAMRA guide to brewery visits and attractions)		£3.99	
The CAMRA Guide to Cellarmanship		£6.99	
Room at the Inn (The CAMRA guide to pub accommodation)		£8.99	
Good Pub Food (4th edition)		£9.99	
The CAMRA Guide to Real Cider		£7.99	
Known Treasures and Hidden Gems (The CAMRA guide to London pubs)		£7.99	
The CAMRA Guide to Home Brewing		£6.99	
Brew Classic European Beers at Home		£8.99	
The CAMRA Beer and Pubs Quiz Book		£3.99	
Kegbuster Remembers (selection of the best Kegbuster cartoons)		£4.99	
OTHER PRODUCTS			
CAMRA Lapel Badge		£2.50	
CAMRA T-shirt (white: M, L, XL, XXL – state size)		£7.50	
		Total	£

Please send to CAMRA, 230 Hatfield Road, St Albans, Hertfordshire AL1 4LW (cheques made payable to CAMRA must accompany all orders). Allow 21 days for delivery.

To place a credit card order, phone (01727) 867201 and ask for the Products Secretary.

Name
Address
Post Code

READERS' RECOMMENDATIONS

Suggestions for pubs to be included or excluded

All pubs are surveyed by the local branches of CAMRA. If you would like to comment on a pub already featured, or any you think should be featured, please fill in the form below (or a copy of it) and send it to the address indicated. Your views will be passed on to the branches concerned.

Pub Name:

Address:

Reason for recommendation/criticism:

Pub Name:

Address:

Reason for recommendation/criticism:

Your name and address:

Please send to: Good Beer Guide, CAMRA, 230 Hatfield Road, St Albans, Hertfordshire AL1 4LW